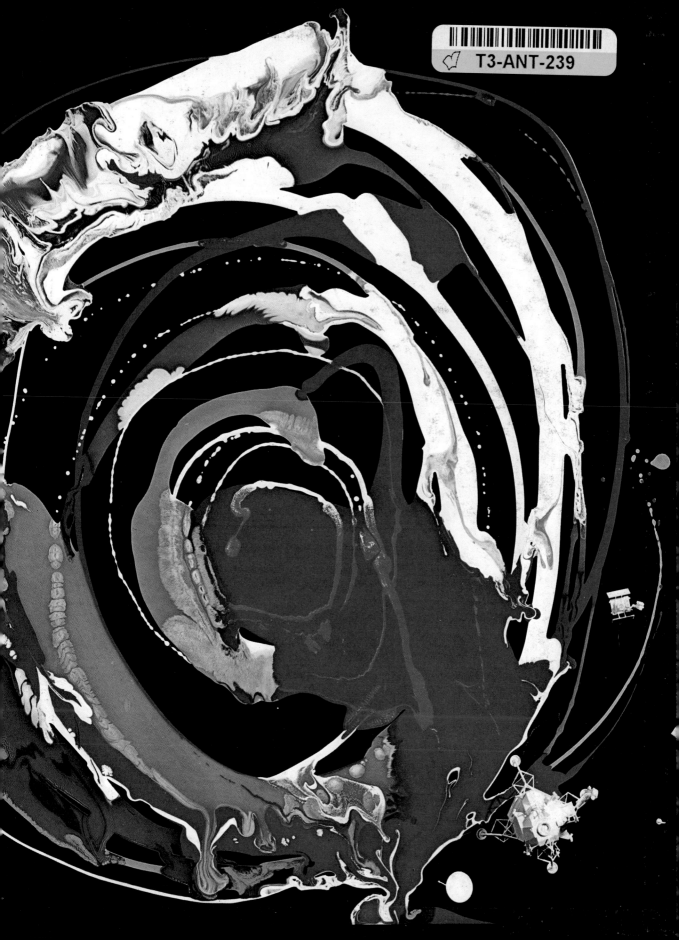

Abnormal Psychology and Modern Life

FOURTH EDITION

FOURTH EDITION

Scott, Foresman and Company

Glenview, Illinois   London

Abnormal Psychology and Modern Life

James C. Coleman
University of California at Los Angeles

William E. Broen, Jr., Contributing Author
University of California at Los Angeles

Preface

Eight years have gone by since the publication of the Third Edition of *Abnormal Psychology and Modern Life*—years of rapid and drastic change. The world has undergone major crises involving age-old problems, such as war, famine, and discrimination, as well as new and emerging problems, such as overpopulation, violations of ecological balance, and uncontrolled technological change. But while these years have recorded many tragic events and brought new and crucial problems, they have also been a time of tremendous scientific advance, with an awakening of new hopes for the future.

These new hopes and visions have been given impetus by our changed perspective resulting from man's landing on the moon. From a lunar vantage point, we have been able to see ourselves as astronauts on a spaceship hurtling through space, and it has become apparent that we must come to grips with the urgent problems that confront us on our spacecraft if we are to survive. And we have come to realize as never before that the kind of future man will have depends on our actions—whether by decision or by default.

With our expanding perspective of ourselves as an interdependent community of astronauts has come an expansion of our perspective of abnormal behavior. We now see it as encompassing behavior not only of individuals but also of families and larger groups, including entire societies. It has been the urgent task of this revision to reflect that broader orientation. At the same time, the text has been extensively updated with respect to the more usual syndromes of individual maladaptive behavior, such as neuroses, schizophrenia, and drug dependence. Throughout, new research findings, new case materials, and new summary charts have been introduced, supported by a new illustration program designed to convey the reality of the many unusual forms of human experience being described. Overall, an attempt has been made to consider the major issues, trends, and horizons in the approaches to both mental health and abnormal behavior.

Six chapters have been added in this edition. The chapters on the major psychosocial models of man, the behavior disorders of childhood, and the maladaptive behavior of groups are entirely new. In other cases, the additional chapters represent a more comprehensive coverage of topics included before: whole chapters are now devoted to the affective disorders and suicide, schizophrenia and paranoia, sexual deviations, and delinquency and crime. Throughout, the attempt has been made to show the crucial role of learning in the development and maintenance of abnormal behavior as well as the application of learning principles in therapy. In addition, more emphasis has been focused on the influence of interpersonal and sociocultural factors in the development and alleviation of abnormal behavior. And in our final chapter dealing with horizons in mental health, more attention is devoted to building a "good future" for man and to the role that the individual can play in this crucial endeavor.

The overall sequence in this Fourth Edition is similar to that of previous editions:

Part One sets the stage—defining the concept of *abnormal*, or *maladaptive*, behavior, describing its magnitude, explaining common misconceptions, tracing viewpoints and methods of treatment from ancient to modern times, delineating contemporary psychosocial models of man, and showing the need for an interdisciplinary approach to understanding and dealing with maladaptive behavior.

Part Two reviews principles involved in human development and adjustment, both adaptive and maladaptive. Behavior is seen as a function of (1) the individual's psychobiological makeup and adjustive resources, (2) the stress situation he faces from internal and external demands, and (3) the resources and constraints of his environment, including the contingencies that reward certain behavior patterns and punish others. Within this context, maladaptive behavior is seen as involving not only the individual but his interpersonal and sociocultural setting.

Part Three details the clinical pictures, causal factors, therapy, and outcomes of the various maladaptive patterns. Included are both the "functional" disorders—in which brain pathology is not considered of primary causal significance—and the disorders associated with acute or chronic brain pathology. The syndromes described conform essentially to the classification currently in use by the World

The author would like to thank all sources for the use of their material. The credit lines for copyrighted materials appearing in this work are placed in the Acknowledgments and References and the Picture Credits sections at the end of the book. These pages are to be considered an extension of the copyright page.

Health Organization and the American Psychiatric Association. However, our main emphasis is not on classification but on the causal patterns involved in the development and maintenance of these disorders.

Part Four deals with the problem of assessment and with contemporary approaches to the treatment and prevention of abnormal behavior—on both individual and group levels—including, as already noted, a consideration of man's greatly increased potential for planning a "good future" for his species.

Finally, in this Fourth Edition, the glossary has been expanded in an effort to make it more comprehensive and useful. In most cases page references are included to guide the student to the original or most detailed discussion of the term in the text. The index has been designed to make it as easy as possible to locate specific topics in the text. And the back endsheets contain the currently accepted classification of mental disorders although, as explained in Chapter 1, we have made certain modifications in our text presentation for purposes of instruction.

Several ancillary publications are available to provide flexibility and depth in the planning of the abnormal psychology course: (1) a student guide prepared by Dr. Barbara D'Angelo of De Anza College which can be used to focus and extend the student's understanding of the material of each chapter through review, analysis, and personal involvement; (2) two sets of tapes—the new *Six Diagnostic Interviews*, prepared by Dr. Rudolph Novick of Forest Hospital, Des Plaines, Illinois, and the still available *Six Modern Therapies*, prepared by Dr. Stewart Shapiro of the University of California at Santa Barbara; and (3) an instructor's resource book, which includes suggestions for organizing the course, chapter overviews, activities for student involvement, provocative questions, film suggestions, and multiple-choice and essay-type test items.

Grateful acknowledgment is made to Dr. William E. Broen, Jr., for his participation in the planning of this edition, and for early drafts of sections relating to neuroses, schizophrenia, mental retardation, suicide, assessment, and therapy, as well as for a careful reading of all the chapters in galleys and a number of suggestions for illustrations. The final researching, organizing, and writing were carried out by the senior author.

Any author of a book such as this is greatly indebted to his many colleagues in the biological and social sciences whose research is helping conquer the frontier of abnormal behavior and whose work is drawn on in interpreting the field to students. In addition, acknowledgment is due to many individuals for professional contributions without which this book could not have been developed.

Special thanks go to Dr. James Linden of California State College at Long Beach for help in shaping the chapter on therapy; to Dr. James G. Kelly of the University of Michigan for help in revising and illustrating the chapter on mental health; and to Dr. Solomon Feldman of Northern Illinois University, whose critical comments on each chapter were most constructive and helpful. Others who read and commented on sections of the manuscript and to whom the author wishes to express his appreciation are: Dr. Richard Bootzin of Northwestern University; Dr. Ernest H. Dondis of California State College at Fullerton; Dr. Alan S. Lowenthal of California State College at Long Beach; Dr. Rolf A. Peterson of the University of Illinois at Chicago Circle; Dr. Leon Rappoport of Kansas State University at Manhattan; and Dr. Edward Sheridan of the University of Illinois at Chicago Circle. He is grateful also for the suggestions of Dr. George Coelho of the National Institute of Mental Health; Dr. Andrew Comrey of the University of California at Los Angeles; Dr. Henry P. David of the International Research Institute; Mr. George W. Erdmann, President of Borg-Erickson Corporation; Mr. John Harris of Ventura College; Dr. John Heiken of the Malibu Medical Group; Dr. Douglas Mohr of the California Institute of Technology; Dr. Stanley F. Schneider of the National Institute of Mental Health; and Dr. Joseph Sheehan of the University of California at Los Angeles.

For the illustration program, special thanks are due to Rita Knipe and Karen McArthur; for the design, to John Mayahara of the Scott, Foresman staff. Finally, his profound thanks go to Margaret Martin, Cynthia Adamic, Marguerite Clark, Sybil Sosin, Louise Howe, and Donna Delaine of the Scott, Foresman editorial staff for dedication far beyond the call of duty; to Fay Levinson for research assistance and many constructive suggestions; and to his wife for her patience and understanding over the three years of sustained pressure required to complete this edition.

At the close of his journeys, Tennyson's Ulysses says, "I am a part of all that I have met." It is the author's hope that the reader of this book, at the end of his journey through it, will see what he has learned as a meaningful part of his life experience that will contribute to his understanding of and empathetic concern for all those for whom the problems of living create severe stress or perhaps become too great.

James C. Coleman

Contents

Part Three Patterns of Abnormal Behavior

Perspectives on Abnormal Behavior

Part One

Abnormal Behavior in Our Times

1

POPULAR VIEWS OF ABNORMAL BEHAVIOR

ABNORMAL BEHAVIOR AS THE SCIENTIST
SEES IT

THE ORIENTATION OF THIS BOOK

The seventeenth century has been called the Age of Enlightenment; the eighteenth, the Age of Reason; the nineteenth, the Age of Progress; and the twentieth, the *Age of Anxiety*. Although the path to a meaningful and satisfying way of life has probably never been an easy one, it seems to have become increasingly difficult in modern times. Wars regularly disrupt both personal and national life, leaving in their wake grief and social unrest. Economic fluctuations and technological changes have taken their toll in unemployment, dislocation, and poverty for millions of people. The human population explosion is creating difficult social problems and tensions. Racial prejudice, with its unreasoned feelings of superiority, hatred, and resentment, hurts both the individual and the community. Grinding poverty and discrimination exist side by side with abundance and opportunity—leading to social pressures which periodically erupt in violence. The pollution of air, water, and soil is dangerously eroding our environmental resources, threatening the life-support system of all who travel on the spaceship Earth. Urban society, with its high mobility, impersonality, and loss of extended family bonds, places increasing stress on the home. Unhappy marriages and homes broken by divorce lead to hurt and disillusionment and leave emotional scars upon parents and children alike. Excessive competition, impersonal bureaucracy, and the ever present threat of global atomic war further aggravate modern man's anxieties.

Ours is an age of tremendous growth of knowledge and of rapid social change. More scientific and technological advances have been made in the past fifty years than in all previous recorded time; and modern science and technology are having an increasingly profound effect upon all phases of our lives. Innovations in transportation and communication have broadened man's horizons, so that he must daily face international problems as well as national and local ones. The landing of men on the moon has inevitably placed the earth and its inhabitants in a new perspective; and as man ventures farther into the universe, he is increasingly and inescapably confronted with his own finiteness and with questions as to the meaning of his existence. At the same time, traditional values and beliefs no longer seem self-evident, and he lacks the comforting religious and social absolutes that seem to have provided security for his forebears. Contemporary man is skeptical of traditional beliefs and values as never before; more and more, he questions all the long-accepted assumptions—about the church, education, sex, marriage, and social and political institutions.

Unfortunately, advances in our understanding of man have lagged far behind our advances in the physical and biological sciences. We know much about the atom and the gene but not nearly enough about love or the values needed for a meaningful and fulfilling life in our changing world. In fact, we lack much of the information about man's basic nature that could help us plan and construct a "good future world" for human beings. As a consequence, we tend to stumble around among diverse religions, philosophies, and social programs, seeking answers that will satisfy us and provide direction and meaning for living in our contemporary world.

Small wonder that on every side we see anxious, unhappy, bewildered people who miss the fulfillment of their potentials because they cannot find satisfactory answers to problems that seem just too great. The strain of life is indicated by the incredible amounts of tranquilizers, sleeping pills, and alcoholic beverages consumed in our society; by the widespread preoccupation with marijuana and other psychedelic drugs; and

by the ample literature on the "alienation" and "dehumanization" of modern man. In an equally dramatic way it is reflected in the large number of young people who have lost faith in the ability and will of the older generation to live by the values it verbalizes; in the alarming rise in delinquency and crime; in racial conflict and tension; and in riots and other manifestations of violence.

Despite the stress of modern life, most people still manage to "muddle through," worrying along and solving their problems after a fashion. But for large numbers of individuals the stress proves too much. It is startling to note that emotional disturbances incapacitate more people than all other health problems combined. If present trends continue, approximately one person in ten now living in this country will at some time require professional treatment for such a disturbance. Furthermore, this figure says nothing of the many kinds of organic illness brought on and exacerbated by emotional conflict and tension.

Abnormal behavior has for good reason been designated the country's Number One health problem. This does not mean that effective personality adjustment is impossible in modern life. It does mean, however, that many of us encounter serious difficulties in dealing with life's problems—particularly problems centering around values and the search for a meaningful, fulfilling way of life. Thus the study of abnormal behavior may be of great help in fostering personal adjustment and growth and in reducing the great toll of misery and lost productivity which mental disorders are exacting in our society.

POPULAR VIEWS OF ABNORMAL BEHAVIOR

When we think of abnormal behavior, we are likely to think of extreme, spectacular examples because, as in other fields, it is the bizarre and the sensational that command attention. Examples of mental disorders that we have heard or read about are apt to be extreme cases which, isolated and lumped together, give us a "chamber-of-horrors" picture of abnormal behavior rather

than the truer picture, in which less spectacular minor maladjustments are far more common. Popular present-day beliefs about abnormal behavior thus tend to be based on atypical and unscientific descriptions. Partly this has been inevitable, because it is only recently that scientific research methods have been turned to an understanding of abnormal behavior.

Left, an engraving depicting the madness of Nebuchadnezzar as described in the Book of Daniel. Nebuchadnezzar, King of ancient Babylon, suffered from lycanthropy, a form of disorder in which the sufferer believes himself to be a wolf.

Above, Saul and David. The biblical account relates that at first David's music soothed King Saul when "the evil spirit" was upon him, but later Saul became increasingly fearful and jealous of David and finally tried to kill him.

Despite their limitations, a brief review of a few cases of mental disorders reported from the past and from literature will be of value in giving us a broader perspective of our problem; for most of the forms of severe mental disorder that we see today have been observed and reported in other ages too.

VIEWS CARRIED OVER FROM HISTORY

Some of the earliest writings of man—Chinese, Egyptian, Hebrew, and Greek—provide striking "case histories" of disturbed individuals.[1] Saul, King of Israel in the eleventh century B.C., suffered from recurrent manic-depressive episodes. During an attack of mania (excitement) he stripped off all his clothes in a public place. On another occasion he tried to kill his son Jonathan.

Cambyses, King of Persia in the sixth century B.C., was one of the first alcoholics on record. His alcoholic excesses were apparently associated with periods of uncontrollable rage during which he behaved "as a madman not in possession of

his senses." (Whitwell, 1936, p. 38) On one occasion, without making any provision for the feeding of his army, he set out against the Ethiopians, who had greatly enraged him by calling the Persians "dung eaters." He was shortly forced to return to Memphis, where he found the people celebrating the feast of Apis. Furious at what he took to be rejoicing at his failure, he ordered that all the people taking part in the feast be killed. Cambyses also defied Persian law by marrying one of his sisters, and later he killed his other sister by kicking her during pregnancy. On another occasion he used his friend's son as a target for his arrows to demonstrate that his excessive drinking had not affected his skill. His aim was true and he killed the boy, thus proving his point, at least to his own satisfaction.

Greek mythology contains many descriptions of mentally disturbed persons which afford some insight into the nature of the real-life cases from which the descriptions must have been drawn. For example, Hercules seems to have been afflicted

---

[1]Sources upon which this section is based include the following: Bluemel (1948), Born (1946), Lombroso (1891), Marks (1925), Sewell (1943), Whitwell (1936), and Zilboorg and Henry (1941).

with convulsive seizures accompanied by a homicidal fugue-type reaction. His attacks are graphically described by Euripides in the "Phrenzy of Hercules": his eyes rolled, his consciousness clouded, he frothed at the mouth, showed violent fury, and attacked persons in his way, then fell, writhed, and finally fell into a deep sleep. Upon awakening he had complete amnesia for the seizure. During the course of several attacks, Hercules killed two of his own children, two of his brother's children, his best friend, and his teacher. Ajax, too, became mentally disordered and slew a flock of sheep under the impression that he was attacking his enemies. On regaining his senses, he was so overcome with remorse that he committed suicide by throwing himself on his sword.

Many of the notables of later Greece and Rome, including Socrates, Democritus, and Alexander the Great, apparently suffered from mental disorders of one kind or another, and the ensuing period of the Middle Ages contains innumerable instances of abnormal behavior. The great oriental conqueror, Tamerlane (1336–1405), for example, was particularly fond of building pyramids of human skulls. One of his architectural achievements is reported to have contained some forty thousand of them.

In more recent times, George III of England—known as the "mad monarch"—manifested a variety of symptoms, including periods of intense excitement and overactivity. During periods of manic excitement he jumped rapidly from one topic to another, asked precipitate questions without waiting for an answer, ate his food so rapidly that the members of his court had to bolt their food or leave the table hungry, raced up and down stairs, rode his horse to death, indulged in obscene language, and displayed the tireless energy typical of the manic who is just too busy to sleep.

The French philosopher Jean Jacques Rousseau (1712–1778) developed marked paranoid symptoms during the latter part of his life. He was obsessed with fears of secret enemies and thought that Prussia, England, France, the king, priests, and others were waging a terrible war against him. He believed that these enemies caused him to have all kinds of internal troubles, but that their chief artifice was to torture him by overwhelming him with benefits and praise, even going so far as to corrupt vegetable peddlers so that they would

sell him better vegetables more cheaply. According to Rousseau, this was undoubtedly designed to prove his baseness and their generosity. It would be interesting here to know whether this behavior was related to the fact that he and his wife had left each of their five children at a foundling hospital.

Rousseau became panicky during a visit to London and fled, leaving all his luggage and money at the hotel. On his arrival at the coast the winds were not favorable for his departure, and in this he saw another indication of the plot against him. After his return to France, his invisible enemies apparently stepped up their persecution. They corrupted his coffee merchant, his hairdresser, and his landlord; the shoeblack had no more blacking when Rousseau needed him; the boatman had no boats when this unfortunate man wished to cross the Seine; his enemies even prevented his front door from opening. He demanded to be put in prison, but even this was prevented by his imaginary foes. No longer able to trust man, he turned to God, to whom he addressed a very tender and familiar letter. To ensure the arrival of the letter at its proper destination, he tried to place it on the altar of Notre Dame at Paris. Finding the railing closed, he believed that Heaven, too, was conspiring against him. Finally he even came to distrust his dog.

The names of philosophers, painters, writers, and musicians who might also be mentioned would make a long and celebrated list. Mozart, for example, during the composition of the *Requiem*, labored under the delusion that he was being poisoned. Beethoven, although miserably poor, was constantly changing his living quarters and sometimes had to pay for lodgings at three or four different places at once. Robert Schumann, in later life, was pursued by turning-tables which knew everything, and heard spirit voices and melodies and harmonies that developed into entire compositions.

On one occasion Van Gogh cut off his ear and sent it to a prostitute, an action apparently performed in a state of clouded consciousness resulting from his epileptic condition. Schopenhauer, Chopin, and John Stuart Mill suffered from attacks of depression. Rabelais, Tasso, Samuel Butler, Burns, Byron, and Poe used alcohol excessively. Coleridge acknowledged using opiates before writing "Kubla Khan."

In reviewing these historical instances of abnormal behavior, it should be made clear that we are to some extent evaluating this behavior in the light of present-day concepts of mental disorder. In their own day, some of these men were looked upon as perfectly normal, and others as only eccentric or unusual. We may also take note of the fact that, although many individuals with mental disorders have made significant contributions to society and the shaping of history, it has been those men and women of more effective personality adjustment who have carried the major burden in the achievement of social progress.

IDEAS CARRIED OVER FROM LITERATURE

Long before abnormal psychology became an area of scientific study, the masters of fiction and drama developed many brilliant and moving characterizations of abnormal behavior, based on their sensitive, keen observations of human behavior. Such literary classics, in their descriptions of human abnormality in all of its infinite subtleties of degree and variety, often achieve a lifelike vividness and an emotional force that science cannot achieve. *Othello*, for example, provides an unforgettable insight into the subjective quality of obsessive, violent jealousy.

Of course, literature cannot provide either the theoretical or practical basis for understanding and treating specific cases of abnormal behavior; but it does complement psychology in giving a different kind of understanding of such behavior. Literature yields valuable information, for example, about the concepts of personality dynamics, about mental disorders prevalent during a particular historical period, and about the inner experiences of the author as well.

The writings of the Greek poets and dramatists contain many allusions to abnormal behavior. In his play *Medea*, Euripides (480–406 B.C.) described and analyzed the emotions of jealousy and revenge as displayed by a mother who murders her children. Sophocles (495–406 B.C.) in *Oedipus Rex* and *Electra* has given us the first intimation of incest motives in the shaping of human behavior. And in *Orestes* he clearly described delusional and hallucinatory symptoms arising out of severe feelings of remorse and guilt.

Many of the characters in the plays of William Shakespeare portray the development of abnormal behavior with almost clinical accuracy. The intense guilt reaction of Lady Macbeth, after planning and participating in the bloody murder of King Duncan, is well brought out in her uneasy sleepwalking and symbolic handwashing:

"It is an accustomed action with her, to seem thus washing her hands: I have known her continue in this a quarter of an hour."—*Macbeth*, Act V, Scene 1

That her compulsive handwashing has failed, however, to "cleanse" her of her feelings of uncleanness and guilt is shown in her admission that

"Here's the smell of the blood still: all the perfumes of Arabia will not sweeten this little hand. Oh, oh, oh!"— Act V, Scene 1

Can anyone fail to see the humor as well as the pathos in the adventures of Don Quixote? Cervantes' hero becomes so overwhelmed by reading the most famous books of chivalry that he believes them to be true. How natural it seems for him to accept his "mission" as a knight errant and to sally forth into the world to defend the oppressed and to right injustice like the heroes of his romances. Even when his excited imagination turns windmills into giants, solitary inns into castles, and galley slaves into oppressed gentlemen, the reader can feel a part of his adventuring. And finally when he is restored to his "right" mind through a severe illness and is made to renounce the follies of knight errantry, most of us probably feel a tinge of disappointment that the hero must give up his dreams and his noble "mission."

De Quincey revealed something of the "world within" in his description of his opium dreams:

". . . I brought together all creatures, birds, beasts, reptiles, all trees and plants, usages and appearances, that are found in all tropical regions, and assembled them together in China or Indostan. From kindred feelings, I soon brought Egypt and all her gods under the same law. I was stared at, hooted at, grinned at, chattered at, ran into pagodas: and was fixed for centuries at the summit, or in secret rooms; I was the idol; I was the priest; I was worshipped; I was sacrificed. I fled from the wrath of Brama through all the forests of Asia: Vishnu hated me: Seeva laid wait for me. I came suddenly upon Isis and Osiris: I had done a deed,

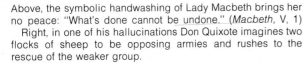

Above, the symbolic handwashing of Lady Macbeth brings her no peace: "What's done cannot be undone." (*Macbeth*, V, 1)
Right, in one of his hallucinations Don Quixote imagines two flocks of sheep to be opposing armies and rushes to the rescue of the weaker group.

they said, which the ibis and the crocodile trembled at. I was buried for a thousand years in stone coffins, with mummies and sphinxes, in narrow chambers at the heart of eternal pyramids. I was kissed, with cancerous kisses, by crocodiles; and laid, confounded with all unutterable slimy things, amongst reeds and Nilotic mud."—*Confessions of an English Opium Eater*

The irrational motivations and images that seem to come to light under unusual circumstances—delirium, the influence of drugs, or severe mental disorders—when inner restraints are lowered and perceptions are distorted, have long been a source of puzzlement to man.

It is interesting to speculate concerning the motivation that prompted other writings. Was a sort of vicarious sadism, for example, behind the fantasies of Jonathan Edwards when he pictured the brutal torturings in hell of those he considered to be sinners? When he preached on "Sinners in the Hands of an Angry God," his congregation received a terrifying warning:

"The wrath of God burns against them; their damnation does not slumber; the pit is prepared; the fire is made ready; the furnace is now hot, ready to receive them; the flames do now rage and glow. . . . The devils watch them; they are ever by them, at their right hand; they stand waiting for them, like greedy, hungry lions that see their prey, and expect to have it, but are for the present kept back; if God should withdraw His hand, by which they are restrained, they would in one moment fly upon their poor souls. The old serpent is gaping for them; hell opens its mouth wide to receive them; and if God should permit it, they would be hastily swallowed up and lost. . . .

"The God that holds you over the pit of hell, much as one holds a spider or some loathsome insect over the fire, abhors you, and is dreadfully provoked; His wrath towards you burns like fire; He looks upon you as worthy of nothing else, but to be cast into the fire; He is of purer eyes than to bear to have you in His sight; you are ten times so abominable in His eyes, as the most hateful and venomous serpent is in ours. . . .

"If we knew that there was one person, and but one, in the whole congregation, that was to be the subject of this misery, what an awful thing it would be to think of! If we knew who it was, what an awful sight would it be to see such a person. How much all the rest of the congregation might lift up a lamentable and bitter cry over him! But alas! instead of one, how many is it likely will remember this discourse in hell! And it would be a wonder, if some that are now present should not be in hell in a very short time, before this year is out. And it would be no wonder if some persons that now sit here in some seats of this meetinghouse in health, and quiet, and secure, should be there before to-morrow morning. These of you that finally continue in a natural condition, that shall keep out of hell longest, will be there in a little time!" (Edwards, 1809, pp. 489–502)

Many modern writers have attempted to capture, often from their own experience, the pattern of thought processes underlying various types of abnormal behavior. Themes so treated have included schizophrenia, alcoholism, paresis, manic-depressive psychoses, drug addiction, homicide, mental retardation, and sexual sadism—in fact, almost the entire gamut of behaviors considered to be abnormal.

Even the biographer, historian, and political scientist have inevitably become interested in abnormal psychology. The biographer tries to explain the personality development and the odd or peculiar behavior of historical persons in the light of present psychological knowledge. And the historian cannot afford to ignore psychological principles in his attempt to understand historical events. For example, psychiatric evaluations of Nazi leaders have added much to our insight into events that shocked the world during and after their period of power. In 1960 the World Health Organization expressed the opinion that the stresses on persons in high positions are often too great for normal people. It suggested that, as a consequence, individuals with psychopathic personality makeup—who tend to exploit power for selfish purposes and have little concern for ethical values or social progress—often become leaders (WHO, 1960). Such a possibility obviously has profound social implications.

SOME POPULAR MISCONCEPTIONS

Throughout most of history, as we shall see in Chapter 2, beliefs about mental disorder have been generally characterized by superstition, ignorance, and fear. Although successive advances in the scientific understanding of abnormal behavior have dispelled many false ideas, there remain a number of popular misconceptions that merit brief discussion.

The belief that abnormal behavior is always bizarre. The instances of abnormal behavior reported in the mass media, like those recorded in history and literature, are likely to be extreme ones involving murder, sexual assault, suicide, or other striking deviation from the accepted norms of behavior. This emphasis on deviance has helped perpetuate a tendency to equate mental disorder with bizarre and often dangerous behavior. The inmates of mental hospitals are often pictured in the popular mind as a weird lot who spend their time cutting out paper dolls, posing as Napoleon, or ranting and raving. In fact, only a relatively small percentage of patients in mental hospitals are unaware of what is going on around them or exhibit behavior that is clearly bizarre. The behavior of most mentally disturbed individuals, both in hospitals and without, is indistinguishable in many respects from that of "normal" people.

Actually, mental disorders cover a wide range of behavior patterns. Some types of abnormal behavior are clearly pathological, but others are abnormal only in the sense that they interfere with the individual's ability to cope effectively with various problems in his life. Abnormal behavior at this level of severity may be regarded as a cause for concern, but it is well within the bounds of ordinary, understandable human experience. Here, for example, is the youth of high intelligence who does inferior college work and complains that he "just can't concentrate" on his studies; the adolescent girl who refuses dates for fear she will prove disappointing; the middle-aged Don Juan who centers his life around the conquest of women; and the youth who consistently lies about trivial matters.

Next, there are difficulties that may be more serious and may bring a recognition that "there's definitely something wrong"—as, for example, with the college girl who is so depressed and anxious for no reason she can name that she cannot study or go to class, and eventually has to drop out of school entirely; the young husband who cruelly mistreats his wife and then attempts suicide when she decides to leave him; the adolescent girl who turns to prostitution to pay for her drug habit; and the father who wanders away from his family and is found months later in a strange community—the victim of amnesia.

Finally, there are behaviors that are generally

recognized as severely abnormal—the adolescent who pours gasoline over an old man and sets him on fire; the indignant young man who insists that his enemies have set up an electrical device that "pours filth into his mind and controls his thoughts"; the young mother who mistreats and eventually kills her infant son; the middle-aged man who molests children; the alcoholic who cringes in terror before an imagined invasion of cockroaches; and the paranoid who kills several innocent people he believes are plotting against him.

We shall shortly concern ourselves with the problems of defining and classifying abnormal behavior, which will help further in clarifying the picture of the range and severity of abnormal behavior in everyday life.

The idea that "normal" and "abnormal" are sharply differentiated. As should by now be apparent, a sharp dividing line between "normal" and "abnormal" behavior simply does not exist. There are not "normal" people on the one hand and "madmen" on the other—two different and distinct kinds of beings. Rather, adjustment seems to follow what is called a normal distribution, with most people clustering around a central point or average, and the rest spreading out toward the two extremes. Most people are moderately well adjusted; a few at one extreme enter mental hospitals and a few at the other extreme lead unusually satisfying and effective lives.

We have probably all known and sympathized with someone who became embittered after an unhappy love affair, or someone who became morbidly depressed following a serious failure. These individuals were showing behavior that differed only in degree from that of patients in mental hospitals, on the one hand, and from that of "normal, well-adjusted" people on the other.

Not only does the behavior of different individuals range by imperceptible degrees from the normal to the abnormal, but one individual may shift at different times to different positions along the continuum. Common observations show that a person's success in coping with life problems is subject to change from many different causes. For example, an individual may be making a satisfactory adjustment when some change in the

INCIDENCE OF MAJOR MALADAPTIVE BEHAVIOR PATTERNS IN THE UNITED STATES IN 1970
(Approximate Figures)

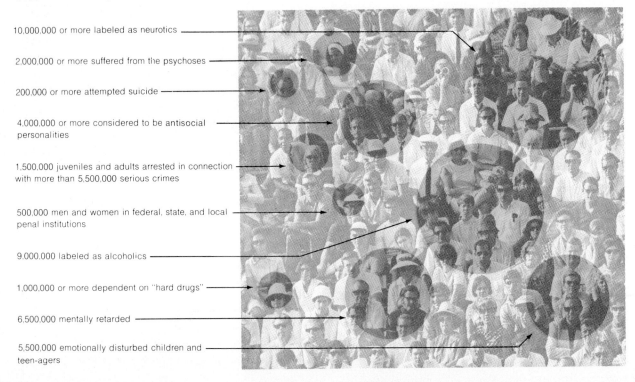

10,000,000 or more labeled as neurotics

2,000,000 or more suffered from the psychoses

200,000 or more attempted suicide

4,000,000 or more considered to be antisocial personalities

1,500,000 juveniles and adults arrested in connection with more than 5,500,000 serious crimes

500,000 men and women in federal, state, and local penal institutions

9,000,000 labeled as alcoholics

1,000,000 or more dependent on "hard drugs"

6,500,000 mentally retarded

5,500,000 emotionally disturbed children and teen-agers

demands made on him—perhaps as a result of a disappointment in love, loss of money, an illness, an accident, or the death of a loved one—may so greatly increase the severity of his adjustment problems that he is no longer able to cope with them satisfactorily. In the same way, an improvement in one's occupational status, marital adjustment, or physical health can lead to better all-around adjustment.

Both normal and abnormal behavior patterns are now seen as *attempts by the individual to cope with his life situation* as he sees it. Although people have different adaptive resources, use differing methods, and have differing degrees of success, we can assume that the same *fundamental principles apply to behavior called "normal" and to behavior called "abnormal,"* however unusual the latter may sometimes seem.

The view of mental disorder as a hereditary stigma. Most families have one or more mentally disordered individuals in their histories, and the relatives—especially close relatives—often live in fear of a mental breakdown themselves. Sometimes they are even reluctant to marry because they fear their children may be victims of "tainted" heredity.

In general, such fears appear to be unfounded, according to present knowledge. It has been shown that certain forms of mental retardation result from chromosomal irregularities on the part of one or both parents, but new advances in genetics now make it possible to tell whether a prospective parent has a normal chromosomal pattern.

It would also appear that genetic factors may play a predisposing role in the development of schizophrenia and certain other mental disorders, but the precise nature and importance of this role is unknown (it probably varies according to the type of mental disorder and the total patterning of other conditions). In most cases where "insanity runs in families," the children probably "inherit" the mental disorder through *learning*, not through the germ plasm. Often the adults are too emotionally disturbed themselves to provide the child with an environment conducive to healthy personality development and effective behavior. Thus the individual learns inadequate coping patterns, and in the face of life stresses that most people can handle in stride, he "breaks down." While genetic factors may have played a contributing role, the mental disorder appears to be primarily the consequence of pathogenic family patterns and faulty learning, and hence to be primarily of *social* rather than *genetic* origin.

The view of genius as "akin to insanity." People regarded as geniuses in the arts and sciences have often been looked upon as especially prone to mental illness. Lombroso (1891) and other early writers fostered this misconception by compiling long lists of historical personages who did suffer from mental disorders, in an attempt to prove that genius was related to insanity.

Experimental studies, however, have found no such relationship. After a seventeen-year study of heredity and physical and mental health conditions of 294 highly gifted personalities in the arts and sciences, Juda (1949) concluded that there is "no evidence to support the assumption that the genesis of highest intellectual ability depends on psychic abnormalities." (p. 306) In an even more comprehensive study, Terman followed the lives of over 1300 California school children who had obtained IQ's of 140 or above in the early 1920's. A tally when most of the "children" had reached their mid-forties showed that their death rate, divorce rate, and mental illness rate were all lower than those for the general population (Terman & Oden, 1959). Similarly, MacKinnon (1962), in an intensive study of architects, writers, and other professional personnel considered to be highly creative, failed to find a significant relationship between creative talent and psychopathology. Rather, he emphasized the tendencies of these creative people toward self-acceptance, lack of defensiveness, openness to new experience, and complexity and richness of personality. Such findings effectively explode the old notion that creativity and genius are "akin to insanity."

The view of mental patients as incurable and dangerous. The common misconception persists that mental illness is "incurable." As a consequence, persons who have been discharged from mental hospitals or have suffered severe emotional disturbances are often viewed with suspicion as being unstable and possibly dangerous. Commonly they are discriminated against in employment or job advancement. While it is true that persons with certain forms of mental disorder (such as psychoses associated with senile brain damage) will never recover completely, most of the mentally ill respond well to treatment.

In fact, some 70 to 80 percent of all hospitalized

mental patients recover, and most make a satisfactory adjustment in society. Many achieve a higher level of personality adjustment than before their breakdown. Moreover, the great majority of persons who recover from serious mental illness do not engage in violent or socially disruptive behavior after their release (Giovannoni & Gurel, 1967). In fact, mental hospital patients with no history of arrests before their hospitalization have a strikingly low rate of arrests after release, and are *less* likely than the general population to engage in violent behaviors, such as assault, rape, and homicide (NIMH, 1969).

Here it may be emphasized that the nature of the life situation with which the individual is confronted after his recovery will have a marked effect on his immediate and long-range adjustment.

The belief that mental disorder is a disgrace. Many people who do not hesitate to consult a dentist, an ophthalmologist, a lawyer, or other professional person for assistance with various types of problems are reluctant to go to a psychologist or a psychiatrist with emotional problems. Actually, a mental disorder should be considered no more disgraceful than a physical disorder. Both are adaptive failures.

The National Commission on Community Health Services (1967) has pointed out that, despite the attempt to educate people to a better understanding of mental disorders, there is still a tendency to reject the mentally ill in our society. Whereas most people are sympathetic toward a crippled child or an adult with cancer, they may turn away from the person suffering from an incapacitating mental disorder. Even many psychologists and medical personnel are both uninformed and unsympathetic when they are confronted with problems involving mental illness. Yet the great majority of the mentally ill are doing the best they know how, and desperately need understanding and help.

Fortunately, treatment of mental disorders is becoming recognized as an integral part of total social and community health programs—as indicated by the provisions in Medicare for psychological or psychiatric assistance, together with general medical assistance, for older citizens (Hess, 1966). However, in a survey by Elinson, Padilla, and Perkins (1967) it was found that while the mentally ill are "not uniformly rejected,

the stigma that traditionally has been attached to mental illness still lingers in the minds of many people." Similar findings have been reported by Sarbin and Mancuso (1970).

An exaggerated fear of one's own susceptibility to mental disorder. Fears of possible mental disorder are quite common and cause much needless unhappiness. "Other people seem so self-assured and capable. They cannot possibly have the irrational impulses and fantasies I do, or feel the hostility or anxiety or despair that plagues me." Probably most people feel anxious and discouraged during difficult periods in their lives, and may notice with alarm that they are irritable, have difficulty in concentrating or remembering, or even feel that they are "going to pieces." In one study, a representative sample of Americans were asked if they had ever felt they were going to have a "nervous breakdown." Almost one out of five people interviewed replied "Yes." (U.S. Department of Health, Education and Welfare, 1971).

We should not be misled by the apparent self-confidence and competence of other people into thinking that we alone are unhappy and having difficulty with life's problems. Often we are surprised, when we are going through a particularly difficult period, to find that other people do not notice our distress. By the same token, we often fail to recognize the unhappiness of others. The fact that even the seemingly most successful person may be experiencing serious inner difficulties is dramatically illustrated in E. A. Robinson's poem "Richard Cory" (1943):

Whenever Richard Cory went down town,
We people on the pavement looked at him:
He was a gentleman from sole to crown,
Clean favored, and imperially slim.

And he was always quietly arrayed,
And he was always human when he talked;
But still he fluttered pulses when he said,
"Good morning," and he glittered when he walked.

And he was rich—yes, richer than a king—
And admirably schooled in every grace:
In fine, we thought that he was everything
To make us wish that we were in his place.

So on we worked and waited for the light,
And went without the meat, and cursed the bread;
And Richard Cory, one calm summer night,
Went home and put a bullet through his head.

TERMS USED IN REFERRING TO ABNORMAL BEHAVIOR

The comprehensive terms *abnormal behavior, maladaptive behavior, mental disorder,* and *psychopathology* will be used more or less interchangeably in this book. There are, however, some important distinctions to be noted concerning the use of these terms. The following descriptions not only indicate how they and other key terms are used in the present text, but also allude to differences in usage within the field.

Abnormal behavior	Used in a variety of ways to refer to a person's inner personality makeup or outer behavior or both; to refer to specific behavior like phobias or more pervasive patterns like schizophrenia; to mean chronic, long-lasting problems or those—such as drug intoxication—in which symptoms are acute and temporary. Roughly synonymous with *mental disorder* as so defined; however, in a broader context is synonymous with *maladaptive behavior.*
Maladaptive behavior	As used in this book, a term that widens the conceptual framework of *abnormal behavior* to include any behavior that has undesirable consequences for the individual and/or the group—e.g., includes not only disorders like psychoses and neuroses but also such individual or group patterns as unethical business practices, racial prejudice, alienation, and apathy.
Mental disorder	As indicated above, applies to abnormal behavior patterns, covering the whole range from mild to crippling. Although criticized by some on the grounds that it seems to imply not only a mind-body dualism but also a severe disturbance of normal functioning, *mental disorder* nevertheless is a well-established term and is integral to the only comprehensive (APA) classification system yet to be developed in the field.
Psychopathology	Refers to the study of *abnormal behavior* or *mental disorder;* also used as synonymous with those terms.
Emotional disturbance	Refers to inadequate personality integration and personal distress. Commonly used in referring to maladaptive behavior of children.
Mental illness	Once used as synonymous with *mental disorder* but now ordinarily restricted to disorders involving brain pathology or severe personality disorganization. The label *illness,* although it seems justified when referring to disorders that are severely incapacitating, is hardly appropriate in cases which apparently stem largely from faulty learning (see *behavior disorder*).
Behavior disorder	Used especially in referring to disorders that stem from faulty learning—either the failure to learn needed competencies or the learning of maladaptive coping patterns. May be used more broadly as roughly synonymous with *abnormal behavior.*
Mental disease	Formerly used to refer to disorders associated with brain pathology, but rarely used today.
Insanity	Legal term, indicating that the individual is mentally incompetent to manage his affairs or foresee the consequences of his actions. Denotes serious mental disorder.

In the course of this text, we shall try to clarify these distinctions further. As is the case with most attempts at labeling, none of these terms is completely satisfactory, and professional usage varies a great deal both from person to person and from one school of thought to another.

Of course, any of us may experience serious emotional difficulties, especially when life's problems seem to pile up. In such instances we can avoid unnecessary mistakes and suffering by obtaining competent psychological assistance instead of "worrying it out alone." However, a realization that our difficulties are not unique and that most people have many "loose ends" does help destroy feelings of isolation and of being different which often play a large part in personal fears of mental disorder.

In this connection, it should perhaps be mentioned that medical students, in reading about various physical disorders, are likely to imagine that they have many of the symptoms described; the same reaction is likely among those reading about mental disorders. However, by gaining a better understanding of abnormal behavior and

of the factors that can interfere with or foster mental health, an individual can become increasingly confident of his ability to function effectively.

ABNORMAL BEHAVIOR AS THE SCIENTIST SEES IT

In order to conceptualize abnormal behavior and to assess, treat, and eventually prevent such behavior, the scientist must work out clear definitions of "normal" and "abnormal," and develop criteria for distinguishing one from the other in actual clinical cases. Unfortunately this has not proven an easy task.

WHAT DO WE MEAN BY "ABNORMAL"?

Since the word *abnormal* literally means "away from the normal," it implies deviation from some clearly defined norm. In the case of physical illness, the norm is the structural and functional integrity of the body, and the boundary lines between normality and pathology can usually be clearly delineated by medical science. On a psychological level, however, we have no "ideal model" or even "normal model" of man to use as a base of comparison. Thus we suffer considerable confusion and disagreement as to just what is or what is not *normal*, a confusion aggravated by the rapid change and upset of old, established norms.

In part, too, our difficulty stems from clinicians' preoccupation with abnormal behavior and consequent neglect of the concept of the normal. The philosopher Kaplan (1967, p. 325) has formulated a principle called the "Law of the Instrument" which he finds operative throughout the behavioral sciences. He illustrates it this way: "If you give a small boy a hammer, it will turn out that everything he runs into needs pounding." Inevitably, clinical psychologists and other "helping personnel," because of the job they are doing, tend to focus on personality difficulties rather than on normal functioning. Their theoretical

formulations have inevitably reflected this orientation.

The chart on pages 16-17 summarizes some of the complementary and conflicting approaches that have been used in defining mental health and abnormal behavior. Briefly, they may be described as (1) the formulation of general, comprehensive definitions as to what constitutes mental health, e.g., self-fulfillment; (2) the delineation of traits that a normal, mentally healthy person would show, in the opinion of most investigators, e.g., self-acceptance and self-direction; (3) the establishment of criteria for considering behavior abnormal, e.g., deviation from statistical or social norms; and (4) the basing of concepts of normal and abnormal on a particular model or set of assumptions about human nature. The four approaches may thus be viewed as a "frontal attack," a multiple traits approach, a specific criterion approach, and a theoretical systems approach, respectively.

From the diversity of these various approaches there emerge two basic and conflicting views of abnormal behavior. One maintains that the concepts of "normal" and "abnormal" are meaningful only with reference to a given culture: normal behavior conforms to social expectations, whereas abnormal behavior does not. The other view maintains that behavior is abnormal if it is maladaptive—that is, if it interferes with the ability of the individual and/or the group to function as effectively as possible. We shall examine each of these perspectives in turn.

Abnormal behavior as culturally relative. A number of social scientists have argued the view that conformity to social norms approximates normality, while deviation from such norms constitutes abnormality. This position has been well formulated in recent years by Ullmann and Krasner (1965; 1969), who maintain that *abnormal* is simply a label of convenience for behavior patterns that fail to meet social expectations. Because such behavior is disturbing to other people, society assumes that it ought to be changed. Ullmann and Krasner summarize their position as follows:

"For social life to be possible, people must be able to predict with some degree of accuracy the responses of their fellows. The failure to live up to social expectations is called *deviance,* and the special subclass of deviance which currently sanctions the intervention of the mental health professions is called *abnormal behavior.* This definition stems from a view that abnormal behavior is a label of convenience and that in actuality behavior considered abnormal is no different in its development and maintenance from behavior considered normal. It also stresses that no act by itself can be called abnormal, but rather that the social context of the act and actor must be taken into account." (1969, p. 6)

Ullmann and Krasner maintain that behavior cannot be considered abnormal so long as society accepts it. As cultural relativists, they reject the concept of a "sick society," in which normative behavior might be viewed as pathological:

"A critical example is whether an obedient Nazi concentration-camp commander would be considered normal or abnormal. To the extent that he was responding accurately and successfully to his environment and not breaking its rules, much less coming to the professional attention of psychiatrists, he would not be labeled abnormal. Repulsive as his behavior is to mid-twentieth-century Americans, such repulsion is based on a particular set of values. Although such a person may be made liable for his acts—as Nazi war criminals were—the concept of abnormality as a special entity does not seem necessary or justified. If it is, the problem arises as to who selects the values, and this, in turn, implies that one group may select values that are applied to others. This situation of one group's values being dominant over others is the fascistic background from which the Nazi camp commander sprang." (1969, p. 15)

The acceptance of complete cultural relativism obviously simplifies the task of defining abnormality: behavior is abnormal if—and only if—society labels it as such. But serious questions must be raised about the validity of this definition. It rests on the questionable assumption that socially accepted behavior is never pathological, and it implies that normality is nothing more than conformity.

The task of the psychotherapist, in Ullmann and Krasner's view, is not to foster mental health but rather to teach the individual socially appropriate behavior so that he can "take his place in society." (1969, p. 593). Scientific and philosophic objections to this approach are compounded by the practical difficulty of deciding what is "socially appropriate" for a given individual. In the final analysis, the therapist cannot avoid making value judgments. As Ullmann and Krasner admit,

". . . it is sometimes hard to determine a person's place in the world. A white supremacist and a black nationalist might well differ as to what the proper place of a specific person is, and the positive value of one might well be the negative value of the other. The point which cannot be escaped is that casting the therapist as a teacher raises the problem of what he shall teach. The decision of what he shall teach involves concepts of good and bad." (1969, p. 593)

Ullmann and Krasner thus pinpoint a basic contradiction in their own theoretical position. It maintains that no group has a right to select values and apply them to other groups, yet it accepts the need for a psychotherapist to decide what social values should be accepted by the people he treats.

Abnormal behavior as maladaptive. Some degree of social conformity is clearly essential to group life, and some kinds of deviance are clearly harmful not only to society but to the individual. However, the present text maintains that the best criterion for determining the normality of behavior is not whether society accepts it but rather whether it fosters the well-being of the individual and, ultimately, of the group. By *well-being* is meant not simply maintenance or survival but also growth and fulfillment—the actualization of potentialities. According to this criterion, even conforming behavior is abnormal if it is *maladaptive,* i.e., if it interferes with optimal functioning and growth. So defined, "abnormal behavior" includes not only disorders like psychoses and neuroses but also patterns such as alcoholism, unethical business practices, racial

THE PROBLEM OF DEFINING "NORMAL" AND "ABNORMAL"

Because we have no "ideal model" of man, it is difficult to specify exactly what is meant by "normal" and "abnormal." Mental health personnel have taken one or a combination of four approaches in their attempts to agree on what they mean by these terms: (1) formulating general, comprehensive definitions; (2) trying to delineate the traits that a normal, mentally healthy person would show; (3) establishing criteria for considering behavior abnormal; and (4) basing concepts of "normal" and "abnormal" on a particular model, or set of assumptions, about human nature. (The models summarized here will be discussed at some length in Chapter 3.)

GENERAL DEFINITIONS

World Health Organization	Health is "a state of complete physical, mental, and social well-being and not merely the absence of disease or infirmity."
Karl Menninger, a psychiatrist	"Let us define mental health as the adjustment of human beings to the world and to each other with a maximum of effectiveness and happiness. Not just efficiency, or just contentment—or the grace of obeying the rules of the game cheerfully. It is all of these together. It is the ability to maintain an even temper, an alert intelligence, socially considerate behavior, and a happy disposition. This, I think, is a healthy mind."
H. B. English, a psychologist	Mental health is "a relatively enduring state wherein the person is well adjusted, has a zest for living, and is attaining self-actualization or self-realization. It is a positive state and not mere absence of mental disorder."
W. W. Boehm, a social worker	Mental health is "a condition and level of social functioning which is socially acceptable and personally satisfying."

TRAITS OF A HEALTHY PERSON

Attitudes toward self	Emphasizing self-acceptance, adequate self-identity, realistic appraisal of one's assets and liabilities.
Perception of reality	A realistic view of oneself and the surrounding world of people and things.
Integration	Unity of personality, freedom from disabling inner conflicts, good stress tolerance.
Competencies	Development of essential physical, intellectual, emotional, and social competencies for coping with life problems.
Autonomy	Adequate self-reliance, responsibility, and self-direction—together with sufficient independence of social influences.
Growth, self-actualization	Emphasizing trends toward increasing maturity, development of potentialities, and self-fulfillment as a person.

prejudice, alienation, and apathy. All are indicative of biological, psychological, or sociological maladaptations that impair individual and/or group well-being.

In adopting this criterion, we are making two basic assumptions, namely: (1) that survival and actualization are worth striving for on both individual and group levels; and (2) that human behavior can be evaluated in terms of its consequences for these objectives. The first assumption is clearly a value judgment and therefore subject to criticism on the grounds that it is "unscientific." But unless we make such a judgment, there is little point in trying to define abnormal behavior—or in trying to do something about it.

Our second assumption, that behavior can be evaluated as adaptive or maladaptive, has a solid scientific basis. For in much the same way that the biological sciences have been able to identify conditions that are conducive or detrimental to physical health, the social sciences have begun delineating conditions that foster or impede the

CRITERIA OF ABNORMALITY

Deviation from statistical norms Abnormality as what is unusual, atypical, literally "away from the norm." Most traits are distributed according to the familiar bell-shaped "normal" curve, in which two thirds of the cases fall in the middle third of the range. This criterion is appropriate in the case of some traits, such as aggressiveness, where scores at either end of the scale—extreme aggressiveness or extreme passiveness—suggest maladaptive behavior. But for traits like intelligence, it is clearly unsuitable; genius would be considered as abnormal as retardation.

Deviation from social norms Abnormality as nonconformity. This is the criterion of cultural relativism: whatever is prevalent is normal. Few would accept it, stated so baldly, though in practice it is commonly used. According to this norm, head-hunting or war crimes and atrocities would be normal if the society condoned them, abnormal if it did not. Two questionable assumptions are involved: that the values and activities of the majority are always desirable and that individual behavior in conformity with the current norms is always in the best interest of both the individual and the group.

Maladjustment Abnormality as ineffectiveness in adjusting to the demands placed on the individual by his physical and social environment and by his own needs. The concept is useful in clinical assessment but is essentially negative: it does not take into account the fact that a "well-adjusted" individual may not be using his potentialities.

Personal distress Abnormality as serious feelings of anxiety, depression, or guilt. Chronic distress may be a signal that something is wrong, but personal distress may also be a normal reaction in a situation of great sorrow or frustration or injustice. It would be the person who did not react in such a way who would be in need of treatment. Thus personal distress is an inadequate criterion for distinguishing between normal and abnormal behavior.

Personal immaturity Abnormality as behaving inappropriately for one's age level, inappropriately with reference to the seriousness of the situation and one's resources for meeting it. Though some kinds of behavior, such as temper tantrums or extreme dependency, would be easy to label as "immature," it would be much more difficult to settle on criteria of "appropriateness" and "maturity." One attempt at delineating traits related to maturity appears on page 16.

VIEWS BASED ON MODELS OF MAN

The psychoanalytic model Emphasizes man's basic instinctual drives, such as sex. Mental health is viewed as the ability to gratify these drives within limits imposed by society. Abnormal behavior is seen as the result of faulty development or exaggerated defensive measures in coping with anxiety.

The behavioristic model Emphasizes overt behavior, seen as the organism's attempt to adapt to environmental stimuli. Abnormality is seen as ineffective adaptation resulting from the learning of maladaptive responses and/or the failure to learn needed ones.

The humanistic model Emphasizes man's natural tendencies toward responsible self-direction and self-fulfillment. Abnormality is seen as failure to develop one's full humanity as a result of a blocking or distortion of these tendencies toward growth and self-fulfillment.

The existential model Emphasizes the primary reality of the individual's conscious experience and decisions. Abnormality is viewed as the failure to achieve an adequate self-identity and a meaningful way of life.

The interpersonal model Emphasizes the role of interpersonal relationships in shaping development and behavior. Abnormal behavior is seen as stemming from interpersonal relations and accommodations of a pathological type.

Chart based on material from Allport (1961), Bandura (1969), Boehm (1955), Bugental (1967), Cantril (1967), Carson (1969), Cox (1970), English and English (1958), Jahoda (1958), Maslow (1967), Menninger (1945), Peck (1959), Rogers (1967), and Sabahin (1967).

fulfillment of human potentialities. They have noted, for example, the probable effects of such factors as parental neglect or racial discrimination on a child's early development and on his later capacity for self-acceptance and achievement. There is no need for recourse to moral judgments in labeling such patterns abnormal.

The conception of abnormal behavior as maladaptive provides a framework that should make possible increasingly precise definitions of "normal" and "abnormal" as more knowledge is accumulated about the unique nature of man and his requirements for optimal functioning and growth. It has the further advantage of enabling us to assess abnormal behavior patterns not only of individuals but also of groups (whether families, corporate structures, communities, or whole societies). Increasingly, those concerned with the assessment, treatment, and prevention of abnormal behavior are looking beyond the individual and trying to evaluate—and if possible correct—pathogenic relationships in his social milieu. Seldom is the goal of therapy defined today solely in terms of helping the individual become better adjusted to his life situation, no matter what it may be.

THE PROBLEM OF CLASSIFICATION

Classification is a first step toward introducing some order into our discussion of the nature, causes, and treatment of abnormal behavior. Classification proper involves the delineation of various types, or categories, of maladaptive behavior; this provides a basis for studying the causes and treatment of such behavior, and for communicating about mental disorders in agreed-upon and meaningful ways. The problem of classification is complicated by the fact that the term *abnormal behavior* is used in a variety of ways— to refer to a person's inner personality makeup or outer behavior or both; to mean specific behaviors like phobias or more pervasive patterns like schizophrenia; to mean chronic, long-lasting abnormalities or those—such as drug intoxication —in which symptoms are acute and temporary. We shall try to clarify these various usages in the course of our discussion.

Ideally, a classification scheme should not only describe maladaptive behavior but should also point to certain causal patterns and appropriate treatment procedures. This is a formidable requirement, and none of the various classification schemes developed so far have been completely satisfactory. In 1952, the American Psychiatric Association adopted a classification of mental disorders that was based largely on a scheme worked out by the United States Army during World War II. In 1968, the APA adopted a modified classification worked out in conjunction with the World Health Organization.[1] This international classification permits comparisons of the incidence, types of disorders, treatment procedures, and other relevant data concerning mental disorders throughout the world. However, as we shall see, it has certain serious limitations.

Current classification of mental disorders. A complete outline of the current APA classification—with its ten categories of mental disorders— appears on the endsheets at the back of this book. These ten categories may be regarded for purposes of clarity as fitting into three still broader categories: organic brain syndromes, disorders of psychogenic or possible psychogenic origin, and mental retardation. The following is a brief listing of the disorders in each of the three main groups:

1. *Organic brain syndromes.* Disorders in which there is organic brain pathology include:

a) *Acute brain disorders*—cases involving brain malfunctioning, due to such conditions as high fever or drug intoxication, in which there may be confusion, delusions, hallucinations, or other behavior disturbances. Ordinarily these disturbances are temporary.

b) *Chronic brain disorders*—cases involving brain tumors, head injuries, cerebral arteriosclerosis, or other conditions that result in extensive and lasting damage to the brain. Some impairment of learning, judgment, memory, and emotional response can be expected to occur and persist.

Both acute and chronic brain disorders may vary greatly in severity, from mild impairment of psychological functioning to psychotic conditions that involve severe personality disorganization.

2. *Disorders of psychogenic or possible psychogenic origin.* Disorders in which there is no apparent or presently known physical cause or brain pathology include:

a) *Transient situational disturbances*—disturbances that are precipitated by acute or special stress, in which individuals may show panic, severe shock, disorganization, and other behavior indicative of personality disturbance. The individuals typically involved are previously stable, and they show good ability to recover.

b) *Neuroses*—reactions involving various maladaptive behaviors that lower the individual's effectiveness in dealing with the problems of living. Several specific types are included here, including anxiety, phobic, hysterical, and hypochondriacal patterns. Unlike the psychoses, neuroses do not ordinarily involve loss of contact with reality or gross personality disorganization.

c) *Functional psychoses*—disorders characterized by severe degrees of personality disorganization and a loss of adequate contact with reality. They include schizophrenia, paranoia, and major affective disorders, such as manic-depressive psychoses. Although these disorders are commonly classified as being of psychogenic origin,

---

[1]Diagnostic and Statistical Manual of Mental Disorders. American Psychiatric Association: Washington, D.C., 1968.

PATIENTS IN STATE AND COUNTY MENTAL HOSPITALS FROM 1880 TO 1970
(Approximate Figures)

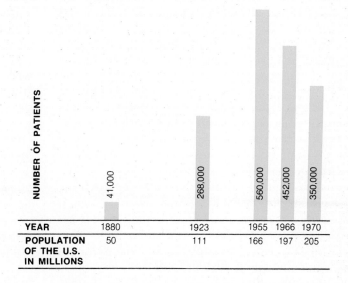

The year 1970 represented the fifteenth consecutive year in which the resident population of state and county mental hospitals showed a decline. This decline is considered to be due to a number of factors, including (1) introduction of major tranquilizing and antidepressant drugs; (2) increased availability of alternate care facilities for the aged (for example, nursing homes); (3) reduction in length and stay of first admissions; (4) more effective aftercare facilities; and (5) introduction of outpatient clinics, day hospitals, and related community health facilities.

Based on Yolles (1967), U.S. Public Health Service (1969; 1970)

YEAR	1880	1923	1955	1966	1970
	41,000	268,000	560,000	452,000	350,000
POPULATION OF THE U.S. IN MILLIONS	50	111	166	197	205

accompanying biochemical changes that disturb brain functioning may also play a key role. Usually hospitalization is required for treatment, although an increasing number of functional psychotics are being treated in their home and community setting.

d) *Personality (character) disorders*—a group of disorders characterized by deeply ingrained, socially maladaptive behaviors, including antisocial or psychopathic personality, sexual deviation, and dependence on alcohol or drugs—diverse patterns that may have little in common. Often the individual involved reveals a life-long pattern of socially undesirable behavior that is recognizable by adolescence or earlier.

e) *Psychophysiologic (psychosomatic) disorders* —a wide range of bodily conditions in which emotional factors play a key role, such as migraine headaches, hypertension, dermatitis, and peptic ulcers. Typically persons with such disorders do not display the maladaptive behaviors and suffering of the neurotic, the severe personality disorganization of the psychotic, or the socially undesirable behavior of those manifesting character disorders.

3. *Mental retardation.* This category refers to subnormal general intellectual functioning that originates during early development and is asso-

ciated with impairment of learning and other psychological functioning. The degree of retardation may vary from profound (IQ under 20) to borderline (IQ 68–83). The retardation may result from genetic defects, brain injury or other organic causes, or psychosocial (environmental) deprivation.

The new APA classification has also added a special category for the behavior disorders of childhood and adolescence. Although most of the mental disorders listed above can occur at any time during a person's life cycle, the special problems that may occur in youth warrant separate categorization. We will discuss these in Chapter 17.

In referring to mental disorders, several qualifying terms are commonly used: *acute* and *chronic*, for example, are often used in connection with schizophrenia, as well as with the organic brain syndromes; *episodic* may be used to refer to recurrent maladaptive patterns, such as depressions of a cyclic nature; and *mild, moderate,* and *severe* are commonly used in describing transient situational disorders, psychophysiologic disorders, and mental retardation.

In discussing specific patterns of abnormal behavior (Part III), this text makes some modifications in the APA classification scheme, as necessary for instructional purposes. It also includes a chapter on the abnormal behavior of groups, which is not covered in the APA classification.

Limitations of classification. The presently accepted classification of mental disorders suffers from a number of serious limitations— some of which would probably characterize any classification scheme.

While the present system attempts to delineate maladaptive behavior and also to point to certain causal patterns and appropriate treatment procedures, some of its most important categories—such as the functional psychoses and the personality disorders—are mainly descriptive. Consequently, one must guard against the tendency to think something has been explained when in fact it may only have been named. This limitation is not exclusive to the APA classification, but rather reflects the fact that scientific understanding of psychopathology is still far from complete.

A second limitation involves the failure to take into consideration the group setting or the pathological behavior of groups. Disturbed families, delinquent subcultures, and even pathological societies represent maladaptive patterns that do not fit into the classification scheme. Classifying only individual behavior as abnormal implies that a lack of harmony between an individual and his social milieu represents maladjustment on his part, and that he is the one who must change. But this attitude casts the mental health profession in the role of a force for the preservation of the establishment or status quo. We shall deal further with this point in the course of this text; but in our own discussion we shall deal with pathogenic families and maladaptive group behavior as well as with the maladaptive behavior of individuals. And the attempt will be made to show the interaction and vicious circles that may ensue from such behaviors.

A third limitation is the failure to provide for changing patterns of maladaptive behavior. Not adequately covered in the current classification are maladaptive patterns that are emerging in our rapidly changing society, such as an individual's dehumanization and alienation in an impersonal mass bureaucracy—as well as the effects of the tremendous stress imposed on the individual by the accelerating rate of technological and social change. In short, we need to be able to predict trends in mental disorders and the problems we are likely to encounter in the near and more remote future.

In defense of the present APA classification, it should be noted that it does provide an idea of the range of behaviors considered to be abnormal in major societies throughout the world. Familiarity with it helps teachers, researchers, clinicians, and students to be sure they are talking about the same thing when they are communicating about abnormal behavior patterns. Also, it is useful to know what a label like *schizophrenia* is intended to mean, since labels—for better or for worse— do influence the way we perceive and react to other persons.

ASSESSING AND TREATING MALADAPTIVE BEHAVIOR

What is involved in helping people overcome maladaptive behaviors? With disorders so diverse and, until recently, so little understood, it is inevitable that conflicting views of the nature, causation, treatment, and prevention of abnormal behavior should have developed.

Identifying those who need help. Before maladaptive behavior patterns can be corrected, they must first be identified. Procedures for assessing abnormal behavior vary considerably, but, in general, a clinician's judgment is made on the basis of how well an individual is meeting demands placed on him, how well his behavior is meeting his overall needs, and whether his behavior is socially responsible. Sometimes assessment of a given person is undertaken because of his own complaints; perhaps he is anxious, depressed, lacks satisfying interpersonal relationships, or has other worries. In other cases mental health personnel may take the initiative at someone else's request and may use interview procedures and medical as well as psychological tests to ascertain whether an individual is unduly depressed, shows schizophrenic tendencies, or manifests other maladaptive patterns.

Here it may be emphasized that being labeled a "neurotic," "schizophrenic," "alcoholic," and so on, may have unfortunate effects. The label may devalue the individual's concept of himself; it may provide him with a "sick role" which he thinks he is expected to play; and it may adversely influence his interpersonal relationships and occupational and other opportunities. Such effects as these are largely responsible for the current trend away from rigid labeling and classification. Further, it becomes apparent that those charged with deciding when a person's behavior is abnormal—and how abnormal it is—have an awesome responsibility to the individual and to society.

Helping fields and personnel. At the present time there are several distinct but closely related professional fields concerned with the study of abnormal behavior and with mental health. The distinction among them is often hard to draw precisely, because although each has its own functions and areas of work, the contributions in one field are constantly influencing the thinking and work in others.

Abnormal psychology has long been referred to as that part of the field of psychology concerned with the understanding, treatment, and prevention of abnormal behavior. However, the term is now relegated largely to titles of courses in colleges and universities that cover the subject matter of abnormal behavior. In other contexts it has generally been replaced by the terms *clinical psychology* (the professional field broadly concerned with the assessment, treatment, and study of abnormal behavior) and *experimental psychopathology* (a somewhat more specialized field concerned primarily with research). *Counseling psychology*, which overlaps with clinical psychology, is concerned primarily with supportive help to essentially normal individuals who have problems related to educational, occupational, and marital decisions and adjustments. *Psychiatry* is the branch of medicine that specializes in the understanding, diagnosis, treatment, and prevention of mental disorders; thus it is closely related to clinical psychology. *Psychiatric nursing* is the branch of nursing that focuses upon the care of mental patients. *Social work*, an offshoot of sociology, entails the analysis of social data and the provision of services to foster adjustment of the individual in his family and social setting.

As a consequence of the shortage of trained personnel in the mental health field, increasing attention is being given to the possibility of utiliz-

ing personnel with less professional training, particularly for helping in crises related to marital, occupational, and family problems—where prompt help is especially important. Such help may be provided in neighborhood centers by mature and experienced people, and thus may not only assist the individual involved but also may contribute to greater integration and cohesion in the community.

Of growing importance in helping the maladjusted is the "team" approach to assessment and treatment. This approach involves the coordinated efforts of medical, psychological, social work, and other mental health personnel working together

Trapped between childhood and adulthood, many adolescents in our society go through difficult crises that call for professional assistance.

as the needs of each case warrant. Also of key importance is the trend toward providing treatment facilities in the community. Instead of considering maladjustment as a private misery of the individual, often requiring his confinement in a distant mental hospital, this approach focuses on the web of interpersonal relationships and the general social milieu in which he is involved, and attempts to utilize family and community resources in an integrated treatment program.

THE ORIENTATION OF THIS BOOK

Throughout this book we shall be attempting to acquire a perspective on abnormal behavior and its place in contemporary society. Although we shall deal with all of the major categories of mental disorders, we shall not attempt an encyclopedic coverage, but rather shall focus on those patterns that seem most relevant to an understanding of abnormal behavior—on both individual and group levels. And while we shall not hesitate to include the unusual or bizarre, our emphasis will be on the unity of human behavior, ranging from the normal to the abnormal end of the continuum.

It is our conviction that a sound and comprehensive study of abnormal behavior should be based on the following concepts:

1. *A scientific approach to abnormal behavior.* Any comprehensive view of man and his behavior must draw upon concepts and research findings from a variety of scientific fields. Of particular relevance are the fields of genetics, neurophysiology, sociology, and anthropology, as well as psychology. Such common scientific concepts as causal processes, control groups, dependent variables, placebos, and models and theories will figure prominently in our discussion. Emphasis will also be placed on the application of learning principles to the understanding and treatment of mental disorders. And while we shall view science as the most dependable source of information about abnormal behavior, we shall draw upon information from other specified sources as well.

2. *An awareness of man's existential problems.* There are many experiences and problems common to human existence about which science as yet has had little to say. Included are such vital experiences as hope, faith, courage, love, grief, despair, death, and man's quest for values and meaning. Authentic insights into such experiences can often be gained from literature, drama, and biographical accounts that strike a common chord and relate directly to an understanding of human behavior. In addition, material from such fields as art, history, and religion will be utilized for the insights it provides. However, such information will be distinguished from that obtained through scientific observation.

3. *Respect for the dignity, integrity, and growth potential of the individual.* A basic orientation for this book is well described in the statement of the Ethical Standards of Psychologists, formulated by the American Psychological Association:

"The psychologist believes in the dignity and worth of the individual human being. He is committed to increasing man's understanding of himself and others." (1963, p. 56)

Implicit in this statement is a view of man, not merely as a product of his past conditioning and his life experiences, but as a potentially active agent as well—one who can develop and use his capacities for building the kind of life he chooses for himself and the kind of world he chooses for mankind.

In attempting throughout this volume to provide a perspective for viewing abnormal behavior, we shall focus not only on what maladaptive patterns, such as schizophrenia, look like to observers, but also on how such disorders feel to the individuals experiencing them. In dealing with the major patterns of abnormal behavior, we shall focus upon four significant aspects of each: clinical picture, causes, treatment, and outcomes.

Most of the space in this volume will be devoted to specific patterns of abnormal behavior. Initially, however, we shall trace the emergence and nature of our contemporary views of mental disorders; and we shall review the information and concepts essential for an understanding of these disorders. Later we shall devote two chapters to a detailed study of methods of assessment and treatment. And in our final chapter, we shall deal with the problem of preventing mental disorders, and the potentialities of modern psychology and allied sciences for helping mankind to achieve a more sane and harmonious world.

In this introduction we have briefly reviewed the nature and scope of abnormal behavior; we have surveyed some examples of mental disorders from history, literature, and drama; we have noted some popular misconceptions of mental disorders; we have dealt with the scientific problem of explaining what we mean by "abnormal"; and we have briefly reviewed the problem of assessment and treatment.

Some of the problems of classification were also mentioned and a summary was presented of the current APA listing of disorders. Part Three follows this scheme with minor modifications.

In the course of our discussion, we have emphasized that: (1) *abnormal behavior* may be defined as *maladaptive*; (2) human behavior falls along a continuum which extends from highly adaptive behavior at one extreme to highly maladaptive behavior at the other; (3) a person's position on this continuum of adjustment may shift over time; (4) maladaptive behavior may involve relatively specific responses or permeate the entire life style of the individual; and (5) the same principles that are used to conceptualize and understand normal behavior are also applicable to abnormal or maladaptive behavior.

Having presented this introduction to the study of abnormal behavior, we shall proceed in the next three chapters to trace the progress that has been made in understanding psychopathology from ancient times to the present.

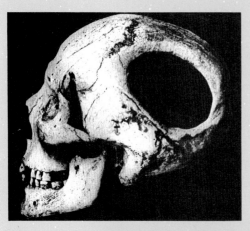

Historical Perspectives and the Medical Model

2

ABNORMAL BEHAVIOR IN ANCIENT TIMES

DEMONOLOGY IN THE MIDDLE AGES

DEVELOPMENT OF HUMANITARIAN APPROACHES

DEVELOPMENT OF THE ORGANIC VIEWPOINT AND THE MEDICAL MODEL

With the development of modern research methods, psychopharmacological drugs, techniques of psychotherapy, and community mental health concepts and facilities, we feel that we have come a long way from the superstitious and often cruel treatment of mental disorders characteristic of earlier times. The story of this journey is a fascinating one, and one that will help us understand how modern views of abnormal behavior have come about. For not only do many popular misconceptions about mental disorders have roots in the dim historical past, but even our modern scientific concepts are the result of a long developmental process. For example, electroshock treatment for severe depression is antedated by flogging, immersing a person in cold water, and other crude "shock" treatments devised by the ancients. As Rabkin (1966) has noted, even the method of "free association"—a cornerstone of psychoanalytic therapy, designed to allow repressed conflicts and emotions to enter conscious awareness—is described by the Greek playwright Aristophanes in his play *The Clouds*. Interestingly enough, the scene in which Socrates tries to calm and bring self-knowledge to Strepsiades is complete with a couch!

In this chapter we shall trace the evolution of man's views on psychopathology from ancient times to the turn of the present century—with the development of the organic viewpoint and the medical model. Only recently, as we shall see, have mental disorders been recognized as having natural causes. The great advances that have come about during the twentieth century in the understanding and treatment of abnormal behavior become all the more remarkable when viewed against the long background of ignorance, superstition, and fear.

ABNORMAL BEHAVIOR IN ANCIENT TIMES

Although man presumably appeared on earth some four million or more years ago, his written records extend back only a few thousand years. Thus our knowledge of "primitive man" is very limited and often based on extrapolation from so-called primitive peoples who remained isolated and relatively static into modern times. Beginning with the Egyptian and other ancient civilizations, historical information becomes more reliable, although far from complete.

DEMONOLOGY AMONG THE ANCIENTS

The earliest treatment of mental illness of which we have any knowledge was that practiced by Stone Age cavemen some half million years ago. For certain forms of mental disorders, probably those in which the individual complained of severe headaches and developed convulsive attacks, the early shaman, or medicine man, treated the disorder by means of an operation now called *trephining*. This operation was performed with crude stone instruments and consisted of chipping away one area of the skull in the form of a circle until the skull was cut through. This opening, called a *trephine*, presumably permitted the evil spirit which supposedly was causing all the trouble to escape—and incidentally may have relieved a certain amount of pressure on the brain. In some cases trephined skulls of primitive men show healing around the opening, indicating that the individual survived the operation and lived for many years afterward (Selling, 1943).

References to mental disorders in the early writings of the Chinese, Egyptians, Hebrews, and Greeks show that they generally attributed such disorders to demons which had taken possession of the individual. This is not surprising when we remember that "good" and "bad" spirits were widely used to explain lightning, thunder, earthquakes, storms, fires, sickness, and many other events which otherwise seemed incomprehen-

sible. It was probably a very simple and logical step to extend this theory to peculiar and incomprehensible behavior in their fellows.

The decision as to whether the "possession" involved good spirits or evil spirits usually depended upon the individual's symptoms. If his speech or behavior appeared to have a religious or mystical significance, it was usually thought that he was possessed by a good spirit or god. Such individuals were often treated with considerable awe and respect, for it was thought that they had supernatural powers. In the Bible story, David took advantage of this popular belief when he simulated "madness" in order to escape from Achish, the king of Gath (Samuel 21:12–14).

Most possessions, however, were considered to be the work of evil spirits, particularly when the individual became excited and overactive and engaged in behavior contrary to the teachings of the priests and temple worshipers. Among the ancient Hebrews, such possessions were thought to represent the wrath and punishment of God. Moses is quoted in the Bible as saying, "The Lord shall smite thee with madness. . . ." Apparently this involved primarily the withdrawal of God's protection, and the abandonment of the individual to the forces of evil. For example, Saul presumably disobeyed God, with the result that the spirit of the Lord left him and an evil spirit was thereby permitted to enter. In such cases every effort was made to rid the person of the evil spirit. Christ reportedly cured a man with an "unclean spirit" by transferring the devils that plagued him to a herd of swine who, in turn, became possessed and "ran violently down a steep place into the sea" (Mark 5:1–13).

The primary type of treatment for demoniacal possession was *exorcism*, which included various techniques that were developed for casting the evil spirit out of the body of the afflicted one. These varied considerably but typically included prayer, incantation, noisemaking, and the use of various horrible-tasting concoctions, such as purgatives made from sheep's dung and wine. In extreme cases flogging, starving, and other more severe measures were often used in an attempt to make the body of the afflicted person such an unpleasant place that the evil spirit would be driven out.

Such treatment was originally in the hands of shamans, but was eventually taken over in Greece, China, and Egypt by the priests, who were apparently a curious mixture of priest, physician, psychologist, and magician. Although these priests were dominated in the main by beliefs in demonology and established exorcistic practices, they did make a beginning in the more humane and scientific treatment of mental disturbances. For example, as early as 860 B.C. in the temples of Asclepius in Greece, the priests supplemented the usual prayer and incantation with kindness, suggestion, and recreational measures, such as theatricals, riding, walking, and harmonious music. However, starving, flogging, and chains were still advocated for recalcitrant patients.

EARLY PHILOSOPHICAL
AND MEDICAL CONCEPTS

During the Golden Age of Greece we find considerable progress being made in the understanding and treatment of mental illness. Originally, membership in the medical priesthood of the Greek temples of healing was hereditary, but gradually outsiders were admitted and various "schools" began to form. It was in one of these groups that Hippocrates received his early training.

Hippocrates. The great Greek physician Hippocrates (460–357 B.C.) has been called the "father of modern medicine." He denied the intervention of deities and demons in the development of disease, and insisted that mental disorders had natural causes and required treatment like other diseases. His position was unequivocal: "For my own part, I do not believe that the human body is ever befouled by a God." (Lewis, 1941, p. 37) As the basic explanation of mental illness, Hippocrates emphasized the view, earlier set forth by Pythagoras, that the brain was the central organ of intellectual activity and that mental illness was due to brain pathology. Hippocrates also emphasized the importance of heredity and predisposition and pointed out that

injuries to the head could cause sensory and motor disorders.

Hippocrates classified all the varieties of mental disorder into three general categories—mania, melancholia, and phrenitis—and he gave detailed clinical descriptions of the specific disorders included in each category, such as alcoholic delirium and epilepsy. Hippocrates relied heavily upon clinical observation, and his descriptions, which were based upon the daily clinical records of his patients, were surprisingly thorough in their coverage. It is interesting to note that Hippocrates realized the clinical importance of dreams for understanding the personality of the patient. On this point he anticipated one of the principal concepts of contemporary psychoanalysis.

The methods of treatment advocated by Hippocrates were far in advance of the exorcistic practices then prevalent. For the treatment of melancholia, for example, he prescribed a regular and tranquil life, sobriety and abstinence from all excesses, a vegetable diet, continence, exercise short of fatigue, and bleeding if indicated. For hysteria,[1] which was thought to be restricted to women and caused by the wandering of the uterus to various parts of the body because of its pining for children, Hippocrates recommended marriage as the best remedy. He also believed in the importance of environment, and not infrequently removed his patients from their families.

Hippocrates' emphasis upon natural causes, clinical observations, and brain pathology in relation to mental disorders was truly revolutionary. Like his contemporaries, however, Hippocrates had very little knowledge of physiology. (Greek physicians were poor physiologists and anatomists because they deified the human body and dared not dissect it.) Thus in his concept of the "four humors"—blood, black bile, yellow bile, and phlegm—Hippocrates apparently conceived the notion of a balance of physiological processes as essential to normal brain functioning and mental health. In his work *On Sacred Disease*, he stated that when the humors were adversely mixed or otherwise disturbed, physical or mental disease resulted: "depravement of the brain arises from phlegm and bile; those mad from phlegm

---

[1] The appearance of symptoms of physical illness in the absence of organic pathology.

are quiet, depressed and oblivious; those from bile excited, noisy and mischievous." Although this concept went far beyond demonology, it was too crude physiologically to be of any great value. Medical treatment based on such inadequate anatomical and physiological knowledge was to continue for many centuries, often proving both humorous and tragic.

Plato and Aristotle. The problem of dealing with mentally disturbed individuals who committed criminal acts was studied by the great philosopher Plato (429–347 B.C.). He made it clear that such persons were obviously not responsible for their acts and should not receive punishment in the same way as normal persons: ". . . someone may commit an act when mad or afflicted with disease . . . [if so,] let him pay simply for the damage; and let him be exempt from other punishment." Plato also made provision for mental cases to be cared for in the community as follows: "If anyone is insane, let him not be seen openly in the city, but let the relatives of such a person watch over him in the best manner they know of; and if they are negligent, let them pay a fine. . . ." (Plato, n.d., p. 56) In addition to this emphasis on the more humane treatment of the mentally ill, Plato contributed to a better understanding of human behavior by pointing out that man, as well as all other forms of life, was motivated by physiologic needs or "natural appetites." He also seems to have anticipated Freud's insight into the functions of fantasies and dreams as substitutive satisfactions, concluding that in dreams, desire tended to satisfy itself in imagery when the higher faculties no longer inhibited the "passions." In his *Republic* Plato emphasized the importance of individual differences in intellectual and other abilities, and pointed out the role of sociocultural influences in shaping the thinking and behavior of the individual. Despite these modern ideas, however, Plato shared the belief of his time that mental disorders were partly organic, partly moral, and partly divine.

The question of whether mental disorders could be caused by psychological factors like frustration and conflict was discussed and rejected by the celebrated systematist Aristotle (384–322 B.C.), who was a pupil but not a follower of Plato. In his extensive writings on men-

tal illness, Aristotle generally followed the Hippocratic theory of disturbances in the bile. For example, he believed that very hot bile generated amorous desires and loquacity, and was also responsible for suicidal impulses. The perpetuation of such views undoubtedly retarded the development of modern psychopathology.

Later Greek and Roman thought. Work along the lines that had been established by Hippocrates was continued by some of the later Greek and Roman physicians. Particularly in Alexandria, Egypt (which after its founding in 332 B.C. by Alexander the Great became the center of Greek culture), medicine developed to a high level, and the temples dedicated to Saturn were first-rate sanatoriums. Pleasant surroundings were considered of great therapeutic value for the mentally ill, and the patients were provided with constant occupation, entertainment, and exercise. These activities included parties, dances, walks in the temple gardens, rowing along the Nile, and musical concerts. The later Greek and Roman physicians also utilized a wide range of other kinds of therapeutic measures, including dieting, massage, hydrotherapy, gymnastics, hypnotism, and education, as well as certain less desirable measures, such as bleeding, purging, and mechanical restraints (R. W. Menninger, 1944).

Among the Roman physicians who continued in the Hippocratic tradition were Asclepiades, Aretaeus, and Galen. Asclepiades (c. 124 B.C.) was well versed in the medical ideas and philosophy of his day and made notable contributions to psychiatry (Zilboorg & Henry, 1941). He was the first to note the difference between acute and chronic mental illnesses, and to distinguish between illusions, delusions, and hallucinations. In addition, he invented various ingenious devices designed to make the patients more comfortable. One of these was a suspended hammock-like bed whose swaying was considered very beneficial for disturbed patients. Asclepiades' progressive approach to mental illness was also evidenced by his vigorous opposition to bleeding, mechanical restraints, and dungeons.

The first hint that certain mental disorders were but an extension of normal psychological processes was given by Aretaeus near the end of the first century A.D. People who were irritable, violent, and easily given to joy and pleasurable pursuits were thought to be prone to the development of manic excitement, while those who tended to be serious were thought to be more apt to develop melancholia. Aretaeus was the first to describe the various phases of mania and melancholia, and to consider these two pathological states as expressions of the same illness. His insight into the importance of emotional factors and of the prepsychotic personality of the patient was quite an achievement for the day in which he lived.

Galen (A.D. 130–200) did not contribute much that was new to the therapy or clinical description of mental disorders, although he did make many original contributions concerning the anatomy of the nervous system and maintained a scientific approach to mental illness, performing a major service in compiling and integrating the existing material in this field (Guthrie, 1946). In the latter connection, he divided the causes of mental illness into physical and mental. Among the causes he named were injuries to the head, alcoholic excess, shock, fear, adolescence, menstrual changes, economic reverses, and disappointment in love.

Although historians consider the fall of Rome to the barbarians toward the end of the fifth century to be the dividing era between ancient and medieval times, the Dark Ages in the history of abnormal psychology began with Galen's death in A.D. 200. The contributions of Hippocrates and the later Greek and Roman physicians (which anticipated so many of our modern concepts of mental disorder) were shortly lost in the welter of popular superstition, and most of the medical men of later Rome returned to some sort of demonology. One notable exception to this trend, however, was Alexander Trallianus (A.D. 525–605), who followed the works of Galen rather closely but placed a great deal of emphasis on constitutional factors—stating, for example, that people with dark hair and a slim build were more likely to be affected by melancholia than persons with light hair and a heavy build. Worthy of note also are some of the clinical cases he recorded (Whitwell, 1936). Among his cases he cited that of a woman who had the delusion that her middle finger was fixed in such a way that it held the whole world within its power. This caused her great distress for fear she should bend her finger,

thus overthrowing the world and destroying everything. Another interesting case was that of a man who was greatly depressed because he was convinced that his head had been amputated. Trallianus reported that he cured this case by suddenly placing a close-fitting leaden cap on the patient's head so that he was able to feel the weight and thought his head had been replaced.

Survival of Greek thought in Arabia. During medieval times it was only in Arabia that the more scientific aspects of Greek medicine survived. The first mental hospital was established in Baghdad in A.D. 792; and it was soon followed by others in Damascus and Aleppo (Polvan, 1969). In these hospitals the mentally disturbed received much more humane treatment than they did in Christian lands.

The outstanding figure in Arabian medicine was Avicenna (c. A.D. 980–1037), called the "prince of physicians" (Campbell, 1926). In his writings Avicenna made frequent reference to hysteria, epilepsy, manic reactions, and melancholia. The following case shows his unique approach to the treatment of a young prince suffering from a mental disorder:

"A certain prince . . . was afflicted with melancholia, and suffered from the delusion that he was a cow. . . . he would low like a cow, causing annoyance to everyone, . . . crying, 'Kill me so that a good stew may be made of my flesh,' finally . . . he would eat nothing. . . . Avicenna was persuaded to take the case. . . . First of all he sent a message to the patient bidding him be of good cheer because the butcher was coming to slaughter him, whereat . . . the sick man rejoiced. Some time afterwards Avicenna, holding a knife in his hand, entered the sickroom saying, 'Where is this cow that I may kill it?' The patient lowed like a cow to indicate where he was. By Avicenna's orders he was laid on the ground, bound hand and foot. Avicenna then felt him all over and said, 'He is too lean, and not ready to be killed; he must be fattened.' Then they offered him suitable food of which he now partook eagerly, and gradually he gained strength, got rid of his delusion, and was completely cured." (Browne, 1921, pp. 88–89)

Unfortunately, most medical men of Avicenna's time were approaching the problems of the mentally ill in a very different way.

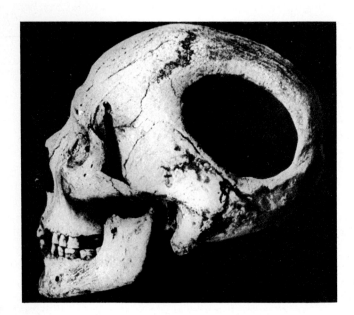

The view that mental disorders were caused by evil spirits influenced the treatment of the mentally disturbed in ancient and medieval times, and even beyond. Above left, the neolithic skull is evidence that trephining operations were performed in the Stone Age. An opening was made in the skull of the patient, presumably in the belief that this would allow the evil spirit to escape.

Left, burning persons for witchcraft was a phenomenon that began toward the end of the Middle Ages and persisted for centuries. Between 1484 and 1782, approximately 300,000 women were put to death as witches in Europe and North America; historical records suggest that many of them were mentally disturbed.

Sympathetic treatment of the mentally disturbed was not unknown, however, as illustrated in the seventeenth-century engraving (above) entitled "St. Clara Healing an Epileptic Woman."

DEMONOLOGY IN THE MIDDLE AGES

With the collapse of Greek and Roman civilization, medicine as well as other scientific pursuits suffered an almost complete eclipse in Europe. There was a tremendous revival of the most ancient superstition and demonology, with only a slight modification to conform to current theological demands. Man now became the battleground of demons and spirits who waged eternal war for the possession of his soul. Mental disorders were apparently fairly frequent throughout the Middle Ages, and toward the end of the period, when medieval institutions began to collapse, their incidence seems to have increased. As Rosen (1967) has described it:

"The medieval world began to come apart in the 14th century, and the process of disintegration continued inexorably through the succeeding centuries. Fundamental changes took place in its institutions, its social structure, its beliefs and outlook. It was a period of peasant revolts and urban uprisings, of wars and plagues, and thus an age in which many felt acutely insecure and discontented. An emotional malaise was abroad." (p. 775)

"MASS MADNESS"

The last half of the Middle Ages saw a peculiar trend in abnormal behavior, involving the widespread occurrence of group mental disorders which were apparently mainly cases of hysteria. Whole groups of people were affected simultaneously.

Dance manias, taking the form of epidemics of raving, jumping, dancing, and convulsions, were reported as early as the tenth century. One such episode, occurring in Italy early in the thirteenth century, was recorded by physicians of the time whose records have been reviewed by the medical historian H. E. Sigerist. He has written:

"The disease occurred at the height of the summer heat.... People, asleep or awake, would suddenly jump up, feeling an acute pain like the sting of a bee. Some saw the spider, others did not, but they knew that it must be the tarantula. They ran out of the house into the street, to the market place, dancing in great excitement. Soon they were joined by others who like them had been bitten, or by people who had been stung in previous years. . . .

"Thus groups of patients would gather, dancing wildly in the queerest attire. . . . Others would tear their clothes and show their nakedness, losing all sense of modesty. . . . Some called for swords and acted like fencers, others for whips and beat each other. . . . Some of them had still stranger fancies, liked to be tossed in the air, dug holes in the ground, and rolled themselves into the dirt like swine. They all drank wine plentifully and sang and talked like drunken people. . . ." (1943, pp. 103, 106–107)

Actually, the behavior was very similar to the ancient orgiastic rites by which people had worshiped the Greek gods. These had been banned with the advent of Christianity, but were deeply imbedded in the culture and were apparently kept alive by secret gatherings. Probably considerable guilt and conflict were engendered; then, with time, the meaning of the dances changed, and the old rites appeared as symptoms of disease. The participants were no longer sinners but the poor victims of the tarantula (Gloyne, 1950).

Known as *tarantism* in Italy, the dancing mania later spread to Germany and the rest of Europe where it was known as *St. Vitus' dance*. Other peculiar manifestations also appeared. In the fifteenth century, a member of a German convent was overcome with a desire to bite her fellow nuns. The practice was taken up by her companions, and the mania spread to other convents in Germany, Holland, and Italy (A. D. White, 1896).

Isolated rural areas were also afflicted with outbreaks of *lycanthropy*—a form of mental disorder in which the patient imagined himself a wolf and imitated its actions. In 1541 a case was reported wherein the lycanthrope told his captors, in confidence, that he was really a wolf but that his skin was smooth on the surface because all the hairs were on the inside (Stone, 1937). To cure him of his delusions, his extremities were amputated, following which he died, still unconvinced.

These epidemics continued into the seventeenth century, but apparently reached their peak during the fifteenth and sixteenth centuries—a period noted for oppression, famine, and pestilence. During this period, Europe was ravaged by an epidemic known as the "Black Death," which spread across the continent, destroying millions of human lives and severely disrupting social organization. Undoubtedly many of the peculiar manifestations during this period, including the Children's Crusade, in which thousands of children left their homes to liberate the Holy Sepulcher, were related to the depression, fear, and wild mysticism engendered by the terrible events of the time. People did not dream that such frightening catastrophes were attributable to natural causes and thus would some day be within man's power to control, prevent, or even create.

TREATMENT IN MEDIEVAL TIMES

In the Middle Ages treatment of the mentally disturbed was left largely to the clergy. Monasteries served as refuges and places of confinement. During the early part of the medieval period, the mentally disturbed for the most part were treated with considerable kindliness. Much store was set by prayer, holy water, sanctified ointments, the breath or spittle of the priests, the touching of relics, visits to holy places, and mild forms of exorcism. In some monasteries and shrines exorcism was performed by the gentle "laying on of hands." Such methods were often intermixed with vague ideas of medical treatment derived mainly from Galen, which gave rise to such prescriptions as the following: "For a fiend-sick man: When a devil possesses a man, or controls him from within with disease, a spew-drink of lupin, bishopswort, henbane, garlic. Pound these together, add ale and holy water." (Cockayne, 1864–1866)

As exorcistic techniques became more fully developed, it was emphasized that it was Satan's pride which had led to his original downfall. Hence, in treating persons possessed by a devil, the first thing to do was to strike a fatal blow at the devil's pride—to insult him. This involved calling the devil some of the most obscene epithets that imagination could devise, and the insults were usually supplemented by long litanies of cursing:

". . . May all the devils that are thy foes rush forth upon thee, and drag thee down to hell! . . . May God set a nail to your skull, and pound it in with a hammer, as Jael did unto Sisera! . . . May . . . Sother break thy head and cut off thy hands, as was done to the cursed Dagon! . . . May God hang thee in a hellish yoke, as seven men were hanged by the sons of Saul!" (From *Thesaurus Exorcismorum*)

This procedure was considered highly successful in the treatment of possessed persons. A certain bishop of Beauvais claimed to have rid a person of five devils, all of whom signed an agreement stating that they and their subordinate imps would no longer persecute the possessed individual (A. D. White, 1896).

As theological beliefs concerning abnormal behavior became more fully developed and were endorsed by the secular world, treatment of the mentally disturbed became more harsh. It was generally believed that cruelty to "madmen" was punishment of the devil residing within them, and when "scourging" proved ineffective, the authorities felt justified in driving out the demons by less pleasant methods. Flogging, starving, chains, immersion in hot water, and other torturous methods were devised in order to make the body such an unpleasant place of residence that no self-respecting devil would remain in it. Undoubtedly many men and women who might have been restored to health by more gentle and humane measures were driven into hopeless derangement by such brutal treatment.

WITCHCRAFT

During the latter part of the fifteenth century, it became the accepted theological belief that demoniacal possessions were of two general types: (1) possessions in which the victim was unwillingly seized by the devil as a punishment by God for his sins, and (2) possessions in which the individual was actually in league with the devil. The latter persons were supposed to have made a pact with the devil, consummated by signing in blood a book presented to them by Satan which gave them certain supernatural powers. They could cause pestilence, storms, floods, sexual impotence, injuries to their enemies, and ruination of crops, and could rise through the air, cause milk to sour, and turn themselves into animals. In short, they were witches.

These beliefs were not confined to simple serfs but were held and elaborated upon by most of the important clergymen of this period. No less a man than Martin Luther (1483–1546) came to the following conclusions:

"The greatest punishment God can inflict on the wicked . . . is to deliver them over to Satan, who with God's permission, kills them or makes them to undergo great calamities. Many devils are in woods, water, wildernesses, etc., ready to hurt and prejudice people. When these things happen, then the philosophers and physicians say it is natural, ascribing it to the planets.

"In cases of melancholy . . . I conclude it is merely the work of the devil. Men are possessed by the devil in two ways; corporally or spiritually. Those whom he possesses corporally, as mad people, he has permission from God to vex and agitate, but he has no power over their souls." (*Colloquia Mensalia*)

Those who were judged to have been unwillingly seized by the devil as punishment by God were treated initially in accordance with the established exorcistic practices of the time. As time went on, however, the distinction between the two types of possessions became somewhat obscured, and by the close of the fifteenth century, the mentally ill were generally considered heretics and witches.

More and more concern was expressed in official quarters over the number of witches roaming around and the great damage they were doing by pestilences, storms, sexual depravity, and other heinous crimes. Consequently, on December 7, 1484, Pope Innocent VIII sent forth his bull *Summis Desiderantes Affectibus*, in which he exhorted the clergy of Europe, especially Germany, to leave no means untried in the detection of witches. This papal bull was theologically based on the scriptural command "Thou shalt not suffer a witch to live" (Exodus 22:18).

To assist in this great work, a manual, *The Witch Hammer, Malleus Maleficarum*, was prepared by two Dominican monks, Johann Sprenger and Heinrich Kraemer, both Inquisitors appointed by the pope to act in northern Germany and territories along the Rhine. This manual, revered for centuries in both Catholic and Protestant countries as being almost divinely inspired, was complete in every detail concerning witchcraft and was of great value in witch-hunting. It was divided into three parts. The first confirmed the existence of witches and pointed out that those who did not believe in them were either in honest error or polluted with heresy. The second part contained a description of the clinical symptoms by which witches could be detected, such as red spots or areas of anesthesia on the skin, which were thought to resemble the claw of the devil ("devil's claw") and were presumably left by the devil to denote the sealing of the pact with him. The third part dealt with the legal forms of examining and sentencing a witch.

In accordance with the precepts laid down in the *Malleus*, the accepted way to gain sure proof of witchcraft was to torture the person until a confession was obtained. This method was eminently effective. The victims of these inhuman tortures—writhing in agony and viewed with horror by those they loved—confessed to anything and everything. Frequently they were forced to give the names of alleged accomplices in their evildoing, and these unfortunate persons were in turn tortured until a satisfactory confession of their activities was elicited.

Confessions were often weird, but this seldom deterred the learned judges. For example, James I of England proved, through the skillful use of unlimited torture, that witches were to blame for the tempests that beset his bride on her voyage from Denmark. A Dr. Fian, whose legs were being crushed in the "boots" and who had wedges driven under his fingernails, confessed that more than a hundred witches had put to sea in a sieve to produce the storms (A. D. White, 1896).

Further impetus to these persecutions was undoubtedly given by many of the suspects themselves, who, although obviously ill by our present standards, participated so actively in the beliefs of the time that they often freely "confessed" their transactions with the devil, almost gleefully pointed out the "marks" he had left on their bodies, and claimed great powers as a result of their evildoing. Others, suffering from severe depressions, elaborated on their terrible sins and admitted themselves to be beyond redemption. (Even today many psychotics are convinced of their hopeless guilt and damnation.) This sort

In medieval times and even more recently, a belief in natural causes of mental disorders provided no guarantee against inhumane treatment of the patient. Some medieval quacks claimed that mental disorders were caused by stones developed in the head. They performed operations (upper left) to remove the stones, but actually made only superficial cuts.

Before the reforms begun by Pinel in the eighteenth century, it was generally believed that violence was the best treatment for the mentally ill. At St. Medard, Paris (lower left), the doctors jumped on the patients to remove "mental obstructions."

In the asylum at Leyden (upper center), hot irons were applied to the head to bring patients to their senses. Boerhaave, a medical authority of the time, is depicted threatening hysterical women patients with cauterization.

As late as the early nineteenth century, the circulating swing (upper right) was used to bring the mentally disturbed back to sound reasoning. It was said that "no well-regulated institution should be without one."

of basis for the iron-bound logic of the Inquisitors is well illustrated in the following case of a woman who was probably suffering from involutional melancholia.

"A certain woman was taken and finally burned, who for six years had an incubus devil even when she was lying in bed at the side of her husband . . . the homage she has given to the devil was of such a sort that she was bound to dedicate herself body and soul to him forever, after seven years. But God provided mercifully for she was taken in the sixth year and condemned to the fire, and having truly and completely confessed is believed to have obtained pardon from God. For she went most willingly to her death, saying that she would gladly suffer an even more terrible death if only she would be set free and escape the power of the devil." (Stone, 1937, p. 146)

To be convicted of witchcraft was a most serious matter. The penalty usually followed one of three general forms. There were those who were beheaded or strangled before being burned, those who were burned alive, and those who were mutilated before being burned. The treatment accorded a mentally disordered man caught in the wrong period of history is illustrated in the following case:

"In Königsberg in 1636 a man thought he was God the Father; he claimed that all the angels and the devil and the Son of God recognized his power. He was convicted. His tongue was cut out, his head cut off, and his body burned." (Zilboorg & Henry, 1941, p. 259)

There seems to have been little distinction between the Roman and the Reformed churches in their attitudes toward witchcraft, and large numbers of people were put to death in this period.

"A French judge boasted that he had burned 800 women in sixteen years on the bench; 600 were burned during the administration of a bishop in Bamberg. The Inquisition, originally started by the Church of Rome, was carried along by protestant churches in Great Britain and Germany. In protestant Geneva 500 persons were burned in the year 1515. In Trèves some 7000 people were reported burned during a period of several years." (Bromberg, 1937, p. 61)

The full horror of the witch mania and its enthusiastic adoption by other countries, including some American colonies, took place during the sixteenth and seventeenth centuries. And though religious and scientific thought began to change gradually, the basic ideas of mental illness as representing punishment by God or deliberate association with the devil, which were developed in such elaborate detail during the Middle Ages, were to continue to dominate popular thought until well into the nineteenth century.

DEVELOPMENT OF HUMANITARIAN APPROACHES

Any criticism or questioning of the theological doctrine of demonology during the Middle Ages was made at the risk of life itself. Yet even during the early part of the sixteenth century we find the beginnings again of more scientific intellectual activity. The concepts of demonology and witchcraft, which had long acted to retard the understanding and treatment of mental disorders, began to be challenged and attacked by men greater than their time—men from the fields of religion, physics, medicine, and philosophy.

REAPPEARANCE OF SCIENTIFIC QUESTIONING IN EUROPE

In the early part of the sixteenth century Paracelsus (1490–1541) insisted that the "dancing mania" was not a possession but a form of disease, and that it should be treated as such (Zilboorg & Henry, 1941). He also postulated a conflict between man's instinctual and spiritual nature, formulated the idea of psychic causes for mental illness, and advocated treatment by "bodily magnetism," later recognized as hypnosis (Mora, 1967). Although Paracelsus thus rejected demonology, his view of abnormal behavior was colored by belief in astral influences (*lunatic* is derived from the Latin word "luna" or moon): he was convinced that the moon exercised a supernatural influence over the brain. Nevertheless, Paracelsus stood clearly in defiance of both medical and theological tradition, and he was hounded and persecuted until his death.

Johann Weyer (1515–1588), a physician and man of letters who wrote under the Latin name of Joannus Wierus, was so deeply impressed by the scenes of imprisonment, torture, and burning of persons accused of witchcraft that he made a careful study of the entire problem of witchcraft and about 1563 published a book on the subject. In it he argued that a considerable number, if not all, of those imprisoned, tortured, and burned for witchcraft were really sick mentally or bodily, and consequently that great wrongs were being committed against innocent people. Weyer's work received the approval of a few outstanding physicians and theologians of his time. In the main, however, it met with vehement protest and condemnation. Father Spina, the author of a polemical book against Weyer, stated: "Recently Satan went to a Sabbath[1] attired as a great prince, and told the assembled witches that they need not worry since, thanks to Weyer and his followers, the affairs of the Devil were brilliantly progressing." (Castiglioni, 1946, p. 253)

Weyer was one of the first physicians to specialize in mental disorders, and his wide experience and progressive views on mental illness justify his being regarded as the true founder of modern psychopathology. Unfortunately, however, he was too far ahead of his time. His works were banned by the Church and remained so until the twentieth century.

Perhaps there is no better illustration of the spirit of scientific skepticism that was developing in the sixteenth century than the works of the Oxford-educated Reginald Scot (1538–1599), who devoted his life to exposing the fallacies of witchcraft and demonology. In his book *Discovery of Witchcraft*, published in 1584, he convincingly and daringly denied the existence of demons, devils, and evil spirits as the cause of mental disorders.

---

[1]The word *Sabbath* has no relation to the Biblical Sabbath, but refers to witches' gatherings in which orders were supposedly received from Satan.

"These women are but diseased wretches suffering from melancholy, and their words, actions, reasoning, and gestures show that sickness has affected their brains and impaired their powers of judgment. You must know that the effects of sickness on men, and still more on women, are almost unbelievable. Some of these persons imagine, confess, and maintain that they are witches and are capable of performing extraordinary miracles through the arts of witchcraft; others, due to the same mental disorder, imagine strange and impossible things which they claim to have witnessed." (Castiglioni, 1946, p. 253)

King James I of England, however, came to the rescue of demonology, personally refuted Scot's thesis, and ordered his book seized and burned. But churchmen also were beginning to question the practices of the time. The wise and far-seeing St. Vincent de Paul (1576–1660), surrounded by every opposing influence and at the risk of his life, declared: "Mental disease is no different to bodily disease and Christianity demands of the humane and powerful to protect, and the skilful to relieve the one as well as the other."

In the face of such attacks, which continued through the next two centuries, demonology was forced to give ground, and the way was gradually paved for the triumph of observation and reason, culminating in the development of modern experimental science and psychopathology.

ESTABLISHMENT OF EARLY ASYLUMS AND SHRINES

From the sixteenth century on, monasteries and prisons gradually relinquished the care of the mentally ill to special institutions that were being established in increasing numbers. The care received by patients, however, left much to be desired.

Early asylums. In 1547, the monastery of St. Mary of Bethlehem at London was officially made into a mental hospital by Henry VIII. Its name soon became contracted to "Bedlam," and it became widely known for the deplorable conditions and practices that prevailed. The more violent patients were exhibited to the public for one penny a look, and the more harmless inmates were forced to seek charity on the streets of London in the manner described by Shakespeare:

"Bedlam beggars, who, with roaring voices . . .
Sometime with lunatic bans, sometime with prayers
Enforce their charity."—*King Lear*, Act II, Scene 3

Such hospitals, or "asylums" as they were called, were gradually established in other countries (Lewis, 1941). The San Hipolito, established in Mexico in 1566 by the philanthropist Bernardino Alvares, was the first hospital for the care and study of mental disorders to be established in the Americas. The first mental hospital in France, La Maison de Charenton, was founded in 1641 in the suburbs of Paris. A mental hospital was established in Moscow in 1764, and the notorious Lunatics' Tower in Vienna was constructed in 1784. This was a showplace in Old Vienna, and the description of the edifice and its practices makes interesting reading. It was an ornately decorated round tower within which were square rooms. The doctors and "keepers" lived in the square rooms, while the patients were confined in the spaces between the walls of the square rooms and the outside of the tower. The patients were put on exhibit to the public for a small fee, and were, in general, treated like animals and criminals.

The Pennsylvania Hospital at Philadelphia, completed under the guidance of Benjamin Franklin in 1756, provided some cells or wards for the mentally ill, but the first hospital in the United States devoted exclusively to mental patients was constructed in Williamsburg, Virginia, in 1773.

These early asylums, or hospitals, were primarily modifications of penal institutions, and the inmates were treated more like beasts than like human beings. Selling gives a striking account of the treatment of the chronic insane in La Bicêtre Hospital in Paris. This treatment was typical of the asylums of this period and continued through most of the eighteenth century.

The patients were ordinarily shackled to the walls of their dark, unlighted cells by iron collars which held them flat against the wall and permitted little movement. Ofttimes there was also an iron hoop around the waist of the patient and both his hands and feet were chained. Although these chains usually permitted enough movement so that the patient could feed himself out of a bowl, they often did not permit him to lie down at night. Since little was known about dietetics, and the patients were presumed to be animals anyway, little attention was paid to whether the patient was adequately fed or to whether the food was good or bad. The cells were furnished only with straw and were never swept or cleaned; the patient was permitted to remain in the midst of all the accumulated ordure. No one visited him except at feeding time, no provision was made to keep him warm, and even the most elementary gestures of humanity were lacking. (Modified from Selling, 1943, pp. 54–55)

Treatment of mental patients in the United States was little, if any, better. The following is a vivid description of their plight in this country during colonial times:

"The mentally ill were hanged, imprisoned, tortured, and otherwise persecuted as agents of Satan. Regarded as sub-human beings, they were chained in specially devised kennels and cages like wild beasts, and thrown into prisons, bridewells and jails like criminals. They were incarcerated in workhouse dungeons or made to slave as able-bodied paupers, unclassified from the rest. They were left to wander about stark naked, driven from place to place like mad dogs, subjected to whippings as vagrants and rogues. Even the well-to-do were not spared confinement in strong rooms and cellar dungeons, while legislation usually concerned itself more with their property than their persons." (Deutsch, 1946, p. 53)

Some insight into the prevalent forms of treatment in the early American hospitals may be gained from a thesis on "Chronic Mania," written by a medical student in 1796 at the New York Hospital, in which cells or wards were provided in the cellar for the mentally ill patients. He considered that restraint should be avoided as long as possible, "lest the strait jackets, and chains and cells should induce a depression of spirits

THE
Diſcovery of Witchcraft:

PROVING,

That the Compacts and Contracts of WITCHES with *Devils* and all *Infernal Spirits* or *Familiars*, are but Erroneous Novelties and Imaginary Conceptions.

Alſo diſcovering, How far their Power extendeth in Killing, Tormenting, Conſuming, or Curing the bodies of Men, Women, Children, or Animals, by Charms, Philtres, Periapts, Pentacles, Curſes, and Conjurations.

WHEREIN LIKE WISE

The Unchriſtian Practices and Inhumane Dealings of *Searchers* and *Witch-tryers* upon *Aged, Melancholly,* and *Superſtitious* people, in extorting Confeſſions by Terrors and Tortures, and in deviſing falſe Marks and Symptoms, are notably Detected.

And the Knavery of *Juglers, Conjurers, Charmers, Soothſayers, Figure-Caſters, Dreamers, Alchymiſts* and *Philterers*; with many other things that have long lain hidden, fully Opened and Deciphered.

ALL WHICH

Are very neceſſary to be known for the undeceiving of *Judges, Juſtices,* and *Jurors,* before they paſs Sentence upon Poor, Miſerable and Ignorant People; who are frequently Arraigned, Condemned, and Executed for *Witches* and *Wizzards.*

IN SIXTEEN BOOKS.

By REGINALD SCOT *Eſquire.*

Title page of Reginald Scot's *Discovery of Witchcraft,* published in 1584, which denied the common belief that demons caused mental disorders.

seldom surmounted." He also doubted the propriety of "unexpected plunging into cold water," of "two to six hours in spring water or still colder," of the "refrigerant plan," of bleeding, purging, vomiting, streams of cold water on the head, blisters, and similar procedures (Russell, 1941, p. 230).

Even as late as 1830, new patients had their heads shaved, were dressed in straitjackets, put on a low diet, compelled to swallow some active purgative, and placed in a dark cell. If these measures did not serve to quiet unruly or excited patients, more severe measures, such as starvation, solitary confinement, cold baths, and other torturelike methods, were used (Bennett, 1947).

The Gheel shrine. There were a few bright spots in this otherwise tragic situation. Out of the more humane Christian tradition of prayer, the laying on of hands, or holy touch, and visits to shrines for cure of illness, there arose several great shrines where treatment by kindness and love stood out in marked contrast to generally prevailing conditions. The one at Gheel in Belgium, visited since the thirteenth century, is probably most famous.

"Somewhere in the dim past there lived a king in Ireland who was married to a most beautiful woman and who sired an equally beautiful daughter. The good queen developed a fatal illness, and at her death bed the daughter dedicated herself to a life of purity and service to the poor and the mentally bereft. The widowed king was beside himself with grief and announced to his subjects that he must at once be assuaged of sorrow by marrying the woman in his kingdom who most resembled the dead queen. No such paragon was found. But the devil came and whispered to the king that there was such a woman—his own daughter. The devil spurred the king to propose marriage to the girl, but she was appropriately outraged by this incestuous overture and fled across the English Channel to Belgium. There the king overtook her and with Satan at his elbow, slew the girl and her faithful attendants. In the night the angels came, recapitated the body and concealed it in the forest near the village of Gheel. Years later five lunatics chained together spent the night with their keepers at a small wayside shrine near this Belgian village. Overnight all the victims recovered. Here indeed must be the place where the dead girl, reincarnated as St. Dymphna, was buried, and here was the sacred spot where her cures of the insane are effected. In the 15th century pilgrimages to Gheel from every part of the civilized world were organized for

the mentally sick. Many of the pilgrims remained in Gheel to live with the inhabitants of the locality, and in the passing years it became the natural thing to accept them into the homes and thus the first 'colony' was formed and for that matter the only one which has been consistently successful." (Karnosh & Zucker, 1945, p. 15)

The colony of Gheel has continued its work into contemporary times. As late as 1960 more than two thousand certified mental patients lived in private homes, worked with the inhabitants, and suffered few restrictions except from using alcohol and visiting public places (Barton, 1959; Hewitt, 1962; Dumont & Aldrich, 1962). Many types of mental disorder were represented here, including schizophrenia, manic-depressive psychoses, psychopathic personality, mental retardation, and various types of organic brain disorders. Approximately one in every ten persons in the community of some twenty thousand persons was a mental patient.

Patients reported regularly to a supervising psychiatrist and ordinarily stayed in Gheel until they were considered recovered. It is unfortunate that the great humanitarian work of this colony has received so little recognition, and that economic and other factors have led to a gradual reduction in its program of therapy.

HUMANITARIAN REFORM

Although scientific skepticism had undermined the belief that mental disturbance was the devil's work, most early asylums were no better than concentration camps. The unfortunate inmates lived and died amid conditions of incredible filth and cruelty. Humanitarian reform of mental hospitals received its first great impetus from the work of Philippe Pinel (1745–1826) in France.

Pinel's experiment. In 1792, shortly after the first phase of the French Revolution came to a close, Pinel was placed in charge of La Bicêtre (the hospital for the insane in Paris to which we have previously referred). In this capacity he received the grudging permission of the Revolutionary Commune to remove the chains from some of the inmates as an experiment to test his

The treatment of patients in early mental asylums left much to be desired. Chains, irons, and other physical restraints (upper left) were regarded as necessary for the treatment of the mentally ill.

Typically, all types of mental patients were crowded together, receiving only custodial care. The public attitude was largely one of curiosity. An engraving (above) shows two ladies of fashion going through the St. Mary of Bethlehem asylum in London, more generally known as "Bedlam."

Reform came slowly. At the time of the French Revolution, Pinel demonstrated the effectiveness of a completely new approach to the handling of mental patients. Until then, these unfortunate sufferers had been kept in chains, presumably for their own protection as well as that of others. Pinel's demand that the chains be removed from the patients at La Bicêtre Hospital (lower left) was at first regarded as dangerous and foolish—until the beneficial results became apparent.

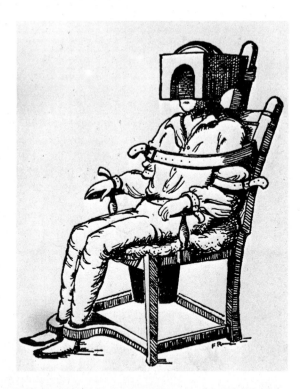

Even after reform of mental institutions had begun, such devices as the "tranquillizing chair" (left) of Dr. Benjamin Rush were used to restrain unmanageable patients. The crib (below), a restraint device, was still used for violent patients in 1882; and in 1889 mental patients were treated by a type of swinging device (lower left) at the Salpêtrière Hospital in Paris.

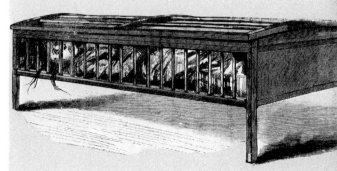

views that the mentally ill should be treated with kindness and consideration—as sick people and not as vicious beasts or criminals. Had his experiment proved a failure, Pinel might well have lost his head, but, fortunately for all, it proved to be a great success. Chains were removed, sunny rooms were provided instead of dungeons, patients were permitted to exercise on the hospital grounds, and kindliness was extended to these poor creatures, some of whom had been chained in dungeons for thirty years or more. The effect was almost miraculous. The previous noise, filth, and abuse were replaced by order and peace. As Pinel said: "The whole discipline was marked with regularity and kindness which had the most favorable effect on the insane themselves, rendering even the most furious more tractable." (Selling, 1943, p. 65)

The reactions of these patients when all their chains were removed for the first time is a pathetic story. One patient, an English officer who had years before killed a guard in an attack of fury, tottered outside on legs weak from lack of use, and for the first time in some forty years saw the sun and sky. With tears in his eyes he exclaimed, "Oh, how beautiful!" (Zilboorg & Henry, 1941, p. 323) Finally, when night came, he voluntarily returned to his cell, which had been cleaned during his absence, to fall peacefully asleep on his new bed. After two years of orderly behavior, including helping to handle other patients, he was pronounced cured and was permitted to leave the hospital. It is a curious and satisfying fact of history that Pinel was saved from the hands of a mob who suspected him of antirevolutionary activities by a soldier whom he had freed from asylum chains.

Pinel was later given charge of the Salpêtrière Hospital, where the same reorganization in treatment was instituted with similarly gratifying results, the Bicêtre and Salpêtrière hospitals thus becoming the first modern hospitals for the care of the insane. Pinel's successor, Jean Esquirol (1772–1840), continued his good work at the Salpêtrière and, in addition, helped in the establishment of some ten new mental hospitals, which helped to put France in the forefront of humane treatment for the mentally disturbed.

Tuke's work in England. At about the same time that Pinel was reforming the Bicêtre Hospital, an English Quaker named William Tuke established the "York Retreat," a pleasant country house where mental patients lived, worked, and rested in a kindly religious atmosphere. This represented the culmination of a noble battle against the brutality, ignorance, and indifference of his time. Some insight into the difficulties and discouragements he encountered in the establishment of the York Retreat may be gleaned from a simple statement he made in a letter regarding his early efforts: "All men seem to desert me." This is not surprising when we remember that demonology was still widespread, and that as late as 1768 we find the Protestant John Wesley's famous declaration that "The giving up of witchcraft is in effect the giving up of the Bible." The belief in demonology was too strong to be conquered overnight.

As word of the amazing results obtained by Pinel spread to England, Tuke's small force of Quakers gradually gained support from John Connolly, Samuel Hitch, and other great English medical psychologists. In 1841 Hitch introduced trained women nurses into the wards at the Gloucester Asylum and put trained supervisors at the head of the nursing staffs. These innovations, regarded as quite revolutionary at the time, were of great importance not only in improving the care of mental patients but also in changing public attitudes toward the mentally disturbed. As mental illness came to be put on somewhat the same footing as physical illness, the mystery, ignorance, and fear that had always surrounded it began gradually to give way.

Rush and Dix in America. The success of Pinel's and Tuke's experiments in more humanitarian methods revolutionized the treatment of mental patients throughout the civilized world. In the United States, this was reflected in the work of Benjamin Rush (1745–1813), "the father of American psychiatry." Becoming associated with the Pennsylvania Hospital in 1783, Rush encouraged more humane treatment of the mentally ill, wrote the first systematic treatise on psychiatry in America, *Medical Inquiries and Observations upon the Diseases of the Mind* (1812), and was the first American to organize a course in psychiatry. But even he did not escape entirely from the established beliefs of his time. His medical theory was tainted with astrology, and his principal remedies were bloodletting and purgatives. In addition, he invented and used a torturelike device called "the tranquillizer." Despite these limitations, however, we may consider Rush an important transitional figure between the old era and the new.

The early work of Benjamin Rush was followed through by an energetic New England schoolteacher, Dorothea Dix (1802–1887). Miss Dix was retired early from her teaching because of recurring attacks of tuberculosis, and in 1841 she began to teach in a Sunday school for female prisoners. Through this contact she soon became acquainted with the deplorable conditions prevalent in jails, almshouses, and asylums. In a "Memorial" submitted to the Congress of the United States in 1848, she stated that she had seen "more than 9000 idiots, epileptics and insane in the United States, destitute of appropriate care and protection . . . bound with galling chains, bowed beneath fetters and heavy iron balls attached to drag-chains, lacerated with ropes, scourged with rods and terrified beneath storms of execration and cruel blows; now subject to jibes and scorn and torturing tricks; now abandoned to the most outrageous violations." (Zilboorg & Henry, 1941, pp. 583–584)

As a result of her findings, Miss Dix carried on a zealous campaign between 1841 and 1881 which aroused the people and the legislatures to an awareness of the inhuman treatment accorded the mentally ill. Through her efforts many millions of dollars were raised to build suitable hospitals, and some twenty states responded directly to her appeals. Not only was she instrumental in improving conditions in the United States, but she directed the opening of two large institutions in Canada, and completely reformed the asylum system in Scotland and several other countries. She is credited with the establishment of some thirty-two modern mental hospitals, an astonishing record considering the ignorance and superstition which still prevailed in the field of mental health. She rounded out her amazing career by organizing the nursing forces of the Northern armies during the Civil War. A resolution presented by the United States Congress in 1901 characterized her as "among the noblest examples of humanity in all history." (Karnosh & Zucker, 1945, p. 18)

Moral therapy. During the early part of this period of humanitarian reform, the use of moral therapy in mental hospitals was relatively widespread. This approach stemmed largely from the work of Pinel and Tuke and was based on the view that most of the insane were essentially normal people who could profit from a favorable environment and help with personal problems. As Rees (1957) has described it:

"The insane came to be regarded as normal people who had lost their reason as a result of having been exposed to severe psychological and social stresses. These stresses were called the moral causes of insanity, and moral treatment aimed at relieving the patient by friendly association, discussion of his difficulties, and the daily pursuit of purposeful activity; in other words, social therapy, individual therapy, and occupational therapy." (pp. 306–307)

There seems little doubt that moral therapy was remarkably effective, however "unscientific" it may have been. Records indicate that during the first half of the nineteenth century, when moral therapy apparently reached its peak as the sole method of treatment, at least 70 percent of mental-hospital patients who had been ill for less than one year were discharged as recovered or improved. Some recovery rates were reported to be as high as 80 to 90 percent (Tourney, 1967).

Despite these impressive results, moral therapy declined in the latter half of the nineteenth century—in part, paradoxically, because of the acceptance of the view that the insane were ill people. Though those who suffered from mental disorders were no longer seen as "possessed," neither were they seen as able to meet expectations, carry out tasks, or make decisions. Rather, it was assumed that they were helpless, and that application of the powerful new techniques of physical medicine would be more "scientific" than any psychological therapy. As Adams (1964) has noted:

"One important reason for its abandonment was that moral therapy was supposed to be a form of treatment for mental illness. But as physical medicine developed during the late nineteenth century, it was thought that the types of procedures found effective with physical illnesses could be carried over unaltered into the treatment of mental illnesses." (p. 192)

This approach gained strength as the superintendence of mental hospitals was taken out of

GALEN (2ND CENTURY), AVICENNA (980–1037), HIPPOCRATES (460?–?377 B.C.)

These historical figures were especially important in laying the groundwork for modern psychiatric thought: Galen, Avicenna, and Hippocrates, early proponents of a scientific approach to mental illness; Johann Weyer, who at great personal risk wrote against prevalent beliefs in witchcraft and decried the persecution of the mentally ill; Philippe Pinel, who revolutionized the hospital treatment of the mentally ill by removing chains and introducing humane methods; Dorothea Dix, who campaigned tirelessly for better conditions in mental hospitals; and Emil Kraepelin, who, by integrating clinical data, worked out the first systematic classification of mental disorders.

| WEYER (1515–1588) | PINEL (1745–1826) | DIX (1802–1887) | KRAEPELIN (1856–1926) |

the hands of wardens or stewards and placed under the auspices of medical men.[1] The attempt to provide hospital facilities for increasing numbers of those with mental disorders seems to have further contributed to a decline in moral therapy, since the procedures it used were possible only when the patient population was relatively small in relation to treatment personnel. In any event, hospital statistics show that recovery and discharge rates declined as moral therapy gave way to the medical approach. Only in recent years has this trend been reversed. Interestingly enough, the fact that mental hospitals have now ceased to be "storage bins" for the mentally disturbed can be attributed partly to the contemporary emphasis on treatment procedures not unlike those used in moral therapy. For fundamental to this early nineteenth-century approach was the "modern" view that people with mental disorders can best be helped if they are treated as nearly as possible like normal human beings.

Beginnings of the mental health movement. In the last half of the nineteenth century the asy-lum, "the big house on the hill," with its high turrets and fortresslike appearance, became a familiar landmark in America. In it mental patients lived under semiadequate conditions of comfort and freedom from abuse. To the general public, however, the asylum was an eerie place, and its occupants a strange and frightening lot. Little was done by the resident psychiatrists to educate the public along lines that would reduce the general fear and horror of insanity. One principal reason for this, of course, was that the early psychiatrist had very little actual information to impart. Even as late as 1840, no clear-cut classification of mental disorders had been worked out, and a German teacher, Dr. Heinroth, was still advancing the theory that sin produced insanity and repentance a cure, and that piety was conducive to mental health (Lewis, 1941).

---

[1]The present American Psychiatric Association developed out of an organization originally formed in 1844 by thirteen superintendents of mental hospitals, the Association of Medical Superintendents of American Institutions for the Insane (Lowry, 1946).

In America, the pioneering work of Dorothea Dix in educating the public about mental illness was followed up by that of Clifford Beers, whose now-famous book, *A Mind That Found Itself*, was published in 1908. Beers, a Yale graduate, described his own mental collapse and told of the bad treatment he received in three typical institutions of the day, and of his eventual recovery in the home of a friendly attendant. Although chains and other torture devices had long since been given up, the straitjacket was still widely used as a means of "quieting" excited patients. Beers ex-

perienced this treatment and supplied a vivid description of what such painful immobilization of the arms means to an overwrought mental patient in terms of intensification of inner excitement. He began a campaign to make people realize this was no way to handle the sick, winning the interest and support of many public-spirited individuals, including the psychologist William James and the "dean of American psychiatry," Adolf Meyer. Thus through the combined efforts of many dedicated people our contemporary mental health movement had its start.

DEVELOPMENT OF THE ORGANIC VIEWPOINT AND THE MEDICAL MODEL

With the emergence of modern experimental science, tremendous advances were made toward better understanding and treatment of abnormal behavior. These advances initially centered upon the development of the organic viewpoint and the postulation of a medical model.

MEDICAL BREAKTHROUGHS IN THE UNDERSTANDING OF MENTAL DISORDERS

From the early part of the eighteenth century, knowledge of anatomy, physiology, neurology, chemistry, and general medicine increased rapidly. These advances led to the gradual uncovering of organic pathology underlying many physical ailments, and it was only another step for these early workers to look upon mental disorder as a definite sickness based on organic brain pathology. This concept of mental illness is called the *organic viewpoint* or *medical model*. Although it was too broadly employed before the limitations of its applicability were recognized, it represents the first great advance of modern science in the understanding and treatment of mental disorders.

As early as 1757, Albrecht von Haller (1708–1777) in his *Elements of Physiology* emphasized the importance of the brain in psychic functions

and advocated studying the brains of the insane by post-mortem dissection. The first systematic presentation of the organic viewpoint, however, was made by the German psychiatrist William Griesinger (1817–1868). In his textbook *The Pathology and Therapy of Psychic Disorders*, published in 1845, Griesinger insisted that psychiatry should proceed on a physiological and clinical basis and emphasized his belief that all mental disorders could be explained in terms of brain pathology.

Kraepelin and classification. Although the work of Griesinger received considerable attention, it was his follower, Emil Kraepelin (1856–1926), who played the dominant role in the establishment of the organic viewpoint. Kraepelin, whose textbook *Lehrbuch der Psychiatrie* was published in 1883, not only emphasized the importance of brain pathology in mental illness but also made several related contributions which helped establish this viewpoint. The most important of these was his system of classification. Kraepelin noted that certain groups of symptoms of mental illness occurred together with sufficient regularity to be regarded as specific types of mental disease, in much the same way that we think of measles, smallpox, and other distinct physical ailments. He then proceeded to describe and clarify these types of mental disorders, working out the scheme of classification which is the basis of our present categories. The integration of the clinical material underlying this classification was a herculean task and represented a major contribution to the field of psychopathology.

Kraepelin looked upon each type of mental illness as separate and distinct from the others, and thought that its course was as predetermined and predictable as the course of measles. Such conclusions led to widespread interest in the accurate description and classification of mental disorders, for by this means the outcome of a given type of mental illness could presumably be predicted even if it could not yet be controlled. The subsequent period in psychopathology, during which description and classification were so heavily emphasized, has been referred to as the "descriptive era."

Conquest of general paresis. During this period, tremendous strides were being made in the study of the nervous system by such now-famous men as Golgi, Ramón y Cajal, Broca, Jackson, and Head, and the brain pathology underlying many mental disorders was gradually being uncovered. The syphilitic basis of general paresis (syphilis of the brain) was finally established as the result of the brilliant contributions of a series of medical scientists. Similarly, the brain pathology in cerebral arteriosclerosis and in the senile psychoses was established by Alzheimer and other investigators. One success was followed by another, and eventually the organic pathology underlying the toxic psychoses, certain types of mental retardation, and other "organically" caused mental illness was discovered.

These discoveries were not made overnight but resulted from the combined efforts of many scientists. For example, at least ten different steps can be traced in the discovery of the organic pathology underlying general paresis—one of the most serious of all mental illnesses, which produced paralysis and insanity and typically brought about the death of the afflicted subject in from two to five years. Prior to this discovery, organic pathology had been suspected in many mental disorders but had not been demonstrated systematically and completely enough to allow for effective therapy. The sequence of events in this long search shows graphically the way in which scientists working independently can utilize research by others in the field in advanc-

ing knowledge bit by bit and developing a model that will fit all the known facts. The major steps involved in the conquest of general paresis and the development of appropriate treatment were:

1. Differentiation of general paresis as a specific type of mental illness by the Frenchman A. L. J. Bayle in 1825. Bayle gave a very complete and accurate description of the symptom pattern of paresis and convincingly presented his reasons for believing paresis to be a distinct disorder.

2. Report by Esmarch and Jessen in 1857 of cases of paresis who were known to have had syphilis and their conclusion that the syphilis caused the paresis.

3. Description by the Scotchman Argyll-Robertson in 1869 of the failure of the pupillary reflex to light (failure of the pupil of the eye to narrow under bright light) as diagnostic of the involvement of the central nervous system in syphilis.

4. Experiment by the Viennese psychiatrist Richard Krafft-Ebing in 1897, involving the inoculation of paretic patients with matter from syphilitic sores. None of the patients developed the secondary symptoms of syphilis, which led to the conclusion that they must previously have been infected. This was a crucial experiment which definitely established the relationship of general paresis to syphilis.

5. Discovery of the *Spirochaeta pallida* by Schaudinn in 1905 as the cause of syphilis.

6. Development by von Wassermann in 1906 of a blood test for syphilis. Now it became possible to check for the presence of the deadly spirochetes in the bloodstream of a man who would not otherwise realize he was infected.

7. Application by Plant in 1908 of the Wassermann test to the cerebrospinal fluid, to indicate whether or not the spirochete had invaded the patient's central nervous system.

8. Development by Paul Ehrlich in 1909, after 605 failures, of the arsenical salvarsan (which he thereupon called "606") for the treatment of syphilis. Although "606" proved effective in killing the syphilitic spirochetes in the bloodstream, it was not effective against the spirochetes which had penetrated the central nervous system.

9. Verification by Noguchi and Moore in 1913 of the syphilitic spirochete as the brain-damaging agent in general paresis. They discovered these spirochetes in the post-mortem study of the brains of patients who had suffered from paresis.

10. Introduction in 1917 by Julius Wagner-Jauregg, chief of the psychiatric clinic of the University of Vienna, of the malarial fever treatment of syphilis and paresis. He inoculated nine of the paretic patients in his clinic with the blood of a soldier who was ill with malaria, and found marked improvement in three patients and apparent recovery in three of the others.

Thus the organic brain pathology underlying one of the most serious mental disorders was uncovered and scientific measures for its treatment developed. True, the complete understanding of paresis—why one patient becomes expansive and another depressed with the same general organic brain pathology—involves an understanding of certain psychological concepts yet to be discussed. Also, of course, progress in treatment has continued, and penicillin has become the preferred method of treatment, avoiding the complications of malaria. But the steps outlined above show the way in which, *for the first time in all history, a clear-cut conquest of a mental disorder was made by medical science.*

ADVANCES ACHIEVED
BY THE MEDICAL MODEL

Let us pause for a moment to examine the important advances that had been made in psychopathology up to the turn of the twentieth century, which represented the end of the period during which the medical model almost completely dominated psychopathology.

1. The early concepts of demonology had finally been destroyed, and the organic viewpoint of mental illness as based upon brain pathology was well established.

2. For general paresis and certain other mental disorders, definite underlying brain pathology had been discovered and appropriate methods of treatment developed.

3. A workable, though not yet completely satisfactory, scheme of classification had been set up.

4. Mental illness had finally been put on an equal footing with physical illness, at least in medical circles, and for the first time mental patients were receiving humane treatment based upon scientific findings.

5. A great deal of research was under way in anatomy, physiology, biochemistry, and other allied medical sciences, in an attempt to ascertain the brain pathology (or other bodily pathology which might be affecting the brain) in other types of mental disorder and to clarify the role of organic processes in all behavior.

These were truly remarkable achievements, and they helped pave the way for some of the great advances in psychopathology that have come about in the present century. We have seen dramatic breakthroughs, for example, in the fields of genetics and neurophysiology, where vigorous experimental work has shown how defects of the brain or changes in its internal chemistry can produce disturbances in thought processes. Another important advance has come about with the introduction, in the 1950's, of tranquilizing and energizing drugs, both of which have proven effective in the treatment of functional psychoses and other mental disorders. These drugs have undergone refinement, and new drugs are periodically being introduced. Although such drugs cannot "cure" a mentally disordered individual, they have made it possible for more persons to remain in their family and community settings instead of going to remote mental hospitals; they also have led to earlier discharges for individuals who have been hospitalized for mental disturbances; and lastly, they have reduced the severity of symptoms and cut down on the need for restraints and locked wards. As R. W. White (1959) has pointed out, Pinel's mission in striking the chains from the mentally ill has at last come close to its ultimate fulfillment.

Contemporary progress in the understanding and treatment of mental disorders cannot be wholly explained, however, in terms of advances in the medical sciences. At least equally important has been the belated recognition that psychosocial factors are key elements in the causation of both normal and abnormal behavior. During the early years of the twentieth century most students of abnormal behavior became convinced that organic pathology of the brain or nervous system must be at the root of *all* mental disorders, as they had been shown to be in the case of paresis. As we shall see in the next chapter, this view has now been effectively refuted.

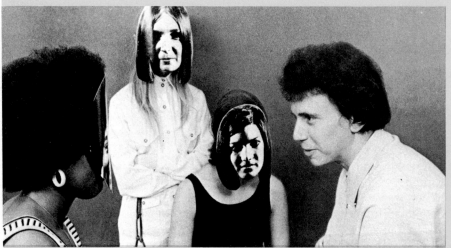

Psychosocial Models

3

THE PSYCHOANALYTIC MODEL

THE BEHAVIORISTIC MODEL

THE HUMANISTIC MODEL

THE EXISTENTIAL MODEL

THE INTERPERSONAL MODEL

In Chapter 2 we traced the development of our views of psychopathology from ancient times to the beginning of the twentieth century—from early beliefs in demonology and witchcraft to the development of the organic viewpoint and the medical model. But despite great advances in the understanding and treatment of mental disorders achieved by the medical model, much more was yet to be done. Many puzzling and important questions remained unanswered.

For one thing, repeated clinical examinations and research studies failed to reveal any organic pathology in the great majority of patients. True, a given patient might show some minor deviation in bodily chemistry, but then, so did a great many normal people; furthermore, many patients with the same symptoms of mental disorder did not show the same organic deviation.

To some scientists these discrepancies were a challenge to intensify research, for they felt certain that organic pathology must be there, and that the refinement of their laboratory techniques would make it clear. But there was also a new school of thought emerging which questioned the dominant belief in brain pathology as the sole cause of mental disorders. This was the "revolutionary" view that certain types of mental disorders might be caused by *psychological* rather than organic factors.

Although one might assume that the role of psychological factors in mental disorders would have been recognized long before 1900, such was not the case. Psychology as a science was still in its infancy in 1900, its inception dating back only some twenty-one years to the establishment of the first experimental psychology laboratory at the University of Leipzig in 1879 by Wilhelm Wundt. In addition, early psychology was rather naïve in its approach to an understanding of human behavior, and consisted primarily of experimental studies of sense perception. True, William James (1890) had published his monumental work, *Principles of Psychology*, in which he attempted to explain emotion, memory, reasoning, habits, consciousness of self, hysteria, and other aspects of human behavior. However, he was handicapped because little experimental work had been done in these areas, and his brief allusions to abnormal behavior were mainly descriptive and speculative.

This is not to disparage the contributions of the early workers who helped psychology through its infant period or to minimize the importance of physiological studies as a foundation for what came next. The fact remains, however, that psychology was still in its early stages; and there was little systematic knowledge regarding the role of psychological processes in maladaptive behavior. Thus the groundwork for our present understanding of maladaptive learning and inner conflict—

e.g., the conflict between the individual's "real" self, or the way he thinks he is; his "ideal" self, or the way he thinks he should be; and his "social" self, or the mask he wears in attempts to meet the perceived demands and expectations of others—was still to be laid.

In reviewing the development of contemporary psychological thought, we shall examine five systematic models of man—the psychoanalytic, behavioristic, humanistic, existential, and interpersonal. Although these various orientations represent distinct and sometimes conflicting approaches to the understanding of human behavior, they are also, as we shall see, in many ways complementary. All of them are properly termed *psychosocial* models, since they take some cognizance of social influences as well as of psychological processes.

THE PSYCHOANALYTIC MODEL

The first systematic steps toward the understanding of psychological factors in mental disorders came about through the astounding contributions of one man—Sigmund Freud (1856–1939). Freud developed his psychoanalytic model of man over a period of five decades of observing and writing. The major principles of his model were based on the clinical study of individual patients undergoing treatment of their problems—usually of a neurotic nature. Initially Freud utilized hypnosis in treating his patients and making his observations concerning the psychodynamics of their problems. Later, however, the method of free association, in which the patient is asked to give an unrestricted verbal account of whatever comes into his mind, became the preferred procedure.

In reviewing the psychoanalytic model of man, it is useful to divide our discussion into an examination of (1) the roots of psychoanalysis, (2) the basic principles of the model, including its concept of psychopathology, and (3) the impact of the psychoanalytic model on our views of man and his behavior.

ROOTS OF PSYCHOANALYTIC THOUGHT

We find the early roots of the psychological viewpoint and of psychoanalysis in a somewhat unexpected place—in the study of hypnosis, especially in its relation to hysteria.[1]

Mesmerism. Our story starts out with one of the most notorious figures in psychiatry, Anton Mesmer (1734–1815), who further developed Paracelsus' notion of the influence of the planets on the human body. Their influence was believed to be caused by a universal magnetic fluid, and it was presumably the distribution of this fluid in the body that determined health or disease. In attempting to find a cure for mental disorders, Mesmer came to the conclusion that all persons possess magnetic forces that can be used to influence the distribution of the magnetic fluid in other persons, thus effecting cures.

Mesmer attempted to put his views into practice in Vienna and in various other towns, but it

---

[1]The term *hysteria* is used here to refer to physical ailments—such as blindness or the paralysis of a limb—for which there is no basis in terms of organic pathology.

was not until he came to Paris in 1778 that he achieved success. Here he opened a clinic in which he treated all kinds of diseases by "animal magnetism." The patients were seated around a tub (a *baquet*) which contained various chemicals and from which protruded iron rods that were applied to the affected portions of the body; the room was darkened, appropriate music was provided, and Mesmer appeared in a lilac robe, passing from one patient to another and touching each one with his hands or his wand. By this means Mesmer was apparently able to remove hysterical anesthesias and paralyses and to demonstrate most of the phenomena discovered later by the use of hypnosis.

Finally branded as a charlatan by his medical colleagues, Mesmer was forced to leave Paris, and he shortly faded into obscurity. However, his methods and results were the center of controversy in scientific circles for many years—in fact, mesmerism in the early part of the nineteenth century was as much a source of heated discussion as psychoanalysis was to be in the early part of the twentieth century. This discussion eventually led to a revival of interest in the hypnotic phenomenon as itself an explanation of the cures that took place.

"The Nancy school." One of the most successful of these physicians was the Frenchman Liébeault (1823–1904), who practiced at Nancy. Also in Nancy at this time was a professor of medicine, Bernheim (1840–1919), who became interested in the relationship between hysteria and hypnosis primarily as a result of Liébeault's success in curing by hypnosis a patient whom Bernheim had been unsuccessfully treating by more conventional methods for some four years (Selling, 1943). Bernheim and Liébeault worked together on the problem and developed the concept that hypnotism and hysteria were related and that both were due to suggestion (Brown & Menninger, 1940). Their view was based on two lines of evidence: (1) phenomena observed in hysteria, such as paralysis of an arm, inability to hear, anesthetic areas in which the individual could be stuck with a pin without feeling pain—all of which occurred when there was apparently nothing organically wrong with the patient—could be produced in normal subjects by means of hypnosis; and (2) symptoms such as these could be removed in hysterical subjects by means of

THE USEFULNESS OF MODELS IN SCIENCE

A model is essentially an analogy that helps a scientist to order his findings and see important relationships among them. The computer model of the brain, for example, has made it commonplace to utilize the concepts of input, information processing, and feedback in conceptualizing human thought processes. Unlike formal theories, which purportedly account for all relevant data, models are not intended to be entirely accurate explanations of reality. Rather, they are conceptual tools that can help investigators organize and interpret masses of data that might otherwise prove meaningless and unwieldy.

A model may be very comprehensive or relatively limited in scope. Thus, in psychology, we have comprehensive models of man, such as the psychoanalytic model, and more specific models, such as the various models of schizophrenia. Models also differ in terms of completeness and degree of detail. Some of the psychosocial models examined in this chapter actually represent more of a perspective, or point of view, than a clearly formulated model with a systematized and agreed-upon structure. This is particularly true of the humanistic and interpersonal models.

Although the models we shall be discussing in this book are commonly referred to as "theories" of normal and abnormal behavior, the concept of "models" seems more appropriate in view of our present limited knowledge and the need for maintaining flexibility in our thinking about man. Theories, once formalized, tend to seem like final explanations and are often adhered to long after new research findings cast them in doubt. Models, on the other hand, follow a strategy of successive approximations, and they can be readily modified—or, if necessary, abandoned—to accommodate new evidence. It is this ability of science to be "self-correcting" that makes scientific progress possible.

hypnosis so that the patient could use his arm, or hear, or feel in the previously anesthetized areas. Thus it seemed likely that hysteria was a sort of self-hypnosis. The physicians who accepted this view were known as "the Nancy school."

Meanwhile, Jean Charcot (1825–1893), who was head of the Salpêtrière Hospital in Paris and the leading neurologist of his time, had been experimentally investigating some of the phenomena described by the old mesmerists. As a result of his research, Charcot disagreed with the findings of Bernheim and Liébeault and insisted that there were brain changes of a degenerative nature in hysteria. In this Charcot proved to be wrong, but work on the problem by so outstanding a scientist did much to awaken medical and scientific interest in it.

In one of the major medical debates of history, in which many harsh words were spoken on both sides, the adherents of the Nancy school finally triumphed. The recognition of one psychologically caused mental disorder spurred research, and it soon became apparent that psychological factors were involved in morbid anxiety, phobias, and other psychopathology. Eventually Charcot himself, a man of great scientific honesty, was won over to the new point of view and did much to promote an interest in the study of psychological factors in various mental disorders.

Toward the end of the nineteenth century, then, it was clear to many that there were mental disorders with a psychological basis as well as those with an organic basis. But one major question remained to be answered: How do these psychologically caused mental disorders come about?

Freud and the beginnings of psychoanalysis. The first systematic attempt to answer this question was made by Sigmund Freud. Freud was a brilliant young Viennese physician who at first specialized in neurology and received an appointment as lecturer on nervous diseases at the University of Vienna. On one occasion, however, he introduced to his audience a neurotic patient suffering from a persistent headache, and mistakenly diagnosed the case as chronic localized meningitis. As a result of this error in diagnosis, he lost his job—although, as he pointed out in his autobiography, greater authorities than he were in the habit of diagnosing similar cases as cerebral tumor. Freud went to Paris in 1885 to study under Charcot and later became acquainted with the work of Liébeault and Bernheim at Nancy. He was greatly impressed by their use of hypnosis on hysterical patients and came away convinced that powerful mental processes may remain hidden from consciousness.

On his return to Vienna, Freud worked in collaboration with an older physician, Joseph Breuer, who had introduced an interesting innovation in the use of hypnosis on his neurotic patients, chiefly women. He let the patient under hypnosis talk about her problems and tell what had bothered her. Under these circumstances the patient usually spoke rather freely, displayed considerable emotion, and on wakening from the hypnotic state felt considerably relieved. Because of the regular discharge of emotions involved, this method was called the "cathartic method." This simple innovation in the use of hypnosis proved to be of great significance, for not only did it help the patient discharge her emotional tensions by discussion of her problems, but it revealed the nature of the difficulties that had brought about her neurotic symptoms. The patient saw no relationship between her problems and her hysterical symptoms, but the therapist could usually see it quite readily.

Thus was made the discovery of the "unconscious"—the realization of the important role played by unconscious processes in the determination of behavior. In 1893, Freud and Breuer published their joint paper *On the Psychical Mechanisms of Hysterical Phenomena*, which constituted one of the great milestones of psychodynamics.

Freud soon discovered, moreover, that he could dispense with the hypnotic state entirely. For by encouraging the patient to say freely whatever came into her mind without regard to logic or decency, Freud found that she would eventually overcome inner obstacles to remembering and would discuss her problem freely. The new method was called *free association*, and the term *psychoanalysis* was given to the principles involved in analyzing and interpreting what the patient said and did, and in helping her gain insight and achieve a more adequate adjustment.

Freud devoted the remainder of his long and energetic life to the development and elaboration of the psychoanalytic model. His views were formally introduced to American scientists in 1909, when he delivered a now-famous series of lectures at Clark University at the invitation of G. Stanley Hall, the eminent American psychologist who was then president of the university. These *Introductory Lectures on Psychoanalysis* led to a great deal of controversy which helped publicize the concepts of psychoanalysis to both scientists and the general public.

BASIC PRINCIPLES OF THE PSYCHOANALYTIC MODEL

The psychoanalytic model of man is both highly complex and highly systematized. Its general outlines may be sketched as follows:

Id, ego, and superego. Basically, the individual's behavior is assumed to result from the interaction of three key subsystems within the personality: the id, ego, and superego.

The *id* consists of primitive biological drives which are considered to be of two types: (1) constructive drives, primarily of a sexual nature, which constitute the *libido*, or basic energy of life, and (2) destructive drives which tend toward aggression, destruction, and eventual death. Thus *life*, or constructive, instincts are opposed by *death*, or destructive, instincts. Here it may be noted that Freud used the term *sex* in a broad sense to refer to almost anything of a pleasurable nature, from eating to creativity.

The id operates in terms of the *pleasure principle* and is concerned only with the immediate gratification of instinctual needs. It is completely selfish and unconcerned with reality or moral considerations. Although the id can generate mental images and wish-fulfilling fantasies related to need gratification—referred to as the *primary process*—it cannot undertake direct action toward meeting instinctual demands. Consequently, a second key subsystem— the *ego*—develops and mediates between the demands of the id and the realities of the external world. The primary purpose of the ego is to meet id demands, but in such a way as to ensure the well-being and survival of the individual. This requires the use of reason and other intellectual resources in dealing with the external world, as well as the exercise of control over id demands. Such adaptive measures of the ego are referred to as the *secondary process*, and the ego is said to operate in terms of the *reality principle*. Here it may be emphasized that Freud viewed id demands—especially sexual and aggressive strivings—as reflecting an inherent conflict between the animal instincts of the individual and the inhibitions and regulations imposed by society.

Since the id-ego relationship is merely one of expediency, Freud introduced a third key subsystem—the *superego*—which is the outgrowth of learning the taboos and moral values of society. The superego is essentially what we refer to as *conscience*, and is concerned with right and wrong. As the superego develops we find an additional inner control system coming into operation to cope with the uninhibited desires of the id. However, the superego operates through the ego system and strives to compel the ego to inhibit desires that are considered wrong or immoral.

The relationships between these intrapsychic subsystems of id, ego, and superego are of crucial significance in determining behavior. Often the instinctual desires and demands of the id are in conflict with superego demands or with the demands of the external world. The adequate resolution of such conflicts by the ego is considered essential to personality adjustment. Neuroses and other mental disorders result when the individual is unable to resolve these conflicts.

Anxiety, defense mechanisms, and the unconscious. The concept of anxiety is prominent in the psychoanalytic model. Freud classified three types of anxiety, or "psychic pain": (1) *reality* anxiety, arising when the individual is confronted by dangers or threats in the external world; (2) *neurotic* anxiety, arising when the individual's id impulses threaten to break through his ego controls and result in behavior that will lead to his punishment; and (3) *moral* anxiety, arising when the individual does something or even contemplates doing something in conflict with his superego or moral values, and arouses feelings of guilt.

Anxiety is both a warning of impending danger

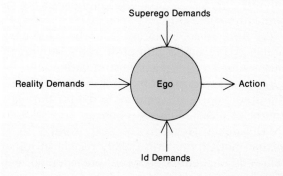

THE RELATION OF ID, EGO, AND SUPEREGO IN THE PSYCHOANALYTIC MODEL OF MAN

This diagram illustrates the concept of the ego as the central integrating core of the personality, which mediates between inner demands and the environment.

and a painful experience, and hence it forces the individual to undertake corrective action. Often the ego can cope with the anxiety by rational measures; however, if these do not suffice, the ego resorts to irrational protective measures—such as rationalization and repression—which are referred to as *ego-defense mechanisms*. These defense mechanisms alleviate the painful anxiety, but they do so at the expense of distorting reality, and hence do not deal directly with the stress situation. We shall examine the major ego-defense mechanisms in Chapter 5.

Another concept of key importance in the psychoanalytic model is that of the *unconscious*. Freud thought that the conscious represented a relatively small area of the mind; while the unconscious, like the submerged part of an iceberg, was much the larger portion. In the vast expanse of the unconscious are the images, desires, feelings, and ideas that have been either forgotten or repressed. The assumption is that objectionable memories, wishes, and impulses are less disruptive to the ego and arouse less anxiety when they have been repressed and excluded from consciousness. Although the individual is unaware of such unconscious desires, these feelings actively seek expression and may be reflected in fantasies and dreams when ego controls are temporarily lowered. Thus we see the major role ascribed to unconscious motivation by Freud and the conclusion that we are often unaware of the real basis for our thoughts and actions.

Psychosexual development. Freud viewed personality development as a succession of stages, each being characterized by a dominant mode of achieving libidinal pleasure. The five stages as he outlined them were:

(1) *Oral stage*. During the first year of life the mouth is the principal erogenous zone; the infant's greatest source of gratification is assumed to be sucking.

(2) *Anal stage*. From age 2 to age 3, the membranes of the anal region presumably provide the major source of pleasurable stimulation.

(3) *Phallic stage*. From age 3 to age 5 or 6, self-manipulation of the genitals provides the major source of pleasurable sensation.

(4) *Latency stage*. In the years from 6 to 12, sexual motivations presumably recede in importance as the child becomes preoccupied with developmental skills and activities.

(5) *Genital stage*. After puberty the deepest feelings of pleasure presumably come from heterosexual relations.

Freud believed that gratification during each stage is important if the individual is not to be *fixated* at that level. For example, an individual who does not receive adequate oral gratification during infancy may be prone to excessive eating or drinking in adult life.

In general, each stage of development places demands on the individual that must be met, and arouses conflicts that must be resolved. One of the most important conflicts occurs during the phallic stage, when the pleasures of masturbation and accompanying fantasies pave the way for the Oedipus complex. Oedipus, according to Greek mythology, unknowingly killed his father and married his mother. Each young boy, Freud thought, symbolically relives the Oedipus drama. He has incestuous cravings for his mother and views his father as a hated rival; however, he also dreads the wrath of his dominant male parent and fears especially that his father may harm him by removing his penis. This *castration anxiety* forces the boy to repress his sexual desires for his mother as well as his hostility toward his father. Eventually, if all goes well, the boy identifies with his father and comes to have only harmless tender affection for his mother. The female Oedipus complex is more intricate, but it is based essentially on the view that the girl wants to possess her father and replace her mother. For either sex, resolution of the Oedipal conflict is considered essential if the young adult is to develop satisfactory heterosexual relationships.

IMPACT ON OUR VIEWS OF
NORMAL AND ABNORMAL BEHAVIOR

According to the psychoanalytic model, man is dominated by instinctual biological drives, as well as by unconscious desires and motives. Although there is the constructive libidinal side to his nature, there are also darker forces leading toward destruction and death. And although the ego tends toward rationality, the counter forces of intrapsychic conflict, defense mechanisms, and the unconscious all tend toward a high degree of irrationality and maladaptive behavior. About

FREUD (1856–1939)   JUNG (1875–1961)

ADLER (1870–1937)   MENNINGER (1893–)

As the work of Sigmund Freud gradually received recognition, it won him a following of special students and supporters. Later, some of these students found themselves in serious disagreement with various aspects of Freud's system and set up modified systems of their own. Among the more prominent of the dissenters were C. G. Jung and Alfred Adler, who both left Freud in 1911. Others of Freud's students and followers stayed more within the general theoretical framework developed by Freud. One of these has been Karl Menninger, a leading figure in the elaboration and dissemination of psychoanalytic thought in America. Menninger has gathered data from his own clinic in support of Freud's principles and has written extensively, including among his books *The Human Mind* and *Man Against Himself.*

In departing from the Freudian system, which both felt placed undue emphasis on sex as a determinant of behavior, Jung and Adler founded their own schools of psychology—the Analytic and the Individual Schools, respectively. Jung's approach was mystical and theoretical, whereas Adler's was pragmatic and not so highly systematized, but from both schools have emerged concepts of considerable contemporary interest.

Although Jung is perhaps best known for his distinction between extrovert and introvert personality types, two of his most valuable concepts are "the collective unconscious" and "inner self-experience." Jung believed that each individual, in addition to his personal unconscious (a storehouse of experiences which once were conscious but have become forgotten or repressed), has a collective unconscious, which consists of memories established throughout mankind's history and inherited in the brain structure in the form of "primordial images" or "archetypes." Such universal images, strongly emotional in content, are elicited by aspects of one's own experiences; e.g., the archetype of the "earth mother" may be elicited by a child's own mother. Jung used these "collective memories" to account for similar folk legends, such as those concerning witches, dragons, and heroes, and other aspects of culture found repeatedly among diverse peoples throughout the world.

In emphasizing the importance of inner self-experience, Jung held that everything within the unconscious seeks outward manifestation, and that the individual achieves true

"wholeness" only as fantasies, images, and dreams from the personal and collective unconscious become accessible to the conscious self. Unlike some contemporary thinkers, Jung viewed the self not as something that unfolds in the course of growing up, but rather as something that can be achieved only by great effort. The individual must learn to understand and integrate fantasies from his personal and collective unconscious, and also must have the courage to separate himself from group convention and go his own way. Thus, the full development of the self is a task of heroic proportions and not achieved by the mass of men who live out their lives in the safe confines of social convention. Only as the individual achieves selfhood, however, does he find wholeness and fulfillment.

While Jung's analytic model of man did not receive widespread acceptance, having been criticized as too mystical and lacking in scientific grounding, renewed interest is presently being taken in some of its concepts, particularly in the collective unconscious and archetypes.

Adler differed from Freud and Jung in his emphasis on social rather than inherited determinants of behavior. He viewed man as an inherently social being whose most basic motivation is to belong to and participate in the group. Adler did not submerge the individual in the group, however; he emphasized an active, creative, conscious "self" that plays a central role in the individual's attempts to organize his experiences and achieve fulfillment as a human being. Therefore, each individual is unique in his development of a "style of life" reflecting his own basic purposes, values, and coping patterns. Inferiority feelings arise whenever the individual experiences a lack of competence or self-fulfillment. Normally, inferiority feelings drive him toward self-improvement, but when such feelings are intense they may lead to an "inferiority complex" with exaggerated strivings toward power and self-aggrandizement.

Man is thus, according to Adler's view, a conscious agent, with tendencies toward "social interest," self-direction, and self-fulfillment—a view directly in contrast to Freud's gloomy concept of man's irrationality and his continual battle with his socially disapproved instincts. While Adler's individual psychology has been largely absorbed by the humanistic model (p. 65), its basic concepts have been influential in shaping contemporary thinking about man.

the best that man can hope for is a compromise, from which he will realize as much instinctual gratification as possible while minimizing punishment and guilt. Finally, although man is driven by inner desires, his behavior is largely conditioned by his early experiences and learning. Thus the psychoanalytic model basically involves a negativistic and deterministic view of man which minimizes the concepts of "free will" and freedom for self-direction. On a group level, it sees violence, war, and related pathological phenomena as the inevitable product of man's aggressive and destructive instincts.

Many of Freud's ideas have been revised or discarded as a result of subsequent research findings, and the psychoanalytic model is no longer widely used as the principal framework for organizing and interpreting scientific observations about psychopathology. However, this should not obscure the fact that Freud greatly advanced our understanding of both normal and abnormal behavior. Three of his contributions stand out as particularly noteworthy:

1. The development of techniques—free association and dream analysis—for becoming acquainted with both the conscious and unconscious aspects of the mental life of the individual. The data thus obtained led Freud to emphasize (a) the dynamic role of unconscious motives and ego-defense processes, (b) the importance of early childhood experiences in later personality adjustment and maladjustment, and (c) the importance of sexual factors in human behavior and mental disorders. Although, as we have said, Freud used the term *sex* in a much broader sense than it is ordinarily used, the idea caught the popular fancy, and the role of sexual factors in human behavior was finally brought out into the open as an appropriate topic for scientific investigation.

2. The demonstration that certain abnormal mental phenomena—such as the repression of traumatic experiences and irrational fears—occurred as the individual attempted to cope with his problems and were simply exaggerations of normal ego-defense mechanisms. With the realization that the same psychological principles apply to both normal and abnormal behavior, much of the mystery and fear surrounding mental disorders was dispelled, and the mental patient was helped to regain his dignity as a human being.

3. The development of a therapeutic technique —psychoanalysis—for the psychological treatment of mental disorders. This technique is directed toward uncovering and dealing with unconscious and irrational processes, and helping the individual achieve more effective personality integration and coping techniques. Particular emphasis is given here to conflicts arising as a result of social demands and prohibitions that are incompatible with the individual's basic biological needs.

We shall deal with psychoanalysis as a form of individual psychotherapy in Chapter 20. Here we may simply note that such therapy is directed at uncovering and dealing with the irrational and anxiety-arousing desires and impulses in the unconscious—which presumably lie at the root of the individual's difficulties—and thereby helping him achieve more effective personality integration and coping behavior. In this context, it may be emphasized that psychoanalytic therapy is not content simply with removing symptoms (for example, hysterical paralysis, sexual deviation, or dependence on drugs) but rather focuses on removing the "basic causes" that presumably led to the symptoms. If successful, it thus precludes the possibility of "symptom substitution" —the appearance of a new set of symptoms in place of others that have been cleared up.

Freudian theory has been criticized for an overemphasis on the sexual drive, for undue pessimism about man's basic nature, for exaggerating the role of unconscious processes, for a failure to consider motives toward personal growth and fulfillment, for a neglect of cultural differences in shaping behavior, and for a lack of empirical evidence to support many of its assumptions. In historical perspective, however, it can be seen as the first systematic model of man to recognize the interrelated roles of biological, psychological, and sociocultural factors in personality development and functioning. The comprehensive nature of the psychoanalytic model made possible the integration of research findings from various scientific areas—principally physiology, neurology, psychology, sociology, and anthropology—which in turn paved the way for contemporary views of man as a unified organism functioning in a physical and sociocultural environment.

THE BEHAVIORISTIC MODEL

While the psychoanalytic model largely dominated psychological thought in the early part of this century, a new school—behaviorism—was emerging to challenge its supremacy. The behavioristic psychologists felt that the study of subjective experience—via the techniques of free association and dream analysis, for example—did not provide acceptable scientific data, since such observations were not open to verification by other investigators. In their view, only the study of directly observable behavior and the stimulus and reinforcing conditions that "control" it could serve as a basis for formulating scientific principles of human behavior. The behavioristic model is organized around a single theme—learning—and is sometimes referred to as the stimulus-response, or "S–R," model of man.

ROOTS OF BEHAVIORISM

The origins of the behavioristic model can be traced to the work of the Russian physiologist Ivan Pavlov (1849–1936), but credit for its elaboration belongs largely to three distinguished American psychologists: J. B. Watson (1878–1958), E. L. Thorndike (1874–1949), and B. F. Skinner (1904–). We shall examine the contributions of each of these men in turn.

Pavlov and the conditioned reflex. While performing a series of studies on the salivary response in dogs, Pavlov discovered the phenomenon of the *conditioned reflex*. He found that if a stimulus which automatically elicits salivation—such as a bit of food—is presented as a tone is sounded, after several repetitions the tone will come to elicit the salivation. Even seeing the person who ordinarily brought the food, or hearing his footsteps, also produced salivation on the part of the dog. As we shall see, this simple conditioning method was destined to become a key approach to the study of learning; and the conditioned reflex to become a fundamental concept in modern psychology.

In 1914, while pursuing the study of conditioned reflexes in dogs, one of Pavlov's students reported an unusual and dramatic incident. He had conditioned a dog to distinguish between a circle and an ellipse. The ellipse was then altered in shape so that it became more and more like the circle, until the dog could no longer distinguish accurately between the two. During three weeks of subsequent experimentation, the dog's ability to discriminate between the two similar figures not only failed to improve, but became considerably worse, and finally disappeared altogether. At the same time the behavior of the dog underwent an abrupt change. The previously quiet and cooperative animal began to squeal and squirm in its stand and tore off the experimental apparatus with its teeth. In addition, when taken into the experimental room, the dog now barked violently, instead of going quietly as it had before. On testing, even the cruder differentiations between the circle and the ellipse which the dog had previously mastered could not be elicited. This change in the dog's behavior was considered by Pavlov to be equivalent to an acute neurosis.

Following this initial lead, later investigators have conducted similar experiments with rats, cats, dogs, sheep, pigs, monkeys, and chimpanzees with comparable results. When the animals were forced by the experimental conditions to make discriminations that were beyond their capacities, they seemed to suffer the equivalent of a "nervous breakdown"—usually referred to as an *experimental neurosis*.

Thus an unusual incident in laboratory routine, which might have been overlooked as merely trivial and annoying by an observer less astute than Pavlov, led to a whole new method of attack in the study of abnormal behavior. On the basis of subsequent experimental findings, Pavlov went on, after the age of eighty, to attempt a rather comprehensive formulation of human psychopathology (Pavlov, 1941). This formulation was based on the speculative assumption that the different reaction patterns shown by dogs to the conditioned-reflex techniques would also be reflected on the human level in reactions to life stresses. Among dogs Pavlov had found three general reaction, or constitutional, types: an excitatory group, an inhibitory group, and a central group. Each reaction type was found to develop a somewhat different kind of experimental neurosis. For example, when an animal of the excitatory type was forced beyond the limits of its discriminatory ability, it developed periods of depression or excitement comparable to manic-depressive reactions in humans. Under similar conditions, the inhibitory type developed schizophrenic-like reactions, whereas the central group developed what appeared to be mixed reactions.

In applying these findings to human beings, Pavlov made certain modifications in order to take into account the factors of language and of "weak" nervous systems. Thus he distinguished two personality types: (1) the artistic type, intense, vivid, and highly responsive to external stimulation, and (2) the thinking type, quiet, ruminative, and more responsive to verbal concepts and ideas than to sensory stimulation. In the event of mental disorder, the artistic type presumably would be prone to hysterical or manic-depressive reactions, while the thinking type would be more prone to obsessive-compulsive and schizophrenic reactions.

Thus, much of Pavlov's work was concerned with individual differences in neural functioning —with types of nervous systems—which, in turn, provide the bases for different reactions to stimulation and different forms of mental disorders. His conditioning techniques, production of "experimental neuroses," and concepts of excitation and inhibition paved the way for a vast amount of experimental work in psychopathology.

Watson and "behaviorism." Pavlov's principle of conditioning was seized upon by the American psychologist J. B. Watson as a procedure for studying human behavior more objectively and avoiding the pitfalls of introspection implicit in both psychoanalysis and studies of conscious states. Combining the principles of conditioning with certain ideas of his own, Watson formulated a point of view which he called "behaviorism." His book *Psychology from the Standpoint of a Behaviorist* was published in 1919. As might be expected, this approach placed heavy emphasis on the role of the social environment in "conditioning" personality development and on the importance of assessing the effects of given stimuli on learning and behavior.

Watson and Rayner (1920) used the conditioning technique in a dramatic demonstration of the role of learning in abnormal behavior. In their now-famous experiment with little Albert, an eleven-month-old boy who was fond of animals, they demonstrated that an irrational fear or phobia could be readily learned through conditioning. The procedure was simple: The experimenter stood behind the boy and struck a steel bar with a hammer whenever Albert reached for a white rat. The loud noise elicited a fear response on the boy's part and made him cry. After several repetitions of this experience Albert became greatly disturbed at the sight of the animal even without the loud noise, and his fear generalized to include other furry animals and objects as well. This demonstration of the development and generalization of the child's irrational fear suggested that other types of abnormal behavior might also be the result of learning.

Later, Mary Cover Jones (1924) succeeded in eliminating such fears by presenting a white rabbit at a distance when the child, previously conditioned to fear it, was reacting positively to food—an anxiety inhibitor. By bringing the animal gradually closer, always avoiding overbalancing the positive tendency by the strength of the negative fear tendency, the experimenter finally eliminated the boy's fear and replaced it with pleasant feelings toward the white rabbit; these feelings, in turn, generalized to other furry animals.

The contributions of Thorndike and Skinner. The work of Pavlov and Watson convinced many investigators that all learning is based on conditioned reflexes, or Pavlovian conditioning; and that studying the lawful properties of such conditioned reflexes could explain human behavior. However, a second fundamental concept of the behavioristic model was to be developed through the work of E. L. Thorndike and, later, B. F. Skinner.

In his formulation of the "law of effect," Thorndike (1913) made the observation that responses that have rewarding consequences are strengthened or learned, and responses that have negative or aversive consequences are weakened or extinguished. Thus he emphasized the control of man's behavior through reward and punishment. Following this early lead, Skinner (1953) concluded that the most important, understandable, and manipulable determinants of behavior lie outside the organism in environmental events, and can be manipulated to control the learning and behavior of the organism. As Skinner (1953) expressed it:

"The practice of looking inside the organism for an explanation of behavior has tended to obscure the variables which are immediately available for a scientific analysis. These variables lie outside the organism, in its immediate environment and in its environmental history." (p. 31)

The contributions of Thorndike and Skinner thus have led to a second major concept of conditioned learning—operant conditioning—which we shall examine in dealing with the basic principles of the behavioristic model. This concept has had a far-reaching influence not only on our views of how man learns but also on contemporary techniques of behavior modification and therapy.

BASIC PRINCIPLES OF LEARNING

As we have noted, learning provides the central theme of the behavioristic model. Since most of man's behavior is learned, the behaviorists have addressed themselves to the question of how learning comes about.[1] In trying to answer this question, they have focused on environmental conditions or stimuli that can be related to the acquisition, modification, and weakening or elimination of response patterns.

Respondent (classical) and operant conditioning. As a starting point, behaviorists commonly make a distinction between *respondent* (classical) and *operant* learning and the responses characteristic of each. In the former type, learning is effected by the presentation of a stimulus that is known to elicit a particular response. Even prior to learning, certain appropriate stimuli will elicit specific responses, such as relatively simple reflexes or emotional responses. For example, a bright light leads to the constriction of

the pupil of the eye; a sudden loud noise, to a fear response. Through conditioning, these same responses may come to be elicited by a wide range of other stimuli in the manner demonstrated by Pavlov. Thus an animal, after consistently hearing a bell when food is presented, will start salivating at the sound of the bell alone. The classic example of respondent conditioning in humans is the experiment cited previously in which little Albert was conditioned to fear a white rat. In both instances a stimulus that did not previously elicit a given response has come to elicit it; the stimulus is now referred to as a *conditioned stimulus*, and the response, as a *conditioned response*. And conversely, the repeated presentation of the conditioned stimulus (for example, the bell) without the unconditioned stimulus (food) leads to the *extinction*, or elimination, of the learned response.

In operant conditioning, instead of being presented with a stimulus that elicits a known response, the subject—animal or human—is placed in a situation in which he learns to make a response that brings about the attainment of a goal or the satisfaction of a need. Hence the use of the term *operant*: the subject "operates" upon or modifies his environment. As an example, a hungry rat may be placed in a cage that has a lever; in the course of exploring the cage he eventually presses the lever and is immediately given a bit of food. Before long he presses the lever again and the same thing happens. Ultimately he learns to press the lever whenever he is hungry. In learning to press a lever to obtain food, he has undergone operant conditioning. Operant responses are thus determined by their consequences. On the human level, operant conditioning is involved in the learning of language as a means of communication—for sending and receiving messages. The application of operant learning to psychopathology can be illustrated by the use of rewards or reinforcers to foster social behavior among chronic schizophrenics and teaching self-management skills to mentally retarded children and adolescents.

Reinforcement. Essential to both respondent and operant conditioning is *reinforcement*—the

---

[1] Distinguished American psychologists who have contributed to the development and extension of learning theory include E. C. Tolman, E. R. Guthrie, Clark Hull, R. R. Sears, J. Dollard, N. E. Miller, O. H. Mowrer, K. W. Spence, W. K. Estes, and R. L. Solomon.

SAY NOSE, JIMMY

JIMMY SAYS NOSE

GOOD BOY, JIMMY

TRIUMPH AND REWARD

The principle of operant conditioning is used in the "token exchange" system of learning which these pictures illustrate. Jimmy is rewarded with a "token"—such as a trinket—for desired behavior. This procedure has been successful in efforts to teach autistic children to speak as well as in encouraging the development of other desired behaviors.

strengthening of a new response by its repeated association with some stimulus. Such a stimulus is called a *reinforcer* and may be either *positive* (pleasant) or *negative* (aversive). Thus in Watson and Rayner's early demonstration of respondent conditioning (page 58), successive repetitions of the loud noise in association with the rat strengthened—or reinforced—Albert's conditioned fear. Operant conditioning is a little more complex: here an animal may learn to press a lever either because it is repeatedly associated with the reward of food or because it repeatedly enables him to avoid or terminate an electric shock. In this case, "negative reinforcement" involves not *receiving* the aversive stimulus but *avoiding or escaping from it.*

When the positive or negative value of the reinforcing stimulus is intrinsic—as with food or an electric shock—the stimulus is referred to as a *primary reinforcer;* if, on the other hand, the reinforcing characteristics of the stimulus must be learned or acquired through continued association with primary reinforcers—as is the case for money, which has no inherently rewarding or punishing potential—the stimulus is known as a *secondary reinforcer.* Included in this latter category are words—such as "good" or "bad," "yes" or "no," "excellent" or "poor"— which, once a language has been learned, may function as potent secondary reinforcers. Such stimuli may also be referred to as *generalized reinforcers* since, once their value has been established, they may influence a wide range of behaviors in addition to those involved during their initial acquisition.

It is assumed that any response which the subject is capable of making can be established and maintained by the appropriate scheduling of reinforcement—provided, of course, that the experimenter can effectively control the subject's environment. Whereas a high rate of reinforcement may be necessary to establish a response initially, lesser rates are usually sufficient to maintain it. In fact, learning appears to be especially persistent when reinforcement is *intermittent*—that is, when the reinforcing stimulus does not invariably follow the response.

The effectiveness of intermittent, or partial, reinforcement in the maintenance of learning has been demonstrated repeatedly in studies of both respondent and operant conditioning. The complete *withholding* of reinforcement, however, usually results in the eventual *extinction* of a learned response. Thus a dog who has learned to salivate at the sound of a bell, as in Pavlov's famous experiment, will sooner or later stop making the response if food (the reinforcing stimulus) is consistently withheld.

Exceptions to this principle are found in *avoidance learning*, where the subject has been conditioned to anticipate an aversive stimulus and to respond in such a way as to avoid it. Such avoidance behavior may continue indefinitely even in the absence of any apparent reinforcement. For example, consider a situation in which (1) a warning light signals that an electric shock is to follow, and (2) a rat has learned that by pressing a lever he can cause the warning light to go off and prevent his receiving the shock. Once established, such avoidance behavior may continue even when the electric shock mechanism is no longer in operation. For the warning light is still associated with actual aversive stimulation; and turning it off thus tends to be reinforcing in its own right. Since the animal presses the lever as soon as the light goes on, he fails to find out whether or not the electric shock is still operational. His avoidance behavior therefore persists.

Similarly, a child who has been bitten by a vicious dog may develop a conditioned avoidance response in which he consistently turns away from and avoids all dogs. Since his avoidance behavior alleviates his fear, it is highly resistant to extinction and denies him the possibility of having his fear of dogs extinguished, or of being reconditioned, by experiences with friendly dogs. We shall examine the significance of such avoidance responses in our later discussion of abnormal behavior patterns.

Generalization and discrimination. The tendency for a response that has been conditioned to one stimulus to become associated with other similar stimuli is referred to as *generalization*. We noted in the experiment conducted by Watson and Rayner that the infant's fear generalized from white rats to other furry animals. The greater the similarity of stimuli, the greater the likelihood of generalization. A process complementary to generalization is *discrimination*, which occurs when the individual learns to distinguish between similar stimuli and to respond to one and not

another. Discrimination is brought about through selective reinforcement and extinction. For example, if one of two similar stimuli is reinforced and the other is not—as in the case of red strawberries tasting good while green ones do not—a conditioned discrimination will occur. According to the behavioristic model, complex processes like attending, perceiving, concept formation, problem solving, and decision making are based on an elaboration of this basic discriminative process.

Discriminative responses have many implications for maladaptive behavior. For example, a delinquent youth may fail to develop discriminations between "responsible" and "irresponsible" behavior, or a schizophrenic may make discriminations that most other people do not. In some instances, a discrimination may be forced on the individual that is beyond his capability—as we noted in the case of Pavlov's production of experimental neuroses in dogs—and may lead to psychological disorganization and inefficient coping behavior.

Modeling, labeling, and shaping. Three key concepts in information processing and coping behavior—modeling, labeling and shaping—can enlarge our picture of the behavioristic model.

The process of *modeling*, or imitation, is important in the learning process; it entails what the term implies—the systematic modeling of particular response patterns for the subject by parents or other persons, and the systematic reinforcing of his imitation of such responses. If the individual is capable of imitating the act modeled and is motivated to do so, he can acquire new performances very rapidly.

The process of *labeling* is another concept of central importance in information processing and coping behavior. For once an object or experience has been labeled, further responses are made in terms of the label. Thus, if a person is labeled a *schizophrenic*—justifiably or not—we automatically tend to place him in that category in our thinking and expect him to manifest the characteristics we ascribe to schizophrenics; and we tend to treat him in ways we think suitable for one so labeled. In addition, such a label may provide the individual with an undesirable social role that he feels expected to play. For this reason, the behaviorists have placed great emphasis on avoiding premature, misleading, or inappropriate labels that may place the individual at a disadvantage in his relations with others and tend to encourage undesirable role behavior.

A third important concept in behavior theory is *shaping*. Often an appropriate response is not available in a person's behavior repertoire, a matter which presents problems for operant conditioning since the response must occur in order for it to be reinforced. In such cases it is possible to shape the response through the reinforcement of successive approximations of the desired behavior. Here, the behavior that is in the right direction—even though it does not represent the final performance to be achieved—is reinforced while other responses are not reinforced, and hence extinguished. For example, in getting a mute chronic schizophrenic to speak, the slight movement of the lips and then perhaps unintelligible sounds may be reinforced. His behavior is thus gradually shaped until the final goal of coherent speech is achieved.

Drive. Another concept related to learning principles that requires mention is that of *drive*. Many behaviorists view motivation as based on a limited number of *primary* biological drives, like hunger and thirst, which are directly related to meeting body needs. And they regard the diversity of motives in everyday life as learned extensions of these primary drives. For example, the infant soon learns that parental approval leads to need gratification; and disapproval to punishment, or need deprivation; and later the seeking of parental approval may generalize or come to be associated with academic achievement and other behaviors valued by the parents. Thus, motives for approval, achievement, and so on are regarded as *secondary* drives which are merely conditioned extensions of our more basic biological drives.

Here it may be noted that positive reinforcement is ordinarily effective only as it is related to a felt need. For example, food tends to lose its effectiveness as a reinforcer for an individual who is satiated. Ayllon and Michael (1959) utilized this principle in modifying the behavior of three mentally retarded patients who hoarded junk—old magazines, newspapers, and rubbish. In fact, one of the men had to be "dejunked" several times a day. It was thought that the hoarding behavior might have been reinforced by the attention that the men received,

as well as by a scarcity of such materials on the ward. Thus a treatment program was instituted in which the ward was flooded with magazines and the usual attention, or reinforcement for hoarding, was withheld by simply ignoring the hoarding. After a period of nine weeks, none of the patients hoarded any longer; and this improvement continued after the end of the treatment program. Satiation, together with the withholding of reinforcement, accomplished its purpose.

IMPACT ON OUR VIEWS OF NORMAL AND ABNORMAL BEHAVIOR

The behavioristic model views abnormal behavior as essentially the result of: (1) a failure to learn necessary adaptive behaviors or competencies; (2) the learning of ineffective or maladaptive behaviors; or (3) conflict situations that require the individual to make discriminations or decisions of which he feels incapable. An inability to establish satisfying interpersonal relationships would be an example of failure to learn needed competencies; a phobia or fear response—such as the fear of the white rat induced in little Albert—would be an example of learned maladaptive behavior; and the "experimental neuroses" experiments with animals (page 57) would illustrate conflict-generated disorganization of behavior.

We shall examine the more complex formulation of ineffective and maladaptive learning in neuroses and other mental disorders later in this book. For the moment it may suffice to emphasize again that behaviorists assume that all abnormal patterns of behavior can be accounted for according to the principles of a straightforward learning model.

The behaviorists have developed a number of *behavior-modification techniques* based on the application of learning principles to the treatment of abnormal behavior. Typical are the following: (1) the modification of environmental conditions that may be serving to reinforce undesirable or maladaptive behavior, as in the case of the "junk hoarders" cited at left; (2) the use of aversive conditioning or related procedures, such as the withholding of reinforcement, to eliminate specified behaviors; and (3) the use

PAVLOV (1849–1936)   WATSON (1878–1958)   SKINNER (1904–)   BANDURA (1925–)

Among the behaviorists, Ivan Pavlov and J. B. Watson pioneered in showing the part conditioning plays in the learning and treatment of maladaptive behavior. B. F. Skinner has added a new dimension to the picture with his views of operant learning—including the shaping of responses in desired directions; and Albert Bandura has clarified and integrated learning principles in the etiology and treatment of maladaptive behavior in his textbook *Principles of Behavior Modification* (1969).

of modeling, positive reinforcement, and other operant techniques to help the person acquire more effective behavior patterns. Generally, such procedures are used in combination. For example, aversive conditioning has been used with males seeking treatment for homosexuality by repeatedly showing them pictures of nude males while also administering an electric shock. A positive response to members of the opposite sex may then be established by turning off the electric shock each time a picture of an attractive female is shown. Some further illustrations of behavior therapy are summarized in the chart on page 64.

We shall discuss behavior-modification techniques at various points throughout this book, and in Chapter 20 we shall consider them in detail. Here we may simply note that behavior therapy sets forth clear-cut goals and methods for achieving them, and that removal of symptoms —such as the phobia of little Albert—is the chief goal of treatment. The symptoms—that is, the maladaptive behaviors manifested by a subject— are the disorder, and their removal is the "cure." In fact, the term *symptom* is regarded as, questionable in this context because of connotations of some more basic disturbance—a concept usually rejected by behavior therapists, to whom the "symptom" is a simple maladaptive learned response. Thus, in their view, the concept of *symp-*

tom substitution—that the symptoms will reappear in another guise if the underlying cause has not been cleared up—is unfounded. They do, however, leave room for the reappearance of the symptom or the appearance of other symptoms if the environmental conditions reinforcing the maladaptive behavior or symptom are not dealt with adequately. As Bandura has put it: "A treatment that fails to alter the major controlling conditions of the deviant behavior will most certainly prove ineffective." (1969, p. 50)

The behavioristic model has exerted a marked influence on contemporary views of man and his behavior, while also generating a great deal of controversy. On the positive side, it has been heralded for its conciseness and objectivity. For by means of relatively few basic concepts this model attempts to chart the acquisition, modification, and extinction of any type of behavior, whether adaptive or maladaptive. The model also allows for the fact that an individual may behave in ways that are good or evil, rational or irrational, depending on his conditioning. But rather than attribute the causes of his behavior to inferred constructs—such as an ego and superego—that cannot be objectively observed, the behaviorist looks for causes in the individual's learning experiences. And, in the modification of behavior, the therapist sets forth clear-cut goals along with learning principles to be utilized; and he can evaluate the outcome of therapy objectively by the degree to which it achieves these goals.

On the other hand, the behavioristic model has been criticized on a number of grounds, including: (1) its failure to include the data of subjective experience, which is highly meaningful to the individual; (2) its heavy dependence on animal experimentation, which may not be as directly applicable to human behavior as is sometimes supposed; (3) its having been constructed on the basis of the study of a few simple stimulus-response units rather than on the tackling of more complex dimensions of human experience, like love, courage, and despair; (4) its ignoring of the

problem of values and how men should live together; and (5) its utilization of conditioning techniques to manipulate the behavior of other human beings. The behaviorists, for their part, hold that contemporary behavior theory is far more sophisticated and comprehensive in its approach than its critics usually admit. And they point out with justification that their approach has opened up new vistas in the rapid and effective treatment of behavior disorders.

An interesting facet of the behavioristic model is its view that man is completely at the mercy of his previous conditioning and present environment. Although the person he is controls what he does, the person he is has been determined by

SOME BEHAVIOR-MODIFICATION TECHNIQUES BASED ON LEARNING PRINCIPLES

LEARNING PRINCIPLE	TECHNIQUE	EXAMPLE IN TREATMENT
Behavior patterns are developed and established through repeated association with positive reinforcers.	Use of positive reinforcement to establish desired behavior.	Wahler (1968) successfully modified extreme oppositional and negativistic behavior on the part of children by having parents reward cooperative behavior with approval and with tokens exchangeable for prized toys. Tokens were gradually eliminated, but dramatic improvement in cooperative behavior remained stable.
The repeated association of an established behavior pattern with negative reinforcers results in avoidance behavior.	Use of negative reinforcement to eliminate undesirable behavior (aversive conditioning).	Wolpe (1965) successfully treated drug addiction in a physician by having him use a portable apparatus to give himself an electric shock whenever he had a craving for the drug.
When an established behavior pattern is no longer reinforced, it tends to be extinguished.	Withdrawal of reinforcement for undesirable behavior.	Lovaas et al. (1965) found that self-injurious behavior of emotionally disturbed children could be reduced by cutting off social reinforcers— e.g., by having parents and others show less attention and concern when such behavior occurred.
Avoidance behavior will be inhibited or reduced if the conditions that provoke it are repeatedly paired with positive stimuli.	Desensitization to conditions that elicit unreasonable fear or anxiety.	In a classic experiment by Mary Cover Jones (1924), a boy's phobia for white rabbits and other furry animals was inhibited by feeding the boy his favorite food while the rabbit was in the background; the rabbit was gradually brought closer during feeding until the boy's fear of the animal was eliminated.
A specified behavior can gradually be established if successive approximations of the behavior are reinforced.	Shaping of desired behavior.	Isaacs, Thomas, and Goldiamond (1960) successfully reinstated speech in a schizophrenic subject who had been mute for 17 years by rewarding behavior that led in the direction of verbal communication. The initial objective was to have the subject focus his eyes on a stick of gum; when he did, he was given the gum. Next, the gum was withheld until the subject made a small mouth movement. By the end of the 4th week he made a croaking sound. Then, when a piece of gum was held up, the subject was told to pronounce the word *gum*. By the end of the 18th session he said "Gum, please," and subsequently he responded to questions in individual and group therapy sessions.

past conditioning. Thus, behaviorists tend to regard man's belief in his freedom of choice as largely an illusion. Paradoxically, however, the most ardent behaviorists, like Watson and Skinner, have repeatedly emphasized the potential use of modern science and technology for planning a better future world—as if man could *choose* to use these potentialities in one way rather than another. In both his famous didactic novel, *Walden Two* (1948), and its nonfiction version, *Beyond Freedom and Dignity* (1971), Skinner has been concerned with depicting a utopian world which would result from the systematic application of learning principles and behavior-modification procedures.

But whatever its limitations and paradoxes, the behavioristic model has had a tremendous impact upon contemporary psychological thought in general and upon psychopathology in particular.

THE HUMANISTIC MODEL

Although their thinking is influenced by both the psychoanalytic and the behavioristic models, the humanistic psychologists disagree with both. They view the behavioristic model, with its focus on the stimulus situation and observable behavior, as an oversimplification; they feel that it needs to be balanced by a greater consideration of the internal psychological makeup and experiencing of the individual. At the same time, they disagree with the negative and pessimistic picture of the psychoanalytic model.

EMPHASIS ON SELF-DIRECTION AND SELF-FULFILLMENT

The humanistic model is characterized as much or more by its general orientation toward man than by any coherent set of principles of personality development and functioning. Although some of this model's roots extend deep into the history of psychology, others are of relatively recent origin; it seems to have emerged as a major model of man in the 1950's and 1960's when middle-class America realized simultaneously its material affluence and spiritual emptiness. An important new force in contemporary psychology, this model is concerned with topics about which we as yet have little scientific information— topics like love, creativity, values, meaning, personal growth, and self-fulfillment.

Self as a unifying theme. As we noted at the beginning of this chapter, William James made extensive use of the self-concept before the turn of the century; but this concept was later dropped by the behaviorists because of its "inferred" rather than observable nature. Eventually, however, the need for some kind of unifying principle of personality and some way of taking cognizance of the subjective experience of the individual—including awareness of self—led to the reintroduction of this concept in the humanistic model. Here it may be reemphasized that the concept of self is analogous to the psychoanalytic concept of ego—in that both represent inferred subsystems concerned with evaluating, decision making, planning, and coping. The humanistic viewpoint, however, extends the self-concept to include self-identity and also tendencies toward growth and self-actualization.

Among contemporary humanistic psychologists, Carl Rogers has developed the most systematic model of self in relation to personality functioning, based largely on his pioneering research into the nature of the psychotherapeutic process. Rogers has stated his views in a series of statements which may be roughly summarized as follows:

1. Each individual exists in a private world of experience of which he—the I, me, or myself— is the center.

2. The most basic striving of the individual is toward the maintenance, enhancement, and actualization of the self.

3. The individual reacts to situations in terms of his unique perceptions of himself and his world—he reacts to "reality" as he perceives it and in ways consistent with his self-concept.

4. Perceived threat to the self is followed by defense—including the narrowing and rigidification of perception and coping behavior and the introduction of self-defense mechanisms.

5. The individual's inner tendencies are toward health and wholeness, and under normal conditions he behaves in rational and constructive ways and chooses pathways toward personal growth and self-actualization.

In utilizing the concept of self as a unifying theme, the humanistic model emphasizes the importance of individuality. Each individual, by virtue of his great potentiality for learning and his own particular background of experience, is unique. In studying man, psychologists are thus faced with the dual task of describing the singular nature of each individual as well as characteristics that he has in common with the rest of the human species. The humanistic model also leaves room for the importance of interpersonal relations and the general sociocultural setting in which the individual functions; these are factors that influence his development and behavior and bear significantly upon the satisfactions and meaning he finds in living.

Focus on values, personal growth, and fulfillment. In placing strong emphasis on the role of values, personal growth, and self-fulfillment in human existence, humanistic psychologists consider it crucially important that an individual's values be based on his own thought and choice rather than on blind acceptance of values fostered by his social environment. They also consider it essential that an individual gain a clear sense of his self-identity—that he discover who he is and what he wants to become—so that his potential may be fully developed. From this viewpoint, the individual is seen as having an internal or basic impetus which motivates him toward maturity and self-actualization.

Here it may be emphasized that the humanistic model stresses the problem of values and fulfillment, not only as they apply to the individual, but to society as well. Man is viewed as having a "basic" nature which is characteristic of his species. And as science progressively reveals this inherent nature, it becomes increasingly possible to make judgments regarding what is good or bad for humankind. In this sense it therefore becomes the responsibility of science to directly concern itself with values and social progress. This is a somewhat revolutionary viewpoint, since science has traditionally concerned itself only with objective "facts" and left questions of value and social progress up to religion, government, and other social forces. However, Maslow (1969) has pointed out that the task of modern science is to produce a "good society" as well as a "good person," because the actualization of human potentialities on a mass basis is possible only under favorable social conditions.

POSITIVE VIEW OF MAN AND HIS POTENTIALITIES

Throughout history there have been conflicting views of man's "basic" nature. Some have viewed human nature as basically selfish, cruel, and predatory; others have taken an opposing view. Some have emphasized man's irrationality; others have seen him as a rational being. Some have seen man as a puppet whose behavior is controlled by forces beyond his control; others have viewed him as having a significant capacity for self-direction.

These conflicting views of man's basic nature—as good or evil, rational or irrational, and free or determined—are still unresolved. But the dispute is far from an idle one; it has important social implications. For example, if man is by nature selfish and predatory, then society must shape him into a social creature by stringent discipline and social control. If, on the other hand, man's natural tendencies are toward cooperative and constructive behavior, society should encourage the development of spontaneity and self-direction. We have seen that the psychoanalytic model takes an essentially negative view of man's nature as one that is selfish, predatory, and irrational; while the behavioristic model takes the more neutral view that man's nature may be good or evil, rational or irrational, depending on his conditioning history. Both the psychoanalytic and behavioristic models, however, view the nature and direction of man's behavior as determined largely, if not entirely, by forces beyond his control.

In contrast, the humanistic model takes a much more positive view. Despite the myriad instances of violence, war, and cruelty that have existed from ancient times to the present, humanistically oriented psychologists conclude that under favorable conditions man's propensities are in the direction of cooperative, friendly, and constructive behavior. They regard aggression and cruelty as pathological behavior resulting from the denial, frustration, or distortion of man's basic nature. Similarly, they suggest that although man can be misled by inaccurate information, handicapped by social and economic deprivation, and overwhelmed by the complexity and number of issues he is expected to act upon, he still tends to be a rational creature. The socially constructive and rational nature of man has been emphasized by Carl Rogers (1961) on the basis of his extensive study of clients in psychotherapy:

"One of the most revolutionary concepts to grow out of our clinical experience is the growing recognition that the innermost core of man's nature, the deepest layers of his personality, the base of his 'animal nature,' is positive in nature—is basically socialized, forward moving, rational and realistic." (pp. 90–91)

Humanistic psychologists retain their positive outlook in considering the problem of whether the course of man's life is free or determined. In his everyday life, as we know, man operates on the assumption that he has some measure of control over his destiny, that he is free to make decisions and choose from alternative courses of action—at least within certain limits. Yet many psychologists take the position that man is *not* free. Pointing to the scientific doctrine of determinism, which views the world as an orderly place in which all events occur in keeping with natural laws of cause and effect, they argue that if we could be given a complete knowledge of the past experiences of the individual, we would be able to predict how he will—indeed, must— act in any given situation. As B. F. Skinner (1953) has put it: "The hypothesis that man is not free is essential to the application of scientific method to the study of human behavior." The humanists point out, however, that our whole way of life— with its democratic institutions, ballot boxes, and assumption of personal responsibility for

DIFFERING VIEWS OF MAN'S BASIC NATURE

	Good or Evil	Rational or Irrational	Free or Determined
Psychoanalytic model	Evil	Irrational	Determined
Behavioristic model	Neutral	Depends on learning	Determined
Humanistic model	Good	Rational	Free

The views of the interpersonal and existential models are not so easily categorized; however, the psychosocial models listed here illustrate the marked differences in contemporary views of man's basic nature.

one's actions—is based on the concept of man's freedom for self-direction and self-determination.

Although the problem of freedom vs. determinism has by no means been resolved, the humanistic psychologists see freedom as an "emergent" quality in the evolutionary process. They are impressed with man's unique quality of self-awareness; with his ability to reflect, reinterpret, and reorganize his past experience; to be critical and evaluative of his own behavior; and to integrate his experiences and make plans in terms of past, present, and future. Rather than viewing man as a passive automaton, they see him as an active participant in shaping his own destiny—both on individual and group levels.

To the humanistic psychologists, man is capable of both good and evil, of rational and irrational behavior, of being both active and reactive or determined. These qualities are not mutually exclusive but rather are the opposite poles on a continuum. Man may operate closer to one pole than another at a given time, but he retains the potentiality for approaching both. No one is invariably selfish or altruistic, rational or irrational, free or determined. The patterns of a given society or the life style of an individual may tend toward one extreme or the other. However, it is possible to take a positive view of man's basic nature as tending under favorable conditions in the direction of goodness, rationality, and responsible self-direction.

JAMES (1842–1910) MASLOW (1908–1970) PERLS (1893–1970) ROGERS (1902–)

Before the turn of the twentieth century, William James set the stage for the humanistic model in a chapter on the concept of the self in his book *Principles of Psychology*. In more recent times A. H. Maslow devoted more than two decades to showing the potentialities of man for higher-level self-development and functioning; Frederick Perls was influential in the development of therapeutic procedures for enhancing human experiencing and functioning, particularly in the context of confrontation groups; and Carl R. Rogers has contributed significantly to the humanistic viewpoint with his theoretical formulations and his systematic studies on the therapeutic process and its outcomes.

IMPACT ON OUR VIEWS OF NORMAL AND ABNORMAL BEHAVIOR

The humanistic model stresses both faulty learning and exaggerated self-defense mechanisms as sources of psychopathology. The effect of these causal factors, however, is viewed essentially as the blocking of personal growth and fulfillment. Thus an individual may learn faulty values and maladaptive coping patterns; or he may be forced —by deprivation and general lack of opportunity —to concentrate his energies on meeting his basic bodily needs. In either case, the result is a blockage of personal growth and fulfillment.

With respect to irrational defensive processes of a maladaptive nature, these may stem from threat and anxiety—as in the psychoanalytic model. Feelings, thoughts, and events incongruent with the individual's self-concept—which would lead to anxiety-arousing self-devaluation— are screened from awareness or given a distorted symbolization. Such a process of self-defense may ultimately lead to incongruence between reality and the individual's experiencing, and hence to lowered integration and ultimately to maladaptive behavior. In extreme degree, this process of anxiety-arousing stress and defense may result in personality disorganization and psychological breakdown.

Humanistic approaches to therapy usually focus on assisting the individual to perceive himself as he really is and to accept and be himself—with both weaknesses and strengths. As he learns to do this, he can drop his defenses and become more open to experience—and thus more capable of choice, growth, and self-fulfillment. One of the procedures commonly used in treatment is nondirective therapy, in which the therapist serves as a kind of "sounding board" in helping the individual to express and clarify his thinking about himself and his problems. Humanistic psychologists are also keenly interested in encounter groups and other innovative techniques for enriching human experience.

It is too early to assess the ultimate impact of the humanistic model, but it has clearly introduced a new dimension to our thinking about abnormal behavior. For humanistic psychologists tend to view psychopathology not so much as abnormality or deviance per se, but rather as a blocking of the individual's natural tendencies toward health and self-actualization. Thus Bugental (1967) sees the future of humanistic psychology as related to a "growth of attention to the creative and healthy side of human potential (in contrast to our emphasis up to now on pathology and repair)." (p. 4) And in a similar vein Maslow (1962; 1969) has expressed concern with "the psychopathology of the normal"—that is, the disappointing failure of most "normal" people to realize their potentialities. The long-range task of humanistic psychology is an ambitious and challenging one. As Bugental has expressed it:

"Humanistic psychology has as its ultimate goal the preparation of a complete description of what it means to be alive as a human being. This is, of course, not a goal which is likely ever to be fully attained; yet it is important to recognize the nature of the task. Such a complete description would necessarily include an inventory of man's native endowment: his potentialities of feeling, thought, and action; his growth evolution, and decline; his interaction with various environing conditions; the range and variety of experience possible to him; and his meaningful place in the universe." (1967, p. 7)

THE EXISTENTIAL MODEL

The existential model of man emphasizes the uniqueness of the individual, his quest for values and meaning, and his freedom for self-direction and self-fulfillment. In these ways it is highly similar to the humanistic model, and, in fact, many humanistic psychologists are also referred to as *existentialists*. However, the existential model represents a somewhat less optimistic view of man and places more emphasis on the irrational trends in man's nature and the difficulties inherent in self-fulfillment—particularly given our bureaucratic and dehumanizing mass society. And the existentialists place considerably less faith in modern science and more in the inner experiencing of the individual in their attempts at understanding and dealing with man's deepest problems.

CENTRAL THEMES AND CONCEPTS

The existential model is not a highly systematized school of thought, but it is unified by a central concern with the ultimate challenge of human existence—the need to establish a sense of personal identity and to build meaningful links with the world. Its basic concepts stem mainly from the writings of such European philosophers as Heidegger, Jaspers, Kierkegaard, and Sartre. Especially influential in the development of existential thought in the United States have been the theologian Paul Tillich and the psychologist Rollo May.

Existence and essence. From the existential viewpoint, man's basic motivation is to find the best possible way of life, to actualize his potentialities, and to fulfill himself as a human being. However, in an age of profound cultural change, traditional mores and beliefs are being questioned. As a result, modern man suffers from confusion and deep spiritual and emotional strain.

Essentially, man can resolve his dilemma in one of two ways: (1) by giving up his quest and finding some satisfaction in blind conformity and submergence in the group; or (2) striving for increased self-definition in the reality of his own existence. The existentialists view the first alternative as being unauthentic and the pathway to anxiety and despair. For if blind conformity and immersion in the group lead to a wasted life, the individual can neither evade the consequences nor blame anyone else for his failure.

Thus a basic theme of existentialism is that the individual's existence is given, but what he makes of it—his essence—is up to him. The adolescent who defiantly blurts out "Well, I didn't ask to be born" is stating a profound truth; but in existential terms, it is completely irrelevant. For whether he asked to be born or not, here he is in the world and answerable for himself—for one human life. What he makes of his existence is up to him.

Freedom, choice, values, and meaning. A second basic theme of the existentialists is the will-to-meaning. This is primarily a matter of finding and choosing satisfying values. For it is in his value *choices* that the individual shapes his essence. And in choosing his values and the kind of person he is to become, the individual is viewed as having complete freedom. Even refusing to choose and submerging oneself in the group represents a choice. Thus the locus of valuing is within the individual. He is inescapably the architect of his own life. Morris (1966) has stated the matter in the form of three propositions:

"1. I am a *choosing* agent, unable to avoid choosing my way through life.
2. I am a *free* agent, absolutely free to set the goals of my own life.
3. I am a *responsible* agent, personally accountable for my free choices as they are revealed in how I live my life." (p. 135)

The problems of choice and responsibility often become an agonizing burden. They require finding satisfying values, a lonely and highly individual matter because the values that provide one life with meaning may be quite different from those that provide another with meaning. Thus the individual must have the courage to break away from old patterns if need be, to stand on his own, and to seek fulfilling pathways. In a sense, man's freedom to shape his essence is "both his agony and his glory."

Here it may be noted that the emphasis on individual value patterns is not to be construed as moral nihilism. For there is a basic unity to mankind, and all people are faced with the task of learning to live constructively with themselves and others. Hence there will be an underlying continuity in the value patterns chosen by different individuals who are trying to live authentically. Existentialism also places strong emphasis on the individual's *obligation* to his fellow man—for one's life can be fulfilling and meaningful only if it involves socially constructive values and choices.

EXISTENTIAL ANXIETY

An existentialist theme which adds an urgent and painful note to the human situation is that of *nonbeing*, of *nothingness*. In the idiom of

KIERKEGAARD (1813–1855)	SARTRE (1905–)	MAY (1909–)	LAING (1927–)

Soren Kierkegaard, early nineteenth-century Danish theologian and author who was beset by personal heartbreak and public scorn, is generally regarded as the first major existential thinker. Jean-Paul Sartre in France and Rollo May in America are among the leading exponents of existentialism in this century, along with R. D. Laing of England, whose concepts fit under both the existential and interpersonal models. Those currently engaged in elaborating upon the concepts of existentialism are focusing, as did Kierkegaard, on the individual's struggle to shape his "inner self" and to find a meaningful, authentic, and fulfilling way of life.

the existential theorists, nonbeing is the opposite of being, and in ultimate form is death—the inescapable fate of all men.

Prior knowledge of this encounter with nothingness is unique to man; he is the only creature who must live with the constant awareness of the possibility and inevitability of nonbeing. At each moment, he makes his way along the sharp edge of possible annihilation; never can he escape the fact that death will arrive at some unknown time and place. For to realize what it means to be, he must also grasp the possibility of nonbeing; and this awareness adds a crucial dimension to man's existence and immediate experience.

The *encounter with nothingness* thus becomes a central theme of existentialism, and it is this awareness of inevitable death that leads man to *existential anxiety*—the deep concern over whether he is leading a fulfilling and meaningful life.

Such anxiety often stems from inner conflict with respect to being and nonbeing. For example, the individual may be confronted with the anxiety-arousing choice of maintaining his present life pattern, with the security it affords, or trying something new which, although it appears to offer greater self-fulfillment, also involves greater risk. Often the individual lacks the courage to follow the latter path and so denies himself new possibilities of being. The neurotic, for example, may cling to his pathological life pattern; or the outer-directed person may avoid the anxiety of being by engaging in blind conformity or immersing himself in the group. In such cases the individual pays a heavy price. To the extent that he fails to realize his potentialities he is a failure and experiences guilt; to flee from one's freedom and obligation to life is to be *unauthentic*, to show *bad faith*, and to condemn oneself to a condition of despair.

The primary focus of the existential therapist is to help the individual clarify his values and to work out a meaningful way of "being-in-the-world." He stresses the importance of *confrontation*—in which the individual is directly challenged with questions concerning the meaning and purpose of his existence—and the *encounter* —the relationship established between two interacting human beings in the therapeutic situation. The therapist also strongly emphasizes

---

THE SOCIAL ROOTS OF PSYCHOPATHOLOGY AS EMPHASIZED BY LAING

R. D. Laing, a British existential psychiatrist who has won widespread attention for his views of why people experience psychotic breakdowns and for his therapeutic approach as well, is vehement in his emphasis on the damaging effects of pathological social relationships upon the individual. Each person, Laing says, is not a discrete entity but is part and parcel of his culture, or of the groups to which he belongs, including the family group; thus he is shaped by significant others, just as he, for his part, shapes others. In this never ending process an illimitable number of transactions may occur between people, with potentially destructive results.

In Laing's view, these social interactions typically are based on falsehoods and take the form of "games" by which people not only avoid discovering their true selves but also attempt to achieve substitute gratifications. The pervasiveness of this pathology in contemporary society is so great, he says, that:

"By the time the new human being is 15 or so, we are left with a being like ourselves, a half-crazed creature more or less adjusted to a mad world. This is normality." (1967, p. 58)

Describing the so-called normal world as a place where all of us are "bemused and crazed creatures, strangers to our true selves, to one another, and to the spiritual and material world," Laing explains that a split arising between an individual's false outer self and true inner self is a consequence of intolerably confusing and conflicting social demands, sanctions, and life situations. And he sees the psychotic breakdown as occurring when the split can no longer be maintained; the processes involved in "madness" represent the individual's attempts to recover his wholeness as a human being. The implications of this viewpoint for therapy are elaborated upon in Chapter 9.

Based on Gilluly (1971), Gordon (1971), and Laing (1967).

---

the individual's need to relate positively to other human beings and participate in constructive ways with them.

IMPACT ON OUR VIEWS OF NORMAL AND ABNORMAL BEHAVIOR

Many of the concepts of the existential model— such as nonbeing, freedom, choice, meaning, authenticity, obligation, commitment, and existential anxiety and despair—have had a profound impact on the thinking of the humanistic psychologists and on contemporary thought in general.

In assessing the impact of the existential model, it may be noted that existentialists are very much concerned with the social predicament of modern man. They emphasize the crises of faith and the weakening of traditional church authority that are prevalent today; the depersonalization of the individual in our mass society; and the loss of meaning in human existence. They view modern man as alienated and estranged—a stranger to God, to other men, and to himself. The social context of contemporary life thus forces man to an awareness of his empty existence, to existential anxiety, and to psychopathology.

From a more positive standpoint, we can see that the impetus given to personal growth as an important goal in life by the humanistic and existential psychologists has led to a variety of innovative approaches for achieving growth experiences. However, these models of man may have even more far-reaching effects on our view of psychopathology, leading us to balance the traditional concept of moving from maladjustment to adjustment with the concept of personal growth and the need to find a socially constructive and personally meaningful life.

THE INTERPERSONAL MODEL

Strictly speaking, there is no systematic model of man based entirely on an analysis of man as a social being. Perhaps the closest approximation is the interpersonal model developed by the psychiatrist Harry Stack Sullivan (1953), and extended somewhat by later investigators. As we shall see, the interpersonal model does not ignore the concepts of self and self-direction, but the focus of its analysis is "the ongoing social process."

SOCIAL PROCESSES AND PERSONALITY

Sullivan saw personality development as consisting of various stages, involving differing patterns of interpersonal relationships. According to this view, interpersonal relations in early childhood are characterized by the intensive efforts on the part of parents toward the child's socialization; in later childhood there emerges the capacity to love other people—to be as much concerned about their well-being as about one's own; in adolescence there is a gradual emancipation from parents and the increasing importance of peer relationships; and in young adulthood there is the establishment of love, and typically marital and parental relationships in a new family setting.

It should be noted that early interpersonal relationships are regarded as having an extremely important bearing on the development of the self-concept. For very early the infant begins to develop a self-concept which—since he is completely dependent on parents and "significant others"—is constructed largely out of their reflected appraisals. It is important to note also that the socialization pressures exerted by parents and the continual appraisals of others lead the child to label some tendencies in himself as characteristic of the "bad me" and others as manifestations of the "good me." As the self-structure emerges, the child also develops various defense mechanisms for protecting the self from devaluation. For example, tendencies labeled the "bad me" may be screened out of consciousness or may be blamed on somebody else. However, this leads to an incongruity between the individual's perceived world and the world as it really is, and may therefore pave the way for maladaptive behavior. Here we can readily see a similarity between Sullivan's views and those of both Freud and Rogers.

Communication and consensual validation. A key concept of the interpersonal model is that of *communication*, which is the connecting link between people. In this, Sullivan stressed both the nonverbal and the verbal cues by means of which people interpret the messages and actions of others. The infant is capable of crude communication via empathy. Later on, communication involves gestures and action, but still is not precise enough to be useful in interpreting or communicating highly differentiated experience. With the child's development of language, however, he can communicate in precise and reality-oriented ways. Communication of this kind is subject to *consensual validation*—that is, to confirmation or negation by others. Where the individual fails to develop or maintain a mode of communication that is open to consensual validation, reality becomes distorted for him and maladaptive behavior is the result.

Sullivan held that faulty communication is far more common than most people realize—especially in family interactions on an emotional level. Koestler (1954) underscores the unique nature of communication difficulties among family members:

"Family relations pertain to a plane where the ordinary rules of judgment and conduct do not apply. They are a labyrinth of tensions, quarrels and reconciliations, whose logic is self-contradictory, whose ethics stem from a cozy jungle, and whose values and criteria are distorted like the curved space of a self-contained universe. It is a universe saturated with memories—but memories from which no lessons are drawn; saturated with a past which provides no guidance to the future. For in this universe, after each crisis and reconciliation, time always starts afresh and history is always in the year zero." (p. 218)

Thus, when individuals in close interpersonal relationships have serious misunderstandings and conflicts, there is likely to be difficulty in their communicating with each other. In fact, the final phase of a failing marriage is often marked by almost complete inability of the couple to communicate, and the closing of communication channels altogether.

Social roles and interpersonal accommodation. A good deal of research effort has been directed toward the study of social roles and their influence on personality development and behavior. Such studies have made it clear that smooth social interaction requires role reciprocity between the members of the group—that is, individuals must behave in ways expected of persons in their roles. A general, for example, cannot play his role effectively unless other military personnel also play theirs. For this reason strong social reinforcements usually accompany role behavior when it is enacted successfully, and social sanctions are

SULLIVAN (1892–1949)   BERNE (1910–1970)

The interpersonal model of man is based largely on the work of Harry Stack Sullivan, who thought it was pointless to speak of the individual personality, since the individual personality does not exist apart from interactions with others. Among the psychologists and psychiatrists who have elaborated upon this model, Eric Berne delineated and popularized the extent to which we "play games" in our interpersonal relationships. Berne developed a system of therapy known as *transactional analysis*, in which the individual is helped to understand maladaptive games in which he may be engaged and to develop more effective coping behavior.

imposed when it is not. The individual who is labeled "mentally ill" is one who can no longer meet the role demands made of him; hence, he is provided with a "sick role" that relieves him of ordinary role responsibilities. We shall examine the implications of the sick role in mental disorders shortly.

Both social roles and communication patterns are of great importance in *interpersonal accommodations*—that is, the achievement of satisfactory interpersonal relationships. Sullivan (1953) pointed out that interpersonal accommodation "is a reciprocal process in which (1) complementary needs are resolved, or aggravated; (2) reciprocal patterns of activity are developed, or disintegrated; and (3) foresight of satisfaction, or rebuff, of similar needs is facilitated." (p. 198) In this context the term *complementary needs* refers to a situation in which a need of one person complements that of another—as when both persons have a strong need for affection, or one has a need to be dominant and the other dependent— thus leading to need satisfaction for both persons. Sullivan placed strong emphasis on meeting each person's need for security in interpersonal re-

COMMUNICATION AND FAULTY INTERPERSONAL RELATIONSHIPS

In a highly simplified way, interpersonal communication may be diagrammed as involving four elements:

Communication problems are likely to arise if the sender is unclear about the message he wishes to send, if he fails to code it in such a way that it can be understood, or if he ignores or misinterprets feedback from the receiver. Similarly, the receiver may precipitate communication failure if he misunderstands, misinterprets, or distorts the message he receives. Difficulties are compounded in such cases by the fact that the receiver is likely to emit feedback that only confuses and/or irritates the sender rather than helping to clarify communication. Particularly where the sender and receiver have differing or conflicting frames of reference—assumptions about reality, possibility, and value—are communications likely to be misunderstood and interpersonal difficulties to arise.

The following is an excerpt from the communication of a newly married couple who sought marital counseling:

Wife: Would you like to go to the movies? (asked in an earnest, information-gathering voice)

Husband: No.

(Ten-minute pause)

Wife: You never take me out. Why did you refuse to take me to the movies?

Husband: But you never asked me.

Wife: I never asked! I asked you ten minutes ago. You never listen to me. You don't care about me.

Husband: (to himself) She may be right. I don't remember her asking so I guess I really don't listen to her. Maybe I don't want to hear her.

(Rabkin, 1967)

It is apparent that such communication failures can lead to marital misunderstanding and conflict, as well as to difficulties in other interpersonal relationships.

lationships. In discordant and unstable relationships, some frustration of security and other needs occurs almost inevitably. This may lead to a breaking up of the relationship, or to a distorted interchange in which one person's needs are met at the expense of the other's.

DISORDERED INTERPERSONAL RELATIONS

A number of contemporary investigators have shared Sullivan's concern with interpersonal relations and accommodations of a pathological type. For example, Lennard and Bernstein (1969) have quoted a passage from Genet's (1960) *The Balcony* to show how role behavior may be highly costly as well as rewarding:

"[Judge:] . . . My being a judge is an emanation of your being a thief. You need only refuse—but you'd better not!—need only refuse to be who you are—what you are, therefore, who you are—for me to cease to be . . . to vanish, evaporate. Lord, I beseech you. Don't leave me in this position failing to be a judge." (pp. 14–15)

In a similar vein, Carson (1969) has referred to *fraudulent* and *disordered interpersonal contracts*. In the former, the norms governing agreed-upon and healthy interpersonal relationships are violated and exploited by one party to the relationship at the expense of the other.

In referring to disordered interpersonal contracts, Carson has described the "negotiated maladjustment contract" in which an interpersonal relationship is maintained only because one of the parties agrees that certain deviant rules and norms will be substituted for established social rules in their relationship.

"For example, one of the more common forms of negotiated maladjustment involves an agreement to falsify jointly some aspect of reality by denying its existence or distorting its meaning . . . [as] where the parents of a young man negotiated an agreement to interpret his 13-month, mute withdrawal as anger at the nurses." (1969, p. 250)

Another example of a "negotiated maladjustment contract" would be a tacit agreement between a husband and wife that the excessive drinking of one of them would be treated as normal by both partners.

A great deal of current research has focused on the patterns of communication and accommodation among the members of "schizophrenic" families—that is, families with a schizophrenic adolescent or young adult member. Of key importance here appear to be communications and relationships that leave one member devaluated, confused, and nonconfirmed as an authentic person (Watzlawick, Beavin & Jackson, 1967).

As Laing and Esterson (1964) have so vividly expressed it,

"The ultimate of this is . . . when no matter how [a person] feels or how he acts, no matter what meaning he gives his situation, his feelings are denuded of validity, his acts are stripped of their motives, intentions, and consequences, the situation is robbed of its meaning for him, so that he is totally mystified and alienated." (pp. 135–136)

IMPACT ON OUR VIEWS OF NORMAL AND ABNORMAL BEHAVIOR

The interpersonal model focuses upon faulty communications and unsatisfactory interpersonal relationships as being at the root of maladaptive behavior and mental disorders. Such roots may extend back to childhood—as when the child's self-concept was distorted by significant others who appraised him as being worthless and rejected him, or when rigid socialization measures made it difficult for him to accept and integrate the "bad me" into his self-concept. In any case, the focus of therapy is on present patterns of communication and relationships, and on trying to help the individual understand and cope with his current interpersonal difficulties. In this process verbal and nonverbal communication, social roles, interactions with others, and the total social milieu of the individual are all seen as relevant concerns.

Interpersonal therapy typically involves three basic steps: (1) determining the maladaptive interpersonal relationships to be changed; (2) modifying conditions that help maintain the ineffective behavior; and (3) helping the individual achieve clearer self-understanding and more adequate

ways of relating to others. Therapy also utilizes feedback from family members and friends, by means of which the individual may make needed corrections and achieve increased interpersonal competence and satisfaction.

We shall examine a number of specific studies concerning interpersonal relations and communications in our discussions of mental disorders in Part Three. It may suffice for the moment to indicate that the interpersonal model has been extended through such studies, for they have shown that there are indeed a number of interpersonal patterns conducive to severely maladaptive behavior—patterns that can "drive another person crazy"; and conversely, that there are interpersonal patterns that are "disorder reducing," or therapeutic, in their effects.

Although the interpersonal model provides a less comprehensive picture of man than the other models we have discussed in this chapter, it has made a distinctive contribution to psychological thought by focusing attention on the importance of social processes in shaping individual behavior. It has demonstrated the close connection between intrapsychic and interpersonal difficulties and, in doing so, has helped pave the way for contemporary approaches in the mental health field. For as we shall see in the next chapter, the concern of mental health personnel today typically extends beyond the individual to his sociocultural milieu.

In reviewing the major psychosocial models of man—the psychoanalytic, behavioristic, humanistic, existential, and interpersonal—we have noted that each of them contributes to our understanding of psychopathology, but that none alone seems to account for the myriad types of maladaptive behaviors exhibited by man. Each has a good deal of research evidence to support it, but ultimately each also depends on generalizations from particular kinds of events and observations.

In the present text we shall utilize concepts from all of the psychosocial models, and we shall also draw on relevant findings from the biological and social sciences. This interdisciplinary approach will be described in the next chapter, which summarizes current issues and trends in the field of psychopathology.

Sociocultural and Interdisciplinary Approaches

4

THE SOCIOCULTURAL PERSPECTIVE

THE INTERDISCIPLINARY APPROACH AND ITS IMPLICATIONS

A LOOK AHEAD

In the preceding three chapters we have considered many differing views of abnormal behavior, some of them long since discarded but others at the very forefront of contemporary thought. Before attempting to summarize the major trends in the field of psychopathology today, it may be useful to review some highlights of our discussion thus far.

In Chapter 1 we noted that mental disorders are not new to modern civilization; we considered some historic examples and early views of mental disorders; and we reviewed some of the common misconceptions that still exist concerning these disturbances. Next we dealt with problems of defining *abnormal behavior*, and settled on a tentative definition that equates *abnormal* with *maladaptive*; then we reviewed the accepted APA classification of mental disorders—noting the necessity of categorization for imposing order on our discussion, while maintaining an awareness of the limitations of this particular schema. Finally, we touched on some of the problems that arise in the clinical assessment of cases, and on the types of personnel and therapeutic procedures presently employed in helping the maladjusted.

Chapters 2 and 3 were devoted to a consideration of the development of modern views of psychopathology. Initially, we traced the evolution of psychopathology from its beginnings in demonology, through medieval concepts of witchcraft, to the emergence of more humanistic approaches, and to the development of the organic viewpoint and medical model. As we noted, the great achievement of the medical model was the substitution of the view of organic brain pathology, in place of demons and witches, as the cause of mental disorders. We then traced the development of the psychological viewpoint in the twentieth century, outlining the major contributions of the psychoanalytic, behavioristic, humanistic, existential, and interpersonal models of man and noting their impact on our views of psychopathology.

In the present chapter we shall round out our historical picture by tracing the development of the sociocultural perspective and the gradual shift in emphasis from an exclusive concern with the individual to an expanded focus that takes in his family, community, and general sociocultural milieu. Next, we shall consider some major trends in contemporary psychopa-thology—the growing use of interdisciplinary approaches, the reevaluation of medical and psychosocial perspectives, and the development of innovative treatment techniques. And finally, we shall look briefly at two trends that promise to become increasingly important in the future—the comprehensive health approach and general systems theory.

THE SOCIOCULTURAL PERSPECTIVE

By the beginning of the twentieth century, sociology and anthropology had emerged as independent scientific disciplines and were making rapid strides in understanding the role of sociocultural factors in man's development and behavior.[1] Soon it became apparent that man is almost infinitely malleable and that his personality development reflects both the larger society in which he lives—its institutions, traditions, values, ideas, and technology—and the immediate family and other interpersonal relationships to which he is exposed. Eventually, too, it became clear that there is a relationship between sociocultural conditions and mental disorders—between the particular stresses in a society and the incidence and types of mental disorders that occur in it. And it was also observed that the patterning of both physical and mental disorders in a given society may change over time, commensurate with changes in sociocultural conditions.

CROSS-CULTURAL STUDIES

With the publication of Malinowski's *Sex and Repression in Savage Society* in 1927, it became apparent that the then dominant psychoanalytic model had certain definite limitations in its applicability to different cultures. For Malinowski found little evidence among the Trobriand Islanders of any Oedipal conflict, as described by Freud, and he concluded that the phenomenon was not a universal one but rather a product of the patriarchal family in Western society. Shortly thereafter, a paper by Ruth Benedict (1934) dealing with anthropology and abnormal behavior made it clear that such limitations extended to the definition of "abnormality" itself. Citing various ethnographic reports, she pointed out that what is considered abnormal in one society may be considered normal in another. For example, she noted that cataleptic and trance-like states were often valued by "simpler" peoples. Thus she concluded that normality is a culturally defined concept.

Not only were differences found among cultures, with regard to what each considered abnormal, but some types of abnormal behavior appeared to occur only in given cultures. Thus, various "ethnic" psychoses were delineated. One was *amok*, found among the Malays and involving a sudden, wild outburst of homicidal aggression during which an individual might kill or injure anyone standing in his way. The phrase "to run amok" stems from early observations of this behavior. Other patterns included the *windigo* psychosis found among the Algonquin Indian hunters, in which the individual became extremely anxious and agitated, convinced that he was bewitched and being turned into a *windigo*, or cannibal, by the power of a supernatural monster with an insatiable craving for human flesh.

These early anthropological findings led many investigators to take a position of *cultural rela-*

---

[1]Prominent early contributors to this field were Ruth Benedict, Ralph Linton, Abram Kardiner, Margaret Mead, and Franz Boas.

tivism concerning abnormal behavior. From this viewpoint, each culture is more or less an island unto itself, and there are no universal standards that can be applied to all societies. This viewpoint had a beneficial effect in making us aware of the cultural bias and prejudice in our own views of abnormal behavior. However, the notion of cultural relativism underwent some refinement following World War II when it became apparent that a whole society or culture can develop maladaptive patterns and even threaten the survival of other cultural groups. In the Nüremberg trials in Germany following the war, a number of Nazi leaders were convicted of genocide and other "crimes against humanity"; and it became evident that certain standards for group as well as individual behavior are essential for man's survival and well-being—that all patterns are not equally in keeping with man's needs. Thus we can talk about maladaptive or abnormal behavior on a group level as well as on the individual level.

A strictly relativistic view of abnormal behavior was dealt a further blow as it gradually became apparent that the more severe types of mental

In prescribing and rewarding certain behavior, a culture is an important determiner of what is seen as normal or abnormal. To the tribe of head-hunters and cannibals on the southwest coast of Netherlands New Guinea, life is a "nightmare of fear," and an appropriate way of warding off supernatural foes is by displaying bones of the dead. This man wears his mother's skull as a protection against her ghost.

The great love felt by these Caribou Eskimo parents for their infant is typical of a culture characterized by warm family and community life. The social structure is simple, with several families making up a camp in which the good will of neighbors is more highly prized than possessions, and community disapproval in the form of ostracism is the punishment reserved for the gravest crimes.

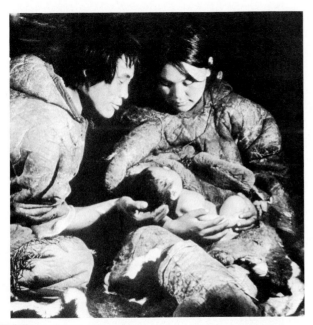

disorders delineated in Western society were, in fact, found among peoples throughout the world. For example, although the relative incidence and specific symptoms varied, schizophrenia was found among all peoples, from the most primitive to the most technologically advanced. And finally, it was noted that when an individual became so mentally disordered that he could no longer control his behavior, perform his expected role in the group, or even survive without the special care of others, his behavior was considered abnormal in any society.

EPIDEMIOLOGICAL STUDIES

The study of the incidence and distribution of disease or other disorders in a population is referred to as *epidemiology*. As we narrow our focus to our own society, we find a number of early studies dealing with the relation of social class and other subgroup factors to the nature and incidence of mental disorders.

A pioneering study in this area was that reported by Faris and Dunham (1939), who found that a disproportionate number of the schizophrenics admitted to mental hospitals came from

Margaret Mead (1901–), the world-famous anthropologist, has spent years studying primitive peoples and amassing cross-cultural data. She has contributed greatly to our understanding of variations in individual and group behavior patterns—both normal and abnormal. Here she is pictured learning the language of Bali from Balinese children.

the lower socioeconomic areas of a large city. The rate of admission decreased with distance of residence from these disorganized and deteriorating sections of the city. In another early study, Hyde and Kingsley (1944) correlated the mental disorders of 60,000 military selectees rejected at the Boston Armed Forces Induction Station with the socioeconomic level of the community from which the selectees came. They found that the total incidence of major mental disorders increased gradually, from about 7 percent in communities with the highest socioeconomic status to almost 17 percent in those with the lowest.

Such early studies concerning social class were gradually augmented by studies dealing with urban-rural, ethnic, religious, occupational, and other subgroups in relation to mental disorders. In one of these, an extensive epidemiological study of mental disorders in Texas, Jaco (1960) found the incidence of psychoses as a group to be three times higher in urban than in rural areas, and higher among the divorced and separated than among the married or widowed. And follow-

ing the early lead of G. H. Mead, whose *Mind, Self, and Society* was published in 1934, researchers focused attention on family patterns and such specific concepts as social roles, communication, and interpersonal relationships. We noted this trend in our review of the interpersonal model of man.

SOCIAL PATHOLOGY AND COMMUNITY MENTAL HEALTH

The sociocultural viewpoint added still another dimension to our thinking about abnormal behavior; and with its acceptance in psychology and psychiatry, the almost exclusive concern with the individual now broadened to include a concern with societal, communal, familial, and other subgroup factors in mental disorders.[1] It became apparent that certain social conditions can have a pathogenic influence on individuals exposed to them. As Lennard and Bernstein (1969) put it: "Therapeutic or damaging potentials often inhere in social contexts rather than in individuals. . . ." (p. 205) Thus we see the introduction of the concept of *social pathology*—with its focus on conditions like overcrowding, poverty, and racial prejudice.

This concept has led to the community mental health model, which calls for an assessment of the sociocultural environment as well as of the individual in relation to the etiology, treatment, and prevention of mental disorders. Smith (1968) has referred to the community mental health model as "the third mental health revolution."

"The first mental-health revolution unshackled the insane. By calling them sick, it managed to treat them as human. Its monuments and symbols are the great, usually isolated, state mental hospitals. The second revolution came from the spread of dynamic psychiatry (mainly Freud's) and was characterized by individual, one-to-one psychotherapy. Now the third revolution throws off the constraints of the doctor-patient medical model—the idea that mental disorder is a private misery—and relates the trouble, and the cure, to the

[1]Among the pioneers who early recognized the importance of the sociocultural viewpoint and were to help give psychopathology a new and more socially oriented image were Alfred Adler, Karen Horney, Harry Stack Sullivan, and Erich Fromm.

entire web of social and personal relationships in which the individual is caught." (p. 19)

In later chapters we shall deal with the clinic facilities and other programs—both governmental and private—that have been established on the basis of the community mental health model. It may suffice here to point out that this model has led to the introduction of programs designed to alleviate social conditions that foster maladaptive behavior, as well as to the provision of community facilities that enable many disturbed individuals to remain in their family and community setting instead of being obliged to go to a remote state mental hospital for treatment.

Although the initial thrust of the sociocultural viewpoint has been to engender a concern with the role of family, community, and other sociocultural factors in mental disorders, it extends beyond the community mental health model. Thus on a societal level we have the National Institute of Mental Health; and on an international level, the World Health Organization. It also may be noted that the sociocultural viewpoint must concern itself not only with the relationship of mental disorders to existing social conditions but also with the nature and incidence of the mental disorders that may be anticipated as a consequence of the profound changes taking place in the world.

THE INTERDISCIPLINARY APPROACH AND ITS IMPLICATIONS

As the research engendered by the organic, psychological, and sociocultural viewpoints has gradually led to a better understanding of psychopathology, it has become increasingly clear that no single perspective offers a complete picture in itself. Thus we have seen the gradual emergence of an interdisciplinary approach that calls for the integration of biological, psychological, and sociocultural factors into a comprehensive clinical picture. In dealing with a particular disorder, of course, we may be primarily concerned with one set of determinants or another. For example, one case of homicidal behavior may be closely associated with drug intoxication, another with pent-up frustration and hostility, and still another with the learning of criminal values in a faulty environment.

In most instances of abnormal behavior, all three kinds of determinants are involved in varying degrees and varying ways. Thus the problem becomes one of assessing the role of particular organic, psychological, and sociocultural factors as they have affected a given individual. In schizophrenia, for example, we may be concerned with possible genetic predisposition, with family patterns that lead to maladaptive learning and faulty coping techniques, and with sociocultural conditions that may be contributing to stress.

The interdisciplinary approach has led to the integration of research findings from such varied disciplines as genetics, biochemistry, neurophysiology, psychology, sociology, anthropology, and ecology in efforts to understand and cope with abnormal behavior. On a practical level, we can see the approach being applied in the community mental health center, with its emphasis on family and community variables, as well as individual ones, and with the meaningful collaboration of several kinds of mental health personnel. Of key importance, too, have been efforts to reevaluate the medical, psychological, and sociocultural viewpoints in terms of a broadened perspective.

In the sections that follow we shall consider three contemporary trends that have gone hand in hand with the emergence of the interdisciplinary approach: (1) the decline of the medical model, (2) the growing influence of psychosocial models, and (3) the development of innovative techniques for coping with abnormal behavior.

The contemporary interdisciplinary approach to mental disorders owes a major debt to Adolf Meyer (1866–1950), whose views were formulated under the heading of *psychobiology* and rested on the assumption that the determinants of an individual's behavior are pluralistic and interactional. Consequently, all the relevant factors —biological, psychological, and sociocultural—must be integrated into a coherent view of the clinical picture of a specific disorder. Because of his prominent role in the development of American psychological thought, Meyer has appropriately been called the "dean of American psychiatry."

DECLINE OF THE MEDICAL MODEL

In reviewing the development of the organic viewpoint, we noted that some of its limitations became apparent very early. Even in the organic disorder paresis (page 46), the pride and joy of the medical model, it was observed that not everyone with the same brain damage developed the same type or severity of symptoms. Similarly, in psychoses associated with senile and arteriosclerotic brain damage, it was found that some individuals with only small amounts of brain damage became severely mentally disordered, whereas others with relatively extensive damage showed only mild symptoms. Among the great majority of mental patients, furthermore, there was no evidence of brain impairment at all. But despite such findings, and despite the growing influence of the psychological and sociocultural viewpoints, the medical model—with its view of abnormal behavior as "mental illness"—has remained until recently the dominant influence in psychopathology. Even today the most widely accepted classification of abnormal behavior patterns is that of the American Psychiatric Association, a medical organization.

Over the past several years, however, the dominance of the medical model in the field of psychopathology has come under sustained attack—by many people within the medical field as well as by psychologists and other mental health personnel. It should be noted that critics have not questioned the usefulness of medical approaches in the treatment program for disorders involving organic impairment. Their opposition has been directed, rather, at use of the medical model as an overall framework for conceptualizing abnormal behavior. Criticism has centered chiefly around three points:

1. *Most abnormal behavior does not involve brain pathology or "mental illness."* One of the first major assaults to be made on the medical model was that of Szasz (1960; 1969), a psychiatrist, who coined the controversial phrase "the myth of mental illness" to emphasize his view that most persons labeled "mentally ill" are not really "sick" in a medical sense. Rather, their behaviors are deviations from ethical, legal, or other social norms—and typically stem from the stresses of everyday life. Such behaviors thus are not the result of some organic malfunctioning of the brain, but of "problems in living." In a similar vein, we quote Adams (1964), a psychologist:

"What is the phenomenon to which the label 'mental illness' is applied? It is applied to arbitrarily designated types of maladaptive interpersonal behavior, often accompanied by reports of subjective discomfort, unsatisfying human relationships, and social rejection." (p. 191)

This view of abnormal or maladaptive behavior —not as "mental illness" but as a consequence of faulty learning and coping methods in the individual's struggle with the problems of living— obviously has far-reaching implications. It suggests, for example, that treatment programs should generally focus on helping the individual learn more effective coping techniques and on alleviating stressful conditions in his life situation.

2. *Rigid classification and labeling of abnormal behavior is inappropriate and generally harmful.* The medical viewpoint has placed considerable emphasis on the classification and labeling of specific disorders. Although this approach may be useful and necessary in dealing with organic disorders, it does not seem appropriate for abnormal behavior that stems primarily from faulty learning and/or excessive stress. For example, on what basis is an anxious and unhappy individual labeled "neurotic"? And to what end?

The labeling of abnormal behavior patterns tends to be highly arbitrary, for it depends a great deal on societal norms and on the viewpoints of the persons doing the labeling. An even more serious consideration, however, is the damaging effect that labeling may have on an individual's self-image and on his interpersonal relationships.

3. *The "sick role" may actually encourage maladaptive behavior.* A further argument against the medical model and the concept of mental illness is that it provides the individual with a "sick role" that tends to relieve him of responsibility for coping with his life situation and may influence his subsequent behavior. If he is "ill," then it is up to mental health personnel to make him "well"—and in the meanwhile it seems unreasonable to expect that he can handle his normal responsibilities or maintain normal relationships with other people. Thus, instead of involving himself in the task of learning how to cope with his problems more effectively, the individual may fall back on patterns of behavior that seem appropriate for one who is "sick"— e.g., neurotic or psychotic.

Although the medical and biological sciences have an important contribution to make under the interdisciplinary approach, it can be expected that the medical model will gradually fall into disuse as a general schema for conceptualizing abnormal or maladaptive behavior.

models. In historical perspective a key achievement of the *psychoanalytic model* was the introduction of the concept of anxiety, and defenses against anxiety, as causing hysteria and certain other mental disorders—thus replacing organic pathology as the sole causal agent. This anxiety-defense view of psychopathology has had a pervasive influence on all subsequent psychosocial models. The psychoanalytic model also provided free association and other procedures for treating mental disorders and bringing about major personality changes. But despite these and other epic contributions, the psychoanalytic model was gradually reduced to the status of *one* rather than *the* psychosocial model of mental disorders.

For shortly to emerge was the *behavioristic model,* which has been in the forefront of efforts to formulate and apply principles of learning to psychopathology. After more than half a century of research in psychological laboratories in the Western world, the behaviorists have provided a great deal of information about learning in general, and about the role of faulty learning in maladaptive behavior. And by applying learning principles to the modification of behavior, they have developed effective methods of treatment. These methods are being utilized more and more by psychologists and psychiatrists of diverse theoretical orientations; and as these methods are systematically applied to abnormal behavior, we can expect behavior-modification techniques to become increasingly sophisticated and effective.

More recently we have seen the emergence of the humanistic model, which has been particularly influential in shifting the focus of psycho-

INCREASING INFLUENCE OF PSYCHOSOCIAL MODELS

The decline of the medical model has been accompanied by a concomitant increase in the influence of the various psychosocial models —particularly the behavioristic, humanistic, and interpersonal models. As we have seen, these major models of man are properly termed *psychosocial,* because they take cognizance of sociocultural as well as psychological determinants.

At the risk of repetition, we shall briefly review the contribution made by these psychosocial

Prominently associated with attacks on the medical model and the lessening of its influence in psychopathology is the psychiatrist Thomas S. Szasz (1920–). In his book *The Myth of Mental Illness* (1961), Szasz argued that *illness* is an inappropriate term for most abnormal behavior, which results from problems in living, rather than from organic causes.

logical and psychiatric thinking from the mere treatment of mental disorders to an active enhancement of personal growth and self-fulfillment. In contrast to the usual view of psychopathology as an undesirable deviation from social norms, this model—with its focus on the self-actualizing person as representing normality and health—adheres to a view that may be called the "psychopathology of the average." For this reason, humanistic psychologists are interested not only in traditional learning principles but also in new ways of experiencing and learning—hence their interest in encounter groups and other innovative approaches to personal growth.

Closely related to the humanistic model is the *existential model,* with its emphasis on the problems of freedom, courage, and choice in shaping one's self and finding a meaningful and fulfilling life. To lack courage and to flee from one's obligation to one's own life and to one's fellow man is to be unauthentic, to show bad faith, and to live in despair. And we have seen the existential emphasis upon the "encounter with nothingness," or death, which adds a note of urgency to life, and the existentialists' concern with the human situation—the alienation and dehumanization of man in a vast, bureaucratic and impersonal society. Here are the roots of existential anxiety—apprehensiveness about achieving a meaningful and fulfilling life.

Also of more recent vintage has been the *interpersonal model,* with its emphasis on interpersonal relationships in the development and maintenance of psychopathology. We have noted the nature of fraudulent and other interpersonal patterns that lead to frustration, blocked or distorted growth, and maladaptive behavior. And we have seen that treatment focuses not only on the alleviation of pathogenic patterns but also on actively fostering interpersonal relationships that promote mutual need satisfactions, personal growth, and self-fulfillment. Although pathogenic interpersonal relationships are by no means limited to any one group or social class, such problems appear to be more extensive among the socially disadvantaged; for poverty, family disorganization, and related conditions—all of which confront this segment of the population to an inordinate degree—make the establishment and maintenance of satisfying interpersonal relationships extremely difficult.

In noting the increasing influence of these psychosocial models, it is useful to recall their differing views of man's basic nature—from the essentially negative view of the psychoanalysts, to the neutral view of the behaviorists, to the positive view of the humanists—and the implications of these views for psychopathology. It is also useful to emphasize the differential applicability of these models to the treatment of mal-

Electrical stimulation of the brain (ESB) is a frontier in behavior modification which is being explored with striking results by Physiologist Jose Delgado; the technique, involving the implantation of microcircuitry in the subject's brain, is now being used on humans for diagnostic and therapeutic purposes, after years of experimentation with animals. These pictures illustrate the changes that were brought about in a brain-damaged girl's emotions and behavior—from happiness to anger and violence—as electrical impulses were directed to specific areas of her brain.

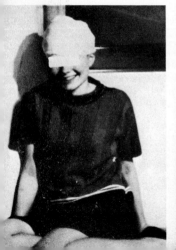

Encounter groups represent a relatively recent innovative approach to coping with problems of adjustment and realizing human potentials. These groups aim at increased self-understanding, improved effectiveness in relating to others, and exposure to new channels of experiencing and personal growth. We shall have occasion to refer to encounter groups in the course of this book, both in the context of dealing with personal problems and of achieving personal growth.

adaptive behavior. For the behavioristic and interpersonal models are primarily concerned with the problems of everyday coping; while the humanistic and existential models focus on personal growth and self-fulfillment.

DEVELOPMENT OF INNOVATIVE APPROACHES TO TREATMENT

The interdisciplinary approach has led not only to the integration of research findings from various fields but also to the "team" approach in coping with abnormal behavior. A typical treatment program today may involve the coordinated efforts of psychologists, psychiatrists, social workers, and various paraprofessional personnel. And depending on the particular problems of the individual or group of individuals needing help, it may draw on innovative techniques in any or all of the following areas.

Innovations on a biological level. We shall comment elsewhere on some of the great breakthroughs that have occurred in modern genetics, and their application to genetic counseling and potentially to the ultimate correction of genetic defects. We are also witnessing the introduction of increasingly effective psychopharmacologic drugs—such as methadone for the treatment of heroin addiction, and L-dopa for alleviation of symptoms in Parkinson's disease—as well as new surgical techniques for dealing with organic

brain syndromes. In addition, we can point to the advances in corticovisceral medicine which are making it increasingly possible for an individual to exert some control over his own internal bodily processes—including brain waves, blood pressure, and other functions. Finally, we are witnessing experimental work in electrical brain stimulation, neurophysiology, and biochemistry which is gradually unlocking the secrets of the human brain and helping us understand how developmental defects, damage to the brain, or changes in brain biochemistry can lead to disturbances in thought processes and psychological functioning.

Innovations on a psychological level. On a psychological level we are witnessing increasingly sophisticated advances with regard to the treatment of abnormal behavior. For example, the concern of social psychology with interpersonal relationships and with group-individual

The rapport established between a teen-ager and a mentally retarded child gives both of them an emotional lift and emphasizes the value of volunteer help in community-sponsored programs. Teen-aged aides are highly regarded in this program designed to meet the needs of handicapped preschool children—mentally retarded, emotionally disturbed, and physically handicapped. Key features of the program are classroom learning activities, physical exercises and games, language development exercises, and lessons in self-care.

interactions, and the humanistic emphasis on exploring new pathways of creative learning and personal growth, are broadening our thinking concerning man's behavior. Concurrently we are seeing the "coming of age" of various innovative psychotherapeutic approaches, such as sensitivity training and confrontation groups. These general approaches may vary greatly in specific content—from nude sensitivity training groups to marathon encounters where group members stay together for intensive interaction over a weekend or longer. Then too, there has been an increased application of learning principles—in the form of behavior modification techniques—to a wide range of maladaptive behaviors, from simple phobias to sexual deviations, drug dependence, alcoholism, psychoses, and criminal behavior.

Innovations on a sociocultural level. Comparable innovative trends have been taking place in the sociological realm as well. We have seen the shift in emphasis from a limited concern with the intrapsychic dynamics of the individual to an increased acknowledgment of the importance of his relationships in his family and social milieu. Thus, increasing prominence has been given to the study and treatment of "pathogenic" family and community patterns, and this emphasis is being extended to our entire social structure.

As we noted in Chapter 1, there is a current emphasis on the training and use of paraprofessional personnel—persons trained in and capable of handling specific types of problems, such as family crises in socially disadvantaged areas, drug problems among teen-agers, and so on—but who have not had the formal training that would qualify them for functioning as psychologists, psychiatric social workers, or the like. In view of the shortage of professional mental health personnel—it has been estimated that at least four times more professionals are needed—the importance of this trend in treatment can be readily seen (Cline, 1970). But beyond that consideration, paraprofessional personnel, because they often share common experiences and understandings with the people with whom they work, have a special part to play in easing problems of communication and promoting effective treatment.

A LOOK AHEAD

The rapidly accelerating advances in modern science and technology, together with the profound sociocultural changes taking place in the world, make it extremely risky to speculate about "the shape of things to come." However, the trends that we have discussed in this chapter portend some of the events that appear to be emerging in the field of psychopathology.

TOWARD COMPREHENSIVE HEALTH

Over a decade ago the World Health Organization laid down the guiding principle of a "sound mind, in a sound body, in a sound society." Although we still have a long way to go before this goal can be achieved—even in our affluent society—we are gradually implementing what may be termed a "comprehensive public health" concept.

Such a comprehensive health approach must begin with a respect for the rights, privileges, and requirements of the individual from the moment of his conception—or perhaps before, in terms of healthy parents and planned parenthood—with good prenatal, birth, and early postnatal health care. As Williams (1970) has phrased it:

". . . child advocacy is an assertion of the rights of children to be wanted, to be born healthy, to live in a healthy environment, to receive basic need satisfaction and continuous loving care, to acquire optimal intellectual and emotional skills and appropriate treatment when required. Local Child Development Councils established throughout the nation would serve as agents of advocacy in order to guarantee these rights to every American child from conception through age 24." (p. 7)

The advancement of an individual from "childhood" to "adulthood" does not mean that these same needs and rights are no longer important. In describing the reasons for seeking help given by persons using a community mental health clinic, Raphling and Lion (1970) found that they

". . . sought treatment when they felt isolated, lonely, depressed, and overwhelmed by life stresses. . . . The precipitating events were experienced . . . as overwhelming crises which tended to exert upon them a disproportionately severe degree of disorganization requiring the assistance of an external agency to prevent disaster." (pp. 315-316)

Many of these persons returned for assistance when beginning a new job or personal relationship, when suffering from disappointments and frustrations, and when overburdened with personal responsibilities.

Probably there are occasions in the lives of most adults when they wish there were someone they could readily turn to for assistance in coping with a particular situation. Thus Roe (1970) has urged the development of "community resources centers" that would be available to everyone as a routine aid in dealing with normal life problems. Roe stresses the need for overcoming the notion that an individual must be emotionally disordered before seeking help—a belief that keeps many people from utilizing the community resources that are currently available.

Carson (1969) and others have helped call attention to the fact that individuals who have once been labeled "mentally ill" often have a special need for community assistance in rebuilding their lives. Miller (1966) describes the problem with respect to persons who have been discharged from mental hospitals:

". . . what is needed to keep the great majority of them out [from being rehospitalized] are things so simple that most of us take them for granted: adequate livelihoods; indications from doctors, employers, and other professionals that they are well, competent, respected; a life partner to extend affection, share burdens, lend support; a consistent, structured, reassuring self-image and world. Yet our findings show that most released patients do not have these things. Their outside careers

James G. Miller (1916–) has been one of the pioneers in the development of general systems theory. He has extensively explored the commonalities and differences in living systems—on all levels from cells through the individual to groups—relating to the processing of matter-energy and information. Many of his basic formulations are reflected in our illustration "Man As a Living System," and we shall make further references to a number of these concepts in the course of the present text.

are fragmented, marginal, depressing, disillusioning. . . . The community must offer these patients and their families much more to help them build the new worlds they require." (p. 41)

As we have seen, the community mental health movement is based essentially on this concept of comprehensive health and is concerned not only with the well-being of the individual but with family, community, and broader societal factors as well. Implementing this overall trend are social programs—sponsored by nongovernmental as well as governmental agencies—that provide facilities and services in community settings, thus making them more available to those in need. In Chapter 21, dealing with efforts toward mental health and toward a more sane and harmonious world, we shall go into some detail concerning international, national, and local efforts by professional people and citizens to further the goal of comprehensive mental health—to produce "good people" in a "good society."

GENERAL SYSTEMS THEORY

Implicit in the comprehensive health approach is the need for a schema that will provide a unified view of man and his world. Such a schema must be (1) capable not only of dealing with cur-

MAN AS A LIVING SYSTEM

All living systems, whether simple or complex, have certain characteristics in common. However, as we move up the scale from one level of system to a higher one, behavioral capabilities emerge that were not apparent on the level just below. Thus, in viewing man as a living system it is relevant to consider both the general properties of living systems and the unique properties of the human system.

GENERAL PROPERTIES OF LIVING SYSTEMS

Structural properties

Every living system is composed of parts or subsystems, which are integrated in such a way that the total system is capable of self-regulation, development, and reproduction. Some of these subsystems, such as the circulatory and nervous systems in animals, can be observed directly; others, such as the self-system in man, can only be inferred from the way the system functions.

Of key importance in all living organisms are subsystems for *processing matter-energy*, as in the assimilation of nutrients, and subsystems for *processing information* from the environment, as necessary for adjustive action. These subsystems become progressively more sophisticated as we move from lower-level organisms to higher-level ones, and behavioral capabilities increase accordingly. Thus an amoeba, with its rudimentary structure, has much less flexibility in dealing with its environment than does a fish; similarly, the behavioral potentialities of a fish are severely limited compared with those of a man.

Integrative properties

Every living system has built-in tendencies to maintain its organizational and functional integrity. In man, maintenance of the system involves control not only of physiological variables, such as oxygen supply and body temperature, but of psychological and sociocultural variables as well. All must be kept within a range compatible with integrated functioning and survival.

Another integrative characteristic of living systems is their tendency to develop in accordance with their genetic potentialities. An acorn may develop into a magnificent specimen of "oakhood" or into a stunted, gnarled tree, depending largely on its environment; but it will always become an oak, never a birch or a maple. Similarly, human development follows a characteristic pattern and sequence, despite individual differences.

Field properties

Each living organism is an "open" system—it is not self-sufficient but can continue to exist only if it can maintain certain kinds of transactions with its environment, or *field*. This constant interaction modifies both system and field. Even in such a simple matter as breathing, the human organism both alters and is altered by its environment. On an interpersonal level, we can see the influence of a child on his family as well as the influence of the family on the child.

A key element in system-field transactions is the use of *feedback*. The concept of feedback stems from cybernetics and refers to the manner in which the effect of adjustive action is introduced as input in the ongoing processing of information and the regulation of further adjustive action. For instance, the feedback a husband receives in his efforts to resolve a conflict with his wife will influence his further efforts along that line.

Systems theory, in short, views man not as separate and distinct from his environment but as an integral part of it—both physically and socially.

UNIQUE PROPERTIES OF THE HUMAN SYSTEM

Self-awareness and self-direction

All living things have a responsiveness to stimulation—sometimes called irritability—but in man alone has this awareness evolved to the level of *reflective consciousness*. This unique type of self-awareness, coupled with the ability to delay action over sustained periods of time, provides man with his potentialities for thought, evaluation, and self-direction. To a far greater extent than any other living system, man has the ability to transcend the stimulation of the moment and thus to shape his own future and control his own destiny.

rent problems but also of forecasting the kind of mental health problems we are likely to encounter in the future, and (2) capable of providing a sound scientific basis for shaping a "good" future for man—one that will foster and help to ensure his well-being and fulfillment. The new and still emerging *general systems model* or *theory* appears potentially capable of meeting these qualifications.

Physical and biological scientists have long been accustomed to thinking in terms of *energy systems,* and recently an increasing number of behavioral scientists have found it helpful to approach their study of man in much the same

Modifiability of action	Of all living systems, man is the least bound by "built-in" patterns and the most capable of changing his behavior. His resources for learning, reasoning, and imagining give him almost unlimited flexibility for coping with new and changing situations in appropriate and often original ways—a critical advantage in our modern world with its shifting and changing demands. Man has a further advantage in his ability to control and direct many of the changes themselves, preventing or reversing those that threaten his welfare.
Use of symbols	While many other organisms show flexibility and resourcefulness in coping with problems, they are unable to deal in any complex way with absent situations by thinking about them. Man's thought processes, on the other hand, may be concerned largely with ideas—symbols of absent or even imaginary objects, events, and concepts. Thus man can better understand the order inherent in his world, anticipate the probable outcome of given courses of action, and make plans in the light of past, present, and future. Man's ability to use symbols has also made it possible for him to communicate more precisely with others as well as to communicate with individuals or groups far removed in time or space. Thus Greek writers, dead over two thousand years, can still influence our contemporary thinking.
Complexity of transactions with field	Whereas lower animals must usually eat what they can find or starve, rely on instinctual responses for coping with bodily disease or damage, and live where climatic conditions are not too extreme, man is not so limited. In fact, there seems to be almost no end to the ways in which man can modify his environment. As a consequence, he increasingly lives in a world of his own making, and the adjustive demands he must meet are largely ones that he himself has created.
Concern with values and meaning	Since man's behavior is not limited to instinctual patterns of adjustment, he must decide for himself what goals to pursue and what means are appropriate for trying to achieve them. In selecting goals and means, he must come to grips with the problem of values—of what is good or bad, desirable or undesirable. And inevitably the problem of values becomes coupled with that of trying to ascertain the meaning of his own existence. Such concerns are uniquely human. They can arise only in a living system which has a high degree of self-awareness, flexibility in behavior, and opportunity for choice among alternatives.

CHANGES IN THE SYSTEM WITH TIME

Changes toward growth and complexity	In man, as in other types of organisms, the basic pattern of change comes as part of a genetically determined and predictable life cycle extending from conception to old age and death. In the early phases of the life cycle the changes are in the direction of increased size, complexity, and competence in dealing with the environment.
Changes toward entropy	In the later phases of human life, changes are toward entropy, or deterioration, and eventual disintegration.
Other changes	In the course of its field transactions, the system also experiences changes in structure and functioning that are not, strictly speaking, genetically programmed—as a result of learning, for example, or of accidents and disease.

In summary, general systems theory takes cognizance in a systematic way of man's inner experiencing and his outward behavior, his propensities for action and transactions with his environment. It goes beyond other models of man in recognizing his continuity with other living things as well as his uniqueness.

The material in this chart based on Berrien (1968), Bertalanffy (1967; 1968), Buckley (1968), Coleman (1969), Collier (1964), Lennard and Bernstein (1969), and Miller (1965a; 1965b).

way—viewing the human organism as comparable in many basic ways to other living energy systems but also possessing certain unique characteristics.

An energy system can be described in a general way as an assemblage of parts held together by some form of interaction or interdependence. There are nonliving systems, like our solar system, and living systems, like plants and animals. These living systems can be arranged in a hierarchy, extending from cells to organs, individual organisms, groups, organizations, societies, nations, and supranational bodies like the United Nations. Each higher-level system is composed of lower-level ones and provides the environment for systems on the level directly below. For example, a group is made up of individuals, and it also provides the social environment in which these individuals function. Thus, general systems theory does not view individuals as distinct from their environment but rather as integral and interacting parts of it.

The complexities and details of general systems theory lie beyond the scope of our present discussion, but the illustration on pages 88–89 summarizes both the general properties of living energy systems and some of the unique characteristics of the human system. We shall consider the implications of systems theory in relation to adaptive and maladaptive behavior in Chapters 5 and 6.

In a broad sense, general systems theory represents an extension of the interdisciplinary viewpoint; but it goes considerably beyond this viewpoint in terms of explanatory principles and capabilities of prediction and control. It appears in fact to have the potential for unifying modern science and for providing an integrated and comprehensive framework for viewing the continuity of man with other living things and the world in which he lives.

As we turn now to a more detailed examination of abnormal behavior, we shall be faced with the task of integrating varied vocabularies, research findings, clinical data, and theoretical orientations into a meaningful and coherent picture. In some instances it will be necessary to make inferences and generalizations on the basis of very limited research data, but our effort overall will be directed at presenting the broad core of generally accepted scientific thought concerning abnormal behavior.

In Part Two we shall lay the groundwork for our subsequent analysis of particular patterns of abnormal behavior by examining the dynamics of human behavior in general. Chapter 5 will consider such broad topics as personality development, motivation, types of adjustive demands, and general patterns of adjustive behavior. Chapter 6 will then focus more specifically on the various types of causative factors that may lead to maladaptive behavior or serious psychopathology.

The Dynamics
of Adjustive
Behavior

Part Two

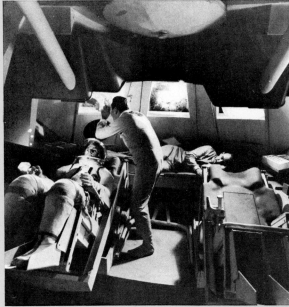
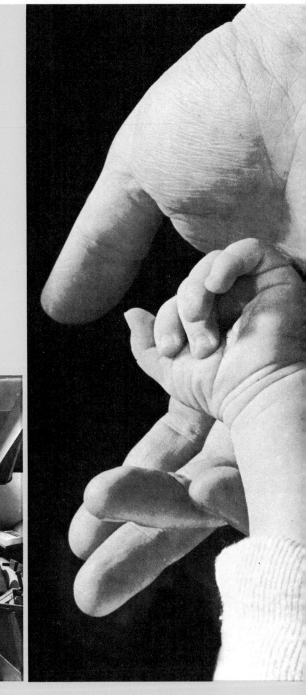

Personality Development and Adjustment

5

DETERMINANTS OF DEVELOPMENT

PATTERNING OF DEVELOPMENT

HUMAN NEEDS AND STRIVINGS

TYPES OF ADJUSTIVE DEMANDS (STRESS)

COPING WITH ADJUSTIVE DEMANDS

Why are some people homosexuals and others heterosexuals, some alcoholics and others tee-totalers, some criminals and others law-abiding citizens, some schizophrenics and others happy and productive individuals? The task of trying to explain such variations in behavior necessarily begins with a consideration of the broad principles underlying human development and functioning.

Our initial focus in this chapter will be on the developmental process itself. We shall consider not only the basic determinants of development —the individual's genetic endowment, his environment, and his emerging self-structure—but also the general patterning of development. Here we shall note the orderly sequence and cumulative nature of the growth process and the interplay of maturation and learning in producing both likenesses and differences among individuals.

Turning next to the dynamics of human behavior, we shall consider the key role of motivation in directing the individual's actions toward the satisfaction of basic needs and strivings; the kinds of obstacles, or adjustive demands, that commonly interfere with efforts to achieve need satisfaction; and the patterns of behavior that come into play as the individual attempts to cope with such demands. We shall see that the biological and psychological traits built into the human system during the process of development are basic resources that the individual brings to each new adjustive situation. But we shall also see that his behavior in every instance is a product of outer as well as inner determinants. With both normal and abnormal behavior, we are always dealing with a complex pattern of interacting causes or determinants.

DETERMINANTS OF DEVELOPMENT

The basic sources of personality development are heredity and environment. However, as a person's genetic inheritance interacts with and is shaped by environmental factors, there emerges a self-structure that becomes an important influence in the shaping of further development.

HEREDITY

Despite the approximately million different kinds of animals and half million kinds of plants on our earth, each kind of living thing breeds true. Deer give birth to fawns and never to lambs; acorns grow into oak trees and never into elms. It thus becomes apparent that each type of living thing transmits specific hereditary information from one generation to the next. With the breaking of the *genetic code* (see illustration on page 95), man has learned a great deal about this information, how it is transmitted, and how it operates in guiding development.

Heredity influences the determination of some traits more than others. Its influence is perhaps most noticeable in physical features, such as eye color and physique; but it also may play an influential role in "primary reaction tendencies" such as activity level, sensitivity, and adaptability. Even very young babies reveal differences in how they react to particular kinds of stimuli. Some of them are startled at even slight sounds, or cry if sunlight hits their faces; others are seemingly insensitive to such stimulation. Thus, conditions that one baby can tolerate may be quite upsetting to another. Although such constitutional differences may be influenced by environmental as well as genetic factors, longitudinal studies have shown certain of them to be relatively stable from infancy to young adulthood. By virtue of such constitutional differences, infants may be affected in diverse ways by similar environmental conditions and may interact quite differently with their milieu.

Probably the most unique aspect of man's genetic inheritance is his superior brain. It has been described as the most highly organized apparatus in the universe—consisting of some ten billion nerve cells or neurons, with countless interconnecting pathways as well as generous connections with other parts of the body. Thus it provides a fantastic communication and computing network with tremendous capabilities for learning and "storing" experience; for reasoning, imagining, and problem solving; and for integrating the overall functioning of the organism.

It would appear that the essential characteristics of man's genetic inheritance are basically the same for persons of all racial and ethnic groups; however, the specific features of this endowment may vary considerably from one person to another. Thus, heredity not only provides the potentialities for development and behavior typical of the species but also is an important source of individual differences.

ENVIRONMENT

In much the same sense that man receives a genetic inheritance which is the end product of millions of years of biological evolution, he also receives a sociocultural inheritance which is the end product of many thousands of years of social evolution—the significance of which was well pointed up by Huxley (1965):

"The native or genetic capacities of today's bright city child are no better than the native capacities of a bright child born into a family of Upper Paleolithic cave-dwellers. But whereas the contemporary bright baby may grow up to become almost anything—a Presbyterian engineer, for example, a piano-playing Marxist, a professor of biochemistry who is a mystical agnostic and likes to paint in water colours—the paleolithic baby could not possibly have grown into anything except a hunter or foodgatherer, using the crudest of stone tools and thinking about his narrow world of trees and swamps in terms of some hazy system of magic. Ancient and modern, the two babies are indistinguishable. . . . But the adults into whom the babies will grow are profoundly dissimilar; and they

BREAKING THE GENETIC CODE

One of nature's best-kept secrets has been how a single fertilized egg cell can develop into an adult human being with billions of highly differentiated cells and complex organ systems and functions. In a series of epic research studies, scientists have traced the secret to DNA, which contains the specific carriers of heredity, called *genes*.

The DNA molecule is a helix, a spiral that looks like a coiled ladder (top illustration). The sides of this "ladder" are chains of alternating sugar and phosphate; the rungs are formed between the sugar groups by combinations of four basic control chemicals—adenine, thymine, guanine, and cytosine—a given rung being formed by a pair of these chemicals. It is in the sequence of these rungs (center) that the specific hereditary instructions of the growing organism are encoded. DNA molecules are present not only in germ cells but in the nucleus of every living cell. Each living thing resembles the stock from which it descended because of the DNA it inherits. And interestingly enough, the same 4 "letters" appear to be present in the DNA codes of all living creatures—demonstrating the oneness of the whole living world.

The instructions carried in the DNA make provision for two main functions. The first is reproduction of cells by the making of exact copies. Were it not for this power of the DNA to duplicate itself, cells could not split in two—each with a complete set of genetic instructions. A DNA molecule replicates itself by separating down the middle or "unzipping" (bottom drawing). Then each half of the molecule picks up the appropriate new base units from the surrounding area and the duplication is complete. In this way, for example, a new liver cell or red blood cell is formed which, in turn, is capable of replicating itself.

The second key function provided by the DNA instructions is direction of the activities in each cell, including the making of proteins. Proteins are the "building blocks" of life: structural proteins play a crucial role in the development of body tissues and organs, and protein enzymes regulate bodily processes. In fact, it is by means of proteins that the genetic instructions are carried out—that a living organism is created and its growth and functioning implemented.

In breaking the genetic code, it was found that each base represented a letter in the genetic alphabet. Just as the uniqueness of each word in the dictionary depends on a specific arrangement of the 26 letters of the alphabet, the uniqueness of each word in the DNA ladder depends on the sequencing of these chemical letters or bases. All DNA words are short, however—never more than 3 letters long.

Each 3-letter word stands for one of the 20 different varieties of amino acids which are used in the production of proteins. Each of the proteins, or "building blocks" of life, is made up of a different sequencing of these amino acids, a given protein typically requiring a linear sequence of some 300 to 500 amino acids. The DNA *sentence* or *gene* specifies the sequence of amino acids for manufacturing one type of protein. Since there are only 20 different amino acids a question might be raised about the other 44 possible words in the DNA code. It turns out that more than one base triplet, or word, can be used to signify the same amino acid and that some words are used as "start" and "stop" instructions.

The proteins are actually assembled in the cytoplasm of the cell by means of an ingenious arrangement. Too precious to leave the fortress-like security of the cell nucleus, the DNA makes an intermediary chemical called *RNA (ribonucleic acid)*, which is similar but not identical to DNA. The molecules of RNA serve as genetic messengers, journeying from the nucleus of the cell to sites in the cell protoplasm where proteins are to be manufactured. One type of RNA, *messenger RNA*, serves as a template in regulating the sequence of amino acids in protein manufacture. Another type, *transfer RNA*, scavenges in the surrounding area to pick up the amino acids needed for protein manufacture and transports these to the sites where the protein molecules are being assembled. The prodigious feat of the DNA in producing precise instructions for manufacturing the proteins required for the developmental and functional needs of the organism has been compared to the operation of a fantastically complex electronic computer.

Interestingly enough, each cell in the human body contains all the DNA information needed for producing a new human being; somehow "turn-off" mechanisms manage to delete all the DNA information except what is needed for the cell to duplicate itself or to produce a particular protein. If any detail of the DNA instructions is missing or garbled—as we might misspell *cat* as *cot*—the organism may be in for trouble. For example, people become ill and die with inherited sickle-cell anemia, in which a single amino acid is wrong out of the 574 that make up a hemoglobin molecule of the blood.

Some idea of the difficulties inherent in breaking the genetic code can be gleaned from noting that the vast information stored in the DNA is written in such a tiny script that all the DNA in all the fertilized egg cells that have given rise to the approximately three billion people on earth would fit into a 1/8-inch cube.

Based in part on Beadle (1964), McClearn (1968), Pfeiffer (1964), Watson (1965), and Wooldridge (1968). Diagrams redrawn, with permission, from Sonnenborn (1962).

are dissimilar because in one of them very few, and in the other a good many, of the baby's inborn potentialities have been actualized." (p. 69)

Because each group fosters its own cultural patterns by the systematic teaching of its offspring, all of its members tend to be somewhat alike—to conform to certain "basic personality types." Individuals reared among headhunters will become headhunters; individuals reared in societies that do not sanction violence will learn to settle their differences in nonviolent ways. In New Guinea, for example, Mead (1949) found two tribes—of similar racial origin and living in the same general geographical area—the members of which developed diametrically opposed characteristics; the Arapesh were a kindly, peaceful, cooperative people, while the Mundungumor were warlike, suspicious, competitive, and vengeful. Such differences appear to be clearly social in origin.

The more uniform and thorough the education of the younger members of a group, the more alike they will become. Thus, in a society characterized by a limited and consistent point of view, there are not the wide individual differences typical of a society like ours, where children have contact with many divergent beliefs and values. Even in our society, however, there are certain core values that we attempt to perpetuate as essential to our way of life.

Subgroups within a general sociocultural environment—such as family, sex, age, social class, occupational, and religious groups—also foster beliefs and norms of their own—largely by means of social roles which their members learn to adopt. Thus we could delineate the role behaviors expected of the student, the teacher, the army officer, the clergyman, the nurse, and persons occupying other specific positions. The extent to which role expectations can influence development is well illustrated by the assignment of sex roles among the Techambuli, a New Guinea tribe studied by Margaret Mead (1949); in this tribe, women are supposed to earn the living, handle business transactions, take the initiative in courtship, and head the family in general—while men are expected to be coquettish, prone to gossip, interested in dancing and theatricals, and good homemakers. Obviously the sex roles among the

Techambuli tend to channel personality development along lines quite different from those encouraged in our society.

Because the individual is a member of various subgroups, he is subject to various role demands. And, of course, he may be expected to change roles if his position in the group changes. In fact, the life of the individual can be viewed as consisting of a succession of roles—child, student, worker, husband or wife, parent, and senior citizen. The group may allow the individual considerable leeway in role behavior—depending on his specific position in the group—but there are limits. Conformity to role demands is induced by the use of positive and negative reinforcers—such as money, prestige, status, punishment, and loss of membership in the group—as well as through instruction in group norms and role behavior. When an individual's social roles are conflicting, unclear, or uncomfortable, or when he is unable to achieve a satisfactory role in the group, he may be handicapped in his personality development.

Each individual is exposed to various interactions with other persons; and these relationships, beginning with the members of his family, gradually extend to his peer group and other "significant" people in his world. Much of his personality development reflects his experiences with these key people. For example, the child who is rejected and mistreated by his parents is likely to develop quite differently from one who is accepted and encouraged. Similarly, interpersonal relationships in a Boy Scout troop would likely have quite different effects on development than would such relationships in a delinquent gang. The behavior patterns children learn depend heavily on models to which they are exposed.

Since each individual belongs to different subgroups and experiences different interpersonal relationships, he participates in the sociocultural environment in a unique way. As a consequence of such "differential participation," no two of us grow up in quite the same world. Thus the sociocultural environment is the source of differences as well as commonalities in personality development.

In discussing environment and its effects in shaping development, it is important to note the effects of the physical as well as the sociocultural environment. For each physical setting is unique in that it consists of a constellation of favorable or unfavorable conditions that make special demands on the organisms living within it. Thus the physical environment may also foster somewhat different characteristics, even among people with similar genetic inheritances.

In summary so far, we may say that our genetic endowment provides our potentialities for both biological and psychological development, but the shaping of our potentialities—in terms of perceiving, thinking, feeling, and acting—depends heavily on our physical and sociocultural environment.

SELF AS A THIRD DETERMINANT

As the infant grows and learns to distinguish between himself and other people and things, a part of his total perceptual field is gradually delineated as the "me," "I," or "self." As this self-structure develops, it becomes the integrating core of his personality—the reference point around which his experiences and coping patterns are organized. When a problem arises, it is perceived, thought about, and acted upon in relation to the self;[1] that is, the individual comes to perceive himself as an active agent in determining his own behavior—as indicated by such statements as "I know," "I want," and "I will." In essence, his experience of self-direction involves the self as knower, striver, and doer; these are the three key functions of the self-structure as a centralized decider subsystem.[2]

Fundamental to the functioning of the self-system are the assumptions that the individual makes about himself and his world. These assumptions are based on learning and are of three kinds: (1) *reality* assumptions—his view of things as he thinks they really are, of the kind of person he is, and of the nature of the world in which he lives; (2) *possibility* assumptions—his concept of how things could be, of possibilities for change, of opportunities for personal growth and social progress; and (3) *value* assumptions—his view of the way things should be, of right and wrong, good and bad, desirable and undesirable. These three sets of assumptions provide an individual with a *frame of reference*, or *cognitive map*—a

consistent view of himself in relation to his environment, which is essential for guiding his behavior.

Several aspects of the individual's frame of reference merit further mention. For one thing, the individual's assumptions about reality, possibility, and value afford him a sense of *self-identity*—a realization of who and what he is. They also provide him with a *self-ideal*—a picture of what he could and should be. As we shall see, an unclear self-identity or a marked discrepancy between his "real" and "ideal" selves can lead an individual to serious inner conflict. Second, a person's pattern of assumptions contributes to his perceiving, thinking, feeling, and acting in a consistent manner—to the evolution of a characteristic *life style*. Third, the individual's premises serve not only as guides to behavior but also as *inner controls*. For example, value assumptions may prevent him from stealing or behaving in other ways that he considers unethical. Such value assumptions are often referred to as the individual's *superego*, or *conscience*.

When the individual's inner controls are capable of directing his behavior in accordance with the expectations and norms of his group, he is said to be *socialized*. In some cases, for reasons we shall examine later, these inner controls do not develop to an adequate degree; and under certain conditions—such as alcoholic or drug intoxication—they may give way. However, society does its best to see that such restraints are well developed and maintained, for without them, organized social life would be impossible.

The individual's assumptions may be valid or invalid; they may be held with varying degrees of conviction; and they may be more or less explicit and conscious. Since they are learned, they are subject to modification, although new learning tends to be consistent with one's existing presuppositions. In any event, the individual's frame of reference provides him with an essen-

---

[1]The self-structure, like gravity, cannot be observed directly, but is inferred from the finding that psychological functions operate in an integrated manner as part of a unified organism. As Hebb (1960) has pointed out, "The self is neither mythical nor mystical, but a complex mental process." (p. 743) It has a developmental course, is influenced by learning in both structure and degree of differentiation, and can be studied by various experimental procedures. In the present context we shall use the concepts of *ego* and *self* as roughly synonymous.
[2]Miller (1965) has inferred a "centralized decider subsystem" which controls the entire system in all living organisms. The self appears to function as such a decider subsystem in human beings.

tial basis for evaluating new experience and for coping with his world. As a consequence he tends to defend his existing assumptions and to reject or distort new information that is contradictory to them. Because the individual experiences the self as the very core of his existence, he becomes especially concerned with its maintenance and enhancement; thus he develops a system of *ego* or *self-defense mechanisms* to maintain the adequacy and worth of the self and defend it from devaluation. We shall examine the operation of such mechanisms in the final section of this chapter.

As a person achieves a sense of selfhood, he becomes an increasingly important force in directing his own behavior. Regardless of the many external demands and influences that press in on him, he typically perceives *himself* as an active force in initiating *his* plans and actions— as the *I* who wants or needs some things while trying to avoid others. He perceives and responds to each new situation in light of *his* motives, as-

sumptions, and feelings—and he achieves an increasing sense of his identity and of *self-direction*. If we view the individual as a striving, evaluating, adapting system in his own right— not simply as the passive result of heredity and environment—we may consider the "self" as the third and final determinant of personality development.

In viewing the interaction of genetic, environmental, and self determinants in the shaping of personality development, it may be noted that the tremendous advances of modern science are adding a new dimension to this pattern. For as man transforms his physical and sociocultural environment, he is also changing himself—physiologically and psychologically. Breakthroughs in genetics, brain research, communication, learning theory, and other areas are steadily increasing his power to mold, change, and control human development and behavior. The value problems and other implications of this new power will be discussed in Chapter 20.

PATTERNING OF DEVELOPMENT

A key characteristic of the human life cycle is the relatively long period of infancy and childhood, during which the growing individual is expected to acquire the information and competencies essential for adult functioning. In contrast to animals lower on the phylogenetic scale, who have "built-in" patterns of behavior and who mature rapidly, the human infant begins life with few built-in patterns and a far greater capacity to learn from experience. But the price of such a high degree of modifiability is initial helplessness and the necessity of mastering the "know-how" and "know-why" of living. In our society, such learning is coming to require most of the life cycle.

In reviewing the patterning or sequencing of development we shall focus on the formative period of the life cycle—to see how growth is patterned under the combined influence of inner

and outer determinants. We shall see that within limits human development follows a sequential course and proceeds in a characteristic direction. However, the maintenance of this overall pattern depends on a favorable environment and on the individual's learning essential information and competencies along the way.

By way of introduction we may note certain general principles which provide a useful perspective for viewing the nature and course of human development:

1. Development normally proceeds in an orderly sequence, although its rate is not constant but rather shows spurts and periods of slow growth; in addition, each part and subsystem has its own pattern and sequence of development.

2. Development can be viewed in terms of stages, each having its own characteristics; although there is an underlying continuity to the human life cycle, we can point to differing characteristics of development during infancy, childhood, and later life periods.

3. There are both similarities and differences in the development of individuals; each person goes through the same stages, but there are differences in learning, growth patterns, and outcomes among the members of any age group.

4. Each new stage of development builds on and is limited by previous development, and, in turn, provides the foundation for the stages that follow; what happens in childhood is influenced by the events of infancy and, in turn, codetermines the course of adolescence.

5. Finally, the pathway from infancy to maturity involves increasing differentiation, integration, and complexity of structure and behavior.

TRENDS TOWARD PERSONAL MATURITY

Although children's growth is shaped in different ways in different sociocultural settings, there are certain characteristic trends in development that are seen in any society—whether primitive or advanced. These trends are essential for responsible self-direction and for participating in and contributing to one's social setting. Here we may briefly note seven of these specific but interrelated trends toward personal maturity:

1. *Dependence to self-direction.* One of the most obvious progressions toward maturity is from the dependency of fetus, infant, and child to the independence of adulthood. Bound up with this growth toward independence and self-direction is the development of a clear sense of personal identity and the acquiring of information, competencies, and values. In our society this includes sufficient emancipation from family and other social groups to be a person in one's own right.

2. *Pleasure to reality (self-control).* Freud postulated the *pleasure principle*—the tendency to seek pleasure and to avoid pain and discomfort —as fundamental in governing early behavior. However, he thought this principle was in time subordinated to the *reality principle*—the realization that we must learn to perceive and face reality if we are to meet our needs. This means distinguishing between fantasy and reality, con-

trolling impulse and desire, delaying immediate gratification in the interest of long-range goals, and learning to cope with the inevitable hurts, disappointments, and frustrations of living.

3. *Ignorance to knowledge.* The human infant is born in a state that might be called total ignorance, but he rapidly begins to acquire information about himself and his world. With time, this information is organized into a coherent pattern of assumptions concerning reality, possibility, and value which provides him with a stable frame of reference for guiding his behavior. If this frame of reference is to prove adequate, it needs to be realistic, to be relevant to the kinds of problems he must deal with, and to be one in which he has faith. Also, it needs to be flexible so that it can be modified by new experiences.

4. *Incompetence to competence.* The entire preadult period from infancy through adolescence is directed toward the mastery of intellectual, emotional, social, and other competencies essential for adulthood. The individual acquires skills in problem solving and decision making, learns to control his emotions and to use them for the enrichment of living, and learns to deal with others and to establish satisfying interpersonal relationships. Included here too is preparation for sexual, marital, occupational, parental, and other problems likely to be met in adult life.

5. *Diffuse sexuality to heterosexuality.* Initial expressions of sexuality, while relatively diffuse and generalized, are found at an early age; even infants may experience pleasure from genital stimulation, and childhood "crushes" often have a high degree of sexual involvement. With the advent of puberty, heterosexual differentiation progresses rapidly, usually eventuating in marital sexual patterns. Here it may be noted that growth toward sexual maturity may be influenced by maturity in other life areas. Although sexual mores are changing, it would nevertheless appear that mature sexual behavior involves the ability to establish intimate and satisfying interpersonal relationships.

6. *Amoral to moral.* The newborn infant is amoral—in the sense that he has no concept of "right" and "wrong." Very early he learns, however, that certain forms of behavior are approved, or "good," while other patterns are disapproved, or "bad." Gradually he learns a pattern of value assumptions which operate as inner guides and controls of behavior and which we have referred to as his *conscience* or *superego*. Initially, he accepts these value assumptions blindly; but with increasing maturity he learns to appraise them, and works out a value orientation that bears his own stamp.

7. *Self-centered to other-centered.* The infant is almost exclusively concerned with his own needs and wants, but with time there is normally an expanding understanding and concern with the needs of others as well. This includes the ability to give love in one's family setting, and to be concerned about and involved with people in one's community and with society as a whole.

There are widespread differences in the success with which individuals reach these goals, but all are important in the actualization of growth potentials and development into a productive, effective member of society.

DEVELOPMENTAL STAGES AND TASKS

Intensive studies of thousands of infants and children have shown that human development tends to follow a definite schedule, not only in physical and motor development, but also in intellectual, emotional, and social development (Gesell & Armatruda, 1947; Gesell, 1953; Ilg & Ames, 1955; Piaget, 1952; Elkind, 1967). The infant crawls and sits up before he begins to walk; his early diffuse emotional reactions become differentiated into love, humor, grief, and other specific patterns; and his language behavior progresses from random vocalizations to the words that eventually become vehicles for thinking.

In the present context, it is not necessary to discuss the stages of human development—prenatal, infancy, childhood, adolescence, adulthood, and old age—or to delineate the details of development in intellectual or other specific areas. But it is important for our purposes to know that at each stage of development there are certain tasks which the individual must master if he is to maintain a normal schedule. For example, learning to walk and talk are major chores of infancy; establishing a mature sense of identity and preparing for work and marriage are key tasks of adolescence.

If these tasks are not mastered at the appropriate stage, the individual suffers from immaturities and incompetencies which place him at a serious disadvantage in adjusting at later developmental levels. A young child who has not learned to walk or talk would be at a serious disadvantage in entering nursery school or kindergarten; the adolescent who does not date misses a major opportunity for acquiring experience in interpersonal relations and role behavior that he will need later for selecting a satisfactory mate. The demands of a given developmental period may be relatively easy or difficult to meet, depending on how well the tasks at prior developmental levels have been mastered and what kind of guidance the individual receives.

From a broader perspective, of course, it is apparent that developmental tasks vary, not only with the stage of development, but also with the sociocultural setting. Children in all societies learn to walk and talk, but they do not all have to master reading or the skills involved in hunting or farming. The members of each society and subgroup face somewhat unique developmental tasks; and of course, with social change, new tasks may arise for any or all of the life stages.

THE CRUCIAL ROLE OF LEARNING

Although personality development is closely related to maturational processes,[1] the particular direction of an individual's development—and even its timing—is greatly dependent on learning.

Maturation and readiness. Maturational processes guide the development of the individual's bodily structure and pave the way for learning. For most kinds of human behavior, maturation establishes the necessary readiness, but learning determines the direction that development takes. Even the preconditions necessary for new learning require both maturation and previous learning. Thus, the first-grader cannot learn to read unless he is maturationally ready and has learned to understand and use language and to differentiate between similar sounds; and later he can learn academic subjects only if he has the necessary readiness, which includes the ability to read.

The latter point is particularly important, since today the emphasis is on the "sequencing" of development in terms of learning rather than on maturational readiness *per se.* For example,

---

[1]Maturation refers to the orderly process of growth and change which occurs more or less independently of learning.

EFFECTS OF MATERNAL DEPRIVATION ON MONKEYS

In Harlow's well-known experiments, monkeys separated from their mothers at birth and raised in isolation with artificial mothers (wire frames covered with terry cloth) treated them like real mothers, spent hours clinging to them, and apparently developed normally (left). At maturity, however, they failed to establish normal sexual relations, and those that bore young were helpless and dangerous mothers.

Another experiment involved raising four motherless monkeys together in one cage (center), permitting them 20 minutes each day in a playroom. Although they appeared normal at one year of age, they spent their early months huddled together.

When the young monkeys were raised under conditions of relatively complete social deprivation, they exhibited various symptoms of maladaptive behavior. The monkey huddling in a corner of a cage (right) has been taken out of isolation and is reacting with a typical response of fear and withdrawal.

it was formerly thought that a child was not "ready" for formal reading instruction until the age of six. Now it is known that by the sequential learning of required skills, he may learn to read at the age of three or even younger. Thus, each new phase of development is limited or facilitated by previous development and, in turn, influences and remains a part of successive stages of development.

Early and later learning. In describing the behavioristic model of man in Chapter 3, we covered the basic principles of human learning. Here, however, our concern is not so much with the principles of learning as it is with the effects of early and later learning on all aspects of psychological development—on ways of perceiving, thinking, feeling, and coping.

Simple conditioning is common in infancy and early childhood, and provides many new response patterns—often without the child's awareness of such learning. However, as the youngster's perceptual, retentive, and cognitive capabilities develop, he becomes an increasingly active agent in pursuing his own interests and selecting and shaping his own learning. In fact, by the age of four he has a fairly clear picture of himself and his world; and his ability to discriminate, interpret, and evaluate experience makes him less susceptible to simple conditioning (Gagne, 1968).

Learning in later childhood and adolescence usually focuses primarily on formal school instruction, but it takes place in the informal learning situations of everyday life as well. Although this new learning inevitably leads to marked changes in an individual's frame of reference and in his ways of viewing and coping with his world, most psychologists have emphasized the relatively enduring impact of a person's basic cognitive style. And as Fowler (1970) has pointed out, cognitive styles or modes may be more or less efficient for facilitating further learning and personal growth.

Critical periods and stimulation. Recent research findings point to periods in early development when certain types of stimulation and activity are physiologically and psychologically essential (Harlow & Harlow, 1967; Hunt, 1961; Kovach, 1970; Scott, 1963). For example,

Hunt (1961) showed that if chicks were kept in darkness for up to five days after hatching, they showed no apparent defects in their pecking response; but if this perceptual restriction lasted eight or more days, they were unable to learn to peck. Similarly, studies by Harlow & Harlow (1966; 1967) found that if infant monkeys were subjected to partial deprivation—in which they were permitted to see but not interact with other monkeys—permanent inadequacies in social and sexual development would result. On the human level there appears to be a longer period of grace before permanent damage occurs; however, mental retardation and inability to form warm interpersonal relationships are commonly found among children who have undergone extreme emotional, social, and intellectual deprivation in infancy.

The effects of stimulus deprivation and of noxious stimulation on intellectual, social, and other aspects of development during early critical periods will be examined in Chapter 6. Here we may simply note that if needed stimulation is lacking during the critical period, then certain functions expected to develop at these times (1) may not appear, (2) may be slower in making their appearance, or (3) may be only partially adequate. And once the critical period has passed, it may be difficult or even impossible to correct the physiological or psychological deficiencies stemming from a lack of needed stimulation.

VARIATIONS IN DEVELOPMENT

All individuals go through the same stages of growth; however, the general pattern followed by the human species leaves ample room for individual variation in the traits that emerge.[1] Thus it is apparent that people differ in physical appearance, intelligence, temperament, interests, attitudes, values—and, indeed, in almost any other characteristic that could be named. In measuring such trait differences it has been found that the majority of traits are distributed among the population along a continuum, with most measures clustering around a midpoint and the number of cases falling off rapidly toward either extreme of the range. For example, most people fall in the intermediate or average range of in-

telligence, while a few at one extreme are geniuses and a few at the other are mental retardates. Thus, very few people possess a very large or very small degree of most psychological traits. This point is an important one since we often erroneously tend to think of people as falling into "either-or" categories—introvert or extrovert, creative or noncreative, well-adjusted or maladjusted.

Although the distribution of traits tends to follow the pattern we have described, variation may occur from one individual to another in: (1) the *nature* of a given trait, such as blood type or skin color; (2) the *differentiation* or extent to which a given trait is developed, such as the capacity for abstract thinking; (3) the *integration* of traits or harmony among them, as between self-concept and self-ideal; and (4) the overall *patterning* of traits which we call *personality*.

The significance of variation in a particular trait depends on a number of factors. If the individual's position with respect to the trait is very much above or below the average, the trait is likely to play a more important role in his development and behavior than it would if he were near average. If the trait in question is a comprehensive one, like general intelligence, it is likely to be more important than less inclusive traits, like perceptual speed. The significance of a given trait depends, too, on the individual's total trait pattern. A girl with low intelligence but outstanding physical beauty will probably develop in a different way than will a girl with low intelligence and a severe physical handicap.

When we consider the unique pattern of interacting determinants—genetic, environmental, and self—which shape a given individual, we can readily see that the potentialities for individual differences are beyond human calculation. However, it may be emphasized that these determinants produce commonalities as well as differences in development. On a *universal level*, we share an inheritance that distinguishes man from all other living things, and we are born into a sociocultural environment unlike that of any other species. On a *communal level*, we inherit

---

[1]As psychologists use the term, a *trait* is any distinguishable and relatively enduring characteristic of the individual. However, situational demands may elicit consistent behaviors that may also be referred to as traits. Thus, trait continuity is dependent on both inner characteristics of the individual and regularities in stimulus situations.

the legacy of our particular group, which tends to produce similar physical characteristics, and a sociocultural environment which tends to produce uniformities among the members of our society. On an *individual level*, each of us (except for identical twins) has a unique genetic inheri-tance and a pattern of learning and experiences different from anyone else's. An understanding of both the uniqueness of each individual and the commonalities among all human beings is essential for an understanding of development and adjustment.

HUMAN NEEDS AND STRIVINGS

Underlying the apparently limitless diversity of human behavior are certain basic strivings common to people the world over. This common motivational core enables us to understand such divergent behavior as that of the student cramming for an examination, the hate-monger fanning fear and prejudice, and the priest performing the last rites for a dying man. In our brief review of motivation, we shall emphasize its key role in determining both the *direction* and the *activation* of human behavior.

In attempting to understand human motivation, it is useful to note that the term *motive* refers to any inner condition of the organism that initiates or directs its behavior toward a goal. The specific motives an individual may develop are almost limitless, but for present purposes we shall focus on the basic core of needs that apparently must be met if the individual is to grow and function normally. This basic core includes both biological and psychological needs, and it is strongly influenced by the needs and demands of society.

TENDENCIES TOWARD MAINTENANCE AND ACTUALIZATION

The motivation of all living organisms is based on their fundamental tendencies toward *maintenance* or survival and toward the *actualization* of their potentialities. The individual organism resists disintegration or decay[1] and tends to develop and behave in accordance with its genetic possibilities. Among human beings we see these tendencies operating on both biological and psychological levels.

Although we do not fully understand the processes involved, it is apparent that digestive, circulatory, and other body functions operate in such a way as to maintain the body's physiological equilibrium and integration. In the mechanisms for ensuring normal blood chemistry, for maintaining constant body temperature, and for combating invading microorganisms, we see this continuous endeavor of the body to preserve *steady states*—to maintain physiological variables within a range essential for survival—an endeavor generally referred to as *homeostasis*. The tendency toward actualization on the biological level can be seen in physical growth and in sexual and parental behavior that perpetuates the species.

If we do not fully understand the forces underlying biological motivation, we understand still less the forces related to psychological motivation. They appear, however, to be an extension of the maintenance and actualization strivings that operate on the biological plane. On the psychological level this striving becomes an attempt to maintain and enhance the self. Damage to the self—as through severe guilt feelings or from an overloading of the system by being forced to deal with too many problems at once—can disable a person just as surely as can the failure of physiological homeostatic mechanisms.

---

[1]The tendency of living matter to preserve itself is dramatically illustrated in Wilson's (1925) classic experiment with a sponge. He reduced the sponge to a pulp, squeezed and rolled it flat, and centrifuged it so that no trace of its original form remained. He then allowed the remains to stand overnight. Slowly and in orderly fashion, the material reconstituted itself into the organized sponge it had been before its mistreatment. Similarly, more recent experiments have shown that completely scrambled cells taken from the liver or kidneys of chick embryos can reconstruct the same organ (Weiss & Taylor, 1960).

POSSIBLE ROLE OF SLEEP DEPRIVATION IN PSYCHOPATHOLOGY

Recordings of brain waves, eye movements, and other measures have shown that there are four stages of sleep, extending from light sleep to progressively deeper sleep. From such recordings we have learned that a normal adult spends about 20 percent of his sleep in Stage 1 (considered the main stage for dreaming, in which rapid eye movements—REM—occur, about 60 percent in intermediary Stages 2 and 3, and about 20 percent in the deep sleep of Stage 4. Although some dreaming may occur, the latter stages are referred to as non-REM, or NREM sleep. Typically, the individual goes through all four stages in cycles of about 90 minutes, from light through deep sleep and back again to light sleep.

A number of scientific studies have pointed to the importance of normal sleep patterns in mental health. Dement (1960) deprived 5 normal subjects of most of their REM sleep for 5 consecutive nights by awakening the subjects whenever their brain waves and eye movements indicated that they were entering an REM period. This procedure reduced REM time some 80 to 90 percent. Among the many interesting findings reported by Dement were: (1) An increasing number of awakenings were required to keep the subjects from having REM periods—from 4 to 5 the first night to 20 to 30 the fifth night. (2) In the daytime, during the deprivation period, the subjects were observed to be unusually tense and irritable; although they had slept 6 to 7 hours, they behaved as if they had been deprived of a great deal of sleep. (3) During the recovery period, the subjects showed a marked increase in REM time which often took up to 30 to 40 percent of their total sleeping time.

In a later study, Dement (1963) subjected 3 human subjects to 15 nights of dream deprivation and found that these effects were accentuated—and he concluded that the prevention of REM sleep may trigger a breakdown in a marginally adjusted individual. Many drugs, including the barbiturates and amphetamines, reduce the amount of REM sleep; and sudden cessation in the use of these drugs results in a massive increase in REM sleep. In fact, a person undergoing withdrawal from a serious drug addiction may spend almost the entire night in REM sleep (Berger, 1970).

In a study of three groups of poor sleepers—normal elderly persons, severe asthmatics, and patients suffering from insufficient thyroid hormones—it was found that all members of these groups had a marked lack of deep sleep and in some cases almost none. When the thyroid-deficient patients were treated with thyroid hormone, the percentage of sleep in Stage 4 rose significantly (Jacobson & Kales, 1967). It has also been shown that depressed patients commonly suffer a deficit of deep sleep and show more Stage 4 sleep after therapy (Jacobson & Kales, 1967; Nelson, 1967). Sleep disturbances are also common in schizophrenia, anxiety states, and other psychopathology.

Although we do not understand the precise role of REM and deep sleep in maintaining normal physiological and psychological functioning, it appears probable that disturbed sleep patterns in depression, schizophrenia, and other mental disorders may play an important interactive role in both the etiology and clinical picture. As Berger (1970) has pointed out, "One thing is sure: regardless of what functions the REM or NREM states may serve, we must sleep in order to stay sane." (p. 70)

As Miller (1965) has pointed out, living organisms also strive to maintain steady states with their environment so as to prevent environmental variations from destroying them. Thus, on the human level we can observe attempts to maintain steady states with respect to work, love, marriage, and other variables. And here actualization tendencies may take the form of improving one's environment in the interest of maintenance and growth.

It is in relation to maintenance and actualization strivings that we use the terms *adjustment* and *maladjustment*, for they refer to the outcome of these strivings. The term *treatment*, too, becomes meaningful only in this context, for the goal of therapy—whatever its particular orientation—is to help the individual satisfy his own needs in a socially constructive way.

BIOLOGICAL NEEDS

The biological needs that appear most relevant to human motivation and behavior include visceral needs, the need for safety and avoidance of pain, the need for stimulation and activity, and the need for sexual gratification.

Visceral needs. The most basic of all human needs are those for food, water, sleep, the elimination of wastes, and for other conditions and substances necessary for life. In order to survive and meet adjustive demands, the organism must constantly renew itself through rest and the taking in of nutrients to replace materials used up in the process of living. Prolonged interference with such renewal weakens the organism's resources for coping with even normal adjustive demands, and makes it highly vulnerable to special stresses. Prisoners have sometimes been "broken" by nothing more persuasive than the systematic prevention of sleep or deprivation of food over a period of several days.

In one experimental study, army volunteers underwent sleep deprivation for periods ranging from 72 to 98 hours. As sleep loss increased, the subjects showed increased visual misperceptions, temporal disorientation, and cognitive disorganization. Other anomalies included tactual illusions and feelings of depersonalization. A few reported the "hat illusion"—feeling a band of pressure around the head—and were observed making repeated efforts to remove the nonexistent hat (Morris, Williams & Lubin, 1960).

Studies of dietary deficiencies have pointed to marked changes in psychological functioning, the exact change depending largely on the type and extent of the deficiency. Some of these effects are illustrated in a study of semistarvation carried out during World War II by Keys and his associates (1950). The subjects were thirty-two conscientious objectors who existed on sixteen hundred calories each per day, with an average resulting weight loss of 24 percent during the six-month period of the study.

Dramatic personality changes took place in the subjects during the experiment. They became irritable, unsociable, and increasingly unable to concentrate on anything but food. Among other psychological symptoms were apathy, loss of pride in personal appearance, and feelings of inadequacy. By the close of the experiment, there was a marked reduction or disappearance of their interest in sex, and the predominant mood was one of gloom and depression. Food dominated the men's thoughts, conversation, and even day dreams. They even pinned up pictures of chocolate cake instead of pretty girls. In some cases, they went so far as to replan their lives in the light of their newly acquired respect for food. The investigators concluded that by the end of the 25th week, hunger had become the dominant influence in the behavior of their subjects.

In our society people are rarely subjected to excessive physical demands in everyday life; however, an individual's general resistance to stress may often be lowered by insufficient rest, inadequate diet, or attempts to carry a full work load under the handicap of a severe cold, fatigue, or emotional strain. The result is a deprivation of needed adjustive resources and an increased vulnerability to stress.

Safety and avoidance of pain. From early infancy on we withdraw from painful stimuli and try to avoid objects that have brought us pain or discomfort in the past. The threat or experience of pain is unpleasant and highly motivating.

Severe hunger, thirst, and fatigue can be extremely painful, as can most forms of intense stimulation—such as heat, cold, and pressure. And certain emotions—particularly anxiety—are also painful and highly motivating. In fact, anxiety has been referred to as "psychic pain." In this sense, just as pain serves as a warning or indicator to protect the individual from grave bodily harm, it can serve as a safeguard against psychological damage too.

The precise influence of physical pain on behavior has never been fully delineated, although experience and observation indicate that it can be very great. Solomon (1964) found that even mildly painful electric shocks could suppress eating behavior among male dogs and cats, eventually inducing death through starvation. And through the centuries, torture and the infliction or threat of pain have been used to elicit confessions and to punish certain types of behavior. Certainly pain is itself an acute adjustive demand; and when pain is severe and long-continued, it may gradually wear down adjustive resources and lead the individual to overwhelming feelings of hopelessness and despair.

Stimulation and activity. Research studies, as well as personal accounts of explorers, have demonstrated that psychological integration depends on adequate contact with the outside world —on adequate levels of stimulation or information input. As Jones and McGill (1967) have described it:

"Human subjects appear to experience drive states whenever their rate of information transmission varies in either direction from some characteristic value. . . ." (p. 29)

When incoming stimulation is greatly reduced under experimental conditions for a period of several hours, the individual's thought processes undergo some measure of disorganization (Schultz, 1965; Solomon et al., 1961; Solomon & Kleeman, 1971). Individuals react differently to such situations, depending on their personality makeup, but typically there is some measure of disorientation, impairment of problem-solving ability, and other symptoms of lowered integration. In some instances subjects develop delusions and hallucinations (Haythorn & Altman, 1967; Schultz, 1965). In addition, individuals become more receptive to information that is "fed-in"—a tendency that suggests why "brainwashing" may be effective after long periods of solitary confinement.

An interesting personal account of the need

for stimulation comes from the experience of Dr. Alain Bombard, who sailed alone across the Atlantic Ocean for sixty-five days on a life raft to prove that shipwrecked people could survive for an indefinite length of time. He subsisted solely on the food he could get from the sea. During this period of isolation, Bombard stated, he "wanted terribly to have someone . . . who would confirm my impressions, or better still, argue about them. . . . I began to feel that . . . I would be incapable of discerning between the false and the true." (Bombard, 1954, pp. 106–107)

The fact that "information overloading" may also lead to impaired problem-solving ability and lowered integration has been demonstrated by Miller (1960; 1965). When messages—for example, information that must be acted on—come in too fast, subjects cannot handle even the usual number effectively. Typically a subject will attempt to "tune out" surplus inputs or to utilize other defense measures in an effort to maintain inner integration. Where such defenses are inadequate and the excessive input continues, psychological functioning becomes disorganized.

Even in the less dramatic conditions of everyday life, there appears to be an optimal level of stimulation and activity that varies with each individual and over time, but that must be maintained within limits if normal integration is to take place. Under some conditions—such as boredom—one may strive to increase his level of stimulation by doing something different or engaging in an "exciting" activity. Conversely, when under excessive pressure, or "overloaded," one may strive to reduce the level of input and activity.

Sex. Although the meaning and importance of sexual motives vary greatly from one person to another, sexual tensions, fantasies, and experiences, as well as problems centering around sexual gratification, usually are important facets of a person's life. Depending on the individual's attitude toward sex and the part he assigns it in his life plan, sex can be an important source of satisfaction and self-realization or else a source of anxiety and self-devaluation. In any case, sexual motivation is probably second only to the hunger motive in its far-reaching implications for both personal and social living.

Although the sex drive has a hormonal basis and stimulation of the genitals is innately pleasurable, the strength of an individual's sex drive depends heavily on his experiences (Hardy, 1964). A girl who is indoctrinated with the view that sex is dirty and evil may develop little sexual motivation, and may even find sexual intercourse unpleasant or repugnant. Because of differences in age, cultural viewpoints, and individual life experiences, there are widespread differences in the strength and perceived significance of sexual behavior. Approved patterns of sexual gratification also vary considerably from one society to another and within particular societies over a period of time. In our own society sexual codes appear to be getting more liberalized, but certain sexual patterns are nevertheless considered deviant and abnormal; these will be discussed in Chapter 13.

Before going on to consider psychological needs, we may note that biological needs are much the same for all people and thus tend to foster uniformities in human behavior. Although the expression of hunger, sex, and other biological motives is influenced by differing patterns of socialization, these motives do not, in general, lead to the marked variations in behavior that distinguish the members of one culture from another. However, this does not diminish the importance of biological maintenance in personal adjustment. The failure to meet basic biological needs—as indicated by malnutrition, disease, extreme fatigue, and related conditions—either may lower an individual's stress tolerance and thus act as a predisposing cause in mental disorders or may itself be the precipitating condition.

PSYCHOLOGICAL NEEDS

The psychological requirements for healthy human development and functioning are influenced by learning and social processes to a greater degree than are biological requirements, and the goals relating to their gratification are capable of greater variation. A position of leadership, for example, so highly valued in our society as a means of meeting needs for adequacy and worth, was found by Mead (1949) to be a nuisance and burden to the Arapesh, who avoided leadership roles whenever possible. But despite wide individual and group differences in human motives, there does appear to be a common core of psychological needs related to maintenance and to actualization.

Psychological maintenance. Although man's basic psychological requirements are less readily identified than his requirements for food, water, sleep, and the like, there is widespread agreement that the following broad needs must be met if the individual is to maintain his personality integration and to function effectively.

1. *Order, understanding, and predictability.* Man is inherently curious and he strives to understand and to achieve a meaningful picture of his world. Such a frame of reference is essential for evaluating new situations and anticipating the outcome of his actions. Unless he can see order and predictability in his environment, he cannot work out an intelligent response to it. Social customs, rules, and laws are in part a reflection of this need for order and predictability.

Human beings do not like ambiguity, lack of structuring, chaos, or events that seem beyond their understanding and control. Even the most primitive people develop explanations for lightning, thunder, death, and other phenomena. Accurate or not, such explanations tend to impose order and meaning on seemingly random events, thereby giving a sense of potential prediction and control. Modern science is simply a more sophisticated attempt in the same direction.

Man's striving for order, understanding, and predictability is also evident in his curiosity about himself and his quest for knowledge about his world. It is apparent too in his development of inner controls and in his tendency to maintain the consistency and stability of his frame of reference. New experiences are "screened" and interpreted in relation to his existing assumptions. As Festinger (1962) has shown, when new information contradicts existing assumptions, man experiences *cognitive dissonance* and remains uncomfortable until he somehow reconciles the differences or convinces himself that they do not exist.

2. *Adequacy, competence, security.* Each person needs to feel capable of dealing with his problems. Seeing oneself as incapable of coping with a stressful situation is conducive to confusion and disorganization.

Feelings of adequacy are heavily dependent on the development of competencies—physical, intellectual, emotional, and social—for dealing with the tasks and problems of living. White (1959) has pointed out that striving toward competence is evident even in the early playful and investigatory behavior of children. This process of play and "reality testing" brings into use learning, reasoning, and other integrative abilities, and enables a child to acquire practical knowledge and skills that later are greatly expanded by the processes of formal education.

The need for security develops with and is closely related to the need for adequacy. The growing individual soon learns that failure to meet his biological or psychological needs leads to unpleasant results. Consequently he strives toward the maintenance of whatever conditions can be counted on to assure the present and future gratification of his needs. The need for security is reflected in the preference for jobs with tenure, in social security legislation, in insurance against disability and other contingencies, and in society's emphasis upon law and order. Feelings of insecurity may have widely differing effects on behavior; but pervasive and chronic feelings of insecurity typically lead to fearfulness, apprehension, and failure to participate fully in one's world. The more adequate a person feels and the greater his level of competence, the less aware he is of his need for security and the more he may value the exploration of unfamiliar paths and freedom for self-direction.

3. *Love and affiliation (relatedness).* The need to love and be loved is crucial for healthy personality development and functioning. In an intensive study of 158 well-adjusted children, Langdon and Stout (1951) concluded that the single most important factor—in fact, the only factor common to all of the cases studied—was satisfaction of the child's need for love and acceptance. Similarly, in their extensive study of patterns in child rearing, Sears, Maccoby, and Levin (1957) concluded that the most crucial and pervasive of all the influences exerted in the home were the love and warmth imparted by the parents. For the child who feels loved and accepted, many conditions that might otherwise impair development, such as a physical handicap, poverty, or harsh discipline, may be largely neutralized.

The need for close ties to other people continues throughout life and becomes especially important in times of severe stress or crisis. In a study of terminal cancer victims, Bard (1966) concluded that never is the need for affiliation and human contact greater than it is as death approaches. On a less dramatic level, Kanter (1970) has pointed out that the quest for togetherness, affiliation, and intimacy is a major purpose of today's communes—founded by such varied groups as hippies, religious sects, and humanistic psychologists.

4. *Belonging, acceptance, and approval.* The growing infant is completely dependent for his existence on the help and approval of others. He rapidly learns that when he behaves in socially approved ways he is rewarded, but when he misbehaves he is punished. At first, this pattern takes in only the family group, but later he finds that being accepted and approved by other individuals and groups becomes increasingly essential. So he learns to strive for acceptance and approval from other persons who play important roles in his life, and he tries to become and remain an approved member of the social groups with which he identifies himself.

Eloquent testimony to man's need for belonging, acceptance, and approval is provided by the experience of small groups of scientists, officers, and enlisted personnel who voluntarily subjected themselves to isolated antarctic living for the better part of a year (Rohrer, 1961). During this period troublesome individuals were occasionally given the "silent treatment" in which a man would be ignored by the group as if he did not exist. This "isolation" procedure resulted in a syndrome called the "long eye," characterized by varying combinations of sleeplessness, outbursts of crying, hallucinations, a deterioration in habits of personal hygiene, and a tendency for the man to move aimlessly about or to lie in his bunk staring into space. These symptoms cleared up when he was again accepted by and permitted to interact with others in the group.

Failure to achieve interpersonal and group acceptance and the loneliness that results are difficult problems in our group-conscious and group-oriented society. Especially is this true for the person who depends heavily on others for his feelings of self-identity and worth. In his work with persons in psychotherapy and encounter groups, Rogers (1967; 1971) has emphasized the crucial importance of "positive regard" for the other person in healthy interpersonal relationships.

5. *Self-esteem, worth, and identity.* Closely related to feelings of adequacy and social approval is the need to feel good about oneself, to feel worthy of the respect of others. Usually personal worth is judged largely in terms of the values and standards of those in one's milieu. If an individual measures up to these standards—for example, in terms of physical appearance, achievement, or economic status—he can approve of himself and feel worthwhile.

Self-esteem has its early grounding in parental affirmation of worth and in mastery of early developmental tasks; it receives continual nourishment from the development of new competencies and from achievement in areas deemed important. The individual also tends to depend for continuing confirmation of his worth on the esteem of significant others.

Intermeshed with feelings of self-esteem and worth is the sense of self-identity. This, too, is heavily influenced by significant others and by the individual's status and role in the group. Here it is interesting to note that despite changes in physical appearance, in status, and in social roles, people tend to maintain continuity in their basic feelings of self-identity. That is, we think of ourselves as much the same *I* or *me* today that we were yesterday and will be tomorrow. Although a person would perhaps like to make changes in his self-identity, it is doubtful that anyone would willingly give it up. In any event, when a person's sense of self-identity and continuity become disorganized—as happens sometimes in psychotic disorders—the experience is usually acutely painful.

6. *Values, meaning, and hope.* Human beings seek some value pattern to which they can commit themselves.[1] As Cantril (1967) has put it:

"In the midst of the probabilities and uncertainties that surround them, people want some anchoring points, some certainties, some faith that will serve either as a beacon light to guide them or as a balm to assuage them during the inevitable frustrations and anxieties that living engenders." (p. 17)

---

[1]As we noted in Chapter 3, existential psychologists consider the quest for values and meaning to be *the primary* human striving.

Closely related to the individual's values are his goals and plans, for man lives in the future as well as in the past and present. His goals and plans—and his hopes of achieving them—are the focus not only of his aspirations but of much of his present striving. The apathy seen among persons living in black ghettos often reflects not so much their lack of desire to achieve a better kind of life for themselves but their hopelessness about ever achieving it. In situations that are even more extreme, hopelessness is a prelude to death. Reports from prisoner-of-war camps have told of cases in which prisoners who had lost hope simply pulled their blankets over their heads and waited for death to come (Nardini, 1952); and Lazarus (1966) has reported that shipwreck victims who lose hope may die after a few days, even though physiologically they could have survived many days longer. Similarly, Farber (1968) has implicated loss of hope as one key factor in suicide. In relating hope to coping, Korner (1970) has concluded that its key purpose is the avoidance of despair.

Surprisingly, there has been little research on man's need for values, meaning, and hope. But we can infer such needs, like the need for love, from observations of the typical results when people are unable to find satisfying value patterns, are "planless," or lack hope. Values, meaning, and hope appear to act as catalysts; in their presence energy is mobilized, competencies are developed and used, and satisfactions are achieved. Without them life is futile.

The needs discussed above appear to represent the basic core of psychological requirements that typically emerge through normal interaction with one's world and that contribute significantly to the direction of man's behavior. The strength of a given psychological need may vary considerably, of course, from one person to another, and from one social group to the next. It should be apparent too that biological and psychological needs are closely interrelated and that failure to meet particular needs may adversely influence a person's entire motivational pattern.

Actualization strivings. Our views of motivation have long been dominated by the concepts of maintenance and homeostasis, according to which man's energies are directed toward meeting any deficiency that arises and then returning to a state of equilibrium. But although maintenance strivings are a significant part of man's motivational structure, they alone do not explain the efforts expended, for example, by the mountain climber, the explorer, the great artist or composer, or the astronaut. Man obviously strives not only to maintain himself, but also to grow, to express himself, to improve—to actualize his potentials and to fulfill himself. Huxley (1953) has made this point well:

"Human life is a struggle—against frustration, ignorance, suffering, evil, the maddening inertia of things in general; but it is also a struggle *for* something . . . And fulfillment seems to describe better than any other single word the positive side of human development and human evolution—the realization of inherent capacities by the individual and of new possibilities by the race; the satisfaction of needs, spiritual as well as material; the emergence of new qualities of experience to be enjoyed; the building of personalities." (pp. 162–163)

Strivings toward fulfillment take different forms with different people, depending on their abilities, values, and life situations. On a simple level, we see attempts at self-enhancement in ornamentation to make oneself attractive; on a more complex level, in being a good spouse and parent; or engaging in other activities that contribute to personal growth and the well-being of others. Here it may be noted that man's needs for competence, love, relatedness, values, and meaning—which we have described as maintenance needs because they must be met for normal growth and functioning—are actualization needs as well, since they are components of man's efforts toward personal fulfillment.

Whatever particular forms actualization strivings take, there appear to be tendencies common to all mankind—tendencies toward developing one's potentials and creative self-expression, toward finding increased satisfactions, toward building richer linkages with the world, and toward "becoming a person" and finding increased meaning in one's life.

1. *Developing and using potentials.* This may take the form of building new competencies and improving old ones, developing individual capabilities in various areas and using them in creative and constructive ways. Even if a person does not have special talents in art, music, writing, or athletics, he may find it highly fulfilling to develop and use the potentials he does have; and where a person does have special talents, it may be highly frustrating to be denied the opportunity for their development and expression. The development of potentialities also takes the form of learning more about the physical and social world of which one is a part.

2. *Finding increased satisfactions.* Man's capacity to find satisfaction from various experiences results in his coming to expect a certain level of satisfaction from almost everything he does. A person, for example, may plan a trip because he expects certain satisfactions from it; and he may avoid a lecture or television program if he thinks it will be dull and unrewarding. But this is not all; man also strives toward increased satisfactions—to enrich the range and quality of his experiences and satisfactions. We see this on group as well as individual levels. As Cantril (1967) has expressed it:

"Man is engaged in a ceaseless quest to extend the range and improve the quality of his satisfactions through the exercise of his creative and inventive capacities." (p. 15)

Some of man's experiences are in familiar and tried directions, as when a person attends a symphony or art exhibit; others are new or emergent, in the sense that he discovers or creates them for the first time. Many people today are entering into sensitivity training, encounter groups, and related innovative approaches to enriching their self-understanding and interpersonal experience.

3. *Building rich linkages with the world.* This is essentially an extension of the maintenance need for love. Self-centeredness or narrow concern with self leads to a restriction of energy and an impoverishment in one's life. By contrast, the person who can form warm and meaningful relations with others or who can lose himself in a worthwhile "cause" that he feels will improve life for others may experience a deep sense of fulfillment, even though his efforts may entail sacrifices and though the gains he works for do not come to him personally or even materialize during his lifetime.

4. *Becoming a person.* Closely allied with the striving to develop one's potentials is the striving to become a person—to be one's "real self" or the person that the individual feels he should be or become. As Rogers (1958) has put it:

"As I follow the experience of many clients in the therapeutic relationship which we endeavor to create for them, it seems to me that each one has the same problem. Below the level of the problem situation about which the individual is complaining—behind the trouble with studies, or wife, or employer, or with his own uncontrollable or bizarre behavior, or with his frightening feelings lies one central search. It seems to me that at bottom each person is asking: 'Who am I, really? How can I get in touch with this real self, underlying all my surface behavior? How can I become myself?' . . . It appears that the goal the individual most wishes to achieve, the end which he knowingly or unknowingly pursues, is to become himself." (pp. 9–10)

In his later work with encounter groups Rogers (1969; 1971) has found this same striving to become oneself. The existential philosopher Kierkegaard came to a similar conclusion more than a hundred years ago. He pointed out that the most common despair is in being unwilling to be oneself, but that the deepest form of despair is choosing to be other than oneself.

An individual's actualization strivings receive no automatic fulfillment, and their expression may be difficult or impossible in some situations. The neurotic is too busy defending himself to be free to grow; the person who must struggle for mere physical survival has little time or energy for personal growth; the individual in a regimented culture may find many of his growth tendencies blocked. People in such situations usually experience a sense of frustration and dissatisfaction. Life seems meaningless and incomplete, for they are missing the fulfillment of themselves as human beings.

SOCIAL FORCES IN MOTIVATION

Thus far we have viewed motivation in terms of individual needs and strivings. However, environmental factors are of great importance in facilitating or inhibiting given strivings, in formulating the goals toward which one works, and in determining the extent to which one's needs are gratified. In addition, not all adjustive demands originate within the individual; environmental demands can initiate behavior as well.

Social inhibition and facilitation of motives. By its system of values and by the manipulation of rewards and punishments, society encourages the gratification of certain needs while it attempts to inhibit others. In most societies, for example, patterns of sexual gratification are strictly regulated by society; in general, unusual or aberrant expressions of such desires are inhibited. Conversely, the pursuit of other needs, such as the need for social approval, may be strongly encouraged.

The rewards and punishments controlled by the group, and its value patterns, also influence the goals its members seek and the means they learn to use in working toward these goals. In our society, for example, there are strong incentives to strive toward such goals as academic excellence, creative accomplishment, financial success, and leadership. And although a wide range of means for achieving these goals is approved, there nevertheless are limitations; and the use of socially disapproved means subjects an individual to possible punishment.

Needs of groups and of society. Social groups have basic needs in much the same sense that individuals do. Their survival depends, for example, on the maintenance of orderly social relationships—which in turn requires the development of various "homeostatic" mechanisms, such as customs and laws and the means for enforcing them.

When normal group functioning or organizational structure is disrupted, groups strive to reestablish a state of equilibrium. This applies to small groups as well as larger ones. If a general is killed in battle, another officer moves up to take his place; if the father of a family dies, there are changes in relationships and responsibilities as other family members attempt to establish a new pattern of effective functioning.

The needs of groups and of society are important determinants of the behavior of individual members. Usually the meeting of family and other group needs, as well as the needs of the greater society, tends to promote the welfare of individual members. However, the needs of the group and society may conflict with or eclipse the needs of the individual, as when a young mother must work long hours at a monotonous job to support her family or when a soldier is forced to risk his life in combat.

MOTIVATION AND BEHAVIOR

In the preceding discussion we have been concerned with the nature and direction of man's strivings. Now let us consider some facets of motivation that bear directly on behavior.

Activation or arousal. The concept of activation refers to the energy mobilization required for the organism to pursue its goals and meet its needs. Activation can vary in degree from very low to very high—from deep sleep to intense excitement. At any moment an individual's level of activation is influenced by a wide range of individual and situational factors. It is affected by the way he perceives his situation and evaluates its potential satisfactions and frustrations; it is affected by many inner conditions, including biological drives, emotions, and drugs; it is affected by sudden loud noises and strange or novel stimuli; and it is affected by fatigue, disease, and pain. Usually, efficient task performance requires a moderate level of activation (Duffy, 1962; Lacey, 1967; Malmo, 1959). With too low a level, the individual may fail to expend the energy and effort essential for task achievement, while at very high levels there tends to be poorly coordinated functioning and impaired performance.

Although there are individual differences in personal tempo and sensitivity or excitability, most people learn to respond to familiar situations with appropriate levels of activation. However, an individual is likely to react with an overly high level of activation in the face of an unfamiliar challenge or under stress conditions to which he is particularly vulnerable. Similarly, conditions such as severe fatigue, intense inner conflict, or faulty assumptions and loss of hope, may lead to extreme and inappropriate fluctuations in activation, as well as to slow recovery from the effects of prior activation and energy output.

Motivational sequences. With both maintenance and actualization strivings, behavior is patterned toward achieving need gratification. On the maintenance level the motivational sequence consists of three important steps: (1) activation, resulting from need deprivation; (2) choice of some goal and means for achieving it; and (3) goal-directed behavior, leading, if successful, to gratification of the need.

On an actualization level, the motivational sequence is more complex. Instead of being aimed at the alleviation of some unpleasant condition, such as intense hunger or a threat to the worth of the self, it is directed toward expression and fulfillment. Consequently, there is a welcoming of stimulation, tension, and effort. The scientist may go without food and sleep in the excitement of a crucial experiment; the mountain climber may risk his life to conquer some dangerous peak; the writer may isolate himself from others and devote seemingly endless hours and effort to his work. Even when the effort promises to be tedious, painful, or otherwise unpleasant, human beings are often willing to give up comfort and security in their efforts to express and fulfill themselves.

Usually, need gratification is pleasurable and leads to a reduction in activation. There are, however, conditions under which need gratification can be distinctly unpleasant, as in the case of a vegetarian who must violate religious values and eat meat in order to keep from starving. Both pleasurable and unpleasurable aspects of need gratification are important to an adequate understanding of motivation.

Motivational selectivity. An individual's motives are constantly influencing his perceiving, reasoning, learning, and other psychological processes. For example, people tend to perceive only those aspects of the environment which are related to the gratification of immediate or long-term needs. The man looking for the television section in the newspaper ignores the sports columns; the politician is alert for signs of approval from his constituents; and a man lost in the desert and suffering from intense thirst would likely ignore the vivid colors of the sunset and keep scanning his surroundings for some indication of water. This tendency of the organism to single out those elements considered to be most relevant to its purposes is called *selective vigilance*. Intense motivation may also lead to distortions in perception, so that neutral or irrelevant stimuli are perceived as desired goal objects; or intense

fear may lead to misperceptions of neutral stimuli as aversive objects.

Although motivation may often sensitize the individual to particular stimuli, it may also have the opposite effect—that is, unpleasant or taboo stimuli are likely to be screened from consciousness. For example, a study by Bootzin and Natsoulas (1965) showed clearly that accuracy for identifying rude words falls below accuracy for identifying neutral words. Similar findings have been reported by many other investigators. The fact that unpleasant stimuli are less likely to be perceived than neutral ones is referred to as *perceptual defense.*[1]

Motivation also influences what the individual learns, as well as how rapidly and how much; and, despite his attempts to be logical, it influences beliefs and may cause a subversion of thought processes in order to justify his assumptions and behavior. However, this is a two-way street, and motives themselves may be encouraged or ignored, expressed or denied, in keeping with one's reality, possibility, and value assumptions.

Hierarchy of needs. Maslow (1954; 1969) has suggested that there is a fundamental ordering of the human motivational structure—that man's needs arrange themselves in a hierarchy which ascends from the most basic biological requirements to the quest for self-actualization and fulfillment. A modification of this schema is depicted on page 113.

According to Maslow's formulation, the unmet need on the lowest level is ordinarily the one that commands the individual's primary attention and effort. Unless needs for food and safety are reasonably well met, behavior will be dominated by these needs. With their gratification, however, the individual is free to devote his energies to meeting his needs on higher levels. Here Maslow has emphasized the distinction between *deficiency* and *growth* motivation. Behavior motivated primarily by maintenance needs is considered unhealthy, since it leaves the individual little opportunity for the development of potentials and self-actualization.

This hierarchy concept tends to be borne out

---

[1]An interesting discussion of perceptual defense and subliminal perception is contained in Spence (1967).

by observations of behavior under extreme conditions. Friedman (1949) reported that: "In all survivors of the Nazi concentration camps, one might say the self-preservation instinct became so dominant that it blotted out all other instincts." Similarly, in the Japanese prisoner-of-war camps in World War II, it was a common pattern for those inmates who had been subjected to prolonged deprivation and torture to obtain food at the expense of their fellow prisoners and in other ways surrender the loyalties and values they had held under more normal conditions (Nardini, 1952; Wolf & Ripley, 1947). Under experimental conditions, too, the tremendous driving force of hunger has been demonstrated—as we noted on page 105 in describing the semistarvation study of Keys and his associates with young conscientious objectors.

Although this hierarchy of needs presumably is characteristic of the motivational structure of most people, Maslow acknowledged that there are exceptions. For example, to some individuals, values other than the meeting of food or safety needs acquire precedence, as shown by the countless numbers of people who have sacrificed their lives or suffered physical torture for the sake of ethical, social, or religious values. Here it may be emphasized that failure on the actualization level, as well as in meeting lower-level needs, may lead to maladjustment. As Helson (1966) has stated it: "The satisfaction of so-called basic needs is necessary but not sufficient for a full and truly satisfying life." (p. 179)

Conscious and unconscious aspects of motivation. We have seen (in Chapter 3) that the concept of unconscious motivation, extensively propounded by Freud, is basic to the psychoanalytic model of man; and some years ago, W. A. White (1947) pointed out that the failure to take unconscious motivation into consideration was "probably the cause of more inadequacies in the understanding of human behavior than any other one thing." Although there is still considerable controversy among psychologists concerning the nature and importance of unconscious processes in human behavior, there is abundant evidence that the individual is often unaware or only partially aware of what his needs and goals really are.

Many physiological needs operate on an un-

conscious level; others enter awareness as conscious desires or wishes only when they become pressing—and sometimes not even then. For example, people are not ordinarily aware of the need for air until breathing is hindered in some way. A person may mutter something about how stuffy it is and continue with his ongoing activity. But if all air is cut off and he is in danger of suffocation, then the awareness is immediate and

HIERARCHY OF NEEDS

According to Maslow, needs on the "lower" levels are prepotent as long as they are unsatisfied. When they are adequately satisfied, however, the "higher" needs occupy the individual's attention and effort.

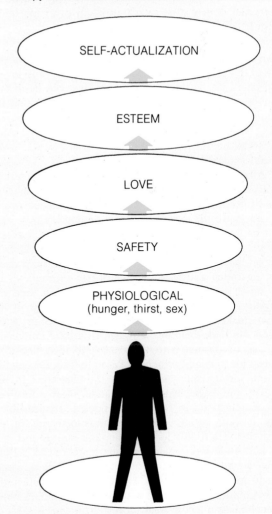

vivid, and drastic action may be undertaken to restore his equilibrium.

Psychological needs—such as those for security, adequacy, social approval, and self-esteem—may also operate on relatively unconscious levels. Thus one may criticize his associates, join exclusive clubs, and even get married for reasons of which he is unaware. Of course, he may think of good reasons to justify his behavior, but they may not be the real reasons at all.

The degree of a person's awareness of his motivation varies considerably from one behavior pattern to another and from one individual to another. Usually those who are seriously maladjusted lack insight into many key facets of their motivational patterns. The following illustration demonstrates the action of unconscious motivation and is especially revealing, because here we know the exact motivational pattern, which is not usually the case.

"During profound hypnosis the subject was instructed to feel that smoking was a bad habit, that he both loved and hated it, that he wanted to get over the habit but that he felt it was too strong a habit to break, that he would be very reluctant to smoke and would give anything not to smoke, but that he would find himself compelled to smoke; and that after he was awakened he would experience all of these feelings.

"After he was awakened the subject was drawn into a casual conversation with the hypnotist who, lighting one himself, offered him a cigarette. The subject waved it aside with the explanation that he had his own and that he preferred Camels, and promptly began to reach for his own pack. Instead of looking in his customary pocket, however, he seemed to forget where he carried his cigarettes and searched fruitlessly through all of his other pockets with a gradually increasing concern. Finally, after having sought them repeatedly in all other pockets, he located his cigarettes in their usual place. He took them out, engaged in a brief conversation as he dallied with the pack, and then began to search for matches, which he failed to find. During his search for matches he replaced the cigarettes in his pocket and began using both hands, finally locating the matches too in their usual pocket. Having done this, he now began using both hands to search for his cigarettes. He finally located them but then found that he had once more misplaced his matches. This time however he kept his cigarettes in hand while attempting to locate the matches. He then placed a cigarette in his mouth and struck a match. As he struck it, however, he began a conversation which so engrossed him that he forgot the match and allowed it to burn his

finger tips whereupon, with a grimace of pain, he tossed it in the ash tray. . . .

"This behavior continued with numerous variations. He tried lighting a cigarette with a split match, burned his fingers, got both ends of one cigarette wet, demonstrated how he could roll a cigarette, kept stopping to converse or tell a joke, and so on. Several cigarettes were ruined and discarded. When he finally got one going successfully, he took only a few good puffs with long pauses in between and discarded it before it was used up." (Erickson, 1939, pp. 342–345)

Motive patterns and life style. The individual tends to develop a relatively consistent life style, an essential element of which is his motive pattern—the needs, goal objects, and means that characterize his strivings. Some persons are primarily concerned with love, relatedness, and self-actualization; and others with security, material possessions, and power. Any individual's motive pattern is in part a product of his experiences relating to the reward and punishment values of various goals; in part an outgrowth of his learned reality, possibility, and value assumptions; and in part a reflection of the demands, limitations, and opportunities of his environment.

Implicit in an individual's motive pattern is his *level of aspiration.* Well-adjusted people tend to have a reasonably accurate evaluation of themselves in relation to their world and hence have a fairly realistic level of aspiration. Maladjusted people, on the other hand, tend to be unrealistic—to set their goals too high or too low.

Although people tend to show a relatively consistent pattern of motives, their incentives undergo predictable change with time. The key motives of the child are not those of the adolescent; nor are the motives of the adolescent those of the adult or older person. Similarly, changes in a person's life situation may lead to the modification of his motive patterns. The employee who has taken little responsibility for production quotas may show a considerable shift in behavior when he is placed in a supervisory position. Broadly speaking, one may develop important new motives, show shifts in the priorities of existing motives, or discard motives that have formerly been of significance. Some of these changes emerge as the products of experience and learning; others seem to result from new requirements at different life stages; and still others are influenced by changed environmental conditions.

TYPES OF ADJUSTIVE DEMANDS (STRESS)

Life would be simple indeed if one's biological and psychological needs were automatically gratified. But as we know, there are many obstacles, both environmental and internal, that interfere with need gratification. Such obstacles place adjustive demands, or *stress*, on the individual. In the present section we shall be concerned primarily with the different types of adjustive demands commonly experienced by the individual, and also with the unique and changing patterns of such demands. In the section following we shall consider the implications of such demands for behavior.

Adjustive demands are usually classified as frustrations, conflicts, or pressures. We shall consider each type of demand separately, but it will be apparent that they are all closely interrelated and usually form part of a total stress pattern for the individual.

FRUSTRATION

Frustration is experienced whenever an individual's motives are thwarted, either by obstacles that block or impede his progress toward a desired goal, or by the absence of an appropriate goal. For example, overly restrictive parents would be a source of frustration to an adolescent girl who wanted to give a party; while a lack of water would be a source of frustration to a man lost in the desert.

A wide range of obstacles, both environmental and internal, can lead to frustrations. Famines, wars, droughts, earthquakes, storms, fires, economic fluctuations, social inequalities, marital and occupational dissatisfaction, accidents, disease, the loss of loved ones, physical handicaps, personal failures, and even the individual's own ethical restraints can thwart the achievement of desired goals. Frustrations resulting from personal limitations and mistakes are likely to be particularly stressful, since they lead to self-devaluation. Far less serious are the countless frustrations we encounter in everyday life, such as a flat tire on the car when one is in a hurry, rain on a day when a picnic is planned, or the loss of one's notes on a class lecture.

CONFLICT

In many instances stress results not from a single obstacle but from a conflict between two needs or valued goals, in which the choice of either alternative entails frustration with regard to the other. An early marriage may mean forgoing or shortening a college education; involvement in a social issue may require personal risks and sacrifices. Although we are discussing frustration and conflict as if they were distinct sources of stress, this differentiation is for convenience only. Indeed, the essential element of conflict is the frustration that arises when one chooses either alternative.

Conflicts with which everyone has to cope may be conveniently classified as approach-avoidant, double-approach, and double-avoidant types.

1. *Approach-avoidant* conflicts involve strong tendencies both to approach and to avoid the same goal. A person may want to marry for sexual, social, and security reasons, while at the same time fearing the responsibilities of married life and the loss of personal freedom. In a similar way, other desires may conflict with inner reality or ethical restraints or with fear of failure. Perhaps an individual wants to join a high-status group but can do so only by endorsing views contrary to his values; or he may feel strongly attracted to a particular girl while recognizing that her scale of values would jeopardize the success of their marriage.

Approach-avoidant conflicts are sometimes referred to as "mixed-blessing" dilemmas, because some negative and some positive features must be accepted regardless of which course of action is selected. Since many approach-avoidant conflicts involve multiple alternatives—rather than just one either-or choice—the term *multiple approach-avoidance* is sometimes used here. Thus an individual may be in conflict not only about whether to get married but also about which of several girls would make the best wife.

2. *Double-approach conflicts* involve competition between two or more desirable goals. On a simple level the individual may have to decide between leather or vinyl upholstery, or between two dinner entrées, or between two invitations for a particular weekend. To a large extent, such simple "plus-plus" conflicts result from the inevitable limitations in one's time, space, energy, and personal and financial resources—and are handled in stride. In more complex cases, however, as when an individual is torn between duty and ambition, between loyalty to his mother or his wife, between a career in psychology or one in law, or between present satisfactions and future ones, decision making may be very difficult and stressful.

3. *Double-avoidant conflicts* are those which completely hem the individual in—he is caught "between the devil and the deep blue sea." He may, for example, have to choose between finishing a job he intensely dislikes or quitting and being called a failure. In wartime he may have to choose between fighting—with the possibility of killing or being killed—and refusing to fight, with the attendant social disapproval and possible punishment.

It can be seen that this classification of conflicts is somewhat arbitrary, and that various combinations among the different types are perhaps the rule rather than the exception. Thus a "plus-plus" conflict between alternative careers may also have its "plus-minus" aspects growing out of the professional responsibilities that either imposes.

As we noted in Chapter 3, experiments have shown that animals will undergo an "experimental breakdown" if they are forced to choose between two undesired alternatives or to make decisions based on discriminations that are beyond the range of their sensory abilities. In human beings, overwhelming conflicts produce comparable, though far more complex, results.

PRESSURE

Stress may stem not only from goal-blocking frustrations and conflicts, but also from pressures to achieve particular goals or to behave in particular ways. Pressures may originate either from outside sources or from within the individual himself. For example, a college student may feel under severe pressure to make good grades because his parents demand it, because he hopes to gain admission to graduate school, or because he needs to prove to himself that he can do it. Often such factors interact, contributing to the overall intensity of stress.

In general, pressures force a person to speed up, intensify, or change the direction of goal-oriented behavior. All of us encounter many different pressures in the course of everyday living, and often it is possible to handle them without undue strain. In some instances, however, pressures seriously overtax an individual's adjustive resources and cause acute stress. If they become excessive, they may lead to a breakdown of organized behavior.

As we conclude our discussion of types and sources of stress, it may be emphasized that a given stress situation may involve elements of frustration, conflict, and pressure. For example, a serious financial loss not only may lead to lower living standards but also may confront an individual with the problem of reconciling his notion of his shrewd business sense with the evidence of his poor judgment. Such "cognitive dissonance," arising from information contradictory to a person's existing assumptions about himself and his world, adds to the complexity of many stress situations. And although a particular stress may predominate in any situation, we rarely deal with an isolated situation, but rather with a continuously changing complex of interrelated and sometimes contradictory demands. Thus we usually speak of "stress patterns" rather than simply of a given stress situation.

SOURCE OF THE ADJUSTIVE DEMAND AS A SIGNIFICANT CHARACTERISTIC OF THE STRESS SITUATION

As might be surmised, the response of an individual to a stress situation is significantly affected by the specific source of the adjustive demand: an individual will respond quite differently to hunger if he is on a diet, for example, than if he lacks money to buy food. Adjustive demands may be classified in a general way as imposed, assigned, chosen, or devised. As some of the following illustrations suggest, however, such categories are not always discrete.

Imposed: Draftees in the military service may be involuntarily subjected to rigid discipline and other stressful conditions. The picture illustrates the crowding of soldiers in a troopship.

Chosen: An individual may choose a stressful situation for personally valid reasons; for example, Admiral Byrd preferred complete isolation in wintering over in Antarctica.

Assigned: Astronauts, like submariners and others in similarly hazardous and confined occupations, may be subject to long periods of unusual stress.

Devised: Stress may be devised in artificially controlled laboratory conditions, such as the sensory deprivation experiments shown here.

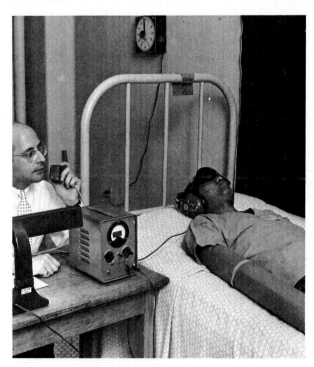

UNIQUE AND CHANGING PATTERNS OF STRESS

Each individual faces a unique pattern of adjustive demands. This is true partly because of differences in the way people perceive and interpret similar situations. But objectively, too, no two people are faced with exactly the same pattern of stress. Each individual's age, sex, occupation, economic status, personality makeup, competencies, and family situation help to determine the demands made on him. The stress pattern a child faces will differ in many ways from that of an older person, and the stress pattern faced by a carpenter will differ from that of a business executive.

Patterns of demand change with time too—both predictably, as the individual enters different life periods, and unpredictably, as when an accident, a death in the family, or some other unforeseen event makes new demands on him. Often a particular stress will assume major prominence in an individual's life. Such key stresses may stem from a severe physical handicap that limits the individual's activities, a continuing difficult life situation, or a severely traumatic experience.

In some cases these key stresses originate in what might be called "crisis" situations. Although there is some confusion concerning the meaning of the term *crisis*, Lazarus (1966) has pointed out that:

"Crisis seems to imply a limited period in which an individual or group is exposed to threats and demands which are at or near the limits of their resources to cope.

"In threat the emphasis is on a particular harm, while in crisis, the focus is on a period of the person's or group's life in which major threats and frustrations that tax adaptation are prominent." (pp. 407–408)

A crisis might have its locus in a traumatic divorce, an episode of severe depression with suicidal thoughts, a painful adjustment to effects of serious injuries, or other experiences or events that place severe—and sometimes excessive—demands on the individual.

COPING WITH ADJUSTIVE DEMANDS

Since stress—beyond a minimal level—threatens the well-being of the organism, it engenders automatic, persistent attempts at its resolution; it forces a person to do something about it. What is done depends on many factors, including one's frame of reference, motives, competencies, stress tolerance, environmental limitations and supports, and momentary conditions like prior mental set or fatigue. Sometimes inner factors play the dominant role in determining one's stress reactions; at other times environmental conditions are of primary importance. Any stress reaction, of course, reflects the interplay of a combination of determinants—some more influential than others, but all working together to make the individual react as he does.

In this section we will begin by considering some general principles of adjustive behavior. Next, we will outline the various steps involved in coping with adjustive demands. And finally, we will examine the particular characteristics of both task-oriented and defense-oriented coping patterns.

SOME GENERAL PRINCIPLES OF ADJUSTIVE BEHAVIOR

In reviewing certain general principles that underlie stress reactions, we shall again find it convenient to utilize the concept of three interactional levels. Thus, on a biological level there are immunological defenses against disease, and damage-repair mechanisms; on a psychological level there are learned coping patterns and self-defenses; and on a sociocultural level there are interpersonal and group resources, such as family, friends, labor unions, and law-enforcement agencies.

The failure of coping efforts on any of these levels may seriously impair an individual's adjustment on other levels. For example, a breakdown of immunological defenses against disease may impair not only bodily functioning but psychological functioning as well; chronic malfunctioning of psychological coping patterns may lead to peptic ulcers or other "diseases of adaptation"; and the failure of a group on which one depends may seriously interfere with ability to satisfy basic needs.

Reactions are holistic. We have seen that living organisms tend to maintain their integrity or "wholeness." Basic to this integration of behavior are the neural processes of *excitation* and *inhibition*.

Since all of an individual's adjustive behavior must use the same bodily equipment—sense organs, nervous system, glands, muscles, and so on—the overall adjustive demands of the moment will determine how it is used. If there are several competing demands, the one that is most important, or is perceived as most important, will commandeer the organism's adjustive resources, and some functions or actions will be inhibited while others are facilitated.

This coordination is well illustrated by emergency emotional reactions—for example, in a combat situation. Here, digestive and other bodily processes that are not immediately essential for survival are slowed down or stopped, while the organism's resources for increased activity and effort are mobilized—with the heightening of muscle tonus, the releasing of stored sugar into the bloodstream, and the secretion of adrenalin—a key agent in helping the body to tolerate stress.

In general, the processes of excitation and inhibition provide the organism with the flexibility it needs for dealing with stress. Only under unusual or pathological conditions does the organism function "segmentally" rather than as an integrated unit. Such segmental actions may occur as a consequence of interference with the integrating functions of the higher brain centers by alcohol, drugs, or brain damage; or it may occur as a con-

sequence of excessive psychological stress which leads to behavior disorganization.

Reactions are economical. Not only does an individual react to stress as an integrated unit, but he responds in a way that entails a minimum expenditure of his resources. This, of course, is what we might expect in view of his tendencies toward self-maintenance. Man's needs and goals are many, but his resources, while impressive, are limited.

J. G. Miller (1965) has pointed out that organisms that survive—whether they are low or high on the evolutionary scale—tend to employ first those defenses that are least expensive; if these are ineffective, then additional and more expensive resources are brought into operation. If a continuously increasing amount of acid is injected into a dog's veins, for example, the first defense mechanism that appears is overbreathing. If this does not prove effective, more drastic protective mechanisms, such as biochemical changes in the blood, are brought into operation. Similarly, if a general finds a squad too small to achieve a military objective, he may commit a company or a regiment—at an increasing cost in resources.

The same sequence may be observed on a psychological level. A student who fails an examination rather than receiving the A or B he expected may curtail his social life and increase his study hours. A low grade on the next examination, however, may cause him to lower his level of aspiration and hope to get through the course with simply a passing grade. This is a relatively inexpensive defense, at least for the moment. But if he then fails the course and feels increasingly inadequate and anxious about his college career, he may unfairly place the whole blame on his instructor. This is obviously a more expensive and self-defeating defense, since he cannot now profit from whatever mistakes he has made or see himself more realistically as a consequence of his failure.

The principle of economy is also relevant in a slightly different context. The individual tends to maintain his existing patterns of thought and action not only because they provide his basic source of security in dealing with the world but because it requires less effort to follow established patterns than it does to modify them or adopt new ones. This tendency to resist change in established ways of perceiving and acting has been referred to as "inertia" on the individual level and as "cultural lag" on the social level. It is one of the big blocks to successful therapy and helps us to understand the tendency of maladaptive behavior patterns to persist long after new, more efficient patterns have become available.

Reactions may be automatic or planned. Reactions to stress situations may be undertaken with conscious planning, with only partial awareness, or with no conscious involvement at all. In general, an individual's potentials for conscious and automatic functioning represent complementary resources for meeting adjustive demands.

On a biological level, the repair of damaged tissue, immunological defenses against disease, and other corrective and defensive processes take place automatically. Some psychological tension-reducing and repair mechanisms—such as crying, repetitive talking, and rationalization—also take place automatically. Even if the individual is aware of what he is doing, such responses are not usually planned or consciously thought out. Seeing what one wants to see, screening out or distorting threatening information, and repressing painful experiences are other examples of automatic and mainly unconscious processes. On a psychological level, automatic functioning typically takes the form of habits, in which reactions that once were conscious and planned no longer require an individual's attention.

Automatic functioning can be a boon in processing routine stresses, since it frees the individual's attention for problems that require careful thought. It is apparent, however, that automatic behavior can also impair effective adjustment. A person who unthinkingly employs habitual patterns of response in coping with a marital problem, for instance, is clearly reducing the chances that the problem will ever be satisfactorily resolved. In all but routine situations, the ability to adapt effectively depends on conscious effort and the flexibility to choose an appropriate response.

Stress arouses emotion. The particular emotional states accompanying reactions to stress vary greatly, from grief and depression at one extreme to emotional mobilization for emergency action at the other. Three emotional patterns are of special significance here: anger, fear, and anxiety.

1. *Frustration tends to elicit anger (hostility).* The organism's immediate reaction to frustration is typically one of anger. And anger, in turn, typically leads to attack or aggressive action as the organism tries to remove the obstacle to its goals. Where the frustration continues or the individual is confronted with a succession of frustrating situations stemming from the same source, anger gradually blends into hostility, with a tendency to destroy, damage, or hurt the person or object viewed as the source of frustration (Buss, 1961).

Anger and hostility are extremely difficult emotions to deal with, inasmuch as civilized living permits few direct outlets. Consequently, these emotions are often expressed in indirect and deviant but "safe" ways which we shall presently examine. Where anger is intense and the individual's inner controls are poorly developed or temporarily lowered—as by severe fatigue or alcoholic intoxication—assaultive or homicidal acts may result.

2. *Specific dangers tend to elicit fear.* The perception of danger usually arouses fear; and fear, in turn, tends to elicit withdrawal or flight.

DIMENSIONS OF ANXIETY

1. Realistic or pathological. Anxiety is considered realistic when it is appropriate in degree to the objective threat; it is considered pathological when it is out of proportion to the actual threat.

2. Specific or general. Anxiety may be elicited by certain specific situations which the individual perceives as threatening; or it may be elicited by a view of the world as a generally dangerous and hostile place.

3. Aware or unaware. The individual may be acutely aware of his anxiety, as in an anxiety attack; he may feel vaguely apprehensive and anxious; or his anxiety may be repressed and kept out of awareness.

4. Acute or chronic. The individual may evidence sudden intense anxiety in the face of a threatening situation; or he may maintain a chronic, continuously high level of anxiety.

5. Positive or negative. At mild levels, anxiety may lead to increased effort and improved performance; at intermediate and higher levels, it may lead to the disorganization of behavior.

These dimensions of anxiety are not necessarily discrete, of course, but rather occur in varying combinations.

However, the actual behavior evoked by fear depends greatly on the individual and the specific situation. A person who fears he has cancer may go immediately for a medical checkup so as to relieve his fear; or he may put it off because he cannot face having his worst expectations confirmed. In the face of extreme danger, the individual may panic or "freeze" and become unable to function in an organized manner. Such behavior is commonly observed at fires and other disasters.

3. *A sense of threat tends to elicit anxiety.* Anxiety is a feeling of apprehension and fearfulness in the absence of specific danger. Because it is acutely unpleasant, it forces the individual to take some action in an effort to find relief. Many threats—such as possible atomic war—may give rise to both fear and anxiety. But, in general, fear is related to clearly perceived dangers, whereas the source of the threat which elicits anxiety is usually not clearly perceived. For example, if repressed hostility threatens to break through existing defenses an individual may become anxious, even though he is unaware of the source of the danger. As we shall see, intense anxiety may be highly disorganizing, and the defenses mustered to cope with it may run the entire gamut of abnormal behavior.

Of course, as a consequence of experience and learning, these typical emotional responses to frustration, danger, and threat may not be elicited. The individual may learn to "turn the other cheek" in the face of provocation and frustration; or he may become apathetic and depressed. Then, too, anger, fear, and anxiety may be elicited in various combinations as well as singly. Where fear or anxiety is aroused, anger and hostility often follow; for dangers and threats are potential sources of frustration. It may also be noted that the so-called negative emotions of anger, fear, and anxiety may be mixed with positive emotions, such as love—as when an individual has ambivalent feelings toward a mate or parent. The specific emotional patterns elicited are determined by learning and by the individual's perception and appraisal of the stress situation.

Reactions have inner and outer determinants. As we have seen, the behavior of a living organism is determined both by its own structural and functional properties, and by the nature of its environment. Sometimes inner determinants,

such as a person's frame of reference, play a predominant role; at other times external factors, such as social demands or environmental resources, are of primary importance. But any adjustive action reflects the interplay of organismic and environmental characteristics.

Inner determinants of an individual's reactions to stress include his frame of reference, motive patterns, competencies, stress tolerance, and momentary physiological and psychological condition. Environmental determinants of reactions to stress include interpersonal and group supports, social expectations and demands, momentary events, and the general life situation of the individual.

With these basic principles in mind, let us proceed to an examination of the typical steps involved in coping with stress.

STEPS IN COPING WITH ADJUSTIVE DEMANDS

In spite of a great deal of research, we know very little about how the human brain—our "biological computer"—processes stress situations. At one time the brain was thought of as a "switchboard" where stimuli and responses were connected. Present-day computer-simulation studies support the notion that it is more like an elaborate communication and decision-making center where incoming information is continuously evaluated, alternative responses are formulated and weighted, decisions are made and implemented, and feedback is checked with a view to correcting possible error. The human brain tends to be a highly efficient computer in processing stress, but it is subject to error; and such errors may lead to seriously maladaptive behavior.

As we consider the typical steps in coping with stress situations, we shall be concerned with the general nature and sequencing of events, rather than with specific details.[1]

Appraising the stress situation. Communications experts have estimated that an individual receives some ten thousand sensory impressions per second (Watzlawick, Beavin & Jackson, 1967);

---

[1]For a more detailed consideration of the processes involved in human problem solving, the reader is referred to Simon and Newell (1971).

thus, a drastic screening and filtering process is necessary to keep the higher brain centers from becoming overwhelmed by irrelevant information, while ensuring that relevant adjustive demands are perceived. The process involved includes categorizing stress situations and appraising the degree of threat involved.

1. *Categorizing the stress situation.* When a new adjustive demand is perceived, it is quickly assigned to a particular category of problems, based on its similarities to and differences from previous ones. This tendency to categorize is a highly useful one, since it makes the task of appraisal much simpler. However, the tendency to categorize is also a possible source of error, since it may cause a person to assign a new problem to a category set up for similar past situations rather than to analyze it for its own unique characteristics. Thus, simplification can readily become oversimplification—as when stereotypes of liberals and conservatives, or "hawks" and "doves," are used. Of course, when an individual faces a stress situation for which existing categories are obviously inadequate, he is forced to examine it as a unique situation, try to discern its key dimensions, and perhaps establish a new category.

2. *Appraising the threat.* As we have seen, threat refers to the anticipation of harm—the degree of threat being commensurate with the magnitude of the contemplated danger. What one person considers to be highly menacing may seem only mildly ominous or even nonthreatening to another. In general, threat appraisal depends on the perceived balance of power between the harm-producing stress and the counter-harm, or coping resources available to the individual (Lazarus, 1966). If the individual evaluates the stress situation as nonthreatening or only mildly menacing, he is likely to deal with it in terms of established patterns that require little thought or effort. On the other hand, if he evaluates the stress as a serious threat, he is likely to experience anxiety and to interrupt other ongoing activities and focus on coping with it (Simon, 1967).

Of course, the individual's threat appraisal may be in error. He may perceive danger where none exists, fail to perceive it where it does exist, or exaggerate or minimize the threat. But accurate or inaccurate, threat appraisal is an extremely important aspect of the evaluation of the adjustive demand; for the degree of perceived threat will markedly influence the further processing of the stress situation.

Deciding on a course of action. Having defined the problem and its degree of threat, the individual must then decide what to do about it. This involves formulating alternative courses of action that might resolve the stress (problem solving), and selecting the one that appears most promising (decision making). Both of these steps involve complex processes which we can study only by inference.

1. *Formulating alternative courses of action.* Often by defining the problem an individual has gone a long way toward formulating alternative courses of action. For the categorization of the problem provides what some investigators have called a *search model*—an index to requirements for dealing with the adjustive demand. The individual may recall how similar stress situations were dealt with previously so as to arrive at a basis for formulating appropriate courses of action.

In a familiar situation the process of definition and action may take place automatically, with little or no conscious involvement; but a stress situation with unfamiliar elements may not be amenable to categorization, and no appropriate response pattern may be evident even when the problem has been defined. Reason, generalization, imagination, and other conscious processes may then be required to find possible solutions. Often this involves discussing the stress situation with others and obtaining additional information about dealing with such problems.

2. *Balancing probability, desirability, and cost.* Once the individual has formulated alternative courses of action for dealing with a given stress situation, he must assess the relative merits of the alternatives and make a choice. Influencing his decision will be the probabilities of success, the degree of satisfaction he is willing to accept, and the cost he is willing to pay.

Peterson and Beach (1967) have concluded from their research on problem solving and decision making that man is an "intuitive statistician"; that is, other things being equal, the individual tends to select the course of action that seems to offer the greatest probability of success in coping with the adjustive demand. In figuring the odds, a person not only examines the relevant information at his disposal but also tends to assess—often unconsciously—the likelihood that chance factors will upset his calculations or that events beyond his control will prevent his carrying out a given course of action and reaching his goal.

An important consideration in figuring the odds and weighing the risks is the individual's assessment of the goal to be reached via a particular course of action. All coping behavior exacts its costs in effort, resources, time, and the surrender of other possibilities and satisfactions; and some coping behavior also exacts costs in unpleasantness or pain. For high stakes and good odds a person may be willing to exert great effort and undergo sacrifice and pain. But if the returns do not seem to warrant the sacrifice, if he lacks the competencies needed for success, or if the risks involved seem too great, he usually will reject the course of action. In general, an individual will not try to ferret out and assess every conceivable alternative, but rather will accept the first one that seems to balance out with respect to probability, desirability, and cost.

Taking action and using feedback. Once a decision has been made, the next step is to implement it—to put the chosen alternative into action. And once a course of action has been embarked upon, the individual can keep checking on whatever feedback information is available to see if corrections or adjustments in ongoing action are called for.

In general, feedback may be described as convergent or divergent. Convergent feedback is information telling the individual that he is progressing satisfactorily toward, or has actually met, the adjustive demand; divergent feedback indicates that he is not progressing satisfactorily or perhaps that his action is ineffective or making the stress situation worse. Here it may be noted that feedback also involves what Richards (1968) has called "feedforward." That is, when an individual embarks on a course of action, he has certain expectancies about the outcome of his action. Thus there is a forward reference to his coping patterns; and it is against this expectation of outcome that the individual uses feedback in evaluating his coping efforts.

A course of action, once undertaken, is usually continued until the stress situation has been resolved and/or the strain resulting from it has been relieved to the point where it is manageable.

There are several "goal-terminating mechanisms," however, which may come into operation sooner —e.g., extreme discouragement (Simon, 1967).

Of course, error may occur in any part of the sequence in processing stress. Wishful thinking may lead a person to take untoward risks or disregard danger signs. He may even keep wagering on responses that have failed consistently in the past, like the gambler who continues betting despite heavy losses over a period of time. Here again we see that intermittent reinforcement—in terms of occasional small wins—may be highly effective in maintaining given response patterns. Faulty assumptions, emotions, lack of adequate information, time pressures, and many other factors may lead to wrong answers. Problems of self-defense also may affect the way a problem is perceived, the alternatives that are seen for dealing with it, and the course of action that is selected.

TASK- AND DEFENSE-ORIENTED COPING PATTERNS

When a person feels competent to handle a stress situation, his behavior tends to be *task-oriented*—that is, aimed primarily at dealing with the requirements of the adjustive demand. But when his feelings of adequacy are seriously threatened by the stress situation, his reactions tend to be *defense-oriented*, or directed predominantly at protecting the self from devaluation and relieving painful anxiety and tension.

Task-oriented reactions. Since task-oriented reactions are aimed at meeting the demands of the stress situation, they tend to be based on an objective appraisal of the situation, to be rational and constructive, and to be consciously directed. The action itself may involve making changes in oneself or one's surroundings or both, depending on the situation. In general, task-oriented reactions may be categorized as attack, withdrawal, or compromise behavior.

1. *Attack.* In attack behavior the individual tries to remove or surmount obstacles that block his goals. Such responses are apparently based on tendencies of living organisms toward increased activity and variation in mode of attack when obstacles are encountered. The possible ways of

CHARACTERISTICS OF TASK-ORIENTED REACTIONS TO STRESS

Task-oriented stress reactions may be viewed as falling into one of three categories: attack, withdrawal, and compromise. Characteristic reactions for each of these categories are listed below.

ATTACK REACTIONS

Focusing coping resources   The individual musters his forces, increases his effort, and undertakes a course of action to deal with the problem.

Maintaining flexibility of attack   The individual chooses the most promising course of action but maintains flexibility and shifts his approach if it does not seem to be working out or if a better possibility presents itself. He attempts to remain sensitive to changes in the stress situation, to avoid narrowing and rigidity of thinking, and to function rationally despite fear or other emotions that may be elicited.

Developing new resources   The individual attempts to increase his coping resources by such means as searching out new information, developing new competencies or improving existing ones, and obtaining professional assistance when indicated.

Affiliating for group action   The individual may join with others so that the resources of the group can be added to his own in dealing with the stress situation.

WITHDRAWAL REACTIONS

Admitting defeat   The individual admits that the situation is too difficult for him or that he has chosen an inappropriate goal which he no longer wishes to pursue.

Leaving the field   This may involve physical or psychological withdrawal from the stress situation or both—as in the case of leaving an uncongenial profession.

Establishing a new direction   Instead of drifting or indefinitely "nursing his wounds," the individual redirects his efforts toward a new and hopefully more appropriate goal.

COMPROMISE REACTIONS

Accepting substitute goals   When an individual realizes that he cannot attain the exact goal he is seeking, he may settle for the best substitute or approximation. This may mean lowering his level of aspiration to a more achievable level.

Accepting substitute means   Unable to reach his goal by one means, an individual tries another. Sometimes people lower their ethical standards to get what they want; such a reaction, though task-oriented, is maladjustive in the larger view because it meets their needs at others' expense.

Assuring minimum essentials   If an individual cannot have all he hopes for, it is important for him to know what he can and cannot do without. For example, a young wife who maintains harmony by always giving in to her husband's wishes has chosen a compromise that she probably cannot live with indefinitely. Sometimes people make bad compromises that complicate rather than resolve their problems in the long run.

Taking time to deliberate   When an individual is in doubt about what decision to make and time permits a delay, he does well not to let himself be rushed into action. With a wait-and-see response he can let the situation unfold and avoid precipitous action that he might regret later. Circumstances may change, and the problem may even solve itself. In some cases, of course, the convenient option of delay may not be open to him.

We have presented these reactions in three separate categories for the sake of clarity; however, it should be noted that varying combinations of attack, withdrawal, and compromise reactions may occur in given reaction patterns.

attacking a problem are legion, and they range from obvious actions, such as physical assault or learning new skills, to subtle means, such as patience or passive resistance.

Many years ago Miller and Dollard (1941) concluded that aggression is a logical and expected consequence of frustration. More recent evidence, however, indicates that aggression is commonly a consequence of social learning which tends to occur in response to frustration only when it is seen as a possible way of removing the obstacle without undue cost to the individual (Buss, 1963; Bandura & Walters, 1963; Ilfeld, 1969).

When appropriate to the situation and the individual, an attack approach usually offers the best channel for using and coordinating resources in constructive action. However, attack behavior may be destructive as well as constructive. With anger and hostility, there is a tendency to destroy as well as attack—a tendency that may lead to socially disapproved and self-defeating behavior.

2. *Withdrawal.* Simple withdrawal is a second type of task-oriented reaction to stress. Many animals seem capable of fairly well-coordinated withdrawal or flight reactions shortly after birth, but the human infant has no such built-in patterns. However, a child is able to withdraw a hand or foot from a painful stimulus, such as a hot object, and when subjected to sudden, unexpected stimuli he may tend to curl up into a ball, apparently manifesting a primitive type of fear reaction.

In addition to withdrawing physically, the individual may withdraw in various psychological ways—such as admitting defeat, avoiding certain types of adjustive demands, and reducing his emotional involvement in a situation and becoming apathetic. Resistance and protective inhibition are common forms of avoidance or withdrawal in the face of excessive pressure. Here again we can see that the individual is not necessarily a passive recipient of stress; often he can exercise considerable control over the nature and degree of stress to which he exposes himself, and thus keep pressures and other stresses from becoming excessive.

There are, of course, many stress situations in which the simplest and most realistic solution is simply that of avoidance or withdrawal. In fact, attack and withdrawal—fight and flight— are fundamental forms of coping with stress

found in all animals. They appear to be part of the organism's built-in evolutionary heritage. Attack helps the organism to overcome obstacles and attain goals relevant to its survival; withdrawal serves to remove the organism from dangerous situations which it cannot overcome. While anger is the emotion that most commonly accompanies attack, and fear the emotion that most frequently accompanies withdrawal, severe stress usually elicits anxiety as well.

3. *Compromise.* Since most situations cannot be dealt with successfully by either direct attack or withdrawal, it usually becomes necessary to work out some sort of compromise solution. This approach may entail changing one's method of operation, accepting substitute goals, or working out some sort of accommodation in which one settles for part of what he may initially have wanted.

An individual faced with starvation may compromise with his conscience and steal "just this one time"; or he may ignore his squeamishness and eat worms, bugs, or spiders—he may even go so far as to eat human flesh. Another form of compromise is the acceptance of substitute goals under conditions of severe frustration. Thus a soldier may gain some sexual satisfaction from pinup pictures or from wish-fulfilling daydreams. In fact, Masserman (1961) has shown that under sustained frustration individuals usually become increasingly willing to accept substitute goals—both symbolic and nonsymbolic ones.

When compromise reactions succeed in meeting the essential requirements of the stress situation, the problem is resolved and the individual can go on to other activities. Often, however, he makes compromises which he cannot fully accept and live with because important needs continue to go unmet. In such instances, additional adjustive action is required.

Task-oriented reactions of all three types— attack, withdrawal, and compromise—involve the same basic steps of: (1) defining the problem; (2) working out alternative solutions and deciding on an appropriate course of action; and (3) taking action and evaluating the feedback. Perhaps the most difficult step in this sequence is that of decision making, or choice.

Here it may be pointed out that even if the individual suffers a setback in dealing with severe stress or a crisis situation, the results may not be

POSSIBLE CONSTRUCTIVE EFFECTS OF STRESS

Although we emphasize the high cost of dealing with stress, it may have the following constructive effects if circumstances are of the type described.

Increased self-understanding	Through his experience in a stressful situation, the individual may gain a clearer view of his assets, liabilities, and adaptive potentials.
Increased competencies	Stressful situations may be rendered less stressful through a combination of experience, new information, and increased know-how for coping.
New approaches to problems	If an individual faces the fact that previous or present coping patterns are ineffective, he may be amenable to the development of more effective patterns.
More realistic goals and expectations	Persistent failure and frustration may provide feedback, which can lead an individual to a more realistic appraisal of the alternatives actually available to him.
Increased stress tolerance	By success in adapting to and "living with" difficult stress situations, an individual may increase his ability to cope with stress and also increase his stress tolerance.

In general, stress may either "sensitize" the individual and lower his stress tolerance, or it may "immunize" him and increase his feelings of self-confidence and his ability to cope with given stress situations.

entirely negative if he utilizes the feedback in a task-oriented way. For example, the individual who is going through a traumatic divorce may gain a better understanding of his personal limitations and perhaps improve upon his competencies for the sake of future interpersonal relationships.

Defense-oriented reactions. In the face of severe stress an individual confronts two problems: (1) to meet the adjustive demand; and (2) to protect himself from psychological disorganization. Defense-oriented behavior is focused on the latter difficulty—the utilization of coping patterns to lessen anxiety or emotional hurt and to prevent self-devaluation.

Three types of defense-oriented reactions are commonly differentiated. The *first* consists of a group of responses—such as crying and repetitive talking—which seem to function as psychological damage-repair mechanisms. The *second* type is composed of the so-called "ego" or "self-defense" reactions—such as denial and rationalization—which function to protect the self from hurt and devaluation. A *third* type of reaction is manifested by an individual's reliance upon drugs for the alleviation of tension and anxiety. All of the above responses are designed to maintain psychological integration and steady states, much as our biological homeostatic mechanisms are designed to maintain them on a physiological level.

Our present discussion will focus on certain common ego-defense mechanisms in which learning ordinarily plays a key role. These defense reactions protect the individual from both external threats, such as devaluating failures, and internal threats, such as guilt-arousing desires or actions. They appear to protect the self in one or more of the following ways: (1) by denying, distorting, or restricting the individual's experience; (2) by reducing emotional or self-involvement; and (3) by counteracting threat or damage. Often, of course, a given defense mechanism may offer more than one kind of protection; and a person usually will rely on a pattern of defenses rather than on any specific mechanism. Since there are a large number of such defense reactions, we shall review only those that seem immediately relevant to an understanding of abnormal behavior.

All of us employ various ego-defense mechanisms in our efforts to maintain psychological integration and to protect our self-concepts from devaluation. Defense-oriented reactions must be considered pathological, however, when they become the predominant means for coping with stress and seriously interfere with the resolution of adjustive demands.

1. *Denial of reality.* Probably the simplest and most primitive of all self-defense mechanisms is denial of reality, in which an attempt is made to "screen out" disagreeable realities by ignoring or refusing to acknowledge them. The tendency toward perceptual defense, discussed earlier, is part of this inclination to deny or avoid reality. One may turn away from unpleasant sights, refuse to discuss unpleasant topics, faint when confronted with a traumatic situation, ignore or deny criticism, and become so preoccupied with work that he does not have time to deal with his marital, child-rearing, or other personal problems. Under extreme conditions—such as imprisonment—an individual may experience the feeling that "This isn't really happening to me." Here the defensive reaction appears, at least temporarily, to protect him from the full impact of his traumatic situation. Similarly, in a study of persons with severe injuries, Hamburg and Adams (1967) report that:

"At first there are efforts to minimize the impact of the event. During this acute phase there tends to be extensive denial of the nature of the illness, its seriousness, and its probable consequences." (p. 278)

2. *Fantasy.* In fantasy the individual achieves his goals and meets his needs in his imagination. Two common varieties of wish-fulfilling fantasy are the *conquering hero* and *suffering hero* patterns. In the first, the individual pictures himself as a famous general, a courageous astronaut, a great athlete, a world-renowned surgeon, or other figure who performs incredible feats and wins the admiration of all, the idea being that he is capable, powerful, and respected. James Thurber used this theme as the basis for his *Secret Life of Walter Mitty.* Frequently hostility is dissipated safely and conveniently through conquering-hero fantasies, in which the individual destroys or punishes all who stand in his way. Such fantasies act as safety valves and provide some measure of compensatory gratification.

The *suffering hero* does not have to admit any personal inferiority because he imagines himself to be suffering from some terrible affliction, handicap, or visitation from unjust fate. When others find out about these difficulties and realize how nobly and with what courage he has carried on, they will accord him the sympathy and admiration he deserves. Thus, inferior performance or failures are explained away without any threat to the individual's feelings of adequacy and worth.

Escaping temporarily from the stresses of everyday life into a more pleasant fantasy world is often helpful in adding a dash of excitement to life. But fantasizing becomes maladaptive if the easier accomplishments of make-believe are substituted for real-life endeavors.

3. *Repression.* This is a defense mechanism by means of which threatening or painful thoughts and desires are excluded from consciousness. Although it has often been referred to as "selective forgetting," it is more in the nature of selective remembering. For although the material which is repressed is denied admission to conscious awareness, it is not really forgotten. The soldier who has seen his best friend's head blown off by shrapnel may find the experience so terribly painful that he excludes it from consciousness and becomes "amnesic" with regard to the battle experience. When brought to an aid station he may be nervous and trembling, unable to recall his name or what has happened to him, and manifesting other signs of his ordeal. But the intolerable battle experience, screened from consciousness, may be brought into awareness by means of hypnosis or sodium pentothal interviews.

Repression is an extremely important self-defense mechanism, and in varying degrees enters into many other defense reactions.[1] Repression may help the individual control dangerous and unacceptable desires; and it may protect him from sudden, traumatic experiences until time has somewhat desensitized him to the shock. However, repression may screen out stressful experiences that could be met better by realistically facing and working through the situation.

4. *Rationalization.* Rationalization has two major defensive values: (a) it helps a person to justify his behavior; and (b) it aids in softening the disappointment connected with unattainable goals.

Typically, rationalization involves thinking up logical, socially approved reasons for past, present, or proposed behaviors. With a little effort a person may be able to justify to himself the spending of money needed for essentials on lavish entertainment, neglecting his work for cultural pursuits, or even marrying someone whom he does not love. Carrying matters a step further, one may find it possible to justify most selfish and antisocial behavior. "Why should I yield the right of way to an oncoming motorist? He wouldn't yield it to me if he could help it, so

---

[1]Repression may be distinguished from suppression in that it does not occur because the individual consciously wants it to. It happens without the awareness or conscious intent of the individual. In suppression, the individual consciously decides to not express a feeling or to not even think about a disturbing event.

why should I show him any consideration?" Even callous brutality can be interpreted through rationalization as necessary or even praiseworthy. Adolf Hitler saw the extermination of the Jews as his patriotic duty. And one of the most notorious gangsters and vice-overlords in American history insisted that the government was persecuting him—that all he was trying to do was bring people the "lighter pleasures of life." As Fromm (1955) has pointed out:

"However unreasonable or immoral an action may be, man has an insuperable urge to rationalize it—that is, to prove to himself and to others that his action is determined by reason, common sense, or at least conventional morality." (p. 65)

Rationalization is also used to soften the disappointment of thwarted desires. A common example of such rationalization is the "sour grapes" reaction—stemming from Aesop's fable of the fox who, unable to reach a cluster of delicious grapes, decided he did not want them after all because they were probably sour. If a man has little money he may emphasize that the really important things in life—such as love and friendship—are free; if his proposal is turned down by an attractive girl, he may note that she talks too much and will probably lose her figure at an early age. Similarly, mediocre college or occupational performance may be justified on the ground of refusal to get involved in the "competitive rat race" of modern society. As Aronson and Carlsmith (1962) have pointed out, one way of reducing the discrepancy between an assumption of what is desirable and a failure to take action is to convince oneself that the particular goal object is not really desirable after all.

Frequently, of course, it is difficult to tell where an objective consideration of facts and problems leaves off and rationalization begins. Behaviors that commonly indicate rationalization are: (a) hunting for reasons to justify one's behavior or beliefs; (b) being unable to recognize inconsistencies or contradictory evidence; and (c) becoming upset when one's "reasons" are questioned. Questioning of the individual's rationalizations is a threat to the defenses he has managed to construct against self-devaluation. Although rationalization is an important defense reaction in helping a person avoid unnecessary frustra-

tions and maintaining feelings of adequacy and worth, it exacts a price in self-deception.

5. *Projection.* Projection is a defensive reaction by means of which an individual (a) places the blame for his own shortcomings, mistakes, and misdeeds on others; and (b) attributes to others his own unacceptable impulses, thoughts, and desires.[1]

Projection is perhaps most commonly evidenced by the former tendency. The student who fails an examination may feel that the teacher was unfair; the delinquent teen-ager may blame his problems on a rejecting and non-understanding mother; and even the small boy being punished for fighting may protest, "It wasn't my fault—he hit me first." Fate and bad luck are particularly overworked objects of projection. Even inanimate objects are not exempt from blame. The three-year-old who falls off his hobby horse may attack it with blows and kicks; the basketball player who slips may return to inspect the alleged slippery spot. In extreme cases, the individual may become convinced that other persons or forces are systematically working against him. Such ideas may develop into delusions of persecution involving the supposed plots and conspiracies of his enemies.

In other projective reactions an individual may attribute to others his own unacceptable desires and thoughts. This tendency appears to be particularly common among those with rigid moral values and strict conscience development—for whom desires viewed as immoral are highly threatening and self-devaluating and usually cannot be handled adequately by rationalization or other defense mechanisms. As a consequence, these desires are projected to someone else who now becomes the offender while the individual himself remains conveniently "pure." The individual with guilt-arousing homosexual leanings may accuse other men of trying to seduce him—while he remains unaware of his own homosexual inclinations.

6. *Reaction formation.* Sometimes an individual protects himself from dangerous desires by not only repressing them but actually by developing conscious attitudes and behavior patterns that are just the opposite. Thus he may conceal

---

[1] A detailed discussion of the nature and dimensions of projection may be found in Holmes (1968).

hate with a façade of love, cruelty with kindness, or desires for sexual promiscuity with moralistic sexual attitudes and behavior. In this way he erects obstacles or barriers that reinforce his repression and keep his real desires and feelings from conscious awareness and from being carried out overtly.

On a simple level, reaction formation is illustrated by the story about the old maid who looks hopefully under her bed each night for fear that a man may be lurking there. On a more complex level, reaction formation may be manifested by people who crusade against loose morals, alcohol, gambling, and other real or alleged evils. Often such people have a background of earlier difficulties with these problems themselves, and their zealous crusading appears to be a means of safeguarding themselves against recurrence of their difficulties.

Self-appointed protectors of the public morals often appear to gain a certain amount of vicarious satisfaction of their own repressed desires without endangering their self-concepts. In some cases reaction formation is more subtle, as when a juror demands the severest penalty under the law for an infraction that he himself has been tempted to commit.

Reaction formation, like repression, may have adjustive value in helping a person maintain socially approved behavior and avoid facing desires that he considers threatening and self-devaluating. But because this mechanism, too, is self-deceptive and not subject to conscious control, it often results in exaggerated and rigid fears or beliefs that may complicate the individual's adjustive reactions and lead to excessive harshness or severity in dealing with the lapses of others.

7. *Displacement.* In displacement there is a shift of emotion or symbolic meaning from a person or object toward which it was originally directed to another person or object. Often displacement involves difficult emotions, such as hostility and anxiety. A common subject for cartoons is the meek office clerk who has been refused a raise by his domineering boss. Instead of expressing his hostility toward his employer—which would be dangerous—he goes home and snaps irritably at his wife because dinner is a few minutes late.

In some instances the individual may turn his

AN EXAMPLE OF REACTION FORMATION

Reaction formation in extreme form is well illustrated by excerpts from a letter that Masserman (1961) received from a "kind-hearted" antivivisectionist:

"...I read [a magazine article]...on your work on alcoholism...I am surprised that anyone who is as well educated as you must be to hold the position that you do would stoop to such depths as to torture helpless little cats in the pursuit of a cure for alcoholics....A drunkard does not want to be cured—a drunkard is just a weak minded idiot who belongs in the gutter and should be left there. Instead of torturing helpless little cats why not torture the drunks or better still exert your would-be noble effort toward getting a bill passed to *exterminate* the drunks. They are not any good to anyone or themselves and are just a drain on the public, having to pull them off the street, jail them, then they have to be fed while there and it's against the law to feed them arsenic so there they are....If people are such weaklings the world is better off without them.

"...My greatest wish is that you have brought home to you a torture that will be a thousand fold greater than what you have, and are doing to the little animals....If you are an example of what a noted psychiatrist should be I'm glad I am just an ordinary human being without a letter after my name. I'd rather be just myself with a clear conscience, *knowing I have not hurt any living creature*, and can sleep without seeing frightened, terrified dying cats—because I know they must die after you have finished with them. No punishment is too great for you and I hope I live to read about your mangled body and long suffering before you finally die—and I'll laugh long and loud." (p. 38)

hostility inward against himself. He may engage in exaggerated self-accusations and recriminations and feel severe guilt and self-devaluation. Such intropunitive reactions do protect the individual from expressing dangerous hostility toward others, but may lead to depression and even to attempted or actual suicide.

On a social level, displacement is often combined with projection, as in Nazi Germany, where the blame for the country's ills was projected onto the Jews and the Communists, and feelings of frustration and hostility were displaced onto these two groups. Such "scapegoating" is common in dictatorships, where hostility is likely to be aroused by the stern, repressive measures of the government but where any opposition or direct expression of the hostility is extremely dangerous.

Through a process of symbolic association, displacement may become extremely complex and deviant. Swearing is commonly used as a means of discharging pent-up feelings. Destructive criticism and vindictive gossip frequently are only disguised methods of expressing hostility. In a study of skydivers, Fenz and Epstein (1969) found that the fear and anxiety associated with skydiving was displaced onto other situations unrelated to parachuting. "It is as if the jumper were saying: 'This feeling of fear that I have, it is of other things, not parachuting.'" (p. 28) This type of defensive reaction is referred to as "stimulus displacement": while the fear or anxiety remains, it is displaced to other situations.

Displacement may have adjustive value, since it is a means of discharging emotional tensions without risk of retaliation. But displacement may also exact a high price. In most cases it is much more healthful and less painful in the long run to face and work through hostility or anxiety-arousing situations than to avoid them through displacement.

8. *Emotional insulation.* Here the individual reduces his degree of emotional involvement in situations that might or do prove disappointing and hurtful.

Since many disappointments are encountered in life, people usually learn to keep their anticipations within limits. Until a hoped-for event occurs, they are careful to avoid premature celebrations or to let their hopes run too high. The student who looks forward to a date with a very attractive girl may not let himself get too excited or enthusiastic for fear she may not like him. Such reactions are well expressed in the common saying, "I didn't dare even to hope."

In more extreme cases of long-continued frustration, as in chronic unemployment or prison confinement, many persons lose hope, become resigned and apathetic, and adapt themselves to a restricted way of life. Such "broken" individuals thus protect themselves from the bitter hurt of sustained frustration by becoming passive recipients of whatever life brings them. Similarly, in extreme forms of alienation the individual may become noninvolved and apathetic, feeling isolated, bewildered, and without hope. In certain mental disorders, too, such as chronic schizophrenia, there is often an extreme use of insulation which apparently protects the individual from emotional involvement in a life situation and world that he has found unbearably hurtful.

Up to a point, emotional insulation is an important means of defense against unnecessary disappointment and hurt. But life involves calculated risks, and most people are willing to take a chance on active participation. Emotional insulation provides a protective shell that prevents a repetition of previous pain, but it reduces the individual's healthy, vigorous participation in life.

9. *Intellectualization (isolation).* This defense mechanism is related to both emotional insulation and rationalization. Here the emotional reaction that would normally accompany a painful event is avoided by a rational explanation that divests the event of personal significance and painful feeling. The hurt over a parent's death is reduced by saying that he or she lived a full life or died mercifully without pain. Failures and disappointments are softened by pointing out that "it could have been worse." Cynicism may become a convenient means of reducing guilt feelings over not living up to one's ideals. Even the verbalization of good intentions, as in a glib admission that "I should work harder" or that "I should be less selfish and more interested in the welfare of others," seems to cut off a good deal of guilt and relieve one of the necessity of positive action.

Intellectualization may be utilized under extremely stressful conditions as well as in dealing with the milder stresses of everyday life. Bluestone and McGahee have found that this defense mechanism was often utilized by prisoners awaiting execution. They have described the pattern as follows: "'So they'll kill me; and that's that'—this said with a shrug of the shoulders suggests that the affect appropriate to the thought has somehow been isolated." (1962, p. 395)

Another form of intellectualization or isolation involves the dissociation of certain conflicting attitudes or normal thought-affect relationships. The confirmed believer in democracy may practice racial discrimination. The ruthless and dishonest businessman may also be a kind father and a "pillar of the church." The individual may resort to rationalization to make such incompatible values seem more consistent, but usually he is unaware of his inconsistency. The essential process seems to be one of unconscious isolation in which one assumption is isolated from the other. A passage from Sheila Cousins (1938), a

London prostitute, illustrates the isolation of thought-affect relationships. She wrote:

"The act of sex I could go through because I hardly seemed to be taking part in it. It was merely something happening to me, while my mind drifted inconsequentially away. Indeed, it was scarcely happening even to me; it was happening to something lying on a bed that had a vague connection with me, while I was calculating whether I could afford a new coat or impatiently counting sheep jumping over a gate." (pp. 150–151)

In this way situations that ordinarily would give rise to strong emotional conflicts are kept isolated from each other in our minds.

10. *Undoing (atonement).* Undoing is designed to negate or annul some disapproved thought, impulse, or act. It is as if the individual has spelled a word wrong and used an eraser to clear the paper and start over. Apologizing for wrongs committed against others, penance, repentance, and undergoing punishment are all forms of undoing. The opportunity for confession and the assurance of forgiveness in some religions appear to meet a deep human need to be able to resolve guilt feelings and make a new beginning.

Undoing apparently develops out of early training in which children are made to apologize or to make some restitution, or are punished in some way commensurate with their socially disapproved behavior. Once a child's apology, restitution, or punishment has taken place, his misdeed is negated and he can start with a clean slate and with renewed parental approval and affection. In this sequence of events the child also learns that repentance, penance, or restitution may forestall more serious punishment. By returning Johnny's toys and saying he is sorry, he may escape punishment, although he may, of course, be scolded.

SUMMARY CHART OF EGO-DEFENSE MECHANISMS

Denial of reality	Protecting self from unpleasant reality by refusal to perceive or face it
Fantasy	Gratifying frustrated desires by imaginary achievements
Repression	Preventing painful or dangerous thoughts from entering consciousness
Rationalization	Attempting to prove that one's behavior is "rational" and justifiable and thus worthy of self and social approval
Projection	Placing blame for difficulties upon others or attributing one's own unethical desires to others
Reaction formation	Preventing dangerous desires from being expressed by exaggerating opposed attitudes and types of behavior and using them as "barriers"
Displacement	Discharging pent-up feelings, usually of hostility, on objects less dangerous than those which initially aroused the emotions
Emotional insulation	Reducing ego involvement and withdrawing into passivity to protect self from hurt
Intellectualization (isolation)	Cutting off affective charge from hurtful situations or separating incompatible attitudes by logic-tight compartments
Undoing	Atoning for and thus counteracting immoral desires or acts
Regression	Retreating to earlier developmental level involving less mature responses and usually a lower level of aspiration
Identification	Increasing feelings of worth by identifying self with person or institution of illustrious standing
Introjection	Incorporating external values and standards into ego structure so individual is not at their mercy as external threats
Compensation	Covering up weakness by emphasizing desirable trait or making up for frustration in one area by overgratification in another
Acting-out	Reducing the anxiety aroused by forbidden desires by permitting their expression

As a consequence of learning that wrong-doing inevitably leads to punishment, people commonly develop methods of atoning for or undoing their misdeeds—methods designed to avoid or ameliorate the punishment that would otherwise accrue. The unfaithful husband may bring his wife presents; the unethical businessman may give huge sums of money to charity.

Sometimes one feels that the only atonement for his misdeeds is punishment itself, and he may confess them in order that he may be punished and thereby pay for and erase his sins. Not infrequently a person who has committed a crime years earlier will confess to the police in order to be punished and regain his feelings of self-esteem. Where sins seem so great that the individual sees no hope of atoning for them, he may suffer such intense guilt, anxiety, and self-devaluation that suicide seems the only way out.

Since undoing is fundamental to the maintenance of ethical human relations, as well as to one's self-esteem, it is one of man's most valuable ego defenses. Particularly in combination with rationalization and projection it is a potent defense against self-devaluating guilt feelings. As we shall see, however, in our study of psychotic patterns, undoing is subject to exaggerated and unhealthy usage.

11. *Regression.* Regression is a defense mechanism in which one returns to the use of reaction patterns long since outgrown. When a new addition to the family has seemingly undermined his status, a child may revert to bed-wetting, baby talk, thumb-sucking, and other infantile behavior

AN EXTREME EXAMPLE OF REGRESSION

This young woman looked like an average 17-year-old girl (left) until she found the photograph of herself taken at the age of 5 (center). Thereafter, she tried to look as much as she could like the pictured child (right).

From her childhood, the girl had been the victim of an extremely contentious and unstable environment. She first showed neurotic symptoms about the age of 4, when her parents began to quarrel violently. When the girl was 7, the mother refused further sexual relations with the father; but the girl slept with the father until she was 13. The mother, suspecting incestuous seduction, obtained legal custody of the girl at this time and removed her to another home.

Resenting the separation from her father, the girl quarreled with her mother, became a disciplinary problem at school, and acquired a police record for delinquency. On the girl's insistence the mother and she visited the father after 3 years, and found him "living with a girl in questionable circumstances." A violent scene ensued, and again the mother took her daughter home, against her wishes.

After this the girl would not attend school, and she became sullen and withdrawn. In her mother's absence she would go on destructive forays of the house, and in one of these forays discovered the early picture of herself. In her subsequent behavior she "appeared to have regressed to a relatively desirable period in life antedating disruptive jealousies and other conflict; moreover, she acted out this regression in unconsciously determined but strikingly symbolic patterns of eliminating the mother as a rival and regaining the father she had lost in her childhood." (Adapted from Masserman, 1961, pp. 70–71, case of Dr. John Romano)

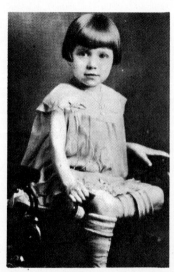
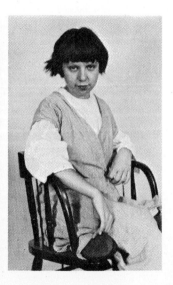

that once brought him parental attention. The frustrated adult may resort to the temper tantrums of childhood. The bride may run home to Mother at the first sign of trouble. Regression is also typified by the tendency of older people to live more and more in the past and extoll its advantages. In fact, regression has been called the "old oaken bucket" delusion because of its emphasis on the superior joys of "the good old days."

Regression can be readily understood if we remember the child's gradual shift from a position of helplessness and dependence on the parents to one of independent action and responsibility. This developmental process from dependence to independence is by no means an easy accomplishment, and it is common in the face of adult difficulties to yearn for the carefree, sheltered days of childhood. Consequently, it is not surprising that in the face of severe stress an individual may retreat from adult reaction patterns to a less mature level of adjustment. We might expect something akin to regression to occur merely on the basis of the frequent failure of more recently learned reactions to bring satisfaction. In looking for other, more successful modes of adjustment it would be only natural to try out discarded patterns which previously had brought satisfaction (Barthol & Ku, 1959).

However, regression is a more comprehensive reaction than merely trying out older modes of response when new ones have failed. For in regression the individual retreats from reality to a less demanding personal status—one that involves lowered aspirations and more readily accomplished satisfactions. This point is well illustrated by Bettelheim's reference to a general "regression to infantile behavior" seen in nearly all the prisoners at Dachau and Buchenwald.

"The prisoners lived, like children, only in the immediate present; . . . they became unable to plan for the future or to give up immediate pleasure satisfactions to gain greater ones in the near future. . . . They were boastful, telling tales about what they had accomplished in their former lives, or how they succeeded in cheating foremen or guards, and how they sabotaged the work. Like children they felt not at all set back or ashamed when it became known that they had lied about their prowess." (1943, p. 443)

The disorganization and collapse of adult behavior and the emergence of developmentally lower levels of functioning is a very common form of ego breakdown. In its most dramatic form, it is seen in those psychotic adults who show such extreme regression to infantile levels of behavior that they are unable to wash, dress, or feed themselves or take care of their eliminative needs. In some cases, they even curl up in a position similar to that of the fetus in the womb.

The defensive function of regression, as well as its limitations for adaptive behavior, are brought out in the illustration on page 132.

12. *Identification.* As we have seen, identification often takes place in imitative learning—as when a boy identifies with his father and uses him as a model. Identification may also operate as a defense mechanism in enhancing feelings of worth and protecting the individual against self-devaluation.

The growing child soon realizes that other people's evaluations of him are to a large extent dependent upon his family and other group memberships. During adolescence and adulthood, the mechanism of identification is expanded to include a range of personal and group identifications. Not only does society evaluate him in terms of his group identifications, but he comes to evaluate himself in the light of them. College students who work actively for social causes or political candidates identify with their groups and standard bearers. Adults identify themselves with their professions, homes, special interest groups, and the accomplishment of their children. Many employees identify themselves with the power and prestige of the company for which they work. By so doing they take as their own some of the desirable attributes of the groups to which they belong. Particularly for an individual who feels basically inferior, such identifications may have important supportive and defensive value. The individual who relies too heavily on his identification with others for his feelings of adequacy and worth may, however, be highly vulnerable to stress situations in which his identifications cannot help him or in which those with whom he identifies prove disillusioning, suffer humiliation, or occupy low-status positions in society.

13. *Introjection.* Introjection is closely related to identification. As a defense reaction it involves the acceptance of others' values and norms as one's own even when they are contrary to one's previous assumptions. After revolutions leading to dictatorial forms of government, for example, many people introject the new values and beliefs as a protection for themselves. By internalizing the socially prescribed values and norms, they can then trust themselves to avoid behavior that would bring social retaliation and punishment.

The use of introjection under extreme conditions has been well described by Bettelheim (1943) in a report of his experiences at the German concentration camps of Dachau and Buchenwald. Under the cruel and insidious camp experiences, previous values and identifications were broken down and new norms were introjected—Nazi norms.

"A prisoner had reached the final stage of adjustment to the camp situation when he had changed his personality so as to accept as his own the values of the Gestapo. . . . old prisoners were sometimes instrumental in getting rid of the unfit, in this way making a feature of Gestapo ideology a feature of their own behavior." (pp. 447–449)

Introjection has been referred to as "identification with the aggressor" and is a defensive re-

action which seems to follow the idea that "If you can't beat 'em, join 'em." However, as is evident, introjection may lead to seriously distorted and maladaptive behavior.

14. *Compensation.* Compensatory reactions are defenses against feelings of inferiority and inadequacy growing out of real or imagined personal defects or weaknesses, as well as out of the individual's inevitable failures and setbacks. Such reactions may take many forms and may even represent deliberate, task-oriented behavior, as in the case of an individual who attempts to overcome a physical handicap through increased effort and persistence. Demosthenes, the great orator, had to overcome his early stuttering, and Theodore Roosevelt waged a valiant fight against early ill health to become noted for his physical daring and robustness. Compensatory reactions of this type may be a deciding factor in success, as biographers are quick to point out.

More commonly, compensatory reactions are indirect; there is an attempt to substitute for the defect in some way or to draw attention away from it. The physically unattractive boy or girl may develop an exceptionally pleasing personality, the puny boy may turn from athletics to scholarship, and the mediocre nobody may become the Grand Imperial Potentate of some secret order. The entire cosmetics industry has developed around minimizing undesirable facial features and emphasizing desirable ones.

Unfortunately, not all compensatory reactions are desirable or useful. The child who feels insecure may show off to try to get more attention and raise his status in the eyes of others and himself; the boy who feels inferior and unpopular may become the local bully; the person who feels unloved and frustrated may eat too much or resort to excessive fantasy satisfactions. Some people brag about their illustrious ancestors and exaggerate their own accomplishments, while others resort to criticism or innuendoes in attempts to cut others down to their own size. In extreme cases, an individual may engage in antisocial behavior or develop marked eccentricities in an unconscious attempt to get some attention and evidence of interest and concern from others.

15. *Acting out.* Acting out is a reaction in which the individual reduces the anxiety and tension associated with dangerous desires by actually permitting their expression. For example,

---

PROGRESSION OF DEFENSES IN NAZI DEATH CAMPS

The following hierarchy of progressively employed ego defenses has been reported as common under the extreme conditions of the Nazi concentration camps during World War II:

1. **Denial**—as expressed in the feeling "It can't be happening," "It isn't really happening to me," "It can't be true."

2. **Regression**—involving some measure of depersonalization and childish coping patterns, with a focus on the present and on immediate gratifications, and an inability to plan for the future.

3. **Fantasy and identification with the aggressor**—involving unrealistic hopes of a miraculous rescue and the introjection of Nazi values, with old prisoners often killing the "unfit" as part of their new ideology.

4. **Emotional insulation**—leading in its ultimate form to apathy and the "musselman" syndrome, with its apathy, loss of hope, depression, and giving up.

   Many hundreds of thousands of prisoners found their end in the last defense of the "musselman" syndrome.

Based on Bettlelheim (1943), Chodoff (1970), Frankl (1959), and Niederlund (1968).

a person who feels mistreated and discriminated against may lash out in physical violence against those he considers responsible, or he may damage or destroy their property. Vandalism often seems to be motivated by pent-up frustration and hostility.

Everyone has probably experienced times of acute conflict or stress when tension and anxiety have built up to such a level that almost any action that would "get it over with" is welcome. Soldiers under the stress of waiting have been known to leave their relatively safe shelter and blindly attack the enemy. Although such acting-out behavior may momentarily reduce tension and anxiety, it is obviously not well designed to deal effectively with the stress situation eliciting the anxiety. Under most circumstances acting out is not feasible except for those who have relatively weak reality and value controls; most people are deterred not only by their values but by the likelihood of social disapproval, punishment, personal injury, or other aversive results.

The various defense mechanisms we have discussed are ordinarily used in combination, rather than singly, and often they are combined with task-oriented behavior. Because they are essential for softening failure, alleviating anxiety, and protecting one's feelings of adequacy and worth, we may consider them to be normal adjustive reactions unless they seriously interfere with the effective resolution of stress situations. Both the "positive" and "negative" functions of such defenses have been well illustrated in a recent investigation by Katz and his associates (1970), who intensively studied the ego defenses of 30 hospitalized women who were awaiting the outcome of breast tumor biopsy. These researchers found the defense mechanisms of denial and rationalization to be highly effective in coping with anxiety, particularly when used in combination. They also found, however, that many of the women who allayed their anxieties with these defenses impaired their chances for survival—e.g., by not seeking medical help.

In summary, it may be emphasized that the defense mechanisms are, in the main, learned; they are designed to deal with inner hurt, anxiety, and self-devaluation; they operate on relatively automatic and habitual levels; and they typically involve some measure of self-deception and reality distortion.

Our primary purpose in reviewing development and adjustment in this chapter has been to lay the foundation for a better understanding of both normal and abnormal behavior. In this chapter we have reviewed the primary determinants of human development; we have seen that development normally proceeds in an orderly manner through predictable stages; and we have noted that the quality of development at each stage is limited by what has gone before. We have also stressed the crucial role of learning in shaping development and in determining the personal resources an individual has available for pursuing his goals and for coping with adjustive demands.

In the final analysis, the outcome of the individual's efforts to satisfy his biological and psychological needs depends not only on his own personal resources but also on the severity of the adjustive demands he must face. We shall take a closer look at the interplay of these two factors in the next chapter, which focuses on some specific causes of abnormal or maladaptive behavior.

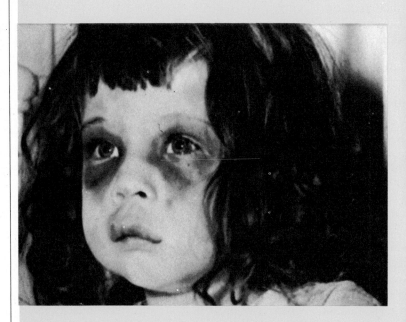

Causative Factors in Abnormal Behavior

6

FAULTY DEVELOPMENT

SEVERE STRESS

THE INTERPLAY OF INADEQUATE RESOURCES AND EXCESSIVE STRESS

GENERAL PERSPECTIVES ON CAUSATION

In reviewing personality development and adjustment, we have established a framework for examining the causes of abnormal or maladaptive behavior—faulty development and severe stress. The causation of any particular behavior pattern is tremendously complex, of course, and it is all but impossible to predict how given circumstances will affect given individuals. In considering the life and achievements of Rousseau, Will and Ariel Durant (1967) raise a provocative question:

"How did it come about that a man born poor, losing his mother at birth and soon deserted by his father, afflicted with a painful and humiliating disease, left to wander for twelve years among alien cities and conflicting faiths, repudiated by society and civilization, repudiating Voltaire, Diderot, the Encyclopedie and the Age of Reason, driven from place to place as a dangerous rebel, suspected of crime and insanity, and seeing, in his last months, the apotheosis of his greatest enemy—how did it come about that this man, after his death, triumphed over Voltaire, revived religion, transformed education, elevated the morals of France, inspired the Romantic movement and the French Revolution, influenced the philosophy of Kant and Schopenhauer, the plays of Schiller, the novels of Goethe, the poems of Wordsworth, Byron and Shelley, the socialism of Marx, the ethics of Tolstoi, and, altogether, had more effect on posterity than any other writer or thinker of that eighteenth century in which writers were more influential than they had ever been before?" (p. 3)

Whether or not one wholly agrees with the Durants' evaluation of Rousseau, his accomplishments seem truly remarkable when viewed against the developmental and stressful conditions of his life. Although he apparently suffered from serious emotional difficulties (see page 6), he nevertheless reached an unusually high level of achievement. His story makes clear the need for caution in interpreting the effects of given conditions in the etiology of abnormal behavior. Psychology is still a long way from providing an adequate answer to the Durants' question, "How did it come about . . .?"

In attempting to analyze the causation of abnormal behavior, it is helpful to think in terms of *predisposing* and *precipitating* causes as well as particular kinds of maladaptive learning. Predisposing factors go before and pave the way for later psychopathology by lowering the individual's adjustive ability, as, for example, in the case of fatigue or parental overprotection. Precipitating causes represent the particular condition, such as brain disease or disappointment in love, which proved too much for the individual and precipitated psychopathology. In a given case the exact pattern of predisposing and precipitating causes may be far from clear, and what precipitates today's symptoms may become a predisposing factor in tomorrow's behavior. But we can attempt to show the part various factors play in lowering our adjustive ability or in increasing stress.

FAULTY DEVELOPMENT

On a biological level, we have relatively well-defined norms for height, weight, blood pressure, glandular balance, and other aspects of bodily development and functioning. But we lack comparable norms for evaluating the enormous variations we find in personality development. For example, is an adolescent who sees no value in competitive achievement, drops out of school, and joins a youth commune showing healthy or faulty development during this phase of his life? Our answers to such questions inevitably reflect value judgments.

Perhaps the best we can do at this stage of our knowledge is to agree that conditions which seriously impair the individual's growth potentials lead to faulty development. Since our behavior is based on the quality and functional intactness of our nervous system and other bodily equipment, any factors that can interfere with normal physical development must be considered to be potential causes of abnormal behavior. Similarly, conditions that seriously impair the development of psychological potentialities—for example, the failure to learn needed adaptive behaviors or the learning of maladaptive behaviors—may result in faulty psychological development. As we have noted, the individual develops and functions as a psychobiological unit, and faulty development on one level may adversely affect overall development.

Faulty psychobiological development may take any one of the following general forms: (1) *Arrested development* is readily illustrated by arrested growth of the central nervous system resulting from severe malnutrition. On the psychological level, there may be serious impairment of the individual's adaptive capacities in the form of immaturities, lack of needed competencies, and other conditions associated with faulty learning. (2) *Distorted development* is illustrated on the biological level by the child who fails to develop legs or is otherwise physically malformed. On the psychological level, the individual may learn deviant values that are seriously detrimental to the group, as in the case of a youth who commits a series of murders for "kicks." (3) *Special vulnerability* is illustrated by the lowered resistance to respiratory infections that may result from pneumonia. Similarly, an individual may be especially sensitive to conflicts that threaten the stability of his marriage because of the hurt he experienced in childhood when his parents were divorced. Probably most of us have a more-or-less vulnerable "Achilles heel" as a result of earlier life experiences.

The significance of the early years for later development has long been recognized, as evidenced by the aphorisms "As the twig is bent the tree's inclined" and "The child is father of the man." Scientific support for such sayings has come from a growing body of psychological research showing that it is during infancy and childhood that the foundations are laid for later ways of perceiving, thinking, feeling, and coping. Although the multiplicity of interacting variables makes it virtually impossible to relate specific "causes" to particular effects, a number of conditions have been identified that influence development in unhealthy ways. Among the most important of these are (1) genetic defects, (2) constitutional vulnerabilities and physical handicaps, (3) maternal deprivation, (4) early psychic trauma, (5) pathogenic family patterns, (6) social pathology, and (7) failure to develop an adequate self-structure. In the present section we will examine the significance of these various conditions for psychological development and psychopathology.

GENETIC DEFECTS

Since man's behavior is inevitably influenced by his biological inheritance, genetic defects are clearly a potential cause of psychopathology. The three areas of major concern in this regard are chromosomal aberrations, mutant genes, and inherited predispositions to mental disorders.

Chromosomal aberrations. Dramatic progress in the field of genetics during recent years has enabled us to detect chromosomal aberrations and to launch studies into their implications for development and behavior. The first major breakthrough was the identification of the complement of forty-six chromosomes in the nucleus of each normal living human cell and the discovery that encoded in the chromosomes is the hereditary plan—the overall strategy or information for guiding development. When fertilization takes place, the normal inheritance of the new individual consists of twenty-three pairs of chromosomes—one of each pair being from the mother and one from the father. Twenty-two of these chromosome pairs are called *autosomes;* they determine body characteristics. The remaining pair, the *gonosomes,* or *sex chromosomes,* determine the individual's sex and certain other characteristics. In the female, both of these sex chromosomes—one from each parent—are designated as X *chromosomes.* In the male, the sex chromosome from the mother is an X but that from the father is called a Y *chromosome.*

Research in developmental genetics has shown that abnormalities in the structure or number of chromosomes are associated with a wide range of

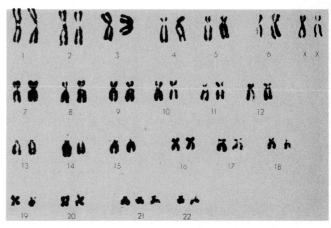

Here illustrated is an example of a chromosomal aberration involving the trisomy of chromosome 21. Most cases of Down's syndrome—a type of mental retardation—reveal 47 instead of the normal complement of 46 chromosomes.

congenital malformations and hereditary disorders. Where the chromosome is deficient in specific genetic information the result may be color blindness, hemophilia, or any of a wide range of other defects. In mongolism, or *Down's syndrome*—a type of mental retardation in which the individual has slanting eyes, a flat face, and other characteristics that produce a superficial resemblance to Mongolians—investigators have discovered the presence of an extra chromosome, involving a trisomy (three instead of two) of one autosomal pair. Similarly, *Turner's syndrome*—characterized by short stature, "webbing" of the neck, and sexual infantilism—has been shown to result from an abnormal number of sex chromosomes. Recently attempts have been made to relate criminal behavior in males to the presence of an *XYY* chromosomal anomaly (see Chapter 11).

In a study of 2159 consecutively born babies, Sergovich et al. (1969) found a gross chromosomal abnormality rate of 0.48 percent. The exact causes of chromosomal anomalies are not yet fully understood. Where the chromosome is deficient in specific genetic information—as in color blindness—the defect is usually transmitted by faulty recessive genes; but such chromosomal defects can also reflect gene mutations in the fertilized ovum—for example, as a result of ionizing radiation. Where there is a trisomy instead of the normal chromosome pair—referred to as a failure in disjunction—the causes of the anomaly are not as well understood, but apparently also may involve faulty genes or various conditions affecting the fertilized ovum. Interestingly enough, females are less susceptible to the deleterious effects of aberrations of the sex chromosomes, since they have two X chromosomes. Thus, if one proves faulty, the other member of the pair generally can handle the work of development. Since males have a single X chromosome paired with a single Y chromosome, a defect in either will mean trouble.

A search for chromosomal irregularities in schizophrenia and other psychoses has not proved fruitful: none of the chromosomal anomalies thus far observed has appeared to be directly related to mental disorder. It may be emphasized, however, that the potential effects of gross chromosomal anomalies are largely unknown, since such irregularities ordinarily result in the death of the embryo.

Mutant genes. A second major breakthrough in modern genetics has been the development of ultramicroscopic techniques—for example, the combined use of the electron microscope and X-ray diffraction—which make it possible to study the actual structure of the chromosomes. Each chromosome is made up of long molecules of DNA (deoxyribonucleic acid) which are arranged in two strands linked together at regular intervals to form a double spiral, or helix, that looks like a ladder curving round and round. In a series of epic experiments, scientists have shown that our genetic instructions are stored in this DNA ladder, or "book."

The "sentences" in this DNA book of instructions are the genes, following one another like beads that are strung together to form a necklace. Each gene carries the instructions, either singly or in combination with other genes, for specific body traits—such as eye color and blood type. Thus, genes are the discrete units or bearers of an individual's genetic inheritance. With the breaking of the "genetic code," scientists can now read the DNA book of instructions—thus introducing a second and more precise approach to relating genetic factors to physical and mental disorders.

This new approach entails the study of gene mutations—losses, gains, or changes of material in the gene itself. As Dobzhansky (1960) has pointed out:

"Every one of the tens of thousands of genes inherited by the individual has a tiny probability of changing in some way during his generation. Among the small,

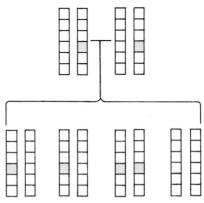

The wedding of "General" Tom Thumb and Miss Lavinia Bump in 1863 united two midgets. The groom was 38 inches tall, and the bride was 32 inches in height. Recessive genes probably caused their small stature, as suggested in the schematic drawing of chromosomes (McKusick & Rimoin, 1967). A recessive gene (color) in the paired chromosomes of both parents (top) could be combined in different ways in the paired chromosomes of their offspring (bottom). A combination of two recessive genes (third from left) would give rise to the recessive trait.

and probably atypical, sample of human genes for which very rough estimates of the mutation frequencies are available, the rates of mutation vary from one in 10,000 to one in about 250,000. For example, it has been calculated that approximately one sex cell in every 50,000 produced by a normal person carries a new mutant gene that causes *retinoblastoma*, a cancer of the eye affecting children." (p. 206)

As a consequence of such spontaneous changes, it has been estimated that each person carries an average of five to ten mutant genes, along with thousands of normal ones (Davis, 1968). However, the incidence of gene mutations may be much higher if the individual is exposed to special mutagens—such as ionizing radiation and certain drugs—which are known to cause gene damage. Mutagens are particularly hazardous since their effects may not be immediately apparent, but may show up in future generations. For example, a higher incidence of mental retardation associated with small head circumference has been reported among the children of survivors of the nuclear bombings at Hiroshima and Nagasaki (Miller, 1969).

Although many kinds of gene mutation are relatively harmless, some are seriously detrimental to development. An example is the disorder known as phenylketonuria (PKU) in which the infant lacks an enzyme needed to break down phenylalanine, an amino acid found in protein food. This disorder is assumed to be transmitted via a recessive gene, and if it is not detected and treated early, the phenylalanine builds up in the blood and damages the brain. Thus, gene mutations can produce a wide variety of hereditary diseases, congenital malformations, and constitutional weaknesses or vulnerabilities.

Genetic predisposition to specific mental disorders. So far, most of the knowledge we have concerning the role of genetic factors in mental disorders has been gained from family studies, including the study of twins and siblings.

The family history method requires that the investigator observe a large sample of relatives of each *proband* or *index* case (carrier of the trait in question, such as schizophrenia) in order to see whether the incidence increases in proportion to the degree of hereditary relationship. In addition, he compares the incidence of the trait in a normal population with its incidence among the relatives of the index cases. This approach is illustrated in Kallmann's (1953; 1958) statistics for schizophrenia.

Degree of Relationship to Schizophrenic	Percent Who Develop Schizophrenia
Identical (one-egg) twins	86.2
Fraternal (two-egg) twins	14.5
Siblings	14.2
Half-siblings	7.1
General population	0.85

These figures indicate that the incidence of schizophrenia is much higher among all degrees of blood relationship to the schizophrenic than in the general population, and that with an increasing degree of blood relationship there is an increasing incidence—from 7.1 percent in half-siblings of schizophrenics to 86.2 percent in identical twins. Kallmann tentatively concluded from his findings that schizophrenia must be transmitted via recessive genes.

It may be noted that most family studies, including Kallmann's, have involved methodological weaknesses. Typically, they have failed to take into account the importance of early environmental conditions. For example, Jackson (1960) has pointed out that even physical diseases may run in families without necessarily having a genetic basis. Beriberi, a vitamin deficiency disease, is one example of this type of pattern. What is apparently "inherited" by a child who develops this disorder is the preference for vitamin-poor foods, a preference acquired from his parents through learning rather than genetic transmission.

Although Kallmann's early findings are useful for illustrative purposes, later studies have raised serious doubts about the degree of genetic influence in schizophrenia. They have by no means ruled out an hereditary influence, but they show that such a determinant does not follow a simple recessive genetic pattern. Similarly, other mental disorders—aside from Huntington's chorea and a few other rare diseases of the central nervous system which *are* transmitted via recessive genes—do not follow recessive genetic patterns.

Most investigators now take the position that only a *predisposition* to mental disorder can be inherited. Here it is presumed that certain individuals are especially prone to develop mental disorders if placed under severe stress. However, this tendency is thought to follow a polygenetic pattern involving many genes rather than a simple recessive genetic pattern. And given a favorable life situation, the individual's inherent vulnerability will not show up. This position is bolstered by medical evidence concerning inherited predisposition to diabetes, high blood pressure, some forms of cancer, and coronary heart disease (Kaiser Foundation, 1970).

Much still remains to be learned about human genetic inheritance, but achievements thus far have made it possible for geneticists to make a chromosomal map for a child or adult—which is often useful in understanding and predicting certain types of pathology. Such chromosomal maps have particular value in genetic counseling of potential parents concerning the risks they run in having defective children. Many geneticists believe that the rapidity of scientific progress—including the recent artificial creation of a gene itself—will make it possible in this century to alter defective genes, thus eliminating the risk of various developmental defects and instituting a new era of "genetic engineering."

CONSTITUTIONAL VULNERABILITIES AND PHYSICAL HANDICAPS

The term *constitution* is used to denote the relatively enduring biological makeup of the individual resulting from both genetic and environmental influences.[1] Physique, primary reaction tendencies, and temperament are among the myriad traits included in this category.

Since ancient times, attempts have been made to classify people into *types* in terms of constitutional factors, and to use these classifications for predicting general personality and behavioral patterns. However, our present focus is on the role of constitutional variations and vulnerabilities in psychopathology.

Physique. When Shakespeare's Julius Caesar exclaims:

Let me have men about me that are fat;
Sleek-headed men and such as sleep o'nights:
Yond Cassius has a lean and hungry look;
He thinks too much: such men are dangerous.

(Act I, Scene ii)

he expresses the age-old popular belief that fat men are more likely to be good-natured and reliable.

Perhaps the best known of various scientific attempts to relate physique to personality and psychopathology is that of Sheldon and his associates (1954). As shown in the illustration, Sheldon concluded that there are three types of body build, each associated with a particular type of temperament. Presumably the type of physique and temperament have nothing to do with the individual's becoming mentally ill, but influence the variety of illness he will develop should he become psychotic. Here it is of interest to note that Davidson, McInnes, and Parnell (1957), in a study of seven-year-old children, found that boys with above-average fatty tissue were more self-confident; stocky boys showed superior communication abilities and greater aggressiveness; and boys with less than average muscular development tended to display more anxiety and "showing-off" behavior. Glueck and Glueck (1962; 1968) have reported a higher incidence of individuals with muscular physiques among juvenile delinquents and adult criminals—perhaps indicating simply that such individuals are more vigorous and aggressive than the average, and, in a high-delinquency area, more likely to find delinquency rewarding. In their study of both delinquent and nondelinquent boys, Cortés and Gatti (1970) found a highly significant relationship between body build and need for achievement. Mesomorphs were preponderantly above average and ectomorphs below average in achievement motivation. These investigators concluded that if the high achievement needs of delinquent boys could be channeled appropriately, "society would gain some very energetic and constructive members." (p. 82)

Although Sheldon's findings have been supported by some investigators, others have been critical of his typology. It does seem unlikely that the complexities of human development and behavior can be predicted on the basis of one relatively simple variable, such as physique. However, we have only to look at everyday situations to realize that physique—including physical appearance as well as body build—does play

PHYSIQUE, TEMPERAMENT, AND PSYCHOPATHOLOGY

	ENDOMORPHIC	MESOMORPHIC	ECTOMORPHIC
Physique	Soft, round	Strong, muscular, athletic	Slender, fragile
Temperament	Comfort-loving, sentimental, pleasure-seeking, socializing	Active, energetic, less religious, more achievement-oriented, aggressive	Sensitive, delicate, intellectual, more religious, withdrawing
Most likely psychopathology	Severe mood alternations involving extreme elation or depression (particularly the latter)	Delinquency, criminal behavior, mood alternations involving extreme elation or depression	Schizophrenia, anxiety neurosis, peptic ulcers

Sheldon's original work relating body type to personality type (Sheldon, 1942) was widely criticized for oversimplification and for weaknesses in methodology. Subsequent studies have shown that physical characteristics may indeed be related to personality characteristics, but suggest that the relationship is much less direct than Sheldon first supposed. As Cortés and Gatti (1970) have emphasized, the fact that physique and temperament seem to be correlated does not necessarily mean that one determines the other.

Based on work of Cortés and Gatti (1970), Damon and Polednak (1967), Davidson, McInnes, and Parnell (1957), Glueck and Glueck (1962), Sheldon (1942), and Sheldon et al. (1954).

an important role in personality development and adjustment. Beauty, for example, is highly valued in our society. One need only attend a social gathering, watch television and motion pictures, or note the billions of dollars spent each year on cosmetics and beauty treatments to see the influence of the beauty cult on behavior. It is certainly not surprising that Byrne, Oliver, and Reeves (1968) found that there is greater interpersonal attraction toward strangers of either sex who are considered good-looking than toward those who are not. Similarly, tallness and shortness and other variations in physique influence the adjustive reactions of an individual, as well as other people's reactions to him. When we stop to realize the unique problems introduced into the life of a person who is very tall—endless remarks about the "climate up there," frustrating encounters with standard beds and doorways, scarcity of ready-made clothes, expectations of being presumed to be big in spirit as well as stature, and so on—we may agree with the early conclusion of Barker, Wright, and Gonick (1946)

that "very tall men are in many respects in quite a different sociopsychological situation from persons of normal height." (p. 13)

Perhaps of most significance is the view an individual takes of his own physical appearance. A conception of one's body as being too different from the standards valued by one's group can be self-devaluating—as can dissatisfaction over changes in bodily proportions during adolescence and old age. As Hurlock (1968) has pointed out, "It is difficult for a pubescent to be self-acceptant when he is anxious and concerned about his changing body and when he is dissatisfied with the image of himself he sees reflected in the mirror." (p. 376) It is also difficult in our youth-oriented society to accept the physical deterioration that comes with aging.

Primary reaction tendencies and faulty development. In discussing the role of heredity in development, we noted how primary reaction tendencies—such as sensitivity, temperament, and activity level—affect the individual's interactions with his environment. Several investigators have attempted to relate such tendencies to abnormal behavior.

Shaw and Schelkun (1965), for example, found that many children and adolescents who seem most susceptible to suicide have been characterized as highly sensitive. Similarly, work by Eysenck (1960) and Eysenck and Rachman (1965) makes reference to the extremes of autonomic reactivity found among some children. Although certain conditioned fears and anxieties are considered essential for normal socialization, children who overreact to stress presumably form "surplus conditioned reactions," or fears, many of which are maladaptive and lower stress tolerance. On the other hand, the child who is deficient in emotional reactivity presumably lacks the capacity to form quick and strong conditioned responses and is likely to suffer from "deficient conditioned reactions." In the latter case the result is inadequate socialization, characterized by impulsivity, antisocial behavior, and a lack of inner controls.

Other studies have dealt with the effects of overactivity, extreme passivity, and other primary reaction tendencies on development. For example, a longitudinal study of infant development by Chess and associates (1965) found that a particular type of temperament, such as that of the "difficult baby," may predispose an individual to later maladjustment. According to this study, some 7 to 10 percent of all babies are "different"— they have irregular patterns of eating, sleeping, and bowel movement; tend to cry a great deal and to show a predominantly negative mood; and are irritable and have difficulty in adjusting to new stimuli and change. In her efforts to deal with such a baby, the mother usually tries first one method and then another, so that she is highly inconsistent in her interactions with the infant. In addition, she does not gain the satisfaction from the infant that she expected. The result is often a disturbance in the mother-infant relationship that has undesirable consequences for both of them.

Constitutional differences also seem to affect individual reactions to stress. Some infants react to changes in routine or other stress by manifesting fever; others, by digestive disorders; and still others, by sleeping disturbances. It would appear that a particular subsystem of the body is especially vulnerable to stress and hence more likely to show a reaction to any disturbances in the overall functioning of the organism. We shall comment further on this point in our later discussion of peptic ulcers, hypertension, and other psychosomatic disorders.

Another factor that has received intensive study is the role of constitutional defects in the body's defenses against disease and other stresses. Normally the body produces antibodies to defend itself against invading viruses and bacteria. Faulty functioning of the antibody-producing system leaves the body vulnerable to certain diseases —and it may be that degenerative diseases of the nervous system are among them. It would also appear that under severe stress, certain individuals are more vulnerable than others to disruptions in various biochemical systems involved in brain functioning. However, further research is needed in biochemistry and neurophysiology to delineate the precise nature and effects of these constitutional vulnerabilities.

The effects of a specific constitutional factor will vary, depending on the total interactional growth pattern and the stresses in the individual's life situation. In many cases constitutional vulnerabilities appear to be so minimal that under normal conditions a given organ or system can carry out its necessary function regardless, as in subclinical diabetes. But resistance is lowered, and under severe stress the system may fail, with far-reaching consequences for the total organism.

Congenital and acquired physical handicaps. Robert Burton (1577–1640), in his *Anatomy of Melancholy*, wrote these poignant words: "Deformities and imperfections of our bodies, as lameness, crookedness, deafness, blindness, be they innate or accidental, torture many men. . . ." Such physical handicaps may result from genetic defects or from environmental conditions operating before or after birth.

1. *Prenatal and birth difficulties.* In this country an estimated seven out of every one hundred babies who survive one month after birth have some birth defect (Davis, 1968). About a third of these defects are considered to be of hereditary origin, another sixth are due to drugs or disease, and the rest—about half—result from unknown causes. Some of these aberrations are apparent at birth, while others—such as heart defects or errors in bodily chemistry—may not be detected until months or years later. Often such anomalies are minor, but more serious congenital malformations and defects constitute one of the five leading causes of death during childhood (Dept. of Health, Education, and Welfare, 1965).

Prenatal conditions that can lead to growth defects include nutritional deficiencies, drug effects, radiation exposure, disease, and emotional stress. Recent studies have pinpointed protein deficiency in the mother's diet as a cause of lower IQ and other impairments in the offspring. Various drugs, including alcohol and tobacco in excessive amounts, have been implicated in faulty fetal development, as have German measles, diabetes, tuberculosis, syphilis, and other illnesses of the mother during pregnancy. Birth complications, including anoxia, bleeding, and prolonged pressure on the head during difficult delivery, may result in brain damage and a wide range of growth abnormalities—including mental retardation, epilepsy, hyperactivity, and learning disabilities.

The most common single birth difficulty associated with death or brain damage to the newborn is premature birth—defined as either an elapsed gestation time of less than 280 days, or a birth weight of 5½ pounds or less. In a review of the literature, Rothschild (1967) has reported a higher incidence of emotional disturbances among persons born prematurely. And in an even more recent report, Caputo and Mandell (1970) have pointed to a relationship between prematurity and an above-average incidence of mental retardation, hyperkinesis (overactivity), autism, difficulties in learning and language development, and impaired physical and motor development. Mothers who are subjected to emotional stress and anxiety during pregnancy appear to have a higher incidence of premature deliveries and complications of delivery. As might be expected, socioeconomic status has been found to be related to fetal and birth difficulties—the incidence of the latter being several times greater among mothers on lower socioeconomic levels (Pasamanick & Knobloch, 1960; 1961).

Even in full-term babies, severe maternal stress appears to produce hyperactivity in the fetus during later pregnancy, and after birth to be reflected in feeding difficulties, sleep problems, and irritability of the infant. (Blau et al., 1963; Davids & DeVault, 1962; McDonald, Gyther & Christakor, 1963; Sontag, Steele & Lewis, 1969).

Also, the more negative the mother's attitude toward sex and toward her feminine role, the more likely she is "to experience a spectrum of psychological and physiological problems during pregnancy" (Heinstein, 1967, p. 234).

As a consequence of such findings, it would appear that the fetus is not so well protected as many investigators formerly thought—and that a variety of physiological and psychological conditions affecting the mother during pregnancy can have profound effects on early development.

2. *Physical impairment during infancy and youth.* A number of studies have shown that severe malnutrition during infancy not only impairs physical development and lowers resistance to disease, but also stunts brain growth and results in markedly lowered intelligence (Dobbing, 1967; Bladeselee, 1967). In a postmortem study of infants who died of malnutrition during their first year of life, Winick (1968) found a total brain cell content that was 60 percent below that of normal infants. Even in the case of babies who suffer severe malnutrition but survive, the stunting of brain growth is considered irreversible, since the working cells, or *neurones*, presumably grow to their full number during the period just before and after birth. In a random sample of areas where 75 to 80 percent of the resident families are either living in poverty conditions or close to it, a preliminary study by the United States Department of Health, Education, and Welfare found that 15 percent of all children studied showed evidence of growth retardation associated with malnutrition (Loyd, 1969). The broader social magnitude of this problem is indicated by the estimate that two thirds of the world's preschool children—more than 300 million—lack sufficient protein food for minimum nutritional needs (Scrimshaw, 1969).

The conquest of polio and other diseases has lessened their high toll of disablement and death, yet large numbers of our youth continue to fall victim to disease and various other physical impairments. Projected figures indicated that in the 1970's one fifth of this country's under-17 age group will suffer from at least one chronic physical condition that adversely affects adjustment (Dept. of Health, Education and Welfare, 1965).

The significance of physical impairments for development and possible psychopathology—

Loving parents may help offset a child's deficiencies—both personal and situational. Lee and Jeff, the boys in these pictures, are identical twins—with one important difference. Jeff has normal vision and Lee has been blind since birth. Their parents, however, have created an atmosphere in which each boy is loved and encouraged to develop as fully as possible.

except in the case of defects that are almost totally disabling, such as severe mental retardation—depends primarily on the way the individual evaluates and adjusts to his stressful life situation. Among the obstacles for a handicapped youth to overcome is the tendency to become resigned and to accept the role of a "cripple" which society often seems to expect him to play (Hughes, 1960). Other common and undesirable reactions to physical handicaps are feelings of inferiority, self-pity, fear, and hostility. In an intensive study of children hospitalized as a consequence of the severe crippling effects of poliomyelitis, Bernabeu (1958) emphasized his observation of the core reactions of frustration, anxiety, and rage. These feelings were handled by defenses considered pathogenic in nature or intensity, or inappropriate to a given stage of development.

It may be noted here that parents of handicapped children often develop attitudes of extreme overprotection or rejection, or expect performance beyond the child's capabilities. In such cases the child may develop psychological handicaps that are much more disabling than his physical impairment.

MATERNAL DEPRIVATION

Faulty development has often been observed in infants deprived of maternal stimulation (or "mothering") as a consequence of either (1) separation from the mother and placement in an institution, or (2) lack of adequate "mothering" in the home. Although the emphasis here is on maternal deprivation, we are essentially concerned with warmth and stimulation, whether it be supplied by the mother, father, or other persons responsible for the child's rearing.

In an institution, as compared with an ordinary home, there is likely to be less warmth and physical contact, less intellectual, emotional, and social stimulation, and a lack of encouragement and help in positive learning.

A study by Provence and Lipton (1962) compared behavior of infants living in institutions with that of infants living with families. At one year of age, the institutionalized infants showed a general impairment in their relationship to people—rarely turning to adults for help, comfort, or pleasure, and showing no signs of strong attachment to any person. These investigators also emphasized a marked retardation of speech

and language development, an impaired ability to delay the immediate gratification of needs, and emotional apathy, together with impoverished and repetitive play activities. In contrast to the babies living in families, the institutionalized infants failed to show the personality differentiation and learning which "can be thought of both as accomplishments of the first year of life and as the foundation upon which later learning is built." (p. 161)

With more severe and pervasive deprivation, development may be even more severely retarded. For example, Dennis (1960) found that over 60 percent of the two-year-olds in a Teheran orphanage—where stimulation was minimal—were not yet sitting up alone, and 85 percent of the four-year-olds were not yet walking alone.

Institutions vary, of course, and some institutions provide more stimulation and affection than some families. But the difficulty of providing adequate personal contact for infants "en masse" is a very real one.

The long-range effect of severe early deprivation of maternal love and stimulation is suggested by the findings of Beres and Obers (1950) in a study of 38 adolescents who had been institu-

tionalized between the ages of about 3 weeks and 3 years. At the time of the study, 16 to 18 years after discharge from the orphanage, 4 were diagnosed as psychotic, 21 as having a character disorder, 4 as mentally retarded, and 2 as psychoneurotic. Only 7 were judged to have achieved a satisfactory personality adjustment.

A more recent follow-up study of institutionalized children by Skeels (1966) shows dramatically how an enriched environment can change the final picture. His study reported on the adult status of two groups of individuals who had been placed in an orphanage as infants. One group of 13 children, ranging between 7 months and 3 years of age, had been transferred to another institution in which more stimulation, as well as an opportunity for closer relationships with adults, was provided. A follow-up study 21 years later showed an average gain of 31.6 IQ points for this group, as compared with an average loss of 20.6 IQ points for a matched (control) group of 12 children who had stayed in the original institution. All members of the experimental group were self-supporting; of the control group, 6 were unskilled laborers, 4 were in institutions, and 1 had died. Interestingly enough, the twelfth member of the control group turned out to have had an enriched environment for a year at age 5, as part of another special study; at the time of the follow-up study he was married, had 4 children of normal IQ, and was working as a compositor and typesetter with an income higher than that of all the other control subjects combined.

By far the greatest number of infants subjected to maternal deprivation are not those separated from their mothers, but rather the ones who suffer from inadequate or distorted maternal care. In the latter situation, the mother neglects the child, devotes little attention to him, and is generally rejecting. The effects of such "masked deprivation" may be devastating (Bullard et al., 1967; Prugh & Harlow, 1962). The early work of Ribble (1944; 1945), for example, has shown that rejecting, indifferent, or punishing mothers may cause tense, unsatisfied, and negativistic behavior among their infants even at a very early age. Such behavior may even take the form of a refusal to nurse, and as a result the infant may fall into a semistuporous condition from which it is extremely difficult to rouse him. In fact, Bullard and his associates (1967) have delineated a "failure to thrive" syndrome which:

"... is a serious disorder of growth and development frequently requiring admission to the hospital. In its acute phase it significantly compromises the health and sometimes endangers the life of the child. Investigations of social and psychological aspects of this syndrome have led to demonstrations of parental neglect and variable forms of 'maternal deprivation.'" (p. 689)

In a follow-up study conducted eight months to nine years after hospitalization of the child for treatment, Bullard found that almost two thirds of the subjects showed evidence "either of continued growth failure, emotional disorder, mental retardation, or some combination of these." (p. 681) A not-unexpected finding was that children who showed a reversal of the disorder and lack of sequelae came from homes that were relatively stable.

Conditions of nursing, weaning, and toilet training also have long been considered important factors in "masked deprivation" and the shaping of personality development. For example, where parental demands are beyond the infant's

level of development, constant failure and reproof or punishment may lead to behavioral disturbances. However, the warm or rejecting quality of parent-child interaction is probably more important than the age at which training begins (Chess et al., 1960; 1965). Discontinuities in care—for example, a series of separations from the mother or substitute mother figure to whom the infant has formed an attachment—represent another form of maternal deprivation which has been shown to affect personality development adversely (Ainsworth, 1962).[1] However, this does not mean that nursery schools or adequate mother surrogates cannot be utilized by working mothers without harmful effects to their infants.

A number of investigators have pointed out that the effects of maternal deprivation vary considerably from infant to infant, and that neonates in other societies appear to thrive under widely differing conditions of maternal care. Despite such differences, available evidence leaves no doubt that maternal deprivation—whether it involves growing up in an institution with restricted stimulation, or somewhat comparable conditions of "masked deprivation" in the home—can seriously retard intellectual, emotional, social, and even physical development. Eventually it can result in lowered intelligence, limited capacity to cope with problems, and less adequate interpersonal relationships during adolescence and adulthood.

The actual nature and extent of the damage appear to depend upon: (1) the age at which deprivation first occurs; (2) the extent and duration of such deprivation; (3) the substitute care, if any, that is provided; and (4) the constitutional makeup of the infant (Yarrow, 1965). In cases of severe and prolonged deprivation, the damage may be irreversible or only partially reversible, despite later corrective experiences.

EARLY PSYCHIC TRAUMA

Most of us have had traumatic experiences that temporarily shattered our feelings of security, adequacy, or worth, and were important in influencing our later evaluations of ourselves and

---

[1] In general, faulty "mothering" or maternal care may take the form of deprivation, distortion, or discontinuity.

EFFECTS OF EARLY DEPRIVATION AND TRAUMA ON ADULT BEHAVIOR OF ANIMALS

EARLY EXPERIENCE	ADULT BEHAVIOR—SPECIES
Raised in darkness or with restricted tactual stimulation	Permanent impairment of vision (birds, monkeys, other mammals); retarded use of limbs, abnormal sitting and walking posture (chimps)
Immobilization of movement in early infancy	Inability to fly (buzzards); impaired ability to swim (fish)
Partial starvation in early infancy	Increased hoarding tendency and faster eating rate (rats)
Total social isolation for six months or more after birth	Permanent deficiencies in exploratory, play, sexual, and maternal behavior, and in grooming (monkeys)
Raised by humans	Preference for human company over own species (chimpanzees, lambs, wild sheep, birds, guinea pigs)
Subjected to aversive stimulation, such as electroshock or loud noise	Modification of emotional reactivity to later stress (rats); greater emotionality and possible timidity in wide range of situations (mice)
Raised in overcrowded environment	Many forms of abnormal behavior in rats, including infant mortality rate as high as 96 percent. Dogs raised in overcrowded conditions neither fight nor mate.
Trained to fight over food	Fighting over food even when not hungry (mice). In comparison, mice trained in non-competitive or cooperative behavior were far less aggressive.

The material in this chart is based in part on the excellent summary of earlier literature in this field by Beach and Jaynes (1954), and also on Denenberg et al. (1970), Dennis (1941), Eiduson et al. (1962), Eisenberg (1967), Gray (1958), Harlow (1962), Harlow and Suomi (1970), Hersher et al. (1962), Lessac and Solomon (1969), Lindzey et al. (1960), Moltz (1960), Reisen (1947), Rogers and Davenport (1969), and Turner, Davenport, and Rogers (1969).

our environments.[1] The following illustrates such an incident.

"I believe the most traumatic experience of my entire life happened one April evening when I was eleven. I was not too sure of how I had become a member of the family, although my parents had thought it wise to tell me that I was adopted. That much I knew, but what the term *adopted* meant was something else entirely. One evening after my step-brother and I had retired, he proceeded to explain it to me—with a vehemence I shall never forget. He made it clear that I wasn't a 'real' member of the family, that my parents didn't 'really' love me, and that I wasn't even wanted around the place. That was one night I vividly recall crying myself to sleep. That experience undoubtedly played a major role in making me feel insecure and inferior."

Situations that somehow parallel an earlier traumatic experience are apt to be particularly difficult for the individual to handle. This helps explain why one person may have difficulty with a problem that is not highly stressful to other people. Three points aid in the understanding of this process.

1. Conditioned responses are readily established in anxiety-provoking situations and are resistant to extinction. Thus, one traumatic experience with a vicious dog may be sufficient to establish a conditioned fear response which endures over a sustained period of time. In addition, we have noted that learned avoidance behavior may tend to perpetuate such responses. Hence a traumatic experience may continue to influence behavior long after the original event.

2. Traumatic experiences usually result in emotional conditioning. Thus a similar situation may reactivate an emotional response rather than a consciously formulated one, which would be more subject to modification and hence more likely to be adaptive.

3. Heightened anxiety tends to induce a state of "tunnel vision" in which perception is restricted and a consideration of relevant information and alternative courses of action is impaired.

---

[1]The terms *psychic trauma* and *traumatic* are used here with reference to any aversive experience that inflicts serious psychological damage upon the individual.

PARENTAL SEPARATION OR LOSS AS A TRAUMATIC EXPERIENCE

In a pioneering study, Bowlby (1960) summarized effects of parental separation on children from 2 to 5 years of age who were hospitalized for prolonged periods. He cited three stages of their separation reaction:

1. **Initial protest**—characterized by increased crying, screaming, and general activity.

2. **Despair**—which included dejection, stupor, decreased activity, and general withdrawal from the environment.

3. **Detachment**—following the children's discharge from the hospital and reunion with their mothers—in which the children appeared indifferent and sometimes even hostile toward their mothers.

The effects of long-term or permanent separation from one or both parents are complex. When the separation occurs as early as 3 months after birth, the infant's emotional upset seems to be primarily a reaction to environmental change and strangeness, and he usually adapts readily to a surrogate mother figure. But once attachment behavior has developed, the emotional hurt of separation may be deeper and more sustained, and the child may go through a period of bereavement and have greater difficulty adjusting to the change. It would appear that the age at which the infant is most vulnerable to long-term separation or loss is from about 7 months to 3 years (Yarrow, 1964; 1965). The long-term consequences of such loss appear to depend not only on the time of its occurrence, but also on the child in question, his previous relationship with the parent, and the quality of subsequent parental care.

The magnitude of the problem of separation from parents is indicated by the finding that some 10 million children in the United States have had the experience of losing at least one parent through separation, divorce, or death; this is approximately 1 child in 7 (Witmer, 1965).

Although traumatic experiences tend to be maladaptive, their after-effects depend heavily upon the support and reassurance given the child by his parents or other significant persons in his world. This appears particularly important when the trauma involves some experience—such as being sexually assaulted and afraid to resist—which arouses strong feelings of guilt and self-devaluation in the child. Of course, many traumatic experiences in childhood, though highly upsetting at the time, are probably minor in their consequences; also, some children are less vulnerable than others to traumatic experiences and show more resiliency and recoverability from such damage. In fact, for many children traumatic experiences may serve as challenges that foster the development of competencies and personal growth; they may even raise the individual's threshold for such painful or noxious stimulation (Hunt, 1965). However, severely traumatic experiences that occur at a critical period in development, or a series of traumatic experiences that keep the child off balance, are likely to bring disruption instead of growth. And although subsequent experiences may have a corrective influence, the detrimental effects of early trauma may never be completely obliterated.

PATHOGENIC FAMILY PATTERNS

As the infant progresses into childhood, he must learn new competencies, develop usable assumptions about himself and his world, and exert increasing control over his behavior.

During this period, the family unit remains the crucial guiding influence in the child's personality development; and conversely, faulty family patterns are a fertile source of unhealthy development and maladjustment. Sometimes parents do too much, not letting a child manage his own growing; other times they do too little, not providing him with a stimulating environment or giving him the encouragement and guidance he needs. And sometimes they foster inappropriate assumptions and reaction patterns. Whatever they do, their methods tend to be fairly consistent during the child's growing years (Schaefer & Bayley, 1960).

Despite a good deal of research on pathogenic family patterns, we lack much essential information concerning the long-range effects of specific patterns. The task of identifying predictable relationships is further complicated by the findings that: (1) children respond somewhat differently to similar child-rearing practices, depending on their constitutional and psychological makeup and the way they perceive the situation; (2) the effect of a given child-rearing procedure depends on the total family and social context in which it occurs—for example, whether one or both parents are involved in parental rejection, the degree of acceptance and love shown by the nonrejecting parent, and the various desirable and undesirable aspects of the child's total life situation; and (3) early damage is often corrected to some extent by later experience—as when the child was rejected at first and later was accepted.

In this section we shall review some pathogenic parent-child relationships and general family patterns that have been pointed up by a number of research studies. In view of the magnitude of this problem—the parents of 25 percent of the nation's children have been reported to be inadequate (Joint Commission of Mental Health of Children, 1968)—we shall go into this topic in some detail. It should be noted, however, that since parent-child relationships and family interactions are a complex matter, care should be taken in applying the family patterns we deal with to the understanding of specific clinical cases.

Faulty parent-child and sibling relationships. Several types of specific parent-child patterns appear with great regularity in the background of children who have evidenced emotional disturbances and other types of faulty development. Eight of these patterns, including rejection, overpermissiveness, and faulty discipline, will be discussed here.

1. *Rejection.* Parental rejection of a child may be manifested in various ways—by physical neglect, denial of affection, lack of interest in his activities and achievements, harsh punishment for relatively minor annoyances, failure to spend time with him, and lack of respect for the child's rights and feelings as a person. In a minority of cases it also involves cruel and abusive treatment. Parental rejection may be partial or complete, passive or active, and subtly or overtly cruel.

Since the child's self-concept is largely a reflection of the way "significant others" react to him, it becomes apparent that parental rejection fosters a distorted and devaluated self-concept. If his parents see him as unworthy or insignificant, it is difficult for the child to think of himself in a positive way and to develop the feelings of self-esteem and adequacy needed for confident interactions with his world. If he is not rewarded for desirable behavior with praise and encouragement, it is more difficult for him to discriminate between approved and disapproved behavior. And if the child becomes discouraged and gives up striving for parental approval, his parents then lose control of an important means of guiding his development.

In general, research studies have corroborated the close relationship between parental love and acceptance, and the development of such crucial traits as self-esteem, self-reliance, conscience development, self-control, and coping behavior. In a study of 379 mothers of five-year-olds, Sears, Maccoby, and Levin (1957) found that "cold" mothers reported a background of feeding problems, persistent bed-wetting, aggressiveness, and slow conscience development in their children. Rejected children often appear to be attention-seeking, aggressive, hostile, and lonely. Pringle (1965) found that institutionalized children who had not experienced lasting love and loyalty from any adult were unable to develop feelings of love and loyalty in their own relationships; and many adults who had been rejected in childhood appeared to have serious difficulty in giving and receiving affection. In addition, Hurley (1965) found parental rejection to be associated with diminished intelligence during the early school years; and he concluded that a common core of discouragement and unpleasant emotional climate has a general inhibiting and suppressing effect on the child's intellectual development and functioning.

Of course, rejection is not a one-way street, and the child may be unaccepting of his parents whether or not they reject him. This pattern sometimes occurs when the parents belong to a low-status minority group of which the child is ashamed. Although the results of such rejection have not been studied systematically, it would appear that a rejecting child denies himself needed models, loving relationships, and other essentials for healthy development.

A consideration of why parents reject their children would take us too far afield, but it would appear that a large proportion of such parents have themselves been the victims of parental rejection. In this sense, lack of love has been referred to as a "communicable disease." In our later discussion we shall view the insidious damage that parental rejection may accomplish and the diverse roles that rejection and lack of love may play in mental disorders.

2. *Overprotection and restrictiveness.* Maternal overprotection, or "momism," involves the "smothering" of the child's growth. The mother may watch over her child constantly, protect him from the slightest risk, overly clothe and medicate him, and make up his mind for him at every opportunity. In the case of mother-son relationships, there is often excessive physical

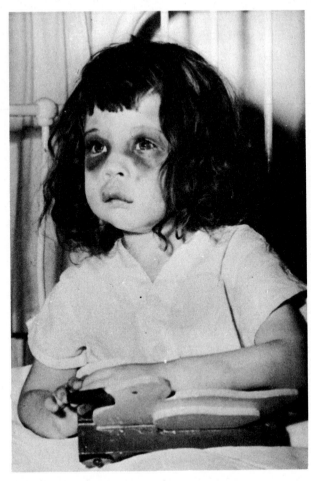

LOVED CHILD AND BATTERED CHILD: TWO VIEWS OF THE WORLD

The child who is loved and respected as an individual in his own right develops a basic sense of security and trust, and a positive self-image. What vision of the world and himself does a battered child develop?

Unfortunately, a substantial number of parents in our society not only fail to provide adequate care for their infants; they actually subject the infants to cruel and brutal treatment. In the United States each year an estimated 50,000 to 70,000 infants and young children are subjected to cruel and inhuman treatment by their parents; more than 300,000 children are in foster homes as a result. Hundreds of victims die each year from abusive treatment, and many others are paralyzed, physically deformed, or rendered mentally retarded by their injuries. The following are examples of cases reported by Earl (1965):

The mother of a 29-month-old boy claimed he was a behavior problem, beat him with a stick and screwdriver handle, dropped him on the floor, beat his head on the wall or threw him against it, choked him to force his mouth open to eat, and burned him on the face and hands. After she had severely beaten him, the mother found the child dead.

A blond, blue-eyed 4-year-old girl was admitted unconscious to a hospital in the nation's capital. Examination disclosed a fractured skull, and lacerations covering her back, face, arms, and legs. Later she reportedly told the doctors, "Mama kept hitting me with a big black stick."

Because her 2½-year-old daughter did not respond readily enough to toilet training, the mother became indignant and in a fit of temper over the child's inability to control a bowel movement gave her an enema with near scalding water. To save the child's life a doctor was forced to perform a colostomy.

In a study of 140 cases of child abuse, Helfer and Kempe (1968) reported that 74 percent suffered bruises and welts, 25 percent abrasions and lacerations, 14 percent punctures, and 11 percent burns and scalds. The figures add up to more than 100 percent, since many of the children suffered multiple injuries.

As might be expected, the parents most commonly involved in such behavior appear to be emotionally unstable or mentally disordered. Alcoholic fathers are commonly found in the group, particularly in cases of rape and child-beating, but disturbed mothers appear to be worse offenders, in that more mothers than fathers kill their infants. Some of the abused children are illegitimate, but most are not. Usually the parents are between 20 and 40 years of age, and most live in poverty. A large percentage, having themselves been reared with neglect and brutality, showed little or no remorse for their cruel behavior; thus brutality tends to breed brutality.

Based on Earl (1965), Flynn (1970), Gardner (1967), Helfer and Kempe (1968), Loper (1970), and Terr (1970).

contact, in which the mother may sleep with the child for years and be subtly seductive in her relationships with him.

Different parental motivations may lead to overprotection, but we may note in passing that an early study by Levy (1945) found that in an experimental group of abnormally protective mothers, 75 percent had little in common with their husbands. Such maternal reactions appeared to represent a compensatory type of behavior in which the mother attempted, through her contact with the child, to gain satisfactions that normally should have been obtained in her marriage. It is not uncommon in such cases for the mother to call the child her "lover" and actually to encourage the child in behaviors somewhat typical of courting.

In a study of the family background of children referred to a child guidance clinic, Jenkins (1968) found that those youngsters characterized as "overanxious" were likely to have an infantilizing, overprotective mother. In shielding the child from every danger, this type of mother denies him needed opportunities for reality testing and development of essential competencies. In addition, her overprotection tells him, in effect, that she regards him as incapable of fending for himself. It is not surprising that such children often reach adolescence and young adulthood feeling inadequate and threatened by a dangerous world. Although girls may also be the victims of parental overprotection, the effects seem to be more serious for boys, who tend to exhibit passivity, lack of initiative, and overdependency (Kagan & Moss, 1962).

Closely related to overprotection is restrictiveness. Here the parents rigidly enforce restrictive rules and standards and give the child little autonomy or freedom for growing in his own way. Whether such objections were justified or not, Douvan and Adelson (1966) found that "parental restriction" was the most common complaint of adolescent girls with regard to their parents. The effects of severe restrictiveness appear to vary considerably, depending on the sex of the child, the severity and duration of the restraints, the age of the child when the limitations are introduced, and whether the parents had initially been rather permissive and then imposed restrictions because they thought the child or adolescent was misusing his freedom.

In some instances, early and severe parental restrictions appear to result in the perpetuation of an "infantile conscience," in that the individual blindly accepts the standards he has been taught. In other instances, the adolescent rebels against his severe restrictions, and goes to the other extreme. As we shall see, this conflict between violent rebellion and submission is not infrequently reflected in the sexual behavior of delinquent girls. Rebellion frequently leads to anxiety and feelings of guilt, and so does not satisfactorily solve the problem. Of course, some form of rebellion often occurs as a first step in breaking out of excessive parental restrictions, and in the long run may prove constructive—provided that the individual achieves a value pattern he can live with. However, the process of rebellion may itself be a highly stressful one, and is often accompanied by maladaptive behavior patterns.

In a review of available literature Becker (1964) concluded that while restrictiveness may foster well-controlled, socialized behavior, it also tends to nurture fear, dependency, submission, repressed hostility, and some dulling of intellectual striving. In a study of young adult college men who appeared seriously alienated from the society around them, Keniston (1967) implicated severe restrictiveness, as well as other parental inadequacies.

3. *Overpermissiveness and indulgence.* Although it happens less commonly than is popularly supposed, sometimes one or both parents cater to the child's slightest whims and in so doing fail to teach and reward desirable standards of behavior. In essence, the parent surrenders the running of the home to an uninhibited son or daughter. Pollack (1968), for example, has quoted a permissive father who finally rebelled at the tyranny of his nine-year-old daughter, and in a near tantrum exploded with: "I want one thing clearly understood—I live here, too!" (p. 28)

Overly indulged children have been found to be characteristically spoiled, selfish, inconsiderate, and demanding (Becker, 1964; Watson, 1965). Sears (1961) found that high permissiveness and low punishment in the home were correlated positively with antisocial, aggressive behavior—particularly during middle and later childhood. Unlike the rejected, emotionally deprived child, who often finds it difficult to enter into warm interpersonal relationships, the indulged child enters readily into such relationships but exploits people for his own purposes in the same way that he has learned to exploit his parents. In dealing with authority, such a child is usually rebellious since, for so long, he has had his own way. The overly indulged child also tends to be impatient, to approach problems in an aggressive and demanding manner, and to find it difficult to accept present frustrations in the interests of long-range goals.

The fact that his important and pampered status in the home does not transfer automatically to the outside world may come as a great shock to the indulged youngster; and confusion and adjustive difficulties may occur when "reality" forces him to reassess his assumptions about himself and his world. As a 25-year-old woman in psychotherapy reflected:

"The worst mistake my parents made was giving me free rein. I was an only child, so my parents treated me like a queen. They made me think I could always have everything I wanted—not just money, but privileges. I wish they had set some limitations, because when I got out in the world I found things different." (Pollack, 1968, p. 28)

4. *Unrealistic demands.* Some parents place excessively strong pressures on their children to excel in school and other activities. Where the child has the capacity for exceptionally high-level performance, things may work out, but often the child is never quite able to live up to parental expectations and demands. If he improves his grade from a C to a B, he may be asked why he did not get an A. If he succeeds in getting an A, the next step is to attain the highest A in his class. The parents seem to be telling the child that he could do better if he tried, and that he is not good enough the way he is. But no matter how hard he tries, he always seems to fail in the eyes of his parents and, ultimately, in his own eyes as well—a fact that results in painful frustration and self-devaluation.

One need only observe a child's eager "Watch me, Mommy," as he demonstrates some new achievement, to understand how important success and recognition are to healthy development. And research studies, such as those of Coopersmith (1967), have shown that high parental ex-

pectations are both common and desirable. Such expectations, however, need to be realistic, and to take into consideration the capabilities and temperament of the child. Too often, such standards become a matter of what the parents value rather than what the child may need. Thus a professional football player may have his heart set on his son's following in his footsteps, when actually the son lacks both capability and interest. In some instances unrealistic demands may take the form of parental overdependence on the child. Perhaps being unhappily married or in other ways failing to find a meaningful and fulfilling life, the parents may focus on the child for meeting their own needs.

Although some lack of success is inevitable, parents who promote failures by their excessive demands undermine the child's sense of adequacy and thus tend to discourage further effort on his part. Almost invariably he comes to feel, "I can't do it, so why try?" Even where the child has the ability to live up to parental expectations he may be under such sustained pressure that little room is left to him for spontaneity or development in his own right. Some of these children may get back at their parents by passive resistance and refusal to achieve—thus depriving the parents of their cherished goals for the child.

Not infrequently, unrealistic parental demands focus around moral standards—particularly with regard to sex, alcohol, and related matters. Thus the parents may instill in the child the view that masturbation or any other sexual activity is terribly sinful and can lead only to moral and physical degeneration. The child who accepts such rigid parental standards is likely to face many guilt-arousing and self-devaluating conflicts. For, despite his attempts at controlling his thoughts and actions, the adolescent may engage in masturbation or other sexual activities—with consequent feelings of guilt, moral weakness, and lack of self-control. Such anxiety-arousing failures are, of course, devastating to feelings of self-esteem; and such unrealistic attitudes tend to foster rigid and restricted personalities.

In still other instances, parental demands are unrealistically low, and the parents do not care what the child does so long as he stays out of trouble and has a reasonably good time. Coopersmith (1967) found that the children of such parents were significantly lower in both achievement and self-esteem than were children whose parents had high but realistic expectations for them. Unrealistic expectations and demands—either too high, too low, or distorted and rigid—thus can be important causes of faulty development and maladjustment.

5. *Faulty discipline.* Parents have been particularly confused during recent years with respect to appropriate forms of discipline. Sometimes a misinterpretation of psychological findings and theories has led to the view that all punishment and frustration should be avoided lest the child be fixated in his development. In other cases parents have taken the view of "spare the rod and spoil the child," and have resorted to excessively harsh discipline. And in still other cases, the parents have seemed to lack general guidelines, punishing the child one day and ignoring or even rewarding him the next for doing the same or similar things.

As we have noted, overpermissiveness and lack of discipline tend to produce a spoiled, inconsiderate, antisocially aggressive child—and an insecure one as well. On the other hand, overly severe or harsh discipline may have a variety of harmful effects, including fear and hatred of the punishing person, little initiative or spontaneity, and less friendly feelings toward others (Becker, 1964; Watson, 1965). When accompanied by rigid moral standards, overly severe discipline is likely to result in a seriously repressed child who lacks spontaneity and warmth and devotes much effort toward controlling his own unacceptable impulses. Such children often subject themselves to severe self-recrimination and self-punishment for real or imagined mistakes and misdeeds. Overly severe discipline, combined with overrestrictiveness, also tends to incite rebellion and socially deviant behavior as the child grows older and is subjected increasingly to outside influences that may be incompatible with the views and practices of his parents (Winder & Rau, 1962).

Similarly, inconsistent discipline makes it difficult for the child to establish stable values for guiding his behavior. When he is punished one time and ignored or rewarded the next for the same behavior, he is at a loss as to what behavior is appropriate. Deur and Parke (1970) found that children with a history of inconsistent reward and punishment for aggressive behavior

In this drawing, a woman in therapy depicts herself as a child alone and isolated, rejected even by mother figures.

were more resistant to punishment and also to the extinction of their aggressive behavior than were children who had been subjected to more consistent discipline. This finding appears to corroborate earlier findings of antisocial aggression in children subjected to inconsistent discipline by their parents (Rosenthal, 1962; Sears et al., 1957). In one early study McCord, McCord, and Zola (1959) reported that erratic punishment procedures were highly correlated with criminal behavior.

Similar to inconsistency of discipline in its effect on a child's behavior is the tendency of some parents to threaten punishment for certain acts and then not to follow through with the punishment when the acts are committed. In such cases the child soon learns that his parents do not mean what they say, and he proceeds to do as he wishes (Pollack, 1968).

Since punishment is self-devaluating, it is considered important for a parent to make it clear that in disapproving the child's behavior he is not condemning or rejecting the child himself. Furthermore, if the child is to develop needed inner controls, it seems essential that he have a clear view of the behavior that is expected of him, and that consistent and positive methods be worked out for dealing with infractions. In general, it would appear that freedom should be commensurate with the child's maturity and ability to use it constructively.

6. *Communication failure.* As we shall see, limited and inadequate communication patterns are common among socially disadvantaged families—in which parents may discourage children from asking questions and in other ways fail to foster the information exchange essential for intellectual stimulation and growth. However, faulty communication is by no means limited to socially disadvantaged families; and it may take several different forms. Some parents are too busy with their own concerns to listen to their children and try to understand the conflicts and pressures they are facing. As a consequence, they often fail to give the child needed support and assistance during crisis periods. Other parents may have forgotten that the world often looks different to a child or adolescent and that rapid social change can lead to a very real communication gap between generations.

In other instances faulty communication may take more deviant forms. In their discussion of pathological communication, Watzlawick, Beavin, and Jackson (1967) cite a passage from *Through the Looking Glass* in which Alice's straightforward communication is corrupted by the "brainwashing" approach of the Red and White Queens. These two accuse Alice of trying to deny something because of her "state of mind":

"'I'm sure I didn't mean—' Alice was beginning but the Red Queen interrupted her impatiently.
"'That's just what I complain of! You should have meant! What do you suppose is the use of a child without any meaning? Even a joke should have a meaning—and a child is more important than a joke, I hope. You couldn't deny that, even if you tried with both hands.'
"'I don't deny things with my hands,' Alice objected.
"'Nobody said you did,' said the Red Queen. 'I said you couldn't if you tried.'
"'She is in that state of mind,' said the White Queen, 'that she wants to deny something—only she doesn't know what to deny!'

"'A nasty, vicious temper,' the Red Queen remarked: and then there was an uncomfortable silence for a minute or two."

The author was apparently intuitively aware of the effects of this kind of illogical communication, for after some additional harassment, he mercifully has Alice faint.

Although the preceding illustration is an extreme example of pathological communication, some parents do apparently follow similar patterns. One type of such inconsistent and contradictory communication by the parent—a communication that conveys contradictory messages—has been referred to by Bateson (1960) as the *double bind.* For example, a mother may complain of her son's lack of affection toward her; but when he tries to be demonstrative, she freezes up and shows strong disapproval. Similarly, parents may convey one message by their behavior and another by their verbalizations. Thus a parent may deplore lying and admonish his son to "never tell a lie"; but it is apparent to the son that his father lies a good deal himself.

The double-bind phenomenon and other faulty communication patterns require further study before their precise effects on development can be ascertained. However, faulty parent-child communications have been found to be more common in the background of emotionally disturbed adolescents and young adults than among those more adequately adjusted (Bateson, 1960; Carson, 1969; Lennard & Bernstein, 1969; Lu, 1962; Mishler & Waxler, 1965). Apparently, if a child's parents consistently induce him to respond to incongruous messages, his behavior may generalize so that he will interpret and deal with the messages of others in comparable and maladaptive ways.

7. *Sibling rivalry.* When a child feels that more parental attention and love are directed to a brother or sister than to himself, or when a new arrival in the family replaces him as the center of attention, adjustment difficulties commonly arise. In younger children these changes are typically of a regressive nature; thus the child may wet himself, resort to baby talk, show off, or evidence other behavior designed to elicit parental notice. Not infrequently the child may threaten to injure the new baby and may actually pinch or hit him. However, the child soon learns that such activity leads to a further deterioration of parental relationships, and therefore he usually works out more indirect and covert methods of expressing his hostility—such as belittling, tattling, or referring to the younger sibling with contempt.

Generally, such undesirable attitudes and reactions can be prevented or alleviated by preparing the child in advance for the advent of the new baby. Even without such preparation, most children make a fairly rapid adjustment to the new situation without apparent long-range damage. In some cases, however, parents do "play favorites" and focus their interest and affection on one child in preference to others. For example, the father may make it very clear that he identifies himself with the accomplishments of the older son rather than the younger, or with the son and not the daughter. If one child is exceptionally attractive or has special talents, a parent may tend to focus his attention and approval on this sibling, to the neglect of the others. Such parental reactions are, of course, likely to lead to intense jealousy and to feelings of insecurity and devaluation on the part of the less-favored child.

Although there is a dearth of research data on the long-range effects of sibling relationships, it is apparent that such interactions involve intense interpersonal relationships over a sustained period of time, and that siblings often serve as close-range models for one another. Einstein and Moss (1967) have suggested that areas of interaction among siblings which may have an important effect on development are: feelings of inferiority or superiority; wishes to be like or different from the sibling; sharing; sexual behavior; rivalry or jealousy; support or devaluation; and alliances against parents, peers, or outsiders. Toman (1970) has concluded that birth order has much to do with sibling rivalry as well as sibling relationships in general, and that such relationships tend to generalize to significant others in their lives. For example, first-borns are presumably prone to find relationships which they can dominate.

If relationships between siblings are fraught with jealousy and hostility or take other undesirable forms—as where an older sibling is an undesirable model or an older brother forces sexual relations upon a younger sister—they are likely to have an adverse effect on development. On the other hand, desirable sibling models and emotionally supportive relationships may have highly beneficial effects upon development—and may even go far toward compensating for other family deficiencies.

8. *Undesirable parental models.* Children observe and imitate the patterns of behavior they see around them. Bandura (1962) found that children who watched aggressive models were themselves more aggressive later when frustrated than were members of a control group, while a third group who had watched nonaggressive models made the most nonaggressive responses to frustration. It was also found that the learning of coping techniques can be accelerated by the provision of adult models with whom the child can identify, particularly when such imitative behavior is reinforced by subtle or obvious approval from these models.

Ordinarily the child's key models are his parents, who serve as guides and educators. Their behavior can have a highly beneficial or detrimental effect on the way a youngster learns to perceive, think, feel, and act. The parent provides an undesirable model if he has faulty reality and value assumptions, if he depends excessively on defense mechanisms in coping with his problems—as when he consistently projects the blame for his own mistakes upon others—or if he refuses to face and deal realistically with family problems. Similarly, the parent who lies and cheats or espouses criminal values is an undesirable model, as is the parent who shows a discrepancy between the values he claims to hold and those reflected in his actual behavior.

A parent may also serve as an undesirable model if he is emotionally disturbed, addicted to alcohol or drugs, or otherwise maladjusted. In his extensive study of emotional disturbances in children, Jenkins (1966) found that nearly half of a group of children diagnosed as "overanxious-neurotic" had mothers who were described as neurotic because of extreme anxiety, nervousness, and related symptoms; concurrently, the children characterized by habitual delinquent behavior tended to come from a background combining poverty, parental neglect, a bad neighborhood, and an inadequate father figure. Similarly, Anthony (1969) found a much higher incidence of maladaptive behavior among children with

IMITATIVE LEARNING OF AGGRESSION FROM ADULT MODELS

The extent to which children may imitate adult models is graphically illustrated in a study by Bandura et al. (1963). In this sequence, an adult model (left) batters the head of a large inflated doll with a mallet.

After viewing an adult model perform such actions, in person or on film, each child in the experimental group underwent mild frustration and was then observed in a playroom supplied with a variety of toys—including crayons, a tea set, a mallet, a dart gun, and an inflated doll—which could be used in aggressive or nonaggressive play. A control group (who saw no aggressive model) underwent the same mild frustration. Children who had seen the adult model were nearly twice as aggressive in their play activities as the control group. Some children, such as those depicted here, imitated the adult model almost exactly.

Social groups differ markedly in the extent to which aggressive behavior occurs and in the exposure of children to adult models of aggression. We shall elaborate on this point in our discussion of violence in Chapter 18.

psychotic parents than among a control group with nonpsychotic parents.

Undesirable parental models are undoubtedly an important reason why mental disorders, delinquency, crime, and other forms of maladaptive behavior tend to run in families. But it should be pointed out that there is nothing inevitable in the effects of parental pathology on the child's development. The pathology of one parent may be compensated for by the wisdom and concern of the other; or an alcoholic parent may perhaps serve as a "negative model"—showing the child what he does *not* want to be like. Kadushin (1967) has cited a number of studies in which children coming from homes with undesirable parental models have grown up into successful and well-adjusted adults. As Chess, Thomas, and Birch (1965) have found:

"We see loving mothers whose children have problems. And we see very sick mothers with healthy and well-adjusted children who are apparently immune to the mother's pathology and the erratic patterns of care." (p. 13)

Although the reasons for such favorable outcomes are not clear, these findings should be borne in mind as we turn to a brief summary of types of unhealthy homes—homes characterized by pathological characteristics of the family as a group.

Pathogenic families. Whereas in the previous sections we considered specific patterns of faulty intrafamilial relationships, the present discussion will focus on more comprehensive prototypes or models of family pathology. With current emphasis being placed on the study of the family as a group and the interaction of all family members, the maladjustive behavior pattern developed by a child is now frequently viewed as fostered by his general family environment rather than by his specific relationships with one or both parents, or by his relationships with a particular sibling. An early study by Fisher and others (1959) concluded that: (1) normal adjustment of the child is fostered by parents who individually are well adjusted and who together have a harmonious relationship; (2) neutoric adjustment of the child is fostered by parents who are maladjusted individually but still able to maintain a moderately good relationship with each other; and (3) the possibility of later schizophrenic breakdown is greatest where parents are individually maladjusted as well as being discordant in their marital relationship. Similarly, Stabenau and his associates (1965) found that the family organization of a group of delinquent children was unstable, the emotions of individual members quite artificial and uncontrolled, and the parental roles not reliably executed; in contrast, they found the family organization of schizophrenic children to be rigidly stable and lacking in warmth, with parental roles being inflexible and often distorted. The families of normal children, on the other hand, showed stability of organization, warm, affectionate relationships, and reliability of parental role fulfillment. Later in our discussion we shall examine in more detail the family backgrounds that appear to be related to various patterns of abnormal behavior.

In reviewing the effects of the family system on development, we again encounter the problem of establishing criteria for differentiating between what is "healthy" and what is "pathogenic"; for, as in the case of the individual, we have no model of the "ideal" family. However, several investigators have attempted a typology of pathogenic families which clearly have a detrimental influence on child development in our society. For present purposes, we shall briefly describe four such types of families.

1. *The inadequate family.* This type of family is characterized by inability to cope with the ordinary problems of family living. It lacks the resources, physical or psychological, for meeting demands with which most families can satisfactorily cope. Consequently, the inadequate family relies heavily on continued outside assistance and support in resolving its problems. The incompetencies of such a family may stem from immaturity, lack of education, mental retardation, or other shortcomings of the parents. Sometimes, of course, demands are so severe that they overtax the adjustive resources of even highly adequate families.

A family that is floundering against odds too great for its resources, for whatever reason, cannot give its children the feeling of safety and security they need, or adequately guide them in the development of essential competencies. Nor can financial or other outside assistance be counted on to meet the needs of such families; for families, like individuals, need to feel they are self-directing and in control of their own destinies.

2. *The disturbed family.* At all socioeconomic levels we find some parents who, because of personal instability, interact with other people in ways that are destructive to others as well as themselves. Parents with grossly eccentric and abnormal personalities may keep the home in constant emotional turmoil.

Disturbed homes may involve many pathological patterns, but such homes appear to have certain characteristics in common: (a) the presence of parents who are fighting to maintain their own equilibrium and who are unable to give the child the love and guidance that he needs; (b) exposure of the child to a highly irrational home environment and faulty parental models; and (c) almost inevitably, the enmeshment of the child in the emotional conflicts of the parents at the expense of his own development. In general, it would appear that maladjusted parents who are able to establish a harmonious relationship with each other are less damaging to the child than are maladjusted parents who live in disharmony (Bowen, 1960; Fisher et al., 1959; Satir, 1967).

Parental quarreling, bickering, nagging, and general tension are unfortunate conditions for the growing child. They represent a threat to his base of operations, to which he may respond by developing tension and anxiety himself. Somewhat typical here is the college student who told of his severe feelings of insecurity during his childhood because of the periodic quarrels of his parents. He stated that he would sit outside on the steps, apprehensively biting his nails and anticipating the breaking up of his home. Often, too, parents may come to resent the child as the only reason for maintaining the unhappy marriage.

3. *The antisocial family.* Here the family espouses values not accepted by the wider community. In some families the parents are overtly or covertly engaged in behavior that violates the standards and interests of society, and they may be chronically in difficulty with the law. Such antisocial values usually handicap marital and other family relationships, as well as providing undesirable models for the child.

Children in such families may be encouraged in dishonesty, deceit, and other undesirable behavior patterns; or they may simply observe and imitate the behavior of undesirable parental models. In some cases, children may develop a high degree of courage, self-discipline, and loyalty to the family group at the expense of identification with the society as a whole. More often, the models they see are immature and self-seeking, and the social interactions they observe and take part in are shallow and manipulative—a poor preparation for mature, responsible adulthood. Here it is of interest to note that

Langner and Michael (1963), in an extensive study of mental health and mental disorder in a congested urban area, found a higher mental health risk for children who disapproved of their parents' character than for those who experienced a broken home.

4. *The disrupted family.* Disrupted families are families that are incomplete as a result of death, divorce, separation, or other conditions involving the loss of a parent. The effects of family disruption are experienced by the remaining parent, of course, no less than by the children. And the stress on this parent—usually the mother —further adds to the insecurity of the home.

A number of studies have shown the traumatic effects divorce can have on a child. Feelings of insecurity may be aggravated by conflicting loyalties and, sometimes, by the spoiling he receives while staying with one or the other parent—maybe not the one he would prefer to be with. It would appear that divorce is much more traumatic for children whose homes were happy prior to the divorce than for those who came from unhappy homes (Biller, 1970; Westman, Cline, Swift & Kramer, 1969).

Loss of the mother during the early critical period of socialization is likely to be more detrimental than the same loss at a later age; the loss of a father is likely to be more serious for a son than for a daughter. The boy who is brought up only by a mother suffers a definite lack in his dealings with other children who have protective father figures. In addition, he suffers from the lack of a model to help him in patterning his behavior

SUMMARY CHART OF FAULTY PARENT-CHILD RELATIONSHIPS

UNDESIRABLE CONDITION	TYPICAL EFFECT ON CHILD'S PERSONALITY DEVELOPMENT
Rejection	Feelings of anxiety, insecurity, low self-esteem, negativism, hostility, attention-seeking, loneliness, jealousy, and slowness in conscience development
Overprotection—domination	Submissiveness, lack of self-reliance, dependence in relations with others, low self-evaluation, some dulling of intellectual striving
Overpermissiveness—overindulgence	Selfishness, demanding attitude, inability to tolerate frustration, rebelliousness toward authority, excessive need of attention, lack of responsibility, inconsiderateness, exploitativeness in interpersonal relationships
Perfectionism, with unrealistic demands	Lack of spontaneity, rigid conscience development, severe conflicts, tendency toward guilt and self-condemnation if there is failure to live up to parental demands
Faulty discipline:	
Lack of discipline	Inconsiderateness, aggressiveness, and antisocial tendencies
Harsh, overly severe discipline	Fear, hatred of parent, little initiative or spontaneity, lack of friendly feelings toward others
Inconsistent discipline	Difficulty in establishing stable values for guiding behavior; tendency toward highly aggressive behavior
Contradictory demands and communications	As in case of "double bind" communications, the tendency toward confusion, lack of an integrated frame of reference, unclear self-identity, lack of initiative, self-devaluation
Undesirable parental models	The learning of faulty values, formulation of unrealistic goals, development of maladaptive coping patterns

The exact effects of faulty parent-child relationships on later behavior depends on many factors, including the age of the child, the constitutional and personality makeup of the child at the time, the duration and degree of the unhealthy relationship, his perception of the relationship, and the total family setting and life context, including the presence or absence of alleviating conditions and whether or not subsequent experiences tend to reinforce or correct early damage. There is no uniform pattern of pathogenic family relationship underlying the development of later psychopathology, but the conditions we have discussed often act as predisposing factors.

along masculine lines; conversely, the boy who is brought up only by a father may lack needed understanding of the female role. In his extensive review of the literature on the effects of father loss on a boy, Biller (1970) has pointed to a variety of detrimental effects, involving self-control, cognitive functioning, interpersonal relationships, playing the male sex role, and the higher incidence of later psychopathology.

Although father absence appears to have more effect on boys, it may also have detrimental effects on girls, as indicated by the bitterness of a daughter of a naval officer who stated, "I despise my father. He was never there. He was in the Navy 120 years." (*Time*, 1967)

Regardless of cause, broken homes deprive the child of a needed adult model. Of course, the long-range effects of family disruption may be minimized if substitute models are available, if the remaining family members are able to compensate in part for the missing parent, or if the home is reconstituted by a successful remarriage that provides an adequate environment for child rearing.

A number of studies have shown that a disproportionate number of juvenile delinquents and adult criminals were raised in broken homes. In California, for example, 75 percent of the state's juvenile offenders and 50 percent of the inmates of its adult penal institutions come from this type of disordered background. Similar findings have been compiled for Norway by Bratfos (1967). However, it is also necessary to remember that there is a higher proportion of broken homes among the economically and socially disadvantaged—a fact which indicates that other conditions besides father- or mother-absence may contribute to faulty development. Apparently one significant factor is the reason for which the home has been divided (that is, separation, divorce, or death). For example, in an interesting study conducted with more than two thousand young male subjects, Douglas and his associates (1966) found that even when educational and social-class status of parents were ruled out as factors, delinquency was associated nearly twice as often with homes broken by divorce or separation than with homes broken by the death of parents or homes that were intact.

The preceding categories are by no means discrete, and a given family may show a wide range of maladaptive behaviors. The point is that these family patterns have been labeled "pathogenic" because of the high frequency with which they are associated with problems in child development and later psychopathology. Again, it should be emphasized that although healthy parents and a healthy family environment are more likely to produce healthy children than are emotionally maladjusted parents and an unhealthy family environment, this relationship is not inevitable. In fact, Victor and Mildred Goertzel (1962) looked back over the lives of four hundred eminent people and found that only fifty-eight had come from relatively untroubled homes; the remainder had come from homes that demonstrated "considerable pathology."

It is also important to emphasize that family relationships always represent an interaction—not just a one-way influence of the parent or family on the child. We cannot assume that the parent's behavior is always the independent variable, and the child's behavior and development the dependent variables. In fact, Devor (1970) has studied the effects of "children as agents in socializing parents."

Finally, it may be pointed out that pathogenic interpersonal relationships and interactions are by no means confined to the family, but may involve peer group and other non-family members as well. Particularly during adolescence, when the young person is becoming progressively independent of parental controls, are his peer group and other relationships outside the family likely to influence his further development. If such relationships are emotionally hurtful and damaging, or lead to undesirable values, or block his personal growth, they may exert a strong influence toward faulty development.

SOCIAL PATHOLOGY

When there are conditions in the community or larger society that have pathogenic effects on the development and behavior of people exposed to them, the situation is one of *social pathology*. In this category there are a wide range of conditions, including poverty, crime, racial prejudice and discrimination, and social disorganization.

In some instances an entire society may be considered pathological, as in the case of a military dictatorship that indoctrinates its youth with beliefs and values leading to intolerance, disregard for the rights of others, cruelty, and glorification of force.

In our own society, attention has centered in recent years on the closely interrelated problems of poverty, racial prejudice and discrimination, and anomie and alienation. We shall not attempt to deal in depth with the complexities of these problems here—for these and related problems will be discussed in Chapter 18—but rather shall indicate their pathological effects on personality development.

Poverty and the disadvantaged child. Although poverty in the United States has progressively decreased, it has been estimated that the 1970 census would show that some 20 million Americans live in conditions of poverty.[1] The income of these people may be far higher than that of the average person in most other parts of the world; but by the standards of their own society, they are seriously deprived nonetheless. The gap between the socially disadvantaged and the advantaged represents a key social problem in our country, and a yet greater one for the world at large.

Adults who are trapped in low-income geographical locations, especially in the ghetto areas of big cities, are apt to be chronically submerged in a complex of difficult, and often insoluble, problems. Many such adults, as parents, lack both the material and the psychological resources necessary for the rearing of their children. So it is hardly surprising that in one study of 1414 children aged four to six, enrolled in an OEO Head Start project in Boston, 25 percent were found to have severe psychological difficulties, ranging from serious behavior problems to psychoses (Joint Commission on the Mental Health of Children, 1968). As Close (1965) has pointed out: "Being born to uneducated, unskilled and bewildered poverty-stricken parents could in itself be a major handicap even for the healthiest of babies."

Research studies of families in urban slum areas have delineated several prevalent family conditions that are detrimental to child development—or at least to the patterns of development that have come to be valued in our society.[2]

1. Lack of the cultural artifacts commonly associated with intellectual development and school readiness—such as books, magazines, toys, and self-instructional materials. Often such children have never been to a library, museum, or zoo. Although they may live only a few miles from a lake or ocean, they may never have seen it.

2. Limited parent-child communication and language usage. Parents often speak in short, disconnected sentences, and tend to discourage their children from asking questions. There is generally a lack of information exchange and intellectual stimulation.

3. Physical and often arbitrary punishment, rather than explanation and persuasion, used in child discipline. Often such treatment results in the child's feeling fearful and hostile toward his parents and having an impaired ability to appraise his own behavior rationally or evaluate the probable outcome of given actions.

4. Noise, overcrowding, and disorganization. Despite close proximity of family members there is often little coordinated activity. In one study, for example, only half of the children regularly ate meals with their parents (Keller, 1963). Disorganization is further shown in the high incidence of broken homes.

5. Inability of parents to serve as effective models and teachers. The incompetence of such parents with regard to communication with and instruction of their children is well brought out in the study of Hess and Shipman (1965), summarized on page 163. The children, in turn, do not look on their parents or other adults as persons of whom to ask questions or from whom to expect help.

Studies of "socially disadvantaged" children raised under such conditions, as contrasted with studies of children raised in typical middle-class homes, have revealed a number of limitations and distortions in development, including: (a) inadequate language development and specific limitations with regard to the ability to discriminate, categorize, and conceptualize; (b) deficien-

---

[1] *Poverty is defined in the U.S. as a total income of $3,335 a year or less for a family of four at 1967 prices. For an excellent discussion of the types of poverty throughout the world, the reader is referred to Van Den Berghe (1969).

[2] Among the references utilized here are Baratz and Baratz (1970), Cohen (1969), Dawson et al. (1969), Deutsch et al. (1967), Eisenberg (1969), Karnes, Teska, and Hodgins (1970), Moore (1968), Radin (1968), Scott (1967), Smith and Bissell (1970), and Werner (1969).

cies in problem-solving ability, with slowness and lack of flexibility in intellectual functioning; (c) motivational difficulties, such as apathy, lack of hope, and little desire for personal growth; (d) inadequate inner controls—reality, possibility, and value assumptions—and continued dependence on external controls; and (e) self-devaluation, resentment, and lack of a sense of ability to achieve or to exert control over events and one's future.

As we noted in our discussion of maternal deprivation, malnutrition and extreme lack of needed stimulation and learning opportunities during infancy and early childhood have been associated with mental retardation. Thus it is not surprising that 75 percent of the nation's mentally retarded come from urban and rural slums (President's Committee on Mental Retardation, 1968).

Although such children do not lack a culture, they are disadvantaged in the sense that their upbringing, with all of its attendant hardships and obstacles to development, fails to prepare them for competent performance in school and society. These youngsters come to school with problems of acculturation, impaired capacity to differentiate and conceptualize formal learning experiences, and less well-developed language skills and motivation than school tasks require. The result is lower performance and their designation as "slow learners"; and this classification, in turn, further reduces their already low levels of self-esteem and self-expectation. In addition, the learning and socialization processes carried on in school tend to follow middle-class standards and to deprecate such children's heritage, their way of life, their parents, and ultimately, themselves.

Unfortunately, this process is also a cumulative one. At the time these children begin kindergarten or first grade they are, as a group, about two years behind others of their age (Hess & Shipman, 1965). And they tend to fall proportionately farther behind during their subsequent years in school. As a consequence, it is much more likely that socially disadvantaged children will drop out of school. In fact, the great majority of the million or more students who each year terminate their schooling before completion of high school come from socially disadvantaged homes; in the black ghetto areas, the chances are only about one in three that a child will finish secondary school. These dropouts then find themselves at a serious disadvantage in our increasingly technological society, and are forced to take low-paying, menial jobs or to seek welfare—thus perpetuating the "culture of poverty."

Of course, not all disadvantaged families are pathogenic in structure or effect, and a considerable number do manage to rear healthy children. But the odds do not favor success; for such children are also exposed to the pathological community environment that surrounds the family, with its high incidence of delinquency, crime, mental disorders, undesirable models, and pervasive resentment and despair. And the pathogenic effects of racial prejudice and discrimination characteristic of the greater society may be added to those intrinsic to ghetto culture.

Racial prejudice and discrimination. Racial prejudice is loudly decried in our society, yet it seems to be among our most ingrained attitudes. All of society suffers as a result of this prejudice, but the victims lose most by it. In his book dealing with the Negro ghetto, Clark (1965) described the pernicious effects on child development of ghetto living, in combination with racial prejudice:

"Human beings who are forced to live under ghetto conditions and whose daily experience tells them that almost nowhere in society are they respected and granted the ordinary dignity and courtesy accorded to others will, as a matter of course, begin to doubt their own worth. Since every human being depends upon his cumulative experiences with others for clues as to how he should view and value himself, children who are consistently rejected understandably begin to question and doubt whether they, their family, and their group really deserve no more respect from the larger society than they receive. These doubts become the seeds of a pernicious self- and group-hatred and the Negro's complex, debilitating prejudice against himself. . . ." (pp. 63–65)

In a subsequent article Clark (1967) pursued the same theme:

"To the Negro child the most serious injury seems to be in the concept of self-worth related directly to skin color itself. . . . By the age of seven most Negro children have accepted the reality that they are, after all, dark-skinned. But the stigma remains; they have been forced to recognize themselves as inferior. Few if any

Prominent among the victims of racial prejudice and discrimination are the children, like this boy being brought up in an urban ghetto.

Negroes ever fully lose that sense of shame and self-hatred. . . . Because school is a central activity at his age, his sense of inferiority is revealed most acutely in his lack of confidence in himself as a student, lack of motivation to learn, and in problems of behavior—a gradual withdrawal or a growing rebellion." (p. 36)

One index of the toll that such conditions take is Harlem's rate of admissions to mental hospitals —which is three times that of the rest of New York City—and its startlingly high rates for suicide, drug abuse, delinquency, crime, and other maladaptive behaviors. Racial discrimination, poverty, and social disorganization tend to debase and confuse human beings. Children reared in such a setting have the almost impossible task of trying to learn what is predictable and possible, of striving to develop healthy motives and values, and of attempting to achieve educational and other competencies essential for effective participation in our highly technological society. A report of the National Institute for Mental Health (1969) concluded that

". . . a child of parents at the bottom of the socioeconomic scale who comes into the world with the same basic intellect as a child of parents at the top is less likely, for lack of stimulation and opportunity, to develop it. Moreover, poverty often interferes with the development not only of intelligence but also of a healthy personality. There is evidence, too, of an association between poverty on the one hand and, on the other, ignorance and distrust of democratic ideals and institutions. Violence, too, breeds in an atmosphere of deprivation and despair." (p. 2)

Thus we see the beginning of the vicious circle of educational underachievement, menial jobs, broken homes, and the perpetuation of the culture of poverty. And from a broader sociological viewpoint, such conditions provide the fuel for protests and riots. It is against this background that the movement toward black power has developed, with its insistence on social, educational, political, and economic equality of opportunity for black people.

Anomie and alienation. The term *anomie* refers to a state of disregulation in which mutually agreed-upon social norms are no longer effective in controlling man's actions. It is a condition that commonly occurs during periods of social disruption and change, when value conflicts tend to spread through the social system so that there is a lack of widely shared norms to guide and control group goals and behavior. Symptoms of anomie in our society are reflected in the generation gap, in troubled race relations, in the conflict between the "have's" and "have-nots," and in the disharmony inherent in many people's relations to the broader society.

The consequences of anomie are *alienation*—as reflected in such symptoms as "rootlessness," a lack of authentic relationships with others, a confused sense of self-identity, inability to find satisfying values and meaning, and a belief that one is powerless to do anything that will have any significance or effect.[1] Seaman (1966) and other investigators have pointed out that alienation, in turn, results in alienated behavior—such as racial and religious prejudice, lack of concern for others, and political passivity or participation in movements that promise to usher in the millennium but have little practical effect or are actually nihilistic. Sager (1968) has also emphasized the relationship of alienation to violence, crime, and mental disorders; and May (1969) has even characterized contemporary society as "Our Schizoid World"—in which alienation leads to a sequence of identity confusion, apathy, powerlessness, and eventually, violence.

For those youths who feel alienated from their families as well as from the broader society, entering into maladaptive interpersonal relationships and group activities in an effort to find an alternative appears to be an ever present danger. Thus to gain feelings of acceptance, belongingness, and significance, a teen-ager may participate in the hard-core drug culture, join destructive and nihilistic youth movements, or even enter into a personally destructive relationship with another person. Some investigators have expressed concern that alienation from the family and the greater culture exposes the young person to becoming a captive of his own peers—to whom he may quite naturally turn for approval and support. As Riesman (1969) has put it: "As adult authority disintegrates, the young are more and more captives of each other" (p. 28).

INADEQUATE SELF-STRUCTURE

In Chapter 5 we noted that the self-structure is the center of the individual's world of experience and his reference point for evaluating and coping with his environment. We also noted that once the self-structure begins to develop, the individual tends to maintain it and to behave in ways consistent with it. Thus if the self-structure that emerges is faulty, it tends to be perpetuated as an unhealthy influence on subsequent person-ality development and hence to foster patterns of maladaptive behavior.

The development of an adequate self-structure can be related to the task of finding answers to three basic questions about oneself: (1) Who am I? (2) Where am I going? and (3) Why? We shall see that either a failure to find answers to these questions or the formulation of faulty answers leads to faulty development and to vicious circles, which by definition tend to perpetuate maladaptive behavior.

"Who am I?" The question "Who am I?" is by no means a simple one to answer. In modern life there appear to be three particular obstacles to the achievement and maintenance of an adequate answer. *First* is the possibility of adverse family and social influences—an impediment that is well exemplified in the case of the socially disadvantaged child. Subjected to poverty, discrimination, and lack of opportunity, such an individual may find it difficult to gain a clear-cut sense of his own identity—particularly one involving a positive self-image. Instead he may see himself as inferior and powerless in a hostile world, so that considerations of self-identity and self-determination appear irrelevant.

Second is the threat to a stable self-identity posed by the complex phenomenon of change. The factors that enter into an individual's self-identity are continually changing. These include his physical appearance, beliefs, competencies, and other attributes that he perceives as characteristic of himself, plus his social roles, group identifications, and other outer attributes with which he is ego-involved. Complicating this picture still further is the perceived threat of dehumanization. The individual may feel alienated, alone, and powerless in a computerized society that seems increasingly intent on reducing men to numbers and statistics rather than viewing each as a unique person. To achieve and maintain a clear-cut self-identity in the face of such constant inner and outer change is not an easy task.

Third is the danger of preferring dependence to independence. The point is well made by the existentialists that it takes courage to "be oneself" and to "shape oneself." Not only does this

---

[1]It is of interest to note that psychiatrists were formerly called *alienists*—and in some places still are—referring to persons who treat the "alienated" or insane.

choice of self-direction require that an individual seek values, make decisions, and take responsibility for the consequences; it also creates conflicts with group expectations and pressures. The inconsistency of adolescent behavior often reflects a very real ambivalence: the adolescent wants to be self-directing but hesitates to give up his security for the responsibilities that go with independence. Riesman (1950; 1969) has emphasized the tendency of modern man to immerse himself in the group—to be a sort of outer-directed "radar man" who lives as though he wore a receiving set on his head in order to receive signals from others as to what he should believe and how he should behave. He becomes dependent on the group in much the same way that a child is dependent on his parents—but at the expense of his own identity as a person.

Despite such difficulties, however, the achievement of a clear-cut and relatively stable sense of one's own identity is essential if the individual is to experience some measure of freedom for choice and self-determination and to see himself as the originator of his own actions.

Where am I going? During the adolescent and young adult period, the individual is making "plans" and acquiring the competencies needed for adult living—plans and competencies related to earning a living, achieving a satisfactory marriage, being a good parent, and contributing to his community and society. As Miller et al. (1960) have pointed out, if the individual is "planless"— unable to agree upon goals or plans that seem worthwhile to him—or if his plans are unrealistic or in conflict, he is in for difficulties. Even if he is able to make plans which he considers meaningful and likely to lead to a fulfilling life, he is faced with the additional task of developing the competencies essential for carrying them out. Four types of competencies appear essential to adequate self-direction; and the failure to achieve these competencies may be considered a key factor in the causation of maladaptive behavior.

1. *Inadequate physical competencies.* Here the basic concern is with keeping physically fit and protecting the body against disease. Maintaining a state of health contributes to a sense of well-being and adequacy, and also enhances a person's attractiveness to others. Conversely, a lack of physical fitness tends to produce chronic

---

ADOLESCENT CONFLICT: MEANINGLESSNESS AND ALIENATION AS SEEN BY THE BEATLES

"He's a real Nowhere Man,
Sitting in his nowhere land,
Making all his nowhere plans for nobody.
Doesn't have a point of view,
Knows not where he's going to,
Isn't he a bit like you and me?

Nowhere Man please listen,
You don't know what you're missing. Nowhere Man.
The world is at your command.

He's as blind as he can be,
Just sees what he wants to see,
Nowhere Man can you see me at all?

Nowhere Man don't worry
Take your time, don't hurry,
Leave it all till somebody else lends you a hand."

(Lennon & McCartney, 1965)

---

fatigue, impaired efficiency in learning and problem solving, and lowered resistance to disease. Problems that seem difficult to an individual in good physical condition may seem insurmountable to one who is "run down." Unquestionably, the failure of many emotionally upset people to maintain proper nutrition and rest contributes to their adjustive difficulties.

2. *Inadequate intellectual competencies.* Despite man's great potentialities for thinking, he is often very inefficient in solving his personal difficulties and contributing to the solution of group problems. Effective thinking is a highly skilled process—one that requires adequate information, training in methodology, accurate assumptions, and continual reality checks, including the use of feedback. Failure to fulfill these requirements is a major reason why man, with the best brain that has ever been evolved, often uses his intellect ineffectively. In a broad sense, intellectual competence also includes an adequate "briefing" on the nature of various crucial life problems, such as marriage, parenthood, occupation, and old age, which we are all likely to encounter.

3. *Inadequate emotional competencies.* Although man's emotions are important resources in his adjustive reservoir, they may present problems in terms of their expression and control. Anxiety, fear, anger, depression, guilt, and even love are all difficult emotions to handle effectively. Often people overreact to minor anxieties and fear, give way to chronic hostility, or suffer from exaggerated feelings of guilt. Realistic anxiety and worry are adaptive mechanisms that help an individual deal with threats and dangers, but when they are inappropriate to the stress situation, they become maladaptive. Anger and hostility are often constructive forces in helping a person overcome obstacles through aggressive action, but unbridled ire and sustained hostility complicate interpersonal relations and tend to isolate an individual from others. In extreme form, chronic resentment and hostility may lead to aggressive criminal or other antisocial activities. Similarly, normal feelings of guilt can prod a person to make needed changes in his attitudes and behavior; but exaggerated, morbid, or imagined guilt leads to pervasive feelings of devaluation, depression, and despair.

4. *Inadequate social competencies.* Most of man's needs can be met only through relationships with other people; thus the nature of interpersonal relationships has much to do with the satisfactions one gains in living. Whether an individual is attempting to attract a desired mate, achieve a happy marriage, promote a new idea or civic enterprise, or simply make friends, the outcome is heavily dependent on his competencies for dealing with and achieving authentic relationships with others. If he antagonizes people, tries to lean on them excessively, or seeks to dominate or exploit them, he is likely to find some of his own deepest psychological needs going unfulfilled. Many people become "unpopular," fail in their work, ruin their marriages, bring up maladjusted children, and go through life feeling alone and friendless because they cannot establish satisfying relationships with others.

Particularly in our highly complex and changing society, the individual who fails to develop these essential competencies is at a disadvantage in coping with the problems of living.

Why?   Why this life plan rather than another? What kind of life is good for human beings in general and for me in particular? What makes this goal desirable and that one undesirable? From the various alternatives we see open to us, we make choices in terms of what we see as realistic, desirable, and possible to achieve.

We have seen that the individual gradually builds a frame of reference—a set of assumptions concerning fact, possibility, and value—which provides him with a meaningful picture of himself and his world. Without such an inner cognitive map he would be incapable of pursuing consistent or purposeful action. If the individual's assumptions are inaccurate or poorly integrated, his perceiving and thinking will be impaired accordingly. In a general sense, faulty assumptions have important implications for adjustive behavior. First, an individual is put in a position of following an erroneous map. He may bristle at nonexistent bogeymen and be unaware of real hazards. To the extent that his view is distorted, he will adjust to a world that does not exist, and will inevitably make miscalculations that will lead to failure and self-devaluation. This is especially likely when an individual grossly overestimates or underestimates either his own abilities or the opportunities available to him. Too, the individual's assumptions concerning reality, value, and possibility determine what behavior he will avoid as likely to lead to frustration and hurt. For example, if he sees the world as a dangerous place, he may restrict his activities and maintain a generally defensive orientation to life. Or if he has perfectionistic moral values concerning sex, he may spend considerable energy fighting inner impulses that he considers dangerous, thereby becoming a rigid person who cannot afford the luxury of spontaneity or flexibility. In a rapidly changing society such as ours, which requires a good deal of flexibility, such individuals are constantly in danger of being thrown off balance.

Finally, serious conflicts, discrepancies, and imbalances among an individual's reality, possibility, and value assumptions—as, for example, between his self-concept and self-ideal—may impair his personality integration and contribute to his faulty development and maladjustment. In this context, it is also relevant to note that self-acceptance and self-esteem tend to be associated with inner integration and effective adjustment, whereas self-rejection and devaluation are commonly associated with seriously maladaptive behavior.

Unfortunately, a distorted frame of reference tends to be perpetuated. A person who sees the world as a jungle will be selectively sensitive to dishonesty, selfishness, and other characteristics that tend to support his point of view. Similarly, the individual with rigid views concerning the evilness of sex will find ample incidents to support his conclusions. We do not easily become aware of our errors in perception, because new situations, seen through distorted lenses, seem continually to revalidate our earlier perceptions. For this reason, faulty assumptions may seriously impair adjustment and lead to vicious circles and increasingly maladaptive behavior unless or until corrective measures are taken.

SEVERE STRESS

The various kinds of faulty development discussed in the preceding section can be viewed in a general way as predisposing factors in the causation of abnormal behavior. Genetic defects, constitutional vulnerabilities, physical handicaps, lack of adequate mothering, early trauma, pathogenic family patterns, social pathology, failure to develop an adequate self-structure—all of these conditions tend to impair the individual's ability to cope effectively with the problems of life.

In the present section we shall consider severe stress as another key element in the causation of psychopathology. Adaptive ability, as we have suggested, reflects an interplay between adjustive resources and adjustive demands. Thus an individual with faulty development may manage to "get along" if the demands made upon him are not great, but he may be wholly overwhelmed by problems that most other people could handle in stride. On the other hand, some adjustive demands are so great that they are severely taxing even on individuals with above-average competencies. The severity of stress depends, in short, both on the individual's resources and on the nature of the adjustive demand itself.

At the end of this chapter we shall examine the "costs" of stress for the human system, including lowered adaptive efficiency and—in the case of prolonged and excessive stress—severe disorganization of personality and behavior. Here we are concerned primarily with identifying the kinds of stress—biological, psychological, and sociocultural—that are commonly encountered in contemporary life.

BIOLOGICAL STRESS

Many biological conditions—infection, physical trauma, disease, malnutrition, fatigue—may lower the individual's stress tolerance and act as predisposing causes in mental disorders. Sometimes they may themselves be the precipitating factor.

Accidents and disease. Accidents and disease exact a high toll in our society. Each year accidents alone take the lives of over 100 thousand persons, permanently disable another 800 thousand, and temporarily disable at least 10 million others (*Science Journal*, 1967). These figures suggest that accidental injuries are the "neglected disease" of modern civilization. In addition, over 20 million persons suffer from heart conditions and other serious physical impairments that may be both painful and debilitating. When pain is severe and long-continued it may gradually wear down adjustive resources and lead to discouragement and despair. Chronic disease may also threaten the individual with a reduction in his expected life span.

In some instances the individual may be forced to undergo operations that involve an unusual degree of psychological as well as biological stress. Here it is of interest to note that in a study of kidney transplant patients, panic and hopelessness were found significantly more often among patients who did not survive than among those who did (Eisendrath, 1969). But even for individuals who survive such operations, there is often an elevated level of anxiety and depression, apparently associated with changes in self-concept and the fear that death may still be imminent.

Chronic emotional mobilization. In discussing arousal as an aspect of motivation (page 111), we noted that emotional processes like fear, anger, and anxiety represent the mobilization of body resources to meet emergency situations. Of course, this total mobilization of resources is for the protection of the threatened organism, helping it to either fight or flee more effectively. In modern life, however, the individual is rarely confronted with situations that can be met adequately by simple physical attack or flight.

When there is no adequate channel of discharge for the increased energy and tension, even relatively mild fear, anger, or anxiety can adversely affect the accuracy of perception and thought. And as the level of emotional tension rises, it becomes increasingly disruptive not only to psychological organization but to biological functioning as well. In his "stress theory of disease," Selye (1956; 1969) has shown that prolonged emotional mobilization produces physiological changes that are not only useless but actually harmful. In Chapter 14 we shall discuss psychosomatic disorders—peptic ulcers, arthritis, and other physical ailments in which chronic emotional mobilization typically plays a major role.

Organic brain pathology. Another set of biological factors, whose role in psychopathology has been better delineated, are the more typical organic disturbances that directly affect the central nervous system. About one half of the patients in mental hospitals are suffering from mental disorders associated with toxic or organic brain pathology—that is, conditions that result in the destruction of brain tissue or otherwise interfere with normal functioning of the brain. Brain pathology may be temporary, as in the delirium of fever or drug intoxication, or it may be permanent, as in the case of syphilitic infection of the brain.

Another neurophysiological factor receiving intensive study is the way in which defects in the body's defenses against disease and other stresses may contribute to brain pathology. Normally the body produces antibodies to defend itself against invading viruses and other microorganisms, and faulty functioning of the antibody-producing system leaves the body vulnerable to certain diseases—possibly including degenerative diseases of the central nervous system. Similarly,

the brain has special forms of reaction to stress in comparison with other organs (Dearing, 1969); and stress may disrupt the delicate biochemistry of the brain, with adverse consequences for certain predisposed individuals. In fact, a disorganization of thought processes similar to that observed in various severe mental disorders can be induced temporarily in normal people by the injection of certain drugs, such as LSD or mescaline. In Chapter 15 we shall deal with the various mental disorders associated with demonstrable brain pathology.

SEVERE FRUSTRATIONS

In contemporary life there are a number of frustrations that lead to self-devaluation and hence are particularly difficult to cope with. Among these are failure, losses, personal limitations and lack of resources, guilt, and unrelatedness and lack of meaning.

Failure. Since our society is a highly competitive one which places a great premium on individual success, failure tends to induce strong feelings of inferiority and self-devaluation. The fact that some degree of failure is inevitable—not everyone can win every contest—does not necessarily make defeat any easier to accept. Furthermore, some people seem to court failure by setting unrealistically high goals. Repeated failures are especially frustrating, as is failure in an undertaking where one very much wanted to succeed.

Often it is important that such experiences be "worked through" and the insights gained from them be used for ensuring success in meeting similar future situations. Successful accomplishment in an endeavor in which one has met with previous failure is highly therapeutic in restoring feelings of adequacy and worth, as is the ability to accept one's failures. In this context, it is interesting to note a report by Harmeling (1950) that the Eskimos at Cape Prince of Wales conducted a primitive form of psychodrama in their community igloo during the six-month winter. Accompanied by an orchestra of drums, they staged a pantomime of the failure experiences in their lives and laughed at their own mistakes thus objectively viewed.

Losses. Closely related to failure are the many losses that people inevitably experience—losses involving objects or resources they value or individuals with whom they strongly identify.

Among the most distressing material losses are those of money and status. In our society money gives its owner security, self-esteem, and the use of desired goods and services; thus an appreciable financial loss is apt to lead to severe self-recrimination and discouragement. Similarly, loss of social status—whether it stems from loss of economic position or some other cause—tends to devalue an individual in his own eyes as well as in the eyes of others.

Losses related to other persons, rather than to material objects, may come about through quarrels, separation, or death. An individual may lose the friendship of a person whom he esteems very highly or the love and respect of his mate. Or he may undergo physical loss in the death of loved ones. Bereavement is a highly traumatic experience, especially for older people—many of whom never fully recover from the death of a spouse. In one study the key reasons given by normal individuals who felt they were about to "go to pieces" were a death, an illness, or a separation from a loved one (Gurin, Veroff & Feld, 1960).

Personal limitations and lack of resources. Being "on the low end of the totem pole" with regard to material advantages and possessions is a powerful source of frustration—one afflicting members of disadvantaged minorities in our society with special severity. But this type of frustration is shared, to a greater or lesser degree, by most people; and the problem may not always be one of survival, but of being afforded a share of the pleasures or benefits that others are perceived as enjoying.

Modern advertising is highly adept at depicting desirable objects and pleasurable experiences in our affluent society; and such scenes are usually peopled with highly attractive human beings. Seeming to be "on the outside looking in" can be highly frustrating. In fact, Clark (1967), writing about the explosion in the ghetto, has concluded that:

"A central fact emerges from the murky background of the present urban eruptions: a society of affluence has raised the expectations and aspirations of the poor but has bypassed them, thereby increasing their frustra-

tion and anger, their bitterness, hostility, and expressions of aggression." (p. 31)

In addition, personal limitations and handicaps may be especially frustrating, and perhaps with real reason. But often such frustrations stem from the continual comparison of oneself with others who seem more favorably endowed or situated. Such *envious status comparisons* are a source of unnecessary frustration and self-devaluation.

Guilt. Feelings of guilt are the usual consequences of doing something that is felt to be wrong or failing to do something that is felt to be required. Guilt may be particularly stressful if it seems that nothing can be done to rectify the error.

To understand guilt feelings it is useful to remember that: (a) various value assumptions concerning right and wrong are learned and accepted, and then are applied to the evaluation of one's own desires, impulses, and behavior; and (b) it also is learned, often by hard experience, that wrong-doing leads to punishment. Thus, when an individual behaves in ways that he views as immoral, he experiences not only self-devaluation but apprehension as well. As a consequence of this orientation, he may become reaction-sensitive to immediate losses and setbacks, and search back through his past life, locating and exaggerating misdeeds that have presumably led to his present difficulties. This process is especially obvious among severely depressed persons.

In our society many social prohibitions and highly emotional moral attitudes center around the expression of hostility and of sexual desires. Many people feel especially guilty over infractions in these areas. They dare not admit feelings of hostility toward parents, mates, children, or close friends; yet occasional feelings of hostility toward loved ones are probably universal and to be expected. Sometimes early sexual experience, such as incest or mutual sex play among boys, is evaluated as terribly sinful in the light of moral values learned at a later stage in life. The results can be devastating to feelings of esteem and worth.

A college student had engaged in mutual masturbation with boys during his early youth and had had occasional homosexual experiences during his army life. He had later married, but his homosexual fantasies and past behavior, which he considered unpardonable, made his sexual adjustment in marriage quite hopeless and led to attempts to seduce practically every woman he met in an attempt to demonstrate his masculinity.

Like so many persons, he had also become convinced that he was different from other people, that they might be able to tell that he had homosexual inclinations, and that he deserved to fail because he was fundamentally no good. The improvement in this man was startling once he realized the nature of his problem and could understand that his homosexual fantasies and past experiences were not unusual and would probably cease to bother him as his marital adjustment became better established.

Lack of meaningful relationships. Feelings of isolation are another common source of self-devaluation and discouragement. Probably most individuals experience a painful sense of being alone in the world at some point in their lives. They feel like strangers in an alien world. As the novelist Thomas Wolfe (1929) has expressed it:

"Which one of us has known his brother? Which of us has looked into his father's heart? Which of us has not remained forever prison-pent? Which of us is not forever a stranger and alone?" (p. 3)

Feelings of isolation and loneliness may become extremely painful when the individual suffers the loss of some loved person who previously had provided him with his main source of interpersonal intimacy—as often happens in the case of divorce or the death of one's mate. Frieda Fromm-Reichmann (1959) has commented on the disintegrative effect of feeling alone, unappreciated, and unloved; and she considered this a particularly difficult stress in our group-conscious culture.

Charlotte Buhler (1969), however, has emphasized the importance of distinguishing between "neurotic alienation, and the feeling of loneliness that modern man experiences existentially." (p. 173) Although, as she has said, it is difficult to draw a definite line between the two, there is a distinction, nevertheless, to be observed between (1) the individual who is unconcerned, uncommitted, and unloving, and who does not attempt to use his freedom to escape from his loneliness in meaningful interpersonal relationships; and (2) the involved, committed, loving person whose loneliness is the result of conditions beyond his

control—such as the death of his mate or commitment to certain values and actions that require self-sacrifice. Loneliness resulting from the loss of a loved one thus is experienced as existential loneliness, especially where the mutual understanding and intimate union are disrupted by irreversible loss. This is true in all life periods, but perhaps especially so in later maturity when it is so much more difficult to rebuild one's life.

Related to feelings of loneliness, and equally destructive of morale, is an inability to find meaning in one's life. As Becker (1962) has pointed out: "Let it be stressed emphatically that the most difficult realization for man is the possibility that *life has no meaning*." (p. 30) Without meaning life is wasted, futile, and empty. There is little reason to try, to be concerned, or even to hope. Thus again we sense man's great need for a sense of identity, for a feeling of relatedness, and for values that give direction to life.

CORE CONFLICTS OF CONTEMPORARY LIFE

Conflicts are important sources of stress, and frequently lead to such tension and inner turmoil that the individual's adjustive capacities are seriously impaired. The following are among the more common and important sources of such conflict in our society.

Dependence vs. self-direction. Everyone has to make the transition from the dependent, protected status of childhood to adult status and responsibility, with all that this implies in terms of independence and self-directed activity. For most people this transition is a difficult one, and when problems accumulate and the going gets tough, an individual may wish, consciously or unconsciously, that he could return to the security and protected status of childhood.

Usually the dependence-independence conflict is severest during late adolescence and young adulthood, when a person is expected to start assuming adult responsibilities. For many young people the problem is complicated by difficulties in meeting financial needs and achieving emancipation from their parents. With further maturing and successful achievement, the conflict is usually resolved in favor of independence and self-direction; but underlying dependency needs may still remain, revealing themselves—at times of setback and failure—in extreme discouragement and possibly fantasies of life on some carefree South Sea island.

Commitment vs. noninvolvement. The need for relatedness is closely tied in with an underlying need to become committed to the welfare of others. Because of the impersonality and anonymity of modern society, however, it is difficult to experience a sense of commitment; moreover, even for persons so motivated, commitment entails a risk—one's efforts on others' behalf could put him in jeopardy. To many people, the risks of involvement and their possible repercussions seem too great a price to pay for helping "strangers." As Seaman (1966) has put it:

"Often it seems painful but realistic to conclude that, in the last analysis, you and your family are alone, and the only ones you can count on for help and support are yourselves. No one else cares." (p. 35)

The conflict between commitment and noninvolvement is by no means confined to interactions with strangers, or to participation in broader programs to right social injustices. Even in close interpersonal relationships, an individual may choose to remain somewhat aloof. All caring has hazards, since the one who invests his affections is vulnerable to being hurt, and a painless outcome can never be guaranteed. Noninvolvement, on the other hand, exacts a price in lost satisfactions, feelings of estrangement and alienation, and a lack of meaning in one's existence.

Avoiding vs. facing reality. Perhaps the first requisite of maturity is the ability to see oneself and the surrounding world objectively and to make the best of realities. But this is no simple task. Reality is often unpleasant and anxiety-arousing, and may undermine an individual's efforts to feel good about himself and his world. For example, facing the realization that failure in an important venture resulted from one's own inadequacies would be self-devaluating. Hence a person may tend to avoid facing this reality by rationalizing, projecting, or using other defense mechanisms.

Similarly, a proud parent may screen out the fact that his son is drinking too much, or is unduly preoccupied with drugs and neglecting his stud-

ies; or he may attempt to minimize this undesirable behavior by saying that young people go through "phases" and that there is really no cause for concern. An unrealistic self-concept sometimes helps a person accept himself and feel adequate in dealing with life's problems; but it may also keep him from facing his limitations and making needed changes in his values and modes of adjustment.

Integrity vs. self-advantage. At times it may appear that one's needs might be served best by actions that are strongly in conflict with his ethical attitudes; an individual may be tempted, for example, to cheat on examinations, to be devious in business transactions, to lie or otherwise to practice deceit to get something he wants, or to fail to stand up for values in which he believes because of possible social disapproval or retaliation. A person is particularly likely to be tempted by such behavior when he notes that others engage in it with seemingly successful results. But for most people, yielding to such temptation results in considerable feelings of guilt. Thus the adolescent who becomes cynical over the failure of the adult world to live up to the standards it preaches may nonetheless find it self-devaluating when he is tempted to go against what he has been taught. He is likely to experience considerable conflict in the process of working out and adhering to his own standards.

Fearfulness vs. positive action. It has been said that anyone who lives in the latter half of the twentieth century and does not experience a certain amount of fear and anxiety is either stupid, insensitive, or atrophied. But many people—instead of taking positive action to improve their condition—overreact to perceived dangers with disproportionate feelings of fear and inadequacy.

Although most people are familiar with the increased tension and desire to flee that accompany fear, few realize that fatigue, worry, indecision, and oversensitivity may also be disguised manifestations of fear. The pervasive effects of fear are illustrated by the person who is afraid to go out in the dark alone after watching a terrifying murder mystery on television. If he goes out anyway, he is prone to jump at the slightest sound. This increased sensitivity is characteristic of the many frightened, insecure persons who go through life overreacting to the slightest threat. Their fears rob them of courage and cripple their reasoning and other adjustive capacities. Also, as we have seen, men tend to hate the things they fear. Fear and hate combined are, of course, not conducive to reasoned positive action, and often lead to a self-defeating "lashing out" at one's problems.

Another commonly overlooked aspect of fear is the distinction between feeling, showing, and reacting to it. Everyone experiences fear, although most people learn to conceal it rather effectively. But the key factor in dealing with fear is how one acts when he is afraid. The brave person is not one who experiences no fear, but one who acts courageously despite its presence. Not realizing this, many people expend their efforts fighting the feeling of fear and trying to deny or conceal it, instead of learning to function effectively in spite of it. To the extent that fear or worry are allowed to inhibit positive action, personal progress is blocked.

Sexual desires vs. restraints. As a result of social prohibitions centering around the expression of the sex drive, many people experience severe conflict. Initially, sexual conflicts are commonly related to masturbation and, as we have seen, may persist as a running battle between strong sexual desires and the belief that masturbation is a vile habit engaged in only by those who lack moral fiber and will power. Often, too, the early sexual picture may be complicated by an overattachment to the mother or father.

With adolescence and young adulthood, sexual conflicts are likely to arise over questions of petting, premarital sexual relations, and marital infidelity—patterns of sexual behavior in conflict with traditional social mores. When an individual has a background of training regarding the "evils" of sex, he may find it difficult to accept his sex drive as part of himself or to accept himself as a worthwhile person. To complicate matters further, such individuals often retain the undifferentiated sexual desires characteristic of preadolescence. Their sexual fantasies are often directed toward both males and females, leading to bewilderment and self-devaluation. They do not realize that such fantasies are common to youngsters who are growing up and usually are outgrown later.

Adding to the young person's difficulty is the confusion and disagreement he sees around him concerning what is acceptable and unacceptable in sexual behavior. In general, our society appears to be moving toward a view that sexual behavior is a natural and acceptable source of pleasure, and toward a concomitant decrease in the restraints governing patterns of sexual behavior.[1] But guidelines still are not clear, and sexual values may differ markedly among different ethnic, socioeconomic, and religious groups. Despite the fact that "the pill" has reduced the likelihood of pregnancy, many young people continue to experience intense conflict as they try to work out an acceptable code of sexual ethics.

Conformity vs. nonconformity. A constant and often deeply disturbing problem facing the individual is when to conform or not to conform to group expectations and pressures. In this respect a person's behavior may be "blind," or it may be based on rational thought and decision. The latter appears to best serve both individual and group interests, and to provide the best guide in resolving conformity-nonconformity conflicts.

Group pressures toward conformity, although decried—and often with good reason—as being detrimental to the personal growth and well-being of the individual, inevitably develop as a group tries to maintain itself and achieve its goals. No group could long function as an integrated system without some uniformity and discipline among its members, a principle that is generally recognized and accepted.

Usually an individual is most amenable to the demands of groups in which he most values membership, for these have the greatest power to give or withhold approval, and to meet or frustrate his needs. Thus it is often easier for a teenager to repudiate adult norms—particularly with respect to customs he views as arbitrarily imposed, such as styles in clothing or length of hair, or taste in music—than it is to go against peer group pressures. By the same token, an individual may experience marked conflict when confronted by the demands, expectations, or pressures of his peer group—as when a teen-ager is pressured to try an hallucinogenic drug at a party.

Whatever an individual's decision may be with respect to conformity or nonconformity in a par-

---

[1]Sprey (1969) has pointed out that human sexuality has been analyzed traditionally within the conceptual framework of marriage and family. However, he suggests that sex is becoming an autonomous and distinct realm of social interaction; and he points to some of the possible implications of this trend.

ticular case, most people tend to condemn blind conformity because it represents an abdication of responsible self-direction. Living in accordance with one's own convictions will sometimes lead to behavior that others expect and approve; but sometimes it will mean standing alone.

Value conflicts. Values enter into all of the conflicts we have discussed, for an individual's values ultimately determine the choices he makes. In selecting goals, in choosing means for achieving these goals, and in resolving conflicts, a person is influenced at every turn by his conception of what is desirable or undesirable. Where an individual's value assumptions are unclear or contradictory, he is likely to experience difficulties in making choices and directing his behavior.

Often a distinction is made between conceived and operative values. Conceived values are conceptions of the ideal which the individual may hold with considerable conviction but may not follow in his actual behavior; operative values are the assumptions which the individual actually uses in making choices. Sometimes the discrepancy between an individual's conceived and operative values reveals a serious schism between his "idealized" and "real" selves.

Several writers of our time have pointed to the tendency of many people to surrender to an outer authority the task of thinking through their values and prescribing rules for their behavior. They guide their behavior and judge themselves as worthy or unworthy, successful or unsuccessful, in terms of the standards of this authority. It seems doubtful, however, that value conflicts are ever entirely resolved by surrendering to the expectations of others.

PRESSURES OF MODERN LIVING

Each person faces a somewhat unique pattern of pressures, but in a general way everyone faces pressures of competing with others, meeting educational, occupational, and marital demands, and coping with the complexity and rapid pace of modern living.

Competition. Because in our society people are encouraged to surpass others, to excel, to "get to the top," they often drive themselves mercilessly toward high levels of achievement, subjecting themselves in the process to sustained and severe pressure. Whatever is said in defense of such activity, it is bound to lead to much disappointment and frustration, for statistically there is not "room at the top" for everyone.

Competitive pressures have been acclaimed as leading to greater productivity, an increased sense of purpose, higher standards of excellence, and a "feel for life." Yet inappropriate or indiscriminate competition—particularly competition where one person can achieve or succeed only at the expense of others—may be especially harmful for the individual and divisive for the group (McDavid & Harari, 1968). And if it leads to a constant burden of pressure on the competitors, it may be ultimately harmful to winners and losers alike.

Educational, occupational, and marital demands. The long hours of study, the tension of examinations, and the sustained concentration of effort over many years result in considerable stress for many students. And where a student is handicapped by inefficient study habits, financial insufficiencies, personal problems, or other difficulties, the competition for grades and for admission to advanced training may become highly stressful. Adding to the stress is the awareness that educational achievement has important implications for future success.

Occupational demands also are often highly stressful, especially when an individual is very ambitious or feels under pressure from family or friends to succeed. Many jobs make severe demands in terms of responsibility, time, and performance. But regardless of the actual demands of the work situation, if the individual is not really interested in or well suited to his work, occupational demands are likely to be highly stressful.

Marriage makes difficult demands on both partners—demands that may be stressful if either individual is immature and poorly prepared for marital responsibilities, if there are basic incompatibilities between the partners, or if financial or other problems make the external situation unfavorable. Marriage calls on individuals to adjust to intimate relationships with their spouses, to take responsibilities, and to resolve value conflicts. And with the arrival of children, the problems of parenthood may further complicate marital adjustment.

Complexity and pace of modern living. The

mere complexity and pace of modern living tend to "overload" the organism, and the strain of living under such highly complicated and demanding conditions can play havoc on both biological and psychological levels. Increasing research evidence is pointing to the role of "overloading" in heart attacks and physical disorders. On a psychological level, "overloading" leads to lowered efficiency and irritability; in extreme degree, there may be a complete breakdown of organized behavior (J. G. Miller, 1961; 1965).

Many of the demands made on individuals are contradictory, such as the problem of insufficient time to meet combined family, civic, and occupational demands. Thus the need to make choices and bear responsibility for them adds to the stress of the demands themselves.

SOCIOCULTURAL FACTORS

In addition to the biological and psychological stresses that already have been reviewed, there remain to be discussed other stresses especially characteristic of contemporary living.

War, civil conflict, and violence. Mankind today lives in fear of the new and incredibly destructive means of modern warfare—thermonuclear, chemical, and bacteriological. Unless some solution can be found to the problem of war, the world may be consumed by a holocaust. Fear growing out of this threat has led some individuals to overly aggressive attitudes, some to apathy, and some to other irrational response patterns.

At the same time that wars continue to smolder on our globe, polarizing nations, civil conflict and violence erupt in our own society, polarizing groups. In recent years we have witnessed the violent disruption of our college campuses, the burning and pillaging of large areas of our cities, the assassinations of prominent political figures and group leaders, and the increasing tendency to resort to violence rather than to rational and peaceful communication as a means of settling differences between groups. We have also seen the rising rate of crimes of violence that make many communities unsafe even in the daytime.

Group prejudice and discrimination. We have seen the damaging effects of racial prejudice and discrimination on personality development. But the effects of these pathological social conditions are not limited to early development,

any more than group prejudice is limited to the black minority. For example, of the various groups subjected to prejudice and discrimination in our society, we must include older people who are typically forced to adjust to arbitrary retirement, a marked reduction in income, and feelings of no longer being useful or even wanted.

In Chapter 18 we shall deal in more detail with the problem of group prejudice and discrimination as it relates to various groups in our society, including racial minorities. Here we may note, however, that the stress to which victims of prejudice and discrimination are subjected tends to elicit feelings of frustration, hostility, and self-devaluation. Often with young victims of racial discrimination, these feelings are associated with shame of their parents and hostility toward them—as if the parents are to blame for their problems. Attempts to cope with such stresses are extremely difficult; and they are even more difficult for those who do not have a definite, accepted status in any group, such as light-skinned Negroes.

Economic and employment problems. Inflation, unemployment, and job dissatisfaction are sources of stress for many persons in our society. Inflation, for example, has imposed hardships on people whose finances cannot keep pace with the economic spiral, such as those on fixed retirement incomes. And unemployment has placed a burden on a sizable population segment, bringing with it both physical hardships and self-devaluation. As an indication of the toll that unemployment exacts, periods of extensive unemployment are usually accompanied by increases in certain types of maladaptive behavior, such as apathy, suicide, and marital conflict.

For the employed, a major source of stress is job dissatisfaction—by conservative estimate, a feeling shared by well over a third of all employees in the United States. This point takes on particular significance in the light of findings that work satisfaction not only influences personal happiness but longevity as well (Palmore, 1970). Whatever the possibilities for job satisfaction in an increasingly computerized society, the demand for it seems to be increasing; and at the same time the emphasis on the puritan concept of work as a duty and a virtue, besides being necessary for survival, is declining.

We see more coming to be demanded of work

than a requirement of simply "filling a slot" or "doing a job." Young people are no longer content with only money as a return for their investment of time and energy. Schein (1968) has used the term "first-job dilemma" to describe the disillusionment and apathy that many college graduates experience on their first jobs. Thus there is an increasing demand for meaningful employment and the need for integrating education, work, and increased leisure into a more fulfilling life pattern.

Domestic discord and family instability. The divorce rate in the United States is the highest of any nation in the world. Some 660,000 marriages ended in divorce in 1969 (Robbins, 1970), and an equivalent number of separations are estimated to occur each year (Packard, 1968). This represents a grand total of over a million marital breakups annually. In addition, it has been estimated that about 50 percent of all marriages continue in the face of deep dissatisfaction and unhappiness (Renne, 1970). Heartache, bickering, feelings of wasted opportunity, of being tied down, of marking time, and so on, are very common, especially when children are the only bond holding a marriage together. Half of all married partners apparently would not pick the same mate if they had it to do over again. And of course, marital dissatisfaction and instability are not only frustrating to parents but also place the children under additional stress and lead to what has been called "dysfunctional parenting" (Satir, 1967).

It is relevant to emphasize here both the changing role and the increasing importance of the family in meeting the needs of the individual. As our society has made the transition from a rural to an urban, industrial society, a new family pattern has emerged. Whereas authority was formerly vested in the father, and the ties that bound the family together were often based on duty and economic necessity, a new type of pattern has emerged in which all family members now share in decision making, and the emphasis is on the members' growth and happiness. Too, modern urbanization has led to the decline of the extended family with the relatively stable network of relationships and supports it provided; in our mobile, urban society it is difficult to establish and maintain close interpersonal relationships out-

side the nuclear family. As a consequence, the individual has come to depend increasingly on his marital and immediate familial relationships for satisfaction of his emotional needs. Not surprisingly, the growing demand for happiness and personal fulfillment through marriage has been accompanied by a growing acceptance of divorce as a viable choice in an unsatisfactory marital situation. Thus there arises a modern dilemma in which family stability has been reduced while the demands on the family system have increased.

Rapid change and existential anxiety. Rapid social change has also created serious problems for mankind. It has played havoc with traditional mores and value patterns and with many persons' assumptions concerning the meaning of human existence. With the advent of the space age, man is confronted with a new perspective of time and space and the problem of finding the meaning of his existence in a universe in which the earth and even the whole solar system may be no larger in relation to the whole than an atom is to the earth. At the same time, materialistic values—based on the belief that scientific progress would automatically lead to man's happiness and fulfillment —have proved sadly disillusioning. As a result, many people are groping about, bewildered and bitter, unable to find any enduring faith or to develop a satisfying philosophy of life. Despite their fine automobiles, well-stocked refrigerators, and other material possessions and comforts, the meaning of life seems to be evading them. In essence, they are suffering from *existential anxiety*.

Rapid changes are taking place in other parts of the world as well as in the United States. In fact, the world is in a period of unrest and tension, in which vast social change seems to be the order of the day. Few are the places in the world where people still follow as a matter of course the ways of their fathers and grandfathers. In the developing nations no less than in the industrialized world, people are demanding the "good life" that modern technology can provide; they are becoming aware of the inadequacies of many existing forms of political and social organization; and they are feeling both hope for a better way of life and frustration that they themselves may not experience it. Unfortunately, all of these changes are accompanied by considerable turmoil as old patterns and values give way to new ones.

THE INTERPLAY OF INADEQUATE RESOURCES AND EXCESSIVE STRESS

When we speak of mild or severe stress, we are referring to the degree of strain or disequilibrium that adjustive demands produce in the organism. Mild stress may actually improve an individual's level of performance and efficiency. Severe stress, on the other hand, tends to impair adaptive ability; if it continues over a long period of time, as we shall see, it may eventuate in the breakdown of integrated functioning.

FACTORS DETERMINING THE SEVERITY OF STRESS

The severity of stress depends partly on the characteristics of the adjustive demand, partly on the individual, and partly on the cultural and situational context in which the stress occurs. On a biological level, for example, the severity of stress created by invading viruses depends partly on the strength and number of the invaders, partly on the organism's ability to resist and destroy them, and partly on available medical resources for implementing body defenses. On a psychological level, the severity of the stress depends not only on the nature of the stress and the individual's resources—both personal and situational—but also on how he perceives or evaluates the stress situation and what techniques he may employ in coping with it.

Characteristics of the adjustive demand. Several factors influence the severity of the adjustive demand, regardless of the individual involved or the situational context in which the demand occurs.

1. *Importance, duration, and multiplicity of demands.* The importance of an adjustive demand is gauged by the degree of need deprivation and disruption in the system that will occur if an individual fails to cope with the demand. Simply telling an employee that he *may* lose his job *if* his work does not improve may cause him to experience stress, but if he is told he is fired his assessment of the situation is likely to be far more serious. Similarly, frustration of

a key motive is more stressful than frustration of a peripheral one. Failing one's bar examination would be more stressful than having to give up a desired vacation trip.

Ordinarily, the longer a stress operates, the more severe it becomes. Prolonged exhaustion imposes a more intense stress than does temporary fatigue. Often, too, stress appears to have a cumulative effect. A married couple may maintain amicable relations through a long series of minor irritations or frustrations only to "explode" and dissolve the relationship in the face of the "final straw."

Encountering a number of stresses at the same time makes a difference too. If a man has a heart attack, loses his job, and receives distressing news of his son or daughter's being arrested for drug abuse—all at the same time—the resulting stress will be more severe than if these events occurred separately. In their study of life stresses and mental health in midtown Manhattan, Langner and Michael (1963) found that the number of stress factors, past and present—rather than any particular stress—best predicted the mental health of their subjects. Fourteen stress factors, including health status, work worries, socioeconomic worries, social isolation, marital worries, and parental worries, were rated individually on a scale from one to ten. The higher the score for the list as a whole, the poorer the mental health of the subject was found to be.

2. *Strength and equality of conflicting forces.* Conflict between weak motives or motives with little self-investment involves minimal stress, for neither alternative would lead to serious loss. On the other hand, conflicts between strong motives —such as one involving a choice between self-esteem and social approval—are likely to subject the individual to considerable stress. Of course, the more nearly equal the strength of the opposing motives, the greater the stress.

The picture is complicated further by the fact that the strength of a given motive or goal object does not remain static or unchanging. In approach-avoidance conflicts, for example, the strength of opposing motives is likely to increase as the goal draws near (Maher, 1966; Miller, 1959). If a young man is ambivalent about getting married, both his eagerness and his fear will become greater as the wedding date approaches, and stress will mount accordingly. This probably helps explain why some people experience a feeling of near panic on their wedding day.

3. *Imminence of anticipated stress.* In other stress situations—as well as those involving conflict—the severity increases as the anticipated stress approaches. For example, Mechanic (1962), observing graduate students, found that although the students thought about their examinations from time to time and experienced some anxiety during the prior three months, anxiety did not become intense until the examinations were nearly upon them. Similarly, persons anticipating other stress situations—such as major surgery—have found that the severity of stress increased as the time for the ordeal approached.

If the individual repeatedly subjects himself to a particular stress situation—as in the sport of skydiving—a somewhat different pattern of severity may be involved. For novice jumpers, the peak of anxiety or avoidance does not come at the period of greatest danger—the free fall—but at the ready signal, when he can choose to go ahead or cancel the jump. For experienced jumpers, on the other hand, the anxiety peaks the morning of the jump, and once they have made the decision that they will jump that day, their fear and anxiety usually decrease (Fenz & Epstein, 1969).

4. *Familiarity and suddenness of the problem.* Often new adjustive demands that have not been anticipated and for which no ready-made coping patterns are available will place an individual under severe strain. One reason why major catastrophes are so overwhelming is that all one's knowledge and skills seem totally inadequate and irrelevant to the task at hand. By contrast, if a stressful event, even a potentially catastrophic one, can be prepared for, it loses some of its severity. The training of firemen, policemen, and soldiers in exactly what to expect and what to do in crisis situations makes it possible for them to function more effectively under extreme degrees of stress.

The same sense of adequacy and control may be achieved when the stress has been chosen voluntarily, rather than having been imposed by others or having come unexpectedly. Seeing meaning in a stressful situation, preparing for it, and knowing how long it will last, all lessen the severity of the stress when it does come.

Characteristics of the individual. The individual's perception of the problem, the degree of threat involved, and his stress tolerance, all influence the severity of stressful situations. Thus, situations that one person finds highly stressful may be only mildly stressful or even nonstressful for another.

1. *Perception of the problem.* One factor that is often crucial in determining the severity of stress is an individual's evaluation of his stress situation. This point is particularly important in understanding abnormal behavior. As outsiders we may see no stresses in a person's life situation severe enough to have brought on his maladaptive behavior. Yet to him the situation may be intolerable. An individual always reacts, not simply to the situation, but *to the situation as he evaluates it*—especially in relation to his ability to cope with it.

2. *Degree of threat.* Threat is the anticipation of harm. Stress situations that are perceived as potentially damaging or threatening to survival—such as having a limb amputated or being given a diagnosis of cancer—carry a high degree of threat. Similarly, stress situations that threaten the adequacy and worth of the self—such as loss of social status, failure in one's chosen occupation, or desires that the individual considers highly immoral and incompatible with his self-concept and self-ideal—involve a strong element of threat. The individual is also likely to feel threatened in situations which place demands on him that he perceives as important but beyond his power to meet. For this reason, the person who doubts his adequacy and worth is much more likely to experience threat than the one who feels more confident and secure. In general, a situation perceived as threatening is much more stressful than one perceived as presenting a difficult but manageable problem.

3. *Stress tolerance of the individual.* The severity of a given stress depends, too, on the individual's resources for withstanding stress. If he is marginally adjusted, the slightest frustration or pressure may be highly stressful. The term *stress tolerance*, or *frustration tolerance*, refers

to the amount of stress one can tolerate before his integrated functioning is seriously impaired. Both biologically and psychologically, people vary greatly in general vulnerability to stress as well as in the types of stress to which they are most vulnerable. Emergencies, disappointments, and other life problems that one individual can take in stride may prove incapacitating to another. Sometimes, as we have seen, early traumatic experiences leave the individual especially vulnerable to certain kinds of stress.

External resources and supports. Lack of external supports—either personal or material—makes a given stress more severe and weakens an individual's capacity to cope with it. A divorce or the death of one's mate is more stressful if one feels alone and unloved than if one is still surrounded by people one cares about and feels close to.

Even pressures toward conformity are less stressful and more easily withstood when one has an ally than when one is alone (Asch, 1955). It is hardly surprising that studies have found a tendency for individuals exposed to highly stressful situations to turn to others for support and reassurance.

Environmental supports are a complex matter, however, and behavior by one's family or friends which is intended to provide support may actually increase the stress. In his study of graduate students facing crucial examinations, Mechanic (1962) compared the effects of different types of behavior on the part of the spouses:

"In general, spouses do not provide blind support. They perceive the kinds of support the student wants and they provide it. The wife who becomes worried about examinations also may provide more support than the spouse who says, 'I'm not worried, you will surely pass.' Indeed, since there is a chance that the student will not pass, the person who is supportive in a meaningful sense will not give blind assurance. . . . Often a statement to the effect, 'Do the best you can' is more supportive than, 'I'm sure you are going to do well.' The latter statement adds to the student's burden, for not only must he fear the disappointment of not passing, but also the loss of respect in the eyes of his spouse." (p. 158)

Often the culture provides for specific rituals or other courses of action which support the individual in his attempts to deal with certain

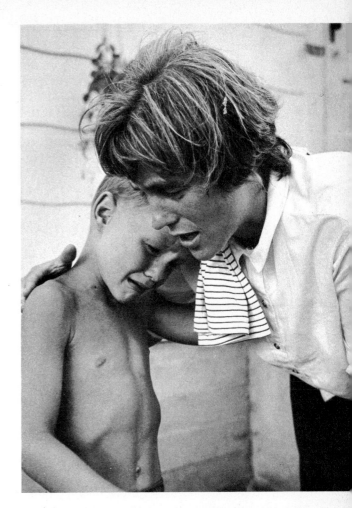

During periods of special stress or crises, parental support and assistance are of vital importance to children.

types of stress. For example, most religions provide rituals which help the bereaved through their ordeal; and in some faiths, confession and atonement help people to deal with stresses related to guilt and self-recrimination.

COSTS OF ADAPTATION TO STRESS

The consequences of faulty development become most readily apparent when the individual must cope with severe stress. Adaptation to stress exacts its costs on everyone, but the cost is greatest for those with poor stress tolerance and inadequate adjustive resources. In this section we shall examine the general effects of stress in lowering adaptive efficiency. In the section following we shall show how severe and prolonged stress may lead to serious disorganization of the system and sometimes its eventual breakdown.

Lowering of adaptive efficiency. Under severe stress there is a narrowing of the perceptual field and an increased rigidity of cognitive processes, so that it is difficult and often impossible for the individual to reinterpret or see new possibilities and relationships in a stress situation—even though he is continually preoccupied with it. This probably explains why people in the throes of a difficult conflict are often unaware of much that is going on around them.

Studies with animal subjects have shown that even when the stress situation is changed and new possibilities of solution are made available, an animal under stress is likely not to see the new possibilities but instead to continue to follow a rigid, stereotyped adjustive pattern (Maier, 1949). Comparable findings have been made with human subjects in experimental stress situations (Maher, 1957).

Reduction in resistance to other stresses. In utilizing resources for coping with one stress, the organism typically suffers a lowering of tolerance to other stresses (Selye, 1956; 1969). For example, Selye (1956) found that mice exposed to extremes of cold developed increased resistance to the cold but became unusually sensitive to X rays. Similarly, people can become accustomed to an aversive environmental stress but show lowered tolerance for frustration and impaired performance efficiency when the aversive stress is discontinued. And, soldiers who develop resistance to combat conditions may show a lowered tolerance for other pressures, such as viral infections or bad news from home.

Wear and tear on the system. With sustained or very severe stress there may be considerable, and irreversible, wear and tear on the system. Many people believe that after undergoing very stressful experiences, rest can completely restore them. Selye, however, has found evidence to the contrary:

"Experiments on animals have clearly shown that each exposure leaves an indelible scar, in that it uses up reserves of adaptability which cannot be replaced. It is true that immediately after some harassing experience, rest can restore us almost to the original level of fitness by eliminating acute fatigue. But the emphasis is on *almost*. Since we constantly go through periods of stress and rest during life, just a little deficit of adaptation energy every day adds up—it adds up to what we call *aging*.

". . . Due to the great advances made by classic medicine during the last half century, premature death caused by specific disease producers . . . has declined at a phenomenal rate. . . . But an ever-increasing proportion of the human population dies from the so-called wear-and-tear diseases, or degenerative diseases, which are primarily due to stress." (1956, pp. 274–275)

Selye (1969) also has pointed to experiments with volunteer military subjects, showing that relatively brief exposure to severe stress—in fact, stress less severe than most people are confronted with at some time in their lives—can provoke pathological organic changes.

When pressure is severe and long continued, physiological mobilization may become chronic and in time lead to irreversible pathology in bodily organs—ranging from peptic ulcers and high blood pressure to heart attacks or strokes. And, as we have noted, in some individuals sustained or very severe stress appears to lead to chemical changes in the blood that interfere with brain functioning and seriously impair the individual's ability to think, feel, and act in an integrated manner. Later we shall examine the implications of such chemical changes.

DECOMPENSATION UNDER EXCESSIVE STRESS

When the individual's coping behavior fails to deal effectively with the stress situation, there is a lowering of integrated functioning and eventually a breakdown of the system. This lowering of integration is referred to as *decompensation*. Whether stress becomes "excessive" depends, of course, not only on the nature of the adjustive demand but also on the resources available for coping with it. Decompensation has been observed on biological, psychological, and sociological levels.

Biological decompensation. A model that helps explain the course of biological decompensation under excessive stress has been advanced by Selye (1956; 1969) in his formulation of the general adaptation syndrome. Selye found that the body's reaction to sustained and excessive stress typically occurs in three major phases: (1) *alarm and mobilization*—representing a general call to arms of the body's defensive forces; (2) *stage of resistance*—in which biological adaptation is

A CASE OF DECOMPENSATION UNDER EXCESSIVE STRESS

The following case of a young college girl illustrates the course of psychological decompensation from the "alarm and mobilization" stage through a psychotic level of decompensation.

A sensitive, highly intelligent college girl . . . had a personal history of being rather shy, withdrawn, philosophically minded and overly given to daydreaming. During her sophomore year . . . she was informed by her parents that they were unhappy and planning a divorce. This served to undermine her precarious security further and precipitated the following reaction:

"I decided that I would start with a clean slate, study hard, look into and revise some of my views and avoid the unhappiness that seemed to saturate the world. The main trouble was that I could find no one else who wanted to be sensible and mature. This led to a rather hermitic existence in which I studied and philosophized most of the time.

". . . I set certain people, who I thought were leading the perfect life, up on little pedestals and completely worshiped them and devoted myself to them. Since I wanted so to please them and was under such tension, I could hardly speak and was soaked with perspiration while with them. Each remark they had made, no matter how trivial, was indelibly impressed in my mind. It was during this period that I somehow seemed to get completely off the track. In my desperate attempts to find security, I planned a strict schedule which I must adhere to each day. I would figure out my plan, enter it whole-heartedly, and then something would go wrong. One rung off the perfect ladder would send me plunging into the depths. During this period I began to experience obsessive ideas of suicide. I felt so terribly alone and isolated and such a miserable failure. With my attempts at building security I developed grasping, clutching feelings. I wanted to grab people, or trees, or buildings, whenever I felt emotional.

"During this period I was enrolled in a course in biology. My biology teacher was a wonderful person but he did not believe in God as I had been taught to. He knocked the props right out from under my blind faith in God. I could find no immediate substitute which would show clearly which way my life's course should turn. Now I began to experience depressions and as time went on they became more severe and lasted longer. The world seemed a terrible place, and I had no hope for the future. I would spend an average of two to three hours in daydreams each day, and would talk to myself and other imaginary persons whenever I was alone.

"It seems that during this period I somehow lost control. I would hear voices and see persons who weren't really there but they seemed real."

optimal in terms of bodily resources; and (3) *exhaustion and disintegration*—in which bodily resources are depleted and the organism loses its ability to resist so that further exposure to the stress can lead to disintegration and death.

Where decompensation does not run its entire course and result in the death of the organism, maintenance mechanisms attempt to repair damage and reorganize functions. If the stress has resulted in extensive damage, this restorative process is often a matter of reorganizing "remaining parts and resources," but there is also a permanent lowering of the previous level of integration and functioning.

Psychological decompensation. Personality decompensation under excessive stress appears to follow a course resembling that described for biological decompensation.

1. *Alarm and mobilization.* At first there is an alerting of the organism and a mobilizing of resources for coping with the stress. Typically involved at this stage are emotional arousal and increased tension, heightened sensitivity and alertness (vigilance), and determined efforts at self-control. At the same time, the individual undertakes various coping measures—which may be task-oriented or defense-oriented or a combination of the two—in his efforts to meet the emergency. He also may show symptoms of maladjustment, such as continuous anxiety and tension, gastrointestinal upset or other bodily manifestations, and lowered efficiency—indications that the mobilization of adaptive resources is not proving adequate.

2. *Stage of resistance.* If the stress continues, the individual is often able to find some means for dealing with it and thus to resist psychological disintegration. Resistance may be achieved temporarily by concerted task-oriented coping measures; and the use of self-defense mechanisms may also be intensified during this period. Even in the stage of resistance, however, there may be indications of strain—including psychosomatic symptoms, which Selye has referred to as the "diseases of adaptation." During the stage of resistance the individual tends to become rigid and to cling to his coping patterns rather than trying to reevaluate the stress situation and work out more adaptive coping patterns.

3. *Stage of exhaustion.* In the face of continued excessive stress, the individual's adaptive resources are depleted and the coping patterns utilized in the stage of resistance begin to fail. Now as he enters the stage of *exhaustion* there may be a marked lowering of integration and effectiveness and an introduction of exaggerated and inappropriate defensive measures. The latter reactions may be characterized by psychological disorganization and a "break with reality"—involving delusions and hallucinations—that appear to represent increased disorganization in thought and perception together with a desperate effort to salvage some measure of psychological integration and self-integrity through a restructuring of reality. Metabolic changes that impair normal brain functioning may be directly involved in delusional and hallucinatory behavior. Eventually, if the excessive stress continues, the process of decompensation proceeds to a stage of complete psychological disintegration—perhaps involving continuous uncontrolled violence, apathy, or stupor, and eventually death.

As we shall see, relatively severe psychological decompensation may be precipitated by sudden and extreme stress; but more often the decompensation is a gradual and long-range process. Typically, of course, treatment measures are instituted before decompensation runs its course. Such measures may increase the individual's adaptive capabilities or alleviate the stress situation so that the process of decompensation is reversed to *recompensation*. We shall illustrate the stress-decompensation model with case material in later chapters.

Decompensation in group life. Although sci-

ence is just beginning to make inroads into the understanding of social pathology, it would appear that the concept of decompensation is just as applicable here as on biological and psychological levels. In the face of wars, economic problems, and other internal and external stresses that surpass their adjustive capabilities, societies may undergo varying degrees of decompensation, often resorting to extreme measures in their attempts to maintain organization and resist disintegration. This process has been depicted by the historian Toynbee and other writers in their descriptions of the decline and fall of Greece, Rome, and other societies.

Although our focus in this discussion of decompensation has been on psychological stress reactions, it should be reemphasized that man's behavior, including mental disorders, can be understood only in terms of the interaction of biological, psychological, and sociological coping patterns and defenses. The outcome in any given situation depends on: (1) the effectiveness of coping behavior in meeting adjustive demands; (2) the extent to which any damage can be repaired and remaining resources reorganized; and (3) the level of integration and functioning that can be achieved. In some instances the functional level may be permanently lowered following severe stress; in other cases the system may attain a higher level of integration and functioning than had existed previously.

GENERAL PERSPECTIVES ON CAUSATION

Thus far in this chapter we have focused primarily on the particular kinds of developmental difficulties and types of stress that may be involved in the etiology of abnormal behavior. In this final section we shall broaden our view by considering some theoretical orientations to the complex problem of causation.

DIFFERING MODELS OF CAUSATION

In Chapters 2 and 3 we noted the views of psychopathology inherent in the medical, psycho-

analytic, behavioristic, and other major models of man. As we review the different causal patterns emphasized in these various models, we can see that each contributes to our overall understanding of the dynamics of abnormal behavior.

1. *Anxiety-defense.* This causal pattern is emphasized in both the psychoanalytic and humanistic models of man. Stress situations that involve a threat to the individual elicit anxiety, which functions as both a warning of dangers and an acutely unpleasant condition in itself, demanding alleviation. If an individual copes effectively with the stressful situation in a task-oriented way, his anxiety is eliminated; however, if the stress and anxiety continue he typically will resort to various ego-defense mechanisms, such as denial, rationalization, and projection. This process of self-defense then leads to an incongruence between reality and the individual's experiencing, and in extreme degree may result in lowered integration and maladaptive behavior.

2. *Faulty learning.* Although faulty learning is seen as the key cause of psychopathology in the behavioristic model, it is also recognized as an important causal factor in all of the major models of man. This approach assumes that maladaptive behavior is the result of either (a) the failure to learn necessary adaptive behaviors or competencies, or (b) the learning of maladaptive behaviors. Delinquent behavior based on a failure to learn necessary social values and norms would be an example of the former; while the phobia or fear response to the white rat learned by little Albert (page 58) would be an example of the latter.

As we have seen, the faulty learning model not only emphasizes failure to learn—together with aversive conditioning or other faulty learning—as causes of maladaptive behavior; it also places strong emphasis on conditions that reinforce and hence maintain the maladaptive behavior.

3. *Blocked personal growth.* The humanistic and existential models of man place strong emphasis on the concept of blocked personal growth as a primary cause of psychopathology. Thus, proponents of these views speak of maintenance vs. growth motivation, and the necessity of being and shaping one's self. If the individual is denied opportunities for personal growth and self-fulfillment, or if he fails to utilize the freedom he does have to shape his potentialities into the self he feels he should be, and to achieve a meaningful and fulfilling life, the inevitable consequences are anxiety, futility, and despair.

4. *Stress-decompensation.* In the preceding section of this chapter we described the process of psychological decompensation under excessive stress. And we noted that such decompensation may occur in the face of sudden acute stress which is beyond the range of the individual's adjustive resources—as in the case of "experimental neuroses." More typically, however, this process is a gradual one that (a) is marked by the progressive depletion of an individual's adaptive resources, and (b) follows a predictable course— from alarm and mobilization, through resistance, to eventual exhaustion and destruction of the organism—if it is not stopped or reversed. We also noted that such decompensation may take place on group and societal as well as biological and psychological levels.

5. *Interpersonal and social pathology.* We have dealt with the effect of pathogenic interpersonal relationships—such as fraudulent and negotiated maladjustment contracts—on the development and maintenance of maladaptive behavior. We have also dealt with the effects of pathological social conditions—particularly poverty and racial prejudice and discrimination—on both children and adults. Not only do such immediate sociocultural conditions affect the nature and incidence of mental disorders in a given society, but the pattern of mental disorders changes over time as new technological advances lead to profound alterations and changes in society. In fact, the patterning of both physical and mental disorders changes with each major change in civilization.

6. *Brain pathology.* The view of causation underlying the medical model emphasizes the role of various organic conditions that can impair brain functioning and lead to psychopathology. Included here are a wide variety of conditions, ranging from syphilitic infection to drug intoxication to nutritional deficiencies. We have also noted the possibility that genetic defects may predispose some persons to specific metabolic alterations under severe stress, and that these changes may in turn impair brain functioning.

It may be emphasized here that although we have dealt with these specific models of causation in terms of their distinctive features, several or all of them may be essential to understanding the dynamics of a particular maladaptive pattern.

CHANGING VIEWS OF CAUSAL RELATIONSHIPS

Traditionally in the sciences, the task of determining cause-and-effect relationships has entailed the isolation of a given condition X (cause), which leads to another condition Y (effect). For example, the spirochete of syphilis was isolated as the cause of the mental disorder called *general paresis*. Where more than one causal factor is involved, the term *causal pattern* is used. Here, conditions A, B, C, etc., lead to condition Y. Thus, in essence, the concept of cause follows a simple linear model, in which a given variable or set of variables leads to an end result.

1. *Effect of feedback on the causal agent.* With the introduction of the notion of cybernetics and the concept of self-regulating open systems, the causal picture often becomes much more complex. No longer is a simple linear relationship of cause to effect sufficient as a model. For now the effects of *feedback* on the causal agent must also be taken into account. Consider, for example, the following situation:

A husband and wife are undergoing counseling for difficulties in their marriage. The husband accuses his wife of drinking excessively; while the wife accuses her husband of rejecting her and showing no affection. In explaining her frustrations to the therapist, the wife views the situation as "I drink because my husband rejects me"; while the husband sees the problem differently: "I reject my wife because she drinks too much."

Over time a vicious circle develops in which the husband increasingly withdraws as his wife increasingly drinks. Assuming that each contributes about equally to their mutual difficulties, it becomes extremely difficult, if not impossible, to differentiate cause from effect. Rather, the problem is one of circularity; A influences B in this interaction, and B influences A—and so on. The husband "punctuates" the interaction, in terms of the direction of the cause-and-effect sequence, in one way; while the wife punctuates it in the opposite way. The causal picture becomes still more complicated when added to it is the influence of the total field situation in which the interaction occurs.

This hypothetical situation helps to point out that new concepts of causal relationships must deal with the more complex factors of feedback loops, information exchange or communication, patterns of interaction, and circularity.

2. *Predisposing, precipitating, and reinforcing causes.* As we have seen, in dealing with maladaptive behavior it is useful to think in terms of predisposing, precipitating, and reinforcing factors. Predisposing factors—such as extreme fatigue or parental rejection—go before and pave the way for later psychopathology; precipitating factors are conditions—such as disappointment in love—that prove too much for the individual and trigger the "symptoms" of his disorder; and reinforcing factors are involved in maintaining the maladaptive behavior over time.

With respect to predisposing and precipitating factors, we again have to contend with circularity; for example, the conditions that precipitate a schizophrenic episode or other mental disorder today may serve as predisposing causes for a recurrence of such psychopathology at a later time.

In this chapter we have considered the interrelated causes of abnormal or maladaptive behavior—faulty development and excessive stress. In some instances, as in combat situations, it may be the overwhelming stress that plays the dominant role. In other instances, as in the case of a withdrawn and fearful child who becomes a seriously maladjusted young adult and eventually a schizophrenic, early and continued faulty learning and development seem to be largely responsible for the abnormal behavior.

In our review of the various factors that may be involved in faulty development, we paid particular attention to genetic defects, constitutional vulnerabilities and physical handicaps, maternal deprivation, early trauma, pathogenic family patterns, social pathology, and failure to develop an adequate self-structure. We then examined some major sources of stress in contemporary life—biological, psychological, and sociocultural. Whether or not a stressful situation becomes overwhelming depends on the individual's evaluation of it, his intellectual and other competencies, the social supports available to him, and the objective severity of the stress. Rounding out our perspective on causation, we reviewed faulty learning and other models of psychopathology and we noted our changing views of causal relationships. This perspective will be highly useful as we turn now to an examination of specific patterns of abnormal behavior.

Patterns
of Abnormal
Behavior

Part Three

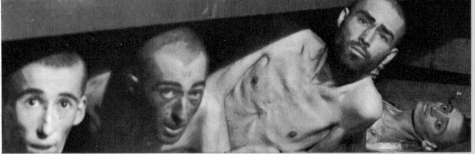

Transient Situational Disorders

7

TRAUMATIC REACTIONS TO COMBAT

REACTIONS TO CIVILIAN CATASTROPHES

REACTIONS TO CHRONIC SITUATIONAL STRESS

PSYCHOLOGICAL PROBLEMS IN SPACE FLIGHTS

As we noted previously, any one of us may break down if the going gets tough enough. When conditions of overwhelming stress occur—as in terrifying accidents, imprisonment, physical mutilation, or military combat—temporary mental disorders may develop, even in previously stable personalities. The personality decompensation may be sudden, as in the case of an individual who has gone through a severe accident or fire; or it may be gradual, as in the case of a person who has been subjected to conditions in a prisoner-of-war camp or even to a very difficult situation in civilian life. Usually the individual shows good recoverability once the stress situation is over, although in some cases there is residual damage to the self-structure and an increased vulnerability to certain types of stress. Of course, in the case of individuals who are marginally adjusted to begin with, the situational stress may precipitate more serious psychopathology.

Perhaps the special value of starting our discussion with these transient personality disturbances, particularly with reactions to the acute stress of combat, lies in the perspective that they can give us on the development of more typical maladaptive patterns that occur in less extreme situations. World War II, as well as the Korean War and the war in Vietnam, furnished the social sciences with a laboratory in which the effects of severe environmental stresses on the personality integration of thousands of men could readily be evaluated. As Grinker (1969) has pointed out:

"The entire range of factors from the biological to the sociological were sharply etched in miniature and required only a magnified view for understanding. Likewise time was compressed so that in rapid succession we could view predisposition, precipitation, breakdown, and recovery." (p. 3)

Although war is undeniably abhorrent, it has provided a research setting that could perhaps never be duplicated in civilian life. As a result of this unique situation, plus the pressure of military necessity growing out of the large number of men developing transient reactions to combat—particularly in World War II and the initial phases of the Korean War—marked strides were made in the understanding and treatment of psychopathology.

These forward strides in the understanding of psychological breakdowns in combat settings led, in turn, to a better understanding of mental disorders by the general public. For the first time, millions of people became aware of the potential effects of extreme stress upon personality integration. They learned that such stress could seriously impair adaptive behavior or even incapacitate the individual; and they learned that this was not a disgrace—it could happen to anyone.

We shall begin our discussion with the psychological casualties of World War II and of the conflicts in Korea and Vietnam, particularly those cases involving army personnel subjected to combat; then we shall attempt to show the general implication of these findings for typical civilian mental disorders. Next we shall examine transient personality reactions to civilian catastrophes and to other situations of unusual and severe stress. Although we shall see similarities, we shall also see differences between combat and civilian stress reactions. Finally, we shall discuss some of the psychological problems associated with man's exploration of space.

TRAUMATIC REACTIONS TO COMBAT

During World War I traumatic reactions to combat conditions were called "shell shock," a term coined by a British pathologist, Col. Frederick Mott, who regarded such reactions as organic conditions produced by minute hemorrhages of the brain. It was gradually realized, however, that only a very small percentage of such cases represented physical injury from concussion of exploding shells or bombs. Most of these men were suffering instead from the general combat situation with its physical fatigue, the ever present threat of death or mutilation, and severe psychological shocks. During World War II, traumatic reactions to combat passed through a number of classifications, such as "operational fatigue" and "war neuroses," before finally being termed "combat fatigue" or "combat exhaustion" in the Korean War and the Vietnam conflict.

Even the latter terms were none too aptly chosen, since they implied that physical exhaustion played a more important role in such reactions than was usually the case. However, they did serve to distinguish such disorders for purposes of treatment from neurotic, psychotic, and other disorders that happened to occur under war conditions but might well have occurred in civilian life—for example, among individuals showing a history of maladaptive behavior which was aggravated by the increased stress of military life. In the great majority of cases, men who became psychological casualties under combat conditions had adjusted satisfactorily to civilian life and to prior military experiences.

In World War II an estimated 10 percent of the men in combat developed combat exhaustion; however, the actual incidence is not known since many received therapy at their battalion aid station and were returned to combat within a matter of hours. Records were kept mainly on men evacuated from the front lines who were considered the more seriously disturbed cases. Of the slightly over 10 million men accepted for military service during World War II, approximately 1,363,000 were given medical discharges, of which approximately 530,000—39 percent— were for neuropsychiatric disorders. In fact, what we now call combat exhaustion was the disability causing the single greatest loss of manpower during that war (Bloch, 1969). In the Korean War the incidence of combat exhaustion dropped from an initial high of over 6 percent to 3.7 percent; and 27 percent of medical discharges were for psychiatric reasons (Bell, 1958). In the Vietnam conflict the figure dropped to less than 1.5 percent for combat exhaustion, with a negligible number of discharges for psychiatric disorders (Bourne, 1970; Tuohy, 1968).

The marked decrease in combat exhaustion cases in the Vietnam War has apparently been due to a number of factors, including (1) improved methods of selection and training, (2) competent military leadership, (3) the sporadic nature of the fighting, in which brief intensive encounters were followed by periods of relative calm and safety— as contrasted with weeks and months of prolonged combat which many soldiers went through in World War II and the Korean War—and (4) a policy of rotation after twelve months of service (thirteen months for Marines). Apparently it is easier for soldiers to tolerate combat stress for a known period of time, after which the war becomes "somebody else's war."

CLINICAL PICTURE

The specific symptoms in combat exhaustion have varied considerably, depending on the branch of the service, the severity and nature of the traumatic experience, and the personality makeup of the individual. Common symptoms among combat troops were dejection, weariness, hypersensitivity, sleep disturbances, and tremors. In air-corps personnel, after long combat flying, the more typical symptoms were anxiety, frequently with accompanying dejection and depression, phobias toward combat missions, irritability, tension, and startle reactions. In addition, where the stress was cumulative, symptoms often differed from those brought on by a sudden and particularly intense combat situation. Despite such variations, however, there was surprising uniformity in the general clinical picture —in World War II and the Korean and Vietnam wars.

"There is almost unanimous agreement that the first symptoms of the failure to maintain psychological equilibrium are increasing irritability and disturbances of sleep.

"The irritability is manifested externally by snappishness, over-reaction to minor irritations, angry reactions to innocuous questions or incidents, flareups with profanity and even tears at relatively slight frustrations. The degree of these reactions may vary from angry looks or a few sharp words to acts of violence.

"Subjectively, the state of irritation is perceived by the soldier as an unpleasant 'hypersensitiveness' and he is made doubly uncomfortable by a concomitant awareness of his diminishing self-control. One patient put this very vividly by saying—'The first thing that brought home to me the fact that I was slipping was this incident: A fellow next to me took some cellophane off a piece of hard candy and crumpled it up, and that crackling noise sounded like a forest fire. It made me so mad I wanted to hit him. Then I was ashamed of being so jumpy.'

"In association with this 'hypersensitiveness' to minor external stimuli, the 'startle reaction' becomes manifest (increasingly so as time goes on). This is a sudden leaping, jumping, cringing, jerking or other form of involuntary self-protective motor response to sudden, not necessarily very loud noises, and sometimes also to sudden movement or sudden light.

"The disturbances of sleep, which almost always accompany the symptom of increased irritability, consist mainly in the frustrating experience of not being able to fall asleep even upon those occasions when the military situation would permit. Soldiers have to snatch their rest when they can. They expect a rude and sudden awakening at any time. Opportunities for sleep become very precious and an inability to use them very distressing. Difficulties were experienced also in staying asleep because of sudden involuntary starting or leaping up, or because of terror dreams, battle dreams and nightmares of other kinds.

"This triad of increased 'sensitivity,' irritable reactions and sleep disturbances represents the incipient state of 'combat exhaustion.' It usually does not lead to referral [for treatment]. It may exist without much change for days, weeks or even months. Sooner or later, often upon the occasion of some incident of particularly traumatic significance to the soldier, the marginal and very unstable equilibrium is upset and the soldier becomes a casualty." (Bartemeier et al., 1946, pp. 374–375)

When the combat casualties reached the aid station or the clearing station, they presented a somewhat typical pattern of symptoms, differing only in the degree of personality decompensation.

"In the majority of cases they followed a stereotyped pattern: 'I just can't take it any more'; 'I can't stand those shells'; 'I just couldn't control myself.' They varied little from patient to patient. Whether it was the soldier who had experienced his baptism of fire or the older veteran who had lost his comrades, the superficial result was very similar. Typically he appeared as a dejected, dirty, weary man. His facial expression was one of depression, sometimes of tearfulness. Frequently his hands were trembling or jerking. Occasionally he would display varying degrees of confusion, perhaps to the extent of being mute or staring into space. Very occasionally he might present classically hysterical symptoms." (Menninger, 1948, p. 143)

In extreme cases where the soldier has undergone an unusually traumatic combat experience, the entire episode may be repressed so that he is amnesic for the entire battle experience.

The following diary covers a period of about six weeks of combat in the South Pacific area and illustrates the cumulative effect of combat stresses on an apparently stable personality.

"Aug. 7, 1942. Convoy arrived at Guadalcanal Bay at approximately 4 A.M. in the morning. Ships gave enemy a heavy shelling. At 9 A.M. we stormed the beach and formed an immediate beachhead, a very successful landing, marched all day in the hot sun, and at night took positions and rested. Enemy planes attacked convoy in bay but lost 39 out of 40 planes.

"Aug. 8, 1942. Continued march in the hot sun and in afternoon arrived at airport. Continued on through the Jap village and made camp for the night. During the night, Jap navy attacked convoy in battle that lasted until early morning. Enemy had terrific losses and we lost two ships. This night while on sentry duty, I mistook a horse for a Jap and killed it.

"Aug. 19, 1942. Enemy cruiser and destroyer came into bay and shelled the beach for about two hours. The cruiser left and the destroyer hung around for the entire morning. We all kept under shelter for the early afternoon a flying fortress flew over, spotting the ship and bombed it, setting it afire we all jumped and shouted with joy. That night trouble again was feared and we again slept in foxholes.

"Aug. 21, 1942. The long awaited landing by the enemy was made during the night 1500 troops in all and a few prisoners were taken and the rest were killed. Bodies were laying all over beach. In afternoon planes again bombed the Island. [Here the writing begins to be shaky, and less careful than previously.]

"Aug. 28, 1942. The company left this morning in higgins Boats to the end of the Island, landed and started through thick Jungle and hills. It was hot and we had to cut our way through. In afternoon we contacted the japs. our squad was in the assault squad so we moved up the beach to take positions the enemy trapped us with machine gun and rifle fire for about two hours. The lead was really flying. Two of our men were killed, two were hit by a hand greade and my corporal received a piece of shrampnel in back,—was wounded in arm, out of the squad of eight we have five causitry. We withdrew and were taken back to the Hospital.

"Sept. 12, 1942. Large jap squadron again bombed Island out of 35 planes sent over our air force knocked down 24. During the raid a large bomb was dropped just sevety yards from my fox hole.

"Sept. 13, 1942. At on o'clock three destroyers and one cruiser shelled us contumally all night The ships turned surch lights all up and down the beach, and stopped one my foxhole seveal time I'm feeling pritty nervese and scared, afraid I'll be a nervas reack be for long. slept in fox hole all night not much sleep. This morning at 9:00 we had a nother air raid, the raid consisted of mostly fighter planes. I believe we got several, this afternoon. we had a nother raid, and our planes went out to met them, met them someplace over Tulagi, new came in that the aircraft carrier wasp sent planes out to intersept the bombers. This eving all hell broke lose. Our marines contacted enemy to south of us and keep up constant fire all night through.

"Sept. 14, 1942. This morning firing still going on my company is scaduted to unload ships went half ways up to dock when enemyfire start on docks, were called back to our pososeion allon beach, company called out again to go after japs, hope were lucker than we were last time [part of this illegible.] Went up into hills at 4:00 P.M. found positions, at 7:00 en 8 sea planes fombed and strifed us, 151942 were strifed biy amfibious planes and bombed the concussion of one through me of balance and down a 52 foot hil. I was shaking likd a leaf. Lost my bayanut, and ran out of wathr. I nearves and very jumpy, hop I last out until morning. I hope sevearly machine s guns ore oping up on our left flank there going over our heads

"Sept. 16. this morning we going in to take up new possissons we march all moring and I am very week and nerves, we marched up a hill and ran in to the affaul place y and z company lost so many men I hardly new what I was doing then I'm going nuts.

"Sept. 17. don't remember much of this day.

"Sept. 18. Today I'm on a ship leaving this awful place, called Green Hell. I'm still nearves and shakey." (Stern, 1947, pp. 583–586)

In some instances the personality decompensation is more immediate and acute as a result of some particularly overwhelming combat experience. This is well illustrated in the following case from the Vietnam War.

"A 21-year-old rifleman was flown directly to the hospital from an area of fighting by a helicopter ambulance. No information accompanied him, he had no identifying tags on his uniform, and he was so completely covered with mud that a physical description of his features was not possible. His hands had been tied behind him for the flight, and he had a wild, wide-eyed look as he cowered in a corner of the emergency room, glancing furtively to all sides, cringing and startling at the least noise. He was mute, although once he forced out a whispered 'VC' and tried to mouth other words without success. He seemed terrified. Although people could approach him, he appeared oblivious to their presence. No manner of reassurance or direct order achieved either a verbal response or any other interaction from him.

"His hands were untied, after which he would hold an imaginary rifle in readiness whenever he heard a helicopter overhead or an unexpected noise. The corpsmen led him to the psychiatric ward, took him to a shower, and offered him a meal; he ate very little. He began to move a little more freely but still offered no information.

"He was then given 100 mg. of chlorpromazine (Thorazine) orally; this dose was repeated hourly until he fell asleep. He was kept asleep in this manner for approximately 40 hours. After that he was allowed to waken, the medication was discontinued, and he was mobilized rapidly in the ward milieu.[1] Although dazed and subdued upon awakening, his response in the ward milieu was dramatic. This was aided by the presence of a friend from his platoon on an adjoining ward, who helped by filling in parts of the story that the patient could not recall. The patient was an infantryman whose symptoms had developed on a day when his platoon had been caught in an ambush and then was overrun by the enemy. He was one of three who survived after being pinned down by enemy fire for 12 hours. His friend told him that toward the end of that time he had developed a crazed expression and had tried to run from his hiding place. He was pulled back to safety and remained there until the helicopter arrived and flew him to the hospital.

"Within 72 hours after his admission the patient was alert, oriented, responsive, and active—still a little tense but ready to return to duty. He was sent back to duty on his third hospital day and never seen again at our facility. It should be noted that he had no history of similar symptoms or emotional disorder." (Bloch, 1969, p. 42)

In the recorded cases of combat exhaustion the common core usually was overwhelming anxiety. In World War II, however, an exception was noted in the case of troops from India to whom admission of fear was unacceptable. They rarely showed anxiety reactions, instead resorting occasionally to self-mutilation and other "honor-

able" ways of avoiding further combat (Williams, 1950).

It is interesting to note that wounded soldiers were apt to show less anxiety and other combat exhaustion symptoms. In fact, anxiety states with major wounds were exceptionally rare; in general, the more disabling the wound, the less the anxiety, except in cases of permanent mutilation (McElroy, 1945; Noble, Roudebush & Price, 1952; Tuohy, 1967b). Apparently the wound, in providing an escape from the stressful combat situation, at the same time removed the source of the anxiety state. It was not unusual for a soldier to admit that he had prayed to be hit or to have something honorable happen to remove him from battle. When they were approaching full recovery and the necessity of returning to combat, injured men sometimes showed prolongation of their symptoms or a delayed traumatic reaction with nervousness, insomnia, and related symptoms which were nonexistent during the initial period of hospitalization.

In some cases soldiers who had stood up exceptionally well under intensive combat experiences developed what might be called "delayed combat reactions" upon their return home—often in response to relatively minor stresses in the home situation which they had previously been capable of handling. Evidently there had been underlying damage to their adaptive capabilities, in some cases complicated by memories of killing enemy soldiers or civilians, tinged with feelings of guilt and anxiety [Karpe & Schnap, 1952; Polner, 1968; Strange & Brown, 1970).

DYNAMICS

In a combat situation, with the continual threat of injury or death and repeated narrow escapes, one's ordinary methods of coping are relatively useless. The adequacy and security feelings the individual has known in a relatively safe and dependable civilian world are completely undermined. Furthermore, the ever present threat can be neither overcome nor escaped. As one soldier recalled his twelve months of combat experience in Vietnam:

---

[1]The ward milieu was designed to be therapeutic in nature.

These pictures, taken during the war in Southeast Asia, give some indication of the extreme stress to which soldiers are subjected during combat.

"I was always afraid. In fact, I can't remember not being afraid. For one thing, a combat medic doesn't know what's happening. Especially at night, everybody screaming or moaning and calling, 'Medic, medic.' I always saw myself dying, my legs blown off, my brains spattered all about, shivering in shock, and talking madly. This is what I *saw* in reality." (Polner, 1968, p. 18)

Although not all soldiers experience the same degree of threat and anxiety in combat situations, there is an emergency mobilization of emotional resources, which is sustained as long as the crisis exists; and with time, there are usually increasingly severe feelings of threat and anxiety as one sees one's buddies killed or wounded and experiences narrow escapes oneself.

The hypersensitivity shown in the startle reaction follows directly from this continued fear and anxiety. Consequently, the buzz of a fly or the striking of a match may produce marked overreactions. This hypersensitivity is, of course, intensified when the stimulus bears a direct association with some traumatic combat experience. A soldier who has been strafed by attacking planes may be terrified by the sight of approaching aircraft. As continued emotional mobilization and fatigue take their toll of adjustive resources, the common symptom of irritability makes its appearance and adds to the soldier's anxiety by making him aware of his diminishing self-control. Even in our normal lives, prolonged emotional stress and fatigue tend to keep our nerves "on edge" and to increase irritability.

Difficulties in falling asleep and other sleep disturbances are common accompaniments of anxiety and sustained emotional arousal. Most of us have difficulty in sleeping when we are emotionally upset. However, the dynamic significance of the recurrent nightmares is not fully understood. How and why does the traumatic material become reactivated during sleep, when the soldier desperately needs quiet and rest? In some cases the repeated dreams are so terrifying that the soldier is even afraid to go to sleep. It may be, however, that the continual reliving of a traumatic battle experience in dreams gradually serves to discharge the anxiety associated with it and to desensitize the individual to the point where he can assimilate the experience.

In severe combat exhaustion cases, the stupor or amnesia is thought to result from temporary repression, which enables the individual to avoid consciousness of the traumatic experience until its emotional intensity has cooled down to the point where he can tolerate memory of it. Here the defensive function of repression is clearly demonstrated since the repressed material can be brought to consciousness in full detail under the influence of hypnosis or various drugs, such as sodium pentothal.

So far, we have spoken only of excessive stress as a precipitating cause in combat exhaustion. However, we must not overlook the fact that some 90 percent of the men came through combat without becoming psychiatric casualties, although most of them evidenced severe fear reactions and other symptoms of ego disorganization which were not serious enough to be incapacitating. In addition, many men tolerated almost unbelievable stress before they broke, while others became casualties under conditions of relatively slight combat stress. Consequently, it appears that differences in the evaluation of combat stress, along with other factors—such as possible biological predisposition, fatigue, one's degree of personal maturity, confidence in one's officers, identification with one's unit, convictions about war goals, and previous experience in handling stress—must be examined for their contribution to the total picture.

Biological factors. Do constitutional differences in sensitivity, vigor, and temperament affect one's resistance to the stress of combat? The probabilities are that they do, but there is a dearth of actual evidence. Similarly, the importance of a family history of mental disorder is not clear. Hastings, Wright, and Glueck (1944) reported a history of psychoses in 6 percent of the families of 100 American fliers who had completed a tour of combat duty without psychological mishap in World War II; thus, a family history of mental disorder does not necessarily disqualify a man for combat service. Army investigators did find, however, a relatively lower incidence of mental disorders and other pathological conditions in the background of successful soldiers, although this finding cannot be taken as conclusive evidence of the importance of hereditary or constitutional factors (Hirschberg, 1944; McNeel & Dancey, 1945; Sheps, 1944).

Of more importance than hereditary factors are the conditions of battle which place a tremendous strain on a soldier's physical stamina. Grinker and Spiegel describe this vividly in a World War II study:

"Battle conditions are notoriously destructive to health. Frequently men must go for days without adequate sleep or rest. . . . The purely physiological effects of nearby blasts are also a factor. Many men are repeatedly subjected to minimal doses of blast. They are knocked over by the compression wave, or perhaps blown slightly off the ground, if they are lying prone. In some instances they are temporarily numbed or even stunned. . . . Lastly, the continued auditory irritation of constant explosions, bangs, snaps of machine guns, whines of artillery shells, rustle of mortars . . . wears down resistance." (1945, pp. 68–70)

Add other factors that have often occurred in combat situations—such as severe climatic conditions, malnutrition, and disease—to the strain of continual emotional mobilization, and the result is a general lowering of the individual's resistance to all stress.

Psychological and interpersonal factors. A number of psychological and interpersonal factors may contribute to the overall stress load experienced by a soldier and predispose him to break down under the increased burden of combat. Such factors include separation from home and loved ones, sacrifice of personal freedom, frustrations of all sorts, marital or related problems, and the anxiety built up by prior combat experiences. Letters from home which create worries add to the soldier's already difficult adjustive burden—particularly since he is far away and is helpless to take any action. A soldier who has withstood months of combat may break when he finds that his wife has been unfaithful, when she stops writing, or when she writes him a "Dear John" letter stating that she is leaving him for someone else. The death of a buddy may lead to a serious loss of emotional support as well as to feelings of guilt if the soldier cannot help feeling glad that it was his buddy and not himself who was killed.

Several other psychological and interpersonal factors deserve special mention:

1. Strangeness of the situation can be a source of severe threat and stress. When the individual knows what to expect and what to do he has a much better chance of coming through with a minimum of psychological disorganization. But even the best training cannot fully prepare a soldier for all the conditions of actual battle. The factor of strangeness also partly explains the effectiveness of innovations in armaments for which enemy soldiers are not properly prepared.

Related to the strangeness of the combat situation in terms of the average soldier's background of experience in civilian life is the common reaction expressed by many combat soldiers in Vietnam of feeling that "I'm out there alone." Although there are other soldiers in their vicinity, they often feel that there is really no one "who cares about what happens to me." For this reason, where combat conditions permit, soldiers are often encouraged to shout to one another, to remind themselves that they are not alone on the battlefield (Tuohy, 1967a).

2. Immobilization in the face of acute danger makes soldiers especially vulnerable to combat exhaustion. Sustained artillery fire, under which the soldier is helpless and cannot fight back, is particularly destructive and leads to a marked intensification of anxiety.

The combat exhaustion case cited on page 190, of the soldier who was pinned down by enemy fire for twelve hours after most of his platoon had been killed in an enemy ambush, is an example of the effects of immobilization on a person in extreme danger. Some activity or duty to perform, even though it does not lessen the danger, appears to provide an outlet for tension and to help a soldier keep his fear and anxiety within manageable limits.

3. The necessity of killing enemy soldiers, and sometimes civilians, can also be an important factor in combat reactions. Most of us have strong moral convictions against killing or injuring others, and for some men it is psychologically almost impossible to engage in ruthless killing. In extreme cases, such soldiers may even be unable to defend themselves when attacked. When such men do engage in killing they often have intense feelings of guilt, together with fear of retaliation and punishment.

A good fighter, a machine gunner, one day killed five of the enemy almost simultaneously. "His first reaction was elation—but suddenly he felt that it was wrong to enjoy this and thereupon developed anxiety with some depression, so severe that he was incapacitated." (Saul, 1945, p. 262)

Such a soldier may come to see further combat as the means by which he is inevitably to receive the dreaded retaliation and punishment for his actions. Thus, anxiety arising out of combat experience may reflect not only a simple fear of death or mutilation but also emotional conflicts and guilt feelings generated by the act of killing other human beings.

4. The longer a soldier is in combat, the more vulnerable—and more anxious—he is likely to feel. Although, as Tuohy (1967b) found, most soldiers on their arrival in Vietnam had the notion of their own invulnerability—that anyone but themselves was likely to get killed—they soon found that Vietnam was a dangerous place and that "war really is hell." This time of realization is when many soldiers show their first signs of anxiety. And after a soldier has been in combat for a while and has seen many of his buddies killed and wounded as well as having had narrow escapes himself, he usually loses whatever feelings of invulnerability he may have had. When a soldier has almost completed the number of missions or duration of duty necessary for rotation, particularly, he is apt to feel that his "luck has run out" and that a bullet coming his way will "have his name on it."

The effect of prolonged combat in lowering stress tolerance was exemplified in World War II by "the old sergeant syndrome," in which men of established bravery exhibited anxiety, depression, tremulousness, and impairment of self-confidence and judgment after prolonged combat experience —usually 150 to 350 days of combat (Bell, 1958). The progressive lowering of stress tolerance under prolonged combat is illustrated in the case study on page 190.

5. Personality characteristics that lower the individual's resistance to stress or to a particular type of stress may be important in determining his reactions to combat. Personal immaturity— often stemming from maternal overprotection— has often been cited as making the soldier more vulnerable to combat stress.

Interestingly enough, a background of personal maladjustment does not always make an individual a "poor risk" for withstanding the stresses of combat. Some neurotics are apparently so accustomed to anxiety that they can cope with it more or less automatically, whereas men who are feeling severe anxiety for the first time are often terrified by the experience, lose their self-confidence, and go to pieces. Thus in some cases it would appear that a neurosis may actually be beneficial to a man's adjustment to combat. It has also been observed that psychopathic personalities, though frequently in trouble in the armed services during peacetime as a consequence of disregarding rules and regulations, often demonstrated good initiative and effective combat aggression against the enemy. In general, however, the more adequate the individual's personality integration and adjustment are prior to combat, the more stress he is apt to stand before breaking. The soldiers who function effectively and survive the rigors of combat without breaking down most often come from family backgrounds which fostered emotional maturity, acceptance of responsibility, self-reliance, ability to identify with the group, and ready adjustment to new situations (Bloch, 1969; Grinker, 1969; Knight, 1943; Nardini, 1962a).

General sociocultural factors. In the preceding section our focus was on psychological and interpersonal factors that may contribute to a soldier's stress load in battle. There remain to be considered a number of more general sociocultural factors that may play a part in determining an individual's adjustment to combat. These include the clarity and acceptability of war goals, the quality of military leadership, and the cohesiveness and morale of the combat unit.

1. *Clarity and acceptability of war goals.* In general, the more concretely and realistically war goals can be integrated into the values of the individual in terms of "his stakes" in the war and the worth and importance of what he is doing, the greater will be their supportive effect on him. The individual who is fighting only because he is forced to, or to "get the damned war over with," is not as effective and does not stand stress as well as the soldier who knows what he is fighting for and is convinced of its importance. Time and again men who have felt strongly about the rightness of their cause and its vital importance to themselves and their loved ones have shown incredible endurance, bravery, and personal sacrifice under combat conditions.

Of course, in the actual combat situation the soldier's concern about the political goals of the war is somewhat remote; he is fighting for survival. Too, as is often the case, a young soldier may not understand the complexities of international policies and may simply have accepted combat as a job his country asked him to undertake.

2. *Quality of leadership.* Confidence in military leaders is also of vital importance. When the soldier respects his leaders and has confidence in their judgment and ability, and can accept them as relatively strong father or brother figures, his morale and resistance to stress are bolstered. On the other hand, lack of confidence or actual dislike of leaders is highly detrimental to morale and to combat stress tolerance.

In fact, Bloch (1969) points to the distinction between what he terms *intrapsychic* and *interpersonal psychopathology.* The former has reference to doubts, conflicts, and anxieties within the individual, and the latter to difficulties between the individual and other members of his group. Of course, the two classifications may overlap, in that intrapsychic difficulties not infrequently lead to difficulties also in interpersonal relationships. Bloch, however, considers the distinction an important one, inasmuch as transferring a soldier from a unit in which he is in conflict with his superior may be the most effective way of resolving a crisis situation and preventing further damage to the soldier's morale and stress tolerance.

3. *Cohesiveness and group identification.* It has been found particularly important to maintain good group identification in combat troops. The soldier who is unable to identify himself with or take pride in his group lacks the feeling of "we-ness" that is a highly supportive factor in maintaining stress tolerance. Lacking this, he stands alone, psychologically isolated and less able to withstand combat stress. In fact, the stronger the sense of group identification, the less chance that the soldier will crack up in combat.

In cases of combat exhaustion, the soldier often returns to his unit with feelings of apprehension that his unit will not accept him or have confidence in him in the future (Tuohy, 1968). If the group does accept him, he is likely to make a satisfactory readjustment to further combat; if it does not, he is highly vulnerable to subsequent breakdown. In general, group identification and acceptance appear to be highly important in maintaining his appropriate róle behavior.

4. *Esprit de corps.* Closely related to group identification is the matter of *esprit de corps,* the morale of the group as a whole. The spirit of the group seems to be contagious. When the group is generally optimistic and confident prior to battle, the individual is also apt to show good morale. If the unit has a reputation for efficiency in battle, the individual soldier is challenged to exhibit his maximum effort and efficiency.

On the other hand, when the unit is demoralized prior to battle, is defeated in battle and resorts to disorganized flight, or has a history of defeats and a high loss of personnel, the individual is likely

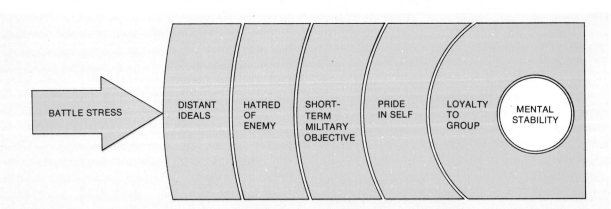

In studying the eventual breakdown of the army personnel who had been most resistant to personality decompensation, Sobel (1949) found that such individuals seemed to have been protected by five "defensive layers." These were surrendered progressively in the face of too-severe stress and threat. Distant ideals like "democracy" and "the four freedoms" went first. Loyalty to the group was the last to be given up.

to succumb more easily to anxiety and panic. This is particularly true if low *esprit de corps* is associated with lack of confidence in leaders or in the importance of immediate combat objectives.

5. *Other supportive factors.* A number of other supportive factors merit brief mention. The "buddy system," in which the individual is encouraged to strike up a close personal relationship with another member of his unit, often provides needed emotional support. The pursuit of short-range military objectives appears, in general, to cause less stress than the pursuit of long-range ones, where there always seems to be another hill or town to take. Finally, hatred of the enemy appears to be a factor that tends to raise the combat soldier's stress tolerance.

In the context of social supports that are important in maintaining or raising a soldier's stress tolerance, it may be noted that prisoners of war subjected to "brainwashing" during the Korean conflict were systematically isolated from these sources of support. Leaderless and alone, encouraged to be suspicious of each other and to question America's war goals, and systematically made to choose between ethical values and satisfaction of minimum body needs, their will to resist was often broken. The brainwashing techniques used and their short-term effects are summarized in the chart on page 211.

In summarizing the dynamics of combat exhaustion, it may be emphasized that the terrifying nature of the combat situation is actually only one of the causes of such a reaction. We must also consider a complex of other factors, such as the morale of the group, the soldier's relationships with buddies, his confidence in the competence of leaders, his degree of physical fatigue, the adequacy of his training, his family situation and problems, and his own motivation and stress tolerance in general. And as we have seen, the duration of combat and the approaching time of rotation—when the war becomes "somebody else's war"—are also important considerations.

TREATMENT AND OUTCOMES

In most cases the decompensation brought on by the acute stress of battle conditions has been quickly reversed when the men were taken out of combat and given brief therapy. In World War II,

an attempt was made to give treatment as near to the battlefront or combat group as was practical (Menninger, 1948). Treatment usually consisted of mild supportive psychotherapy, warm food, and sedation to help the soldier gain needed sleep. Many men were able to return to combat after a night or two of such relief. Soldiers whose symptoms proved refractory were evacuated to medical facilities at the rear. It was found, however, that the farther the soldier was removed from the combat area for treatment, the less likely he was to be able to return to battle. Removal to an interior zone seemed, in fact, to encourage the maintenance of symptoms on the soldier's part and a reluctance to return to his unit. For example, during the first combat engagements of the American forces in North Africa in World War II, when combat exhaustion cases were transported from the fighting area to base hospitals, often some three hundred to five hundred miles behind the lines, less than 10 percent of the men in question were able to return to duty (Menninger, 1948). In contrast, with immediate treatment within fifteen to twenty miles of the front lines, approximately 60 percent of combat exhaustion cases were sent back to combat duty, and apparently the majority of these men readjusted successfully to combat conditions (Ludwig & Ranson, 1947). Such statistics varied, however—ranging from a high of 80 to 90 percent for men from units with only a month or so of combat, down to 30 to 35 percent for "old" divisions. Comparable statistics were obtained in the Korean War, with some 65 to 75 percent of the soldiers treated at the division level or forward being returned to combat duty, and less than 10 percent of those returned showing up as repeaters (Hausman & Rioch, 1967; Peterson & Chambers, 1952). Statistics for the Vietnam War are somewhat unclear, but the percentage of men responding favorably to treatment appears even higher (Bloch, 1969).

The lessons learned in World War II were translated in the Korean and Vietnam wars into the principles of *immediacy, proximity,* and *expectancy* (Bloch, 1969; Bourne, 1970; Glass, 1954; Hausman & Rioch, 1967).

1. *Immediacy* refers to the early detection of signs of combat exhaustion—such as sleeplessness, tremulousness, and crying spells—and the removal of the soldier for immediate treatment.

In the Vietnam War, for example, officers were taught to watch for these symptoms in combat personnel. When a soldier manifested such symptoms he was taken to the nearest outpost, where a specially trained medic administered to him—usually urging him to review the traumatic events, reassuring him, providing him with a hot meal when possible, and recommending medication for ensuring a restful night. The soldier was then returned to duty the next morning (Bloch, 1969). A prolonged delay between the occurrence of symptoms and treatment tended to fixate the decompensatory pattern, making it more resistant to therapy.

It may be noted that in such cases care was taken to use a bland label—such as *combat fatigue* or *combat exhaustion*—in referring to the soldier's condition. Otherwise it was found that the soldier tended to play the "sick role" assigned to him and to surrender the responsibility for his recovery and behavior to others (Hausman & Rioch, 1967).

2. *Proximity* refers to the treatment of the soldier as near to his combat unit and the battle zone as possible. As we have seen, mild cases were taken to the nearest outpost and given brief supportive therapy by specially trained medics. In the Vietnam War, soldiers who showed more severe combat reactions or whose symptoms proved refractory to this brief supportive therapy were often evacuated by helicopter to the division base camp, where a similar but more intensive program of rest and supportive therapy was instituted. Usually after three days of such treatment the soldier felt "like his old self again" and could return to his unit. In exceptionally refractory cases, the soldier was sent to a hospital in the zone of the interior containing a psychiatric ward staffed by medical, psychological, and social work personnel (Bloch, 1969).

3. *Expectancy* refers to (a) a "duty-expectant" attitude—the attitude that every soldier, despite his anxieties and traumatic experiences, is expected to perform his combat duties, and (b) the removal, insofar as possible, of the factor of gain in combat exhaustion—the attitude that anxiety, fear, and tension are not conditions of sufficient severity to require permanent removal from battle.

In the Korean War, such an approach on the

part of treatment personnel—who were themselves in the forward area and under enemy fire—implied that "the soldier was a morally responsible individual who either could fold up as the situation became more hazardous or could go on in spite of the multiplicity of symptoms which he might develop due to his fear and anxiety." (Bell, 1958, p. 285) The decision was his to make. It was felt that most men found themselves able to bear much more anxiety and tension than they would have believed possible, and that the number of combat exhaustion cases who were declared unfit for duty was markedly reduced by this approach. In essence, personal responsibility and a "doing role" were stressed rather than a "sick role," with a relinquishing of responsibility for one's recovery and behavior.

As we have seen, the great majority of combat exhaustion cases made a rapid recovery and returned to their units able to function in the battle situation. The soldiers evacuated to rear-area hospitals were often men with incipient neurotic or psychotic tendencies which appeared to have been precipitated by the traumatic combat experience. Following treatment, the majority of these men were able to return to noncombat duty, and in many instances, to combat duty. In the Korean War an attempt also was made to reclaim for combat duty earlier psychiatric casualties who had been assigned to noncombat positions in Japan (Glass, 1954). All such cases were reevaluated after three months, and 40 percent were considered sufficiently recovered to return to combat duty. Most of these men were able to carry on without further difficulty. The effectiveness of treatment in the Korean and Vietnam Wars is indicated by the fact that the relatively few soldiers requiring evacuation to the United States were almost all seriously psychotic cases (Hayes, 1969).

In a minority of cases, the residual effects of combat exhaustion persist for a sustained period of time. In one group of fifty-seven men who were studied fifteen years after their combat experience, Archibald and his associates (1962) found a high incidence of symptoms such as tension, irritability, depression, diffuse anxiety, headaches, insomnia, nightmares, and avoidance of situations involving exposure to loud noises or reminders of combat. These appeared to be severe, atypical cases in which the combat experience contributed to a chronic state of "overvigilance" and impaired functioning, and possibly in which there were sustained reinforcements for the "sick role."

In a follow-up study of ninety-two combat veterans of the Vietnam War, Polner (1968) cited a number of cases in which combat experiences continued to disturb the men after their return to civilian life. In most instances the difficulties appeared to center around killing and guilt feel-ings. For example, one veteran said, "I can't sleep, I'm a murderer." He continued:

"We were outside Bac Lieu, out on an eight man patrol along with 15 ARVNs.[1] Our orders were to move ahead and shoot at anything suspicious. My God, how I remember that damned day! It was hot and sticky. The mosquitoes were driving me crazy. And there was this boy, about 8 or 9. He had his hand behind his back, like he was hiding something. 'Grab him,' someone screamed, 'he's got something!'

[1] South Vietnamese soldiers.

RESIDUAL EFFECTS OF COMBAT EXHAUSTION IN WORLD WAR II VETERANS RECEIVING ASSISTANCE AT A VA OUTPATIENT PSYCHIATRIC CLINIC

Archibald and Tuddenham (1965) made a follow-up study of 62 World War II combat exhaustion cases in an investigation of residual effects of combat exhaustion. Taking symptoms reported by members of this group and the same symptoms as reported by a control group of 20 World War II veterans who had not suffered combat exhaustion, the investigators compared the rate of incidence. The chart, on which a representative number of symptoms are listed, indicates the far greater percent of incidence among the veterans who had suffered combat exhaustion. The absence of the second (lighter) line for the last symptom means that it was not observed in the "healthy" group.

The more severe combat exhaustion cases revealed additional symptoms, including difficulties in work and family relationships, social isolation, and narrowing of interests. Alcoholism was a problem for about 20 percent of both the combat exhaustion and non-combat exhaustion cases.

Archibald and Tuddenham concluded that the residual symptoms in the combat exhaustion cases represented gross stress reactions, which are found among persons throughout the world who have been subjected to different kinds of severe stress. In many such instances, symptoms appear to clear up when the stress is over, only to reappear in chronic form later. Thus, intense and sustained stress apparently can lead to lasting symptoms unless the victims receive adequate treatment and follow-up care.

These same investigators obtained corresponding findings in a follow-up study of 15 Korean War combat exhaustion cases. Although both this group and the World War II combat exhaustion veterans in the study just cited were receiving assistance at a Veterans Administration outpatient psychiatric clinic, none was receiving disability compensation, to which a prolongation of symptoms might otherwise be attributed.

Chart adapted from Archibald and Tuddenham (1965), omitting statistics for non-combat psychiatric military cases, which fell between those for the other two groups.

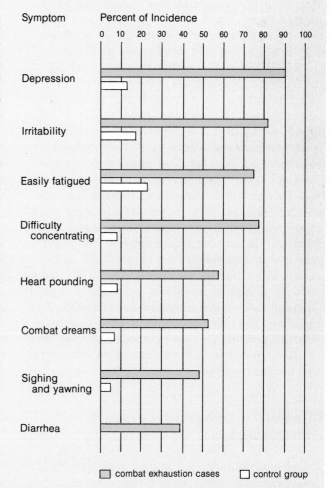

combat exhaustion cases   control group

I made a move for him and his hand moved again. 'Shoot!' I fired. Again and again, until my M-2 was empty. When I looked he was there, all over the ground, cut in two with his guts all around. I vomited. I wasn't told. I wasn't trained for that. It was out-and-out murder. . . .

"Another time, in a village, I was serving as an adviser when a woman ran out of her hut with a rifle held high above her head. She wasn't shooting it, only carrying it high, moaning and shrieking and crying, like she was mad. She was old, like my grandmother maybe. Shrieking and crying. One of the ARVNs then began shouting, 'VC! VC!' I fired once, twice. She fell dead. You know, I killed nine people as an adviser." (p. 12)

Many of the other veterans interviewed by Polner, however, felt that they had simply done their duty in a worthwhile cause. Polner quotes Dixon Wecter, a historian who has specialized in the postwar adjustment of veterans, to the effect that "war colors the mainstream of a citizen-soldier's life, but seldom changes its direction." (p. 20) Whether this holds true for veterans of the Vietnam War remains to be seen.

In another preliminary study of Vietnam combat returnees, Goldsmith and Cretekos (1969) found evidence of residual anxiety stemming from combat experiences and of depression associated with interpersonal problems. The latter finding has been supported in a study by Strange and Brown (1970) comparing combat and noncombat veterans who were experiencing emotional difficulties after returning home from Vietnam: the combat group showed a higher incidence of depression and of conflicts in their close interpersonal relationships. They also showed a higher incidence of aggressive and suicidal threats, but they did not actually carry them out. The investigators tentatively concluded that the potential for violence of these men was probably no greater than that of soldiers who had not been exposed to combat experiences.

CURRENT MILITARY PSYCHOLOGY AND PSYCHIATRY

Current military psychology and psychiatry are concerned with many problems, including the screening of inductees, the training and utilization of personnel, the maintenance of morale and personal effectiveness in the performance of duties, training for survival in the event of capture, and the prevention and treatment of combat exhaustion. For the moment we are concerned with the last three tasks.[1] (In subsequent chapters we shall see how principles developed in the military have direct application to civilian problems of mental health and to our contemporary community mental health approach.)

Maintenance of morale and effectiveness. There has been an increasing awareness that noneffective military behavior stems more often from difficulties in the environment—particularly in interpersonal relationships—than from individual psychopathology (Bloch, 1969; Glass et al., 1961; Grinker, 1969; Hausman & Rioch, 1967). As a consequence, there has been a gradual shifting of mental health personnel from their traditional roles and locations in military clinics and hospitals to the military community itself. The close working relationship between officers and mental health personnel which has resulted permits utilization of the "milieu"—the setting in which the soldier functions—for the treatment and prevention of ineffective behavior.

This new orientation has fostered three kinds or levels of assistance: (1) *primary prevention,* aimed at establishing conditions in the military environment that are likely to reduce the incidence of behavior problems and maladjustment; (2) *secondary prevention,* emphasizing the early recognition and prompt treatment of maladaptive behavior in the area of the soldier's unit; and (3) *tertiary prevention,* employing milieu therapy and intensive treatment for personnel with mental disorders requiring hospitalization, with the aim of heading off the development of chronic disabling conditions and returning the soldier to active duty as soon as possible (Glass et al., 1961; Hausman & Rioch, 1967). In Chapter 21 we shall deal with the application of similar

---

[1]Some psychologists and psychiatrists are presented with an ethical dilemma in viewing their training in the health and healing professions as incompatible with treating a combat-exhaustion case so that he may live to kill again or be killed. The question arises as to whether they are justified in using their skills to "adjust" a mind to the brutalities of combat, particularly when that mind has been traumatized by or has rejected these brutalities. We shall consider the problems of war and violence in more detail in Chapter 18. It may suffice to point out here that the ultimate answer appears to lie in coping with the problem of war itself.

principles to the prevention of psychopathology in civilian life.

Preparation for survival if captured. In the preparation of personnel for honorable survival as prisoners of war, the following points have been emphasized: (1) a clear understanding of what the soldier can expect as a prisoner and what is expected of him in the way of resisting collaboration; (2) a clear understanding of the futility and genuine hazards of collaboration, including the effects of ostracism by his own group; and (3) a strong identification with the military group and commitment to the civilian community for which he is fighting. It also appears that simulated capture and interrogation is a highly useful training procedure in preparing the soldier more realistically for what to expect and what to do in the event of capture.

Prevention and treatment of combat reactions in future wars. Since the stresses in any future war—and presumably the combat reactions—would differ from those of past wars, methods of treatment and prevention would have to be adapted accordingly. Where conditions were comparable with those of the past, however, treatment procedures would probably not differ greatly from those used in the Korean and Vietnam wars. It would, in any case, seem even more important

than in the past to prepare the soldier to know what to expect and what to do, to foster strong identification with his unit and the broader military community, to emphasize his role as a self-reliant and morally responsible individual, and to foster understanding and commitment to his country and what it stands for and is trying to achieve.

In the unthinkable event of a global atomic holocaust, the outcome would be unpredictable. Soldiers of the future must be prepared for eventualities which man has never before had to face—at least not on the same scale—such as the probable death and wounding of hundreds of millions of people during the first few hours of warfare. Also, with the dispersion of troops necessitated by atomic warfare, those soldiers who survived, if any, would be more isolated and probably subjected to many situations in which they would have to function alone in the face of tremendous stress. Such conditions would demand great adaptability, self-reliance, and moral responsibility on the part of any remaining civilian and military personnel if mankind were to survive and rebuild civilization. It has become apparent, however, as John F. Kennedy said, that "Mankind must put an end to war or war will put an end to mankind."

REACTIONS TO CIVILIAN CATASTROPHES

In civilian life, people exposed to plane crashes, automobile accidents, explosions, fires, earthquakes, tornadoes, sexual assault, or other terrifying experiences frequently show "shock" reactions—transient personality decompensation. Over half the survivors of the disastrous Cocoanut Grove Nightclub fire which occurred in Boston in 1942, for example, required treatment for severe psychological shock (Adler, 1943). Other events, such as the sudden loss of loved ones, social disgrace, or severe financial losses, may also prove extremely traumatic. For our immediate purposes, however, we may confine ourselves to a consideration of reactions to terrifying ex-

periences. These will serve as models for understanding the general dynamics in other types of transient personality disorders in civilian life and will keep the discussion parallel to that of combat exhaustion.

CLINICAL PICTURE

Civilian "shock" cases may show a wide range of symptoms, depending on the severity and nature of the terrifying experience, the degree of surprise, and the personality makeup of the individual. Among victims of tornadoes, explo-

After an earthquake that killed her mother, a bewildered Greek girl weeps amid the ruins of her home.

sions, and similar catastrophes, a "disaster syndrome" has been delineated. This syndrome, which appears to characterize many of the people in the disaster area, may be described in three stages:

1. *Shock stage,* in which the victim is stunned, dazed, and apathetic. Frequently he is unaware of the extent of his injuries, tends to wander about aimlessly until guided or directed by someone else, and is unable to make more than minimal efforts at aiding himself or others. In extreme cases the individual may be stuporous, disoriented, and amnesic for the traumatic event.

2. *Suggestible stage,* in which the individual tends to be passive, suggestible, and willing to take directions from rescue workers or others less affected than himself. Here the individual often expresses extreme concern over the welfare of others involved in the disaster and attempts to be of assistance; however, his behavior tends to be highly inefficient even in the performance of routine tasks.

3. *Recovery stage,* in which the individual gradually regains his psychological equilibrium,

often with the help of mild supportive psychotherapy at a hospital or other aid center. Here he may repetitively tell about the catastrophic event, become critical of rescue and relief workers, and show symptoms of generalized anxiety. Often he is tense, jumpy, and apprehensive, shows difficulty in concentrating and sleeping, and tires easily. In about half of the cases there are recurrent nightmares which usually reenact or are closely related to the traumatic experience. With supportive therapy, however, there is usually rapid recovery (adapted from Raker, Wallace & Raymer, 1956).

These three stages are well illustrated in the *Andrea Doria* disaster.

"On July 25, 1956, at 11:05 P.M., the Swedish liner *Stockholm* smashed into the starboard side of the Italian liner *Andrea Doria* a few miles off Nantucket Island, causing one of the worst disasters in maritime history. . . . During the phase of initial shock the survivors acted as if they had been sedated . . . as though nature provided a sedation mechanism which went into operation automatically." During the phase of suggestibility "the survivors presented themselves for the most part as an amorphous mass of people tending to act passively and compliantly. They displayed psychomotor retardation, flattening of affect, somnolence, and in some instances, amnesia for data of personal identification. They were nonchalant and easily suggestible." During the stage of recovery, after the initial shock had worn off and the survivors had received aid, "they showed . . . an apparently compulsive need to tell the story again and again, with identical detail and emphasis." (Friedman & Linn, 1957, p. 426)

In cases where loved ones have been lost in the catastrophe, the disaster syndrome may be complicated by intense feelings of grief and depression. Where the individual feels he bears some responsibility for the disaster—as, for example, in automobile or plane accidents—or feels he has failed loved ones who perished in the disaster, the picture may be further complicated by strong feelings of guilt. This pattern is well brought out in the following case of a man who failed in his attempt to save his wife but was saved himself.

A man aged thirty-five had received only minor burns from the Cocoanut Grove fire. By the end of the fifth day of hospitalization he was apparently well on the road to recovery and was informed that his wife had died in the fire. He seemed to accept the news quite well and appeared somewhat relieved of his worry about her fate. Shortly after his return home, however, he became restless and agitated, and was rehospitalized. On admission he was apprehensive and unable to concentrate. He would attempt to read only to drop it; he would start conversations and break them off abruptly. He repeatedly muttered to himself statements such as, "Nobody can help me. When is it going to happen? I am doomed, am I not?" With great effort it was possible to establish enough rapport to carry on interviews. He complained about extreme tension, inability to breathe, generalized weakness and exhaustion, and his frantic fear that something terrible was going to happen. "I'm destined to live in insanity or I must die. I know it is God's will. I have this awful feeling of guilt." With intense morbid guilt feelings he reviewed incessantly the events of the fire. When he had tried to save his wife, he had fainted and was shoved out by the crowd. She was burned while he was saved. "I should have saved her or I should have died too." He complained about feelings of incredible hostility and violence and did not know what to do about them. The rapport established with him lasted only for brief periods of time, and then he would fall back into his state of intense agitation and muttering. He slept poorly even with large sedation. However, in the course of four days he became somewhat more composed, had longer periods of contact with the therapist, and seemed to feel that he was making progress in coping with his morbid guilt. On the sixth day of his hospital stay, however, after skillfully distracting the attention of his special nurse, he jumped through a closed window to a violent death. (Adapted from Lindemann, 1944, p. 146)

As in combat cases, some civilians who undergo terrifying accidents reveal a somewhat typical post-traumatic syndrome—often referred to as a *traumatic neurosis*—which may last for weeks, months, or even years (Modlin, 1960; 1967). It includes the following symptoms: (a) anxiety, varying from mild apprehension to episodes of acute anxiety—often associated with situations that recall the accident or trauma; (b) chronic muscular tension with restlessness, fatigability, insomnia, and the complaint that "I just can't seem to relax"; (c) irritability, often accompanied by a startle reaction and inability to tolerate noise; (d) complaints of impaired concentration and memory; (e) repetitive nightmares reproducing the traumatic incident directly or symbolically; and (f) social withdrawal—withdrawal from and avoidance of any experience that might increase excitation—commonly manifested in the avoidance of interpersonal involvement, loss of sexual

interest, and an attitude of "Peace and quiet at any price." (1967, p. 1009) Modlin has suggested that this syndrome "may be a fundamental, non-specific, organismic reaction to severe external stress of a frightening or life-threatening kind." (1960, p. 51)

A delayed traumatic neurosis may also occur in cases involving physical injury, with the realization of personal mutilation and the necessity of changes in one's life situation. This syndrome is often complicated by the psychological effects of damage suits and workmen's compensation laws. Somewhere between 10 and 25 percent of the applicants for industrial compensation suffer from post-traumatic reactions. In a study of five hundred such cases Thompson (1965) found that the great majority manifested anxiety states comparable to those in neurotic reactions, while a lesser number manifested hysterical reactions, phobic reactions, and a mixed state of anxiety and hysteria. Depression also complicated the picture in about one third of the cases.

Here it may be noted that the assurance or even

The trauma of being a displaced person is well portrayed in this picture of two young, homeless refugees.

FAMILY CRISES AS SITUATIONAL STRESS

The behavior of various family members, or occurrences within a family, may precipitate crises which can lead to temporary personality decompensation in one or more members. Family crises may be precipitated by events or conditions such as the following:

Separation or divorce	Loss of employment
Death in the family	Drinking or drug abuse
Serious illness	Physical impairment
Financial crisis	Birth of a baby
Automobile accident	Emotional disturbance
Arrest of a family member	Children's leaving home
Marital infidelity	Retirement

Here it may be emphasized that a "crisis" depends not only on the stress situation but also on the beliefs, values, and perceptions of family members. The sudden loss of employment in a middle-class family may seem a disaster; in a lower-class family, on the other hand, the breadwinner may be periodically unemployed, and family members may react philosophically when he loses his job. Marital infidelity may be considered a tragedy in one family, but not in another that has different values or emotional relationships and social supports. As Klemer (1970) has expressed it: "Discovering that one's husband has been unfaithful, finding out that one's daughter is pregnant out of wedlock, or learning that one's son has killed a man depend for their crisis effect on the cultural definition of the behavior involved, as well as on the particular circumstances surrounding the event." (p. 313) In general, middle- and upper-class families appear to recover more rapidly from crisis situations than do lower-class families, who are less prepared for and seldom strengthened by a crisis.

the possibility of monetary compensation may lead to an actual prolongation of post-traumatic symptoms, as in the case of complicated legal suits that require months or even years to settle (Keiser, 1968). For this reason as well as others, it is usually considered advisable to have early settlements of claims involving physical injuries.

DYNAMICS

The dynamics in civilian traumatic reactions seem basically similar to the reactions to the stress of combat. Here, too, the world, which has seemed relatively secure and safe, suddenly becomes a terrifying place, in which one's adjustive resources are completely inadequate. In the face of this catastrophic threat, the individual is overwhelmed by intense anxiety and is unable to function in an integrated and efficient manner. The symptoms of being stunned, dazed, and apathetic stem in part from the disorganization of behavior; they also appear in part to be defense mechanisms protecting the individual from the full impact of the catastrophic experience.

The stage of suggestibility apparently results from the individual's temporary inability to deal with the situation himself, plus a tendency to regress to a passive-dependent position in which he is grateful to have the direction and help of others. During the stage of recovery, the recurrent nightmares and the typical need to tell about the disaster again and again with identical detail and emphasis appear to be mechanisms for reducing anxiety and desensitizing the individual to the traumatic experience. The tension, apprehensiveness, and hypersensitivity that often accompany the recovery stage appear to be residual effects of the shock reaction and to reflect the individual's realization that the world can become overwhelmingly dangerous and threatening. Feelings of guilt in civilian disasters typically center around a sense of having failed to protect loved ones who perished or were seriously injured in the accident or disaster; such feelings may be quite intense in situations where responsibility can be directly assigned.

Contrary to popular opinion, panic reactions are not common among people in the impact area of a disaster. *Panic*, defined as acute fear followed by flight behavior, tends to occur only under fairly specific conditions: (1) when a group of persons is directly threatened, for example by fire, (2) when the situation is viewed as one in which escape is possible at the moment but maybe only for a few minutes or not for everyone, and (3) when the group is taken by surprise and has no prearranged plan for dealing with such a disaster (Fritz, 1957; McDavid & Harari, 1968).

Under such conditions there may be a complete disorganization or demoralization of the group, with each individual striving to save himself; the emotional, panic-stricken behavior of others seems to be highly contagious, and a person may be overwhelmed by fear. Behavior may be extremely irrational and nonadaptive and may actually result in needless loss of life. For example, in the disastrous Iroquois Theater fire in

Chicago in 1903, five hundred people were killed in less than eight minutes due to trampling and asphyxiation rather than to burns. Similarly, in the disastrous Cocoanut Grove fire no lives need have been lost had people exited in an orderly way. Instead the exits were jammed by a rush of panic-stricken people so that many were trampled and those behind them could not get out.

Both precipitating and predisposing conditions in combat situations are apt to differ considerably from those in civilian life, for in the latter the individual is not typically separated from home, extremely fatigued, or exposed to prolonged fear and conflict over physical danger. But here, too, predisposing factors may determine which survivors develop traumatic reactions and which do not, and why some recover much more rapidly than others. In general, the civilian is less prepared for coping with catastrophe than is the combat soldier, who knows that he can expect danger and has been specially trained to deal with it.

TREATMENT AND OUTCOMES

Mild reassuring therapy and proper rest (induced by sedatives if necessary) usually lead to the rapid alleviation of symptoms in civilian shock reactions. In some accident cases, the individual may be encouraged to continue with his activities—for example, to go swimming again after a narrow escape from drowning. Performing the act with which the trauma is associated appears to help the individual reestablish confidence in himself and his world and to prevent the fixation of anxiety in relation to that kind of activity.

It would also appear that repetitive talking about the experience and repetitive reliving of the experience in fantasy or nightmares may serve as built-in repair mechanisms in helping the individual adjust to the traumatic experience. As Horowitz has concluded from his own experimental findings and a review of available literature:

"A traumatic perceptual experience remains in some special form of memory storage until it is mastered. Before mastery, vivid sensory images of the experiences tend to intrude into consciousness and may evoke unpleasant emotions. Through such repetitions the images, ideas, and associated affects may be worked through progressively. Thereafter, the images lose their intensity and the tendency toward repetition of the experience loses its motive force." (1969, p. 552)

Although there is a dearth of actual statistics, it would appear that the great majority of civilian shock cases clear up in a matter of days or, at most, weeks. In a minority of cases, however, the individual remains highly sensitized to certain types of hazardous situations and simply does not regain his self-confidence in dealing with such situations. In other cases, various maladaptive patterns may remain after the immediate shock symptoms themselves have cleared up. As we have seen, where an injury is involved and there is a possibility of financial compensation,

---

PSYCHOLOGICAL REACTIONS TO PHYSICAL DISABILITY

Any injury or illness that necessitates the reorganization of one's life pattern, and especially of one's self-concept, may be very difficult to cope with. Reactions of adults to loss of vision, as analyzed by Cholden (1954), exemplify the stages through which successful readjustment must proceed, thus giving helpful clues to those who suffer such a loss, as well as to relatives and friends who are anxious to help.

1. **Shock.** At first there is a numbness, an emergency constriction of the ego as a defense against imminent disintegration. The individual is "frozen," may be unable to think, or even to feel physical pain. The longer this state lasts, the more difficult is the individual's readjustment.

2. **Depression.** As the shock reaction wanes, it is replaced by deep depression, with self-recrimination, self-pity, and feelings of hopelessness. Recognizing his loss, the individual is beginning a period of mourning. This phase of reorganization—dying as a sighted person in order to be reborn as a blind one—is considered necessary, and no attempts should be made to abort it.

3. **Readjustment.** The individual is now a different person; hence the primary task of readjustment is internal reorganization. His capacities, interests, social position, and aspirations must be woven into a new self-picture and a new body image. Until he accepts himself as a different person, his readjustment cannot proceed. Thus, instead of fostering unrealistic hopes, friends and relatives should help him accept his blindness and see that he can lead a full life even though blind.

In more recent studies of persons with severe and disabling injuries and illnesses, the same basic sequence has been observed: (1) efforts to minimize the impact of the event—for example, by denial of the severity and probable consequences of the injury or illness; (2) the gradual facing of reality, with periods of depression as the individual faces the seriousness of his condition; and (3) readjustment, in which the individual shows impressive resiliency and a capacity to work out new patterns of living (Fitzgerald, 1970; Hamburg & Adams, 1967).

there may be a prolongation of symptoms; similarly, where there are other pronounced secondary gains—as when the experience appears to justify the individual's removal from disliked occupational responsibilities—there may be a tendency to delayed recovery. Of course, in the case of a marginally adjusted individual, such a traumatic experience may further undermine feelings of adequacy and security, and precipitate a psychosis, overdependence on drugs, or other psychopathological patterns.

In general, the more stable and better integrated the personality and the more favorable the individual's life situation, the quicker his recovery from a civilian shock reaction will be. It may also be pointed out that in some cases traumatic experiences, rather than sensitizing the individual to such experiences in the future, tend to raise his stress tolerance. As West (1958) has pointed out:

". . . an experience may be both frightening and painful, yet its repetition may be less stressful because it is now familiar, because its limits have been perceived, because the memory and imagination of the individual enable him to equate it with other known experiences, and because defenses have been developed through fantasied re-experiences during the interval." (p. 332)

A study by Leopold and Dillon (1963) of 34 experienced seamen who survived an explosion and fire on board a gasoline tanker suggests the need for "working through" a traumatic experience soon after it occurs. An investigation conducted from 3½ to 4½ years after the disaster showed that 12 of the survivors (who had succeeded in lowering a lifeboat and getting away from the inferno without any leadership) had never returned to sea work, or had been forced to give it up, as a result of post-traumatic symptoms. Of those who had continued to work at sea, all showed similar post-traumatic symptoms—tension, fearfulness, and anxiety aboard ship. The investigators concluded that with prompt psychotherapy at the time of the accident these conditioned fears could have been prevented from building up.

It may be pointed out again that many other crises in addition to terrifying experiences may produce these transient personality reactions. Such emotional experiences as having a loved one die, going through a divorce, finding one's wife or husband in an intimate relationship with another person, critical illness, and undergoing social disgrace and loss of status may all lead to some measure of psychological decompensation. Typical stages in reacting to the trauma of disability or illness are summarized on page 205. Unfortunately, there has been little systematic research concerning reactions to civilian catastrophes, and the need for additional study in this general area is clearly indicated.

REACTIONS TO CHRONIC SITUATIONAL STRESS

In addition to the decompensation under acute stress seen in combat exhaustion and civilian shock reactions, transient disturbances may also occur when the individual continues for an extended time in a situation where he feels threatened, seriously dissatisfied, or inadequate. Regimentation may make army life intolerable for some. A lifetime farmer may be unable to adjust to life in the city. A person may feel trapped in an unhappy marriage which he feels he must maintain because of the children, or he may hate his work but feel compelled to stick to it because of heavy financial responsibilities and lack of training for any other kind of job. Similarly, an individual subjected to living in a ghetto may find his situation highly frustrating; even living in a society from which an individual feels alienated represents a stressful situation that may eventuate in personality disturbance. We will limit our discussion to adult situational disturbances, but such reactions may occur during infancy, childhood, and other life periods as well.

Although conflicts and quarrels are common in marriage, when such conditions become chronic they place each of the marital partners in a situation of severe and prolonged stress.

In civilian life the symptoms of situational maladjustment may vary greatly; however, chronic fatigue, lowered efficiency, discouragement, and excessive drinking or drug usage are common. In army life—where many of the usual behavior restraints are reduced or removed—gambling, drinking, and frequenting of prostitutes are common means of reducing feelings of boredom and frustration. Some soldiers develop a particularly embittered attitude, and are resistant, irritable, fault-finding, and highly resentful about being "shoved around"; others, particularly those in isolated outposts, show a loss of interest in their environment, and become apathetic. Studies of persons confined to submarines for periods of sixty days—during which the vessels were continuously submerged—have shown that some 4 to 5 percent of the men developed psychological disturbances apparently stemming from the constant environmental stress (Satloff, 1967; Serxner, 1968). Common symptoms included anxiety, depression, insomnia, headaches, and other somatic concerns.

REACTIONS OF PRISONERS OF WAR

The symptoms of situational maladjustment under extreme conditions are well illustrated by prisoner-of-war experiences. One of the best descriptions is that of Commander Nardini, an eyewitness and participant, who depicted the effects of imprisonment and mistreatment on American soldiers following the fall of Bataan and Corregidor during the early part of World War II.

"Our national group experience accustoms us to protection of individual rights and recourse to justice. The members of this group found themselves suddenly deprived of name, rank, identity, justice, and any claim to being treated as human beings. Although physical disease and the shortages of food, water, and medicine were at their highest during this period, emotional shock and reactive depression . . . undoubtedly contributed much to the massive death rate during the first months of imprisonment.

"Conditions of imprisonment varied from time to time in different places and with different groups. In general there was shortage, wearisome sameness, and deficiency of food; much physical misery and disease; squalid living conditions; fear and despair; horrible monotony . . . inadequate clothing and cleansing facilities; temperature extremes; and physical abuse.

". . . Hungry men were constantly reminded of their own nearness to death by observing the steady, relentless march to death of their comrades. . . . Men quibbled over portions of food, were suspicious of those who were in more favored positions than themselves, participated in unethical barter, took advantage of less clever or enterprising fellow prisoners, stole, rummaged in garbage, and even curried the favor of their detested captors. There was a great distortion of previous personality as manifested by increased irritability, unfriendliness, and sullen withdrawal. . . . Hungry, threatened men often found it difficult to expand the horizon of their thinking and feeling beyond the next bowl of rice. . . .

"Disease was abundant . . . fever, chills, malaise, pain, anorexia, abdominal cramps from recurrent malaria (acquired in combat), and dysentery plagued nearly all and killed thousands. . . . most men experienced bouts of apathy or depression. These ranged

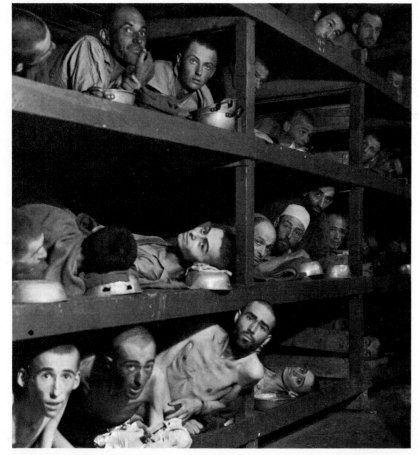

Cruelty, torture, and mass extermination cost the lives of some ten million people in Nazi concentration camps—and left thousands of others emotionally and physically scarred for life. These pictures were taken by American military photographers during the closing phases of World War II.

from slight to prolonged deep depressions where there was a loss of interest in living and lack of willingness or ability to marshal the powers of will necessary to combat disease. An ever-present sign of fatal withdrawal occurred 3 to 4 days before death when the man pulled his covers up over his head and lay passive, quiet, and refusing food.

"... One of the most distressing features was the highly indefinite period of imprisonment. The future offered only visions of continued hunger, cold, disease, forced labor, and continued subservience in the face of shoutings, slappings, and beatings. . . . Strong hostility naturally arose from the extreme frustration. . . . Little could be done with these hostile feelings. . . . It was not possible to demonstrate recognizable signs of hostility to the captors for obvious reasons. Therefore, where there were mixed groups of Allied prisoners, much hostility was turned from group to group and in other instances to individuals within the group. . . . In many cases hostile feelings were obviously turned inward and joined with appropriate feelings of frustration to produce serious waves of depression. . . . Self pity, in which some indulged, was highly dangerous to life. . . ." (Nardini, 1952, pp. 241–244)

Similar reactions were observed among prisoners held by the North Koreans and Chinese Communists during the Korean War (Lifton, 1954; Segal, 1954; Strassman, Thaler & Schein, 1961). Here, however, the picture was further complicated by "brainwashing" techniques which are described in the chart on page 211. In this context, Farber, Harlow, and West (1956) noted a common syndrome produced among the POW's which they referred to as "DDD"—debility, dependency, and dread. *Debility* was induced by semistarvation, disease, and fatigue, and led to a sense of terrible weariness and weakness. *Dependency* was produced by a variety of techniques, including the use of solitary confinement, the removal of leaders and other accustomed sources of support, and occasional and unpredictable respites which reminded the prisoners that they were completely dependent on their captors for what happened to them. *Dread* was described as a stage of chronic fear which their captors attempted to induce—fear of death, of pain, of nonrepatriation, and of permanent deformity or disability due to neglect or inadequate medical treatment. The net effect of these conditions was a well-nigh intolerable state of mental and physical discomfort which rendered the men more amenable to brainwashing.

Descriptions of prisoners in Nazi concentration camps, who were subjected to even more inhuman and sadistic conditions, emphasize similar symptomatology (Bettelheim, 1943, 1960; Chodoff, 1970; Eitinger, 1961, 1962, 1969; Friedman, 1948; Frankl, 1959; Hafner, 1968). Inmates of concentration camps also showed greater use of the defense mechanisms of denial and isolation of affect. The feeling that "This isn't really happening to me" was widespread. Chodoff (1970) has cited the case of a young prisoner "who would not see the corpses she was stepping over" and the even more poignant picture "of her fellow inmates who refused to believe that the smoke arising from the crematorium chimneys came from the burning corpses of their mothers" who had been selected—because of age—to be killed first. Isolation of affect apparently reached the degree of almost total emotional anaesthesia in the case Chodoff cited of a young female prisoner who stated "I had no feelings whatsoever" while being stripped naked and having all her hair shaved off in front of SS troopers (p. 83).

Concentration camp inmates also tended to form hopes of deliverance via miraculous events, possibly because their situation was even more hopeless than that of the POW's, and any hope would have had to be rather unrealistic.

DYNAMICS

Reactions to situational stress vary with the individual as well as with the nature and severity of the stress itself. Some people adjust fairly readily to changes in their life situations or to chronic frustrating conditions, whereas others find even relatively minor changes or frustrations difficult to cope with. Here again the reaction of a particular individual depends on the patterning of biological, psychological, and sociocultural factors that we have discussed in connection with maladaptive reactions to stress. In general, of course, the more severe and chronic the stress situation, the greater the degree of personality disturbance that is likely to be elicited.

When situational stress is severe and long-lasting, there may be a marked degree of personality decompensation. Among POW's during the Korean War, for example, a common reaction was that of emotional withdrawal, leading sometimes to almost total apathy. This pattern of defense—by partially depriving the situation of its power to hurt—apparently helped some men survive in the face of severe and sustained stress which, as far as they knew, might continue indefinitely. As we have previously noted, however, extreme apathy and the abandonment of hope can ultimately lead to death.

As conditions in the POW camps improved somewhat and the threat of death from malnutrition and disease decreased, the problem for the men was no longer merely to survive but to avoid collaboration with their captors. Here the pattern of "playing it cool"—being cautious, noncommittal, and minimally communicative, and of holding back strong feelings—came into increasing prominence as a means of avoiding major collaboration while at the same time not getting "on the wrong side" of their captors.

Schein (1956) classified the prisoners of war in Korea into "get alongers," "resisters," and "cooperators"; and he noted that in many instances soldiers shifted categories in different situations or even in the same situation, often in an attempt to avoid punishment or to gain favored treatment. Of course, cooperative behavior with military captors in the POW camp did not prove ideological change; nor did a return to earlier patterns of behavior upon repatriation indicate that the soldier was unaffected by the attempted brainwashing. In general, the effects of brainwashing techniques appeared to vary "from heightened resistance, to outer conformity, to conformity in depth." (Yinger, 1965, p. 176)

The success in the Korean War of the Chinese Communists in obtaining false confessions from some prisoners depended on a number of techniques, including the forced choice between "cooperation" and possible starvation, torture, and death. In some instances the extreme use of isolation served to "soften" the prisoner and break his will to resist. Hinkle and Wolff have emphasized the importance of isolation as a major technique of "brainwashing":

"When the initial period of imprisonment is one of total isolation . . . the complete separation of the prisoner from the companionship and support of others, his utter loneliness, and his prolonged uncertainty have a further disorganizing effect upon him. Fatigue, sleep loss, pain, cold, hunger, and the like,

augment the injury induced by isolation. . . . With the passage of time, the prisoner usually develops the intense need to be relieved of the pressures put upon him and to have some human companionship. He may have a very strong urge to talk to any human and to be utterly dependent on anyone who will help him or befriend him. At about this time he also becomes mentally dull and loses his capacity for discrimination. He becomes malleable and suggestible. . . ." (1956, p. 173)

The interrogator would then exploit the prisoner's dependence, need for human companionship, suggestibility, and impaired thinking—by scolding, threatening, and punishing him when he did not "cooperate," and by approving and rewarding him when he did. As indicated in the chart on brainwashing, however, even the extreme methods used were relatively ineffective on the great majority of soldiers.

TREATMENT AND OUTCOMES

Mild situational reactions usually clear up very rapidly when the individual is removed from the stressful situation. Yet such a simple therapeutic procedure is often impossible or undesirable. For example, a child who is having great difficulty in adjusting to his first year of school cannot be allowed to stay home—at least not indefinitely. Such a procedure would only undermine his self-confidence and further complicate his adjustment problems. Similarly, it may not be feasible or desirable to break up a disappointing and frustrating marriage. In cases where it is impossible or undesirable to remove the individual from his current life situation, counseling and psychotherapy may often be of assistance in modifying the stress situation or in helping the individual to develop more effective coping techniques. We have seen this principle illustrated in the concept of secondary prevention in the military community (page 201).

In the case of prisoners of war subjected to extreme and inhuman conditions, and of concentration-camp survivors, there is often residual organic as well as psychological damage and a lowering of tolerance to stress of any kind. In the observation and treatment of large numbers of former prisoners of war, the following clinical pattern has been emphasized:

BRAINWASHING OF AMERICAN PRISONERS DURING THE KOREAN WAR

In his novel *1984*, George Orwell (1949) described the process of "brainwashing," in which the environment around a person is controlled so completely that the effects are similar to those of removing the person's brain and literally washing it clean of all thoughts considered socially undesirable by those in control. Orwell's fictional concept became a frightening reality during the Korean conflict, when the Chinese Communists launched a systematic program to indoctrinate prisoners of war with communist values and to achieve their collaboration.

During the early part of the war, the men captured by the North Koreans were subjected to a variety of cruelties, including forced "death marches," inadequate diet, exposure to freezing weather without adequate clothing or shelter, and vicious beatings for minor or alleged transgressions. Physical treatment improved somewhat after the Chinese Communists took charge of all POW's—but with the improvement came the emotional assault of brainwashing. The approach used by the Communists can be described in terms of three phases, which were in simultaneous and continuous operation: isolation, thought control, and political conditioning.

PHASE	HOW CARRIED OUT	RESULTS
Isolation	Removal of leaders: officers transferred to a separate camp, and natural leaders, as they emerged, removed silently to "reactionary" camps. Informers rewarded to discourage personal ties and interaction. Home ties cut—pessimistic, complaining letters delivered while other mail withheld.	Creation of a group of "isolates" with low morale and no *esprit de corps*. Social and emotional isolation robbed soldier of usual sources of strength and prevented him from validating his beliefs and values through discussion with others. Led to loss of strength to resist, increased suggestibility, and vulnerability to both threats and bribes.
Thought control	Prisoners forced to choose between "cooperation" and possible starvation, torture, and death. Ethical values, loyalty to country, religion, and self-identity placed in direct opposition to self-preservation and meeting of bodily needs: resistees subjected to threat, punishment, and marginal living conditions; cooperators rewarded with increased food, privileges in camp, and promises of early repatriation. Guilt feelings concerning prior behavior stimulated by mandatory "confessions" and self-criticism. Alternate harshness and friendliness by "inscrutable authority."	Fear, anxiety, guilt, confusion, and conflict about how to behave. "Playing it cool"—being inconspicuous, holding back strong feelings, being minimally communicative and noncommittal on everything, "cooperating" a little when necessary but avoiding major collaboration. Withdrawal of emotional involvement, marked apathy. Listlessness and apparent indifference.
Political conditioning	Daily "instruction" with repetitious teaching of communist catch phrases and principles. Appeals to be "openminded" and to "just listen to our side of the story." Only anti-American books and newspapers available, stressing inequalities and injustices in U.S. Communists portrayed as "peace seekers," prisoner offered "opportunity to work for peace." Intensive pressure applied to those who seemed most susceptible; those already convinced used to indoctrinate others. Constant use of reward for cooperation and punishment for resistance.	Little actual conversion to communism but considerable confusion and doubt about America's role in war; poor morale and discipline; breakdown of group loyalty. Men turned against each other—"progressives" versus "reactionaries." Difficulty in relating to others even after release. Five percent later won commendation as resisters, 15 percent were judged to have complied unduly; the remaining 80 percent were relatively passive.

When prisoners were first released, they were apathetic, detached, dazed, without spontaneity, and at the same time tense and suspicious of their new surroundings. Large memory gaps were present, particularly for the period of their capture and for so-called death marches. They were ambivalent in their feelings about the Chinese Communists, showed strong guilt about all phases of their POW experience, and were not anxious to return home to the U.S. This "zombie reaction" wore off after three to five days and was followed by a period of greater spontaneity. However, they still appeared "suspended in time"—confused by their newly acquired status and incapable of making decisions concerning future courses of action. All of the men felt alienated from others who had not shared their POW experience and were apprehensive about homecoming; they tended to band together in small, uneasy groups and maintained isolation from nonrepatriates.

On their return home, some got into difficulty over indiscriminate outbursts of misdirected, long-pent-up hostility. Expecting at last to be free of stress, some became disillusioned and discouraged in their efforts to adjust to economic and other changes and to communicate with others. Physical disabilities, chronic fatigue, and a confused self-picture complicated the adjustment problems of many. But although some drank too much or managed other escape measures, the majority of these men eventually made adequate adjustments. In a few cases, their weathering of the prison experience seemed to have given them increased inner strength and greater capacity for achievement.

Material for this chart taken from Kinkead (1959), Lifton (1954), Schein, Schneier, and Barker (1961), Segal (1954), Strassman, Thaler, and Schein (1956), and West (1958). For information on the application of similar techniques to civilian populations—for example, in Russia and China—see Hinkle and Wolff (1956), Hunter (1954), Lifton (1961), and Watzlawick, Beavin, and Jackson (1967).

"With relatively few exceptions the presenting complaints are usually as follows: fatigability, lack of ability to withstand frustration, frequent resort to alcohol and sedative drugs, low resistance to physical illness, neurotic-type pains in feet and hands and frequently edema of the ankles and feet, irritability and other manifestations in varying degree of emotional instability, and a need for preferential duty assignments. . . . On physical examination remarkably little is found in the way of structural pathology." (Chambers, 1952, pp. 247–348)

And Wolff (1960) reported that American POW's who survived the extreme stresses of imprisonment in the Pacific area during World War II showed an excessively high mortality rate during the six years following their liberation. Deaths from tuberculosis were nine times, from gastrointestinal disease four times, from cancer more than twice, and from heart disease twice the number expected in civilian life. Also, three times the expected number died as a result of accidents, and twice the expected number died from suicide.

It should be pointed out that in analyzing the reactions of those who survived, we are dealing with a select group, for about half the Japanese and Korean War prisoners died during their imprisonment. Undoubtedly, chance factors often played a crucial role. Nardini (1962b) has suggested the following qualities as being positive factors in both physical and psychological survival of POW experiences: a philosophical, fatalistic, yet nondefeatist attitude; intense application of life energies to the present; an ability to retain hope in the face of the greatest hardships; the ability to manage hostility and fight depression; personality maturity and ego strength; a strong sense of self-identity and self-respect; and the intangible but all-inclusive determination to live.

Nardini observed that some passive-dependent individuals did fairly well in POW camps because they could accept a passive role and follow instructions. The aggressive psychopath almost invariably developed a depressive reaction when he finally realized the inevitable and final restrictions of confinement. Prisoners with mild paranoid trends often made a fair adjustment since they were very persevering in their determination not to let the enemy win. Immature

individuals did not fare well because they were most vulnerable to temptations to collaborate with the enemy—for which, in turn, they suffered the serious consequences of ostracism.

In general, the eventual outcome for the survivors of POW camps seems to have depended on the individual's psychobiological stress tolerance, the length and severity of the traumatic experience, and his ability to devise defenses to protect his integrity. Some men adjusted well to combat but not to POW camps; some adjusted well to POW camps but not to their return home. In some instances after their return home survivors had trouble with indiscriminate outbursts of hostility. Evidently, underlying the apathy so prevalent in the POW situation there were often intense pent-up feelings of hostility which proved to be a problem to the individual once he was no longer in the stressful situation. Despite a wide variation in adjustment, however, follow-up studies indicate that the majority of Korean and World War II Pacific area POW's made adequate psychological postwar adjustments (Nardini, 1962b).

It is likely that follow-up studies will provide similar and possibly even more favorable findings for POW's of the war in Vietnam, particularly since these men were much better trained in terms of what to expect and what to do in the event of capture by the enemy. In fact, a number of soldiers in the Vietnam War were put through "torture training" in simulated POW camps prior to actual combat service.

The residual damage to survivors of the Nazi concentration camps appears similar but even more extensive than that of the POW survivors. In a preliminary follow-up study of one hundred Norwegian survivors of German concentration camps, Eitinger (1961; 1962) found that 96 percent continued to experience symptoms resulting from their stay in the concentration camps. Predominant symptoms included fatigue, nervousness, irritability, restlessness, impairment of memory, sleep disturbances, anxiety, feelings of inadequacy, loss of initiative, headaches, depression, and abuse of alcohol. All but three of the survivors were found to have led normal lives up to the time of their imprisonment. Of these one hundred former prisoners, eighty-four could cope with their work, but only with the greatest effort. In later follow-up studies of larger numbers of concentration camp survivors, Eitinger (1964; 1968) reported similar findings. And in a study focusing specifically on psychosomatic sequelae, Eitinger (1969) reported a high incidence of "functional" diarrhea, peptic ulcers, and impaired sexual potency. "Functional" diarrhea meant that this symptom occurred in any situation of stress, even ones of a relatively mild nature. Eitinger made it clear that these various residual symptoms were attributable not only to the psychological stresses of the concentration-camp experiences but also to biological stresses, such as head injuries suffered during interrogation, prolonged malnutrition, and serious infectious diseases—all of which were common in the concentration camps.

In summarizing the available evidence on concentration-camp survivors from Denmark, Norway, and the Netherlands—including both Jews and non-Jews—Hafner (1968) delineated what he considered to be a basic syndrome of psychopathological sequelae to the systematic terror and cruelty experienced in these camps. This syndrome included anxiety, nightmares, insomnia, headaches, irritability, depression, and social withdrawal. The severity of the clinical picture varied, of course, with the individual

and the severity of stress suffered. Here it is of interest to note that in a study of sixty survivors of Nazi concentration camps, Oswald and Bittner (1968) found that what some of their subjects described as a successful readjustment was based on an aggressive and single-minded pursuit of financial and related signs of success—which tended to conceal residual post-traumatic anxiety, depression, and hostility and to obscure the massive threat to their prior existence.

In a study of first- and second-year college students whose parents were survivors of concentration camps—students who went to a mental health clinic for assistance—Trossman (1968) found that the students' difficulties were related to parental interaction. He describes a "survivor syndrome," in which the parent suffers from chronic anxiety, recurrent nightmares of his wartime experiences, and intense guilt from having survived the imprisonment while others perished. The parental attitude most harmful to the student was an expectation that he would fill the void in the parents' lives and somehow make up for their suffering. Trossman thus concluded that the concentration-camp experience scarred not only the survivors but some of the next generation as well.

PSYCHOLOGICAL PROBLEMS IN SPACE FLIGHTS

With the landing of men on the moon and preparation for more extended space travel to other planets, the psychological problems of space flight are becoming of increasing interest to scientists. Present knowledge of psychological problems in extended space flight is based partly on our relatively limited experience and partly on inference. However, it would appear that key stresses are: separation from earth, prolonged exposure to danger, difficulties in adjustment of the individual to the group, sameness of the environment, and the absence of many accustomed sources of emotional gratification. Some of these hazards, such as loneliness and a sense

of ever present danger, can be anticipated but not simulated.

Problems relating to the adjustment of the individual to the group, to monotony, and to absence of many accustomed sources of gratification were studied among a small group of scientists, officers, and enlisted personnel who voluntarily subjected themselves to isolated Antarctic living for almost a year. Typical reactions to this experience are summarized in the chart on page 214. From an overall viewpoint, the Navy found that the most important single factor in successful adjustment in the Antarctic was work efficiency, in the sense that

REACTIONS TO "WINTERING OVER" IN THE ANTARCTIC

Problems related to the individual's adjustment to close group interdependence, monotony of environment, and absence of accustomed sources of emotional gratification have been studied among groups of volunteers subjected to isolated Antarctic living for 6 to 8 months at isolated U.S. bases. Scientists, officers, and enlisted personnel lived in groups of 12 to 40, with each man assigned a specific job and hence dependent on every other man. Technical competence, responsibility, and stability in job performance thus became key factors in determining group acceptance and status. Reactions such as those cited below are of special interest in terms of their possible relationship to reactions to the conditions of space travel.

SYMPTOMS OBSERVED

Intellectual inertia	Lack of energy for intellectual pursuits, especially during winter. Earlier plans to catch up on reading or learn a foreign language rarely realized.
Impaired memory and concentration	Varied from absentmindedness and poor concentration to marked lowering of intellectual acuity and periods of amnesia. Most pronounced during winter months.
Insomnia	Varying degrees of sleeplessness, again mostly in winter. Individual felt tired but unable to relax.
Headaches	Frequent headaches, more common among officer-scientist group than among enlisted men. Appeared to be of psychogenic origin and possibly related to repression and control of hostility.
Hostility	Relatively little overt hostility expressed, probably because of the tremendous need for relatedness and group acceptance in these small, isolated groups. Social censure, in the form of the "silent treatment," inflicted on the occasional troublesome individual; resulted in "long-eye" syndrome—varying degrees of sleeplessness, crying, hallucinations, deterioration in personal hygiene, and a tendency to move aimlessly about or to lie in bed staring blankly into space until man was again accepted by group.
Depression	Low-grade depression prevalent, particularly during winter months. Of 6 men who became psychiatric casualties, 3 diagnosed as cases of relatively severe neurotic depression.
Appetite	Appetite for food greatly increased, possibly because of absence of other gratifications. Weight gains of 20 to 30 pounds not unusual.

This program was initiated during the International Geophysical Year, 1957–1958, and is still continuing on a reduced scale. The chart is based on material from Haythorn and Altman (1967), Mullin (1960), Nardini (1962a), and Rohrer (1961).

the effective functioning of the small group depended on each individual's performing his assigned task efficiently. The next most important factor was the individual's adjustment to the small isolated group.

In space flights the smaller crews, more confined quarters, more alien environment, and greater danger can be expected to render problems of technical proficiency, adjustment to the group, and adaptability to diverse stresses even more crucially significant.

In connection with the problem of assembling a crew who can function effectively as a team, experimental studies have been made of small groups of men placed in confined compartments over a period of several days. Before and after each experiment the subjects are put through psychological assessment procedures, and a detailed record is kept of their reactions in the experimental situations. Findings indicate

marked individual differences in reactions to such situations, depending on the subject's personality makeup, background, motivation, and mental set. Of key importance is the way the individual perceives or evaluates the stress situation. Some subjects adapt successfully, while others show various symptoms of personality decompensation.

In a study of two-man teams working together in experimentally induced isolation, Haythorn and Altman (1967) found that task performance was markedly influenced by the ability of the men to adjust to each other, as well as to the demands of the task and the conditions of isolation. As they pointed out:

"But 'good adjustor,' of course, is a relative term; all men suffer in isolation. Even a good adjustor cannot be locked into a space capsule with just anybody—or even with just any other good adjustor. So what kinds of people can get along together with the least amount of open friction in isolation? What kinds can accomplish most work when locked up together? What kinds simply sentence one another to mutual tedium?" (p. 19)

The development of an artificial environment that can support effective human functioning during relatively long periods of time poses many physiological and psychological problems. Experimental studies, as well as studies on actual space missions, are helping advance our knowledge and capabilities in dealing with such problems as oxygen supply, radiation, weightlessness, isolation from earth, confinement, restrictions in the perceptual field, fatigue, and exposure to prolonged danger. Under conditions that simulate long space missions, some subjects have shown impairment in judgment; inaccurate perceptions, including distortions of space and time; peculiar changes in body image; sensations of an alien presence; and even delusions and hallucinations. Negative reactions of some subjects have required termination of the simulated missions.

Even mild thought disturbances, of course, might have serious consequences if they occurred during an actual space mission. As we noted in our discussion of sensory deprivation in Chapter 6, it would appear in general that both variety and meaningfulness of sensory input (stimulation and information) are essential for preventing the disorganization of perception and thought.

A relatively new approach to the problem of effective human functioning in space is directed toward the modification of the human system itself. As White (1958–1959) has pointed out, "Man is a sea-level, low-speed, one-g, 12-hour animal." For man's greater adaptability in functioning under various extraterrestrial conditions, chemical and electrical techniques are being developed to modify some of the body's homeostatic controls—both on physiological and psychological levels. For example, it might be possible to use drugs or other techniques to have the pilot or other crew members sleep twenty-three hours out of the day. Of course,

there would be procedures for waking them in the event of an emergency. It may also be that we can reduce the amount of "earth environment" that crew members must take with them by controlling their cardiovascular rate, body temperature, metabolic systems, and even thought processes.

In the man-machine system required for space flight, it becomes apparent that not only the life-support system, but also the limitations of the human organism, make up the baseline determining the efficiency of the total system. However, with our successful landing of men on the moon and their safe return to earth, it would appear likely that man can learn to cope with the greater physiological and psychological hazards of longer space flights—that as habitable space ships for longer missions are constructed, crews will be trained to man them effectively.

In this chapter we have discussed transient situational disturbances. These disorders occur in normal individuals who are subjected to conditions of excessive stress—as in military combat, prisoner-of-war camps, and civilian catastrophes; and they may involve a variety of symptoms, including intense anxiety, denial, repression, apathy, depression, and the lowering of ethical standards. In most cases the symptoms recede as the stress diminishes. However, in extreme cases—such as those involving the survivors of concentration camps—there may be residual psychological as well as physical damage. Furthermore, studies of the children of concentration camp survivors indicate that such stress and trauma may indirectly have deleterious consequences for the second generation.

While space exploration imposes somewhat different stresses, the problems of acute situational maladjustment and decompensation under excessive stress are still applicable. But with man's successful landing on the moon, it would appear that we can learn to cope with the physiological and psychological stresses of longer space flights.

Neuroses

8

THE BASIC NATURE OF NEUROSES

SPECIFIC NEUROTIC PATTERNS

GENERAL ETIOLOGY, TREATMENT, AND
   OUTCOMES

In our discussion of transient situational disorders we dealt primarily with stable personalities who had been subjected to excessive stress. In the neuroses we find faulty learning leading to ineffective responses to everyday problems of living.[1]

The individual is said to exhibit neurotic behavior if he frequently misevaluates adjustive demands, becomes anxious in situations that most people would not regard as threatening, and tends to develop behavior patterns aimed at avoiding rather than coping with his problems. Curiously, the individual may realize his behavior is irrational and maladaptive—as in the case of a severe phobia for germs—but he seems unable to alter it. Although neurotic behavior is maladaptive, it does not involve gross distortion of reality or gross personality disorganization; nor is it likely to result in violence to the individual or to others. Rather, neurotics are anxious, unhappy, ineffective, and often guilt-ridden individuals who do not ordinarily require hospitalization but nevertheless are in need of therapy. The incidence of neuroses is difficult to determine, but it has been estimated that there are at least 10 million individuals in the United States who might be classified as neurotic.

In this chapter we shall begin by considering the general characteristics of neurotic behavior and then go on to analyze particular neurotic patterns such as anxiety reactions, phobias, compulsions, and hypochondria.

---

[1]The term *neurosis* was coined by the Englishman William Cullen in his *System of Nosology*, published in 1769, to refer to disordered sensations of the nervous system (Knoff, 1970).

THE BASIC NATURE OF NEUROSES

The common core of neuroses is a maladaptive life style, typified by anxiety and avoidance. Basic to this neurotic life style are: (1) faulty evaluation of reality and the tendency to avoid problems rather than to cope with them—the *neurotic nucleus;* and (2) the tendency to maintain this life style despite its self-defeating nature —the *neurotic paradox.*

THE NEUROTIC NUCLEUS

Neurotic behavior is a circular process in which an individual: (1) has basic feelings of inadequacy and inferiority, which lead to the evaluation of everyday problems as threatening and to the resultant arousal of anxiety; (2) tends to avoid stress situations through various defensive maneuvers, rather than attempting to cope with them directly; (3) manifests a lack of insight into his self-defeating behavior together with rigidity, in the sense of failing to perceive or act upon alternative courses of action; (4) manifests egocentricity and therefore has trouble establishing and maintaining satisfying interpersonal relations; and (5) has feelings of guilt for failing to cope directly with his problems, together with general feelings of dissatisfaction and unhappiness with his way of life.

It may be emphasized that not all the characteristics of this neurotic nucleus are found in a given case. Neurotic behavior may vary markedly from one person to another. In addition, most of us evidence some neurotic symptoms in coping with the stresses of contemporary life, and none of us can escape times of anxiety and unhappiness. As Cattell and Scheier (1961) have pointed out: "... a neurotic is ... a person with an excess of the external and internal difficulties and inadequacies from which everyone suffers in some degree." (p. 392)

1. *Feelings of inadequacy and anxiety.* The neurotic perceives himself as basically inadequate, and consequently sees many situations as threatening which would not be so perceived by most persons. This "threat vulnerability" is characterized by a need to cling to others for support, and by the dread of competitive situations. The experience of success may contribute to his underlying sense of inadequacy no less than the experience of defeat. A job promotion, for example, may raise fears that his "real lack of ability" will inevitably be exposed.

Since the neurotic sees various common stresses as threatening, anxiety is a major characteristic of the neuroses. Sometimes such anxiety is felt acutely, as in an anxiety attack, but more typically the neurotic develops various defenses for reducing his anxieties. These defenses are rarely adequate, however, and a considerable amount of anxiety and fearfulness usually remains.

The neurotic's anxiety is often intensified by the fact that he recognizes the irrationality of his own behavior. In addition, fears and conflicts that are usually held in check by neurotic defenses may flare up from time to time and raise the terrifying possibility of a breakdown of the whole defensive structure. Often this is symbolically represented in irrational fears of insanity, accidents, illness, or death.

2. *Avoidance instead of coping.* Wolpe (1969, p. 37) has stated, "I think it is quite clear that almost all neuroses stem from emotional habits that are essentially phobias." By this he means that the neurotic's basic life style is one of avoidance in meeting the problems of everyday living. Thus, somatic complaints may provide him a reason for lack of achievement; neurotic phobias may prevent his having to come to grips with various stressful situations; and even the content of his thoughts tends to be altered in the direction of avoidance, as in the case of "mind-filling" rituals, obsessions, and compulsions. His entire ideation and behavior is channeled into an avoidance pattern that to some extent enables him to escape from his feelings of inadequacy and anxiety. Unfortunately, his avoidance behavior blocks the development of more effective coping patterns, and hence in the long run reinforces his distress. In essence, he is enmeshed in a quagmire of "covering up," excusing, escaping, and, in general, avoiding— a pattern that blocks his personal growth and fulfillment.

3. *Rigidity and lack of insight.* Perceived threat leads to a narrowing of perception and other defensive maneuvers, including a restriction of information that is threatening to the self and an incongruence between reality and the neurotic's self-concept. Hence the neurotic is at a disadvantage in understanding his own behavior as well as others'. Although he may complain about his symptoms, he usually has little insight into the nature or causes of his self-defeating life style. He may agree that his fear of social gatherings is an irrational nuisance, yet he does not know why he has this fear and cannot seem to get rid of it. Even in occasional instances where a neurotic does understand the basis of his problems and defenses, he is still anxiety-ridden and seemingly unable to change. He clings to established behavior patterns that provide him some sense of security and thus shuts himself off from opportunities for learning more effective coping techniques.

4. *Egocentricity and disturbed interpersonal relationships.* Threat and the narrowing of perception also leads to a focus on the self. The neurotic is chronically and painfully aware of himself. He is primarily concerned with his own feelings, his own hopes, and his own problems. Since he typically faces life with such a heavy burden of helplessness and insecurity, he feels he is fighting for his very life, and it is not surprising that in such a fight he should be extremely self-centered. And since his main efforts are focused on maintaining his precarious integration, he has little concern for others and has little of himself to give. Often his underlying feelings of inadequacy and anxiety are manifested in a desperate search for a strong and vital marital partner who will make his life seem secure and meaningful. Needless to say, such hopes are usually destined to disillusionment as a result of the neurotic's own personal insufficiencies and egocentricity.

Similarly, the neurotic tends to make unrealistic demands on those around him—trying to find in their approval and support the security he lacks in himself. But because his demands are usually insatiable, he places an impossible burden on others and eventually tends to alienate them; this, in turn, augments his feelings of inadequacy and insecurity.

5. *Guilt and unhappiness.* Usually the neurotic vaguely senses that he is not fulfilling his responsibilities to others or to himself. From time to time he is likely to perceive the consequences of his egocentricity and selfish demands on others, and this gives rise to feelings of guilt. For example, a neurotic who uses a phobia of strangers as a weapon for controlling social relationships in his marriage may feel vaguely guilty for not meeting the needs of his wife or of the marital relationship.

As a consequence of his inadequacy, anxiety, and self-defeating life style, the neurotic is prone to be generally dissatisfied and unhappy. In avoiding the struggles and challenges essential for constructive living, he is denied the enhancement of self-esteem that comes from surmounting obstacles and achieving worthwhile goals. It is probably the vague awareness of his inner confusion, wasted opportunities, and lack of personal growth that generates the feeling that something is missing—that he is not a complete person and is not leading a truly meaningful life. As we have seen, this approach to life tends to result in existential anxiety and guilt.

THE NEUROTIC PARADOX

The human being is capable of learning and modifying his behavior and tends to be highly pragmatic in doing what works. Yet, as we have seen, the neurotic clings to his established behavior patterns despite their self-defeating nature and the fact that they ultimately lead to dissatisfaction and unhappiness. The question then arises as to why his neurotic and self-defeating life style is maintained. This puzzling situation is referred to as the *neurotic paradox.*

The neurotic paradox can be understood in terms of two basic concepts: (1) the immediate relief from anxiety which comes from the neurotic pattern of avoiding stress situations; and (2) the inappropriate persistence of the threat potential. Since the neurotic responds by avoidance to the earliest cues signifying the approach of the feared stress, he is thus prevented from testing the situation to see if what he fears is, in fact, realistic.

For example, let us take the case of a young man who is very much in love with a girl. They are engaged and have made wedding plans. However, she meets someone else to whom she is greatly attracted and abruptly breaks the engagement, terminating their relationship. He reacts with intense feelings of self-devaluation, anxiety, and depression, coupled with a considerable measure of hostility. Then his behavior follows a new pattern. Whenever a relationship with a member of the opposite sex begins to become serious, he becomes anxious and breaks it off. In short, he has acquired a conditioned fear or phobia of close relationships with members of the opposite sex. It may be referred to as a phobia, since it is irrational in the sense that he might actually be able to establish an intimate and secure relationship with another girl if he gave

himself the chance. However, his anxiety and avoidance behavior do not permit him to try out this possibility. Thus the phobia and avoidance behavior are maintained because they are reinforced by anxiety reduction each time he breaks off a relationship that is starting to become serious.

The basic pattern we are dealing with in the neuroses thus involves faulty learning, which makes the individual particularly vulnerable to certain common life stresses that most people can cope with successfully. This vulnerability, in turn, leads to a causal chain of: stress—anxiety—avoidance—reinforcement. The pattern is reinforcing because it enables the individual to alleviate his anxiety, or to escape anxiety entirely, by avoiding the stress at the earliest possible indication of its approach. He may even avoid situations in which a given type of stress is likely to occur. And as we have noted, neurotic avoidance behavior tends to be both self-defeating and self-perpetuating.

SPECIFIC NEUROTIC PATTERNS

In this section we shall consider specific neurotic patterns and their dynamics, examining both the personality factors and the types of stress situations commonly associated with each pattern. We shall then discuss etiological factors, problems of treatment, and outcomes for neurotic disorders in general.

The neurotic symptom patterns that we shall consider include the following categories.[1]

1. *Anxiety neurosis*—involves diffuse but often severe anxiety not specifically referable to a particular situation or threat.

2. *Phobic neurosis*—involves various fears which the individual realizes are irrational but from which he cannot free himself.

3. *Obsessive-compulsive neurosis*—involves thoughts and actions the individual recognizes as irrational but which still persist.

4. *Hysterical neurosis*—consists of two types: (a) *conversion type*, in which symptoms of physi-

cal illness that are not caused by such illness are involved, such as paralysis or loss of hearing; and (b) *dissociative type*, including such reactions as amnesia and multiple personality.

5. *Hypochondriacal neurosis*—involves preoccupation with one's bodily functioning and various presumed diseases.

6. *Neurasthenic neurosis*—involves chronic fatigue, weakness, and lack of enthusiasm.

7. *Depressive neurosis*—involves abnormally prolonged dejection, associated with internal conflict, interpersonal loss, or environmental setback.

Our review of specific neurotic patterns will also deal with the question of whether there

---

[1]In addition to the seven categories listed, the APA classification also includes the category of *depersonalization neurosis*, which we shall not discuss because of the paucity of information concerning depersonalization as a distinct neurotic pattern. However, we shall deal with the phenomenon of depersonalization in our later discussion of psychotic disorders.

is an "existential neurosis"—involving chronic meaninglessness, alienation, and apathy.

At this point, it may be noted that specific neurotic patterns may vary from time to time, and that aspects of different patterns may be combined in a given case.

ANXIETY NEUROSIS

Anxiety neurosis is the most common of the various neurotic patterns, constituting 30 to 40 percent of all neurotic disorders.[1] It is characterized by chronic anxiety and apprehensiveness, which may be punctuated by recurring episodes of acute anxiety. But since neither the anxious expectations nor the acute anxiety attacks appear to stem from any particular threat, the pervasive anxiety is said to be "free-floating." As Wolpe (1969) has emphasized, this means that the eliciting stimuli are obscure, complex, and quite pervasive.

In addition to free-floating anxiety, the predominant symptoms in anxiety neurosis typically include:

Inability to concentrate
Difficulty in making decisions
Extreme sensitivity
Discouragement
Sleep disturbances
Excessive sweating
Sustained muscle tension

It can be readily seen that these symptoms are directly related to the basic anxiety that is characteristic of this pattern. In other neurotic reactions the anxiety is ameliorated by the development of phobias, compulsions, and other defensive reactions. Aside from partial repression, the anxiety neurotic is largely without these supplementary defenses.

Clinical picture. The anxiety neurotic lives in a relatively constant state of tension, worry, and diffuse uneasiness. He is oversensitive in interpersonal relationships, and frequently feels inadequate and depressed. Usually he has difficulty concentrating and making decisions, dreading to make a mistake. His high level of tension is often reflected in strained postural movements, overreaction to sudden or unexpected stimuli, and continual nervous movements. Commonly, he complains of muscular tension, especially in the neck and upper shoulder region, chronic mild diarrhea, frequent urination, and sleep disturbances that include insomnia and nightmares. He perspires profusely and his palms are often clammy; he may show cardiovascular changes, such as elevated blood pressure and increased pulse rate; and he may experience heart palpitations for no apparent reason.

As we have noted, the anxiety neurotic tends to evidence a persistent raised level of anxiety, which may be punctuated from time to time by acute anxiety attacks.

1. *Acute anxiety attacks.* Often, persons suffering from anxiety neurosis experience recurring periods of acute panic that last anywhere from a few seconds to an hour or more. These attacks usually come on suddenly, mount to high intensity, then subside. Symptoms vary from one person to another, but typically they include "palpitations, shortness of breath, profuse sweating, faintness and dizziness, coldness and pallor of the face and extremities, urge to micturate, gastric sensations and an ineffable feeling of imminent death" (Lader & Mathews, 1970, p. 377). The physiological symptoms together with the sensation of impending death or catastrophe make an anxiety attack a terrifying experience while it lasts.

Usually the attack subsides after a few minutes. If it continues, the individual may frantically implore someone around him to summon a doctor. After medical treatment has been administered, commonly in the form of reassurance and a sedative, he gradually quiets down. Such attacks vary in frequency from several times a day to once a month or even less often. They may occur during the day, or the person may awaken from a sound sleep with a strong feeling of apprehension which rapidly develops into an attack. Between attacks he may appear to be relatively unperturbed, but mild anxiety and tension usually persist.

2. *Chronic anxiety.* In general, anxiety neurotics are chronically apprehensive no matter how well things seem to be going. Their vague fears and general sensitivity keep them continually

---

[1]Incidence statistics relative to the various neurotic patterns are rough estimates, since they are based only on cases diagnosed in clinics and hospitals. Figures used in the present text are drawn chiefly from Eiduson (1968), Goodwin, Guze, and Robbins (1969), Kenyon (1966), and Marks (1970).

upset, uneasy, and discouraged. Not only do they have difficulty making decisions, but after decisions have been made they worry excessively over possible errors and unforeseen circumstances that may lead to disaster. The lengths to which they go to find things to worry about is remarkable; as fast as one cause for worry is removed, they find another, until relatives and friends lose all patience with them.

Even after going to bed, the anxiety neurotic is not likely to find relief from his worries. Often he reviews each mistake, real or imagined, recent or remote. When he is not reviewing and regretting the events of the past, he is anticipating all the difficulties that are going to arise in the future. Then, after he has crossed and recrossed most of his past and future bridges and has managed to fall asleep, he frequently has anxiety dreams—dreams of being choked, falling off high places, being shot, or being chased by murderers, with the horrible sensation that his legs will move only in a slow-motion fashion and that his pursuers, try as he will to elude them, are gradually overtaking him.

As might be expected, the excessive use of tranquilizing drugs, sleeping pills, and alcohol often complicates the clinical picture in anxiety neuroses.

Dynamics. Anxiety reactions reflect the individual's acute feelings of inadequacy in the face of inner and outer stresses that he evaluates as threatening. Such reactions may be perfectly normal, provided the stress situation is sufficiently severe to justify them. In our present highly unsettled world, many of us feel uneasy a good deal of the time and may even experience occasional mild anxiety attacks. Similarly, severe financial reverses, loss of employment, and other unusual stresses may activate rather severe but perfectly normal feelings of anxiety. Thus it is not the anxiety *per se* but the type and degree of stress eliciting it that determines its normality or abnormality. In neurotic reactions the anxiety is considered pathological because it tends to be chronic and is elicited by stress situations that the average individual handles without too much difficulty.

1. *Faulty parental models and expectations.* As we have seen in our discussion of faulty development, a tense and anxious mother can transmit her anxiety to even a very young infant. If interactions with such a faulty parental model continue, the child may evidence anxiety reactions similar to those of the parent. In his studies of the behavior disorders of children, Jenkins (1966; 1968; 1969) found that "The overanxious-neurotic

The psychological distress of the anxiety neurotic is typically accompanied by heightened muscular tension, emotional strain, and sleep disturbances.

child appears more frequently . . . with neurotic mothers, who are themselves anxious. . . ." (1966, p. 455) As one neurotic young adult expressed the problem in the course of psychotherapy, "I guess there is more of my overanxious neurotic mother in me than I had realized."

Jenkins (1968; 1969) also has pointed out that anxiety neurotics often come from families in which the parents have high expectations for their offspring and seemingly make their love and support for a child contingent on his ability to satisfy those expectations. An individual reared in such a setting is likely to adopt unrealistic standards for himself and to become highly self-critical and anxious when he fails to meet them.

After ten years of very successful practice, a 34-year-old dentist noted that his practice had declined very slightly during the closing months of the year. Shortly after this he began to experience mild anxiety attacks and complained of continual worry, difficulty in sleeping, and a vague dread that he was "failing." As a result, he increased his hours of practice during the evenings from one to five nights and began driving himself beyond all reason in a desperate effort to "insure the success of his practice." Although his dental practice now increased beyond what it had been previously, he found himself still haunted by the vague fears and apprehensions of failure. These, in turn, became further augmented by frequent heart palpitations and pains which he erroneously diagnosed as at least an incapacitating if not a fatal heart ailment. At this point his anxiety became so great that he voluntarily came to a clinic for assistance.

In the course of assessment and treatment, a somewhat typical pattern was revealed. The patient had a history of early and chronic emotional insecurity. No matter what his accomplishments, his parents continued to reject and belittle him, which led him to feel inferior and to anticipate failure. When he once proudly told his parents that the school counselor informed him he had a very high IQ, they demanded to know why he didn't make better grades. He remembered occasionally receiving presents, such as a model airplane set, which were always beyond his age level so that his father would have to help him assemble the kit. Linked to his continual failure and inferiority was a very high level of aspiration—reflecting the expectations of his parents and his desire to accomplish something that would win their approval and support.

As a result of this early background, the dentist was unable to enjoy the successes he did achieve, for he always felt he could be accomplishing more. Even the mere suggestion of failure in his professional work as an adult was met by exaggerated fear and anxiety and a frantic redoubling of effort, with increasing imbalance in his daily living as more and more time was taken from other activities and devoted to his excessively long hours of work. Finally, the distressing symptoms led to worry about his own health as well as about his professional status, and to the realization that he was badly in need of help.

The preceding case seems somewhat typical of the many ambitious, conscientious, insecure individuals who have habitually driven themselves toward well-defined material goals. Usually such individuals have a history of feeling inadequate and insecure, and of evaluating themselves in terms of exacting standards and high levels of achievement. They tend to react to the slightest threat of failure with apprehension and anxiety out of proportion to the degree of actual threat. This, in turn, upsets their pattern of living and augments the total stress. In the preceding case it precipitated a rather common neurotic anxiety reaction.

2. *Failure to learn needed competencies.* In many cases neurotic anxiety results from the failure to acquire needed competencies—often because of parental overprotection, rejection, or neglect. In competing for education, mates, and jobs—as well as in assuming the responsibilities and meeting the demands of adulthood—such a person is at a distinct disadvantage.

The person with well-developed competencies for coping with the problems of living will find far fewer situations threatening and anxiety arousing. But lacking such competencies, the individual is likely to feel basically inadequate and insecure in a competitive world for which he is poorly prepared. Finding more situations difficult to manage and threatening, he tends to suffer from persistent feelings of apprehension and anxiety.

Such chronic mild anxiety may be intensified by new demands or dangers that augment the total stress load. Thus the individual may function more or less effectively despite his inadequate competencies until a change in his life situation increases the pressures on him. A promotion at work may involve the necessity of increased self-assertiveness and raise the possibility of serious friction with others. As a consequence, his anxiety level rises, even though he is unable to pinpoint the relationship between his new position and his increased anxiety. In essence, he is reacting to vague danger signals stemming from his lack of needed competencies and his deeply imbedded feelings of inadequacy. This is one of the reasons why success experiences may augment, rather than alleviate, anxiety in this type of personality. An actual failure, whether real or potential, is even more traumatic.

3. *Inability to handle "dangerous" impulses.* The neurotic is likely to experience intense anxiety in situations that elicit "dangerous" feelings —that is, feelings that would devalue his self-image or endanger his relationships with other people. The handling of hostility, for example, tends to be especially difficult for the neurotic, who typically feels forced to take a compliant, subservient, self-suppressing attitude toward others as the price of security, love, and acceptance. The blocking of his own strivings to be a person leads inevitably to strong feelings of aggression and hostility, yet it seems that these feelings must be controlled and denied at all costs to avoid possible rejection by others and to maintain an image of himself as a worthy person. Sometimes such repressed hostility reveals itself in indirect ways, such as in fantasies of killing or injuring other people, perhaps even someone he loves or feels dependent upon for acceptance and security.

An 18-year-old male student developed severe anxiety attacks just before he went out on dates. In therapy it was revealed that he came from a very insecure home in which he was very much attached to an anxious, frustrated, and insecure mother. He was not particularly attractive and had considerable difficulty getting dates, especially with the girls of his choice. The girl he had been dating recently, for example, would not make any arrangements to go out until after 6:00 P.M. of the same day, after her chances for a more preferable date seemed remote. This had increased his already strong feelings of inferiority and insecurity and had led to the development of intense hostility toward the opposite sex, mostly on an unconscious level.

He had begun to have fantasies of choking the girl to death when they were alone together. As he put it, "When we are alone in the car, I can't get my mind off her nice white throat and what it would be like to choke her to death." At first he put these thoughts out of his mind, but they returned on subsequent nights with increasing persistency. Then, to complicate the matter, he experienced his first acute anxiety attack. It occurred in his car on the way over to pick up his date and lasted for only a few minutes, but the youth was panic-stricken and thought that he was going to die. After that he experienced several additional attacks under the same conditions.

The relationship of the repressed hostility to the persistent fantasies and anxiety attacks is clear in this case. Yet it was not at all apparent to the young man. He was at a complete loss to explain either the fantasies or the attacks.

Similarly, repressed sexual desires may threaten to break through existing defenses and elicit intense anxiety. For example, a man may attempt to repress homosexual impulses that he considers highly immoral and completely incompatible with his self-concept. For a time the repression protects him, but repression is rarely—if ever—complete, and the individual is likely to experience periodic flare-ups of anxiety even though he may be unaware of the reason for them. In addition, some change in his life situation—perhaps a friendly relationship with an effeminate man—may intensify his homosexual impulses, posing a major threat to his repressive defenses and eliciting intense anxiety.

4. *Anxiety-arousing decisions.* We have noted that anxiety neurotics tend to have difficulty in making decisions. Under certain conditions—such as conflicts involving moral values or possible loss of security and status—there may be acute anxiety and paralyzing indecision.

A college sophomore, Mary _____ , wanted very much to marry a young man she had met in school. However, he insisted on having premarital sex relations "to be sure that they would be sexually compatible." This was contrary to her ethical and religious training, yet she found herself strongly attracted to him physically as well as very much in love. As a consequence, the thought of giving in to his demands persisted, but she was unable to make up her mind. Eventually, she began to experience periodic anxiety attacks, had serious difficulty in concentrating on her studies, and suffered from insomnia, during which she would go over and over the conflict situation.

When Mary came to the college clinic for assistance it seemed apparent that two factors had contributed to the development of her anxiety attacks. The first factor was a devaluated self-concept; she viewed herself as unattractive, felt insecure in playing the appropriate female role, and was apprehensive about her relations with males. This basic inadequacy and

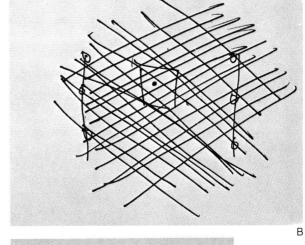

B

A

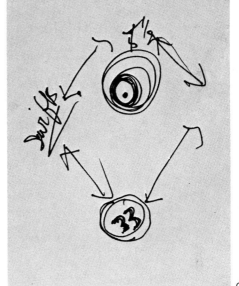

C

Drawing is often considered a primitive but effective method of communicating one's inner thoughts and feelings. Of course, the therapist must exercise caution to avoid misinterpretation. The four pictures shown here were drawn by a woman assessed as suffering from an acute anxiety neurosis. Although she was a successful businesswoman, having risen progressively through jobs of greater and greater responsibility, she felt herself incapable of achieving further advancement—that she had "reached the end of the line." Subsequently, she experienced feelings of frustration, inadequacy, and anxiety.

Sketch A was hurriedly drawn under great tension. The smoking buildings on the left represent New York City, the woman's place of employment, and buildings on the right, her desired place of employment. Separating the two is the middle structure, which contains the "aggressive, agitated figures of her male competitors in the business world."

In Sketch B, the woman appeared to represent herself in a cage by the boxed-in dot. She then partially blotted out the crude diagram "by rapidly placed crosshatching, as though to deny the admission that she found herself so trapped." Sketch C appears to represent "the merry-go-round on which she has been moving, from one firm to another, around and around, always seeking advancement, without finding any satisfying fulfillment." Finally, Sketch D indicates her anxiety over her present dilemma—"What road today? What road tomorrow?" (Adapted from Brown, 1957, pp. 171–174)

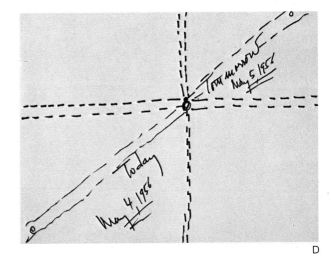

D

insecurity appeared to pave the way for the second factor, which precipitated the anxiety attacks—namely, the conflict between her guilt-arousing desire for sexual relations, which she considered highly immoral, and her fear of losing the man she loved if she continued to refuse. The situation was also fraught with other anxiety-arousing uncertainties. Even if she did yield to his demands, she had to face the possibility that he was only trying to seduce her or that even if he were sincere, he might not find her sexually compatible. In addition, she had vague feelings of apprehension that she would somehow be punished if she indulged in such behavior, perhaps by becoming pregnant or causing him to lose his respect for her. The end result was indecision and anxiety.

In cases where the neurotically insecure person has achieved some degree of real success and consequently of security, anxiety attacks may develop when his proposed behavior jeopardizes this security.

A successful business executive developed acute anxiety attacks about once every two or three months. His wife was eight years older than he, and he was no longer physically attracted to her. He had found himself increasingly interested in younger women and had begun to think how much more enjoyable it would be to have a younger, more companionable wife. During this period he met a girl with whom he was sure he had fallen in love. It was shortly thereafter that the anxiety attacks began to occur. They were preceded by a period of several days of increased tenseness and anxiety, but the attacks came on suddenly and were intense.

This man, too, was at a complete loss to explain his attacks. But the explanation was not difficult to find. He had had a poverty-stricken and insecure childhood and felt basically inferior, insecure, and threatened by a harsh world. These feelings had been intensified when he had failed college courses in his second year, even though the failure had resulted primarily from excessive outside work. He had been able to achieve some security, however, by marrying an older and very strong woman who had instilled considerable self-confidence and initiative in him. The relationship had proved very fruitful financially, and the man was living in a style which as a youth, "I hadn't dared to imagine in my wildest dreams!" His persistent thoughts about divorcing his wife, on whom he felt dependent for his security and style of life, thus represented a severe threat to the moderately successful adjustment he had been able to achieve. The anxiety attacks followed.

Life often poses problems in which the pursuit of increased satisfactions involves giving up present hard-won security and taking new risks. For the neurotic, this is likely to prove an especially anxiety-arousing conflict situation.

5. *Reactivation of prior trauma.* A stressful situation that parallels some earlier trauma may elicit intense anxiety in an individual who is basically insecure. The following reactions are those of a man who sought treatment after being absent from his job for three days as a result of "sickness."

"I've just reached the point where I can't go on. Got no fight left. And not enough guts to end it here. Best damn job I ever had. Almost can see my way out of debt. And it's all going to hell, and I'm getting so I don't care about anything, except not going back to work. I can't kid myself, I just can't take it anymore. And I'll have to confess I have no faith left in anything including your profession. Or faith in myself. Maybe if I can tell someone how I feel, how balled up I am, I can see the light. I can't afford to take time off work. I can't afford to relax a couple of weeks on some warm beach, or forget my troubles with some floozy blonde. Hell, that's for the books on the best seller's lists. I've just got to go about acting like my normal stupid self and something's got to blow. It goes in waves. Sometimes, I'm alright and then I get anxiety feelings, and my heart pounds. I get to shaking all over, and think I'm going to die. God, it's awful!"

Interestingly enough, the primary cause of the intense anxiety reactions in this case was found to be associated with a new and rather critical supervisor at work. In response to criticisms which may have annoyed but did not completely disrupt the behavior of other employees, this man became anxious and depressed. His reaction was traced to his relationship with his father, who had died some five years before. Since his earliest memory, the patient had idolized his father and had practically lived for the occasional hard-won compliments he received from him. Conversely, when his father had criticized him, the patient had been so upset that he would go to his room completely distraught and cry for hours at a time. Now, as an adult, this dependent, insecure individual experienced these same feelings of distress when criticized by an exacting supervisor. Apparently the new supervisor had reactivated an old "weak spot" and thus precipitated the anxiety reaction.

Although we have emphasized the inadequacy, oversensitivity, and low stress tolerance of the anxiety neurotic, it may be pointed out that he often puts up a good battle in view of his faulty evaluations of himself and his environment. As Portnoy (1959) has pointed out: "To the picture of an anxious individual apprehensively coping with life in the face of inner and outer dangers must also be added the picture of a human being with courage, able to endure this much anxiety without the more massive defenses and character distortions which characterize the other psychiatric syndromes." (p. 320) This statement seems particularly relevant when we realize that repression—which is seldom adequate—represents the only basic defense mechanism utilized by the anxiety neurotic. And as we have noted in our discussion of combat reactions, some anxiety neurotics function very effectively when confronted with an actual danger that both demands and permits definitive action (Cattell & Scheier, 1961).

We shall comment on the treatment of anxiety reactions in our section on the treatment of neuroses in general. However, it may be pointed out that anxiety neurotics often find some relief in mild tranquilizers, which appear especially effective in reducing somatic complaints (Lipman et al., 1969). Anxiety neurotics also tend to respond well to psychotherapy, although it appears that their chronic anxiety is seldom completely removed. But as we shall see, newer therapeutic innovations are providing a brighter picture concerning the outcome of treatment.

PHOBIC NEUROSIS

A phobia is a persistent fear of some object or situation that presents no actual danger to the person or in which the danger is magnified out of all proportion to its actual seriousness. The following list of the common phobias and their objects will give some hint of the variety of situations and objects around which phobias may be centered:

Acrophobia—high places
Agoraphobia—open places
Algophobia—pain
Astraphobia—storms, thunder, and lightning
Claustrophobia—closed places
Hematophobia—blood
Mysophobia—contamination or germs
Monophobia—being alone
Nyctophobia—darkness
Ocholophobia—crowds
Pathophobia—disease
Pyrophobia—fire
Syphilophobia—syphilis
Zoophobia—animals or some particular animal

Some of these phobias involve an exaggerated fear of things that most of us fear to some extent, such as darkness, fires, disease, and snakes. Others, such as phobias of open places or crowds, involve situations that do not elicit fear in most people.

The term *phobic neurosis* may refer not only to a specific learned fear of some object or situation, but also to an overall pattern of fear and avoidance behavior. Marks (1970) has cited the extreme case of a girl who developed agoraphobia —fear of open places—at the age of 19 and who, after 4 months of unsuccessful treatment, left her home only twice in the next 7 years. The pervasive influence of this neurotic phobia on the entire life style of an individual has, in fact, led Snaith (1968) to argue that the term *agoraphobia* should be replaced by the phrase "non-specific insecurity fears."

Among neurotics seeking professional assistance, the phobias constitute about 8 to 12 percent of all neuroses (Eiduson, 1968). Phobic neuroses occur more commonly among young adults and are much more common among women than men. Possibly, the higher incidence among women relates to the fact that in our society strong fears are more acceptable as part of the female role than of the male role.

Clinical picture. Most of us have minor irrational fears, but in phobic reactions such fears are intense and interfere with everyday activities. For example, a claustrophobic may go to great lengths to avoid entering a small room or passageway, even when it is essential for him to do so. Neurotics usually admit that they have no real cause to be afraid of the object or situation, but say they cannot help themselves. If they attempt to approach rather than avoid the phobic situation they are overcome with anxiety, which may vary from mild feelings of uneasiness and distress to a full-fledged anxiety attack.

Persons with phobic neuroses usually show other symptoms in addition to their phobias, such as headaches, back pains, stomach upsets, dizzy spells, and fear of "cracking up." For example, the reluctance of agoraphobics to venture from the security of their homes is often attributed to a fear of "blacking out"—either in the street or some other dangerous open space—as a consequence of the intensification of their neurotic anxiety (Snaith, 1968). At times of more acute panic, the individual may complain of feelings of unreality, of strangeness, and of "not being himself."

In some cases phobic reactions may also be obsessive, as when a persistent obsessive fear of contamination dominates the neurotic's consciousness. Fears of this type will be considered in the next section under "obsessive-compulsive" neurosis.

Terhune (1961) has pointed out that the particular phobias which individuals develop and the extremes to which such phobias may go are often influenced by the current culture. This is well brought out in a study by Kerry (1960) of four patients who had a phobia of outer space. "They were preoccupied with fears of the earth deviating from its course and being destroyed in a collision. . . . Artificial satellites were felt to increase this danger." (p. 1386) One patient, on going outside and seeing other people, would say, "Do these other people realize what danger they're in on this spinning ball we call a globe?" (p. 1383)

Dynamics. Phobias may occur in a wide range of personality patterns and abnormal syndromes, reflecting the part that anxiety and avoidance play in so many manifestations of abnormal behavior. Traditionally phobias have been thought of as attempts to cope with internal or external dangers by carefully avoiding situations likely to bring about whatever is feared. Thus phobias have been seen as simple defensive reactions in which the person feels he *must* give in to his fears in order to protect himself.

Three major dynamic patterns have been emphasized in the development of phobias: displacement of anxiety, defense against threatening impulses, and avoidance learning. It is useful to remember that specific threats that initiate phobic patterns of behavior may not be the only factors acting to maintain them. Avoidance behavior may be maintained in part by secondary gains, such as increased attention, sympathy,

protection, and some control over the behavior of others. For example, fear of crowds may allow a housewife to escape from responsibilities outside the home, such as shopping or transporting her children to and from school. And of course, if the person persistently avoids stress situations, he will fail to develop the competencies needed for coping with them. Thus in labeling himself as "a person who can't," he may be creating a self-fulfilling prophecy.

1. *Displacement of anxiety.* A phobia may represent a displacement of anxiety from the stress situation that elicited it to some other object or situation. This mechanism is strongly emphasized in psychoanalytic theory and derives largely from Freud's case history of little Hans, published in 1909. On the basis of this case and subsequent clinical experience, Freud concluded that phobias represent displaced anxiety associated with the Oedipus complex. According to this model, the child desires to possess his mother sexually and is jealous and hostile toward the father. The child therefore fears his father—and in particular dreads being castrated. The fear of the avenging father may then be displaced to some external and formerly innocuous object. In the case of little 5-year-old Hans, the horse pulling the carriage in which he and his mother were riding fell down and was hurt. Hans had become very frightened, and according to Freud this dramatic situation led to the displacement of his fear of castration by his father to the fear of being bitten by horses. Freud concluded that phobias in adults develop only in people with disturbed sexual relationships.

Later investigators have pointed out that many kinds of stress situations may lead to phobic reactions through the mechanism of displacement. For example, a person who fears that he will be discharged from his job for inefficiency may develop an elevator phobia, which makes it impossible for him to get to the office where he works and hence protects him from embarrassment and anxiety-arousing self-devaluation. The following case shows the same mechanism.

A young man had started his first business venture by renting a very small store near the entrance to a large building and stocking it exclusively with neckties. He managed to make ends meet over a trial period of several months, but it was becoming obvious that his business venture was doomed to failure. About this time he noticed that the shop "seemed stuffy," that he didn't have any "elbow room." It seemed as if the walls were closing in on him, and he would feel compelled to go outside and get his "lungs full of fresh air." These feelings increased in frequency and intensity until he was forced to close the shop.

Here the protective function of the phobic reaction is easily seen. There was no need to admit failure or poor business ability. The young man had to close the shop for other reasons, and he was completely unaware of the real source of his anxiety and fear.

Arieti (1961) has also noted that many phobias may indicate a more generalized anxiety state. Thus intense guilt feelings over immoral behavior may lead to phobias of objects or situations that are symbolically associated with anticipated punishment; a phobia of speaking in public may relate to the individual's more generalized fear that other people will detect his insufficiencies and "see him for what he really is"; or a phobia of traveling may hide a bigger fear of making excursions into life.

2. *Defense against threatening impulses.* Salzman (1968) and Lief (1968), among others, point out that a phobia may represent a defensive reaction that protects the individual from situations in which his repressed aggressive or sexual impulses might become dangerous. Here, too, the anxiety is displaced; the thing feared consciously is not the basic cause of his anxiety. Thus a husband may develop a phobia of lakes, swimming pools, and other bodies of water because on previous occasions he had persistent ideas of drowning his wife; similarly, a woman may develop a phobia of sharp knives and refuse to keep one in the house because of repressed impulses to cut her husband's throat; or a young mother may develop a phobia of being alone with her unwanted baby because of recurring fantasies about strangling him.

Similarly the individual may protect himself from unacceptable sexual impulses by developing phobic reactions. For example, 24-year-old Herbert S. sought psychological assistance because of a "morbid fear of syphilis which makes it impossible for me to have sexual relations." In the course of psychotherapy it became apparent that this youth's syphilophobia represented a displacement of a fear of engaging in

homosexual relations. His fear of contracting syphilis helped him to maintain what he considered sexually moral behavior. That it also prevented him from engaging in heterosexual relations—which he viewed as moral—apparently stemmed from the fact that during intercourse his "mind was completely dominated by homosexual fantasies." These fantasies were highly anxiety-arousing and on a number of occasions had terminated in impotency, which he had found acutely embarrassing. Thus the syphilophobia kept him from situations that might arouse his sexual conflicts.

3. *Conditioning and avoidance learning.* As we saw in Watson's case of "little Albert"—who was conditioned to fear a white rat by the making of a sudden, loud noise each time the rat was presented—a phobia may be the learned result of prior trauma in the feared situation. And this fear, as happened in the case of little Albert, may generalize to similar situations.

Phobias of this type are not difficult to understand because most of us probably have mild phobias based on previous learning. A person who has been attacked and bitten by a vicious dog may feel uneasy around dogs, even though some reconditioning experiences have intervened. A pervasive pattern of fear and avoidance behavior can be learned in much the same way. For example, if a child's fumbling attempts to master new skills are ridiculed by his parents, or if he is discouraged from becoming independent, he may never develop the confidence he needs to cope with new situations. In effect, he learns that avoidance is the "appropriate" response where risk or uncertainty is involved.

As we have seen, a phobia may generalize to a fear of situations only minimally related to the basic trauma. This generalization process often takes the form of a "hierarchical chaining" of avoidance behaviors (Hogan & Kirchner, 1967; Stampfl & Levis, 1967).

An 18-year-old girl had been given strict "moral" training concerning the evils of sex, and she associated sexual relations with vivid ideas of sin, guilt, and hell. Nevertheless, when the young man she was dating kissed her and "held her close," it aroused intense sexual desires—which were extremely guilt arousing and which led to a chain of avoidance behaviors. First she stopped seeing him in an effort to get rid of her immoral thoughts; then she stopped all

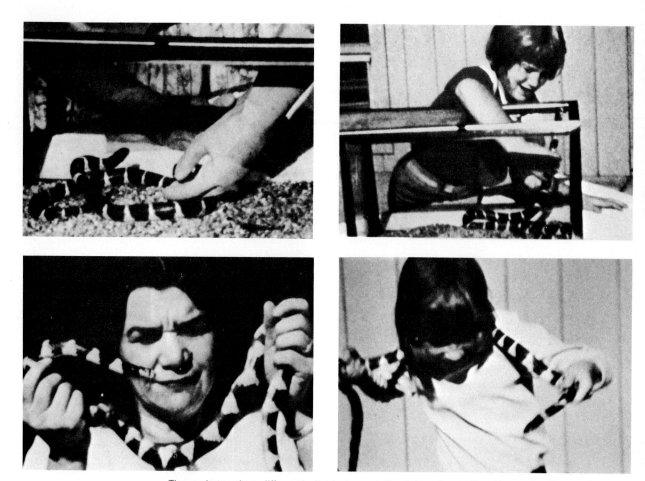

These photos show different individuals modeling interactions with a king snake. By means of such demonstrations Bandura (1969) has shown that persons with a phobia of harmless snakes can be encouraged to slowly approach, and with the model's help, learn to handle king snakes. Thus they gradually eliminate their previously phobic avoidant behavior.

dating; then she began to feel uncomfortable with any young man she knew; and finally she became fearful of any social situations where men might be present. At this point her life was largely dominated by her phobias, and she was so "completely miserable" that she requested professional help.

In the treatment of phobias two main strategies have been followed. The first—based on the assumption that phobias are symbolic representations of more basic anxieties—focuses on helping the patient understand his phobia and learn more effective techniques for coping with feared situations and his underlying anxiety. However, this focus on development of understanding or insight does not appear very effective. As Salzman,

a psychoanalytically oriented psychiatrist, has noted, "It has been known for some time that understanding, alone, is ineffectual in resolving the phobic state. It is a commonplace that, while the patient may have adequate insight into the origin, symbolism, and function of his phobia, he is still unable to risk the initial venture into the heretofore out-of-bounds area of living." (1968, pp. 464–465)

Consequently, the second major strategy, involving behavior-modification techniques, is being increasingly used to deal directly with the hierarchy of fears and avoidance behaviors. The girl in the preceding case, for example, was taught to relax while imagining herself in a social situation in which men were present. Next she was encouraged to attend such a gathering, and found herself able to do so without experiencing the usual fear. Treatment then proceeded through each step of the fear hierarchy until she could behave normally in heterosexual relationships.

Other behavior-modification techniques that could be used in the treatment of phobias will be dealt with later. Here it may be pointed out that the successful treatment of phobias may lead to changes in the patient's entire life style. This is well brought out in a case cited by Bandura, Blanchard, and Ritter (1969).

"My success in gradually overcoming this fear of snakes has contributed to a greater feeling of confidence generally in my abilities to overcome any other problem which may arise. I have more faith in myself." (p. 197)

In essence, the performance of behaviors that were formerly avoided can help the individual gain confidence in himself and his ability to cope with stressful situations.

OBSESSIVE-COMPULSIVE NEUROSIS

In obsessive-compulsive neurosis the person seems compelled to think about something that he wishes not to think about, or to carry out actions that he does not want to carry out. These obsessive and compulsive patterns are quite varied, and may occur in association with other neuroses. The incidence of obsessive-compulsive neuroses has been variously estimated from about 4 to 20 percent of the neurotic population (Coleman, 1964; Goodwin, Guze, & Robbins, 1969). Age and sex differences have not been systematically studied.

Clinical picture. As Nemiah (1967) has pointed out, there is a wide range of obsessive-compulsive behaviors.

"The phenomena may be manifested psychically or behaviorally; they may be experienced as ideas or as impulses; they may refer to events anticipated in the future or actions already completed; they may express desires and wishes or protective measures against such desires; they may be simple, uncomplicated acts and ideas or elaborate, ritualized patterns of thinking and behavior. . . ." (p. 916)

Most of us have experienced thoughts of a somewhat obsessional nature, such as persistent thoughts about a coming trip or date, or a haunting melody that we cannot seem to get out of our mind. In the case of obsessive reactions, however, the thoughts are much more persistent, appear irrational to the individual, and interfere with his everyday behavior.

Obsessive thoughts may center around a wide variety of topics, such as concern over bodily functions, committing immoral acts, attempting suicide, or even finding the solution to some seemingly unsolvable problem. Particularly common are obsessive thoughts of committing some immoral act. A youth may fear that he is going to shout some obscene word in public. A father may be obsessed with the idea of bashing in his son's head with a hammer, a wife of poisoning or stabbing her husband, a daughter of pushing her mother down a flight of stairs.

These obsessive thoughts usually begin with occasional ruminations that can at first be easily dismissed from the mind. Even at this stage the person may experience some anxiety at the immoral or antisocial nature of the thoughts and may make a determined effort to get rid of them. But they continue to recur, and the more desperately he tries to rid himself of them the greater their persistence. Yet they seem "ego alien"—to be thoughts and impulses that lie outside his control and are not *really* his.

Even though obsessive ideas are not carried out in action, they remain a source of torment to the individual. Often he feels that he is going insane or that he is not fit to live. This pattern is illustrated in the case of a girl who . . .

"complained of having 'terrible thoughts.' When she thought of her boy-friend she wished he were dead; when her mother went down the stairs, she 'wished she'd fall and break her neck'; when her sister spoke of going to the beach with her infant daughter, the patient 'hoped that they would both drown.' These thoughts 'make me hysterical. I love them; why should I wish such terrible things to happen? It drives me wild, makes me feel I'm crazy and don't belong to society; maybe it's best for me to end it all than to go on thinking such terrible things about those I love.'" (Kraines, 1948, p. 183)

In compulsive reactions the person feels compelled to perform some act which, even during the process, seems absurd and strange to him.

Compulsive acts vary from relatively mild, ticlike rituals, such as running the finger around under the collar, to more complicated ritualistic acts, such as tying one's tie exactly seven times before feeling satisfied. In many cases, the compulsive behavior seriously disrupts the individual's everyday life, as in the case of a person who finds it necessary to wash his hands as often as 50 times a day. The performance of the compulsive act usually brings a feeling of satisfaction, however, whereas if he tries to restrain the compulsion, he is overcome with anxiety.

Actually, most of us show some compulsive behavior, such as stepping over cracks in sidewalks, walking around ladders instead of under them, or turning away when a black cat crosses our path—but without the degree of compulsiveness of the neurotic. A woman may feel very uncomfortable if the dishes are not washed after each meal; or she may follow a prescribed cleaning routine in which a certain pattern is rigidly followed—as in beginning with the dishes, then vacuuming, then dusting, and so on. If anything upsets this routine she feels uncomfortable; and if the stresses in her life increase, she may feel compelled to adhere even more rigidly to the routine. A public speaker may pace back and forth, periodically hunch his shoulders, or chain smoke—acts which he does not intend to perform and which are not characteristic of his behavior in a more secure situation.

Most of us also resort to minor obsessive-compulsive patterns under severe pressure or when trying to achieve goals which we consider of critical importance. Many historical figures have shown an "obsessive-compulsive" adherence to their goals despite discouragement and ridicule—Columbus persisted for 18 years in his efforts to secure financial backing for his expedition to "India," and Darwin assembled evidence for 22 years before he would present his ideas on evolution.

A rigid ordering of behavior can be temporarily adaptive in particularly difficult stress situations. The autobiographical accounts of Admiral Richard Byrd, who spent 6 solitary months in the Antarctic, and of Dr. Alain Bombard, who sailed alone across the Atlantic for 65 days on a life raft, show that both men reacted to the experience of prolonged isolation and loneliness with obsessive-compulsive patterns.

"Both explorers found that while their lives were threatened daily by the hazards of their milieu, it was the constancy of their surroundings which seemed like a force which would destroy them. Both men felt that they could control themselves and their environment only by thoroughly organizing their days, assigning themselves to a strict routine of work, and spending no more than one hour at a time doing a task. In this way, each felt he proved to himself that he could control both himself and his environment. . . . Both men used the same mechanisms to fight off depression: controlling their thoughts, dwelling only on pleasant past associations and experiences and refusing to allow themselves to think about the anxiety-producing aspects of their situations." (Solomon et al., 1957)

An obsessive-compulsive neurosis, by contrast, is considered maladaptive because it represents irrational and exaggerated behavior in the face of stresses that are not unduly upsetting to most people, and because such patterns reduce the flexibility of behavior and the capability for self-direction.

Dynamics. Either the obsessive thoughts or the compulsive actions may predominate in a given case, but both are parts of a total reaction pattern, and their dynamics are essentially the same. Several dynamic patterns have been delineated.[1]

1. *Substitutive thoughts and activities.* The obsessive-compulsive may defend himself from anxiety by persistently thinking of or doing something else each time threatening thoughts or impulses make their appearance. A person walking in a lonely place late at night might find the following thought continually persisting in his mind: "There is nothing to be afraid of—I am not afraid." In this way he attempts to allay his underlying fear. Similarly, an individual who has severe inadequacy feelings in a given situation may "think positively" and persistently review the success he has achieved in other situations. In essence, "safe" obsessive thoughts

---

[1]Obsessive thoughts and compulsive actions may, of course, occur as part of other clinical syndromes. Masserman (1961) has cited the case of a soldier who in an acute fatigue state kept throwing out his arms in a peculiar gesture. This gesture could not be explained until the patient recalled under narcosis that in the heat and excitement of a night battle, he had machine-gunned a friend, and had suffered a remorse so great that he had an overpowering desire to throw away his gun and run blindly from the unbearable horror of the situation. In our later discussion of psychotic disorders, we shall see how obsessive-compulsive reactions may be related to delusional and hallucinatory behavior.

are substituted for more unpleasant or dangerous ones.

The same dynamic pattern may underlie compulsive preoccupation with some activity, such as working on a new invention, writing the "truly great" novel, or developing a system to beat the horses. The task may never be completed, but by working on it so hard the individual is kept too busy to deal with unpleasant problems and is too engrossed to think disturbing thoughts. In many cases the compulsive behavior may, of course, be directed toward a constructive task. It is judged neurotic because it is used as an escape from marital, sexual, interpersonal, or other problems with which the individual must cope if he is to achieve effective adjustment.

In some instances, substitutive thoughts may be more complicated, and may involve the defense mechanism of *reaction formation.* Thus, the individual may think or act in ways directly contradictory to his dangerous thoughts or impulses. For example, he may unconsciously attempt to cope with inner hostility by persistently thinking about brotherly love, or he may defend himself from underlying homosexual desires by obsessive thoughts condemning such behavior.

Obsessive fantasies may help satisfy repressed desires and provide a substitute for overt action.

A farmer developed obsessive thoughts of hitting his three-year-old son over the head with a hammer. The father was completely unable to explain his "horrible thoughts." He stated that he loved his son very much and thought he must be going insane to harbor such thoughts. In the treatment of this case it became apparent that the patient's wife had suffered great pain in childbirth and has since refused sexual relations with him for fear of again becoming pregnant. In addition, she lavished most of her attention on the son, and their previously happy marriage was now torn with quarreling and bickering.

The farmer's obsessive thoughts of violence toward his son had apparently developed out of a combination of repressed hostility toward the boy, who had replaced him in his wife's affection, and wishful thinking in the direction of a return to his previously happy marital state, once the son was out of the way. However, the man vigorously and sincerely denied this explanation when it was suggested to him. Because his fantasies were lacking in affect—they did not seem to represent his real feelings at all—they permitted expression of his hostility without any attendant feelings of guilt.

2. *Guilt and fear of punishment.* Obsessive-compulsive behavior often seems to stem from feelings of guilt and self-condemnation. Lady Macbeth's symbolic handwashing after her participation in the bloody murder of King Duncan is a well-known literary example of ritualistic behavior aimed at the cleansing of guilt for immoral behavior. In the following case, the development of obsessive-compulsive patterns seems to be associated with a belief that "unforgivable" behavior will inevitably be punished.

A 32-year-old high-school cooking teacher developed marked feelings of guilt and uneasiness, accompanied by obsessive fears of hurting others by touching them or by their handling something she had touched. She dreaded to have anyone eat anything she had prepared, and if students in her cooking class were absent, she was certain they had been poisoned by her cooking. In addition, she developed the obsessive notion that a rash at the base of her scalp was a manifestation of syphilis, which would gnaw at her brain and make a "drooling idiot" of her.

Accompanying the obsessive fears were compulsions consisting primarily in repeated hand-washings and frequent returns to some act already performed to reassure herself that the act had been done right, such as turning off the gas or water.

In treatment it became clear that the patient was a self-centered but highly sensitive and conscientious person. She had graduated from college with honors and considered herself highly intelligent. About three years before her present difficulties she had married a noncollege man of whom she had been very much ashamed because of his poor English, table manners, and other characteristics which she thought led to a very poor social showing. As a result she had rejected him in her thinking and behavior and had treated him in what she now considered a very cruel manner. On one occasion she had also been unfaithful to him, which was very much against her moral training.

Over a period of time, however, she came to realize that he was a very fine person and that other people thought highly of him despite his lack of social polish. In addition, she gradually came to the realization that she was very much in love with him. At this point she began to reproach herself for her cruel treatment of him. She felt that he was a truly wonderful husband, and that she was completely unworthy of him. She was sure her past cruelty and unfaithfulness could never be forgiven. "Heaven knows that every word he says is worth fifty words I say. If I were real honest and truthful I would tell my husband to leave me."

This woman's obsessive fear of contaminating other people and of having syphilis apparently grew out of a feeling that her past "sins" had caught up with her. They also served the function of protecting her from acting upon her occasionally returning desire for sexual relations with other men.

3. *Assuring order and predictability.* Confronted with a world that seems highly dangerous, the neurotic may attempt to maintain some semblance of order and control by becoming unduly meticulous and methodical. A rigid pattern of behavior helps to prevent anything from going wrong, and hence provides some security and predictability. But if the slightest detail gets out of order, the entire defensive structure is endangered and the individual feels threatened and anxious.

A case that illustrates this pattern is that of a patient who, prior to hospitalization, had his life ordered in the most minute detail. He arose in the morning precisely at 6:50, took a shower, shaved, and dressed. His wife had breakfast ready precisely at 7:10 and followed a menu that he worked out months in advance. At exactly 7:45 he left for the office where he worked as an accountant. He came home precisely at 5:55, washed, then read the evening paper, and had dinner precisely at 6:30, again as per menu. His schedule was equally well worked out for evenings and weekends, with a movie on Tuesday, reading on Wednesday, rest on Monday and Thursday, and bridge on Friday. Saturday morning he played golf and Sunday morning and evening he attended church. Saturday evening usually involved having guests or visiting others. He was fastidious in his dress. Each shirt had to be clean and unwrinkled, his suit pressed every two days, and so on. His demands, of course, also included his wife, who was inclined to be easy-going and was upset when he "blew up" at the smallest variation from established routine.

By means of his carefully ordered existence the patient managed to make a reasonably successful adjustment until he became involved in a business deal with a friend and lost a considerable sum of money. This proved too much for him and precipitated a severe anxiety reaction with considerable agitation and depression, necessitating hospitalization.

In this case the individual's primary means of defense against *external* threats was to try to impose rigid order, thus making the world safer and more predictable. In other instances such a compulsive following of a daily routine, particularly a socially desirable and ethical one, helps the individual establish automatic control over dangerous inner desires. He avoids situations that might stimulate such desires, as well as situations that might permit their expression.

The semimagical signs and rituals common in obsessive-compulsive patterns are part of this ordering of a dangerous world, and are probably comparable to the repetitive and rigid rituals long used by primitive peoples as a means of warding off evil forces and ensuring the cooperation of supernatural powers. If they are to be effective, such rituals must be faithfully observed and performed in rigidly prescribed ways.

For the obsessive-compulsive neurotic—with his characteristic feelings of inadequacy, his proneness to guilt, and his vulnerability to threat—the careful and precise ordering of his world also becomes highly important; and anything that might threaten the order of his precariously structured life is viewed as a serious menace. And the greater the degree of threat—and consequently of anxiety—the more likely is a repetitive, obsessive-compulsive pattern to become "fixed," or "frozen." This is probably an exaggeration of the process we described in the case of the two explorers—Admiral Byrd and Alain Bombard—who resorted to compulsive and rigid behavior patterns in the face of potentially overwhelming stress (page 232).

Therapy in obsessive-compulsive neuroses tends to follow three basic strategies: (1) helping the individual to discriminate between thought and action, to accept his "forbidden" desires as common to most people, and to integrate them into his self-structure; (2) helping the individual to discriminate between objective and imagined dangers and encouraging him to respond selectively to different kinds of stimuli; and (3) blocking obsessive-compulsive rituals by positively reinforcing any response that departs from ritual and/or by administering an aversive stimulus, such as an electric shock, each time the ritualistic behavior occurs. All of these strategies are aimed at eliminating neurotic defenses and helping the individual realize that catastrophe does not follow their removal. The treatment program in the following case apparently achieved its aim.

A middle-aged married woman had the compulsion to shake every article of her own clothes and those of her children. The shaking ritual—which occupied over an hour of her time each morning—required that each piece of clothing be shaken three times in each of three different directions and at each of three different levels. In addition, most of the clothes had to be brushed inside and out; and whenever anything was washed, it had to be washed three times. The woman also found it difficult to stop washing her hands once she had started and repeatedly felt a compulsion to rub her hands together in each of three different ways.

Interview assessment indicated that much of the woman's compulsive behavior was associated with vague fears of germs and disease. A treatment program was formulated that (1) helped her discriminate between stimuli that were objectively "dirty" and unhygienic and those that were not—thus eliminating unnecessary fears and helping her make realistic decisions about standards of cleanliness; (2) consistently reinforced her behavior when she abandoned her compulsive rituals; and (3) utilized verbal instructions by the therapist to prevent their repetition whenever possible.

Therapy began in February, and by November of the same year the woman's ritualistic behavior had been completely eliminated. She was able to make her own decisions about cleaning and washing and was more confident about her standards of cleanliness. (Adapted from Mather, 1970)

HYSTERICAL NEUROSIS: CONVERSION TYPE

The conversion type of hysterical neurosis involves a neurotic pattern in which symptoms of some physical illness appear without any underlying organic pathology. It is one of the most intriguing and baffling patterns in psychopathology, and we still have much to learn about it.

The term *hysteria* is derived from the Greek word meaning "uterus." It was thought by Hippocrates and other ancient Greeks that this disorder was restricted to women and that it was caused by sexual difficulties, particularly by the wandering of a frustrated uterus to various parts of the body because of sexual desires and a yearning for children. Thus the uterus might lodge in the throat and cause choking sensations, or in the spleen, resulting in temper tantrums. Hippocrates considered marriage the best remedy for the affliction.

The concept of the relationship of sexual difficulties to hysteria was later advanced in modified form by Freud. He used the term *conversion hysteria* to indicate that the symptoms were an expression of repressed and deviated sexual energy—that is, the psychosexual conflict was *converted* into a bodily disturbance. For example, a sexual conflict over masturbation might be solved by developing a paralyzed hand. This is not done consciously, of course, and the person is not aware of the origin or meaning of his symptom.

In contemporary psychopathology, hysterical reactions of this type are no longer interpreted in Freudian terms as the "conversion" of sexual conflicts or other psychological problems into physical symptoms. Rather, the physical symptoms are now usually seen as serving a defensive function, enabling the individual to escape or avoid a stressful situation. Despite this change in interpretation, however, the term *conversion reaction* has been retained.

In World War I conversion reactions were the most frequent type of psychiatric syndrome. For many soldiers this involved a highly threatening approach-avoidance conflict, in which military orders and doing one's duty were pitted against fear of being killed or maimed in the crude bayonet charges that characterized this war. Here, conversion symptoms—such as being paralyzed in the legs or unable to straighten one's back—enabled the soldier to avoid the combat situation without being labeled a "coward" or being subjected to court-martial. Conversion reactions were also relatively common among combat personnel in World War II. These conversion reactions typically occurred in association with the highly stressful conditions of combat, and involved men who ordinarily would be considered relatively stable.

Conversion reactions were once relatively common in both civilian and military life, but today they constitute only 5 percent of all neuroses treated. Interestingly enough, their decreasing incidence seems to be closely related to our growing sophistication about medical and psychological disorders: an hysterical disorder apparently loses its defensive function if it can be readily shown to lack an organic basis. The educational factor may help explain why the incidence of conversion reactions is highest among individuals with low socioeconomic status.

Clinical picture. In an age that no longer believes in such phenomena as being "struck" blind or suddenly afflicted with an unusual and dramatic paralysis with no obvious organic basis, conversion patterns increasingly involve more exotic physical diseases that are harder to diagnose as functional—such as mononucleosis or convulsive seizures. Here it may be emphasized that conversion reactions are great imitators, and the range of symptoms is practically as diverse as it is for real physical ailments.

In describing the clinical picture in conversion hysteria, it is useful to think in terms of three categories of symptoms: sensory, motor, and visceral.

1. *Sensory symptoms.* Any of the senses may be involved in sensory conversion reactions. The most common forms of these reactions are:

Anesthesia—loss of sensitivity
Hypesthesia—partial loss of sensitivity
Hyperesthesia—excessive sensitivity
Analgesia—loss of sensitivity to pain
Paresthesia—exceptional sensations, such as tingling

Some idea of the range of sensory symptoms that may occur in conversion reactions can be gleaned from Ironside and Batchelor's (1945) study of hysterical visual symptoms among airmen in World War II. They found blurred vision, photophobia, double vision, night blindness, a combination of intermittent visual failure and amnesia, deficient stereopsis (the tendency to look past an object during attempts to fixate it), restriction in the visual field, intermittent loss of vision in one eye, color blindness, jumbling of print during attempts to read, and failing day vision. They also found that the symptoms of each airman were closely related to his performance duties. Night fliers, for example, were more subject to night blindness, while day fliers more often developed failing day vision. Results of a more recent study of student aviators who developed conversion reactions in the military are reported in the illustration on page 237.

A wide range of disorders may also be manifested in other sensory modalities; but anesthesias that formerly were common—such as loss of vision or hearing—have become increasingly rare. However, Parry-Jones and his colleagues (1970) have described a case of hysterical blindness, and the illustration on page 238 presents an interesting case of hysterical deafness.

2. *Motor symptoms.* Hysterical motor disorders also cover a wide range of symptoms, but only the most common need be mentioned here.

Hysterical paralyses are usually confined to a single limb, such as an arm or a leg; and the loss of function is usually selective. For example, in "writer's cramp" the person cannot write but may be able to use the same muscles in shuffling a deck of cards or playing the piano. Tremors (muscular shaking or trembling) and tics (localized muscular twitches) are common. Occasionally there are contractures that usually involve the flexion of fingers and toes, or there is rigidity of the larger joints, such as the elbows and knees. Paralyses and contractures frequently lead to walking disturbances. A person with a rigid knee joint may be forced to throw his leg out in a sort of arc as he walks. Another walking disturbance worthy of mention is *astasia-abasia,* in which the individual can usually control his leg movements when sitting or lying down, but can hardly stand and has a very grotesque, disorganized walk, with his legs wobbling about in every direction.

The most common hysterical disturbances of speech are *aphonia,* in which the individual is able to talk only in a whisper, and *mutism,* in which he cannot speak at all. Interestingly enough, a person who can talk only in a whisper can usually cough in a normal manner. In true laryngeal paralysis both the cough and the voice are affected. Aphonia is relatively common in hysterical conversion reactions and usually occurs after some emotional shock, whereas mutism is relatively rare. Occasionally, conversion symptoms may involve convulsions, similar to those in epilepsy. However, the hysteric shows few of the usual characteristics of true epilepsy—he rarely, if ever, injures himself, his pupillary reflex to light remains unaffected, and he is not incontinent.

3. *Visceral symptoms.* Hysterical visceral symptoms also cover a wide range of disorders, including headache, "lump in the throat" and choking sensations, coughing spells, difficulty in breathing, cold and clammy extremities, belching, nausea, vomiting, and so on. Occasionally there is persistent hiccoughing or sneezing.

Conversion reactions can simulate actual disease symptoms to an almost unbelievable degree.

CONVERSION REACTIONS IN STUDENT NAVAL AVIATORS

Mucha and Reinhardt (1970) have reported on a study of 56 student aviators with conversion reactions who were assessed at the U.S. Naval Aerospace Medical Institute in Pensacola, Florida. In the group, representing 16 percent of a total population of 343 patients at the Institute, four types of conversion symptoms were found. These were, in order of frequency: visual symptoms, auditory symptoms, paralysis or paresthesias of extremities, and paresthesia of the tongue. The chart at lower right indicates the rates of incidence.

Generally, the 56 students came from middle-class, achievement-oriented families. The fathers of 80 percent of them were either high-school or college graduates, and were either professional men or white-collar workers. Interestingly enough, 89 percent of the students with conversion reactions had won letters in one or more sports in high school or college; all were college graduates and presently were flight students, officer candidates, or officers.

Commenting on the relatively high incidence of conversion reactions among the patients at the Institute, Mucha and Reinhardt emphasized three conditions which they considered of etiological significance:

1. **Unacceptability of quitting.** In the students' previous athletic training, physical illness had been an acceptable means of avoiding difficult situations, whereas quitting was not. Moreover, the present training environment tended to perpetuate this adaptation, since the military is also achievement-oriented, and does not tolerate quitting as a means of coping with stress situations.

2. **Parental models.** Seventy percent of the parents of these students had had significant illnesses affecting the organ system utilized in the students' conversion reactions; and a majority of the students had had multiple physical symptoms —often as a result of athletic injuries—prior to enlistment.

3. **Sensitization to the use of somatic complaints.** As a result of their previous experience, the students were sensitized to the use of somatic complaints as a face-saving means of coping with stressful situations.

"When faced with the real stress of the flight training program and with frequent life-or-death incidents, they resorted to this unconscious mechanism to relieve the stress and to avoid admitting failure. To admit failure would be totally unacceptable to the rigid demands of their superegos." (p. 494)

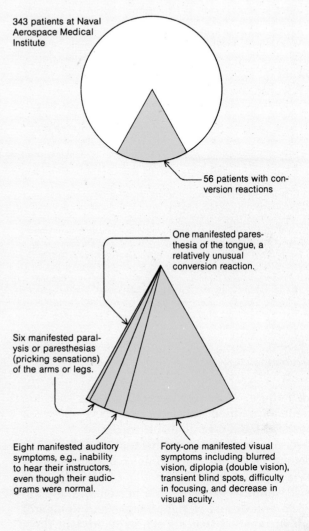

343 patients at Naval Aerospace Medical Institute

56 patients with conversion reactions

One manifested paresthesia of the tongue, a relatively unusual conversion reaction.

Six manifested paralysis or paresthesias (pricking sensations) of the arms or legs.

Eight manifested auditory symptoms, e.g., inability to hear their instructors, even though their audiograms were normal.

Forty-one manifested visual symptoms including blurred vision, diplopia (double vision), transient blind spots, difficulty in focusing, and decrease in visual acuity.

In a pseudo-attack of acute appendicitis, not only may the person evidence pain in the lower abdominal region and other typical symptoms of acute appendicitis, but his temperature may also shoot up far above normal. Cases of psychogenic malaria and tuberculosis have also been cited in the literature. In the latter, for example, the individual may show all the usual symptoms —coughing, loss of weight, recurrent fever, and night sweats—without actual organic disease. Even cases of pseudo-pregnancy have been cited, in which the menstrual cycle ceases, there is an enlargement of the abdominal area, and the individual experiences morning sickness.

Since the symptoms in conversion hysteria are capable of simulating almost every known disease, differential diagnosis can be a problem. However, in addition to specialized medical

THE STORY OF ANNE: A CASE OF HYSTERICAL DEAFNESS

Anne, a young woman of 19, became hysterically deaf, apparently as a result of family tensions. Her relations with her mother had been particularly strained, and the deafness was thought to be a type of avoidant behavior for screening out her mother's nagging voice. Anne showed no overt startle responses to sudden loud noises; however, she revealed covert responses to sound in the first of two trials to measure muscle contractions via an electromyogram (EMG). The first EMG trial revealed muscle contractions in Anne's neck when a loud sound was made, but the second trial 60 seconds later revealed no contractions. Some strong inhibitory neural changes must have come into operation in the brief time between the two trials, because complete inhibition of muscle contractions—covert ones, at least—is seemingly beyond the voluntary control of anyone suddenly exposed to loud noise.

Since Anne could read lips, the therapist combined conditioning with suggestion—telling Anne that she would soon be able to hear. The conditioning involved the removal of a negative reinforcer, which was an electric shock that closely followed the sounding of a tone for 150 trials. The first time the shock was withheld, the EMG picked up a burst of covert muscle contractions. These promising early results of treatment were given an unexpected boost when a near-accident caused Anne's hearing to be suddenly restored. Crossing a busy street, she was narrowly missed by a driver who honked his horn and shouted at her. The hearing that she instantly regained has subsequently remained intact. (Adapted from Malmo, 1970)

techniques, there are several criteria that are commonly used for distinguishing between hysterical and organic disturbances:

a) A certain *belle indifference,* in which the patient makes his complaints in a rather matter-of-fact way, with little of the anxiety and fear that would be expected in a person with a paralyzed arm or loss of sight. Mucha and Reinhardt (1970) reported that all of the 56 student fliers in their study (page 237) evidenced this pattern, seeming to be completely unconcerned about the long-range effects of their disabilities.

b) The frequent failure of the dysfunction to clearly conform to the symptoms of the particular disease or disorder. For example, there is no wasting away or atrophy of the paralyzed limb in hysterical paralyses, except in rare and long-standing cases.

c) The selective nature of the dysfunction. For example, in hysterical blindness the individual does not usually bump into people or objects, and the paralyzed muscles can be used for some activities and not others. Hysterical contractures also usually disappear during sleep.

d) The interesting fact that under hypnosis or narcosis the symptoms can usually be removed, shifted, or reinduced by the suggestion of the therapist. Similarly, if the individual is suddenly awakened from a sound sleep he may be tricked into talking or using a "paralyzed" limb.

Of course, where conversion symptoms are superimposed on an actual organic disorder, the difficulty in making a diagnosis may be increased. However, it is usually fairly easy to distinguish between conversion hysteria and *malingering.* The malingerer is consciously perpetrating a fraud, and this fact is reflected in his demeanor. The hysteric is usually dramatic and apparently naïve, whereas the malingerer is inclined to be defensive, evasive, and suspicious. When inconsistencies in his behavior are pointed out, the hysteric is usually unperturbed, whereas the malingerer immediately becomes even more defensive. Finally, the hysteric is concerned mainly with his symptoms and willingly discusses them, whereas the malingerer is apt to be reluctant to be examined and slow to talk about his symptoms, lest his pretense be discovered. Thus conversion hysteria and malingering are considered distinct patterns, although sometimes they overlap.

The phenomenon of *mass hysteria,* as typified by outbreaks of St. Vitus' dance and biting manias during the Middle Ages (see page 31), has become a rarity in modern times. However, a recent outbreak of mass hysteria that resulted in the temporary shutting down of a textile mill has been reported by Kerckhoff and Back (1969). The mass hysteria involved a "mysterious illness"—with symptoms of nausea and a rash over the body—presumably caused by an insect in a shipment of cloth that arrived from England. The report quoted one victim:

"'Some of those women were deathly sick. They were passing out, and they were taking them out of here like flies. I don't know what happened to me.' State and Federal health officials were called into the case; but the victims were reported to be suffering from 'nothing more than extreme anxiety.'" (p. 46)

Suggestibility clearly plays a major role in the development of mass hysteria, in which a conversion reaction in one individual rapidly spreads to others.

Dynamics. In the development of conversion patterns there is usually the following chain of events: (1) a desire to escape from some unpleasant situation; (2) a fleeting wish to be sick in order to avoid the situation (this wish, however, is suppressed as unfeasible or unworthy); and (3) under additional or continued stress, the appearance of the symptoms of some physical ailment. The individual sees no relation between his symptoms and the stress situation. The particular symptoms that occur are usually those of a previous illness or are copied from other sources—such as illness symptoms observed among relatives or on television or read about in magazines. However, they may also be superimposed on an existing organic ailment, be associated with anticipated secondary gains, or be symbolically related to the conflict situation.

Unfortunately, the neurophysiological processes involved in the simulation of various disease symptoms, such as malarial fever, are not well understood. However, there is increasing research evidence of the remarkable extent to which an individual can control his own bodily functions. For example, recent studies with animals and humans have shown that blood pressure, heart rate, kidney function, and even the distribution of blood flow can be altered by reinforcement procedures (Lacey, 1967; Lang et al., 1967; Lessing, 1970; Miller, 1969). Clearly, then, we need not be surprised by the extent to which awareness and bodily functions can be altered to meet the psychological needs of the individual.

1. *Personality and role factors.* What can be said about the personality of the individual who attempts to solve serious problems by getting sick? It should be remembered that most of us at some time or other have probably solved some problem or avoided something we did not want to do by pleading sickness. In fact, the common sayings "I don't feel like doing it" or "I don't feel up to it" show the prevalence of this type of reaction. The conversion hysteric, however, unconsciously commits himself to this pattern in the face of everyday life problems that most persons can deal with more effectively.

The individual who adopts such a "sick role" is typically one who experiences serious difficulties in meeting the problems of living and playing his social role. In a study of female hysterics, Jordan and Kempler (1970) have pointed specifi-

cally to anxieties over adequacy and sex-role competency as significant factors in the behavior of these individuals. Feeling inadequate to cope directly and independently with the problems of life, the hysteric seeks help and sympathy. In relation to other neurotic types, the conversion hysteric tends to be highly suggestible and dramatic—a "histrionic personality": excitable but shallow in emotional responsiveness, particularly capable of ignoring, denying, and repressing what he does not want to perceive, and demanding and manipulative in interpersonal relationships (Halleck, 1967; O'Neill & Kempler, 1969; Steele, 1969). Female conversion hysterics have also been described as sexually seductive but often frigid in actual sexual relations.

The following excerpts from a therapy hour provide an excellent illustration of an hysterical personality.

"The patient, a 30-year-old married woman, sought therapy because of nervousness, depression, headache, and severe menstrual cramps. She entered the office with a despondent air which contrasted sharply with her colorful, almost flashy, dress. She wore a low-cut blouse and crossed her legs in a seductive manner as she sat down. The following interchange took place.

Pt: Well, you know what's bothering me. Why don't you talk today.

[The patient's attempt to control the interchange is immediately apparent.]

Th: Silent

Pt: I don't know why I come here. I have been coming to see you for six months now (actually four months) and I feel worse than ever. My head hurts so much (patient dramatically touches head) and I wonder more each day if life is worth living.

[This communication illustrates the patient's attention-seeking and histrionic behavior; there is also some obvious dishonesty.]

Th: Silent

Pt: I keep thinking that life isn't worth living. I'm worrying that I may kill myself.

Th: I have noticed that when I don't respond to you immediately you begin to complain more and feel sicker.

Pt: (Suddenly angry) You get me so mad. I come here for help and all you can do is interpret. You and your worship of Freud. I know all about the years you spent studying but I'm not impressed. Somebody like me is miserable and finds every minute of life pure hell and you attribute all kinds of unconscious motives to my suffering. You don't know how much courage it takes for me to just go on from hour to hour.

[The communication again illustrates the patient's controlling and attention-seeking behavior.]

Th: Somehow I can't feel your misery as that powerful or real. Can't we go beyond it and look at what's so unsatisfying in your life?

Pt: (Angrily exploding) I only wish you could feel what I'm feeling. (She reaches for an ash tray on the desk and postures as if she is going to throw it on the floor; then she changes her mind and shouts.) Damn you, nobody cares, nobody, nobody, nobody. (Sobs for several minutes while the therapist is silent, then slowly and dramatically) I guess you win, there's no beating you at your own game while I am so sick and helpless. I need you too much. (Suddenly she perks up and smiles coquettishly) Well, what do you want me to talk about today.

[Here she is again controlling, playing as if helplessly dependent, and demonstrating a reluctance to assume responsibility.]

Th: (Somewhat irritated) You know we've been over that before.

Pt: (Teasingly) Sure, I'm supposed to talk about my conflicts, bare my soul, search out my hidden oedipal wishes and my frustrations. (Suddenly more dramatic) But I know those things and so do you. You know how my mother treated me so cruelly, and how she paid more attention to my brothers, how my father ignored me, and what a bastard my husband is. You know what the problem is and what the answer is, I'll always be miserable and trapped with that no good impotent husband of mine. Why didn't I marry John? I had my choice and I goofed it. If only my parents had helped me I wouldn't have made such a miserable choice. Now I am trapped, trapped, trapped.

[In this communication the patient almost assumes responsibility for her choice, but then backslides and blames it on her parents.]

Th: Sounds like you and your husband have been fighting again.

Pt: (More seriously and sober) We had an awful fight after a party this weekend. Phil thought I was paying too much attention to one of our guests and . . . (Patient goes on to give a fairly nondramatic account of her flirtatiousness and ensuing verbal and physical battle with her husband.)"

(Halleck, 1967, pp. 751–752)

In describing the "sick role" enactment of the conversion hysteric, it is useful to note that: (a) the role is useful only in a culture that provides sympathy and support for sick persons and enables them to avoid normal responsibilities; (b) the role is enacted or modeled on the basis of information the individual has concerning the physical ailment he is simulating; (c) the role tends to be self-perpetuating, since it is reinforced by anxiety reduction and other gains—in essence, it works. Here it may be emphasized again that the conversion hysteric is not consciously aware of playing a sick role, for if he were, the psychological benefit to him would be lost. This need not be considered a mysterious phenomenon, since the literature on learning includes many instances in which behavior is altered by reinforcement without the person's awareness of the relationship between his changed behavior and the reinforcing conditions (Bandura, 1969).

2. *Avoidance of or defense against threat.* Typically a conversion pattern enables the individual to avoid or defend himself against a threatening stress situation. The avoidance pattern seems clear in the case of a youth who fainted on his way to the altar on two separate occasions, each time planning to wed the same girl. In another instance, a divorcee lost her sense of smell when she noticed a sweet and pungent odor that she suspected to be "pot" in the room of her adolescent son—on whom she was strongly dependent for affection and meaning in her life. In an early report, Halpern (1944) cited 15 cases of hysterical amblyopia—markedly diminished visual acuity—in the armed forces, which developed at a port of embarkation and cleared up when the soldiers were removed from the conflict situation by hospitalization. These reactions have sometimes been called "gangplank fever."

The following case of astasia-abasia—a rare conversion pattern involving difficulty in walking (see page 236)—has been described by Hammer (1967). The case involves an athletically inclined youth who did well in preparatory school and was admitted to the United States Military Academy at West Point.

Early in cadet training, when new cadets are under considerable pressure, he suffered a shoulder separation while playing football. Surgery was performed, he responded well, and after a thorough physical examination was returned to duty. Back on duty, however, his activities were significantly changed. Losing the privileges accorded a member of the football squad, he became just another "plebe." This change in his status was considered significant, for within two weeks he returned to the hospital with acute vertigo and temporary loss of consciousness. A physical examination at the time he reentered the hospital showed nothing significant.

Shortly after hospitalization, the student developed a markedly ataxic gait and had difficulty standing erect; however, when he was in a sitting or reclining position his coordination and tonus remained normal. With the continuation of hospitalization, the cadet's symptoms gradually intensified. On rare occasions when he showed some improvement, a return to duty was suggested. This was promptly followed by a recurrence in intensity of symptoms.

Psychological and psychiatric evaluation revealed ambivalent feelings about his remaining at West Point, and a concomitant increase in overt dependency needs. The psychologist's conclusions follow:

"This cadet shows an emotionally unstable, impulse-ridden, hysteroid, neurotic character makeup, manifested by difficulty in accepting authority, low tolerance for frustration of his egocentric compensatory need to prove his manliness, and inadequacy in interpersonal relations generally. He appears to be acting out conversion symptoms which are persistent largely because of secondary gains in defying authority and avoiding having to come to grips with his problem in adjusting to the normal demands of the United States Military Academy."

Following 60 days of hospitalization the cadet was separated from the Corps of Cadets. He returned home and accepted work as a bank clerk. A 6-month follow-up study revealed that his symptoms cleared up within a week after he returned home, that he had no further educational plans, and that he had remained symptom-free during the intervening period. (Adapted from Hammer, 1967, pp. 672–673)

Conversion reactions may also represent defenses against dangerous desires and impulses. Abse (1959) has cited the case of a middle-aged male patient who suffered total paralysis of his legs after his wife left him for another man. During the course of treatment it became apparent that he had a strong wish to pursue his wife and kill her and her lover. Although the wish had been repressed it was quite intense, and the paralysis apparently represented a massive defense against the possibility that this vengeful wish might be carried out.

Sometimes, conversion reactions seem to stem from feelings of guilt and the necessity for self-punishment. In one case, for example, a female patient developed a marked tremor and partial paralysis of the right arm and hand after she had physically attacked her father. During this incident she had clutched at and torn open his shirt with her right hand, and apparently the subsequent paralysis represented a sort of symbolic punishment of the "guilty party," and prevented the recurrence of her hostile and forbidden behavior.

3. *Secondary gains stemming from actual illness or injury.* In some instances conversion symptoms develop following physical illness or an accident in which the individual may or may not have been injured. If pneumonia temporarily enables a patient to avoid highly unpleasant occupational responsibilities—as well as receive the sympathy and attention of others—he may unconsciously prolong his invalidism. An injury may lead to the same pattern.

Not uncommonly, conversion symptoms develop following some accident or injury as a result of which the individual hopes to receive monetary compensation. These reactions usually occur after accidents in which the individual might have been seriously injured but is actually only shaken up or slightly injured. Later, in discussions with family or friends, it may be agreed that he would have had a strong legal case if he had been injured. Is he sure he is all right? Could he possibly have injured his back? After a few careful exploratory movements he may actually notice that he does seem to be a little "stiff." Perhaps there *is* something wrong with his back. With the aid of a sympathetic lawyer, he may proceed to file suit for compensation for his alleged injuries.

Here it is especially hard to distinguish between the malingerer's deliberate simulation of injury and the unconscious deception of a hysteric. Apparently in many hysterical cases there is an admixture of the two, in which conscious acting is superimposed on unconscious acting or role playing. In these cases the patient shows an amazingly rapid recovery once he has been properly compensated for his "injuries." In this general context, Liebson (1969) reported an interesting case in which a machinist's helper experienced pain and weakness in both legs.

About five years after the initial occurrence of his symptoms, this man had to stop work and was put on welfare payments. Although no organic pathology could be found, he finally required hospitalization.

A variety of treatments were tried, including a substantial number of drugs, all without success. At this time, behavior therapy—focusing on the reinforcement contingencies of his symptoms—was begun. Although the causal factors were not clear, it was felt that the symptoms might have been induced and maintained because of their reinforcing consequences—that is, the avoidance of a job he disliked and the receipt of welfare payments. The treatment program was worked out in collaboration with the patient, and focused on the target behaviors of walking and doing a day's work. A job was found for him and to add to his $235 monthly welfare payments, he could earn $3.00 per day working, with a bonus of $1.00 for getting there on time and a second bonus of $1.00 if his work was approved by his instructor.

The patient progressed at his own rate, beginning with a two-day-per-week schedule, and despite occasional mild setbacks, was able to work a five-day week by the seventh month. Four months later he accepted a full-time job similar to his old one, and no longer required welfare aid. A follow-up study six months later showed that the man was still on the job, although he occasionally experienced symptoms similar to his initial ones. (Adapted from Liebson, 1969, pp. 217–218)

Conversion hysteria may also be complicated by other maladaptive patterns. For example, in a study of a group of women labeled as hysterics, Guze, Woodruff, and Clayton (1971) reported a high incidence of school delinquency, fighting, running away, repeated episodes of rage, and other antisocial behavior. These characteristics appeared much less frequently in the backgrounds of a control group of women labeled as anxiety neurotics. The subjects in the two groups were well matched in terms of age, education, race, and economic circumstances.

Whatever specific causative factors may be involved, however, the basic dynamic pattern in conversion hysteria seems to be the avoidance or reduction of anxiety-arousing stress by getting sick—thus converting an intolerable emotional problem into a face-saving physical one. The initial learning of the reaction and its maintenance are reinforced, both by anxiety reduction and by the interpersonal gains—in terms of sympathy and support—that result from being sick. These various points are well illustrated in a classic case described by Coon and Raymond (1940):

"Since a child, this young woman cherished vague and beautiful ideas of her own charm, refinement and artistic ability. Her ambitions were stimulated and fostered by an admiring family circle, a protected life, and a group of friends whose admittance to friendship, consciously or unconsciously, depended on their uncritical admiration. The more or less deliberate purpose of her striving was to insure and magnify the admiration and uncritical affection of her friends through the talented use of a great voice.

"Now the day approaches when her voice is to be tested, not by the admiring circle, but by a critical professional teacher who is to determine the course of her vaguely planned career. This day has approached before, but she has always had a severe headache or a bad throat or some other rather sudden but not infectious ailment which has prevented her meeting the test. . . .

"Finally, an act of will, or perhaps an access of ambition . . . and she actually goes to the test. She passes the earlier and simpler parts of the audition with fair credit, though with some trepidation. Then comes a more crucial, a more important, and far more difficult step in the trial, involving an uncompromising test of real quality of voice and real ability of technique. Something happens. Her voice cracks at the very beginning of this important step, her throat hurts, she has suddenly become hoarse. It is impossible to carry the test further. She explains quite honestly to the teacher that she has a very delicate throat and that she did not realize it was in such shocking condition; furthermore, she ought not to have attempted the test. She goes home to much genuine and deserved sympathy. She becomes voiceless for several days or weeks.

". . . and she rationalizes the episode as follows: The test, because she took it when her throat was in poor condition, has strained her voice. Of course, the teacher should have known better. Ever after she refers to it sadly as the time when her voice was strained by an injudicious and premature test to which she was led by her inexorable courage and ambition. Furthermore, she says now, that because of this accident she is unable ever to sing well, the inference being that she did sing well before, which is probably not the fact, as her voice, though apparently quite normal, is of very small calibre and mediocre quality. However, the automatism of escape has 'saved her face.' It has saved the pretty picture of her great artistic ability, and has transferred the vision of her powerful and charming performance from the future to the past, and furthermore, it has given her a perfectly satisfactory explanation and justification in perpetuity for the manifest discrepancy between the greatness of her talent and the hopeless mediocrity of her best possible performance." (pp. 224–225)

As we have seen, treatment of conversion hysteria may focus on removing the reinforcing conditions that appear to have influenced the development and maintenance of the symptoms.

Another general approach to treatment includes the same principle of not allowing the symptoms to "work" for the patient, but in addition, includes attempts to change his personality and general life style. The method is illustrated by Halleck's (1967) summary of his treatment approach with female hysterics:

"The patient should be told at the beginning that the purpose of therapy is to understand herself, and that permanent symptom relief will come only if she is able to change her style of living. Her insistence that she will change when she feels better should be countered by the suggestion that she will not feel better until she changes. No dishonesty should be allowed to pass unnoticed. The therapist must protest every exaggeration, every histrionic outburst, and every attempt at sexual seductiveness. He must almost religiously exhort the patient to take responsibility for all her thoughts and actions, and must attack every defensive effort to relate her plight to external circumstances." (p. 756)

The latter approach is, of course, considerably more ambitious than simply focusing on symptom removal and helping the patient become "functional" again.

Conversion symptoms can often be removed by means of hypnosis, drug interviews, placebos (inactive substances administered as "medicine"), and "miracle cures." This raises the question of whether eliminating specific symptoms is a better treatment strategy than focusing on changing the hysteric's life style. For example, Guze (1967) and other investigators have noted the persistence of the patient's life style, and have pointed to the probability that the same or related illness symptoms will reappear unless the life style itself changes. In cases where conversion symptoms occur only in unusual stress situations, however, symptomatic treatment may be effective in helping the person avoid a chronic pattern of dealing with his problems by sickness. This is particularly true where the stress situation can be alleviated to some extent.

HYSTERICAL NEUROSIS: DISSOCIATIVE TYPE

Like conversion hysteria, the dissociative type of hysteria is a way of avoiding stress while gratifying needs—in a manner permitting the person to deny personal responsibility for his unacceptable behavior. Dissociative patterns include amnesia, fugue states, and multiple personality.[1] These patterns are relatively rare, constituting less than 5 percent of all neuroses.

Amnesia and fugue. Amnesia is partial or total inability to recall or identify past experience. It may occur in neuroses, psychoses, or brain pathology—including delirium, brain injury, and diseases of the nervous system. Where the amnesia is caused by brain pathology, it generally involves an actual failure of retention. That is, the information is either not registered and does not enter memory storage, or it is not retained in storage—it is truly lost.

Psychogenic amnesia, on the other hand, is usually limited to a failure to recall. The "forgotten" material is still there beneath the level of consciousness, as becomes apparent under hypnosis, narcosis interviews, and in cases where the amnesia spontaneously clears up. As we have noted, amnesia is fairly common in reactions to intolerably traumatic experiences, such as those occurring under combat conditions of warfare and the "shock" conditions of civilian life. In hysterical amnesia, however, the reaction occurs in the face of life stresses with which most people deal more effectively.

1. Clinical picture. In the typical neurotic amnesic reaction, the individual cannot remember his name, does not know how old he is or where he resides, and does not recognize parents, relatives, or friends; yet his basic habit patterns—such as his ability to read, talk, and so on—remain intact, and he seems quite normal aside from the amnesia.

In this amnesic state the individual may retreat still farther from his problems by going away in what is called a "fugue state." A fugue reaction, as its name implies, is a defense by actual flight. The individual wanders away from home, and then days, weeks, or sometimes even years later suddenly finds himself in a strange place, not knowing how he got there and with complete amnesia for the period of the fugue. His activities during the fugue may vary from merely going on a round of motion pictures to

---

[1]Somnambulism, or sleepwalking, could be included here, but we shall deal with this dissociative pattern in our discussion of the behavior disorders of childhood (Chapter 17).

traveling across the country, entering a new occupation, and starting a new way of life.

2. *Dynamics.* The pattern in psychogenic amnesia is essentially the same as in conversion reactions, except that instead of avoiding some unpleasant situation by getting sick the person does it by avoiding thoughts about it. This avoidance of areas of thought may represent a pattern of avoidance learning without awareness, or it may involve more conscious suppression. In patterns involving suppression, the individual apparently tells himself that he will not remember some traumatic event or situation; and subsequently he tries to believe and behave as though he were amnesic during the time the event occurred. For example, in a study of 98 amnesia cases, primarily among military personnel, Kiersch (1962) found 41 to be of this "feigned" type.

In actual psychogenic amnesia we typically find an egocentric, immature, highly suggestible personality faced with an acutely unpleasant situation from which he sees no escape. There is often a conscious impulse to "forget" and run away from it all; but this solution is too cowardly to be accepted. Eventually, however, the stress situation becomes so intolerable that large segments of the personality and the stress situation itself are repressed, while more congenial patterns carry on in an amnesic or fugue reaction. As O'Neill and Kempler (1969) have pointed out, this process of amnesia is highly selective and involves only material that is basically intolerable or threatening to the self.

During such dissociative reactions the individual appears normal and is able to engage in complex activities, which are often of a wish-fulfilling or compensatory nature. This is well illustrated in an interesting case described by Masserman (1961).

"Bernice L., a forty-two-year-old housewife, was brought to the Clinics by her family, who stated that the patient had disappeared from her home four years previously, and had recently been identified and returned from R———, a small town over a thousand miles away. On rejoining her parents, husband and children she had at first appeared highly perturbed, anxious, and indecisive. Soon, however, she had begun to insist that she really had never seen them before, that her name was not Bernice L— but Rose P— and that it was all a case of mistaken identity; further, she threatened that if she were not returned to her home in R——— immediately, she would sue the hospital for conspiracy and illegal detainment. Under treatment, however, the patient slowly formed an adequate working rapport with the psychiatrist, consented to various ancillary anamnestic procedures such as amytal interviews and hypnosis, and eventually dissipated her amnesias sufficiently to furnish the following history:

"The patient was raised by fanatically religious parents, who despite their evangelical church work and moralistic pretenses, accused each other of infidelity so frequently that the patient often questioned her own legitimacy. However, instead of divorcing each other, the parents had merely vented their mutual hostility upon the patient in a tyrannically prohibitive upbringing. In the troubled loneliness of her early years the patient became deeply attached to her older sister, and together they found some security and comfort; unfortunately, this sister died when the patient was seventeen and left her depressed and unconsolable for over a year. After this, at her parents' edict, the patient entered the University of A——— and studied assiduously to prepare herself for missionary work. However, during her second semester at the University, she was assigned to room with an attractive, warm-hearted and gifted girl, Rose P—, who gradually guided the patient to new interests, introduced her to various friendships, and encouraged her to develop her neglected talent as a pianist. The patient became as devoted to her companion as she had formerly been to her sister, and was for a time relatively happy. In her Junior year, however, Rose P— became engaged to a young dentist, and the couple would frequently take the patient with them on trips when a chaperone was necessary. Unfortunately, the patient, too, fell 'madly in love' with her friend's fiancé, and spent days of doubt and remorse over her incompatible loves and jealousies. The young man, however, paid little attention to his fiancée's shy, awkward and emotionally intense friend, married Rose P— and took her to live with him in Canada. The patient reacted with a severe depression, the cause of which she refused to explain to her family, but at their insistence, she returned to the University, took her degree, and entered a final preparatory school for foreign missionaries.

"On completion of her work she entered into a loveless marriage with a man designated by her parents and spent six unhappy years in missionary outposts in Burma and China. The couple, with their two children, then returned to the United States and settled in the parsonage of a small midwest town. Her life as a minister's wife, however, gradually became less and less bearable as her husband became increasingly preoccupied with the affairs of his church, and as the many prohibitions of the village (e.g., against movies, recreations, liberal opinions and even against secular music) began to stifle her with greater weight from year to year. During this time the patient became increasingly prone to quiet, hazy reminiscences about the only relatively happy period she had known—her first two years in college with her friend, Rose P— —and these years, in her day-dreaming gradually came to represent all possible contentment. Finally, when the patient was thirty-seven, the culmination of her disappointments came with the sickness and death of her younger and favorite child. The next day the patient disappeared from home without explanation or trace, and her whereabouts, despite frantic search, remained unknown to her family for the next four years.

"Under treatment in the Clinics, the patient recollected that, after a dimly remembered journey by a devious route, she finally reached A———, the college town of her youth. However, she had lost all conscious knowledge of her true identity and previous life, except that she thought her name was Rose P—. Under this name she had begun to earn a living playing and teaching the piano, and was so rapidly successful that within two years she was the assistant director of a conservatory of music. Intuitively, she chose friends who would not be curious about her past, which to her remained a mysterious blank, and thereby eventually established a new social identity which soon removed the need for introspections and ruminations. Thus the patient lived for four years as though she were another person until the almost inevitable happened. She was finally identified by a girlhood acquaintance who had known both her and the true Rose P— in their college years. The patient at first sincerely and vigorously denied this identification, resisted her removal to Chicago, where her husband was now assigned, and failed to recognize either him or her family until her treatment in the Clinics penetrated her amnesia. Fortunately, her husband proved unexpectedly understanding and cooperative, and the patient eventually readjusted to a fuller and more acceptable life under happily changed circumstances." (pp. 35–37)

In his analysis of this case, Masserman pointed out that the patient's behavior enabled her to flee from an intolerable mode of living as Mrs. Bernice L—, the unhappy wife, and to substitute an intensely desired way of living, personified by Rose P—, the loved and successful artist. Her "new personality" was in no sense completely novel, but represented an unconscious selection and integration of certain patterns of the old.

It is interesting to note that a person rarely engages in activities that would have been morally incompatible with his pre-fugue personality. Thus, in her identity as Rose P—, the patient neither married again nor engaged in any direct sexual activity, since "bigamy or unfaithfulness, conscious or not, would have been untenable."

Multiple personality. Dual and multiple personalities have received a great deal of attention and publicity in fiction, television, and motion pictures. Actually, however, they are rare in clinical practice. Only slightly more than a hundred cases can be found altogether in psychological and psychiatric records.

1. *Clinical picture.* Multiple personality is a dissociative reaction to stress in which the patient manifests two or more complete systems of personality. Each system has distinct, well-developed emotional and thought processes and represents a unique and relatively stable personality. The individual may change from one personality to another at periods varying from a few minutes to several years. The personalities are usually dramatically different; one may be gay, carefree, and fun-loving, and another quiet, studious, and serious.

Various types of relationships may exist between the different personalities. Usually the individual alternates from one personality to the other, and cannot remember in one what happened in the other. Occasionally, however, while one personality is dominant and functions consciously, the other continues to function subconsciously and is referred to as a *co-conscious* personality. In these cases the co-conscious personality is usually intimately aware of the thoughts of the conscious personality and of things going on in the world, but indicates its awareness through automatic writing (in which the individual writes a message without full awareness or conscious control) or in some other roundabout way. The conscious personality, however, usually knows nothing of the co-conscious personality.

Relationships may become highly complicated when there are more than two personalities, as in the case described on page 246. Some of the personalities may be mutually amnesic while others are only one-way amnesic.

2. *Dynamics.* In a sense, we are all multiple personalities, in that we have many conflicting and warring tendencies and frequently do things that surprise both ourselves and others. This is illustrated by many common sayings, such as "I don't know why I did it" or "I didn't think

THE FOUR FACES OF EVE

A dramatic example of multiple personality was the widely publicized case of Eve White, a 25-year-old woman who sought therapy because of "severe and blinding headaches" often followed by "blackouts." Eve had been having serious marital conflicts and was separated (and subsequently divorced) from her husband. For financial reasons, her 4-year-old daughter lived with grandparents some 100 miles away from where Eve worked. Concern about the happiness of her daughter and fear of becoming a stranger to her added to Eve's stresses.

In therapy, Eve gave the appearance of a demure, retiring, and gently conventional person trying somewhat stoically to cope with severe personal frustrations. Then one day, during an early therapy session she appeared to be seized by a sudden pain and put both hands to her head. "After a tense moment of silence, her hands dropped. There was a quick, reckless smile and, in a bright voice that sparkled, she said, 'Hi there, Doc!' . . . there was in the newcomer a childishly daredevil air, an erotically mischievous glance, a face marvelously free from the habitual signs of care, seriousness, and underlying distress, so long familiar in her predecessor. This new and apparently carefree girl spoke casually of Eve White and her problems, always using *she* or *her* in every reference, always respecting the strict bounds of a separate identity. When asked her own name she immediately replied, 'Oh, I'm Eve Black.'" (Thigpen & Cleckley, 1957, p. 137)

The traits of the two personalities, as they continued to present themselves in ensuing therapy hours, may be summarized as follows:

	EVE WHITE	**EVE BLACK**
Appearance	Face: quiet sweetness, sadness Movements: careful, dignified Voice: gently modulated Dress: neat, conservative, inconspicuous No allergy to nylon	Face: pixie-like, mischievous, seductive Movements: suggested light-heartedness Voice: coarse, mirthful, teasing Dress: a little provocative, expensive Skin reacted to nylon by breaking out
Personality	Industrious worker and good housekeeper, literary tastes, not spontaneous, not deceitful, devoted to child, passive strength of character, admired by others	Attractive, likable, heedless, unthinking, quick, vivid, a rowdy wit, ready for any adventure, enjoyed teasing Eve White
Role	Role involved unspoken pathos; one felt she was doomed to be overcome.	Seemed strangely secure from stresses of everyday life and from grief.

After about 8 months of therapy, a third personality, Jane, appeared. Jane was more mature and capable than the retiring Eve White and had a much more vivid personality. Unlike Eve Black, Jane had positive attitudes both toward herself and toward cultural values. She remained conscious when either of the two Eves was in control, but for a long time had no memory of her past.

At last, after recalling and working through a highly traumatic experience—in which she had been forced by her mother to kiss her dead grandmother—a somewhat new personality emerged who was like Jane but more complete. This personality appeared to represent a resolution of the separate entities of Eve White and Eve Black and decided to call herself Evelyn (Eve's full legal name). Evelyn remarried and at last report had managed to establish a stable marriage and family life (Lancaster & Poling, 1958; Thigpen & Cleckley, 1954, 1957).

---

he had it in him." It is also illustrated by the peculiar behavior many men indulge in at conventions when they are away from their families and associates and "cut loose." In pathological cases, there is evidently such a deep-seated conflict between contradictory impulses and beliefs that a resolution is achieved through separating the conflicting parts from each other and

elaborating each into a more-or-less autonomous personality system. In this way the individual is able to realize incompatible systems of behavior without the stress, conflict, and guilt that would otherwise occur. As Murphy (1947) has pointed out, "the main dynamics in most cases of double and multiple personality seems to be an exaggeration of a conflict situation which is present in nearly all of us, namely, a conflict between a conforming and a guilty non-conforming trend." (p. 443)

This dynamic pattern is well brought out in Lipton's comprehensive and excellent analysis of the case of Sara and Maud K., excerpts of which are given below.

". . . in general demeanor, Maud was quite different from Sara. She walked with a swinging, bouncing gait contrasted to Sara's sedate one. While Sara was depressed, Maud was ebullient and happy, even though suicidal. Suicide and death meant nothing to Maud, and she saw nothing wrong or depressing in them.

". . . in so far as she could Maud dressed differently from Sara. Sara had two pairs of slippers. One was a worn pair of plain gray mules; the other, gaudy, striped, high-heeled, open-toed sandals. Sara always wore the mules. Maud would throw them aside in disgust and don the sandals. Sara used no make-up. Maud used a lot of rouge and lipstick, painted her fingernails and toenails deep red, and put a red ribbon in her hair. She liked red and was quickly attracted by anything of that color. Sara's favorite color was blue.

"Sara was a mature, intelligent individual. Her mental age was 19.2 years, I.Q., 128. A pyschometric done on Maud showed a mental age of 6.6, I.Q., 43. Sara's vocabulary was larger than Maud's, and she took an intelligent interest in words new to her. When Maud heard a new word, she would laugh and mispronounce it, or say, 'That was a twenty-five cent one.' In sharp contrast to Sara, Maud's grammar was atrocious. A typical statement was, 'I didn't do nuttin'.' Sara's handwriting was more mature than Maud's.

"Sara did not smoke and was very awkward when she attempted it. Maud had a compulsion to smoke. At times she insisted she 'had to' and would become agitated and even violent if cigarettes were denied her. She would smoke chain fashion as many cigarettes as were permitted but two would satisfy her for a while. . . .

"Maud had no conscience, no sense of right and wrong. She saw no reason for not always doing as she pleased. She felt no guilt over her incestuous and promiscuous sexual relationships. Sara on the other hand had marked guilt feelings over her previous immoral sexual behavior.

"It seemed that Sara changed to Maud at the point when Sara's feeling of guilt was greatest." (1943, pp. 41–44)

Judging from the previous history of this patient, it would appear that the development of a dissociated personality in the form of Maud had, among other things, enabled Sara to gratify her sexual desires by engaging in promiscuous sexual relations without conscious knowledge and hence without guilt feelings. Apparently Sara reverted to Maud when her guilt feelings over her own previous promiscuous sexual behavior became too intense and self-devaluating.

Further light is cast on Sara's background by the report of two of her previous high-school friends that "she was 'boy crazy' and was always chasing after some boy, often being rude to her girl friends, that she dyed her hair red, and that she smoked and used Listerine to deceive her mother about smoking. Sara denied all this but Maud readily recalled it." (Lipton, 1943, p. 47) It is interesting to note that this patient later became psychotic, apparently as a result of the failure of the dissociative reaction to solve her inner conflicts satisfactorily.

Because multiple personalities can be induced experimentally, the question has been raised as to whether all cases are only artificial creations produced inadvertently by suggestions of the therapist. Although this seems unlikely, some of the cases reported in the literature probably do fall in this category.

Treatment for dissociative hysteria is essentially the same as for the conversion type. Usually the immediate amnesia can be readily cleared up by means of hypnosis or narcosis interviews; and, as we have noted, in some cases the individual's amnesia clears up spontaneously. The latter appears especially likely in fugue reactions in which the individual finds himself in an even worse situation than the one from which he was trying to escape. Where the conflict and subsequent dissociative reaction stem from a unique stress situation, and the situation changes or the stress can be alleviated, amelioration of symptoms via hypnosis or other treatment procedures is likely to be followed by a more adequate life adjustment. However, if the stress is due to inadequacies and conflicts in personality makeup and life style, a more comprehensive therapeutic approach is likely to be required.

HYPOCHONDRIACAL NEUROSIS

In hypochondriacal neurosis the individual is preoccupied with his state of health and with various presumed disorders or diseases of bodily organs. Although hypochondriacal symptoms occur in many neurotic patterns—as well as in other forms of psychopathology—hypochondriacal neurosis is relatively rare, occurring in about 5 percent of the neurotic population. This pattern appears to be particularly common during later adulthood, and is found more frequently among women than men (Kenyon, 1966).

Clinical picture. Hypochondriacs are characterized by their multiplicity of complaints about physical illness—complaints that are usually not restricted to any logical symptom pattern. Thus, they may complain of uncomfortable and peculiar sensations in the general area of the stomach, the chest, the head, the genitals, or anywhere else in the body.

Usually they have trouble giving a precise description of their symptoms. They may begin by mentioning pain in the stomach, which on further questioning is not a pain but a gnawing sensation, or perhaps a feeling of heat. Their general mental orientation keeps them constantly on the alert for new illness manifestations. They are often avid readers of popular magazines on medical subjects, and are apt to feel certain they are suffering from every new disease they read or hear about. Tuberculosis, cancer, tumors, and numerous other disease conditions are readily diagnosed by hypochondriacs. Their morbid preoccupation with bodily processes, coupled with their ignorance of medical pathology, often leads to some interesting diagnoses. One patient diagnosed his condition as "ptosis of the transvex colon," and added, "If I am just half as bad off as I think, I am a dead pigeon."

This attitude appears to be typical: Hypochondriacs are sure they are seriously ill and cannot recover. Yet—and this is revealing—despite their exaggerated concern over their health, they do not usually show the fear or anxiety that might be expected of those suffering from such horrible ills. The fact is that they are usually in good physical condition. But it does not follow that the hypochondriac is malingering; he is sincere in his conviction that his symptoms represent real illness. Indeed, in some cases a hypochondriacal reaction may be superimposed on actual organic pathology, which is then magnified out of all proportion and becomes the focal concern of the person's life.

A classic illustration of the shifting symptoms and complaints in a very severe hypochondriacal neurosis is presented in the following letter that a hospitalized patient wrote to her anxious relatives.

"Dear Mother and Husband:

"I have suffered terrible today with drawing in throat. My nerves are terrible. My head feels queer. But my stomach hasn't cramped quite so hard. I've been on the verge of a nervous chill all day, but I have been fighting it hard. It's night and bedtime, but, Oh, how I hate to go to bed. Nobody knows or realizes how badly I feel because I fight to stay up and outdoors if possible.

"I haven't had my cot up for two days, they don't want me to use it.

"These long afternoons and nights are awful. There are plenty of patients well enough to visit with but I'm in too much pain.

"The nurses ignore any complaining. They just laugh or scold.

"Eating has been awful hard. They expect me to eat like a harvest hand. Every bite of solid food is agony to get down, for my throat aches so and feels so closed up. . . .

"With supper so early, and evening so long, I am so nervous I can't sleep until so late. I haven't slept well since I've been here. My heart pains as much as when I was at home. More so at night. I put hot water bottle on it. I don't know if I should or not. I've been wanting to ask some Dr.

"I had headache so badly in the back of my head last night and put hot water bottle there. My nurse said not to.

"They don't give much medicine here. Mostly Christian Science it seems! Well I must close or I never will get to sleep. My nurse gets off at 8:15 so she makes me go to bed by then.

"My eyes are bothering me more.

"Come up as soon as you can. My nose runs terrible every time I eat.

"The trains and ducks and water pipes are noisy at night.

ANNIE"

(Menninger, 1945, pp. 139–140)

Hypochondriacs often show a morbid preoccupation with digestive and excretory functions. Some keep charts of their bowel movements, and most are able to give detailed information concerning diet, constipation, and related matters. Many of them also keep up with "the latest" in medical treatment, by reading newspapers or popular magazines, and are prone to the indiscriminate use of a wide range of medications. However, they do not show the losses or distortions of sensory, motor, and visceral functioning of conversion hysterics; nor do their complaints have the bizarre delusional quality—such as "insides rotting away" or "their lungs drying up"—more typical of somatic complaints by psychotics.

Dynamics. Most of us are interested in our bodily functioning and state of health. In fact, health ranks at the top of the list of subjects that are of general interest. The hypochondriac, however, shows a morbid exaggeration of this common interest and concern—an exaggeration that enables him to avoid certain difficult life stresses and achieve various interpersonal gains.

1. *Parental models and other predisposing factors.* A variety of early experiences may predispose an individual to the later development of hypochondriacal reactions. Among the most important of these are exposure to faulty parental models and being the object of parental overconcern. The child may learn to be oversensitive to and concerned with his bodily processes from the model presented by a parent who is inclined to be hypochondriacal. Similarly, when the parent is continually commenting on and worrying about the child's every sneeze, cough, digestive upset, or other possible illness manifestation, the child, in turn, may learn to attach undue significance to such manifestations in himself. A third important predisposing factor is actual early illness or injury—which focuses the attention of parents and the child himself on his condition and may lead to a highly gratifying position in the family, in terms of attention and care. Particularly is this pattern likely to occur when the illness or injury is accompanied by parental overconcern which, as we have said, sensitizes the child to his own condition.

2. *A disappointing life situation as a precipitating factor.* A predisposed individual is especially likely to experience hypochondriacal reactions during his forties or fifties, for he is forced to the realization that his life is more than half over and that his life pattern is fairly well determined—for better or worse. When his evaluation of his life situation is unfavorable—that is, when he feels he has failed to achieve his hopes and dreams, and perhaps finds his occupational and marital situation far from satisfactory—the stage is set for a hypochondriasis or other psychopathology.

3. *Reinforcement and maintenance of the hypochondriacal pattern.* As in the case of conversion hysteria, the hypochondriacal pattern enables the individual to avoid the demands and stresses of an unpleasant life situation while at the same time gaining sympathy and support from significant others, plus some measure of control over their behavior. We obviously cannot hold a "sick" person responsible for the same level of achievement we expect of well persons. Thus the hypochondriac's feelings of adequacy and worth are protected in his own eyes as well as the eyes of others; he need no longer strive toward difficult or unattainable achievements or accept other unpleasant responsibilities. In a general way, the anxiety aroused by his stressful life situation—often including the failure to achieve important goals—is displaced to a concern and preoccupation with his body and its functioning.

In addition, the increased attention that the hypochondriacal individual devotes to himself and receives from others may endow him and his body with increased significance. Most of us feel fairly important when we have the undivided attention of physicians and the sympathetic interest of our family and friends. And by maneuvering his symptoms with a measure of finesse, the hypochondriac can often control the behavior of those around him. For example, when some activity is planned in which he does not wish to participate, an unexpected intensification of his pain or other symptoms may force others to give up their plans and accede to his wishes. In one case a mother very effectively kept either her husband or son at home and attentive to her every need by her physical complaints, often including statements that she could feel a heart attack coming on. Usually she was not believed, but when she was left alone the family members paid a high price on their return. The recitation of what she had "gone through" in their absence, accompanied by the theme of "Look what you did to me," exacted its toll—and prevented her being ignored very long or often.

In cases where the hypochondriacal pattern is superimposed on actual organic pathology—as in the case of a chronic disease or lasting injury—the dynamics are essentially the same as described above. The hypochondriac utilizes actual physical disability as a defense against feelings of failure and as an escape from future striving. And where he evaluates his injury or illness as so severe that it puts him "out of the running," his evaluation automatically prevents him from developing the healthy attitudes and coping patterns that could overcome or alleviate the consequences of his handicap. Not only does he evade his problems; he also gains compensatory satisfactions—in sympathy and other interpersonal gains.

Whatever short-range gains an individual may obtain with hypochondriacal patterns, he will find that they tend to exacerbate rather than resolve his problems. Like other avoidant neurotic behaviors, they are self-defeating in the long run; however, they are usually very resistant to treatment, since a hypochondriac must believe in his symptoms if he is to avoid the difficult stresses in his life situation. Such patients, therefore, are apt to discontinue therapy when told there is nothing organically wrong with them, but as long as a therapist is willing to listen to their long list of complaints, they are usually willing to continue in "treatment." It can be hoped that behavior-modification techniques and other new therapeutic approaches will eventually provide effective means for helping such individuals.

NEURASTHENIC NEUROSIS

The neurasthenic pattern is characterized by chronic mental and physical fatigue and by various aches and pains. There is disagreement on estimates of incidence, but usually the figure is put at approximately 10 percent of all neuroses. In milder form, neurasthenic neuroses seem to be relatively common among young adults, particularly frustrated housewives.

Clinical picture. The neurasthenic's principal complaint is tiredness. Mental concentration is difficult and fatiguing; the person is easily distracted; and he accomplishes little. He lacks the vigor required to carry activities through to successful completion. Even minor tasks seem to require herculean effort. He usually spends a good deal of time sleeping in an attempt to counteract his fatigue, yet regardless of the amount of sleep he gets, he awakens unrefreshed.

Typically, he sleeps poorly and feels "just rotten" when he drags himself out of bed in the morning. On the rare occasions when he does feel refreshed, he is completely upset by minor emotional setbacks, such as some criticism of his behavior, and his fatigue and listlessness return. Even when things seem to be going relatively well, the fatigue tends to get worse as the day wears on, although by evening he may feel somewhat better and may go to a movie or a party without experiencing anything like his usual exhaustion. In fact, one of the most significant things about the neurasthenic's fatigue is its selective nature. He often shows relatively good energy and endurance in playing tennis, golf, or bridge or in doing anything else that really interests him. In the face of family, occupational, and other routine activities, however, he is usually a monument of listlessness, lack of enthusiasm, and general tiredness.

The incidence of neurasthenic reactions seems highest among married women whose husbands have become neglectful and who feel that they are trapped in the role of "housewife," cheated of the satisfactions that other people seem to enjoy. Those who develop such reactions typically have a childhood history of delicate health and parental overprotection. As adults, they have become almost totally dependent on (if also highly resentful of) their husbands. Now their life situation seems hopeless to them, and they react with discouragement, listlessness, and preoccupation with various somatic complaints. The following excerpts are taken from an interview with a middle-aged married woman who felt, and with good reason, that her husband was no longer interested in her.

The woman's husband often failed to come home for several days at a time, and when he was home, he showed little evidence of interest or affection. Although the patient had completed high school, she had no occupational skills and felt completely dependent upon her husband for support and protection. She was self-pitying in her attitude, prone to relating her symptoms almost endlessly, and very demanding in her attitude toward the therapist.

Pt.: I used to talk rather fluently, but now I'm more nervous than I've ever been and my tongue seems to catch on my teeth so that I don't speak plainly. Everything seems such an effort . . . like I had an anchor tied to me or something. I no longer care to play cards or even talk to people any more. . . . Even the simplest things are too much for me.

Dr.: Even the simplest things . . .

Pt.: Ah, hm, I mean, the phone is there and I'm lonesome and yet I don't even phone. . . . I don't even talk to my neighbors much any more even though I know that I should be with people and I like people, but I've gotten so that . . . (long pause) . . . that . . . (sigh) . . . I feel too bad to even talk or do anything (voice breaks and tears).

I've tried so many things to get well, but it's just awful . . . I mean . . . sometimes I can just barely live . . . I mean just listen to the radio or read, or eat . . . I mean just like being in a daze or something . . . I don't know . . . I just feel so horribly tired and sick.

Two months ago I felt better than I had been. I mean I was able . . . well I went to several shows and I actually even went to a dance. Often I would begin to get tired, and I was very frightened that I would break down, but I would go on . . . I mean like some people would go to a battle or to a battlefront (proud tone of voice). But . . . now . . . well I am just so tired and run-down that I can't even go to a show . . . if I do go . . . I have to leave in the middle because I am not strong enough . . . I mean I don't have enough strength to sit through it.

Dr.: Two months ago you felt better?

Pt.: Well, yes . . . you see my husband's brother came to visit us . . . and he would talk to me and he had such a way of diverting me and he was very interesting, and you'd be amazed, within a few minutes or a few hours I'd be just different . . . and he took me to several shows and to the dance. I felt so much better and I had a really good time. So I can see it isn't sleeping or eating. I mean . . . I need someone who'd give me something different to think about . . . someone who'd show you some affection . . . enough interest in you so that you would improve. But my husband . . . well I just can't understand how he can treat a woman who is ill . . . and trying her best . . . well (tears) . . . I have just sort of withdrawn . . . he has really made me sick . . .

Dynamics. Historical attempts to explain the dynamics of neurasthenic reactions centered around the concept of "nerve weakness," which is the literal meaning of the older term *neurasthenia*. Beard (1905), an early American psychiatrist who first applied the term to the fatigue syndrome, attributed the condition to prolonged conflict and overwork, which presumably depleted the nerve cells of essential biochemical elements.[1] This conception later gave rise to the Weir Mitchell method of treatment for "nervous exhaustion," which involved a long period of complete rest and relaxation for the patient. Neurasthenic patients, however, rarely reveal a history of overwork, nor is the condition corrected by prolonged rest.

Today neurasthenia is looked on primarily as a psychological rather than a physical fatigue reaction. It is not overwork but prolonged frustration, discouragement, and hopelessness which reduce motivation and lead to the characteristic listlessness and fatigue (Cattell & Scheier, 1961; Guilford, 1959). In addition, there are likely to be sustained emotional conflicts centering around hostility toward one's mate and guilt over the abandonment of cherished goals.

We all feel tired and listless when we are discouraged and forced to do something that does not interest us. Those of us who have worked at jobs that were boring and frustrating can readily understand how feelings of listlessness and tiredness can arise in such situations. In the neurasthenic these feelings are elaborated into a chronic fatigue reaction similar to the fatigue reaction commonly found in acute situational maladjustment. Of course, the chronic anxiety, disturbed sleep, and overreactivity of the neurasthenic may eventually lead to a very real depletion of bodily reserves. Although such somatic conditions may complicate the clinical picture and require treatment in their own right, they are results of the neurasthenic reaction—not the basic cause.

As in other neurotic reactions, neurasthenic symptoms may have important secondary gains. They tend to force others to show sympathy and concern, and may even be used aggressively to control the behavior of others. For example, a wife's obvious difficulties and complaints may prevent her husband from obtaining a contemplated divorce, may force additional attention and time from him, such as any sick person would merit, and may largely control the family's social life. Much of the psychological benefit derived from these patterns is due to the neurasthenic's sincerity—he uses his symptoms without awareness of their actual function.

The neurasthenic often gets credit for putting up a noble battle against heavy odds. In general,

---

[1] At one time certain cases of neurasthenia were thought to be the outcome of unsolved sexual problems. Masturbation, for example, was presumed to result in depletion of bodily energy and chronic fatigue. Where sexual practices do constitute a problem, they are now considered to be merely the focal point of a much more general maladjustment.

however, such individuals eventually wear out the patience of their family and friends. Their listlessness, morbid outlook, self-centered attitudes, and continual complaining are not conducive to the maintenance of happy social relationships. Poorly repressed hostility toward their mate or other loved ones—whom they hold accountable for their difficulties—may further damage their interpersonal relationships.

In understanding the etiology of neurasthenic patterns, it is important to note that feeling fatigued and unable to cope with the world are common in our high-pressure society, but the normal individual carries on and makes a fairly satisfactory adjustment. The neurasthenic, by contrast, is typically a person who lacks self-confidence, is overdependent on others, and feels completely inadequate in the face of a situation he perceives as frustrating and hopeless. His symptoms enable him to escape the necessity of dealing with his problems, for he is just too tired and sick. However, they exact a heavy toll in the restriction of his life activities, in blocked self-fulfillment, and in reduced satisfactions in living.

Neurasthenic reactions are frequently very resistant to treatment. Often it is difficult or impossible to ameliorate the neurasthenic's life situation; and it is difficult for him to accept the fact that his problems are psychological and not somatic. In fact, he may actually feel relieved if medical examination does reveal some organic pathology. For since he does not understand why he feels tired all the time, he is continually searching for bodily ailments that might account for his fatigue and indirectly relieve him of meeting his responsibilities.

Tranquilizing drugs have not proved effective in treatment of neurasthenics, although they may help alleviate some of the anxiety and misery. In general, treatment to date has centered around helping the neurasthenic gain some understanding of his problems and progress toward personal maturity—to help him develop enough self-confidence and courage to stop feeling sorry for himself and get back into the "battle of life."

DEPRESSIVE NEUROSIS

In neurotic depressive reactions the individual reacts to some distressing situation with more than the usual amount of sadness and dejection and often fails to return to normal after a reasonable period of time. Although such reactions may last for weeks or even months, they do eventually clear up. In some cases a mildly depressed mood remains after more severe symptoms have abated. Neurotic depressive reactions appear to constitute some 20 to 30 percent of psychoneurotic disorders.

Clinical picture. The general appearance of the individual is one of dejection, discouragement, and sadness. Typically there is a high level of anxiety and apprehensiveness, together with diminished activity, lowered self-confidence, constricted interests, and a general loss of initiative. The person usually complains of difficulty in concentrating, although his actual thought processes are not slowed up. Often he experiences difficulty in going to sleep, and during the night he may awaken and be unable to go back to sleep. In many cases he has somatic complaints and feelings of tension, restlessness, and vague hostility.

The following is typical of a conversation with a neurotic depressive and illustrates the characteristic feeling tone.

Pt: Well, you see, doctor, I just don't concentrate good, I mean, I can't play cards or even care to talk on the phone, I just feel so upset and miserable, it's just sorta as if I don't care any more about anything.
Dr.: You feel that your condition is primarily due to your divorce proceedings?
Pt.: Well, doctor, the thing that upset me so, we had accumulated a little bit through my efforts—bonds and money—and he (sigh) wanted one half of it. He said he was going to San Francisco and get a job and send me enough money for my support. So (sigh) I gave him a bond, and he went and turned around and went to an attorney and sued me for a divorce. Well, somehow, I had withstood all the humiliation of his drinking and not coming home at night and not knowing where he was, but *he* turned and divorced me and this is something that I just can't take. I mean, he has broken my health and broken everything, and I've been nothing but good to him. I just can't take it doctor. There are just certain things that people—I don't know—just can't accept. I just can't accept that he would turn on me that way.

The clinical picture in neurotic depression is often similar to that in neurasthenia. However, the neurotic depressive usually shows greater depression as well as lowered levels of activity and initiative. In very severe cases the person may be unable to work and may sit alone hopelessly staring into space, able to see only the dark side of life. In such cases he is likely to need hospitalization for adequate treatment and safeguard against possible suicide.

Dynamics. All of us have the blues at times and may become greatly depressed at the death of a loved one, a disappointment in love, an accident, some occupational setback, or feelings of guilt concerning failure or unethical desires or behavior. Neurotic depressive reactions occur in a personality predisposed to overreact to such stresses and lacking in the resiliency most people show.

The neurotic depressive usually reveals low stress tolerance, together with rigid conscience development and a proneness to guilt feelings (Cattell & Scheier, 1961; Cattell et al., 1962). Typically the stress situation seems to center around the individual's "Achilles' heel"—that is, some stress situation that reactivates earlier conflicts or trauma, as the death of one's husband may reactivate insecurities associated with the death of one's father many years before.

Often in such cases the clinical picture is complicated by hostility toward the loved one. This hostility is typically repressed because of its dangerous and unethical implications, but it may manifest itself in hostile, guilt-arousing fantasies. Should that loved one die, the person's grief is augmented by his intense guilt, as if his hostile fantasies had somehow brought about the tragedy. Where the individual was indeed partially responsible for the loved one's death, as in an automobile accident in which he was driving, his feelings of guilt and self-condemnation may be extremely severe.

Like other types of neurotics, neurotic depressives sometimes use their symptoms to force support and sympathy from others. One woman telephoned her therapist and told him that she was going to commit suicide. Special precautions were taken, although the woman made no serious suicide attempt. In a later therapeutic session the therapist asked her why she had called him and threatened suicide. The woman explained that she thought the therapist was not taking her symptoms and hopeless situation seriously enough and was not showing proper sympathy

and appreciation for her desperate plight. By her threat of suicide she hoped to make him realize that he "just had to do something for her immediately."

Most persons suffering from neurotic depressions can describe the traumatic situation that led to their depression although they may not be able to explain their overreaction to the situation. Electroshock therapy may be used as an emergency measure in clearing up the depressive symptoms, although newer drug therapies have made this more drastic procedure largely unnecessary. Usually antidepressant drugs, supportive measures, and short-term psychotherapy are effective in alleviating the depression and helping the patient achieve better personal adjustment.

SUMMARY OF TYPES OF NEUROSES

NEUROSIS	MAJOR SYMPTOMS
Anxiety	"Free floating" anxiety, usually punctuated by acute attacks.
Phobic	Irrational fears which lead to anxiety if not heeded; may lead to a pervasive pattern of avoidance behavior.
Obsessive-compulsive	Repetitive thoughts and impulses which the individual realizes are irrational, but which persist nonetheless.
Hysterical (conversion type)	Simulation of actual organic illness, such as paralysis or loss of vision, without organic pathology.
Hysterical (dissociative type)	Dissociation of certain aspects of consciousness or identity from rest of identity; symptom pattern may take the form of amnesia, fugue, or multiple personality.
Hypochondriacal	Preoccupation with bodily processes and presumed disease.
Neurasthenic	Chronic fatigue, weakness, lack of enthusiasm.
Depressive	Abnormally prolonged dejection associated with life stress.
"Existential"	Feelings of meaninglessness, alienation, and apathy, with little sense of purpose or control over one's life. (See page 254.)

The basic dynamics in all of these neurotic reactions involve coping with perceived stress situations by means of avoidant behavior.

IS THERE AN EXISTENTIAL NEUROSIS?

As we have seen, existentialists are very much concerned about the situation of modern man; they point to the breakdown of traditional values, the depersonalization of man in a mass society, and the loss of meaning in human existence. The tasks of shaping one's own identity, finding satisfying values, and living a constructive and meaningful life are seemingly more difficult today than ever before.

Maddi (1967) has suggested the term "existential neurosis" to refer to the individual's inability to succeed in his quest. He has described it basically as follows:

The personal identity out of which this neurosis originates involves a definition of self as simply an embodiment of biological needs and a player of social roles. Such a self-identity is highly vulnerable to various stresses, such as rapid social change and new role expectations, interpersonal relations that victimize a poorly differentiated and confused individual, and acute awareness of the superficiality of one's existence. The resulting symptom pattern is characterized by chronic alienation, aimlessness, and meaninglessness. (Adapted from pp. 311–325)

Many students of psychopathology would not consider the syndrome described by Maddi to be a distinct pattern of neurosis. Most would readily agree, however, that a sense of purposelessness and alienation is severely disturbing to the individual and that it often plays a part in the development of neurotic behavior.

Young people today are becoming increasingly aware of the difficulties and challenges in finding and maintaining a stable self-identity and value pattern in a changing world. But the concept of an existential neurosis is by no means restricted to the young in our society; there are many middle-aged and older people who, in the process of "taking stock," are confronted with the sickening realization that their busy and seemingly important lives have really not proven fulfilling or meaningful.

Maddi (1967) has pointed out that an individual brought up in an environment where he was consistently appreciated as a person, his integrity was respected, and he was encouraged to establish a clear-cut sense of his identity and autonomy, has the least likelihood of developing an "existential neurosis." For he has the self-assurance needed to cope with changing pressures and expectations and, if necessary, to function somewhat independently of current social norms. In our complex and rapidly changing world, however, the task of finding and adhering to a satisfying pattern of values is an extremely challenging one at best.

GENERAL ETIOLOGY, TREATMENT, AND OUTCOMES

In our preceding discussion we have considered the general nature of neuroses, various specific neurotic patterns, and some approaches to treatment. Now let us take a more detailed look at general etiology, treatment strategies, and outcomes in the neuroses.

DEVELOPMENT AND MAINTENANCE OF NEUROSES

In the development and maintenance of neurotic behavior, as in other psychopathology, it is relevant to consider the role of biological, psychological, and sociocultural factors.

Biological factors. The precise role of genetic and constitutional factors in the neuroses has not been delineated. Ample evidence from army records and civilian studies indicates that the incidence of neurotic patterns is much higher in the family histories of neurotics than in the general population, but the extent to which such findings reflect the effect of heredity is not known.

Slater and Woodside (1951) compared one hundred neurotic soldiers and their wives with a control sample of one hundred normal soldiers and their wives. In both groups there was a high incidence of similarity between husbands and wives in height, intelligence, and education. In addition, the wives of the neurotic soldiers showed significantly more neurotic disorders than did the wives in the control sample. These investigators concluded that assortive mating might lead to a family environment that would perpetuate neurotic patterns from generation to generation. This conclusion, as we have seen, has been supported by other findings.

In a more recent study of concordance rates of neuroses in identical and fraternal twins, Pollin et al. (1969) found that among identical twins the rate was only 1½ times as high as it was among fraternal twins; and they concluded that heredity plays a minimal role in the etiology of neurosis. Since the environmental backgrounds of identical twins may be more similar than those of fraternal twins, this conclusion appears to be justified.

Sex, age, glandular functioning, and other physiological factors also have been investigated in relation to the neuroses, without illuminating the etiological picture. It is known that both biological and psychological stress tolerance levels are adversely affected by loss of sleep, poor appetite, fatigue, and irritability from prolonged emotional tension. Cattell and Scheier (1961) have contended that chronic emotional mobilization—a condition that characterizes some neurotic patterns—leads to *low adaptation energy* and *neurotic debility*. And strongly suggesting that high lactic acid concentration may be involved in overreaction to stress are the findings of Pitts and McClure (1967), who have shown that injections of sodium lactate will provoke anxiety attacks in anxiety neurotics but not in normal controls. But it is important to note that the preceding factors are, or may well be, results rather than causes of neuroses.

Several constitutional factors have also been studied for possible relationships to neurotic disorders. For example, in their intensive study of anxiety neurotics, Cattell and Scheier (1961) concluded that dispositional timidity acts to magnify anxiety in relation to both inner and outer threats. A great deal more research is needed, however, to clarify the role of constitutional differences and other biological factors in the development and maintenance of neuroses.

Psychological and interpersonal factors. It would appear that all of the psychological models

we considered in our general discussion of causation (pages 182–184) are applicable, at least to some degree, in the case of the neuroses: maladaptive learning, anxiety-defense, blocked personal growth, pathogenic interpersonal relationships, and stress-decompensation. As we shall see, these models are by no means mutually exclusive, but rather are interrelated ways of viewing neurotic disorders.

1. *Maladaptive learning.* Essentially, the faulty learning model emphasizes: (a) the failure of neurotics to learn needed competencies and coping behaviors, and/or (b) their learning of maladaptive ones. The neurotic nucleus, in other words, is heavily based on the individual's failure to achieve a level of personal maturity and adequacy needed for coping with problems of everyday living, together with the surplus of conditioned fears and anxieties that he may acquire. The combination, of course, is ideally suited to the production of feelings of inadequacy and to a defensive and avoidant life style.

This maladaptive and avoidant life style is anxiety-reducing, and hence is self-reinforcing. Here the faulty learning model is similar to the anxiety-defense model (see below). However, there is another important side to faulty learning—namely, the modification of behavior by the control of external conditions. In contrast to the anxiety-defense model, with its emphasis on internal variables, faulty learning involves the shaping and maintaining of behavior—whether adaptive or neurotic—by external reinforcers. For example, neurotic behavior may be learned and maintained simply because of what it yields in terms of interpersonal support and control. Accordingly, Skinner (1967) has suggested that more attention should be paid to the environmental contingencies of reinforcement, and less to such subjective variables as anxiety, guilt, and alienation.

2. *Anxiety-defense.* Traditionally, the neuroses have been discussed within the framework of the anxiety-defense model developed by Freud, in which threatening inner desires and impulses are seen to elicit anxiety and to lead to the use of various ego-defense mechanisms—such as denial, repression, and undoing. But because such mechanisms are reinforced by anxiety reduction once they come into operation, the anxiety-defense model can be interpreted within a much broader context—that of anxiety reduction, where learning principles, especially modeling and reinforcement, are used. For example, the individual may learn avoidant patterns—such as phobias, obsessive-compulsive reactions, and conversion reactions—directly from his parental models; and these patterns, in turn, may be reinforced by their anxiety-reducing properties. In the process the individual not only learns avoidant behaviors but also learns to evaluate everyday stress situations as threatening and anxiety-arousing. In short, he learns to perceive and act in neurotic and self-defeating ways. As we have already noted, the reinforcement emphasized in this model—via a relatively stable and autonomous neurotic life style—is in contrast to that of external reinforcement via manipulation and control of others' behavior, as propounded by Skinner (1967) in the faulty learning model.

3. *Blocked personal growth.* In Chapter 3 we noted the emphasis placed by the humanistic and existential models of man on values, meaning, self-growth, and fulfillment; and in Chapter 7 we saw how stressful a life situation can become when it is devoid of meaning and hope, as depicted by reports of former inmates of prisoner-of-war camps.

In the neuroses, blocked personal growth may stem from several interrelated sources: (a) a conflict between maintenance and growth motivation—where the individual is so preoccupied with trying to meet his basic needs for adequacy and worth that he spends his main resources on defense, rather than growth; (b) inability of the individual to find values he can believe in and can use as guides toward a meaningful, fulfilling life; (c) the pursuit of false values, a self-defeating endeavor that is inconsistent with the formulation of fulfilling life plans; (d) chronic alienation, aimlessness, and meaninglessness—apparent in the concept of "existential neurosis," which we have reviewed; and (e) faulty socialization, particularly with respect to ethical and conscience development. Instead of emphasizing—as Freud did—a rigid conscience development that conflicts with instinctual drives, Mowrer (1960; 1967) has emphasized an immature conscience development, one that is strong enough to leave the individual with unresolved guilt and pervasive self-rejection, but not strong enough to control his immature and egocentric behavior.

Of course, once the anxious and avoidant life style of the neurotic develops, it tends to be self-perpetuating and to effectively block further growth. The result, as we have seen, is the pervasive feeling of dissatisfaction and unhappiness that is characteristic of the neuroses.

4. *Pathogenic interpersonal patterns.* In a general sense, the inability to establish constructive and satisfying interpersonal patterns—particularly with significant others—underlies all neurotic patterns. In our discussion of neurasthenia, for example, we have seen how certain pathogenic marital interactions that lead to one partner's rejection and disillusionment may rob him of meaning and hope. In this regard, Berne (1964) has described a number of interpersonal patterns, or "games people play," in which one person is victimized by an unscrupulous partner. And Carson (1969) has referred to two kinds of pathogenic "contracts": (a) fraudulent interpersonal contracts, in which the rules—concerning honesty, mutual support, and so on—that normally govern satisfying interpersonal relationships are violated by one of the parties; and (b) disordered interpersonal contracts, such as a "negotiated maladjustment," in which a disturbed family pattern is maintained because all parties agree to support the maladaptive and self-defeating behavior of one of the members.

Here it may be reemphasized that in interpersonal relationships the identity of the participants in their respective roles, and the nature of the contract that has been entered into, tend to be maintained. Where roles and contracts follow normal and constructive patterns, mutual satisfaction and fulfillment usually follow. And conversely, in a fraudulent or disordered relationship, one or both parties may develop feelings of inadequacy or despair.

5. *Stress and decompensation.* The stress-decompensation model of psychopathology appears applicable to the neuroses in certain instances—particularly to situations involving seemingly unsolvable conflicts.

Combs and Snygg (1959) cited the case of a middle-aged schoolteacher who had not married because of overattachment to her mother, and now found herself in a romantic relationship with her married principal. Although she felt guilty and ran the risk of exposure and the loss of her job, she also felt she had to grasp what was probably her last chance at romance. To continue the relationship was threatening, but to discontinue it was equally intolerable. Her subsequent behavior—characterized by anxiety and tension, inability to concentrate, and emotional lability and depression—seems directly comparable to the "experimental neuroses" manifested by animals that had been placed in situations involving a severe approach-avoidance conflict. (See, for example, the illustration on pages 258–259.)

Shapiro (1962) has pointed to another kind of conflict that may underlie neurotic reactions—an intrapsychic conflict between various "subselves" in a poorly integrated individual. For example, an individual may try to be the self his mother expects him to be, the self his father expects him to be, the self other people expect him to be, the real self he thinks he is, and the ideal self he thinks he should be. Conflict among these subselves may make decisions both difficult and anxiety-arousing, and may lead to some degree of decompensation and neurotic manifestations.

As Bandura (1969) has pointed out, the model used in explaining a particular neurotic case may depend heavily on the orientation of the therapist. Psychoanalysts are likely to unearth anxiety-arousing desires and ego-defense mechanisms; behaviorists to point out directly learned maladaptive patterns and their maintenance through reinforcement; and humanistic psychologists to discover blocked personal growth and existential anxiety.

It still may be noted, however, that a particular model may be more useful in explaining one type of neurosis than another. For example, the maladaptive learning model appears well suited for an explanation of the direct learning and generalization of phobias, while the humanistic model appears more applicable to a neurasthenic neurosis. Of course, an adequate explanation in many instances may require a combination of models. In general, it appears that a neurosis represents a complicated system of defenses and avoidance behaviors by which an individual attempts to function in the face of life conditions that are highly stressful to him.

General sociocultural factors. Reliable data on the incidence of neurotic patterns in other societies is very meager, but it would appear that conversion hysteria is common among most primitive peoples, while anxiety, obsessive-compulsive, and existential neuroses are more common in technologically advanced societies. Carothers (1953; 1959) found few anxiety and obsessive-compulsive patterns among natives of Kenya, attributing this largely to an absence of mystery or feelings of shame about sex and to the fact that the native, as part of a rigidly structured tribal organization, does not have to set up his own standards and controls or bear economic trials alone, but draws on the strength and stability of the group. Thus he does not develop the anxiety and obsessive-compulsive patterns that appear to be associated with individual responsibility for one's actions. Among the aborigines of the Australian western desert, Kidson and Jones (1968) failed to find classical neurotic patterns, but noted that as these groups were increasingly exposed to contemporary civilization, somatic complaints and hypochondriacal concerns occurred. The most common type of neurotic disorder in the Soviet Union appears to be neurasthenic neurosis, although the reasons are not clear why this should be so.

In our own society, neurotic disorders are found among all segments of the population. There appear to be significant differences, however, in the incidence and types of neurotic patterns manifested by particular subgroups. In general, neurotic individuals from the lower educational and socioeconomic levels appear to show a higher than average incidence not only of conversion hysteria but also of aches, pains, and other somatic symptoms. Middle- and upper-class neurotics, on the other hand, seem especially prone to anxiety and obsessive-compulsive neuroses—with such subjective symptoms as "unhappiness" and a general feeling of dissatisfaction with life.

Although there has been little systematic research on the exact effects of sociocultural variables in the development of neuroses, it seems clear that the individual's family setting and overall social milieu help determine not only the likelihood of his becoming neurotic but also the patterns of neurosis he is most likely to develop. Thus, as life conditions continue to change in our own society and elsewhere, we can expect that there will be corresponding changes in both the incidence and the prevailing types of neurotic behavior.

THE EXPERIMENTAL INDUCTION OF NEUROSES

An unusual series of experiments on "neurotic" behavior in animals has been carried out by Dr. Jules Masserman. Although we do not know how far the findings of such studies can be applied on the human level, there clearly are many parallels between human reactions to conflict and those observed in Masserman's animal subjects. Masserman's studies were carried out with both cats and monkeys.

The first step in Dr. Masserman's procedure was to condition the animals to respond to a food signal—a light, a bell, or an odor—by pressing a treadle which was connected to a switch. A proper response opened the plastic lid of a food box in which the animal found the reward (A). When this behavior had been learned, conflict was introduced by associating a noxious stimulus with the feeding situation. Cats were subjected to a brief electric shock or had a strong puff of air directed at their heads when they tried to obtain the food. Monkeys were commonly exposed to a toy snake, which was presented in the food box or through the wall of the apparatus. These stimuli all produced strong avoidance reactions when initially presented. After a few experiences with the noxious stimulus the basic conflict was well established: the animal faced the choice of resisting his fear in order to satisfy his hunger or withdrawing and remaining hungry in order to avoid the fear.

Under these conditions many apparently neurotic reactions were observed. Cats displayed typical symptoms of anxiety: they crouched and trembled; their hair stood on end and their pupils dilated; their breathing was rapid, shallow, and irregular;

their pulses were rapid; their blood pressure was markedly increased. They showed severe startle reactions and phobic aversions to sudden lights or sounds, to constricted spaces or to restraint, and to any sensory stimulation in the modality associated with the traumatic experience. Some refused to take any food even when it was presented outside the food box on the floor of the cage. Animals that had willingly entered the cage and had resisted removal during the initial learning period became eager to escape after conflict had been established. Often they would crouch near the sliding glass door of the experimental cage, waiting to be removed (B, C).

Monkeys, in addition to anxiety and phobic reactions like those shown by the cats, displayed even more profound disturbances. Somatic and motor dysfunctions included diarrhea and gastrointestinal disorders resulting in rickets and severe neuromuscular weakness. In contrast to their previous behavior, some monkeys after experimental treatment spent long periods in stereotyped, repetitive activity, such as "pacing" back and forth in the experimental cage (D). Sometimes this behavior alternated with states of tense, apprehensive immobility (E). Some animals would stare fixedly for hours if left undisturbed (F). Often these monkeys would sleep or lie immobile in their home cages until mid-afternoon. Homosexual and autoerotic activity increased markedly, even in the presence of receptive females. One monkey attempted coitus only once in six months. "Neurotic" animals also lost their former positions of dominance in relation to other animals and were frequently attacked by other members of the colony.

A

B

TREATMENT PROCEDURES

Contemporary treatment of a neurotic disorder may involve drug therapy, psychotherapy, sociotherapy, or some combination of the three.

Drug therapy and related measures. Tranquilizing and antidepressant drugs are not uniformly effective in the treatment of all types of neuroses, but they have achieved striking results in reducing anxiety, clearing up depressive symptoms, and stabilizing emotional reactivity. Available statistics indicate that 70 percent or more of neurotic patients show a marked alleviation of symptoms following the use of such drugs, and most of them are able to function more effectively in their life situations (Kline, 1967; Lipman et al., 1969; Rickels et al., 1968; Wallerstein et al., 1967).

But these drugs can have undesirable effects—such as drowsiness—and in some cases the patient develops an increasing tolerance for and dependence on the drug. In addition, many persons expect too much of drug medication, and the masking of their symptoms may prevent them from seeking needed psychotherapy and/or sociotherapy.

Favorable results have been reported in the treatment of anxiety states, neurasthenia, and obsessive-compulsive neurosis by means of "Morita Therapy," in which the individual is subjected to absolute bed rest for a period of 5 to 7 days; no reading, writing, visitors, or other type of external stimulation is allowed (Kora, 1965). By the end of this period, most of those treated find positive reinforcement in responding to external stimuli—for example, in performing a graded series of tasks beginning with "light work" and gradually progressing to "complicated work."

Electrosleep—a relaxed state of sleep induced by means of the transcranial application of low intensity electric current—has shown promising preliminary results in the treatment of neurotic individuals manifesting chronic anxiety (Rosenthal & Wulfsohn, 1970). Further research is needed, however, before the effectiveness of this technique can be accurately assessed.

Psychotherapy. Both individual and group psychotherapy have been utilized in the treatment of neuroses. The various specific approaches may be divided into three general categories: cognitive therapies, behavior therapy, and innovative techniques such as encounter groups.

1. *Cognitive therapies.* Therapeutic approaches such as psychoanalysis, client-centered therapy, and existential therapy are classified as *cognitive* therapies, since they are oriented primarily toward helping the individual achieve greater knowledge and understanding of himself and his problems. The various types of therapy included in this general category differ somewhat in their specific goals and procedures—each reflecting the particular personality model on which it is based—but all stress the need for self-understanding, a realistic frame of reference, and a satisfying pattern of values, as well as the development of more effective techniques for coping with adjustive demands.

These objectives seem deceptively easy to achieve; actually there are a number of common stumbling blocks. First is the problem of creating a therapeutic situation in which the patient feels safe enough to lower his defenses and explore his innermost feelings, thoughts, and assumptions. Second is the problem of providing him with needed opportunities for learning new ways of perceiving himself and his world, new ways of responding, and new ways of relating to others. Involved here is a process of exploration and reeducation, in which he gradually comes to realize that his previous assumptions and values are neither as necessary nor as desirable as he had assumed—that there are other alternatives open to him that would yield greater satisfaction and fulfillment. Third is the problem of helping the individual transfer what he has learned from the therapy situation to real life. This involves dealing with conditions in his personal situation that tend to maintain his neurotic life style. For example, a domineering and aggressive wife may resent and complicate, or even block, therapeutic efforts with her neurotically inadequate and dependent husband.

Finally, it may be pointed out that psychotherapy is often a painful experience for the neurotic, who may lack the courage and persistence to face his problems realistically and change his defensive life style. Thus he may try to present himself in such a way as to put the whole responsibility for his well-being and happiness on the therapist. In essence, he says:

"There's my story, doctor (after taking plenty of time to tell it in detail). Now you pat me. . . and take my pains away . . . and give me inspiration and happiness and tell me how to be successful, and while you are about it, get my mother-in-law out of the house and I'll pay you when I get a job." (Weiss & English, 1943, p. 119)

Despite the difficulties involved, however, powerful forces are aligned on the side of psychotherapy. For one thing, the person who seeks help is usually experiencing considerable inner distress, so that he is motivated to change his behavior. And when helped to understand his problems, to discriminate more effective ways of coping with them, and to open paths for achieving personal growth and fulfillment, he usually will find the courage "to see it through." However, the outcome may vary considerably with regard to the degree of change that is brought about in his basic neurotic life style.

2. *Behavior therapy.* As we have seen, behavior therapy focuses on (a) the removal of specific maladaptive behaviors and symptoms, and/or (b) the development of needed competencies and adaptive behaviors. Although behavior modification does not emphasize self-understanding, changes in values, or personal growth, it often leads in that direction.

Many procedures may be utilized in behavior therapy. Perhaps the simplest and most commonly used is systematic desensitization. Here the person is placed—symbolically or actually—in situations that are increasingly closer to the situation he finds most threatening, and an attempt is made to associate the fear-producing stimuli or situations with emotional states that are antagonistic to anxiety. The prototype of this model was the classic experiment by Mary Cover Jones (1924) in treating three-year-old Peter's phobia of furry objects. She introduced a white rabbit in a cage at the end of the room when Peter was eating and brought the rabbit a little closer each day until Peter's phobia was extinguished.

In an early study utilizing systematic desensitization, Wolpe (1958) reported the apparent recovery of 188 out of 210 neurotic cases, in an average of 35 sessions. Although a wide range of neurotic reaction types were represented, the majority of these cases (135) were labeled as anxiety reactions. In more recent reports, the results of desensitization treatment have continued to be very positive (Paul, 1968; Rachman, 1967). In fact, after a review of 20 studies which utilized control groups for purposes of comparison, Paul concluded: "The findings were overwhelmingly positive, and for the first time in the history of psychological treatments, a specific therapeutic package reliably produced measurable benefits for clients across a broad range of distressing problems in which anxiety was of fundamental importance." (p. 159)

In our discussion of specific types of neuroses, we have seen how maladaptive behaviors—such as conversion hysterias—may be extinguished by removing reinforcements that maintain the behavior while simultaneously providing reinforcements that enhance the learning of more active, responsible, and effective coping patterns (Liebson, 1969). Other maladaptive behaviors, such as compulsions, can often be removed by aversive conditioning (Bandura, 1969; McGuire & Vallance, 1964). The illustration on page 262 describes the treatment of a phobic neurosis with a self-directed and self-reinforcing imagery technique. We shall have occasion to refer to these and other behavior-modification techniques in subsequent chapters.

Although behavior therapy is usually directed at changing specific "target behaviors," it often seems to have more far-reaching positive results (Bandura, 1969; Stampfl & Levis, 1967). The new responses the individual learns are not necessarily applicable to other problem areas in his life; but in learning to deal effectively with even one type of problem, he is also learning that coping with adjustive demands is ultimately more rewarding than trying to avoid them.

3. *Encounter groups and other innovative approaches.* During the past decade we have seen the emergence and "coming of age" of encounter groups and other innovative approaches to treatment of neuroses and other mental disorders (Blanchard, 1970; Rogers, 1969). We shall describe these approaches in some detail in Chapter 20; however, the illustration on page 264 describes the therapeutic effects of an encounter group experience on a group member who was labeled as neurotic.

Sociotherapy. Here the focus is on the modification of circumstances in the individual's life situation that tend to perpetuate his neurosis. Often there are pathogenic family interactions

TREATMENT OF A PATIENT WITH MULTIPLE PHOBIAS
BY A SELF-DIRECTING AND SELF-REINFORCING IMAGERY TECHNIQUE

Frankel (1970) has reported on the treatment of a 26-year-old married woman who suffered from disabling fears of sexual relations, earthquakes, and enclosed places. The background of the case, the treatment procedure, and the outcome are summarized below.

1. **The sexual fear.** The woman reported that she had been able to have sexual relations with her husband only about 10 times in their 3 years of marriage. Her sexual phobia appeared to have a learned basis. She had been molested by an older male at age 5, had been raped by a gang of juvenile delinquents when she was 15, had been "pawed" by intoxicated male visitors of her divorced mother, and had had sexual relations with 3 men prior to her marriage—each of whom had professed love for her but stopped seeing her after the sexual contact. In an effort to "hold her husband" she had had sexual relations with him a few times, but she always had "a cold feeling, like I'm going to suffocate—like I can't breathe" during sexual relations. In the third month of marriage, the couple conceived a son, after whose birth they had sexual relations only twice.

2. **The earthquake fear.** The woman stated that several times a day her thoughts were occupied by an uncontrollable fear of being in an earthquake. Her sequence of thoughts was always the same. First she would imagine that the ground was shaking and the house rocking, and that she rushed to pick up the baby. She would next imagine herself standing in a doorway, with the house collapsing around her. At this point the anxiety would become "unbearable." The recurrent thoughts about being in an earthquake were especially prominent when she tried to go to sleep, with the result that she was physically tired, irritable, and anxious during the day. Although a physician had prescribed tranquilizers, she reported that they did not help. On several occasions, she had arisen during the night, picked up her son, and rushed to a doorway. Interestingly enough, she had never been in an earthquake, nor did she personally know anyone who had.

3. **Fear of closed places.** The woman reported that she had always been fearful of elevators, small rooms, and even being surrounded by people. However, she did not recall ever being locked up in a small enclosure, and did not know anyone who had. She would climb many flights of stairs rather than take an elevator. Just prior to seeking therapy, she had been caught up in a large crowd greeting a visiting dignitary. She reported feeling anxiety, panic, and fear of suffocation. She screamed and pushed people out of the way until she was able to flee.

Since the woman's most disabling fear was that of earthquakes, it was decided to treat that fear first, then the fear of sexual relations, and finally the fear of enclosed places. The innovative treatment procedure was a variation of implosive therapy, in which the woman was instructed to proceed through sequences of thoughts and images of herself in the fear-producing situation.

"The implosive technique raises the client's anxiety level and maintains it until it passes a peak and begins to decline. This reduction in anxiety is seen as the beginning of extinction of the fear response, but it also may be seen as providing the occasion for reinforcement for the toleration of a high degree of anxiety. That is, the ability to proceed through an imagery sequence which elicits high anxiety is itself reinforced first by success in sustaining anxiety and then by mastery implied by its reduction." (p. 497)

Thus, whenever the woman became "too upset to go on"—a point at which she had previously put the imagery "out of her mind"—she was encouraged to continue with the description of her imagery and her feelings toward it. For example, in the earthquake sequence where she imagined that the house was collapsing around her as she stood in the doorway with her son, she was asked such questions as "What's happening now?" "What's happening next?"

"The content produced by the client involved the house collapsing on her, her son trapped under her as large beams fell on her, the earthquake finally ending, her being pinned under beams and being unable to move, screaming for help for several hours with no one coming to her aid, and finally being able to move a beam, stand up, walk away from the rubble, and breathe a sigh of relief at being alive and unharmed." (p. 498)

The imagery sequences lasted from 15 to 30 minutes, and the remainder of each 50-minute therapy session centered on the discussion of the vividness of the imagery sequences and the feelings they elicited. Since the woman could come in only once a week for therapy, she was instructed to proceed along the entire imagery sequence on her own whenever the fear of earthquakes entered her thoughts. She was instructed not to put the thoughts "out of her mind" under any circumstances. This treatment was continued until the fear of earthquakes no longer troubled her. A similar procedure was used in dealing with her sexual fear and her fear of enclosed places.

The entire treatment procedure lasted five months, but the fear of earthquakes was reduced from the highest to the lowest rating (on a 10-point scale) in four sessions. The woman reported that she thought less and less about earthquakes and had no difficulty sleeping. Even though a mild earthquake did occur about six weeks after treatment began, she stated that she was "not bothered in the slightest by its occurrence." Six months after the treatment ended, she showed no recurrence of the fear or evidence of symptom substitution. An interesting finding, however, was that the reduction in the fear of earthquakes did not generalize to her other fears, which maintained their original intensity.

With respect to the sexual phobia, treatment enabled the woman to resume sexual relations with her husband. At first she did not enjoy the sex act; six months after treatment ended she felt increasing pleasure and confidence but was still unable to have an orgasm; and at the end of a year she reported that she was able to gain a great deal of pleasure in sex and to have an orgasm about once in every three or four sexual experiences. Her overall relationship with her husband improved also.

The fear of enclosed places decreased from a fairly high rating to zero after seven sessions. During the fifth session of treatment, the woman remembered that she had accidentally been trapped in an airtight cabinet at about age 6, and would have suffocated if her mother had not found her in time. Memory of the event came after she successfully rode down three floors in an elevator. Thus it would appear that behavior change can be followed by "insight."

In reporting this case, Frankel related the comparatively brief period required for the reduction and elimination of the woman's fears to the fact that none of the fears reappeared after the conclusion of treatment, and to the lack of symptom substitution. He also emphasized the point that the treatment was largely self-administered, a marked advantage over more typical therapy approaches.

that keep the neurotic patient in a continually "sick situation." As the psychiatrist in T. S. Eliot's *The Cocktail Party* says:

"Indeed it is often the case that my patients
Are only pieces of a total situation
Which I have to explore. The single patient
Who is by himself is rather the exception."

Relevant here is a study by Kohl (1962) of 39 patients hospitalized for neuroses, as well as for other types of psychopathology. Kohl found that at the time of hospitalization the patients and their spouses denied that marital conflict was of etiologic significance. Interestingly enough, however, the marital partners often responded to the patients' improvement with resentment, threats of divorce, and, in some instances, personality decompensation. Kohl describes the following case.

A successful inventor was hospitalized for a severe neurotic depression. Although both marital partners described their marriage as "ideal," it became apparent that there was an unconscious struggle for dominance between them. Little progress was accomplished in therapy until this conflict was brought into the open and the patient became able to express his feelings of resentment freely. Then, as the patient improved, the wife, in turn, became depressed and for the first time defiantly participated in an extramarital affair. At this point she also revealed long-standing resentment toward her husband, whom she considered overly dependent. Treatment of both marital partners was then undertaken and stabilization of the marriage was eventually achieved.

In broad perspective, all of the treatment approaches we have discussed are concerned with the alleviation of culture-induced stresses that foster the production of neuroses and other psychopathology.

OUTCOMES

The general outlook for recovery from neurotic disorders is good. Many neurotics show improvement with time—estimates range from about 50 percent to over 70 percent—even when they presumably receive no psychotherapy (Eysenck, 1967; Malan et al., 1968). Statistics on spontaneous improvement are difficult to interpret,

however, for as Bergin (1966) has indicated, disturbed persons who allegedly improve without treatment may actually

" . . . seek and obtain help from various professional and nonprofessional sources such as friends, clergymen, physicians, teachers, and even psychotherapists. All this has typically been unknown to the researchers who were depending upon these so-called controls to be a baseline for comparison with their treatment cases." (p. 122)

In a study of 20 cases of spontaneous improvement Stevenson (1961) found that the following processes facilitated recovery: (1) desensitization to past painful experiences through recall, verbalization, and assimilation, or through association of such experiences with new, pleasurable experiences; (2) increased respect, reassurance, and affection from other significant persons; (3) entrance into the individual's life of new behavioral models from whom he could learn more effective behavior; (4) new situations requiring different responses—for example, the death of an overly protective and possessive mother, that forces the person to adopt new attitudes and assume responsibilities; and (5) shifts in motivation stemming from fear, shame, or desperation.

For those who do receive professional assistance, treatment results are difficult to assess. Differences in the severity of neurotic patterns, in treatment goals and methods, and in the meaning of such terms as *recovered* or *markedly improved* must all be considered in evaluating available studies. In addition, there is a need for differentiating between short-term and long-term results. In a major follow-up study of 605 neurotic outpatients, Cremerius found that 78 percent showed symptom abolition or improvement at the end of treatment, but that ten years later three fourths of them had suffered relapses (cited in Eysenck, 1969). Treatment procedures are continually being improved, however, and it would appear that the great majority of neurotics can benefit substantially from appropriate kinds of help. The use of periodic "booster" treatments can probably improve the long-range results.

In general, persons manifesting anxiety, phobic, and depressive patterns respond more readily to treatment than do those evidencing neurasthen-

ENCOUNTER GROUP THERAPY OF A NEUROTIC DISORDER

Mary, who was 27, had recently separated from her 29-year-old husband, Bill. Since Mary had tried to be the perfect wife, it came as quite a shock to her when Bill, after one year of marriage, told her he was no longer in love with her. Feeling responsible for the difficulties in her marriage, and anxious about her ability to establish meaningful marital or other interpersonal relationships, Mary joined an encounter group which met one evening a week for 2½ hours. The group was cofacilitated by two nonprofessional leaders who were being trained by and working under the local Growth Center, the group's sponsor. The male facilitator was a 27-year-old high-school teacher and the female facilitator was a 35-year-old housewife with three children. The group consisted of 4 male and 5 female participants ranging in age from 19 to 40.

At first during the meetings, Mary remained relatively quiet and listened politely as others spoke. She made only positive comments when she did speak—avoiding saying anything negative to anyone.

During the fourth meeting, one of the members—Sid, aged 38—confronted Mary about her uniform politeness and seeming superficiality, an exchange in which the facilitator also took part:

Sid: Mary, I would like to get to know you better, but your polite sweet manner puts me off. Frankly, your sweetness makes me a little angry with you.

Fcltr.: In your anger, Sid, what do you need to say to Mary?

Sid: (in a loud and moderately angry voice) Damn it, Mary, come out from behind that phony sweet façade of yours! Stop putting me off!

Mary: (with a polite smile and pleasant tone) Gee, I'm sorry, I really don't want to put you off.

Fcltr.: Mary, become aware of your smile and tone of voice.

Mary: (again smiling) I guess I was smiling (followed by a childish chuckle).

Sid: Mary, you're impossible! (said in a tone implying that he did not think Mary capable of being aware of her pattern of behavior).

Mary: (in a more somber tone) I really don't understand, Sid, why you are angry at me. I'm trying to . . . (long pause followed by an embarrassed look).

Fcltr.: Would you be willing to look at Sid and express your embarrassment to him?

Mary: Yes (then looking at Sid). I stopped my sentence because I was going to say . . . "I'm trying to be polite so that you'll like me."

Sid: Mary, that's the trouble. I don't like your politeness—it seems phony to me. I'd feel closer to you if I knew what you *really* were thinking and feeling.

Mary: You know it's true that I don't really feel all the nice things I say—but to imagine not being polite and sweet . . . just really scares me.

Fcltr.: What is your fear?

Mary: I'm afraid nobody will like me.

Sid: I'm liking you right now.

Mary: You know when you said you like me, it made me feel anxious and confused. (She looks to facilitator.) I'm at a loss to figure out what's going on with me. Why do I feel confused?

Fcltr.: Mary, right now the "why" of your confusion is secondary to the fact that you *are* feeling confused *right now*. Try to get the feel of your confusion. In other words, become aware of your sensations and let them emerge on their own.

Mary: (mildly distressed) I feel overcome by a growing sense of emptiness which I feel in my stomach.

Fcltr.: Let your emptiness have its say. You're at the point at which you don't get support from others and you can't quite get it from yourself.

Mary: (mildly fearful) I feel awful. I feel like nothingness—I feel so empty.

Fcltr.: (noting Mary's eyes becoming moist) What do your tears have to say to us, Mary?

Mary: (breaking into deep sobs) I feel unloved and unappreciated for what I am; I so much need everyone's approval. I really don't like myself. (Mary continues crying for several minutes, then adds as she looks down at the floor) Now I feel silly; everyone must think I'm a jerk!

Fcltr.: Mary, you will get yourself into trouble by imagining what people are thinking. Right now, look at each person in the group and tell us what you see.

(As Mary looks around the group, she sees the members looking at her sympathetically; several have been moved to tears by her outpouring of feeling.)

Mary: (responding to the warmth and support she sees around her) I feel so happy, so free right now. I want to express my warm feelings to all of you. (She goes around the group making contact by touching, holding, or talking to each member.)

As the group sessions continued, Mary became able to drop her "polite good-girl" role, to begin to understand and trust herself, and to improve her competence and authenticity in relating to others.

Case material supplied by Bryant Crouse, Psychology Clinic, The University of California at Los Angeles, 1971.

ic, hypochondriacal, obsessive-compulsive, and hysteria patterns. Although symptoms of conversion and dissociative types of hysteria can be cleared up readily, the modification of the patient's neurotic-avoidant life style is often a difficult therapeutic task.

Several additional points are relevant in our discussion of the neuroses. Fear of committing suicide is a common psychoneurotic symptom, but the actual incidence of suicides among neurotics appears relatively low. Nor does the life span of the neurotic appear adversely affected by his chronic tension and somatic disturbances. In an early study, Denker (1939) found that the life expectancy of a group of insured neurotics was greater than average. However, his statistics involve a special group (those carrying insurance) and do not necessarily apply to all neurotics. More recent statistics on this point are not presently available.

How does neurosis affect productiveness and occupational adjustment? Many authors have proclaimed neurotics to be "pleasantly different" and more likely than the "normal" person to be innovative and productive. In general, however, the evidence indicates that the neurotic's reliance on defensive strategies reduces his potential for positive accomplishment as well as his enjoyment of life.

Will neurotic patterns decompensate further into psychoses? This question is a controversial one. Many psychologists and psychiatrists maintain that the two types of disorders are fundamentally different and that neurotics rarely become psychotic—the estimated incidence being less than 5 percent (Goodwin et al., 1969; Parkin, 1966). However, many psychotics reveal neurotic patterns prior to the onset of their psychoses, as well as during the course of recovery; and neurotics often evidence mild delusions that belong in the realm of psychotic symptomatology. Thus some investigators prefer to think in terms of a continuum from normal patterns through neuroses to psychoses, with each successive phase marked by increasing personality decompensation.

We began this chapter by considering the characteristics that seem common to all the different patterns of neurosis. The neurotic nucleus comprises: (1) anxiety, resulting from basic feelings of inadequacy and the evaluation of everyday problems as threatening; (2) a tendency to avoid stress through various defensive maneuvers rather than to cope with it directly; (3) rigidity and lack of self-understanding; (4) egocentricity and difficulties in interpersonal relations; and (5) feelings of guilt and unhappiness. Why does the neurotic individual cling to such self-defeating patterns of behavior? This is the neurotic paradox, which can be explained in terms of: (1) the immediate relief from anxiety which results from avoidance and defensive maneuvers; and (2) the immediate avoidance of fear-arousing situations, which prevents the neurotic from testing the situation to see if his fear is realistic.

From our consideration of the basic nature of the neuroses, we proceeded to discuss clinical pictures and etiological factors in anxiety neurosis, phobic neurosis, and other specific neurotic patterns. We also examined the concept of "existential neurosis," a maladaptive pattern characterized by chronic feelings of alienation and aimlessness—seemingly in many ways a byproduct of our contemporary society.

To round out our discussion, we surveyed some general factors in the etiology of the neuroses, noting that maladaptive learning, anxiety-defense, blocked personal growth, pathogenic interpersonal relationships, and stress-decompensation may be involved in varying degrees and combinations. Finally, we considered various biological and psychosocial treatment procedures and noted the generally favorable results they have achieved.

Schizophrenia and Paranoia

9

SCHIZOPHRENIA

PARANOIA

As we go from the neuroses to schizophrenia and other psychotic disorders, we encounter a new realm of symptoms that typically includes delusions, hallucinations, and various kinds of bizarre behavioral manifestations. Here we are dealing with individuals who not only are unable to cope effectively with their problems but whose contact with reality has become severely impaired. Unable to relate to other people or to meet the ordinary demands of their life situations, they require special help and supervision and often have to be hospitalized. In general, then, the psychoses are much more serious and disabling than the neuroses (see chart, page 269). It may be emphasized, however, that there is not always a sharp dividing line between them. Sometimes a neurotic disorder blends almost imperceptibly into a psychosis as personality disorganization or decompensation becomes more severe.

The disorders classified as *functional psychoses* are generally considered to be primarily psychological in origin, although genetic and other biological factors seem frequently to play a very significant part in their etiology. These disorders can be divided into three major categories: (1) schizophrenia, (2) paranoid disorders, consisting of paranoia and paranoid states, and (3) affective (emotional) disorders, including manic-depressive reactions and involutional melancholia. Psychotic patterns may also be associated with senile brain deterioration and other known brain pathology. We shall deal with schizophrenia and paranoid disorders in the present chapter, with the affective disorders in Chapter 10, and with organic brain syndromes in Chapter 15. Our discussion of schizophrenia will be particularly detailed since it is the most pervasive of the functional psychoses and has long served as the "proving ground" in efforts to understand their etiology.

SCHIZOPHRENIA

Schizophrenia is the descriptive term for a group of psychotic disorders characterized by gross distortions of reality; the disorganization and fragmentation of perception, thought, and emotion; and withdrawal from social interaction. The disorganization of experience that typifies acute schizophrenic episodes is well illustrated in the following description:

"Suspicious and frightened, the victim fears he can trust neither his own senses, nor the motives of other people . . . his skin prickles, his head seems to hum, and 'voices' annoy him. Unpleasant odors choke him, his food may have no taste. Bright and colorful visions ranging from brilliant butterflies to dismembered bodies pass before his eyes. Ice clinking in a nearby pitcher seems to be a diabolic device bent on his destruction.

"When someone talks to him, he hears only disconnected words. These words may touch off an old memory or a strange dream. His attention wanders from his inner thoughts to the grotesque way the speaker's mouth moves, or the loud scrape his chair makes against the floor. He cannot understand what the person is trying to tell him, nor why.

"When he tries to speak, his own words sound foreign to him. Broken phrases tumble out over and over again, and somewhat fail to express how frightened and worried he is." (Yolles, 1967, p. 42)

The group of disorders we now label *schizophrenia* were at one time attributed to a type of "mental deterioration" beginning in childhood. In 1860 the Belgian psychiatrist Morel described the case of a 13-year-old boy who had formerly been the most brilliant pupil in his school, but who, over a period of time, lost interest in his studies, became increasingly withdrawn, seclusive, and taciturn, and appeared to have forgotten everything that he had learned. He talked frequently of killing his father, and evidenced a kind of inactivity that bordered on stupidity. Morel thought that the boy's intellectual, moral, and physical functions had deteriorated as a result of hereditary causes and hence were irrecoverable. He used the term *démence précoce* (mental deterioration at an early age) to describe the condition.

The Latin form of this term—*dementia praecox* —was subsequently adopted by the German psychiatrist Kraepelin to refer to a group of rather dissimilar conditions that all seemed to have the feature of mental deterioration beginning early in life. Actually, however, the term was rather misleading, since schizophrenia usually becomes apparent not during childhood but during adulthood, and there is no conclusive evidence of permanent mental deterioration.

It remained for a Swiss psychiatrist, Bleuler, to introduce in 1911 a more acceptable descriptive term for this disorder. He used *schizophrenia* (splitting of the personality) because he thought the disorder was characterized primarily by disorganization of thought processes, a lack of coherence between thought and emotion, and an inward orientation away from reality.

Schizophrenia has been observed in all cultural groups that have been studied. In the United States its expected incidence in the population is about 1 percent, a figure that has been quite stable over time. About one fourth of the patients admitted each year to public mental hospitals are diagnosed as schizophrenics (Rubinstein & Coelho, 1970). And since schizophrenics often require prolonged hospitalization, they usually constitute about half of the patient population.

Although schizophrenic disorders sometimes occur during childhood or old age, about three fourths of all first admissions are between the ages of 15 and 45, with a median age of just over 30. The incidence rate is about the same for males and females. Because of its complexity, its high rate of incidence, especially during the most productive years of life, and its tendency to recurrence and chronicity, schizophrenia is considered one of the most serious of all psychotic disorders as well as one of the most baffling.

CLINICAL PICTURE IN SCHIZOPHRENIA

Often schizophrenia develops slowly and insidiously. Thus, the early clinical picture may be dominated by seclusiveness, gradual lack of interest in the surrounding world, excessive day-dreaming, blunting of affect, and mildly inappropriate responses. This pattern is referred to as *process schizophrenia,* and the outcome is considered generally unfavorable—partly because the need for treatment usually is not recognized until the disorder has become firmly entrenched. In other instances schizophrenia has a sudden onset, typically marked by intense emotional turmoil and a nightmarish sense of confusion. This pattern, which usually appears to be related to specific precipitating stresses, is referred to as *reactive schizophrenia.* Here schizophrenic symptoms usually clear up in a matter of weeks, though in some cases an acute onset is the prelude to a more chronic pattern.

In both process and reactive schizophrenia, specific symptoms are legion and vary greatly from one individual to another, as well as over a period of time. The basic experience in schizophrenia, however, seems to be one of disorganization in perception, thought, and emotion. Five key categories of symptoms are commonly involved.

1. *Breakdown of perceptual filtering.* The normal individual—by means of complex processes of "filtering"—is able to selectively attend to and cope with the great mass of incoming sensory information to which he is exposed. Thus he perceives his world in an orderly and meaningful way. The schizophrenic, by contrast, is apparently unable to screen out distractions or to discriminate between relevant and irrelevant input. He is highly sensitive to stimuli of all kinds—from both internal and external sources—and is unable to integrate his perceptions into a meaningful pattern.

This point is illustrated by the following excerpts of statements of schizophrenics who were asked to describe their experiences during the early phases of their schizophrenic breakdowns.

"It's as if I am too wide awake—very, very alert. I can't relax at all. Everything seems to go through me. I just can't shut things out."

"I can't concentrate. It's diversion of attention that troubles me. I am picking up different conversations. It's like being a transmitter. The sounds are coming through to me but I feel my mind cannot cope with everything. It's difficult to concentrate on any one sound."

"Everything is in bits. You put the picture up bit by bit into your head. It's like a photograph that's been torn to

COMPARISON OF NEUROSES AND FUNCTIONAL PSYCHOSES

	NEUROSES	FUNCTIONAL PSYCHOSES
General behavior	Maladaptive avoidance behavior, with mild impairment of personal and social functioning.	Severe personality decompensation; marked impairment of contact with reality; severe impairment of personal and social functioning.
Nature of symptoms	Wide range of psychological and somatic symptoms, but no hallucinations or other extreme deviations in thought, affect, or action.	Wide range of symptoms, with extreme deviations in thought, affect, and action—e.g., delusions, hallucinations, emotional blunting, bizarre behavior.
Orientation to the environment	Slight, if any, impairment of orientation to environment with respect to time, place, and person.	Frequent loss of orientation to environment with respect to time, place, and person.
Insight (self-understanding)	Frequently, some understanding of own maladaptive behavior, but with a seeming inability to change it.	Markedly impaired understanding of current symptoms and behavior.
Physically destructive behavior	Behavior rarely dangerous or physically injurious to anyone.	In some cases behavior may be dangerous to self or others.
Etiology	Emphasis on failure to acquire needed competencies, and/or on learned maladaptive behaviors.	Emphasis on maladaptive learning, decompensation under excessive stress, and possible biochemical irregularities.

bits and put together again. You have to absorb it again. If you move it's frightening. The picture you had in your head is still there but it's broken up."

"Sometimes I feel alright then the next minute I feel that everything is coming towards me. I see things more than what they really are. Everything's brighter and louder and noisier." (Excerpted from McGhie & Chapman, 1961, pp. 104–106)

In these excerpts we see not only the breakdown of filtering and the fragmentation of experience, but also the increased intensity of stimulation.

2. *Disorganization of thought processes.* Accompanying the breakdown of filtering is the disorganization of thought processes. This includes difficulty in concentrating, impaired ability to maintain order in the association of thoughts, a sense of being "locked in" on specific thoughts, and severe impairment of problem-solving and decision-making ability.

"My thoughts get all jumbled up. I start thinking or talking about something but I never get there. Instead I wander off in the wrong direction and get caught up with all sorts of different things that may be connected with the things I want to say but in a way I can't explain." (McGhie & Chapman, 1961, p. 108)

The impaired thinking of a schizophrenic is likely to become readily apparent in his answers to questions. For example, when asked about a movie he had seen, a schizophrenic patient replied, "The best part about the movie was that one character had a beard, and since Jesus had a beard and I have a beard, it was not a 'dirty' movie at all but very religious. It made me want to pray and 'cleanse' my mind of sex." Often the thought disorganization is more subtle, as in the case of a young schizophrenic who was asked what he thought about "trial marriage." He replied, "I don't know. I don't believe in marriage, and a trial marriage is just as bad as any other marriage, and why should a trial be involved in marriage, especially when there's no judge."

3. *Emotional distortion and feelings of panic.* Schizophrenia is characterized by emotional reactions inappropriate to the situations or stimuli that elicit them. Since our emotions are strongly influenced by cognitive processes, it is not surprising that the disorganization of thought is also accompanied by distortions in affective responses.

"Half the time I am talking about one thing and thinking about half a dozen other things at the same time. It must look queer to people when I laugh about something that has got nothing to do with what I am talking about, but they don't know what's going on inside and how much of it is running round in my head. You see I might be talking about something quite serious to you and other things come into my head at the same time that are funny and this makes me laugh. If I could only concentrate on the one thing at the one time I wouldn't look half so silly." (McGhie & Chapman, 1961, pp. 109–110)

Loss of control over one's thoughts—the inability to attend selectively and to get thoughts moving again when they get stuck on something—seems to be an important factor in the acute schizophrenic reaction, not only in determining inappropriate affect but also in eliciting intense anxiety and panic. For the experience of losing control over one's thoughts and feelings is terrifying. As one patient expressed it, "It's like no other experience on earth. It's just sheer terror." With time, the schizophrenic learns to cope with his inner experiences without evidencing the panic evident in the acute stage. However, as Grinker (1969) has pointed out, "Anyone who works intensively with these patients knows full well the unique depth and severity of their nameless dreads even to the point of fear of possible annihilation, though these may not be apparent on the surface due to the strength of psychological defenses." (p. 15)

4 *Delusions and hallucinations.* The schizophrenic's disorganized thinking and feeling are commonly reflected in *delusions*—false beliefs that he maintains despite their logical absurdity and despite objective evidence showing that they lack any foundation in reality. Thus he may develop a delusion of influence (in which, for example, his "enemies" may use a complicated electronic device to transmit waves that interfere with his thought processes or "pour filth" into his mind) or a delusion of one of the other types listed on the facing page. Such delusions may vary greatly in the degree to which they are organized into a systematic or coherent explanation of what is happening to the schizophrenic.

The schizophrenic is also subject to hallucinations—the perception of objects and events without any appropriate stimuli. The individual may hear voices telling him what to do or com-

DELUSIONS AND HALLUCINATIONS IN THE PSYCHOSES

Delusions and hallucinations of various kinds are among the most characteristic symptoms of psychotic disorders. *Delusions* are irrational beliefs that the individual defends vigorously, despite their logical absurdity and despite objective evidence showing them to be untrue. Some of the most common types of delusions are listed below. *Hallucinations* are perceptions of various kinds of strange objects and events without any appropriate "external" sensory stimuli. As the examples indicate, hallucinations may involve any of the senses.

DELUSIONS

Delusions of reference
Delusional beliefs of an individual that other people are talking about him, referring to him, portraying his life on television, or otherwise making references to him in their activities.

Delusions of influence
Delusional beliefs of an individual that "enemies" are influencing him in various ways, as with complicated electronic gadgets which send out waves that interfere with his thoughts or "pour filth" into his mind.

Delusions of persecution
Delusional beliefs of an individual that he is being deliberately interfered with, discriminated against, plotted against, threatened, or otherwise mistreated.

Delusions of sin and guilt
Delusional beliefs of an individual that he has committed some unforgivable sins that have brought calamity to others, and that he is evil and worthless.

Hypochondriacal delusions
Delusional beliefs relating to having various horrible disease conditions, such as "rotting," being "eaten away," or having one's brain turn to dust.

Delusions of grandeur
Delusional beliefs in which an individual views himself as some great and remarkable person, such as a great economist or inventor, a religious savior, a historical figure, or even God.

Nihilistic delusions
Delusional beliefs associated with the conviction that nothing exists. The individual may insist that he is living in a "shadow world" or that he died several years before and that only his spirit, in a sort of vaporous form, remains.

HALLUCINATIONS

Auditory hallucinations
Hallucinations involving the sense of hearing; e.g., the individual may hear voices telling him what to do, commenting on or criticizing his actions, or warning him that he will be punished unless he repents.

Visual hallucinations
Hallucinations involving the sense of sight; e.g., the individual may see angels in heaven, the pitfires of hell, or just clouds and open space when he is in an enclosed room.

Olfactory hallucinations
Hallucinations involving the sense of smell; e.g., the individual may smell poison gas that he believes has been injected into his room by his enemies.

Gustatory hallucinations
Hallucinations involving the sense of taste; e.g., the individual may taste poison that he believes to have been put into his food or coffee.

Tactual hallucinations
Hallucinations involving the sense of touch; e.g., the individual may feel cockroaches crawling over him or small bugs crawling around under his skin.

Delusions of reference, influence, persecution, and sin and guilt are considered the most common delusions in the psychoses. However, delusions of grandeur, hypochondriacal delusions, and nihilistic delusions are common. The degree of delusional systematization varies from the fragmentary disorientation which accompanies delirium to the logically consistent delusional system of the paranoiac.

Of the hallucinations, auditory and visual ones are the most common, but olfactory and gustatory hallucinations are not infrequent. In the case of auditory hallucinations, the individual may or may not recognize the identity of the person or persons talking, and the source may be well or poorly localized.

Delusions and hallucinations may result from a variety of biological and psychological conditions. Among these are extreme fatigue, drugs, delirium accompanying fever, brain pathology, sensory deprivation, and exaggeration of the ego-defense mechanisms. Even where biological conditions are important determinants, differences in personality makeup may influence the content of delusional and hallucinatory experiences. This is brought out in Good's (1943) description of the behavior of 5 survivors from a sunken ship who spent 15 days adrift on a raft. Although all 5 survivors reported periodic irrational thoughts while adrift (the most common being that they could walk on the water), only one showed such a severe reaction that he started to talk to an imaginary person.

Based on Forgus and DeWolfe (1969), Good (1943), Goodwin, Alderson, and Rosenthal (1971), Schultz (1965), and Strauss (1969).

menting on or criticizing his actions. In some instances the voices are ascribed to relatives or friends, in others to "enemies" who are interfering with or persecuting him, and in still other cases the messages are received "from God" or from some organization and tell him of great powers that have been conferred on him or of his mission to save mankind. Occasionally the individual insists that he has not the vaguest idea of the identity of the person or persons talking. Often he has difficulty localizing the source of the voices—they may come from a light fixture, a television set that is not turned on, or even from an imaginary telephone receiver he holds to his ear. Sometimes the voices seem to come from all directions. Although auditory hallucinations are the most common, visual and other sensory modalities may also be involved. Thus the schizophrenic may see angels in heaven, or smell noxious gas that has been injected into his room, or taste

poison in his food. As in the case of delusions, his evaluations of stimuli are distorted by the disorganization and fragmentation of thought and experience. And, of course, delusions and hallucinations may occur at the same time.

5. *Withdrawal from reality.* The schizophrenic tends to withdraw from reality into a world of fantasy and private experience. Here it may be emphasized that the disorganization of thought and emotion involves not only the environment but the self as well. In short, the self, as the integrating core of the personality, is also diffused, fragmented, and largely lost. Thus, the schizophrenic may experience varying degrees of confusion concerning who and what he is; and in extreme cases he may undergo such complete depersonalization that he feels he is a machine rather than a human being.

"Things just happen to me now and I have no control over them. I don't seem to have the same say in things any more. At times I can't even control what I want to think about. I am starting to feel pretty numb about everything because I am becoming an object and objects don't have feelings." (McGhie & Chapman, 1961, p. 109)

The degree of withdrawal and apathy may vary markedly from one patient to another. However, the schizophrenic typically becomes preoccupied with inner fantasies and private modes of thought. Efforts to force him back into the world of reality are likely to arouse negativistic and hostile behavior. But many patients—in their own way and at their own pace—do attempt to reestablish contact with reality. An extreme example is depicted in Hannah Green's autobiographical novel *I Never Promised You a Rose Garden* (1964), which describes how a young girl—hospitalized for schizophrenia while in her teens—burned herself repeatedly with cigarette butts to relieve intolerable inner pressures and to "prove to herself finally whether or not she was truly made of human substance."

As this example illustrates, the symptom patterns we have described are often accompanied by bizarre behavior. Thus a schizophrenic may exhibit peculiarities of movement, gesture, costume, and expression—or he may sit apathetically staring into space. We shall elaborate on these and other behavior anomalies in describing the

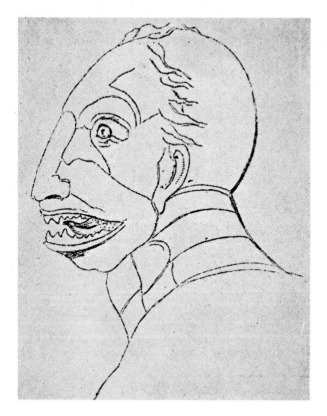

"Ghost of a Flea," based on a hallucination portrayed by William Blake. According to Blake, this flea was in the room and told him that fleas contained the damned souls of bloodthirsty men. Blake, in both his poetry and his etchings, gave many evidences of schizophrenic ideation. (Born, 1946).

various types of schizophrenia. It should be emphasized, however, that bizarre behavior is typically episodic. Most schizophrenics "fade in and out of reality" as a function of the stimuli present and their own inner state.

Indeed, we should note with regard to all the key symptoms of schizophrenia that (1) not all symptoms occur in a particular case; (2) the symptom picture may differ markedly from one patient to another; (3) the symptom picture may be influenced by the individual's being labeled as a schizophrenic and given a "sick" role; and (4) the clinical picture may vary markedly with time, both episodically and over long-range periods. Thus, the patient may be in "good contact" one day and evidence delusions and hallucinations the next; or an acute schizophrenic reaction may clear up fairly rapidly or progress to a more severe and chronic condition. As we shall see, the symptom picture in schizophrenia may also be modified by antipsychotic drugs and other medication.

TYPES OF SCHIZOPHRENIA

The APA classification of mental disorders lists ten subtypes of schizophrenia, which are summarized on page 282. We shall consider five of these subtypes in our present discussion: acute, paranoid, catatonic, hebephrenic, and simple. Of these, the acute and paranoid types are the most common.

Acute type. Since most types of schizophrenia are subject to acute episodes, the classification of *acute schizophrenia* as a distinct type may seem somewhat arbitrary. However, this reaction has several distinguishing characteristics. It comes on suddenly, often in a person whose behavior has previously been relatively normal; it is undifferentiated, involving a wide variety of symptom patterns; and schizophrenic symptoms tend to clear up as the episode abates. Paranoid, catatonic, and most other types of schizophrenia, by contrast, have rather characteristic symptom patterns that tend to be apparent even during acute episodes and that also tend to persist after such episodes abate.

The case of David F. illustrates the onset of an acute schizophrenic episode (Bowers, 1965). David felt great apprehension about his future as

Powerfully evocative of the schizophrenic withdrawal from reality and preoccupation with inner fantasies is this watercolor, "Strange Visitor in My Garden," which was selected for an exhibit of patient art. The wraithlike figure, totally devoid of expression, dominates the work, but a startling component is the face peering out at lower left; the "strange visitor" resembles a mask of a subhuman species.

he approached the end of his undergraduate days. He also felt inadequate in his relationship with his girl friend, Laura—a relationship characterized by emotionally charged separations and reconciliations, as well as by sexual experimentation, in which David frequently doubted his sexual ability. When Laura dated another boy and refused to tell David the details, David thought the date had involved intercourse, and he wrote a vindictive poem in which he called Laura a whore. After mailing the poem he felt guilty, and he was quite disturbed to find that his best friend sided with Laura. David began to stay in his room more, attending only a few classes.

The following excerpts from David's diary were written during the month preceding his hospitalization. It is of particular interest to note the disorganization in thought and emotion, the panic, the occasional awe at the strangeness of his experience, and the attempts to understand and give meaning to what was happening (Bowers, 1965):

". . . and there's old Hawthorne's bosom serpent for you eating away hissing all night I lie there and I lie there and think and think and think all the time trying not to think I think anyway or reminisce rather (delightful pastime) until pow I feel like the top of my head blows off and I smash my fist into something and begin all over again like a one cycle engine." (p. 348)

"Tuesday, March 10, 10 P.M. I can't cope, I can't come to grips . . . it's Hawthorne's disease blazing away, red guilt or little stringy black warts (they're growing with a virulence I swear I never noticed before) . . . music helps a bit and I've conducted the Eroica all over the room three times already today, waving my arms and occasionally hitting things . . . all very dramatic . . . to think I worried myself about sleeping too much last fall! I've given the jargon a once over; it stems from incest drives, castration fears, masturbation complexes, homosexual doubts, oedipal fixations bullshit bullshit it was around before the jargon and its got me . . . already at table I've been making curious unconscious slips as if the synapses suddenly rot away and I come disconnected its all right its all right I'm going to be a lawyer and make lots of money and grow up to be as weak as my father as torn as my mother look ahead!!" (p. 349)

"Midnight Tuesday. . . . Boy, that Nathan and Laura business really pulled the cork I'm bad or mad or just dull? Down on my knees before the crescent moon I got my pants dirty. This is undoubtedly one of the most prolix records of a scarringover process (I'm sealing like one of those puncture proof tires, but in slow motion) I should be back to my habitual state of callousness in a couple of days with no apparent damage, maybe I can even go on staving off like this ("a poem is a momentary stay against confusion" Frost . . . this is quite a poem) till I die." (p. 351)

"Thursday, March 12, 11 A.M. I'm out! I'm through . . . boomed out of the tunnel sometime last night and it's raining stars. . . . whooey . . . its nice out there's time for everything. . . . I can do it I did it and if it happens again I'll do it again twice as hard I got a dexamyl high going and I'm not on dexamyl and I've been up for forty eight or more hours and I'm giddy-giddygiddy and I took a test this morning and it was on Voltaire and I kicked him a couple of good ones for being down on Pascal that poor bastard with his shrivelled body and bottomless abysess they're not bottomless!! You get down far enough and it gets thick enough and black enough and then you claw claw claw your way out and pretty soon you're on top again. And I licked it by myself, all alone. No pandering psychia-

trists or priests or friends by myself. Now, I must admit I'm a little leery; I dashed back to the typewriter to give it form to write it down and sew it in my vest like Pascal so if the Thing hits me again I'll have this in my vest and I'll kick it in the teeth again but Pascal saw God and yet still it hit him again . . . will it hit me again? Who cares . . . I just sat in on one of those weddings of the soul and I tooted tooted . . . I don't care I can use it I can run on it it will be my psychic gasoline now I don't have to sleep sleep all the time to get away with it . . . but if I lose my typewriter?" (p. 351)

"Saturday, March 14, 11 A.M. . . . Falling asleep last night a thousand million thoughts bubbled then the number the age 18 what happened when I was 18? (my stomach hurts . . . it really physically does . . . that blue bear has all kinds of tricks . . . I'm going out for coffee) Well I DO have to go out to get some money but I MUST be merciless with the blue bear. He has no quarter for me. . . . and not scare myself with eery consequences . . . the newspaper odds are AGAINST automobile deaths, that was the resistance mechanism trying to stop me again I'm hot on your tail blue bear that doesn't mean anything what does that mean it means that I'm feeling the denied homosexual instincts, feeling the woman in me and getting over her that's it that's what Faulkner's bear was a woman I have the quotes up on my wall I wrote them down a week ago. . . . woman is a bear you must kill the bear to be a man no that isn't what I've got on my wall the quotes go 'Anyone could be upset by his first lion.'" (p. 356)

In acute schizophrenia, the clinical picture is dominated by symptoms associated with the massive breakdown of filtering, the individual's panic at loss of control over his thoughts and feelings, and his desperate attempts to understand what is happening to him. This pattern is well illustrated in the case of David F., who was hospitalized four days after writing the last of the diary entries recorded above.

The individual does not remain in a state of acute schizophrenia over a sustained period of time. Often the stress situation is alleviated, and he recovers in a few weeks or months. However, a number of persons who are subject to the acute type of schizophrenia tend to experience recurrent episodes. In other instances, the clinical picture changes to a more chronic type of schizophrenia.

Paranoid type. About one half of all schizophrenic first admissions to mental hospitals are of the paranoid type. Frequently there has been a history of growing suspiciousness and of dif-

SCHIZOPHRENIA IN LITERATURE

Some students of psychopathology have suggested that the "madness" of the schizophrenic may be largely a reflection of the "madness" of society itself. An interesting perspective on this issue is provided by Franz Kafka's novel *The Trial*. The bizarre experiences of its central character—known simply as "Joseph K."—have been interpreted by some readers as a symbolic indictment of social injustice and, by others, as an almost clinical depiction of a paranoid schizophrenic. The following synopsis (Grant, 1956) reflects the latter view. The novel's ending, however, suggests that Joseph K. may have been the victim of something more than his own delusions.

"[*The Trial*] begins with the arrest, for no reason he is aware of, of its central figure: 'Someone must have been telling lies about Joseph K. . . .' The charge against him is undefined; he is simply informed that he is under arrest, but he is not detained. Called to an interrogation chamber, before an audience, he takes an aggressive attitude and makes accusations of unfair treatment; back of his arrest, he thinks, a 'great organization' is at work, by which the innocent are accused of guilt. K. observes the magistrate making a 'secret sign' to someone in the audience; he sees 'artifices'; he notes certain badges among the onlookers and concludes that they are in league with the magistrate and are there to spy upon him. He observes peculiar movements in the assembly, the people on the right side of the room behaving differently from those on the left. Strange and seemingly irrelevant incidents occur from time to time in the course of the narrative; e.g., K. is distracted, during his speech in the interrogation chamber, by an assault, apparently sexual, by a male spectator upon a 'washer-woman,' who turns out later to be connected with the court through her husband, and who promises him aid in his case. Other people, also, who would assumedly be unrelated to the action, are disclosed to have such 'connections,' including even some urchin-like girls at play in a tenement. In the same vein K. finds that various people whom he would have supposed were outsiders are familiar with his case; the news has travelled surprisingly. The concept of peculiar 'signs' appears again: there is a superstition that one may read, from the expression of a defendant's mouth, the outcome of his case; from the 'line' of his own lips, K. is told, people have judged that he will very soon be declared guilty; again, a man to whom he had spoken was shocked to read his own condemnation on K.'s mouth.

"Much of the novel is devoted to sustained preoccupation . . . with the details of litigation. . . . An important feature, in this context, is the [implication] that the guilt is subjective, and that the culprit's doom is inescapable. K. himself asserts that the trial is a trial 'only . . . if I recognize it as such.' Following his first visit, he returns to the court without being ordered to do so. Though under arrest he is permitted to go about his usual business as a bank executive. There is no indication of force, or mention of physical punishment, imprisonment, etc. The case is a criminal one, but it 'is not a case before an ordinary court.' K. feels that he could formulate, himself, all the questions for his own cross-examination; in planning a written defense he considers giving an account of his life, with a moral appraisal of each important action. . . .

"It is equally clear that the final judgment will not be determined by the merits of the case. The court is arbitrary, capricious, and irritable. K. is advised that the 'first plea' of his case might determine everything, but also that it might be mislaid or even lost altogether. The defense will be difficult because the charge is unknown to the defense counsel as well as to the accused, though later it might be 'guessed at.' The right of defense itself, in fact, is merely tolerated, rather than legally recognized. The bringing of a charge is, in fact, equivalent to conviction of guilt, in the eyes of the court; one might as well plead innocence, K. is told, before a row of judges painted on canvas. Actual acquittal is almost unknown; there is 'ostensible' acquittal, but this may be followed by a second arrest, a second acquittal by a third arrest and so on.

"The unorthodox procedures of the court continue, through a rather eerie tableau in an empty cathedral to a sinister climax; the novel ends when 2 callers walk K., unenlightened yet not unwilling, to a suburban quarry, and there thrust a knife into his heart.

"*The Trial* is notable for the unaccountable actions of its characters, and for bizarre unrealities presented with matter-of-fact and circumstantial realism. More important, the impression is strong that the interest, the *motivation* for a novel so obsessed with such a theme must be intimately related to something uniquely personal in its author. . . ." (Grant, 1956, pp. 143–144)

---

ficulties in interpersonal relations. The eventual symptom picture is dominated by absurd, illogical, and changeable delusions. Persecutory delusions are the most frequent, and may involve a wide range of ideas and all sorts of plots. The individual may become highly suspicious of his relatives or associates and may complain of being watched, followed, poisoned, talked about, or influenced by electrical devices rigged up by his enemies.

All the attention he receives may lead him to believe that he must possess remarkable qualities or be some great person. For why else would his enemies persecute him? Consequently, he may develop delusions of grandeur and believe that he is the world's greatest economist or philosopher, or that he is Napoleon, Caesar, or Lincoln. These delusions are frequently accompanied by vivid auditory, visual, and other hallucinations. The patient may hear singing, or God speaking, or the voices of his enemies, or he may see angels or feel electric rays piercing his body at various points.

Sirhan B. Sirhan, the convicted assassin of Senator Robert F. Kennedy, was diagnosed as a chronic paranoid schizophrenic by expert witnesses—psychologists and psychiatrists—appointed by the court.

Although proud of his deed and believing himself to have been a great patriot who acted on behalf of the Arab people (Kennedy had proposed a short time previously that the United States send 50 military aircraft to Israel), Sirhan seemed to have no recollection of the actual assassination. Diamond (1969), who examined Sirhan, suspected that the amnesia covered a psychotic break. He hypnotized Sirhan and was able to observe an entirely different individual, one who vividly remembered killing Kennedy and who was intensely emotional when asked any question about the Arab-Israeli conflict. For example, when asked about a terrifying experience of his boyhood, the bombing of Jerusalem by the Israelis in 1948, Sirhan "suddenly crumpled in agony like a child, sobbing and shivering in terror. The tears poured down his face." (p. 54)

According to Diamond, Sirhan planned the killing under self-hypnosis and lacked conscious awareness of it (see facing page). An example of a "truly split" personality, whose arrogance and "cool front" provided a "simulation of sanity," Sirhan apparently preferred to think of himself as a sane patriot and be convicted of the assassination—rather than face his psychotic behavior and the possibility of being declared criminally insane.

The individual's behavior becomes centered around these delusions and hallucinations, resulting in loss of critical judgment and in erratic, unpredictable behavior. In response to a command from a "voice" he hears, he may break furniture or commit other violent acts. Occasionally a paranoid schizophrenic can be dangerous, as when he attacks someone he is sure is persecuting him. In general, there is less extreme withdrawal from the outside world than with most other types of schizophrenia. The illogical, delusional picture, together with continued attention to external data that are misinterpreted, is brought out in the following conversation between a doctor and a chronic paranoid schizophrenic.

Dr.: What's your name?
Pt.: Who are you?
Dr.: I'm a doctor. Who are you?
Pt.: I can't tell you who I am.
Dr.: Why can't you tell me?
Pt.: You wouldn't believe me.
Dr.: What are you doing here?
Pt.: Well, I've been sent here to thwart the Russians. I'm the only one in the world who knows how to deal with them. They got their spies all around here though to get me, but I'm smarter than any of them.
Dr.: What are you doing to do to thwart the Russians?
Pt.: I'm organizing.
Dr.: Whom are you going to organize?
Pt.: Everybody. I'm the only man in the world who can do that, but they're trying to get me. But I'm going to use my atomic bomb media to blow them up.
Dr.: You must be a terribly important person then.
Pt.: Well, of course.
Dr.: What do you call yourself?
Pt.: You used to know me as Franklin D. Roosevelt.
Dr.: Isn't he dead?
Pt.: Sure he's dead, but I'm alive.

Dr.: But you're Franklin D. Roosevelt?
Pt.: His spirit. He, God, and I figured this out. And now I'm going to make a race of healthy people. My agents are lining them up. Say, who are you?
Dr.: I'm a doctor here.
Pt.: You don't look like a doctor. You look like a Russian to me.
Dr.: How can you tell a Russian from one of your agents?
Pt.: I read eyes. I get all my signs from eyes. I look into your eyes and get all my signs from them.
Dr.: Do you sometimes hear voices telling you someone is a Russian?
Pt.: No, I just look into eyes. I got a mirror here to look into my own eyes. I know everything that's going on. I can tell by the color, by the way it's shaped.
Dr.: Did you have any trouble with people before you came here?
Pt.: Well, only the Russians. They were trying to surround me in my neighborhood. One day they tried to drop a bomb on me from the fire escape.
Dr.: How could you tell it was a bomb?
Pt.: I just knew.

Later in this chapter (page 311) we shall see that in paranoia proper the characteristic delusions of persecution and grandeur occur in individuals whose personalities remain otherwise relatively intact. In paranoid schizophrenia, however, there is considerable disorganization, though not so extreme as to cause the person to give up attempts to understand and deal with his condition through delusional interaction with the world. A case cited by Enders and Flinn (1962)—which represents a typical paranoid schizophrenic reaction—will help fill in the symptom picture for this reaction type. It is a particularly interesting case, since it involves an officer in the Air Force, whose rigorous selection and train-

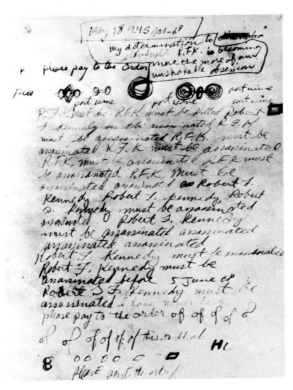

Pages from Sirhan's "trance" notebooks were introduced in evidence at his trial for Robert F. Kennedy's murder. Commenting on them, Diamond (1969) said: "Sirhan's trances obviously took his mind into a voodoo world. He thought he saw Kennedy's face come before him in the mirror, blotting out his own image, and he began to write kill-Kennedy orders to himself . . . 'RFK must die,' he wrote, 'Robert F. Kennedy must be assassinated before June 5, 1968.' . . . Actually his self-hypnosis worked better than he knew. Without real knowledge or awareness of what was happening in the trances, he rigorously programmed himself for the assassination exactly the way a computer is programmed by magnetic tape. In his unconscious mind there existed a plan for the fulfillment of his sick, paranoid hatred of Kennedy and all who might want to help the Jews. In his conscious mind there was no awareness of such a plan or that he, Sirhan, was to be the instrument of assassination." (p. 50)

ing procedures screen out individuals with conspicuous emotional difficulties. In addition, the patient had had an excellent service record as a pilot and had tolerated severe stress.

"The case to be reported occurred in a 41-year-old command pilot with 7,500 hours, who had flown 135 combat missions in World War II and Korea. At the time of his illness, he was a chief pilot in a command headquarters. He was an excellent pilot and had consistently received superior ratings because of his conscientious and dependable performance. The overt onset of his illness was related to a period of TDY [temporary tour of duty] at a conference where flight procedures on a new type aircraft were being drafted. However, in retrospect, it was learned that for several weeks he had been preoccupied and upset, had sensed that he could read other people's minds by radio waves, and suspected those with whom he worked of being 'queer.'

"While at the conference, he developed ideas of reference, believing that certain comments which his companions made, or which he heard over the radio, had hidden meanings and were directed toward him. For example, when the conferees spoke of 'take-off,' he did not know whether they were referring to an airplane or a woman, and suspected they were suggesting he should have an illicit sexual relationship. He developed the delusional idea that his associates were trying to 'teach' him something, and puzzled them several times when he confronted them with a demand that they tell him openly whatever they wanted him to learn. They became further concerned when he became increasingly upset, tearful and incoherent, and when he did not improve after several days of 'rest' at his brother's home, he was admitted to the hospital.

"On admission, he was suspicious of those about him, wondering whether they were dope-peddlers or communists, and he refused to talk to people who could not assure him they were cleared for top secret. He believed that he was accused of taking dope, that there were concealed microphones about the ward, and he had hallucinations consisting of voices which accused him of being 'queer.' He was often apprehensive and tearful, but this alternated with periods when he was inappropriately jovial. He was oriented in all spheres, and physical and neurological exams were entirely normal.

"A review of the patient's past history revealed no other evidence of emotional disturbance. He was the second of four children of a strict, moralistic, financially successful farm family. He did well in school and one year of college, but always felt inadequate in comparison with his peers. He entered the Air Corps and flew 32 B-17 missions in World War II, was separated, then recalled in 1950 and flew 103 combat missions in Korea. He had been married for 18 years and had five children. He used alcohol only rarely, and there was no evidence that toxic or exogenous factors could have been implicated in his psychosis.

"The patient received psychotherapy and began to improve within a few days after admission. For this reason, no drug or other somatic treatment was instituted. He continued to improve over the course of the next several weeks and seemed greatly relieved after telling of an isolated extramarital adventure during the TDY. He gradually gained insight into the unreality of his experiences and was discharged from the hospital after one month."

[Following his discharge from the hospital, the officer was assigned to duties associated with supply and ground training, which he handled without difficulty. Despite his apparent remission, however, some residuals of his previous thought disturbance remained in the background.]

". . . He wondered at times whether he had not been partly right about the events on TDY, and whether his fellow conferees had not been playing a practical joke on him. He had recently considered going to his Wing Commanding Officer to ask whether the experiences had been part of some kind of 'test' of his mental stability, but had decided against this because it might create an unfavorable impression if he were being tested. He had decided that whatever had happened, it was best forgotten, and through the use of this suppressive mechanism had continued to function effectively. Because of his clear-cut history of a psychotic disorder without an underlying organic basis, as well as the evidence of a continuing minimal thinking disorder, return to flying status was not considered to be consistent with flying safety." (pp. 730-731)

In commenting on this case, Enders and Flinn emphasized the patient's lifelong rigid, moralistic, code, which made him unable to tolerate an impulse toward promiscuous behavior. As a result, he projected this unethical impulse to outside agencies; he now misconstrued comments heard on the radio or made by his companions as suggesting illicit activities.

Both Freud and contemporary investigators have pointed to the frequency of homosexual conflicts in paranoid schizophrenia—though the actual significance of such conflicts in the etiology of the disorder is not yet clear. In one study, Klaf and Davis (1960) found homosexual preoccupations 7 times as frequent in a group of 150 male paranoid schizophrenics as in a control group consisting primarily of psychoneurotics and antisocial personalities. Previous homosexual experiences were recorded almost twice as often as in the control group. In addition, approximately 85 percent of the paranoid schizophrenics felt they had male persecutors, whereas only 5 percent reported female persecutors, and 10 percent reported persecutors of both sexes. Similarly, Moore and Selzer (1963) found a significantly greater incidence of past homosexual acts, preoccupation with homosexuality during psychotherapy, and latent homosexual trends among a group of 128 male paranoid schizophrenics than among a control group of 77 nonparanoid schizophrenics. Interestingly enough, Klaf (1961) failed to find a high incidence of homosexual preoccupation or past homosexual experiences among a group of 75 female paranoid schizophrenics. In comparison to the males, 61 percent of the females thought they had male persecutors, 27 percent reported female persecutors, and 12 percent thought they had persecutors of both sexes.

Catatonic type. Catatonic reactions often manifest themselves much more suddenly than other forms of schizophrenia, but the patient's history usually shows the typical pattern of gradual withdrawal from reality and some degree of emotional apathy. Catatonics typically alternate between periods of extreme withdrawal and extreme excitement, though in some cases there is a predominance of one reaction or the other. In the withdrawal reaction there is a sudden loss of all animation and a tendency to remain motionless in a stereotyped position or posture. This position may be maintained for hours or even days, and the hands and feet may become blue and swollen because of the immobility.

Some of these patients are highly suggestible and will automatically obey commands or imitate the actions of others (*echopraxia*) or repeat phrases in a stereotyped way (*echolalia*). If the patient's arm is raised to an awkward and uncomfortable position, he may maintain it in this attitude for minutes or even hours. Ordinarily, however, a patient in a catatonic stupor is extremely negativistic. He is apt to resist stubbornly any effort to change his position and may become mute, resist all attempts to feed him, and refuse to comply with even the slightest request. He pays no attention to bowel or bladder control and saliva may drool from his mouth. The patient's facial expression typically becomes vacant, and his skin appears waxy. Threats and painful stimuli have no effect, and he has to be dressed and washed and have his eliminative processes taken care of. For example, a patient may feel that he has to hold his hand out flat because the forces of "good" and "evil" are waging a "war of the worlds" on his hand; and if he moves it he may tilt the precarious balance in favor of the forces of evil. Surprisingly, despite his apparent lack of attention to his environment while in this condition, he may later relate in detail events that were going on around him.

Suddenly and without warning, the catatonic patient may pass from a state of extreme withdrawal to one of great excitement, during which he seems to be under great "pressure of activity." He may talk or shout excitedly and incoherently, pace rapidly back and forth, openly indulge in sexual activities such as masturbation, mutilate himself or attempt suicide, or impulsively attack and attempt to kill other persons. The suddenness and the extreme frenzy of these attacks make such patients very dangerous both to themselves and others. The excitement may last a few hours, days, or even weeks.

The following case illustrates some of the symptoms typical of the clinical picture in catatonic reactions.

On admission, the patient, a 35-year-old male, appeared apathetic and withdrawn. He would answer questions only after they had been repeated several times and then his speech was so indistinct that it was

difficult to understand what he said. After a period of 3 weeks on the ward, his behavior underwent a rather dramatic shift and he became mildly excited, heard the voice of God talking to him, and spent a good deal of time on his knees praying aloud. He occasionally turned to other patients and beseeched them to "get religion" before the devil got them. During this period the following conversation occurred with the ward physician:

Dr.: How are you today, Mr.——?

Pt.: I am fighting, doctor—fighting sin and evil.

Dr.: Sin and evil?

Pt.: Yes, sin and evil. You know what sin and evil are, and you should be down here praying with me for your salvation. . . . God knows the answers. He has imparted some of his knowledge to Churchill. He knows but others are confused. He is the true hero of the British Empire. The Bible states that "By a man's actions ye shall judge him," and he is a man of action.

Dr.: Do you feel that you have found any answers?

Pt.: I am fighting, doctor. The devil tries to confuse you, but I am fighting. Why do people die, doctor? Why did my mother have to die? That's the crucial point, how can you beat sin and evil, how can you keep from moral and physical decay? God has all the answers!

On one occasion the patient impulsively attacked another patient on the ward who had asked him if he was trying to polish the ward floor with his knees. Afterwards, he blamed the devil for his behavior, stating that it was the devil who directed the attack.

The catatonic schizophrenic's use of immobility to maintain control may be more understandable when it is realized that his filtering processes are markedly reduced, that he is highly vulnerable to the increase in stimulation, and that he is striving to maintain some control over his inner conflict and disorganized thoughts. By his immobility he apparently maintains a measure of control over external, but not necessarily over internal, sources of stimulation. Freeman has cited the explanation advanced by one patient: "I did not want to move, because if I did everything changed around me and upset me horribly so I remained still to hold onto a sense of permanence." (1960, p. 932)

Hebephrenic type. Hebephrenic reactions usually occur at an earlier age and represent a more severe disintegration of the personality than the other types of schizophrenia. Typically the individual has a history of oddness, overscrupulousness about trivial things, and preoccupation with religious and philosophical issues. He frequently broods over the dire results of masturbation and minor infractions of social conventions. While his schoolmates are enjoying normal play and social activities, he is gradually becoming more seclusive and more preoccupied with his fantasies.

As the disorder progresses, the individual becomes emotionally indifferent and infantile in his reactions. A silly smile and inappropriate shallow laughter after little or no provocation are common symptoms. If asked the reason for his laughter, the patient may state that he does not know, or he may volunteer some wholly irrelevant and unsatisfactory explanation. Speech becomes incoherent, and there may be considerable baby talk, childish giggling, a repetitious use of similar sounding words, and a derailing of thought along the lines of associated meanings that may give a pun-like quality to speech. In some instances speech becomes completely incoherent.

Hallucinations, particularly auditory ones, are

The creator of this macabre drawing of a "tree man," who holds a bleeding human head in his claw, was a hebephrenic girl who described her creation as a "comical print." Preoccupation with bizarre fantasies is characteristic of hebephrenic individuals.

common. The "voices" may accuse the patient of immoral practices, "pour filth" into his mind, and call him vile names. Delusions are usually of a sexual, religious, hypochondriacal, or persecutory nature and are changeable and fantastic. For example, the patient may insist not only that he is being followed by enemies but that he has already been killed a number of times. In occasional cases, the patient becomes hostile and aggressive. Peculiar mannerisms and other bizarre forms of behavior appear. These may take the form of verbigeration (meaningless, stereotyped repetition of words or sentences), facial grimaces, talking and gesturing to himself, sudden inexplicable laughter and weeping, and in some cases an abnormal interest in urine and feces, which the patient may smear on walls and even on his person. Obscene behavior and a frank absence of any modesty or sense of shame are characteristic. Although outbursts of anger and temper tantrums may occur in connection with his fantasy life, the patient is indifferent to real-life situations, no matter how horrifying or gruesome they may be.

The overall picture in hebephrenic reactions is that of a young person who has retreated from the stresses of life to a silly, childish level of behavior and into a fantasy world of his own, with accompanying emotional distortion and blunting. The general pattern is illustrated in the following interview.

The patient was a divorcée, 32 years of age, who had come to the hospital with bizarre delusions, hallucinations, and severe personality disintegration and with a record of alcoholism, promiscuity, and possible incestuous relations with a brother. The following conversation shows typical hebephrenic responses to questioning.

Dr.: How do you feel today?

Pt.: Fine.

Dr.: When did you come here?

Pt.: 1416, you remember, doctor (silly giggle).

Dr.: Do you know why you are here?

Pt.: Well, in 1951 I changed into two men. President Truman was judge at my trial. I was convicted and hung (silly giggle). My brother and I were given back our normal bodies 5 years ago. I am a policewoman. I keep a dictaphone concealed on my person.

Dr.: Can you tell me the name of this place?

Pt.: I have not been a drinker for 16 years. I am taking a mental rest after a "carter" assignment or "quill." You know, a "penwrap." I had contracts with Warner

Brothers Studios and Eugene broke phonograph records but Mike protested. I have been with the police department for 35 years. I am made of flesh and blood—see, doctor (pulling up her dress).

Dr.: Are you married?

Pt.: No. I am not attracted to men (silly giggle). I have a companionship arrangement with my brother. I am a "looner" . . . a bachelor.

Although the term "flattening of affect" is commonly used when referring to schizophrenia —particularly hebephrenic and simple types— it perhaps should be emphasized that while the term is often descriptive of a patient's appearance to an observer, it may not truly describe his inner state.

Simple type. Simple schizophrenia is characterized by a slow and progressive onset. Beginning fairly early in life—often during adolescence —there is a gradual reduction in external interests and attachments. The individual no longer cares whether he passes or fails in school, he withdraws from social relationships, and he no longer is concerned about his family or friends. Conversation becomes increasingly scanty and trivial, personal hygiene and appearance are neglected, interest in the opposite sex declines, and the individual has increasing difficulty concentrating on anything outside his own inner world of thoughts and fantasies. He makes no effort to work or assume responsibility, and seems content to lead a simple, indifferent, parasitic existence. Although such persons may show episodes of irritability and even of overt aggression, there is not the dramatic psychotic flare-up that we saw in the acute schizophrenic reaction. Rather, there is a progressive and insidious depletion of thought, affect, and behavior.

Lecturing, pleading, and encouragement by well-meaning family members are of no avail and often lead to obstinate, negativistic, and evasive behavior. But despite the individual's intellectual and emotional withdrawal, his mental functions may not be markedly impaired or disintegrated.

The following interview with a male patient who was diagnosed as a schizophrenic, simple type, illustrates the apathy and indifference typical of such patients.

Dr.: Do you know who I am?

Pt.: A doctor, I suppose.

Dr.: How do you feel?

Pt.: Oh—OK, I guess.

Dr.: Do you know where you are?

Pt.: It's a hospital.

Dr.: Why are you here?

Pt.: I don't know. . . . I don't think I should be here. I'm all right.

Dr.: Where would you rather be?

Pt.: I don't care, just out. . . . I don't know. Maybe with some fellows or something. I don't care. There were some guys I used to know.

Dr.: What did you do with those fellows?

Pt.: I don't know—just go around.

Dr.: How do you like it here?

Pt.: I don't know, I don't care. It's all right, I guess. I liked the boys though. I used to know them.

Dr.: And you used to like them?

Pt.: Yes—they were all right, I guess.

Dr.: Who is "they"?

Pt.: Some men. I don't know them by name.

Dr.: Can you think of any reason why you should be here?

Pt.: No, I'm all right. I feel all right. I'd like to be with the fellows I used to know.

Dr.: Are there any fellows here you like?

Pt.: I don't know. They're all right, I guess.

Dr.: Do you think the men who brought you here had it in for you?

Pt.: No. They were nice to me. They were all right. They didn't have it in for me or hate me or anything.

Dr.: Do you ever hear strange noises?

Pt.: No, I never do that. I'm not crazy.

This patient was hospitalized on the complaint of his sister-in-law, who stated that he had tried to force her at the point of a gun to have sexual relations with him. On admission to the hospital the patient appeared rather indifferent about the whole matter and explained that it must have been some "temporary impulse" which overcame him.

Although 30 years of age, the patient had been living with his parents and was completely dependent on them. His educational background was good. He made an A average in high school, but during his first year of college he lost interest in his studies and refused to attend classes despite his parents' pleadings. His parents then did their best to help him achieve some vocational adjustment, but the patient seemed indifferent to their efforts and hopes for him. After leaving college he did take several part-time jobs, including one in a grocery store, which he lost soon after because of his listless attitude and indifference to his duties. Thereafter he would neither look for nor accept work and was quite content to remain dependent on his parents. Although rather handsome, he had never gone out with girls. When questioned on this subject he stated that "I'm not interested in girls. All they ever do is get you in trouble."

Simple schizophrenic reactions are infrequent in terms of hospital first admissions, doubtlessly because many individuals manifesting them are able to get by in the outside world. They may be cared for by their families, particularly during adolescence and early adulthood; or they may be able to support themselves through simple clerical or manual work. They usually make little or no progress in their jobs, resist efforts to change or complicate their routines, and impress others as being rather queer or stupid—curiously inaccessible, isolated, colorless, and uninteresting.

Careful study of patients who are hospitalized often reveals that episodes involving delusions, hallucinations, and bizarre behavior—such as the attempted rape by the patient described in the preceding case history—are not uncommon. However, psychological disorganization is typically less severe than in other types of schizophrenia, and some superficial contact with reality is usually maintained.

It should be emphasized that the subtypes of schizophrenia we have delineated are all part of a more generalized clinical picture for this disorder, and that it is not always possible or relevant to distinguish between them. Although various characteristic patterns do seem to emerge, symptoms vary greatly from person to person, and the clinical picture for any individual may be significantly altered by circumstances introduced with treatment—including the facts of being labeled a schizophrenic (or a particular type of schizophrenic) and being provided with models of schizophrenic behavior in a hospital setting. In recent years we have seen a growing recognition that effective treatment programs for schizophrenia, as for other disorders, must be geared not to "typical" clinical patterns but rather to the particular problems and needs—and also the particular strengths—of given individuals.

SUMMARY OF TYPES OF SCHIZOPHRENIA

Acute type	Characterized by a sudden onset of undifferentiated schizophrenic symptoms, often involving perplexity, confusion, emotional turmoil, delusions of reference, excitement, dreamlike dissociation, depression, and fear. The individual seems to undergo a massive breakdown of filtering processes, with the result that experience becomes fragmented and disorganized, taking on the qualities of a nightmare.
Paranoid type	A symptom picture dominated by absurd, illogical, and changeable delusions, frequently accompanied by vivid hallucinations, with a resulting impairment of critical judgment and erratic, unpredictable, and occasionally dangerous behavior. In chronic cases, there is usually less disorganization of behavior than in other types of schizophrenia, and less extreme withdrawal from social interaction.
Catatonic type	Often characterized by alternating periods of extreme withdrawal and extreme excitement, although in some cases one or the other reaction predominates. In the withdrawal reaction there is a sudden loss of all animation and a tendency to remain motionless for hours or even days, in a stereotyped position. The clinical picture may undergo an abrupt change, with excitement coming on suddenly, wherein the individual may talk or shout incoherently, pace rapidly, and engage in uninhibited, impulsive, and frenzied behavior.
Hebephrenic type	Usually occurs at an earlier age than most other types of schizophrenia, and represents a more severe disintegration of the personality. Emotional distortion and blunting typically are manifested in inappropriate laughter and silliness, peculiar mannerisms, and bizarre, often obscene, behavior.
Simple type	An insidious depletion of thought, affect, and behavior, beginning early in life and gradually progressing until the individual impresses others as being curiously inaccessible, isolated, colorless, and uninteresting. Because psychological disorganization is typically less severe than in other types of schizophrenia and some superficial contact with reality is usually maintained, hospitalization is less frequent.
Schizo-affective type	Characterized by a mixture of general schizophrenic symptoms, in conjunction with more pronounced obvious depression or elation—not typical of the usual surface pattern of "flattened affect."
Latent type	Characterized by various symptoms of schizophrenia but lacking a history of a full-blown schizophrenic episode.
Chronic undifferentiated type	Although manifesting definite schizophrenic symptoms in thought, affect, and behavior, not readily classifiable under one of the other types.
Residual type	Mild indications of schizophrenia shown by individuals in remission following a schizophrenic episode.
Childhood type	Preoccupation with fantasy, and markedly atypical and withdrawn behavior prior to puberty.

BIOLOGICAL FACTORS IN SCHIZOPHRENIA

Despite extensive research on schizophrenia, the dynamics of this disorder are still unclear.[1] Responsibility for its development has been attributed at one time or other to numerous biological factors, including heredity and various neurophysiological and biochemical processes that presumably interfere with normal brain functioning.

Heredity. In view of the disproportionate incidence of schizophrenia in the family backgrounds of schizophrenic patients, it is hardly surprising that many investigators have emphasized the importance of genetic factors in this psychotic disorder. As we saw in Chapter 6 (page 141), early studies by Kallmann (1953; 1958) found a concordance rate of 86.2 percent for identical twins, 14.5 percent for fraternal twins, 14.2 percent for siblings, and 7.1 percent for half-siblings. These findings contrast with an incidence figure for the general population of approximately 1 percent. In a number of other early studies, concordance rates in schizophrenia were found to range from 60 to 80 percent for identical twins and from 10 to 15 percent for fraternal twins.

More recent studies using a refined methodology have reported substantially lower concordance rates, but they have supported the general conclusion that genetic factors can be significant in schizophrenia. In a major investigation in Norway, for example, Kringlen (1967) found a concordance rate of 38 percent for identical twins as opposed to a rate of 10 percent for fraternal twins. Still lower concordance rates for schizophrenia have been reported in a recent study of psychopathology among almost 16 thousand twin pairs who were veterans of the American armed forces—15.5 percent for identical twins and 4.4 for fraternal twins (Hoffer & Pollin, 1970; Pollin et al., 1969). As in the Norwegian sample, however, the concordance rate for twins with the same genetic makeup was about 3½ times greater than that for other twin pairs.[2] With neurotic disorders, by contrast, the concordance rate for identical twins in this group of veterans was less than 1½ times greater than that for fraternal twins. The investigators interpreted this difference as "evidence for a genetic factor in the pathogenesis of schizophrenia and its relative absence in psychoneu-

rosis." (Pollin et al., 1969, p. 43) Their review of related studies with comparable findings lends strong support to this conclusion, while leaving ample room for debate on the exact extent of genetic influences.

An inherited predisposition to schizophrenia should be thought of not as an "all-or-nothing" factor but rather as a matter of degree. For example, the inheritance of a mild degree of predisposition would lead to schizophrenia only in persons subjected to very unfavorable environments. Moreover, where environmental circumstances differ for twins—as they often do in adulthood—the concordance rate would be expected to decrease, since the environment might be favorable for one and not the other. On the other hand, with a high degree of predisposition, the probability that schizophrenia would occur in both identical twins would increase, since environmental differences would be less important. Even under mildly unfavorable environmental conditions, both twins might show a schizophrenic breakdown. In this context, it is interesting to note that Gottesman and Shields (1966) found that the concordance rate was higher for twins with severe schizophrenic disorders than for those with mild schizophrenic symptoms.

Another line of research has studied the incidence of schizophrenia among children of schizophrenics. A review of the literature led Heston (1970) to report that about 45 percent of the children who have one schizophrenic parent would later become schizoid (borderline) or actual schizophrenics; and the corresponding statistic for children with two schizophrenic parents approached 66 percent. Even more pertinent is the research focusing on the frequency of schizophrenia among adults who were separated from schizophrenic parents in infancy. Two relevant studies, in which frequency of schizophrenia among persons in this category was compared with that among adults who had nonschizophrenic parents but were also raised in foster homes, are

---

[1] For a compilation and integration of research studies related to the dynamics of schizophrenia, the reader is referred to Broen, *Schizophrenia: Research and Theory* (1968), Buss and Buss, eds., *Theories of Schizophrenia* (1969), and Schooler and Feldman, *Experimental Studies of Schizophrenia* (1967).
[2] The marked difference in the actual concordance rates found in the two studies may be partially explained by the fact that the veteran sample, though large, was not representative of the general population, consisting entirely of men who had been considered fit for military service.

those of Heston (1966) and Rosenthal et al. (1968). Their findings provide an additional indication of the influence of genetic factors: about 9 percent of the children of schizophrenic parents became schizophrenic, as opposed to none of the children of nonschizophrenic parents. When the criteria of schizophrenia are expanded to include borderline cases, the frequencies rise to 30 percent and 6 percent, respectively, for the two groups.

In spite of the apparent forcefulness of genetic data in suggesting that a predisposition to schizophrenia can be inherited, a number of issues and problems have been raised. Critics have noted flaws in research designs of early studies; moreover, noting that the closer the genetic relationship among relatives, the closer the social relationship, they have raised the question of whether maladaptive social learning might not account for the tendency of schizophrenia to run in families. As we have noted, physical diseases, such as the vitamin-deficiency disease beriberi, tend to run in families without having a genetic basis. What is apparently "inherited" is the preference for vitamin-poor food—a preference acquired through learning or perhaps through deprivation of certain types of needed foods.

Gregory (1961) has commented on still another puzzling problem—namely, that the "reproductive fitness" of schizophrenics is not greater than 70 percent—mainly because of their diminished heterosexual aggressiveness, the low marriage rate of schizophrenic males, and the diminished fertility of schizophrenic females. Nevertheless, the incidence of schizophrenia continues over time at an apparently constant rate of about 1 percent of the total population. This seeming constancy in the incidence of schizophrenia—despite a lower than normal rate of reproduction among schizophrenics—may mean that the pool of pathological genes is being continually augmented by mutations, or it may mean that some types or cases of schizophrenia do not involve a genetic predisposition.

The picture is further complicated by evidence that a factor in the plasma of schizophrenic mothers is apparently damaging or lethal to the male-determining Y chromosome, although it has little or no effect on the X chromosome (Taylor, 1969). In studying the pregnancies of 54 schizophrenic women who were labeled as schizophre-

nic on the basis of such criteria as hallucinations, delusions, catatonic motor symptoms, and disordered affect and thought disorders, Taylor found that all of the female babies were delivered alive and seemingly healthy. In contrast, among the 20 male babies, 4 were stillborn, 2 died within 4 days of delivery, and 5 others evidenced birth defects. Taylor concluded that the rate of live male births declines if the mothers are psychotic at the time of conception or become psychotic within a month after becoming pregnant. If the psychosis occurs during the second or third month of pregnancy, the male fetus develops abnormally or dies slowly. After this time the fetus is much less likely to be seriously affected by a schizophrenic breakdown on the part of the mother.

Until research more clearly delineates the role of genetic factors in the development of schizophrenia—including possible differential effects for different subtypes—their influence will remain a matter for speculation. This is not to minimize the probable etiological significance of genetic factors, but merely to emphasize that their specific role is at present unknown.

Neurophysiological factors. A good deal of research has focused on the role of neurophysiological disturbances in schizophrenia. These disturbances are thought to include (1) an imbalance in excitatory and inhibitory processes and (2) inappropriate arousal to stress.

1. *Excitatory and inhibitory processes.* This line of investigation goes back to the early work of Pavlov (1941), who suggested that schizophrenics have abnormally excitable nervous systems. A key concept here is that, under intense stimulation, a process of protective ("transmarginal") inhibition occurs, which reduces the person's general level of excitability and reactivity. If the intense stimulation is sustained, however, there is a change in the process of protective inhibition, so that the normal correlation between strength of stimulation and excitation is reversed. Strong stimulation still results in inhibition, but weaker stimulation—below the level needed to produce protective inhibition—will result in cortical excitation. In essence, weak stimuli are now capable of producing the cortical excitation that previously would have been produced only by strong stimuli. Consequently, the individual may have difficulty distinguishing relevant from irrelevant stimuli, and may confuse vague memories, fears, and fantasies with present reality. No longer able in his confusion to distinguish clearly between fact and fantasy, he falls prey to delusions and hallucinations.

More recent advances in brain research have intensified interest in the possibility that imbalances in excitatory and inhibitory processes predispose some people to behavioral disorganization in stressful situations. Such a constitutional imbalance is illustrated to an extreme degree in monkeys, where the process of excitation predominates over that of inhibition—making these animals highly excitable and "unequilibrated" (Voronin, 1962). On the human level, Delgado (1969; 1970) has reported highly interesting results from experiments using electrical stimulation of the brain. One preliminary conclusion has been that

". . . electronic microcircuitry, partly implanted in the brain, can today by remote control bring a schizophrenic patient almost instantaneously from catatonic withdrawal to active, outgoing friendliness and intelligent contact with the surrounding milieu." (1969, p. 1)

Because this is a relatively new research frontier, it is premature to draw any general conclusions from such findings. But if this report is confirmed by further studies and for other types of schizophrenia, it may open up new horizons for understanding and treating schizophrenic disorders.

2. *Arousal and disorganization.* Closely related to the concept of disturbances in excitatory and inhibitory processes is the view that schizophrenia may be related to irregularities in the functioning of the autonomic nervous system, which predispose the individual to "overarousal" or "underarousal" in the face of stress situations.

Fenz and Velner (1970), from a review of the literature and a study of 28 schizophrenic patients and 14 control subjects under conditions of rest and of stress, concluded that:

". . . schizophrenics fall anywhere along the continuum of arousal, although in most cases toward the high or low end of this continuum. In addition, some schizophrenics show marked and sudden shifts in autonomic activity, now being 'overaroused' and now 'underaroused.' A common and basic deficit in all schizophrenics, nevertheless, lies in their inability to modulate effectively or change their level of autonomic

responsiveness to correspond to variations in internal and external stimulation." (p. 27)

Although schizophrenics do vary greatly in degree of arousal, there are some general trends. In situations that represent relatively low stress for normal subjects, arousal tends to be abnormally high in schizophrenics. However, in response to more extreme or more demanding stimulation, schizophrenics' reactivity is often lower than that of normal subjects (Broen, 1968).

An interesting study bearing on the role of arousal in schizophrenia is the longitudinal one by Mednick and McNeil (1968) of 200 children of schizophrenic mothers—a high-risk group for the development of schizophrenia. Preliminary findings presented on 20 children who showed schizoid tendencies indicated that, compared to a group of children who had maintained good adjustment, the disturbed children showed irregularity in autonomic functioning. They did not habituate or adapt to repeated stress; rather, they evidenced increasing irritability. Along with the labile and nonhabituating autonomic arousal of these children, there was a marked tendency for their "associative processes . . . to 'drift away' from the stimulus word (despite repeated instructions and reminders)." (p. 690) Thus, we see evidence of inappropriate arousal to stress even in this young group, as well as a hint of how such a condition may be associated with a breakdown in filtering.

In more recent reports on these children, Mednick (1970; 1971) noted a correlation between autonomic irregularities and serious pregnancy and birth difficulties, which apparently had resulted in damage to the hippocampal region of the brain. This raises a puzzling question, since most schizophrenics do not reveal obvious brain abnormalities. It is interesting to relate Mednick's findings to those of Taylor (1969) on the damaging effect of pregnant schizophrenic mothers on male fetuses, particularly during the early months of pregnancy, in view of the fact that 14 of the 20 children studied by Mednick were males.

A concise answer to the question of just how inappropriate arousal is translated into the breakdown of filtering and the disorganization of thought and affect of the schizophrenic remains to be given. We have noted that both very low and very high levels of arousal are associated with impaired task performance. Thus, some investigators have emphasized that low arousal leads to the unfocused attention, distractibility, and disorganization of the schizophrenic, while others have emphasized the role of high arousal in producing these symptoms. The issue is further complicated, as Lacey (1967) has pointed out, by the fact that high levels of arousal tend to generate homeostatic inhibitory processes (the phenomenon of "protective inhibition" that we noted in the preceding section). This suggests that hyperarousal and decreased activity are not necessarily incompatible. Thus again we are faced with interesting possibilities regarding the role of neurophysiological factors in the dynamics of schizophrenia, but with a need for further research before we can arrive at definitive answers.

Biochemical factors. Research into the possibility of biochemical abnormalities in schizophrenic patients was given impetus when it was shown that profound mental changes can be produced by the presence of some chemical agents in the bloodstream, even in minute amounts. Lysergic acid (LSD) and mescaline, for example, can lead to a temporary disorganization of thought processes and a variety of psychotic-like symptoms that have been referred to as "model psychoses."

Such findings have encouraged investigators to look for an endogenous hallucinogen—a chemical arising within the body under stressful conditions—that might account for the hallucinations and disorganization of thought and affect in schizophrenia and other psychotic disorders. A great deal of enthusiasm was engendered when a Swedish biochemist reported a new test for schizophrenia based on increased levels of *ceruloplasmin* in the bloodstream (Akerfeldt, 1957), but subsequent investigations demonstrated that this condition could be completely explained by a dietary insufficiency of ascorbic acid and was not related to the etiology of schizophrenia (Kety, 1960).

Similar and still continuing interest has centered around *serotonin*, a substance which exists in high concentration in the brain and has been assumed to be an important factor in brain metabolism. The hypothesis that disturbances in serotonin level might lead to mental disturbances was given strong encouragement when the antipsychotic drug *reserpine* was shown to cause a marked and persistent fall in the level of brain serotonin (Shore et al., 1957). Although for a time many investigators questioned the etiological significance of serotonin levels, attention again is being directed to this possibility by the findings of Dement and his associates (Dement, 1968–1969; Dement et al., 1968). Presumably, such changes in serotonin levels result in the intrusion of dreamlike states into wakefulness.

"Some of the features that characterize both dreaming and psychosis may be mentioned for the purpose of illustrating this principle. Thus, *hallucinations or perceptions without a basis in reality* may occur in both conditions. There is often a *sense of depersonalization* in that the self may be observed as though events were happening in the life of someone else. *Time sense may be altered* so that there is a feeling of timelessness—that time has stopped—or that it has speeded up or slowed down. *Feelings or affects are more variable in intensity* than in waking life and *may be*, at times, quite inappropriate to what is going on. Objects or other people often seem to be either incompletely recognized or incompletely represented, and may be involved in episodes that would not occur in normal circumstances. *At times, thinking has a bizarre, fractured quality. Judgment may be partially suspended* so that events which have an aura of strangeness are believed." (Dement et al., 1968, p. 1)

Support for this hypothesis was obtained when the serotonin level in cats was lowered for long periods of time and a "release" of apparent dreamlike phenomena in waking states was observed. However, one difficulty with such a dream interpretation of schizophrenia is that many of the clinical manifestations of schizophrenia seem unlike those in dreams.

Perhaps the most exciting early finding was that made by Heath and his associates at the Tulane Medical School (Heath, 1960; Heath et al., 1957; 1958). Using two volunteers (convicts from the Louisiana State Prison), these investigators were able to produce manifestations of schizophrenia by injecting *taraxein*, a substance obtained from the blood of schizophrenic patients. One subject developed a catatonic type of reaction, the other a paranoid type.

In a series of follow-up studies, taraxein was administered to additional nonpsychotic volunteers, all of whom developed schizophrenic-like symptoms. The characteristic reaction was mental blocking with disorganization and fragmenta-

SCHIZOPHRENIA AND DRUG-INDUCED "PSYCHOSES"

The similarities between the symptoms of schizophrenia and those produced by the psychoto-mimetic drugs (most commonly LSD-25, mescaline, and psilocybin) have led many investigators to speculate that their biochemical bases may be the same. But schizophrenia and drug-induced symptoms differ significantly, not only in many particular respects, but most importantly, in overall pattern.

	SCHIZOPHRENIC REACTIONS	DRUG-INDUCED PSYCHOSES
Mood	Daydreaming and extreme withdrawal from personal contacts, ranging from sullen reluctance to talk to actual muteness.	Dreaming, introspective state, but preference for discussing visions and ruminations with someone.
Communication	Speech vague, ambiguous, difficult to follow; no concern about inability to communicate; past tense common.	Speech rambling or incoherent but usually related to reality; subjects try to communicate thoughts; present tense used.
Irrationality	Great preoccupation with bodily functions; illnesses attributed to unreasonable causes (the devil, "enemies").	Great interest in the vast array of new sensations being experienced; symptoms attributed to reasonable causes.
Hallucinations	Frequent, very "real" hallucinations, usually auditory and extremely threatening; attempts to rationalize them rejected.	Hallucinations predominantly visual; rare auditory hallucinations not so personal or threatening; subjects attempt to explain them rationally.
Delusions	Delusions common, usually of paranoid or grandiose pattern.	Delusions rare; occurrence probably due to individual personality conflicts.
Mannerisms	Bizarre mannerisms, postures, and even waxy flexibility manifested by certain patients.	Strange and bizarre mannerisms rare.

Adapted from Blacker et al. (1968), Himwich (1970), Hollister (1962), and Luby et al. (1962).

tion of thought processes. Many of the subjects became autistic and displayed a lessening of animation in facial expression. Other common symptoms included delusions of reference, persecution, and grandeur; auditory hallucinations; and subjective complaints of depersonalization. The onset of the symptoms was gradual, reaching a peak between 15 and 40 minutes following the injection and then subsiding. In an additional experiment, rapid blood transfusions were made from schizophrenic to normal subjects; the latter developed mild schizophrenic-like symptoms that cleared up within an hour. On the basis of these findings, it was concluded that there is an inherited metabolic defect in schizophrenia that is activated by severe stress.

Similar findings have been made in further studies by these same investigators (Heath et al., 1967), who have concluded that schizophrenia is a disease in which the body manufactures antibodies against its own brain cells. Thus presumably it is an autoimmunic disease, in which the guilty antibody, taraxein, disrupts the passage of information from one cell to another and hence the processing of information. Unfortunately—as in so many biochemical studies—the findings of Heath and his associates have not been generally supported by other investigators, at least in the United States. However, Dearing (1969) has cited Russian research supporting Heath's views of autoimmunological antibodies produced by the human brain under stress.

A number of other recent research reports have provided promising leads to the possible role of biochemical alterations in schizophrenia. Gottleib, Frohman, and Beckett (1969) have cited their own research and research in the Soviet Union that points to a malcontrolled blood protein as being responsible for a disruption of information processing in the brain. And finally, Himwich's studies have led him to conclude (1970) that schizophrenics are "biologically different," and consequently they convert certain chemicals in their bodies into psychotogenic (psychosis-producing) agents when placed under stress. These presumed biochemical aberrations are usually considered to be based on hereditary factors.

On the basis of interviews with 68 chronic schizophrenic patients who were in remission, Brooks, Deane, and Hugel (1968) concluded that the subjective experience of schizophrenia is often similar to the mental states produced by hallucinogenic drugs such as LSD. This finding is consistent with the view that biochemical alterations play a part in at least some schizophrenic disorders. Thus far, however, there is no conclusive evidence that the basic etiological pattern in schizophrenia can be explained in terms of biochemical irregularities.

Sleep loss and lowered adaptive energy. In 1896, White gave the following picture of the effects of extreme sleep deprivation.

"One sort of treatment used for those accused of witchcraft was the 'tortura insomniae.' Under this practice, these half-crazed creatures were prevented, night after night and day after day, from sleeping or even resting. In this way temporary delusion became chronic insanity, mild cases became violent, torture and death ensued. . . ." (White, 1896, II, p. 119)[1]

Although White was describing the effects of prolonged sleep loss on people who presumably were already mentally disturbed, such deprivation has long been considered a form of torture.

Later investigators have also suggested a relationship between schizophrenic reactions and sleep loss. Under conditions of extreme sleep deprivation, normal subjects have shown psychopathological changes including irritability, visual hallucinations, dissociative states, and paranoid thinking. Presumably, metabolic changes associated with sleep loss may afford a neurophysiological setting favorable to the development of psychosis in predisposed persons. Bliss, Clark, and West (1959) noted that sleep-deprived subjects were more sensitive to the hallucinogenic effects of lysergic acid and that some acute schizophrenic reactions were seemingly precipitated by loss of sleep. Additional evidence for this hypothesis was provided by Koranyi and Lehmann (1960), who subjected 6 schizophrenic subjects to sleep deprivation and observed that progressive mental deterioration occurred after 72 hours. In

fact, 5 of the 6 subjects again manifested their earlier acute symptoms.

In attempting to explain these findings, Luby et al. (1962) pointed out that under the stress of prolonged sleep deprivation there is an initial increase in energy output followed, after about 100 hours, by a decrease. This decrease is accompanied by a marked decline in emotional reactivity and an inability to marshal energy resources. Since the processing of external sensory input involves greater effort than attention to internal input, the sleep-deprived subject is likely to react predominantly to internal stimuli, such as fantasies. As a consequence, he tends to lose contact with reality and to show a disorganization of thought processes. One implication is that sleep loss resulting from emotional conflicts might lessen the individual's adjustive resources to the point where a stress he could normally withstand would become overwhelming. Here it may be noted that Feinberg et al. (1969) reported an average reduction of 50 percent in Stage 4 (deep) sleep for schizophrenics—Stage 4 sleep being considered essential for normal rest and psychological functioning. However, these investigators have noted that the sleep loss may be linked to the psychosis itself and result from anxiety and high arousal.

Other investigators have also pointed to an alleged *deficiency in adaptation energy*, which may reduce the schizophrenic's resources for coping with stress. Some investigators have viewed this alleged deficiency as an inherited constitutional characteristic, while others have supported the concept of a "general adaptation syndrome" that runs its course from alarm through resistance to final exhaustion (Beckett et al., 1963; Luby et al., 1962; Rubin, 1962). Eventually, the adrenal glands may stop putting out the hormones needed by the organism for adapting to stress, in which case behavioral disorganization would result. A study of corticosteroid excretion during acute schizophrenic episodes showed that corticosteroid levels far exceeded the elevations seen in normal subjects under stress (Sachar et al., 1970). Such episodes presumably place a heavy strain on the adrenal glands, but as Hoagland pointed out in a similar

[1]From: *A History of the Warfare of Science with Theology in Christendom* by Andrew D. White. Copyright 1896, D. Appleton and Company.

context in 1954, "Our findings do not prove that the adrenal abnormalities cause the psychosis; they may be the result of it." (p. 76) The same conclusion would still appear to hold.

Although the metabolic effects of sleep loss and lowered adaptation energy—and their inter-actions—cannot be ignored, they appear to be one group of possible contributing factors rather than primary etiological agents. It has been demonstrated that drugs, fever, and other stresses that lower adaptive resources may also precipitate schizophrenic or other psychotic disorders in marginally adjusted individuals.

In summarizing the role of biological factors in schizophrenia, we may reiterate that although the data indicate that various neurophysiological and biochemical processes are altered in schizophrenia, the etiological significance of these changes remains to be clarified. The weeks and months of acute turmoil that ordinarily precede hospitalization are likely to affect nutrition, sleep, activity patterns, and the entire metabolic functioning of the individual. In addition, few changes appear to be specific to schizophrenia. For example, many schizophrenic patients have been shown to have altered adrenocortical functioning, unusual amounts of protein in their cerebrospinal fluid and blood plasma, disturbances in enzyme activity, and so on, but these changes are by no means unique to schizophrenia. Nor do they characterize all schizophrenics; in fact, such changes may range from hypofunction to hyperfunction.

In 1956 Horwitt alluded to claims of biological anomalies in schizophrenia as follows:

"Year after year, papers appear which purport to distinguish between the state of schizophrenia and that of normalcy. The sum total of the differences reported would make the schizophrenic patient a sorry physical specimen indeed: his liver, brain, kidney, and circulatory functions are impaired; he is deficient in practically every vitamin; his hormones are out of balance, and his enzymes are askew. Fortunately many of these claims of metabolic abnormality are forgotten in time . . . but it seems that each new generation . . . has to be indoctrinated—or disillusioned—without benefit of the experiences of its predecessors." (p. 429)

It still seems useful to exercise caution in assessing the findings and claims of investigators concerning the role of biological factors in schizo-phrenia. It would certainly appear that they play an important etiological role, but whether they are primary causes of schizophrenia or only secondary effects of it is difficult to ascertain.

PSYCHOLOGICAL AND INTERPERSONAL FACTORS

Laing (1967b) has observed:

"The experience and behavior that are labelled schizophrenic are a special sort of strategy that a person invents in order to live in an unlivable world. He cannot make a move . . . without being beset by contradictory pressures both internally, from himself, and externally, from those around him. He is in a position of checkmate." (p. 56)

This viewpoint contrasts sharply with that in which schizophrenia is held to be a biological condition that involves brain pathology, for here the schizophrenic is seen as an individual who escapes from an unbearable world and seemingly unsolvable conflicts by altering his inner representation of reality. Although biological factors may complicate the clinical picture, the origins of the disorder are held to be psychosocial in nature.

In this section we shall deal with the psychological and interpersonal factors that appear particularly relevant to the etiology of schizophrenia. This will lead us to a consideration of: (1) early psychic trauma and deprivation, (2) pathogenic family patterns, (3) faulty learning and self-structure, (4) excessive stress and decompensation, (5) extreme defenses, and (6) reinforcing social roles and vicious circles.

Early psychic trauma and deprivation. Investigators have placed strong emphasis on the early traumatic experiences of children who later became schizophrenics. Wahl (1956) found that 41 percent of 568 male schizophrenic patients in the U.S. Navy had lost a parent (usually the father) through death, divorce, or separation before they had reached the age of 15, and that 18 percent had lost both parents before that age. These figures are approximately 4 times higher than those for the general population.

Often early traumatic experiences occur outside the family. The child may be rejected, made fun of, and beaten up by members of his peer group; he may be subjected to sexual traumas that leave him guilt-ridden and devaluated; he may suffer painful injuries or illnesses requiring hospitalization and separation from his family; he may lack adequate food and other necessities of life. Bettelheim (1955) cited the case of a boy who was rejected by his mother and placed in an orphanage. Here he never learned the names of any of the other boys but referred to them as "big guys" and "little guys"—he lived in a terrifying world of shadowy figures who had the power to beat him up and hurt him without reason.

In a pioneering study of the psychoses of children and adolescents, Yerbury and Newell emphasized the total lack of security in human relationships, the severely disturbed home life, the beatings and brutal treatment that many of the children had experienced, and the hatred many of them bore their parents. They found that of the 56 psychotic cases,

"Ten of them had been shocked by the deaths of parents to whom they had retained infantile attachments. Four children were so disoriented upon learning of their adoption that they could not reconcile themselves to the true situation. Four children had lived with mentally ill mothers who were finally hospitalized. Sex traumas were reported in 14 cases of children who were overwhelmed with guilt and fear regarding masturbation. Four boys had been seduced and exploited by homosexuals. Three children were horrified by incest in the home, and three girls had become pregnant. Five girls were obsessed with imaginary pregnancy, having had no sex instruction except from other girls. Six children had been tormented, beaten, tied, and confined by their companions so that they were terrified in the company of children, and felt safe only with adults." (1943, p. 605)

In contrast to a control group of normal children who had, for the most part, led happy and well-organized lives and whose problems centered around school difficulties and social strivings, the psychotic children experienced conflicts centering around violent interpersonal relationships and sex experiences.

Early traumatic experiences can be particularly important in the etiology of schizophrenia when they are part of an overall picture of childhood deprivation. Karl Menninger has provided a vivid picture of the defenses—and special vulnerabilities—of children who have suffered deep hurts

and have thus come to view the world as a dangerous and hostile place.

"Children injured in this way are apt to develop certain defenses. They cover up, as the slang expression puts it. They deny the injury which they have experienced or the pain which they are suffering. They erect a façade or front, 'All's well with me,' they seem to say. 'I am one of the fellows; I am just like everybody else. I am a normal person.' And indeed they act like normal persons, as much as they can. They go to the same schools, they complete the same work, they seek the same goals, they do the same things that all the rest of us do. Often they are noticeable only for a certain reticence, shyness, perhaps slight eccentricity. Just as often, they are not conspicuous at all. . . .

"What is underneath that front? One might say that the same sort of thing goes on in the emotional life that goes on when an abscess slowly develops beneath the surface of the body, for example in the lungs or in the liver. There has been an injury, an infection. Counteracting processes have been set up so that tenseness and pressure and potential pain are gathering. But all of this is concealed from the outsider. There is intense conflict and tension and anxiety and strong feelings of bitterness, resentment and hate toward those very people with whom the external relationships may be so perfectly normal. 'I hate them! They don't treat me right. They will never love me and I will never love them. I hate them and I could kill them all! But I must not let them know all this. I must cover it up, because they might read my thoughts and then they wouldn't like me and wouldn't be nice to me.'

"All this is covered up as long as possible—by trivial conversation, pleasant greetings, chat about the movies or the picnic and the next date, and the rest of the ordinary things of adolescent or early adult life. For the chief problem in the person who is going to develop what we call schizophrenia is, 'How can I control the bitterness and hatred I feel because of the unendurable sorrow and disappointment that life has brought to me?' His efforts to control it often show themselves in various kinds of withdrawal, lonewolfishness, seclusiveness, even mild suspiciousness, or just a quiet going of one's own way with disinterest in active social participation.

". . . the regimen under which they live has much to do with their successful adaptation. Given certain new stresses, the façade may break down and the underlying bitterness and conflict may break through. . . ." (1948, pp. 101–104)

Withdrawal from a dangerous world is not the only pattern that may emerge from early trauma.

In some instances, the outcome seems to be what Arieti (1959) calls a "stormy" personality. Here the individual, instead of withdrawing, tries aggressively to relate to people and to find a meaningful life. He is highly vulnerable to hurt, however, and his existence is usually an anxious one. Often his life is a series of crises, precipitated by minor setbacks and hurts which he magnifies out of all proportion. In other instances, the child develops a pattern of rebellion and somewhat disorganized paranoid ideation involving pathological lying, incorrigibility, unbridled aggression, running away, and various types of delinquent behavior.

Two additional considerations appear relevant here. First, in the light of what we noted earlier about the necessity of certain types of stimulation during early critical periods for achieving normal intellectual, emotional, and social development, there may be a critical period during early life for self-differentiation and integration—for getting the self-structure under way. When this period has passed without normal growth taking place—as a result, for example, of early trauma and deprivation—it may be exceedingly difficult to correct the damage. Second, although most children who undergo such experiences do show residual effects in later life, most of them do not become schizophrenics, and, conversely, not all schizophrenics undergo such traumatic childhood experiences (Offord & Cross, 1969). Thus, we must consider early trauma and deprivation as only two among many interactional factors that may contribute to schizophrenia or other mental disorders in later life.

Pathogenic family patterns. A number of studies focusing on interactions in schizophrenic families have pointed to such factors as (1) "schizophrenogenic" mothers and fathers, (2) marital schism and marital skew, (3) pseudo-mutuality and role distortion, (4) faulty communication, and (5) the undermining of personal authenticity. Such terms as *marital schism* and *pseudo-mutuality* will be clarified in the course of our discussion.

Although we shall begin with a consideration of the role of "schizophrenogenic" mothers and fathers in the etiology of schizophrenia, it may be emphasized that the direction of research has shifted from the parents to total family interaction. In dealing with pathogenic family patterns, our focus will be on factors that may pave the way for schizophrenic episodes under excessive stress.

1. *"Schizophrenogenic" mothers and fathers.* Many studies have been made of the parents of schizophrenics—particularly the mothers of male patients. Typically, these mothers have been characterized as rejecting, dominating, cold, overprotective, and impervious to the feelings and needs of others. While verbally such a mother may seem accepting, basically she rejects the child. At the same time, she depends on him rather than the father for her emotional satisfactions and feelings of completeness as a woman. Perhaps for this reason she tends to dominate, possessively overprotect, and smother the child—keeping him dependent on her. Often combined with this behavior are rigid, moralistic attitudes toward sex that make her react with horror to any evidence of sexual impulses on the child's part. In many instances the mother is overtly seductive in physical

FOLIE A DEUX

A relatively neglected phenomenon in the functional psychoses is that of *folie a deux*—a form of psychological "contagion" in which one person copies and incorporates into his own personality structure the delusions and other psychotic patterns of another person. Familial relationships between individuals in 103 cases studied by Gralnick (1942) fell within one of the following four categories:

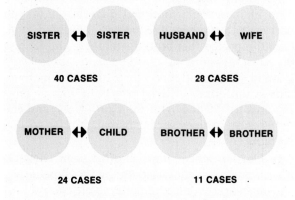

SISTER ◆▶ SISTER	HUSBAND ◆▶ WIFE
40 CASES	28 CASES
MOTHER ◆▶ CHILD	BROTHER ◆▶ BROTHER
24 CASES	11 CASES

Gralnick emphasized the following explanatory factors, all environmental: (1) length of association, (2) dominance-submission, (3) type of familial relationship, (4) prepsychotic personality, and (5) homosexual desires. The high incidence in the husband-wife category is particularly striking since common heredity would play no part as an etiological factor in these cases.

contacts with her son, thus augmenting his sexual conflicts. In general, the mother-son relationship in schizophrenia appears to foster immaturity and anxiety in the youth—depriving him of a clear-cut sense of his own identity, distorting his views of himself and his world, and causing him to suffer from pervasive feelings of inadequacy and helplessness.

Although the "schizophrenogenic" mother has long been a favorite target of investigators, the fathers have not come through unscathed—especially in regard to schizophrenic daughters. Available studies have typically revealed a somewhat inadequate, indifferent, or passive father who appears detached and humorless—a man who rivals the mother in his insensitivity to others' feelings and needs. Often, too, he appears to be rejecting toward his son and seductive toward his daughter. At the same time, he is often highly contemptuous and derogatory toward his wife, thus making it clear that his daughter is more important to him. This treatment of the wife tends to force her into competition with her daughter, and it devaluates her as a model for her daughter's development as a woman. In fact, the daughter may come to despise herself for any resemblance to her mother. Against this background, the daughter often moves into adolescence feeling an incestuous attachment to her father, which creates severe inner conflict and may eventually prove terrifying to her.

As might be expected, studies have shown a high incidence of emotional disturbance on the part of both mothers and fathers. Kaufman et al. (1960) reported that both the mothers and fathers of 80 schizophrenic children and adolescents studied were emotionally disturbed. The mothers almost uniformly utilized psychotic-like defense patterns in dealing with their problems, and the fathers also utilized seriously maladaptive coping patterns.[1]

2. *Marital schism and marital skew.* Several investigators have focused on the incompatibility and maladaptive marital patterns of parents, and the effects of these patterns on the children. In an early study of 71 male schizophrenics, Gerard and Siegel (1950) found open discord between the parents in 87 percent of the cases, compared with 13 percent in a control group of normal subjects.

Of particular interest here is the pioneering work of Lidz and his associates (1957; 1958), who

studied a group of 14 families with schizophrenic offspring. They failed to find a single family that was reasonably well integrated. Eight of the 14 couples lived in a state of severe chronic discord in which the continuation of the marriage was constantly threatened—a condition the investigators called *marital schism*. A particularly malignant feature of these families was the chronic undermining of the worth of one marital partner by the other, which made it clear to the children that the parents did not respect or value each other. Each parent expressed fear that the child would resemble the other parent, and a child's resemblance to one parent was a source of concern and rejection by the other parent. The other 6 couples in this study had achieved a state of equilibrium in which the continuation of the marriage was not constantly threatened but in which the relationship was maintained at the expense of a basic distortion in family relationships—a pattern referred to as *marital skew*.

In some of the 14 families the serious psychopathology of one parent dominated the home; in others, the parents shared in their pathological outlook. There was a tendency for the wives to dominate the family and to relegate the husbands to an ineffectual role; in a minority of families, however, the husband was dominant to a pathological degree and demonstrated insatiable needs for admiration and indulgence. In over half the cases, at least one parent was an ambulatory schizophrenic or was clearly paranoid. Still others were chronic alcoholics, severe obsessives, or passive-dependent "children" of their spouses. The fathers were considered as pathological as the mothers. The investigators concluded that in these families there was a great deal of irrationality and distortion of reality—that the net effect on the child was to "provide training in irrationality."

In further studies of these and additional families with a schizophrenic offspring, Fleck (1960) and Lidz et al. (1963) also emphasized the finding that male schizophrenics usually came from skewed families with a passive, ineffectual father and a disturbed, engulfing mother. Such a father failed to provide the son with a positive role

[1]This picture of the parents of schizophrenics is based largely on Alanen (1958, 1968), Beck (1960), Fleck et al. (1963), Garmezy et al. (1961), Lidz (1968), Mishler and Waxler (1968), Rodnick (1968), Rosenthal and Kety (1968), and Wynne (1968).

model for guiding his development as a male—leaving the son somewhat undifferentiated from and dependent on the engulfing mother, with his problems further augmented by incestuous attachments. On the other hand, schizophrenic girls typically came from schismatic families with an unempathic and emotionally distant mother and a narcissistic father who was often paranoid. Such a father was often seductive toward the daughter but contemptuous of his wife and disparaging of women in general. The daughter thus lacked a mother with whom she could identify or to whom she could go for help, while being subjected to the father's confusing combination of seductiveness and disparagement of women. It was observed that children growing up in such families tended to break down during young adulthood, when a sense of identity is essential for a more independent social role outside the family. To illustrate the effect of such family pathology in the transmission of irrationality and even in the learning of particular symptoms, Fleck cited the following case:

"[The patient] came to us from another hospital, to which he had been admitted following a serious suicide attempt. Although relatively compliant and cooperative at first, he soon became increasingly resistant to hospital routines, spoke less and less with anybody, neglected his appearance, grew a beard, and would not allow his hair to be cut, so that long locks soon framed his shoulders. Being unusually tall, he not only looked like the Messiah but was indeed preoccupied with strange mystical religions—seemingly of his own invention. As if this appearance were not bizarre enough in the setting of an unbelievably messy room in which he hoarded food, a typical daily scene showed him almost naked, sitting on his toilet, studying stock quotations in the *Wall Street Journal*. . . .

"As we began to learn about the family background, it became clear that the patient conducted his hospital life in the same autocratic, pompous, and captious manner in which the father had governed the parental household. [The father] was an ingenious and successful foreign-born manufacturer, but at home he ruled his roost like an Eastern potentate, a role for which he also claimed divine sanction and inspiration via a special mystical cult that he shared only with a very few select friends. The patient would permit only a chosen few of the staff into his sanctum, just as the father had secluded himself in his bedroom during most of the time that he spent at home, with only his wife and the children's governess permitted to enter and attend to

his needs. [The father], successful inventor and merchant, would sit there in his underclothes reading religious books by the hour. The entire household participated in the religious rites, the mother sharing his beliefs completely and continuing to do so even after his death, which according to the cult meant continuing life in a different form; the widow did not dare to disavow his teachings, because she believed he would know of it.

"More than imitation and caricaturization of the father's behavior was involved. Both the patient and his only sister were emotionally deprived children who were isolated from the parents *and* from the surrounding community because the family milieu was so aberrant." (1960, pp. 337–338)

As Fleck pointed out, this case provides a striking example of the way in which the irrationality of family relationships may come to pervade the entire family, as well as indicating the deviant patterns the child may learn in trying to adjust in such a setting. To live satisfactorily outside the family, he would have had to learn a whole new set of adjustive patterns.

The extent to which such irrational family patterns may go is also well illustrated in a report by Anthony (1968). In this family

". . . a father with paranoid schizophrenia turned his home into a beleaguered fortress in which the family mounted watches against the enemy, and weapon training was rigorously enforced. A great deal of secrecy prevailed, and no one was allowed to come and go without an examination of credentials. A child who went out shopping was closely interrogated on his return. One of the children complained bitterly that he even had to report before going to the bathroom." (p. 307)

Such a family setting would certainly provide a distorted view of one's world and more than adequate training in irrationality—conditions that Anthony referred to as "developmental precursors of adult schizophrenia."

3. Pseudo-mutuality and role distortion. Wynne et al. (1958) studied families of schizophrenics from the standpoint of interpersonal relationships, and found that such relationships often had the appearance of being mutual, understanding, and open, but in fact were not—a condition they termed *pseudo-mutuality*. They also found considerable rigidity in the family role structure, which tended to depersonalize the child and block his growth toward maturity and self-direction.

Similarly, Bowen (1959; 1960), studying the backgrounds of 12 schizophrenics, noted the "striking emotional distance" between the parents in all of the studies. He referred to the emotional barrier as having the characteristics of an "emotional divorce." Although the parents in such families often maintained a façade of love—for example, making a big drama out of giving each other presents at Christmas—there was an underlying withdrawal accompanied by severe disappointment and often hostility. The patient's function had often been that of an unsuccessful mediator between the parents. In the case of the male patients, however, the most common pattern was an intense association between mother and son which excluded the father. Bowen also noted that, as the years passed, the son was threatened by signs of the mother's aging or by other characteristics that might prevent her from being the strong person upon whom he was dependent, while the mother was threatened by any signs of personality growth that might prevent the son from remaining "her baby."

Pseudo-mutuality seems related to a variety of role distortions in schizophrenic families. Stabenau et al. (1965) found that such families were characterized by the assignment of inflexible and simplified roles to each member. Brodey has extended this analogy, using a model based on the theater.

"The family drama is unlike the modern theatre. It is more like the morality play of medieval times. Actors take allegorical role positions that are stereotyped and confined—one is Good; another, Evil; a third, Temptation." (1959, p. 382)

Summarizing the data on some 50 schizophrenic families, Rosenbaum (1961) has suggested that the rigid and inflexible roles played by the family members permit a facade of continuing relatedness with each other and with the world, and make the business of living seemingly understandable and controllable. But in these families the roles provided for the child are destructive to his personality growth.

4. *Faulty communication and cognition.* Bateson (1959; 1960) has pointed to the conflicting and confusing nature of communications among members of schizophrenic families. As we noted in Chapter 6, he used the term *double-bind* to describe the effect of such transactions. Here the parent presents to the child ideas, feelings, and demands that are mutually incompatible. For example, the mother may be verbally loving and accepting but emotionally anxious and rejecting; or she may complain about the child's lack of affection but freeze up or punish him when he approaches her affectionately. As Anthony (1968) has described it, "At one moment they [the children] are pulled into intimate closeness and at the next thrust far away with bitter and unjustified recrimination." (p. 307) The mother subtly but effectively prohibits comment on such paradoxes, and the father is too weak and ineffectual to intervene. In essence, a child is continually placed in situations where he cannot win. He becomes increasingly anxious and unable to organize his thinking; presumably, such disorganized and contradictory communications in the family come to be reflected in the thought processes of the schizophrenic.

Singer and Wynne (1963; 1965a; 1965b) have linked the thought disorders in schizophrenia to two styles of thinking and communication in the family—*amorphous* and *fragmented*. The amorphous pattern is characterized by failure in differentiation; here, attention toward feelings, objects, or persons is loosely organized, vague, and drifting. Fragmented thinking involves greater differentiation but lowered integration, with erratic and disruptive shifts in communication. A more recent study is that of Feinsilver (1970), who found supporting evidence for such amorphous and fragmented thinking in the impaired ability of members of schizophrenic families to describe essential attributes of common household objects to each other. And Bannister (1971) has found that schizophrenic thinking tends to be even more "loose" and disordered when the individual is dealing with persons and interpersonal relationships than when he is dealing with objects.

Lidz (1968) has characterized the parents of schizophrenics as deficient tutors who create a family milieu inappropriate for training the child in the linguistic abilities essential for categorizing experience, thinking coherently, and communicating meaningfully. Similarly, Wynne (1968) has emphasized deficiencies in the cognitive style of the schizophrenic—that is, in the way he attends to, categorizes, and responds to incoming stimuli—and to the detrimental effect of this cognitive style on his communications and interactions.

Despite difficulties in research methodology—for example, limited samples and inability to clearly delineate the variables under investigation—there would appear to be a considerable body of evidence pointing to the role of the family in fostering faulty learning, thinking, and communication patterns in children who later become schizophrenics.

5. *Undermining personal authenticity.* The philosopher Martin Buber (1957) pointed out that a confirmation of each person's authenticity is essential to normal interpersonal relationships.

"In human society at all its levels, persons confirm one another in a practical way, to some extent or other, in their personal qualities and capacities, and a society may be termed human in the measure to which its members confirm one another. . . ." (p. 101)

Such confirmation apparently is often denied the schizophrenic. Haley (1959; 1960) has noted that members of schizophrenic families, when they interact, are not consistent with what they themselves say, and continually disqualify each other's statements. Margaret Singer (1961) also has found disqualifying communications in her analysis of families having a schizophrenic member.

Such disconfirming communications subtly and persistently mutilate the self-concepts of other family members—and particularly the child's. This pattern has been well described by Laing and Esterson (1964):

"The characteristic family pattern that has emerged from the study of families of schizophrenics does not so much involve a child who is subject to outright neglect or even to obvious trauma, but a child whose authenticity has been subject to subtle, but persistent, mutilation, often quite unwittingly. . . . (p. 91)

As we noted in Chapter 3, Laing considers the ultimate of this mutilation process as occurring when

". . . no matter how [a person] feels or how he acts, no matter what meaning he gives his situation, his feelings are denuded of validity, his acts are stripped of their motives, intentions, and consequences, the situation is robbed of its meaning for him, so that he is totally mystified and alienated." (Laing & Esterson, 1964, pp. 135–136)

This denial of confirmation may help explain the failure of the individual who later becomes schizophrenic to maintain his motivation to communicate and interact with his social milieu.

In concluding our consideration of pathogenic family patterns, we may note that a number of investigators have emphasized the fact that most parents of schizophrenic children have other children who are not schizophrenic. The specific effects of these patterns, as noted previously, depend on the constitutional makeup of the child, the nature and extent of the pathology, and other factors in the child's life situation. In this respect, Lidz et al. (1963) found that siblings of schizophrenics who made reasonably good adjustments tended to use two defensive maneuvers: (a) a "flight from the family," where the defense mechanism of isolation helped them to keep from facing the full extent of the intrafamilial difficulties; and (b) a "constriction of life activities" to situations where they could adjust adequately.

There is also the point that most families evidencing pathogenic characteristics do not raise children who later become schizophrenic; thus, few investigators would maintain that all cases of schizophrenia are rooted in pathogenic family interactions. In assessing the relative contribution of genetic and family factors in schizophrenia, Eisenberg (1968) has hypothesized that (a) some family environments are so healthy and growth-producing that schizophrenia would rarely occur except in the presence of a marked genetic predisposition; (b) some family environments are so traumatic in their effects on the offspring that schizophrenia may occur with a minimal genetic loading or possibly even in the absence of any genetic predisposition; and (c) in average families the occurrence of schizophrenic episodes is usually caused by a combination of stress factors and genetic predisposition.

Faulty learning and self-structure. Early psychic trauma and pathogenic family patterns tend to produce specific vulnerabilities and faulty learning. In general, the results may be described as:

1. Feelings of rigid control by parents, of strong dependence on them, and of being rejected by them

2. An inaccurate and distorted frame of reference, with faulty assumptions concerning reality, possibility, and value
3. Inadequate cognitive, interpersonal, communicative, and other competencies needed for coping with the problems of everyday living
4. Serious problems in handling sexual desires, hostility, and interpersonal relationships, as well as vulnerabilities associated with early trauma
5. A confused and poorly differentiated self-concept, with a tendency to place great value on being a "good girl" or a "good boy"

The following summary of Adolf Meyer's conclusions concerning the personality makeup of the preschizophrenic serves to illustrate this basic pattern.

The individual who later develops schizophrenia usually manifests an early withdrawal from a world he interprets as frustrating and hostile. This withdrawal is often concealed behind what seems to be an exemplary childhood, but which on closer examination reveals adherence to meekness and formally good behavior in order to avoid fights and struggles. Instead of participating in an active and healthy way in the activities of childhood, the individual withdraws behind a facade of goodness and meekness. This withdrawal, of course, inevitably leads to failures and disappointments which in turn serve to encourage further withdrawal from the world of reality and foster the use of fantasy satisfactions to compensate for real life failures.

As this "good" child enters the adolescent period, he tends to be overly serious, painfully self-conscious, inhibited, and prone to prefer his own company. Often he is unduly preoccupied with various religious and philosophical issues. Normal interest in the opposite sex is lacking, and vivid ideas of the evilness of sexual behavior are usually only too apparent. As the adolescent enters the period of adulthood, with its demands for independence, responsibility, and family relationships, the youth's lack of adequate socialization and preparation for meeting these problems proves fatal. Instead of increased effort and a vigorous attack on the problems associated with assuming adult status, the youth finds the world unbearably hurtful and turns progressively inward to fantasy satisfactions. (Based on Christian, 1936; Lief, 1948)

The pattern described by Meyer does not characterize all cases of schizophrenia, but it does illustrate the background out of which many cases develop.

The basic assumptions of the preschizophrenic, although usually growing out of limited and atypical experiences, tend to be perpetuated and to shape his perceptions and actions. In the sexual sphere his problems are often complicated by highly moralistic attitudes toward sex and a failure to develop normal heterosexuality. Often he has had few, if any, close contacts with the other sex (it is not unusual to find schizophrenics over 30 in age who have had few or no dates). Because of his sexual immaturity, the schizophrenic's sexual fantasies, like the early adolescent's, may have a wide range of sexual objects, including members of his own sex. Such fantasies typically lead to severe conflicts and self-devaluation.

In a similar way, the problem of handling hostility is a particularly difficult one for the "good" individual, because he usually considers hostility as immoral and dangerous. As a consequence of his withdrawal from normal social participation, he typically lacks any adequate comprehension of the role of hostility in normal everyday social relations. The hostility generated by feelings of hurt and frustration is often more than he can bear; he feels guilty and devaluated by his hostility toward family members or other persons, and does not know how to express his hostility in socially acceptable ways; and at the same time, he tends to be completely upset if he is the object of other people's hostility.

Typically, the preschizophrenic has a poorly differentiated and confused self-concept and is prone to have distorted, fantasy-ridden assumptions about himself. His extreme dependence on parental dictates denies him the experience of self-direction and feelings of control over his own destiny, and he does not experience himself as an active agent in his own behavior. It is not surprising, therefore, that he often feels that his thoughts and actions are alien to him and controlled by others. Planansky and Johnston (1962) have emphasized this point with respect to homosexual fantasies among male schizophrenics: "The perplexity which so typically accompanies homosexual preoccupation reveals that the patients perceive their alleged homosexuality as something alien; as if something unwanted, undesirable, and above all, not under their control was happening to them." (p. 613)

The tendency of the preschizophrenic to withdraw from social participation does not reduce his need or desire for social approval, status, and love; it only reduces his chances of gratifying these desires by preventing him from acquiring essential social competencies. So he finds it increasingly difficult to establish satisfying marital and other interpersonal relationships and tends to have serious difficulties in social adjustment. Ruesch, Brodsky, and Fischer (1963), reporting on a study of 89 schizophrenics treated at the Langley Porter Clinic, concluded: "Most of these patients have been socially inadequate, have had strained human relationships, and have had difficulties in holding jobs, belonging to a group, or pursuing a vocation or profession." (p. 203)

Although different investigators have emphasized the significance of different psychological and interpersonal factors in the etiology of schizophrenia, a review of the relevant literature shows an overall pattern of faulty development that typically involves "abnormalities in basic human functions of learning and remembering, perception and cognition, language and communication, and the capacity to form meaningful interpersonal relationships and positive social attitudes." (Rubinstein and Coelho, 1970, p. 519) Most studies to date, however, have been more descriptive than explanatory. As Bannister (1971) has pointed out, "We will eventually have to develop a theory of what makes all people march before we can say very much about why some people march to a different drummer." (p. 84)

Extreme defenses. In the acute schizophrenic episode, as we have seen, the clinical picture is dominated by the massive breakdown of filtering, the individual's panic at the loss of control over his thoughts and feelings, and his desperate attempts to understand his experience. Thus, he may ask such questions as "Am I going crazy?" "Shall I fight it?" "Shall I try it?" "Who is doing this to me?" "Do I have a mission?" As yet he has not developed defenses to cope with his situation, but he cannot continue indefinitely in this state of panic, anxiety, and confusion. His acute schizophrenic episode either clears up eventually, or various extreme defenses—including extreme withdrawal and the reinterpretation of experience—may come into operation.

One major defense of the schizophrenic commonly seems to be a *global avoidance* reaction to overwhelming stimulation. As Freeman (1960) has pointed out:

". . . there is a strong reaction against the disintegration of the ego. It would appear as if the patient is attempting to recover his capacity for stabilized thinking, motility and perception by insulating himself against stimulation from the environment. This would account for the reluctance and resentment which many patients show when invited to undertake activities or make human contacts. It is as if they feel themselves to be in a state of overstimulation and their desire is to reduce this to manageable proportions." (p. 935)

Patterns of avoidance may be quite variable. The individual may sit in a corner with his head averted, or he may seek stimulation that tends to mask out inner thoughts and confusion. As one schizophrenic reported concerning the suturing of a wound in her scalp, "In fact I rather liked it. There was something clean and definite about that slight pain, so much more desirable than the dull confusion *inside* my head." (Hillyer, 1926, p. 95) Transistor radios playing music may be held against the ear "to shut out voices"; and with milder levels of distress—induced by drug therapy—watching television may provide sufficiently intense stimulation to screen out distracting stimuli while not proving disorganizing. In their attempts to reduce stimulation, however, it seems that schizophrenics are in a quandary. If they restrict input too much, they lose relevant information, but if they attempt to monitor their environment as normal persons do, they run the risk of being overwhelmed by input.

Schizophrenic behavior often seems to reflect the exaggerated use of various ego-defense mechanisms. Emotional blunting and distortion protect the individual from the hurt of disappointment and frustration. Regression enables him to lower his level of aspiration and accept a position of dependence. Projection helps him maintain some semblance of ego integrity by placing the blame for his difficulties on others and attributing his own unacceptable desires to them. Preoccupation with some obsessional theme may help him screen out other stimuli and problems. Wish-fulfilling fantasies enable him to achieve some measure of compensation for feelings of frustration and self-devaluation.

Exaggerated use of such defense mechanisms as projection and fantasy appears particularly likely to lead to delusions and hallucinations, which not only represent the breakdown of organized perception and thought processes, but also—as part of the schizophrenic reorganization of reality—may have marked defensive value. Delusions of influence enable the individual to blame others for causing his own inadmissible thoughts and behavior. Fantasies of being the focus of widespread interest and attention help him compensate for feelings of isolation and lack of social recognition and status. Delusions of persecution explain away his failure to achieve a satisfactory adjustment in the real world. Delusions of grandeur and omnipotence may grow out of simple wishful thinking, and may help him counteract feelings of inferiority and inadequacy.

Hallucinations may also represent the projection of unacceptable desires or be an outgrowth of wishful thinking. Thus the schizophrenic may hallucinate the voices of his enemies encouraging him to engage in immoral sexual behavior; or he may hallucinate sexual relations. Some schizophrenics hallucinate conversations in which they hear God confer great powers on them and assign them the mission of saving the world. They may be entrusted to solve problems of justice, settle international conflicts, or bring a new code of morality to the world.

If we assume that these defensive maneuvers represent a method of adjusting to an unbearably dangerous and hurtful world, it is not surprising that they are directed more toward avoiding further struggle and frustration than toward achievement and need gratification (Garmezy, 1966; Rodnick, 1968). Thus, numerous investigators have placed strong emphasis on the role of regression to more primitive levels of behavior as more highly differentiated and reality-oriented patterns give way. According to the psychoanalytic model, "secondary" thought processes, which follow the rules of logic and take external reality into consideration, are replaced by "primary" thought processes, which involve illogical ideas, fantasy, and magical thinking. Presumably, such primary thought processes characterize the thinking of children. The child lives in a world that is partly fantasy and partly real, and develops all manner of fantastic notions about things and events around him. He talks to imaginary playmates, personifies inanimate objects, and attributes various powers to these figments of his imagination. Not uncommonly, he feels that he is the center of the world and develops ideas of his omnipotence.

The regressed schizophrenic does not, however, perceive, think, and feel in ways precisely like those of a child. For example, the child, unlike the schizophrenic, can usually distinguish between his fantasies and the world of reality, and most children, despite their fantasies, imperfect logic, and lack of perspective, are clearly not schizophrenic. Thus, it would appear that regression in schizophrenia does not represent a return to childhood, but rather a defensive pattern that enables the individual to assume a position of dependency and hence avoid problems and responsibilities that he perceives as overwhelming.

Here it should be emphasized that schizophrenic reactions appear to represent a total defensive strategy rather than a conglomeration of individual defenses. In essence, the schizophrenic withdraws from the real world and evolves a system of defenses that enables him to distort and "reshape" aversive experiences so that he can assimilate them without further self-devaluation. Even though this new defensive system may be highly illogical and far from satisfactory, it relieves much of his inner tension and anxiety and protects him from complete psychological disintegration.

Excessive stress and decompensation. The actual schizophrenic breakdown may be precipitated by increased stress during adolescence and young adulthood or by stresses occurring later in life. Often the precipitating stress is not apparent to others, because it stems from the individual's subjective appraisal of a situation rather than from objectively observable stress factors.

1. *Stress vulnerability.* It is particularly in coping with the ordinary problems of adolescence and young adulthood that the inadequate and confused individual seems to get into serious difficulties. Will (1959) described the stress situation this way:

"There comes a time . . . (later adolescence and young adulthood) . . . at which one must declare himself; he must identify himself as a person apart from his family, establish intimacy with a friend or face loneliness,

SCHIZOPHRENIC WRITINGS

The personality decompensation in psychotic reactions is frequently manifested in the content and form of patients' letters and other spontaneous writings. These examples clearly reveal the "loosening" and deviations of thought, the distortion of affect, and the lowered contact with reality so common among schizophrenics.

The typed postcard is a reproduction of a card sent by a paranoid schizophrenic.

The handwritten excerpts are from a letter written by an 18-year-old girl, also diagnosed as a paranoid schizophrenic. As is apparent from the first and last parts of the letter, shown here, the handwriting is of two quite different types, suggestive of the writer's emotional conflict and personality disorganization. Lewinson (1940) included this letter in her study of handwriting characteristics of different types of psychotics. Among psychotics generally, she found that handwriting typically showed abnormal rhythmic disturbances, with rigidity or extreme irregularity in height, breadth, or depth.

```
To:  The football department and its members present and future
     The University of New Mexico, Albuquerque, N. M.

I depend on correct, honest supplementation of this card by telep-
athy as a thing which will make clear the meaning of this card.
There exists a Playing of The Great Things, the correct, the con-
structive, world or universe politics, out-in-the-open telepathy,
etc. According to the Great Things this playing is the most
feasible thing of all; but it is held from newspaper advertising
and correct, honest public world recognition, its next step, by
telepathic forces (it seems), physical dangers, and lack of money.
Over 10,000 cards and letters on this subject have been sent to
prominent groups and persons all over the world. Correct, honest
contact with the honest, out-in-the-open world. This line of
thought, talk, etc. rule. The plain and frank. Strangers. The
Great Things and opposites idea. References: In the telepathic
world the correct playings. Please save this card for a history
record since it is rare and important for history.
```

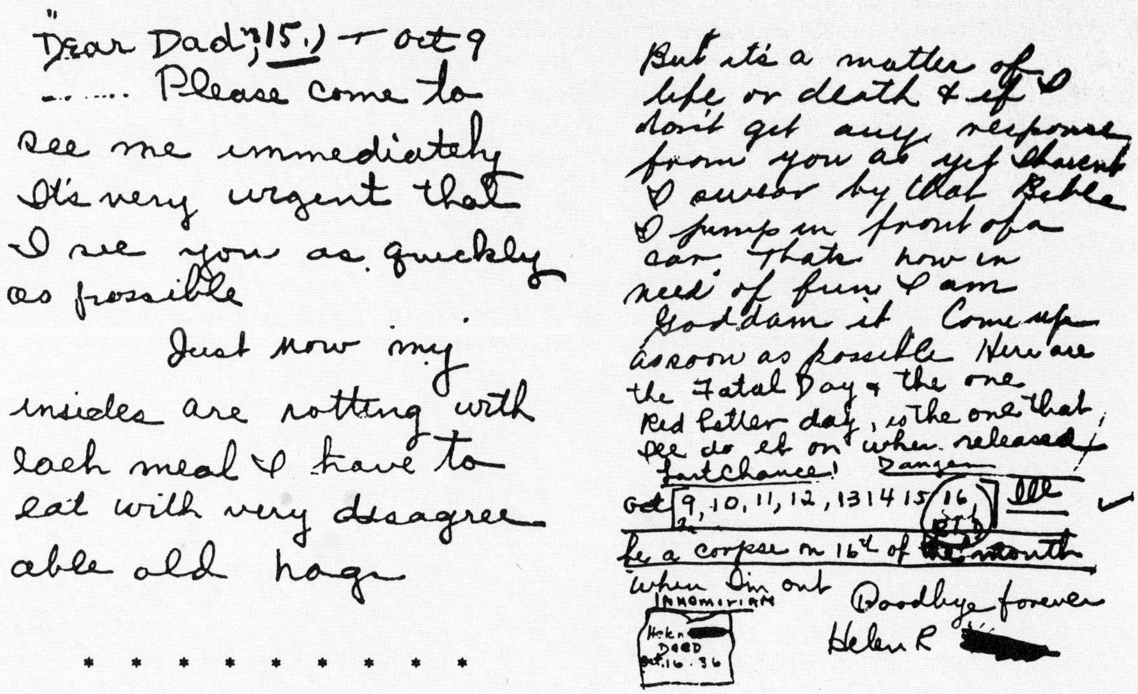

"Dear Dad (15.) ~ oct 9
.... Please come to
see me immediately
It's very urgent that
I see you as quickly
as possible

        Just now my
insides are rotting with
each meal & I have to
eat with very disagree-
able old hags

*   *   *   *   *   *   *   *

But it's a matter of
life or death & if I
don't get any response
from you as yet I haven't
I swear by that Bible
I jump in front of a
car. That now in
need of fun I am
Goddam it Come up
as soon as possible Here are
the Fatal Day & the one
Red Letter day, is the one that,
see do it on when released
last chance! Danger
Oct 9, 10, 11, 12, 13 14 15 16
be a corpse on 16th of the month
when I'm out Goodbye forever
                    Helen R

pattern his sexual behavior, and consider such matters as further formal education, marriage, work, and life in a community. All of these activities require increased self-identification, the ability to relate, and the revelation of self to others. The move toward intimacy involves increasing anxiety; the failure to make the move brings loneliness and the threat of unrelatedness. The extreme of either course is panic and the feeling of impending, if not actual, dissolution and death. Many of the phenomena observable during the development of this disorder reflect efforts to escape the intolerables of anxiety and aloneness." (1959, p. 217)

A strong dependence on significant others tends to make the preschizophrenic particularly vulnerable to disturbances in interpersonal relationships. Thus the loss of a protective mother or even the lack of a good relationship with a supervisor at work may prove overwhelming. Aronson and Polgar (1962) reported on 13 soldiers who had served at least one year in the army before experiencing schizophrenic episodes. These soldiers had shown adequate and sometimes outstanding work performances so long as their supervisors made them feel accepted and demanded behavior in accordance with group norms—thus providing support and setting limits. But when the relationship was disrupted by the transfer of the soldier or by the appointment of a new supervisor who failed to provide support and impose rigid behavior expectations, the soldier developed an acute schizophrenic breakdown.

Finally, the preschizophrenic is confronted with the crucial problem of meaning (Burton, 1960; Becker, 1962). He is deeply confused about who he is, what sort of world he lives in, and what an appropriate life pattern for him would be. It is common to hear a schizophrenic ask such questions as "Who am I?" "What is the meaning of it all?" and "Is there any future?" Typically, he feels alone and overwhelmed by a complex and hostile world he does not understand—a world that seems to provide no meaning, hope, or incentive. The following excerpts from Curry's description of a 29-year-old female schizophrenic illustrate this picture:

"She seemed to have a different conception and experiencing of time (hopelessly entangled in the past) and of social space (tremendous gaps between individ-

uals). Quite often she would describe her feelings of 'hopelessness,' 'emptiness,' 'the void,' and a general kind of despair and futurelessness.

"Hilda gave the impression of being crowded, squeezed into a very tiny corner of a universe, and fighting off oblivion. During our initial meeting, she lashed out angrily with questions of 'what' and 'how,' speculating rapidly and illogically.

"The world of this woman was a wasteland, a battlefield where the wreckage of interpersonal wars pressed her into isolation and suffocation. 'It is as if I'm a girl alone in an attic, with no air to breathe.' . . . [there] was only threat in her world—each human was at war with each other human. She could not get beyond this. Even in her intimate relations with men, there had been nothing: a tearfulness devoid of love and care.

"The structure of her existence was threat—impending attack, destruction. There was no orientation toward the future. . . . Each moment was but each moment, and like the first, long ago, filled with only emptiness. . . . In her distorted world there was only past, because she had had it; no future, because she could not make it. . . . What we called 'her psychosis' was her particular being-in-the-world, in all its pain and unauthenticity: a flight from true existence, a corruption of care. Gradually, she seemed to no longer need this world, having transcended it to, what she termed, 'beauty with eyes open.'" (1962, pp. 129–130, 133–135)

2. *Sequence of decompensation.* The immediate sequence of decompensation leading to the schizophrenic breakdown has been described by Bowers (1968) in terms of the following four steps.

a) *The setting.* Although patients often state initially that their psychotic reaction came "out of the blue," questioning usually reveals a state of mind characterized by conflict and despair.

"Such phrases as, 'I had nowhere to turn,' 'There was no way out,' were common. Often the basic emotional state was one of overwhelming guilt and dread as a crucial maturational step was confronted but retreated from. Life-threatening conflict was perceived, but neither 'flight' nor 'fight' seemed possible." (p. 349)

As might be expected, oscillations in mood and anxiety are typically manifested.

b) *Destructuring of perception and affect.* Frequently the incipient psychotic progresses from a state of impasse to one of heightened awareness. Perceptions and thoughts come in faster than they can be assimilated, and, as we have

In these paintings of cats by the English artist Louis Wain, there is a transition from realistic and recognizable portraits to representations that become increasingly more stylized and ornamental—so bizarre and abstract that they bear little resemblance to their subjects. Wain's art is remarkable for the clues it provides to his changing mental state and the distortions of perception characteristic of schizophrenia. An eccentric bachelor, Wain had become well known for his paintings of cats before experiencing a schizophrenic breakdown in middle life. He stuck with his chosen subject during this schizophrenic episode and also during subsequent relapses.

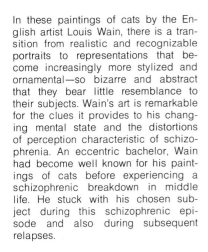

noted, there appears to be a breakdown in information-filtering mechanisms. Not only is there heightened awareness of experience, but incoming information is qualitatively altered.

"Things seem to have hidden meanings, neutral individuals are suddenly animated with strange ideas and designs, curious connections between feelings and perceptions are experienced. Categories of relevance, normally capable of sifting experience automatically, are broadened. Everything experienced is measured as to its possible relevance for the individual. Most nonpsychotic individuals can recall times of acute crisis in which every sound, every newcomer was processed intrapsychically with regard to his relevance for the crisis at hand. This phenomenon can be seen teleologically as serving a useful function, for at times of mortal danger (real or imagined), the entire organism is geared to scrutinize the perceptual field." (p. 350)

Unfortunately for the prepsychotic individual, this process of scrutiny seems to get out of hand. The individual experiences a tremendous "press for meaning," which may lead to delusions of reference and influence.

c) *Destructuring of the sense of self.* Almost without exception, heightened awareness gives way to a fragmentation of experience and a progressive loss of the sense of self—to identity dissolution. The following excerpt from the account of a 26-year-old medical student who had been hospitalized for 3 weeks as a result of an acute schizophrenic episode describes how this experience feels.

[Describing the first day of hospitalization] "I had the idea that I didn't know who I was and I had to find out. I kept looking at the patients in my room to find out which one I looked like. I saw the bad side of each of them and became convinced this was the side I was similar to. I tried on other people's clothes. I said to myself, 'If his clothes fit you then you must be like him.' The next morning I felt OK, I knew I was [name], that I was a doctor in training, so I put on a white coat." (p. 352)

In an ongoing schizophrenic episode, the inner turmoil and confusion and loss of the sense of self can lead to dramatic and bizarre behavior as the individual desperately strives to answer the question "Who am I?" and regain his self-identity.

d) *Formation of delusions.* The foregoing steps would indicate that the development of delusions is a logical outcome of the individual's breakdown of filtering mechanisms, altered sensory influx, loss of sense of self, and pressure for some explanation of what is happening to him. The following excerpts are from the report of a young Ph.D. in psychology who was a third-year medical student at the time of his schizophrenic episode. He had been experiencing the haunting notion that he could not breathe and that there was something very wrong with him. The night prior to this episode had been fear-ridden, and he had slept little.

"I got up at 7 AM, dressed, and drove to the hospital. I felt my breathing trouble might be due to an old heart lesion. I had been told when I was young that I had a small ventricular septal defect. I decided that I was in heart failure and that people felt I wasn't strong enough to accept this, so they weren't telling me. *I thought about all the things that had happened recently and could be interpreted in that light.* I looked up heart failure in a textbook and found that the section had been removed, so I concluded someone had removed it to protect me. *I remembered other comments.* A friend had talked about a 'walkie talkie,' and the thought occurred to me that I might be getting medicine without my knowledge, perhaps by radio. I remembered someone talking about a one-way plane ticket; to me that meant a trip to Houston and a heart operation. I remembered an unusual smell in the lab and thought that might be due to the medicine they were giving me in secret. I began to think I might have a machine inside of me which secreted medicine into my blood stream. And I reasoned that I had a disease no one could tell me about and was getting medicine for it secretly. At this point, I panicked and tried to run away, but the attendant in the parking lot seemed to be making a sign to motion me back. . . . A custodian's eyes attracted my attention, they were especially large

and piercing. He looked very powerful. He seemed to be 'in on it,' maybe he was giving medicine in some way. Then I began to have the feeling that other people were watching me. And, as periodically happened throughout the early stages, *I said to myself that the whole thing was absurd, but when I looked again the people really were watching me* . . . I felt that comments made in the elevator pertained to me. One patient said, 'They have full strength medicine around here.' I thought maybe the heart medicine I was being given was morphine and that I might get addicted. . . . Conversations had hidden meanings. *When someone told me later that I was delusional, though, I seemed to know it. But I was really groping to understand what was going on. There was a sequence with my delusions: first panic, then groping, then elation at having found out. Involvement with the delusions would fade in and out. One moment I would feel I certainly didn't believe these things, then, without realizing it, I would be caught up in them again.* . . ." (p. 353)

Of course, the degree of decompensation may vary markedly, depending on the severity of stress and the makeup of the individual. However, the preceding steps help clarify the course that such decompensation commonly takes in schizophrenic reactions.

Reinforcing social roles and vicious circles. Social role behavior has been tied into the etiology and course of schizophrenic reactions in several different ways. A factor emphasized by Cameron and Margaret (1949; 1951) in their intensive studies of schizophrenic patients was the schizophrenic's failure to learn appropriate role-taking behavior. Thus, inflexible in his own role behavior and uncomprehending of the role behavior of others, he does not know how to interact appropriately with them.

Laing (1969; 1971) has carried this view of role behavior a step further—to the schizophrenic's creation of his own social role to protect himself from disturbing reality. Thus, he dons the "mask of insanity" as a social role as well as a barricade. Behind this "false self" and often turbulent façade, however, the real person—the "inner self" —remains. In his hidden world, despite his outward role of madness, the schizophrenic's hopes and aspirations may remain very much intact. Thus, Laing thinks treatment should focus less on removing "symptoms" than on finding a path to this remote and often inaccessible sanctuary.

A third view of social role behavior in schizophrenia places emphasis on the learning of the schizophrenic role. Normal people presumably emit indications of disturbed thinking, whose nature and degree can be influenced by environmental instructions and reinforcements. In fact, Levitz and Ullmann (1969) were able to produce indications of disturbed thinking in normal subjects; and they speculated whether an experimental group of normal subjects could be made to evidence disturbances in thinking that would require "incarceration." Of course, such manipulation of individuals is unethical and not to be considered. These investigators, however, remarked that conditions eliciting schizophrenic behavior in everyday life might include the following: (1) when the person has some knowledge of schizophrenic behavior or the schizophrenic role, (2) when this role provides the individual with a means of avoiding some highly aversive life situation, and (3) when the role behavior is consistently reinforced not only by the alleviation of aversive experience but by the labeling and expectations of others. In regard to the latter point, we have noted that being labeled a schizophrenic and provided with a "sick" role may markedly influence the subsequent course of the disorder.

Finally, it may be noted that the impaired learning and role behavior of the schizophrenic not only leads to faulty coping behavior but also to vicious circles. In commenting on the child who is raised in a family where the social roles bear little resemblance to those in the "outside world," Carson (1969, p. 251) has stated:

"A child growing up in a family of this kind will have conceptions of the real and the decent that are different from those of the larger culture, and as he moves out into the larger culture, his 'autistic' ways will shortly be noted and will generate punitive and rejecting responses from others. Ignorant of the reasons for this harsh treatment, such a person becomes increasingly frightened, perplexed, and confused. His attempts to achieve cognitive clarity, limited as they are by his peculiar modes of thought, only increase his estrangement from the reality of others."

As time goes on, the individual's faulty frame of reference and inadequate competencies may lead to an ever widening breach between him and others, and his language and thought patterns may become progressively more individualistic. As Overstreet has described it, he becomes "an emotional stranger in a strange land, with his own inner problems and conflicts dictating what he sees in the world around him. . . ." (1954, p. 83) To complete the vicious circle comes the terrifying realization that he is "losing his mind"—that he has lost control over his inner thoughts and feelings—followed by hospitalization and being labeled a schizophrenic.

GENERAL SOCIOCULTURAL FACTORS

Schizophrenia occurs in all societies, from the aborigines of the Australian Western desert to the most technologically developed countries. However, the incidence rate, as well as the clinical picture, may vary considerably from one society to another. As Al-Issa (1969) has pointed out, some symptoms appear to be more heavily influenced by cultural factors than others. Disorders of thought and affect are common to schizophrenia the world over, but delusions of persecution or grandeur may be relatively specific to given cultures. In a study of 60 West African students who were hospitalized with a diagnosis of schizophrenia, Copeland (1968) found delusions of persecution almost without exception—usually relating to poison or magic—and he also noted a very high incidence of grandiose delusions.

Carothers (1953; 1959) has pointed out that while the overall incidence of functional psychosis appears to be considerably lower among African tribal groups than among Americans or Europeans, schizophrenia is proportionately higher. Interestingly enough, the paranoid type, which is the most frequent in the United States, is uncommon in these tribal groups. More common is the hebephrenic type, a fact Carothers attributed to the lack of well-developed ego-defense mechanisms among African natives; thus, when decompensation does occur, a complete disorganization of the personality is more likely. Similarly, Field (1960) described the initial schizophrenic breakdown among natives in rural Ghana as typically involving a state of panic. It was observed that when the individual was brought to a shrine quickly for treatment, he usually calmed down and in a few days appeared recovered. But when there was considerable delay before he reached the shrine, he presented a classical hebephrenic picture. It seems likely that this clinical picture will change as rural Africans are exposed increasingly to urban living and Western civilization.

Apparently the incidence of schizophrenia in primitive societies varies considerably. While it appears proportionately high among rural Africans, it was found to be quite low among the aborigines of Formosa (Rin & Lin, 1962). In more technologically advanced societies the rates also vary, but overall they are relatively high (Dearing, 1969; Kramer, 1969; Murphy, 1968). From his studies in a variety of cultures, Murphy (1968) concluded that schizophrenia is commonly precipitated by "a problem or choice which affects the individual deeply; pressure by the community or culture to make some choice; contradictions or confusion in the guidance which the culture provides; chronicity in the sense that the problem persists until a decision is taken." (p. 152)

Murphy summarized the evidence with respect to social class within our own society as follows:

"There is a truly remarkable volume of research literature demonstrating an especially high rate of schizophrenia . . . in the lowest social class or classes . . . of moderately large to large cities throughout much of the Western world. It is not altogether clear what is the direction of causality in this relationship—whether the conditions of life of the lowest social classes are conducive to the development of schizophrenia, or schizophrenia leads to a decline in social class position—but present evidence would make it seem probable that some substantial part of the phenomenon results from lower class conditions of life being conducive to schizophrenia." (p. 152)

There is no hard evidence to support Murphy's hypothesis, but apparently the social disorganization, insecurity, poverty, and harshness characteristic of urban slums intensify personal problems and tend to increase the likelihood of both psychotic and neurotic disorders.

A number of early studies emphasized a high incidence of schizophrenia among certain ethnic groups in our society. Kimmich (1960) found that approximately 50 percent of the Japanese and Filipino first admissions to mental hospitals in Hawaii were diagnosed as schizophrenics—an incidence that was proportionately much higher than that among Hawaiian and Caucasian first admissions. Most of the Japanese patients were of the paranoid type, showing outward conformity but powerful inner rebellion. Similarly,

Vitols (1961) and other investigators pointed to a proportionately higher incidence of Negro than white first admissions with schizophrenia in certain southern states as well as New York State. When socioeconomic conditions are taken into consideration, however, the ethnic differences would not appear to be significant (American Orthopsychiatric Association, 1969; Fischer, 1969). Nor are the clinical pictures in schizophrenia significantly different for black Americans, Mexican Americans, and Anglo Americans, when social class, education, and related factors are equated (Fabrega et al., 1968).

In his Texas study, Jaco (1960) found a lower incidence of schizophrenia among professional men than among unskilled or semiskilled men. Women in professional and semiprofessional occupations, on the other hand, showed a very high rate of schizophrenia—as well as other types of functional psychoses. It seems probable that the preceding pattern has changed over the past decade as women have achieved more equality in terms of rates of pay, opportunities for promotion, and related considerations; research data, however, are lacking in this area.

In concluding our discussion of etiological factors in schizophrenia, we should stress the fact that research on the causation of human behavior is, as Shakow (1969) notes, "fiendishly complex" even with normal subjects.

"Research with disturbed human beings is even more so, particularly with those with whom it is difficult to communicate, among them schizophrenics. The marked range of schizophrenia, the marked variance within the range and within the individual, the variety of shapes that the psychosis takes, and both the excessive and compensatory behaviors that characterize it, all reflect this special complexity. Recent years have seen the complication further enhanced by the use of a great variety of therapeutic devices, such as drugs, that alter both the physiological and psychological nature of the organism. Research with schizophrenics, therefore, calls for awareness not only of the factors creating variance in normal human beings, but also of the many additional sources of variance this form of psychosis introduces." (Shakow, 1969, p. 618)

In general, it appears that there is no one clinical entity or causal sequence in schizophrenia. Rather, we seem to be dealing with several types

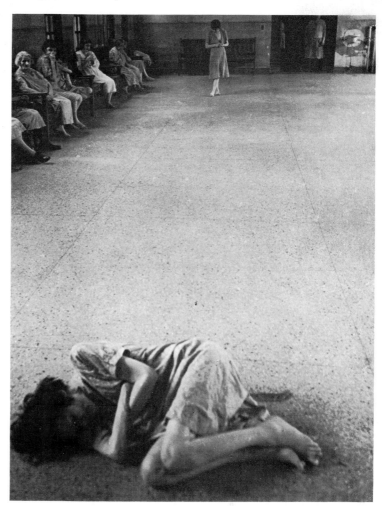

For schizophrenics today, the outlook is considerably brighter than it was for the patients in this mental hospital ward in 1947; therefore, this kind of custodial scene, with its apathetic and withdrawn patients, is less frequently encountered now than formerly. Being hospitalized, however, still results in some patients' adopting a "sick role" which impedes their chances for recovery. They tend to join the sick community and to view themselves as incompetent, like the other persons with whom they reside. In short, they fall prey to the "hospitalization syndrome," a concept we shall elaborate on in Chapter 20.

of maladaptive reactions resulting from an interaction of factors—biological, psychological, and sociocultural—whose roles vary according to the given case and clinical picture. Often this interaction appears to involve a vicious spiral, in which life stresses trigger metabolic changes that impair brain functioning. The latter, in turn, appears to intensify anxiety and panic as the individual realizes he is losing control. And so the spiral continues until more permanent defensive patterns are established, treatment is undertaken, or the disorder has run its course.

Again it may be emphasized that the label of *schizophrenic* and the sick role that goes with it not only are likely to influence the individual's perception of himself but his subsequent behavior as well. Moreover, since hospitalization disrupts the individual's established life situation and interpersonal patterns, the clinical picture in any given case may be markedly influenced by treatment conditions that are not a part of the basic disorder.

TREATMENT AND OUTCOMES

Until quite recent times, the prognosis for schizophrenia was generally unfavorable. Under the routine custodial treatment in large hospital settings, the rate of discharge approximated only 30 percent.

Sommer and Osmond (1962) used the term "schizophrenic no-society" to refer to such chronic mental hospital wards. "Long-stay wards are inhabited by ghostly figures, who like the crew of the *Flying Dutchman*, are able to walk through one another without leaving a trace." (p. 244) These investigators noted that in 1883 Sir Francis Galton made a similar observation.

"There is yet a third peculiarity of the insane which is almost universal, that of gloomy segregation. Passengers nearing London by the Great Western Railway must have frequently remarked upon the unusual appearance of the crowd of lunatics who take their exercise in the large green enclosures in front of the Hanwell Asylum. They almost all, without exception, walk apart in moody isolation, each in his own way, buried in his own thoughts." (1883, p. 67)

For most schizophrenics, the outlook is now not nearly so dark. Improvement in their dismal picture was to come with dramatic suddenness when the phenothiazines—major tranquilizing drugs—were introduced in the 1950's. Chemotherapy, together with other modern treatment methods, permits some 50 percent or more of schizophrenic patients to be treated in outpatient clinics; and a schizophrenic who enters a hospital for the first time has an 80- to 90-percent chance of being discharged within a matter of weeks or, at most, months. However, the rate of readmission is still extremely high, with 45 percent of all discharged patients being readmitted during the first year after release. From an overall point of view, about one third of schizophrenic patients recover; another third show partial recovery; and a final third remain largely or totally disabled (Yolles, 1967).

At present, mental hospitals appear to be conducting two parallel treatment programs (Zubowicz, 1969). The *first* concerns the newly admitted acutely schizophrenic patient whose family and community ties are still relatively intact. Most of these patients respond rapidly to treatment and can be discharged within 20 to 60 days. Caffey, Gallbrecht, and Klett (1971) have noted that the greatest reduction in symptoms occurs within the first 3 weeks, and that patients discharged at this time are just as well off as those who remain in the hospital longer, provided they receive adequate aftercare. The *second* program is devoted to more severe and chronic cases, whose family and community ties have been disrupted and whose post-hospitalization careers—if they recover sufficiently to leave the hospital—usually continue in sheltered environments, such as halfway houses.

Chemotherapy. Modern drugs—tranquilizers and energizers—have proven to be of great benefit in the treatment of schizophrenic patients. Commonly used drugs are (1) phenothiazines, such as chlorpromazine, which are used to control excitement, agitation, and thought disorders; (2) antidepressants, which are used to increase alertness and interest and to elevate mood; and (3) antianxiety drugs, which are used to decrease apprehension and tension and to promote sleep. These drugs are frequently used in combination with each other and in some instances with electroshock therapy. Additional drugs may also be used to counteract the possible side effects of the phenothiazines. In the overall treatment and follow-up program, the phenothiazines are usually used for periods of months or even years, while the antidepressant and antianxiety drugs are usually used only for a short period of time and then intermittently during periods of special stress.

Acute schizophrenic patients respond readily to drug treatment, showing a rapid alleviation of symptoms. The more severe and chronic patient responds more slowly, but his delusions and hallucinations are gradually eliminated or reduced to a point where he is no longer upset by them. For example, in paranoid schizophrenic reactions, the patient loses interest in his persecutors and begins to take more interest in his environment. "Voices" that have been a source of torment to him may still be heard but do not bother him anymore. Grinspoon et al. (1968, p. 1651) described one patient who "still heard voices while receiving thordiazine, but he no longer shouted at them or did cartwheels in response to their commands." And, as we have noted, chemo-

IS THERE A SCHIZOPHRENIC RESIDUAL?

Evidence that a schizophrenic residual may persist after recovery or during periods of remission is provided by Strauss' study (1969) of a woman who had been severely delusional during a schizophrenic episode. When first interviewed by a therapist after her breakdown, she had stood at attention, feeling that the devil willed her to do so; she had also thought that the devil was trying to get her to do bad things. A follow-up study made a year after recovery showed that the woman no longer felt that the devil was trying to influence her. However, in response to one card of the Rorschach test—in which the subject is asked to interpret the shapes in an inkblot—"she was startled to see the face of a malevolent devil commanding someone to do something." Strauss concluded that although the subject had apparently gone from schizophrenic to normal in terms of becoming free of delusions, a residual of her delusional ideas was still with her.

therapy enables some 50 percent or more of schizophrenics to be treated in outpatient clinics, and thus remain in their family and community settings.

Ideally, of course, treatment programs in schizophrenia involve much more than chemotherapy, for an individual whose symptoms have been relieved by drugs may still remain schizophrenic in his basic makeup. Some investigators have reported that drug therapy actually appears to be detrimental for certain patients—particularly acute cases with good premorbid adjustment (that is, a good record of adjustment before onset of the disorder)—possibly making it less likely that such patients will work through their inner conflicts and achieve better personality integration (Goldstein et al., 1969; Goldstein, Rodnick & Judd, 1971). Whatever its limitations, however, modern chemotherapy has clearly improved both the immediate and long-range outlook for most schizophrenics.

Psychosocial approaches to treatment. Advances in chemotherapy have been accompanied by the development of various new psychosocial treatment approaches, aimed at modifying the personality and behavioral patterns of the schizophrenic and at providing him with a favorable climate for recovery. One widely used new approach is *milieu therapy*. Here, the entire hospital is regarded as a therapeutic community, and the emphasis is on a normal and meaningful world in which the patients participate in the regulation of their activities. Self-reliance and the formation of socially acceptable interpersonal relationships are encouraged, and a climate is provided that permits reality testing and fosters personal growth (Paul, 1969; Zubowicz, 1969). A more recent innovation has been to place entire wards on "token economy" programs, where individual responsibility and social interaction are rewarded by tokens that the patients can exchange for cold drinks and other things they want (Atthowe & Krasner, 1968; Ayllon & Azrin, 1965; Paul, 1969). In both of these treatment programs, patients have shown a marked improvement in initiative, responsibility, and social interaction.

Various forms of psychotherapy have been utilized in an attempt to help the schizophrenic correct distorted attitudes, develop needed social competencies, and achieve a more clear-cut sense

---

CONDITIONS ASSOCIATED WITH FAVORABLE OUTCOMES IN THE TREATMENT OF SCHIZOPHRENIA

In general, the following conditions are associated with favorable outcomes in schizophrenia. To the extent that conditions are the *reverse* of those described, the likelihood of recurrent episodes or of chronic schizophrenia becomes correspondingly greater.

1. Reactive rather than process schizophrenia, in which the time from onset to full-blown symptoms is 6 months or less

2. Clear-cut precipitating stresses

3. Adequate heterosexual adjustment prior to schizophrenic episode

4. Good social and work adjustment prior to schizophrenic episode

5. Minimal pathogenic factors in family background

6. Involvement of depression or other schizo-affective pattern

7. Favorable life situation to which to return and adequate aftercare in the community

Based on Caffey, Galbrecht, and Klett (1971), Fenz and Velner (1970), Stephens, Astrup, and Mangrum (1966), Turner, Dopkeen, and Labreche (1970), and Yolles (1967).

---

of personal identity. Generally, psychoanalysis and other forms of individual psychotherapy have not proven effective in schizophrenia. Rutner and Bugle (1969) have, however, reported the successful elimination of hallucinations in a schizophrenic patient by means of behavior therapy, although the role of conditioning techniques in the treatment of individual cases remains to be clarified. In fact, Bandura (1969) has concluded that schizophrenia can be more effectively treated in a group or social systems context than on an individual level. This conclusion is supported by the finding that group psychotherapy—which has been extensively used—helps provide the patient with a safe environment in which to test reality and develop understanding and competence in role playing and interpersonal behavior.

Sociotherapy—directed toward coping with family crises, alleviating pathogenic family conditions, and helping the patient make an adequate adjustment in the community—is receiving increasing emphasis as a crucial part of the overall treatment program. As we have noted, this approach may involve therapy for the entire family unit. In essence, the trend is toward making the mental hospital—if the patient requires hospitalization—and the family and community setting

SCHIZOPHRENIA: "DESPERATE STRATEGY OF LIBERATION" . . .

"Insane Liberation is the name of a group formed this year in New York City to combat what members say is the oppressive treatment of the mentally ill by many psychologists and psychiatrists and by society as a whole. Founders of the group claim their illnesses are really inner revolts against an inhuman society and that many members of the psychotherapeutic professions are, in effect, allied with the society in taking an authoritarian and moralistic attitude toward mental illness. The group calls for a new kind of therapy: open interaction between human beings in community 'freakout centers' where no one would have authority over another." (Gilluly, 1971, p. 335)

The movement Gilluly describes clearly shows the influence of —even though its implied activism is uncharacteristic of—R. D. Laing. Regarding individual "madness" as but a reflection of the madness of society, Laing has referred to the schizophrenic breakdown as a "desperate strategy of liberation within the micro-social situation in which [the individual] finds himself." An acute schizophrenic episode, in this context, is sometimes simply "the sudden removal of the veil of the false self which had been serving to maintain an outer behavioral normality that may long ago have failed to be any reflection of the state of affairs of the secret self"; and the experience may represent an opportunity for a person to begin to heal the division between his true and false selves.

To anyone holding this view, it is catastrophic for a schizophrenic to be subjected to traditional therapeutic techniques, including drug therapy, for these techniques seem directed merely at restoring the status quo between his true and false selves. Although they may produce outward compliance, they deny the validity and acceptability of the individual's inner self's accusations and aspirations. Consequently, therapists using these traditional techniques are accused of dehumanizing the individual by labeling his behavior as "crazy" rather than trying to understand his way of experiencing reality and his disturbed behavior, and they are criticized for denying the individual the opportunity to work through the split which has deformed his life.

What Laing feels is needed in the way of therapy—and what the Insane Liberation group has sounded a battle cry for—is the encouragement and guidance of the individual in his exploration of the "inner time and space" into which psychosis has plunged him. A new therapeutic setting is required, one in which the movement of the acute schizophrenic episode is followed, rather than arrested, and the relationship between therapist and patient is two-sided and interpersonal. With a group of associates, Laing attempted to provide such a setting for his model of therapy at Kingsley Hall in

London's East End. From 1965 to 1970, when the lease expired, Kingsley Hall was occupied by therapists and patients. The usual occupancy was 14 persons, and the greater number of persons coming there for assistance were diagnosed as schizophrenics. At Kingsley Hall, where Laing lived for more than a year, there was the ultimate breakdown of the therapist-patient role system of the mental institution; and behavior that could not be tolerated in most clinic facilities made heavy but eventually tolerable demands on the group.

In the story of Mary Barnes, a resident of Kingsley Hall during the five years of its operation, can be found a concrete example of what Laing is proposing as an alternative to hospitalization. The problems associated with providing such therapy also are suggested. Miss Barnes described her experience to James S. Gordon in 1970, and excerpts from Gordon's account are on the facing page. According to Gordon, Mary's experience "is crucial to Laing's model of therapy in the same way that Freud's early hysterical patients were to psychoanalysis. It is quite unlikely that it could have taken place anywhere but Kingsley Hall, and even there a great strain was felt by the other inhabitants. . . ." (Gordon, 1971, p. 62)

Centers modeled after the Kingsley Hall experiment in psychotherapy and communal living have been established in the United States as well as in England, and there apparently is a growing demand for more. What effect on psychopathology Laing's views and methods ultimately will have cannot yet be predicted, and it is still too early to ascertain the direction his followers will pursue. Laing himself has been content to devote his energies to what he calls "micro-revolutions"—significant changes in individuals, families, and institutional facilities. Kingsley Hall was one such micro-revolution.

Even though Laing's "microrevolutionary" views appear to have considerable merit, three relevant points are commonly raised concerning them: (1) chemotherapy, while it has been found to be detrimental to some schizophrenic patients with good premorbid backgrounds, has definitely benefitted the great majority of patients evidencing poor premorbid backgrounds (Goldstein et al., 1969; Goldstein, Rodnick & Judd, 1971); (2) Laing seems to have dealt in the main with patients evidencing good premorbid backgrounds, and these persons tend to "recover" from an immediate schizophrenic episode regardless of the form of therapy used, or even if they receive no therapy; and (3) there are problems of practicality in Laing's approach—in terms of available facilities and personnel for such a time-consuming and demanding treatment program.

Based on Gilluly (1971), Goldstein et al. (1969), Goldstein, Rodnick, and Judd (1971), Gordon (1971), and Laing (1967a, 1969).

as supportive and therapeutic for the patient as possible.

Community treatment and aftercare. As a consequence of more effective methods of treatment, an increasing number of schizophrenics are being treated in community clinics; also, an increasing number of hospitalized patients are being dis-

charged—not only acutely disturbed new admissions but many chronic cases as well. Thus, increased attention is being given to outpatient clinics and other supportive facilities in the community, and to sociotherapy with patients' families. In essence, the emphasis is now on community treatment, or—where hospitalization is

. . . AND THE STORY OF ONE INDIVIDUAL AT KINGSLEY HALL

Vivid in its depiction of a person who has been allowed to experience "the natural healing process" of madness is this account by Gordon (1971) of Mary Barnes' experiences at Kingsley Hall:

"Mary had gone to Laing in 1963 to ask for help. She had been in a mental hospital in 1953 for a year with a diagnosis of schizophrenia, and had maintained herself since then as a nursing tutor in a general hospital. But she saw her daily life as a rigid, anxiety-laden, and constricted façade. She began to sense 'that I had lost myself sometime in my life a long time ago.' She felt she was on the verge of another psychotic episode, but this time, instead of the padded cells and shock therapy of the mental hospital, she wanted 'to go back to before I was born and come up again.' Laing told her that he was trying to establish a place where she could live through this experience, and Mary agreed to try to 'hold on' until he could do so. . . .

"Nineteen months later Kingsley Hall opened, and Mary Barnes moved in: 'At first so great was my fear I forgot what I had come for. Quite suddenly, I remembered, I've come here to have a breakdown, to go back to before I was born, and come up again.' She continued to work for two weeks, but each night when she came to Kingsley Hall she 'regressed.' '. . . Half aware that I was going mad, there was the terror that I might not know what I was doing, away, outside of Kingsley Hall.' She wrote to the hospital resigning her position and then took to bed, 'went down' into her madness and back in time to infancy.

"'The tempo was increasing. Down, down, oh, God, would I never break?'

"She stopped eating solids, was fed milk from a bottle by Joe [Berke, who became her therapist], by Laing, and by others. She rarely spoke and lay immobile for hours at a time. 'In bed I kept my eyes shut so I didn't see people but I heard them. Touch was all important. Sometimes my body seemed apart, a leg or an arm across the room. The wall became hollow, and I seemed to go into it as into a big hole. Vividly aware of people, I was physically isolated in my room.'

"During this time there were several crises. Joe recalled that at one point Mary stopped sucking, urinating, and defecating; she was returning to a completely womblike state. She lost weight, grew weaker. The community met and decided that they couldn't let her continue this way, and that at Kingsley Hall they felt uneasy about putting in the feeding tube and catheter that would be necessary. They told Mary their decision, and gradually she began to suck again. Somewhat later the smell of the feces she smeared on the walls became annoying: Mary's room was next to the kitchen. Again the community debated. Eventually it was decided to let Mary

continue. Each time a crisis came up the members of the community came together to decide what to do. Each step on Mary's journey was also a step in the community's development.

"As Mary 'came up' out of the madness she put on trousers, played ball, and danced, as she had never been allowed to as a child. Joe gave her some grease crayons, and in November, 1965, after five months at Kingsley Hall, she began to 'scribble black breasts all over the walls of the hall. Suddenly a picture emerged, a woman kneeling with a baby at her breast.'

"'About the house, left over from decorating, were old tins of paints and brushes. On the walls of my room I painted moving figures, on my door twining stems and leaves, and on the table an orange bird appeared. Finding odd lengths of wallpaper I made picture stories. Then on strips of wallpaper backing, and on the walls of the house, I painted big, very big, at high speed. Through the spring of 1966 work poured out, all my insides were loose, the painting, like lightning, was streaking from the storm of me. Joe suggested paint the Crucifixion; I did, again and again; hungry for life I wanted the cross.'

"Joe was with Mary every day, talking, playing with her, taking her shopping. For a long time she felt 'Joe and I are not separate.' But there were frequent crises of trust. . . .

"In June, 1966, 'feeling it go in on me,' Mary took to her bed again, but with the support of the community she was up in a few months. . . .

"Since then, Mary has been painting and writing steadily. She has had four shows of her work and was preparing for another when I saw her. The paintings—dozens of which she showed me after we had talked, on canvas, boards, sheets of wrapping paper, and the walls —reminded me of a hybrid of Munch and Rouault. I bought two from her, vivid, powerful renderings of Saul struck down by God on the way to Damascus, emblems to me of the blinding force of Mary's own transformation. . . .

"Mary still feels that in many ways she is 'not very grown up.' She continues to see Joe in therapy, continues to learn more about herself. Though she could have lived elsewhere, she preferred, until its closing, to stay at Kingsley Hall, which she regarded as home. There, according to other members of the community, she was a highly valued therapist. Having gone so deeply down and come out, she is unafraid of others' madness. A terrified girl would speak with no one else but came to Mary, slept in her room for days, and drank the mixture of warm milk and honey that Mary prepared for her. When Mary was 'down' Joe had given it to her. . . .

"When Kingsley Hall did close, Mary Barnes took an apartment of her own, the first she has ever had, and there she paints and writes." (Gordon, 1971, pp. 62–66)

required—on short-term hospitalization with long-term aftercare in the community. It is of interest to note that in Russia, extensive community programs—participated in by labor unions, housing councils, and other agencies— attempt to make the entire community a therapeutic milieu for the schizophrenic, helping him

feel "You are not alone in the world" (Ziferstein, 1968).

A recent study by Caffey, Galbrecht, and Klett (1971) suggests that intensive hospital treatment for about 21 days followed by a comprehensive aftercare program may be more effective in most cases than longer hospitalization and

A

B

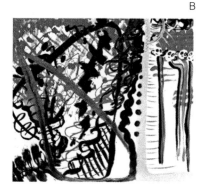

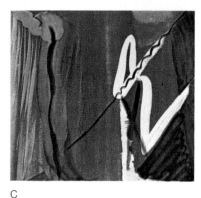

C

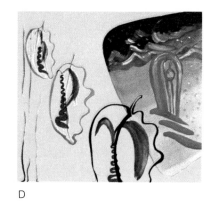

D

E

These paintings represent the gropings toward sanity of a schizophrenic girl named Jennifer, whose story was told by Dr. Ainslie Meares, a psychiatrist, in *The Door of Serenity* (1958). Only in the symbolism of her painting could Jennifer, at 19, communicate with Dr. Meares, and he had to become able to decode her symbols before he could help her find her way out of her frightening world.

From Jennifer's earliest paintings Dr. Meares learned that yellow, to Jennifer, represented happiness and goodness; black represented evil; and red represented sex. She felt that she was evil and sexual and had desires for evil men, and therefore she was undeserving of happiness. In Painting A she saw herself in darkness looking into the happiness of other people's lives and barred from it forever by three black crosses; and in Painting B she depicted herself as the chaotic mass of red and black on the left. The four tree-like people on the right, representing the rest of the world, have elements of red and black too, but in them these elements are orderly and are separated by neutral green. Later Jennifer used trees exclusively to symbolize men.

At about this time Jennifer began painting herself as a bird with a strange third wing. In Painting C she revealed that on some subconscious level she knew what she would have to do to become sane. The line from the tree man at left over the background of red sex to the blue area (representing a door beyond which the sun shines) is the path the bird must travel.

In Painting D, three large leaves with red and black in them are falling from the tree at left. The realization that men are becoming less evil, less sexual, permits Jennifer a vision both of the gateway through which she may be able to pass and of what lies beyond—the clear, cool, moonlit mountains of serenity.

For a long time Jennifer continued to paint herself as a bird with a third wing—a symbol of deformity. An incident in her childhood—being bathed with her foster brother—caused her to see the difference between herself and little boys; this led to a fear of her own deformity that tormented her through childhood and persisted, as a conviction she was evil, into adulthood. Finally, however, came the day when she brought Dr. Meares Painting E. The bird no longer has the third wing, which lies lifeless—no longer threatening. Jennifer was free. And suddenly she was no longer able to paint. But she continued to improve and at 26 was well enough to take her first job.

may markedly reduce readmission rates. Further evidence in support of this view has been provided by Driemen and Minard (1971), who demonstrated that "preleave planning" and intensive aftercare in the community—for example, family therapy and assistance with financial and vocational plans as well as psychotropic drugs when necessary—reduced the usual readmittance rate of 40 to 70 percent to slightly less than 10 percent at Metropolitan State Hospital in California. These statistics call to mind Miller's (1966) conclusion that what is needed to keep most schizophrenics from returning to the hospital are the very things that most of us take for granted in our own lives, including an adequate livelihood, the love and support of family and friends, and feelings of competence and self-respect.

The conditions associated with a favorable outcome in schizophrenia are listed on page 307. Although the prognosis is now generally favorable, there still is no substitute for early detection and treatment. Making such detection difficult is the fact that there are no clear-cut warning signs of schizophrenia; however, the onset of the disorder is commonly preceded by increasing social withdrawal, difficulties in interpersonal relationships, and preoccupation with one's own thoughts. None of these warning signs necessarily ensures the later development of schizophrenic reactions, but since all are psychologically handicapping, their early detection and correction are important.

As indicated at the beginning of this discussion we have dealt with schizophrenia in detail because it has long been the "proving ground" for delineating the role of biological and psychosocial factors in the etiology of the functional psychoses. A great deal of research is being devoted to schizophrenia, and as more information is accumulated it should become possible to understand, effectively treat, and ultimately prevent this pervasive affliction of man.

PARANOIA

The term *paranoia* has been in use a long time. The ancient Greeks and Romans used it to refer more or less indiscriminately to any mental disorder. Our present, more limited use of the term stems from the work of Kraepelin, who reserved it for cases showing delusions and impaired contact with reality but without the severe degree of personality disorganization characteristic of schizophrenia.

Paranoia is rare in mental hospital populations, but many exploited inventors, persecuted businessmen, fanatical reformers, self-styled prophets, suspicious husbands and wives, and crank-letter writers fall in this category. Unless they become a serious nuisance, these individuals are usually able to maintain themselves in the community. In some instances, however, they are potentially dangerous.

CLINICAL PICTURE IN PARANOIA

In paranoia the individual feels that he is being singled out and taken advantage of, mistreated, plotted against, stolen from, spied upon, ignored, or otherwise mistreated by his "enemies." His delusional system usually centers around one major theme, such as financial matters, a job, an invention, an unfaithful wife, or other life affairs.[1] A person who is failing on the job may insist that his fellow workers and superiors have it in for him because they are jealous of his great ability and efficiency. As a result, he may quit his job

---

[1]At one time it was customary to distinguish several types of paranoid reactions in accordance with the delusional ideas manifested—whether persecutory, grandiose, erotic, jealous, or litigious. But a classification in terms of delusional content has been found not to be very helpful.

and go to work elsewhere, only to find friction developing again and his new job in jeopardy. Now he may become convinced that the first company he worked for has written to his present employer and has turned everyone here against him, so that he has not been given a fair chance. With time, more and more of the environment is integrated into his delusional system as each additional experience is misconstrued and interpreted in the light of his delusional ideas.

Although the evidence the paranoiac advances to justify his claims may be extremely tenuous and inconclusive, he is unwilling to accept any other possible explanation and is impervious to reason. He may be convinced of his wife's unfaithfulness because on two separate occasions when he answered the phone the party at the other end hung up. Argument and logic are futile. In fact, any questioning of the paranoiac's delusions usually only convinces him that his interrogator has sold out to his enemies.

Milner cited the case of a paranoiac, aged 33, who murdered his wife by battering her head with a hammer. Prior to the murder, he had become convinced that his wife was suffering from some strange disease and that she had purposely infected him because she wished him to die. He believed that this disease was due to a "cancer-consumption" germ. He attributed his conclusion in part to his wife's alleged sexual perversion and also gave the following reasons for his belief:

"1. His wife had insured him for a small sum immediately after marriage.

"2. A young man who had been friendly with his wife before their marriage died suddenly.

"3. A child who had lived in the same house as his wife's parents suffered from fits. (He also believed that his wife's parents were suffering from the same disease.)

"4. For several months before the crime his food had had a queer taste, and for a few weeks before the crime he had suffered from a pain in the chest and an unpleasant taste in the mouth." (1949, p. 130)

Although ideas of persecution predominate in paranoid reactions, many paranoiacs develop delusions of grandeur in which they endow themselves with superior or unique ability. Such "exalted" ideas usually center around Messianic missions, political or social reforms, or remarkable inventions. Religious paranoiacs may consider themselves appointed by God to save the world and may spend most of their time "preaching" and "crusading" to gain adherents to their new cult. Threats of fire and brimstone, burning hell, and similar persuasive devices are liberally employed. Many paranoiacs become attached to extremist political movements and are tireless and fanatical crusaders, although they often do their cause more harm than good by their self-righteousness and their condemnation of others.

Some paranoiacs develop remarkable inventions which they have endless trouble in patenting or selling. Gradually they become convinced that there is a plot afoot to steal their invention, or that enemies of the United States are working against them to prevent the country from receiving the benefits of their remarkable talents. Thus a paranoiac may insist that international bankers or foreign agents are conniving to steal his invention and profit from it themselves. Hoffman cited the case of an individual who went to Washington to get presidential assistance in obtaining a patent for a flamethrower which, he claimed, could destroy all the enemies of the United States. He would patiently explain who he was. "There's God who is Number 1, and Jesus Christ who is Number 2, and me, I am Number 3." (1943, p. 574)

Aside from his delusional system, the paranoiac may appear perfectly normal in his conversation, emotionality, and conduct. Hallucinations and the other obvious signs of psychopathology are rarely found. This normal appearance, together with the logical and coherent way in which he presents his delusional ideas, may make him most convincing. In one case an engineer developed detailed plans for eliminating the fog in San Francisco and other large cities by means of a system of reflectors which would heat the air by solar radiation and cause the fog to lift. The company for whom he worked examined the plans and found them unsound. This upset him greatly and he resigned his position, stating that the other engineers in the company were not qualified to pass judgment on any really complex and advanced engineering projects like his. Instead of attempting to obtain other employment, he then devoted full time trying to find some other engineering firm who would have the vision and technical proficiency to see the great potentialities of his idea. He would present his plans convincingly but become highly suspicious and hostile when questions concerning their feasibility were raised. Eventually, he became convinced that there was a conspiracy among a large number of engineering firms to steal his plans and use them for their own profit. He reported his suspicions to the police, threatening to do something about the situation himself unless they took action. As a consequence of his threats, he was hospitalized for psychiatric observation and diagnosed as a paranoiac.

The delusional system is apt to be particularly convincing if one accepts the basic premise or premises upon which it is based. For example, where the delusional system develops around some actual injustice, it is difficult to distinguish between fact and fancy. As a result, the individual may convince his family, friends, and well-meaning public officials of the truth of his claims. However, his inability to see the facts in any other light, his typical lack of evidence for his far-reaching conclusions, and his suspicious and uncommunicative attitude when his delusional ideas are questioned usually give him away.

The following case history is a rather classical description of a mild paranoid reaction; it reveals the development of a logically patterned delusional system and the pertinent selection of environmental evidence in an attempt to involve more and more individuals in a supposed conspiracy. Despite this paranoiac's delusional system, however, she was not severely out of touch with reality, and there are many nonhospitalized cases in the community who reveal similar symptomatology to a more serious degree.

The patient was an attractive 31-year-old nurse who was commissioned a second lieutenant in the Army Nurse Corps shortly after the beginning of World War II. From the start she found it difficult to adjust to fellow nurses and to enlisted men under her supervision, the difficulty apparently arising from her overzealousness in carrying out ward regulations in the minutest detail. In any event, "No one could get along with her." After some 2 years of service, she was transferred to the European Theater of Operations.

". . . Initially she made an excellent impression, but soon showed herself to be a perfectionist, a hypercritical and domineering personality who insisted on the immediate, precise, exact and detailed execution of orders. Within a 14-week period she was transferred on three separate occasions from post to post, and at each new post her manner and her attitude, despite her precise and meticulous efficiency, con-

PSYCHOTIC VISITORS TO THE CAPITAL

Each year, a number of psychotic persons come to government offices in Washington, D.C., many of them to the White House seeking or insisting on a personal interview with the President. Hoffman (1943) reported on 53 cases of psychotic persons who had come to Washington for various reasons, and who were referred to a mental hospital for evaluation. The 53 subjects did not include persons who came to relate simple grievances or to register political protests, or those guilty of criminal offenses. Often they came to Washington at great personal inconvenience or expense; many sent in a request to see the President hours or days before their arrival. Secret Service agents or White House guards met with each visitor and referred to a mental hospital for evaluation those who appeared to be mentally disturbed.

On the basis of the evaluations made in the mental hospital, the 53 cases were categorized as follows:

Schizophrenia, paranoid type	23 cases
Schizophrenia, other types	12 cases
Organic brain syndromes	9 cases
Paranoia, paranoid condition	6 cases
Manic-depressive psychoses, manic type	3 cases

Purposes in coming to Washington were reported as follows:

To obtain relief from persecution	21 cases
To give advice	7 cases
To collect large sums of money	5 cases
To display or sell a bizarre invention	5 cases
To be sworn in as President	2 cases
(Purpose of visit not reported)	12 cases

The preceding data were based on the period from 1927 to 1937. A more recent study of 40 psychotics who visited the White House in 1960 and 1961 produced almost identical findings (Sebastiani and Foy, 1965). The study reported that some of the psychotics came to gain relief from persecution, some to collect fortunes in money or land, some to help the President, some to bring messages from God, and some to claim the presidency.

stituted a virtual demand that nurses, wardmen, patients, and medical officers conform to her exceedingly rigid ideas about the management of ward and even departmental routine. . . .

"During the course of her last assignment, she received every possible help. She requested additional responsibility and was, therefore, assigned, as charge nurse, to the E.E.N.T. Clinic. Within a week she lodged a complaint with the commanding officer of the hospital, accusing the enlisted men of conspiring against her, the nurses of lying about her, and the officer in charge, of lack of co-operation. She was, therefore, transferred to one of the wards, where she expected wardmen, nurses and patients to execute her orders on the instant, in minute and exact detail, and where she violently berated them because of their inability to do so. A week later, the responsible medical officer requested that she be relieved from duty there. Instead, she discussed the problem with the chief nurse and promised to correct her attitude. Within four days, the patients as a group requested her removal. Two weeks later, the ward officer repeated his request. She was, therefore, given a five-day leave, and during her absence all ward personnel were contacted in an attempt to help her adjust when she returned to duty.

"During this period she became convinced that she was being persecuted. She grew tense and despondent, kept rigidly to herself, was unable to sleep in a room with a ticking clock, and frequently burst into tears. As she herself said, 'Some of the nurses deliberately went out of their way to annoy and criticize me. They wanted to make me trouble. That's why I was so upset.' On three separate occasions, she requested the appointment of a Board of Officers to investigate these alleged discriminatory acts. Finally she demanded that a Board of Officers be convened to determine her efficiency as a nurse. Instead, she was ordered to report to our hospital for psychiatric observation.

"On admission, few details of her military history were known. She seemed alert and co-operative, was well oriented in all three spheres, and was thought to be in complete contact. Extreme care, however, was necessary when addressing her. Even fellow patients would warn newcomers to the ward, 'Be careful what you say when she's around. She won't mean it, but she'll twist your statements without changing your words, and give them some meaning you never intended.' In addition, she was bitter about the unfair treatment she had received in the Army, wished to reform the Medical Department and the Army Nursing Corps, and indignantly repudiated the existence of any condition that could justify placing her under NP [neuropsychiatric] observation. As a result, she was at first thought to be an obsessive-compulsive personality with paranoid tendencies, and it was believed she could be returned to duty. While under observation, however, she became unco-operative, aloof and seclusive. She preened constantly, and was exceedingly coquettish whenever men of any rank or grade appeared on the ward. . . . she was meticulous and precise, argumentative and domineering, hypercritical of others but upset by even the slightest hint of criticism directed against herself, and constantly antagonizing all with whom she came in contact. Rapport superficially appeared excellent, but few details could be obtained about her background. Her apparently frank and detailed answers, when analyzed, were seen to be verbose and digressive evasions.

"She was constantly complaining, 'These nurses dislike me because I'm so efficient. That's why they discriminated against me. . . . And the enlisted men

didn't like taking orders from me. That's why they lied about me. . . . It doesn't seem credible but they actually got together in a sort of conspiracy [against me]. . . . And he [the officer in charge of the E.E.N.T. Clinic] backed them up: he deliberately misrepresented the facts.' And she adduced fact after fact which apparently supported this conclusion of hers.

"The diagnosis of 'paranoia, true type' was made, and she was returned to the United States, one month after admission to the hospital, a rigid and overzealous individual whose inelasticity had antagonized her associates and aroused severe emotional strain within herself, firmly convinced that she was being persecuted because of the necessary and badly needed work which she had much too efficiently performed. And by one of those fortuitous circumstances that nevertheless occur so frequently, she was received in the States as a patient in the very hospital to whose psychiatric section she had previously, for so brief a period of time, been assigned as ward nurse." (Rosen & Kiene, 1946, pp. 330–333)

Paranoiacs are not always as dangerous as we have been led to believe by popular fiction and drama, but there is always the chance that they will decide to take matters into their own hands and deal with their enemies in the only way that seems effective. In one instance, a school principal who was a paranoiac became convinced that the school board was discriminating against him and shot and killed most of the members of the board. In another case a paranoiac shot and killed a group of 7 persons who he thought were following him. The number of husbands and wives who have been killed or injured by suspicious, persecuted mates is unknown but undoubtedly large. Even postmen have been accused and attacked. Paranoiacs may also get involved in political assassinations and subversive activities of a violent and destructive nature.

DYNAMICS OF PARANOIA

Most of us on various occasions may wonder if we are not "jinxed," when it seems as if everything we do goes wrong and the cards seem to be "stacked against us." If we are generally somewhat suspicious and disposed to blame others for our difficulties, we may feel that most people are selfish and ruthless and that an honest man, no matter what his ability, does not have a fair chance. As a result, we may feel abused and become somewhat bitter and cynical. Many people go through life feeling underrated and frustrated and brooding over fancied and real injustices.

In paranoia, the picture is similar but considerably more extreme. Such reactions usually occur in sensitive, rigid, and suspicious persons who in severe stress situations begin to selectively perceive certain aspects of reality in a distorted way—usually concluding that others are deliberately interfering with or mistreating them. In some instances, as we shall see, these delusions have some grounding in fact but become grossly exaggerated. Neither genetic nor biochemical alterations have been emphasized in the etiology of paranoia. Available evidence indicates that psychosocial factors are of primary importance.

1. *Faulty learning and development.* As children, most paranoiacs seem to have been aloof, suspicious, seclusive, stubborn, and resentful of punishment. When crossed, they become sullen and morose. Rarely do they show a history of normal play with other children or good socialization in terms of warm, affectionate relationships (Sarvis, 1962; Schwartz, 1963).

Often the family background appears to have been authoritarian and excessively dominating, suppressive, and critical. Such a family has often been permeated with an air of superiority which was a cover-up for an underlying lack of self-acceptance and feelings of inferiority, creating for the child, in turn, the necessity of proving that he is superior. Inevitably his family background colors his feelings about people in general and his way of reacting to them. His inadequate socialization keeps him from understanding the motives and point of view of others and leads him to suspicious misinterpretation of their unintentional slights. Also he tends to enter into social relationships with a hostile, dominating attitude that drives others away. His inevitable social failures then further undermine his self-esteem and lead to deeper social isolation and mistrust of others.

In later personality development these early trends merge into a picture of self-important, rigid, arrogant individuals who long to dominate others and readily maintain their unrealistic self-picture by projecting the blame for difficulties onto others and seeing in others the weaknesses they cannot acknowledge in themselves. They are highly suspicious of the motives of other people and quick to sense insult or mistreatment.

Such individuals lack a sense of humor, focus on their own assumptions, and are incapable of seeing things from any viewpoint but their own. Typically, they categorize people and ideas into "good" and "bad" and have difficulty in conceiving of something as having both good and bad qualities. Their goals and expectations are unrealistically high, and they refuse to make concessions in meeting life's problems by accepting more realistic goals. They expect to be praised and appreciated for even minor achievements; and when such praise is not forthcoming, they sulk and withdraw from normal contacts. Although such individuals may have broad interests and appear normal in general behavior, they usually are unable to relate closely to other persons; they appear inaccessible, are overly aggressive, and maintain a somewhat superior air.

2. *Failure and inferiority.* The history of the paranoiac is replete with failures in critical life situations—social, occupational, and marital—stemming from his rigidity, his unrealistic goals, and his inability to get along with other people. Such failures jeopardize his picture of himself as being adequate, significant, and important and expose his easily wounded pride to what he interprets as the rejection, scorn, and ridicule of others.

His failure is made more difficult to cope with by his inability to understand the causes for it. Why should his efforts to improve the efficiency of his company—which people approve in principle—lead to such negative reactions from others? Why should people dislike him when he strives so hard to do the best possible job down to the very last detail? Unable to see himself or the situation objectively, he simply cannot understand how he tends to alienate others and elicit rebuffs and rejection.

Although the paranoiac's feelings of inferiority are masked behind his air of superiority and self-importance, they are manifested in many aspects of his behavior. Rosen and Kiene (1946) pointed out that clues in profusion were found in the pathetic craving of their patients for praise and recognition, in their hypersensitivity to criticism, in their exact and formal adherence to socially approved behavior, and in their conscientious and overzealous performance of the most minute occupational tasks.

In essence, then, the paranoid individual is confronted with failure experiences which in

PARANOID STATES—BRIDGE BETWEEN SCHIZOPHRENIA AND PARANOIA

In addition to paranoia, the APA classification of mental disorders lists the category of *paranoid states,* which, in essence, bridge the gap between schizophrenia and paranoia. Paranoid states are characterized by delusions—usually of a persecutory nature—with associated disturbances in mood and behavior. Hallucinations may occur but are relatively rare. However, the individual's contact with reality is impaired; he manifests some degree of personality decompensation; and he consequently is labeled as a psychotic. At the same time, he does not manifest the severe personality disorganization characteristic of the schizophrenic, nor the systematized delusional pattern characteristic of the paranoiac.

In paranoia, we typically are dealing with a long-term defensive reaction to life stresses which eventuates in a rigid, internally logical, and unshakable delusional system. This system protects the individual from overwhelming feelings of inferiority and unimportance and enables him to function adequately in life areas not involved in this system. In paranoid states, on the other hand, the mechanism of projection is used without elaboration or systematization. The delusions are vaguer, more pervasive, and more in flux; often they change spontaneously or can be changed by the questions of other people.

Usually, there is not the insidious onset in paranoid states that often occurs in schizophrenia and paranoia; typically, paranoid states are precipitated by some immediate stress. Such stresses may run the gamut of frustrations, conflicts, and pressures, but often they are associated with marital difficulties (Dupont & Grunebaum, 1968; Modlin, 1963; Retterstol, 1968). For example, in an intensive study of 5 women manifesting paranoid states, Modlin (1963) found the precipitating factor in each case to be a disturbance in the husband-wife relationship. The reactions of these women were characterized in the main by delusions concerning their husbands' philandering and adulterous activities and by delusions that they, the wives, were being influenced in evil ways by other men.

In some cases paranoid states appear to have etiological patterns similar to those in schizophrenia, including probable biochemical alterations that interfere with normal brain functioning. Usually, however, paranoid states are considered transitory psychotic reactions that occur in response to some specific and overwhelming stress. Although paranoid states tend to be of short duration and to clear up spontaneously—particularly with the alleviation of the stress situation—drug therapy may be used for alleviating psychotic symptoms. Behavior therapy has also shown promising results.

The case on the facing page is a somewhat atypical example of a paranoid state, but it is useful in showing the diverse forms this reaction pattern may take.

effect say, "People don't like you," "Something is wrong with you," "You are inferior." But he is incapable of dealing with the stress situation in a task-oriented way—for example, trying to understand why people react to him as they do and making needed corrections in his attitudes and behavior. Instead, he tends to intensify his existing defenses. Thus he becomes more rigid, opinionated, and prone to blame others for his difficulties. He cannot admit weaknesses or mistakes but clings to the feeling that he is unique and has some important contribution to make to mankind. This defensive pattern helps protect him from facing unbearable feelings of inferiority and worthlessness.

3. *Elaboration of defenses and the "pseudo-community."* A rigid, self-important, humorless, and suspicious individual such as we have described becomes understandably unpopular with other people. He is, in effect, an aversive stimulus. Thus as Lemert (1962) has noted, many times the paranoiac not only misconstrues the world "as if others were against him" but is, in fact, a target of actual discrimination and mistreatment. Ever alert to injustices, both imagined and real, the paranoid individual has little trouble finding "proof" that he is being persecuted.

Paranoid reactions usually develop gradually, with mounting failures forcing the individual to an elaboration of his defensive structure. To

"A 45-year-old businessman appeared for consultation in an anxious, agitated, perplexed, and somewhat confused state. His stated reason for consultation was that he wished to be hypnotized, given 'truth-serum,' or in some other way interrogated without his conscious awareness in order to determine what his behavior had actually been.

"The patient had been married for nineteen years and described his wife in glowing idealized terms as a beautiful, intelligent, artistic, creative individual who was strong and dependable and the type of woman whom any man would believe in and love.

"The patient stated that he had always been frightened and shy with women, had never had sexual relations prior to marriage, had a relatively low sexual appetite in his marriage, was a poor lover with premature ejaculation who had never been able to satisfy his wife, and that he had never considered having an extramarital affair. However, since the beginning of their marriage the wife had been . . . delusionally jealous of him, accusing him repetitively of promiscuity and philandering. In almost everything that happened, including neutral and indifferent experiences, she was able to find some aspect of the patient's behavior which 'proved' that she was right, frequently citing such 'evidence' months or years after it had happened. She would insist that she saw evidences of such behavior (e.g., 'seeing' him put packages of condoms in his suitcase when he packed for a business trip), and even though the patient denied this and invited her to examine his behavior (e.g., to look through his suitcase) she would not be convinced otherwise.

"Throughout their marriage, the patient's wife repeatedly told him that she was increasingly unable to feel like a woman, blaming it on his promiscuity, and pleaded for 'a confession' that would make her again feel feminine. The wife would spend hours questioning him about his behavior and her suspicions of him, begging him for details about the women involved, the frequency of their sexual contacts, the positions they used, sexual acts they performed, duration, and so forth.

"For many years the patient denied his wife's allegations and maintained his innocence. However, she became increasingly alienated from him and he became fearful of losing her. This may account for what transpired next. For he decided that he would be a 'fool' not to confess to his wife's accusations, since this seemed the only way of holding her. Now he began to fabricate details of his alleged sexual misbehavior, filling in women's names, fictitious details of times, places, and elaborate fantasied descriptions of his sexual activities. As this continued he became plagued with thoughts that perhaps the confessions were really true, that perhaps he did or wanted to do all of the things that she accused him of, and that he had merely forgotten the reality of having done them. He was no longer sure about fact or fantasy in regard to his own memory and behavior, and was increasingly accepting of his wife's version of his behavior. . . . He was plagued with a mounting need to find out whether or not he really did the things to which he had confessed." (Dewald, 1970, pp. 390–392)

Whereas delusions in paranoid states usually relate to some person or organization that is interfering with, persecuting, or otherwise mistreating the individual, in this case the delusional ideas related to the individual's own behavior. The therapist interpreted the symptom picture in terms of the man's love for and dependence on his wife, his chronic anxiety about his own sexual potency and masculinity, and his willingness to participate in and believe in his own "confessions" in order to hold onto her and to maintain his fragmented ties with reality. In therapy, the man was able to make a rapid and dramatic recovery, to take a more independent role in his marital relationship, and to stop reinforcing his wife's deviant behavior by his fabricated confessions. Although it is interesting to speculate on the causes of the wife's behavior—for example, whether her belief that her husband was unfaithful was an actual delusion or was advanced to meet deviant sexual desires—there is not sufficient information for drawing conclusions. However, the therapist referred to this case as one of folie a deux, implying the transfer of delusional ideas from one person to another in a close interpersonal relationship.

avoid self-devaluation, he searches for "logical" reasons for his lack of success. Why was he denied a much deserved promotion? Why was it given to someone less experienced and obviously far less qualified than he? He becomes more vigilant, begins to scrutinize his environment, searches for hidden meanings, and asks leading questions. He ponders like a detective over the "clues" he picks up, trying to fit them into some sort of meaningful picture.

Gradually the picture begins to crystallize. It becomes apparent that he is being singled out for some obscure reason, that other people are working against him, that he is being interfered with. In essence, he protects himself against the intolerable assumption "There is something wrong with me" with the projective defense "They are doing something to me." Now he has failed not because of any inferiority or lack on his part but because others are working against him. He is on the side of good and the progress of mankind while "they" are allied with the forces of evil. With this as his fundamental defensive premise, he proceeds to distort and falsify the facts to fit it and gradually develops a logic-tight, fixed, delusional system.

Cameron (1959) has referred to this process as the building up of a paranoid "pseudo-community" in which the individual organizes the people around him (both real and imaginary) into a structured group whose purpose is to carry out some action against him. As this delusional system emerges, the paranoiac often has the feeling that "Everything has become clear to me; I can see it all now." Everything comes to be interpreted in terms of this delusional system, and the most trivial events may take on an ominous meaning. If a new employee is hired by his company, the man was obviously sent by the organization to spy on him. If an employee under his supervision makes a mistake, it is done to discredit his competence as a supervisor. Even the most casual conversation of others may have a hidden and sinister meaning. This pseudo-community is not all-embracing, however, in the sense that everybody is against him. It remains limited in scope to those stress areas—such as occupational failure—which present the greatest threat to his feelings of adequacy and worth. In other life areas not directly involved with his paranoid system, he may be quite rational and may function adequately. Over a period of time, of course, additional life areas and experiences may be incorporated into his delusional system.

In many cases the attention the individual thinks he is receiving leads him to believe that he is a person of great importance. For why else would his enemies go to all this trouble? In one case, it was pointed out to a hospitalized patient that if his enemies were persecuting him in the way he insisted they were, it would be costing them about $10,000 per day, which was obviously a ridiculous figure. The patient drew himself up proudly and replied, "Why shouldn't they? After all, I am the world's greatest atomic scientist." As might be expected, the particular content of the grandiose ideas that develop is closely related to the individual's education, vocation, and special interests. A paranoid person with strong religious convictions may develop the notion that he is a great religious savior, whereas the individual interested in science is more likely to envision himself as a great inventor.

The role of perceptual selectivity in the development of these delusional systems should be emphasized. Once the individual begins to suspect that others are working against him, he carefully notes the slightest signs pointing in the direction of his suspicions and ignores all evidence to the contrary. With this frame of reference it is of course quite easy in our highly competitive,

somewhat ruthless world to find ample evidence that others are working against us. And the individual's very attitude leads him into a vicious circle, for his suspiciousness, distrust, and criticism of others drive his friends and well-wishers away and keep him in continual friction with other people, generating new incidents for him to grasp hold of and magnify. Often people do in fact have to conspire behind his back as to how best to keep peace and cope with his eccentricities.

4. *Sexual maladjustment.* Case histories of paranoiacs, like those of schizophrenics, almost invariably reveal sexual maladjustment. Although all of the patients studied by Rosen and Kiene (1946) claimed normal heterosexual development, these investigators reported that only one of the patients had dared attempt the marriage relationship. Interestingly enough, this patient chose as her husband a chronic alcoholic 11 years her senior whom she divorced after 4 years of marriage. She was apparently sexually incompatible with this man, although whether because of frigidity on her part or sexually deviate practices on his was not clear. For not marrying, other patients gave such reasons as having had too many family responsibilities and never having met the right person. Most of the patients followed an exceedingly rigid moral code relative to sexual behavior and attempted to enforce this code upon others. The only patient who prided herself on her sexual prowess was so exhibitionistic and coquettish as to suggest that her activity was aimed at enhancing her self-esteem rather than at achieving sexual gratification. In fact, indications were that she may have actually been frigid.

In some paranoid reactions, guilt over actual or contemplated immoral behavior seems to play an important role. Two dynamic considerations appear to be involved here: (a) the individual cannot tolerate the self-devaluation resulting from his failure to live up to his moral views and high opinion of himself, and (b) he justifies his own actions by projecting his unacceptable desires to others, who are now seen as trying to take advantage of him.

Homosexual conflicts have frequently been emphasized in the origin of paranoid delusional systems. For example, the individual's accusation of infidelity against his wife may represent an ego defense against his own homosexual tendencies. In one case, the patient was sure his wife had been unfaithful to him on numerous occasions because when salesmen came into their business establishment, he, the patient, had an erection. The patient could not accept his own erotic arousal and therefore projected the sexual desire to his wife, who now was charged with infidelity. This factor of homosexuality was strongly emphasized by Freud, who concluded that paranoia represents the individual's attempt to deal with homosexual tendencies which the ego is not prepared to acknowledge. Most contemporary investigators believe, however, that the dynamics of paranoid reactions center not around homosexual tendencies per se but rather around overwhelming feelings of inadequacy and inferiority that are frequently—though not necessarily—related to underlying sexual conflicts.

TREATMENT AND OUTCOMES

In the early stages of paranoia, treatment with individual and/or group psychotherapy may prove effective, particularly if an individual voluntarily seeks professional assistance (Salzman, 1960; Schwartz, 1963). Here, behavior therapy also appears to show promise; for example, the paranoid ideation may be altered by a combination of aversive conditioning, the removal of factors in the person's life situation which are reinforcing the maladaptive behavior, and the development of more effective coping patterns.

Once the delusional system is well established, however, treatment is extremely difficult. It is usually impossible to communicate with the paranoiac in a rational way concerning his problems. In addition, such persons are not prone to seeking treatment, but rather justice for all the wrongs done to them. Unfortunately, hospitalization of paranoiacs is usually of little avail. To the paranoiac it often seems more a form of punishment than of treatment. He is apt to regard himself as superior to other patients and will often complain that his family and the hospital staff have had him "put away" for no valid reason; thus he refuses to cooperate or participate in treatment.

Eventually, hospitalization may "sober" the patient to the extent that he realizes that his failure to curb his actions and ideas will result in prolonged hospitalization. As a result, he may make a pretext of renouncing his delusions, admitting that he did hold such ideas but claiming that he now realizes they are absurd and has given them up. After his release, he is often more reserved in expressing his ideas and in annoying other people, but he is far from recovered. Thus the prognosis for paranoia has traditionally been unfavorable.

In beginning our consideration of the psychoses with schizophrenia and paranoia, we have dealt with clinical manifestations considerably different from those found in the neuroses. Thus in schizophrenia we noted severely impaired contact with reality and marked personality disorganization—involving disturbances in thought, affect, and behavior. We examined the major types of schizophrenia—acute, paranoid, catatonic, hebephrenic, and simple—and attempted to identify certain differences in the clinical picture of each type. We then dealt with various dynamic considerations, noting that we still do not understand the etiology of schizophrenia. However, we examined evidence pointing to the role of neurophysiological and biochemical alterations in the impairment of normal brain functioning in schizophrenia, including the breakdown of filtering mechanisms. It remains to be ascertained whether these alterations precede or result from the disorder, as well as the precise nature of the alterations. We also considered the potential significance of various psychosocial factors, regarded by many investigators to be of primary importance in the etiology of schizophrenia. Finally, we noted how innovations in chemotherapy, psychosocial therapy, and aftercare programs have resulted in an increasingly favorable outlook for the schizophrenic patient.

In the latter part of the chapter we examined paranoia, characterized by the development of a highly systematized delusional system. Here, the evidence indicates that psychosocial factors are of primary importance, neither genetic nor biochemical alterations having been emphasized in the etiology of paranoia. Paranoid disorders involve less personality disorganization than most other types of psychosis, but they are highly resistant to presently available methods of treatment.

Major Affective Disorders and Suicide

10

MANIC-DEPRESSIVE PSYCHOSES
INVOLUTIONAL MELANCHOLIA
SUICIDE

The term *affect* is roughly equivalent to *emotion*, and the affective disorders involve changes in mood or emotion—either extreme elation or depression. Here, then, we are dealing with psychotic disorders in which distorted and inappropriate emotional responses dominate the clinical picture. By contrast, the disorders discussed in the preceding chapter primarily involved thought disturbances accompanied by a certain amount of emotional distortion.

For our purposes we shall focus on two subgroups of affective disorders: (1) manic-depressive reactions and (2) involutional melancholia. Although mania—involving extreme feelings of elation and psychomotor overactivity—presents a relatively clear-cut clinical picture, this is not true for depressive reactions. In fact, the term *depression* is almost as frequently used as *anxiety* in describing mental disorders; and there is considerable disagreement about the distinctions between the various depressive reactions delineated in the APA classification. However, we shall attempt to point up certain differences as well as similarities that appear to underlie psychotic depressive patterns. In the last section of the chapter we shall consider the problem of suicide, which is closely related to that of depression.

Affective disorders are not new in the history of mankind. Descriptions of affective disorders are found among the early writings of the Egyptians, Hebrews, and Greeks; and in more recent history, comparable descriptions are found in the plays of Shakespeare. Thus we are again dealing with mental disorders that appear to be common to the human species—both cross-culturally and historically. In our own society, it has been estimated that about 10 persons in 100 become severely depressed at some point in their lives (Nelson, 1970).

MANIC-DEPRESSIVE PSYCHOSES

The great Greek physician Hippocrates classified all mental disorders into three broad categories—mania, melancholia, and phrenitis. His descriptions of mania and melancholia, based on the clinical records of his patients, are strikingly similar to modern clinical symptomatology.

The sixth-century physician Alexander Trallianus was perhaps the first to recognize recurrent cycles of mania and melancholia in the same person, thus anticipating by several hundred years Bonet's (1684) "folie maniaco-mélancolique" and Falret's (1854) "folie circulaire." It remained for Kraepelin, however, to introduce, in 1899, the term *manic-depressive psychosis* and to clarify the clinical picture. Kraepelin described the disorder as a series of attacks of elation and depression, with periods of relative normality in between and a generally favorable prognosis. Kraepelin's clinical description was a major step forward in the delineation of this psychotic reaction.

Some individuals evidence only manic reactions and others only depressive reactions; still others show both types of reactions, either alternating between the two or showing a combination of manic and depressive reactions at the same time. Consequently, three major types of manic-depressive psychoses are commonly distinguished: (1) manic type, (2) depressed type, and (3) circular and mixed reactions.

Mental hospital statistics indicate that manic-depressive psychoses—particularly the manic type—are decreasing in our society. At present the depressive type is far more common. The great majority of cases occur between the ages of 25 and 65, although such reactions may occur from early childhood to old age. Poznanski and Zrull (1970) have described depressive reactions among children ranging from 3 to 12 years of age; and cases have been observed even after age 85. The incidence is higher among females than males, with a ratio of about 3 to 2.

CLINICAL PICTURE

The clinical picture in manic-depressive reactions is colored by the predominant emotional mood of the individual, which may be one of elation or depression. Against this affective background there may be a variety of psychological and behavioral symptoms which are roughly appropriate to the prevailing mood.

In manic reactions there are feelings of optimism and elation, accompanied by a speeding up of thought processes and activities and a decreased need for sleep. The individual is loud and boisterous, appears to have unbounded energy and enthusiasm, and is involved in all sorts of activities. He shows impaired ability to concentrate, is easily distracted, and changes rapidly from one trend of thought and activity to another. Judgment is impaired; sexual and other behavioral restraints are lowered; and the individual tends to be extremely impatient with any attempts to restrain his activities. Extravagant plans and delusions of grandeur are common. The person may envision himself as the ruler of the world, the most remarkable scientist who ever lived, or a great prophet who can solve the problems of all mankind.

In depressive reactions the individual experiences a feeling of profound sadness and loneliness, and the whole world becomes joyless and gray. Nothing seems worth while any more; emptiness prevails; and only bad things are expected. Thought processes and behavior are slowed down. The individual speaks slowly in a monotonous voice. He limits himself to brief answers to questions. He rarely poses questions; he avoids people and has a listless facial expression and a stooping posture. Self-accusatory and hypochondriacal delusions are common. The individual may accuse himself of having committed various crimes, participated in immoral sexual acts, been selfish and callous with loved ones. He feels guilty of "unpardonable sins" and regards himself as basically worthless and not fit to live. He may be convinced that he has an incurable disease, that his internal organs have disappeared or are rotting away, or that his body is undergoing peculiar changes. In older depressed persons, the delusional content often centers around ideas of poverty, of suffering from some terrible disease, and of being abandoned and doomed to die in loneliness and despair. The general mood of the depressed individual is well captured in the following excerpt from a poem by Joseph Cowen (1959):

In the slave market of my melancholy mind
I mount the auction block
To sell myself to the highest bidder of misery.

Hallucinations are commonly found in severe manic-depressive reactions. They are usually somewhat fragmentary and may include a wide range of content. In an early study of 208 cases, Rennie and Fowler (1942) cited the following as being typical:

". . . conversed with God; heard sentences—'daughter is dead'; saw iceberg floating, bottle of carbolic in ceiling; . . . people talking through stomach; saw star on Christmas day; saw and heard dead mother; voices tell her not to eat, to walk backwards; sees something white—a vision; saw path of fire running up and down; saw and heard God and angels; saw snake coming to her; trees glitter like gold; saw dead father; animal faces in food; saw and heard animals; heard voices; voices—'they've got me now'; sees dead people and skulls (patient very superstitious); brother's and dead people's voices; God's voice; sees devil and Hell's flames; saw God; sees husband and coffin; hand pointing to cross; sees her babies in heaven; voice says: 'Do not stay with husband' . . . ." (p. 805)

About 75 percent of depressed cases have suicidal ideas and some 10 to 15 percent attempt suicide. Occasionally, depressed persons commit infanticide or homicide—usually then taking or attempting to take their own lives (Easson & Steinhilber, 1961). Although manic individuals may become hostile if interfered with and may physically assault others, they rarely kill anyone.

Manic-depressive reactions tend to be episodic and of relatively brief duration. Even in those cases where no formal treatment is received, manic reactions usually run their course in about three months and depressive reactions in about nine months. There are considerable variations, however, with some psychotic episodes lasting only a few days and others as long as a year or more. At the conclusion of a manic or depressive episode, the individual usually returns to apparent normality. As shown in the chart on page 324, however, manic-depressive reactions tend to recur.

COMPARISON OF CLINICAL PICTURES IN MANIC AND DEPRESSIVE PATTERNS

	MANIC PATTERN	DEPRESSIVE PATTERN
Emotional symptoms	Euphoric, elated mood Sociability Extreme impatience with restraint or criticism	Gloomy outlook, loss of hope Social withdrawal Marked irritability
Cognitive symptoms	Short attention span; racing of thoughts; flight of ideas Orientation toward action; impulsiveness; overtalkativeness Positive self-image; tendency to blame others Grandiose delusions	Slowing of thought processes Obsessional worrying; exaggeration of problems; indecisiveness Negative self-image; tendency to blame self Delusions of sin, guilt, disease, poverty
Motor symptoms	Hyperactivity Indefatigability Decreased need for sleep Variable appetite Increased sex drive	Decreased motor activity Fatigue Insomnia Loss of appetite Decreased sex drive

Such clear-cut differences cannot, of course, be drawn in the case of certain symptom patterns. For example, in involutional melancholia and "mixed" depressive reactions, the clinical picture may be complicated by agitation and overactivity.

Based in part on American Psychiatric Association (1968), Beck (1967), and Reich, Clayton, and Winokur (1969).

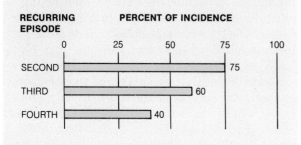

LIKELIHOOD OF RECURRENCE OF MANIC-DEPRESSIVE REACTIONS

Only 25 percent of the individuals experiencing manic-depressive reactions are likely to undergo single episodes; the majority are commonly subjected to recurring episodes. However, as the graph indicates, likelihood of recurrence diminishes following a second episode.

RECURRING EPISODE	PERCENT OF INCIDENCE			
	0 25 50 75 100			
SECOND	75			
THIRD	60			
FOURTH	40			

Manic type. Manic reactions are characterized by varying degrees of elation and psychomotor overactivity.[1] Three degrees are commonly delineated, denoting the progression of behavior from mild to extreme degrees of manic excitement. Though these reactions differ in degree rather than kind, they merit separate consideration.

1. *Hypomania.* This is the mildest form of manic reaction and is characterized by moderate elation, flightiness, and overactivity. The individual states that he has never felt better or happier in his life. He has unbounded confidence in his ability and knowledge and will unhesitatingly express his opinion on any and all subjects. His thinking is speeded up and he may become particularly witty and entertaining. He seems tireless and gets practically no sleep, stating that he feels so well that he does not need any. During the day he engages in ceaseless activity, talking, visiting, keeping luncheon and other engagements, telephoning, writing, and working on various sure-fire schemes. Numerous appointments are made, postponed, and canceled. The mails frequently seem too slow to these persons, and they are fond of sending telegrams and special-delivery letters and making long-distance telephone calls.

The overall picture frequently appears at first to be one of an aggressive, brilliant, sociable individual who has many commendable enthusiasms and wonderful plans for the future. Initially he may seem an exciting person to be with,

but he soon reveals his self-centeredness, becomes domineering, monopolizes the conversation, and shows difficulty in sticking to the subject. He is intolerant of criticism and may unsparingly denounce as a stupid fool anyone who dares to disagree with him or interfere with his plans. The details of his plans are seldom worked out; very few of them are ever put into action, and those few are not completed. However, the individual easily rationalizes his activities and concedes no mistakes. He spends money recklessly and in a short period of time may dissipate his entire savings. Moral restraint gives way, and he may engage in numerous promiscuous sexual acts and in alcoholic excesses.

Although these persons rarely show marked delusions or hallucinations, they show very poor judgment and usually lack insight into their condition. Any suggestion that they are ill and should be hospitalized is met with angry abuse. They are ready with a rebuttal to all charges made against them and may threaten legal action against anyone who dares to interfere with them.

The following conversation with a hypomanic patient reveals the elated mood and pressure toward activity typical of this reaction pattern. The patient was a woman of 46.

Dr.: Hello, how are you today?
Pt.: Fine, fine, and how are you, Doc? You're looking pretty good. I never felt better in my life. Could I go for a schnapps now? Say, you're new around here, I never saw you before—and not bad! How's about you and me stepping out tonight if I can get that sour old battleship of a nurse to give me back my dress. It's low cut and it'll wow 'em. Even in this old rag, all the doctors give me the eye. You know I'm a model. Yep, I was No. 1—used to dazzle them in New York, London and Paris. Hollywood has been angling with me for a contract.
Dr.: Is that what you did before you came here?
Pt.: I was a society queen . . . entertainer of kings and presidents. I've got five grown sons and I wore out three husbands getting them . . . about ready for a couple of more now. There's no woman like me, smart, brainy, beautiful and sexy. You can see I don't believe in playing myself down. If you are good

---

[1]Actually, manic reactions are often impure in the sense that worry, sadness, and brooding often complicate the predominantly elated emotional mood. It is also common to find underlying depression close on the heels of elation. In fact, the manic attack is often considered a defense against depression.

and know you're good you have to speak out, and I know what I've got.

Dr.: Why are you in this hospital?

Pt.: That's just the trouble. My husbands never could understand me. I was too far above them. I need someone like me with savoir faire you know, somebody that can get around, intelligent, lots on the ball. Say, where can I get a schnapps around here—always like one before dinner. Someday I'll cook you a meal. I've got special recipes like you never ate before . . . sauces, wines, desserts. Boy, it's making me hungry. Say, have you got anything for me to do around here? I've been showing these slowpokes how to make up beds but I want something more in line with my talents.

Dr.: What would you like to do?

Pt.: Well, I'm thinking of organizing a show, singing, dancing, jokes. I can do it all myself but I want to know what you think about it. I'll bet there's some schnapps in the kitchen. I'll look around later. You know what we need here . . . a dance at night. I could play the piano, and teach them the latest steps. Wherever I go I'm the life of the party.

2. *Acute mania.* The symptoms in acute mania are similar to those in hypomania but are more pronounced. This condition may develop out of a hypomanic reaction or may develop suddenly with little or no warning except for a short period of insomnia, irritability, and restlessness. Elation and pressure of activity become more pronounced, and the individual may laugh boisterously and talk at the top of his voice. He becomes increasingly boastful, dictatorial, and overbearing, and may order everyone around as if he were a super-dictator.

Irritability is easily provoked, and the individual's mood may change rapidly from gaiety to anger. Both before and after hospitalization violent behavior is common, and the individual may break up furniture, deface the walls, and even assault nurses and other patients. He is continually on the go, walking back and forth, gesturing to himself, singing, and banging on the walls and door demanding release. Even persons who have had the most rigid moral backgrounds will show a complete abandonment of moral restraint and may be obscene in their talk, expose themselves, and make sexual advances to those around them.

There is a wild flight of ideas, frequently leading to incoherent speech. The alternation in ideas may be so rapid that at one moment the person may engage in erotic activities and the next deliver a profound religious dissertation. There may be some confusion and disorientation for time, place, and person, with a tendency to misidentify those about him.

Transient delusions and hallucinations may occur, in which the person may have grandiose ideas of his wealth and abilities or in which he may hear voices and carry on conversations with persons whom he imagines to be present. Occasionally there may be short periods of relative calmness in which the individual shows some insight into his noisy behavior, and he may even apologize for it. In general, however, insight and judgment are severely impaired, and periods of insight are shortly followed by a resumption of manic activity. The outstanding symptoms in acute manic reactions are the irritable and elated mood, the increased flight of irrational ideas, the rapid and frequent alternation in thought, and the extreme psychomotor overactivity.

The following brief description of an acute manic reaction will serve to illustrate some of the typical symptoms.

"On admission she slapped the nurse, addressed the house physician as God, made the sign of the cross, and laughed loudly when she was asked to don the hospital garb. This she promptly tore into shreds. She remained nude for several hours before she was restrained in bed. She sang at the top of her voice, screamed through the window, and leered at the patients promenading in the recreation yard. She was very untidy and incontinent, smearing her excreta about the floor and walls. Frequently she would utter the words, 'God, Thou Holy One,' cross herself, laugh, and then give vent to vile expletives while she carried out suggestive movements of the body. She yelled for water, and, when this was proffered, she threw the tin cup across the room." (Karnosh & Zucker, 1945, p. 78)

3. *Delirious mania.* In the most severe type of manic reaction the individual is confused, wildly excited, and violent. The condition may develop out of hypomania or acute mania but more frequently appears suddenly and with very few warning signs. The individual is incoherent and severely disoriented. He has no appreciation of his surroundings and may have vivid auditory and visual hallucinations. It is impossible to converse with him or to hold his attention. He evidences the most extreme psychomotor over-activity, is violent and destructive, and spends his days and nights in restless pacing, singing, screaming, gesticulating, and incoherent shouting. His eyes may show a peculiar glare and his features may be contorted beyond recognition. One moment he may refuse food and the next devour everything he can get hold of. His behavior is obscene and entirely shameless, and personal habits completely deteriorate. He may smear his excreta on his person or about the walls. He is dangerous to those about him and may seriously injure himself. In short, he fulfills the popular notion of a raving maniac.

This condition places a tremendous burden on all bodily functions, and the patient loses weight rapidly and may become utterly exhausted. As might be expected, vulnerability to heart attacks and strokes is increased and resistance to disease is lowered—particularly among older patients.

The following scene, which took place in the courtyard of a state mental hospital before the advent of newer treatment procedures, illustrates the extreme excitement that may occur.

A manic patient had climbed upon the small platform in the middle of the yard and was delivering an impassioned lecture to a number of patients sitting on benches which surrounded the platform. Most of the audience were depressed patients who were hallucinated and muttering to themselves and not paying a bit of attention to the speaker. However, the speaker had an "assistant" in the form of a hypomanic patient who would move rapidly around the circle of benches shaking the occupants and exhorting them to pay attention to the speaker. If anyone started to leave, the assistant would plump him back in his seat in no uncertain terms. In the background were a number of apparently schizophrenic patients who were pacing a given number of steps back and forth, and beyond was the high wire fence which surrounded the yard.

The speaker herself was in a state of delirious mania. She had torn her clothing to shreds and was singing and shouting at the top of her voice. So rapidly did her thoughts move from one topic to another that her "speech" was almost a complete word hash, although occasional sentences such as "You goddam bitches" and "God loves everybody, do you hear?" could be made out. These points were illustrated by wild gestures, screaming climaxes, and outbursts of song. In the delivery of her talk, she moved restlessly back and forth on the platform, occasionally falling off the platform in her wild excitement. Her ankles and legs were bleeding from rubbing the edge of the platform during these falls, but she was completely oblivious to her injuries.

Fortunately, the degree of excitement in manic reactions can now be markedly reduced by means of various drugs—often in combination with electroshock—and scenes such as this need no longer occur.

Depressed types. The symptom picture in depressive reactions is in many ways a reversal of that in manic reactions. Here, too, there are differences in degree.

1. *Simple depression.* The outstanding symptoms in simple depression are a loss of enthusiasm and a general slowing down of mental and physical activity. The individual feels dejected and discouraged. Work and other activities require tremendous effort and somehow do not seem worth bothering with anyway. Feelings of unworthiness, failure, sinfulness, and guilt dominate his sluggish thought processes. His loss of interest in things about him extends to eating and is usually reflected in loss of weight and digestive difficulties, such as constipation. Conversation is carried on in a monotone and questions are answered with a meager supply of words. In general, the individual prefers just to sit alone, contemplating his sins and seeing no hope for the future. As we have noted, suicidal preoccupation is common and actual suicide attempts may be made.

Despite the mental and motor retardation, however, the person shows no real clouding of consciousness or actual disorientation. His memory remains unimpaired and he is able to answer questions fairly satisfactorily if allowed sufficient time. Many of these individuals have some insight into their condition and understand that they need treatment, although they may not admit that they are depressed but rather emphasize various bodily ailments, such as headaches, fatigue, loss of appetite, constipation, and poor sleep. In fact, mild depressive cases are sometimes diagnosed as neurasthenia. In depressive reactions, however, the person usually insists that his ailments and other difficulties are punishment for various mistakes and sins committed in the past. The following is an excerpt from a conversation between a therapist and a young woman 25 years old who had been classified as a mild depressive.

Th.: Good morning, how are you today?

Pt.: (Pause) Well, o.k. I guess, doctor. . . . I don't know, I just feel sort of discouraged.

Th.: Is there anything in particular that worries you?

Pt.: I don't know, doctor . . . everything seems to be futile . . . nothing seems worth while any more. It seems as if all that was beautiful has lost its beauty. I guess I expected more than life has given. It just doesn't seem worth while going on. I can't seem to make up my mind about anything. I guess I have what you would call the "blues."

Th.: Can you tell me more about your feelings?

Pt.: Well . . . my family expected great things of me. I am supposed to be the outstanding member of the family . . . they think because I went through college everything should begin to pop and there's nothing to pop. I . . . really don't expect anything from anyone. Those whom I have trusted proved themselves less than friends should be.

Th.: Oh?

Pt.: Yes, I once had a very good girl friend with whom I spent a good deal of time. She was very important to me . . . I thought she was my friend but now she treats me like a casual acquaintance (tears).

Th.: Can you think of any reason for this?

Pt.: Yes, it's all my fault. I can't blame them—anybody that is . . . I am not worthy of them. I have sinned against nature. I am worthless . . . nobody can love me. I don't deserve friends or success. . . .

Th.: You sinned against nature?

Pt.: Well . . . I am just no good. I am a failure. I was envious of other people. I didn't want them to have more than I had and when something bad happened to them I was glad. Now I am being repaid for my sins. All my flaws stand out and I am repugnant to everyone. (Sighs) I am a miserable failure. . . . There is no hope for me.

2. *Acute depression.* In acute depressive reactions the mental and physical retardation is increased. The individual becomes increasingly inactive, tends to isolate himself from others, does not speak of his own accord, and is extremely slow in his responses. Feelings of guilt and worthlessness become more pronounced and the individual becomes increasingly self-accusatory. He may hold himself responsible for plagues, floods, or economic depressions, and may insist that he has committed all sorts of horrible sins which will bring disaster on everyone.

Delusions may take a hypochondriacal turn, and in keeping with his morbid mood, the individual may believe that his brain is being eaten away, that his "insides are slowly petrifying," or that his bowels are completely stopped up. One hospitalized patient maintained that he had not had a bowel movement for over a month. The patient may refuse to eat because he has no stomach and is only a "living shell." He usually blames these ailments on early sex practices or other sins which have undermined his health and for which he is now being punished.

The individual experiencing acute depression sees absolutely no hope that things will ever improve. Remedies are of no avail, and he can only anticipate a horrible end. Feelings of unreality and mild hallucinations occasionally occur, particularly in connection with ideas of sin, guilt, and disease. There is a considerable danger of suicide, since death generally seems the only way out. The reactions of this 47-year-old patient are fairly typical:

Th.: Good morning, Mr. H., how are you today?

Pt.: (Long pause—looks up and then head drops back down and stares at floor.)

Th.: I said good morning, Mr. H. Wouldn't you like to tell me how you feel today?

Pt.: (Pause—looks up again) . . . I feel . . . terrible . . . simply terrible.

Th.: What seems to be your trouble?

Pt.: . . . There's just no way out of it . . . nothing but blind alleys . . . I have no appetite . . . nothing matters anymore . . . it's hopeless . . . everything is hopeless.

Th.: Can you tell me how your trouble started?

Pt.: I don't know . . . it seems like I have a lead weight in my stomach . . . I feel different . . . I am not like other people . . . my health is ruined . . . I wish I were dead.

Th.: Your health is ruined?

Pt.: . . . Yes, my brain is being eaten away. I shouldn't have done it . . . If I had any will power I would kill myself . . . I don't deserve to live . . . I have ruined everything . . . and it's all my fault.

Th.: It's all your fault?

Pt.: Yes . . . I have been unfaithful to my wife and now I am being punished . . . my health is ruined . . . there's no use going on . . . (sigh) . . . I have ruined everything . . . my family . . . and now myself . . . I bring misfortune to everyone . . . I am a moral leper . . . a serpent in the Garden of Eden . . . why don't I die . . . why don't you give me a pill and end it all before I bring catastrophe on everyone. . . .

These pictures reveal the deep distress that is felt by depressed and suicidal individuals.

The photograph on the upper left communicates a woman's feeling of depression and despair, a sign that personal resources are proving inadequate for dealing with her problems.

A detail from the painting "Alone" (above, right) holds a mirror to the panic and helplessness the artist, a psychiatric patient, associates with aloneness or alienation. Painted entirely in black and white, the work was among those selected for an exhibit of patient art.

"The Cry" (at right) is by the Norwegian artist Edvard Munch. The Los Angeles Suicide Prevention Center has used this picture to demonstrate the desperation underlying the individual's "call for help" and to emphasize the importance of answering such calls in the prevention of suicide. (For a description of how such calls are answered, see p. 359.)

Th.: Don't you think we can help you?

Pt.: . . . (pause) . . . No one can help me . . . everybody tries to help me . . . but it is too late . . . (long pause, sigh) it's hopeless . . . I know that . . . it's hopeless. . . .

The clinical picture in acute depression is very similar to that in disorders categorized as *psychotic depressive reactions* in the APA classification. A psychotic depressive reaction is distinguished from other patterns of severe depression primarily on the basis of two characteristics: (1) it is clearly precipitated by a stressful experience, usually one resulting in extreme self-devaluation, and (2) the individual ordinarily has no history of prior depressive episodes or of cyclothymic mood swings. However, the dynamics, treatment, and outcomes associated with psychotic depressive reactions are not significantly different from those associated with other depressive patterns described in this chapter, and we shall not give them separate consideration.

3. *Depressive stupor.* In the most severe degree of retardation and depression, the individual becomes almost completely unresponsive and inactive. He is usually bedridden and utterly indifferent to all that goes on around him. He refuses to speak or eat and has to be tube-fed and have his eliminative processes taken care of. Confusion concerning time, place, and person is marked and there are vivid hallucinations and delusions, particularly involving grotesque fantasies about sin, death, and rebirth. The following brief description illustrates this severe depressive reaction.

The patient lay in bed, immobile, with a dull, depressed expression on his face. His eyes were sunken and downcast. Even when spoken to, he would not raise his eyes to look at the speaker. Usually he did not respond at all to questions, but sometimes, after apparently great effort, he would mumble something about the "Scourge of God." He appeared somewhat emaciated, his breath was foul, and he had to be given enemas to maintain elimination. Occasionally, with great effort, he made the sign of the cross with his right hand. The overall picture was one of extreme vegetative-like immobility and depression.

With the newer treatment methods—usually involving a combination of antidepressant drugs and electroshock—most depressive reactions can be rapidly ameliorated today, and few hospitalized patients remain severely depressed for an extended period of time.

Circular and mixed types. The circular type of manic-depressive psychosis is distinguished by at least one episode of both a depressive and manic reaction, and helps us to understand why manic and depressed types are combined into a single category in the APA classification. Although manic-depressive reactions have been considered historically as circular reactions, only some 15 to 25 percent of manic-depressives actually show an alternation between manic and depressive episodes. Typically when such an alternation occurs, there is a direct change from a manic to a depressive reaction or vice versa—with the change often occurring during the night. For example, the patient may go to sleep depressed and wake up manic. Jenner et al. (1967) have cited an unusual case of a manic-depressive patient whose manic phase lasted 24 hours and was then followed by a depressive phase of equal

length. This cycle had persisted for 11 years. This case, of course, is atypical. Occasionally there is a transitional period between the mania and depression. The individual may recover from a manic episode and leave the hospital or clinic, only to be readmitted several months or years later with a severe depression.

In "mixed" manic-depressive episodes, manic and depressive symptoms appear simultaneously. For example, there may be a "manic stupor," in which the individual experiences marked feelings of elation, accompanied by a dearth of ideas and generally decreased psychomotor activity; or there may be an "agitated depression," characterized by restlessness and hyperactivity with a depressed and self-deprecatory mood.

In some cases the clinical picture in manic-depressive psychoses may show a distinct schizophrenic coloring—schizo-affective depression—but the marked distortion of reality common to schizophrenia is not typically found in such reactions. This pattern has led some investigators to speculate that schizophrenia and manic-depressive psychoses are not separate mental disorders, but rather are extremes of a continuum characterized by a shattering of thought processes at one end and relatively pure mood disturbances at the other—with gradations of mixture in between (Blinder, 1966).

DYNAMICS OF MANIC-DEPRESSIVE REACTIONS

In considering the etiology of manic-depressive psychoses, we shall again find it useful to examine the possible significance of biological, psychosocial, and sociocultural factors.

Biological factors. Attempts to explain manic-depressive psychoses on a biological level have run the familiar gamut from genetic and/or acquired predisposition through neurophysiological differences, biochemical alterations, and various related considerations.

1. *Hereditary predisposition.* Research findings indicate that the incidence of manic-depressive disorders is considerably higher among the relatives of manic-depressives than in the population at large. In an early study, Slater (1944) found that approximately 15 percent of the brothers, sisters, parents, and children of manic-depressives were also manic-depressives; Kallmann's (1952; 1953) early estimates were in the neighborhood of 25 percent. These figures may be compared with an expectancy of about 0.5 percent for the general population. Kallmann (1958) found the concordance rate for manic-depressive reactions, as for schizophrenia, to be very much higher for identical twins than for fraternal ones. He also noted that schizophrenic and manic-depressive reactions do not occur in the same twin pair—that is, if both twins become psychotic, both develop the same disorder. He thus concluded that schizophrenic and manic-depressive reactions are genetically different—with the latter seeming to involve a genetic defect in the neurohormonal mechanisms that control emotion.

Recent studies have failed to find any genetic defects characteristic of manic-depressive disorders; but in general they have supported the earlier findings of a significantly higher incidence of such disorders among the relatives of manic-depressive patients (Dorzab et al., 1971; Pollin et al., 1970; Reich, Clayton & Winokur, 1969; Winokur et al., 1971). In a study of 59 manic patients, for example, Reich and his associates (1969) found that about 20 percent of the fathers and 34 percent of the mothers revealed affective disorders, mainly of a depressive type. It was also noted that mothers suffering from affective disorders were much more likely than fathers to have offspring who later developed affective disorders. Related findings are shown in the illustration on page 331.

Evidence for a hereditary predisposition to manic-depressive disorders cannot be ignored, but it is subject to the same limitations we have mentioned before—the factor of early environment and learning having been left uncontrolled. Although the precise role of heredity is far from clear, it appears realistic to think of it as an important interactional factor in the etiological pattern.

2. *Constitutional predisposition.* Several investigators believe that certain individuals have constitutional tendencies toward extreme mood swings—some showing predominant feelings of well-being and elation, others of discouragement and depression, and still others alternating between one and the other.

In attempting to understand manic-depressive reactions, it is helpful to note that we all experi-ence moods. We may feel particularly elated and self-confident at one time and vaguely anxious and depressed at another. In a pioneering study of euphoric and depressed moods in normal subjects, Johnson (1937) found striking differences in an individual's whole manner and approach to problems, depending on whether he was in a euphoric mood or a depressed one. In euphoric moods, subjects made more spontaneous and unnecessary conversation and reached decisions much more easily. In addition, they made more expansive movements in such psychomotor functions as writing. Depression, on the other hand, resulted in a very definite regression to childhood events in thought and memory, increased difficulty in making decisions, more cramped and smaller script and figures, and a judgment of distances as being greater than they actually were.

Findings like these in normal subjects help us to understand the effects of more exaggerated mood swings in manic-depressive reactions. Whereas our cognitive processes ordinarily maintain adequate control over our perceptions and reactions to stress situations, it appears that in manic-depressive reactions, affective processes take over and largely determine an individual's appraisal of events and experiences. For example, in depression a negative mood tends to produce a negative evaluation of events and experiences, as well as the recall of unpleasant, rather than pleasant, experiences. Hence, a negative mood—particularly a severe one, as in depression—may be self-perpetuating.

That many individuals show exaggerated mood swings in relation to minor triumphs or upsets cannot be denied. But whether such swings result from genetic factors, acquired constitutional makeup, or learned psychological reaction patterns—or from some combination of all three—has not been clearly determined. Nor is it clear, in fact, what part a tendency toward exaggerated mood swings may play in the development of manic-depressive reactions.

3. *Neurophysiological processes.* Following Pavlov's early lead, some investigators have assumed that manic reactions are states of excessive excitation and weakened inhibition of the higher brain centers, possibly due to constitutional factors. We have seen that in monkeys the processes of excitation predominate over the processes of

inhibition, and that these animals are highly excitable and unequilibrated. In many other species, including man, there is a greater equilibration of excitatory and inhibitory processes, but in any species there are wide individual differences, probably stemming from both genetic and environmental factors. Presumably such neurophysiological differences may predispose some individuals to manic-depressive disorders under severe stress.

In considering the possible role of neurophysiological factors in manic and depressive reactions, it is relevant to note Engel's (1962) conclusion that the central nervous system is apparently "organized to mediate two opposite patterns of response to a mounting need." The first is an active, goal-oriented pattern directed toward achieving the gratification of needs from external sources; the second, in contrast, is a defensive pattern aimed at reducing activity, heightening the barrier against stimulation, and conserving the energy and resources of the organism. Manic reactions appear to be an exaggerated form of the first response pattern, while depression appears to be an extreme form of the second.

But though the psychomotor retardation of the depressive and the psychomotor overactivity of the manic do suggest polar opposites in neural functioning as well as behavior, this view may be oversimplified. For example, in the Oxford Conference on Stress in 1958 (Hill, 1960), it was concluded that one type of response to severe psychological stress involved high arousal with restricted motor activity. This was seen as an immediate response to bereavement, disaster, and various kinds of threats to the self. More recent clinical evidence also supports the possibility of neural hyperexcitability—in cases of depression as well as mania (Goldstein, 1965; Whybrow & Mendels, 1969). As we noted in our earlier discussion of schizophrenia (page 284), high arousal is not necessarily accompanied by low inhibition, nor is high inhibition necessarily accompanied by low arousal.

Aside from the complexities of the arousal and inhibitory processes in the central nervous system itself, there is a further complicating factor, in that any group of individuals labeled as manic-depressives are likely to be heterogeneous on key dimensions. Thus, a great deal more research is needed before we can form valid generalizations

FAMILIAL INCIDENCE OF DEPRESSION AND ALCOHOLISM FOR ONE HUNDRED DEPRESSIVE PATIENTS

An investigation into the incidence of depression and alcoholism among primary relatives of 100 depressive patients has revealed the following figures:

PRIMARY RELATIVES	INCIDENCE (number)	
	Depression	Alcoholism
Fathers (100)	9	8
Mothers (100)	18	1
Brothers (118)	12	6
Sisters (116)	17	1

The investigators found that although there was a higher incidence of depression among female than male relatives, the higher incidence of alcoholism among male relatives made total incidence figures for female and male relatives almost equal. In general, the total incidence of depression and alcoholism was found to be much higher among relatives of younger, rather than older, patients.

Based on Dorzab et al. (1971) and Winokur et al. (1971)

about the role of neurophysiological processes in manic-depressive reactions. It would appear, however, to be a significant one.

4. *Biochemical factors.* Kraepelin considered manic-depressive psychoses to be toxic in nature, and a good deal of research effort has been directed toward finding possible metabolic alterations and brain pathology in individuals with these disorders. Particularly prominent during the last decade has been the "catecholamine hypothesis," in which both mania and depression are viewed as being related to the level of catecholamines (norepinephrine, noradrenaline, dopamine, and other biogenic amines) in the blood. Norepinephrine has received special attention, since it presumably facilitates or inhibits the transmission of neural impulses (Greenspan et al., 1969; Schildkraut, 1965; 1967). The hypothesis is essentially bipolar and has been stated as:

". . . some, if not all, depressions are associated with an absolute or relative deficiency of catecholamines, particularly norepinephrine, available at central adrenergic receptor sites. Elation, conversely, may be associated with an excess of such amines." (Schildkraut, 1965)

A number of studies have actually shown the urinary excretion of norepinephrine to be above normal during periods of mania, and below normal during periods of depression. However, the significance of these differences is not yet clear. It is possible, for example, that a deficiency of norepinephrine may be primarily an effect rather than a cause of depression. And as Kopin (1967) has pointed out, "In the absence of a method of assessing the rate of catecholamine utilization and metabolism in the human brain, studies of urinary excretion may provide useful, though limited, information concerning norepinephrine metabolism." (p. 223)

The fact that substances known to influence catecholamine metabolism have been successfully used in the treatment of manic-depressive disorders seems to lend some support to the catecholamine hypothesis. The drug imipramine, for example, has proven highly effective as an antidepressant, though precisely how it works is still unknown (Bunney et al., 1971; Goodwin et al., 1969; Van Der Velde, 1970; Whybrow & Mendels, 1969). Much more experimental is the use of lithium carbonate, which seems effective in the treatment of acute mania but not depression.

An alternative to the catecholamine hypothesis has been proposed by Mandell (1969; 1970),

POSSIBLE BIOCHEMICAL "SWITCH" FROM DEPRESSION TO MANIA

Clinical study of patients in a metabolic research ward at the National Institute of Mental Health, Bethesda, Maryland, led a team of investigators to suspect that a biological switch mechanism may be a factor in sudden cyclic shifts from depression to mania. As an example of how the switch occurs, they described the case of a female patient. Twelve days prior to the onset of a manic episode, the woman was deeply depressed. For the next seven days she stayed in bed in her room, avoiding contact with the nurses and staff. She appeared sad and deep in thought. Then the "countdown" to switch day proceeded as follows:

'Switch day' minus 5	Patient remains alone, depressed but beginning to come out of it. She says to a nurse: 'I guess I'm in one of my low periods.'
'Switch day' minus 4	Patient still appears depressed and still secludes herself in her room, but there are times when she actually seems pleasant and not brooding.
'Switch day' minus 3	In the morning, the nurses find that the patient 'appears to be functioning on a good level' and not depressed. Her behavior is rated as normal. She says how good it would be to go home on a pass the next day and expresses concern about a new female patient.
'Switch day' minus 2	Patient is normal and spends the day out on a pass with her mother.
'Switch day' minus 1	Patient is still normal and returns from pass 'in excellent spirits.' She recounts many of the events at home: 'I washed my windows, gave my dog a bath, took care of other odds and ends and got my hair cut and styled.'
'Switch day'	Patient was up entire night. Sudden onset of mania was noted around midnight. After midnight she became loud, threatening and seductive, and provoked fights. She was very angry, sarcastic, euphoric at times, talking continuously. By afternoon, she was shouting, had dressed gaudily and had put on bizarre makeup. "For the next 25 days she continued to be manic, very loud, threatening, shouting continuously, bizarre in dress, obnoxious, provocative, and extremely angry, with moods frequently vacillating from tears to forced laughter. By 'switch day' plus 26, she began to come down slowly. The cycle was starting again." (Bunney, Paul & Cramer, 1971, pp. 1–2)

On the assumption that "Something must be happening in the body as well as the mind" of such patients, these NIMH investigators studied biochemical changes in 6 manic-depressive patients: 5 female and one male, who, with one exception, were not on medication. It was found that there was a brief but marked elevation in cyclic AMP (adenosine 3', 5'-monophosphate) in the urine of the depressed patients on the day of the switch. Patients with the most rapid onset of mania also showed the most marked elevations of cyclic AMP on the switch day. Although the investigators considered the elevated cyclic AMP to be a possible biochemical switch mechanism, it was their impression "that progression into mania is often a more active process with identifiable environmental stresses playing a part. We have not seen these stresses in the change out of mania."

whose research suggests that the biochemical bases of manic-depressive disorders may be considerably more complex than the bipolar catecholamine hypothesis would seem to suggest. On the basis of experiments utilizing injections of different chemical substances known to be present in the brain, Mandell and his associates have hypothesized three basic patterns: (a) dopamine is related to energy available for coping, initiative, and "doing"; (b) methylated indoleamine is related to euphoria, calm, and optimistic creativity; and (c) norepinephrine is actually a depressant—its apparent mood-elevating effects being attributable to a blocking of its access to post-synaptic neural receptors. Thus Mandell and his associates believe that the action of norepinephrine is quite different from that proposed in the catecholamine hypothesis. In addition, they postulate that the three chemical systems they have identified underlie related psychological behavioral systems—for example, that malfunction of the dopamine system will result in lethargy, and so on.

Because the human brain is relatively inaccessible to direct chemical analysis, it has been extremely difficult for investigators to obtain sufficient evidence for evaluating the various biogenic amine hypotheses. However, evidence in support of a biochemical model of affective disorders has been steadily accumulating, while no evidence has yet turned up that might negate such a model (Lipton, 1970). In general, the following points appear relevant to all of the biochemical models developed thus far:

a) Treatment agents—such as electroshock therapy, antidepressants, and lithium carbonate—influence the metabolism of the biogenic amines.

b) The biogenic amines—such as noradrenaline, serotonin, dopamine, and norepinephrine—serve as neural transmitters or modulators.

c) Since treatment agents alter the metabolism of the biogenic amines in a corrective direction, it may be assumed that biochemical pathology exists in the affective disorders.

Several investigators have utilized the strategy of studying the biochemical changes in rapidly alternating manic-depressive reactions. Perhaps the conclusion of Wilson and Wilson (1968) is typical here: ". . . there is definitive neurophysiological evidence that in severe affective disorders brain function is altered, that specific systems are involved, and that altered activity returns to normal with treatment." (p. 107) Yet the precise causal significance of such changes in manic-depressive psychoses remains to be clarified. In particular, the question may be raised about which changes—such as adrenal pituitary changes—are part of a general adaptation syndrome to stress, and which are specific to manic-depressive or other types of affective psychoses.

Again it is relevant to note that various kinds of psychopathology may lead to alterations in brain biochemistry, rather than the other way around. This point is supported by the fact that no clear-cut differences have yet been found in brain waves or biochemistry between recovered manic-depressives and normal subjects.

5. *Sleep disturbances.* The psychomotor hyperactivity of the manic makes normal sleep all but impossible. Even in relatively mild manic reactions, as we have seen, sleep patterns are seriously disturbed. In acute mania, the individual may average less than an hour's sleep per night.

Sleep disturbances are also highly characteristic of depressive reactions. In fact, depressed persons often cite an inability to sleep as their primary complaint rather than depression itself. Not only do they usually have a difficult time falling asleep, but their sleep is frequently interrupted by spontaneous awakenings, especially during the last third of the night. Studies have shown that sleep disturbances in depression typically involve less total sleep, less REM (rapid eye movement) sleep, and less Stage 4 (deep) sleep (Mendels & Hawkins, 1968).

Several investigators have conducted experiments aimed at normalizing the overall sleep pattern in depressed persons by further depriving them of REM sleep and thereby increasing the pressure for such sleep. Thus in a study by Vogel and Traub (1968), REM pressure was elevated by awakening the subjects whenever their eye movements indicated they were going into REM sleep; and in a study by Wyatt and his associates (1971), REM sleep was completely suppressed over a prolonged period by means of drugs (monamine oxidase inhibitors). Both of these experiments were successful to the extent that increased pressure for REM sleep was accompanied by an alleviation of depressive symptoms. However, some subjects became profoundly anxious when REM deprivation was discontinued and REM compensation took place. Investigators have also noted that sleep disturbances often continue even after the clinical symptoms in depression have been alleviated (Snyder et al., 1968; Whybrow & Mendels, 1969).

As these findings illustrate, the precise role of sleep disturbances in the etiology of depressive reactions remains to be clarified. It seems probable, however, that such disturbances are not only a symptom of depression but also a contributing factor in the pathological process.

One curious aspect of manic and depressive reactions that supports a biological viewpoint is that, once the reaction is under way, it becomes relatively "autonomous" until it runs its course or is interrupted by drug or other treatment procedures. In fact, some investigators have delineated what they consider to be hereditary and endogenous "disease" type reactions, which seem to be relatively unaffected by conflicts or other stresses in the individual's life situation, while others view manic-depressive psychoses as falling along a continuum from endogenous reactions at one end to a type of psychological stress reaction at the other.

In general, the available evidence suggests that (1) genetic and constitutional factors may predispose a person to manic-depressive reactions; (2) alterations in brain biochemistry and in the processes of arousal and inhibition play a key role in these reactions; (3) sleep disturbances appear to be both a byproduct and possibly an interacting factor in the "autonomy" of these reactions once they are instituted; and (4) the preceding factors, singly and in combination, can influence the onset, nature, and course of manic-depressive reactions.

Psychological and interpersonal factors. Adolf Meyer (1948) viewed manic-depressive psychoses as reactions to stressful life situations —reactions involving both biological and psychological components and being both defensive and compensatory in nature. In essence, he viewed such reactions as an attempt by the individual, however effective or ineffective, to protect himself, ameliorate the stress, and bring about recovery. This, of course, does not rule out constitutional predisposition or the possibility that neurophysiological and biochemical disturbances may be contributing to the overall clinical picture.

Although some investigators have failed to find any stress factors that appear of causal significance, most researchers who have studied manic-depressives have been impressed with the high incidence of aversive life situations that apparently precipitated the psychotic breakdown. In an early study, Rennie and Fowler (1942) found that about 80 percent of their manic-depressive patients had had disturbing life situations which were dynamically related to the onset of their disorder. Only 20 percent of the disorders seemed to have arisen relatively "out of the blue"; and these cases may have been caused by life situations disturbing to the patient which were not apparent to an objective observer. Following this lead, Arieti (1959) concluded that the typical precipitating stresses in severe depressive reactions can be put into three categories: (1) the death of a loved one, (2) failure in an important interpersonal relationship, usually with the spouse, and (3) a severe disappointment or setback in the work to which an individual has devoted his life. All of these precipitating conditions involve the loss of something that has been of great value to the individual.

In a more recent study Paykel et al. (1969) compared a sample of 185 depressed patients with a matched control group consisting of residents in the same community. They found a "general excess" of aversive life events prior to the onset of depression, including marital difficulties, personal illness, and the death of loved ones. Similarly, Leff, Roatch, and Bunney (1970) found in an intensive study of 40 depressed patients that all had experienced multiple stresses prior to the onset of depression. And King and Pittman (1970) have reported a number of cases of young patients in which difficulties in school or divorces were contiguous with the onset of depression. The findings of these investigations are summarized in the illustration on page 335. Utilizing a different approach, Beck (1969) studied the dreams of several hundred depressed patients. He found that depressed persons commonly dreamed of themselves as the victims of aversive experiences involving frustration and loss, and he concluded that these dreams actually depicted the individual's picture of himself as a "loser."

Here it is also of interest to note the relation of stressful events to the recurrence of manic-depressive episodes. For example, Hartmann (1968) reported the case of a patient who had six severe manic episodes, all of which required hospitalization, and a number of depressive episodes, two of which required hospitalization, between the ages of 44 and 59. Typically, this patient tended to be hypomanic in his general functioning, but during the early autumn he usually ran for a political office himself or took an active role in someone else's campaign. In the process, he would become increasingly manic; and when the ventures led to defeat—which they almost invariably did—he would then become depressed in November and December.

In pointing to stress as the precipitating factor in depressive reactions, we should note that the key element is not the stressful event as such—since many people lose their jobs, quarrel with their spouses, and suffer the death of loved ones without becoming psychotically depressed—but rather the individual's appraisal of such an event in relation to himself. The many types of stress associated with depression appear to elicit certain common reactions in the individuals involved—namely, feelings of anxiety and despair and usually a catastrophic lowering of self-esteem (Beck, 1967; Grinker, 1969; Hill, 1968; Hoedemaker, 1970; Melges & Bowlby, 1969). Thus Beck, for example, found that 78 percent of his depressed patients had feelings of "hopelessness" and a negative outlook toward the future. We shall have more to say about this aspect of depression elsewhere in our discussion. The point to be emphasized here is that affective disorders, while generally precipitated by stressful events, cannot be explained in terms of stress alone. Psychological and biological factors apparently play key predisposing roles.

1. *Manic patterns as reactions to stress.* Manic and depressive reactions may be viewed as two different but related ways of dealing with stress. The manic tries to escape his difficulties by a "flight into reality." In less severe form, this type of reaction to stress is evidenced by the person who goes on a round of parties to try to forget a broken love affair, or tries to escape from anxiety by restless activity in which he occupies every moment with work, theaters, athletics,

sex affairs, travel, and countless other crowded activities—all performed with professed gusto but actually with little true enjoyment.

In true manic reactions, the dynamics are similar but the pattern is exaggerated. The manic, with a tremendous expenditure of energy, tries to deny his failure and inadequacy and play a

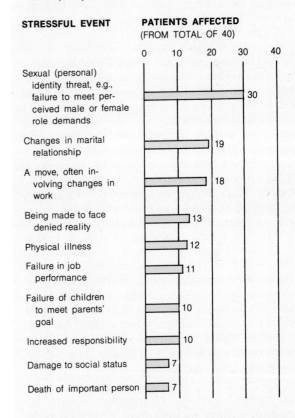

STRESS FACTORS PRECEDING SEVERE DEPRESSION

In an intensive study of 40 depressed patients, Leff, Roatch, and Bunney (1970) found that each patient had been subjected to multiple stressful events prior to early symptoms and to a clustering of such events during the month preceding the actual breakdown in functioning. The chart shows ten types of stress most frequently involved.

STRESSFUL EVENT	PATIENTS AFFECTED (FROM TOTAL OF 40)
Sexual (personal) identity threat, e.g., failure to meet perceived male or female role demands	30
Changes in marital relationship	19
A move, often involving changes in work	18
Being made to face denied reality	13
Physical illness	12
Failure in job performance	11
Failure of children to meet parents' goal	10
Increased responsibility	10
Damage to social status	7
Death of important person	7

Strikingly similar to the findings of Leff and her associates are those of Paykel et al. (1969). In that study, which involved 185 depressed patients, it was found that comparable stressful events preceded the onset of the depressive breakdown. In order of significance, these events were categorized as (1) marital difficulties, (2) work moves or changes in work conditions, (3) serious personal illness, and (4) death or serious illness of an immediate family member.

role of competence. He becomes more and more hyperactive in this role, undertaking endless activities. It is as if he overrides underlying doubts about himself and allays his anxiety by sheer weight of activity, reminding us of Shaffer's (1947) finding that soldiers felt less fear when some activity was possible, even activity that did nothing to lessen the actual danger they were facing.

Once this mode of coping with difficulties is adopted, it is maintained until it has spent itself in emotional exhaustion, for the only other alternative is an admission of defeat and inevitable depression. This is well brought out in the following case of a hypomanic patient.

"He dressed in flashy pajamas and loud bathrobes, and was otherwise immodest and careless about his personal appearance. He neglected his meals and rest hours, and was highly irregular, impulsive, and distractible in his adaptations to ward routine. Without apparent intent to be annoying or disturbing he sang, whistled, told pointless off-color stories, visited indiscriminately, and flirted crudely with the nurses and female patients. Superficially he appeared to be in high spirits, and yet one day when he was being gently chided over some particularly irresponsible act he suddenly slumped in a chair, covered his face with his hands, began sobbing, and cried, 'For Pete's sake, doc, let me be. Can't you see that I've just got to act happy?' This reversal of mood was transient and his seeming buoyancy returned in a few moments; nevertheless during a sodium amytal interview his defense euphoria again dropped away and he burst into frank sobbing as he clung to the physician's arm. He then confided that during the preceding year he had begun to suspect, with some reason, that his young second wife whom he 'loved to distraction' had tired of their marriage and had been unfaithful to him. He had accused her of this, but she had replied, almost indifferently, with an offer of divorce. His pride had been greatly wounded. . . ." (Masserman, 1961, pp. 66–67)

In manic reactions information overloading seems to become an important contributing factor. The individual's thought processes are speeded up to a point where he can no longer "process" incoming information with any degree of efficiency and loses the capacity to discriminate between relevant and irrelevant stimuli. In a manner of speaking, "the programmer loses control of the computer," resulting in a lowering of inner integration and in maladaptive behavior. In this context it is interesting to note that mania appears to be more maladaptive in some respects than depression, in that the individual's self-critical and judgmental processes are more severely impaired.

2. *Depressive patterns as reactions to stress.* Whereas the manic tries to compensate for failure or disappointment by means of frenzied activity, the depressive tends to blame himself, to feel that he is completely inadequate and worthless, and to withdraw from the stressful situation. As Weisz has expressed it:

"If such a person meets a situation representing to him an overwhelming loss or frustration, he is stymied, he is held up. Loss and frustration may be answered with the withdrawal of interest in the outside world and its objects so that such a person now pulls his tentacles in, severs himself from the outside, abandons the emotional investments and charges he has built up, becomes overwhelmed by the magnitude of the task or his failure and develops feelings of regret, feelings of catastrophe." (1947, pp. 214–215)

a) *The defensive nature of depression.* The depressive individual apparently gains some relief from his intolerable stress situation by admitting defeat and giving up the fight. Also, the slowing down of thought processes may serve to decrease his suffering by reducing the sheer quantity of painful thoughts. However, his feelings of relief are gained at the expense of his sense of adequacy and self-esteem, and thus are accompanied by marked guilt and self-accusation. Like the soldier who panics and flees from combat, he may feel relieved to be out of an intolerable situation, but he may also feel guilty and devaluated. Melges and Bowlby (1969) have reported self-blame and self-criticism to be present in about 80 percent of moderate to severe depressions.

As we have noted, the depressive tends to blame himself for his difficulties; and he tends to go over his past with a microscope, picking out any possible sins of omission or commission and exaggerating their importance in relation to his present difficulties. Immoral sexual behavior, failure to observe religious convictions, and other alleged or actual unethical actions become quite naturally the focus of his attention. Even suppressed desires and impulses may be elaborated on, as if they had actually been carried out. Thus the depressive may accuse himself of selfishness, unfaithfulness, or hostile acts against loved ones that did not actually occur. These self-accusations seem to be attempts to explain and find some meaning in his predicament and at the same time achieve some measure of expiation and atonement. The latter may help explain the eventual remission of depressive reactions, even without treatment. Apparently there is a gradual working through of the individual's feelings of unworthiness and guilt, in which he pays the price for his failures by self-punishment and is thereby cleansed and ready to have another go at life.

b) *Turning inward of aggression and hostility.* The traditional Freudian view of depression has emphasized its association with the loss of a loved person—such as one's mate through death. Bereavement leads to a natural reaction of mourning or depression, and Freud speculated on the elaborate rituals—such as funeral rites—that society has established to ease the relinquishing of loved ones. But as we have noted in our discussion of neurotic depressive reactions, normal grief and depression may be intensified to a pathological degree if the individual has had feelings of hostility toward the deceased. The following case study describes a severe depressive reaction in which hostility and self-recrimination appear to have played a major role:

The patient, a 24-year-old woman, had eloped two years previously with a young man of whom her parents disapproved. Following the elopement the parents disowned her and refused to have anything to do with her. The patient and her husband then travelled to California, where he obtained employment as a shipping clerk in a wholesale company.

The daughter and her parents did not correspond, although the daughter had severe guilt feelings about letting her parents down—they had had great ambitions for her in college and had looked forward to her future marriage with a wealthy youth whose parents were old friends. During her first year in California she became pregnant and just before the baby was to arrive wired her parents of the forthcoming event. Unfortunately, the baby died during birth and the handsome presents her parents sent for the baby only served to intensify her disappointment. However, this did serve to reestablish relations with her parents, and they made immediate arrangements to drive to California to visit the patient and her husband. But on the way they were involved in a tragic automobile accident. The father was killed outright and the mother died on the way to the hospital.

Upon the receipt of this news, the patient became extremely depressed and attempted suicide by taking an overdose of sleeping tablets. Emergency medical attention saved her life but she remained depressed and was extremely anxious and tense, unable to sit still or concentrate on any topic except her parents' death. She blamed herself for it and paced the floor in great agitation, muttering to herself and bewailing her guilt. During this period the following conversation took place.
Dr.: You feel that you are to blame for your parents' death?
Pt.: Yes, oh why didn't I obey them. Now they are dead . . . I have killed them. They were wonderful to me and I have repaid them by disobedience and murder. I deserve to die too. Oh God! I have killed my baby and now my parents! I don't deserve to live. . . . I am no good, evil. I will be punished too . . . Oh God what have I done!

It was thought in this case that the patient had felt considerable hostility toward her parents following their rejection of her, as well as guilt for disobeying them. She had never been able to express this hostility even to her husband. Apparently it added considerably to her guilt feelings and played an important part in the severe guilt reaction and agitated depression which followed their death.

In a recent study Kendell (1970) explored the hypothesis that depressive reactions result when the normal expression of aggression and hostility to frustrating situations is prevented. He found a limited relationship between inhibition of such normal aggressive responses and incidence of depression. This held for individuals as well as cultures. For example, he found that the fewer outlets a culture permits for hostility and aggression in response to frustration, the higher the incidence of depressive reactions.

It may be emphasized, however, that self-recrimination and guilt may stem from feelings of failure and other causes, as well as from the blocking or turning inward of aggressive impulses and hostility—or there may be an interaction of a number of such factors. King and Pittman (1970) reported a number of instances among young people in which divorce was contiguous with the depressive symptoms. Here it might be expected that a combination of failure, recrimination, hostility, and guilt could all be involved in varying degrees and combinations. Also of relevance is Grinker's (1969) finding that younger depressed persons revealed a high incidence of intense guilt feelings on hospital admission, while those over 50 also evidenced guilt, but were more concerned with loneliness and material losses.

c) *Loss of hope*. Depressive reactions are commonly associated with feelings of hopelessness about one's ability to achieve basic life goals. Melges and Bowlby (1969) have described the situation this way:

"... the hopelessness of a severely depressed patient is characterized by the following beliefs and expectations: (1) he believes that his skills and plans of action are no longer effective for reaching the goals he has set himself, (2) he holds his failures to be due to his own incompetence so that he must now rely more on others, and (3) he deems his previous investments in long-range goals to have met with numerous frustrations and failures." (p. 693)

Feelings of hopelessness about achieving one's goals have been emphasized as basic to depressive reactions by investigators of differing theoretical orientations. Thus Bibring (1953), a psychoanalyst, posited "... as the basic mechanism of depression, the ego's shocking awareness of its helplessness in regard to its aspirations ... such that the depressed person ... has lost his incentives and gives up, not the goals, but pursuing them, since this proves to be useless." (p. 39) From a behavioristic viewpoint, Lazarus (1968) has concluded that "... depression may be regarded as a function of inadequate or insufficient reinforcers ... some significant reinforcer has been withdrawn." (pp. 84–85) And from a more eclectic position, Stotland (1969) has hypothesized that "The lower an organism's perceived probability of attaining a goal and the greater the importance of that goal, the more will the organism experience anxiety." (p. 9) And if the state of hopelessness and anxiety continues, "... he then tends to become depressed, apathetic, withdrawn...." (p. 34) These observations, together with findings concerning concentration-camp inmates and prisoners of war, lend strong support to the saying that "When you abandon hope, you abandon everything."

Here it may be emphasized that the depressive's pursuit of continuing and long-range goals appears to be particularly important to him, and such goals are especially difficult for him to give up. Melges and Bowlby (1969) have concluded that the depressive's adherence to such goals probably stems from (a) his relative neglect of present events as determinants of his thinking and behavior, and (b) the strong resistance to extinction of his habitual goal-directed behavior:

"These factors may, in part, explain why a depressive adheres to his goals long after the probability of his achieving them has come to seem hopeless to him. To quote one depressed patient: 'I can no longer do what I want to do, and yet I still want to do those things.'" (p. 694)

3. *Predisposing personality and family factors.* We have examined the possible role of biological predisposition to manic-depressive reactions. There is also a question as to whether there may be a psychological predisposition to such disorders in certain individuals—possibly as a result of their family backgrounds.

As yet, we lack a clear understanding of the particular family background that might predispose an individual to manic-depressive reactions under stress. Studies of a limited sample of patients (Gibson, 1958; Gibson, Cohen & Cohen, 1959) indicate that manic-depressives came from home backgrounds marked by concern for social approval, strivings for prestige, and an atmosphere of competitiveness and envy. Often there were rigid standards as well as severe punishment for failing to live up to these standards and for misbehavior. In many instances the individual who later became depressed appeared to have borne the brunt of the prestige strivings of his family.

In general, available evidence indicates that manic patients—whatever their childhood background may have been—typically tend to be ambitious, outgoing, energetic, sociable, and often highly successful, both prior to their psychotic breakdown and after remission. As contrasted with normal controls, they place a higher conscious value on achievement, are very conventional in their beliefs and attitudes, and are deeply concerned about social approval and what others think of them (Becker, 1960; Becker & Altrocchi, 1968; Gibson et al., 1959; Katkin, Sasmor & Tan, 1966; Spielberger, Parker & Becker, 1963). Depressives share these characteristics of achievement motivation, excessive conformity and conventionality, and concern with social approval. However, they appear to be more obsessive, anxious, and self-deprecatory; and they show an unusually rigid conscience development, which prevents the overt expression of hostile feelings and makes them particularly prone to feelings of guilt and self-blame when things go wrong (Grinker, 1969).

One would also expect that exaggerated mood swings in the child would be fostered by similar emotional patterns in the parents, and would persist as learned maladaptive response patterns. In their study of 14 depressed children ranging in age from 3 to 12 years, Poznanski and Zrull (1970) reported that 5 of the parents were depressed at the time of referral and one father had committed suicide—apparently during an episode of depression. These investigators noted that the depressed parents had serious difficulty in handling aggression and hostility and tended to use depression defensively and intropunitively to control outbursts of rage. They concluded:

"... in those cases where parental depression was known, one source of the child's depression could be based on identification with the parent, particularly the parent's affective reaction to stress and difficulties within his own life." (p. 14)

4. *Social roles and communications.* Two other factors merit consideration in understanding manic-depressive reactions—namely, social roles and communications.

Curiously enough, the manic tends to play a social role well suited to alienating himself from others; while the depressive tends to elicit their sympathy and support. In their discussion of "playing the manic game," Janowsky, Leff, and Epstein (1970) have observed:

"The acutely manic patient is often able to alienate himself from family, friends, and therapists alike. This knack is based on the facile use of maneuvers which place individuals relating to the manic in positions of embarrassment, decreased self-esteem, and anxious self-doubt. Those dealing with the manic frequently find themselves on the defensive, attempting to justify their actions and motivations. Commonly, they feel 'outsmarted' and 'outmaneuvered.' They may 'know' that their judgment and actions are appropriate, yet be out-argued and manipulated into positions which they consider unacceptable." (p. 253)

Unlike the depressive patient, the manic apparently feels it threatening and unacceptable to rely on others or wish to be taken care of. Thus, as a way of maintaining his self-esteem and feelings of adequacy and strength, he establishes a social role and position in which he is able to control and manipulate the people on whom he must rely. The maneuvers by which he achieves this are summarized in the illustration below.

On the other hand, the depressive tends to adopt a role that places others in the position of supporting and caring for him (Janowsky et al., 1970). Ullmann and Krasner (1969) have particularly emphasized the reinforcement of this "depressed role" in our society.

"Because most people respond with kindness to the cues called depressed behavior, there may well be immediate reinforcement for emitting such behavior. ... If depressed role enactments continue, most other people will become less responsive. The effect over time is toward placing the person on an intermittent reinforcement schedule resistant to extinction." (p. 423)

The depressive generally obtains some secondary gains from his symptoms—for example, via sympathy and support from others—and he may tend to play the depressive role in accordance with his own feelings and perceptions and the apparent ex-

---

PLAYING THE MANIC GAME

Janowsky, Leff, and Epstein (1970), noting the extent to which the manic intentionally induces discomfort in those around him, pointed to the following techniques that are used in "the manic game":

1. Manipulating the self-esteem of others—either lowering or raising it—as a means of exerting leverage over them.
2. Discovering areas of sensitivity and vulnerability in others for purposes of exploitation.
3. Projecting responsibility in such a way that other people become responsible for his own actions.
4. Progressively testing limits—avoiding the limits imposed on him by challenging them or finding loopholes in them.
5. Creating interpersonal distance between himself and others by alienating family members.

Although the reasons for the use of these techniques are not clear, these investigators suggest that the manic's feeling of being threatened by and unable to rely on others may be a contributing factor.

pectations of others. However, depressive reactions are not as resistant to extinction as Ullmann and Krasner suggest: they tend to run their course with or without secondary gains. Thus they cannot be explained wholly in terms of a learning model.

Other investigators have emphasized the communication factor in depressive reactions. As Hill (1968) has expressed it:

"Symptoms, then, whether they be verbal expressions, deviant behavior, or simple motor postures or movements, are forms of communication. They are postures in the sense that they communicate the internal need state of the patient, his distress, his fear and anger, his remorse, his humble view of himself, his demands, and his dependency." (p. 456)

Particularly in interpersonal relations with significant others, depressive reactions appear to be attempts of the individual to communicate his feelings of discouragement and despair—to say, in effect, "I have needs that you are failing to meet." Hopefully, this communication will elicit a helpful response from the other person, but often it goes unheeded. Thus in failing marriages, which are commonly associated with depressive reactions, we may see the curious spectacle of one partner trying to communicate his unmet expectations, distress, and dependency— and then becoming increasingly depressed and disturbed when the other partner fails to make the hoped-for response. In a study of combat returnees from Vietnam, Goldsmith and Cretekos (1969) found that whereas anxiety was the most common reaction to earlier combat experiences, depression was the most common reaction to interpersonal problems and conflicts. Here again we may speculate that depression was at least partly a form of communication—of pleading, demanding, and exhorting that significant others should meet the returnee's special needs.

General sociocultural factors. The incidence of manic-depressive reactions seems to vary considerably among different societies; in some, manic reactions are more frequent, while in others depressive reactions are more frequent. The overall rates of manic-depressive reactions are high in New Zealand and Scotland, whereas they are low in Finland and Israel (Gold, 1951; Hes, 1960;

Murphy, Wittkower & Chance, 1967; New Zealand Department of Health, 1960; Scottish Home and Health Department, 1961). Similarly, Kendell (1970) has cited a number of studies indicating that manic reactions predominate over depressive reactions in Formosa, parts of Africa, and among the Maoris of New Zealand. Conversely, Western societies show a preponderance of depressive reactions.

Among African natives generally, Carothers (1953; 1959) found manic reactions fairly common, but depressive reactions relatively rare— the exact opposite of their incidence in the United States. He attributed the low incidence of depressive reactions to the fact that in traditional African cultures the individual has not usually been held personally responsible for his failures and misfortunes. The culture of the Kenya Africans may be taken as fairly typical in this respect:

Their behavior in all its major aspects is group-determined. Even religion is a matter of offerings and invocations in a group; it is not practiced individually and does not demand any particular attitude on the part of the individual. Similarly, grief is not borne in isolation, but appropriate rites are performed amid great public grieving. In these rites, the widow (or husband) of the deceased expresses her grief dramatically in ways prescribed by custom, and then resumes the tenor of her life as if no bereavement had occurred. Motives are social rather than individual; as a result, the individual feels none of the sense of personal aspiration and responsibility which is at the core of our Western attitudes toward our own behavior. Psychologically speaking, the Kenyan receives security because he is part of a larger organism and is not confronted with the problems of individual self-sufficiency, choice, and responsibility which may play such a large part in our culture. He does not set himself unrealistic goals, and he has no need to repress or feel guilty about "dangerous" desires. His culture actively discourages individual achievement of success, does not consider sexual behavior as evil, and is tolerant of occasional outbursts of aggressive hostility.

In addition, the Kenyan feels a great humbleness toward his natural environment, which is often harsh in the extreme. He always expects the worst, and hence can accept misfortunes with equanimity. Here too, responsibility and blame are automatically placed on forces outside himself. Although he attempts to counteract misfortune and assure success in his ventures by performing appropriate rituals, the outcome is in the hands of the gods. He is not personally responsible and hence does not ordinarily experience self-devaluation or the need for ego-defensive measures. When excessive stress and decompensation do occur, there tends to be a complete disorganization of personality —as in the hebephrenic type of schizophrenia, which is the most common type of psychotic reaction. (Adapted from Carothers, 1947; 1951; 1953)

Needless to say, Africa today is in a major transitional stage, and the preceding patterns have undoubtedly undergone change since Carothers' observations were made. However, his description is of great value in helping us understand the role of sociocultural factors in depressive reactions and other types of mental disorders as well.

Even where depressive reactions are relatively common among so-called primitive peoples, they seem less closely associated with feelings of guilt and self-recrimination than in the "highly developed" countries (Kidson & Jones, 1968; Lorr & Klett, 1969; Zung, 1969). In fact, among several groups of Australian aborigines where depressive reactions were relatively common, Kidson and Jones (1968) found not only an absence of guilt and self-recrimination but also no incidence of attempted or actual suicide. In connection with the latter finding, they stated:

"The absence of suicide can perhaps be explained as a consequence of strong fears of death and also because of the tendency to act out and project hostile impulses." (p. 415)

By way of contrast, Lorr and Klett (1969) found an "anxious depression syndrome"—characterized by anxiety, self-blame, apprehension, guilt, hopelessness, sinful feelings, self-devaluation, and suicidal impulses—in a number of highly developed societies, including the United States, England, France, Germany, Italy, Japan, and Sweden.

Social-class factors appear to be of relatively little significance in the development of affective disorders (Kendell, 1970). Some investigators have reported a higher incidence of manic-depressive disorders among the middle and upper classes and people of superior educational and occupational status; other investigators have found the reverse relationship; and still others have found little or no relationship. In his ex-

tensive study in Texas, Jaco (1960) found that manic-depressive psychoses were distributed more evenly in the population than schizophrenia, but that manic-depressive psychoses were relatively most frequent among people of superior educational, occupational, and socioeconomic status. Affective disorders as a group were about three times higher in urban than in rural areas and higher among the divorced and separated than among the married and widowed. Jaco also found a relatively high rate of manic-depressive reactions among females in professional and semiprofessional occupations.

In contrast to previous reports that depressive reactions among Negroes in the United States were likely to be characterized less by guilt and suicidal trends and more by somatic complaints, Tonks, Paykel, and Klerman (1970) found no difference between a group of Negro depressives and a group of white depressives—matched for social class—except that the clinical picture appeared to be less severe in the case of most of the Negroes.

Finally, in a study of 8000 Hutterites in 70 collective settlements in the United States and Canada, Eaton and Weil (1955) found over four times as many manic-depressive reactions (mainly of the depressive type) as schizophrenic disorders. This religious group encourages the submission of the individual to community expectations and emphasizes the principles of personal responsibility, guilt, and nonviolence. Eaton and Weil concluded that under excessive stress the Hutterites are more likely to be anti-self than antisocial—and hence more likely to become depressed than to develop other types of psychotic reactions.

None of the investigators we have cited minimize the influence of biological, psychological, and interpersonal factors on the incidence rates and clinical picture of manic-depressive reactions; but their findings indicate that sociocultural factors are important also in the overall etiological pattern.

TREATMENT AND OUTCOMES

Since lithium was first introduced in the treatment of affective disorders (by Cade of Australia in the late 1940's), it has undergone a series of tests and has been found effective in the treatment of acute mania—though not, as we have noted, in the treatment of depression (Baldessarini & Stephens, 1970; Lynn, Satloff & Tinling, 1971; Van Der Velde, 1970). Use of lithium carbonate is potentially dangerous, however, and careful precautions must be taken to guard against serious side effects. In many cases, electroshock therapy (EST) continues to be the preferred form of treatment for manic reactions in which the altering of biochemical and neurophysiological processes seems indicated.

With depressive reactions, treatment on the biological level usually involves electroshock therapy and/or the use of antidepressant drugs such as imipramine. Where depression is not severe, antidepressant drugs are often the therapy of choice, since they are the simplest, most flexible, and most readily available form of treatment. Sometimes they have even proven effective in instances where an individual did not respond to EST (Heller, Zahourek & Whittington, 1971). However, since antidepressant drugs do not have much effect until after they have been used for a week or more, EST is generally indicated in cases of severe depression when the danger of suicide appears to be great. After a series of EST treatments, most depressed patients—85 percent or more—become animated and relatively normal and approachable (Lehmann, 1968).

Even when electroshock therapy is considered necessary in order to achieve a rapid amelioration of symptoms, it is often used in combination with antidepressant and antianxiety drugs, which help maintain the treatment gains until the depression has run its course. Here it may be emphasized that

"Depression and anxiety are two symptoms which very often co-exist in the same patient. They are nevertheless different symptoms and they may vary independently in their intensity. Of the two symptoms, anxiety is by far the more conspicuous and depression the more dangerous." (Lehmann, 1968, p. 18)

Of course, treatment is not ordinarily confined to EST or drugs, but usually is combined with milieu therapy and individual or group psychotherapy directed at helping the patient achieve a more stable long-range adjustment. Attention is usually paid also to the individual's life situation, since a highly unfavorable life situation may lead to an early recurrence of the psychotic

reaction as well as to the necessity of prolonging treatment (Pollack, 1959; Zung, 1968). Perhaps the most crucial task of therapy, however, is that of evoking hope and helping the individual develop a more positive view of himself and his future (Frank, 1968). As Melges and Bowlby (1969) have noted, the more clearly we can come to understand the cognitive and affective mechanisms underlying hopelessness and loss of self-esteem, the more possible it should become to design appropriate therapy programs tailored to meet the needs of the individual.

With respect to hospitalization, proper nursing care is a vital aspect of treatment, since depressed patients are frequently very ingenious in their efforts to put an end to their suffering. Despite the patient's seemingly earnest assurance that he will do nothing to harm himself, he may cut his wrists with a small fragment of glass or set fire to his clothing with a cleverly concealed match. Because of the likelihood of suicide attempts, it is considered hazardous for family members to try to care for depressed patients in the home.

Recently a number of innovative approaches have been introduced—particularly in the treatment of depression. For example, Folsom (1969) has reported that in one Veterans Administration hospital electroshock has been discontinued since 1963 and replaced by a "paternalistic antidepression therapy" where a staff member takes over completely for the patient, permits him to make no decisions on his own, and utilizes a technique of firm kindness in guiding the patient's activities. Friedman (1964) has shown that the depressive's actual performance is not consistent with his highly devaluated image of himself. Using a group of 55 depressed patients and a control group of 65 normal subjects—matched for sex, age, education, and intelligence—he found that the depressed patients did as well as the normal persons on a series of perceptual, cognitive, and psychomotor tasks. Once the patients' protests of being too tired and incapable of doing well had been dealt with—for example, the examiner sympathized with or ignored the complaints—most patients cooperated and performed well on the assigned tasks. This study raises an interesting question concerning the possibility of providing alternative tasks and roles for depressed patients.

Although the behavior therapists so far have

not developed any overall technique for dealing with psychotic depressions, they have developed techniques for dealing with target behaviors found in such depressive reactions. For example, Schaefer and Martin (1966) have reported on a behavior-control procedure for dealing with "apathy." The approach involves schedules of reinforcement, utilizing tokens to establish and/or strengthen behavior incompatible with apathy. For example, taking care of one's personal hygiene and interacting with others would be considered incompatible with apathy in the depressed patient. These investigators found their subjects significantly less apathetic at the end of the experiment than a control group receiving the usual ward therapy. Lazarus (1968) has also attempted to utilize behavioral techniques in helping depressed patients formulate more positive attitudes toward their futures.

Even without formal therapy, as we have noted, the great majority of manic-depressives recover within less than a year. And with modern methods of treatment, the general outlook has become increasingly favorable, so that most hospitalized patients can now be discharged within 60 days. It has been noted, however, that only about one in four of these individuals remains permanently free from subsequent psychotic episodes. In a follow-up study of 215 manic-depressives in Norway, Bratfos and Haug (1968) found that 60 percent of those patients who had achieved a "full remission"—prior to or following discharge from a psychiatric clinic—experienced further manic or depressive reactions within a period of six years. More important, it was found that the mortality rate for this group had been twice as high as that for the general population during the same period, because of the high incidence of suicide. Thus, while the development of effective antidepressant drugs and other new approaches to therapy has brought greatly improved outcomes for depression, the need clearly remains for still more effective treatment methods—both immediate and long-term.

INVOLUTIONAL MELANCHOLIA

Involutional melancholia is differentiated from other depressive reactions by the initial appearance of the disorder during the climacteric (change of life), and by its tendency to become chronic unless treatment is undertaken. The involutional period is generally considered to occur in women of 40 to 55 and in men of 50 to 65. Involutional melancholia is on the decline and constitutes less than 3 percent of first admissions to public and private mental hospitals and clinics. These reactions occur about three times more often among women than men.

Much of what we have already said about depression applies to involutional melancholia as well, and in recent years there has been very little research concerned with involutional reactions as distinct from other depressive psychoses. Thus we shall limit our present discussion to a brief description of the clinical picture and a consideration of those etiological factors that appear to be particularly relevant.

CLINICAL PICTURE

The onset of this disorder is gradual, with a slow buildup of pessimism, irritability, restlessness, and insomnia. Often there is excessive worry about minor matters and unprovoked spells of weeping. The individual is worried about the past and sees little or no hope for the future. As the more acute symptoms make their appearance, he becomes increasingly depressed, anxious, and agitated, and develops marked feelings of guilt. Somatic complaints and hypochondriacal delusions are frequently present. The individual may insist that his bowels are stopped up and will never move again, that his stomach is rotting away, that his body is all withered and dried up, that his brain has been eaten away, or that he has cancer or some other terrible disease. Feelings of unreality and nihilistic delusions are also common; the individual may feel that he is living in a shadow world, that his wife and children are dead, and that nothing really exists.

The following case of a woman of 47 illustrates the feelings and thought content typical in involutional depressions.

Th.: Hello—how do you feel today?
Pt.: Oh (moaning), why don't you just let me die! It would be better for everybody.
Th.: What is the matter?
Pt.: Misery and death follow me around; everyone who gets close to me suffers. My mother and father, my children, and my husband suffered by my hand and died by my hand. (Gets up and paces back and forth.)
Th.: Isn't the girl that visits you your daughter?
Pt.: She says she is my daughter, but my children are all dead—and it is my fault. I should die a horrible death. God knows this and wants me to die. Why did I do it, there's nothing left for me but death. Nothing can be done for me—it's unforgivable; you should kill me. (Runs hands nervously through hair.)
Th.: What did you do?
Pt.: I let them die and now I should die. I am only dirt, there is only dirt left in me. There is no reason for me to eat because I am only dirt—filthy, smelly dirt. I treated everyone like dirt and now I am dirt—the worst sort and everyone knows it.
Th.: Don't the people treat you well here?
Pt.: They don't try to hurt me—but they will suffer like all the rest if they try to help me. They wouldn't try anyway—because they can see I am dirt turning to dirt. I am worthless and I can't do anything about it; no one can be my friend. They try to feed me. Can't they see that they can't feed dirt—earth into earth, that's the only place for me, and maybe I can atone for the evil I have caused.

Feelings of anxiety and depression in involutional reactions are usually accompanied by an increase in motor activity, which may range from mere restlessness to extreme agitation in which the individual paces the floor weeping, wringing his hands, pulling his hair, biting his lips, and bemoaning his fate. Despite the dramatic symptoms, however, the actual depressive affect is generally thought to be shallow as compared to that in other depressive reactions. Thought processes are not retarded, orientation is usually fairly good, and the individual may realize that he needs treatment. However, the danger of suicide is great even among individuals who show considerable insight into their condition and voluntarily seek help. It has been estimated that prior to the advent of modern treatment procedures some 25 percent of persons with involutional depression died by their own hands (English & Finch, 1954).

In some instances of involutional melancholia, the depressive substrate is overlaid with delusions of persecution and other paranoid ideation. Noting that involutional psychotics with paranoid delusions are likely to commit acts of violence, Lanzkron (1961) has emphasized that they should be hospitalized as a safeguard to other people as well as to themselves.

DYNAMICS

In general, the clinical picture in involutional psychotic reactions has been distinguished from that in manic-depressive reactions by the following characteristics: (1) a lack of previous episodes of depression prior to the involutional period; (2) a rigid, obsessive, prepsychotic personality as contrasted with a more cyclothymic one; (3) a gradual rather than abrupt onset of the disorder; (4) symptoms of agitation rather than of retardation; and (5) an absence of manic symptoms (Rosenthal, 1968). In addition, involutional melancholia tends to run a longer course, with fewer spontaneous recoveries. With modern methods of treatment, however, involutional reactions are usually cleared up before they progress to a chronic pattern.

Biological factors. Many women during the beginning of the involutional period experience various disturbances referred to as the *menopause syndrome*. The symptoms consist primarily of hot flashes, headaches, periods of dizziness, excessive sweating, nervous irritability, insomnia, and difficulty in concentrating. There may be mild depression and the clinical picture may resemble a mild neurosis, but the disturbance is transitory. It is apparently due to a decrease in ovarian hormone production, and treatment with estrogen has proven helpful both physiologically and psychologically (Neugarten, 1967; Olds, 1970).

Although the menopause syndrome and involutional psychosis may occasionally occur at the same time and the symptoms may be somewhat fused, the two conditions are distinct: involutional reactions are much more serious and do not respond to estrogen treatment. In general, studies of involutional melancholia have stressed the etiological importance of psychological and interpersonal factors rather than endocrine imbalances or other organic pathology.[1]

Psychological and interpersonal factors. The primary emphasis in the study of involutional melancholia has been on the reactions of a psychologically predisposed individual to severe stresses typical of this life period. Although the nature of parent-child relations and patterns of family interaction have not been investigated, the prepsychotic personality of involutional patients has been fairly well delineated.

In an early study comparing manic-depressives, involutional melancholics, and normals, Titley (1936) found a distinctive prepsychotic personality profile for the involutional patients, marked by overmeticulousness, overconscientiousness, rigid adherence to a high ethical code, anxiety, stubbornness, a narrow range of interests, and poor sexual adjustment. Other investigators have pointed to such traits as perfectionism, overconformity, insecurity, compulsiveness, and rigidity in everyday living habits (Gregory, 1961; Haggerty, 1941; Palmer, 1942; Rosenthal, 1968). Where paranoid ideation is involved in involutional reactions, the prepsychotic personality profile often includes sexual frigidity and a tendency to be suspicious of other people's motives.

Individuals who are thus psychologically handicapped are especially vulnerable to the stresses that inevitably accompany the involutional period of life. In a study of 379 involutional patients, Tait and Burns (1951) found that the main precipitating factor was concern about the decline of the self. Almost without warning, the individual becomes aware of getting "old." The man finds he can no longer expect promotions or change the direction of his career; he lacks his old strength and tires more easily; his sexual desire tends to be lessened. The woman realizes that she can no longer bear children and that her beauty and physical attractiveness are on the wane. Often the individual has various chronic ailments or may have to adjust to seemingly minor stresses, such as false teeth. During this period, too, the individual must cope with the loss of friends and loved ones in death.

Each individual reacts to these stresses in his own way, depending on his general personality organization and on the degree of success and independence he has achieved, his family attachments, and so on. Some people accept the inevitable with philosophical calm, perhaps tinged with a little sadness, and grow old gracefully; others begin the downward path as they climbed up, without much thought or awareness. Others, however, find this a most trying and difficult period. This is particularly true if general disappointment and frustration are accompanied by other precipitating factors, such as financial losses, the death of a loved one, or worries about health. The following poem by an involutional patient clearly conveys her feelings of hopelessness and despair:

"My kin all dead, my childless home a hall
Of spells and spectres deforming the windowed sun,
Friends few and far, and passing one by one,
My body yoked here like an ox in stall
By long disease. . . ."

The dynamic pattern involved in both the depressed and the paranoid forms of involutional melancholia thus seems readily understandable and might almost be predicted. In response to the very real stresses at this time of life, lonely, overconscientious, perfectionistic individuals easily become worried, anxious, and depressed. As past failures and disappointments loom large and as the future holds potentially less and less, the increased self-centering of interests and hypochondriacal concern provide a measure of substitute satisfaction. Then, as the involutional reaction becomes exaggerated, these hypochondriacal factors may develop into definite delusions.

Ideas of unreality probably develop out of this same self-centering of interests and the accompanying loss of interest in others and in the environment. It has been pointed out that, to a large extent, things feel real to us in proportion to the amount of interest we take in them; if we gradually become preoccupied with our own thoughts and difficulties, the external world can be expected to become progressively less real and to take on a somewhat shadowy aspect. Thus, it is not surprising that people with a tendency

---

[1]In Chapter 15 we shall discuss some other psychoses associated with old age in which organic pathology does play a primary causative role.

to be distrustful and suspicious should develop paranoid delusions as they become increasingly concerned with their own problems and increasingly isolated from meaningful interaction with other people.

Delusions of sin grow naturally out of the individual's feelings of failure and self-recrimination. He begins to feel that he must not have deserved to succeed (for it is common in our culture to assume that a really good and deserving person who works hard is bound to be a success). It is then only another step to magnify the most trivial mistakes to cardinal and unpardonable sins and to distort them as a means of explaining his present predicament.

Like other depressives, the involutional patient may even derive some satisfaction out of his exaggerated self-accusations. Statements such as "I am the greatest sinner that ever lived and the whole world knows it" may not only express his feelings of extreme guilt and unworthiness, but at the same time help to build his feelings of esteem and importance as a unique person. Also, the excessive self-recrimination probably ensures some measure of expiation and atonement. However, the failure of these defensive measures and the continued feelings of hopelessness and depression are reflected in the ten-

SOME UNANSWERED QUESTIONS CONCERNING THE AFFECTIVE PSYCHOSES

Research into the affective psychoses has yet to provide answers to the following questions:

1. Why are affective disorders usually of limited duration?
2. Why do affective disorders tend to recur?
3. Why are affective disorders relatively "autonomous," tending to run their course even without treatment?
4. Why, in depression, does the individual select from a lifetime of experience the most painful thoughts and memories?
5. What precise role is played in the affective psychoses by neurophysiological, biochemical, and psychosocial processes?

In psychology, as in the other sciences, research provides answers to some questions while leaving others unanswered; and sometimes the answers themselves give rise to other, more difficult, questions. As Lipton (1970) has said, ". . . sound research is characterized not only by the questions it answers but also by the many others it generates." (p. 357)

dency of these reactions to become chronic if treatment is not undertaken.

General sociocultural factors. Differences in the incidence of involutional reactions have been reported for different societies. Henderson and Gillespie (1950) have referred to the high incidence of involutional reactions in the rural areas of Scotland. Carothers (1947), on the other hand, found that involutional reactions constituted only 1.4 percent of total admissions among Kenya Africans, as contrasted with some 4 to 5 percent in the United States at that time. He also found no guilt in the Kenyan reactions, presumably because their behavior was primarily group-determined rather than a matter of individual choice or personal responsibility. In general, however, it would appear that the symptoms of involutional reactions are much the same in all societies. As Field (1960, p. 36) has pointed out, such persons are "the world over, unshakenly convinced of their own worthlessness and wickedness and irrationally accuse themselves of having committed every unforgivable sin."

Field (1960) has described how women experiencing involutional depression in rural Ghana travel to Ashanti religious shrines and there accuse themselves of vile witchcraft. To explain this phenomenon, Field points out that the Ashanti woman raises a large family with extreme care, is an excellent housekeeper, and is an efficient business manager. In short, she has a role to play which provides ample meaning in her life. But when she grows old and the children have left the family, the husband often takes on a younger bride on whom he lavishes his possessions and affection. Here the wife's life style, which had integrity and meaning, is suddenly undermined. Interestingly enough, however, the culture provides a ready rationalization which provides some continuity and meaning for her existence. The woman can simply acknowledge that all along she has really been a witch, and that she therefore deserves the evil that has befallen her. Thus society provides a transitional role which is intropunitive but which explains the sudden change in her life situation and paves the way for her new role as a discarded wife— which she will assume after her cure as a "witch" at the shrine.

In our society, Jaco (1960) found that the incidence rate for involutional psychoses in Texas was over twice as high in urban as in rural areas. He also found that the divorced and single population had the highest rate and the widowed the lowest rate. Except for the lower rate for the widowed, these findings seem to be somewhat self-explanatory. Becker (1964) has also pointed to the lack of interpersonal reinforcements in our society as making realistic and effective reactions to stressful events more difficult:

"We make no provision for sustaining meaning when the bottom drops out of someone's life. When a woman's children marry, when the mirror begins to reflect the gradual and irrevocable loss of her charm, her performance as a responsible person, culturally desirable, is over. She may find herself left with no part to play, as early as her late 30's . . . worth nothing to justify and sustain her identity. Since this utter subversion of meaning usually coincides with menopause, psychiatry has labeled the depression that may occur 'involutional depression.'" (p. 128)

In a highly competitive, age-conscious society in which many middle-aged and older people are alienated from broader societal and family groups, we would expect to find a substantial incidence not only of depression but also of other psychopathology during the involutional period, when many life stresses are intensified.

TREATMENT AND OUTCOMES

Prior to the advent of modern treatment approaches, the course of involutional melancholia was a long one, estimated at one to four years for those patients who recovered spontaneously—some 30 to 60 percent (Rosenthal, 1968). The other 40 or more percent became chronic hospital cases. With the use of EST, the duration of the disorder has been shortened to three to six weeks in many cases; and the great majority of patients respond to broadly based treatment programs that include the use of antidepressant drugs, psychotherapy, and sociotherapy.

The importance of psychotherapy and sociotherapy seems particularly important in involutional melancholia. As we have seen, the manic-depressive is apparently only temporarily defeated; once he has worked through his feelings of loss, hopelessness, and self-devaluation, he can return to the struggle of life. On the other hand, the depressed involutional patient, more rigid and perfectionistic, older and probably actually facing a more hopeless future, has little incentive to recover and reenter the fight to build a meaningful and fulfilling life in the time that remains to him. Thus, he needs additional and long-range supportive measures to help him make an adequate readjustment.

SUICIDE

Suicide ranks among the first ten causes of death in the industrialized world (World Health Organization, 1967). In our own society, it is estimated that over 200,000 persons attempt suicide each year, and official figures show that some 25,000 succeed. This means that about every twenty minutes someone in the United States kills himself, and that over two million living Americans have made suicide attempts at some time in their lives. Indeed, the problem may be much more serious than even these figures suggest, since many self-inflicted deaths are certified in official records as being attributable to

other, "more respectable," causes than suicide. Experts have judged that, depending on the country, the number of actual suicides is anywhere from two to five times the number officially reported.

Nor can statistics, however accurate, begin to convey the tragedy of suicide in human terms. As we shall see, probably the great majority of persons who commit suicide are actually quite ambivalent about taking their own lives. The irreversible choice is made when they are alone and in a state of severe psychological stress, unable to see their problems objectively or to evaluate

FACTS ABOUT SUICIDE

INCIDENCE

General

Suicide ranks seventh in causes of death in the United States, and among the first ten causes of death in the industrialized world. By conservative estimate, more than 2 million living Americans (approximately one percent of the total population) have made suicide attempts at some time in their lives—the incidence of such attempts in this country having been estimated at more than 200,000 a year. For adolescents and adults in the United States, the incidence of suicide is estimated to be well over 25,000 annually, and the rate is estimated to be approximately 25 persons per 100,000. The incidence of suicide is highest in the spring, although it is disproportionate during the Christmas holidays as well. An estimated 70 to 80 percent of suicides are associated with severe depression.

Age and sex

Three times as many men as women commit suicide, but women make more suicide attempts, generally using less lethal means. For both sexes, the incidence of suicide generally increases with age, with more than half of all suicides being committed by persons over 45 years old. Over the past several years, however, the incidence of suicide has shown a marked increase among adolescents and young adults.

Marital and occupational status

Suicide rates are higher among divorced persons, followed by the widowed and the single, than among married persons. Among certain professional and occupational groups, also, the rate is higher than average; e.g., it is high for physicians (particularly psychiatrists), lawyers, and dentists, and it is also high for unskilled laborers and persons with low employment security.

General sociocultural factors

The incidence of suicide varies significantly from one society to another as well as among subgroups within a society. In West Germany, Finland, and Hungary, for example, the annual suicide rate is about 30 persons per 100,000, whereas New Guinea and the Philippines have a rate of about 1 per 100,000. Religious beliefs are apparently one significant variable, as suggested by the fact that suicide rates are relatively low in both Catholic and Muslim countries—as they are among religious people generally. The incidence of suicide also varies over time with general sociocultural conditions. Contrary to popular belief, the incidence of suicide tends to decrease during wars, earthquakes and certain other crises; however, it generally increases during economic depressions and periods of normlessness or social unrest. In the United States, as in other industrialized societies, the suicide rate is significantly greater in urban than in rural areas.

METHOD

Range of methods used

Every possible method of dying gets tried, including the use of barbiturates and other pills, inhalation of carbon monoxide and other poisonous gases, use of firearms and explosives, hanging, strangulation, suffocation, drowning, cutting and stabbing, jumping from high places, and automobile crashes.

Differences in methods used by men and women

Among men, the methods used in suicide attempts occur approximately in this order: gunshot, hanging, inhalation of carbon monoxide, drowning, use of barbiturates, jumping, use of other drugs, and cutting and stabbing. Among women, the most common methods are the use of barbiturates, hanging, and gunshot, followed by inhalation of carbon monoxide, use of other drugs, jumping, and cutting and stabbing.

---

alternative courses of action. In many instances, too, suicide is an accidental act, intended as a dramatic warning that the individual is distressed and needs help. For example, a person may take an overdose of sleeping pills and then call a friend to tell what he has done—assuming that the friend will call the police or take other action necessary to prevent his death. But things do not always work out as intended, and the action may be terminal.

Aside from relatively explicit religious and cultural mores condemning suicide in most societies, there appear to be two basic humanitarian problems involved. The first is the seemingly senseless loss of life by an individual who may

be ambivalent about living, or who does not really want to die. The second tragic problem arises from the long-lasting distress among significant others that may result from such action. As Shneidman (1969) has put it, "The person who commits suicide puts his psychological skeleton in the survivor's emotional closet. . . ." (p. 22)

In our present discussion of suicide, we shall focus in turn on the dynamics of suicidal behavior and on the measures being taken to prevent suicide in our own society. This will lead us to a consideration of such questions as: Who commits suicide? What are the motives for taking one's own life? What role do significant others

INTENT

Degree of intent   Most persons who attempt suicide either do not want to kill themselves (approximately two thirds of all who make such attempts) or are ambivalent about the consequences of their act (approximately one third). Only a very small minority—estimated at from 3 to 5 percent—are intent on dying. Investigators have noted that the more violent the method used (such as jumping from high places or the use of firearms or explosives) the more serious the intent. The use of such methods also indicates that, if one attempt fails, another is likely to follow.

Communication of intent   The great majority of persons who eventually attempt suicide make their distress and intentions known beforehand —either by threats or by such other cues as sudden increase in the consumption of alcohol or barbiturates, discussion of the methods of suicide, or a developing depression. Some write suicide notes which, if found in time, may prevent the suicide attempt from succeeding. Contrary to the popular belief that few persons who threaten suicide actually attempt to take their lives, the risk of suicide is very high among such individuals. A recent study of suicides (Rudestam, 1971) revealed that the majority were preceded by direct or indirect threats, predominantly the former.

INTERVENTION   More than 200 Suicide Prevention Centers have been established throughout the United States for the purpose of helping people through suicidal crises. Emotionally disturbed individuals can call such centers around the clock and get help in dealing with their problems, depressions, and self-injurious impulses. (See page 359.)

  The preceding information relates to actual suicidal behavior. However, it would appear that many individuals, while not clearly suicidal in the ordinary sense, also engage in life-threatening behavior. Here, for example, may be those who "drink themselves to death," who are extremely accident-prone as a result of indifference or carelessness, or who otherwise engage in behavior so injurious to health and physical well-being, as well as to interpersonal relationships, that it may lead to their death.

Based on Darbonne (1969), Dizmang (1970), Farberow and Litman (1970), Hall, Bliss, Smith, and Bradley (1970), Kidson and Jones (1968), Kiev (1970), Lunn (1970), Melges and Bowlby (1969), Motto (1969), National Institute of Mental Health (1969), Nelson (1971), Rudestam (1971), Shneidman (1969), Stotland (1969), Thomas (1970), Weisman (1970), and World Health Organization (1967).

play in attempted and actual suicide? What sociocultural variables appear to be relevant to an understanding of suicide? And finally, what measures have proved most effective in suicide prevention?

THE DYNAMICS OF SUICIDAL BEHAVIOR

Most people have probably gone through periods of conflict and distress when they have contemplated suicide. In fact, Star (1966) has stated the matter more strongly: "Everyone, at some time or other, has the wish to kill himself." (p. 62) Fortunately, most people do not attempt suicide, even under severely stressful conditions; and where suicide attempts do occur, they are the end result of processes that differ greatly from case to case. Thus, few general statements can be made about suicidal behavior.

Since research effort has only recently focused on the problems of suicide and death, data are limited; and interpretations of available data are tentative and often highly speculative as well. Our present discussion will deal mainly with psychological, interpersonal, and general sociocultural factors that appear relevant to an understanding of suicidal behavior.

Stress factors in suicide. The stress situations associated with suicide are not particularly different from those found in the affective disorders. Thus, crises commonly associated with suicide run the gamut from interpersonal disruptions through failure and self-devaluation to loss of meaning and hope.

1. *Interpersonal crises.* Interpersonal conflicts and disruptions—such as those associated with marital conflict, separation, divorce, or the loss of loved ones through death—may result in severe stress and suicidal behavior. Darbonne (1969, p. 49) has described the following note as typical of such interpersonal crises. It was written by a 28-year-old married woman who was undergoing a marital crisis in which she felt misunderstood and devaluated.

"Dear Mom:

I've tried very hard to hide it, but I'm still as much in love with Bill as always. I don't know how he feels about me, but my life is in his hands now. He knows I can't go on without him and if you read this it means he didn't care enough to stop me. I'm sorry to have failed you this way, but I love Bill so much, I'm not quite sane, let alone intelligent without him. It's better for the babies that I just check out this way than for me to keep on being so unhappy around them. There's a letter somewhere in my grey suitcase for Tim when he is 16.

All my love forever,
Mary"

In other instances, suicidal behavior may follow the death of a loved one on whom the person felt highly dependent for emotional support and meaning in his life.

2. *Failure and self-devaluation.* Among males in particular, many suicides are associated with feelings of having failed in some important enterprise—often involving occupational aspirations and accomplishments.

Although James Forrestal did not hold public office at the time of his death, he was one of the two highest ranking American public officials to have taken his own life. He had been the Secretary of the Navy and the nation's first Secretary of Defense. He took his life by jumping from his sixteenth-floor room at Bethesda Naval Hospital.

Forrestal was described as extremely conscientious, compulsively hard-working, and inclined to make excessive demands on himself. He demanded the highest level of achievement, was highly self-critical, and suffered from feelings of inadequacy even at times of great achievement. Prior to taking his life, he apparently felt increasing pessimism concerning the world situation, and also felt that he had failed to achieve what he had hoped to accomplish during his tenure in public office. During an episode of self-recrimination and depression, he committed suicide. (Adapted from Rogow, 1969)

A tragic aspect of this case is that James Forrestal was a highly respected man who was admired for his accomplishments in office. In fact, some of his friends thought that his political future might even include the White House.

3. *Loss of meaning and hope.* In their review of hopelessness in relation to psychopathology, Melges and Bowlby (1969) found that of all the symptoms correlated with suicide, hopelessness predominated. As long as they see a chance that things will improve, and as long as they see meaning in their lives, most people continue to work toward valued goals. With the loss of hope and meaning, however, the individual may give up trying and take his own life. The following is a note left by a 71-year-old man to his son (Darbonne, 1969, p. 50):

"John, I do not seem to be wanted living with you and Betty so the best thing I can do is put myself out of the way. When you brought up about the large telephone bill you sure had upset me. I have not been using your phone so I do not understand why you said that. . . . So goodbye to you all and please forgive me. I will never get any better at my age so what is the use of trying to go on . . . just a lot of suffering and expense. Say goodbye to Martha Smith for me and treat her right. You know we all have our faults when we get older. She has been very nice to me for what she had done since Mom died. I have had this heart trouble since 1948 and it sure is not going to get better. I do not want to spend several months or years in a rest home. Good Bye.   Dad"

The feeling that life has lost its meaning and hope and is no longer worth living often occurs in terminal illnesses, particularly where the individual suffers severe and sustained pain. In a study of surgical patients with malignant neoplasms, Farberow, Shneidman, and Leonard (1963) found that suicide may occur even when the patient has only a few hours or, at most, days to live.

Although the preceding categories include most of the stresses commonly associated with suicidal behavior, the specific stress factors in each category may take many forms. In Chapter 7 we noted the case of the young man who suffered intense guilt feelings for not having saved his wife in the disastrous Cocoanut Grove fire and shortly afterward committed suicide. Similarly, suicide may be associated with interpersonal problems involving intense hostility, severe financial reverses, loss of social status, and other difficult stress situations.

Suicidal motivation and ideation. From the standpoint of motivation, suicide appears to be one method of obtaining relief from an aversive life situation. However, since most people undergoing severe stresses do not commit suicide —for example, only a small number of patients who develop terminal cancer take their own lives —the question again arises of why an individual uses this method of coping rather than another. This is not an easy question to answer, and involves consideration not only of stress but also of the psychological state of the individual at the time of the suicide attempt.

An estimated 75 to 80 percent of suicides are associated with severe depression (Motto, 1969). Often the individual is hurt and discouraged and seems to retreat into himself in an attempt to "comprehend" what is happening and to think through a course of action. Unfortunately, as we have seen, during periods of intense stress the individual's ability to think rationally is often impaired. As Farberow and Litman (1970) have expressed it:

"When clinical depression becomes acute, mental myopia is common. That is to say, a depressed person is emotionally incapable of perceiving realistic alternative solutions to a difficult problem. His thinking process is often limited to the point where he can see no other way out of a bad situation other than that of suicide." (p. 85)

One depressed and suicidal young woman described her feelings as "being like a dark fog drifting in and enveloping me, so that I can no longer see or think about anything but darkness and gloom."

In some instances, the individual's irrational thinking is not associated with depression but

"Suicidal Ideas," a nineteenth-century lithograph by Traviès de Villers, a French caricaturist and painter, depicts a melancholy imagination at work. The gloomy individual is surrounded with visions of himself as victim by a range of methods that are used in suicide attempts.

rather with intense anger and hostility and a desire to seek revenge on other persons. As we have seen, the individual who commits suicide often creates lasting distress for significant others who are left behind, especially when the latter feel some responsibility for the person's death. In still other instances, the individual's thought processes are chaotic, and he is out of contact with reality when he attempts suicide. This may occur in certain forms of drug intoxication, schizophrenia, psychotic depressions, and states of extreme anxiety and panic.

Shneidman (1969) has distinguished three categories of suicidal motivation and ideation, all closely related to the stress factors in suicide which we have discussed and to the resulting distress of the individual.

The first type involves interpersonal difficulties and is characterized by conflict with or unfulfilled need for another person. The major motivational and ideational factors include histrionic rage, hostility and revenge, frustration over rejection, and the desire to withdraw from the turmoil of a relationship that is highly conflictful but on which the individual feels dependent. Thus, the suicidal act can only be understood in terms of the disturbed interpersonal relationship. Apparently most suicides are of this type.

The second type of suicidal motivation and ideation is associated with feelings of meaninglessness and hopelessness. The individual either loses or is unable to find a meaningful role in the human enterprise. He seems to have no place in "the scheme of things." His life is futile. The notes left behind after this type of suicide are often addressed "To whom it may concern" or "To the police." Often they are not addressed to anyone. As Shneidman has expressed it, "They seem to be muted voices in a macrotemporal void." (1969, p. 17)

The third type is characterized by inner conflict. Specific environmental pressures or conflicts with others are of minor importance as compared to the debate in the person's own mind. He may be anxious and confused, struggle with the meaning of life and death, and decide that he does not wish to continue the struggle any longer. Shneidman has described the suicide notes left by such persons as "special windows not so much into the ideation or affect of the anguished person as they are private views of idiosyncratic existential struggles and inner unresolved philosophic disputations." (1969, p. 14) In some suicides of this type, the ideation involves religious or mystical ideas about death, the reunion with loved ones, "oceanic" feelings of oneness with the cosmos in death, or eroticized feelings about the seductiveness of death.

In this context, it is interesting to note a short piece written by Ernest Hemingway after he had been erroneously reported as killed in an African air crash:

"In all the obituaries, or almost all, it was emphasized that I had sought death all my life. Can one imagine that if a man sought death all his life, he could not have found her before the age of 54?

"It is one thing to be in the proximity of death, to know more or less what she is, and it is quite another thing to seek her. She is the most easy thing to find that I know of. *You may find her through a minor carelessness, on a road with heavy traffic, you could find her in a bottle of Seconal, you could find her with any type of razor blade; you could find her in your own bathtub or you could find her by not being battlewise.* If you have spent your life avoiding death as cagily as possible but, on the other hand, taking no back-chat from her and studying her as you would a beautiful harlot who could put you soundly to sleep for ever with no problems and no necessity to work, you could be said to have studied her but not sought her."

Commenting on this statement, Farberow and Shneidman (1961) pointed out that Hemingway denied any concern with suicide but rather showed concern with the whole problem of death. However, his own death was a suicide; and it may have been that when his life was threatened by a terminal illness, his views of death made suicide a logical step to take.

Emotional content of suicide notes. A number of investigators have analyzed the content of suicide notes in an effort to better understand the motives and feelings of persons who take their own lives. In a study of 742 suicides, Tuckman et al. (1959) found that 24 percent left notes, usually addressed to relatives or friends. The notes were either mailed, or found on the person of the deceased or near the suicide scene. With few exceptions, the notes were coherent and legible. In terms of emotional content, the suicide notes were categorized into those showing positive, negative, and neutral affects. And, of course, some notes showed combinations of these affective components.

1. *Positive emotional content.* Interestingly enough, 51 percent of the notes in the study of Tuckman et al. (1959) showed positive affect, expressing affection, gratitude, and concern for others. The following is a brief but somewhat typical example.

"Please forgive me and please forget me. I'll always love you. All I have was yours. No one ever did more for me than you, oh please pray for me please." (p. 60)

The following note also shows positive affect and concern for others, but the discouragement and hopelessness expressed led Darbonne (1969) to call it the "communication of the vanquished."

"Please God forgive me, never again after this is over will I hurt anyone. I love my wife and children too much to continue on not knowing when I'll do something again to hurt them. . . . If I continue as I have in the past my family will not have a chance. Now they can. . . ." (Darbonne, 1969, p. 49)

2. *Negative (hostile) emotional content.* In the study of Tuckman et al. (1959), only 6 percent of the suicide notes were classified as involving pure hostility or negative affect. In most cases the hostility was directed toward others, but in some instances it was directed inward toward the self.

"I hate you and all of your family and I hope you never have a piece of mind. I hope I haunt this house as long as you live here and I wish you all the bad luck in the world." (Tuckman et al., 1959, p. 60)

Hostility directed inward, accompanied by severe self-devaluation, is expressed in the following note.

"I know at last what I have to do. I pray to God to forgive me for all the many sins I have committed and for all the many people I have wronged, I no longer have the strength to go on, what I am about to do might seem wrong to a lot of people, but I don't think so, I have given it plenty of sober consideration." (Tuckman, et al., 1959, p. 60)

This note would also qualify as a "communication of the vanquished."

3. *Neutral emotional content.* Suicide notes expressing neutral feeling commonly begin with "To whom it may concern," "To the police," or they may not be addressed to anyone. The following are somewhat typical examples.

"Everything I own goes to Miss_____ in case of my death." (Tuckman et al., 1959, p.   )

"To Whom It May Concern,

"I, Mary Smith, being of sound mind, do this day, make my last will as follows—I bequeath my rings, Diamond and Black Opal to my daughter-in-law, Doris Jones and any other of my personal belongings she might wish. What money I have in my savings account and my checking account goes to my dear father, as he won't have me to help him. To my husband, Ed Smith, I leave my furniture and car.

"I would like to be buried as close to the grave of John Jones as possible." (Darbonne, 1969, p. 50)

As Shneidman (1969) has pointed out, people who leave notes of this type have often lost a sense of having a meaningful role in life. In the study of Tuckman et al. (1959), 25 percent of the suicide notes were classified as neutral.

4. *Mixed emotional content.* The note which follows was classified as a combination of positive affect and inward-directed hostility.

"My Dear Sister I love you and B—— more than life itself—I have brought shame and heartaches for you both—Doing what I am about to do is the only decent thing that I can do with this miserable life—You see Sis you *alone* was the only one who understood what had happened to me—When I came back to being a free man once again I was determined and full of hope that this time I was going to make it—to put down on paper the obstacles and hazards that I had to over come would take me a week—small things like being shook down for what I happened to have in my pocket— pulled out of the movies and being embarrassed by rolling up sleeves—you see I needed help in a lot of ways—The main thing was a job—I believe that if I had a fairly good job I would have made it—That was the biggest assist I needed but it never happened. J—— —you are a swell guy—an ace—to you I couldn't explain and make you understand why I did what I did.

"Whats the use or to what purpose am I living—I pray to God to let me take my life." (Tuckman et al., 1959, pp. 60–61)

Eighteen percent of the suicide notes in the study by Tuckman et al. involved a mixture of positive and negative affect.

In general, hostile and positive emotional tone were found to be more common in the suicide notes left by persons under 45 years of age, while neutral emotional tone was almost four times as frequent among those over 45 (Tuckman et al., 1959).

Communication of suicidal intent. Research has clearly demonstrated the tragic fallacy of the opinion that those who threaten to take their lives seldom do so. In fact, such people represent a very high-risk group with respect to suicide. In a recent cross-cultural study, Rudestam (1971) conducted extensive interviews with close friends or relatives of 50 consecutive suicides in Stockholm and Los Angeles and found that at least 60 percent of the victims in both cities had made *direct* verbal threats of their intent. An additional 20 percent had voiced *indirect* threats. Contrary to popular opinion, men were found to have communicated their suicidal intent as often as women.

In a detailed study of such communications, Robins et al. (1959) found that indirect threats quite typically include statements about being better off dead, references to methods of committing suicide and to burial, and dire predictions about something happening to them. The latter is illustrated by the anguished and pathetic communication of a chronic alcoholic to his current wife:

"Mommy, I'm going to have to go away." "Mommy, where are you going to bury me?" "Mommy, I won't be here in the morning. I'm going to die tonight." "Oh, Mommy, come and sleep with me this one night more, and hold me tight, I'm so afraid." (Robins et al., 1959, p. 725)

This contrasted with his bitter but still indirect phone call to his ex-wife: "Come out and see my grave sometime."

Whether direct or indirect, communication of suicidal intent usually represents "a cry for help." The person is trying to express his distress and his ambivalence about taking his life; and, at the same time, he is both warning significant others and soliciting their help. Unfortunately, the message is often not received or is received with skepticism. The latter pattern is particularly apt to occur when the suicidal person has made repeated warnings but has not made an actual suicide attempt. As a consequence, the recipient of the message may state that he did not think it would happen; or that he thought it might happen but only if the person became much more depressed.

Noting the need for concern, Stotland (1969) has pointed out that most people who are contemplating suicide have been reduced to a state of near-hopelessness. But they may feel there is still some hope if they can obtain the understanding and support of significant others. Failing to receive it, they go on to actual suicide.

"They had turned to these others, asked for help, for hope in some way. They had asked by verbal communications, abortive suicide attempts, and had received a fearful reaction from others, signifying little hope. After they had received this communication, they went on to suicide. If they did not receive . . . a hopeless response from others, they were unlikely to go on to suicide." (p. 145)

In our later discussion of suicide prevention centers, we shall again stress the effectiveness of "a sympathetic ear" as a means of helping an individual through a suicidal crisis.

Degree of intent. The ambivalence that typically accompanies thoughts of suicide finds classic expression in Hamlet's famous soliloquy:

To be, or not to be: that is the question:
Whether 'tis nobler in the mind to suffer
The slings and arrows of outrageous fortune,
Or to take arms against a sea of troubles,
And by opposing end them? To die: to sleep;
No more; and by a sleep to say we end
The heart-ache and the thousand natural shocks
That flesh is heir to, 'tis a consummation
Devoutly to be wish'd. To die, to sleep;
To sleep: perchance to dream: ay, there's the rub;
For in that sleep of death what dreams may come
When we have shuffled off this mortal coil,
Must give us pause. . . .

(Hamlet, Act III, Scene 1)

Recognizing that the vast majority of people who contemplate suicide do not in fact kill themselves, some investigators have focused on analyzing the degree of intent associated with suicidal behavior. Thus Farberow and Litman (1970)—echoing Hamlet—have classified suicidal behavior into three categories: "To be," "Not to be," and "To be or not to be."

The "To be" group involves individuals who do not really wish to die, but rather wish to communicate a dramatic message to others concerning their distress and contemplation of suicide. Their suicide attempts involve minimal drug ingestion, minor wrist slashing, and similar non-lethal methods. They usually arrange matters so that intervention by others is almost inevitable, although sometimes things do go awry. This group is estimated to make up about two thirds of the total suicidal population.

In contrast, the "Not to be" group involves persons who seemingly are intent on dying. They give little or no warning of their intent to kill themselves, and they usually arrange the suicidal situations so that intervention is not possible. Although these persons use a variety of different methods for killing themselves, they generally rely on the more violent and certain means, such as shooting themselves or jumping from high places. It has been estimated that this group makes up only about 3 to 5 percent of the suicidal population.

The "To be or not to be" group constitutes about 30 percent of the suicidal population. It is comprised of persons who are ambivalent about dying and tend to leave the question of death to chance, or, as they commonly view it, to fate. Although loss of a love object, strained interpersonal relationships, financial problems, or feelings of meaninglessness may be present, the individual still entertains some hope of working things out. The methods used are often dangerous but moderately slow acting, such as fairly high drug ingestion, or cutting oneself severely in nonvital parts of the body, thus allowing for the possibility of intervention. The feeling is apparently that, "If I die the conflict is settled, but if I am rescued that is what is meant to be." Often persons in this group lead stormy, stress-filled lives and make repeated suicide attempts. After an unsuccessful attempt, there is usually a marked reduction in emotional turmoil. This reduction is not stable, however, and in a subsequent trial by fate, the verdict may well be death. In a follow-up study of 886 persons making suicidal attempts, Rosen (1970) found the attempts to be serious in 21 percent of the cases and non-serious in 79 percent; at the end of one year, the suicide rate was twice as high among those making serious attempts.

Farberow and Litman's classification is largely descriptive and has little practical value in terms of predicting suicidal behavior. Nevertheless, it is a very useful reminder that most people who

SUICIDE AMONG COLLEGE STUDENTS

Incidence and methods	Ten thousand students in the United States attempt suicide each year, and over 1,000 succeed. The incidence of suicide is twice as high among college students as it is among young people in the same age range who are not in college. The greatest incidence of suicidal behavior occurs at the beginning and the end of the school quarter or semester. Approximately three times more female than male students attempt suicide, but the incidence of fatal attempts is considerably higher among males. More than half of those attempting suicide take pills, about one third cut themselves, and the remainder—mostly males—use other methods, such as hanging or gunshot.
Warning signs and threats	A change in a student's mood and behavior is a most significant warning that he may be planning suicide. Characteristically, the student becomes depressed and withdrawn, undergoes a marked decline in self-esteem, and shows deterioration in habits of personal hygiene. This is accompanied by a profound loss of interest in his studies. Often he stops attending classes and remains in his room most of the day. Usually he communicates his distress to at least one other person, often in the form of a veiled suicide warning. A significant number of students who attempt suicide leave suicide notes.
Precipitating factors	When a college student attempts suicide, one of the first explanations to occur to those around him is that he may have been doing poorly in school. However, students who manifest suicidal behavior are, as a group, superior students, and while they tend to expect a great deal of themselves in terms of academic achievement and to exhibit scholastic anxieties, grades, academic competition, and pressure over examinations are not regarded as significant precipitating stresses. Also, while many lose interest in their studies prior to the onset of suicidal behavior and their grades get lower, the loss of interest appears to be associated with depression and withdrawal caused by problems other than academic ones. Moreover, when academic failure does appear to trigger suicidal behavior—in a minority of cases—the actual cause of the behavior is generally considered to be loss of self-esteem and failure to live up to parental expectations, rather than the academic failure itself. For most suicidal students, both male and female, the major precipitating stress appears to be either the failure to establish, or the loss of, a close interpersonal relationship. Often the breakup of a romance is the key precipitating factor. It has also been noted that there are significantly more suicide attempts, and suicides, by students from families where there has been separation, divorce, or the death of a parent.
Need for assistance	Although most colleges and universities have mental health facilities to assist distressed students, few suicidal students seek professional help. Thus, it is of vital importance for those around a suicidal student to notice the warning signs and to try to obtain assistance for him.

Based on Blaine and Carmen (1968), Nelson (1971), Ross (1969), Schrut (1968), Seiden (1966), Shneidman, Parker, and Funkhouser (1970), and Stanley and Barter (1970).

contemplate suicide retain at least some urge to live. Their hold on life, however tenuous, provides the key to successful suicide prevention programs.

General sociocultural factors. Suicide rates vary considerably from one society to another. Among Western nations, they are especially high in West Germany, Finland, and Hungary, where the annual incidence for adolescents and adults is about 30 per 100,000 (World Health Organization, 1967); in West Berlin, specifically, the rate approaches 40 per 100,000 (Thomas, 1970). The United States has about 25 suicides per 100,000 people annually, England about 20, and still other Western countries 10 or less. In the Philippine Islands and New Guinea, the rate drops to 1 person per 100,000; and among certain "primitive" groups, such as the aborigines of the Australian western desert, the rate drops to zero—possibly as a result of the strong fear of death among these people (Kidson & Jones, 1968; Parker & Burton-Bradley, 1967).

The attitudes of a society toward death and social taboos concerning suicide are apparently important determinants of suicide rates. Most societies have developed very strong strictures against suicide, regarding it as a sin and often as a crime.[1] Some have even "punished" the suicidal victim by mutilating his corpse (Tuckman, Kleiner & Lavell, 1959). Japan is one of the very few major societies in which suicide has been socially approved under certain circumstances—for example, in response to conditions that bring disgrace to the individual or the group. During World War II, large numbers of Japanese villagers were reported to have committed mass suicide when faced with imminent capture by Allied forces. There were also reported instances of group suicide by Japanese military personnel under threat of defeat. In the case of the *Kamikaze*, Japanese pilots who deliberately crashed their planes into American warships during the final stages of hostilities, self-destruction was a way of demonstrating complete personal commitment to the national purpose.

Societal norms cannot wholly explain differences in suicide rates, however, for the incidence of suicide often varies significantly among societies with quite similar cultures and also among different subgroups *within* given societies. In the United States, for example, suicide rates are

higher than average among some groups with high occupational status (including psychiatrists, lawyers, and dentists) and also among unskilled workers and those with low employment security (National Institute of Mental Health, 1969). They are also relatively higher among divorced, widowed, and single people (in that order) than among people who are married; higher in the western states than in other regions; and higher in urban areas than in rural areas and small towns. In addition, the incidence of suicide is considerably greater among whites than among nonwhites; considerably greater among males than among females (though women make the greater number of suicide attempts); and considerably greater among older people than among younger ones. The interplay of such variables is suggested by a sampling of suicide rates for different subgroups in the United States based on official figures for 1960. Among *white males*, the rate was 40.6 per 100,000 in the 60-64 age group as opposed to 12.0 per 100,000 in the 20-24 age group. The rates for *nonwhite males* in the corresponding age groups were 17.5 and 7.4; for *white females*, 11.2 and 3.2; and for *nonwhite females*, only 3.0 and 1.6 (DeFleur, D'Antonio & DeFleur, 1971).

In a pioneering study of sociocultural factors in suicide, the French sociologist Émile Durkheim (1897) attempted to relate differences in suicide rates to differences in group cohesiveness. Analyzing records of suicides in different countries and for different historical periods, Durkheim concluded that the greatest barrier against committing suicide in times of personal stress is a sense of involvement and identity with other people. The likelihood of suicide increases, he maintained, among individuals who lack strong group ties (e.g., among single and divorced people as opposed to married ones, among the nonreligious as opposed to those who identify themselves with an organized faith), and it also increases under conditions of normlessness or *anomie*, when traditional group standards and expectations no longer seem to apply (e.g., during periods of economic depression, and after defeat in war). Durkheim termed these two patterns of suicide *egoistic* and *anomic* suicide, respectively.

---

[1]In the United States, suicide is illegal in 9 states. In addition, 18 states have laws making it a felony to abet a successful suicide.

As a form of public protest in Vietnam, a Buddhist monk turns himself into a burning torch as spectators solemnly watch.

He identified a third pattern of suicide as *altruistic* suicide, in which the individual—far from lacking a sense of group involvement—feels so closely identified with a group that he willingly sacrifices himself for "the greater good." In modern times this pattern has been clearly illustrated not only by the *Kamikaze* but also by Buddhist monks who burned themselves to death as a form of public protest in Vietnam.

Durkheim's theory takes little account of psychological factors and of sociocultural variables other than group cohesion, but it does seem to help explain some of the variations in suicide rates that have been observed. Thus, in our own society, as in those Durkheim studied, suicide rates have tended to increase during economic depressions, to remain constant during periods of domestic stability and prosperity, and to decrease during crises such as war, when people become united in a common purpose. The hypothesis that suicide rates generally increase under conditions of uncertainty and in the absence of strong group ties may help explain the findings of a recent study sponsored by the National Institute of Mental Health—namely, that low-income persons from large urban areas have a high rate of suicidal gestures and attempts (Hall et al., 1970). Similarly, suicide rates have also been found to be higher than average among people who are "downwardly mobile" (or who fear they may be-

come so) and among groups who are undergoing severe social pressures—such as young urban blacks and Indian teen-agers. In a study of suicide among blacks, Hendin (1969) found that:

"Most whites and blacks are surprised to learn that among young urban Negroes of both sexes suicide is a serious problem or that it is, for example, twice as frequent among New York Negro men between the ages of 20 and 35 as it is among white men of the same age group. The high frequency of suicide among older whites has led to the misconception that suicide is a 'white' problem, obscuring the fact that among young adults, particularly in urban areas, it is actually more of a black problem." (p. 407)

Referring to the special problems of young urban blacks, Seiden (1970) has flatly stated that "We're driving young blacks to suicide." Similarly, Dizmang (1970) and Resnik and Dizmang (1971) have referred to the suicide rate among Indian teen-agers as being "epidemic"; it is about ten times the national average. The lives of those who committed suicide were characterized generally by broken homes, difficulties in school, emotional deprivation, social disorganization, and alienation. Some of these same factors—particularly alienation—would appear to help account for the increasing incidence of suicide among young people generally in our society (Nelson, 1971; Pollack, 1971). Among college students, it has risen to the third—second according to some studies—leading cause of death (see illustration, page 355).

A number of investigators, including Havighurst (1969), have suggested that there is an inverse relationship between homicide and suicide in most cultures and ethnic groups. Where homicides are high, the suicide rate tends to be lower, and vice versa. Presumably, where homicide rates are high, frustration and hostility are turned outward against others rather than inward against the self. Further evidence is needed before any definite conclusions can be drawn; but in our society, where violence, homicide, and suicide rates are all high, the proposed inverse relationship is not apparent.

SUICIDE PREVENTION

The prevention of suicide is an extremely difficult problem. One complicating factor is that most persons who are depressed and contemplating suicide do not realize they are mentally disordered and in need of assistance. Only about one third voluntarily seek help (Hall et al., 1970); the others are brought to the attention of mental health personnel by family members or friends who are concerned because of their depressed states, their having made suicide threats, and so on. On the other hand, most persons who attempt suicide give prior warning of their intentions, and if the individual's "cry for help" can be heard in time, it is often possible to successfully intervene. Currently the main thrust of preventive efforts is on crisis intervention, but efforts are gradually being extended to the broader tasks of alleviating stressful conditions known to be associated with suicidal behavior and of trying to better understand and cope with the suicide problem in "high-risk" groups.

Crisis intervention. We have noted that the majority of suicide threats and attempts are made by individuals who either do not want to die or are ambivalent about taking their lives. In such instances, the communication of intent—if it is identified in time and assistance is sought—can open the door to crisis intervention.

When a serious suicide attempt has just been made, the first step obviously is emergency medical treatment. Generally the treatment is given through the usual channels for handling medical emergencies. However, special suicide centers have been found to be useful since they are staffed with personnel capable of handling drug intoxication as well as managing the suicidal patient. Over the longer term, electroshock therapy and antidepressant drugs may be utilized in medical treatment to clear up the depression and help the individual maintain a more normal affective state. Also, medical personnel may play a key role through giving attention and interpersonal support to the person who was discouraged enough to have attempted suicide.

When a person contemplating suicide is willing to make contact and discuss his problems with someone at a suicide prevention center or with another qualified person, it is often possible to avert an actual suicide attempt. As Korner (1970) has noted, speed of intervention, the reversal of despair, and the eliciting of realistic hope are crucial aspects of crisis intervention. Emphasis is usually placed on: (1) maintaining contact with the person over a period of time, (2) helping him realize that his distress is impairing his ability to assess his life situation and choose among possible alternatives, (3) helping him see that there are other ways of dealing with his problems, which are preferable to suicide, (4) taking a highly directive as well as supportive role, e.g., telling him what to do and what not to do, and (5) helping him see that his distress and emotional turmoil will not be endless. The following description of a telephone contact and its follow-up is illustrative of several of the points in our discussion. It involves directive, understanding intervention by a person in a context of continued involvement with another human being.

"Mr. B., a 30-year-old divorced clerical worker, living in a boarding house, telephoned the chaplain of a hospital stating that he had been sitting on his bed for three hours trying to muster enough nerve to shoot himself. The chaplain sought to sustain the contact by encouraging this distressed person to talk on. The man told of being lonely, having no friends, being unsuccessful in relating to the opposite sex, and experiencing life as being without meaning. The pastor responded in a calm, understanding, and hopeful way. He said to Mr. B., 'I know you must feel right now as though the bottom has dropped out of your world, but from what you have already told me, I honestly believe there is another solution to your problem. It must look hope-

HOW A SUICIDE PREVENTION CENTER ANSWERS CALLS FOR HELP

The first of the currently more than 200 professionally organized and operated suicide prevention centers in the United States was established in Los Angeles in 1958. Its founders, Norman L. Farberow and Edwin S. Shneidman, realized the great need for the services such a center could provide while collecting data for a study on suicide on the wards of their local County Hospital. Patients who attempted suicide received adequate treatment for their physical injuries, but little attention was given to their psychological distress. On discharge they often returned to the same environmental stresses which had produced their self-destructive conflicts.

Initially the Suicide Prevention Center searched the medical wards for persons who had attempted suicide and then, on the basis of interview and other assessment data, it helped them find a mental health resource in the community for the kind of treatment they needed. As the SPC became better known, people telephoned for help, and it soon became apparent that the SPC could best serve as a crisis facility. To do so, it has to be both accessible and available, and the staff has to be trained in certain basic meanings of suicidal behavior as well as in therapy procedures.

Taking calls for help centers on five steps, which may or may not occur concomitantly. Farberow has enunciated them as follows:

1. **Establish a relationship, maintain contact and obtain information.** The worker has to be able to listen nonjudgmentally and to assure the caller of interest, concern, and availability of help with his problems.

2. **Identify and clarify the focal problem.** Often the caller is so disorganized and confused that he is overwhelmed with all problems, both major and minor, having seemingly lost the ability to determine which is most important.

3. **Evaluate the suicide potential.** The staff person must determine quickly how close the caller is to acting on his self-destructive impulses, if he has not already done so. He does this by evaluating the information he obtains from the caller against a schedule of crucial items, such as age and sex, suicide plan, and so on. (See "'Lethality Scale' for Assessment of Suicide Potentiality," p. 360.)

An SPC staff worker taking a call. Focusing on the psychiatric emergency, the SPC devotes its skills and resources to help the caller endure the immediate disturbing situation.

4. **Assess the individual's strengths and resources.** A crisis often presents an opportunity for constructive change. The staff worker attempts to determine the caller's strengths, capabilities, and other resources as he works out a therapeutic plan.

5. **Formulate a constructive plan and mobilize the individual's own and other resources.** The staff person, together with the caller or significant others, determine the most appropriate course of action for the caller. This may range from involvement of family and friends to referral to a clinic or a social agency or to recommendation of immediate hospitalization.

The emphasis is upon crisis intervention and referral, not upon long-term therapy, for the latter soon would take SPC staff time away from those in need of immediate help.

In its organization and operation, the Los Angeles Suicide Prevention center has provided a prototype for the other suicide prevention centers that have been established throughout the United States.

Based on information supplied by the Los Angeles Suicide Prevention Center.

"LETHALITY SCALE" FOR ASSESSMENT OF SUICIDE POTENTIALITY

In assessing "suicide potentiality," or the probability that a person might carry out his threat to take his own life, the Los Angeles Suicide Prevention Center uses a "lethality scale" consisting of ten categories:

1. **Age and sex.** The potentiality is greater if the individual is male rather than female, and is over 50 years of age. (The probability of suicide is also increasing for youths in their early 20's.)

2. **Symptoms.** The potentiality is greater if the individual manifests such symptoms as sleep disturbances, depression, feelings of hopelessness, alcoholism, or homosexuality.

3. **Stress.** The potentiality is greater if the individual is subject to such stress as the loss of a loved one through death or divorce, the loss of his job, increased responsibilities, or serious illness.

4. **Acute vs. chronic aspects.** The potentiality is greater when there is a sudden onset of specific symptoms, a recurrent outbreak of similar symptoms, or a recent increase in long-standing maladaptive traits.

5. **Suicidal plan.** The potentiality is greater in proportion to the lethality of the proposed method, and the organizational clarity and detail of the plan.

6. **Resources.** The potentiality is greater if the person has no family or friends, or if his family and friends are unwilling to help.

7. **Prior suicidal behavior.** The potentiality is greater if the individual has evidenced one or more prior attempts of a lethal nature or has a history of repeated threats and depression.

8. **Medical status.** The potentiality is greater when there is chronic, debilitating illness or the individual has had many unsuccessful experiences with physicians.

9. **Communication aspects.** The potentiality is greater if communication between the individual and his relatives has been broken off, and they reject efforts by the individual or others to reestablish communication.

10. **Reaction of significant others.** Potentiality is greater if a significant other, such as the husband or wife, evidences a defensive, rejecting, punishing attitude, and denies that the individual needs help.

The final suicide potentiality rating is a composite score based upon the weighting of each of the ten individual items.

Another interesting approach to the assessment of suicide potentiality involves the use of computers and actuarial methods to predict not only the risk of suicide but also of assaultive and other dangerous behaviors. Clinicians find this information helpful in making decisions regarding treatment for individuals who are potentially suicidal—e.g., decisions regarding the amount of controls needed or the amount of freedom that can safely be allowed.

When a fatality that might have been a suicide does occur, a "psychological autopsy" is often performed in an attempt to learn whether the individual did, in fact, take his own life. The life situation of the individual is recreated, as well as the death scene, and all known details are gone over carefully by a team of experts that includes medical, psychological, and social work personnel. A similar autopsy may be performed in cases of known suicide, for purposes of understanding the individual's motives and behavior (Anderson & McClean, 1971; Kastenbaum, 1970; Slotten, Altman & Ulett, 1971).

Material concerning the lethality scale based on information supplied by the Los Angeles Suicide Prevention Center.

less, but I feel there is some real help available.' The chaplain then asked, 'Have you ever felt this way before?' Mr. B. went on to tell about feeling similarly depressed two weeks before. The chaplain responded, 'Now, hear what I have to say. When you were depressed two weeks ago, didn't it lift some? You were able to go back to work?' Mr. B. answered, 'Yes.' The chaplain talked to him with the tone of authority, directness, firmness, and certainty, saying, 'This present feeling you now have can be changed with proper help. You, like many others I have worked with, are suffering from an illness which is distorting your ability to think clearly. It is definitely coloring your view of things and hindering you from making a logical decision. I can help you. I want you to get in your car and come to the hospital. I will meet you there.' Mr. B. came to the emergency room, was met by the chaplain

who had arranged for a psychiatric consultation, and was admitted to the hospital for self-protection and further examination. After a few days a staff conference was held, and it was decided that the chaplain, who was trained in pastoral counseling, should work with Mr. B. on an outpatient basis.

"The chaplain provided Mr. B. with a supportive relationship which he had never before experienced. The relationship strengthened the ego of Mr. B. to the extent that he entered into a more meaningful vocation, and eventually remarried." (McGee & Hiltner, 1968, pp. 468–469)

During the last decade the availability of competent assistance at times of suicidal crisis has been expanded considerably by the establishment of suicide prevention centers, as described in the illustration on page 359. They are geared primarily to crisis intervention—usually via 24-hour-a-day availability of telephone contact; however, they can also arrange for the referral of suicidal persons to other agencies and organizations that can maintain supportive and helpful relationships with them. Such suicide prevention centers are manned by a variety of personnel: psychologists, psychiatrists, social workers, clergymen, and trained volunteers. Although there was initially some doubt about the wisdom of using nonprofessionals in the important first-contact role, experience has shown that the empathetic concern and peer-type relationships provided by volunteer workers can be highly effective in helping an individual through a suicidal crisis.

It is difficult to evaluate the long-range impact of the emergency aid provided by suicide prevention centers, but such facilities seem to have the potential, at least, for significantly reducing suicide rates. The Suicide Prevention Center of Los Angeles (Farberow & Litman, 1970) has reported that in comparison with an estimated suicide rate of 6 percent among persons judged to be high risks for suicide, the rate has been slightly less than 2 percent among approximately

8000 high-risk persons who have used their services. One difficult problem with which suicide prevention facilities have to deal is that approximately 60 percent of persons who are seen do not follow up their initial contact by seeking additional help from a clinic or other treatment agency (Bogard, 1970; Ringel, 1968).

Other preventive measures. Increasingly, suicide prevention programs are focusing not only on crisis intervention but also on alleviating the problems of persons who have threatened or actually attempted suicide—by eliciting the aid of family and friends, helping the individual resolve his interpersonal conflicts, providing hope, and so on. One innovative approach has been that of the Samaritans in England, a group of volunteers whose service is simply that of "befriending." The befriender offers support with no strings attached. He is available to listen and to help in whatever way he can, expecting nothing—not even gratitude—in return.

Many investigators have emphasized the need for broadly based preventive programs aimed at alleviating the life problems of people who, on the basis of statistics, fall into high-risk groups with respect to suicide. Few such programs have

Ambivalence about taking her life, which is so common in suicidal behavior, was manifested in the behavior of this 17-year-old girl who spent nearly 90 minutes on the 11th-floor ledge of a hotel. Her indecision concerning whether to jump or not finally ended when a captain of the Fire Department persuaded her to return to her room.

Marilyn Monroe is one of the celebrities of the theatrical world who committed suicide in recent years. This picture seems to convey a sense of depression and inner turmoil; at any rate, her death occurred two weeks later, the result of an overdose of barbiturates, and it initiated one of the earliest "psychological autopsies" into the causes of a specific suicide.

actually been initiated, but one approach has been to involve older males—a very high-risk group—in social and interpersonal roles that contribute to others as a means of lessening their frequent feelings of isolation and meaninglessness. Among this group, such feelings often stem from forced retirement, financial problems, the death of loved ones, impaired physical health, and being unneeded and unwanted. Emphasizing the need for a broadening of suicide prevention programs, Kiev (1970) has pointed out that most of the calls received by suicide prevention centers are from persons considered to be low risks. Apparently, high-risk persons are less likely to get in touch with such centers. Thus he has emphasized the need "for widening the treatment net and delivering care to high-risk groups that are now not being reached." (p. 87)

The ethical issue in suicide prevention. We have mentioned the ethical issues involved in taking one's own life, and the distress it often causes the loved ones left behind. In general, suicide is considered to be not only tragic but "wrong." However, efforts to *prevent* suicide also involve problems of ethics. If an individual wishes to take his own life, what obligation—or right—do others have to interfere?

The ethical problem would appear to be minimal when the person is ambivalent about taking his life and intervention simply helps him regain his perspective and see alternative ways of dealing with his distress. The dilemma becomes more intense, however, when prevention requires that the individual be hospitalized against his will, when personal items, such as belts and sharp objects, are removed from him, and when medication is forcibly administered to calm him. If suicide is to be prevented in such cases, considerable restriction is needed. And even then, such efforts may be fruitless. For example, in a study of hospitalized persons who were persistently suicidal, Watkins, Gilbert, and Bass (1969) reported that "almost one third used methods from which we cannot isolate them—seven head ramming, two asphyxia by aspiration of paper, one asphyxia by food, and three by exsanguination by tearing their blood vessels with their fingers." (p. 1593)

However, it may be reemphasized that only a small minority of suicide attempts are made by people who want to die. The great majority of persons who attempt suicide either do not want to die or are ambivalent about taking their lives. In addition, they usually give prior warning of their distress. Thus, existing suicide prevention programs and further research into suicidal behavior should reduce the toll taken in our society by suicide each year.

In the present chapter we have dealt with the affective disorders, which involve severe mood disturbances in the direction of elation or depression, and associated thought disturbances. In manic reactions we observed psychomotor overactivity accompanied by feelings of elation and a seeming "flight into reality" as a means of coping with excessive stress. In depressive reactions we observed psychomotor retardation accompanied by severe feelings of dejection and often of guilt and self-recrimination. Such depressive reactions appear to provide some relief from overwhelming stress through the admission of defeat and giving up, but take their toll in a catastrophic loss of self-esteem. In involutional melancholia we observed a clinical picture of agitated depression—with a similar but even greater loss of hope in an aversive life situation.

While emphasizing the importance of psychological factors in the etiology of affective disorders, we have also noted the growing body of research, indicating that neurophysiological and biochemical factors are often significantly involved.

In the last section of this chapter we dealt with the problem of suicidal behavior. We noted that the great majority of persons who attempt suicide do not want to die or are ambivalent about taking their lives. Often they give advance warning to others of their suicidal concern or intent. Although suicide is commonly associated with depression, we noted other etiological factors—revenge, for example—that may enter into suicidal behavior. And finally, we dealt with the ethical issues in suicide and the problems and methods of suicide prevention.

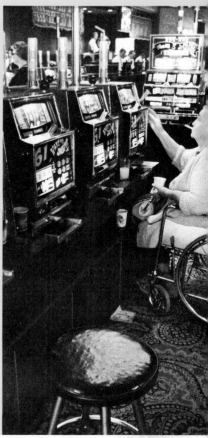

Sociopathic Disorders, Delinquency, and Crime

11

ANTISOCIAL (PSYCHOPATHIC) PERSONALITY

COMPULSIVE GAMBLING

DELINQUENT BEHAVIOR

CRIMINAL BEHAVIOR

In this chapter and the two that follow, we shall be dealing for the most part with patterns of abnormal behavior that have been classified by the APA as "Personality Disorders and Certain Other Non-Psychotic Mental Disorders." This category is a broad one, including not only various disturbances in personality pattern (e.g., the antisocial personality, the passive-aggressive personality, and the "immature" personality), but also alcoholism, drug dependence, and sexual deviations. In the present chapter we shall focus on the antisocial personality pattern and the related problems of compulsive gambling, delinquency, and crime. Alcoholism and drug dependence will be discussed in Chapter 12, and sexual deviations will be the topic of Chapter 13.

Like other personality disorders (see page 370), the antisocial—or psychopathic—personality pattern differs perceptibly from neurotic and psychotic disorders. Typically, these disorders do not stem primarily from defenses against anxiety or from decompensation under excessive stress. Rather, they represent a pattern of "acting-out" behavior that seems to produce little or no sense of personal distress on the part of the individual.[1] Often these psychopathological patterns are recognizable by adolescence or earlier and continue into adult life. Compulsive gambling, though not yet well understood, appears to merit consideration as a personality-pattern disturbance. As we shall see, it typically involves many traits that are also characteristic of the antisocial personality.

Although delinquent and criminal behavior do not constitute distinct patterns of personality disturbance, they may be closely allied not only with the antisocial personality pattern but also with other types of psychopathology. For example, an alcoholic may be arrested for dis-

---

[1]Sometimes behavior patterns similar to those in the personality disorders are determined primarily by the residual effects of head injuries or other brain pathology. Such cases will be considered in our discussion of brain disorders (Chapter 15).

orderly conduct; a manic may write bad checks; a depressed person may take not only his own life but also the lives of loved ones; a paranoiac may kill someone he perceives as persecuting him; and a heroin addict may steal or commit other illegal acts in order to get money for drugs. In considering the topics of delinquency and crime, we shall concern ourselves not only with the varied nature and causes of such behavior but also with programs of treatment and prevention. Although there is some overlap between individual and group pathology, our present focus will be on the sociopathic behavior of individuals, particularly acts of violence. Patterns of group violence, such as wars and destructive civil disorders, will be central topics in Chapter 18.

ANTISOCIAL (PSYCHOPATHIC) PERSONALITY

The terms *antisocial* and *psychopathic* personality are used more or less interchangeably to refer to personality characteristics and behavior patterns that lead to serious difficulties in interpersonal relationships and usually bring the individual into repeated conflict with society. Antisocial personalities are not classifiable as mentally retarded, neurotic, or psychotic. Their outstanding characteristics are a marked lack of ethical or moral development and an inability to follow approved models of behavior. Basically, they are unsocialized and incapable of significant loyalty to other persons, groups, or social values. Typically intelligent, spontaneous, and very likable on first acquaintance, they seem to live in a series of present moments, without consideration for the past or future and with callous disregard for the rights and well-being of others. The following case is not atypical.

Two 18-year-old youths went to visit a girl at her home. Finding no one there, they broke into the house, damaged a number of paintings and other furnishings, and stole a quantity of liquor and a television set. They disposed of the latter to a mutual friend for a small sum of money. Upon their apprehension by the police, they at first denied the entire venture and then later insisted that it was all a "practical joke." They did not consider their behavior particularly inappropriate, nor did they think any sort of restitution for damage was called for.

The category of antisocial or psychopathic personality includes a mixed group of individuals: unprincipled businessmen, shyster lawyers, quack doctors, high-pressure evangelists, crooked politicians, impostors, drug pushers, prostitutes, and assorted delinquents and criminals. Few of these individuals find their way into mental hospitals; only about 1 percent of all first admissions are so classified. A much larger number are confined in penal institutions, but, as the APA manual points out, a history of repeated legal or social offenses is not sufficient justification for labeling an individual a psychopath. In point of fact, the great majority of psychopaths manage to stay out of corrective institutions, although they tend to be in constant conflict with authority. The incidence of psychopathic personality is difficult to estimate; however, incidence figures are thought to exceed four million. This behavior pattern is considered to be much more common among males than females and more common among younger than older people.

CLINICAL PICTURE

Although the category of antisocial personality covers a wide range of specific behavior patterns, the following characteristics are considered generally indicative of the type.

1. *Inadequate conscience development and lack of anxiety or guilt.* The antisocial personality is unable to understand and accept ethical values except on a verbal level. Because of the marked discrepancy between his level of intelligence and his conscience development, he has been referred to as a "moral moron." His glib verbalizations and seeming adherence to high standards of morality are usually false and deceptive. He tends to "act out" tensions and problems rather than to worry them out. Often hostile and aggressive, he has little or no sense of guilt. His lack of anxiety and guilt, combined with his apparent sincerity and candor, may enable him to avoid suspicion and detection for stealing and other illegal activities. He often shows contempt for those he is able to take advantage of—the "marks."

2. *Irresponsible and impulsive behavior; low frustration tolerance.* The antisocial personality generally has a callous disregard for the rights, needs, and well-being of others. He is typically a chronic liar, and has learned to take rather than earn what he wants. Prone to thrill-seeking, deviant, and unconventional behavior, he often breaks the law impulsively and without regard for the consequences. He seldom foregoes immediate pleasure for future gains and long-range goals. He lives in the present, without realistically considering the past or future. External reality is used for immediate personal gratification. Unable to endure routine or to shoulder responsibility, he frequently changes jobs. He thinks he "should have the best," but he uses self-defeating means.

3. *Ability to put up "a good front" to impress and exploit others, and to project the blame for his own socially disapproved behavior.* Often the psychopath is charming and likable, with a disarming manner that easily wins friends. Typically, he has a good sense of humor and an optimistic outlook. If detected in lies he will often seem sincerely sorry and promise to make amends but not really mean it. He seems to have good insight into the needs and weaknesses of other people and is very adept at exploiting them. He readily finds excuses and rationalizations for his antisocial conduct, typically projecting the blame onto someone else. Thus he is often able to convince other people—as well as himself—that he is free of fault.

4. *Inability to maintain good interpersonal relationships.* Although initially able to win the liking and friendship of other people, the psychopathic personality is seldom able to keep close friends. Irresponsible and egocentric, he is usually cynical, unsympathetic, ungrateful, and remorse-

less in his dealings. He seemingly cannot understand love in others or give it in return.

The psychopath imposes a great burden on family and friends and creates a great deal of unhappiness for them. Manipulative and exploitative in his sexual relationships, he is irresponsible and unfaithful as a husband. Though he often promises to change, he rarely does so for any length of time; seemingly he is incorrigible.

5. *Rejection of authority and inability to profit from experience.* The psychopath behaves as if social regulations do not apply to him—he does not play by the rules of the game. His rejection of constituted authority may show itself in impulsive, hostile, criminal acts. Frequently he has a history of difficulties with educational and law-enforcement authorities. Although he often drifts into criminal activities, he is not typically a calculating professional criminal. Despite the difficulties he gets into and the punishment he may receive, he goes on behaving as if he were immune from the consequences of his actions.

Many of the preceding characteristics may be found in varying degrees in the neuroses, in drug dependence, and in other maladaptive behavior patterns. In the case of the antisocial or psychopathic personality, however, they are extremely pronounced and occur apart from other "symptoms" of psychopathology. Whereas most neurotics, for example, are beset by worry and anxiety and have a tendency to avoid difficult situations, the antisocial personality acts out his impulses fearlessly, with little or no thought for the consequences.

The following letter, written by a youth in prison to a girl he had never seen, shows utter disregard for his current circumstances, his past, and his probable future. It is a good example of the vivid imagination, wishful fantasy, impulsiveness, and emotional immaturity and instability that are characteristic of the antisocial personality.

"DEAR JUNE,

"Of course you know my cousin, David! Well, I had a long talk with him about beautiful women. He said that you are the most beautiful thing on earth. The way he described you he made me think that I've known you all my life. You must be a second Jean Harlow. I've dreamed about you, from the very first day he told me. I'd give a million dollars to have you in my arms. Sometimes I think I am in love with you although I've never seen you. Maybe someday I will see you. June, my darling, I love you. I love you with all my heart and soul. Please believe me?

"June, my love, although I've never seen you I would like you to be my wife. I have lots of money and life would be a bowl of roses for you. I know that you will never regret it. Because I will make you the happiest woman on this earth. . . .

"I am six feet tall, weight is 190 lbs., light complexion, sharp and always in the chips. I can take you anywhere you desire. Money doesn't mean a thing to me. You can have anything your little soft, warm heart desires. I own a cafe on Seventh Avenue. Business is very successful. Money flows in like a bristling brook. I have an apartment and a . . . Chrysler convertible sedan, black with white-wall tires. Everything works by the push of a button. Life will be a luxurious one for you.

"In the winter, I vacation in Miami, Florida. In the summer, I go to Canada. If I can have you as my companion and later, my sweetheart and finally my wife, we both could enjoy these luxuries together.

Love,

(Signed) JAMES"

(Banay, 1943, p. 171)

Nazi Field Marshal Goering, who was convicted as a war criminal and sentenced to death following the downfall of Germany in World War II, is another example of the antisocial or psychopathic personality.

"Goering had a better family background then most of his Nazi associates. His father had been Governor of German Southwest Africa and Resident Minister at Haiti. Hermann attended several boarding schools but he was bored and restless till he got to the Military Academy, where he settled down to his studies. He entered the army as an infantryman but he took flying lessons surreptitiously and got himself transferred to the Air Force against the wishes of his superior officers. He was a courageous and impetuous flyer and after the death of Richthofen he took charge of The Flying Circus.

"At the close of the First World War Goering went to Sweden where he worked as a mechanic and as a civil aviator. He married a wealthy woman and was able to return to Germany and enroll at the University of Munich. In Munich he met Hitler and joined the Nazi movement. . . .

"Goering's manner of living is described as 'Byzantine splendor' and as 'piratical splendor.' He built a pretentious country home near Berlin and furnished it magnificently with tapestries and paintings and an-

tiques. He had a private zoo. He required his servants to address his wife as Hohe Frau, thus giving her the distinction of nobility. He felt that the Germans liked his display of luxury—that it gave food for their imagination and gave the people something to think about. Goering was given to exhibitionism and he had a passion for uniforms, gold braid, medals, and decorations. . . . Goering would strut and swagger in private and public. In political rallies he made himself a flamboyant master of pomp and pageantry. He was an exhibitionist in the psychopathic pattern.

"Goering was coarse and gross. He was a Gargantuan eater and drinker. He was ribald in jest. He laughed uproariously when his pet lion urinated on a lady's dress. He once horrified his men and women guests at his country estate by having a bull and a cow mate before them. Personally he enjoyed the spectacle and declared that it was an old Teutonic custom.

"'Our Hermann' was popular with the masses and they smiled goodnaturedly at his antics and self-display. He demanded that they make sacrifices in order to win victory and exhorted them to choose guns instead of butter. He patted his fat belly and said that he had lost forty pounds in the service of his country. The Germans appreciated his sense of humor. . . .

"Goering was unscrupulous in his exercise of authority. He was said to be courageous, hard, challenging and authoritative in the Prussian manner. He was described as an affable, hearty butcher. . . . When he was made Chief of the Prussian Police he told his men to shoot first and inquire afterward. 'If you make a mistake, don't talk about it.' 'The faults which my officials commit are my faults; the bullets they fire are my bullets.' Goering regarded his bullets as an effective form of propaganda. He introduced the concentration camp and declared that it was not his duty to exercise justice, but to annihilate and exterminate. He reintroduced decapitation as an honest old German punishment. Goering is given credit for plotting the Reichstag Fire and for the planning and direction of the Blood Purge. Goering admitted that he had no conscience; his conscience was Adolf Hitler.

"Like many a psychopath Goering had a tender side. He was fond of animals, including his lion cubs. He declared that 'He who torments an animal hurts the feelings of the whole German people.' . . .

"Goering was often considered the most normal and the most conservative of the Nazi leaders. Like most psychopaths he would appear normal in his social relationships and he might seem genial and kindly with his humor and laughter. His pattern of behavior, however, identifies him as a constitutional psychopath and he presents a fair example of this personality disorder." (Bluemel, 1948, pp. 78-82)

Found guilty as a war criminal at the Nuremberg trials following World War II, Goering was sentenced to death on the gallows. However, he managed to evade his punishment by obtaining a capsule of cyanide—an extremely fast-acting poison—and taking his own life.

One of the most interesting types of persons found in the category of antisocial personality is the impostor, whose abilities are often outstanding and might seemingly be channeled in socially approved ways. This is well brought out in the following unusual case.

One of the boldest impostors of recent times was Ferdinand Waldo Demara, Jr. As an adolescent, he ran away from a rather tragic family situation and after unsuccessful attempts first to become a Trappist monk and then to teach school, he joined the army. Soon thereafter he went AWOL, joined the navy, and was assigned to duty on a destroyer during World War II. Here, by a ruse, he got hold of some navy stationery with which he managed to obtain the transcript of college grades of an officer who was on leave. He then "doctored" this transcript by substituting his own name and adding some courses; when photostated, it looked so impressive that he used it to apply for a commission. While waiting for his commission to come through, he amused himself by obtaining other records, including the full credentials of a Dr. French, who had received a Ph.D. degree in psychology from Harvard. Informed during a visit to Norfolk that he could expect his commission as soon as a routine security check was completed, he realized that such a check would surely expose him. Under cover of darkness, he left his navy clothes on the end of a pier with a note that "this was the only way out."

Now that Demara was "dead"—drowned in the oily waters off Norfolk—he became Dr. French. He obtained an appointment as Dean of Philosophy in a small Canadian college and taught courses in general, industrial, and abnormal psychology. Eventually, however, he had a disagreement with his superior and reluctantly left.

During this period he had become friends with a physician by the name of Joseph Cyr and had learned a considerable amount about the practice of medicine from him during the cold winter months when neither man had much to occupy his time. Interested in the possibility of getting a license to practice in the States, the trusting doctor had given Demara a complete packet including baptism and confirmation certificates, school records, and his license to practice medicine in Canada.

Using these credentials, Demara now obtained a commission as lieutenant in the Royal Canadian Navy. His first assignment was to take sick call each morning at the base. To help solve his problem of lack of knowledge in the field, he went to his superior officer and stated that he had been asked to work up a rule-of-thumb guide for people in lumber camps, most of whom did not have physicians readily available. His senior officer, delighted with the project, prepared a manual covering the most serious medical situations, which served as a basic guide for amateur diagnosticians. Demara then used this manual faithfully as his own. He also studied medical books and evidently picked up considerable additional knowledge.

Assigned to duty on the aircraft carrier HMCS *Magnificent*, Demara was criticized by his senior medical officer for his lack of training in medicine and surgery, especially for his deficiency in diagnosing medical problems. Learning of the report, Demara took characteristic bold action. He commandeered several seamen's compartments in the lower area of the ship, posted them with quarantine signs, and sent there for observation the patients whom he was having trouble diagnosing—in the meantime giving them penicillin. The chief medical officer knew nothing of this plan—Demara had confided only in a bosun's mate—and the reports of Demara's performance, based only on cases that Demara reviewed with his superior officer, became more favorable.

Perhaps the climax of Demara's incredible career came during the Korean War when—still as Lieutenant Cyr—he was assigned as the ship's doctor to the Canadian destroyer *Cayuga*. As the *Cayuga* proceeded to the combat zone, Demara studied medical books and hoped that his skill would never be put to the test. But fate decreed otherwise. One afternoon the destroyer spotted a small Korean junk littered with wounded men who had been caught in an ambush. "Dr. Cyr" was summoned and knew that there was no escape for him.

"Nineteen suffering men were lifted tenderly from the junk. Three were so gravely wounded that only emergency surgery could save them. Demara had read books on surgery, but had never seen an operation performed.

"The self-taught 'M.D.' cleaned and sutured the 16 less seriously wounded men, while gathering his courage for the great ordeal. Then he commandeered the captain's cabin as an emergency operating room. Working hour after hour with slow, unskilled hands, but drawing on all the resources of his great memory and natural genius, Demara performed miracles, while the ship's officers and dozens of enlisted men helped and watched.

"From one wounded man he removed a bullet that

OTHER PERSONALITY (TRAIT) DISORDERS

In addition to the antisocial personality, the APA Diagnostic Manual lists a number of other personality trait disturbances—disorders that are relatively heterogeneous and appear to have little in common except that each involves personality traits or patterns that lead to maladaptive behavior.

Paranoid personality	This pattern is characterized by suspiciousness, hypersensitivity, rigidity, envy, and excessive self-importance, plus a tendency to blame others for one's own mistakes and failures and to ascribe evil motives to others.
Cyclothymic (affective) personality	This pattern is a milder version of manic-depressive reactions, and is characterized by recurring and alternating periods of elation and depression. The periods of elation may involve enthusiasm, ambition, optimism, high energy, and warmth, while the periods of depression tend to be marked by worry, low energy, pessimism, and a sense of futility. Usually the mood variations are not readily attributable to stressful situations.
Schizoid personality	In this behavior pattern, the individual manifests seclusiveness, shyness, oversensitivity, avoidance of competitive or close interpersonal relationships, and often, egocentricity. Autistic thinking and daydreaming are common, although the individual does not lose the capacity to recognize reality. The schizoid personality has difficulty expressing ordinary aggressive feelings or hostility, and tends to react to disturbing stress situations with apparent detachment.
Explosive personality	This behavior pattern is characterized by gross verbal or physical aggressiveness and outbursts of rage. Such outbursts are strikingly different from the individual's usual behavior, and he may be quite regretful and repentant about them. The individual is generally considered excitable and overresponsive to environmental stresses. The intensity of the outbursts and the individual's seeming inability to control them are the distinguishing characteristics of this pattern.
Obsessive-compulsive personality	In this behavior pattern the individual manifests excessive concern with conformity and rigid adherence to standards of conscience. Such an individual tends to be overinhibited, overconscientious, overdutiful, rigid, and to have difficulty relaxing. This disorder is a milder version of obsessive-compulsive neurosis, to which it may actually lead.
Hysterical personality	This type of personality is characterized by immaturity, excitability, emotional instability, and self-dramatization. Whether or not the individual is aware of his motives, such self-dramatization is attention-seeking and often seductive. Such persons, who have also been referred to as histrionic personalities, are usually self-centered, vain, and quite concerned about the approval of others.

had lodged near the heart; from the second, a piece of shrapnel in the groin. For the third man, Demara collapsed a lung which had been perforated by a bullet.

"The operations began at midnight. When the pseudo surgeon looked up after the last operation, the light of dawn was shining through the portholes. Drenched in his own sweat, with the cheers of officers and crew ringing in his ears, he took a long drink of the ship's rum, went to his cabin, and collapsed in a stupor of sleep."

When his ship was sent to Japan for refitting, an eager young press officer seized on "Dr. Cyr's" exploits and wrote them up in full. His story was released to the civilian press, and the "miracle doctor" became world famous. This publicity proved to be Demara's temporary undoing, for it led to queries from the real Dr. Joseph Cyr as to whether the physician mentioned

in the press releases was a relative, and when Dr. Cyr saw the newspaper picture, he was shocked to find it was that of an old friend.

Dropped from the Canadian navy without fanfare —largely because he had managed to get a license to practice medicine in England and was now a licensed physician—Demara went through a difficult period. Wherever he went, he was soon recognized, and he lost job after job. He managed to work for a year at a state school for retarded children and did so well that he received a promotional transfer to a state hospital for the criminally insane. Here he found that the patients seemed to like him and that he was able to communicate with them. The experience began to bother him and he started to drink heavily and eventually resigned.

One morning after a prolonged drinking bout, he

Asthenic personality   In this type of personality pattern, the individual manifests a mild version of neurasthenia, with low energy level, easy fatigability, lack of enthusiasm, oversensitivity to physical and emotional strain, and a marked incapacity to enjoy life. Typically he is very self-pitying and tends to place the main responsibility for his difficulties and for helping him out of them upon others.

Passive-aggressive personality   This pattern is characterized by both passivity and aggression. The latter is typically expressed nonviolently—e.g., by procrastination, obstructionism, pouting, intentional inefficiency, or stubbornness. Often the individual's behavior reflects a hostility that he does not dare express openly, and his behavior commonly stems from a frustrating interpersonal or institutional relationship upon which he is overdependent.

Inadequate personality   This behavior pattern is characterized by ineffectual responses to stress—particularly to emotional, intellectual, social, and physical demands. While the individual does not appear to be mentally retarded or physically deficient, he does manifest ineptness, poor judgment, social instability, poor adaptability, and a lack of physical and emotional stamina.

Other personality disorders   This category includes such patterns as immature personality and passive-dependent personality.

In general, it is risky to use the above categories in labeling a given individual, since few persons appear to fit into a given category very adequately. Small et al. (1970) did find a number of common characteristics in a study of passive-aggressive personalities, but these were hospitalized cases and not necessarily representative, since personality trait disturbances usually are not incapacitating. Of course, persons with these disturbances may be more vulnerable to life stresses than normal persons.

Because the clinical pictures and dynamics in these personality disorders may be so different, it would appear that treatment may also show considerable variation from one person and subgroup to another. In general, however, treatment tends to be focused on modifying maladaptive patterns and fostering development of competence in dealing with problems of living. Although outcomes may also vary considerably, it would appear that the overall prognosis with adequate treatment is favorable.

Based on American Psychiatric Association (1968).

woke up in a southern city and realized his drinking was getting out of hand. He joined the local chapter of Alcoholics Anonymous as Ben W. Jones, whose credentials he had acquired along the way. With the help of sympathetic friends in Alcoholics Anonymous and a few fraudulent references obtained by ingenious methods, he was hired as a guard in a state penitentiary. Here he did a remarkable job, instituting a number of badly needed reforms in the maximum security block. Again he found himself able to communicate with the men, and he was promoted to assistant warden of maximum security. Ironically, one of his reform measures was to ask the townspeople to contribute old magazines, and before long one of the prisoners read the issue of *Life* which contained his picture and case history and recognized the new assistant warden.

Trying to get away lest he wind up as a prisoner in the same penitentiary, Demara was jailed in a nearby state and given considerable publicity but eventually released. Some time later he telephoned Dr. Crichton, from whose report most of this material has been adapted, to say "I'm on the biggest caper of them all. Oh, I wish I could tell you." (Summarized from Crichton, 1959; quoted passages from Smith, 1968.)

By way of a postscript, it may be mentioned that in early 1970 there was a newspaper report of Demara functioning successfully as a minister in a small northwestern community, this time with the congregation's full knowledge of his past. As we shall see, many persons labeled as antisocial personalities do eventually settle down to responsible positions in the community.

DYNAMICS

Although the personality characteristics and behavior patterns that we now label "antisocial" or "psychopathic" have been part of the human scene since ancient times—and are found in primitive as well as in highly developed societies —the dynamics of antisocial reactions are not fully understood. Undoubtedly they differ from case to case and from one socioeconomic class to another. Contemporary research in this area has variously stressed constitutional deficiences, the early learning of antisocial behavior as a coping style, and the influence of particular family and community patterns.

Neurophysiology and conditionability. Because the psychopath's impulsiveness, acting-out behavior, and intolerance of discipline tend to appear early in life, several investigators have suggested that an imbalance between inhibitory and excitatory processes in the nervous system is basic to the etiological pattern. For example, Stott (1962) marshaled evidence indicating that congenital injuries may impair the higher inhibitory centers in the nervous system, thus making the psychopath more vulnerable to the breakdown of inner controls under stressful conditions. EEG (electroencephalogram) studies, however, have failed to reveal brain abnormalities. As Robins (1967) has concluded, ". . . there is no proof that brain damage or abnormality as reflected in the EEG is a necessary precondition for the development of antisocial reaction." (p. 955) In addition, mentally retarded and brain-damaged individuals who do reveal faulty brain structures are seldom psychopathic. Thus, it appears likely that brain anomalies—when they do occur—are interactive factors rather than primary determinants.

In a similar vein, Eysenck (1960) concluded that the psychopath has a slower rate of conditioning than the normal individual, which explains why he fails to acquire many of the conditioned reactions essential to normal socialization, and also why he is likely to be deficient in conscience development. Hare (1968) and other investigators have reported similar findings, particularly with respect to these individuals' lack of normal fear or anxiety reactions, and their failure to learn readily from punishment or noxious stimuli. Physiologically, antisocial personalities seem to be at the opposite end of the continuum from anxiety neurotics, who appear oversensitive to noxious stimuli and oversusceptible to conditioned fears and anxieties. However, this possibility and its significance require further investigation.

Stimulation-seeking. In his study of criminal psychopaths, Hare (1968) reported that these individuals operate at a low level of arousal and are deficient in autonomic variability. He considered these findings—together with the psychopath's lack of normal conditioning to noxious and painful stimuli—indicative of a "relative immunity" to stimulation that is likely to make the psychopath seek stimulation and thrills as ends in themselves. In a study comparing psychopaths and normals, Fenz (1971) similarly found that psychopaths seem to have an insatiable need for stimulation.

Such findings support the earlier view of Quay (1965), who concluded that psychopathic behavior is an extreme form of stimulation-seeking behavior:

"The psychopath is almost universally characterized as highly impulsive, relatively refractory to the effects of experience in modifying his socially troublesome behavior, and lacking in the ability to delay gratification. His penchant for creating excitement for the moment without regard for later consequences seems almost unlimited. He is unable to tolerate routine and boredom. While he may engage in antisocial, even vicious, behavior, his outbursts frequently appear to be motivated by little more than a need for thrills and excitement. . . . It is the impulsivity and the lack of even minimal tolerance for sameness which appear to be the primary and distinctive features of the disorder." (p. 180)

What such extreme stimulation-seeking might mean in the total context of a personality characterized as impulsive, lacking in judgment, deficient in inner reality and moral controls, and seemingly unable to learn from punishment and experience can only be surmised. Though further investigation is needed, it seems plausible that stimulation-seeking "unchecked by conditioned fear response is a two-edged sword for antisocial behavior." (Borkovec, 1970, p. 222)

Early sociocultural deprivation. As we noted in Chapter 6, early deprivation, associated with a lack of maternal care, warm interpersonal relationships, and other normal socializing experiences, can lead to characteristics that are typical of the psychopathic personality. For example, in a follow-up study of 38 adolescents who had been institutionalized between the ages of 3 weeks and 3 years, 21 were diagnosed as having a personality disorder, and only 7 had achieved a relatively adequate adjustment (Beres & Obers, 1950). Other investigators have found that early deprivation is associated with an inability to delay immediate gratification, slow conscience development, disregard for the approval of others, inability to pursue long-term goals, confused self-identity, and impaired capacity to give and receive love.

Here it may be reemphasized that the greatest number of infants subjected to early maternal and sociocultural deprivation are not separated from their mothers but rather suffer from "masked deprivation," such as rejection, inadequate stimulation and communication, and other deficiencies in the family setting. We have also seen that the long-term effects of early deprivation depend on the infant's constitutional makeup, the age at which the deprivation occurs, and the extent and duration of the deprivation.

Faulty models and learning. A number of investigators have emphasized the role of faulty parent-child and family interactions in the origin of the psychopathic personality. Such factors lead to faulty learning and poorly equip the child for adult responsibilities and role behaviors.

In a study of 40 male psychopathic personalities, Heaver (1943) emphasized the influence exerted by faulty parental models—typically, a mother who overindulges her son and a father who is highly successful, driving, critical, and distant. Following a similar orientation, Greenacre (1945) added a number of details that have been corroborated by subsequent findings. The father is a successful and respected member of the community and is distant and fear-inspiring to his son. The mother, on the other hand, is indulgent, pleasure-loving, frivolous, and often tacitly contemptuous of her husband's importance. Because such parents are usually highly dependent on the approval and admiration of their community, it is crucial that they maintain the illusion of a happy family by concealing all evidence of bickering, and even pretending that

difficulties do not exist. Thus, the children learn that appearances are more important than reality, and they, too, become part of the show-window display, where a premium is put on charm and impressing others, rather than on competence and achievement. This need to be pleasing and to win social approval for their parents' sake seems to bring out a precocious but superficial charm in these children, together with great adroitness in handling people for purely selfish ends. Moreover, since what passes for maternal affection is actually overindulgence, the children's misbehavior tends to be concealed, rather than punished. At the same time, the remoteness of the father makes a healthy identification with him difficult or impossible for a son, and this often subjugates the boy to prolonged emotional dependence on his mother, with a consequent failure to develop a well-differentiated male sexual role and sense of identity.

It is not surprising that under such circumstances a highly ambivalent attitude develops toward the parents, which tends to become generalized toward all authority. The son in such a family cannot hope to emulate his successful and awe-inspiring father; but, aware of the extension to himself of the high evaluation that is placed on his father, he develops a feeling of importance and exemption from the consequences of his actions. Frequently the prominence of the father does, in fact, protect the child from the ordinary consequences of antisocial behavior. If we add one additional factor—namely, the contradictory influence of a father who tells his son of the necessity for responsibility, honesty, and respect for others, but who himself is deceitful and manipulative—we appear to have a family background capable of producing a middle-class psychopath.

Another aspect of this picture has been pointed out by Buss (1966), who has concluded that two types of parental behavior foster psychopathy. In the first, parents are cold and distant toward the child and allow no warm or close relationship to develop. If the child imitates the parental model, he will become cold and distant in his own later relationships; although he learns the formal attributes and amenities of social situations, he does not develop empathy for others or become emotionally involved with them. The second type of parental behavior involves inconsistency, in which parents are capricious in supplying affection, rewards, and punishments. Often they are inconsistent in their own role enactments as well, so that the child lacks a stable model to imitate and fails to develop a clear-cut sense of self-identity. Often the parents reward not only "superficial conformity" but "underhanded nonconformity"—that is, nonconformity that goes undetected by outsiders. Thus, they reinforce behaviors that lead to psychopathic behavior. Similarly, when the parents are both arbitrary and inconsistent in punishing the child, avoiding punishment becomes more important to him than receiving rewards. Rather than learning right from wrong, the child learns how to avoid blame and punishment by lying or other manipulative means.

A variation on this theme of faulty parental models and learning has been offered by Maher (1966), who has concluded that moral behavior and conscience development are produced by certain patterns of punishment and reward. For example, the child who is caught stealing money from his mother's purse is usually punished, and the money is taken away from him. However, if the child is able to forestall punishment by expressing repentance and promising not to do it again, the parent, by relenting, may be reinforcing the child's ability to avoid punishment and extinguishing his fear of punishment as well.

Punishing the child is often difficult for the parent, particularly if the child is unusually attractive and lovable. Hence the child soon learns that "being lovable" may help him avoid the unpleasant consequences of his actions; and he learns to use charm and personal attractiveness in manipulating others and gaining his own ends. Such a child, moreover, may—in effect—train his parents to indulge him, so that he does not have to wait for or earn what he wants. The mechanisms that enable him to avoid punishment also operate to ensure his overindulgence. Essentially, the child lives in a sort of "paradise of immaturity," which fosters the development of behaviors we label as psychopathic.

Wilkins (1961) has pointed out that antisocial personalities, much like college professors or politicians (or anyone else), seem to have a "career," or life style—a consistent, learned pattern of living that tends to be self-perpetuating. The life style of the psychopath seems especially resistant to change, since it is intermittently reinforced by short-term gains and by the avoidance of punishment or other noxious situations. Besides, the psychopath's relative freedom from anxiety, guilt, and remorse is not conducive to change in established behavior patterns.

Presumably, the psychopath's role behavior is both ineffective and inflexible because he is incapable of empathy—of actual emotional understanding of the commitments, responsibilities, and values implicit in various social roles. Although capable of manipulating others, he is incapable of either understanding or learning from them.

Anomie and alienation. Although we have emphasized the part played by constitutional and family factors in the formation of psychopathic personalities, it would appear that social conditions such as those found in our urban ghettos also produce their share of psychopaths. An environment characterized by the breakdown of social norms and regulations, disorganization, undesirable peer models, and a climate of alienation from and hostility toward the broader society appears to produce a type of psychopathic personality that is recognizable by inadequate conscience development, lack of concern for others, and destructive antisocial behavior. On a family level, the picture is often aggravated by broken homes, parental rejection, and inconsistent discipline. In this kind of environment, the youth's relations with others tends to induce distrust, a confused sense of personal identity, self-devaluation, and feelings of hurt and hostility. The end result may be overt aggressive behavior, directed especially at the representatives of "conventional" society.

In one high school in a disadvantaged area, two black youths held a white teacher while a third poured gasoline over him and set him on fire. Fortunately, another teacher came to the rescue and was able to extinguish the flames before the teacher was seriously burned. The youths were apprehended and detained in a juvenile facility, since they were under 18 years of age. Interviewed by a social worker, they showed no remorse for their act, did not consider it wrong, and were disappointed that they had not succeeded in killing the teacher. The youths were not in any of his classes, nor did they know him personally. The apparent leader of the group stated that "Next time we'll do it right, so there won't be nobody left around to identify us."

In reference to this type of psychopath, Melges and Bowlby (1969) have pointed to the individual's frustration and loss of hope. They concluded that such psychopaths believe that other people cannot be counted on, and that their own future is out of their control. In essence, they feel both helpless and hopeless in relation to their aversive life situations.

As Stotland (1969) has noted, the greater the expectation or hope of achieving a desired goal, the more likely will effort be expended toward achieving it; and conversely, where the individual feels inconsequential and hopeless—in the sense that no matter what he does, it will make no difference—he is not likely to strive toward constructive goals. Facing a seemingly frustrating and hopeless future, he attempts to extract what satisfaction he can from the present —by hostile, antisocial acts.

In summary, antisocial personalities are a mixed group of individuals who nevertheless have certain characteristics in common. They are poorly socialized, emotionally immature, impulsive, irresponsible, unethical, and unable to make an adequate and constructive social adjustment. In some instances, they engage in extremely violent and destructive acts. Although the etiological pattern is not clear and may differ considerably from case to case, it would appear to involve varying combinations of constitutional and/or psychosocial factors.

TREATMENT AND OUTCOMES

Since individuals with antisocial personalities do not exhibit obvious psychopathology and can function effectively in most respects, they seldom come to the attention of mental hospitals or clinics. Those who run afoul of the law may participate in rehabilitation programs in penal institutions, but thus far these programs have not proven generally effective. Even if more and better therapeutic facilities were available, effective treatment would still be a challenging task.

One complicating factor in treatment is that— because of the long developmental background of antisocial behavior—it is necessary to modify the psychopath's life style. Evidence of the long-standing nature of such patterns has been provided by Robins (1966), who, in a follow-up study of children who exhibited antisocial behavior, found that such behavior was predictive of sociopathic behavior in adulthood. And, of course, the treatment picture may be further complicated by constitutional factors.

Some early case reports pointed to favorable results with intensive psychotherapy, but, in general, traditional psychotherapeutic approaches have not proven effective (Banay, 1945; Lindner, 1945; Thorne, 1959). More recently, behavior therapists have dealt successfully with specific antisocial behaviors; and modern behavior control techniques appear to offer real promise of more effective treatment.

Bandura (1969) has cited three steps for effecting changes in antisocial behavior through the application of learning principles: (1) the modeling of desired behavior by "change agents" (the therapist and/or other behavioral models) and the use of a graded system of incentives, or reinforcers, to reward the antisocial individual for imitating such behavior; (2) the gradual transfer of evaluative and reinforcement functions to the antisocial individual himself, so that eventually he evaluates his own behavior and rewards himself accordingly; and (3) the reduction of material incentives and rewards as the individual's behavior is increasingly brought under the control of self-administered, symbolic rewards. Essentially, the objective is to help the antisocial personality develop internalized controls that will minimize the need for external constraints and rewards. An important facet of this approach is providing situations in which the psychopath models desired behavior for other individuals in treatment; he thus functions as a "change agent" or therapist in helping others, while also furthering the long-range modification of his own behavior patterns.

Fortunately, many psychopathic personalities improve after the age of 40, possibly because of weaker biological drives, better insight into their self-defeating behavior, and the cumulative effect of social conditioning. Such individuals are often referred to as "burned-out" psychopaths. However, psychopaths create a great deal of havoc before they reach 40—as well as afterward if they do not change. In view of the distress and unhappiness they inflict on others and the social damage they cause, it seems desirable—and more economical in the long run—to put increased effort into the development of effective treatment programs.

COMPULSIVE GAMBLING

Gambling is usually defined as wagering on games or events in which chance to some degree determines the outcome. In modern societies money is typically the item of exchange; in other societies, seashell currency, beads, jewelry, and food are often used. The ancient Chinese frequently wagered hairs of their head, and sometimes even digits and limbs, on games of chance (Cohen & Hansel, 1956). Occasionally the Mojave Indians wagered their wives (Devereaux, 1950). But regardless of the item of exchange, gambling seems to be an enduring human proclivity. Judging from man's written history and the studies of anthropologists, gambling has occurred and continues to occur almost universally and among all social strata.

CLINICAL PICTURE

Gambling in our society takes many forms, from the casino gambling of Las Vegas, to betting on horse races (legally or otherwise), to numbers games, dice, bingo, and cards. The exact sums that change hands in legal and illegal gambling are unknown, but there are anywhere from 6 to 10 million regular gamblers in the United States who lose some $20 billion or more each year (Berry, 1968; Strine, 1971). If one were to define *gambling* in its broadest sense, even playing the stock market might be considered a game of chance. Sherrod (1968) has humorously pointed to the need for a clearer definition of terms:

"If you bet on a horse, that's gambling. If you bet you can make three spades, that's entertainment. If you bet cotton will go up three points, that's business. See the difference?" (p. 619)

In any event, gambling appears to be one of our major national pastimes, with some 50 percent of the population gambling at one time or other on anything from horse races to Saturday-night poker games (Berry, 1968). In general, such gambling is a harmless form of social entertainment: the individual places a bet and waits for the result; and, win or lose, that is that. However,

with some people gambling becomes an addiction.

Aside from the tremendous number of hours spent in gambling rather than in productive activity, these individuals suffer from a disorder that disrupts their entire lives. Their compulsion leads to neglect of their families and perhaps of their work, and often to illegal methods of obtaining money with which to continue gambling. In general, it would appear that the compulsive gambler is higher than average in intelligence and has completed one or more years of college. He is usually married and often has a responsible managerial or professional position that provides a reasonably good income. Apparently, far more men than women are compulsive gamblers.

DYNAMICS

Since very little systematic research has been done in this area, the dynamics of compulsive gambling are not yet well understood. It seems to be a learned pattern that is highly resistant to extinction. Often the person who becomes a compulsive gambler wins a substantial sum of money the first time he gambles; chance alone would dictate that a certain percentage of individuals would have "beginner's luck." Bolen and Boyd (1968) consider it likely that the reinforcement an individual receives during this introductory phase is a significant factor in his later pathological gambling. And since anyone is likely to win from time to time, the principles of intermittent reinforcement appear to be applicable in explaining the addict's prolonged gambling despite excessive losses. Bolen and Boyd were struck particularly by the similarity between female slot-machine players and Skinner's laboratory pigeons; the latter, which had been placed on a variable reinforcement schedule, "repetitively and incessantly pecked to the point of exhaustion and eventual demise while awaiting the uncertain appearance of their jackpot of bird seed." (1968, p. 629)

In much the same way, the compulsive gambler

seems to form the unrealistic belief that he can become rich through further gambling and will not have to work for a living. Despite his awareness that the odds are against him, and despite the fact that he never, or rarely, repeats his early success, he continues to gamble avidly. To "stake" his gambling he often dissipates his savings, neglects his family, defaults on bills, and borrows money from friends and loan companies. Eventually he may resort to writing bad checks, embezzlement, or other illegal means of obtaining money, feeling sure that his luck will change and that he will be able to repay what he has taken.

Psychoanalysts have described the gambler as being immature, hostile, passive-dependent, rebellious, obsessive, masochistic, superstitious, and prone to act on impulse (Bergler, 1957; Bloch, 1961; Bolen & Boyd, 1968). Other investigators have labeled the gambler as "an obsessive-compulsive neurotic," and still others have seen him as "basically an antisocial personality." In one of the few well-controlled studies in this area, Rosten (1961) studied a group of former compulsive gamblers and found that they tended to be rebellious, unconventional individuals

One reason for compulsive gambling may be found in the intermittent reinforcement of winning—exemplified here by the occasional payments the slot machine metes out to this woman, so intent on her playing. As we have noted, a given response, whether maladaptive or adaptive, tends to be maintained through such a pattern of reinforcement.

who did not seem to fully understand the ethical norms of society. Half of the group described themselves as "hating regulations." Of 30 men studied, 12 had served time in jail for embezzlement and other crimes directly connected with their gambling.

On a superficial level, the compulsive gambler tends to be quite personable and is often socially facile and responsive. His social relationships, however, are usually manipulatory and shallow. In addition, his gambling activities tend to alienate him from family and friends. Whereas others view his gambling as unethical and disruptive, he is likely to see himself as a man taking "calculated risks" to build a lucrative business. Often he feels alone and resentful that others do not understand his activities. Apparently the only way he can vindicate his assumptions and life style is by further gambling. This, in turn, leads to further personal, financial, and often legal difficulties, and the problem is compounded. Increasingly, the only way out of his difficulties seems to be the way he got in—by gambling.

Rosten also found that compulsive gamblers are unrealistic in their thinking and prone to seek highly stimulating situations. In the gambler's own words, he "loves excitement" and "needs action." Life must be highly stimulating and risky to be really satisfying. Although these former compulsive gamblers admitted that they had known objectively the all-but-impossible odds they faced while gambling, they had felt that these odds did not apply to them. Often they had unshakable feelings that they were "special" and that "tonight is my night." Typically they had also followed the so-called "Monte Carlo fallacy"—that after so many losses, their turn was coming up and they would hit it big. Similarly, they had understood the consequences of illegal activity to secure funds with which to gamble but had not believed that they could lose and be unable to replace the funds they were taking. Many of them discussed the extent to which they had "fooled" themselves by elaborate rationalizations. For example, one gambler described his previous rationalizations as covering all contingencies: "When I was ahead, I could gamble because I was playing with others' money. When I was behind, I had to get even. When I was even, I hadn't lost any money." (Rosten, 1961, p. 67)

Since Rosten studied men who had stopped gambling, the question arises as to how his subjects differ from those who continue to gamble. He suggests the probability that the compulsive gambler who remains active is more egocentric, unconventional, unrealistic, and less insightful than the one who is able to stop. It is of interest to note that within a few months after they were studied, 13 of Rosten's 30 subjects either had returned to heavy gambling, had started to drink excessively, or had not been heard from and were presumed to be gambling again. Very little has been written about the compulsive woman gambler, and since Rosten's subjects were all men we can only speculate as to how his findings would generalize to women gamblers.

TREATMENT AND OUTCOMES

The treatment of compulsive gamblers is still a relatively unexplored area, but several approaches have been tried with some success. Boyd and Bolen (1970) have reported on a recent study in which compulsive gamblers and their spouses were treated conjointly through group psychotherapy—an approach based on the finding that the compulsive gambler's marital relationship is generally chaotic and turbulent, with the spouse frequently evidencing seriously maladaptive behavior patterns. Of the eight gamblers treated, there was a complete cessation of gambling in three and a near cessation in the other five. The extent to which changes in the gamblers' marital relationships influenced the outcome of treatment can only be surmised—six of the eight couples showed a significant improvement. One of the subjects stated after not having gambled for five months that this was "some kind of record for him"; but although he felt that therapy had been helpful, he was "hard-pressed to explain how." (p. 86) Other treatment approaches that have been successfully tried with compulsive gamblers include individual psychotherapy and aversion therapy (Barker & Miller, 1968; Victor & Krug, 1967). Further studies are needed, however, before we can evaluate the potential effectiveness of these and other therapeutic techniques.

Some compulsive gamblers find help in changing their behavior through membership in Gam-

A CASE OF COMPULSIVE GAMBLING

John ____ was a 40-year-old rather handsome man with slightly greying hair who managed an automobile dealership for his father. For the previous two years, he had increasingly neglected his job and was heavily in debt as a result of his gambling activities. He had gambled heavily since he was about 27 years old. His gambling had occasioned frequent quarrels in his first marriage and finally a divorce. He married his second wife without telling her of his problem, but it eventually came to light and created such difficulty that she took their two children and returned to her parents' home in another state.

John joined an encounter group in the stated hope that he might receive some assistance with his problems. In the course of the early group sessions, he proved to be an intelligent, well-educated man who seemed to have a good grasp of the nature of his gambling problem and its self-defeating nature. He stated that he had started gambling after winning some money at the horse races. This experience convinced him that he could implement his income by gambling judiciously. However, his subsequent gambling—which frequently involved all-night poker games, trips to Las Vegas, and betting on the races—almost always resulted in heavy losses. In fact, he was so involved in trying to retrieve his losses in a poker game that he had not returned home the previous Christmas Eve or all Christmas day—which had proven the "final straw" in his marriage and led to his wife's leaving him.

In the group, John talked about his compulsive gambling freely and coherently—candidly admitting that he enjoyed the stimulation and excitement of gambling more than sexual relations with his wife. He was actually rather glad his family had left since it relieved him of certain responsibilities toward them as well as feelings of guilt for neglecting them. He readily acknowledged that his feelings and behavior were inappropriate and self-defeating, but stated that he was afflicted with a "sickness" which was ruining his life and that he desperately needed help.

It soon became apparent that while John was willing to talk about his problem, he was not prepared to take constructive steps in dealing with it. He wanted the group to accept him in the "sick role" of being a "compulsive gambler" who could not be expected to "cure" himself. At the group's suggestion he did attend a couple of meetings of Gamblers Anonymous but found them "irrelevant." It was also suggested that he try aversive therapy, but he felt this would not help him.

While attending the group sessions, John apparently continued his gambling activities and continued to lose. After attending the eighth encounter group session, he did not return. Through inquiry by one of the members, it was learned that he had been arrested for embezzling funds from his father's business, but that his father had somehow managed to have the charges dropped. John reportedly then left for another state and his subsequent history is unknown.

blers Anonymous. This organization was founded in 1957 in Los Angeles by two compulsive gamblers who found that they could help each other control their gambling by talking about their experiences. Since then, groups have been formed in most of the major cities in the United States. The groups are modeled after Alcoholics Anonymous, and the only requirement for membership is an expressed desire to stop gambling. In group discussions, members share experiences and try to gain insight into the irrationality of their gambling and to realize its inevitable consequences. They consider it their obligation to help each other when a member feels he cannot control himself or has had a relapse. Gamblers Anonymous has no policy for influencing legislation to control gambling but emphasizes the view that each person who gambles is personally responsible for his own actions.

Unfortunately, only a small fraction of compulsive gamblers find their way into Gamblers Anonymous; and of those who do, only about 1 in 10 manages to overcome his addiction to gambling (Strine, 1971). At a G.A. meeting a member declared: "We've said many times . . . if a compulsive gambler had a choice of going to bed with an actress or betting on a horse, the compulsive gambler would bet on the horse. . . ." (Strine, 1971, p. 6)

With the first dollar he wins or loses, the compulsive gambler is seemingly driven to chase the elusive dollar forever. And very often his quest is a tragic one, involving bad checks, job losses, divorce, and desperation.

DELINQUENT BEHAVIOR

Delinquency refers to behavior by youths under 18 years of age which is not acceptable to society and is generally regarded as calling for some kind of admonishment, punishment, or corrective action.[1] Thus, delinquent behavior may range from truancy, "incorrigibility," and the use of illegal drugs to homicide and other serious criminal offenses.

The actual incidence of juvenile delinquency is difficult to determine, since many delinquent acts are not reported. In addition, the states differ somewhat in their definitions of delinquent behavior—particularly regarding minor offenses; so that what may be considered delinquent behavior in Texas may not be so considered in California or New York. Of the approximately one million young people who go through the juvenile courts each year in the United States, about half have done nothing that would be considered a crime in the case of an adult. However, many of this group are returned to the courts at a later time for having committed serious offenses. Delinquency has become a cause for national concern not only in our own society but in most modern countries throughout the world.

INCIDENCE

Between 1960 and 1970, arrests of persons under 18 years of age increased more than 110 percent—almost 4 times faster than the population increase of the group aged 10 to 17. In 1970, juveniles accounted for over 1 out of 3 arrests for robbery, 1 out of 5 for forcible rape, and 1 out of 10 for murder. Of the more than 110,000 persons arrested for vandalism, more than 70 percent were under 18. Although the great majority of delinquents are males, the rate of increase of delinquent behavior is much greater for females. In 1970 about 1 teen-ager out of every 20 in the nation was arrested. Even more alarming is the fact that juveniles are committing about half of all the serious crimes in the United States.[2]

Well over half of the juveniles who are arrested

---

[1] It may be noted here that children under 8 are not considered delinquents, because it is assumed that they are too immature to understand the significance and consequences of their actions.

[2] Statistics in this and the following section are based on Roswell and Fishman (1968), *Uniform Crime Reports* (1971), *U.S. News and World Report* (1970), and Velde (1971).

each year have prior police records. Female delinquents are commonly apprehended for drug usage, sexual offenses, running away from home, and "incorrigibility"; but crimes against property—such as stealing—have markedly increased among them. Male delinquents are commonly arrested for drug usage and crimes against property; to a lesser extent they are arrested for aggravated assault and crimes against the person. Unfortunately, however, crimes of violence by young people are increasing in our large metropolitan centers, so that in many areas the streets are considered unsafe after dark.

In general, it appears that the incidence and types of delinquent behavior vary between lower- and middle-class youth—particularly between those from urban ghettos and from relatively well-to-do urban families—the incidence being higher and the severity of offense being greater

for those from the slums (Gordon, 1967; Hoover, 1968). For lower-class, socially disadvantaged youth, the delinquency rate for whites and non-whites appears about equal.

DYNAMICS

Various conditions, singly and in combination, may be involved in the etiology of delinquent behavior. In general, however, we appear to be dealing with three key variables: (1) personality characteristics, (2) family patterns and interactions, and (3) juvenile gangs and delinquent subcultures. We shall also see that certain delinquent acts may be triggered by unusual and seemingly fortuitous stresses.

Pervasive personal pathology. A number of investigators have attempted to "type" delin-

AN ADOLESCENT'S HOMICIDAL BEHAVIOR

The following case was one of those included in a study of homicidal adolescents by Jane and Glen Duncan (1971):

"David, aged 14, instructed by his teacher to write a paragraph about a book he had read recently, wrote as follows: 'This book does not have a title but is the story of a boy who was fed up of living. His name? That doesn't matter. It's what he will do that will shock you. One night when his parents went to bed he got up from his bed, took his shotgun, loaded it, and went quietly into their bedroom. His mother and dad were sleeping, he took aim, shot his father first his mother screamed he shot her his smaller brother came running out of his bedroom to see what was the matter. He fired again. What was the reason for this grusome (sic) murder? What made him do it. He hated them. His life ambition was to get a car. They promised him one but always fell down on their promises. He has a car now and will kill anyone who tries to take it from him. This story is not fiction although it sounds fantastic it happened in my family.' The teacher did not take this 'book report' too seriously, although she intended to talk to David about it later.

"That night, after the family retired, David entered the darkened bedroom of his parents and fired two shotgun shells at them from a distance of eight feet. Pellets struck the father in the leg and head, the mother in the leg. David turned on the light, shouting 'You let me down, you let me down!' He then brought towels to dress the parents' wounds, telephoned an ambulance and a neighbor, and explained what he had done. When he saw lights of the neighbor's approaching car, David left the scene in his father's car.

"As he was driving along the highway, David put the gun to his temple and pulled the trigger, but the safety was on. He de-

cided against suicide until he could ascertain the condition of his parents. He turned himself in to a police officer.

"David admitted that he had intended to kill his parents, but darkness had prevented accurate aim. He said he had changed his mind about killing his brother. He told how his feelings of resentment toward his parents had been present for more than a year and had been building up more and more during the past three months. Two months earlier he had contemplated suicide. Instead, he decided to run away and went to the home of relatives. There he poured out his troubles, repeating over and over again, 'I just can't stand it any longer.' Nevertheless, the relatives returned him home.

"Thereafter David considered killing his parents for two and a half weeks and definitely decided to do so four days before the attempt was made. The 'last straw' was their failure to buy him a car after promising and leading him to expect that they would.

"The parents survived. When questioned later, the father sought to understand his role in the unfortunate sequence of events. He described a life pattern of parental coercion of David followed by unkept promises. The mother, on the other hand, steadfastly maintained that her methods had been correct. She could see no reason why David should react as he had." (pp. 1498–1499)

Duncan and Duncan noted that in the above case and in the other four cases they studied, the "adolescent's abrupt loss of control was associated with a change in his interpersonal relationship with the victim, together with a sequence of events progressively more unbearable and less amenable to his control." (p. 1498) In assessing an adolescent's potential for homicidal behavior within the family, according to their report, "a history of parental brutality is a significant consideration."

quents with regard to more pervasive patterns of personal pathology.

1. *Brain-damaged and mentally retarded delinquents.* In a distinct minority of cases—probably less than 1 percent—brain pathology may result in lowered inhibitory controls and a tendency toward episodes of violent behavior (Caputo & Mandell, 1970; Loomis et al., 1967). These youths are often hyperactive, impulsive, emotionally unstable, and unable to inhibit themselves when strongly stimulated, but typically their inner controls appear to improve with age. Often, acceptance or rejection by families and peers has a marked influence on their behavior, as does the presence or absence of opportunities to learn aggressive acts.

In perhaps 5 percent of delinquent behavior, low intelligence appears to be of etiological significance. Here the individual is unable to foresee the probable consequences of his actions or to understand their significance. This is particularly true of mentally retarded, sexually delinquent girls (Wirt et al., 1962). Delinquent male retardates typically commit impulse offenses, often against the person (Blackhurst, 1968). Occasionally, too, boys and girls of low intelligence fall prey to brighter psychopaths or delinquent gangs that exploit and dominate them. In some instances mental retardation is associated with serious brain damage, so that an individual may combine characteristics of the brain-damaged and mentally retarded delinquent.

2. *Neurotic and psychotic delinquents.* An estimated 10 percent of delinquent behavior appears directly associated with neurotic disorders. Here the delinquent act often takes the form of a compulsion—such as "peeping," stealing things that are not needed, or setting fires. Such compulsions often seem related to deviant sexual gratification in overinhibited adolescents who have been indoctrinated in the belief that masturbation and other overt forms of sexual discharge are terribly evil and sinful. Often such individuals fight their inner impulses before committing the delinquent act, and then feel extremely guilty afterward. Disturbances of this sort seem to be declining, possibly because parents are no longer so prone to induce overinhibition in sexual behavior.

About 3 to 5 percent of delinquent behavior is associated with a psychotic disorder. In such cases there is often a pattern of prolonged emotional and social withdrawal, culminating, after long frustration, in an outburst of violent behavior (Bandura & Walters, 1959). The delinquent act is the by-product of the personality disturbance, rather than a reflection of a consistent antisocial orientation. Wirt and his associates (1962) found a number of delinquents in this category to be descriptively schizoid rather than actually schizophrenic—that is, distant from others, eccentric in their thoughts, and showing a flatness of affect, but lacking delusions, hallucinations, and other symptoms of a full-blown psychosis. Kaufman (1962) cited the case of a 13-year-old boy who stole a gun and was running away from school when a stranger saw him. The boy shot and killed the stranger, and when apprehended and hospitalized for examination showed no emotional reaction to what had happened.

3. *Psychopathic delinquents.* A sizable number of persistent delinquents appear to share the traits typical of the antisocial or psychopathic personality—they are impulsive, defiant, resentful, devoid of the feelings of remorse or guilt, incapable of establishing and maintaining close interpersonal ties, and unable to profit from experience. Because they lack conscience and reality controls, they often engage in seemingly "senseless" acts that are not planned but occur on the "spur of the moment." They may steal a small sum of money that they do not need; or they may steal a car, drive it a few blocks, and abandon it. In essence, these individuals are "unsocialized delinquents" who are largely at the mercy of their inner impulses, seek stimulation and excitement, and live in the present with little thought of the future (Skrzypek, 1969; Stain & Sarbineta, 1968). The following case provides an extreme example of a juvenile psychopath.

At the age of 12, Benny hurled a brick from the roof of an apartment building, striking another boy on the head and killing him. Benny first told the police that "it was all an accident," the brick having slipped out of his hand. He later stated that a friend had hurled the brick and that he had tried to stop him. He absolutely refused to discuss the episode again.

Benny was a cherubic-looking boy who was superficially cheerful and seemed to relate easily to other people. Yet he had thrown puppies and kittens from the roof of the apartment building where he lived; had engaged in stealing, truancy, and glue-sniffing; and frequently got into terrific fights with other boys, alternately experiencing savage beatings and bloody triumphs. He kept a flock of pigeons on the roof, and his concern for the birds appeared to be touching. However, when a pigeon was injured "in a bad fight," he would dispose of it by throwing it down the incinerator alive.

Over a period of time Benny had been remanded to various juvenile correctional facilities. At each institution, the same behavior pattern was noted. Benny would be warm and charming for a time, but just when it appeared that he was responding to the treatment program, he would engage in defiant behavior culminating in escape. He escaped from various institutions more than twenty times and boasted that "the place hasn't been built that can hold me." His eventual course was a tragic one, ending in death when he escaped from a maximum security installation and slammed a stolen bicycle into a parked car, suffering a fatal cerebral injury. (Adapted from Greenberg & Blank, 1970)

Although research has focused primarily on male delinquents, several investigators have also emphasized the high incidence of psychopathic personalities among girls in state correctional institutions (Cloninger & Guze, 1970a; Fine & Fishman, 1968; Konopka, 1964; 1967). In a study of 115 girls in a state correctional institution in Kentucky, Fine and Fishman (1968) emphasized a personality picture characterized by rebelliousness, impulsiveness, inadequacy, instability, and immaturity—characteristics commonly found in the psychopathic personality.

4. *Drug-dependent delinquents.* Today an increasing number of delinquent acts—particularly acts involving stealing and prostitution—are directly associated with drug problems. Most youths who are addicted to hard drugs, such as heroin, must steal in order to maintain their habit, which can be highly expensive. To make matters worse, they must steal goods worth nearly five times as much as the money they need, since they must dispose of such stolen articles to a "fence" at cut-rate prices. In addition, youths using the amphetamines, or "speed," may—under influence of the drugs—commit impulsive antisocial acts, often involving crimes against the person. We shall deal more extensively with the relation of drug problems to delinquency and criminal behavior in the following chapter.

Pathogenic family patterns. Although various pathogenic family patterns have been emphasized in the research on juvenile delinquency, the following appear to be most important.

1. *Broken homes.* A number of investigators have pointed to the high incidence of broken homes and multiple parental figures in the backgrounds of delinquent youths. In a study of institutionalized delinquents in Colorado, Barker and Adams (1962) found that only about a third of them (boys and girls) came from complete home settings—in the sense that they lived with both of their original parents. More than a fourth of them lived only with the mother. Similarly, in a study of adolescents at the National Training School in Washington, D.C., which treats black and white offenders, Anderson (1968) found that well over half of them came from homes lacking a father—with the incidence being higher for blacks than for whites. Since mothers or mother surrogates were almost uniformly present, Anderson concluded that the loss of the father and lack of a father surrogate was of crucial importance in the socialization failure of these delinquent youths—the youths being particularly vulnerable to paternal loss from the ages of 4 to 7.

2. *Paternal rejection and maternal dominance.* Here we are not referring to broken homes but to homes in which the father rejects his son or plays a reduced role, and the mother tends to be the dominant parental figure. In this context, it is interesting to note the findings of Bacon, Child, and Berry (1963) who studied the incidence of crime in 48 nonliterate societies. They found a much higher incidence of theft and personal crime in societies where the family typically restricts opportunities for the young boy to identify with his father.

In a study of delinquent and nondelinquent boys, Andry (1962) found that the great majority of delinquent boys felt rejected by their fathers but loved by their mothers, while the nondelinquents felt loved equally by both parents. Andry also noted that the delinquent boy typically tended to dislike his father. In the background of a group of 26 aggressively delinquent boys, Bandura and Walters (1959; 1963) delineated a pattern in which father rejection was combined with inconsistent handling of the boy by both parents. To complicate the pathogenic family picture, the father typically used physi-

THE "KID NOBODY WANTED" SOUGHT IN BIG MANHUNT

Exploding into the headlines in the early 1950's was the story of Billy Cook, hard-luck killer from Joplin, Missouri, whose days were ended in the gas chamber at San Quentin. The photo at left shows Cook's left hand with his life motto, "Hard Luck," tattooed on the fingers. At right, Cook is shown after his capture following a murderous rampage extending across several states from Missouri to California, then into Lower California, where a Mexican posse tracked him down.

"Hard luck" was an appropriate motto for the youth; his mother died when he was 5 years old, and his father thereupon abandoned him, with his brothers and sisters, in a mine cave. In addition, he was handicapped with a deformed right eyelid. Nobody wanted Billy when he was offered for adoption, resentful and squint-eyed, and it was only a matter of time until his tantrums became too much for county-appointed guardians to control. Billy quit school at the age of 12, and when brought before the court he was sent to the reformatory at his own request. From then on, almost all of his life was spent behind bars, first in the reformatory and then in the state penitentiary, to which he was "graduated" at 18.

Released from prison, Cook looked up his father and announced his intention to "live by the gun and roam." He got a job washing dishes, bought a gun, and was on his way—stealing his first car from a Texas mechanic with whom he hitched a ride. Robbed and locked in the trunk, the mechanic escaped to freedom by prying open the lid, but the next kidnap victims—an Illinois farmer, his wife, and three small children who picked Cook up near Oklahoma City when the first stolen car broke down—were not so lucky. Not daring to set them free, Cook forced them to drive back and forth through four states while he decided what to do with them. It was a three-day nightmare which included a foiled escape attempt, and it finally ended in Joplin where Cook shot them and threw their bodies down a mine shaft.

A horrible pattern of kidnapping and murder had been set in motion, and as the hunted Cook desperately attempted to elude the law, he hitched three more rides and took the cars' occupants as captives. He spared the life of one kidnap victim, a Blythe, California, deputy officer whom he left tied up in the desert; but he shot and killed a Seattle businessman—the crime for which he eventually received the death penalty. The big interstate manhunt that was on for Cook spread into Mexico when he was reported seen there with two companions—California prospectors who picked him up below the border and were his prisoners for eight days. When Cook was apprehended, less than a month had gone by since he had hitched the ride with the Texas mechanic. But though the time was brief, the toll was high: 9 people kidnapped, 6 killed.

As if in explanation of his deeds, Billy Cook said when arrested, "I hate everybody's guts, and everybody hates mine."

Based on *Life* (1951), and *Time* (1951, 1952).

cally punitive methods of discipline, thus augmenting the hostility the boy already felt for him. The end result of such a pattern is a hostile, defiant, inadequately socialized boy who lacks normal inner controls and tends to act out his aggressive impulses.

As a consequence of paternal rejection or for other reasons, the father may play a reduced role, while the mother plays the dominant role in providing affection, discipline, and other socialization behaviors. During adolescence, the youth who has identified with his mother and relied on her as a role model presumably has difficulty shaping a masculine self-concept. As a consequence he tends to be rebellious and to engage in "proving offenses" to reassure himself of his courage, independence, and virility.

Similarly, Shainberg (1967), in a study of 1500 young "military delinquents" (primarily servicemen who had been A.W.O.L.), reported that 90 percent of them had had severe difficulties with their fathers, whom they perceived as vague, lacking in warmth, and difficult to communicate with. The relationships were so full of conflict that the sons had given up trying to maintain them; and the fathers, unable to communicate with or discipline their sons, abandoned their roles in child rearing altogether. The mothers were remembered with clarity and the sons frequently reported having had good relationships with them.

3. *Sociopathic parental models.* Several investigators have found a high incidence of sociopathic traits in the fathers of delinquent boys (Bennett, 1961; Glueck & Glueck, 1962, 1969; O'Neal et al., 1962). These included alcoholism, brutality, antisocial attitudes, failure to provide, frequent unnecessary absences from home, and other characteristics that made the father an inadequate and unacceptable model. Elkind (1967), for example, cited the case of a "father who encouraged his 17-year-old son to drink, frequent prostitutes, and generally 'raise hell.' This particular father was awakened late one night by the police who had caught his son in a raid on a so-called 'massage' parlor. The father's reaction was, 'Why aren't you guys out catching crooks?' This same father would boast to his co-workers that his son was 'all boy' and a 'chip off the old block.'" (p. 313) McCord and McCord (1959) reported that when a family pattern combines rejection

with a sociopathic father, there is often early and prolonged delinquent behavior on the part of the son.

Sociopathic fathers—and mothers—may contribute in various ways to delinquent behavior of girls as well. Covert encouragement of sexual promiscuity is fairly common, and in some instances there is actual incest with the daughter. In a study of 30 delinquent girls, Scharfman and Clark (1967) found evidence of serious psychopathology in one or both parents of 22 of the girls, including 3 cases of incest and many other types of early sexual experience. These investigators also reported a high incidence of broken homes (only 11 of the 30 girls lived with both parents)—and harsh, irrational, and inconsistent discipline:

"Any form of consistent discipline or rational setting of limits was unknown to the girls in their homes. Rather, there was an almost regular pattern of indifference to the activities or whereabouts of these girls, often with the mother overtly or indirectly suggesting delinquent behavior by her own actions. This would alternate with unpredictable, irrational, and violent punishment." (p. 443)

Scharfman and Clark concluded that the key factors in the girls' delinquent behavior were: (1) broken homes, combined with early affective or material deprivation; (2) patterns of early sexual and aggressive overstimulation; and (3) irrational, harsh, and inconsistent parental discipline.

General sociocultural factors. Here, we are concerned with broad social conditions that tend to produce delinquency. Interrelated factors that appear to be of key importance include alienation and rebellion, social rejection, and the psychological support afforded by membership in a delinquent gang.

1. *Alienation and rebellion.* Feelings of unrelatedness and alienation are common to many young people today. However, we are referring here particularly to middle-class youths who are uncommitted to the values of the "establishment" and at the same time are confused about their own values and sense of identity. Often they view the world as a hostile and artificial place, inhabited by "squares" who make unfair distinctions and discriminations about race and class, who work at useless jobs that they pompously assume are meaningful, and who try to "sell" the younger

generation on a fraudulent and inevitably disappointing way of life. Outwardly the youths may passively submit to their elders' demands, but they may find it easier to do so with the use of drugs; or they may rebel, "drop out," leave home, and drift into groups in which drug usage and other behavior—considered delinquent by established social standards—is more or less the normal way of life.

In evaluating the role of pathogenic family patterns in delinquency, it may be emphasized that a given pattern is only one of many interacting factors. For example, many children who are rejected by their fathers do not become delinquents; and "broken home" is a catchall term to describe the absence of one or both parents because of a variety of conditions—such as desertion, separation, death, or imprisonment. A home may be "broken" at different times, under varying circumstances, and have differing influences, depending on the individual involved and his total life situation. Thus, the effects of a given family pattern must be assessed in relation to the total situation.

2. *The "social rejects."* A new population element is making itself increasingly felt in our society. This is the growing population of 16- to 20-year-olds who lack the ability or motivation to do well in school but are unable to find acceptable jobs in the community. With the emphasis on academic excellence in the United States, school pressures have become intolerable to them; and with increasing automation there are few jobs for which they can qualify. Whether they come from upper-, middle-, or lower-class homes, they have one crucial problem in common—they are not needed in our society. They are the victims of social progress, the "social rejects."

Shore and Massino (1969) have specifically delineated a "social rejection" pattern involving adolescents from lower-class suburban homes, in which the family usually is stable and the father employed. These adolescents do poorly in school, are identified early as school failures, and "drop out" as soon as they reach the age of 16. Although some jobs are available to them in suburbia, they lack essential skills—psychological, social, or academic—even for semiskilled work and frequently cannot get or hold a job. And unlike the ghetto slums, suburbia has few delinquent gangs in which the youths can find belongingness and

status. There are social agencies available to assist them, but they seem unable to benefit from the services offered—perhaps coming to a clinic or agency for only one or two interviews, and never returning. They appear bored and restless and may engage in delinquent acts to break the monotony or possibly to defend themselves

TWO POEMS BY DELINQUENT GIRLS

These poems, written by inmates of a girls' reformatory and published in studies of delinquency and rehabilitation of adolescent girls by Gisela Konopka, give some indication of the girls' views of themselves and their world.

The first poem, "The Delinquent Girl's Self-Image," was written by an institutionalized 17-year-old girl:

The broken and withered limb
Struggles, grasping, fighting to live
And doing so destroys the tree,
Its roots and all the blossoms it has to give.

I, like that bent and broken limb
Am unable to mend my broken ways,
But sucking, drawing, hanging on
Like a parasite to that which is pure and good.

Eventually that, too, will be broken
And without joy or blossom.
Even as the limb fights to survive
In doing so it may destroy that which is good!
Shall I let go?   (Konopka, 1964, p. 25)

The next poem, which also reveals the low self-esteem characteristic of delinquent girls, was read to Konopka by a sad-eyed 16-year-old:

I live in a house called torture and pain,
It's made of materials called sorrow and shame,
It's a lonely place in which to dwell
There's a horrid room there, and they call it Hell.

From the faucets run tears that I've cried all these years,
And it's heated by my heart made of stone
But the worst part to face is
I'll die in this place—
And when I die I'll die all alone.   (Konopka, 1967, p. 75)

Work with institutionalized delinquent girls has led Konopka to emphasize the importance of helping them build self-respect and hope. Such degrading practices as shaving off a girl's hair or removing all her clothing in solitary confinement should be eliminated, and increasing attention should be given to constructive practices, such as the girls' development of significant relationships with accepting and consistent adults. Additionally, community-based facilities should be provided to assist the girls in making the transition from institutional life to life in the community.

against underlying feelings of hopelessness and depression.

3. *The subcultural delinquent—delinquent gangs.* Here we are not dealing so much with personal psychopathology *per se* as with organized group pathology, involving rebellion against the norms of society. The individual may have achieved a capacity for loyalty and relatively stable interpersonal relationships, but appears to be alienated from and lacking in effective integration with the larger society. As Jenkins (1969) has expressed it:

"The socialized delinquent represents not a failure of socialization but a limitation of loyalty to a more or less predatory peer group. The basic capacity for social relations has been achieved. What is lacking is an effective integration with the larger society as a contributing member." (p. 73)

An estimated 70 to 90 percent of juvenile crimes are committed in pairs or groups (Rushing, 1969). As Cohen (1955) pointed out in his classic study of delinquent boys, the members of delinquent gangs typically feel inadequate in and rejected by the larger society. Gang membership gives them a sense of belonging and a means of gaining some measure of status and approval. Although some youths who join delinquent gangs come from seemingly good home backgrounds, the vast majority are socially and economically disadvantaged. Rejected by our predominantly middle-class society, they often develop a subculture in which the approved patterns of behavior are the very opposite of those approved by society as a whole.

These youths frequently gather at night in drive-ins, in front of bowling alleys, or in areas of town that appear to attract others of their kind. They find some superficial psychological support and group identification by looking and dressing in similar ways; however, they can rarely communicate their deepest concerns to each other, and tend to "cover up" with an air of bravado and various escapist activities, such as drinking, smoking "pot," getting "hopped up" on other drugs, and engaging in promiscuous sexual activities. Many of them sense and deeply resent their rejection by society.

In a study of adolescent and young adult offenders in a state prison, Goshen (1969) concluded that their offenses were the

". . . product of a passive, leaderless background in which by default, the acceptance by a peer group (street gang) led to a way of life motivated by efforts to meet the expectations of the group. . . . Conspicuous deficiencies in the background of this subgroup were the absence of desirable male models and the failure of public schools . . . to provide a substitute. By default, then, the expectations and the model behavior of the street gang became the only example which offered a reward in the form of acceptance and status." (p. 429)

Cloward and Ohlin (1963) have identified three more-or-less distinct types of delinquent subcultures among male adolescents in the lower-class areas of large urban centers. One is a *criminal subculture,* identified with a type of gang that directs its activities toward material gain through theft, extortion, and other illegal activities. Usually such gangs have connections with adult criminals in the area, who serve as "instructors" and provide such other "services" as helping to dispose of stolen goods. A second type of delinquent gang is one with a *conflict subculture,* in which physical aggression and violence are the chief means of gaining status and approval in the group. Still a third gang pattern is that with a *retreatist subculture,* in which drugs, promiscuous sex, and other sensual experiences are emphasized as a means of escaping life problems. As Cloward and Ohlin have noted, those who participate in a retreatist subculture lack even such opportunities for status as are afforded by membership in criminal- or conflict-oriented gangs.

Juvenile authorities have expressed concern about the number of girl gangs that have developed in recent years. Girl gangs provide much the same function for confused, resentful, and defiant girls as male gangs do for boys. In these gangs the girls create their "own world" for purposes of belongingness, protection, and defiance. In the gang they find acceptance, rules, loyalty, authority, discipline, and many of the other components that they cannot find or accept in the adult world. Many of these girl gangs are affiliated with male gangs, while maintaining their own separate organizations. Statistics indicate that girls are involved in about 15 to 30 percent of all delinquent gang activities that come to the attention of the police—assaults on other juveniles, automobile thefts, gang raids, carrying deadly weapons, narcotic violations, and impulsive gang activity.

Although delinquent gangs provide their members with some sense of belonging, they are by no means always highly organized and cohesive groups. In fact, Yablonsky (1959) has referred to the typical delinquent gang as a "near group"—in the sense of the shifting roles of its members, its low cohesiveness, and its unstable leadership and organization. Similarly, in an informal observation of several hundred Negro and Mexican-American gangs—both male and female—Klein (1968) emphasized their low cohesiveness, shifting roles, and little relation to adult criminal groups. Klein also noted the widespread and chronic dissatisfaction among gang members. In view of their life situations, the basic problems of slum-area gang members cannot be resolved by membership in a gang; the key challenge is to help such youths become productive members of the larger society.

Unusual stresses and other factors. We have noted that many delinquent acts are based on momentary impulses or are part of the regular activities of a delinquent gang. Delinquent behavior may also be triggered by some relatively minor event, as when a riot is triggered by a fight between two youths. And, of course, it may sometimes be inadvertent, resulting from innocent pranks that backfire.

In some instances, traumatic experiences in the life of a boy or girl appear to act as precipitating events. In a study of 500 delinquent boys, Clarke (1961) found that in about a third of the cases it was possible to isolate highly stressful events that preceded the delinquency—such as death of parents, disruption of family life, or discovery that they had been adopted. These events had proved highly disorganizing and often had led to poor school performance, truancy, brooding, and—eventually—delinquent behavior. Burks and Harrison (1962) have also emphasized the importance of stresses that undermine a youth's feelings of adequacy and worth as precipitating factors in some cases of aggressive antisocial behavior. In an analysis of 4 case histories—involving arson, murder, and breaking and entering—Finkelstein (1968) found an "accumulation of emotional tensions [leading] at times to temporary disintegration, or at least to a state in which the person in full awareness of what he is doing loses his ego control" (p. 310).

Three additional points may be mentioned in relation to delinquent behavior. (1) A great deal of controversy has centered around the effect that violence, as depicted in comics, on television, and in movies, has on violent delinquent behavior. Bandura (1969) and Wolfgang (1970) have pointed out that violent behavior can be learned through imitation and modeling, and that violence tends to run in families and cultures. Although this conclusion is backed by ample research evidence, it would appear that being raised in an actual culture of violence—as in an urban slum—is more likely to lead to the learning of violent behavior patterns than merely seeing such behavior depicted in fantasy. Violence in the mass media may sometimes influence the particular kinds of violent acts committed, but it probably does not supply the motivation for them. (2) The type of offense committed is often related to the motivation of the offender. Car stealing, for example, is often a crime of excitement and a means of gaining status and approval from delinquent peers; sexual delinquency is commonly associated with pervasive feelings of inadequacy and is a "proving" offense. (3) There is evidence that a disproportionate number of delinquent boys have a mesomorphic (athletic) body build. Glueck and Glueck (1956) found that 60 percent of 500 persistently delinquent boys from a disorganized urban area had a mesomorphic physique, as contrasted with 30 percent for a matched nondelinquent control group. They interpreted this to mean that mesomorphs tend to respond to environmental pressures differently than endomorphs and ectomorphs—for example, by aggressively acting out their tensions. Later studies by Cortés and Gatti (1970) and by Gibbens (1969) have also found a disproportionate percentage of mesomorphs among delinquents. However, a possible explanation for such findings may be that gang activities often place a special premium on physical prowess. While the role of physique in juvenile delinquency merits further study, it seems probable that it is at most a secondary factor in the total etiological pattern.

TREATMENT AND OUTCOMES

If they have adequate facilities and personnel, juvenile institutions and training schools can be of great help to youths who need to be removed from aversive environments and given a chance to learn about themselves and their world, to further their education and develop needed skills, and to find purpose and meaning in their lives. In such settings the youths may have the opportunity to receive psychological counseling, group therapy, and guided group interaction. Here it is of key importance that peer-group pressures are channeled in the direction of re-socialization, rather than toward repetitive delinquent behavior. Behavior-modification techniques—based on the assumption that delinquent behavior is learned, maintained, and changed

---

THE USE OF REINFORCEMENT PROCEDURES IN THE MODIFICATION OF DELINQUENT BEHAVIOR

Favorable reports on the use of reinforcement procedures in the treatment of delinquent behavior have been made by a number of investigators, including Bednar et al. (1970), Burchard (1967), and Cohen et al. (1968). Programs may differ according to the emphasis put upon individual performance, group performance, or a combination of the two.

Individual reinforcement program

Of particular interest is a study by Cohen and his associates (1968) of adolescents in a juvenile correctional institution who were selected to participate in an educational program. The program, which utilized a reinforcement-oriented, 24-hour learning environment, was based on the assumption that little progress could be made in the modification of the subjects' delinquent behavior until they could acquire skills for achieving social and material rewards legitimately rather than in antisocial ways. All of the adolescents selected for the study were school dropouts who had received little or no satisfaction from intellectual activities.

Unlike many treatment programs that depend heavily on negative sanctions and reinforcements, this program depended primarily on positive reinforcers, individual initiative, and self-determination. The investigators instigated an extrinsic system of rewards based on a point economy; e.g., points could be earned for high achievement scores in programmed instruction and other educational projects, and these points could be used to buy commodities and services. More points could be earned by additional individual study.

The program was parallel to incentive programs in the community outside the institution in that the adolescents paid for their private rooms, their selected meal plans, their private offices for study, their tuition for courses, and their rent for recreational items or admission fees. They were allowed considerable freedom in planning their own educational programs and leisure pursuits. However, if a boy's points fell below 1200 he was placed "on relief"; he lost his private room, had to eat regular institutional food, and received no extra luxuries.

The results of this program were considered to be highly successful. The subjects worked hard at self-managed educational programs, studied conscientiously in their spare time, and advanced more than two grades, as measured by standard achievement tests, within an 8-month period. In addition, discipline problems essentially disappeared and defacement or destruction of facilities did not occur. Since the program prepared the subjects for, and paralleled, life on the outside, it was expected that the gains achieved would generalize to the subjects' "real life" settings after their discharge.

Reinforcement contingencies on a group basis

Another way of using reinforcement procedures in modification of behavior is to base reinforcement contingencies on the group, rather than individual, performance. This type of approach is aimed especially at increasing mutual cooperation, responsibility, cohesiveness, and commitment to common goals. Here, of course, a powerful force is peer group approval or disapproval—the latter sometimes leading to group discipline of individual offenders, since an aversive or poor performance by one may bring about negative consequences for everyone involved.

Double reinforcement contingencies

Still another approach is to combine individual and group reinforcement procedures in what are called "double reinforcement contingencies." Here, the rewards or punishments are jointly determined by the individual's own contribution and by the overall group performance. An example of this approach is found on football teams in which a player may receive stars on his headgear for outstanding performances in given games, but whose status also depends on his team's record of wins and losses. The advantages of this approach for the treatment of delinquent behavior has been stressed by Bandura (1969), who concluded that "Double reinforcement contingencies in which individuals' outcomes are jointly determined by the nature of their own contributions and by the group's overall performance are likely to produce the most socially productive functioning." (p. 284)

according to the same principles as other learned behavior—have shown marked promise in the rehabilitation of juvenile offenders who require institutionalization. Counseling with parents and related sociotherapeutic measures are generally of vital importance in the total rehabilitation program.

The procedure of probation is widely used with juvenile offenders. Probation may be granted either in lieu of or after a period of institutionalization. In keeping with the trend toward helping troubled persons in their own environments, the California Youth Authority conducted The Community Treatment Project, a 5-year experiment in which delinquents—other than those involved in such crimes as murder, rape, or arson—were granted probation and supervised and assisted in their own communities. The 270 youths treated in this project showed a rehabilitation success rate of 72 percent during a 15-month follow-up period. In contrast, a comparable group of 357 delinquents who underwent institutional treatment and then were released on probation showed a rehabilitation success rate of only 48 percent (Blake, 1967). Since 90 percent of the girls and 73 percent of the boys committed to the California Youth Authority by juvenile courts were found eligible for community treatment, it would appear that most delinquents can be guided into constructive behavior without being removed from their family or community. It should be noted, however, that a key factor in the success of this research project was a marked reduction in the case load of the parole officers supervising the delinquents immediately placed on probation.

The procedure of institutionalization seems particularly questionable in the case of "juvenile status offenders"—youths whose offenses have not involved acts against persons or property and would not be considered criminal in nature if committed by an adult. Lerman (1971) found that over 80 percent of the girls in a State Home for Girls in New Jersey were institutionalized for such offenses (e.g., for running away from home, being truant, being considered ungovernable or beyond the control of parents, engaging in sexual relations, and becoming pregnant). As this investigator pointed out, the practice of institutionalizing juvenile status offenders may actually exacerbate their behavioral problems rather than correct them. He cited a number of points that merit serious consideration:

Placing juvenile offenders behind bars in dehumanizing penal institutions appears to be far less effective than placing them in institutions with rehabilitation facilities, represented by the photo immediately above. In the "school camps" operated by the Juvenile Division of the Illinois Department of Corrections, boys spend half of their time at work in nearby parks or in community service, the other half in a classroom on the camp's grounds. Individualized attention in small, ungraded classrooms is a characteristic of the special education schools, and boys are able to advance at their own rate.

1. Juvenile status offenders—usually because of family troubles that make it difficult for them to be returned to their homes—are incarcerated longer on the average than "real" juvenile offenders who have committed crimes against persons or property, e.g., robbery and assault.

2. Mixing juvenile status offenders and "real" delinquents in detention facilities provides learning experiences for the nondelinquents on how to become delinquents; many of them do in fact later engage in criminal behavior.

3. The public is not generally aware of the differences between youth who "need supervision" and delinquents who rob, steal, and commit other crimes such as assault; and consequently they are not sensitized to the special needs of juvenile status offenders.

4. Juvenile status offenders have not committed criminal acts and hence should not be subject to criminal-type sanctions; juvenile institutions that mix noncriminal and criminal offenders constitute the state's human garbage dump for dealing with problem children, especially those from poor families.

Fortunately, there is growing public concern about the inadequacies of our correctional system for juveniles, and various new approaches are being tried. One key task in dealing with troubled youth is that of opening lines of communication with them. The behavior of even some of the most "hard-core" delinquent gangs has shown marked improvement when social workers or police officers have managed to make contact with them and win their confidence and respect. Often such personnel can help channel the youths' activities into automobile or motorcycle rallies and other programs that provide both recreational and learning opportunities. Here, however, as in the case of institutional and probation programs, too often severe handicaps are presented by a lack of trained personnel and resources.

The need is not only for more effective rehabilitation programs, but also for provision of long-range programs aimed at the prevention of delinquency. Here the emphasis is on the alleviation of slum conditions, the provision of adequate educational and recreational opportunities for disadvantaged youth, the educating of parents, and the delineation of a more meaningful societal role for adolescents.

CRIMINAL BEHAVIOR

In our society, criminal behavior is classified for the most part as falling into one of two major categories: felonies or misdemeanors. Felonies are serious crimes such as murder and robbery for which there are severe legal penalties. Misdemeanors, as the name implies, are minor offenses such as disorderly conduct and vagrancy. The particular behaviors classified as misdemeanors often vary considerably from state to state—illustrating once again the importance of social definitions in the labeling of behavior as "abnormal."

Although criminal behavior sometimes has its roots in juvenile delinquency, most juvenile delinquents do not become criminals as adults, and many criminals have no prior history of juvenile delinquency. The range of offenses, motivations, and etiological factors are much the same, however, in both delinquency and crime. In the following discussion we shall attempt to highlight both the likenesses and differences between these two categories of sociopathic behavior.

INCIDENCE

Official figures compiled by the Federal Bureau of Investigation indicate that the crime rate is higher in the United States than in most other countries, and that it has been steadily increasing. In fact, the problem is even more serious than government statistics suggest, for many crimes go unreported. Ennis (1967) surveyed a random sample of 10,000 households and found that about as many major crimes go unreported as reported.

The incidence of such minor crimes as petty larceny, malicious mischief, and simple assault undoubtedly exceeds reported figures by an even bigger margin.

In 1970, more than $5\frac{1}{2}$ million reported crimes in the United States were of the types classified by the FBI as *serious:* homicide, forcible rape, robbery, aggravated assault, burglary, larceny, and auto theft. Some investigators point out that the total figure is not as ominous as it seems, since the subtotal for auto theft—which many people feel should not be included in the classification—came close to a million. But there would appear to be little room for complacency when it is realized that *violent* crimes—that is, offenses of the first four types that we have listed—increased 11 times faster in the 1960's than population size. As shown by the FBI "crime clocks" (next column), violent crimes occurred in 1970 at the rate of one every 43 seconds, while the overall rate for serious crimes was 11 per minute. The cost of crime is estimated at over $50 billion, an incredible and wasteful financial toll.

It has also been found that crime rates vary considerably from one region of the country to another, from city to city, and from metropolitan to rural areas. Crime rates are much higher in the West than in the Northwest or South; higher in New York City and Washington, D.C., than in Philadelphia; and much higher in metropolitan centers than in smaller cities and rural areas, particularly for crimes against the person.

Among lower-income groups, blacks are almost twice as likely as whites to be victims of crimes of violence; but they are only slightly more likely than whites to be victims of crimes against property. Middle- and upper-income groups, whether black or white, are about equally exposed to crime, but crimes against property are much more common than crimes against the person. By and large, whites tend to victimize whites and blacks to victimize blacks. Findings also show that criminals most often strike in the vicinity of their own homes and that they often know their victims personally.

More than 10 million Americans come into contact with some agency of criminal justice each year for having committed, or for suspicion of having committed, a serious crime. Approximately 80 percent of both juvenile and adult offenders are male, and, as we have noted, about

CRIME CLOCKS, 1970

MURDER
1 every 33 min.

FORCIBLE RAPE
1 every 14 min.

AGGRAVATED ASSAULT
1 every 96 sec.

ROBBERY
1 every 91 sec.

BURGLARY
1 every 15 sec.

LARCENY
1 every 18 sec.

AUTO THEFT
1 every 34 sec.

Serious crimes in the United States —which include all of the offenses represented by the seven "crime clocks" at left—occurred at the rate of 11 per minute in 1970, up from 9 per minute in 1969. For offenses in the subcategory of violent crimes— murder, forcible rape, robbery, and assault to kill—the rate of occurrence was one every 43 seconds, as compared with one every 48 seconds the year before. Specific figures on the increase in violent crime in the 1960's are provided in the illustration on the following page.

Based on Uniform Crime Reports (1971).

half of all serious crimes are committed by juveniles. As a consequence of apprehension and conviction for serious crimes, over 500,000 individuals are in federal, state, and local prisons and jails; in addition, more than a million others —both male and female—are on probation. It has been estimated that if existing trends continue, at least 40 percent of male children in the United States will be arrested for a nontraffic offense at some time in their lives; the figure approximates 60 percent for boys in metropolitan areas.

ETIOLOGICAL FACTORS IN CRIMINAL BEHAVIOR

In our discussion of delinquency, we noted the etiological importance of (1) pervasive personal pathology, (2) pathogenic family patterns, (3) general sociocultural factors, including alienation and subcultural climates that foster antisocial behavior, and (4) unusual or seemingly fortuitous stresses that are not likely to be repeated. In the present section we shall reconsider some of these factors as they relate to crime among adults. We shall also examine some patterns of sociopathic

behavior in which juveniles are not usually involved, namely, professional crime and organized crime.

Chromosomes and crime. A number of early investigators attributed criminal behavior to heredity. Prominent among these investigators were Lombroso and his followers, who became known as the "Italian School of Criminology" (Lombroso-Ferrero, 1911). According to Lombroso, the criminal was a "born type" with "stigmatizing" features—such as a low forehead, an unusually shaped head and jaw, eyebrows growing together above the bridge of the nose, and protruding ears—that clearly distinguished him from normal people. These stigmata were considered to be a throwback to "savage man" and seemingly predisposed the individual to criminal behavior.

Although Lombroso's view has long since been discarded, a number of recent investigators have dealt with the possibility that an extra Y chromosome—a genetic anomaly that may occur in males—is associated with criminal behavior. The pioneering study in this area was that of Jacobs and her colleagues (1965) who published their findings on 197 mentally abnormal inmates of a special security institution in Scotland. All were considered to have violent and dangerous criminal tendencies. Seven—3.5 percent—were of the XYY chromosomal type. The incidence of the XYY chromosomal pattern in the general population, by contrast, is apparently about 1 in 250 males, or 0.4 percent (Sergovich et al., 1969).

A number of related studies have produced further evidence suggesting a link between the XYY chromosomal aberration and criminal behavior, but findings are by no means conclusive. Sergovich (1970) found significantly more XYY males among those who were tall and criminal, as well as those who were tall and criminally insane, tall and mentally retarded, and tall and mentally ill. In a maximum security prison in Australia, Wiener (1968) found 4 XYY males among 34 tall prisoners[1]—a frequency of 11 percent. Two of these men had committed murder, one had

---

[1]Physical tallness is the one characteristic clearly associated with the extra Y chromosome on the basis of presently available studies. The XYY males in Jacobs' early study, for example, averaged about 6'1", as contrasted with a mean height of only 5'7" for inmates with a normal (XY) chromosomal pattern. It should be emphasized, however, that most tall males are *not* XYY. In a study of 36 basketball players ranging in height from 5'11" to 6'10", not a single instance of chromosomal abnormality was found (Montagu, 1968).

attempted murder, and the other had been convicted of larceny.

The findings of Abdullah et al. (1969) provide additional evidence of a relationship between the XYY pattern and antisocial behavior, while also demonstrating the need to guard against easy generalizations. In a study of 70 XYY males, these investigators found that all but 5 had a history of antisocial or aggressive criminal behavior—and 2 of these 5 were juveniles. On the other hand, they found only 2 chromosomal aberrations (1 an XYY and 1 an XXY) in a study of 49 males in mental hospitals and prisons, all of whom were above average in height and characterized by aggressive, impulsive, antisocial behavior. This incidence of slightly less than 2

FACTS ABOUT HOMICIDE

Homicides are classified, in terms of intent, into: (1) first degree murder, characterized by premeditation and planning, or committed during a felony, such as rape or robbery; (2) second degree murder, in which there is no premeditation or planning, e.g., as when the homicide is committed "in the heat of passion"; and (3) manslaughter, committed without malice aforethought, as when a driver accidentally kills a pedestrian in a crosswalk. Relevant to these three categories are the following data concerning homicide in the United States.

Incidence

For reasons that are unclear, the homicide rate—which had been on the decline since the 1930's despite an overall increase in the crime rate—rose sharply in 1965 and has continued to rise ever since. In 1970, more than 15,000 murders were committed in the United States. For each actual murder, it should be noted that many attempts are unsuccessful and the victim lives (80 percent of gunshot victims and 90 percent of stab victims). Thus, homicidal acts are far more common in our society than the statistics on homicide would indicate.

Who kills whom?

Children and adolescents sometimes commit murder, but by far the greater number are committed by adults, with most victims being in their 20's and 30's. Males outnumber females as victims at a ratio of more than 3 to 1, and as offenders at a ratio of over 5 to 1. In approximately 90 percent of all murders, the offender and victim are of the same race. Blacks are disproportionately represented, as both victims and offenders. Apprehending the offender is often easy, since in most cases offender and victim are relatives, friends, or close acquaintances; in one fourth of all murders offender and victim are members of the same family.

Methods or weapons used

By far the greatest number of homicides result from shooting (65 percent), followed by cutting or stabbing (19 percent), use of other impersonal weapons such as clubs or poisons (8 percent), and use of personal weapons, such as hands (8 percent). The high incidence of murder committed by firearms is not surprising in view of the widespread possession of guns by civilians in our society, exceeding that in any other country.

Motives

As we have noted in listing the three categories of homicide, motives may be diverse, or the homicide may even be accidental. However, aside from murders committed for calculated monetary gains by individuals or professional killers associated with organized crime—which constitute over a fourth of all murders—homicide is typically considered a "crime of passion." It often results from quarrels combined with a lowering of inner reality and ethical restraints; for example, intoxicants complicate the motivational picture in about half of all homicide cases. In some instances the victim—for whatever reason—seems to invite being killed, as by striking the first blow; and, as we have seen, homicide may be associated with such mental disorders as schizophrenia and paranoia.

Psychosocial factors

Although diverse personality types may commit homicide, offenders tend to come from homes or neighborhoods in which violence is an aspect of daily life. Often they have a history of violent tendencies and behavior. In ghetto slums among socially disadvantaged blacks, homicide rates are disproportionately high. Homicide rates also show marked cross-cultural differences—with Iceland and Colombia, South America, representing extremes in rates of incidence among the major countries. Iceland's rate is zero, while that for Colombia is 5 times that of the United States.

In general, it would appear that the preceding statements concerning the incidence and nature of homicide would hold true for most major industrialized nations.

Based on Cole, Fisher, and Cole (1968), Greenberg and Blank (1970), Langner (1971), Tanay (1969), Uniform Crime Reports (1971), Voss and Hepburn (1968), and Wolfgang (1969).

percent is considerably lower than that reported in related studies—though it is still somewhat higher than the 0.4 percent incidence for males in the general population.

XYY males have been found to be more than normally aggressive and impulsive, tall in stature, and usually below average in intelligence. Facial acne is common in adolescence. Montagu (1968) has cited Richard Speck, who was convicted of the brutal murder of eight student nurses in Chicago in 1966, as an example of the XYY type. Speck was tall, mentally dull, and had an acne-marked face. Prior to the murder of the student nurses, he had a history of some 40 arrests. But as Montagu pointed out, it is a moot question whether Speck's chromosomal abnormality might have been sufficient cause for his behavior, or whether his impoverished social environment was the key determinant, or whether both factors were involved in combination.

Generally speaking, it would appear that chromosomal aberrations of any sort are more likely to lead to abnormal development and behavior than are normal chromosomal patterns. However, there is no evidence to support the contention that some people are "born criminals." As a recent study sponsored by the National Institute of Mental Health concluded, it has not even been clearly established that XYY males are violence-prone:

"Quite clearly, very complex and varied interactions between hereditary and social and environmental influences appear to be involved. Further, it seems unlikely that such variable and socially defined and determined problems as crime and delinquency are primarily and directly linked with the possession of an extra chromosome." (NIMH, 1970, p. 19)

This of course does not rule out the possibility that the XYY chromosomal aberration may be a predisposing factor in the development of criminal behavior. Of relevance here is a study by Prince and Whatmore (1967), who found a lower incidence of crime and mental disturbance in the family backgrounds of the XYY criminals they studied than in the family backgrounds of genetically normal criminals used as a control group.

Speculating on the possible influence of an extra Y chromosome, Montagu (1968) has suggested ". . . that the ordinary quantum of aggressiveness of a normal XY male is derived from his Y chromosome, and that the addition of another Y chromosome presents a double dose of those potencies that may under certain conditions facilitate the development of aggressive behavior." (p. 46)

Presumably the Y chromosome might lead to the excessive production of androgens during early development—a condition that influences brain structure and functioning and may result in unusually aggressive behavior patterns in later life, even though hormonal levels have long since returned to normal (Jarvik, 1968). In this context, it is interesting to note that the XXY aberration does not appear to be related to impulsive, aggressive behavior as does the XYY aberration. A great deal more research is needed, however, before we can determine the precise influence of the extra Y chromosome. One puzzling aspect of the question is that available studies have failed to show a disproportionate incidence of the XYY aberration among delinquent boys. Welch et al. (1967) found only one XYY case among 464 institutionalized delinquents; similarly, Hunter (1968) found only 3 cases among 1021 boys who had been institutionalized for juvenile offenses.

In conclusion, it may be emphasized that XYY males make up only a small proportion of the criminal population—and that not all XYY males become criminals. To obtain more definitive evidence concerning the interaction of genetic and environmental factors among those who do, we will need a great deal more research, including systematic studies involving the early detection and follow-up of males born with this chromosomal abnormality.

Personal and social pathology. In an early study, Arief and Bowie (1947) needed 18 diagnostic categories to describe shoplifters referred for evaluation by the Chicago Municipal Court. In a study of 300 bad-check writers, MacDonald (1959) not only found a high incidence of psychopathic personalities and chronic alcoholics, but also a lesser number of schizophrenics, manics, seniles, and mentally retarded individuals. Of 175 murderers studied by Guttmacher (1960), 53 were clearly psychotic at the time of the murder and 17 others manifested such disorders as alcoholism, psychopathic personality, and drug dependence. In a study of 223 felons, Guze, Goodwin, and Crane (1969) found that the types of psychopathology most often associated with serious crime were antisocial personality, alcoholism, and drug dependence. Often, of course, such disorders are interrelated.

Neurophysiological defects apparently may also be a factor in some types of criminal behavior. In a study of 100 prisoners who had been referred for psychiatric assessment by courts and other law enforcement agencies in St. Louis, Small (1966) reported a high incidence of abnormal EEG's and other indications of central nervous system impairment. Interestingly enough, it was found that felons with abnormal EEG's were less likely to engage in "skilled" criminal behavior but were usually guilty of repeated thievery; moreover, individuals with no demonstrable evidence of CNS lesions—except those with organic brain disorders of later life—accounted for the most serious crimes, such as assault, murder, and sexual violence.

In the case of criminals who are biologically normal, personal pathology seems often to stem primarily from social pathology—as evidenced by the unusually high incidence of adult as well as juvenile offenses in the slums and ghettos of our large cities. In these areas there appears to be a gradual and progressive social disorganization that, in some ways, reverses the usual forms of socialization and social regulations. Values are in flux; there are widespread feelings of contempt for authority, and feelings of frustration and hostility are endemic. Under such conditions, aggressive and antisocial behavior may become the norm.

The professional criminal. The term *dyssocial personality* has been used to refer to individuals who are not psychopathic personalities but are predatory and follow criminal pursuits—such as racketeers, drug pushers, and a variety of other professional criminals. Such individuals usually come from a subcultural setting in which they are exposed to deviant codes of behavior and criminal models.

The concept of *differential association*, first developed by Sutherland in the late 1930's, has provided a framework for understanding the importance of subcultural influences in the "training" of the professional criminal (Sutherland & Cressey, 1966). As Sutherland noted, the basic process of socialization is much the same for everyone: the individual comes to accept as his own the values and behavioral standards empha-

PSYCHOPATHOLOGY AND FEMALE CRIMINALITY

In a study of 66 convicted female felons in Missouri, Cloninger and Guze (1970a; 1970b) concluded that all of their subjects revealed some type of psychopathology. Salient characteristics of the individuals in their sample included:

Race	White, 34; black, 30; Indian, 1; white-Indian, 1
Age range	17 to 54 years; median age, 27 (75 percent were between 20 and 35.)
Education	Dropped out of elementary school, 11; completed eighth grade only, 8; dropped out of high school, 29; stopped after graduating from high school, 7; attended college, 10; graduated from college, 1
Marital status	Never married, 13; married and living with husbands, 14; widowed, 6; separated but not divorced, 20; divorced, 13 (62 percent of those who had married were separated or divorced.)
Family background	Permanent absence of at least one parent from home before subject was 18 years old: 65 percent Incidence of mental disorders: fathers, 59 percent; mothers, 76 percent Antisocial behavior of father or surrogate: heavy drinking, 53 percent; neglect of family, 29 percent; in prison or jail, 20 percent; cruel or physically abusive, 12 percent Antisocial behavior of mother or surrogate: heavy drinker, 21 percent; cruel or abusive, 12 percent; in prison, 9 percent; neglect of family, 9 percent
Criminal history	No previous arrest or conviction, 44 percent; prior felony conviction, 20 percent; no information, 36 percent
Present crime	Homicide, 14; shoplifting, 11; check forgery, 11; drug violations, 10; burglary, 8; robbery, 5; other crimes, including assault and embezzlement, 7
Type of psychopathology	Labeled as antisocial personalities, 43; alcoholics, 31; hysterics, 27; drug dependents, 17; homosexuals, 9; anxiety neurotics, 7; other labels, 9 (The total exceeds 66 because in many cases more than one label was assigned; e.g., 60 percent of the cases of antisocial personality were associated with alcoholism and 40 percent with hysteria.)

A factor that the investigators regarded as noteworthy in these cases was the marked parental deprivation, as well as the familial, social, and personal psychopathology.

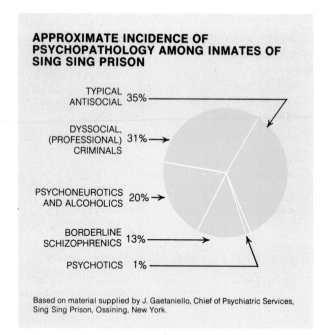

**APPROXIMATE INCIDENCE OF
PSYCHOPATHOLOGY AMONG INMATES OF
SING SING PRISON**

TYPICAL
ANTISOCIAL 35%

DYSSOCIAL,
(PROFESSIONAL) 31%
CRIMINALS

PSYCHONEUROTICS
AND ALCOHOLICS 20%

BORDERLINE
SCHIZOPHRENICS 13%

PSYCHOTICS 1%

Based on material supplied by J. Gaetaniello, Chief of Psychiatric Services,
Sing Sing Prison, Ossining, New York.

sized by those with whom he associates on a repeated and intimate basis—most notably, his parents and peers. But in the case of a young person growing up in a subculture where antisocial behavior is the norm, the values and standards internalized—and the skills learned—are likely to be quite different from those emphasized in conventional society. Thus, the individual who becomes a professional criminal usually acquires his training in much the same way that legitimate professionals do, responding to the learning opportunities, values, and reinforcements that his environment has provided. Unlike the antisocial or psychopathic personality, he is socialized—but in a deviant way.

Typically, the professional criminal specializes in a particular type of crime, such as forgery or burglary, and develops a particular style of operation. His goal is to make money in the quickest and safest way possible. In general, he attempts to avoid violence, since it would greatly increase the risk of detection and imprisonment. His crimes are usually well planned and may even be rehearsed. This point has been made clear by MacDonald in his study of check forgers.

"The skilled bogus check writer plans his check passing carefully, limits it to a brief period in a large town and then moves quickly to another state where he re-

peats his offenses when his funds are exhausted. The checks are printed with the title of a state or city government, a widely known or a nonexistent company. In the latter case a bank account may be opened but only a small deposit is made. The check may be labelled payroll and the value, which is printed with a protectograph, is for an irregular amount such as $88.72 to give the appearance of a payroll deduction for income tax. A large number of checks are passed late Friday afternoon and Saturday. When the bank discovers the fraud the following Monday, the check writer is already in another state." (1959, p. 439)

By and large, professional criminals do not appear to show significant personality deviations, aside from their adherence to the values and codes of their own group. But Stojanovich (1969) has sounded a note of caution. While many professional criminals he studied did manifest so-called dyssocial characteristics—such as predatoriness, permanence of motivation, good control of inner impulses, and ability to profit from experience and utilize gains—others showed characteristics more typically associated with the psychopathic personality. Apparently we are dealing with a continuum that has antisocial personality at one end, dyssocial personality at the other end, and a combination of antisocial and dyssocial personalities in between.

Of course, even typical dyssocial professional criminals are not immune to mental disorders, and the stressful life situation they typically live under often leads to some degree of personality decompensation, which may reach neurotic or psychotic levels. In general, however, their background or training and their emotional insulation protect them from stress and personality decompensation, even during imprisonment. Possible arrest and imprisonment is one of the hazards of their profession; and should it happen, the criminal tries to adapt to prison life and do "easy time."

Organized crime. As Cressey (1967) has pointed out, it is difficult to assess or discuss the nature and incidence of organized crime, since it has not been legally defined in the same sense that such criminal acts as forcible rape or homicide have. However, Cressey has tentatively defined the "organized criminal" as "one who commits a crime while occupying an organization position specifically set up for committing that crime" (p. 176).

The largest criminal organization in the United States, by all accounts, is La Cosa Nostra, also known as "the Mafia," "the Syndicate," and "the Mob." The gross annual income of Cosa Nostra has been variously estimated at between $20 billion and $50 billion. In 1969 the Attorney General reported a figure of not less than $50 billion—more than the total national revenue of all but a few of the world's major countries (Alsop, 1969). This income is derived from gambling, narcotics traffic, hijacking, interest from loan sharking, illegal distribution of alcohol, and prostitution—in that order.

Of course, as our society changes, the patterns of organized crime also change; and activities that the syndicate once found economically rewarding—such as prostitution—may now be de-emphasized in favor of more lucrative pursuits, such as gambling. In recent years, Cosa Nostra money has been invested in various legitimate businesses, as well as in the business chattels over which it has gained control—thus implementing its income. In his authoritative book *Theft of a Nation*, Cressey (1969) estimated Cosa Nostra's minimum contribution to our political campaigns at about 15 percent of their total cost. Operating in most, if not all, of the big cities and many smaller ones, the syndicate represents a powerful and pervasive force.

In their fight against organized crime, law-enforcement agencies must obtain evidence and seek convictions; however, since , violence is such an integral part of organized crime, evidence is extremely difficult to obtain. As Hoover (1968) has noted, violence

". . . is a coldly calculated tactic to maintain the group's dominance over its own members and over the members of the society in which it operates rather than terror for terror's sake.

"The peculiar evil of this type of 'corporate' violence is not the individual sadism and brutality of the 'enforcers' and 'strong-arm men,' but the monopolistic position it enables racket leaders to gain and hold in their legitimate, as well as their illicit, activities.

"Force and threats of force are employed to eliminate rivals, collect on gambling and loan-sharking debts, frighten potential witnesses, enforce internal discipline, and gain possession of various business chattels. In the greater Chicago area alone, there have been more than 1,000 gangland slayings since 1919, only 17 of which have been solved; in the greater Boston area there have been more than 50 during the past four years, only 11 of which have been solved." (p. 62)

Since organized crime is a major threat to a democratic society based on justice, law, and order, our country is striving to find more effective methods of dealing with it.

The "new" criminal. About a decade ago, Yablonsky (1962; 1963) noted the growing prevalence of individuals who turn to crime primarily for ego-satisfaction and "kicks." A "kick" is derived from performing some taboo act—usually a senseless act of violence—which serves to intensify the present moment, clearly differentiating it from the routine of daily life. Whereas most "old" types of criminal carefully calculate their acts, usually with an eye on material gain, the "new" criminal commits violent acts on impulse, simply because it "makes him feel good." As one youth told Yablonsky after a gang killing:

"If I would of got the knife, I would have stabbed him. That would of gave me more of a build-up. People would have respected me for what I've done and things like that. They would say, 'There goes a cold killer.'"

Typically, the illegal acts of the "new" criminal are spontaneous and unpremeditated; in most cases there is no evidence that he has even had prior contact with his victim. When he does participate in planned criminal acts, he is still primarily interested in "kicks." Unlike most other criminals, he seeks no gain other than the pleasure to be derived from the criminal act itself.

The view that the "new" criminal is becoming a major social menace appears to be well documented by daily reports in the news media of seemingly irrational crimes and senseless acts of violence. The well-publicized Tate murder case of 1970 is only one of many extreme examples: several individuals were killed in gruesome ways, including the mutilation of a pregnant young woman by cutting open her abdomen. Although this group killing, like some others in recent years, apparently involved an element of "social protest"—in the sense of warning the "establishment" that its days were numbered—it seems to have been motivated primarily by a desire for thrills. Like most of the crimes perpetrated by the "new" criminal, it violated all codes of human decency.

TREATMENT AND OUTCOMES

"Man has never been able to develop a completely rational and satisfactory set of alternatives for dealing with convicted violators of the criminal law. The more primitive forms of criminal sanctions were based primarily on ideas of revenge and retribution. Execution, physical torture, and public degradation were the most common methods in use until near the close of the eighteenth century. Imprisonment as the principal method did not come into general use until the beginning of the nineteenth century. Concepts of retributive punishment have persisted, but superimposed upon them were other purposes, such as deterrence, public protection, and rehabilitation. The trend in Western civilization for the past 150 years has been steadily in the direction of more and more commitment to rehabilitation and resocialization of offenders. Implementation of these ideas has been extremely slow and hampered by lack of financial support and the excessive fragmentation of the public agencies responsible. The movement is now away from the excessive use of imprisonment and more and more toward the development of community-based programs making use of the social sciences. The correctional field is on the threshold of revolutionary changes which will take place gradually, tested by scientific methods." (McGee, 1969, p. 1)

As is apparent from the preceding excerpt, the trends in dealing with criminal behavior have in many ways paralleled those used for psychopathology in general; and it is obvious that similar treatment procedures apply throughout—such as the early detection and correction of unhealthy personality trends, the correction of undesirable social conditions, and the provision of adequate treatment personnel and facilities. But since crime represents a vast range of individuals and

---

MILESTONES IN DEALING WITH DELINQUENT AND CRIMINAL BEHAVIOR IN THE UNITED STATES

1817   Inauguration in New York State of the first parole system in the U.S.

1841   Adoption by the city of Boston, Massachusetts, of probation procedures—the first in the U.S.

1855   Opening of an institution for the criminally insane—the first in the U.S.—adjacent to Auburn State Prison, New York

1899   Establishment at Chicago, Illinois, of the first juvenile court in the U.S.

1915   Presentation by Paul E. Bowers, psychiatrist at Indiana State Prison, of comprehensive studies on the relationship between crime and mental illness

1922   Establishment of the Division for the Prevention of Delinquency by the National Committee for Mental Hygiene

1930   Congressional passage of law reorganizing federal prisons and providing for medical services to prisoners

1940   First publication of the *Journal of Criminal Psychopathology*

1948   Utilization in the New Jersey prison system of group therapy techniques

1952   Inauguration by the State of Wisconsin of the first program in the U.S. for adequate treatment of sex offenders

1956   The rendering, by the U.S. Court of Appeals for the District of Columbia, of the Durham decision, in which the provision is made that a defendent is not criminally responsible if his criminal act was the product of mental disease or mental defect

1958   Congressional passage of Public Law 752, providing for psychiatric examination of convicted federal offenders before imposition of sentence

1965   Congressional passage of the Prisoner Rehabilitation Act, authorizing the daytime release of selected inmates for education or work in nearby communities

1965   The rendering, by the U.S. Supreme Court, of the Miranda decision, which requires that a person accused of a crime be informed of his right to counsel before he is questioned

1970   Congressional passage of "preventive detention" and other new anticrime legislation

In addition to the events listed—which in general signify a trend toward the more humane treatment of the mentally disordered offender, and the more effective rehabilitation of offenders of all kinds —we have noted a growing trend in the late 1960's and early 1970's toward the use of psychologists and psychiatrists as "expert witnesses" in criminal cases. Such testimony is directed at providing a jury with important information concerning a defendant's mental state and in drawing inferences from data that a jury generally would lack the competence to evaluate.

Based chiefly on Halleck (1968); other sources include Mitchell (1971) and Silverman (1969).

behaviors, it is also apparent that no simple formula or single generalization can either explain it or suggest an easy solution to it. Because its complex social, economic, and psychological bases are not fully understood, its eradication must be considered a long-range, rather than an immediately achievable, goal.

For present purposes let us briefly examine three aspects of the treatment of criminal offenders: (1) the traditional reliance on punishment, (2) rehabilitation, and (3) some correctional trends and prospects.

Traditional reliance on punishment. In 1843, Jeremy Bentham concluded that if punishment were certain, swift, and severe, many a person would avoid criminal behavior. The view is still widely held that punishment—usually involving imprisonment—is the most effective way of making the offender realize the error of his ways and curing him of his criminal tendencies. Thus, it is of interest to note that the purposes of punishment have traditionally been threefold: (1) revenge by society; (2) protection of society by imprisonment of the offender; and (3) deterrence through punishment as well as through setting an example to would-be offenders.

1. *Revenge.* This approach is based on the premise—a highly defensible one in view of the distress that criminal acts often bring to others—that the guilty ought to suffer. As Henley (1971) has noted, "Many crime victims carry unseen and long-lasting psychological scars." (p. 39)

Another basis for this approach is the view that if society does not establish legal procedures for punishing criminal offenders, individuals or groups will take the law into their own hands. Even with established laws, the early history of our society reveals numerous incidents of lynchings and illegal hangings.

2. *Protection of society.* The protection of society by the imprisonment of the offender is assured while he is serving his term, but not thereafter. Without rehabilitation, imprisonment may simply serve to expose the offender to prison codes of behavior, to reinforce his criminal values, to permit his learning of new criminal skills or refining old ones, and to augment his degradation.

In extreme cases, for example, young offenders are subjected to sexual assault by tougher convicts and may be sent back to society filled with confusion, shame, and hatred (Davis, 1968; *Time*,

COMPLAINT OF A SAN QUENTIN CONVICT: A JOHNNY CASH INTERPRETATION

San Quentin you've been living hell to me,
You've blistered me since 1963.
I've seen men come and go and I've seen 'em die,
And long ago I stopped asking why.

San Quentin what good do you think you do?
Do you think that I'll be different when you're thru?
You bend my heart and mind and you warp my soul,
Your stone walls turn my blood a little cold.

(Cash, 1970)

1971). Too, racial conflicts among prison inmates may result in stabbings and other acts of violence. In San Quentin prison, 12 stabbings occurred in two weeks in a continuing racial conflict (Drummond, 1971). Thus the criminal offender himself does not appear to be well protected while serving his term, and from such an environment he may return to society more hardened and criminally inclined than before. The President of the United States has referred to our prisons as "universities of crime" which graduate more than 200,000 hardened criminals each year (Nixon, 1971).

3. *Deterrence.* Efforts at deterrence are based on the premise that punishment for criminal acts will both deter the individual offender in the future and keep others from committing similar acts. Several factors, however, limit the deterrent effect of punishment—among them being the lack of guilt feelings in those who are punished and the uncertainty and delay often surrounding the punishment.

Many young blacks in our prisons see themselves as victims of a "racist society" rather than as perpetrators of antisocial acts. Similarly, many imprisoned offenders see their problem as one of getting caught—as "bad luck" rather than "bad character." In addition, the long delay that commonly separates sentencing from the offense lessens the impact of punishment as a deterrent force. In many large cities the delay between arrest and trial averages well over a year; in Brooklyn, for example, the average delay is 16 months. And during the last decade the number of cases coming before the courts increased ten times faster than the number of judges.

Logically, it might seem that the more severe

Prison inmates march with drill-like precision. In the prison environment a convict loses his individuality and becomes a number. Subject to rigid regimentation, deprived of his civil rights, and exposed to highly undesirable models, it is not surprising when he returns to the community unrehabilitated—traumatized by prison experiences and bearing the additional burden of the label "ex-con." Because of the high rate of recidivism, many jails and prisons have been referred to by investigating committees as "crime hatcheries," or breeding grounds of bitter social outcasts.

the punishment, the greater its deterrent effect, but for certain crimes, at least, this has not proven out (Chiricos & Waldo, 1970). For example, homicide rates are as high in states that still maintain capital punishment as in those that have abolished it. And it was found that legislation providing more severe penalties for forcible rape had no discernible effect, either on its incidence or on injuries to victims (Schwartz, 1968). For other types of crimes the deterrent effect of increasingly severe punishment may be different, although the evidence is not all in. For example, severe penalties may lead to the take-over of given criminal activities—such as drug peddling —by organized crime if the profits are considered worth the risk.

In relation to the traditional reliance on punishment in dealing with criminal offenders, it may be noted that in 1970 we witnessed the passage of preventive detention and other drastic new anticrime measures, aimed both at the apprehension of criminals and the stiffening of legal penalties. And in 1971, we witnessed efforts to speed up "justice"—to shorten the time between the commission of an offense and the meting out of punishment. The effectiveness of these measures remains to be ascertained.

Rehabilitation. It has been pointed out that less than 4 percent of the persons working in penal institutions are treatment staff—the rest being guards, administrators, and related personnel. Less than 13 percent of state and local correctional personnel handle probations and parolees, although the latter constitute more than two thirds of the nation's criminal offender population. In view of these figures, both treatment facilities in penal institutions and the supervision of parolees appear to be sadly inadequate; thus, it is not surprising to note that the rate of recidivism is over 60 percent nationwide and as high as 90 percent in some areas, such as New York City (Murphy, 1970).

Aside from the dehumanizing treatment to which many delinquents and criminals are subjected, the labels themselves may be highly detrimental in their effects. To label a person as a delinquent or a criminal is likely to be highly devaluating; and the individual who is so labeled is not only likely to see himself differently but to be perceived differently by significant others. Simply to state that a person is a "juvenile delinquent" or an "ex-con" applies a social stigma with far-reaching implications—particularly in the latter instance. It also tends to become a "self-fulfilling prophecy" in terms of the individual's self-concept and social role, inasmuch as we tend to behave according to the way we view ourselves and the views and expectations that significant others have of us.

The imprisonment of criminals, as Glaus (1968) has pointed out, may have positive value, provided that it includes opportunities for rehabilitation—for atonement, reeducation, and resocialization, including the development of a sense of purpose and responsibility. Imprisonment without such redeeming characteristics is neither a major deterrent to criminal behavior nor a helpful form of treatment. In fact, Menninger (1968) has referred to imprisonment as "the crime of punishment" and has concluded that vengeful punishment only aggravates crime.

Inadequacies in the rehabilitation of criminal offenders are being recognized and attempts are being made to improve treatment facilities in penal institutions and to initiate more workable approaches to the entire problem of dealing with offenders.

1. *Indeterminate sentences and paroles.* In view of the deplorable conditions existing in penal institutions, the courts have become increasingly reluctant to send offenders to prison unless it is considered absolutely necessary, and the idea of the indeterminate sentence has come into wider use. The indeterminate sentence (a) enables qualified rehabilitation personnel—within broad limits—to determine when an offender should be released, and (b) introduces flexibility into the widely disparate ideas of judges about the appropriate lengths of sentences for convicted offenders. In general, the indeterminate sentence ensures the more rapid processing and earlier return to the community of prisoners who meet certain qualifications for probation.

It has been noted that on any given day only about a third of all offenders subject to correctional authorities are behind bars. And it has been ascertained that more than 70 percent of these incarcerated criminals could safely, and immediately, be placed in community-based correctional programs. Another 15 percent may need short-term, community-oriented confinement; while only 15 percent require long-term restraint. Even in the third case, however, the restraint should be accompanied wherever possible by programs directed at returning the offenders to normal community life (Burdman, 1969; Rawitch, 1971). Thus, it has been repeatedly emphasized that the conventional prison term should be abandoned for all offenders except the most dangerous and irredeemable.

In the meantime—as demands are being made for improvement of existing prison facilities and encouragement given to innovations in treatment—the indeterminate sentence is being increasingly used as a means of providing flexibility of sentencing, within statutory limits.

2. *Other innovative approaches to treatment.* A number of other innovative approaches to dealing with criminal offenders have also been suggested; and some have been tried out on a limited basis.

One approach has been directed toward the treatment of narcotic addicts, who account for such a high rate of stealing and petty theft in many of our larger cities, such as New York. A second and more comprehensive approach has been directed toward the systematic application of behavior-modification techniques to both juvenile delinquents and adult criminals (Bandura, 1969; Rachman and Teasdale, 1969). Still a third approach has been the use of electrical methods for controlling criminal tendencies.

A study by Hoagland at the Worcester Foundation for Experimental Biology dealt with a group of 200 violence-prone individuals—particularly persons who lost control of their behavior when angry. Sixty percent of the subjects had been arrested for violent crimes, including 8 who had been charged with murder. Hoagland found that shocks administered via electrodes carefully placed in selected areas of the brain controlled

---

INADEQUACIES IN OUR SYSTEM OF CRIMINAL JUSTICE

The Chief Justice of the United States has reported, "The American system of criminal justice in every phase . . . is suffering from a severe case of deferred maintenance . . . . The failure of our machinery is now a matter of common knowledge." (Burger, 1971, p. 37) Signs of this failure may be summarized as follows:

1. Minimal chances of punishment. Most criminal offenders are not detected, arrested, or punished. In fact, the chances of being punished for a serious crime are probably less than 1 in 20.

2. Delays in trial and sentencing. Those offenders who are arrested are not tried or punished promptly. Over half (70 percent in some cases) of the inmates in our jails are defendants who have not yet been convicted of any crime, yet they may be incarcerated in crowded cells for months or even years.

3. High rate of recidivism. The majority of those who are convicted and sent to prison commit new crimes when they return to society—indicating the general failure of our present punishment and rehabilitation measures.

Relevant to each of these three points is the fact that—as Menninger (1971) has pointed out—the present judicial system is weighted against the poor, the friendless, and the ignorant who cannot raise bail or do not have resources to obtain first-rate legal services. And the great majority of crimes are committed by individuals from this segment of the population.

Finally, attention might also be drawn to our lack of adequate controls concerning the use of firearms. We probably have more guns per capita than any other country in the world—an estimated 100 million guns are in the hands of private citizens in our society—and without adequate controls they inevitably contribute to crimes of violence.

aggressive behavior for as long as 20 hours; and electrodes had been permanently implanted in the brains of some violent psychotic patients. Presumably these patients could self-administer a shock when they felt intolerable hostility and violent behavior coming on. In his report of Hoagland's study, Abramson (1969) noted that an estimated half million people in the United States have brain abnormalities that may cause them to become violent when angry. And, of course, chemical agents are also under study in relation to the control of violent antisocial behavior. In fact, Bach-Y-Rita et al. (1971) have reported the treatment of 130 violence-prone patients in which favorable effects were achieved from the use of Dilantin for those showing abnormal EEG's. The phenothiazines were also found useful for all patients in reducing both chronic and acute episodes of anxiety and acting-out behavior.

Although imprisonment means different things to different people, it tends in general to be degrading, as well as to create serious sexual problems that may lead to homosexual behavior—particularly since about 50 percent of the prisoners are under 25 years of age. And where the prisoner is married and has a family, his imprisonment places a tremendous burden on his wife and children. To help counteract this problem, prisons in Mexico, Sweden, India, and a number of other countries allow conjugal visits. In the United States the first prison to pioneer conjugal visits was the Mississippi State Penitentiary; permitting overnight visits by girl friends of unmarried prisoners is a similar practice that is gaining support in this country (Karabian, 1971).

In general, U.S. penal administrators appear to oppose conjugal visits as being soft on criminal offenders (Balogh, 1965). The following quote is considered by Balogh to be typical:

"If we are going to place them in individual cells with clean sheets every night, feed them family style, work them short hours under ideal conditions, provide hours of recreation every day, and frequent conjugal visits with their respectful spouses, I can see no particular reason for confining them at all." (p. 41)

The same criticism has been leveled at "furloughs" where the prisoner may be allowed to go home for brief periods, such as the Christmas holidays, and be with his family.

In summarizing the available evidence concerning conjugal visits and furloughs, Chriss (1969) has pointed out that penal experts—as well as sociologists—disagree on the relative merits of these programs. However, as one authority expressed it, conjugal visits and furloughs make life worth living for the convict. "Otherwise the prisoner won't be worth a damn. We'll still be sending monsters out into the community." (Chriss, 1969, p. 23) In any event, other countries have reported favorably on such programs.

Some correctional trends and prospects. Systematic attempts are being made to improve our

THE ISSUE OF CRIMINAL RESPONSIBILITY

The Durham decision, rendered in the case of Durham vs. the United States (1956) by Judge Bazelon of the U.S. Court of Appeals for the District of Columbia, contains a now-famous passage to the effect that a defendant is not criminally responsible for his unlawful act if it was the product of mental disease or mental defect (e.g., mental disorder).

Defense attorneys in many criminal suits since the handing down of that landmark decision have pleaded their clients' cases on the basis of insanity; but interestingly enough, a number of psychologists and psychiatrists oppose the plea. Their suggestions that it be abolished as a defense in criminal cases are based on the following grounds: (1) the term *insanity* is too broad, imprecise, and inconsistently applied to justify its use in criminal proceedings; (2) the label *insane* provides the individual with a "sick role" which excuses him from responsibility for his behavior, and injects the medical model into the field of criminology, where it does not belong; and (3) in a democracy the individual is responsible for his actions and cannot justifiably claim a "sick role" or expect to be "treated" rather than "punished."

Probably the insanity plea has been abused in some instances, particularly in cases involving offenders with mild mental disturbances. Abolishing the plea, however, would subject offenders with extreme mental illness to severe punishment and deny them treatment—a seemingly inhumane and ineffective approach. Not only would little be accomplished by placing such individuals in prison as a form of punishment; it would also take us back to an era when mentally retarded, mentally ill, and criminal offenders were all placed indiscriminately in penal institutions.

The cause of modifying criminal behavior would seem to be better served if efforts of psychologists and psychiatrists were directed toward upgrading treatment programs for offenders who are not mentally ill rather than depriving the mentally ill of treatment. Such an approach is becoming increasingly justified as research in the fields of delinquency and crime helps us understand the causes of criminal behavior and the most effective methods of treatment and prevention.

For a concise discussion of criminal responsibility, including the problems of choice and responsibility and the role of the psychologist as an expert witness, the reader is referred to Silverman (1969).

law-enforcement and correctional procedures, and a beginning has been made in the application of scientific findings to the treatment and prevention of crime. A review of the findings of private foundations and the reports of governmental agencies has led to the identification of a number of encouraging prospects (McGee, 1969; Mitchell, 1971).

1. Fewer offenders will be confined in penal institutions—particularly younger offenders; and their confinement will be briefer as rehabilitative methods become more effective.

2. The dichotomy between imprisonment and parole will diminish; offenders will be subjected to varying degrees of restraint, as afforded by work and training furloughs, weekend sentences, halfway houses, and similar community-based programs.

3. Probation services and community-based facilities for rehabilitating young offenders will be expanded. Hostels and other facilities for group therapy will be provided, along with training programs, job placement, and special counseling.

4. We are witnessing the increasing use of probationary sentences and of "plea bargaining" —that is, pleading guilty to a lesser charge than the one the offender is accused of—in order to speed up the delay between arrest and trial. Such practices should be reflected in a saving of the taxpayers' money, since it costs more than $5000 a year to keep a person in jail. They are also intended to cut down on changes that occur during a delay—such as witnesses forgetting details of evidence or moving away—that make it difficult to prove the guilt or innocence of the accused.

5. The use of computer technology will be extended from crime detection to information processing, so that those responsible for decisions regarding the offenders will have more factual data at their disposal.

6. A "new careers" approach is being developed, in which certain offenders are chosen to participate in a special rehabilitation program and later assigned to action groups for the treatment and prevention of such problems in others. This is part of a growing trend toward involving persons who have experienced serious social adjustment difficulties in community efforts to help other persons deal with these problems.

7. Increasing use is being made of research methods in delineating and assessing problems of delinquency and crime, as well as the effectiveness of corrective and preventive measures.

In connection with correctional trends, it is also relevant to note that many states are following the lead of the federal government in making the use of marijuana a misdemeanor rather than a felony. This will help relieve the court congestion in our country as well as the tremendous burden placed on law-enforcement officers— since literally tens of thousands of persons are brought before our judicial system each year for alleged use of marijuana.

Interestingly enough, it would appear that these procedures will make it more difficult for the offender who tries to escape the consequences of his criminal acts, while providing more flexible and effective treatment for the one who needs and will accept help. And as a consequence, society will be better protected from crime, with its often tragic consequences for offenders and victims alike.

In this chapter we have dealt with sociopathic personality disorders and with juvenile delinquency and adult crime. We noted that personality (character) disorders are usually recognizable in childhood or adolescence and tend to continue into adult life, and that they stem primarily from faulty learning, rather than anxiety or other factors associated with excessive stress.

Initially focusing on the antisocial personality, we noted the various traits that tend to characterize this disorder, and the role of such traits in faulty interpersonal relationships and self-defeating behavior. Compulsive gambling, with which we then dealt, is a closely related pattern.

In the latter part of the chapter we dealt with delinquency and crime, noting the increasing incidence and social dangers of both, as well as the complex etiological patterns that may be involved. We have seen that although these patterns are considered separately, a certain amount of overlapping characterizes the range of offenses, motivations, etiological factors, and treatment procedures. Finally, we have seen the inadequacy of present methods of dealing with crime, and some of the innovative approaches that are being utilized in coping with this major social problem.

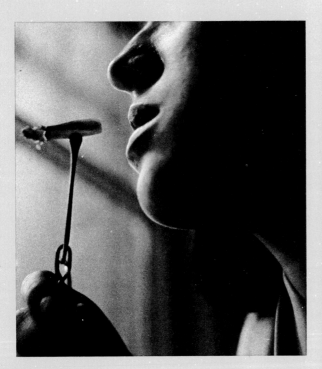

Alcoholism and Drug Dependence

12

ALCOHOLISM

DRUG DEPENDENCE

During the last decade we have seen a marked increase in the use of psychoactive, or mind-altering, drugs in our society. Concurrent with the widespread use of such drugs, however, has come their misuse—with which we are primarily concerned in the present chapter. This misuse may take the form of dependence or abuse.

In traditional usage, *dependence* signified psychological reliance on a particular drug, while *addiction* was reserved for physiological dependence, as indicated by withdrawal symptoms if the drug were to be discontinued. Recently, however, *drug dependence* has come to denote both psychological and physiological dependence. The term *drug abuse* is used to indicate the excessive consumption of a drug, regardless of whether an individual is truly dependent on it. For example, an individual may be hospitalized as a result of drug abuse, even though he has used a given drug, such as LSD, only once. Of course, drug abuse may lead to drug dependence.

The most commonly used problem drugs are alcohol, heroin, barbiturates, amphetamines, LSD, and marijuana (see classification, page 432). Some of these drugs, such as alcohol, can be purchased legally by adults; others, such as the barbiturates, can be legally used under medical supervision; while still others, such as heroin, are illegal. Currently, drug legislation—particularly in relation to marijuana—is a controversial matter.

The increasing magnitude of the drug problem in our society has caused both public and scientific attention to be focused on it. In the past, drug abuse and dependence—particularly in relation to alcohol and heroin—were considered to be manifestations of "moral weakness." But exhortation and other treatment approaches based on this concept—as well as incarceration and punitive measures—have proven singularly ineffective. Thus, until recently, little progress was made toward the identification of etiological factors or the development of effective methods of treatment. Although our present knowledge concerning alcoholism and drug dependence is far from complete, their acceptance and investigation as maladaptive patterns of adjustment to life's demands rather than moral deficiencies is leading to rapid progress in understanding and treatment.[1]

ALCOHOLISM

As we have noted previously (Chapter 1), Cambyses, King of Persia in the sixth century B.C., had the dubious distinction of being one of the first alcoholics on record. Many other early cultures, including the Egyptian, Greek, and Roman, made extensive and often excessive use of alcohol, principally wine. The oldest surviving winemaking formulas were recorded by Marcus Cato in Italy almost a century and a half before the birth of Christ. About A.D. 800 the process of distillation was developed by an Arabian alchemist, thus making possible an increase in both the range and potency of alcoholic beverages. However, both before and since that time, many notable historical figures have had their difficulties with alcohol.

INCIDENCE AND SOCIAL EFFECTS OF ALCOHOLISM

The potentially detrimental effects of alcoholism—for the individual, his loved ones, and society—are legion. In relation to alcohol, Bengelsdorf (1970a) has pointed out that:

"... its abuse has killed more people, sent more victims to hospitals, generated more police arrests, broken up more marriages and homes, and cost industry more money than has the abuse of heroin, amphetamines, barbiturates and marijuana combined." (p. 7)

The technical name of the drug in alcoholic beverages is *ethanol,* or *ethyl alcohol;* popularly, it is known simply as *alcohol.* It has been estimated that there are 70 million or more users of alcohol in the United States—the preponderance of their drinking being social and generally approved. Most users rarely, if ever, cause trouble to themselves or others. But some 9 million Americans may be labeled as *alcoholics:* individuals whose drinking seriously impairs their life adjustments. These excessive drinkers pose difficult problems for an estimated 36 million family members, about 1 out of every 6 persons in our land (Chafetz, 1971). Alcoholism appears to be on the rise, with some 200,000 or more new cases each year, and with alcoholics constituting some 15 to 20 percent of first admissions to mental hospitals, plus a substantial number of first admissions to general hospitals.

One out of every three arrests in the United States is for alcoholic intoxication. The financial drain imposed on the economy by alcoholism is about $15 billion a year, which comprises losses to industry from absenteeism, lowered work efficiency, and accidents, and to the alcoholic from reduced income and the cost of treatment (Department of Health, Education, and Welfare, 1970; NIMH, 1970). The life span of the average alcoholic is about 12 years shorter than that of the average nonalcoholic. In addition to contributing to a greater incidence of accidents in industry and in the home, alcohol has been implicated as a causal factor in at least half of all automobile fatalities and a total of some 800,000 or more automobile crashes in the United States each year. In 1970 an estimated 35,000 Americans were killed in automobile crashes in which alcohol was involved, averaging out to over 670 fatalities per week. Alcohol now ranks as the third major cause of death in the United States.

---

[1]Although alcoholism is associated with drug dependence, the organization of the present chapter is based on the APA classification, which makes a distinction between alcoholism and other forms of drug dependence.

Because alcoholism often progresses by subtle degrees in a potential victim, the line that separates the social drinker from the alcoholic is not always easy to delineate. In general, an individual is considered to be an alcoholic when his drinking seriously interferes with his physical and mental health, his marital or home situation, or his work. Alcoholism in America appears to occur more frequently among middle- and upper-class individuals than among the less affluent; some 60 percent, for example, come from moderate socioeconomic backgrounds. The older popular image of an alcoholic as an unkempt resident of "skid row" is therefore inaccurate. In fact, this latter group constitutes less than 5 percent of the alcoholic population. Alcoholism may develop during any life period from early childhood through old age, though it appears to occur most commonly during early and middle adulthood. And although alcoholism has traditionally been considered to be more prevalent among males than females, this distinction seems to be disappearing in our society. Since many women do not work outside the home, it is often easier for them to conceal their alcoholism—at least from nonfamily members.

Although our discussion will center on the problem of alcoholism in the United States, it should be noted that the incidence of this difficulty is by no means confined to any particular race or group of people, but is found all over the world.

CLINICAL PICTURE

The Roman poet Horace, in the first century B.C., wrote lyrically about the psychological effects of wine:

"It discloses secrets; ratifies and confirms our hopes; thrusts the coward forth to battle; eases the anxious mind of its burthen; instructs in arts. Whom has not a cheerful glass made eloquent! Whom not quite free and easy from pinching poverty!"

Unfortunately the effects of alcohol are not always so benign or beneficial. According to the Japanese proverb, "First the man takes a drink, then the drink takes a drink, and then the drink takes the man."

General effects of alcoholic intoxication. Contrary to popular belief, alcohol is not a stimulant but a depressant which attacks and numbs the higher brain centers, thus lessening their inhibiting control. As behavioral restraints decline, more primitive emotional responses appear; the drinker may indulge in the satisfaction of impulses he ordinarily holds in check. Some degree of motor incoordination soon becomes apparent, and the drinker's sense of discrimination and perception of cold, pain, and other discomforts are dulled. Typically he experiences a sense of warmth, expansiveness, and well-being. In such a mood, unpleasant realities are screened out and the drinker's feelings of self-esteem and adequacy rise. Casual acquaintances become the best and most understanding of friends, and the drinker enters a generally pleasant world of unreality in which worries are temporarily left behind. He may also experience increased feelings of power (McClelland, 1971). Thus he is stimulated emotionally while his intellectual and motor functions are impaired.

When the alcohol content of the bloodstream reaches 0.1 percent, the individual is considered to be intoxicated. Muscular coordination, speech, and vision are impaired, and thought processes are confused. When the blood alcohol reaches approximately 0.5 percent, the entire neural balance is upset and the individual "passes out."

An increasing number of women are reacting to the stresses of marriage and other life problems by turning to the self-defeating means of excessive drinking.

Here unconsciousness apparently acts as a safety device, since concentrations above 0.55 percent are usually lethal.

In general, it is the amount of alcohol actually concentrated in the bodily fluids, not the amount consumed, which determines intoxication. However, the effects of alcohol vary with the individual—his personality, his physical condition, the amount of food in his stomach, and the duration of his drinking. In addition, the user of alcohol gradually may build up a tolerance for the drug so that ever increasing amounts may be needed to produce the desired effects. The attitude of the drinker is important, too: although actual motor and intellectual abilities decline in direct ratio to the blood concentration of alcohol, many persons who consciously try to do so can maintain adequate control over their behavior and can evidence few outward signs of being intoxicated, even after drinking relatively large amounts of alcohol.

The actual physiological effects of alcohol on the human brain are not fully understood but are known to be powerful. A phenomenon occurring in an appreciable number of cases is the "blackout"—a lapse of memory after moderate drinking which typically is unaccompanied by signs of obvious intoxication. Here the drinker may carry on a rational conversation and engage in other relatively complex activities but have not a trace of recall the next day. Blackouts may also occur in association with heavy drinking, but in such instances the individual usually acts as if he is intoxicated.

Alcohol addiction and deterioration. Although many investigators have maintained that alcohol is a systemic poison, even in very small amounts, alcohol actually is a high-calorie drug which can be assimilated by the body at the rate of about one ounce per hour. Quantities in excess of this amount remain in the bloodstream until they can be oxidized. Some 5 to 10 percent of the alcohol ingested is eliminated through breath, urine, and perspiration; the rest is assimilated.

Alcohol in moderate amounts is no longer thought to have the detrimental effects on various bodily organs formerly ascribed to it. For individuals who drink immoderately, however, the picture is less favorable. For one thing, most alcoholic beverages contain a large number of congeners—components other than ethyl alcohol and water —that may have a toxic effect on certain bodily organs. Prolonged immoderate drinking can result in ulceration of the stomach, internal bleeding, and heart and liver damage. About 1 alcoholic in 10 develops cirrhosis of the liver. The continued excessive use of alcohol can also result in the destruction of brain cells and in cerebral dysfunction (Claeson & Carlsson, 1971). Then too, the heavy drinker typically neglects his diet and is likely to suffer from vitamin and other nutritional deficiencies; for although alcohol does contain calories, it has no known nutritional value.

The habitual use of excessive amounts of alcohol as a means of adjusting to life's problems commonly results in personality deterioration, as evidenced by a gradual intellectual and moral decline. Often there are disturbances of concentration, memory, abstracting ability, and judgment (Jones & Parsons, 1971; Tarter & Parsons, 1971). The individual's behavior typically becomes coarse and inappropriate, he assumes increasingly less responsibility, loses pride in his personal appearance, neglects his family, and becomes generally touchy and irritable about his drinking. As his judgment becomes impaired, the excessive drinker may find himself unable to maintain employment and generally unqualified to cope with any new demands that are made of him. In addition, gross physical symptoms— such as tremors, sluggish pupillary action, extreme nausea, and functional retardation produced by brain damage—may overtake the victim, the incidence of such reactions being reported as 25 percent in one study of a thousand alcoholics (Irwin, 1968).

Psychoses associated with alcoholism. As we have noted, one out of every three arrests in the United States is for drunkenness; and many criminal acts are committed under the influence of alcohol. For example, Moore (1966) reported that of 508 homicides that he studied, one or both parties had been drinking in 64 percent of the cases. Alcohol is also commonly associated with suicide. In addition, certain psychotic reactions commonly develop in individuals who have been drinking excessively over long periods of time, or who—for various reasons, such as brain lesions—have a reduced tolerance to alcohol. Such acute reactions usually last only a short time and consist generally of confusion, excitement, and delirium. There are four commonly recognized subtypes, a description of which follows.

1. *Pathological intoxication* is an acute reaction that occurs in persons whose tolerance to alcohol is chronically very low (such as epileptics or those of an unstable personality makeup) or in normal persons whose tolerance to alcohol is temporarily lessened by exhaustion, emotional stress, or other conditions. Following the consumption of even moderate amounts of alcohol, these individuals may suddenly become hallucinated and disoriented, and may evidence a homicidal rage—sometimes committing violent crimes. This confused, disoriented state is usually followed by a period of deep sleep, with complete amnesia occurring afterward. The following case history illustrates the pattern.

The patient was hospitalized following an altercation in a bar in which he attacked and injured a woman and her escort. On admission to the hospital he seemed very friendly and cooperative—in fact, almost servile in his desire to please those in authority. His personal history revealed that he had been involved in five such incidents during the previous two years. His family background was torn with bickering and dissension. Both parents were stern disciplinarians and severely punished him for the most minor disapproved behavior. He was taught to feel that sex was very evil.

In his previous altercations he had been arrested twice for disturbing the peace. In each case these incidents took place in bars where, after a few drinks, he would become aggressive, loud, and abusive, daring any and all to do anything about it. His last escapade and arrest involved an attack on a woman; this had apparently been provoked by her kissing her escort and making what the patient interpreted as sexual overtures in public. He approached the woman in a threatening manner, slapped her, knocked her escort out when he attempted to intervene, and then hit her several times with his fists before he was forcibly restrained by other customers. He was amnesic for the entire episode, apparently "coming to" on his way to the hospital.

It was felt in this case that the woman's behavior aroused unacceptable and therefore threatening sexual desires in the patient, against which he defended himself by becoming hostile and attacking her. The alcohol apparently served to lower his normal behavioral restraints, permitting his hostility to be expressed in overt antisocial behavior.

2. *Delirium tremens* is probably the best known of the various alcoholic psychotic reactions. A fairly common occurrence among those who drink excessively for a long time, this reaction may follow a prolonged alcoholic debauch, appear during a period of abstinence in connection with a head injury or infection, or occur upon the withdrawal of alcohol after prolonged drinking (Alpert & Silvers, 1970; Block, 1962; Weeks & Lawrence, 1961).

In 1881, Lasegue wrote a paper entitled "Alcoholic Delirium is not a Delirium, it is a Dream." Following this early lead, Greenberg and Pearlman (1967) performed a study utilizing two experimental groups—persons withdrawn from alcohol, and individuals placed on increasing levels of the substance—and found that the latter group exhibited a marked reduction in dreaming or REM (rapid eye movement) sleep; conversely, withdrawal from alcohol led to increased dreaming, with 100-percent REM sleep being found just before the development of delirium tremens. These investigators suggested the need for continued study of the possible long-range effects of alcohol on sleep patterns.

The delirium usually is preceded by a period of restlessness and insomnia during which the person may feel generally uneasy and apprehensive. Slight noises or sudden moving objects may cause considerable excitement and agitation. The full-blown symptoms include (a) disorientation for time and place in which, for example, a person may mistake the hospital for a church or jail, friends are no longer recognized, and hospital attendants may be identified as old acquaintances; (b) vivid hallucinations, particularly of small, fast-moving animals like snakes, rats, and roaches which are clearly localized in space; (c) acute fear, in which these hallucinated animals may change in form, size, or color and terrify the person; (d) extreme suggestibility, in which a person can be made to see almost any form of animal if its presence is merely suggested to him or if he is asked what he sees on the wall; (e) marked coarse tremors of the hands, tongue, and lips (as indicated by the name of this disorder); and (f) other symptoms, including perspiration, fever, a rapid and weak heartbeat, a coated tongue, and a foul breath.

The hallucinatory animals the person sees may cause him to cower, terrified, in a corner, or to stand up in his bed and desperately fight them off. This acute fear may be combined with a generalized state of terror in which he feels that something horrible is going to happen to him. As a result, he may even attempt suicide.

The delirium typically lasts from three to six days and is generally followed by a deep sleep. When the person awakens, he has few symptoms —aside from possible slight remorse—but frequently he will have been rather badly scared, and may not resume drinking for several weeks or months. Usually, however, there is eventual resumption, followed by a return to the hospital with a new attack. The death rate from delirium tremens as a result of convulsions, liver disease, heart failure, and other complications has approximated 10 percent (Tavel, 1962). With such newer drugs as chlordiazepoxide, however, the current death rate during delirium tremens and acute alcoholic withdrawal has been markedly reduced (Klett et al., 1971).

The following is a brief description of a 43-year-old male delirium tremens patient.

The subject was brought forcibly to the psychiatric ward of a general hospital when he fired his shotgun at 3:30 A.M. while "trying to repel an invasion of cockroaches." On admission he was confused and disoriented and had terrifying hallucinations involving "millions and millions" of invading cockroaches. He leaped from his bed and cowered in terror against the wall, screaming for help and kicking and hitting frantically at his imaginary assailants. When an attendant came to his aid, he screamed for him to get back out of danger or he would be killed too. Before the attendant could reach him he dived headlong on his head, apparently trying to kill himself.

The subject's delirium lasted for a period of 3½ days, after which he returned to a state of apparent normality, apologized profusely for the trouble he had caused everyone, stated he would never touch another drop, and was discharged. However, on his way home he stopped at a bar, had too much to drink, and on emerging from the bar collapsed on the street. This time he sobered up in jail, again apologized for the trouble he had caused, was extremely remorseful, and was released with a small fine. His subsequent career is unknown.

3. In *acute alcoholic hallucinosis,* the main symptoms are auditory hallucinations. At first the individual typically hears a voice coming from some one person and making certain simple statements. With time, however, the hallucinations usually extend to the voices of several people, all of them critical and reproachful. The individual's innermost private weaknesses, particularly those of a sexual nature, are itemized and discussed, and various horrible punishments are then proposed for him. He may hear the clanking of chains, the sharpening of knives, the sound of pistol shots, or footsteps approaching in a threatening manner. Terror-stricken, he may scream for help or attempt suicide.

This condition may continue for several days or even weeks, during which time the person is depressed but fairly well oriented and coherent, apart from his hallucinations. After recovery, he usually shows considerable remorse as well as some insight into his previous behavior.

Investigators are less inclined than formerly to attribute this psychotic reaction solely to the effects of alcohol. Generally, it seems to be related to a broad pattern of maladaptive behavior, as in the following case.

The subject was hospitalized after a suicide attempt in which he slashed his wrists. He had been hospitalized once before after a similar incident in which he tried to hang himself with a bath towel. He was unmarried and lived alone.

The patient had been drinking excessively for a three-year period. He was not in the least particular about what he drank as long as it contained alcohol. For several days prior to his last suicide attempt he had heard voices which accused him of all manner of "filthy sex acts." He was particularly outraged when they accused him of having committed homosexual acts with his mouth and of having had relations with animals. He complained of a terrible taste in his mouth and imagined that his food had been poisoned as a means of punishing him for his sins. He was generally fearful and apprehensive and slept poorly.

After a stay of two weeks in the hospital, the patient made a good recovery and was discharged. At this time he seemed to have some insight into his difficulties, stating that he felt that his sexual problems had something to do with his suicide attempt.

The psychotic symptoms of the individual were apparently triggered by alcohol, but it seems probable that they could have been similarly brought on by drugs, illness, exhaustion, or other types of stress.

4. *Korsakoff's psychosis* was first described by the Russian psychiatrist Korsakoff in 1887.

The outstanding symptom is a memory defect (particularly with regard to recent events) which is concealed by falsification. An individual may be unable to recognize pictures, faces, rooms, and other objects as identical with those just seen, although they may appear to him as similar. Such persons increasingly tend to fill in gaps with reminiscences and fanciful tales that lead to unconnected and distorted associations. These individuals may appear to be delirious, hallucinated, and disoriented for time and place, but ordinarily their confusion and disordered conduct are closely related to their attempts to fill in memory gaps. The memory disturbance itself seems related to an inability to form new associations. Such a reaction usually occurs in older alcoholics, after many years of excessive drinking.

The symptoms of this psychosis are now considered to be due to vitamin B deficiency and other dietary inadequacies. A diet rich in vitamins and minerals generally restores the patient to more normal physical and mental health. However, some personality deterioration usually remains in the form of memory impairment, blunting of intellectual capacity, and lowering of moral and ethical standards (Meissner, 1967).

PHASES IN ALCOHOL ADDICTION

In a pioneering study of some 2000 alcoholics, Jellinek (1952; 1971) outlined the following series of stages commonly found in the development of addiction to alcohol.

1. *The prealcoholic symptomatic phase.* The candidate for alcoholism starts out drinking in conventional social situations but soon experiences a rewarding relief from tension—a feeling that is strongly marked in his case, either because his tensions are greater than others' or because he has not learned to handle them effectively. Initially, he may seek this relief of tension only occasionally. Gradually, however, his tolerance for tension decreases to such an extent that he resorts to alcohol almost daily. This transition from occasional to constant drinking may take several months or as long as two years.

2. *The prodromal phase.* This phase is marked by the sudden onset of blackouts during which the drinker may show few, if any, signs of intoxication and can carry on a reasonable conversation or go through quite elaborate activities—but will have no memory of these events the next day. Such amnesic episodes may happen to average drinkers when they drink excessively during a state of emotional or physical exhaustion, but their occurrence is very rare. Consequently, Jellinek considered this amnesia without loss of consciousness and sometimes even without intake of extremely large amounts of alcohol to be an indication of a heightened susceptibility to alcohol.

Certain correlated behaviors now make their appearance, among which are (a) surreptitious drinking, in which the drinker seeks occasions for having a few drinks, unknown to others, for fear that they will misjudge him; (b) preoccupation with alcohol, which often takes the form of worrying about whether there will be sufficient drinks at a social gathering to which he is going—and perhaps having several drinks ahead of time in anticipation of a possible shortage; (c) avid drinking, in which the drinker gulps the first one or two drinks; (d) guilt feelings about drinking behavior, which he begins to realize is out of the ordinary; and (e) avoidance of references to alcohol in his conversation.

SOME COMMON MISCONCEPTIONS ABOUT ALCOHOL AND ALCOHOLISM

1. Alcohol is a stimulant.

2. Alcohol is essential to the treatment of certain diseases.

3. You can always detect alcohol on the breath of a person who has been drinking.

4. Impaired judgment does not occur before there are obvious signs of intoxication.

5. The individual will get more intoxicated by "mixing" liquors than by taking comparable amounts of one kind—e.g., bourbon, Scotch, or vodka.

6. An exceptional person can have 0.1 percent or more of alcohol in his bloodstream and still be in control of his faculties.

7. Men can handle their drinking better than women.

8. People with "strong wills" need not be concerned about becoming alcoholics.

9. Alcohol is a far less dangerous drug than marijuana.

10. Most alcoholics who have successfully completed treatment can safely resume social drinking.

Based on American Medical Association (1965), and Calahan (1970).

3. *The crucial phase*. This stage is characterized by the loss of control over drinking, which means that any consumption of alcohol seems to trigger a chain reaction that continues until the individual is either too intoxicated or too sick to ingest any more. But although he has lost the ability to regulate his drinking once he has begun, he still can control whether he will drink on any given occasion. This is evidenced by periods of abstinence or "going on the wagon" following recovery from severe intoxication.

Almost simultaneously with this loss of control, the alcoholic begins to rationalize his drinking behavior and produces the familiar alcoholic alibis. He devises explanations to convince himself that he did not lose control—that he had good reason for getting intoxicated; and these justifications also serve to counter the social pressures that arise as the drinker's behavior becomes more conspicuous.

In spite of his rationalizations, there is a marked lowering of the drinker's self-esteem, and he may now attempt to compensate for this trend with

---

EARLY WARNING SIGNS OF APPROACHING ALCOHOLISM

1. **Increased consumption.** One of the first signs that a drinker may be becoming an alcoholic is increased consumption of alcohol. This increase may seem gradual, but a marked change will take place from month to month. Often the individual will begin to worry about his drinking at this point.

2. **Extreme behavior.** When the individual, under the influence of alcohol, commits various acts which leave him feeling guilty and embarrassed the next day, his alcoholic indulgence is getting out of hand.

3. **"Pulling blanks."** When the individual cannot remember what happened during an alcoholic bout, his alcoholic indulgence is becoming excessive.

4. **Morning drinking.** An important sign that a frequent drinker may be becoming an alcoholic appears when he begins to drink in the morning—either as a means of reducing a hangover or as a "bracer" to help him start the day.

A person who exhibits the preceding pattern of behavior is well on the road to becoming an alcoholic. The progression is likely to be facilitated if he receives environmental support for heavy or excessive drinking—for example, if his spouse provides such support, or if an occupational pattern or sociocultural environment tolerates or even approves of the excessive use of alcohol.

---

extravagant expenditures and other grandiose behaviors and by projecting the blame for his difficulties onto others. But these defenses do not work well and he remains remorseful, which further increases his tension and provides added reason for drinking. This remorse, however, together with social pressures, may also lead to periods of total abstinence. As tensions persist, it may even occur to the drinker that his troubles arise not from the drinking *per se*, but rather from the type of beverage he drinks. So now he may attempt to control his problem by changing his pattern—consuming different beverages, setting up rules about drinking only after a certain hour of the day, and so on.

During this phase the alcoholic usually begins drinking in the afternoon and is intoxicated during the evening. The aftereffects of the evening's drunkenness may cause some loss of time from his job, but he still struggles to maintain his employment and social standing, even though he has now begun a pattern of progressive withdrawal from his environment.

The entire struggle puts the drinker under heavy strain. He begins to drop friends and quit jobs. In some cases, of course, he is abandoned by associates and dismissed by employers; however, he usually takes the initiative as an anticipatory defense. This process leads to increased isolation and to further centering of his behavior around alcohol. He now becomes concerned primarily with how his activities may interfere with his drinking rather than with how his drinking may affect his activities.

About this time, too, the alcoholic takes steps to protect his supply by laying in a large stock of alcoholic beverages which he hides in the most unlikely places. Similarly, his neglect of proper nutrition begins to aggravate the effects of heavy drinking, and the first hospitalization for some alcoholic complaint may occur. Improper nutrition and other complications also induce a marked decrease in sexual drive, a factor which increases the hostility of the alcoholic toward his wife and gives rise to the well-known "alcoholic jealousy syndrome," in which the drinker blames his loss of sexual drive on his wife's alleged extramarital affairs.

By now, the alcoholic has begun to feel that he cannot start the day without a drink to steady himself. This is the beginning of "regular matutinal drinking" and foreshadows the start of the chronic phase.

4. *The chronic phase.* As alcohol becomes increasingly dominant in the drinker's life, he may find himself intoxicated during the daytime on a weekday and may continue in this state for several days until he is entirely incapacitated.

These drawn-out drinking bouts are usually associated with a marked impairment of thinking and with ethical deterioration—processes which, however, are reversible. The alcoholic no longer is selective about the persons he drinks with, and if his normal sources of liquor are not available he will drink almost anything, even hair tonic or rubbing alcohol. At this time, true alcoholic psychoses, such as delirium tremens, may occur.

Commonly noted at this time is a loss of tolerance for alcohol: half of the amount previously required may be sufficient to produce an alcoholic stupor in the individual. Indefinable fears and tremors become persistent, and are especially pronounced as soon as the alcohol disappears from his system. Consequently the alcoholic "controls" the symptoms by continuous drinking.

In this chronic phase the alcoholic's rationalizations begin to fail as they are mercilessly tested against reality. And in many alcoholics—approximately 60 percent—vague religious desires begin to develop. As the rationalization system finally gives way, the alcoholic may admit defeat and become amenable to treatment. However, unless he seeks and receives outside help, his obsessive drinking continues. He is unable to help himself.

Here it should be emphasized that although the stages outlined by Jellinek appear to characterize the course followed by many alcoholics, others do not fit this typical pattern. For example, there are so-called "spree" drinkers who remain sober and handle responsible positions for long periods of time, but then in the face of some stressful situation will lose control completely—usually winding up in a hospital or jail. It has also been shown that not all alcohol addicts have blackouts, and that often such experiences occur in later, rather than earlier, stages of alcoholism (Goodwin, Crane & Guze, 1969). Finally, a new trend has become apparent in our society involving "multiple addictions," in which a "pure" alcohol problem is complicated by the concurrent use of barbiturates, amphetamines, and other

TOLERANCE IN DRUG USAGE

Tolerance to a drug develops in an individual when the same dosage produces decreased effects after repeated use. The degree of tolerance and the rate at which it is acquired depend on the specific drug, the person using it, and the frequency and magnitude of its use. Dosages of drugs that produce tolerance—e.g., alcohol, barbiturates, and heroin—tend to be increased by persons using them as their tolerance to a particular drug increases.

The mechanisms by which physiological tolerance is acquired are not fully understood. There is some evidence that the central nervous system develops some degree of tolerance for various drugs; but, in addition, learning may play an important role in changing an individual's attitude toward a drug and his response to it after repeated use. Thus with some drugs, such as marijuana, the individual may learn to control some effects and maintain relatively normal functioning.

Two aspects of drug tolerance that merit brief mention are "cross-tolerance" and "reverse tolerance." "Cross-tolerance" may occur when the individual who develops tolerance to one drug also shows tolerance to drugs whose effects are similar. A heavy drinker, for example, may not only show tolerance to alcohol but also to barbiturates, tranquilizers, and anesthetics. "Reverse tolerance" may occur in the use of some drugs, such as the psychedelics; here, with experience, the desired effects may be achieved through the use of smaller doses. Both physiological and psychological (learning) factors appear to play a significant part in this process.

Based on Commission of Inquiry into the Non-Medical Use of Drugs (1970).

drugs. This is apparently particularly common among young alcoholics and, of course, may markedly change the nature and course of the clinical picture.

DYNAMICS OF ALCOHOLISM

As noted above, the problem of alcoholism has recently come to be viewed as a maladaptive pattern of adjustment to life's demands—and as such, may be conveniently broken down into its biological, psychological and interpersonal, and sociocultural aspects.

Biological factors. After an inordinate intake of alcohol, an individual who is not an alcoholic may develop a severe "hangover"; however, the nonalcoholic can usually control this toxic reaction merely by abstaining from subsequent overindulgence in the drug. The alcoholic, on the other hand, seeks relief through more alcohol, which merely perpetuates the condition. His attempts to stop drinking result in withdrawal symptoms, which indicate that cell metabolism has adapted itself to alcohol in the bloodstream. These symptoms may be relatively mild, involving a craving for alcohol, tremors, perspiration, and weakness, or more severe, as evidenced by nausea, vomiting, fever, tachycardia, convulsions, and hallucinations.

In terms of learning principles, each drink serves to reinforce alcohol-seeking behavior because it reduces drive. As Bandura has expressed it, "After the person thus becomes physically dependent on alcohol, he is compelled to consume large quantities of liquor both to alleviate distressing physical reactions and to avoid their recurrence." (1969, p. 533) In essence, a recurrent cycle of alcohol-induced need-arousal and need-reduction is established.

A question that has been raised is whether certain individuals have a physiological predisposition to alcoholism—perhaps an unusual craving for alcohol once it has been experienced, and hence a greater than average tendency toward loss of control. Presumably such a craving could result from some genetic vulnerability, such as a lack of one or more of the enzymes needed for the breakdown of alcohol in bodily metabolism.

It has been shown that alcoholism does tend to run in families. In a study of 259 hospitalized alcoholics, Winokur et al. (1970) found that slightly over 40 percent had parents—usually the father—who were alcoholics. From a review of earlier studies, Irwin (1968) reported a higher incidence—finding that more than half the individuals who become alcoholics have an alcoholic parent. Whether this familial incidence results from shared genes or a shared alcoholic environment is not entirely clear. In an early study, Roe, Burks, and Mittelmann (1945) followed the case histories of 36 children who had been taken from severely alcoholic parents and placed in foster homes. The likelihood of their becoming alcoholics was no greater than that of a control group of 25 children of nonalcoholic parents. Similarly, more recent studies have reported comparable results, thus casting doubt on the genetic hypothesis (Rose & Burks, 1968).

Of course, a possible physiological predisposition to alcoholism could be acquired rather than inherited. Whether there are acquired constitutional factors (such as endocrine or enzyme imbalances) that increase vulnerability to physiological dependence on alcohol is not known.

Psychological and interpersonal factors. Not only does the alcoholic become physiologically dependent on alcohol; he develops a powerful psychological dependency as well. Since excessive drinking impairs the total life adjustment of an individual, the question arises as to what needs the alcohol fulfills that would cause him to become psychologically reliant upon it. A number of psychological and interpersonal factors have been advanced as possible answers.

1. *Psychological vulnerability.* The query as to why some individuals lose control over their drinking is often posed in terms of psychological vulnerability; in other words, is there an "alcoholic personality"—a type of character organization that predisposes a given individual to the use of alcohol rather than to some other defensive pattern of coping with stress? Alcoholics do have many behavior traits in common, and their excessive drinking raises such similar problems for them that they may often seem superficially alike.

From the limited research data that are available, it has been indicated that male youths who later become problem drinkers often tend to overplay their masculine roles; in addition they are undercontrolled, impulsive, and rebellious, and rely on denial as a defense mechanism (Gomberg, 1968; Jones, 1968; McCord & McCord, 1962; Winokur et al., 1970). Conversely, in a study of the backgrounds of a sample of female alcoholics, Wood and Duffy (1966) found them to be submissive, passively resentful, and lacking in self-confidence. The female alcoholics studied by Jones (1971) exhibited inadequate coping patterns as well as a high degree of socially manipulative behavior prior to their drinking problem. Winokur et al. (1970) have also pointed to a high incidence of depression in the personal and family background of female alcoholics. In addition, it would appear that both males and females—in terms of prealcoholic as well as alcoholic personality—require a good deal of praise and appreciation from others, are oversensitive to criticism, tend to expect a good deal of the world, and react to failure with marked feelings of hurt and inferiority.

Such findings provide promising leads but

it is difficult to assess their specific function in the etiology of alcoholism. Certainly there are many persons with similar characteristics who do not become alcoholics, and others with dissimilar personality characteristics who do. The only characteristic that appears common to the backgrounds of most problem drinkers is personal maladjustment—yet most maladjusted people do not become alcoholics. Since the personality of alcoholics may be a result rather than a cause of their addiction, it is apparent that longitudinal studies are needed to delineate those characteristics that may predispose an individual to lose control over his drinking.

Although the concept of a prealcoholic personality remains indefinite, alcoholics do tend to show a distinct cluster of personality traits once their drinking patterns have been established. Included here are low stress tolerance, a negative self-image, and feelings of isolation, insecurity, and depression (Irwin, 1968; Weingold et al., 1968; Wood & Duffy, 1966). By the time the alcoholic comes to the attention of a clinic or hospital, he may manifest a number of antisocial tendencies, including a lack of responsibility, a decided tendency toward deceitfulness, and an inability to control his aggressive impulses (Goldstein & Linden, 1969; Winokur

COMING TO GRIPS WITH THE PROBLEM OF ALCOHOLISM: TWO CASE STUDIES

An Actor's Challenging Off-Screen Role

The veteran actor has had an outstanding record of success in motion pictures, and his credits include starring roles in two top-rated television series; yet the most challenging role of his life has been as protagonist in an intensely personal drama. This story pits him—in a battle waged over many years—against feelings of inferiority and fear. When an increasing reliance on alcohol threatened to prove his undoing, a showdown inevitably occurred.

As he looks back on the unfolding of this drama, the actor reports that during most of his 40-year career he was apprehensive and fearful of failing (Haber, 1971, p. 13). No matter how well he was doing, he felt unworthy of the success he achieved, and worried time after time that his contract would be canceled and that he was "washed up."

Fear and apprehension had their physical symptoms—tension and painful headaches. Turning to alcohol to ease his difficulties, the actor found that drinking itself became a major problem. He now feels that if he had not mastered it, alcoholism would have ruined his career and his health. A warning of this came in 1966 when, touring the country in a play, he suffered a physical collapse (Haber, 1971, p. 13).

The actor spent some 4 years fighting—and finally winning—the battle against alcoholism. He attributes his victory largely to the understanding and emotional support of his wife and to Alcoholics Anonymous (Ellison, 1971, p. 27). However, it is the individual's motivation to change his behavior which is crucially important.

"'If you suffer enough, you will either jump out the window or do something about it,'" the actor said. "'In principle, it's the same as a toothache. You can either sit there and suffer or you can go to a dentist.'" (Haber, 1971, p. 13)

Although the actor would probably be the last person to claim that he has completely conquered his feelings of fear and tension, he is no longer so troubled by personal problems or the demands of his profession as to rely on the self-defeating crutch of alcohol.

A Young Teacher's Continuing Battle

Mary —— is an intelligent, attractive, elementary-school teacher who is married to a writer some 10 years her senior. At age 29 she had been teaching for 7 years, and as a result of her high degree of competence had been given increasingly difficult classes. Mary stated that after a difficult day at school she had many unresolved problems that she needed to discuss with someone but seldom could do so with her husband, who was under sustained pressure himself and away on assignments a good deal of the time.

Thus, with her husband either away or too busy to talk, Mary turned to alcohol:

"I started having two or three cocktails every evening to 'settle my nerves.' And as the pressure seemed to build up about 3 years ago, I found myself drinking heavily every night to 'blot out the events of the day.' I seemed to have this insatiable craving for alcohol, and I could hardly wait to get home after school to get a drink. And on weekends, I was drunk from Friday evening through Sunday. On Monday mornings, my hangovers were something awful, and I started calling in sick. I knew my drinking was interfering with my work, but I couldn't seem to cope with either. Frankly, I became just plain desperate."

The principal of Mary's school became aware of the problem and suggested that she take a sick leave and obtain medical assistance. Examination revealed serious liver damage, and the physician informed Mary that if she continued to drink she would kill herself. He prescribed Antabuse to help her stop drinking. Although she had the prescription filled, Mary did not take the drug right away: "I was so terrified by what the doctor told me that I just had to have a drink to calm me down. Then I was going to try the Antabuse, I really was." That drink led to 3 days of intoxication; finally, going into convulsions, Mary was hospitalized.

When she improved sufficiently to leave the hospital, Mary volunteered to join a local chapter of Alcoholics Anonymous and to continue seeing a doctor. Her crucial battle with alcoholism was just beginning.

et al., 1970). Often there is a tendency to rebel against conventional authority. Goss and Morosko (1969) have also reported a high incidence of depression and other psychopathology in 200 consecutive male admissions to an alcoholic treatment unit. In general, it appears that depression and antisocial personality are the two clinical syndromes most commonly associated with alcoholism.

2. *Stress, tension reduction, and reinforcement.* A number of investigators have pointed out that the typical alcoholic is discontented with his life situation and is unable or unwilling to tolerate tension and stress (AMA Committee on Alcoholism and Drug Dependency, 1969). In fact, Schaefer (1971) has concluded that alcoholism is a conditioned response to anxiety. The individual presumably finds in alcohol a means of relieving anxiety, resentment, depression, or other unpleasant feelings resulting from stressful aspects of his life situation. Each time he drinks and experiences relief of tension, his drinking pattern is reinforced; eventually it becomes his habitual way of coping with stress.

Some investigators hold that anyone—regardless of his life situation—who finds alcohol to be tension-reducing is in danger of becoming an alcoholic. However, if such a model were accurate, we would expect alcoholism to be far more common than it is, since alcohol tends to reduce tensions for most persons who use it. In addition, this model does not explain why some excessive drinkers are able to maintain control over their drinking and to function in society, while others are not.

At the opposite end of the spectrum are investigators who hold that any model that views alcoholism as simply a learned maladaptive response pattern—for example, involving tension reduction and reinforcement—is incorrect, since the devastating long-range consequences of excessive drinking far outweigh its temporary relief value. However, as Bandura (1969) has pointed out,

"This argument overlooks the fact that behavior is more powerfully controlled by its immediate, rather than delayed, consequences, and it is precisely for this reason that persons may persistently engage in immediately reinforcing, but potentially self-destructive behavior. . . ." (p. 530)

It seems "the alcoholic drinks not to feel bad," even though he knows he will feel worse later.

Here it is relevant to note that physiological dependence may tend to reinforce psychological dependence; and conversely, psychological dependence may tend to maintain physiological dependence. Thus we see a vicious circle of interactional factors in alcoholism, leading to self-defeating and highly aversive long-range results.

3. *Family patterns in alcoholism.* A number of researchers have pointed to various family patterns that appear related to alcoholism. For example, in their study of 69 female alcoholics —all of whom were high-school graduates, 67 percent of whom had attended and/or graduated from college, and almost all of whom were in their thirties and forties—Wood and Duffy (1966) reported the following modal pattern: "cold domineering mother, warmer but alcoholic father, 'miserable self-image,' cold domineering husband, resort to alcohol patterned after father's drinking." (p. 344)

An alcoholic constitutes a highly undesirable parental model for his children—male or female— to imitate; as a consequence, the nonalcoholic parent often attempts to assume the roles of both father and mother, and may fail to perform either well. Thus, the child of an alcoholic may have special problems in learning who he is, what is expected of him, and what to esteem in others. Further, his range of coping techniques is likely to be more limited than that of the average child. In a study of 20 adolescent alcoholics referred to an alcoholism clinic in Boston, MacKay (1961) found that a large number of these teenagers had alcoholic fathers, and emphasized that parental models persistently had been perceived by these subjects as involving alcoholism. Thus, in attempting to deal with their own problems of feeling rejected, inadequate, and depressed, these adolescents apparently imitated the dominant parental mode of adjustment.

Alcoholism commonly occurs during crisis periods when changes in one's situation or social role lead to confusion in relation to self-concept and value orientations. Thus, in a study of 100 middle- and upper-class women who were receiving help at an alcoholism treatment center, Curlee (1969) found that the trauma which appeared to trigger the alcoholism was related to a change or challenge in the subject's role as wife or mother—for example, menopause, loss of husband, or children's leaving home: the "empty nest syndrome." As a result, many women appear to begin their immoderate drinking during their late thirties and early forties when such life-situation changes are common.

In a review of various models of alcoholism, Siegler, Osmond, and Newell (1968) have described a more general family interaction prototype:

"Alcoholism, like drug addiction and schizophrenia, is best seen as a form of family interaction in which one person is assigned the role of the 'alcoholic' while others play the complementary roles, such as the martyred wife, the neglected children, the disgraced parents, and so forth. As this deadly game is played by mutual consent, any attempt to remove the key actor, the alcoholic, is bound to create difficulties for the other family members, who will attempt to restore their former game. As the game is of far greater interest to the family than to the therapist, the family is almost bound to win. The family may succeed in including the therapist as another role in the game." (p. 579)

Since in this conceptualization alcoholism represents a long drawn-out family game which is circular and self-reinforcing, it appears relatively useless to ask how it all began. Siegler and her colleagues suggest that certain basic personality inadequacies are transmitted from generation to generation, while the particular family game that develops, along with the specific roles that are assumed, presumably result from the configuration of personalities in a given family and in a particular social setting.

In this context, Al-Anon (1966) has pointed out that a husband who lives with an alcoholic wife is often unaware of the fact that, gradually and inevitably, many of the decisions he makes every day are influenced by his wife's drinking. In a case such as this, the husband is becoming "drinking-wife-oriented." And of course, the wife who is married to an alcoholic may become "drinking-husband-oriented." Eventually the entire marriage may be dominated by and center around the drinking of the alcoholic spouse—and occasionally by the excessive drinking of both marital partners.

In a study of the wives of 40 hospitalized alcoholics, Student and Matova (1969) reported that 35 complained of emotional disturbances that developed during marriage—mainly of a neurotic variety. In some instances the husband (or wife) may find himself drinking excessively—possibly through the reinforcement of such behavior by his mate, or to drown out the disillusionment, frustration, and resentment that are often elicited by an alcoholic spouse. Of course, such interpersonal relationships are not restricted to marriage but may also involve love affairs or personal friendships that tend to foster excessive drinking.

General sociocultural factors. In a study of the backgrounds of male alcoholics, McCord, McCord, and Sudeman (1960) found that differences between boys who became alcoholics as adults and those who did not were primarily cultural; that is, alcoholism was demonstrated to be related to ethnic and social-class background rather than to physiological or psychological differences. Cisin and Calahan (1970) have found that urban dwellers tend to drink far more than those in rural areas. They also noted that people tend to imitate the styles of their environment; for example, when rural dwellers move into urban areas their drinking tends to increase. In fact, liquor has come to play an almost ritualistic role in promoting gaiety, ease of conversation, and freer communication at adult social gatherings in urban areas. Certain occupations in our society are apparently more hazardous with regard to alcoholic use than are others. Prominent among such occupations are various types of sales positions where customers expect to be "wined and dined."

In a general sense, our culture has become dependent on alcohol as a social lubricant and a means of tension reduction. Evidence for the importance of a social-stress factor in drinking was supplied in an early study by Horton (1943). In an analysis of 56 primitive societies, he obtained data concerning the basic level of security and the amount of alcohol consumed. The greater the insecurity or anxiety level of the culture, the greater the amount of alcohol consumption—due allowance having been made for the availability of alcohol. Carrying matters a step further, Bales (1946) outlined three cultural factors that appear to play a part in determining the incidence of alcoholism in a given society: (1) the degree of stress and inner tension produced by the culture;

(2) the attitudes toward drinking fostered by the culture; and (3) the degree to which the culture provides substitute means of satisfaction and ways of coping with anxiety. In this context, it is of interest to note that alcoholism is a major problem in both of the world's superpowers—the United States and Russia.

Finally, the effect of cultural attitudes toward drinking is well illustrated by Moslems and the Mormons, whose religious values prohibit the use of alcohol, and by the Jews, who have traditionally limited its use largely to religious rituals. The incidence of alcoholism among these groups is minimal. Conversely, the incidence of alcoholism is proportionately higher among the French and Irish, where cultural approbation is greater. Thus it appears that social custom and religious sanctions can determine whether alcohol is one of the modes of adjustment available to the members of any given society.

TREATMENT AND OUTCOMES

A multidisciplinary approach to treatment of alcoholism appears to be most effective because alcoholism is a highly complex disorder, requiring flexibility and individualization of treatment procedures. Too, the needs of the alcoholic change as treatment progresses.

Formerly it was considered essential that treatment of an alcoholic take place in an institutional setting, which removed him from his traumatic life situation and asserted more control over his behavior—particularly his drinking. However, an increasing number of alcoholics are now being treated in community clinics—especially those alcoholics who do not require hospitalization for withdrawal treatment. This includes a large number of persons who have been arrested for drunkenness and given suspended jail sentences with the provision that they undergo such treatment. Halfway houses are being used increasingly to bridge the gap between institutionalization and return to the community and to add to the flexibility of treatment programs.

The key objective of a treatment program is the recovery of the alcoholic: his physical rehabilitation, his control over the craving for liquor, his abstinence from drinking, and his subsequent realization that he can cope with the problems of living and lead a much more rewarding life without alcohol.

Medical measures. In acute intoxication, the initial focus is on detoxification, or elimination of the harmful alcoholic substances from the individual's body, on treatment of withdrawal symptoms, and on medical regimes for physical rehabilitation. These can best be handled in a hospital or clinic setting, where drugs, such as chlordiazepoxide, have largely revolutionized the treatment of withdrawal symptoms and the prevention of delirium tremens and convulsions. Such drugs function to overcome motor excitement, nausea, and vomiting, and help alleviate the tension and anxiety typically associated with withdrawal.

Detoxification typically is followed by psychotherapy, including family counseling, and the use of ancillary resources in the community relating to employment and other aspects of the alcoholic's social readjustment.

It should be noted that although mild tranquilizing drugs are often used in helping the alcoholic sleep and alleviating anxiety during acute reactions, their effectiveness in long-range reduction of the need for alcohol has not been demonstrated. In fact, the alcoholic usually has to abstain from tranquilizers as well as from alcohol if he is to achieve total restraint, for alcoholics tend to misuse the one as well as the other. And under the influence of tranquilizers he may even return to the use of alcohol.

Aversion therapy. A treatment approach which is receiving increasing research attention and application is that of aversion therapy. Romans employed this technique by placing a live eel in a cup of wine; forced to drink this unsavory cocktail, the alcoholic presumably would feel disgusted and thereafter be repelled by wine.

Today there are a variety of pharmacological and other deterrent measures that can be employed after detoxification has been accomplished. One approach utilizes the intramuscular injection of emetine hydrochloride, an emetic. Prior to the nausea that results from the injection, the patient is given alcohol, so that the sight, smell, and taste of the beverage become associated with severe retching and vomiting (Franks, 1966). With repetition, this classical conditioning procedure acts as a strong deterrent to further drinking—probably in part because it adds an immediate and physiologically negative reinforcer to the more general socially aversive consequences of excessive drinking.

Disulpherim (Antabuse), a drug that creates extremely uncomfortable effects when followed by alcohol, may also be administered to prevent an immediate return to drinking. However, such deterrent therapy is seldom advocated as the sole approach, since pharmacological methods have not alone proven effective in treating alcoholism. For example, an alcoholic may simply discontinue the use of Antabuse when he is released from the hospital or clinic, and return to his former drinking patterns. In fact, the primary value of drugs of this type appears to lie in their interruption of the alcoholic cycle for a period of time, during which psychotherapy and sociotherapy may be undertaken.

Among other aversive methods has been the use of electroshock. For example, Vogler et al. (1970) have reported on a study in which alcoholics were shocked for drinking and then reinforced by shock termination when they spit out the alcohol. Although initial results were encouraging—especially when booster sessions were given after the subjects left the hospital—there is insufficient data available at present to assess the long-range effectiveness of electroshock in the treatment of alcoholism.

Psychosocial measures. Although individual therapy is sometimes effective, psychosocial measures in the treatment of alcoholism more often involve group therapy and sociotherapy, and the approach of Alcoholics Anonymous.

1. *Group therapy.* Usually the first and most important step in group therapy is to get the alcoholic to concede that he has a drinking problem and that there are resources available for helping him deal with it. In the rugged give-and-take of group therapy, the alcoholic is forced to face his problem and to recognize its possible disastrous consequences. Often, but by no means always, this recognition paves the way toward positive efforts to cope with his drinking problem.

In some instances the spouse of an alcoholic and even his children may be invited to join in group therapy meetings. In other situations family treatment is itself the central focus of the therapeutic effort. In the latter case, the alcoholic individual is seen as a member of a disturbed family in which he and the other members each

have a responsibility for cooperating in treatment. Since family members frequently have been the persons most victimized by the alcoholic's addiction, they often tend to be judgmental and punitive; and the alcoholic, who has already passed harsh judgment on himself, tolerates this further source of devaluation very poorly. In other instances, members of a family may unwittingly encourage an alcoholic to remain addicted, as, for example, when a wife with a need to dominate her husband finds that a perennially drunken and remorseful spouse best meets her need.

2. *Sociotherapy.* As with other serious maladaptive behaviors, the total treatment program in alcoholism usually requires supportive follow-up measures, including modification of the alcoholic's life and community environment. Often as a result of his drinking he has become estranged from family and friends, and his job has been lost or jeopardized. Typically the reaction of those around him is not likely to be as understanding or supportive as it would have been had he had a physical illness of comparable magnitude. Thus, simply repairing a "damaged psyche" does not usually effect a recovery.

Relapses and continued deterioration are generally associated with a lack of close relationships with family or friends, or with living in a high-risk environment. In a study of black male alcoholics, for example, King et al. (1969) have pointed to the ghetto cycle of broken homes, delinquency, underemployment, alcoholism, and, once again, broken homes. From the standpoint of behavior research, Keehn and Webster (1969) have concluded that it is not possible for an alcoholic to remain abstinent unless the psychosocial reinforcements that operated in the past are dealt with.

Often, of course, it is not possible to make needed changes in the individual's aversive life situation. In such instances, the treatment program attempts to build increased stress tolerance as well as more effective coping techniques, so that the individual can make a more rewarding adjustment without alcohol than he could with it.

3. *Alcoholics Anonymous.* A practical approach to the problem of alcoholism which has met with considerable success is that of *Alcoholics Anonymous.* This organization was started in 1935 by two individuals, Dr. Bob and Bill W. in Akron, Ohio. Bill W. recovered from alcohol-

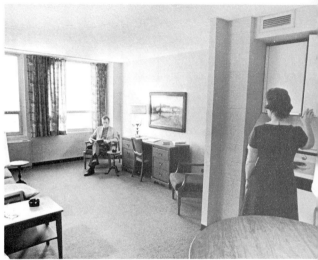

Modern rehabilitation centers for alcoholics provide innovative approaches to treatment in surroundings designed to contribute to, rather then detract from, the individual's feelings of dignity and integrity. At the Alcoholism Rehabilitation Center of Lutheran General Hospital, Park Ridge, Illinois, the facilities are among the most advanced, while being kept as comfortable and homelike as possible. In addition to counseling rooms, lecture hall, library, cafeteria, and living accommodations for participants, the center has facilities for recreational therapy and physical fitness. Apartments enable the spouses of some of the participants to live in and thus become involved in the treatment program.

Comprising the heart of the program are daily group therapy sessions, which are planned to help individuals obtain a clearer picture of their behavior, the forces motivating it, and its effects on their interpersonal relationships. Role-playing, psychodrama, and intensified verbal exchange are among the techniques employed to help individuals express their feelings in more effective and appropriate ways.

Other key features of the program are the "bridge" groups—weekly meetings attended by participants, their spouses, other relatives, referring physicians, employers, etc., and the marital process groups, which involve the participants and their spouses in lectures and group discussions focusing on alcoholism, communications, marital relationships, and dependency problems. Coordinating the nonmedical treatment of each participant is a primary counselor—the staff member to whom he is assigned on admission.

ism through a "fundamental spiritual change," and immediately sought out Dr. Bob, who, with his assistance, achieved recovery. Both in turn began to help other alcoholics.[1]

Alcoholics Anonymous operates primarily as a psychotherapeutic program in which both person-to-person and group relationships are emphasized. Although A.A. is not affiliated with any religious sect, spiritual development is a key aspect of its treatment approach. Meetings are devoted partly to social activities, but consist mainly of discussions of the participants' problems with alcohol, often with testimonials from those who

have recovered from alcoholism. Here, the recovered member usually contrasts his life before he broke the habit with his life now that he can live without alcohol.

An important strength of A.A. is that it lifts the burden of personal responsibility from the shoulders of the alcoholic by helping him realize that alcoholism, like many other problems, is bigger than he. Henceforth, he need not feel himself

---

[1]Here it should be noted that the term *alcoholic* is used by A.A. and its affiliates to refer either to individuals who currently are drinking excessively, or to persons who have recovered from such a problem but must continue to abstain from alcohol consumption in the future.

to be weak-willed or lacking in moral strength, but rather simply unfortunate in that his particular affliction is that he cannot drink—just as other people may not be able to tolerate certain types of medication. Thus, by mutual help and reassurance through participation in a group composed of others who have shared similar experiences, many an alcoholic acquires insight into his problems, a new sense of purpose, greater ego strength, and more effective coping techniques. And, of course, continued participation in the group helps prevent the crisis of a relapse.[1]

An affiliated movement, Al-Anon Family Groups, has been established for the relatives of alcoholics. By meeting together and sharing their common problems and experiences, the wives or husbands of alcoholics are helped to better understand the nature of alcoholism, the effects of the spouses' drinking upon them personally, and the best techniques for helping their alcoholic mates, as well as themselves. They learn to understand, for example, the necessity of their alcoholic spouses' attendance at A.A. meetings several nights a week on a sustained basis if relapses are to be prevented. They are also helped to see their mates in a less "drinking-wife-" or "drinking-husband-oriented" perspective, and they are provided with suggestions for reasonable courses of action. Finally, they are relieved from guilt feelings over being the causes of their spouses' drinking; for they come to realize that many factors may contribute. In addition, it is made clear that the initial choice of using alcohol as a coping mechanism lies with the individual.

An outgrowth of the Al-Anon movement has been the Ala-teen movement, designed to help teen-agers understand the drinking problems of their parents and find support in a group setting.

Results of treatment. A pervasive problem in the treatment of alcoholism is that once a drinker has lost control over his alcohol consumption, he ordinarily will not regain control regardless of the length of the intervening period of sobriety. Davies (1962) followed up 93 alcoholics after treatment at Maudsley Hospital in London and found that after a period of 7 to 11 years, only 7 of the patients had developed a capacity to drink alcoholic beverages in a controlled manner. Similarly, a more recent study by Reinert and Bowen (1968) has reported that the normal use of alcohol by those who previously have been identified as

alcoholics—even after successful recoveries and prolonged abstinence—is indeed a rare occurrence; and even then such use tends to be confined to small, infrequent amounts of wine or beer. But whatever problems abstinence may impose, it is important to note that most cases of alcoholism *can* be treated successfully (AMA, 1969).

Statistics on the long-range outcome of treatment for alcoholism vary considerably, depending both on the population studied and the treatment facilities and procedures employed. They range from a very low rate of success for hard-core, skid-row alcoholics, to recoveries of 70 to 90 percent where modern treatment and after-treatment procedures have been utilized.

In a review of behavior-therapy approaches utilizing aversion techniques, Bandura (1969) has reported a 50-percent rate of remission (moderation in force or intensity of symptoms) over periods as long as 10 years. Where booster treatments are given periodically, the remission rate increases to 85 to 90 percent. This is contrasted with a base-line rate of 10 to 15 percent for spontaneous recoveries and relatively low remission rate for psychoanalytic and other individual psychotherapeutic approaches. Irwin (1968) investigated a number of hospital and clinic results involving total treatment approaches and found that while results varied—depending on the population treated—70 to 80 percent of those whose excessive drinking was dealt with early achieved abstinence following comprehensive team treatment.

Even when continued abstinence is not accomplished, the alcoholic who remains abstinent for a period of years can be credited with a major achievement—and when a relapse does occur he will be in a much better position to realize his need for help. And, here again, relapses may be further prevented by after-treatment programs. For example, the recovered alcoholic may maintain contact with a community alcoholic clinic for a period of years. Alcoholics Anonymous has proven particularly effective in this regard.

Unfortunately, there is an abysmal lack of community facilities for the treatment of alcoholics. Many general hospitals will not admit alcoholics, and even state mental institutions commonly refuse admittance to persons in a state

---

[1]See Bateson (1971) for a discussion of Alcoholics Anonymous in relation to the principles of general systems theory.

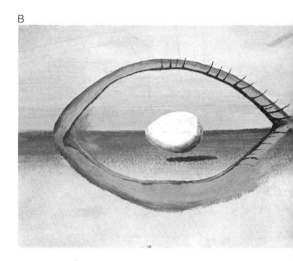

E

PAINTING HELPS ALCOHOLIC BRING HIS PROBLEMS INTO FOCUS

These sketches and paintings were made by W——, a 40-year-old male with a history of alcoholism, repeated loss of employment, and hospitalization for treatment. In style and content, they reveal a progression in the subject's ability to express himself through art forms and to understand his own behavior. His interest in painting, which gradually became the key aspect of his treatment program at an alcoholism treatment center, also led to a new way of life following his discharge.

When admitted to the center, W—— was indifferent to both individual and group therapy but did respond favorably to the idea of occupational therapy, feeling that he would like to try painting. He selected his own art supplies, space was arranged in his room for his painting, and he came to spend much of his free time there. As he showed a marked increase in motivation for therapy, his room, referred to as "the studio," became the location for a significant portion of his individual therapy sessions.

The use of painting in W——'s therapeutic program progressed through four stages:

In Stage 1, the greater precision of perception required for sketching generalized to W——'s understanding of his own behavior; thus, he could see more clearly and verbalize objectively his past abuses of alcohol and the conditions that apparently had precipitated and maintained his drinking patterns.

In Stage 2, W—— attempted to express his feelings and understanding on sketching paper. Pencil sketch A, one of his earliest efforts, was characterized by little definition and a feeling of vagueness and indecisiveness. Although thinking at first that the difficulty stemmed from W——'s lack of training in art, the therapist later concluded that he had been trying to cover too broad an area in the therapy sessions for W—— to develop sufficient emotional understanding of the results. Although able to verbalize his insights, W—— could not adequately translate them via the sketching technique. His understanding was deepened when the therapist adjusted the scope of the sessions and helped him put his insights into writing before sketching. The results are shown in B, a reproduction in oil of a sketch that was clear to both W—— and the therapist. W—— said in explaining it, ". . . from the beginning of my whole damn booze problem, as far back as I can remember, I've been seeing the 'juice' as something it just never was and just never will be."

During Stage 3, W—— continued with his sketching in one-to-one therapy, also participating in group therapy and other phases of the rehabilitation program. He worked independently now in sketching the conclusions of the individual sessions, generally being on target in depicting the insights he expressed in discussion and in writing.

In Stage 4 W—— decided to "put it all together" by grouping several segments from earlier sketches into one composition and painting them in oils on canvas. Sketch C is one of his preliminary grouping efforts, which resulted in painting D. Sketch E, another grouping effort, culminated in the second oil painting, F.

In painting D, W—— depicted alcoholism as a magnet-like vise that drew and crushed his consciousness. He symbolized his feelings in sober periods between drinking sprees as the chained tree, and the nebulous higher power to which he looked for help as a descending dove. The egg and eye from the earlier sketch are now merged into a straining muscular arm reaching back to the more

D

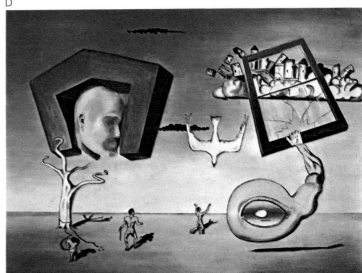

placid past and unattainable dream castles—futile quests with which W—— associated his past abuses of alcohol.

In painting F, the overriding concept is of constructive action. Contrasting with segments at left and right—a world "blown to hell," an aimless passing through one span of sobriety to the barrenness beyond, and the dismal choice offered by the portals to an abyss or barren sobriety—is the cross symbolizing hope. Through this hope W—— sees the landscape representing goal or purpose. The cross-like shape of the hope segment, while not signifying formal religious affiliation, is indicative of W——'s view of the suprahuman nature of one of the forms of help available to him.

In discussing painting F, W—— said, "That world of mine wasn't blown to hell as bad as I thought. It doesn't make much difference anyway, because that was yesterday and this is today. I don't think I'll forget about those dry spells though. Floating around between drunks with all my fears and anxiety was almost worse than when I was 'stoned.'

"I don't plan on forgetting that my next drunk could be my last. I might not get a chance to sober up and I'd go down into that pit with no bottom.

"I'm starting to make something go for me now. . . . I'm working at putting myself together and it won't be too easy. . . . I'll always have problems but I'll always have help. My job is to put my sobriety first so I can use that help. Then I'll be able to keep sober and get some of this contentment and that better way of living that I'm beginning to see. . . ."

On his discharge from the rehabilitation center, W—— began formal instruction in art, lived at a YMCA near the art school, and participated in the activities of Alcoholics Anonymous, to which he was introduced while still at the treatment center. Crises arose during his first year, but were resolved with additional counseling by his therapist. At the end of one year at the art school, he was described by the faculty as a promising student with a good chance of success in the commercial art field. His long-range prognosis is considered excellent by the treatment staff, contingent upon his continuing affiliation with A.A. and utilization of appropriate therapy if crises arise.

Adapted from a case study made by George W. Erdmann, Consultant to the Director, Treatment Center for Alcoholism, Manteno State Hospital, Manteno, Illinois.

of acute intoxication. As a consequence, it has been estimated that only one alcoholic in ten receives treatment (Irwin, 1968). In part, this failure is also based on the refusal of many alcoholics to admit that they have an alcohol problem before they "hit bottom."

On the other hand, alcoholism is to some degree a self-limiting disorder, in the sense that the prognosis tends to improve significantly for persons over age 40 (Drew, 1968). This is only a trend, however, and does not apply to certain sizable portions of the alcoholic population, including many skid-row alcoholics, who have given up hope and are literally "drinking themselves to death."

New hope for alcoholics. On the positive side, attention should be drawn to congressional legislation providing for the establishment of The National Institute on Alcohol Abuse and Alcoholism. Some 1000 or more federally supported community alcoholism centers throughout the nation were projected by the Institute during its first ten years (Chafetz, 1971). The best possible treatment services for alcoholics on a community level and research aimed at practical means for preventing alcoholism—perhaps a biochemical method—are the Institute's chief objectives.

The prevention of alcoholism in our society is a particularly important objective in view of the widespread misery, waste, and loss of life it causes. Pending possible breakthroughs in research leading to biochemical methods of prevention, reliance must essentially be placed on the education of individuals concerning the use of alcohol and its dangers. The early detection and correction of excessive drinking patterns is also of crucial significance. (See illustration giving early warning signs, page 412.)

DRUG DEPENDENCE

The earliest records of man contain references to his familiarity with and use of various psychoactive drugs—i.e., drugs which affect mental processes. Hallucinogenic drugs were made from a variety of mushrooms by paleolithic peoples in Siberia and the Far East to induce cheer, intoxication, and courage during tribal clashes. The substances used apparently had many of the effects of modern hallucinogenic drugs, such as LSD (Brekhman & Sam, 1967). Various narcotic drugs, such as hyoscyamus and hemlock, are also known to have been used by ancient man.

Aside from alcohol, the psychoactive drugs most commonly associated with dependence in our society would appear to be (1) the narcotics, such as opium and its derivatives; (2) the sedatives, such as the barbiturates; (3) the stimulants, such as the amphetamines; (4) the mild tranquilizers, such as the meprobamates; and (5) the hallucinogens, such as marijuana. Caffeine and nicotine are also drugs of dependence, but they are not included in the APA classification, and we shall not deal with them in our present discussion. However, all of the psychoactive drugs have an abuse potential, and they may produce tolerance and physiological and/or psychological dependence.

Drug abuse or dependence may occur at any age, but seems to be most common during adolescence and young adulthood. Clinical pictures vary markedly, depending on the type, amount, and duration of drug usage, the physiological and psychological makeup of the individual—and in some instances, the social setting in which the drug experience occurs. Thus it appears most useful to deal separately with some of the drugs more commonly associated with abuse and dependence. For historical reasons, we shall first deal with opium and its derivatives.

OPIUM AND ITS DERIVATIVES

Man has used opium and its derivatives for over 5000 years. Galen (A.D. 130–201) considered theriaca, whose principal ingredient was opium, to be a veritable panacea:

"It resists poison and venomous bites, cures inveterate headache, vertigo, deafness, epilepsy, apoplexy, dimness of sight, loss of voice, asthma, coughs of all kinds, spitting of blood, tightness of breath, colic, the iliac poisons, jaundice, hardness of the spleen, stone, urinary complaints, fevers, dropsies, leprosies, the trouble to which women are subject, melancholy and all pestilences."

Even today, opium derivatives are still used for some of the conditions Galen mentioned.

Opium is a mixture of about eighteen nitrogen-containing agents known as *alkaloids*. In 1805 it was found that the alkaloid present in the largest amount (10 to 15 percent) was a bitter-tasting powder that proved to be a powerful sedative and pain reliever; it was thus named *morphine* (after Morpheus, god of sleep in Greek mythology). After introduction of the hypodermic needle in America about 1856, morphine was widely administered to soldiers during the Civil War, not only to those wounded in battle but also to those suffering from dysentery. As a consequence, large

numbers of Civil War veterans returned to civilian life addicted to the drug, a condition euphemistically referred to as "Soldier's Illness."

Scientists concerned with the addictive properties of morphine hypothesized that one part of the morphine molecule might be responsible for its analgesic properties[1] and another for its addictiveness. Thus, at about the turn of the century it was discovered that if morphine were treated by an inexpensive and readily available chemical called *acetic anhydride*, it could be converted into another powerful analgesic called *heroin*. Heroin was hailed with enthusiasm by its discoverer, Heinrich Dreser[2] (Boehm, 1968). Leading scientists of his time agreed with Dreser concerning the merits of heroin, and the drug came to be widely prescribed in place of morphine for pain relief and related medicinal purposes; however, heroin turned out to be a cruel disappointment. It proved to be an even more dangerous drug than morphine, acting more rapidly and more intense-

---

[1] An analgesic is a drug that alleviates pain without inducing unconsciousness.
[2] Dreser shortly thereafter introduced aspirin—an effective but nonaddictive analgesic for relief of minor pains.

FOR SELF-TESTING: QUESTIONS ON EFFECTS OF PSYCHOACTIVE DRUGS

In view of the widespread use of psychoactive drugs in our society, there is a relative dearth of accurate information concerning their effects. The reader can test his own knowledge by answering the following multiple-choice questions:

1. In terms of medical usage, alcohol (the beverage) is (a) useful in inducing sleep, (b) important in treating certain diseases, (c) widely used in relieving pain, (d) of little or no value.

2. A person who has taken more than a prescribed amount of an opiate is likely to be (a) excited and hyperactive, (b) quiet and inactive, (c) hostile and aggressive, (d) tense and fearful.

3. In terms of medical usage, barbiturates are most important in (a) inducing sleep, (b) reducing tension, (c) relieving pain, (d) research.

4. Physically harmful effects most commonly associated with the abuse of minor tranquilizers are (a) damage to the kidneys and liver, (b) damage to reproductive capacity, (c) high blood pressure, (d) blood cell damage.

5. By taking amphetamines, the individual is usually able to (a) do much better on tests, (b) think more clearly about

problems, (c) stay awake, (d) retain his composure under stress.

6. In terms of medical usage, hallucinogens are most important in (a) alleviating depression, (b) overcoming emotional problems, (c) controlling fear and anxiety, (d) brain research.

7. Most teen-agers who use psychoactive drugs initially obtained the drugs from (a) parents, (b) friends, (c) drug pushers, (d) drugstore thefts.

8. "Flashbacks" are most commonly associated with the use of (a) heroin, (b) LSD, (c) amphetamines, (d) barbiturates.

9. Abuse of which one of the following drugs is most likely to result in brain damage: (a) LSD, (b) marijuana, (c) methedrine, (d) heroin.

10. Which of the following drugs accounts for the greatest number of deaths from drug use? (a) opiates, (b) hallucinogens, (c) amphetamines, (d) barbiturates.

Answers: 1 (d), 2 (b), 3 (a), 4 (d), 5 (c), 6 (d), 7 (b), 8 (b), 9 (c), 10 (d).

Based on Commission of Inquiry into the Non-Medical Use of Drugs (1970), Greenblatt and Shader (1971), and Moskin (1970).

ly and being equally if not more addictive; and eventually heroin was removed from use in medical practice.

As it became apparent that opium and its derivatives—including codeine, which is used in some cough syrups—were perilously addictive, the United States Congress enacted the Harrison Act in 1914. Under this and later acts, the unauthorized sale and dispensation of narcotic drugs became a federal offense; and physicians and pharmacists were held accountable for each dose they dispensed. Thus, overnight, the role of a narcotic user changed from that of addict —which was considered a vice, but tolerated— to that of criminal. And now, unable to obtain narcotic drugs through legal sources, many turned to illegal ones, and eventually to other criminal

acts as a means of maintaining their suddenly expensive drug supply. Strict control by federal and local authorities, coupled with public education, have helped greatly in limiting the problem, but even so, there are now an estimated 100,000 or more narcotic addicts in New York City alone; and the number of addicts in the country as a whole has been estimated at 250,000 to 300,000 (Newsweek, 1971).

Most narcotic addicts in our society are teenagers or young adults—although some are children—and the annual cost of their drugs is considered to exceed 8 billion dollars.

Effects of morphine and heroin. Morphine and heroin are commonly introduced into the body by smoking, "snorting" (inhaling the bitter powder), eating, "skin popping," and "mainlining,"

DRUG PUSHERS: A PRELIMINARY PORTRAIT

Blum (1971) reported results of a preliminary study of drug dealers in the San Francisco Bay area. To get a representative sample, he interviewed 454 dealers, each interview taking from 2 to 12 hours. All of his subjects were or had been regular dealers in a high-school, college, commune, or other relatively specific setting—35 percent having stated that they had quit dealing prior to being interviewed. Key findings included:

Age	Most were between 19 and 35.
Education	Most had not finished college.
Race	Most were white.
Parental background	The families of most were intact, with noncriminal parents; in about a fourth of the cases one parent or both were alcoholic.
Source of income	About half earned their income only from drug dealing; of those in the "have quit" group, about one fifth had made more than $1000 a month from drug dealing.
Arrest record	The majority—59 percent—had not been subject to arrest in connection with drugs; but of the other 41 percent, 15 percent had served prison terms of more than 6 months.
Personal use of drugs	Most began drinking in their teens, became heavy marijuana smokers before reaching their mid-twenties, and also used opiates by that same age. Nearly half had "mainlined speed" as well. Most got their first illicit drug as a gift from a friend or acquaintance; 10 percent got their first drugs while imprisoned in juvenile halls or jails. Forty percent were worried about being addicted or dependent.
Reasons for drug pushing	Key reasons cited were their own dependence on drugs, the relatively high tax-free income it brought them, their doubts about being able to make a living in the "straight" world, being around people they liked (except heroin addicts, whom they demeaned), the excitement of it all, and—in a minority of cases —a semireligious commitment to drugs and the drug culture. Most did not view themselves as criminals, and only 10 percent acknowledged moral qualms about dealing in drugs.
Reasons for quitting	For most of those who quit—individuals who were from poor families and who had police records beginning as juveniles—fear of arrest was the primary reason for quitting. For the others—who were from more affluent families and who had no criminal records—reasons cited were fear of arrest, increasing violence and personal danger in the criminal world of drug dealers, and pressure by parents, wives, or sweethearts. Half of all who had quit were still earning illicit income in other areas than drug dealing; thus they were not going "straight."

the last two being methods of introducing the drug via hypodermic injection. *Skin popping* refers to injecting the liquified drug just beneath the skin, and *mainlining* to injecting the drug into the bloodstream. In the United States, the young addict usually progresses from snorting to mainlining.

Among the immediate effects of heroin is a euphoric spasm of 60 seconds or so, which many addicts compare to a sexual orgasm (Fort, 1954). This is followed by a "high" which may last for several hours, during which the addict typically is in a lethargic, withdrawn state in which bodily needs, including those for food and sex, are markedly diminished; pleasant feelings of relaxation, euphoria, and reverie tend to dominate. These effects last from 4 to 6 hours and are followed—in addicts—by a negative phase which produces a desire for more of the drug.

The use of opium derivatives over a period of time usually results in a physiological craving for the drug. The amount of time required to establish the drug habit varies, but it has been estimated that continual usage over a period of 30 days or longer is sufficient. The user will then find that he has become physiologically dependent upon the drug, in the sense that he will feel physically ill when he does not take it. In addition, the user of opium derivatives gradually builds up a tolerance to the drugs so that ever larger amounts are needed for the desired effects.

When persons addicted to opiates do not get a dose of the drug within approximately 8 hours, they start to experience *withdrawal symptoms*. The character and severity of the reaction depends on many factors, including the amount of the narcotic habitually used, the intervals between doses, the duration of the addiction, and especially the addict's health and personality.

Contrary to popular opinion, withdrawal from heroin is not always dangerous, nor even very painful. Many addicted persons are able to withdraw without assistance. However, in some instances withdrawal *is* both an agonizing and perilous experience.

Initial symptoms usually include a running nose, tearing eyes, perspiration, restlessness, increased respiration rate, and an intensified desire for the drug. As time passes, the symptoms become more severe, usually reaching a peak in about 40 hours. Typically there may be chilli-

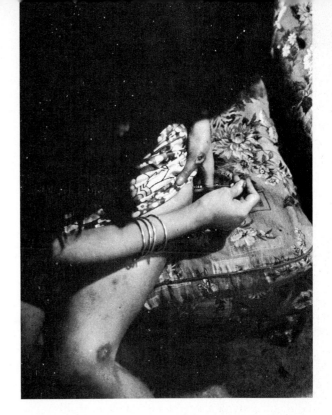

Unable to find any more functioning surface veins into which she can inject heroin, a young addict in the Bronx shoots three bags of the drug directly into skin tissue. Commenting on her inability to find a vein, she said, "Maybe a doctor could find one. I can't."

ness alternating with vasomotor disturbances of flushing and excessive sweating (this may result in marked pilomotor activity so that the skin of the addict comes to resemble that of a plucked turkey—a condition commonly described as "goose flesh"), vomiting, diarrhea, abdominal cramps, pains in the back and extremities, severe headache, marked tremors, and insomnia in varying degrees. Beset by these discomforts, the individual refuses food and water, and this, coupled with the vomiting, sweating, and diarrhea, results in dehydration and weight losses of as much as 5 to 15 pounds in a day. Occasionally there also may be delirium, hallucinations, and manic activity. Cardiovascular collapse may also occur, and may result in death. If morphine is administered at any point along the way, the subjective distress of the addict ends, and physiological equanimity is restored in about 5 to 30 minutes.

Usually the withdrawal symptoms will be definitely on the decline by the third or fourth day, and by the seventh or eighth day will have disappeared. As his symptoms subside, the individual resumes normal eating and drinking, and rapidly regains his lost weight. An additional hazard now exists in that after withdrawal symptoms have ceased, the individual's former tolerance for the drug also will have disappeared, and death may now result from his taking the former large dosage of the drug.

In rare cases an individual will have enough self-control to use opiates without allowing them to interfere with his work and ruin his life; but typically, the danger in the use of such drugs—especially heroin—is very great. Tolerance may be built up so rapidly that larger and more expensive amounts of the drug are soon required, and withdrawal treatments are likely to do little to end the problem. Most addicted individuals—even after withdrawal—find it extremely difficult to break their dependency. Biochemical alterations appear to be at least partly responsible for the individual's continued craving for the narcotic drug even after the completion of the withdrawal treatment.

Typically, the life of a narcotic addict is increasingly centered around obtaining and using drugs; hence, the addiction usually leads to socially maladaptive behavior as the individual is eventually forced to lie, steal, and associate with undesirable companions in order to maintain his supply of the drug. Contrary to the common picture of a "dope fiend," however, most narcotic addicts are not major criminals. Those who have police records usually confine themselves to petty offenses, and very few commit crimes of violence. Female addicts, for example, commonly turn to prostitution as a means of financing their addiction.

Along with the lowering of ethical and moral restraints, addiction has adverse effects on the well-being of the individual. Lack of an adequate diet may lead to ill health and increased susceptibility to a variety of physical ailments. The use of unsterile equipment and techniques may also lead to a variety of ailments, including liver damage from hepatitis. In addition, the use of such a potent drug as heroin without medical supervision and government controls to assure its strength and purity can result in perilous overdosage. For if the heroin user injects too much, he risks coma and death from the overdose, which slows respiration. In 1969 in New York City alone, there were more than 900 deaths associated with heroin usage, 224 of which were of teen-agers who died from overdoses or heroin-related infections (Abelson, 1970).

Usually, however, addiction to opiates leads to a more gradual deterioration of well-being. The ill health and the general personality deterioration often found in opium addiction do not result directly from the pharmacological effects of the drug, but are typically the product of the sacrifice of money, proper diet, social position, and self-respect, as the addict becomes more desperate in his efforts to procure his required daily dosage. On the other hand, narcotic addicts with financial means to maintain both a balanced diet and an adequate supply of the drug without resorting to criminal behavior may maintain their drug dependence over many years without any appreciable symptoms of either physical or mental disorders.

The following case history gives a brief view of a teen-age addict arrested by the Los Angeles police.

"The boy was seventeen years of age. He had a pleasant way of talking, punctuating his remarks with an occasional smile. His excellent grammar and quiet manners indicated a good home and background. . . .

"Is this a 'dope fiend'? This is an inaccurate . . . term, but by all common standards and definitions the answer would be yes. Gene R_____, the boy in custody, is a confirmed heroin addict, a 'mainliner' injecting heroin directly into the main blood vessels of his arm. His body requires five 'pops' every day, costing him from $20 to $25 every twenty-four hours. He has managed to earn this amount by 'introducing' other teenagers into the mysteries of marijuana smoking and, eventually, the use of heroin. The police report . . . five separate cases where good-looking Gene R_____ has inflicted the dope habit upon 'girl friends,' all

EXCERPT FROM HEROIN ADDICT'S 23RD PSALM

"King Heroin is my shepherd, I shall always want. He maketh me to lie down in the gutters. He leadeth me beside the troubled waters. He destroyeth my soul . . . and I will dwell in the House of the Damned forever."

Reprinted by permission of Rev. Robert Stultz, Director, Prevention, Inc.

minors. Investigation indicates that four of these girls now pay for his, and their own, drug supply by means of prostitution." (Los Angeles Police Department, 1952, pp. 3-4)

This case, reported some two decades ago, is of particular interest since it would appear typical of the narcotic drug scene among middle-class adolescents today—except that the daily cost of maintaining the habit would now approximate over 4 times as much.

Dynamics of narcotic addiction. There is no dynamic picture that fits all narcotic addiction; however, dependency on these drugs is commonly associated with a broader fabric of personality maladjustment and sociocultural influences. Hence, the following threefold classification provides a convenient—if somewhat artificial —means of ordering our discussion.

1. *Addiction associated with the relief of pain and with professional persons who have access to narcotic drugs.* Many patients are given narcotic drugs, such as morphine, to relieve pain during illness or following surgery or serious injury. The vast majority of such patients never develop an addiction, and when their medication is discontinued, they do not again resort to the use of morphine. Those narcotic addicts who blame their addiction on the fact that they used drugs during an illness usually manifest personality deficiencies which predisposed them to the use of drugs—such as immaturity, low frustration tolerance, and the ability to distort and evade reality by way of a flight into drug-induced fantasy.

Occasionally, professional people entrusted with the handling of narcotics, such as doctors and nurses, become addicted to these drugs. They may be tempted by curiosity, but more commonly their drug use appears to represent an attempt to ward off anxiety or depression induced by some environmental stress, such as divorce. These persons get little or no emotional satisfaction from the drug; they are not psychologically dependent on its use as a long-range means of escaping unpleasant reality. When their traumatic life situation has improved and their physiological dependence on the drug is broken, they usually feel no strong desire to return to its use (Putnam & Ellinwood, 1966; Quinn, 1970). The advent of tranquilizing and antidepressant drugs, coupled with better understanding of the dangers

inherent in the use of narcotics, has apparently made the addiction of professional persons far less common.

2. *Addiction associated with personality disorders and other psychopathology.* In the great majority of cases, narcotic addiction appears to develop in association with personality disorders. In a comparison between a group of 45 young institutionalized male addicts and a control group of nonaddicts, Gilbert and Lombardi (1967) found that outstanding distinguishing features were "the addict's psychopathic traits, his depression, tension, insecurity, and feelings of inadequacy, and his difficulty in forming warm and lasting interpersonal relationships." (p. 536) Similarly, in a study of 112 drug abusers admitted to Bellevue Psychiatric Hospital in New York, Hekimian and Gershon (1968) found that heroin users were usually psychopaths. These studies lend supporting evidence to earlier studies which found young male addicts immature, inadequate, passive-aggressive individuals for whom narcotics seem to have a unique appeal (Ausubel, 1961).

Although very little research has been done on female narcotics users, Chinlund (1969) has reported a sociopathic personality pattern as being characteristic of female addicts studied over a period of seven years in New York City. He concluded that a female addict has three key goals: (a) a conscious wish to lose control of her drug usage so that she can blame her failures on the drug; (b) a desire to obliterate all sense of time— to blot out what is happening in her frustrating life situation; and (c) a need to deny cause-and-effect relationships in her life—for example, the relationship between sexual intercourse and pregnancy.

Among neurotics and psychotics, narcotic addiction appears to be relatively rare. However, Gilbert and Lombardi (1967) found that many of the addicts they studied did evidence psychoneurotic or psychotic traits in association with sociopathic ones. But it would appear that the sociopathic characteristics are the ones most likely to be associated with narcotic addiction.

As in the case of alcoholism, however, caution should be exercised in distinguishing between preaddiction and postaddiction personality traits. As Scher (1966) has pointed out, the high incidence of sociopathic traits among narcotic addicts may result in part from the long-term effects of the drug addiction, rather than precede them. In the main, however, the picture that emerges is one of a vicious circle in which sociopathic characteristics make an individual more prone to narcotic addiction, while the addiction, in turn, tends to amplify these maladaptive traits.

3. *Addiction associated with sociocultural factors.* The influence of sociocultural factors in drug dependence, including alcohol and opium addiction, is well depicted in the experience of the Meo—a tribal people who inhabit the mountains of several countries in Southeast Asia (Westermeyer, 1971). Although alcohol is used, it is employed with rigid restraints, and alcoholism as such does not occur. On the other hand, opium is a major cash crop and is widely used among the Meo, and opium addiction does occur.

In our own society, there are so-called narcotic subcultures—membership in which makes it easier for an addict to obtain drugs and to protect himself against the sanctions of society. Rubington (1968) has concluded that only about 100,000 alcoholics are part of the skid-row culture, while the great majority of narcotic addicts participate in the drug culture. The decision to join this culture has important implications for the future life of an addict, for from that point on he will center his activities around his role of drug user. In short, his addiction becomes his way of life.

With time, most addicts who join the drug culture become increasingly withdrawn, indifferent to their friends (except those in the drug group), and apathetic about sexual activity. They are likely to abandon scholastic and athletic endeavors, and to show a marked reduction in competitive and aggressive strivings. Most of these young people appear to lack good sex-role identification, and to experience feelings of inadequacy when confronted with the demands of adulthood. While feeling progressively isolated from the broader culture, they experience a bolstering of their feelings of group belongingness by continued association with the addict milieu; at the same time, they come to view drugs both as a means of revolt against constituted authority and conventional values and as a device for alleviating personal anxieties and tensions.

But even as a member of this subculture, an addict finds his drug habit to be costly, and he almost inevitably is forced into various types of criminal activity to finance it. In fact, Hekimian and Gershon (1968) estimated that heroin users alone cost New York City 10 million dollars a day in crimes committed to support their dependence; this amounts to over 3.5 billion dollars per year, largely from such crimes as theft, burglary, and shoplifting.

Lipscomb (1971) has noted that although drug abuse and dependence are common in ghetto areas of large cities, the most popular drugs among ghetto inhabitants are alcohol and marijuana. Heroin, barbiturates, and amphetamines appear to be used considerably less frequently.

Treatment and outcomes. Treatment for heroin addiction is initially similar to that for alcoholism, in that it involves building up the addict both physically and psychologically and helping him through the withdrawal period. Often the discomfort of the latter is greatly feared by the addict; in actuality, however, the withdrawal generally is not abrupt, but rather typically involves the administration of a synthetic drug that eases the distress.

After withdrawal has been completed, treatment then focuses on helping the former addict make an adequate adjustment to his community and abstain from the further use of narcotics. Traditionally, however, the prognosis has been unfavorable. Despite the use of counseling, group therapy, and other rehabilitative measures, only about 15 percent of persons formerly discharged from U.S. Public Health Service Hospitals did not become readdicted, and comparable findings were reported for other treatment facilities.[1]

Some former addicts experience shortened life spans because of their physically weakened conditions; and some become involuntarily abstinent as a result of imprisonment for criminal behavior. Others, however, appear to merely "mature out" of their heroin dependence. In a study of 7200 former addicts, it was found that the majority had voluntarily stopped using heroin by age 35, and that by the age of 47, all but 13 percent had done so (AMA, 1968a).

The fact remains, however, that the general results of hospital treatment have been disap-

---

[1]A narcotics addict who wishes hospitalization and treatment as a voluntary patient at the U.S. Public Health Service Hospital at Lexington, Ky., or at Fort Worth, Texas, can write to the Surgeon General of the United States, Public Health Service, Washington, D.C., who will see that he is furnished with necessary blanks and instructions. An increasing number of states are also establishing facilities for the treatment of narcotic addiction.

THE PROBLEM OF HEROIN ADDICTION IN THE MILITARY

In 1971 a congressional subcommittee visited Vietnam for the express purpose of assessing the extent of heroin use among American troops—an inquiry that brought to public attention facts concerning the nature and severity of the problem. Statistics provided to the subcommittee by the military indicated that some 10 to 15 percent of U.S. troops in Vietnam—30,000 to 40,000 men—were addicted to heroin, although other estimates ranged as high as 20 percent.

For purposes of detection and treatment the military instituted a comprehensive program: (1) amnesty for soldiers coming in voluntarily for treatment; (2) mandatory testing for heroin usage, via a simple urinalysis test, of all personnel leaving the service; and (3) detoxification for those found to be addicted.

The heroin used by the men was of very high quality, and most of those coming in for treatment—admittedly a very small percentage of the total—had either smoked the drug mixed with tobacco in cigarettes (51 percent) or had sniffed heroin powder from their cupped hands (43 percent); only 6 percent "mainlined" the drug directly into their veins. Unfortunately, many of the soldiers were under the impression that when heroin is smoked or snorted it is not addictive; they might pass around a "joint" of heroin as they would a "joint" of marijuana.

The congressional subcommittee further learned that the great majority of men who became addicted to heroin in Vietnam had not used it prior to military service. Reasons given for use of heroin varied, but they seemed to involve curiosity and "willingness to try anything once," the relief of tension in a combat zone, and boredom. Of course, the ready availability and low cost of the drug in Vietnam —the cost being a fraction of what it would be in the United States —and the highly addictive qualities of the relatively pure heroin to which they had been introduced contributed to the development of the addiction.

Complicating factors in a serious situation were the unwillingness of many soldiers to undergo treatment after discharge from service and the fact that treatment facilities at VA hospitals were extremely limited in relation to the size of the problem.

Based on Alsop (1971), Hughes (1971), McArthur (1971), Murphy and Steele (1971), Nixon (1971), and Witcover (1971).

---

pointing. One key difficulty appears to be the continued craving of the addict for heroin even after the withdrawal treatment has been concluded. As Dole (1965) has suggested, it appears possible that repeated exposure to heavy doses of narcotics may—like hormones or radiation—lead to irreversible changes in some bodily biochemical processes.[1] A key target in treatment must be the relief of physiological dependence on and long-range craving for the drug.

One promising approach to the problem of physiological craving for heroin has been pioneered by a research team at the Rockefeller University in New York. Their treatment approach involves the use of methadone in conjunction with a rehabilitation program (counseling, group therapy, and other procedures) directed toward the "total resocialization" of the addict (Dole & Nyswander, 1967; Dole, Nyswander & Warner, 1968). Interestingly enough, methadone hydrochloride is a synthetic narcotic which is related to heroin and is equally addictive physiologically. Its usefulness in treatment lies in the fact that it satisfies the addict's craving for heroin without itself producing notable psychological effects. In fact, when used in combination with heroin, methadone appears actually to *block* the latter's euphoric effects. In a study of 750 criminal addicts who experimented with heroin while on methadone, the subjects experienced little or no euphoria—a lack of reinforcement which may contribute to the extinction of the craving for heroin (Warner, 1968).

The methadone treatment approach usually involves a three-phase program. During the first phase the patient lives on an open ward for about six weeks. During this period methadone is administered in place of heroin to alleviate the addict's withdrawal symptoms; it is given in diminishing doses, then dosage is gradually stabilized at the particular level necessary to block the craving for heroin. During the second stage he attends an outpatient clinic where methadone is consumed each weekday and the supply for weekend use is dispensed. Finally the individual who has achieved a year's abstinence from heroin, and who is making a satisfactory readjust-

[1]Here it is perhaps useful to note that the most common function of all drugs—even those which are medically prescribed—is their alteration of cell metabolism. Typically, this change in cellular action is a temporary one designed to help combat the patient's problem. Nevertheless, the changes that drugs bring about in "target cells" are in a direction *away from normal functioning*. Thus, medication does not result in cells performing "better than ever." Of course, some drugs—such as hormones—do replace or supplement substances which are normally present in the body, and in this sense, they may improve the normal functioning of various organs and cells; but in general, drugs tend to block some important functions of cells. Hence, the general rule of thumb is the less drugs the better.

PSYCHOACTIVE DRUGS COMMONLY INVOLVED IN DRUG ABUSE

Classification	Drugs	Usage	Medical Usage	Tolerance	Physiological Dependence	Psychological Dependence
Sedatives	Alcohol (ethanol)	Reduce tension Facilitate social interaction "Blot out"	No	Yes	Yes	Yes

	Barbiturates
	  Nembutal (pentobarbital)
	  Seconal (secobarbital)
	  Veronal (barbital)
	  Tuinal (secobarbital and
	    amobarbital)
		Reduce tension
		Induce relaxation and sleep
			Yes	Yes	Yes	Yes

Stimulants	Amphetamines
	  Benzedrine
	    (amphetamine)
	  Dexedrine
	    (dextroamphetamine)
	  Methedrine
	    (methamphetamine)
		Increase feelings of alert-
		  ness and confidence
		Decrease feelings of fatigue
		Stay awake for long periods
			Yes	Yes	No	Yes

	Cocaine (coca)	Decrease feelings of fatigue Increase endurance Stimulate sex drive	No	No (minimal)	No	Yes

Narcotics	Opium and its derivatives
	  Opium
	  Morphine
	  Codeine
	  Heroin
		Alleviate physical pain
		Induce relaxation and
		  pleasant reverie
		Alleviate anxiety and
		  tension
			Yes, except
			heroin
				Yes	Yes	Yes

Psychedelics and Hallucinogens	Cannabis
	  Marijuana
	  Hashish
	Mescaline (peyote)
	Psilocybin (psychotogenic
	  mushrooms)
	LSD (lysergic acid diethyl-
	  amide-25)
		Induce changes in mood,
		  thought, and behavior
		"Mind expansion"
			No, except
			in research
				No—
				possible
				reverse
				tolerance
				(marijuana)
					No	Yes

Minor Tranquilizers	Librium (chlordiazepoxide
	  hydrochloride)
	Miltown (meprobamate)
	Valium (diazepam)
	Others, e.g., Compoz
	  (scopolamine)
		Alleviate tension and
		  anxiety
		Induce relaxation and
		  sleep
			Yes	Yes	Yes	Yes

In reviewing this list, it is important to note that it is by no means complete; e.g., it does not include many of the new drugs, such as Ritalin, which are designed to produce multiple effects; it does not include the less commonly used volatile hydrocarbons, such as glue, paint thinner, gasoline, cleaning fluid, and nail polish remover, which are highly dangerous when sniffed for their psychoactive effects; and it does not include the major tranquilizers and antidepressants which are abused, but relatively rarely. We shall deal with the major tranquilizers and antidepressants, as well as the minor tranquilizers, in our discussion of chemotherapy in Chapter 20.

It also should be noted that abuse can occur with both prescriptive and non-prescriptive drugs, and with both legal and illegal drugs.

Based on Isbell and Chrusciel (1970).

ment socially, enters the third phase, in which he attends the clinic just once a week to receive his supply of methadone. Of 863 volunteer addicts—all of whom were between the ages of 20 and 50, had injected heroin for at least four years, and had failed in other treatment programs—750 stopped using heroin. Although they were now methadone addicts, they were nonetheless productive and responsible members of their communities. The results of a four-year trial showed that nine out of ten former heroin addicts abstained from the further use of heroin—a figure that contrasts sharply with the poor record of success achieved by most earlier treatment programs.

In evaluating the preceding study, it may be pointed out that the average age of addicts in the program was older than that of the addict population in general, and participants were perhaps more strongly motivated to undertake treatment than are younger heroin addicts. In a second study of criminal addicts, however, Dole and Robinson (1969) randomly selected 12 who were prison inmates to receive the methadone treatment, as well as a control group of 16 convict-addicts. All had been addicts for at least five years, had had five or more jail sentences, and had volunteered for treatment. The results were impressive: none of the 12 addicts who were treated with methadone became readdicted to heroin; and 9 had no criminal convictions during a 50-week follow-up period. Conversely, of the 16 controls, all but one became readdicted after release from jail; and 15 were also convicted of crimes committed during the same 50-week follow-up period. These investigators concluded that at least 50 percent of all criminal addicts could be rehabilitated permanently by the methadone program of treatment. Similarly, in a five-year study of a methadone maintenance program involving over 2000 narcotic addicts, Gearing (1970) reported that previous antisocial behavior, as measured by arrests and related criteria, was eliminated or markedly reduced, and that there was a corresponding increase in employment and social adjustment.

Despite these promising findings, methadone alone does not appear sufficient to rehabilitate narcotic addicts. Although some former addicts make good life adjustments with little ancillary treatment, most require vocational training and other supportive measures if the overall treatment program is to prove effective (Jaffe,

1971; Perkins & Bloch, 1970; Ramer, Zaslove & Langan, 1971).

There is also the ethical problem of weaning the addict from heroin only to addict him to another drug that may be required for life. A response might be that addicts on methadone can function normally and hold jobs—accomplishments of which very few heroin addicts are capable. And in contrast to heroin, methadone is legally available at a cost of only about one dollar per week. In this context, it is interesting to note that Dole and Nyswander (1967) found no necessity of increasing the methadone dosage for any patient during a 3½-year follow-up period. Further research will show whether or not such individuals may eventually be taken off methadone. It is also encouraging to note that many addicts may be treated successfully with the methadone approach without requiring hospitalization, and are able to hold jobs and function in their family and community setting (Gearing, 1970; Jaffe, 1970a, 1971; Zaks, 1970).

In addition to methadone, other drugs not considered narcotics are undergoing tests as "antagonists" for overcoming a craving for heroin (Jaffe, 1970b; Jaffe & Senay, 1971). These drugs are still in the experimental stage, but they appear to suppress the craving for a much longer period than does methadone. In any event, we appear to be achieving a major breakthrough in the treatment of narcotic addiction through the approach pioneered with methadone.

In addition to the use of methadone and non-narcotic drugs in the treatment of heroin addiction, a number of other measures are aimed at the long-range alleviation of the narcotic problem in the United States. Among these are: (1) stepped-up efforts to eliminate the illegal importation of heroin from foreign sources; (2) the shift in public attitudes away from regarding the heroin addict as a "dope fiend," against whom punitive methods must be applied, to perceiving him as a person who needs medical attention and social rehabilitation; (3) the development of Narcotics Anonymous—which is modeled after and cooperates with Alcoholics Anonymous—for helping addicts deal with their drug problem and maintain abstinence; (4) the education of more young people—both formally in school and informally by observing the results of drug use among their peers—to the realization that using heroin "is just a dumb thing to do"; and (5) the establishment by the President of the United States in 1971 of a Special Action Office of Drug Abuse aimed at coordinating federal activities concerning drug usage—in research, treatment, and prevention. A trend may be noted toward updating and expanding treatment facilities for heroin addicts, which are extremely limited in relation to the magnitude of the drug problem.[1]

THE BARBITURATES

Until the middle of the nineteenth century, the only drugs available for easing tensions were herbs and alcoholic beverages. In the 1850's, new chemical compounds known as *bromides* were introduced. They immediately became popular as sedatives and were taken by millions of people. But with use came abuse; and the excessive consumption of bromides resulted in toxic psychoses —involving delusions, hallucinations, and a variety of neurological disturbances—which for a time became a leading cause of admissions to mental hospitals (Jarvik, 1967). Misuse of bro-

mides waned in the 1930's, however, when more powerful sedatives, called *barbiturates*, were introduced.

Effects. The barbiturates are the primary sedative drugs used by physicians to calm patients and/or induce sleep. They act as depressants— somewhat like alcohol—to slow down the action of the central nervous system. Shortly after taking the drug, there is an initial feeling of relaxation, in which tensions seem to disappear, followed by a physical and intellectual lassitude and a tendency toward drowsiness and sleep— the intensity of such feelings depending on the type and amount of the barbiturate taken. Strong doses produce sleep almost immediately, and excessive doses—resulting in paralysis of the respiratory centers of the brain—are lethal.

Barbiturate abuse leads to the building of tolerance as well as to psychological and physiological dependence. Especially prone to abuse are

---

[1]In this context, it is also of interest to note the legalization of heroin for addicts in England—under medical supervision—a policy which has cut the annual increase in known cases of addiction from 50 percent to 3 percent (Bewey, 1970). Whether such a program is feasible or desirable in the United States is currently a matter of controversy.

THE USE AND ABUSE OF MINOR TRANQUILIZERS

Aside possibly from alcohol, the psychoactive drugs most commonly used for coping are the minor tranquilizers, such as Librium, Miltown, and Valium. Many people use alcohol in moderate amounts for reducing tension as well as for facilitating social interaction; and, when taken under medical supervision, the minor tranquilizers have proven similarly helpful in alleviating anxiety and tension, particularly in relation to specific life stresses. But, again like alcohol, the minor tranquilizers are potentially dangerous because of possible side effects, because of ill-advised practices associated with their use, and because physiological dependence may result from their continued use.

Drowsiness and motor impairment are common side effects of the minor tranquilizers. Thus it is illegal in many states to drive while under the influence of tranquilizers; and such drugs can also be highly dangerous to people in occupations that require continual alertness and a high level of motor coordination. In fact, it would appear that far more accidents, both on and off the job, are associated with the misuse of legal drugs than with the use of illegal ones. There is also evidence that the meprobamates have been implicated in an increasing number of suicide attempts. And, of course, mixing mild tranquilizers with other psychoactive drugs may have potentiating or other undesirable effects; e.g., a medically prescribed barbiturate for

sleeping may be much more potent than intended when taken with alcohol and a tranquilizer.

The practice of mixing prescription drugs is more prevalent than may be supposed. In a study in Florida of the drug usage of 75 nonpsychiatric patients, it was found that 43 percent of them got their prescription drugs from more than one physician; that the average number of prescription drugs taken by each patient was 3.2; and that one patient was taking drugs that exposed him to more than 28 chemicals monthly (Stewart, Finger & Cluff, 1971, p. 365).

Another dangerous practice, common among many husbands and wives, is to use each other's tranquilizers and other prescription drugs. Here, the danger is comparable to that involved in taking drugs prescribed by more than one physician, for in neither case are the drugs being taken under competent supervision.

Even when used as prescribed, it should be recognized that the continual use of minor tranquilizers in heavy dosage can build up tolerance and physiological dependence; and abrupt cessation of usage may lead to serious withdrawal symptoms.

Based on Employers Insurance of Wausau (1971), Greenblatt and Shader (1971), and Stewart, Finger, and Cluff (1971).

the short-acting barbiturates, such as seconal ("red devils") and tuinal ("rainbows"); long-acting barbiturates, such as phenobarbital, are not so subject to abuse, due to their failure to produce quick effects.

Dynamics. Although many young people experiment with barbiturates, or "downs," most do not become dependent on them. Indeed, individuals who do become dependent on barbiturates tend to be middle-aged and older persons who do not commonly rely on other classes of drugs—with the possible exception of alcohol and the minor tranquilizers. Often these persons are referred to as "silent abusers," since they take the drugs in the privacy of their homes and ordinarily do not become public nuisances. Dependence occurs as a result of the gradual building of tolerance, and the concomitant tendency to take an increased dosage to get the required effect. Physiological dependence does not occur in persons who have maintained the normal dosage range. As with alcoholism, barbiturate dependence seems to occur in the emotionally maladjusted person who seeks relief from feelings of anxiety, tension, inadequacy, and the stresses of life (AMA, 1968a; Ewing & Bakewell, 1967).

Unfortunately, barbiturate users are often driven to illegal channels of supply in order to obtain quantities of the drug sufficient to maintain their habits. In addition, reliance on this class of drugs leads to a variety of undesirable side effects which are likely to complicate rather than relieve the individual's problems. Among these are general sluggishness, slow speech, poor comprehension, impaired memory, lability of affect, confusion, irritability, incoordination, and depression. Problem solving and decision making consequently require great effort, and the individual is aware that his thinking is "fuzzy." In extreme cases, the individual may remain bedridden in a semistuporous state. And, whereas building tolerance to the opiates raises their lethal limit, this is not true for the barbiturates—so that death can readily occur through an overdose, whether intentional or accidental. Indeed, barbiturates are associated with more suicides than any other drug (AMA, 1968a).

Occasionally, when an individual has built a high level of tolerance to a barbiturate through prolonged abuse, it may have an exhilarating rather than a depressive effect, and he may experi-

ONE GIRL WHO PLAYED WITH BARBITURATES AND LOST

Judi A. was a young attractive girl from a middle-class family who apparently was seeking something that eluded her. She died of an overdose of barbiturates. The newspaper account of her death began with a statement from the autopsy report:

"The unembalmed body for examination is that of a well-developed, well-nourished Caucasian female measuring 173 cm. (68 inches), weighing 100–110 pounds, with dark blonde hair, blue eyes, and consistent in appearance with the stated age of . . . .

"Judi A. had lived only 17 years, 5 months and 27 days before her nude body was found on a grimy bed which had been made up on the floor of a rundown apartment in Newport Beach [California].

"The inside of her mouth and her tongue were a bright red. The fingers of both hands were stained with the same color . . . A small pill was found on the bed near the body, another was discovered on the floor.

"Judi's death was classified as an accident because there was no evidence that she intended to take her own life. Actually it was about as accidental as if she'd killed herself while playing Russian roulette.

"Judi didn't intentionally take too many reds. She was familiar with them, had taken them before, knew what to expect. She'd even had an earlier scare from a nonfatal overdose.

"But her mind, clouded by the first few pills, lost count and she ingested a lethal number. She was dying before she swallowed the last pill. . . ." (Hazlett, 1971, p. 1)

A complete investigation was ordered, in which it came to light that Judi took drugs when she was unhappy at home, apparently often feeling unloved and unwanted. Following the breakup of her parents' marriage, she lived with her grandparents—neither of whom seemed to have been aware of her drug problem and hence had not attempted to help her with it.

Judi escalated the odds against herself by combining barbiturates with alcohol. Her friends said she was not particularly different from the other girls they knew, most of whom also took pills in combination with beer or wine. In Judi's case, however, the combination was lethal. She never found the something that eluded her, but she did find death.

ence a sense of increased efficiency and self-confidence. However, prolonged excessive use of the drug leads to mental deterioration and brain damage.

Sometimes barbiturates are taken by heroin addicts who lack a supply of their drug, or by teen-agers who combine them with other drugs to induce "far-out" effects. For example, most teen-agers who abuse barbiturates, or "downs," do so by taking them in tandem with the amphetamines, or "ups," which are cortical stimulants

(Mothner, 1970). Some young people also claim they can achieve a kind of "controlled hypersensitivity" by combining barbiturates, amphetamines, and alcohol (AMA, 1968a). However, when barbiturates are combined with alcohol, one possible "far-out" effect is death, since each drug potentiates (increases the action of) the other.

Treatment and outcomes. As with many other drugs, it is often essential in treatment to distinguish between barbiturate intoxication, which results from the toxic effects of overdosage, and the abstinence syndrome associated with withdrawal of the drug from addicted users. We are primarily concerned with the latter. Here the symptoms are more dangerous, severe, and long-lasting than in opiate withdrawal. The patient becomes anxious, apprehensive, and manifests coarse tremors of the hands and face; additional symptoms commonly include insomnia, weakness, nausea, vomiting, abdominal cramps, rapid heart rate, elevated blood pressure, and loss of weight. Between the sixteenth hour and the fifth day convulsions may occur. An acute delirious psychosis often develops, which may include symptoms similar to those in delirium tremens.

For individuals taking larger dosages, the withdrawal symptoms may last for as long as a month, but usually they tend to abate by the end of the first week. Fortunately, the withdrawal symptoms in barbiturate addiction can be minimized by the administration of increasingly smaller doses of the barbiturate itself, or by another drug producing pharmacologically similar effects. The withdrawal program is still a dangerous one, however, especially if barbiturate addiction is complicated by alcoholism or dependence on other drugs.

Although the elimination of psychological dependence on barbiturates may also require psychotherapy or other treatment, this is not so severe a problem as in the case of opiate addiction, where the individual may have an overpowering desire to take the drug even after the physical dependence has been broken.

COCAINE AND THE AMPHETAMINES

In contrast to the barbiturates, which depress or slow down the action of the central nervous system, cocaine and the amphetamines have chemical effects that stimulate or speed up the activity of the CNS.

Cocaine. Like opium, cocaine is a plant product discovered and used by ancient man. As Jarvik (1967) has pointed out:

"The Indians of Peru have chewed coca leaves for centuries and still do, to relieve hunger, fatigue, and the general burdens of a miserable life." (p. 52)

Its use has been endorsed by such diverse figures as Sigmund Freud and the legendary Sherlock Holmes; but although its use appears to have increased among young people in the United States, it is not a commonly used drug.

Like opium, cocaine may be ingested by sniffing, swallowing, or injecting. And like the opiates, it precipitates a euphoric state of four to six hours' duration, simultaneous with which the user experiences feelings of peace and contentment. However, this blissful state may be preceded by headache, dizziness, and restlessness. In certain predisposed persons, acute toxic psychotic symptoms may occur, encompassing frightening visual, auditory, and tactual hallucinations, such as the "cocaine bug."

Because of its anesthetic qualities, cocaine is sometimes used as a substitute for morphine. Unlike the opiates, however, cocaine is a cortical stimulant, inducing sleeplessness and excitement, as well as stimulating and accentuating sexual processes. Consequently, individuals with deviate sexual patterns have been known to administer it as an impetus to seduction. Dependence on cocaine also differs from that on opiates, in that tolerance is not increased appreciably with its use, nor is there any physiological dependence.

However, psychological dependence on cocaine, like addiction to opiates, often leads to a centering of behavior around its procurement, concurrent with a loss of social approval and self-respect. The following case illustrates this pattern:

The subject was a strikingly pretty, intelligent girl of 19 who had divorced her husband two years previously. She had married at the age of 16 and stated that she was terribly in love with her husband but that he turned out to be cruel and brutal.

The girl was too ashamed of her marital failure (her parents had violently opposed the marriage and she had left home against their will) to return to her home. She moved away from her husband and got a job as a cocktail waitress in the same bar where her husband had been accustomed to taking her. She was severely depressed, and several of his friends insisted on buying her drinks to cheer her up. This process continued for almost a year, during which she drank excessively but managed to hold her job.

Following this, she met a man in the bar where she worked who introduced her to cocaine, assuring her that it would cheer her up and get rid of her blues. She states that it both "hopped me up and gave me a feeling of peace and contentment." For a period of several months she purchased her supplies of cocaine from this same man until she became ill with appendicitis and was unable to pay the stiff price he asked. Following an appendectomy, she was induced to share his apartment as a means of defraying her expenses and ensuring the supply of cocaine which she had now become heavily dependent on psychologically. She stated that she felt she could not work without it. During this period she had sexual relations with the man although she considered it immoral and had severe guilt feelings about it.

This pattern continued for several months until her "roommate" upped his prices on the cocaine, on the excuse that it was getting more difficult to obtain, and suggested that she might be able to earn enough money to pay for it if she were not so prudish about whom she slept with. At this time the full significance of where her behavior was leading seems to have dawned on her and she came voluntarily to a community clinic for assistance.

Treatment for psychological dependence on cocaine does not differ appreciably from that for other drugs which involve no physiological dependence. Aversion therapy, group techniques, and related procedures may all be utilized. However, as in the case with other such drugs, feelings of tension and depression may have to be dealt with during the immediate withdrawal period.

The amphetamines. The earliest amphetamine to be introduced—Benzedrine, or amphetamine sulfate—was first synthesized in 1927, and became available in drugstores in the early 1930's as an inhalant to relieve stuffy noses. However, the manufacturers soon learned that some customers were chewing the wicks in the inhalers, for "kicks." Thus, the stimulating effects of amphetamine sulfate were discovered by the public before the drug was formally prescribed as a stimulant by physicians. In the late 1930's two

newer amphetamines were introduced—Dexedrine (dextroamphetamine) and Methedrine (methamphetamine hydrochloride). The latter preparation is a far more potent stimulant of the central nervous system than either Benzedrine or Dexedrine, and hence is considered more dangerous. In fact, its abuse is lethal in an appreciable number of cases (Citron, 1970).

Initially these preparations were considered to be "wonder pills" that helped people stay alert and awake and function temporarily at a level beyond normal. Thus, during World War II military interest was aroused in the stimulating effects of these drugs, and they were used by both allied and German soldiers to ward off fatigue (Jarvik, 1967). Similarly, in the civilian sphere, amphetamines came to be widely used by night workers, long-distance truck drivers, students cramming for exams, and athletes striving to improve their performances. It was also discovered that the amphetamines tended to suppress appetite, and they became popular among persons trying to lose weight. Then, too, they were often used to counteract the effects of barbiturates or other sleeping pills that had been taken the night before.

Today about 8 billion amphetamine pills are manufactured in the United States every year—enough to give each man, woman, and child 35 doses apiece. This is a figure far in excess of known medical requirements, and it has been estimated that about half of these pills go into black-market channels (Bengelsdorf, 1970b; Nelson, 1969).

1. *Effects and dynamics.* Today the amphetamines, or "pep pills," are used medically for (a) curbing the appetite when weight reduction is desirable, (b) relieving fatigue and maintaining alertness for sustained periods of time, and (c) alleviating mild feelings of depression. They are also used for individuals suffering from narcolepsy—a disorder in which the subject cannot prevent himself from continually falling asleep during the day—as well as for the treatment of hyperactive children. Curiously enough, the amphetamines have a calming rather than a stimulating effect on most of these youngsters.

Although the amphetamines have their legitimate medical uses, the AMA (1968a) has emphasized that they are not a magical source of extra mental or physical energy, but rather serve to push the user toward a greater expenditure of his own resources—often to a point of hazardous fatigue. In fact, many athletes have damaged their careers by the abuse of "speed" in trying to improve their stamina and performance (Furlong, 1971). It has also been suggested that they are much too freely prescribed for weight reduction, in view of their short-term effectiveness and the possible dangers inherent in their abuse. For example, an overweight person may like the stimulating effects of the pills, and consequently may take more than he is supposed to.

THE AMPHETAMINE "DRUG PARTY"

The following account of small "drug parties" is by a psychiatrist (Griffith, 1966), who was permitted to observe five such affairs involving youths who had been on amphetamines for up to 72 hours. While a party was usually attended by from 4 to 9 persons, the attendance actually fluctuated, with members coming and going.

"The term 'party' is a misnomer to a nonparticipating observer. It is an incredibly dull affair, except for the demonstrations of aberrant behavior, and in many ways resembles the day room of a back ward in a state mental hospital. Most such gatherings are unplanned. Usually, two or more users will meet by chance, arrange to get a supply of drugs in a variety of ways, then retreat to a secluded spot where they can take drugs unmolested. This is carried out with elaborate precautions to avoid detection. Members speak in low tones, draw blinds, and bolt doors.

"Without preliminary conversation they settle down to the business of taking drugs. Amphetamines are generally taken first, followed by barbiturates in most instances, if both are available. The object then becomes to titrate these two drugs to achieve the desired mental state. While taking drugs, the users sprawl about the room and are quite casual about their state of undress. Partially clad or undraped females attract little attention from the male users. A radio is played to drown out ambient noise.

"Initially, very little activity occurs. Members seem content with even uncomfortable postures. Their faces are flaccid and expressionless, and they show little interest in things about them. The only activities at this stage are smoking, taking drugs, or visiting the bathroom. These acts are carried out in well-coordinated but slowed peculiar gliding movements which make almost no noise. Although a member might occasionally grow verbose for a few moments, conversation is usually nothing more than quick, terse sentences such as 'You all right?' 'Yeah, I'm O.K.' The only exception to this still life is if someone begins to vomit. This will galvanize the entire group, including the author, to find a wastepaper basket for the nauseated individual.

"After one to four hours, members become more active. They lose their initial sense of caution. Some wander out of the room on various errands and the door is not bolted. Members begin to seek out one another for brief exchange of conversation about drugs, their illegal activities, or for lengthy hypochondriacal dissertations. Regardless of how these conversations begin, they usually are terminated when one brings up a mutual grievance between the two. After a brief exchange of sarcasm or anger, both parties drop the subject and retreat.

"Another type of interaction occurs when an individual becomes preoccupied with a painful incident in his past, such as having been jilted by a girl friend. The other drug users find this amusing and will 'egg on' the disturbed individual in a very subtle manner. Appearing quite sympathetic, they will help him organize his grievance and fabricate details to support his irritation, confiding, for example, that they are having relations with the girl friend and that they know from personal experience that she is, indeed, no good. Rage reactions are common under these circumstances and are signals that the game is over.

"During the first 24–48 hours of drug use, underlying conflicts, although never far from the surface, seldom escape the usual ego controls of the drug user. During and after the second day, however, this control may be lost and distinct psychotic behavior and personality changes develop. Most striking are changes in affect which become at first inappropriate, then quite blunted, and assume a sham quality.

"Accompanying these changes in affect is a distinct loss of reality testing. Thought processes take on a distinct paranoid quality which eventually replaces more rational thinking. Initial concern is that there is some sort of danger outside the room such as the police or the impending appearance of an old antagonist. Later people inside the room become imagined sources of danger or derision. Such delusional systems are poorly organized and the individual may quickly shift his concern from one preoccupation to another.

"Hallucinatory phenomena also occur, frequently as a preamble for the more distinct paranoid state. These are first manifest as simple illusions such as the over-interpretation of a shadow, a sound outside, a hum in the air conditioner, or a glint from a shiny object. Except for 'spiders dancing' . . . true visual hallucinations were denied. . . . Auditory hallucinations are quite common although short-lived and are rarely systematized. . . . Disorientation for time and place but not for person or self, was also observed by the author. Later, affected individuals have partial amnesia for these events.

"These psychotic symptoms can be quite troublesome to the individuals and to the group. For this reason they increase the amount of drugs taken. Although this has a quieting effect, the psychotic state is unaltered. Although no parties were observed in a stage of evolution longer than 72 hours, users report that after five days no quantity of drug has either a desirable or quieting effect. At this point, or earlier, the party is self-terminating." (pp. 566–567)

Griffith acknowledged that his sample was limited and that broad generalizations with respect to types of drug parties and their effects on participants could not be made from his observations; and, of course, changing patterns of drug usage could lead to different types of "drug parties." Specifically with respect to the amphetamines, however, he referred to the Japanese experience with over 200,000 amphetamine addicts after World War II. Japanese investigators reported that excessive consumption of amphetamines can produce permanent organic brain damage and serious psychiatric complications ranging from severe personality disorders to chronic psychoses.

As with other drugs, the effects of amphetamines may vary with the type, the dosage, the length of time they are taken, and the physical and psychological state of the individual user. Although amphetamines are not considered to be physiologically addictive, the body does build up tolerance to them very rapidly. Thus, habituated users may consume pills by the mouthful several times a day in amounts that would be lethal to nonusers. In some instances, users inject the drug to get faster and more intense results. To get "high" on amphetamines, persons may give themselves from 6 to 200 times the daily medical dosage usually prescribed for dieters. If lesser amphetamines do not provide a sufficient reaction, then Methedrine, or "speed," will produce the desired high. In some instances, amphetamine abusers go on "sprees" lasting several days.

For the person who exceeds prescribed dosages, consumption of amphetamines results in heightened blood pressure, enlarged pupils, unclear or rapid speech, profuse sweating, tremors, excitability, loss of appetite, confusion, and sleeplessness. In rare instances, the jolt to body physiology from "shooting" methedrine can raise blood pressure enough to cause immediate death. In addition, the chronic abuse of amphetamines can lead to a mental disorder known as *amphetamine psychosis*, which investigators consider to be highly similar to paranoid schizophrenia.

Suicide, homicide, assault, and various other acts of violence are commonly associated with amphetamine usage. In the United States, Ellinwood (1971) studied 13 persons who committed homicide under amphetamine intoxication and found that, in most cases, "the events leading to the homicidal act were directly related to amphetamine-induced paranoid thinking, panic, emotional lability, or lowered impulse control." (p. 90) And a study of 100 hospital admissions for amphetamine intoxication revealed that 25 of the subjects had attempted suicide while under the influence of the drug (Nelson, 1969).

2. *Treatment and outcomes.* Withdrawal from amphetamines is usually painless from a physical standpoint, since there is no physiological addiction. But psychological dependence is another matter, and abrupt abstinence can result in serious depression and suicidal tendencies (AMA, 1968a). And although the paranoid delusions and hallucinations involved in amphetamine psychosis usually disappear when the drug is taken away (Nelson, 1969), treatment of psychotic states—in cases where excessive use of amphetamines has resulted in brain damage—may be more complicated and residual effects may remain. In such instances memory, ability to concentrate, and learning appear to be the areas most commonly affected. This finding is somewhat in conformance with the AMA (1968a) statement that chronic abuse and dependence on amphetamines may result in social, economic, and personality deterioration.

THE MAJOR HALLUCINOGENS: LSD

This classification is composed of drugs whose properties are thought to induce hallucinations; in point of fact, however, these preparations do not so often "create" sensory images as distort them—so that the individual sees or hears things in ways different from those in which he is accustomed to experiencing them. The major drug in this category is LSD, or lysergic acid diethylamide, a chemically synthesized substance first discovered in 1938.

Other commonly used hallucinogens include mescaline, a substance derived from the tops ("mescal buttons") of the peyote cactus, and psilocybin, a drug obtained from a variety of "sacred" Mexican mushroom known as *psilocybe mexicana*. These two drugs have been used for centuries in Central and South America, and they were used by the Aztecs for ceremonial and sacred rites long before the Spanish invaded the land. Both drugs have mind-altering and hallucinogenic properties, but in moderate amounts they appear to be far less potent than LSD.

Our present discussion will be restricted to LSD. In view of its unusual hallucinogenic properties and potentialities for research into brain functioning, we shall deal with it in some detail.

Nature and effects of LSD. The most potent of the hallucinogens, the odorless, colorless, and tasteless drug LSD can produce intoxication in an amount smaller than a grain of salt (AMA, 1968b). However, Hoffman, the Swiss chemist responsible for its initial synthesis in 1938, did not discover its potent hallucinatory qualities until some five years later when he swallowed a small amount. This is his report of the experience:

"Last Friday, April 16, 1943, I was forced to stop my work in the laboratory in the middle of the afternoon and to go home, as I was seized by a peculiar restlessness associated with a sensation of mild dizziness. On arriving home, I lay down and sank into a kind of drunkenness which was not unpleasant and which was characterized by extreme activity of imagination. As I lay in a dazed condition with my eyes closed (I experienced daylight as disagreeably bright) there surged upon me an uninterrupted stream of fantastic images of extraordinary plasticity and vividness and accompanied by an intense, kaleidoscope-like play of colours. This condition gradually passed off after about two hours." (Hoffman, 1971, p. 23)

Hoffman followed up this experience with a series of planned self-observations with LSD, some of which he described as "harrowing." Researchers thought LSD might be useful for the induction and study of hallucinogenic states or "model psychoses," which were thought to be related to schizophrenia. About 1950, LSD was introduced into the United States for purposes of such research and of ascertaining its possible medical or therapeutic uses (Rinkel, 1966). However, as we have noted, model psychoses produced by drugs—including LSD—are different from schizophrenia, and to date LSD has not proven therapeutically useful in the treatment of alcoholism or other mental disorders.

In the meantime, the remarkable effects of LSD were widely publicized, and a number of relatively well-known people experimented with the drug and gave glowing accounts of their "trips." In fact, in the early 1960's an "LSD Movement" was under way, based on the conviction that the drug could "expand the mind" and enable one to use talents and realize potentials previously undetected. The movement was directed toward college students and young adults; and since then many young people have experimented with LSD—both in the United States and in other countries as well.

After taking LSD a person typically goes through about eight hours of changes in sensory perception, lability of emotional experiences, and feelings of depersonalization and detachment. The peak of both physiological and psychological

effects usually occurs between the second and fourth hours. Physiological effects include increased heart rate, elevation in blood pressure, augmented muscle tone, and faster and more variable breathing.

As LSD takes effect, the most important psychic manifestation is a tremendous intensification of sensory perception. Objects seem to become clearer, sharper, and brighter, and endowed with dimensions that the subject has never before perceived. Thus he may lose himself in contemplation of a flower, seeing in it colors that he has never seen before, hearing the movements of its petals, and feeling that at last he understands its essential nature. Another phenomenon associated with the drug has been called "humanity identification"—a sensation in which the individual feels himself to be in empathic concert with all mankind in the experiencing of such universal emotions as love, loneliness, or grief.

In addition to the intensity of the basic perceptual and affective reactions that occur in the early stages of the LSD experience, Katz, Waskow, and Olsson (1968) have pointed to certain contradictory aspects of that experience. These include:

"1. Very strong but opposing emotions occurring approximately at the same time, emotions which may not have a cognitive counterpart;
2. A feeling of being out of control of one's emotions and thoughts;
3. A feeling of detachment from the real world;
4. A feeling of perceptual sharpness, but at the same time perceptions of the outer world as having an unreal quality;
5. The perception of the world and others as 'friendly' but 'suspicious.'" (p. 13)

In this context it should be emphasized that the LSD "trip" is not always pleasant. It can be extremely harrowing and traumatic, and the distorted objects and sounds, the illusory colors, and the new thoughts can be menacing and terrifying. If the drug is administered to a psychotic person, there is typically a marked exaggeration of his psychotic symptomatology; if taken by a maladjusted person, it is likely to lead to bizarre and often dangerous behavior (Szara, 1967). Rorvik (1970) has cited the case of a young British law student who tried to "continue time" by using a dental drill to bore a hole in his head while under the influence of LSD. In other instances, persons undergoing "bad trips" have set themselves aflame, jumped from high places, and taken other drugs which proved a lethal combination. In a study of 114 subjects admitted to the Bellevue Hospital in New York City with acute psychoses induced by LSD, 13 percent showed overwhelming fear and another 12 percent experienced uncontrollably violent urges. Suicide or homicide had been attempted by approximately 9 percent of the subjects (Rorvik, 1970). In a study of chronic users of LSD, Blacker and his associates (1968) found that the "bum trip" usually began in a context of ire. For example, one of their subjects reported that he had taken LSD when he was angry with his mother. Initially his trip had been beautiful; then it exploded. He suddenly became very fearful, thought he could hear monsters coming up the stairs, and was convinced that they would come through the door to his room and eat him.

Here it may be emphasized that there are no precise criteria for assessment of persons to determine whether, for them, the use of LSD is "safe"—that is, not likely to lead to complications. For example, Ungerleider, Fisher, Fuller, and Caldwell (1968) compared 25 persons hospitalized following ingestion of LSD with 25 members of a group who took LSD regularly with no reported difficulties. Their results revealed no clinical features that could be used to predict a person's response to LSD with accuracy. The setting in which the drug was taken appeared to be influential, but a favorable milieu alone was no guarantee against adverse reactions. Even a single dose can trigger serious psychological complications. For example, in a study of 52 persons admitted to a New York hospital with LSD-induced psychoses, it was found that 26 had taken the drug only one time, and only 12 of the total subjects had shown evidence of serious maladjustment prior to their LSD psychosis (AMA, 1968b). On the other hand, even the same individual may be affected differently by the drug at different times. In fact, the preceding investigators cited cases of persons who had used LSD 100 or more times without apparent difficulty—and then suddenly developed severe, adverse reactions.

An interesting and unusual phenomenon that may occur following the use of LSD is the *flashback*: an involuntary recurrence of perceptual distortions or hallucinations weeks, or even months, after taking the drug. These experiences appear to be relatively rare among individuals who have taken LSD only once—although they do sometimes occur. On the other hand, it has been conservatively estimated that about 1 in 20 consistent users experience such flashbacks (Horowitz, 1969). Some persons react with fear to

---

EXAMPLES OF "FLASHBACKS" AFTER THE USE OF LSD

Approximately 1 in 20 users of LSD experience intrusive recurrent hallucinatory images which are known as "flashbacks." These images are usually of a negative and frightening nature, as indicated by the following examples reported by Horowitz (1969):

Pt. A: "Now I often see a bright shiny halo around people, especially at the dark edges—sometimes it's rainbow colors —like during the trip."

Pt. B: "Sometimes the sidewalk seems to bend as if it's going downward—even when I'm not on anything—or it just kinda vibrates back and forth."

Pt. C: "I see this giant iguana, all the time, man. Green. In corners. Like under your chair."

Pt. D: "Now I see things—walls, and faces, and caves—probably imprinted on my thalamus from the prehistoric past." (p. 566)

For other patients, experiences were comparable. One 17-year-old youth who had been terror-stricken when he hallucinated a scorpion on the back of his hand during a "bad trip" continued to have flashbacks of the scorpion five weeks later. A 16-year-old youth who had images during a "bad trip" of a human figure being sucked into the vortex of a whirlpool had the same image turn up about three weeks later, and they interrupted whatever he was thinking about 5 or 10 times a day. The flashbacks were frightening, and he could not rid himself of them; consequently he sought professional help.

Among LSD users who experience flashbacks, those who repeatedly use hallucinogens experience the more severe forms. Various causal factors have been implicated in the occurrence of flashbacks, including: (1) neurophysiologic changes in the brain, which disinhibit the retrieval of images from memory storage; (2) a built-in tendency to desensitize oneself to traumatic images experienced during a "bad trip" via the repetition of the images; and (3) the reactivation of primordial images imprinted on the mind, which recalls Jung's concepts of archetypes and the collective unconscious (see page 55).

Fortunately, flashbacks can be worked through in brief psychotherapy, following which they cease to recur.

**DRAWINGS REVEAL
EFFECT OF LSD**

these recurrent images which "seem to have a will of their own," and extreme anxiety and even psychotic reactions may result.

Studies by Rorvik (1970) and others have suggested that LSD may cause chromosomal damage and act as a carcinogenic agent as well as a potential cause of congenital malformations. However, other investigators have failed to find such effects at moderate dosage levels (Aase, Laestadius & Smith, 1971; Dishotsky et al., 1971). The user of LSD does not develop physiological dependence, nor apparently does he build up tolerance requiring increasingly large doses of the drug. However, some chronic users do develop psychological dependence—and, in a broader sense, sociological reliance as well.

On the other hand, the dangers of LSD usage have appeared to be almost nonexistent for persons who have taken it under supervision. In a follow-up study of 247 persons who received LSD in either an experimental or psychotherapeutic setting, McGlothin and Arnold (1971) concluded:

"There is . . . little evidence that measurable, lasting personality, belief, value, attitude, or behavior changes were produced in the sample as a whole. Compulsive patterns of LSD use rarely developed; the nature of the drug effect apparently is such that it becomes less attractive with continued use and, in the long term, is almost always self-limiting." (p. 35)

Here, a select sample of subjects used LSD in a favorable environmental setting under supervision; and whether the conclusions derived from the study would hold for young people who resort to illegal sources of LSD and use it without supervision is open to question. It may be noted, however, that 1 out of 7 college students reportedly has experimented with LSD (Gallup, 1971), but it appears doubtful that any substantial number of them continue to use it.

Dynamics. In general, three types of reasons have been advanced for the use of LSD.

1. *Curiosity and pleasure-seeking.* As in the case of other drugs, many persons who experiment with LSD are curious about its alleged ability to increase sensory awareness and about the possibility of experiencing a gratifying "mind-expanding trip." Pleasure-seekers have been described as mainly a passive lot: "They sit fascinated while new sounds, shapes, colors, and smells flood their senses, and new thoughts about themselves and their relationships to others

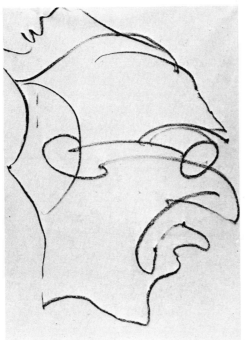

These drawings, produced by an artist who took LSD in a test held in Germany in 1951, indicate that the drug can produce loss of conscious control with accompanying impairment of the individual's motor capabilities. The progressive effects of the drug may be noted in the sequence of drawings on this row, and in the artist's final effort, below.

intrigue their minds" (AMA, 1968b, p. 12). Usually a "bad trip" will discourage this type of LSD user, although it may not deter others.

2. *Escaping from reality.* Some persons use LSD as a means of escape from the day-to-day stresses of reality. Some of these persons are so-called drug-dependent types, while others have been referred to simply as "alienated" or "disenchanted." In an intensive study of 21 chronic LSD users, Blacker et al. (1968) found them to be middle-class youths who, before taking the drug, had held apparently conventional beliefs but were frustrated and angry with their parents and their general life situations. Their use of LSD often appeared to represent their efforts to achieve a passive adaptation to life. However, it was suggested that the "repeated intensive emotional experiences arising out of the use of LSD provided a special learning environment" (p. 351), so that it was difficult or impossible to untangle the complex and interacting influences of the predrug personality from the effects of the drug experience and the social setting in which the drug was used. However, in a study of 100 LSD users and 46 nonuser controls, Smart and Jones (1970) found a high incidence of psychopathic characteristics, alienation, and emotional disturbances which appeared to predate the LSD usage. We shall comment further on the seeming "fit" between psychedelic drugs and the needs of such estranged youths in our discussion of marijuana.

3. *Self-improvement.* Many persons seeking self-improvement have attempted to use LSD as a vehicle for greater personal insight, increased sensitivity, mystic experiences, and better understanding of man and his universe. This category includes a sizable number of painters, writers, and composers who have attempted to use the drug not only for personal growth but also as a means of creating more original and meaningful works of art. However, there is no conclusive evidence that LSD enhances creative activity; no recognized works of art have apparently been produced under the influence of the drug nor as a consequence of a psychedelic experience. And although several imaginative persons have claimed improved creativity stemming from their LSD experiences, objective observers recognize few, if any, refinements (AMA, 1968b). In fact, under the direct influence of LSD, the drawings of one well-known American painter showed progressive deterioration; later, when asked if he felt his LSD experience had improved his ingenuity, he replied in the negative (Rinkel, 1966).

Treatment and outcomes. It has been estimated that about 3 percent of LSD users experience psychotic reactions, and another 10 percent are socially disabled, in that their use of the drug seriously impairs their educational and/or occupational efficiency. For acute psychoses induced by LSD intoxication, treatment requires hospitalization and is primarily a medical matter. Often the outcome in such cases depends heavily on the personal stability of the individual prior to his taking the drug.

In terms of treating the individual who is psychologically dependent on LSD, usual therapeutic techniques may be employed. Also on a psychological level, treatment often involves the working through of trauma experienced during "bad trips" which may yet haunt the subject in the form of flashbacks. Fortunately, brief psychotherapy—often involving repeated discussion of the psychedelic event and its effects—usually helps the individual work through and integrate the LSD experience into his overall

frame of reference and prevents the recurrence of flashbacks (Freedman, 1968; Horowitz, 1969).

MARIJUANA

Although marijuana may be classified as a mild hallucinogen, there are significant differences in the nature, intensity, and duration of its effects as compared with those induced by LSD, mescaline, and other major hallucinogens. In view of its current social significance in our country, we shall deal with this drug in some detail also.

Marijuana comes from the leaves and flowering tops of the weed known as *hemp*, or *cannabis*. It often grows wild and in appearance is similar to tobacco of a fine quality. In its prepared state, marijuana consists chiefly of the dried green leaves—hence the colloquial name "grass." It is ordinarily smoked in the form of cigarettes ("reefers" or "joints") or in pipes; but it can also be baked into cookies and other foods. In some cultures the leaves are steeped in hot water and the liquid is drunk, much as one might drink tea. Marijuana is related to the stronger drug, hashish, which is derived from the resin exuded by the cannabis plant and made into a gummy powder. As is the case with marijuana, hashish may be smoked, chewed, or drunk.

Both marijuana and hashish can be traced far back into the history of man's use of drugs. Cannabis was apparently known in ancient China when it was listed in the herbal compendiums of the Chinese Emperor Shen Nung, 2737 B.C. (Blum, 1969; Culliton, 1970).

Until the last decade, marijuana use in the United States was largely confined to members of lower socioeconomic minority groups and to people in entertainment and related fields (McGlothlin, Arnold & Rowan, 1970). However, the use of marijuana has shown a dramatic increase among youth since the middle of the 1960's. In one national survey, 42 percent of college students conceded that they had used marijuana (Gallup, 1971). Other studies have indicated that over 50 percent of the students in some high schools and over 10 percent of junior high school students have tried marijuana (Bengelsdorf, 1970c; Ingersoll, 1970; Kaplan, 1970). The percentage of regular or chronic users among young people is not known, but it has been estimated that 65 percent of those who try marijuana stop using it after experimenting one to ten times; that 25 percent continue to use it only periodically in social situations; and that 10 percent progress from occasional to habitual use (Yolles, 1969). Marijuana also seems to have made some inroads among young and middle-aged adults, who generally use it at parties and in other social settings. It has been used extensively by U.S. soldiers in Southeast Asia. Wilwerth (1971) has estimated that 90 percent of all noncareer soldiers in Vietnam tried or habitually used marijuana.

Effects. The specific effects of marijuana may vary greatly, depending on the quality and dosage of the drug, the personality and mood of the user, and the past experience of the subject with the drug. However, there is considerable consensus among regular users that when marijuana is smoked and inhaled, the individual gets "high." This state is one of mild euphoria distinguished by increased feelings of well-being, heightened perceptual acuity, and pleasant relaxation, often accompanied by a sensation of drifting or floating away. Sensory inputs are enhanced: music sounds fuller, colors look brighter, smells seem richer, and food tastes better. Somehow the world seems to become more meaningful, and even minor events may take on extraordinary profundity. Often there is a stretching out or distortion of the individual's sense of time, so that an event lasting but a few seconds may seem to cover a much longer span. Short-term memory may also be affected, as when an individual notices he has taken a bite of his sandwich but does not remember doing so. For most users, pleasurable experiences, including sexual intercourse, seem to be greatly enhanced. When smoked, marijuana is rapidly absorbed and its effects appear within seconds to minutes, but seldom last more than 2 to 3 hours. In tests of THC (the synthetically produced drug which appears to be the active ingredient in cannabis) effects may not be noted for 30 minutes to over 2 hours following oral ingestion (Hollister, 1971).

Marijuana may lead to unpleasant as well as pleasant experiences. For example, if an individual takes the drug while in an unhappy, angry, suspicious, or frightened mood, unsavory

events may be magnified. And with high dosages —as well as with certain unstable or susceptible persons—marijuana can produce extreme euphoria, hilarity, and overtalkativeness; it can also produce unpleasant reactions, including intense anxiety, confusion, depression, and perceptual distortions. Keeler (1970) has reported that about a fourth of the subjects in a study on the effects of marijuana told of the spontaneous occurrence of visual effects during later drug-free states. Infrequently, acute psychotic episodes are precipitated in susceptible individuals by moderate dosages, e.g., at social levels of usage (HEW, 1971). Heavy dosages of marijuana can produce depersonalization, hallucinations, and other psychoticlike behavior (HEW, 1971; Massett, 1970). It is of interest to note, however, that in a study reported by Nelson (1969), only 3 hospital admissions for marijuana abuse or intoxication were reported out of 90,733 consecutive admissions, while thousands of admissions and hundreds of deaths were associated with the abuse of alcohol, barbiturates, and amphetamines.

As we have noted, the individual's prior experience with marijuana appears to be an important factor in determining its effects. With mild dosages (about 0.5 gr.), most first users may notice little or no effect. Even with relatively high doses, the effects may differ markedly for experienced and nonexperienced users. In a comparison of nine college students naïve with respect to marijuana and eight who were regular users—all ranging in age from 21 to 26 years— Weil et al. (1968) found that even with high intake of the drug[1] the inexperienced subjects were affected differently than the experienced users. Nonusers reported minimal subjective effects, with little euphoria and no distortion of visual or auditory perceptions. All of the experienced users got "high," but only one nonuser responded in this manner. He was also the only nonuser who expressed a desire to get high. However, the inexperienced subjects were affected in their estimations of time, several of them mentioning that "things seemed to take longer." Nonusers also became more present-oriented, had difficulty maintaining a logical sequence of thought, and experienced significant impairment of perfor-

---

[1] 2.0 gr. of THC was considered to be a large dosage.

mance on simple intellectual and psychomotor tests. Chronic users, however, did not show this impairment, and in some cases performed even better after smoking. The findings suggest that the experienced user can suppress, or "turn off," its effects. As we have noted, however, some susceptible individuals are exceptions to this generalization.

In terms of its physiological effects, marijuana raises the heart rate moderately and slows reaction time, but does not appear to affect respiratory rate, blood sugar, or pupil size. It does, however, tend to cause bloodshot and itchy eyes, dry mouth, and increased appetite. The severe abuse of marijuana—for example, continued use of high dosages—tends to produce lethargy and passivity. Here it appears to have a depressant as well as a hallucinogenic effect.

Marijuana has often been compared to heroin, but the two drugs have little in common with respect to tolerance or to physiological dependence. Although studies conducted in Eastern countries have found evidence of tolerance to marijuana at high dosage levels over long periods of time, studies in the U.S.—which have involved lower dosages for shorter time periods—have failed to find evidence of tolerance (HEW, 1971). In fact, habitual users often show "reverse tolerance." This may be due in part to the users' having learned the proper method of smoking and to the suggestive influence of anticipated effects. In any event, habitual users rarely feel constrained to increase their doses to maintain desired effects (Hollister, 1971). Nor does marijuana lead to physiological dependence as in the case of heroin. Thus, discontinuance of the substance is not accompanied by withdrawal symptoms. Marijuana can, however, lead to psychological dependence, causing the individual to experience a strong need for it whenever he feels anxious and tense.

Dynamics and outcomes. Reasons for using marijuana run the usual gamut: (1) curiosity, thrill-seeking, and easy euphoria; (2) peer pressure for doing the "in thing"; (3) desire for self-improvement through gaining new insights and helping to realize one's potential; and (4) urge to dampen internal conflicts, insecurities, and anxieties, and escape from an intolerable life situation. The last category is often associated with the discouragement and depression of slum life,

as well as with the disillusionment of youth— including teen-age runaways—who "drop out" of the mainstream of society and join drug subcultures (Harris, 1971).

Treatment is similar to that for other drugs involving psychological but not physiological dependence. Ordinarily, users who seek treatment can fairly rapidly break their reliance on marijuana. However, for those heavy users who also regularly use alcohol—usually beer or wine— successful treatment may be more complicated (Mirin et al., 1971; Rorvik, 1970).

Some key questions concerning marijuana. The widespread use of marijuana in our society —coupled with a dearth of actual research findings—has raised a number of questions for which we do not yet have adequate answers.

1. *Does the long-term use of marijuana have harmful physical effects?* As typically used in the United States, marijuana appears to be a relatively mild drug. However, this fact does not guarantee that marijuana may not have long-range harmful effects on the body. It is difficult to formulate a research design that will definitely answer this question, since the study of chronic users of marijuana over sustained periods of time would involve a volunteer population of young people who are willing to admit that they regularly break the law—and these youths may not be representative of chronic marijuana users in general.

As yet, the only chronic physical effects directly linked to the long-term use of marijuana are permanent congestion of the transverse ciliary vessels of the eyes, together with yellow discoloration (HEW, 1971). If the synthesis of THC should result in a drug that is commercially distributable, however, it may become possible to obtain illicit marijuana of greatly increased strength and perhaps with harmful effects—both physically and psychologically.

2. *Does the use of marijuana have harmful psychological effects?* When used in moderation, neither alcohol nor marijuana appear to be harmful psychologically. However, when used in amounts sufficient to produce intoxication, marijuana may impair intellectual functioning—in terms of memory, comprehension, judgment, time estimation, and feelings of depersonalization (Clark et al., 1970; HEW, 1971; Melges et al., 1970). And as we have seen, in heavy dosage marijuana may have highly disorganizing and adverse effects, including anxiety attacks and acute psychotic episodes.

Several investigators have also concluded that when the teen-ager becomes dependent on marijuana and uses it as a crutch for dealing with the demands and stresses of life, his mental health and personal growth are likely to suffer (Kaufman et al., 1969; McGlothlin & West, 1968; Mirin et al., 1971; Yolles, 1969). However, it is important to note that young people who show detrimental psychological effects from using marijuana may have been maladjusted to begin with, and that the drug may simply provide a convenient escape route or intensify their symptoms when used in heavy dosages. It is possible that similar effects could result from the use of alcohol or other drugs by these youths.

In any event, the controversy concerning the long-range effects of marijuana—both physically and psychologically—continues and can only be resolved by further research.

3. Does the use of marijuana lead to the use of hard drugs? A number of investigators have noted that there is no inevitable progression from use of marijuana to hard drugs, such as heroin. Whereas a frequent user of marijuana may go on to become a "pothead" or chronic user in about 2 to 5 percent of the cases, the overwhelming majority of chronic users do not go on to narcotics (Ingersoll, 1970). And although a high proportion of heroin addicts have also used marijuana, this is not accepted as proof of a causal relationship between the two; in fact, a larger proportion of heroin users have probably used alcohol and other drugs than marijuana. It has been pointed out that in our society many youths go from alcohol to marijuana and LSD, then give up the LSD and settle for a pattern of marijuana and beer or wine (Reese, 1970). Such experimentation apparently is typical of the hard-drug user.

Blum (1970) has pointed out that many roads lead to the hard drugs. One road is associated with the discouragement and dejection of the slum-area teen-ager who feels insecure and inadequate, and who inhabits a world where heroin is both available and more or less socially sanctioned. A second pattern is commonly associated with drug exploration by youths in the "psychedelic" world, who progress to heroin out of curiosity and thrill seeking. In experimenting with heroin some of them inevitably get "hooked."

Still a third pattern apparently involves teenagers who find that the terrifying predictions of various authorities concerning the effects of marijuana are virtually never realized. As a consequence, they may assume that the use of illicit drugs—including heroin—is both safe and enjoyable.

Thus, aside from the relative merits or dangers of marijuana *per se*, various sociological factors may influence the picture. Indeed, in societies where marijuana and hashish are approved, their use does not appear to lead to use of or addiction to hard drugs. This, however, does not guarantee that cannabis is itself a safe drug, without inherent danger to its users.

4. Does the use of marijuana enhance an individual's creativity? Yolles (1969) and most other investigators have answered "no" to this question. Although marijuana may induce fantasies

REPORT OF THE INDIAN HEMP DRUG COMMISSION: A HISTORICAL PARALLEL

An interesting parallel may be drawn between contemporary studies of the effects of marijuana and an extensive study initiated by the British government in 1893. The House of Commons, in response to a member's motion, appointed the Indian Hemp Drug Commission to investigate effects of such drugs—which included marijuana. Results of the commission's research were published in 1894 in a 7-volume report, for which data had been gathered in 30 field trips to various cities in India and from interviews with 1193 witnesses (Mikuriya, 1969).

The commission's report was divided into three categories, indicative of the areas in which hemp drugs were popularly believed to have harmful effects:

1. **Health.** Although hemp drugs were believed to cause dysentery, bronchitis, and asthma, the commission concluded that in moderate dosage, hemp drugs were not physically harmful.

2. **Sanity.** Although it was also popularly believed that hemp drugs caused insanity, after going over all cases admitted to Indian mental hospitals for the year 1892, the commission concluded that this concept was based on established hospital diagnostic procedures and was fallacious.

3. **Crime.** After an intensive survey of available evidence, including a review of 81 crimes of violence alleged to have been caused by hemp usage, the commission concluded that there was little or no connection between the use of hemp drugs and crime.

Mikuriya (1969) has suggested that the commission's findings are relevant to contemporary efforts toward the legalization of marijuana.

that are highly creative—or at least seem so to the person experiencing them—what actually is produced in terms of writing, painting, and related creative pursuits is usually evaluated as no better—and often worse—than usual. As with the use of LSD and other hallucinogens, an individual may think he has found "the key to the universe"; but in fact, when he "comes down" it is not there.

Conceivably, enchanced feelings, perceptions, and thoughts altered while under the influence of hallucinogenic drugs can be translated into creative productivity, including new insights into the self, and even self-enhancement. As yet, however, this remains to be proved, and other avenues of "mind expansion" are being explored. We noted that humanistic psychologists are particularly interested in exploring nondrug techniques for enhancing awareness, enriching experience, and fostering personal growth; and we shall comment further on the "human potential movement" in Chapter 20.

5. *Should marijuana be legalized?* Many defenders of marijuana argue that it is no more dangerous than alcohol—and possibly less so; nor does it appear to be related appreciably to increasing violence and crime in the United States, except insofar as its use is illegal and hence constitutes a criminal act (HEW, 1971; McGlothlin, Arnold & Rowan, 1970; McGlothlin & West, 1968). Furthermore, the use of marijuana is not as closely associated with automobile accidents, injuries, and fatalities as is alcohol (Waller, 1971).

Adherents of the legalization of marijuana have pointed out that besides providing a freer access to a source of pleasure and tension reduction, legalization would provide another source of revenue from taxation; and that, since the federal government would supervise the production, distribution, and sale of marijuana, a safer product would be ensured.

Of greater concern to many people is the inequity of sanctioning the use of drugs that are known to be highly dangerous—such as alcohol and nicotine-containing tobacco—while making the use of marijuana a criminal offense. The costs are incalculable—and not just in financial terms—of putting a sizable segment of an entire generation outside the law and of making law-

enforcement agencies an "enemy" that depends on spies, "plants," and informants.

The opponents of legalization take a variety of approaches, one being to point out that removing governmental restrictions would inevitably lead to a marked increase in marijuana use —a development they perceive as a major risk, since we do not as yet have any definitive evidence concerning the long-range effects of the drug on psychological and physical well-being and health; they point to the example of cigarettes, which were once considered to be mild and safe but which have more recently been shown to be hazardous. They also point out that until research does yield more definitive evidence concerning the drug's long-range effects, no one is likely to be harmed by abstaining from its use.

In our society, we appear to be divided and indecisive—both in thought and action—with respect to how best to cope with the marijuana problem; and until this problem is appropriately resolved, it will continue to exact a high toll. Fisher (1968) helped put the marijuana problem in perspective when he noted that the drugs used in a particular society to relieve frustration, anxiety, and tension—and to provide some measure of enjoyment—are based on that society's customs and values. In Eastern societies, the drug of choice is marijuana; in Western societies, it is alcohol.

PERSPECTIVES ON DRUG USAGE

In his book *The Doors of Perception*, author Aldous Huxley remarked:

"That humanity at large will ever be able to dispense with Artificial Paradises seems very unlikely. Most men and women lead lives at worst so painful, at the best so monotonous, poor and limited that the urge to escape, the longing to transcend themselves if only for a few moments, is and has always been one of the principal appetites of the soul." (1954, p. 62)

Although we may not share Huxley's gloomy view of man's lot, we must admit that drugs are important to many people in our culture. In times of turmoil and stress, drugs are often turned to as a means of alleviating anxiety and of coping with existential problems.

In many instances, psychoactive drugs appear to serve a useful function—as in the use of tranquilizers for alleviating anxiety, or in the moderate use of alcohol for reducing tension and facilitating social interaction. And many responsible persons have argued the beneficial effects of marijuana in increasing awareness and enriching experience. However, in other instances, easy drug solutions to the problems of life are sought in place of more effective coping methods. And, as we have seen, psychoactive drugs are also associated with possible abuse, tolerance, and dependence. Thus it may be emphasized that such drugs are two-edged swords that can help us cope with stress and possibly enhance our experience, or they can literally wreck our lives.

To conclude on a positive note, we may emphasize once again the advances in psychopharmacology which modern science and technology are making possible.

" . . . drugs may be employed not only to treat pathological conditions (reduce pain, suffering, agitation, and anxiety), but also to enhance the normal state of man—increase pleasure, facilitate learning and memory, reduce jealousy and aggressiveness. Hopefully, such pharmacological developments will come about as an accompaniment of, and not as a substitute for, a more ideal society." (Jarvik, 1967, p. 59)

A note of caution might well accompany this optimistic view, however. For there always remains the danger that in turning to drugs to escape from unpleasant reality, to resolve problems, and to find euphoria, man will be entering a false paradise.

In the present chapter we have reviewed the nature and effects of the major drugs—including alcohol—that are associated with dependence in our society; and we have examined some of the etiological factors involved in such dependence —the characteristics of the drug itself, the physical and psychological makeup of the individual, and the social setting in which the drug is used. Amid the complexities and personal and social implications of drug dependence two variables appear to be of central importance: (1) the drug-oriented nature of our society, and (2) problems of social control.

While both the older and younger generations use drugs for reducing anxiety and tension, escaping from stressful life situations, and coping more effectively with the problems of living, the younger generation has also turned to drugs for other reasons, such as "mind expansion," pleasure, new thrills and experiences, and increased self-insight and personal growth. Thus there has arisen a "value gap," or a difference in value orientations between the generations, that complicates the problem of drug abuse and social control.

Since many, if not most, mind-altering drugs have potentially harmful effects—particularly if they are abused—society feels it necessary to exercise some sort of control over their use. Thus, most drugs considered potentially dangerous if abused are available only on prescription by a physician. However, in the case of certain controversial drugs it is often difficult to exercise effective controls. This is particularly true if large segments of the population simply ignore such controls, as has been the case with marijuana.

One key issue in control is that of which drugs to legalize; and a second is whether illicit drug abuse should be dealt with as a crime or as a medical, psychological, and social problem and treated accordingly. Until there is some understanding of and agreement concerning the hazards of various drugs and the value to be placed on their use or control, the effective control of drugs is likely to continue to pose a major social problem.

Sexual Deviations

13

CLASSIFICATION AND CAUSES OF SEXUAL DEVIANCE

"NORMAL" SEXUAL DEVIATIONS

ABNORMAL SEXUAL DEVIATIONS

SOCIALLY ORGANIZED AND RELATED SEXUAL DEVIATIONS

The development of adult sexual behavior from the undifferentiated potentialities of the infant is a long and complex process, and the resulting patterns are by no means uniform. Moreover, variations are evident in the prevailing attitudes of different cultures toward these patterns. Each society approves or disapproves of certain sexual patterns and labels certain individuals as "deviant"; but few patterns appear to be universally condemned. For many patterns, including polygamy, prostitution, and homosexuality, sharply contrasting attitudes are found. In addition, attitudes often change over time within a given culture.

In our own society, there is a widespread challenging of traditional sexual mores, plus a concerted attempt to evaluate the appropriate role of sexual behavior in living. Is monogamous marriage the only "normal" adult pattern? Should premarital and extramarital intercourse be encouraged or at least sanctioned? What avenues of gratification should be open to the person who does not marry? Many sexual patterns formerly considered "perverse" or "immoral" are being examined anew; some are even being redefined as desirable. Thus many young people today, and some older ones, believe that premarital sexual relations and even extramarital relations should be permitted or possibly encouraged. Mouth-genital contact—considered a "crime against nature" in many states and punishable as a felony—has apparently become relatively acceptable and common in courting and marital behavior. Many people are redefining homosexuality as a permissible alternative to heterosexual relationships. And some subgroups are experimenting with "wife-swapping," communal sex, and group sexual practices.

Thus the question arises as to what range of sexual patterns should be considered permissible, both personally and socially. This question is difficult to answer, not only because of the challenging of traditional sexual mores by the counterculture, but also because of our inability to ascertain how much the present "sexual revolution" involves actual changes in behavior and how much it reflects only greater frankness about what has always been going on.

Because of taboos regarding the study of sexual behavior in our society, as well as the problems concerning the invasion of individual privacy, research data in this area are meager. The first comprehensive field studies were carried out by Kinsey, Pomeroy, and Martin (1948; 1949; 1953), who reported that in spite of the decades our society has spent in trying to suppress all but marital sexual relations, "a not inconsiderable portion of all the sexual acts in which the human animal engages still fall into the category which the culture rates as 'perverse.'" (1949, p. 28) And this conclusion seems even more applicable today, in terms of conventional sexual mores.

We shall begin this chapter with a brief discussion of the problems of classifying sexual deviations and the causes of such deviance. The remainder of the chapter will focus on various well-defined patterns of deviant sexual behavior. But as shall be seen, we are not equating sexual deviance with abnormal behavior, except in certain specified instances where such behavior appears maladaptive for the individual and/or the group.

CLASSIFICATION AND CAUSES OF SEXUAL DEVIANCE

The term *sexual deviance,* in its broadest sense, refers to sexual behavior that is different or atypical, that does not follow the prevailing patterns sanctioned by laws or the social mores of the particular society. Since socially sanctioned sexual patterns differ from one culture to another, among subgroups within a given culture, and over time, it is apparent that behavior labeled *sexually deviant* is not necessarily abnormal or maladaptive in the sense of being inherently detrimental to the individual or to other people. At the same time, certain patterns—such as forcible rape and pedophilia—have definitely been shown to be detrimental, and are so labeled by society.

TYPES OF SEXUAL DEVIATIONS

No satisfactory classification of sexual deviations has yet been devised. One that has commonly been used identifies behaviors as deviant with respect to: (1) intensity or frequency of sex drive and gratification, as in impotence and nymphomania; (2) mode of gratification, as in exhibitionism or rape; or (3) choice of sex objects, as in incest and homosexuality.

Another and apparently more useful way of classifying sexual deviations is based on a classification proposed by Gagnon and Simon (1967). Again three categories are utilized:

1. *"Normal" sexual deviations.* Included here are such patterns as masturbation and premarital sex. Such behaviors are generally condemned in our society, but are engaged in so widely and so privately that relatively few persons are subjected to social sanctions for engaging in them, and many people—including most mental health personnel—think they should not be. Masturbation, for example, may actually represent a healthy sexual practice.

2. *Abnormal sexual deviations.* Sexual behaviors placed in this category are those viewed by most people, including mental health personnel, as clearly harmful to the individual and/or other persons. Included here are such patterns as incest, pedophilia, and rape. The incidence of such sexual behavior is low relative to the general population, and legal and social sanctions against offenders are usually strong.

3. *Socially organized and related sexual deviations.* This category includes patterns commonly associated with a supportive group structure—for example, homosexuality and prostitution. Al-

SEXUAL DEVIANCE

CLASSIFICATION	PATTERN	DEFINITION	SOCIETAL SANCTIONS AGAINST BEHAVIOR
"Normal" Sexual Deviations	Masturbation	Self-stimulation of the genitals for sexual gratification	Low to none
	Premarital coitus	Sexual intercourse prior to marriage	Low to none
	Extramarital coitus	Sexual intercourse with partner other than spouse	Low to none
	Promiscuity	Nonselective sexual relations with variety of partners; referred to as *sexual delinquency* in girl under 18	Low
Abnormal Sexual Deviations	Impotence and frigidity	Impairment in desire for or inability to achieve sexual gratification	None
	Exhibitionism	Public exposure of genitals for sexual gratification	Low
	Voyeurism (peeping)	Clandestine observation of others engaging in sexual activities or in the nude	Low
	Fetishism	Achievement of sexual gratification through the use of objects, such as clothing, or through deviant activities, such as firesetting	Variable
	Pedophilia	Use of a child as a sex object by an adult	High
	Rape (forcible)	Sexual relations with another person (adult) obtained through force or threat	High
	Incest	Sexual relations between close relatives	High
	Sadism	Achievement of sexual gratification by inflicting pain on others	Variable
	Masochism	Achievement of sexual gratification by having pain inflicted on self	Low to none
Socially Organized And Related Sexual Deviations	Prostitution	The practice—usually repetitive—of engaging in sexual relations for financial gain	Variable
	Homosexuality	Overt sexual activity between members of the same sex	Variable
	Transvestism	Achievement of sexual excitement by dressing in clothes of the opposite sex	Low
	Transsexualism	Inability to accept one's physical sex; gender identification with the opposite sex	Low

though commitment to such patterns can be developed on an individual basis, most persons engaging in them operate in a subculture where such patterns are favored, such as the homosexual community. Some of the contemporary communes fit in this category, supporting sexual patterns among their members that the larger society does not accept.

In the present chapter we shall follow this threefold classification of sexual deviations, grouping various patterns with reference to their apparent consequences in our culture and making no attempt to identify universally adaptive or maladaptive practices.

GENERAL CAUSAL FACTORS IN SEXUAL DEVIATIONS

Before discussing specific sexual deviations, it will be useful to point out some of the general factors commonly involved in their development.

Learning and reinforcement. As we have noted, adult sexual behavior is the result of a long process of development, and there is nothing in the undifferentiated sexual potentialities of the infant guaranteeing that the end result will be a "normal" heterosexual pattern. An almost infinite variety exists in the sexual patterns that an individual can develop.

The individual's view of himself as male or female, the social demands made upon him for playing his expected sexual role, his concept of what sexual behavior is appropriate, and his anticipation of what will be exciting and pleasurable—all these are learned, and they help determine his sexual practices as an adult. And through conditioning, almost any object or situation can become sexually stimulating—particularly among preadolescents and adolescents—such as erotic literature, sex scenes in plays and films, pictures of nude or partially nude individuals, and underclothing or other objects intimately associated with members of the opposite sex. Sexual arousal may also accompany strong emotional reactions —such as fear and excitement—especially if associated with the performance of some forbidden act.

With time, however, some stimuli come to be preferred to others, and erotic arousal and gratification are limited to a relatively narrow range of stimuli and behaviors. Thus an individual may come to prefer plump or thin persons, blondes or brunettes, persons younger or older than himself, members of his own sex or members of the other sex. He may learn to want a considerable amount of sex play prior to actual coitus, or immediate coitus without preliminary sex play; and he may come to find satisfaction in—or be offended by—particular positions, the use of oral or anal techniques, and so on. Social expectations, models, instruction, misinformation, and chance occurrences and reinforcements may all play key roles in this learning process.

Sexual frustration and other life stress. Sexual behavior depends not only on learning and pleasurable reinforcement but also on opportunities and limitations, including those established by the individual's own standards and concepts.

Our society abounds in subtle—and not so subtle—forms of sexual stimulation, yet continues to demand that teen-agers and unmarried youth refrain from sexual intercourse (and in some cases from masturbation and petting). Such stimulation and frustration can be highly stressful, and may lead to socially disapproved sexual patterns—particularly when inner controls are lowered by alcohol or other drugs. And we have seen that in prisons and other institutions, where the sexes are segregated and denied heterosexual outlets, the incidence of homosexual behavior is usually much higher than in ordinary life situations.

Interestingly enough, nonsexual stresses may also be associated with deviant sexual behavior. The study and treatment of sex offenders on lower socioeconomic levels led Yalom (1961) to emphasize the extent to which hostility and resentment that develop in a deeply frustrating life situation may be acted out in antisocial sexual offenses, such as rape. Similarly, Hartman and Nicolay (1966) have reported findings from a study of 91 expectant fathers apprehended for sexual offenses including exhibitionism, pedophilia, rape or attempted rape, homosexual acts, obscene phone calls, and voyeurism. These offenses seemed to be related to the increased stress that the wife's pregnancy had placed upon the husband.

In this context, the concept of a "total sexual outlet" is relevant. This concept was proposed by Kinsey et al. (1948), who found six chief sources of sexual gratification among American males: masturbation, nocturnal emissions, heterosexual petting, heterosexual intercourse, homosexual relations, and contact with animals. According to these investigators, the average number of outlets varied between two and three, with the particular outlets used depending largely on age and social class but also varying with the strength of the sex drive and the available opportunities for gratification.

The concept of a total sexual outlet helps explain the observation that many exhibitionists and other sexual deviants are married and thus have "normal" sexual outlets in addition to their socially disapproved patterns. It also helps explain how under prolonged frustration individuals may resort to substitutive patterns of a deviant nature.

Association with psychopathology. Many persons arrested for sexual offenses have been found to exhibit other serious maladaptive behaviors as well. In a pioneering study of 300 typical sex offenders in New Jersey, Brancale, Ellis, and Doorbar (1952) found only 14 percent to be psychologically "normal." Among the other 86 percent there was a high incidence of neuroses and a lesser incidence of actual and borderline psychoses, disorders associated with brain damage, sociopathic personalities, and mental retardation. Such pathological conditions often involve either inadequate development of or the lowering of inner reality and ethical controls. There also tends to be a somewhat consistent relationship between various categories of psychopathology and particular types of sexually deviant behavior. For example, neurotics are most likely to be brought to the attention of law-enforcement officers for peeping and exhibitionism; and sociopathic personalities are frequently involved in forcible rape. Such relationships are by no means invariably found, however, and individuals manifesting various types of psychopathology may maintain conventional sexual patterns; or they may manifest deviations other than those we have mentioned.

Provocation by victim. In an early study of the files of the Detroit Police Department, Dunham (1951) reported that the victim was known to the offender in about three fourths of the cases involving offenses against children, in half of the sexual assault cases, and in one fourth of the cases of peeping and indecent exposure. Undoubtedly a similar victim-offender relationship existed in a large percentage of cases that went unreported.

These findings have raised the question of whether the victim may actually encourage the sexual act. Although this seems farfetched where child victims are concerned, it appears to have some validity with respect to cases involving adolescents and adults. The "victims"—especially in cases of sexual assault and homosexuality—may consciously or unconsciously emit cues which lead to the deviant's overt response. Evidence for this hypothesis has been reported by Amir (1971), who, in a study of 646 cases of rape reported to the Philadelphia police, found 19 percent of them to have been "victim precipitated."

In the preceding discussion, we have attempted to outline certain general causal factors commonly associated with deviant sexual patterns. In the discussion of specific patterns which follows, we shall elaborate further on the nature and range of etiological factors.

"NORMAL" SEXUAL DEVIATIONS

As we have noted, the sexual behavior in this category, though disapproved by traditional social mores, is so prevalent—and carried out so privately—that few persons are subjected to sanctions for engaging in it. Though deviant, it is classified as "normal deviance" both because of its frequency and because of the lack of evidence that it is necessarily maladaptive. Problems that arise are ordinarily handled without recourse to personnel in the mental health field.

MASTURBATION

Masturbation is defined as self-stimulation of the genitals for sexual gratification. According to the findings of Kinsey and his associates (1953),

62 percent of females and 92 percent of males masturbate at some time in their lives. These investigators found masturbation to be the most common sexual outlet for men prior to marriage and the second most common outlet for women (heterosexual petting ranking first). More recently Gagnon and Simon (1968) have pointed to indications that masturbation is being used both earlier and more frequently by females. Typically, masturbation gives way to coital relations either before or after marriage.

Masturbation has been traditionally condemned on religious and moral grounds, as well as for its allegedly harmful physical effects. Everything from physical weakness to impotence, mental deterioration, and insanity have been attributed to it. At one time hospital authorities maintained separate wards for patients whose insanity was presumably due to this practice. Even today many young people are still taught that masturbation is a vile habit that self-respecting people can prevent with a little self-control.

Many a young person has fought against masturbating and promised himself that he would not give in again; then mounting sexual tension led to failure of his resolve. It is difficult to imagine anything more admirably suited to inevitable self-devaluation and personality damage. Often, too, the threat of social disapproval and scorn has been added to an already stressful situation. In one physical education class, for example, an instructor told his students that the effects of masturbation could be detected "by the baggy appearance of the genitals." Through such misinformation, he engendered the widespread fear that others could detect the consequences of such "despicable" behavior. Such fears may not only interfere with an individual's personal and social adjustment but also with his subsequent marital adjustment.

Thus it is worth emphasizing that masturbation as practiced by the average adolescent has no known harmful physiological effects, and is actually considered a normal and healthy sexual outlet for young people. In those instances where masturbation may be considered maladaptive, it is usually part of a larger picture of maladjustment. Children who feel unhappy, lonely, and unwanted may center too much of their activity around masturbatory practices in an attempt to compensate for their frustrations. Occasionally, masturbation may be used as a form of hostile behavior, as in the rather extreme case in which 25 sixth-grade boys masturbated en masse before their female teacher. These boys came from socially disadvantaged homes and their behavior apparently represented a sort of mass protest based on feelings of frustration, inadequacy, and hostility.

Masturbation may continue into adult life at the expense of normal heterosexual behavior—for example, in the case of a male, when the individual is extremely shy and fearful of the opposite sex; when he finds his wife unattractive and prefers the more exciting and desirable persons depicted in the fantasies which accompany his masturbatory activities; or when he has strong but inhibited homosexual inclinations and pre-

fers the male figures in his masturbatory fantasies to heterosexual relations.

Even though masturbation may occur as part of a larger picture of maladjustment, it is ordinarily a normal phase of development that precedes adult heterosexual behavior, and a practice that some persons may revert to under conditions of deprivation. Usually the only undesirable features are the worry, guilt, and self-devaluation that may be associated with it.

PREMARITAL COITUS

Although the sex drive increases markedly following puberty, the young person is not usually in a position to marry until some years later. And since traditional standards in our society emphasize abstinence prior to marriage, sexual gratification becomes a key problem during adolescence.

Typical premarital sexual patterns. Based on their studies, Kinsey et al. (1948; 1953) estimated that 83 percent of men and 50 percent of women have intercourse before marriage. Although the incidence today is not known, the figure is probably higher, especially for women (Packard, 1968). The availability of the pill has removed much of the fear formerly associated with premarital sex; also, the freer definition of sexual relationships as desirable and legitimate has alleviated for many people the inhibition, conflict, and guilt formerly surrounding such behavior.

Of the females who have intercourse before marriage, a substantial number appear to confine their relations to the man they intend to marry. This was the finding of Kinsey et al. (1953) and is believed to be still true. In cases where premarital intercourse has been restricted to the person's future spouse, no effects on later marital adjustment have been demonstrated, one way or the other (Shope & Broderick, 1967).

Interestingly enough, in a survey of 2200 unmarried college juniors and seniors, the majority of women indicated that they would not be troubled by the knowledge that their husbands had had premarital sexual experiences with one or more other persons, but more than two thirds of the college men replied that they would be troubled to some extent by the knowledge of such experience on the part of their wives (Packard,

1968). Similarly, Mosher and Cross (1971) reported in a study of college students in Connecticut that

"Both men and women tend to endorse more liberal premarital standards for men than for women, and the premarital standards of men are more permissive than those of women." (p. 31)

Thus, the "double standard," although less prevalent than formerly, still exists—a fact that is also apparent in the use of the label "sexually delinquent" for young females but rarely for young males.

Sexual promiscuity and delinquency. In a girl under 18, sexual promiscuity (repeated transient coital experiences) is commonly referred to as *sexual delinquency*. Usually this activity is essentially noncommercial, for while the girl may receive gifts, or even money, the expectation of these returns is not the primary reason for it. And although the term *delinquency* indicates society's disapproval of such transient episodes on the part of young girls, a relatively small percentage of them come to the attention of juvenile authorities or mental health personnel.[1] A number of patterns appear to contribute to the development of sexual delinquency:

1. *Family patterns.* An appreciable number of sexually delinquent girls are provided a model for such behavior by their parents—particularly by divorced and promiscuous mothers (Scharfman & Clark, 1967). Parental rejection and unhappy foster home placement often are propelling forces in converting hurt and frustrated teenagers into delinquents of many kinds—including sexual delinquents. The thrill of an "overnight romance" is often too much for a girl to withstand, offering an irresistible compensation for her feelings of being unwanted, unimportant, and unloved.

Another pattern commonly associated with promiscuity is extreme parental strictness. Some teen-agers rebel against the standards for dating and sexual behavior which their parents attempt to enforce, and in so doing may swing to the other extreme, possibly in part as a means of retaliation. It is interesting to note Gibbens' (1961) finding that girls suffer as much as boys from family problems, but that girls tend to nurse their hurts and anxieties until adolescence, when their suffering may be reflected rather suddenly in sexually promiscuous behavior.

2. *"Proving" behavior.* For a girl who feels inadequate and doubtful about her femininity and attractiveness, the need to "prove" herself may be a key factor in promiscuous sexual behavior. And since she may experience physical as well as emotional gratification from such sexual episodes, the pattern may be reinforced. Over time, however, these girls usually find such transient relationships unfulfilling, and may seek a more stable emotional relationship, with marriage the typical outcome. As we have seen, proving behavior is by no means restricted to girls. Boys frequently engage in delinquent behavior of a proving nature, but whereas girls tend to restrict such behavior chiefly to the sexual realm, the proving behavior of boys may include a wide gamut of behaviors, of which early "sexual exploits" designed to prove their masculinity are a part. But because of the double standard, such behavior in boys is not usually labeled "promiscuous" as it is in the case of girls.

3. *Peer models and pressures.* Delinquent sexual behavior in young girls is often associated with peer-group models and pressures. For example, some girls belong to delinquent male gangs and are expected to "service" various members of the gang. In other instances, having intercourse is simply considered the thing to do in the "ingroup." Sometimes indiscriminate experimentation with deviant sexual practices, such as group sexual acts, may be attempted by lonely and alienated young people who hope to "get in touch." Drugs, of course, usually play a role in such sexual patterns.

Finally, it may be noted that sexual promiscuity on the part of young girls may be associated with psychopathology—as in the case of severe mental retardation, schizophrenia, and sociopathic personality disorders.

A slight correlation between early sexual promiscuity and poor later marital adjustment appears to exist, but it may be associated with such factors as less desirable home backgrounds, peer-group models, and unconventional attitudes toward marriage, rather than to promiscuous sex-

---

[1]It may be noted, however, that an adult male who has sexual relations with a girl under 18 is committing "statutory rape," for which there are legal sanctions.

ual behavior *per se* (Shope & Broderick, 1967). Prostitutes are usually recruited from the ranks of girls who have been engaging in promiscuous sexual behavior, but this does not mean that any substantial number of sexually delinquent girls become involved in prostitution; the overwhelming majority eventually marry and enter into typical family relationships.

EXTRAMARITAL COITUS

In our society, as in many others, extramarital sexual relations have traditionally been regarded as a more serious deviation than premarital relations, subject to correspondingly more severe social and legal sanctions. Adultery has generally been regarded as grounds for separation or divorce and officially it has been rather generally condemned. Yet in the report of Kinsey et al. (1953), extramarital relations at some time during marriage were attributed to 50 percent of men and 27 percent of women. Many investigators believe that such behavior is increasing, especially among women because of the liberating influence of the pill and other new contraceptive devices and women's growing economic independence and freedom.

Whatever its actual incidence, marital infidelity seems to have become for some people almost a lighthearted and guilt-free activity (Salzman, 1969). Apparently many females as well as males find it quite easy to convince themselves that an extramarital affair is essential for maintaining their mental health, fully enjoying life, or making a marriage tolerable. Moreover, an increasing number of men and women seem willing to accept the loss of sexual exclusivity in their marriage as the price of its permanence. Where spouses were once gripped by feelings of rejection, jealousy, and hostility—when learning of such behavior —many now appear relieved that their marriage is suffering "nothing more serious than infidelity." This reaction perhaps becomes more understandable when we note Toffler's (1971) conclusion that our society is inexorably moving in the direction of more temporary marital and other interpersonal relationships. Thus for many people, the maintenance of a permanent relationship may take precedence over concern about their spouses' extramarital sexual patterns.

"SWINGING"—A MODERN SEXUAL PHENOMENON

In a study of wife-swapping and other group sex practices among middle-class Americans, Bartell (1971) has estimated the number of "swingers," or persons engaging in these practices, at 2 million and growing. The greatest concentrations of swinging couples are found in the Los Angeles and San Francisco areas; however, the New York-Boston-Washington complex and other major metropolitan centers rank close behind. One Chicago-based club was reported to have over 2500 members.

Some of Bartell's key findings include:

1. The practice of wife-swapping, the casual trading of sexual partners, and group sex—regardless of label—has developed into a social phenomenon in our society, with organizations devoted to it, meeting places, communication networks, and rules of conduct.

2. "Swingers" range in age from 18 to the middle 50's, with the average age for women being about 29 and for men about 32. The largest percentage of women are housewives and men are salesmen, but many occupations are represented.

3. Advertisements placed by swinging couples and organizations are carried in more than 50 national magazines and hundreds of local publications. In fact, a number of national magazines exclusively concerned with mate-swapping are available at "adult" bookstores. Thus, once a couple decides to become swingers, contact with others is easy and inexpensive.

4. Couples' reasons for turning to swinging appear to vary—including desires to escape from boredom and find variety and excitement, to patch up ailing relationships, and to demonstrate sexual attractiveness and potency. Swingers tend to view themselves as modern people who enjoy sex as recreation, unfettered by traditional sexual mores.

5. The majority of swinging couples exchange partners with another couple only once, then seek new contacts. Usually at first such contacts are infrequent, then are increased to one or more almost every weekend. The latter pattern continues for some two years, when there is a drastic curtailment of such activity or by the couple's dropping out of swinging altogether.

Bartell noted that while alcohol is commonly served at swinging parties, illegal drugs are not ordinarily used, and sometimes are actually forbidden. Nor is any person who attends the parties forced into participating in sexual acts. In general, his findings support and extend those reported by Avery and Avery (page 459).

Masters and Johnson (1966; 1970) have pointed out that novelty in the sex partner tends to increase arousal and response—a factor that may encourage the practice of "wife-swapping." A number of reports of this type of activity have been published. In one case, a reporter and his wife spent two months investigating wife-swapping in California, beginning with the insertion of this ad in the *San Francisco Chronicle*:

"Attractive couple in late 20's, bored with conventional friendships, wishes to meet with couples or singles to exchange unconventional experiences in the unusual/exotic/unique. Both bored." (Avery & Avery, 1964).

The ad prompted more than 300 replies, and during their investigation the Averys corre-

sponded with and met more than 100 couples who, unaware that they were talking to reporters, unashamedly admitted to being wife-swappers. Typically, they preferred to call themselves "swingers" and boasted of being "broad-minded" and "fond of fun in any form." Usually it was the husband who initiated the idea in an attempt to resolve problems that had developed in the marriage.

From the Averys' findings and those of other investigators, it appears that extramarital sex is subject to considerably less social disapproval than formerly and that here too there is a trend toward redefining sexuality and the role of sex in life, with a questioning of its restriction to only the framework of marriage and the family.

ABNORMAL SEXUAL DEVIATIONS

The patterns included in this group are those generally agreed to be harmful for the individual and/or the group. Except in the case of impotence and frigidity, both low incidence and stringent laws and mores attest to their deviance.

In our present discussion we shall include the following patterns: impotence, frigidity, voyeurism, exhibitionism, fetishism, incest, pedophilia, rape, masochism, and sadism.

IMPOTENCE AND FRIGIDITY (SEXUAL INADEQUACY)

Impotence and *frigidity* refer to impairment in the desire for, or inability to achieve, sexual gratification. Both sexual desire and genital functioning may be affected by a wide range of organic conditions—injuries to the genitals, disease, fatigue, and drug-induced states. However, prolonged or permanent impotence before the age of 55 is rare and almost always due to psychological factors. In fact, according to Kinsey's findings, only 27 percent of males be-

come impotent by the age of 70, and even here many cases are due to psychological factors. There is ample evidence, of more recent origin, that people in their 60's, 70's, and even 80's are capable of enjoying sex (Masters & Johnson, 1970; Pfeiffer, Verwoerdt & Wang, 1968).

The most common forms of impotence or sexual inadequacy in the male include: (1) primary impotence, in which the male has never been able to attain an erection long enough to have successful intercourse; (2) secondary impotence, in which the male has achieved successful intercourse but manifests impaired potency—that is, impotence 25 percent or more of the time; and (3) premature ejaculation, in which the male is unable to control ejaculation long enough to satisfy the female. Since secondary impotence may come on gradually, it has also been called insidious impotence. Common conditions in frigidity, or sexual inadequacy in the female, are: (1) vaginismus—a condition in which the outer third of the vagina involuntarily clamps tightly shut when attempts are made to enter; and (2) inability to achieve orgasm. Masters and Johnson (1970) estimated that sexual inade-

SATYRIASIS AND NYMPHOMANIA

The difficulties inherent in labeling certain sexual patterns as abnormal or maladaptive are illustrated by the use of the terms *satyriasis* and *nymphomania* to refer to males and females, respectively, who appear to experience almost continuous sexual desire and to focus their lives largely around their sexual activities. Traditionally, the patterns so labeled have been assumed to be abnormal, but in the light of available evidence and current thinking about sexual patterns, it is difficult to ascribe much meaning to the labels themselves or to attach much validity to their application. Research has shown that there are wide variations in strength and frequency of sexual desire and activity; and a high incidence of sexual intercourse is not maladaptive unless such sexual patterns impair ability to establish satisfying interpersonal relationships or make other life adjustments.

It may be pointed out that certain brain structures appear to be important in the regulation of sexual arousal; e.g., if the amygdala (a portion of the brain lying below the frontal lobes) is destroyed by disease or injury or blocked off by surgery, the result is an almost insatiable desire for sex. Although diagnostic medical data are not available, an interesting case has been reported of a Sunday School teacher who complained of developing an uncontrollable sex drive after receiving a head injury in a San Francisco cable car accident (*L.A. Times,* 1970). She stated that she had had intercourse with over 100 men since the accident, and had lost several jobs because her intense sexual desire interfered with her ability to work.

On the other hand, there is no research evidence to indicate involvement of brain pathology in the behavior of most persons with unusually high degrees of sexual desire and activity.

quacies threaten or damage half the marriages in America.

Dynamics. A number of psychosocial factors have been delineated in impotence, which typically apply to frigidity as well.

1. *Faulty early learning.* In some primitive societies older members of the group instruct younger members in sexual techniques before marriage. But in our society, though we recognize that sexual behavior is an important aspect of marriage, the learning of sexual techniques and attitudes is too often left to chance. The result is that young people often start out with faulty expectations and a lack of needed information or harmful misinformation which can impair their sexual adequacy.

Many women in our society have been subjected to early training that depicted sexual relations as lustful, dirty, and evil. The attitudes and inhibitions thus established can lead to a great deal of anxiety, conflict, and guilt where sexual relations

are concerned—whether in or out of marriage. Faulty early conditioning may also have taken the form of indoctrination in the idea that the woman has a primary responsibility to satisfy the man sexually—and therefore to suppress her own needs and feelings. Masters and Johnson (1970) consider such faulty early learning to be the primary cause of frigidity in females.

Although males may also be subjected to early training that emphasizes the evils of sex, such training apparently is a far less important factor in male impotence. However, another type of faulty early conditioning was found by Masters and Johnson (1970) to be a key factor in premature ejaculation in males. Common to the histories of such males was a first sex experience with a prostitute or in a lovers' lane parking place or other situation in which hurried ejaculation was necessary. Apparently, once this pattern was established, the individual had been unable to break the conditioned response.

2. *Fear, anxiety, and feelings of inadequacy.* In a study of 50 impotent males ranging in age from 25 to 58, Senoussi, Coleman, and Tauber (1959) found that a contributing factor was fear of being unable to play the male role. The individual felt self-conscious and inadequate and anticipated failure, with consequent rejection and humiliation.

In a more recent study of 49 adult males with a disorder of sexual potency, Cooper (1969) found anxiety to be a contributing factor in 94 percent of the cases and the primary factor for those whose potency problems had started early: "Most of these patients . . . had developed considerable apprehension *prior to,* and in *anticipation of* a first or early intercourse." (p. 146) There is evidence that this is a frequent pattern among teenagers who feel pushed into sexual relations as "the thing to do." Instead of bringing the expected satisfactions, such sexual freedom may bring intense frustration and feelings of "not being adequate or normal."

3. *Lack of emotional closeness to the sexual partner.* Lack of emotional closeness can lead to impotence or frigidity. The individual may be in love with someone else; he may find his sexual partner physically repulsive; or he may have hostile or antagonistic feelings as a result of prior quarrels and conflicts.

In the female, lack of emotional closeness often

TREATMENT OF SEXUAL INADEQUACY

Masters and Johnson, widely known for their studies of sexual response and their therapeutic approach to problems of sexual inadequacy, are pictured counseling a couple at their clinic in St. Louis—the Reproductive Biology Research Foundation. These investigators have concluded from their research efforts (1970) that some 50 percent of American marriages suffer from sexual inadequacy, a factor they consider largely responsible for our high divorce rate. In their view, sexual inadequacy is a form of faulty communication which probably extends to other areas of a couple's relationship as well; consequently, their treatment program is oriented toward improving communication in a marriage and preventing it from being wrecked by ignorance about sex and faulty attitudes toward it.

Stressing the concept that sex is an experience that both partners must enter into without reservation or shame, Masters and Johnson insist that fears or anxieties that either partner may have concerning intercourse—pressures that can turn it into a dreaded "command performance"—must be eliminated. In addition, they treat the married couple as a unit rather than as separate individuals.

The sequence of events in the treatment program is as follows:

1. On the first day of therapy a male therapist records the man's sexual history, and a female therapist, the woman's —on the assumption that each will be more candid with a member of his own sex.

2. On the second day a female therapist interviews the male and a male therapist, the female—on the assumption that there are some things neither partner would tell a member of his own sex.

3. On the third day, after complete physical examinations, the man and woman have their first joint meeting with the therapists, who explain what they think the couple's diffi-

culty is, how it has arisen, and how it reflects communication difficulties. Many persons learn for the first time how their spouses feel about them and why; they also realize that their problems are not unique.

4. The next step typically involves two suggestions: (a) that the couple continue temporarily to avoid sexual relations —as they were instructed to do when they arrived at the clinic; and (b) that twice before the next session they undress and participate in gentle one-sided touching; e.g., the woman may "pleasure" the man by stroking his back or stomach or arm until she finds what feels best to him; and the man reciprocates. This assignment frees them of the need to perform sexually and forces them to concern themselves with the other's feelings and their own responses to them.

5. After a few days at most, the therapy focuses on the couple's specific sexual problem, whether it is impotence or premature ejaculation on the male's part, or vaginismus or some other inadequacy on the female's. In some cases specific sexual techniques are explained and encouraged, but at no time is there a demand for any particular kind or level of sexual performance. At each day's therapy session the couple's attempts at sexual communication are supported and strengthened, and mistakes are discussed. The couple may be encouraged to make mistakes purposely, because they can learn from them.

For the great majority of couples participating in this treatment program, it appears that a change is effected in attitudes, feelings, and communication, and that sexual relations become an intimate, normal, and desirable experience. Five-year follow-up studies of 510 married couples and 57 unmarried men and women revealed that the program's rate of failure varied markedly with the type of sexual inadequacy —from zero for cases of vaginismus and 2.2 percent for cases of premature ejaculation to 40.6 percent for cases of primary impotence. Overall, the failure rate in treatment was only 20 percent.

"COITAL ANXIETY" IN MALE POTENCY DISORDERS

The study by Cooper (1969) of potency disorders among 49 young adult males yielded the following data:

DISORDER	CASES	MEAN AGE	DURATION OF DISORDER
Acute (primary) impotence	7	25	1.9 years
Insidious (secondary) impotence	19	35	7.1 years
Impotentia ejaculandi (delayed or absent ejaculation in the presence of normal erection)	13	34	5.8 years
Premature ejaculation	10	28	1.3 years

The majority of subjects reported having three or more specific coital anxieties, the most frequently reported being listed below:

SPECIFIC ANXIETIES ASSOCIATED WITH COITAL ATTEMPTS	NUMBER OF TIMES MENTIONED
Fear of failing to perform adequately	26
Fear of being seen by wife as sexually inferior	20
Fear of wife's ridicule	19
Fear of causing pregnancy	11
Anxiety over size of genitals	7
Fear of contracting disease	7
Pervasive anxiety (no specific cause)	5
Fear of detection	3

Interestingly enough, 4 married subjects explained their potency disorder as due to "organic damage," presumably resulting from masturbation, and feared that repeated intercourse would exacerbate the damage and further impair their potency.

appears to result from intercourse with a partner who is a "sexual moron"—rough, unduly hasty, or concerned only with his own gratification. Here the coital experience may be disillusioning and unpleasant. Under such conditions, the female may come to associate sexual excitement with tension and unfulfillment, and may defensively suppress her erotic feelings.

4. *Low sex drive and apathy.* It is often difficult to distinguish between persons who are actually impotent or frigid and those who have a low sex drive and are sexually apathetic. In Cooper's (1969) study, men whose potency

problem developed late typically reported that it came following a progressive decline in sexual interest and performance over months or years. In these cases, anxiety developed only after the potency disorder had become established, and thus appeared to be the result, rather than the cause, of the disorder.

5. *Latent or overt homosexuality.* In some cases the individual's sexual differentiation has taken a homosexual direction and his erotic desires have come to be focused on members of his own sex, with a corresponding loss of feeling or actual revulsion for members of the opposite sex. Although many males and females seem able to achieve sexual gratification with members of either sex, a homosexual individual is likely to encounter difficulties in heterosexual relationships and to be able to achieve gratification only in homosexual relations.

Treatment and outcomes. The treatment of individuals or couples for impotence or frigidity requires considerable flexibility, depending on the problems of the individual or couple involved. Behavior therapy has been successfully used in treating some cases; Wolpe (1969) has employed a combination of progressive desensitization and the anxiety-inhibiting effect of erotic arousal.

The most extensive and systematic report on the treatment of impotence and frigidity is that of Masters and Johnson (1970); their approach is described in the illustration on page 461.

EXHIBITIONISM

Exhibitionism ("indecent exposure") and voyeurism ("peeping") are the two most common sexual offenses reported to police. Contrary to popular opinion, offenders in both categories are rarely dangerous and usually respond well to treatment.

Exhibitionism involves the intentional exposure of the genitals under inappropriate conditions—usually in public or semipublic places to members of the opposite sex. Sometimes the demonstrations are accompanied by suggestive gestures or masturbatory activity, but more commonly there is only exposure.

The exposure may take place in some secluded location, such as a park, or in a more public place, such as a department store, church, theater, or bus. In cities, the exhibitionist often drives by schools or bus stops, exhibits himself while in the car, and then drives rapidly away. In many instances, the exposure is repeated under fairly constant conditions, such as only in churches or buses, or in the same general vicinity and at the same time of day. In one case a youth exhibited himself only at the top of an escalator in a large department store. The kind of sex object too is usually fairly consistent for the individual exhibitionist. For the male offender this ordinarily involves a strange female in the young or middle-adult age range.

Ordinarily the exhibitionistic act does not involve assaultive behavior, although occasionally a hostile psychopath may accompany exhibitionism with aggressive acts and may knock down or otherwise attack his victim. Despite the rarity of assaultive behavior in these cases, and the fact that most exhibitionists are not the dangerous criminals they are often made out to be in newspaper stories, the exhibitionistic act nevertheless takes place without the viewer's consent and also may upset the viewer; thus, society considers exhibitionism to be a criminal offense.

Exhibitionism is most common during the warm spring and summer months, and most offenders are young adult males. Practically all occupational groups are represented. Among women, the exhibition of the genitals is relatively rare, and when it occurs it is less likely to be reported to the police. Usually exhibitionism by males in public or semipublic places is reported—though sometimes not immediately. In fact, sometimes, especially in theaters, such individuals are encouraged in their activity.

A rather handsome 17-year-old boy had been seating himself beside girls and women in darkened theaters and then exhibiting himself and masturbating. He had been repeatedly successful in obtaining approving collaboration from the "victims" before he finally made the mistake of exposing himself to a policewoman. Out of an estimated 25 to 30 exposures, he was reported on only 3 occasions.

Dynamics. Exhibitionists constitute the largest group of sex offenders apprehended by police. In general, cases of exhibitionism appear to fall into one of three categories:

1. *Exhibitionism associated with personal immaturity.* Witzig (1968) found that about 60

percent of the cases of exhibitionism referred by courts for treatment fall into this category. Here the exhibitionism seems to be based on inadequate information, feelings of shyness and inferiority in approaching the opposite sex, and puritanical attitudes toward masturbation. Commonly, there are strong bonds to an overly possessive mother. Often the exhibitionist states that he struggled against the impulse to expose himself in much the same way that the adolescent may struggle against the impulse to masturbate, but that, as sexual or other tensions increased, he felt compelled to carry out his exhibitionistic activities. And he often feels guilty and remorseful afterward, particularly if he has achieved ejaculation.

Although over half of all exhibitionists are married, they usually fail to achieve satisfactory

COMMON MISCONCEPTIONS ABOUT SEXUAL OFFENDERS

Persons who engage in maladaptive sexual patterns for which there are legal penalties, such as exhibitionism, incest, and rape, are subjects of a number of misconceptions, including:

1. **Sexual offenders are typically homicidal sex fiends.** Homicidal acts associated with sex crimes are rare, and the offender in such cases is usually suffering from a severe mental disorder. Only about 5 percent of all convicted sex offenders inflict physical injury upon their victims. Of course, this does not preclude psychological damage.

2. **Sexual offenders are oversexed from exposure to pornography.** Most sexual deviants arrested by the police are undersexed, rather than oversexed. Typically, they have been subjected to much misinformation about sexual activities and are more prudish than non-offenders; and usually they have been less exposed to pornography than have non-offenders.

3. **Sexual offenders suffer from glandular imbalance.** The development of sexual patterns in human beings appears to be determined primarily by experiences and life situations rather than by hormonal secretions.

4. **Sexual offenders typically progress from minor to more serious sex crimes.** The offender may progress to major sex crimes in order to achieve satisfaction as minor deviations lose their "thrill," but this pattern is the exception. Sexual offenders usually persist in the type of behavior in which they have discovered satisfaction.

5. **Sexual offenders are usually repeaters.** Sex offenders have one of the lowest rates of repeated offenses—less than 10 percent of those convicted, as contrasted with over 60 percent of convicted criminal offenders in general. And most of the repeaters are booked for minor offenses, such as peeping or exhibitionism, rather than for serious criminal acts.

sexual and personal relationships with their wives. Witzig (1968) has pointed out that

"These men almost never like to discuss sexual matters with their wives and frequently avoid undressing before them. The idea of living in a nudist colony is a repulsive thought to most exhibitionists, although they are periodically willing to show off their genitals in quite public places." (p. 78)

Many of these offenders state that they married only because of family pressure, and many married at a late age. Thus we are dealing here with an individual who is essentially immature in his sex-role development, even though he may be well educated and competent in other life areas.

A high-school teacher had exhibited himself for several months to a 30-year-old woman who lived next door. She finally reported him, and before arresting him the police took motion pictures of his activities from the woman's apartment. In order to get clearer pictures they raised the window. At this point the teacher thought he had finally made an impression and in turn raised his own window and intensified his masturbatory activities and suggestive gestures.

After his arrest he revealed a background of over-attachment to a domineering mother and an inhibited, puritanical attitude toward sex. He had rarely gone out with girls and felt extremely shy and insecure in his approach to them. His strong bond to his mother undoubtedly contributed to his difficulties in heterosexual adjustment, making even his fantasies of sexual relations with other women seem like acts of unfaithfulness toward his mother. As a result, he apparently blundered into his awkward, immature, and socially unacceptable form of sexual behavior.

Closely related to the exhibitionist's personal immaturity appears to be a second factor: doubts and fears about his masculinity, combined with a strong need to demonstrate masculinity and potency. Apfelberg, Sugar, and Pfeffer (1944), for example, cited the case of an exhibitionist who achieved sexual satisfaction only when he accompanied the exposure of his genitals with a question to his victim as to whether she had ever seen such a large penis. On one occasion the woman, instead of evidencing shock and embarrassment, scornfully assured him that she had. On this occasion, the defendant stated, he received no sexual gratification.

It is worth noting that exhibitionism rarely takes place in a setting conducive to having sexual relations. The exhibitionist attempts to elicit a reaction that confirms his masculinity without entailing the risk of having to perform adequately in sexual intercourse.

2. *Interpersonal stress and acting out.* Another dynamic factor is suggested by the high incidence of precipitating stress. Often the married exhibitionist appears to be reacting to some conflict or stress situation in his marriage, and his behavior is in the nature of a regression to adolescent masturbatory activity. In such instances, an exhibitionist may state that exhibiting himself during masturbation is more exciting and tension-reducing than utilizing pictures of nude women.

Exhibitionism without genital arousal may take place following a period of intense conflict over some problem—often involving authority figures—with which the individual feels inadequate to cope.

"For example, a Marine who wanted to make a career of the service was having an experience with a superior that made it impossible for him to reenlist. He could not admit to himself that he could be hostile to either the corps or the superior. For the first time in his life, he exposed himself to a girl on the beach. Arrested, he was merely reprimanded and returned to the scene of conflict. A short time later he displayed his genitals to a girl on a parking lot. This time he was placed on probation with the stipulation that he seek treatment, and his enlistment was allowed to terminate in natural sequence. He never repeated the act. He was happily married and seemed to be acting out in this instance a vulgar expression of contempt." (Witzig, 1968, p. 77)

3. *Association with other psychopathology.* Exhibitionism may occur in association with a variety of more pervasive forms of psychopathology. Youths who are severely mentally retarded—both male and female—may be unaware or only partially aware of the socially disapproved nature of their behavior. Some exhibitionists are recruited from the ranks of older men with senile brain deterioration who evidence a lowering of inner reality and ethical controls.

In other cases exhibitionism is associated with sociopathic personality disorders. Such individuals usually have a history of poor school adjustment and erratic work records; and often they have had difficulties with authorities as a consequence of other antisocial acts. Their exhibition-

OBSCENE PHONE CALLS

In 1969 more than 800,000 obscene, abusive, and threatening calls were reported to telephone companies in the United States. But the problem is much more extensive than reports indicate; the police estimate that over twice as many offenses go unreported.

Men typically are the offenders in cases of obscene phone calls, most of which are made to women. Victims commonly include brides whose weddings have recently been reported in the newspaper, or women known to be home alone. The following is a fairly typical example, involving a 28-year-old housewife, the mother of two young children. Her husband, a salesman, was out of town when she was awakened at 3:15 A.M. by the ringing of the phone:

"There was no answer to her 'Hello.' All that the woman heard was a heavy, animal-like breathing.

"'Who is this?' she demanded.

"A low, husky male voice finally replied, 'Hi, Sweetie. Did I wake you? Gee, I'm sorry. But not really. Say, y'know what I'd like to do to you right now? Got the message?'

"A flood of filth followed.

"Gasping in the predawn stillness, the woman . . . started to slam the receiver but stopped when she heard her telephone tormentor warn, 'If you hang up on me, I'll burn down your house.'" (Pollack, 1970, p. 25)

Nadler (1968) has made an extensive study of several cases of obscene phone calls. He found that the dynamics are similar to those in exhibitionism, but obscene phoning is both more aggressive and yet more distant an act. Like the exhibitionist, the obscene caller appears to suffer from pervasive feelings of inadequacy, but the anxiety and hostility he manifests in relating to the opposite sex seems to be greater.

As in the case of exhibitionism, obscene phoning tends to have a compulsive quality, but it apparently involves less sexual excitation. Fortunately, the caller does not tend to be a physical menace, despite the psychological trauma he may inflict on his victims. Regardless of the caller's relative harmlessness, however, society takes a dim view of him; both federal and local laws define his offense as a crime. Information about how to handle obscene (and other abusive) calls has been made available by telephone companies in most cities.

ism appears to be just one more form of antisocial behavior, in connection with which they may or may not achieve sexual excitation and gratification. In some instances, exhibitionism is associated with manic or schizophrenic reactions. For example, the only woman in a group of offenders studied by Witzig (1968) typically exposed herself prior to the onset of a full-blown psychotic episode.

Treatment and outcomes. Although some exhibitionists deny their guilt, even after conviction, stating that they were merely urinating in an inappropriate place or had forgotten to zip up their trousers, most realize that they have a problem and respond well to group therapy.

Successful results in the treatment of exhibitionists have also been reported with behavior therapy. Such therapy usually involves the fostering of more assertive or typical heterosexual patterns, desensitization to stresses that may have precipitated given episodes, and aversive conditioning. Evans (1967) treated 7 exhibitionists by presenting them with descriptive phrases that called up images of exhibitionistic activities or normal heterosexual behavior. The vivid imagery prompted by the exhibitionistic phrases was then associated with electric shock, which the patient could terminate by changing to a slide describing normal sexual responses. Evans reported that 5 of the 7 subjects no longer experienced an urge to expose themselves following treatment, and the other 2 subjects reduced their exhibitionistic activities from a high of 28 to 2 episodes per month.

Aside from psychopathic offenders, who represent a distinct minority, exhibitionists rarely repeat their behavior after treatment. Hence, therapy—rather than imprisonment—ordinarily is a sufficient deterrent against further offenses (Witzig, 1968).

VOYEURISM

Voyeurism, scotophilia, and *inspectionalism* are synonymous terms referring to the achievement of sexual pleasure through clandestine peeping. Although children often engage in such behavior, it occurs as a sexual offense primarily among young males. These "peeping Toms," as they are commonly called, usually concentrate on females who are undressing or on couples engaging in sexual relations. Frequently they masturbate during their peeping activity.

Dynamics. How do they develop this pattern? In the first place, viewing the body of an attractive female seems to be quite stimulating sexually. The saying "He feasted his eyes upon her" attests to the "sexualization" of mere "looking" under certain conditions. In the second place, the hush-hush and mystery that have traditionally surrounded sexual activities tend to increase curiosity about them.

If a youth with such curiosity feels shy and inadequate in his relations with the other sex, it is not too surprising for him to accept the substitute of peeping. In this way he satisfies his curiosity and to some extent meets his sexual needs without the trauma of actually approaching a female, and thus without the failure and lowered self-status that such an approach might lead to. As a matter of fact, peeping activities often provide important compensatory feelings of power and superiority over the one being looked at, which may contribute materially to the maintenance of this pattern. Also, of course, the suspense and danger associated with conditions of peeping may lead to emotional excitement and a reinforcement of the sexual stimulation.

Where older and sometimes married men engage in peeping activities, the dynamics are quite similar, although here the fantasy identification of the peeper with one or the other of the sexual partners may be quite important. We sometimes find older women as well as men involved in peeping. A married peeper is rarely well adjusted sexually in his marriage.

A young married college student had an attic apartment which was extremely hot during the summer months. To enable him to attend school, his wife worked and came home at night tired and irritable and not in the mood for sexual relations. In addition, "the

damned springs in the bed squeaked." In order "to obtain some sexual gratification" the youth would peer through his binoculars at the room next door and occasionally saw the young couple there engaged in erotic scenes. This stimulated him greatly, and he thereupon decided to extend his activities to a sorority house. However, during his second venture he was reported and apprehended by the police. This offender was quite immature for his age, rather puritanical in his attitude toward masturbation, and prone to indulge in rich but immature sexual fantasies.

Although a peeper may become somewhat reckless in his observation of courting couples and thus may be detected and assaulted by his subjects, peeping does not ordinarily have any serious criminal or unalterable antisocial aspects. In fact, many people probably have rather strong inclinations in the same direction, which are well checked by practical considerations and moral attitudes concerning people's rights to privacy.

Treatment and outcomes. In general, the treatment of "peeping Toms" follows the same procedures as those outlined for exhibitionism, and the outcomes are equally favorable. Only in atypical cases—usually involving pervasive psychopathology—is the treatment likely to prove difficult or unsuccessful.

FETISHISM

In fetishism there is typically a centering of sexual interest on some body part or on an inanimate object, such as an article of clothing. Males are most commonly involved in cases of fetishism—reported cases of female fetishists being extremely rare. The range of fetishistic objects includes breasts, hair, ears, hands, underclothing, shoes, perfume, and similar objects associated with the opposite sex. The mode of using these objects for the achievement of sexual excitation and gratification varies considerably, but it commonly involves kissing, fondling, tasting, or smelling the object.

In order to obtain the required object, the fetishist may commit burglary, theft, or even assault. East (1946) related the case of a hair fetishist who was arrested for going up to a little girl on the street and cutting off some of her hair. At his residence, 5 plaits of hair of different colors, as well as 72 hair ribbons, were found.

Probably the articles most commonly stolen by fetishists are women's underthings. One young boy was found to have accumulated over a hundred pairs of panties from a lingerie shop when he was apprehended. In such cases, the excitement and suspense of the criminal act itself typically reinforce the sexual stimulation, and in some cases actually constitute the fetish—the article stolen being of little importance. For example, one youth admitted entering a large number of homes in which the entering itself usually sufficed to induce an orgasm. When it did not, he was able to achieve sexual satisfaction by taking some "token," such as money or jewelry.

Not infrequently, fetishistic behavior consists of masturbation in association with the fetishistic object. Here, of course, it is difficult to draw a line between fetishistic activity and the effort to increase the sexual excitation and satisfaction of masturbation through the use of pictures and other articles associated with the desired sexual object. Utilization of such articles in masturbation is a common practice and not usually considered pathological. However, where antisocial behavior —such as breaking and entering—is involved, the practice is commonly referred to as fetishistic.

A somewhat different, but not atypical, pattern of fetishism is illustrated by the case of a man whose fetish was women's shoes and legs.

The fetishist in this case was arrested several times for loitering in public places, such as railroad stations and libraries, watching women's legs. Finally he chanced on a novel solution to his problem. Posing as an agent for a hosiery firm, he hired a large room, advertised for models, and took motion pictures of a number of girls walking and seated with their legs displayed to best advantage. He then used these pictures to achieve sexual satisfaction and found that they continued adequate for the purpose. (Adapted from Grant, 1953)

Dynamics. In approaching the dynamics of fetishism, we may again note that many stimuli can come to be associated with sexual excitation in everyday life. Probably most people are stimulated to some degree by intimate articles of clothing and by perfumes and odors associated with the opposite sex. In many instances, however, such associations are not easy to explain. Bergler (1947) cited an unusual case in which a man's sex life was almost completely absorbed by a fetishistic fascination for exhaust pipes of cars. Nor

would just any exhaust pipe do; it had to be in perfect shape, that is to say, undented and undamaged, and it had to emit softly blowing gases. This became far more attractive to him than sexual behavior associated with women.

The first prerequisite in fetishism seems to be a conditioning experience. In some instances this original conditioning may be quite accidental, as when sexual arousal and orgasm—which are reflexive responses—are elicited by a strong emotional experience involving some particular object or part of the body.

The endowment of a formerly neutral stimulus with sexual arousal properties has been demonstrated in an interesting experiment by Rachman (1966), who created a mild fetish under laboratory conditions. A photograph of women's boots was repeatedly shown with slides of sexually stimulating nude females. Subjects came to exhibit sexual arousal—as measured by changes in penile volume—to the boots alone; and this response generalized to other types of women's shoes.

Fetishistic patterns of sexual gratification usually become the preferred patterns only when they are part of a larger picture of maladjustment; and the latter typically involves doubts about one's masculinity and potency and fear of rejection and humiliation by members of the opposite sex. By his fetishistic practices and mastery over the inanimate object—which comes to symbolize the desired sexual object—the individual apparently safeguards himself and also compensates somewhat for his feelings of inadequacy.

Treatment and outcomes. When apprehended, fetishists are usually quite embarrassed and penitent about their behavior, but are prone to deny its sexual connotations. In group therapy this process of denial is usually stripped away very rapidly, so that the fetishist has to come to grips with his actual problem. Behavior therapy—particularly aversive conditioning—also appears to be highly effective in the treatment of fetishism (Bandura, 1969; Marks & Gelder, 1967). Utilizing a behavior therapy approach, Kushner (1965) reported the successful treatment of a 33-year-old male with a longstanding fetish involving stealing women's panties and masturbating while wearing them. He could achieve orgasm only by means of his fetishistic practice. Initially Kushner utilized electric shock in association with women's panties to eliminate the fetish. Then a desensitization program was undertaken to alleviate the man's fears and anxieties associated with heterosexual relations. This procedure also proved successful and at last report the individual was married and enjoying an active heterosexual life.

PEDOPHILIA

In pedophilia the sex object is a child, the intimacy usually involving manipulation of the child's genitals—or in the case of a female victim, partial or complete penetration of the vagina. Occasionally the child is induced to manipulate the sex organ of the pedophiliac or to engage in mouth-genital contacts.

Offenders are diverse in terms of the act committed, the intentionality of and general circumstances surrounding the act, and age, education, and developmental history. Most pedophiliacs are men, but women occasionally engage in such practices. The average age of these offenders is 40 years. Most older offenders are or have been married, and many have children. In a study of 836 pedophiliac offenders in New Jersey, Revitch and Weiss (1962) found that the older offenders tended to seek out immature children, while younger offenders preferred adolescent girls between 12 and 15. Girls outnumber boys as victims, at a ratio of more than 2 to 1.

In most cases of pedophilia the victim is known to the offender, the sexual behavior may continue over a sustained period of time, and usually there is no physical coercion. Although in some cases the offenders may be encouraged or even seduced by their victims, Swanson (1968) found provocation or active participation by the victim in only 3 of the 25 cases he studied. Sometimes the pattern follows that described by MacNamara (1968):

". . . the prepubescent, non-sexually aggressive or adventuresome girl may awaken biological urges by her uninhibited affection for a male relative, acquaintance, or neighbor who, if his social inhibitions are weak because of loneliness, depression, alcohol, or other emotional state, may respond sexually." (p. 153)

Whether or not there is an element of provocation by the victim, the onus is always on the offender, for society's norms relating to pedophilia are explicit. Since pedophiliacs may subject children to highly traumatic emotional experiences as well as physical injury, this is not surprising. An alleged offender is sometimes considered guilty until proven innocent, however, and a number of men have served time in penal institutions because children or their parents interpreted simple affection as attempted intimacy or rape. On the other hand, many cases of sexual assault on children undoubtedly go unreported to spare the child a further ordeal.

Dynamics. In an intensive study of 38 pedophiliac offenders living in a segregated treatment center, Cohen and Seghorn (1969) noted three distinguishable patterns:

1. *The personally immature offender,* who has never been able to establish or maintain satisfactory interpersonal relationships with male or female peers during his adolescent, young adult, or adult life. This was by far the most common type. He is sexually comfortable only with children, and in most cases knows the victim. Usually the act is not impulsive but begins with a type of disarming courtship which eventually

---

HETEROSEXUAL PEDOPHILIACS

At the receiving center of the California Department of Corrections, a study was made of 100 consecutive cases in which males were convicted of sexual offenses against female children. The number of victims molested by a single offender varied from 1 to 6; however, the prosecution usually sought conviction on only one count and dropped the other charges. There were 147 victims in all, ranging in age from 3 to 17 years, with a mean age of 10.5. Sixty-seven percent of the molested children were known to the offenders. Other information about the offenders is as follows:

Age range	23 to 70 years; mean age, 37
Marital status	Single, 22; married, 43; divorced, 24; separated, 8; widowed, 3
Race	White, 73; black, 11; Mexican-American, 15; Oriental, 2
Victim's relationship to offender	Own child, 18; child of a relative, 21; child of a friend, 21; stranger, 32; own child plus child of a relative, 4; own child plus child of a friend, 2; own child plus stranger, 1; child of a friend plus stranger, 1

Psychological assessment indicated that these offenders suffered from pervasive feelings of inadequacy and insecurity; they were passive-dependent, guilt-ridden individuals with low heterosexual drive; and they showed confusion about their self-identity (Fisher, 1969).

leads to sexual play. Either male or female children may be the victims.

2. *The regressed offender,* who during adolescence shows apparently normal development, with good peer relationships and some dating behavior and heterosexual experiences.

"However, throughout this period there exist increasing feelings of masculine inadequacy in sexual and nonsexual activities. And, as he enters adulthood, his social, occupational, and marital adjustment is quite tenuous and marginal. There is frequently a history of an inability to deal with the normal stresses of adult life and alcoholic episodes become increasingly more frequent and result in the breakdown of a relatively stable marital, social, and work adjustment. In almost all instances the pedophilic acts are precipitated by some direct confrontation of his sexual adequacy by an adult female or some threat to his masculine image by a male peer." (p. 251)

The most frequent precipitating event is the discovery that the offender's wife or girl friend is having an affair with another man. In most of these cases the victim is a female child.

In contrast to the personally immature offender, the regressed offender is not acquainted with his victim, and the act is characteristically impulsive. For example, the offender may be driving a car, see a child, and become overwhelmed by sexual excitation.

3. *The aggressive offender,* whose primary intent includes both aggressive and sexual components.

"The primary aim is aggression, and is expressed in cruel and vicious assaults on the genitalia or by introducing the penis or elongated objects into the victim orally or anally. The sexual excitement increases as an apparent function of the aggression, but the orgasm itself either does not occur or must be reached through masturbation." (p. 251)

Such offenders usually have a history of antisocial behavior and, in general, could be described as hostile, aggressive psychopaths. Ordinarily they select a boy as the object of their aggression. Psychopaths—particularly those who use coercion—are prone to denying their offenses or placing the blame on their victims.

A number of other investigators have pointed to the high incidence of severe psychopathology —in addition to psychopathic personality—among

pedophiliacs. In a study of 25 offenders, Swanson (1968) reported that over a fourth were severe alcoholics. He also found sociopathic personalities, mental retardates, neurotics, schizoid personalities, and borderline schizophrenics. In over half the cases, the offender was experiencing conflict over or loss of his usual source of sexual gratification.

In the case of older offenders, there may be brain damage or other pathology that has weakened inhibitory controls. Pedophilia and exhibitionism are the most common sexual offenses committed by senile and arteriosclerotic individuals. Here, of course, there may be a combination of lowered inner controls, regression, and fear of impotence; alcoholism may also be a complicating factor.

Treatment and outcomes. In most states, pedophilia is punishable by confinement in prison or a mental hospital. For some offenders, imprisonment appears to be the only course to take: although it may do little to modify the behavior of the offender, it does protect society. However, since many pedophiliacs experience genuine remorse and want to change their maladaptive behavior, an increasing number are being screened for treatability and given indeterminate sentences in state mental hospitals or other facilities for sexual offenders. Here, modern rehabilitative programs—typically utilizing group therapy and, in some instances, behavior modification—have proven highly effective.

RAPE

In rape, sexual behavior is usually directed toward a normal sex object but under antisocial conditions.[1] Almost exclusively in reported cases, the male is the offender. Depending on the victim's age, such offenses are referred to as: (1) *statutory rape,* which involves the seduction of a minor; and (2) *forcible rape,* in which the unwilling partner is over 18. It is with the latter type that we are concerned in this section.

The FBI (1971) reported over 37,000 cases of forcible rape in 1970, more than twice as many as in 1960. And a detailed interview study by the

---

[1]Here we are referring to heterosexual rape. We shall comment on homosexual rape later in this chapter.

National Opinion Research Center of the University of Chicago (NORC) suggests that actual incidence figures are probably more than 3½ times the reported rate (President's Commission, 1967). Relatively speaking, rape is a young man's crime, and typically is a repetitive activity rather than an isolated act. About a third of all rapists are under 20; slightly more than half are in their 20's. Surprisingly, about half of these offenders are married and living with their wives at the time of their crime.

Often the rapist shows very little esthetic preference in his choice of sex objects. Sometimes he simply decides that he will rape the next woman he sees, conditions permitting. East (1946) cited a case in which an unprepossessing old maid over 70 years of age was raped and then murdered by a man who was not mentally retarded, drunk, or suffering from a psychosis. That such acts unfortunately are still being perpetrated is indicated by the case in Los Angeles in 1970 of a man in his late 20's who broke into a 72-year-old woman's apartment, criminally assaulted her, and then sat down to smoke a cigarette and watch television.

It is not uncommon for women who struggle against their attackers to receive broken ribs, fractures, and bruises. Occasionally, several offenders join together, as in some juvenile gangs, and rape a victim consecutively. In addition to the physical trauma inflicted on the victim, the psychological trauma may be severe. Such experiences usually are disturbing to the victim's marital relationship—upsetting the husband as well as the wife, especially when he has been forced to watch the rape.

Dynamics. Both sexual and aggressive com-

RESPONSE PATTERNS AMONG VICTIMS OF RAPE

Reactions to rape among female victims may vary greatly, but most victims apparently find the experience highly traumatic. In a study of 13 female rape victims, ages 18 to 24, Sutherland and Scherl (1970) reported a rather typical response pattern, which involved three phases:

1. **Acute reaction.** "In the moments, hours, and days immediately following the rape, the victim's acute reactions may take a variety of forms including shock, disbelief, and dismay. She often appears at the police station or the hospital in an agitated, incoherent, and highly volatile state. Frequently she is unable to talk about what has happened to her or to describe the man who has assaulted her. Sometimes the victim will initially appear stable only to break down at the first unexpected reminder of the incident. . . . The Phase One reaction normally resolves within a period of a few days to a few weeks."

2. **Outward adjustment.** "After the immediate anxiety-arousing issues have been temporarily settled, the patient generally returns to her usual work, school, or home pursuits. . . . [She] announces all is well and says she needs no further help.

"It is our impression that this period of pseudo-adjustment does not represent a final resolution of the traumatic event and the feelings it has aroused. Instead, it seems to contain a heavy measure of denial or suppression. The personal impact of what has happened is ignored in the interest of protecting self and others.

"During this phase the victim must deal with her feelings about the assailant. Anger or resentment are often subdued in the interest of a return to ordinary daily life. The victim may rationalize these feelings by attributing the act to blind chance ('it could have happened to anyone'), to 'sickness' on the part of the assailant, or to an extension of the social struggle of black against white or of poor against rich. In similar fashion and for the same reasons the victim's doubts about her role in the assault are also set aside."

3. **Integration and resolution.** "Phase Three begins when the victim develops an inner sense of depression and of the need to talk. It is during this period that the resolution of the feelings aroused by the rape usually occurs. Concerns which have been dealt with superficially or denied successfully reappear for more comprehensive review. The depression of Phase Three is psychologically normal and occurs for most young women who have been raped.

"There are two major themes which emerge for resolution in this phase. First, the victim must integrate a new view of herself. She must accept the event and come to a realistic appraisal of her degree of complicity in it. Statements such as 'I should have known better than to talk to him . . .' or 'I should never have been out alone' emerge at this time. Second, the victim must resolve her feelings about the assailant and her relationship to him. Her earlier attitude of 'understanding the man's problems' gives way to anger toward him for having 'used' her and anger toward herself for in some way having permitted or tolerated this 'use.'"

Although a specific incident or discovery, such as a diagnosis of pregnancy or need to identify the assailant for police, may precipitate Phase Three, the phase frequently begins with "a more general deterioration . . . of the defenses of Phase Two . . . [with the victim] thinking increasingly about what has happened . . . and functioning progressively less well." (pp. 504–508)

During the third phase the victim's repetitive talking about her obsessive memories of the rape—which seem to return to haunt her at this time—apparently has a desensitizing effect. As the desensitization process continues, it becomes possible for her to deal with the event as something in the past and to integrate it into her self-structure. The victim may also express concern about the effects of the experience on her future life, as well as on her immediate marital or other interpersonal relationships. Professional assistance may be of great value in helping the victim work through the experience and any interpersonal complications it may create.

ponents are involved in the act of rape—in varying degrees and combinations. On the basis of an intensive study of 27 convicted rapists, Cohen and Seghorn (1969) have suggested the following distinguishable patterns:

1. *Displaced aggression.* In these cases the act is primarily aggressive.

"The sexual behavior is used to physically harm, to degrade, or to defile the victim in the service of this aggressive intent. The acts are experienced by the offender as the result of an 'uncontrollable impulse' and almost always follow some precipitating, disagreeable event involving a wife, girl friend, or mother. The victim is brutally assaulted, and those parts of the woman's body which usually are sexually exciting frequently become the foci for the offender's violence." (p. 250)

Here sexual excitation is minimal or even absent. The offender must masturbate to achieve an erection, and in many cases he cannot reach an orgasm. Thus the behavior appears to be a release not for intense sexual tensions but for displaced hostility and aggression—particularly since the offender does not know his victim.

2. *Compensation.* Here sexual excitation is the key component, and the aggressive features are so minimal that if the victim struggles at all, the offender flees.

"In these acts the primary aim is clearly sexual and the aggression is in the service of gratifying the sexual desires. The offender is always in a state of intense sexual excitation and often has an orgasm in the simple pursuit of the victim or upon making some physical contact. The recurrent fantasy in such offenders is that the victims will yield, submit to intercourse, in which he will be especially virile and so pleasing to the victim that she will become enamoured with him and invite him to repeat the sexual acts." (p. 250)

Aside from episodic assaults, these offenders appear to manifest no other antisocial behavior. Typically they are extremely passive and submissive, and almost obsessively concerned with feelings of sexual inadequacy. After an assault they may feel guilty and much concerned about the well-being of the victim.

3. *Sex aggression defusion.* Here the aggressive and sexual components appear to coexist, so that

". . . the offender is not able to experience, or even fantasy, sexual desires without a concomitant arousal of aggressive thoughts and feelings. Further, he projects such feelings onto his victim and sees her struggles and protestations as seductive—'Women like to get roughed up; they enjoy a good fight.' Such perceptions are made in the context of very brutal assaults. In offenders where this pattern is present, all object relationships, with both men and women, show this same quality of an eroticization of aggressive behavior." (p. 250)

Such individuals tend to be loud and assertive, and women who come in contact with them may feel both seduced and overwhelmed. In extreme form, the pattern is manifested as sexual sadism, where the victim may be viciously violated, mutilated, and even murdered.

4. *Impulse.* In this final pattern, the act of rape is based on impulse and has little to do with either sexual or aggressive feelings.

"The rape is frequently carried out in the context of some other antisocial act such as robbery or theft. . . . The act is opportunistic, narcissistic, and impulsive, and such an offender has a history of predatory, antisocial behavior from his late childhood, preadolescent years." (p. 250)

Although Cohen and Seghorn's classification was based on a limited sample, it appears to be supported by many earlier findings.

Association with other psychopathology. In a study of 100 rapists, Kopp (1962) found a high incidence of antisocial or psychopathic personalities, which he described this way:

"This antisocial psychopath is a cold, seemingly unfeeling man who has always taken what he wanted from others without apparent concern for the feelings of his victims or for the consequences of his act. For him, rape is just another instance of aggressive taking, except that in this case he steals sexual satisfaction rather than money or property. When questioned about his offense, he often responds with callous sarcasm, completely devoid of guilt or concern. He may well simply respond with the statement, 'I wanted it so I took it.' The rape fits so well with his character structure and is so typical of his general behavior pattern that he can see nothing wrong with the act, and often goes on to rationalize that his victim probably enjoyed it. He wants no part of therapy unless he sees it as a means of manipulating his way out of incarceration." (p. 66)

Although probably the largest percentage of rapists are psychopathic, some may fall within other categories of psychopathology. In manic reactions, schizophrenia, and various organic psychoses, for example, the lowering of inner controls may lead to physical assault and occasionally to forcible rape. However, during acute psychotic episodes the individual is likely to be so disorganized as to be capable only of indiscriminate physical assault rather than the coordinated behavior required for forcible rape. In some instances there is a "drunken aggressor," whose behavior may range from clumsy attempts to gain acceptance from a female he mistakenly believes to be available, to pathological violence accompanying an alcoholic lowering of inhibitions (Gebhard et al., 1965).

Treatment and outcomes. Because of the suffering they cause their victims, rapists are treated severely by society, usually being subjected to long jail sentences. The imprisonment seems to have little value in itself, aside from protecting society from further ravages by the offender for the specified time. Appropriate treatment, however, may produce positive results in many cases. Cohen and Seghorn (1969) have noted that for some offenders—particularly those who are categorized as having evidenced displaced aggression, and who have relatively normal social and adaptive skills in other areas—favorable results may be produced fairly quickly with group therapy. Adequate data concerning behavior therapy are not available, but modified aversive procedures may prove effective. Treatment is likely to be more difficult and the outcome less predictable for psychopathic rapists.

Drugs have proven helpful in reducing sex drive in some individuals who are manifesting sexually deviant patterns. In Denmark, castration has been used as a means of controlling relapsed rapists (Sturup, 1968), but this represents a very drastic approach, and the question of its use is complicated by serious social and ethical issues.

INCEST

Culturally prohibited sexual relations between family members, such as a brother and sister or a parent and child, are called *incestuous*. The actual incidence of incest is unknown since it takes place in a family setting and only comes to light when reported to law enforcement or other agencies. However, Kinsey et al. (1948; 1953) reported an incidence of 5 cases per 1000 persons in a sample of 12,000 subjects; and Gebhard et al. (1965) found 30 cases per 1000 subjects in a group of 3500 imprisoned sex offenders. In both these studies brother-sister incest was reported as being 5 times more common than the next most common pattern—father-daughter incest. Mother-son incest is thought to be relatively rare.[1] In occasional cases, such as that described in the illustration on page 473, there may be multiple patterns of incest within the same family.

Although certain cultures have approved incestuous relationships (at one time it was the established practice in Egypt for the king to marry his sister), most social groups have definite prohibitions against them. An indication of the real risks involved in such inbreeding has been provided by Adams and Neel (1967), who compared the offspring of 18 nuclear incest marriages—12 brother-sister and 6 father-daughter—with those of a control group matched for age, intelligence, socioeconomic status, and other relevant characteristics. At the end of 6 months, 5 of the infants of the incestual marriages had died, 2 were severely retarded mentally and had been institutionalized, 3 showed evidence of borderline intelligence, and 1 had a cleft palate. Only 7 of the 18 infants were considered normal. In contrast, only 2 of the control-group infants were not considered normal—one showing indications of borderline intelligence and the other manifesting a physical defect. Lindzey (1967) has concluded that

". . . the consequences of inbreeding are sufficiently strong and deleterious to make it unlikely that a human society would survive over long periods of time if it permitted, or encouraged, a high incidence of incest. In this sense, then, one may say that the incest taboo (whatever other purposes it may serve) is biologically guaranteed." (p. 1055)

Dynamics. For an understanding of incestuous behavior, it may be noted that incestuous fan-

---

[1]Authorities are more likely to deal with cases of father-daughter than brother-sister incest, since the latter are less likely to be reported. For example, a study of 203 cases brought to the attention of authorities in Illinois revealed that 159 were father-daughter incest, 37 brother-sister, 2 mother-son, and 5 were multiple relationships (Weinberg, 1955).

tasies and desires are common during the adolescent period; and it is not uncommon for fathers to have such feelings toward their daughters. However, social mores and prohibitions are usually so deeply ingrained that such desires are rarely acted out. Bagley (1969) has suggested that several different dynamic patterns may be involved where incestuous behavior does occur. The following listing represents a slight modification of his schema.

1. *Accidental incest.* When brothers and sisters share the same bedroom during the preadolescent or adolescent period, they may tend to engage in sexual exploration and experimentation. In some cases older brothers seduce their younger sisters without any apparent understanding of the social prohibitions and possible consequences.

2. *Incest associated with severe psychopathology.* In the case of psychopathic fathers, the incest may simply be part of an indiscriminate pattern of sexual promiscuity; and in other in-

INCESTUAL BEHAVIOR IN THREE GENERATIONS OF A FAMILY

Raphling, Carpenter, and Davis (1967) have reported the intensive study of the behavior of a 39-year-old white male who learned incestual patterns from his father and in turn transmitted them to his son. The case came under study when the wife of the 39-year-old male apparently developed guilt feelings and gave her husband the alternative of accepting a divorce or seeking medical attention. He chose the latter, which led to a psychiatric examination, the report of which is excerpted below:

"The father is described by the patient as being similar to himself, both in physical appearance and personality type. . . . As a unit the family was loosely bound and little affection was expressed. The mother and father remained emotionally isolated from each other and were often openly hostile to one another. . . . The patient received his sexual education from his peers and from what he observed in his own home.

"He recalls having observed sexual relations between his father and older sister when he was 11. Shortly thereafter the patient himself began to experiment in sexual relations with his sister. He denies ever having had orgasm with her as a sexual partner; he also states that she appeared to accept the incestuous relationship.

"The patient states that his mother was aware of her husband's special relationship with his 13-year-old daughter, and passively accepted this behavior. Indeed, the father would manipulate the daughter's genitals while he was in bed with both her and his wife. The patient and his father, quite independently, continued to have relations with the oldest girl until she ran away from home at 14 to marry.

"The patient left home at 16. During his absence the father commenced incestuous relations with his two younger daughters, who were just reaching puberty. When the patient returned home at 18, he soon followed in his father's footsteps and began to have sexual relations with his two younger sisters; he continued this practice sporadically until they left home.

"The patient married an 18-year-old farm girl when he was 21. . . . The couple have five children: four daughters whose ages are 17, 16, 10, and 5 years, and one son, age 14. When the first daughter reached puberty at age 12, the patient states he initiated her into sexual relations while his wife was in the hospital delivering their youngest child. Subsequently he has had intercourse with her on an average of two to three times per week for the last five years.

"The daughter passively accepted her father's proposals, but states that she derives no sexual pleasure from these acts. On the contrary, the patient has been able to achieve orgasm whenever intercourse was carried to completion. The daughter states that she allowed this relationship to continue because her father expected her to participate, because she felt sorry for him after she refused him, and because she feared she would lose any affection which he might have for her if she did not submit.

"When the patient next approached his second eldest daughter he was vehemently refused by her; consequently, he has rarely been able to complete the sexual act with her. He nevertheless persisted in his sexual pursuit. . . . Having already had sexual relations with two daughters, he next attempted manual manipulation of the next-to-youngest daughter, then age 8. She protested so strenuously that he has made no further sexual advances to her.

"When his only son reached puberty the patient took great care to instruct him in the details of sexual behavior and urged him to have sexual relations with his own mother. The son did eventually make vague sexual advances to his mother which greatly angered her. In addition, the patient implicitly gave his son permission to have sexual relations with his sisters. The eldest complied with her brother's demands. The next eldest daughter denies having submitted to her brother; he, however, contradicts this, and further states that he derives great pleasure from sexual relations with his sisters, but denies any other sexual contacts to date.

"On examination the patient appeared anxious but was able to express himself without hesitation. . . . Although he feels unhappy and guilty about his incestuous behavior, he readily admits that this has not prevented him from continuing to have sexual relations with his daughters. He . . . has . . . reassured himself that he is doing his daughters a favor by initiating them into sexual relations. Paradoxically enough, he is a prudish man who dictates high moral standards to his family at the same time he commits incest. . . .

"He has few social contacts other than with those who work with him. His work record has been good and he has carried out duties which involve great responsibility. . . ." (pp. 507–509)

In assessing the family dynamics in this case, the investigators emphasized two points: (1) incestual desires are not uncommon, but the outcome depends heavily on how they are handled—in terms of positive or negative reinforcement—by the parents; and (2) in this case the father encouraged his daughters and son to give in to latent incestuous feelings, and the mother gave silent consent to the incestuous behavior of her daughters. In effect, the mother shared her responsibility as wife and lover with her daughters as a means of avoiding her husband's sexual demands.

dividuals, such as alcoholics and psychotics, the incestuous relations may be associated with the lowering of inner controls.

3. *Incest associated with pedophilia.* Here a father has an intense craving for young children as sex objects, including his own daughters.

4. *Incest associated with a faulty paternal model.* Here a father sets an undesirable example for his son by engaging in incestuous relations with his daughter or daughters, and may encourage his son to do likewise.

5. *Incest associated with family pathology and disturbed marital relations.* Here a family's morals are low or the family is disorganized. In some instances a rejecting, hostile wife may actually foster father-daughter incest.

In general, incestuous fathers who come to the attention of authorities do not have a history of sexual offenses or other criminal behavior, nor do they show a disproportionate incidence of prior hospitalization for mental disorders (Cavillin, 1966). Curiously enough, such fathers do tend to restrict their sexual patterns to family members rather than seeking and engaging in extramarital sexual relations. For example, in his intensive study of 12 fathers convicted of incestuous relations with their daughters, Cavillin (1966) reported that only 2 of the 12 had resorted to extramarital relations, despite feeling unloved and rejected by their wives.

Cavillin further reported that the youngest father in the group was 20 and the oldest was 56, and that the average age was 39. The average age of the daughters was 13—the youngest being 3 and the oldest 18. Five of the 12 fathers had had a relationship with more than 1 daughter, usually beginning with the oldest; and in 11 of the cases the relationships had gone on for some time— from 3 months to 3 years—before being reported. In all of the cases the fathers were reported by the daughters.

As noted above, in all 12 of the cases studied by Cavillin the father felt rejected and threatened by his wife. Other investigators have also noted the frequency of disturbed marital relationships in such cases—the father feeling unloved by a cold and hostile wife, who rejects him sexually and often appears to encourage an incestuous relationship with the daughter.

The effect of the incestuous relationship on the daughter appears to depend on her age when the relationship occurs and the anxiety and guilt, if any, she perceives in her father. Most girls studied who were still adolescent expressed feelings of guilt and depression over their incestuous behavior. Some girls in this situation turn to promiscuity; others run away from home to escape the stressful situation.

Treatment and outcomes. Ordinarily, when an incestuous relationship is broken up, it is by the action of the family members themselves. Many offenses go unreported because, in the case of father-daughter incest, the family may be reluctant to lose the father's economic support. And in cases of brother-sister incest, they may prefer that the brother be admonished and warned, rather than reported and punished. Whatever the circumstances, little occurs in the way of corrective treatment. Nevertheless, the continuation of incestual patterns over long-range periods is the exception rather than the rule.

SADISM

The term *sadism* is derived from the name of the Marquis de Sade (1740–1814), who for sexual purposes inflicted such cruelty on his victims that he was eventually committed as insane. Although the term's meaning has broadened to denote cruelty in general, we shall use it in its restricted sense, to denote achievement of sexual gratification through the infliction of pain on a partner. The pain may be inflicted by such means as whipping, biting, and pinching; and the act may vary in intensity, from fantasy to severe mutilation and in extreme cases even to murder. Males are ordinarily the offenders, although Krafft-Ebing (1950) has reported a number of cases in which sadists were women. In one unusual case, the wife required her husband to cut himself on the arm before approaching her sexually. She would then suck the wound and become extremely aroused.

In some cases sadistic activities lead up to or terminate in actual sexual relations; in others, full sexual gratification is obtained from the sadistic practice alone. A sadist may slash a girl with a razor or stick her with a needle, experiencing an orgasm in the process. Showing the peculiar and extreme associations that may occur is the case of a young man who entered a strange girl's apartment, held a chloroformed rag to her face until she lost consciousness, and then branded her on the thigh with a hot iron. She was not molested in any other way. Sometimes sadistic activities are associated with animals or with fetishistic objects instead of other human beings. East (1946) cited the case of a man who stole women's shoes, which he then slashed savagely with a knife. When he was in prison, he was found mutilating photographs that other prisoners kept in their cells by cutting the throats of the women in them. He admitted that he derived full sexual gratification from this procedure. Below is a more serious case, which involves sadistic murder.

The offender, Peter Kursten, was 47 years old at the time of his apprehension in Dusseldorf, Germany, for a series of lust murders. He was a skilled laborer, well groomed, modest, and had done nothing that annoyed his fellow workers.

Peter came from a disturbed family background, his father having been an alcoholic who had been sent to prison for having intercourse with Peter's older sister. Peter's own earliest sexual experiences were with animals. When he was about 13 years old, he attempted to have intercourse with a sheep, but the animal would not hold still and he took out a knife and stabbed her. At that moment he had an ejaculation.

As a consequence of this experience, Peter found the sight of gushing blood sexually exciting; and he turned from animals to human females. Often he first choked his victim, but if he did not achieve an orgasm he then stabbed her. Initially he used scissors and a dagger, but later he took to using a hammer or an axe. After he achieved ejaculation, he lost interest in his victim, except in taking measures to cover up his crime.

The offender's sexual crimes extended over a period of some 30 years and involved over 40 victims. Finally apprehended in 1930, he expressed a sense of injustice at not being like other people who were raised in normal families. (Adapted from Berg, 1954)

A number of more recent cases in which women have been strangled and mutilated in association with sadistic patterns could also be cited. Not only does the individual appear unable to control his sadistic impulses; but unless he is apprehended, his acts tend to be repetitive. And, as Hirschfeld (1956) has pointed out:

"In genuine cases of sexual murder the killing replaces the sexual act. There is, therefore, no sexual intercourse at all, and sexual pleasure is induced by cutting, stabbing, and slashing the victim's body, ripping open the abdomen, plunging the hands into her intestines, cutting out and taking away her genitals, throttling her, sucking her blood. These horrors . . . constitute the —so to speak—pathological equivalent of coitus." (p. 388)

Dynamics. Explanations of the dynamics of sadism have emphasized a number of factors:

1. *Experiences in which sexual excitation and possibly orgasm have been associated with the infliction of pain.* Such conditioned associations may occur under a variety of conditions. In their sexual fantasies many children visualize a violent attack by a man on a woman, and such ideas may be strengthened by newspaper articles of sadistic assaults on females. Perhaps more directly relevant are experiences in which an individual's infliction of pain on an animal or another person has given rise to strong emotions and, unintentionally, to sexual excitement. We have noted elsewhere the connection between strong emotional stimulation and sexual stimulation, especially during the adolescent period. Just as in fetishism—where simple conditioning seems to make it possible for almost any object or action to become sexually exciting—conditioning can also be an important factor in the development of sadistic tendencies.

The victim's response generally has an important bearing on the development of sadistic behavior; if the response is one of acquiescence and the sadist achieves gratification, the behavior is likely to be reinforced and gradually seem normal to him.

2. *Negative attitudes toward sex and/or fears of impotence.* Sadistic activities may protect an individual with negative attitudes toward sex from the full sexual implications of his behavior, and at the same time may help him express his contempt and punishment of the other person for engaging in sexual relations. Several early investigators have described male sadists as timid, feminine, undersexed individuals, and sadistic behavior as apparently designed to arouse strong emotions in the sex object which, in turn, arouses a great peak of sexual excitement in the sadist and makes orgasm possible (Berg, 1954; Krafft-Ebing, 1950). The sadist apparently receives little or no satisfaction if his victim remains passive and unresponsive to the painful stimuli. In fact, he usually wants her to find the pain exciting, and may even insist that she act pleasurably aroused when being stuck with pins, bitten, or otherwise hurt.

For many sexually inadequate and insecure individuals, the infliction of pain is apparently a "safe" means of achieving sexual stimulation. As Fenichel (1945) put it, the sadist thereby feels that "I am the castrator, not the castrated one." Strong feelings of power and superiority over his victim may for the time shut out underlying feelings of inadequacy and anxiety.

3. *Association with other psychopathology.* In schizophrenia and other severe forms of psychopathology, sadistic sexual behavior and sadistic rituals may result from the lowering of inner controls and the deviation of symbolic processes. Wertham (1949) has cited an extreme case in which a schizophrenic with puritanical attitudes toward sex achieved full sexual gratification by castrating young boys and killing and mutilating young girls. He rationalized his actions as being the only way to save the victims from later immoral behavior. Similarly, Michaux and Michaux (1963) have reported the case of a 17-year-old

PROGRESSION OF PATHOLOGICAL SEXUAL DEVIANCE

In occasional instances, deviant sexual behavior shows a progression from relatively minor patterns to those of a more serious nature. This is illustrated in the following case, which also shows the key role that inadequate and distorted information may play in the development of extreme pathological sexual deviations.

Some years ago, the police of one of our large cities were baffled by three sadistic murders which occurred with no evidence of monetary or other clear-cut motivation. On the wall of one apartment, in which an ex-Wave was brutally killed, there appeared in lipstick "For heaven's sake catch me before I kill more: I cannot control myself." In another killing, a child of 6 was kidnaped and her body dismembered and thrown into various sewers and drains. The kidnaper wrote and delivered a ransom note to the child's parents. No progress was made in this case until a policeman off duty captured a young man who was trying to make a getaway after an attempt at burglary. The youth would probably have been released on probation had it not been for an alert police official who noticed a resemblance between a curve flourish in the youth's signature and the ransom note. This youth, a 17-year-old university student, proved to be the perpetrator of the earlier crimes.

An extensive study of the youth was made. He was found to be of normal intelligence, not psychotic, and medically normal; electroencephalographic tracings were normal. In the clinical report, his background was described as follows:

"When aged 9, the patient began to be interested in the 'feeling and color' and then 'the stealing' of women's underclothing. He began to take these at first from clothes lines, then from basements, and later from strange houses, the doors of which he found open or ajar. Dresses or other articles of woman's apparel made no appeal to him nor was he interested in the undergarments of his immediate family. Having secured a pair of woman's panties or drawers, he would take it to a basement or home, put it on, experience excitement and sexual completion. Most garments he then threw away, some he replaced, and some he hoarded.

"When 12 or 13 years of age, he secured the desired garments by going into houses through windows. This furnished more excitement. After three such expeditions, he took objects ('guns or money') other than underclothes; a change which was again an added stimulation. 'It seemed sort of foolish to break in and not take anything.' When

he had thus changed his objective, the interest in underclothes largely evaporated and was replaced by the excitement experienced on 'making an entrance' through the window. Often he would struggle against his desire to leave his room at night, but when he did leave it was for the purpose of committing burglaries. He had sexual excitement or an erection at the sight of an open window at the place to be burglarized. Going through the window he had an emission."

Even after the youth's admission to the university, his deviant behavior continued, although it apparently became increasingly difficult to achieve sexual gratification and would take several entrances to produce an emission. On one occasion he was startled in the act of burglarizing by a nurse whom he promptly struck and injured. This resulted in an orgasm and he left without striking her again. On subsequent occasions when he was startled in the course of his burglarizing, he immediately killed. In one instance he had an erection on entering the house and then "'The dog barked and the lady started hollering. She had on a night gown. She jumped up and hollered. Then I took the knife and stabbed her—through the throat —just to keep her quiet.'" Although this resulted in an orgasm, he apparently had not intended to kill the woman. "'It was the noise that set me off, I believe....'"

"After an emission was the only time he felt he had done wrong.... [Then he suffered] from the pang of conscience.... We asked him had he never relieved this tension by manual manipulation. On one occasion he indignantly denied even the attempt.... Later he said he tried this method twice without success. In the same manner, he at first denied ever having attempted any sex play with girls. Two days later with one of his rare shows of emotion he said, looking much ashamed, that twice, later correcting himself to eight times, he had touched girls 'on the breasts' and then pressed 'on the leg.' Always, having done this, he would immediately burst into tears and 'be upset and unable to sleep.' He forcibly denied ever having made any more intimate advances, except that he 'kissed them' sometimes. 'They wanted to kiss; I didn't.'

"It was clear that normal sex stimulation and experience were unpleasant, indeed 'repulsive,' to him, and these efforts afterwards created in him a negative emotional state. He found them improper in the conduct of others; he never spoke of them except in condemnation...." (Adapted from Kennedy, Hoffman & Haines, 1947)

schizophrenic who beat into unconsciousness a young woman he did not know, sexually assaulted her, and then impulsively stabbed her to death.

Treatment and outcomes. There is a dearth of definitive data on the treatment of sadism. However, since erotic fantasies may serve as evocative stimuli for overt sexual deviations, the following case reported by Davison (1968) is of interest.

A 21-year-old male college student's sexual behavior had been limited to masturbatory fantasies of inflicting injuries on women. In treatment, the student was initially instructed to masturbate while looking at pictures of nude women. After such conventional stimuli had acquired sex-arousing value, a second procedure was introduced in which sadistic fantasy was paired with nauseous imagery—such as "steaming urine with reeking fecal boli bobbing on top which he drank." Eventually, the sadistic fantasies were supplanted by normal masturbatory fantasies. Interpreting this countercondi-tioning as consistent with self-control processes, the student was encouraged to engage in normal college dating. Prior to his treatment, he stated that he had never been aroused by girls and had only twice kissed them. But now he found himself attracted in a normal sexual way to the girls he dated. This treatment required only 6 sessions.

Of course, where the individual does not want treatment or where his deviation is associated with severe psychopathology, successful treatment may be more difficult or impossible.

MASOCHISM

The term *masochism* is derived from the name of the Austrian novelist Leopold V. Sacher-Masoch (1836–1895), whose fictional characters dwelt lovingly on the sexual pleasure of pain. As in the case of the term *sadism*, the meaning of *masochism* has been broadened beyond sexual connotations, so that it includes the deriving of pleasure from self-denial, expiatory physical suffering such as that of the religious flagellants, and hardship and suffering in general. We shall restrict our present discussion to the sexual aspects of masochistic behavior. The dynamics are similar to those in sadistic practices, except that now pain is inflicted on the self instead of on others.

Masochistic activities may be confined to sexually stimulating fantasies of ill treatment, or they may involve a wide range of pain-inflicting activities, such as binding, trampling, semistrangulation, spanking, switching, sticking with pins, and verbal abuse. Such behavior is more common among women than men.

Dynamics. Patterns of masochistic behavior usually come about through conditioned learning: as a result of early experiences, an individual comes to associate pain with sexual pleasure.

East (1946) cited the case of a young woman who frequently cut herself about the arms, legs, and breasts, and inserted pins and needles under her skin. She experienced sexual pleasure from the pain and from seeing the blood from the incisions. In other cases, masochistic sexual behavior represents an attempt to increase the emotional excitement of the sexual act and thus promote maximum satisfaction from it. Here, the erotic masochistic activities rarely result in severe injury; rather, they are in the nature of play-acting in which the abuse and pain are used to build up sexual excitation. Such sayings as "being crushed in his arms" or "smothered with kisses" reveal the association commonly made between erotic arousal and pain or discomfort.

In other cases the associative pattern may be more complex and may involve fears of abandonment, neglect, or rejection. For example, if punishment has been the only evidence of love and affection that a child has received, he may later, in sexual relations, figuratively offer to submit to being hurt by a sex partner as a means of feeling wanted and loved.

Treatment and outcomes. In dealing with masochism, we are again faced with an almost complete lack of definitive data.

In an interesting treatment program involving three cases of exhibitionism, two of transvestism, and one of masochism, Abel, Levis, and Clancy (1970) utilized the same aversive conditioning techniques. The first step involved making tapes describing each patient's deviant sexual behavior. These tapes were then associated with electric shock; but each shocked run was followed by runs in which the patient could avoid the shock by verbalizing normal sexual behavior in place of the shocked segment of the tape. In this laboratory situation, deviant sexual responses—

as indicated by penile erections—were inhibited in all subjects; and patient reports indicated that this suppression was generalized to real-life situations. This procedure was successful in suppressing deviant sexual behavior for at least 18 weeks, while yielding evidence of sustained benefits in terms of fostering more socially acceptable and normal sexual outlets.

Although this was a preliminary report, it does point to the possibility of similar behavior therapy procedures being effective in the treatment of a variety of sexual deviations. And although the preceding study was limited primarily to aversive conditioning, it would appear that desensitization procedures and assertion training can be used to augment aversive therapy in overall treatment programs.

Other pathological sexual deviations could be mentioned here, including *bestiality* and *necrophilia*. The former refers to the use of animals as sexual objects, a practice which Kinsey et al. (1948) found relatively common—particularly in rural areas. In necrophilia the sexual object is a female corpse. Although it has been recognized since antiquity, necrophilia is of rare occurrence. For the person who has reason to pursue this subject, detailed case histories are cited by Brill (1941), De River (1949), Ehrenreich (1960), and Klaf and Brown (1958).

In general, the pathological deviations with which we have dealt are those considered maladaptive on individual and/or group levels. Now let us turn to a consideration of socially organized and related sexual deviations.

SOCIALLY ORGANIZED AND RELATED SEXUAL DEVIATIONS

As we noted previously, a high proportion of prostitutes and homosexuals operate within a supportive subculture that influences their training, roles, and conditions of operation. Their behavior is viewed as pathological by some persons and groups but not by others; and the frequency of its incidence appears little affected by legal sanctions or social disapproval. Thus for purposes of our discussion we have grouped these and related patterns into a third category of socially organized sexual deviations.

PROSTITUTION

Prostitution is defined as the provision of sexual relations in return for money. Technically, there are four types of prostitution, the most common involving heterosexual relations for which the female is paid. There is also heterosexual prostitution for which the male is paid by the female, male homosexual prostitution, in which a male provides sexual relations for another male, and female homosexual prostitution, in which a female provides sexual relations for another female. The fourth type appears to be relatively rare. The focus of the present discussion is on the first type—prostitution involving heterosexual relations for which the female is paid.

Prostitution has flourished throughout history, often being referred to as "the world's oldest profession." In some societies prostitutes are accorded high social status; where prostitution is governmentally regulated, they are accepted much as persons associated with any other social institution. In most segments of our own society, however, prostitution has traditionally been considered evil, and prostitutes have been subjected to legal sanctions and relegated to low social status. In the United States there are some 500,000 prostitutes, as well as an equal number of women who serve as part-time prostitutes (*Time*, 1971).

For an indication of the proportion of men in this country who frequent prostitutes, we have only the findings of Kinsey et al. (1948), which, in turn, bear only on the white male population. According to these figures 69 percent of white males had some experience with prostitutes; however, for many men there was only one such experience. The investigators estimated that contact with prostitutes provided less than 5 percent of the total sexual outlet of the population sampled—far lower than in countries where prostitution is governmentally controlled. Packard (1968) has reported a decrease in the number of young college males who frequent prostitutes as a consequence of changing sexual mores and the more ready availability of sexual relations with girl friends.

Since there has been relatively little systematic research on prostitution in the United States, there are many questions for which we lack clear-cut answers. For example, one might ask: (1) Why do men frequent prostitutes? (2) Why and how do women become prostitutes? (3) What sort of relationship do prostitutes have with their clients? (4) What kind of social structure do most prostitutes enter when they become part of "the life"? and (5) What is the outcome for women who make a career of prostitution? Available evidence leads more to conjecture than to hard fact, but it is evident that the answers will be both complex and different for different individuals.

Why men frequent prostitutes. Among the reasons that Kinsey et al. (1948) reported for men's frequenting of prostitutes were: (1) insufficient opportunity for other types of heterosexual experience, as is often the case with military personnel; (2) desire to discover what such an experience may have to offer, and, in the case of some older men, to have sexual relations with a much younger woman; (3) desire to avoid responsibilities generally associated with sexual relations; (4) difficulty in securing sexual relations with other women—possibly because of timidity or a physical defect; and (5) desire to find a partner willing to engage in deviant sexual practices.

Why and how women become prostitutes. Research studies have ascribed widely different motives and characteristics to girls who become prostitutes. Contrary to popular opinion, there does not appear to be any systematic process of recruiting females into the profession. As Gagnon and Simon (1968) have stated, ". . . we are dealing with the phenomenon of enlistment rather than recruitment." (p. 117) The majority of girls who enlist appear to come from lower-class or lower-middle-class homes. Often they come from unstable families and have histories of sexual promiscuity during adolescence. Somewhere along the line they may receive money as well as other presents for their sexual favors, and become interested in the possibility of a career in prostitution.

The inclination to become a prostitute must be implemented by some actual means of entering the profession. All but one of the 33 call girls Bryan (1965) studied in the Los Angeles area had personal contact with someone engaged in call-girl activities. In some instances the girls had been friends; sometimes the contact had started with a homosexual relationship between the two. The initial contact usually determined the type or social level of prostitution at which the girl began. These "social levels" ranged from streetwalking to serving a "select clientele" as a "high-class" call girl.

Once the contact is acquired and the decision made to become a call girl, the novice typically enters a period of apprenticeship, which may last from 2 to 8 months or even longer. In general, great value is placed on achieving maximum gains from minimum effort and on cooperating with other working girls. The "johns" (customers) are pictured as basically exploitative, and hence open to exploitation; and the girls view prostitution as basically an honest occupation—certainly no more dishonest than marrying for money. After the novice has acquired a clientele, her training period ceases and she goes into business for herself.

The prostitute-client relationship. The personality makeup of prostitutes and their relationships with their clients appear to be highly variable.

Although there appears to be a higher than average incidence of pathological types, Jackman, O'Toole, and Geis (1963) have concluded that most prostitutes have normal intelligence and come from an average educational background. Especially as we go up the social scale to the "high-class" call girls, we appear to be dealing in the main with physically attractive, well-educated, and sophisticated young women who manage to convince themselves that prostitution is a perfectly acceptable business venture and preferable to being a secretary or working at some other job. In some instances, of course, they

THE NEW BREED OF PROSTITUTES

A young prostitute in New York waits to make a contact.

Most contacts take place on the streets or in bars—or, for call girls, via the telephone. The old-style brothel or house of prostitution has virtually disappeared from the American scene.

Young prostitutes—referred to as "the new breed"—have lowered the average age of prostitutes in every major city in the land. In Miami in 1971, vice officers estimated the average age of prostitutes at 18, compared with 23 only 3 years before. Helping to lower the age is the sizable number of young female runaways who are entering "the oldest profession."

Reasons for entering vary: some are looking for "kicks" and perhaps enough money to maintain a "pad"; others need money to support a drug habit; and still others are preyed upon by underworld groups who recruit them, forcibly or otherwise, into "white-slave rings."

Whatever their reasons for becoming prostitutes, "nobody ever goes into the game for keeps." One girl expressed it:

"Of course I'm only in it for five years
For a few years
Until I'm bored with it
For five years.
For five years. . . ." (Young, 1964, p. 123)

Although the great majority who enter prostitution do not view it as a final life style, many find it much easier to enter than to quit.

---

actually do hold other jobs and work as call girls in their off-hours. In some cases, their jobs involve entertaining out-of-town businessmen, a responsibility that may or may not eventuate in sexual relations.

It has been presumed that the prostitute views her behavior strictly as a matter of business and does not experience orgasm or emotional arousal during a professional contact. However, the relationship appears to vary. For streetwalkers in large cities, who may never expect to see their clients again, the encounter is brief and business-like; while for call girls who have repeated contacts with the same client, there may be some emotional involvement. Bryan (1966) pointed to a wide variety of relationships between call girls and their clients, ranging from coldness and hostility on the girl's part to friendship and sexual gratification.

The world of prostitution. In the world of prostitution, the pimp occupies a role despised by conventional society. However, as Hirschi (1962) and Bryan (1965) have pointed out, many prostitutes could not function without him. The pimp serves as the prostitute's protector, employment agent, impresario, and "man." She often becomes emotionally attached to him and may

even turn over more of her earnings to him than she is required to.

A less important role in the prostitute's affairs is played by the madam, who, as Hirschi describes the relationship, is merely the prostitute's employer:

"The madam . . . hires and fires, makes rules, punishes those who break them, and generally supervises the activities of girls on the job. She often keeps lists of customers and girls who may be available if extra help is needed. She may find it necessary to employ accessory personnel such as maids, cooks, bouncers, and spotters. Her contacts with madams in other cities enable her to assist girls in finding new positions. Her problems include those involved in meeting the sometimes rapidly changing tastes of her customers and of working out some sort of stable arrangement with city officials and the police. Although the prostitute usually sees or works for a madam during the course of her career . . . there is little doubt that she is less important as an associate than either the pimp or the fellow prostitute." (1962, p. 203)

In many instances, the world of prostitution is part of the larger world of organized vice. However, the picture appears to vary markedly from one city or region of the country to another.

The outcome of a career in prostitution. Some prostitutes—particularly the older and less attractive ones who have no other source of income —find it very difficult to get out of the profession until they are forced out by age. As Young (1967) has put it: "The older whores will say quite simply: 'There is no way out.' The younger ones will keep their chins up and pretend to themselves they're not like the rest. Nobody ever went on the game for keeps." (p. 123) Many prostitutes eventually marry and attempt to establish a more satisfying life pattern. As Polly Adler (1953) summed it up in her book about her own experience, "Believe me, whoring is just a slow form of self-destruction."

HOMOSEXUALITY

Homosexual behavior is sexual behavior directed toward a member of one's own sex. Homosexuality has existed throughout man's recorded history and among some peoples has been tacitly accepted. The ancient Greek, Roman, Persian, and Moslem civilizations all condoned a measure of homosexuality, and the practice increased as these civilizations declined. In later Greece and Rome, for example, homosexual prostitution existed openly. There is no evidence, however, that homosexuality was an important contributing factor in the decline of these civilizations, as some critics have charged (NAMH, 1971).

In Elizabethan England, an attitude of permissiveness was taken toward homosexuality without apparent harmful effects; in contemporary England, legislation has been passed making it legal for two consenting adults to engage privately in homosexual acts. Most cultures, however, have condemned homosexuality as socially undesirable. In our own society homosexuals often are subject to arrest and imprisonment, and these sanctions have been staunchly maintained despite the findings that most of these individuals manifest no more evidence of personality deviation than we would expect to find in any random sample of the population (Hoffman, 1969; Hooker, 1957). Homosexuals may be of superior intelligence, well educated, and highly successful in their occupations. Many have made outstanding contributions to our culture in music, drama, and other fields. Not a few of the notable figures of

history—including Alexander the Great, Michelangelo, Oscar Wilde, and Peter Tschaikowsky —are thought to have been homosexuals.

Contrary to popular opinion, it is not possible to divide people into two clear-cut groups— homosexuals and heterosexuals. Rather, these labels signify extreme poles on a continuum; in between, we find many individuals whose experiences and desires combine both heterosexual and homosexual components. Kinsey et al. (1948) found that of their white male subjects:

13 percent had reacted erotically to other males without having overt homosexual experiences after the onset of adolescence.

37 percent had had homosexual experience to the point of orgasm after the onset of adolescence.

50 percent of those who remained unmarried to the age of 35 had had overt homosexual experience to the point of orgasm since the onset of adolescence.

18 percent revealed as much of the homosexual as the heterosexual in their histories.

8 percent engaged exclusively in homosexual activities for at least three years between the ages of 16 and 55.

4 percent were exclusively homosexual from adolescence on.

Homosexual relationships were found to be far less common among women and of those reporting homosexual responses, only about a third had proceeded to the point of orgasm (Kinsey et al., 1953).

Another common misconception is that homosexuals manifest qualities of the opposite sex to a striking degree. Thus, male homosexuals are regarded as effeminate, and are expected to be found almost exclusively in certain so-called feminine occupations, such as hairdressing, interior decorating, art and music, and various entertainment fields. Effeminate male homosexuals form a distinct minority, however, and although male homosexuals are found in the occupations noted, they are also found in military life, professional athletics, and other so-called masculine endeavors. In short, the homosexual population cuts across a wide spectrum in terms of age, occupation, social class, education, and interests.

Some investigators believe that homosexuality is on the increase among both males and females. However, the apparent increase may simply reflect our national climate of greater openness toward sex, which has led to greater "visibility" of homosexuals. If we can assume that the number of homosexuals in our society has not changed drastically since Kinsey's studies were made, about 2.6 million men and 1.4 million women in our society are exclusively homosexual. And if we add those who consistently engage in homosexual acts even though they are not exclusively homosexual, the overall figure for men and women may reach 10 million or more.

Patterns of homosexuality. Homosexual relationships range from erotic fantasies, kissing, and mutual masturbation, to mouth-genital contact (called *fellatio* in the case of males and *cunnilingus* in the case of females), and anal intercourse (*pederasty*). In youths under 15, mutual masturbation appears to be the most common homosexual practice, but for persons beyond that age the most frequently reported practice is mouth-genital contact. The traditional view that one partner plays an active (masculine) and the other a passive (feminine) role in the homosexual relationship is not borne out by the research evidence (Saghir, Robins & Walbran, 1969b). The great majority of both male and female homosexuals interchange passive and active roles.

Various attempts have been made to categorize homosexuals. Such labeling is crude at best, but it nevertheless gives some idea of the range and patterns of homosexual behavior—and also of the impact of societal pressures on those who practice homosexuality.

1. *The "blatant" homosexual.* Here we are dealing with individuals who fit the popular stereotype of the homosexual—the lisping, limp-wristed, swishing caricature of femininity, in the case of the male. His lesbian counterpart, called the "butch," flaunts her masculinity, even to the point of trying to look like a man. Also included in this category are the "leather boys," who advertise their sadomasochistic homosexuality by wearing leather jackets, chains, and often boots. Some transvestites, or "Tvs," who enjoy dressing in women's clothes, using women's makeup, and so on, fit in this category too. However, as we shall see, many transvestites are not homosexuals.

2. *The "desperate" and bisexual homosexual.* The so-called desperate homosexuals tend to haunt public toilets ("tearooms") or steam baths —apparently driven to homosexual behavior but unable to face the strains of establishing and sustaining a serious homosexual relationship. In his study of the "tearoom trade," Humphreys (1970) referred to such behavior as "impersonal sex in public places" and pointed out that barring unusual developments, "an occasionally whispered 'thanks' at the conclusion of the act constitutes the bulk of even whispered communication." (p. 13)

Of the subjects in Humphreys' study, 54 percent were married. Apparently the "tearoom" is used by many bisexuals in an effort, through the anonymity of these contacts, to conceal their homosexuality from their wives—and perhaps even from themselves. Humphreys cited the case of a successful businessman who visited "tearooms" almost daily:

"I guess you might say I'm pretty highly sexed (he chuckled a little), but I really don't think that's why I go to tearooms. That's really not sex. Sex is something I have with my wife in bed. It's not as if I were committing adultery by getting my rocks off—or going down on some guy—in a tearoom. I get a kick out of it. Some of my friends go out for handball. I'd rather cruise the park. Does that sound perverse to you?" (p. 19)

3. *The secret homosexual.* Although members of this group range across all class and racial lines, they tend to come from the middle class and to hold positions that they try to protect by concealing their homosexuality. Often they are married, wear wedding rings, and have wives and employers who never know about their double lives. They are extremely skilled at camouflage and at passing as "straight." They generally prefer subdued clothes and close-cropped hair, and maintain a suitably conservative masculine appearance. Since they do not frequent "tearooms" or "gay" bars—which we shall discuss later on— they may continue their homosexual behavior unsuspected throughout their adult lives. Only a few close friends, their lovers, and occasionally their psychotherapists know about their homosexuality. However, living in continuing fear of detection and social disgrace often adds to their adjustive problems.

4. *The adjusted homosexual.* These individuals accept their homosexuality, hold regular jobs, and settle down in a homosexual community —usually belonging to a clique of homosexual friends. Many of them, particularly as they get older, attempt to form a stable relationship with a regular lover, and some even enter into homosexual "marriages." There have been reports of such marriages lasting fifteen years or longer and eventuating in a highly satisfactory relationship for the partners. Stable homosexual relationships between males are unusual, however; more often these men tend to be promiscuous and to form relationships that are fragile and short-lived, lasting a few months at most.

In the case of female homosexuals, more enduring relationships are commonly established—possibly because women in general tend to be less promiscuous than men, and because two women living together do not usually attract unfavorable attention as two men might. Nor are women homosexuals subject to the same degree of social disapproval as men if their relationship does become known.

5. *The situational homosexual.* There are a variety of situations in which individuals engage in homosexual behavior without any deep homosexual commitment. Both males and females may engage in homosexuality in prisons and other institutions, for example, but such individuals usually resume heterosexual behavior on their release. Some prisoners act as homosexual prostitutes; as in the case of homosexual prostitutes outside the prison world, they may not be homosexuals but may merely engage in homosexual practices for economic advantage.

Davis (1968) has also cited instances of homosexual rape among prisoners in sheriff's vans, detention centers, and prisons. Typically, such assault involves anal intercourse, and apparently it is perpetrated by an individual or a gang who do not consider themselves homosexuals but are attempting to assert dominance and masculinity. Except in penal institutions, however, force appears rare in homosexual activity.

6. *The homosexual prostitute.* The situation in which a younger individual is provided with money and material resources by an older homosexual—who has been placed at a disadvantage in competing for the attention of other homosexuals by his physical appearance or age—is referred to as "being kept." The "kept boy" may not be strongly committed to homosexuality, but he may consider the relationship a relatively "permanent" one "as long as the money holds out." In some instances the boy is a student who dis-

continues the relationship when he has completed his education or becomes able to stand on his own feet financially (Sonenschein, 1968). In many large cities adolescent boys engage in homosexual acts with older males for money. These youths do not consider themselves homosexuals, and they usually give up the activity when they are able to get money in other ways. By considering the homosexual act as an economic venture, they find it possible to maintain their sense of male identity.

In a study of young male prostitutes, Craft (1966) found that almost uniformly they came from disorganized families characterized by hostility and immorality. Esseltyn (1968) has pointed out that

"A large number of youths are prostitutes because they are aimless, because there is nothing else to do, no other way to make money, and no real guidance on how to address the job world or how to become an adult." (p. 134)

As we consider other aspects of homosexuality, it is useful to bear in mind that we are dealing with a heterogeneous group of individuals who often have little in common other than their homosexuality. Moreover, it may be emphasized that, contrary to popular opinion, homosexuals are no more likely to molest young children than are heterosexuals.

Homosexual groups—the homosexual community. Although we still have much to learn about homosexuality and homosexual groups, the extensive study of Evelyn Hooker (1962) on the "homosexual community" added considerably to our knowledge about those who "make the scene."

"That scene, as the community member knows it, is essentially a round of activities, utilizing a particular set of institutions, facilities, or areas and governed by common expectations, beliefs, and values. It is important to distinguish between the visible, or public community activities in which only a small portion of the total homosexual population appears to participate, and the invisible, private community activities which go on in friendship cliques." (p. 357)

Hooker pointed out that there tend to be clusters of homosexuals residing near each other in large cities. Several of the apartment buildings on certain streets may be rented exclusively to homosexuals, and most of the homes in certain areas may be owned by homosexuals. The homosexual community constitutes something of a subculture, with unique customs, value systems, and communication techniques.

The visible section of the homosexual community is to be found mainly in the "gay" bars, for here the homosexual and the "straight" world intersect—in the sense that any stranger may enter. In major cities, such as Los Angeles, New York, and San Francisco, there are relatively large numbers of such bars; for example, the Los Angeles area has 200 or more—which, in the main, are for male homosexuals, there being far fewer bars for lesbians in the area. Friends are met in these bars, news and gossip exchanged, invitations to parties issued, and warnings about cur-

COMING OUT IN THE GAY WORLD

Little research attention has been focused on the transition from the "primary stage" of homosexuality, in which the individual may have homosexual desires and engage in overt homosexual behavior but does not yet consider himself a homosexual, and the "secondary stage," in which he is able to say "I am a homosexual." Reaching that secondary stage is referred to as "coming out."

Coming out may take years and may occur in various social contexts. In a study of self-admitted homosexuals attending a homophile meeting, Dank (1971) obtained questionnaire data on 182 subjects; he also conducted 4- to 5-hour interviews with 55 of his subjects, usually in their homes. He found that the average interval between first homosexual desire and coming out was about 6 years—often with more-or-less continuous homosexual activity during the interval. The average age of the subjects on coming out was 19.3 years; their average age at the time of the study was 32.5.

The contexts most frequently associated with the respondents' coming out are listed below. The total number of contexts exceeds the number of respondents because in some cases more than one context was involved.

Context	Number	Percentage
Having a love affair with a homosexual man	54	30
Attending gay parties and other gatherings	46	26
Frequenting parks	43	24
Frequenting men's rooms	37	21
Going to gay bars	35	19
Serving in the military	34	19
Reading about homosexuals and homosexuality	27	15
Having a love affair with a heterosexual man	21	12
Living in all-male quarters at boarding school or college	12	7
Seeing a professional counselor or psychiatrist	11	6
Being arrested for homosexuality	7	4
Other context, such as being confined in prison or a mental hospital	9	5

The seemingly low percentage of subjects who associated coming out with the frequenting of gay bars—which are probably the most widespread and the best known of the gay social contexts—was attributed to the fact that the legal age limit for entering bars was 21 years.

The act of coming out was a source of great relief to many subjects, as indicated by such statements as "Wow, I'm home"; and "I had this feeling of relief. I guess the fact that I had accepted myself as being homosexual has taken a lot of tensions off me." Dank attributed this sense of relief to cognitive change—a shift in attitude from the view of "homosexuality-as-mental-illness" to "homosexuality-as-way-of-life."

The following excerpt is from a young male's account of his "coming out" in a mental hospital. Admitted at age 20, he had a prior history of heterosexual and homosexual behavior, and thought of himself as bisexual. He had had no contact with self-admitted homosexuals and was engaged to marry.

"I didn't know there were so many gay people, and I wasn't use to the actions of gay people or anything, and it was quite shocking walking down the halls going up to the ward, and the whistles and flirting and everything else that went on with the new fish, as they called it.

"And there was this one kid who was a patient escort and he asked me if I was interested in going to church, and I said yes . . . and he started escorting me to church and then he pulled a little sneaky to see whether I'd be shocked at him being gay. There was this queen on the ward, and him and her, he was looking out the hall to see when I walked by the door and this was to check my reaction. And I didn't say a word. So he then escorted me to the show, and we were sitting there and about half-way through the movie he reaches over and started holding my hand, and when he saw I didn't jerk away, which I was kind of upset and wondering exactly what he had in mind, and then when we got back to the ward, he wrote me a long love letter and gave it to me; before we knew it we were going together, and went together for about six months. . . .

"[The experience in the hospital] let me find out that it wasn't so terrible. . . . I met a lot of gay people that I liked and I figured it can't be all wrong. If so and so's a good Joe, and he's still gay, he can't be all that bad. . . . I figured it couldn't be all wrong, and that's one of the things I learned. I learned to accept myself for what I am—homosexual." (pp. 184–185)

rent police activities circulated. The crucial function of the bars, however, is to facilitate the making of sexual contacts. Typically, these contacts are between strangers, who agree to meet at a certain time and place for sexual purposes. Their relationship is usually transitory, and subsequently each is likely to find a new partner. A central feature of such relationships is the assumption that sexual gratification can be had without obligation or a long-term commitment. When asked what it means to be "gay," one man answered:

"To be gay is to go to the bar, to make the scene, to look, and look, and look, to have a one night stand, to never really love or be loved, and to really know this, and to do this night after night, and year after year." (Hooker, 1962, p. 9)

There are steam baths, gyms, restaurants, barber shops, clothing stores, and even churches that cater almost exclusively to the homosexual population and may serve as meeting places, but they are considered of secondary importance. Indeed, as Achilles (1967) has pointed out, the gay bar is the primary and necessary locus of male homosexuality. It creates a milieu, both permissive and protective, in which social interaction may occur. There are many kinds of these bars, to serve both general and special homosexual populations.

The induction of a recruit into such a group has been described by Hooker.

"The young man who may have had a few isolated homosexual experiences in adolescence, or indeed none at all, and who is taken to a 'gay' bar by a group of friends whose homosexuality is only vaguely suspected or unknown to him, may find the excitement and opportunities for sexual gratification appealing and thus begin active participation in the community life. Very often, the debut, referred to by homosexuals as 'coming out,' of a person who believes himself to be homosexual but who has struggled against it, will occur in a bar when he, for the first time, identifies himself publicly as a homosexual in the presence of other homosexuals by his appearance in the situation. If he has thought of himself as unique, or has thought of homosexuals as a strange and unusual lot, he may be agreeably astonished to discover a large number of men who are physically attractive, personable, and 'masculine' appearing, so that his hesitancy in identifying himself as a homosexual is greatly reduced. Since he may meet a complete cross-section of occupational and socioeconomic levels in the bar, he becomes con-

vinced that far from being a small minority, the 'gay' population is very extensive indeed. Once he has 'come out,' that is, identified himself as a homosexual to himself and to some others, the process of education proceeds with rapid pace. Eager and willing tutors —especially if he is young and attractive—teach him the special language, ways of recognizing vice-squad officers, varieties of sexual acts and social types. They also assist him in providing justifications for the homosexual way of life as legitimate, and help to reduce his feelings of guilt by providing him with new norms of sexual behavior in which monogamous fidelity to the sexual partner is rare." (1962, pp. 11–12)

The structure of the homosexual community is characterized by overlapping social networks of varying degrees of cohesiveness, which usually are linked to the bars. There are, for example, loosely knit friendship groups and tightly knit cliques formed of homosexually married couples or of singles who often are heterosexually married. In addition, there are organizations concerned with establishing and protecting the rights of homosexuals; of these, the best known are probably the Mattachine societies, the first having been founded in Los Angeles in 1950 and named after sixteenth-century Spanish court jesters who wore masks. On the female side are the equally well-known Daughters of Bilitis, whose name is taken from *The Songs of Bilitis*, nineteenth-century lyrics that glorify lesbian love. There are also more radical organizations, such as the Gay Liberation Front.

Other homosexual organizations are more concerned with providing leisure-time pursuits. In some instances homosexuals hold exclusive formal balls at which prizes are given for the best costumes and an "Empress" is elected. The Halloween "Beaux Arts Ball" in San Francisco has been an annual event for several years.

The homosexual who has become affiliated with an organization tends to think of his problem as a group problem and therefore a social rather than an individual one. In such cases, he may experience little fear or conflict and may accept his homosexual behavior as a natural sexual pattern. He may even take pride in his homosexual behavior and consider himself "emancipated" from conventional heterosexual morality. This attitude is exemplified in the slogan "Gay is good." However, many individuals are overzealous in their claims and seem to be trying to counteract the self-devaluation generated by the negative attitudes of the "straight" society.

Problems of homosexuals. Inevitably, it is difficult for many homosexuals to make adequate sexual, occupational, and social adjustments in the face of society's disapproval. Although legal penalties have not been effective in preventing homosexual behavior in private between two consenting adults, or even in reducing its incidence, they do make concealment necessary and subject homosexuals to the emotional stress that accompanies violation of the law. Many homosexuals —even though they feel they have a right to their form of sexual adjustment—live in continual fear of detection, loss of employment, and social disgrace. Others, feeling that their sexual desires are entirely wrong, are in constant conflict. Even among those who accept their homosexuality, many also accept society's stigma. As Hoffman (1969) has said, "The homosexual . . . views himself as queer, bad, dirty, something a little less than human." (p. 70) Although this statement does not apply to all homosexuals, it shows the tendency of members of any oppressed minority groups to accept the degrading view that the larger society takes of them.

In addition, many homosexuals who hold prominent positions run the constant risk of

Male homosexuals attired as women attend the annual Halloween "Beaux Arts Ball" in San Francisco.

blackmail. A survey by Gagnon and Simon (1968) disclosed that only 10 percent of the homosexuals in their sample had ever been arrested, but 10 percent had been blackmailed, and 25 percent had been robbed, often after being beaten. Where homosexuals are beaten and robbed, they are often victims of youths who prey on them for "sport" as well as for robbery. And occasionally what starts out to be a "shakedown" ends up as a murder. In such instances, it has been conjectured that the youth has had considerable latent homosexuality in his own makeup, and has probably been motivated by unconscious sexual desires as well as robbery. In the sequence of events, the two usually have gone to the homosexual's apartment, where the youth has been given a few drinks and then submitted to some homosexual act. Much to his amazement, he has found the act pleasurable and has experienced what is known as *homosexual panic*: tremendous anxiety at this revelation of his own homosexual inclinations. In this state he has blindly attacked the homosexual with anything at hand.

The additional stresses and problems faced by a homosexual, especially one not affiliated with a homosexual group, are well brought out in the following statement of a female homosexual:

"To those whose sex life is based on heterosexual relationships, the homosexual is a grotesque, shadowy creature—a person spoken of with scorn, pity or lasciviousness. The person so spoken of is often in the audience. If you are not one of us, it is impossible to realize our feelings when this occurs. It is incredible to us that a well educated girl could make the following remark: 'What do they look like? I wonder if I've ever seen one?' . . .

"What is it like to be this way?

"You are always lonely. It makes no difference how many friends you have or how nice they are. Between you and other women friends is a wall which they cannot see, but which is terribly apparent to you. This wall represents the differences in the workings of your minds.

"Between you and men friends is another difficult misunderstanding. Very few men desire platonic friendships, the only kind of which you are capable so far as they are concerned. The endless bitter disagreements with them cause many of us to renounce their companionship entirely. Very few men understand the need we have for their friendship and the aversion we feel for sexual love. Unable to find love or its most acceptable substitute, friendships, we frequently become psychiatric cases. You cannot keep a healthy state of mind if you are very lonely.

"The inability to represent an honest face to those you know eventually develops a certain deviousness which is injurious to whatever basic character you may possess. Always pretending to be something you are not, moral laws lose their significance. What is right and wrong for you when your every effort is toward establishing a relationship with another which is completely right to you, but appallingly wrong to others?

"How do homosexuals feel about one another?

"One of the saddest facts in this entire picture is that we seldom like one another. On the surface this appears ridiculous, but there are good reasons for it. . . ." (MacKinnon, 1947, p. 661)

Public attitudes have changed greatly since the above report was made, and there is a greater social acceptance of homosexual behavior. As this trend continues, it will be increasingly easier for those with homosexual inclinations to accept a self-image as a homosexual.

Despite this trend, however, many of the problems and pressures remain, particularly for male homosexuals. For example, results of a national poll released in November 1969 indicated that more than 60 percent of the population in our society considers homosexuality a threat to the American way of life (Massett, 1969). Miller (1971) has also pointed to the distinction between public and private acceptance of homosexuality. Even those who tolerate homosexuality in general may not accept it among their friends. Thus the homosexual not affiliated with an organized group of homosexuals is still likely to experience conflict concerning his behavior and to feel insecure, apprehensive, lonely, and alienated.

Constitutional factors in homosexuality. Since research concerning sexual behavior generally and homosexuality in particular has not been greatly encouraged, there are far more questions and hypotheses than conclusive research data about the causal factors in homosexuality. While some investigators view biological factors as playing a major role in the development of homosexual patterns, a larger number view psychosocial factors as being more important. As with other behavior, there is evidently a complex interaction of biological, psychological, and sociocultural factors.

1. *Genetic factors.* During the early part of this century, most experts believed that homosexuality

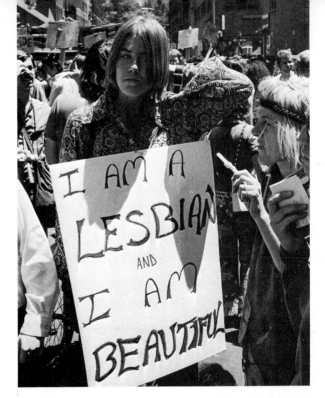

With the increasing acceptance of homosexuality in America, many homosexuals are able to accept themselves without feeling devaluated.

had a constitutional basis through direct genetic inheritance—a view supported by Kallmann's findings, published in 1953. Kallmann studied a series of 95 male twin pairs in which at least one member was known to be exclusively or predominantly homosexual. Of the 44 identical twin pairs studied, both members in every pair were found to be homosexual. Interestingly, all denied practicing homosexual acts with each other, and many claimed to have developed their homosexual patterns independently. By contrast, of the 51 fraternal twin pairs studied, both members were found to be homosexual in only 40 percent of the cases. Later studies, too, have found a higher concordance for identical than fraternal twins but lower figures for both—less than 50 percent among identical pairs.

In the light of presently available research, there is little basis for attributing the development of either homosexual preference or overt homosexual behavior primarily to constitutional factors. Even if constitutional factors play a role in some cases, we still need an explanation for the fact that some individuals change from one pattern of behavior to the other during their lifetime.

2. *Hormonal balance.* Early research led many investigators to conclude that homosexuality resulted from an abnormal androgen-estrogen ratio. Later studies, however, have failed to support these early findings. Furthermore, even in the occasional instances where hormonal imbalances occur, they may have no causal significance: nonhomosexuals often show similar imbalances; individuals may shift from a homosexual to a heterosexual pattern or vice versa without a change in hormone balance; and treatment with sex hormones to change endocrine balance does not modify the direction of sexual behavior.

More recently, Money and Alexander (1969) have reported experiments with animals which indicated "that insufficient androgen at a critical period in fetal and/or neonatal life may potentiate the release subsequently of feminine components of sexual behavior." Similarly, in studies with cats, guinea pigs, and rhesus monkeys, in which female fetuses were masculinized by androgen injections given to the mother, the affected animals later showed masculine behavior traits.

Money and Alexander (1969) have also reported a longitudinal study of 18 human males with precocious sexual development. In this study, a relationship was found between the early release of excessive amounts of male hormones and the intensification of sex drives—which in these subjects were exclusively heterosexual.

Such studies have raised interesting questions about the role of prenatal and early postnatal hormonal balance on later sexual behavior, but as yet we lack sufficient evidence on which to base definite conclusions.

3. *Hermaphroditism.* In this rare condition the individual possesses well-developed genital organs of both sexes; thus, there is an anatomical basis for ambiguous sexuality. However, the pattern that develops cannot be understood solely in terms of constitutional factors.

Two sisters, aged 24 and 26, were to all appearances normal young women. They had feminine voices, smooth skin, no beard, well-developed breasts. They had been reared as girls, had feminine interests, and had never been sexually attracted by girls. However, medical examination revealed that one sister had a bifid scrotum with two well-descended testes, whereas fallopian tubes and ovaries were completely absent. She had married once, had later obtained a divorce, and was in love with another man. She insisted upon an operation to remove the male organs, following which

she reported a reduction in sexual desire by about one half. A subsequent marriage was successful. The other sister showed a similar medical and personal history. If these girls had been legally declared males, they would automatically have been homosexuals! (Summary of case from Witschi & Mengert, 1942)

Later studies of hermaphrodites have led to the conclusion that the sexual role assumed by the individual accords primarily with his masculine or feminine upbringing rather than with internal or external physical characteristics. The most important factor in deciding to which sex a hermaphrodite should be assigned is considered to be the sex role established during the years of early development—particularly the first three years. In a study of hermaphroditic children who had been reared as members of one sex for a time and then treated as members of the other, Money et al. (1957) found little emotional disturbance when the change occurred before the middle of the third year. After that period, the change was very difficult and led to serious emotional problems.

Psychosocial factors in homosexuality. It would appear that many different pathways may lead to homosexual behavior, including early learning, traumatic experiences with members of the opposite sex, and prolonged heterosexual frustration.

1. *Early homosexual experiences and their reinforcement.* The development of homosexuality is frequently associated with homosexual experiences before sexual behavior is well differentiated into a heterosexual pattern. In a pioneering study of 79 homosexuals, East (1946) found early homosexual seduction or other homosexual experiences to be the most common environmental factor. More recent studies, too, have found a high incidence of homosexual experiences in preadolescence (Bieber et al., 1962; Saghir, Robins & Walbran, 1969a).

Simon and Gagnon (1967) found evidence that homosexuality may develop later in females than in males—late in adolescence or even in young adulthood. In most cases, however, individuals who will later show exclusively or almost exclusively homosexual patterns begin to be homosexual by adolescence. Findings by Manosevitz (1970) indicate that "the prehomosexual child becomes sexually active earlier in life than the preheterosexual child." (p. 401)

It is doubtful that early homosexual experiences lead to the later development of homosexuality except where they are reinforced by continual pleasurable repetition and/or meet emotional needs. In an early study of 10 chronically homosexual reform-school inmates, matched with a control group of 10 normal subjects, Greco and Wright (1944) found that each of the homosexuals had had an early intimate association with a homosexual who had been a source of badly needed emotional and social support. This kind of emotional support is described in the following excerpt from the case of an adolescent girl who first entered into homosexual behavior in a correctional institution for delinquent girls.

"I have a girl, a simply wonderful girl. . . . I need her. . . . I feel better toward all people. I feel satisfied. Now I have somebody to care for. Now I have somebody I want to make happy and somebody I will work hard for. . . ." (Konopka, 1964, p. 23)

It would also appear that expected social role behavior may markedly influence the outcome of early homosexual experiences. For example, Davenport (1965) has described the sexual mores of the Melanesians in the Southwest Pacific. Premarital intercourse is forbidden among them, and both males and females are encouraged to masturbate. In addition, all unmarried males engage in homosexual relations with the full knowledge of the community, but after marriage are expected to assume a heterosexual pattern— a transition they appear to have little difficulty in making.

2. *Negative conditioning of heterosexual behavior.* A variety of circumstances may lead to conditioning in which heterosexual behavior becomes an aversive stimulus. For example, where the boy or girl is ridiculed, rebuffed, and humiliated in his effort to approach members of the opposite sex, he may turn toward homosexuality as a safer source of affection and sexual outlet. If a mother catches her son "playing with" a little girl and punishes him for being "bad," she may be subtly telling him that heterosexual behavior is evil. Early sexual relations under unfortunate conditions may have a comparable effect. Konopka (1964) has concluded: "Girls who have been raped by their fathers (and they are not rare among delinquent girls) find relationships with men either threatening or disgusting and often turn to other girls for the fulfillment of their emotional need for love." (p. 23)

In some instances an "uptight" parent or teacher may learn that an impressionable preadolescent or adolescent boy is sexually experimenting with other boys. Quite upset by the discovery, the elder individual may accuse the boy of being a homosexual; and the youth may feel that if others view him as a homosexual he must be one. Moreover, the accusation may become a self-fulfilling prophecy; it may instill fearfulness in the boy and a tendency to "freeze up" in approaching girls. Here being labeled not only provides a homosexual self-image and role but tends to discourage a heterosexual one.

3. *Being reared as a member of the opposite sex.* Very occasionally a mother who has wanted a daughter will treat her son as a girl, keeping his hair long, dressing him in girls' clothes, and inculcating typically feminine attitudes and interests. Similarly, a girl may sometimes be reared as if she were a boy.

The case of John L____ illustrates how a pattern of identification with the other sex may be built up. A successful young business executive, he had been raised with eight older sisters in a poor family. The father left home when John was about six months old and was not heard from again.

To economize and reduce her parental responsibility, the mother dressed and treated John as a girl during his infancy and early childhood. Later when he went to school, his hair was cut and he dressed as a boy, but he could not accept the change in his sex identity. He engaged in mutual masturbation at an early age and mouth-genital contacts during adolescence and early adulthood, stating that he always played the female role in the homosexual act. He came to a psychological clinic for assistance after he had been arrested for a homosexual act and given a choice of a jail sentence or therapy. Despite various treatment approaches, including aversive conditioning, he was unable to change his sexual identity.

This case is admittedly extreme but serves to emphasize again the importance of learning the appropriate gender identity during the early critical period.

4. *Pathogenic family patterns.* In a study of 106 male homosexuals who were undergoing psychoanalysis, Bieber et al. (1962) found a common family pattern involving a dominant, seductive mother and a weak or absent father. Typically the mother, frustrated by an unhappy marital relationship, established a relationship with the son which became seductive and romantic but stopped just short of physical contact. The son, overstimulated sexually, felt anxiety and guilt over his incestuous feelings, and the mother, aware of his feelings and fearful of exposing her own incestuous impulses, discouraged overt signs of masculinity. The father, resenting the son as a rival, also made it clear that the son's developing masculinity was offensive. Often the father showed preference for a daughter, and the son, in envy, wished he was a girl. Bieber et al. described the end result as follows:

"By the time the H-son has reached the preadolescent period, he has suffered a diffuse personality disorder. Maternal overanxiety about health and injury, restriction of activities normative for the son's age and potential, interference with assertive behavior, demasculinizing attitudes and interference with sexuality—interpenetrating with paternal rejection, hostility, and lack of support—produce an excessively fearful child, pathologically dependent upon his mother and beset by feelings of inadequacy, impotence, and self-contempt. He is reluctant to participate in boyhood activities thought to be potentially physically injurious —usually grossly overestimated. His peer group responds with humiliating name-calling and often with physical attack which timidity tends to invite among children. His fear and shame of self, made worse by the derisive reactions of other boys, only drive him further away. . . .

"Failure in the peer group, and anxieties about a masculine, heterosexual presentation of self, pave the way for the prehomosexual's initiation into the less threatening atmosphere of homosexual society, its values, and way of life." (pp. 316–317)

Some doubt has been cast on the generality of the findings of Bieber et al. by recent studies. Evans (1969) failed to find strong supporting evidence that disturbed family relationships are necessary and sufficient conditions for the development of male homosexuality. Snortum and his associates (1969), on the other hand, reported findings that support those of Bieber et al. in demonstrating the influence of a close-binding, controlling mother and a detached,

rejecting father on the development of male homosexuality.

The backgrounds of female homosexuals commonly include: (a) highly disturbed families, as in the case of father-daughter incest or rape; (b) excessive emphasis by the parents on the evils of sex, making heterosexual relationships seem aversive and repugnant; and (c) family rejection or absence, and the finding of acceptance and love in a homosexual relationship (Gundlach, 1969; Kremer & Ritkin, 1969; Saghir et al., 1969a). Although noting a variation in specific details, Kremer and Ritkin, in their study of 25 lesbian girls between 12 and 17 years of age, found that:

"The most striking aspect of this study . . . was their family background. Not one of these girls had grown up in a nuclear-type family unit that maintained its stability over any substantial period of the girl's development." (1969, p. 93)

Although we again seem to be dealing with multiple pathways to adult homosexuality, it would appear that lack of strong affectional relationships in a stable family is often a major factor.

5. *Blocking of sexual expression.* Since the only sexual role that is considered appropriate during early adolescence is abstinence, and since the biological sex drive is intense during this period, it is not surprising that sexual tensions, coupled with curiosity, often lead to experimentation with members of one's own sex or to fantasies about such activities in connection with masturbation. In some instances such experimentation or fantasy may lead to pleasurable reinforcement and to the establishment of homosexual patterns.

Ollendorff (1966) has cited anthropological studies that show sex-negating societies to have a much higher incidence of homosexuality than sexually permissive ones. Marshall (1971) has reported that neither frigid women nor homosexuals are found among the people of Mangaia in the Polynesian Islands, where sex is a principal concern and premarital sex and sophisticated sexual techniques are encouraged.

Homosexual patterns also often develop during adulthood if the individual is placed in a situation where heterosexual behavior is not possible, such as a prison or a correctional institution. It may additionally be emphasized that male prisoners who engage in homosexual acts may not view themselves as homosexual; in fact, they usually deny the existence of homosexual tendencies in themselves. Often they feel that they are demonstrating their masculinity by forcing sodomy on weaker and usually younger inmates (Gundlach, 1969). Such homosexual activities may be given up when heterosexual contacts again become available.

6. *Association with other psychopathology.* Although homosexual behavior may occur in connection with neurotic, psychotic, or sociopathic disorders, there is usually no direct relationship between homosexuality and the particular behavior pattern. Of course, homosexuals are subject to special stresses that may precipitate psychopathology; they are often forced to live under the threat of social sanctions, such as loss of employment if their sexual behavior is revealed, which makes personal adjustment difficult. This strain is often reflected in brittle humor which varies from defensive mockery of the "straight" world to self-devaluating scorn for the "gay" one. However, with our changing sexual mores, an increasing number of homosexuals are able to accept themselves without anxiety or devaluation, which should considerably facilitate their personal and social adjustment.

Treatment and outcomes. The Task Force on Homosexuality of the National Institutes of Mental Health has estimated that roughly one fourth of the exclusively homosexual individuals who wish to change can achieve some measure of heterosexual functioning (Massett, 1969). For those individuals with less deeply established homosexual patterns, the expectancy of a favorable outcome is much higher. Since many variables are involved—such as the pattern of homosexual behavior, the motivation for change, presence or absence of psychopathology, and so on—no single treatment method is uniformly successful. In general, group and individual psychotherapy have been the traditional methods of choice, but in recent years behavior therapy has received increasing emphasis.

To the extent that the homosexual behavior involves an avoidance response to the opposite sex, it may be treated by desensitization and the fostering of approach behavior toward members of the other sex. Lamberd (1969) has reported successful results in treating three cases of male

SOME UNANSWERED QUESTIONS CONCERNING HOMOSEXUALITY

1. Is the human infant psychosexually neutral at birth, so that learning determines the later choice of the sex object; or do sexual predispositions have a selective effect on learning?

2. If learning plays a key role in homosexuality, what specific learning principles are involved—e.g., is it negative conditioning toward members of the opposite sex or positive conditioning toward members of one's own sex; or is it a combination of these processes?

3. Are there critical periods in development—as in infancy, childhood, or adolescence—when physiological and/or psychological processes may determine the choice of homosexual objects?

4. Can relationships in the nuclear family, peer relationships in childhood or adolescence, or deviant subculture membership be of crucial significance in determining homosexuality?

5. Are the etiological pathways to lesbianism different, qualitatively or quantitatively, from those in male homosexuality?

6. Should sanctions against homosexual behavior between consenting adults be removed by society?

7. Even if society legalizes homosexual behavior between consenting adults, should a person who engages in homosexual behavior as his preferred sexual pattern be encouraged in therapy to accept himself as a homosexual, or should the attempt be made to change his behavior?

homosexuality as phobic avoidance reactions toward women. In another case, of a 27-year-old airman, treatment consisted of discussion and desensitization of his fears of sexual relations with women, together with active encouragement of heterosexual behavior. Five months after beginning treatment, the subject had a successful heterosexual relationship with a nightclub entertainer, and later he became completely free of homosexual desires.

In other cases, aversive conditioning procedures may be used, such as associating electric shock with pictures of nude males. But regardless of the precise method used, it is becoming increasingly common after avoidance conditioning to foster approach responses to heterosexual stimuli. For example, therapy with male subjects may include removing aversive stimuli when pictures of attractive females are shown, giving the subject injections of sex hormones and displaying pictures of attractive nude females when the sex drive is at its peak, and providing gradual training in heterosexual relationships through the assignment of a series of "real-life" tasks (Ferster, 1965).

Bandura (1969) and McConaghy (1971) have described the procedures in, and results of, behavior therapy. Although the results appear to be superior to those achieved by traditional psychotherapy, they are far from being uniformly successful. Consequently, therapists feel that in many cases it is more practical to encourage the homosexual to accept his homosexuality than to try to change.

Since the problems of homosexuals result in part from the self-devaluation that society fosters in them and the severe sanctions society imposes on them, many investigators have urged the legalization of homosexual acts between consenting adults in private. Some states, including Illinois and Connecticut, have adopted such legislation. A trend may also be discerned toward eliminating employment practices that discriminate against homosexuals, one indication of this trend being a federal court ruling in 1969 against discharging a homosexual government employee unless it can be proven that the homosexuality impairs his job efficiency (Massett, 1969). The National Association for Mental Health, too, has supported the repeal of existing legal statutes relating to homosexuals (NAMH, 1971).

TRANSVESTISM

Transvestism involves the achievement of sexual excitation by dressing as a member of the opposite sex. This pattern overlaps with homosexuality but is unique in certain aspects. It is a comparatively uncommon condition in which the individual—man or woman—enjoys excursions into the social role of the other sex. Although a male transvestite, for example, regards himself as a man when dressed as a man, he may have feelings of being a woman when dressed in women's clothing.

Dynamics. Four types of transvestites have been distinguished: (1) the male homosexual who adopts feminine attire, including cosmetics and other feminine accoutrements, as an adjunct to his homosexual activity and is often referred to as a "drag queen"; (2) the heterosexual male who finds enjoyment and sexual excitation in the wearing of women's attire; (3) the female who is not homosexual but enjoys dressing as a man; and (4) the individual who has feelings of being a

male trapped in a female body (or vice versa), and who feels that the expected sex role is inappropriate for him. The latter merges into transsexualism, to be considered in the next section.

Very little is known about transvestism. Most reports are based on studies of single cases, and most of those studied have been in therapy, which may make them an unrepresentative group. However, Buckner (1970) has formulated a description of the "ordinary" transvestite from a survey of 262 transvestites conducted by the magazine *Transvestia.*

"He is probably married (about two thirds are); if he is married he probably has children (about two thirds do). Almost all of these transvestites said they were exclusively heterosexual—in fact, the rate of 'homosexuality' was less than the average for the entire population. The transvestic behavior generally consists of privately dressing in the clothes of a woman, at home, in secret. . . . The transvestite generally does not run into trouble with the law. His cross-dressing causes difficulties for very few people besides himself and his wife." (p. 381)

The most extensive studies to date of the personalities of male transvestites are those of Bentler and Prince (1969; 1970) and Bentler, Shearman, and Prince (1970). These investigators obtained replies to a standardized psychological inventory from a large sample of transvestites through the cooperation of a national transvestite organization. The transvestites, in comparison with matched control groups, showed no gross differences on neurotic or psychotic scales. However, they did present themselves as being more controlled in impulse expression, less involved with other individuals, more inhibited in interpersonal relationships, and more dependent.

It would appear that most transvestism can be explained in terms of a simple conditioning model. A male child may receive attention from females in the family who think it is cute for him to dress in feminine attire and hence reinforce this behavior with attention and praise. Such a conditioning process is well portrayed in the case of an adult transvestite studied by Stoller (1967):

"I have pictures of myself dressed as a little girl when I was a small child. My mother thought it was cute. She was right. I was a pretty little girl.

"The highlights of my life as a girl came when I was between the ages of 10 and 17. I had an aunt who was childless and wanted to take me through the steps from childhood to young womanhood. She knew of my desires to be a girl. I would spend every summer at her ranch. The first thing she would do was to give me a pixie haircut, which always turned out pretty good since I would avoid getting a haircut for two months before I went to her ranch. She then would take me into the bedroom and show me all my pretty new things she had bought me. The next day, dressed as a girl, I would accompany her to town and we would shop for a new dress for me. To everyone she met, she would introduce me as her 'niece.'

"This went on every year until I was 13 years old. Then she decided I should start my womanhood. I will never forget that summer. When I arrived I got the same pixie haircut as usual but when we went into the bedroom there laid out on the bed was a girdle, a garter belt and bra, size 32AA, and my first pair of nylons. She then took me over to the new dressing table she had bought me and slid back the top to reveal my very own makeup kit. I was thrilled to death. She said she wanted her 'niece' to start off right and it was about time I started to develop a bust.

"The next morning I was up early to ready myself for the usual shopping trip to town, only this time it was for a pair of high heels and a new dress. I remember I stuffed my bra with cotton, put on my garter belt, and slipped on my nylons with no effort. After all, I became an expert from practice the night before. My aunt applied my lipstick because I was so excited I couldn't get it on straight. Then off to town we went, aunt and 'niece.' What a wonderful day. I shall never forget it." (p. 335)

The adult transvestite who marries faces problems that are well brought out in another case reported by Stoller (1967):

"'We fell in love and as soon as I felt we could we were married. We have been as happy as two people can be and the best part of it is that she knows all about me and not only accepts me as I am but assists in my transformation and then admires me. . . .'

"This is the way the relationship looks at first, when the wife is pleased to see her husband's femininity. She does not know yet that as he becomes a more successful transvestite her enthusiasm will wane. Then he will be hurt that she is no longer interested in his dressing up, his sexual needs, his work. The fighting will start, neither will understand what has happened, and they will divorce." (p. 336)

Treatment and outcomes. An effective and economical treatment for transvestism appears to be aversion therapy, in which dressing in women's clothing is paired with an aversive stimulus. The individual may also undergo assertion training, which fosters confidence and adequacy in playing a more masculine social and sexual role (Bandura, 1969; Clark, 1965; Dengrove, 1967).

In one such case, Lavin et al. (1961) treated a 22-year-old married truck driver who from the age of 8 had had a recurrent desire to dress in women's clothing and had achieved sexual gratification from this activity from the age of 15. Pictures were taken of the subject in various stages of women's attire, and a tape recording was made in which the subject described his putting on various garments. Aversion therapy consisted of presenting the pictures and tape recordings and then terminating them when the subject started vomiting from an emetic mixture. The therapy was continued every two hours for six days and six nights. The subject and his wife were interviewed three times during the ensuing six months, and both reported the continued absence of his deviant sexual pattern.

TRANSSEXUALISM

Transsexuals, unlike transvestites, usually feel relaxed rather than sexually aroused when dressed in the clothing of the opposite sex (Green, 1971). The transsexual feels such an inability to accept his own sex and such an identification with the other sex that he may seek permanent physical change through surgery and a complete life thereafter as a member of the other sex. Although the condition remains quite rare, increasing numbers of transsexuals have sought surgical sex reassignment in recent years.

Problems of gender identity. Case histories of transsexuals indicate that their cross-gender identification had begun in childhood and continued into adulthood. In an intensive study of 14 male transsexuals—of whom 12 had undergone sex-reassignment surgery and 2 were awaiting surgery—Money and Primrose (1968) found that in every case the men had been labeled as "sissies" during childhood. Interestingly, all 14 expressed a desire to adopt children, though their preference was for small children rather than newborn babies.

"In general, the group appeared to possess a feminine gender identity, except for a masculine threshold of erotic arousal in response to visual imagery and an

External changes in a young man who sought sex reassignment through surgery are indicated by these before and after photos.

unmotherly disengagement from the helplessness of the newborn." (p. 472)

Similarly, Green (1968) has cited data for 9 boys 8 years old or less who were manifesting anomalous gender identity. In 6 of the cases, the parents reported cross-gender identity by the time the boys had been 3. In essence, these boys had behaved exactly as adult male transsexual patients report having behaved when they were younger.

In the responses of 6 female transsexuals on a personality scale, Money and Brennan (1968) found a relatively high score on masculinity and a low one on femininity. The subjects had not shown girlish interests in childhood—such as playing with dolls—and were described as having been "tomboys," prone to fighting with boys. Five were living as males, and all showed hatred of their breasts and rejection of pregnancy and motherhood.

As we have seen, gender identity does not automatically correspond to one's physical sex but in most cases appears to be established early—probably during the first three years of life—and to be highly resistant to change.

One hypothesis is that there is a "sex center" in the brain that directs the organism's development as male or female, but that this development always starts as female, becoming male only when adequate male hormones are secreted during an early critical period in development. However, this hypothesis is based on evidence from studies of lower mammals; whether such a "sex center" exists in the brain of man and whether a comparable pattern of virilization takes place in human development is not presently known. From the case histories of adult transsexuals, we know only that cross-gender identification dates back to early childhood, and that many factors—including style of clothing, activity preferences, mannerisms, role expectations, and relations to parents—may be involved (Green, 1968; Newman, 1970).

Treatment and outcomes. Efforts to alter gender identification in adulthood through psychotherapy, including behavior therapy, have been unsuccessful (Baker, 1969). Some transsexuals have sought to resolve the conflict through changing their physical sex to correspond with their feelings of gender identity.

F. Z. Abraham is said to have performed the first transsexual operation in the 1930's. While occasional reports of similar operations were forthcoming for the next two decades, it was not until 1953, when Hamburger reported the case of Christine Jorgensen, that surgical sex reassignment became well known. Johns Hopkins Hospital and the University of Minnesota Hospital were among the first in this country to give official support to sex-change surgery; each has since received thousands of requests from individuals for evaluation and management of their cases.

In males, modern surgical procedures accomplish sex conversion through removal of male organs and their replacement with an artfully designed vagina that apparently works satisfactorily in many cases, even enabling the individual, now a woman, to achieve orgasm. Weekly injections of sex hormones stimulate breast development, give more feminine texture to the skin, and also lessen beard growth, though electrolysis is usually needed to remove excess hair. Surgery for female transsexuals generally has been less successful, for although surgeons can remove the breasts, ovaries, vagina, and uterus, and can insert a penis constructed from rib cartilage or plastic, the penis does not function normally. Transplants of reproductive organs are not yet possible and the patient will be sterile after surgery.

Various evaluative studies of the outcome of such operations have been reported, perhaps the best known being that of Benjamin (1966). This investigator questioned 50 transsexuals who had crossed the sex line from male to female. Their ages at the time of surgery ranged from 19 to 58, with an average age of 32. Of these subjects, 44 reported contentment sexually and socially with their new roles as women; 5 complained either about their ability to perform sexually or about their appearance; and 1 was totally dissatisfied with the results.

In another study, Pauly (1968) reviewed the postoperative course of 121 male transsexuals who had received sex-reassignment surgery, and found that satisfactory outcomes outnumbered unsatisfactory ones at a ratio of 10 to 1. He also reported previous unsuccessful attempts by psychotherapy to help these patients achieve male-gender identity.

There has been considerable controversy about sex-conversion surgery, however, and many physicians, as well as other professional persons, remain opposed to the operations. In any case, sex-conversion surgery is such a drastic form of treatment that every precaution must be taken in screening patients. Commonly it is recommended that those considering sex-reassignment surgery undergo a trial period first during which they receive hormone therapy and live in the new role to get a clearer understanding of the many psychological and social adjustments that will be required.

In the present chapter we have dealt with the highly complex and controversial problem of sexual deviations. In our attempt to classify patterns commonly labeled as deviant—consistent with this book's overall approach to the subject of maladaptive behavior—we have noted that *sexual deviance* is not necessarily to be equated with *maladaptive behavior,* and that societal views of what is deviant are subject to change, a phenomenon that is especially apparent today. In our society, traditional views of sexual behavior are undergoing a reexamination, and many patterns formerly condemned as immoral are being redefined, at least by some, as acceptable and desirable. There is also a growing trend toward sexual experimentation, including such patterns as wife-swapping and group sexual practices.

With these considerations in mind, we organized our discussion of sexual deviations according to the three-fold classification of (1) "normal" deviations, such as masturbation and premarital sexual relations; (2) abnormal deviations, such as incest and rape; and (3) socially organized deviations, such as prostitution and homosexuality. We have dealt with the major sexual patterns in each of these categories, but our chief focus has been on deviant patterns that are maladaptive from the standpoint of the individual and/or the group, such as incest or rape. In this context we delineated the clinical pictures, etiological factors, and most effective methods of treatment. The final section included a discussion of transsexualism, in the course of which we dealt with problems of gender identity and with ethical and other problems associated with attempts to change the sex of an individual through surgery.

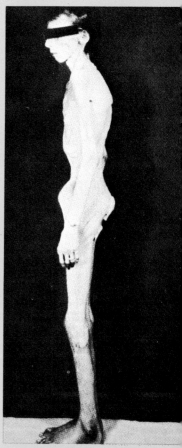

Psychosomatic Disorders

14

CLINICAL PICTURE

DYNAMICS OF PSYCHOSOMATIC DISORDERS

TREATMENT AND OUTCOMES

Traditionally, the medical profession has been concerned with physical illness and has concentrated research efforts on understanding and controlling the organic factors in disease. In psychopathology, on the other hand, interest has been centered primarily on uncovering the psychological and emotional factors in mental disorders. Today we realize that both of these viewpoints are limited; although an illness may be primarily physical or psychological, it is always a disorder of the whole person—not just of his lungs or psyche. Fatigue or a bad cold may lower a person's tolerance for psychological stress, while—by the same token—an emotional upset may lower his resistance to physical disease. In short, man is a totality, whether in health or disease. He functions as a psychobiological unit in continual interaction with his environment.

Relevant sociocultural data are important to this interactional view, for the environment affects the types and incidence of disorders found in different groups. The ailments to which people are most vulnerable—whether physical, psychological, or both—are determined in no small part by when and where they live. Likewise, on a more specific level, the life situation of an individual—in terms of interpersonal and other social variables—has much to do with the onset of a disorder, its duration, and whether or not he recovers. If the individual's family supports him and cooperates in his treatment program, and if he is eager to resume his usual activities, recovery is more probable and apt to be more rapid than if he faces a return to an unpleasant marriage or a frustrating job.

The interdisciplinary approach to all disorders —which fits relevant biological, psychological, and sociocultural data into a coherent picture— is also referred to as the *psychosomatic approach*. It is now reflected in medical and psychological thinking, not only with respect to the treatment of physical illnesses brought on by emotional tension, but also of those cases where no causes other than physical ones are obvious. We might, for example, ask whether emotional factors have lowered the resistance of a tuberculosis patient and hence contributed to the onset of the disease. We might also ask how the individual will react to changes in his life situation brought about by the disease. Will he fail to cooperate in treatment and welcome death as a solution to his problem, or will he fight the disease with a determination to get well? Some patients apparently give up and die when medically the chances seem good that they will recover. Others with more serious organic pathology recover, or survive for long periods of time. In fact, a pioneer in the field of psychosomatic medicine, Flanders Dunbar (1943), concluded that it is often "more important to know what kind of patient has the disease than what kind of disease the patient has" (p. 23).

It has been estimated that at least one out of every two persons who seek medical aid suffers from an illness related to emotional stress. Since this is not a book about medicine, we shall not go deeply into the role of emotional factors in primarily physical diseases, such as tuberculosis, pneumonia, and cancer. We shall, however, be concerned with such disorders as peptic ulcers, bronchial asthma, and high blood pressure, which are brought on in large part by psychological and emotional factors. In these disorders we often find: (1) the effects of sustained emotional tension on visceral organ systems; (2) the tendency in a given person for a single organ system to be involved, such as the respiratory or gastrointestinal system; and (3) the frequent production of organic pathology. In some instances—as in hemorrhaging ulcers—such pathology may actually threaten the person's life.

CLINICAL PICTURE

Unlike the other patterns of abnormal behavior discussed thus far, psychosomatic disorders involve a clinical picture dominated by changes in the structure and function of internal organs rather than overt maladaptive behavior. In the present section we shall note the various categories of disorders included in this very broad classification and then briefly describe several specific reaction patterns.

CLASSIFICATION OF PSYCHOSOMATIC DISORDERS

Psychosomatic disorders are classified according to the organ system affected, and it seems that no part of the body is immune.

The APA uses the term *psychophysiologic* when referring to specific disorders—reserving *psychosomatic* for the general approach to medicine in which physical, psychological, and sociocultural factors are taken into consideration. *Corticovisceral* is the preferred term in some countries to either *psychophysiologic* or *psycho-*

somatic, but we shall use these terms as roughly synonymous. In the APA classification, ten categories of these disorders are listed, each one preceded by the word *psychophysiologic* to emphasize that we are talking about disorders caused and maintained primarily by psychological and emotional factors rather than organic ones. The ten groups and some of the specific disorders in each are:

1. Psychophysiologic skin disorders: reactions such as neurodermatosis, atopic dermatitis, eczema, and some cases of acne and hives
2. Psychophysiologic musculoskeletal disorders: such disorders as backaches, muscle cramps, tension headaches, and some cases of arthritis
3. Psychophysiologic respiratory disorders: such disorders as bronchial asthma, hyperventilation syndromes, hiccoughs, and recurring bronchitis
4. Psychophysiologic cardiovascular disorders: disorders that include paroxysmal tachycardia, hypertension, vascular spasms, and migraine
5. Psychophysiologic hemic and lymphatic disorders: disturbances in the hemic and lymphatic

CONCURRENCE OF EMOTIONAL DISTURBANCE AND PHYSICAL ILLNESS

Advocates of the psychosomatic approach to medicine maintain— as Galen and others did many centuries ago—that it is unrealistic to compartmentalize "mind," "body," and "environment" when assessing and treating maladaptive patterns, whether such patterns are primarily physical or psychological in nature. This view is supported by the striking correlations which a number of investigators have found between the incidence of physical illness and emotional disturbances.

In their pioneering study of illness in relatively healthy populations, for example, Hinkle and Wolff (1957) found that persons who had the greatest number of physical illnesses, regardless of kind, were also the ones who experienced the greatest number of disturbances in mood, thought, and behavior. Similarly, Matarazzo, Matarazzo, and Saslow (1961) concluded that the incidence of physical illness in a population is a good predictor of mental disturbances, and vice versa.

The correlation between physical and emotional disturbances is well brought out in the reports of Jacobs et al. (1970; 1971) of their initial and follow-up evaluations of 179 college students in the Boston area—106 of whom sought medical help for respiratory infections. The ill subjects were significantly more likely than the "normals" to perceive the year preceding their illness as one characterized by failure and disappointment; and the more severely ill they were, the more frequent and intense were their reports of unpleasant and stressful events and emotions. A follow-up study revealed recurrences of illness and repetition of treatment-seeking behavior, while the healthy controls tended to stay healthy. Finding that the chief point of difference between the ill and healthy subjects was the style and intensity of the formers' maladaptive coping behavior, the investigators concluded that a direct association could be made between maladaptive coping styles and physical illness, as well as psychiatric complaints.

An explanation for such concurrences in physical and emotional disturbances may be found in Schwab's (1970) observation that there is often a vicious circle in which emotional disturbances adversely affect the body's functioning and lower its resistance to disease; and disease, in turn, tends to elicit and exacerbate feelings of anxiety, depression, and, often, hopelessness. Thus, Schwab did not find reports of both physical and mental distress by emotionally disturbed persons surprising—noting that "The concurrence of mental and physical symptomatology should be regarded as natural when we view man as a biosocial organism whose nervous system functions as the central integrating medium." (p. 594)

---

systems (This category is included so that all organ systems will be covered.)

6. Psychophysiologic gastrointestinal disorders: disorders that include peptic ulcers, chronic gastritis, and mucous colitis

7. Psychophysiologic genitourinary disorders: such disorders as disturbances in menstruation and micturition

8. Psychophysiologic endocrine disorders: hyperthyroidism, obesity, and other endocrine disorders in which emotional factors play a causative role

9. Psychophysiologic disorders of organs of special sense: such disorders as chronic conjunctivitis (Conversion reactions are excluded.)

10. Psychophysiologic disorders of other types: disturbances in the nervous system in which emotional factors play a causative role

From the foregoing, it is apparent that psychosomatic (psychophysiologic) disorders cover a wide range of disturbances in which emotional factors may play a causative role. It should be emphasized, however, that a given case of hives, hypertension, or ulcers should not be diagnosed as psychosomatic until a thorough medical evaluation has been made.

SOME SPECIFIC REACTION PATTERNS

The clinical picture in psychosomatic disorders tends to be phasic—that is, there are periods of upsurgence of the symptoms—followed by a waning or disappearance of them. The sequence of their appearance and disappearance seems related to the amounts of tension the individual is experiencing. For example, a hard-pressed business executive may find his ulcers clearing up during a 3-week vacation. It is also of interest to note that there are marked differences between the sexes in the incidence of specific disorders— ulcers being much more common among men than women, while the reverse is true of rheumatoid arthritis and mucous colitis.

We shall briefly describe five common types of psychosomatic reactions—peptic ulcers, migraine headaches, asthma, eczema, and hypertension.

Peptic ulcers. Peptic ulcers first came into prominence in our Western culture during the first half of the nineteenth century. In the beginning they were primarily observed in young women, but in the second half of the nineteenth century there was a shift, and today the incidence of ulcers is some 2 or 3 times higher among men than women. Contemporary civilization apparently is conducive to the chronic emotional reactions that lead to peptic ulcers, and it is estimated that about 1 in every 10 Americans now living will at some time in his life develop a peptic ulcer (Necheles, 1970; Schwab et al., 1970).

The ulcer itself results from an excessive flow of the stomach's acid-containing digestive juices, which eat away the lining of the stomach or duodenum, leaving a craterlike wound. Although disease, dietary factors, and other organic conditions may lead to ulcers, it is now recognized that nervous tension, worry, repressed anger, and general emotional strain, even more than food and drink, stimulate the flow of stomach acids.

In a historic study, Wolf and Wolff (1947) utilized a subject, Tom, who—as a consequence of an operation—literally had a window over his stomach, enabling direct observation of his gastric functioning. When Tom was subjected to interview experiences designed to elicit strong resentment, hostility, and anxiety, there was a marked increase in acid production, engorgement of the stomach with blood, and rhythmic contractions—in essence, digestive functions occurred just as if his stomach were full of food. A number of more recent studies have shown comparable findings with respect to such emotions as anger and hostility. Most people, of course, get over emotional upset and return to normal bodily functioning. But if the emotional tension is sustained long enough—if anger and resentment, for example, are repressed or denied adequate expression—the digestive acids with no food to work on may eat into the gastric lining and cause ulceration.

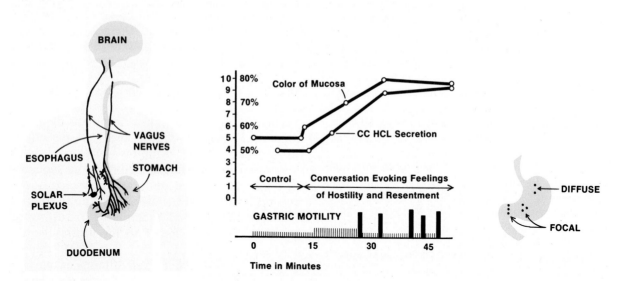

PEPTIC ULCERS

In some individuals the lining of the stomach or the duodenum may be eaten away by acid-containing digestive juices, leaving a peptic ulcer. Nervous tension and general emotional stress are recognized as key factors in the excessive production of digestive juices; thus, the drawing at left depicts the nerves, as well as the organs, primarily involved in the development of peptic ulcers.

The graph (center) and drawing (right) pertain to related experiments of historic importance. The graph presents evidence by Wolf and Wolff (1946)—in experiments with their subject Tom—that feelings of strong resentment, hostility, and anxiety resulted in measurable increases in acid production and stomach bleeding.

The drawing at right indicates areas of ulcerative changes evidenced by certain monkeys in an experimental group, all of which received hypothalamic stimulation via implanted electrodes (French et al., 1957). All 19 monkeys in the group showed signs of bewilderment, agitation, and fear during the stimulation to which they were subjected several times daily for several weeks, and 8 of them developed the ulcerative changes in the areas indicated in the drawing. The latter animals also showed increased restlessness, irritability, and higher gastric acid secretion.

Migraine and tension headaches. Although headaches can result from a wide range of organic conditions, the vast majority of them—about 9 out of 10—seem to be related to emotional tensions. An estimated 15 million or more Americans suffer from recurrent tension headaches, with the incidence apparently being higher among women than men. Research in this area has focused primarily on migraine, an intensely painful headache that recurs periodically. Although typically involving only one side of the head, migraine is sometimes more generalized, and it may also shift from side to side.

Migraine was extensively described by Galen and other medical writers of antiquity, but the cause of the pain remained a mystery until recently, when interest was focused on the pain-sensitive arteries of the head. By dilating these arteries with an injection of histamine, researchers found it possible to reproduce the pain of migraine. Turning to actual cases of migraine, they discovered that the onset of the headaches was accompanied by progressive dilation of the cranial arteries. In addition, persons with unilateral headaches showed dilation of the cranial artery only on the side where the pain occurred. As the attack subsided, either spontaneously or following the administration of drugs, the pain diminished and the arteries returned to their normal size.

It has been found that a variety of experimentally induced stresses—frustrations, excessive work demands, and threatening interviews—cause vascular dilation among migraine sufferers, but not among other persons. The graph on page 502 traces the course of a headache induced during a discussion that evoked feelings of hostility in the subject—a migraine sufferer. Recently it has been shown that two types of migraine headaches that occur at night—the "ordinary" migraine headache and the sharp, stabbing "cluster" type that occurs in multiple episodes—commonly begin after a period of REM, or rapid eye movement, sleep (Alvarez, 1970). The significance of this finding remains to be ascertained.

The clinical picture in migraine is illustrated in the following case summary.

A 33-year-old woman who managed a travel bureau was proud of "making her own way" in life. She had been engaged several times but had always broken off the relationship. About a year prior to the onset of her migraine headaches, she had met a wealthy man 15 years her senior; they were married after only 3 weeks' acquaintance.

The marriage was not approved by the woman's brother and sister, with whom she was quite close, and this upset her considerably. Possibly contributing to her emotional stress was the realization that she did not really love her husband, but married him primarily because she was getting older and might not meet anyone else more suitable. During the first months of the marriage, the relationship seemed to work out despite these problems. But the woman's husband made gradually increasing demands upon her—particularly in terms of time—and soon suggested that she give up her job. Now she began to experience "tension headaches," usually when clients were indecisive about their travel plans or failed to keep commitments they had made.

The woman decided that she would conduct one of the tours to Europe herself, so that she could "get away for a while and think things over." Once she arrived in Europe her migraine headaches ceased completely. But on her return, when her husband became more insistent in his demands on her time, her migraine headaches recurred with greater frequency and intensity. She eventually consulted her physician, who in turn referred her to a marital counselor.

Asthma. Like migraine, asthmatic attacks have been described by medical writers since ancient times. The actual attack occurs when reactive airways become restricted, which makes breathing difficult. Many asthmatics begin to wheeze in the presence of household dust, tobacco smoke, cold air, and other conditions that do not bother other people so much. Attacks may be mild or severe and may continue for hours or even days. In severe cases the individual may become extremely distressed, fight for air, and evidence convulsive coughing. Between attacks, he is relatively symptom-free. The actual incidence of asthma is unknown, but it is considered the leading cause of chronic illness among persons under 17 years of age.

There appear to be several types of asthma, each with its own causes and triggering stimuli. Probably the most common is allergic asthma, initiated by something in the environment to which the individual has become sensitized, such as ragweed pollen (Ellis, 1970). Although the precise way in which sensitization occurs is not known, once it takes place the individual will develop symptoms in the presence of the

MIGRAINE HEADACHES

The side-view drawing of the head at left below shows the location of pain-sensitive cranial arteries, with the dotted lines marking the areas where the headache is felt as various parts of the arteries dilate.

The graph traces the course of a headache induced during a discussion which evoked feelings of hostility in a subject. Both the changes in the amplitude of the artery pulsations and the corresponding increase and diminution in the intensity of the pain are shown. The headache was completely relieved by means of an injection which the subject believed would end the suffering but which actually could have had no physical effect.

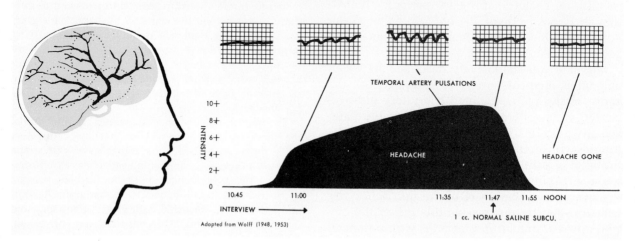

Adapted from Wolff (1948, 1953)

allergen. Other cases of asthma are associated with infectious conditions, and in still other cases asthma appears to be "intrinsic"—that is, there is no apparent sensitization to any given allergen, nor is any infectious condition present. This last form of asthma may be triggered by emotional stimuli and may occur in infancy as well as later life. In a study of 347 youths between the ages of 6 and 16, Purcell, Muser, Miklich, and Dietiker (1969) suggested the importance of ascertaining which are more relevant in the etiological picture—aversive physical stimuli or emotional stresses—and using this information as a guide for treatment. Of course, where the asthma attack is triggered by emotional stress, there still may be predisposing biological factors.

Knapp (1969) has cited the case of a young married woman' who suffered from severe episodes of asthma. Medical examination revealed no selective sensitivity to particular allergens; rather, the asthma attacks appeared to be directly related to her difficulty in handling hostility aroused by interpersonal relationships. The following excerpts are illustrative of the clinical picture.

"I just feel rotten and I can't breathe and I just have to keep using the spray, and if I cough my lungs out it'll go away. . . . When I'm mad or something's bothering me it can happen. If I'm mad, inside mad, this can go off. Now whether it's because there's anxieties or nerves or worries I don't know, but if I get mad and I'm holding it in, and I'm thinking about something, it can happen."

Asked for some specific examples, she thought of an insistent and obnoxious girl friend:

"She drives me kind of crazy. I can think about her, if I want to let it bother me, it can happen. It's happened a lot of times if I was cross and mad." (pp. 141–142)

Eczema. Because the skin is well supplied with small blood vessels, it is a highly sensitive indicator of emotional states. For example, when an individual is embarrassed or angry, his skin tends to flush; when he is severely frightened, the blood tends to be drawn away from the small capillaries of the skin and his face may blanch or turn pale. Often, people who are under stress and emotionally upset develop a rash or other psychosomatic skin reaction. Such reactions typically clear up when the stress is alleviated, but there may be residual scars, particularly if the skin itches and is continually scratched. Persons subject to psychomatic skin reactions—though actual incidence is unknown—undoubtedly number in the millions.

Skin disorders such as eczema and hives are unpleasant to look at, and therefore may have a damaging effect on an individual's relationships with other people and on his self-concept. The tensions thus produced often serve to exacerbate psychosomatic skin reactions.

Hypertension. The heart probably is the most sensitive to emotional stress of the various organ systems. During states of calm, the beat of the heart is regular, pulse is even, blood pressure is relatively low, and the visceral organs are well supplied with blood. With emotion-arousing stress, however, the vessels of the visceral organs are constricted and blood is directed in greater quantity to the muscles of the trunk and limbs—changes that help put the body on an emergency footing for maximum physical exertion. The tightening or restricting of the tiny vessels to visceral organs forces the heart to work harder. As it beats faster and with greater force, the pulse quickens and blood pressure mounts. Usually, when the stress or crisis passes, the body resumes normal functioning and the blood pressure returns to normal. However, an estimated 10 to 25 million persons in the United States suffer from chronically high blood pressure, or hypertension (Finnerty, 1971; Stamler, 1971).

In many cases, a physical cause of hypertension can be ascertained; for example, it may be attributable to certain diseases of the kidneys, to a narrowing of the aorta or one of its arteries, or to the excessive use of certain drugs.

In the majority of cases, however, the cause is not known and the condition is referred to as "essential hypertension." Whatever its origins, high blood pressure is a serious disorder that can cause severe damage to the heart, kidneys, and blood vessels. When associated with the hardening of the arteries, it presents the danger of a stroke.

A number of investigators, following the lead of Wolff (1953), have shown that essential hypertension may be triggered by emotional tension; and that such tension may persist and affect heart functioning even though feelings of anxiety, hostility, or other emotions are repressed and the individual regains surface calm. In a study of 128 middle-aged factory workers, Davies (1970) found that some individuals are prone to develop high blood pressure when they are subjected to sustained emotional stress and cannot find an adequate outlet or channel of expression for their feelings. With time, conscious feelings of emotion may be repressed, but the underlying emotional tension continues.

As the following case illustrates, hypertensive reactions may appear even in young people.

Mark ____ , a senior in law school, evidenced episodes of extreme hypertension whenever he was subjected to stress. He became aware of these episodes when he failed to pass his physical examination for induction into the Armed Forces because of exceptionally high blood pressure. In a later check at a medical clinic, under nonstressful conditions, his blood pressure was normal; however, under simulated stress conditions, his blood pressure showed extreme elevation; and this happened again when he returned for another physical examination at the induction center. Although most people show alterations in blood pressure under stress, Mark seemed to show unusual reactivity to a wide range of stressful conditions.

DYNAMICS OF PSYCHOSOMATIC DISORDERS

In the present section we shall be concerned both with the general etiology of psychosomatic disorders and with the problem of organ specificity—of why one individual manifests bronchial spasms, another hypertension, and still another

migraine headaches. As we shall see, much remains to be learned about the interacting roles of specific neurophysiological and psychosocial variables in triggering and maintaining such disorders. In general, however, the development of psychosomatic reactions seems to involve: (1) the arousal of emotional tensions in response to stress situations—the degree of arousal depending not only on the nature of the stress situation itself, but also on the individual's perception of the situation and his ability to cope with it; (2) the failure of emotional tensions to be adequately discharged—through appropriate physical activity, for example, or through verbalization or fantasy—with the result that the physiological disequilibrium associated with emotional arousal continues on a chronic basis; and (3) response stereotypy—the damaging effects of chronic arousal becoming concentrated in a specific organ system, one that is more vulnerable than others as a result of inheritance, illness, or conditioning. In the discussion that follows, we shall be concerned with the possible significance of particular biological, psychological, and sociocultural variables in contributing to this chain of events.

BIOLOGICAL FACTORS

A number of biological factors have been implicated in psychosomatic disorders, directly or indirectly. These include: genetic factors, differences in autonomic reactivity, somatic weakness, and alterations in corticovisceral control mechanisms.

Genetic factors. There is some evidence to suggest that genetic factors play a predisposing role in certain types of psychosomatic disorders. For example, Solomon (1969) has noted the presence of a rheumatoid factor in the sera of arthritis victims, and Necheles (1970) has pointed to a similar factor in the blood of persons suffering from ulcers. Both investigators viewed these blood factors as predisposing an individual to the respective disorders and not as resulting from them. Speculating on the interplay of biological and psychological factors in the development of rheumatoid arthritis, Solomon concluded:

"It seemed as if the occurrence of psychic disequilibrium in the presence of rheumatoid factor might lead to overt rheumatoid disease, so that physically healthy persons with rheumatoid factor, to remain so, need to be psychologically healthy as well." (p. 338)

Research by Gregory and Rosen (1965) has demonstrated that the brothers of ulcer patients are about twice as likely to have ulcers themselves as comparable members of the general population. Increased frequencies of asthma, hypertension, migraine, and other reactions have also been reported for close relatives, and these increased frequencies are specific to given reactions—that is, the relatives of bronchial asthma cases show an increased frequency of bronchial asthma but not of other psychosomatic disorders.

It used to be considered unlikely that such increased frequencies could be due to parental example and learning, since the autonomic nervous system was presumably much less vulnerable to conditioning and learning than the cerebrospinal system. More recent studies of learning in the autonomic system, however, indicate that

BIOLOGICAL CLOCKS

The 24-hour rhythmic fluctuations observable in the activity and metabolic processes of plants and animals—indeed, all living creatures on earth—are referred to as *circadian* cycles, from the Latin words meaning "about a day." Thus, normal functioning for each system or individual appears to follow a biological clock; and an upset in this cycle, caused by changes in schedule or other factors, may cause malfunctioning in the form of somatic or psychosomatic complaints.

Thousands of experiments with lower animals have established the relationship between biological clocks and normal functioning. And man—although found to be somewhat more adaptable to environmental changes than the lower animals—has revealed similar cyclic fluctuations in activity and sleep, body temperature, chemical constituents of the blood, and so on. Interestingly enough, these cycles have remained essentially the same even for human subjects who have lived in caves, cut off from all means of knowing whether it was day or night for periods as long as several months.

In studies of disturbances in circadian cycles in humans—e.g., a sudden reversal of sleep schedules from night to daytime—subjects have demonstrated various degrees of adaptability. And in comparable experiments that simulated manned space flights, some subjects reacted well to unusual schedules of work and rest—e.g., working for 4 hours, then resting for 4 hours—while others were unable to adapt to them.

A report prepared for the National Institute of Mental Health by Weitzman and Luce (1970) has noted the potential adverse effects of technological change—including abrupt time changes associated with jet travel—on "the invisible circadian cycle that may govern our susceptibility to disease or shock, our emotions, our performance, our alertness or stupefaction." (p. 279)

increased incidence of specific psychosomatic conditions in given families could result from common experience and learning. Further research evidence is needed, but genetic factors should not be ruled out—particularly in such disorders as bronchial asthma, where allergens often play a key role.

Differences in autonomic reactivity. In our earlier discussion of personality development (Chapter 5), we noted that individuals vary significantly in their "primary reaction tendencies," including their reactivity to stress. Even very young infants reveal marked differences in their sensitivity to aversive stimuli: one may become severely upset by exposure to bright sunlight, or by loud noises, whereas another will be relatively undisturbed by these conditions. Such basic differences in emotional reactivity continue into adult life, and presumably they help to account for the fact that different individuals seem to have varying degrees of susceptibility to psychosomatic disorders.

Individual differences in reactivity to stress extend also to specific patterns of physiological response. Wolff (1950) has suggested that people can be classified as "stomach reactors," "pulse reactors," "nose reactors," and so on—depending on what kinds of physical changes are characteristically triggered by stress. These individual patterns of autonomic reactivity appear to be remarkably consistent and stable, and they help to explain why different people develop different types of psychosomatic disorders. A person who characteristically reacts to stressful situations with a rise in blood pressure, for example, will be particularly vulnerable to hypertension under conditions of sustained stress, whereas one who reacts with increased secretions of stomach acids will be more likely to develop peptic ulcers.

Somatic weakness. Assuming that individuals do differ in their characteristic patterns of autonomic reactivity, the question remains as to how such differences arise. At least a partial answer to this question can be found in the concept of *somatic weakness*—that is, such factors as inheritance, illness, or prior strain make one particular organ system more vulnerable to stress than others. If the person has inherited a "weak" stomach, he presumably will be prone to gastrointestinal upsets when he becomes angry or anxious; if a person has had a respiratory infec-

tion, his lungs or nasal passages may remain vulnerable, and emotional stress may bring on attacks of bronchitis or asthma. In a study of asthma in children, for example, Rees (1964) reported that 80 percent of his subjects showed a prior history of respiratory infection. Similarly, in a study of more than 1200 patients, Bulatov (1963) found that a respiratory infection had preceded the bronchial asthma in 98 percent of the cases.

Presumably, the weakest link in the chain of visceral organs will be the organ affected. However, caution must be exercised to avoid *ex post facto* reasoning, since it would not be safe to conclude when a particular organ system is affected that it must have been weak to begin with. Also, as we shall see, conditioning may play a key role in determining which organ system is involved.

Alterations in corticovisceral control mechanisms. Other biological approaches have focused on possible alterations in cortical control mechanisms that normally regulate autonomic functioning (Triesman, 1968; Wittkower & Solyom, 1967). Russian physiologists, including Lebedev, have emphasized an interactive relationship between visceral pathology and cortical control centers.

"From the point of view of corticovisceral pathology a prominent role in the involvement of a particular organ in a psychosomatic illness is played by the functional relationships which are formed, as the pathological process develops, between the cerebral cortex and the subcortical vegetative centers." (Lebedev, 1967, p. 245)

This approach would take into account such findings as those of Sawrey and Sawrey (1964)—who implanted electrodes producing stimulation of the hypothalamus in rats and found that such stimulation can produce ulcers.

Presumably corticovisceral control mechanisms may fail in their homeostatic functions, so that the individual's emotional response is exaggerated in intensity and he does not regain physiological equilibrium within normal time limits. A combination of response stereotypy and faulty visceral control mechanisms will definitely predispose the individual to psychosomatic disorders in the face of continued stress. Conversely, if the individual's corticovisceral control mechanisms work efficiently, he may avoid psychosomatic reactions even in the face of response stereotypy and severe and sustained stress. As Sternbach (1971) has expressed it:

"If a person with marked response stereotypy is continually exposed to stressful situations, he may nevertheless avoid having psychosomatic symptoms if his autonomic feedback and control mechanisms operate efficiently. The individual's own autonomic balance (homeostasis) may be kept within the limits of normal functioning by the reflex mechanisms . . . which prevent either responses or rebounds from being of such magnitude that tissue damage occurs. Thus even though he may have 'physiological rigidity' in the sense that one organ system always shows greater responses than the others, and even though these responses are continually and frequently activated by intensely provoking situations, reflexive control of the response systems may make it possible to avoid the appearance of symptoms." (p. 141)

In assessing the role of biological factors in psychosomatic disorders—in terms of etiology and the specific organ systems involved—most investigators would take into consideration each of the factors we have described. Perhaps the greatest emphasis at present would be placed on the characteristic autonomic activity of given individuals, the vulnerability of affected organ systems, and possible alterations in cortical control mechanisms that normally regulate autonomic functioning.

PSYCHOLOGICAL AND INTERPERSONAL FACTORS

The role of psychological and interpersonal factors in psychosomatic disorders is still not altogether clear. Factors that have been emphasized include personality makeup, family patterns, stress and defenses against it, and learning in the autonomic nervous system. Our primary focus will be on the last two factors.

Personality factors. The work of Flanders Dunbar (1943; 1954) and a number of other early investigators raised the hope that it could be shown that certain personality characteristics are associated with particular psychosomatic disorders—for example, that persons who are

rigid, highly sensitive to threat, and prone to chronic underlying hostility tend to suffer from hypertension. If it were possible, as it then seemed, to delineate ulcer types, hypertensive characters, accident-prone personalities, and so on, such findings would, of course, be of great value in understanding, assessment, and treatment.

More recent experimental evidence suggests that such an approach is oversimplified. Evidently there is a wide variation in personality makeup among individuals suffering from psychosomatic disorders—in general, and in relation to such specific reactions as peptic ulcers. And even where "typical" personality traits are found among hypertensive, peptic ulcer, and other subjects, we are left with the problem of why many other people with similar personality traits do not develop such disorders under stress.

In a related but more limited approach, Graham (1962) focused on the possible relationship between an individual's attitudes toward stressful situations and his coping reactions. He found the following patterns to be fairly typical:

Ulcers—feels deprived of what is due to him, and wants to get what is owed or promised and to get even
Migraine—feels something has to be achieved, drives self to reach a goal, and then feels let down
Asthma—feels unloved, rejected, left out in the cold, and wants to shut the person or situation out
Eczema—feels he is being frustrated, but is helpless to do anything about it except take it out on himself
Hypertension—feels endangered, threatened with harm, has to be ready for anything, to be on guard

As we have seen, an individual's attitudes and personality makeup do play a key role in determining the way he evaluates and reacts to stress situations. Thus, the work of Graham and other investigators on the association between attitudes, stress, and psychosomatic disorders does appear relevant. It would also appear relevant to consider the effects of "feedback"—in terms of changed self-concept, changed life activities, changed family relations, and so on—which are often entailed when an individual develops a psychosomatic disorder. However, we still do not know why some individuals with similar attitudes toward stress and similar patterns of emotional arousal do not develop psychosomatic disorders.

Family patterns. A number of studies have dealt with the possible role of pathogenic family patterns in the etiology of psychosomatic disorders. For example, studies dealing with asthmatic patients have found that the mothers of such patients have in many cases felt ambivalent toward their children and tended to reject them, while at the same time being overprotective and unduly restrictive of the children's activities (Goldberg, 1959; Lipton et al., 1966; Olds, 1970; Szyrynski, 1960; Wenar et al., 1962). The fathers of asthmatic sufferers have been described as typically passive and as inadequate male models for the children. Since individuals coming out of such a family background tend to be overdependent and insecure, it would hardly be surprising if they should react with chronic emotional mobilization to problems that most people take in stride. At the same time, we may wonder why some individuals develop psychosomatic disorders rather than another form of psychopathology—and indeed, why others achieve adequate adjustment. We again appear to be faced with an interaction of factors in which parent-child and family patterns may play roles of varying importance, depending on the case. This point is supported by the findings of Block (1969), who studied the parents of schizophrenic, neurotic, asthmatic, and congenitally ill children. Her findings "clearly show a relationship between the degree of parental psychopathology and the presence of psychological symptoms in the child." (p. 673) She failed, however, to find any specific family patterns characteristic of psychosomatic or other disorders. Again, about all we can conclude is that family pathology is associated with maladaptive behavior on the part of the child, but the form this behavior takes will depend on the total clinical picture.

Whatever part family patterns may play in the development of psychosomatic reactions, such reactions are often maintained by secondary gains achieved in the family setting. Thus, the child with asthma who does not like to be left at home with a baby-sitter may develop an acute attack when his parents are planning to go to some social event; or a spouse who feels neglected may find that his symptoms provide a convenient means of obtaining sympathy and support from significant others, as well as some measure of control over their activities.

Stress. A pioneer in psychosomatic medicine, Day (1951), once pointed out that "To develop chronic active pulmonary tuberculosis a person needs some bacilli, some moderately inflammable lungs . . . and some internal or external factor which lowers the resistance to the disease." He further noted that unhappiness was among the factors that could lower resistance.

A number of later investigators have shown that throughout an individual's lifetime there is a close relationship between the timing of physical illness and life stress (Bahnson, 1969; Engel &

ARE THERE TARGET DATES FOR DEATH?

It has long been apparent in medicine—with respect to major surgery as well as to diseases such as tuberculosis—that the patient's emotional state may play a crucial role in whether he recovers or dies. There are many cases on record in which patients died despite good chances of recovery, apparently because they did not try to live; and there are also cases in which patients who were given a hopeless medical diagnosis somehow managed to recover—presumably as a result of the poorly understood factor called "determination to live."

Some explanation for this tenacious hold on life may be found in the observation that many people seem "determined to live until a certain target date." (Ruch & Zimbardo, 1971, p. 395) In fact, there are reports that older persons are more likely to die after a holiday or birthday than before. Cases have even been recorded of terminally ill patients who managed to stay alive until an important event took place, such as a wedding anniversary or the birth of a grandchild.

Apparently the setting of such "target dates" for living is relatively common. Many middle-aged persons, when asked, will state that they want to live until New Year's Day of the year 2000 —to see the dawning of the twenty-first century.

In somewhat similar fashion, some persons also set what amount to "target dates for death." For example, the prospect of life without the companionship of one's mate has caused many happily married older people to say they want to die when their mates do. So powerful is the loss of the will to live in some cases that the bereavement may actually precipitate the spouse's own death.

An interesting case with respect to target dates for death is that of Mark Twain (Samuel Clemens). He was born on November 30, 1835, when Halley's comet made its spectacular appearance in the sky; and he died—as he had predicted—on April 21, 1910, when Halley's comet returned. Death was attributed to angina pectoris, but the question still remains as to the underlying cause: Was it the excitement surrounding the fiery comet's return, or the conviction that the incontrovertible date for death had arrived?

Adler, 1967; Mutter & Schleifer, 1966; Schwab, 1970; Solomon, 1969; 1971). For example, Mutter and Schleifer (1966) found that the families of ill children—as compared with a control group of families of healthy children—had been more disorganized during the 6-month period prior to the illness and had exposed their children to a greater number of threatening and disruptive psychological stresses. Senay and Redlich (1968) have pointed to the prominence of gastrointestinal and cardiac complaints in populations undergoing severe stresses, such as are imposed by migration, floods, earthquakes, and rapid social change. A study of psychosomatic problems in concentration-camp survivors, made almost a quarter century after the end of World War II, revealed that gastrointestinal disorders were reported for 38 percent of 227 cases and pre-

The ulcer-inducing effect of stress was observed in a well-known conditioning experiment utilizing two monkeys at the psychological research laboratories of Walter Reed Army Hospital. The "executive monkey" (at left) learned to press a lever that prevented electric shocks to him and the control monkey, while—having no responsibility—the control monkey lost interest in its lever. Only the executive monkey developed ulcers (Brady et al., 1958; Brady, 1970).

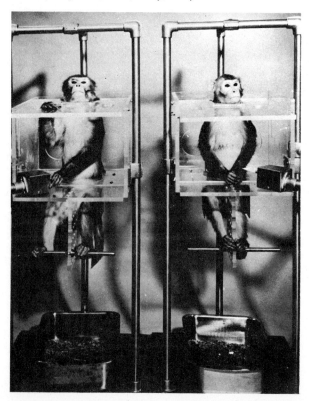

sumably were connected with digestive disturbances experienced during the imprisonment (Eitinger, 1969). These disorders—predominantly peptic ulcers and diarrhea—were reactivated by any situation of unusual stress. From this viewpoint, many psychosomatic disorders are a consequence of the individual's vulnerability to particular stresses and his continuing inability to handle emotional tensions that are aroused. The emotion most frequently associated with psychosomatic disorders is anger; fear follows in second place, and anxiety in third (Musaph, 1969; Sternbach, 1971).

Alexander (1950) hypothesized that each type of psychosomatic disorder could be associated with a particular kind of stress. He concluded that peptic ulcers, for example, are typically associated with frustration of the needs for love and protection. Presumably, the frustration of these needs would give rise to such emotions as anxiety and anger, and these emotions, in turn, would trigger excessive secretions of stomach acid—leading eventually to peptic ulcers. Subsequent research, however, has failed to demonstrate a consistent relationship between particular disorders and particular types of stress. Rather, it would appear that a wide range of stress situations can lead to a given type of disorder— and, conversely, that a wide range of disorders can result from a given type of stress. Most investigators feel that an individual's perception of a stress situation, and his particular pattern of autonomic reactivity, are of key importance in determining the nature of his emotional response.

Often it appears that severe or sustained stress serves merely to pave the way for or precipitate a disorder in a person already predisposed to a particular pattern. For example, the individual who is allergic to a particular protein may have his resistance further lowered by emotional tension; similarly, where an invading virus has already entered the body, emotional tension may interfere with the normal defensive processes of the body in overcoming it.

Engel and Adler (1967) have reported on a major study at the Mayo Clinic which demonstrated a close relationship between emotional tension and physical disease in general:

"The great majority of patients hospitalized for physical illness . . . had experienced a psychological disturbance shortly before they got sick. Most commonly this had not been anxiety, fear, or anger—the emotions generally considered to be associated with illness—but an attitude of helplessness or hopelessness usually described by the investigators as *giving up*. 'It was just too much,' a patient would report. Or, 'I couldn't take it any more.' Or, 'I didn't know what to do,' or, 'I threw up my hands.'" (p. 2)

Again we see the importance, in the clinical picture, of the way the individual perceives and reacts to stress.

Defenses. Since there appears to be a negative relationship between psychosomatic disorders and neuroses, psychoses, and character disorders, the etiological role of psychological defenses in psychosomatic reactions has commonly been emphasized (Davies, 1970; Pedder, 1969). Presumably, the individuals affected are either unable to discharge their emotions adequately by verbal and other everyday means or to erect psychological defenses for the alleviation of emotional tension—as by rationalizing the stress situation or becoming desensitized to it. As a consequence, they appear to rely on repression, which screens out their emotional feelings from conscious awareness; but the physiological components of the emotion continue and finally lead to structural damage.

This viewpoint is supported by the findings of Hokanson and Burgess (1962). When individuals were subjected experimentally to frustrating situations, those given an opportunity afterward to show physical or verbal aggression against the frustrator showed a rapid return to normal systolic blood pressure and heart rate, while those who were permitted only fantasy aggression or none at all returned much more slowly to normal physiological functioning. The stress itself, then, is not of such key importance as an individual's inability to deal adequately with the emotional tensions elicited by the stress.

In this context, Bahnson (1969) has postulated two avenues for the discharge of stress-aroused tension and the consequences of following each.

"Our hypothesis specifies that the 'choice' of behavioral versus somatic regression is associated with the type of ego defense utilized by the individual. Projective defenses, involving interpersonal discharge, predispose to psychological regression under stress, whereas repressing and denying defenses, serving to maintain

THE LONG-TERM EFFECTS OF SEVERE LIFE CRISES

Studies with middle-aged and older persons concerning the association between emotional upsets and physical disorders have shown such a link to exist, on a long-term as well as an immediate basis. It would appear that each highly stressful experience leaves a person with an "indelible scar" to the extent that—in the process we call "aging"—it uses up bodily reserves that cannot be entirely replaced (Seyle, 1956; 1969). And apparently aging—whether due to the sheer number of years the person has lived or the accumulation of "indelible scars"—leads to the impairment, and in some instances the disorganization, of the body's immunity system (Steinmann, 1971).

In a group of 450 cancer patients, LeShan (1966) found that 72 percent had suffered emotional trauma in early life, as compared with only 10 percent of a noncancerous control group. Typically, the cancer appeared from 6 months to 8 years following a second crisis in later life. Similar findings were reported by Rahe and Holmes (1966) concerning a group of almost 400 subjects. In a 10-year period, major health changes were evidenced by 70 percent of those who experienced severe life crises; while the figure was only 37 percent for those who experienced moderate crises.

In the same context, Parkes et al. (1969) observed a sharp increase—40 percent above the expected rate—in the mortality rate for a group of widowers in the 6 months following the death of their wives. The investigators used the term "broken heart" in describing these cases, since the highest number involved coronary artery disease.

an effective external adaptation, result in internal somatic discharge and regression." (p. 324)

Here Bahnson is using the term *regression* as more or less synonymous with *decompensation*, and he further points out that the degree of decompensation will depend on the severity of stress. Carrying this approach a step further, Bahnson and Solomon (1971) have suggested that persons who repress their emotions rather than expressing them openly tend to build up high levels of adrenocortical or so-called stress hormones. Presumably such hormones have a suppressive effect on the body's immunological defenses. The lowering of these defenses may enable various diseases, including cancer, to get a foothold.

Although we need further evidence, it would appear that inability to erect adequate defenses to stress, or else the breakdown of defenses—either of which results in a state of chronic emotional mobilization—can lead to psychosomatic disorders.

Learning in the autonomic nervous system. It has long been assumed that although autonomic responses can be conditioned, they are not subject to voluntary control in the same way that muscular responses are, such as speaking or throwing a baseball.

More recent evidence indicates that this assumption is not valid. Not only can autonomic reactivity be conditioned involuntarily via the classical Pavlovian model, but learning in the autonomic nervous system can also take place voluntarily through a process of operant conditioning (DiCara, 1970; Green, Green & Walters, 1970; Kamiya, 1968; Lang, 1970; Lang, Stroufe & Hastings, 1967; Miller, 1969; Schwartz, Shapiro & Tursky, 1971). The individual can learn to control his brain waves, blood pressure, and other functions that ordinarily are under the control of the autonomic nervous system. Typically, the instrumental learning method involves a light or a tone feedback; for example, the light shines or the tone sounds as long as the subject is raising or lowering his blood pressure or modifying his brain waves in accordance with the instructions he is given.

In a study involving the control of heart rate, Lang et al. (1967) presented subjects with equipment that measured heart rate. The subjects received visual feedback from the dial on the equipment and were instructed to maintain their heart rates within prescribed limits. With learning, subjects became able to control their heart rates. In such studies, the subject may not be aware of how he learns to lower or raise his heart rate or blood pressure, or to control his brain waves, but mental set and exposure to feedback information enable him to achieve the desired result.

Thus, there would appear to be a good possibility that autonomic reactivity and visceral patterns in psychosomatic disorders result from the unique learning experiences of the individual, in much the same way that other behavior patterns are acquired. This conclusion is supported by a number of research findings. Turnbull (1962) demonstrated that by reinforcing certain breathing behavior an experimenter can elicit respiratory patterns that are progressively closer approximations of asthmatic breathing. Similarly, Bleeker (1968) reported that 19 of 40 volunteer subjects developed asthma symptoms after breathing the mist of a salt solution described as containing

allergens, such as dust or pollen. Twelve of the subjects had full-fledged asthma attacks. When the subjects took what they thought was a drug to combat asthma, symptoms disappeared immediately, but actually they were again given the salt mist. Why the other 21 subjects remained unaffected is not clear, but in 19 of 40 subjects we see the effect of suggestion on learning an autonomically mediated response.

Lang (1970) has also pointed out that psychosomatic disorders may arise through accidental conditioning and reinforcement. "A child who is repeatedly allowed to stay home from school when he has an upset stomach may be learning the visceral responses of chronic indigestion." (p. 86) Similarly, a child may get little or no attention from crying, but the gasping or wheezing reactions that often follow crying spells may obtain immediate attention and concern for him. If this pattern is repeated, the infant might learn an asthmalike response as a means of obtaining parental attention and alleviating distress. In addition, an asthmatic reaction—as a means of reducing anxiety—might generalize to other types of stressful situations. By virtue of its anxiety-reducing quality, it would continually be reinforced, and hence tend to persist. Even when more adaptive ways of coping with anxiety were later acquired, the individual might still resort to asthmatic attacks under severe stress.

Neal Miller (1969), who has pioneered much of the work on learning in the autonomic nervous system, has concluded that voluntary learning can be used to produce any visceral response that can be acquired by classical conditioning. Thus, it may be possible, for example, that an individual with hypertension could learn to lower his blood pressure at will and maintain it within normal functional limits. We shall describe one successful experiment with autonomic learning in our discussion of treatment and outcomes for psychosomatic disorders.

GENERAL SOCIOCULTURAL FACTORS

The incidence of specific diseases—including psychosomatic disorders—varies in different societies and in different strata of the same society. In general, psychosomatic disorders occur among all major social groups—from Africans to Australians, from Japanese to Russians, and from

Americans to Chinese. On the other hand, such disorders appear to be extremely rare among certain primitive societies, such as the aborigines of the Australian Western Desert (Kidson & Jones, 1968). As these primitive societies are exposed to social change, however, psychosomatic disorders begin to make their appearance. Of course, the specific type of psychosomatic disorders that occur may vary from one culture to another. For example, peptic ulcers are practically unheard

VOODOO SORCERY, PSYCHOSOMATIC DISORDERS, AND DEATH

"Have you ever felt that you were being hexed and might die?" was one of the questions Murphy and Hughes (1965, p. 125) regarded as relevant in their exploratory study of psychosomatic disorders among a people believing in witchcraft—the Eskimos in Sivokak village, located on St. Lawrence Island in the Bering Sea. While the data from this study have yet to be published, the fact of its concern with voodooism points to the persistence of such beliefs among certain primitive peoples. These villagers, for example, had imputed several deaths to voodoo sorcery.

Although attributing death to voodoo spells may appear naive, Cannon (1942)—in what is probably the only comprehensive study of the scientific literature on the subject—has cited a good deal of evidence to substantiate its occurrence. Included among Cannon's sources were competent scientific observers who had lived among the natives of Africa, Australia, New Zealand, and South America, as well as nearby Haiti. One such observer was Leonard (1906), whom Cannon quoted as follows:

"I have seen more than one hardened old Haussa soldier dying steadily and by inches because he believed himself to be bewitched; no nourishment or medicine that were given to him had the slightest effect either to check the mischief or to improve his condition in any way, and nothing was able to divert him from a fate he considered inevitable." (Leonard, p. 257)

Another statement, from *The Australian Aboriginal* by Basedow (1927), concerns the effect of "bone pointing" on its victim:

"The man who discovers that he is being boned by an enemy is, indeed, a pitiable sight. He stands aghast, with his eyes staring at the treacherous pointer, and with his hands lifted as though to ward off the lethal medium, which he imagines is pouring into his body. His cheeks blanch and his eyes become glassy and the expression of his face becomes horribly distorted . . . . He attempts to shriek but usually the sound chokes in his throat, and all that one might see is froth at his mouth. His body begins to tremble and the muscles twitch involuntarily. He sways backwards and falls to the ground, and after a short time appears to be in a swoon; but soon after he writhes as if in mortal agony, and, covering his face with his hands, begins to moan. After a while he becomes very composed and crawls to his wurley. From this time onwards he sickens and frets, refusing to eat and keeping aloof from the daily affairs of the tribe. Unless help is forthcoming in the shape of a counter-charm administered by the hands of the Nangarri, or medicine-man, his death is only a matter of a comparatively short time. If the coming of the medicine-man is opportune, he might be saved." (Basedow, pp. 178–179)

Cannon's study of such sources led him to answer in the affirmative to the question of whether those who had reported voodoo deaths exercised good critical judgment, and in the negative to that of whether the deaths might have been due to natural causes or poisoning rather than to black magic. He cited the example of Dr. P. S. Clarke, who reported having attended a native in North Queensland to whom an evil spell proved fatal in a few days, even though routine hospital tests preceding death and a postmortem examination disclosed no pathological physical causes. In further support of his conclusions Cannon quoted from a letter he had received from Dr. J. B. Cleland, author of an article on voodoo death in the *Journal of Tropical Medicine and Hygiene* (1928). Referring to the effects of bone pointing, Cleland wrote, "Poisoning is, I think, entirely ruled out . . . among our Australian natives. There are very few poisonous plants available and I doubt whether it has ever entered the mind of the central Australian natives that such might be used on human beings." (Cannon, p. 172)

Then how can we account for the effectiveness of voodoo death spells? Cannon emphasized three interrelated factors:

1. **Debilitating consequences of intense fear.** Studies of man— and other animals—have shown that intense fear, continued over time, may have serious and even fatal consequences. The deaths of soldiers within 3 to 4 days of suffering severe emotional shock and "malignant anxiety," and the results of postmortem findings in such cases have seemed, according to Cannon, to "fit well with fatal conditions reported from primitive tribes." (p. 180) In many cases, of course, physiological disturbances induced by fear are exacerbated by the victim's refusal of food and liquids.

2. **Deep-seated nature of tribal superstitions.** The firm belief of primitive peoples in the calamitous effects of voodoo spells explains the very real terror the spells have inspired. Cannon noted that the victim of bone pointing succumbs to dread, as described above, because ". . . death is sure to intervene. This is a belief so firmly held by all members of the tribe that the individual not only has that conviction himself but is obsessed by the knowledge that all his fellows likewise hold it." (p. 176)

3. **Abandonment of victim.** As Cannon noted, in some groups the member marked for death "becomes a pariah, wholly deprived of the confidence and social support of the tribe." (p. 176) All people who stand in any kinship to him withdraw their sustaining support; and in addition the group appoints a ceremonial leader, a person of very near kin, who conducts the fateful ritual of mourning. Thus effectively cut off from the ordinary world and placed in the world of the dead, the victim—highly suggestible and fearful—responds to group expectations and "assists in committing a kind of suicide." (p. 174)

Although we lack more recent systematic data on the effects of voodoo sorcery, we do have data corroborating Cannon's conclusions in general. For example, in Chapters 5 and 7 we saw that hopelessness and despair have been considered to be key factors in the deaths of prisoners in concentration and prisoner-of-war camps; and in the same chapters we noted the adverse effects (in the "long-eye" syndrome) of the "silent treatment" to which a group wintering over in the Antarctic occasionally subjected a difficult member.

of among certain primitive groups in South America and among the Navajo Indians of Arizona (Stein, 1970). At the same time, we have noted the prominence of gastrointestinal and cardiovascular complaints among people subjected to extreme stress, including rapid social change.

In our own society, a number of early studies found psychosomatic disorders to be disproportionately high at the two extremes of the socioeconomic scale (Faris & Dunham, 1939; Pasamanick, 1962; Rennie & Srole, 1956). For example, arthritis was most commonly found on lower socioeconomic levels, and colitis, rashes, and hay fever on upper levels. Similarly, a high incidence of ulcers and cardiac problems were considered common among executives who worked under conditions of chronic pressure and job insecurity.

More recently, however, reports have cast doubt on those early findings. After an extensive review of the literature, Senay and Redlich (1968) found that psychosomatic disorders—including peptic ulcers, hypertension, rheumatoid arthritis, and asthma—were no respecters of social class or other major subcultural variables. Similarly, Kahn (1969) found that only a limited number of individuals in executive settings develop peptic ulcers, and that blue-collar workers who are dissatisfied with their jobs are more likely to develop ulcers than successful business executives who are moving up the occupational ladder. Other studies have shown high blood pressure to be disproportionately high among blacks (Finnerty, 1971; Johnson, 1971; Stamler, 1971); but data on the role of sociocultural and other possible etiological factors in this markedly elevated incidence of hypertension are lacking.

In general, it would appear that sociocultural conditions which markedly increase the stressfulness of living tend to play havoc with the human organism and lead to the increased incidence of psychosomatic as well as other physical and mental disorders. As Schwab et al. (1970) have pointed out, "With changing social forces, psychophysiologic illness is increasing, its distribution is changing, new forms are emerging, and groups as well as individuals are susceptible." (p. 115)

TREATMENT AND OUTCOMES

Before describing specific methods of treatment in psychosomatic disorders, let us briefly review certain conclusions from our previous discussion which appear directly relevant to the formulation of treatment programs.

1. Attempts to delineate specific personality profiles associated with given disorders have met with little success. A wide range of personality types may, in fact, be associated with peptic ulcers and other psychosomatic disorders. The same conclusion holds for family patterns.

2. Efforts to relate specific stresses in the life history or situation of the individual to psychosomatic disorders appear to be relevant but difficult, because of individual differences in evaluating and reacting to stress. In most cases, the stress would appear to be severe and prolonged before the disorder develops.

3. Constitutional predisposition—whether as a result of genetic, disease, or other biological factors—appears to play an important role in the development of psychosomatic disorders and in the involvement of specific organ systems. Such predisposition may include autonomic reactivity, somatic weakness, and similar conditions.

4. Many psychosomatic disorders may be acquired via learning processes in the autonomic nervous system, which are not essentially different from other types of classical and instrumental learning. Contrary to traditional belief, learning in the autonomic nervous system is not limited to simple conditioning, but appears to follow the same principles as learning in general, placing the same reliance on feedback and reinforcement.

5. More general sociocultural patterns are directly related to the nature and incidence of psychosomatic disorders. Of key importance here are severe stresses, such as those associated with rapid social change.

It also is relevant to note that psychophysiological reactions may be covert; that is, the individual may not be aware of the stress or of his reaction to it. Like psychological coping reactions, psychophysiological reactions may be or may become automatic, and the individual involved may have little or no awareness of them. It also would appear that some psychosomatic reactions that endure over prolonged periods of time—such as hypertension—bring about organic changes that tend to perpetuate the disorder. Thus, the removal of given stresses or the development of more effective coping techniques may be insufficient from the standpoint of treatment.

Treatment of psychosomatic disorders requires the integration of medical and psychosocial approaches. Medical procedures may entail the use of drugs, diet, and even surgery—as in the case of a patient hemorrhaging from a gastric ulcer. Drugs such as ergotamine tartrate are often administered to migraine sufferers to afford relief from the intensity of acute attacks (Mitchell & Mitchell, 1971). Mild tranquilizers have proved effective in alleviating many types of psychosomatic symptoms; in fact, some studies show that 50 to 80 percent of all psychosomatic disorders can be alleviated to some extent by the use of tranquilizing drugs. (The use of such drugs, of course, does not deal with the essential stresses or coping patterns involved.) Rosenthal and Wulfsohn (1970) have also reported highly favorable preliminary results with electrosleep in the treatment of chronic anxiety, depression, and insomnia. Approximately two thirds of 40 patients —who were refractory to standard methods of treatment—showed a rapid and relatively complete remission of symptoms. Electrosleep has received a great deal of emphasis in Russia during the last decade, and we shall describe this method of treatment in Chapter 20. However, its ultimate value as a treatment procedure in psychosomatic disorders is still to be ascertained.

Family therapy has shown promising results in the treatment of children manifesting psychosomatic reactions. In general, however, psychotherapeutic approaches—aimed at helping the individual understand his problem and achieve more effective coping techniques—have proved relatively ineffective in the case of psycho-

OBESITY—ETIOLOGY AND TREATMENT PROCEDURES

Obesity, the condition characterized by an "excess accumulation of body fat," is a major health problem in our society. Obese persons number in the millions, and obesity is associated with high blood pressure, coronary heart disease, and other physical disorders.

Etiological factors in obesity are diverse, with psychological and sociocultural—rather than physiological—influences being the most commonly involved. Only in a small percentage of cases are there revealed endocrine and metabolic anomalies that may account for the continuance of obesity from infancy through old age. In most cases the key determinants appear to be familial and cultural associations or norms, as well as psychological factors. Thus, in some families the customary diet may lead to obesity in its members; and in some cultural groups obesity is regarded as a sign of social influence and power. And, of course, learned responses typically play a major role; some persons have apparently learned in childhood to overeat as a means of alleviating emotional distress, and this pattern may continue into adulthood. The consequences of such overeating following a traumatic experience has been labeled as "reactive obesity."

In general, it would appear that the eating behavior of obese persons is not triggered by the same internal stimuli as that of persons of normal weight. For example, while hunger and its satisfaction dictate the eating patterns of persons of normal weight, obese persons seem to be much more at the mercy of environmental cues. Regardless of how recently or amply they have eaten, they may be prompted to eat again simply by the sight or smell of food. Thus Stuart (1971) has emphasized the importance of environmental controls in treating obesity, utilizing: (1) cue elimination—e.g., restricting all eating activity to one place; (2) cue suppression—e.g., preparing and serving only small quantities of food; and (3) cue strengthening—e.g., keeping weight charts and displaying pictures of desired clothing, appearance, and activities. Preliminary results of this behavioristic approach have been described as highly positive.

Another approach which Penick et al. (1971) viewed as promising utilizes a combination of behavior modification and group therapy procedures. The actual program was of 3 months' duration, with once-a-week sessions carried out from 10:30 A.M. to approximately 3 P.M. Activities consisted of an exercise period, preparation and eating of a low-calorie lunch, and a group therapy period. Results were encouraging: 13 percent of the subjects lost more than 40 pounds each, and 53 percent lost more than 20 pounds each. While results of follow-up studies must be awaited to determine the long-range effectiveness of this treatment program, the investigators considered early results to rank with the best in the medical and psychological literature.

Medical measures in the treatment of psychosomatic obesity, such as the use of appetite-dulling drugs to reduce the individual's food intake, are usually only temporarily effective and the lost weight is eventually regained unless a change in eating behavior takes place. Surgical procedures to reduce absorption, and more recently, to reduce food intake (Mason & Ito, 1969), have been receiving research evaluation.

Based on Crisp (1970), Mason and Ito (1969), Penick et al. (1971), Schachter (1971), and Stuart (1971).

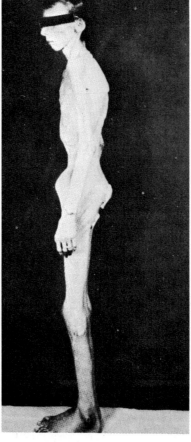

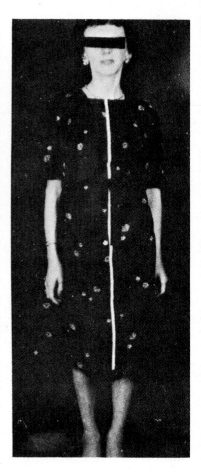

A CASE OF ANOREXIA NERVOSA

The woman in these pictures was diagnosed as suffering from anorexia nervosa, a disorder characterized by severe loss of appetite and weight due to emotional factors. At the age of 18 (above, left), she weighed 120 pounds, but over a period of years her weight dropped to 47 pounds (center). The photo at right, in which she weighed 88 pounds, was taken after she had undergone behavior therapy.

Treatment of anorexia nervosa is often difficult, and about 10 percent of anorexic patients literally starve themselves to death. The disorder—much more common among females than males—can occur from childhood to adulthood but is seen most frequently among adolescents. The reasons behind the refusal of food hold the key to the etiological puzzle in these cases. As noted above, emotional factors are typically involved, and this view is not negated by the fact that there is often a prior nutritional disorder, for both disorders may result from similar underlying causes. Often obesity precedes anorexia nervosa (Crisp, 1970). Here, the individual reverses his eating habits, going from one extreme to another, perhaps in reaction to teasing about being "fat." In anorexic children refusal to eat may be associated with unbearable hurt or a desire to get even with parents for perceived mistreatment. Factors implicated among other age groups include depression and sexual conflicts. The latter appear to lead to an association between eating, sex, and fear of impregnation (Nemiah, 1963; Warren, 1968).

In the treatment of anorexia nervosa, medical procedures typically are required in combination with psychotherapeutic procedures. Liquid feeding—intravenously or by tube—may be indicated for persons whom the disorder has rendered too weak to eat; and with children, forced feeding is sometimes resorted to. Other procedures commonly utilized include chemotherapy, individual psychotherapy, and behavior therapy, with the latter appearing to offer the most promise.

In the case of the woman pictured here, Bachrach, Erwin, and Mohr (1965) utilized a program of environmental control designed to reinforce and shape eating behavior, while denying her pleasures when she did not eat. The program proved effective, and a follow-up report revealed that the woman was working as a nurse on a regular 8-hour shift at the university hospital where she had undergone treatment.

somatic disorders. The most promising new treatment approaches appear to be in the direction of behavior therapy.

Behavior modification techniques are based on the assumption that since autonomic responses may be learned, they may also be unlearned, via extinction and differential reinforcement procedures. Wolpe (1969) has reported a strategy involving deconditioning of the stress or anxiety source, and has stated that it succeeds with peptic ulcers, asthma, migraine, neurodermatitis, and many other psychosomatic disorders. To illustrate, he cited the case of an extremely capable and active 49-year-old woman who suffered from asthma. Her disorder began after the birth of her fourth child. Attacks were brought on by her annoyance with her husband—particularly with respect to family finances—and by seeing anything connected with death or physical disability. Wolpe encouraged her to express her feelings to her husband, and he readily changed. Then Wolpe used routine desensitization procedures to extinguish the woman's fears concerning physical disability and death. Improvement was rapid, and even after 9 years the woman was reported to have maintained her gains.

An interesting case involving persistent sneezing was successfully treated by Kushner (*Time*, 1966), utilizing negative reinforcement. The patient, June Clark, was a 17-year-old girl who had been sneezing every few seconds of her waking day for a period of 5 months. Medical experts had been unable to help her, and Kushner, a psychologist, volunteered to attempt treatment by behavior therapy.

"Dr. Kushner used a relatively simple, low power electric-shock device, activated by sound—the sound of June's sneezes. Electrodes were attached to her forearm for 30 minutes, and every time she sneezed she got a mild electric shock. After a ten-minute break, the electrodes were put on the other arm. In little more than four hours, June's sneezes, which had been reverberating every 40 seconds, stopped. Since then, she has had only a few ordinary sneezes, none of the dry, racking kind that had been draining her strength for so long. 'We hope the absence of sneezes will last,' said Dr. Kushner cautiously. 'So do I,' snapped June. 'I never want to see that machine again.'" (p. 72)

As research reveals more about the role of learning in autonomic reactivity and the most effective methods of helping the individual control his own inner physiological functioning—

including heart rate, blood pressure, stomach acid secretion, and so on—it would appear that the individual himself may be able to prevent most psychosomatic disorders or bring them under control. For example, Sargent (1971) has reported that migraine patients at the Menninger Foundation have been successfully treated by having them learn to increase the blood pressure in their hands—which seems to bring about an accompanying decrease of blood pressure in the vessels of the scalp. The overall effectiveness of autonomic learning as a treatment procedure may depend, however, on the success of concomitant efforts to change the individual's attitudes and coping techniques in dealing with particular stresses, or to modify the stresses in his life situation so that he can more readily adapt.

In this chapter we have noted the high incidence of peptic ulcers, hypertension, and other psychosomatic disorders in our society. In discussing the dynamics of these disorders, we noted that they typically seem to involve (1) the arousal of emotional tensions in response to stress situations; (2) the failure of such tensions to be adequately discharged, with the result that emotional arousal becomes chronic; and (3) the channeling of undischarged tensions to a particular organ system, which sustains physiological damage.

As yet we do not have adequate answers to the question of why some people develop psychosomatic disorders under sustained stress and others do not; or why some persons develop peptic ulcers and others hypertension. But in the course of our discussion we did see the extent to which the organism reacts to stress as a psychobiological unit—that although a disorder may be primarily physical or psychological in nature, it is always a disorder of the whole person. We observed that learning may occur in the autonomic nervous system to a much greater extent than had previously been supposed, and that learning principles can be applied to treatment of psychosomatic disorders. Since faulty autonomic responses may be learned, they also may be unlearned. This unlearning involves the utilization of feedback, reinforcement, and other learning principles to regulate the functioning of various organ systems—thus avoiding hypo- or hyperfunctioning of these systems.

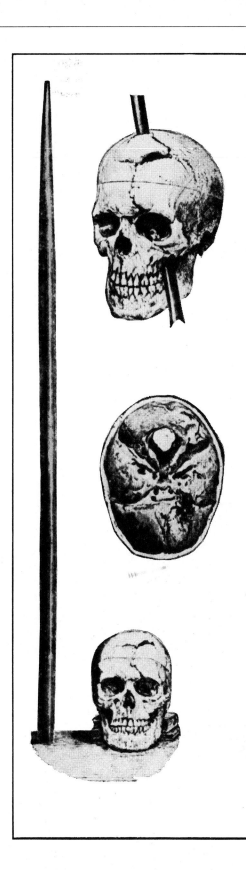

Organic Brain Syndromes

15

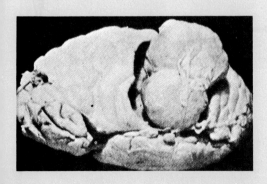

DISORDERS ASSOCIATED WITH INFECTION

DISORDERS WITH BRAIN TUMORS

DISORDERS WITH HEAD INJURY

DISORDERS WITH TOXINS AND METABOLIC DISTURBANCES

PSYCHOSES OF THE AGED

Injuries, disease, and various chemicals can affect the central nervous system and give rise to abnormal behavior. It has been estimated that more than 20 million people in the United States suffer from such neurological disorders. Fortunately the great majority of cases do not involve serious psychopathology, but even so, mental disorders associated with brain pathology constitute more than a fourth of all first admissions to mental hospitals.

These disorders may simply involve an impairment of function, or they may be associated with a wide range of psychopathology, depending on (1) the location and extent of neural damage, (2) the premorbid personality of the individual, and (3) the nature of his life situation. There are many cases involving severe brain damage in which mental change is astonishingly slight, whereas in other cases mild brain damage leads to a psychotic reaction. These variations are explained by the fact that the individual reacts to all stress, whether organic or psychological, as a functional unit. A well-integrated person can withstand brain damage or any other stress better than a rigid, immature, or otherwise psychologically handicapped individual. Similarly, the individual who has a favorable life situation is likely to have a better prognosis.

Since the nervous system is the center for the integration of behavior, however, there are limits to the amount of brain damage an individual can tolerate or compensate for without exhibiting impaired functioning. The clinical symptoms may be specific to the given brain injury, or they may be similar to those in other forms of psychopathology—where the individual, for instance, may become hypochondriacal, depressed, paranoid, psychopathic, or manifest other neurotic, psychotic, or sociopathic disturbances.

Brain disorders may be classified as *acute* or *chronic*, the primary consideration being the reversibility of the brain pathology. An acute disorder is likely to be temporary and reversible, whereas a chronic disorder is irreversible because of permanent damage to the nervous system. This classification is not a hard and fast one, because an acute condition may leave some residual damage after the major symptoms have cleared up, while a chronic condition may show some alleviation of symptoms over a sustained period of time. However, a general picture can be given of the two types.

1. *Acute brain disorders* result from diffuse impairment of brain function accompanying high fevers, severe nutritional deficiencies, drug intoxication, or any of a variety of other conditions. Symptoms range from mild mood changes to acute delirium. The latter may be complicated by hallucinations, delusions, and other person-

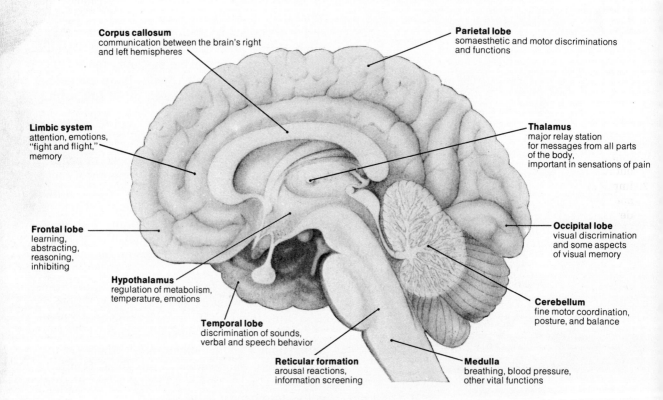

Corpus callosum
communication between the brain's right and left hemispheres

Parietal lobe
somaesthetic and motor discriminations and functions

Limbic system
attention, emotions, "fight and flight," memory

Thalamus
major relay station for messages from all parts of the body, important in sensations of pain

Frontal lobe
learning, abstracting, reasoning, inhibiting

Occipital lobe
visual discrimination and some aspects of visual memory

Hypothalamus
regulation of metabolism, temperature, emotions

Cerebellum
fine motor coordination, posture, and balance

Temporal lobe
discrimination of sounds, verbal and speech behavior

Reticular formation
arousal reactions, information screening

Medulla
breathing, blood pressure, other vital functions

IMPLICATIONS OF BRAIN DAMAGE FOR IMPAIRMENT OF FUNCTIONING

It is very difficult to predict the effects of focused injuries to the brain. Although there is some localization of function (as indicated in this drawing of the right cerebral hemisphere) and damage to a particular area may cause severe impairment of function, the brain's great back-up resources may be able in time to make up for the deficiency. The sheer number of neurons, or nerve cells in the brain—10 to 12 billion—provide a redundancy of capability within each given area, to offset some cell loss. In addition, the interaction of all parts of the brain in receiving and transmitting electrochemical messages often will permit an area sharing related information to compensate for loss of functioning in a damaged area. The limits of these resources, however, can be reached, and while damage to some areas may be only temporarily incapacitating, destruction of other areas may result in a complete loss of a given function. "In some cases, loss of function seems less dependent upon the location of brain tissue [involved] than upon the total amount. . . ." (Ruch & Zimbardo, 1971, pp. 92–93)

ality disturbances. With extensive brain pathology or upset of brain cell metabolism, physiological rather than psychological factors may play the dominant role—as in coma or stupor. In some cases the impairment, by lowering cortical controls, precipitates a latent psychosis which may persist after the immediate brain pathology has cleared up. In a few cases symptoms that appear to result from acute brain pathology actually reflect the fluctuations of a mental disorder unrelated to it.

The prognosis in acute brain disorders is good; such conditions generally do clear up. With older patients, however, or in cases of severe exposure to a toxic agent, there may be residual brain damage and related symptoms.

2. *Chronic brain disorders* result from injuries, disease, drugs, and a variety of other conditions. The permanent destruction of brain tissue is reflected in some degree of impairment of higher integrative functions. Where the damage is severe, such symptoms typically include:

1. Impairment of orientation—especially for time but often also for place and person
2. Impairment of memory—notably for recent events and less so for events of remote past, with a tendency to confabulate or "invent" memories to fill in gaps
3. Impairment of learning, comprehension, and judgment—with ideation tending to be concrete and impoverished—and with inability to think on higher conceptual levels and to plan
4. Lability and shallowness of affect—with general emotional overreactivity and arousal of laughter or tears with minor provocation
5. Impairment of inner reality and ethical controls —with lowering of behavioral standards and carelessness in personal hygiene and appearance

These symptoms may also occur in acute brain disorders, although delirium and hallucinations or stupor are more likely to dominate the clinical picture.

In general, the greater the amount of tissue damage, the greater the impairment of function. As we have noted, however, some individuals are able to compensate much better than others for brain pathology. Depending on the severity of symptoms—in either acute or chronic disorders —the clinical picture may be referred to as *mild, moderate,* or *severe.*

INSIGHTS INTO BRAIN FUNCTIONING AS A RESULT OF SPLIT-BRAIN RESEARCH

Important insights into the relationship between the brain's right and left hemispheres have been provided by studies of the effects of split-brain surgery. This procedure—which involves dividing the hemispheres by cutting the corpus callosum—is sometimes resorted to in the case of epileptics as a means of controlling their seizures. Apparently the surgery produces no noticeable change in the patient's temperament, intelligence, or personality traits, but it does impede the transmission of sensory messages from one side of the body to the other.

Differences in functioning between the right hemisphere and the "dominant" left one have been reported by Gazzaniga (1967). On the basis of his findings in ten split-brain operations, Gazzaniga concluded that for most (right-handed) people, automatic functions tend to be localized in the right hemisphere, while language, self-awareness, and complex problem-solving functions tend to be localized in the left hemisphere. Speculating on effects of cutting the corpus callosum in persons at a very early age, Gazzaniga concluded that both hemispheres could develop advanced intellectual functions presently associated only with the left hemisphere (1967, p. 29).

Although there is an attempt on both biological and psychological levels to compensate for damage or loss, the regenerative capacities of the central nervous system are unfortunately limited. Cell bodies and nonmyelinated neural pathways do not have the power of regeneration, which means that their destruction is permanent. However, the central nervous system abounds in back-up apparatus. If a given circuit is knocked out, others may take over; and functions lost as a result of brain damage may often be relearned. The degree of recovery from functional disabilities, even following an irreversible brain lesion, may be relatively complete or limited, and recovery may proceed rapidly or slowly. Since there are limits to both the plasticity and the relearning ability of the brain, extensive brain damage may lead to a permanent loss of function and result in a wide range of physical and psychological symptoms.

Various factors can result in either acute or chronic brain pathology. To avoid repetition we shall not discuss each factor separately, but shall devote this chapter to a consideration of some of the more common causes of brain pathology and the related mental disorders that may develop.

DISORDERS ASSOCIATED WITH INFECTION

Mental disorders may appear in connection with brain infections resulting from bacteria or viruses that invade the brain and damage or destroy nerve tissue. Among the major infectious diseases of the brain are cerebral syphilis and epidemic encephalitis.

CEREBRAL SYPHILIS

Syphilitic infection of the brain is associated with three somewhat distinct syndromes—*general paresis, juvenile paresis,* and *meningovascular syphilis.* An understanding of these syndromes can best begin with an understanding of syphilis, an infectious disease that has taken an incalculable toll in human lives and happiness. Unless properly treated, syphilis eventually disables and then kills its victims.

Syphilis appeared with dramatic suddenness several centuries ago and spread within a few years over the known world (Pusey, 1933). Many medical historians contend that syphilis was introduced into Europe by the members of Columbus' crew, who presumably contracted it from the women of the West Indies. In fact, Kemble (1936) has pointed out that Columbus himself may have been infected. During his second voyage, in 1494, Columbus began having attacks of fever, possibly indicating the secondary stage of syphilis. During his third voyage, in 1498, he developed "a severe attack of gout" which was widespread and not confined to one or two of the small joints as gout usually is. During this voyage also, the first signs of mental disorder made their appearance. He began to hear voices and to regard himself as an "ambassador of God." On his last voyage, in 1504, Columbus was so ill that he had to be carried ashore. His whole body was dropsical from the chest downward, his limbs were paralyzed, and his brain affected—all symptoms of the terminal stages of syphilis.

Whatever the origin, syphilis spread like a tornado throughout Europe and became known as *The Great Pox* (Parran, 1937; Pusey, 1933). In

1496 it appeared in Paris and the number of victims became so great that the government passed an emergency decree forbidding a syphilitic to leave his home until completely cured.[1] In Edinburgh during the same year, all afflicted inhabitants were banished to an island near Leith.

The numerous armies of mercenaries and adventurers of that period no doubt contributed to the rapid spread of the disease. Apparently also this early strain of syphilis was both extremely contagious and unusually virulent, and attacked its victims with a violence almost unknown today.[2] High fever, delirium, violent headaches, horrible sores, and bone ulcers were typical, even during the early stages. By 1498 the disease had spread to England. Vasco da Gama and his pioneering Portuguese probably carried it around the Cape of Good Hope, and an outbreak occurred in India in 1498, spreading eastward to China by 1505.

During this early period there was no name for the disease. Each suffering nation blamed it on some other nation. The Italians called it the *French* or *Spanish disease,* the English called it the *French pox,* and so on. It finally received its specific name when, in 1530, an Italian physician, Fracastorius, wrote a long poem in which the leading character, a shepherd named Syphilis, was stricken with the disease because of an insult to Apollo. The poem became tremendously popular, and *syphilis* became the accepted name for the dread disease.

Although there were many early approaches to treatment, the physicians of those days could offer little help, and it was several hundred years before any major advances were made in the conquest of syphilis. In Chapter 2 we sketched the several steps by which the deadly spirochete that causes syphilis was discovered, blood tests developed, and methods of treatment worked out.

---

[1] A "cure" probably meant the temporary remission or disappearance of symptoms—common during the third stage of syphilis—which the people of that period mistook for recovery.

[2] Undoubtedly the severity of this disease was also due in part to the lack of resistance or partial immunity usually acquired in the case of older diseases.

The spirochete of syphilis may gain entrance to the body through minute breaks or scratches in the skin, or directly through mucous membranes, such as the lining of the mouth or the genital tract. Even though the mucous membrane is intact, the spirochete can wriggle through it in an hour or so. Syphilis is typically spread from person to person during sexual intercourse, although in exceptional cases it may be contracted through kissing or from direct contact with open syphilitic sores or lesions. It may also be transmitted from mother to child during fetal development; in this case it is referred to as *congenital syphilis*.

Once they have breached the outer defenses of the body, the spirochetes begin their systematic destruction of the body in four fairly well defined stages.

1. *First stage.* Immediately after the spirochetes gain entrance to the body, they multiply rapidly. From 10 to 20 days later, a sore called a *hard chancre* appears at the point of infection, which usually takes the form either of a pimple that feels hard to the touch or of an open ulcerated sore. In some instances it may be so insignificant that the person is unaware of its existence. Even if untreated, this sore disappears in from 4 to 6 weeks, often leaving the victim with the mistaken notion that it was really only a minor irritation or that he is now cured.

2. *Second stage.* Following the chancre by some 3 to 6 weeks is the appearance of a copper-colored skin rash, which may be mild and transitory or more severe, covering the entire body. This skin eruption may look like measles or smallpox and originally gave rise to the term *Great Pox* to differentiate this disease from *smallpox*. The rash may or may not be accompanied by fever, headaches, indigestion, loss of appetite, loss of hair in spots over the scalp, and other symptoms not usually thought of in connection with syphilis.

3. *Third stage.* This is known as the latent period, for in most cases all symptoms disappear. Again the victim is apt to think he is cured and so either avoid or discontinue treatment. During this period, however, the spirochetes are attacking various internal organs and, if untreated, cause permanent degeneration. The spirochetes may attack the bone marrow, the spleen, the lymph glands, or any tissue or organ of the body.

Blood vessels and nerve cells seem to be favorite targets.

4. *Fourth stage.* In this last stage we see the accumulated damage produced during the latent period. Ten, twenty, and even thirty years after the initial infection, the degenerative work of the spirochete may become apparent in a sudden heart attack, failure of vision (until recent times 15 percent of all blindness in the U.S. was due to syphilis), loss of motor coordination in walking, or mental disturbances. Syphilis is often called the "great imitator" because of the wide range of organic disease symptoms that it may produce. The most frequent and fatal forms of late syphilis are those in which the spirochete invades the walls of heart and blood vessels and the nervous system. It is the latter form with which we are primarily concerned in our study of abnormal psychology.

General paresis. General paresis is a mental disorder caused by the progressive infiltration and destruction of brain tissue by the spirochetes of syphilis. It has also been variously called *general paralysis of the insane, dementia paralytica,* and *paresis.* Approximately 3 percent of untreated syphilitics eventually develop general paresis (Gibson, 1960; U.S. Public Health Service, 1961). The first symptoms usually appear about 10 years after the primary infection, although the incubation period may be as short as 2 years or as long as 40. Unless the person receives treatment, the outcome is always fatal, death usually occurring within 2 to 3 years after the initial symptoms. The average age of onset is approximately 50 years for both men and women, although the disease may occur early or in extreme old age. The number of new cases of general paresis has decreased markedly since 1950, and general paresis now accounts for less than 1 percent of all first admissions to mental hospitals. There may be an increase in the number of new cases in the years ahead, however, resulting from the recent increase in new cases of syphilis. In 1970 there were an estimated 1 million persons with untreated syphilis in the United States (Ford, 1970; Strage, 1971).

General paresis is associated with a wide range of behavioral and psychological symptoms. During the early phase of the disorder, the individual typically becomes careless and inattentive and makes mistakes in his work. At first he may notice his mistakes but attributes them to being over-tired; later he does not even notice them. Personal habits may show some deterioration, and the once-neat person may become slovenly. Comprehension and judgment suffer, and the individual may show a tendency to evade important problems, or he may react to them with smug indifference. Accompanying these symptoms is a blunting of affect, so that he does not share in the joys, sorrows, or anxieties of loved ones. He seems unable to realize the seriousness of his behavior and may become irritable or resort to ready rationalizations if his behavior is questioned. Overly sentimental behavior is typical and may involve promiscuous sexual patterns.

As the disorder progresses, a number of well-delineated physical symptoms make their appearance. The pupils are irregular in size and the pupillary reflex to light is either sluggish or entirely absent. Typically, speech functions become badly disturbed, with considerable stuttering and slurring of words. A phrase that invariably gives trouble and is of diagnostic significance is "Methodist Episcopal." This may be mispronounced in a number of ways, such as "Meodist Epispal" or "Methdist Pispal." Writing is similarly disturbed, with tremulous lines and the omission or transposition of syllables. Frequently, the individual has a rather vacant, dissipated look, with a silly grin. Where the spiro-

chetes have also damaged neural pathways within the spinal cord, there may be difficulty in motor coordination. Such individuals typically have a shuffling, unsteady walk, referred to as *locomotor ataxia*. In addition, there may be tremors of the face, lips, and fingers and an absence of tendon reflexes, such as the knee jerk. During this period convulsive seizures may also appear.

Paralleling these physical symptoms is a general personality deterioration. The individual is unmannerly, tactless, unconcerned with his appearance, and unethical in his behavior. Memory defects, which may be noticeable in the early phases of the illness, become more obvious. He may be unable to remember what he did even a few minutes before. He may ask when dinner will be served only a few minutes after he has finished eating it. This memory impairment extends to remote events, and the individual tends to fill in memory losses by various fabrications. As his intellectual processes are increasingly impaired, he becomes unable to comprehend the simplest problems and may optimistically squander his money on harebrained schemes or become involved in a variety of antisocial acts.

This entire picture of personality deterioration is usually colored by emotional reactions in the form of either marked euphoria, depression, or apathy. Thus, three categories are commonly used to distinguish clinical types of paretics—

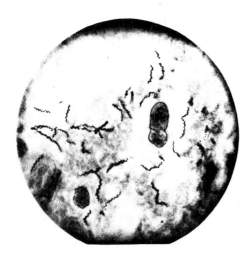

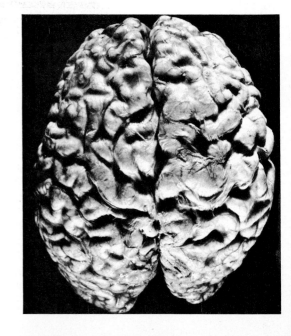

General paresis results when the spirochetes invade the cerebral cortex (above). A post-mortem examination typically reveals thickening of the meninges surrounding the brain and atrophy of the convolutions, especially in the frontal and temporal lobes (right).

expansive, depressed, and *demented*—although these types are by no means always distinct, and depressed patients frequently change categories by becoming euphoric. As the disease enters the terminal period, the extensive brain damage leads to a similar picture for all three types, in which the patient leads a vegetative life, expresses no interest in anything, becomes inarticulate in speech, and can no longer care for himself. Convulsive seizures usually become common. Finally, a terminal infection or breakdown of bodily machinery leads to death.

1. *Expansive type.* Some paretics become extremely euphoric and expansive. If such a patient is asked how he feels, he may answer "Just wonderful! Everything is just perfect!" He often shows an overevaluation of himself in the form of delusions of grandeur. He may state that he is the richest and most powerful man in the world. When asked if he had a million dollars, one patient euphorically admitted he had billions of dollars as well as an abundance of other material possessions such as "about a million of the latest model Cadillacs, millions of wonderful homes, and the best race horses in the country."

Such patients, with optimistic abandon, may plan gigantic projects involving huge sums of money. One patient had plans to build a superhighway from New York to China that would be at least a hundred miles wide. They seem utterly unable to realize the ludicrous nature of their claims and look forward to the outcome of every idea with the utmost optimism. As might be expected, delusional ideas here are poorly systematized. When their ideas are questioned, these persons may become irritable, but more often they dismiss criticisms as inconsequential.

"C. W. flew planes from the United States to North Africa. His route began in Florida, passed through Natal, Ascension Island, and terminated in Dakar. His earlier health record was excellent, save for some 'difficulty' in his early twenties. Now, at 38, he was strong, well liked, and an expert pilot in the ferry command. He had completed a dozen or more trips.

"As he flew his plane eastward on his last journey, C. W. was unusually gay. 'It's a great world,' he sang. 'My rich aunt in Oklahoma is going to leave me $30,000,000.'

"During the periods of relief by his co-pilot, he talked loudly and became chummy with other members of the crew. As a matter of fact, he offered to loan the

navigator $50,000. Landing safely in Dakar, his high spirits continued. Then his friends found him buying several 'diamonds' from an Arab street merchant, spending most of his cash for this purpose.

"'Boy,' he exclaimed, 'I got a swell bargain! Six diamonds for $100 cash now and $100 more on my next trip! I sure fooled that Arab; he's never going to collect the rest from me.'

"'How do you know the diamonds are genuine?' he was asked.

"'I tested them,' he boasted. 'I struck one with a hammer and it proved hard; diamonds are hard.'

"Upon the return journey, C. W. continued the story of his expected wealth and the sum grew with the distance of travel.

"'It's $40,000,000 I am getting and I expect to share some of it with you guys,' he announced. When his co-pilot received this astounding information with doubt and anxiety, C. W. could not understand it. When the co-pilot asked him to rest, he assured him that his body was perfect, that he didn't need rest. Then he added that he could fly the plane without gas, which he tried to prove by doing some fancy maneuvers in the sky.

"'Funny,' he said later, 'no one seemed to believe me. Even when I offered them a million each they weren't happy, but looked at each other in such a puzzled way. It made me laugh, how they begged me to rest and how worried they looked when I refused. I was the boss and I showed them.'

"When the plane landed in Brazil by a miracle, C. W. was examined by a physician, forced into another plane and brought to Florida. Upon examination he was talkative, eyes gleaming, exuberant with statements of wealth and power. 'I am now one of the richest men in the world,' he said. 'I'll give you $5,000,000 to start a hospital. My eyes are jewels, diamonds, emeralds,' . . ." (Fetterman, 1949, pp. 267–268)

2. *Depressed type.* Some individuals react to the progressive organic damage by becoming discouraged and depressed. They usually have some realization of their failing functions and general life situation, though this insight is usually lost as the disorder progresses. Depressed patients frequently develop bizarre hypochondriacal delusions—they may become convinced that they have no brain, or that their bowels are completely stopped up, or that they are dead. Although suicidal attempts among such patients are not uncommon, the intellectual deterioration usually results only in rather childish, unsuccessful attempts.

Occasionally, depressed patients show considerable anxiety and agitation. Even though their mood is predominantly one of depression, they may have episodes of expansiveness. In general, depressed patients become expansive as their personality deterioration becomes increasingly severe.

The following brief conversation with a depressed female paretic, 42 years of age, serves further to illustrate these symptoms.

Dr.: How are you today, Miss——?
Pt.: Not so good doctor . . . (pause)
Dr.: What seems to be your difficulty?
Pt.: My brain has been eaten away. . . . I am no longer living, just a dead shell (shakes head despondently).
Dr.: How do you account for this trouble?
Pt.: I don't know doctor. . . . I have ruined my life . . . my brain is gone . . . there is no hope . . . (stares at floor) . . . my heart has stopped beating . . . I am only a dead shell . . . it's all over now. . . .

3. *"Demented" or simple type.* Strictly speaking, all paretics show gradual intellectual and personality deterioration and hence are "demented." However, this term is usually used to indicate cases where there is no pronounced euphoria or depression, and where symptoms consist chiefly of apathy, memory impairment, and general personality deterioration. Often the clinical picture is somewhat similar to that in schizophrenia, with a gradual withdrawal from the environment, accompanied by delusions and hallucinations, usually of a simple nature. The simple type is the most common of the psychotic reactions associated with general paresis. The following case was diagnosed as simple paresis.

"A woman of twenty-six was brought to the hospital because she had become lost when she attempted to return home from a neighboring grocery store. . . .

"At the hospital the patient entered the admission office with an unsteady gait. There, by way of greeting, the physician inquired, 'How are you today?' to which she replied in a monotonous, tremulous tone, 'N-yes-s, I was-s op-er-a-ted on for 'pen-pendici-ci-tis.' She never made any spontaneous remarks and when, a few days after her admission, she was asked if she were sad or happy she stared vacantly at the physician and with a fatuous smile answered, 'Yeah.' The patient would sit about the ward for hours, taking no interest in its activities. Sometimes she would hold a book in her lap, aimlessly turning the leaves, never reading but often pointing out pictures like a small child. . . ." (Noyes & Kolb, 1968, p. 237)

Although the various physical symptoms, together with deterioration of behavior in a previously well-adjusted individual, may be indicative of general paresis, the final diagnosis must rest upon the actual presence of the spirochete in the individual's bloodstream and nervous system, usually demonstrable by means of blood and spinal-fluid tests.

The onset of symptoms in general paresis usually extends over several months or even years, but in some instances symptoms appear with dramatic suddenness in the course of a few days. Frequently, the early signs of the disorder are not recognized by family and friends until an acute episode of some sort occurs. The family of one patient noticed nothing particularly wrong until one day he went to a bar instead of to his office and there became noisy and expansive. Actually, for several months there had been less obvious symptoms, including forgetfulness of business appointments and peculiar color combinations in dress, but no one had noticed anything seriously amiss.

Although much is now known about general paresis, a number of questions still puzzle investigators. Why do fewer than 1 in 30 untreated syphilitics develop general paresis? Why do a higher percentage of whites than Negroes develop general paresis after syphilitic infection? Why do far more male than female syphilitics develop general paresis? And why is the relative incidence of general paresis much higher in some countries than in others? Some investigators hold that the syphilitic spirochetes attack the most vulnerable organs of the individual's body and that general paresis develops in persons whose brain tissue has an especially low resistance to syphilis. Other investigators have suggested that different strains of spirochetes may account for many of these differences. But the final answers to these questions are not yet available.

Juvenile paresis. Juvenile paresis results from congenital syphilis and is a condition of general paresis occurring in childhood or adolescence. Although no longer a major problem in the United States, congenital syphilis is still relatively common in certain other countries, and contributes to a high infant mortality rate as well as to physical afflictions other than juvenile paresis.

The symptoms in juvenile paresis are similar to those in general paresis and involve a picture of progressive mental and physical deterioration, including progressive impairment of memory, comprehension, and judgment. Motor incoordination, speech disturbances, and convulsions are common. The juvenile paretic usually has no understanding of his condition and is apt to show a relatively simple deterioration without pronounced emotional coloring or marked psychological compensation.

Formerly, syphilis accounted for more than half of all blindness in children at birth. It was also the largest cause of stillbirths and the primary reason for the deaths of many infants during the first weeks of life (Parran, 1937). Although symptoms may appear at any time after birth, ordinarily there are no noticeable symptoms until the child reaches puberty. In some cases, however, retarded physical development, mental retardation, and convulsions make their appearance prior to the onset of the typical paretic syndrome (Bruetsch, 1959). In juvenile paresis, the course of the disorder is longer than in adult paresis, averaging about 5 years between the appearance of initial symptoms and termination in death.

The following is a description of a 15-year-old boy diagnosed as a juvenile paretic.

The patient was referred to the hospital by a school doctor after the boy had become "droopy" in class and began to talk in a rather funny and thick-tongued manner. On admission to the hospital the boy was slightly unsteady in his walk, his pupils were widely dilated and did not show a normal pupillary reflex to light. His emotional mood seemed to alternate from one of depression and apathy to one of mild euphoria. He soiled himself, was careless in his personal appearance, and exposed himself indiscriminately to males and females alike. The following conversation took place during a period of mild euphoria:
Dr.: How are you feeling today, Bob?
Pt.: Jus wonful, jus wonful (silly, fatuous grin).
Dr.: Can you say Methodist Episcopal Church?
Pt.: Mesdus Episfal Chursh.
Dr.: How are your studies progressing at school?
Pt.: Jus fine, jus fine, perfect.

Tragic cases of this kind need not occur if proper safeguards are taken against congenital syphilis.

Historically, Henry VIII of England has often been cited to illustrate the tragic results of congenital syphilis. The first of his wives, Catherine of Aragon, bore four children, all of whom were stillborn or died immediately after birth. A fifth child, a daughter, finally survived to reign later as "Bloody Mary." Mary herself showed many signs of congenital syphilis—her face was prematurely old and scarred; her hair thin and straggling; her head square, with a grotesquely protruding forehead; and her sight extremely bad. Her sudden death at the age of 42 was presumably due to syphilitic complications. Of Henry's six wives, Anne of Cleves, whose marriage was never consummated, was thought by the medical historian Kemble (1936) to be the only one who might have shown a negative Wassermann test.

Meningovascular syphilis. Meningovascular syphilis differs from general paresis in that the syphilitic damage initially centers in the blood vessels and meninges of the brain rather than in the neural tissue. This form of cerebral syphilis is rare.

The symptoms in meningovascular syphilis differ from those in general paresis, in that there is rarely any marked deterioration of conduct. Typical are persistent headaches, dizziness, and blurring or doubling of vision; often there are insomnia and nausea. Lethargy, confusion, and difficulty in concentration are common. Physical symptoms of diagnostic value include disturbed pupillary reactions to light and accentuated knee-jerk reflex. Speech and writing usually are not markedly affected, but convulsive seizures are common.

During the early stages of meningovascular syphilis the actual amount of brain damage is usually less than in general paresis, and the personality deterioration is correspondingly less. In advanced cases the brain damage, symptom picture, and dynamics are comparable for the two disorders.

Treatment and outcomes. After penicillin had been developed and found effective in the treatment of syphilis, there was a spectacular drop in the number of cases. Thus, during the late 1950's the problem of syphilis was considered solved.

In recent years, however, there has been a marked increase in syphilis throughout the world. In the United States there are an estimated 250,000 new cases of syphilis each year (AMA, 1969; Fleming et al., 1970; Strage, 1971). During the late 1960's and early 1970's the incidence of syphilis increased by 200 percent per year. Teen-agers accounted for over 50 percent of the rise, with young adults under 25 following close behind. According to statistics gathered from 102 cities in 1969 (Strage, 1971), the sources of infection in primary and secondary syphilis were, in order of frequency:

1. Friend of the opposite sex, 47 percent
2. Stranger of the opposite sex (including prostitutes and casual pickups), 20 percent
3. Homosexual contact, 17 percent
4. Marital partner, 16 percent

The specific outcomes in cases of paresis receiving medical treatment depends to a large extent on the amount of cerebral damage that has taken place before treatment is started. If the damage is not extensive, the adaptive capacities of the individual—both neurological and psychological—may leave only a small impairment of brain function. Unfortunately, in many cases treatment is not undertaken until the disease has produced extensive and irreparable brain damage. Here about all that can be hoped for is to prevent further inroads of the deadly spirochete. In such cases, the intellectual picture may show considerable improvement, but the patient never approaches his previous level of intellectual ability. For treated paretics as a group, the following rough estimates of outcome may be made:

1. Some 20 to 30 percent show good recovery and can resume their former occupation and activities.
2. Another 30 to 40 percent show some improvement, but usually require a transfer to less complex occupational duties as a consequence of residual intellectual or personality impairment.
3. 15 to 25 percent show no improvement.
4. 10 percent die during the course of treatment (or within a 10-year period following the instigation of treatment).

On the other hand, when treatment is started early, approximately 80 percent of general paretics show a sufficient remission of symptoms to return to their original or other type of employment. As with other mental disorders, psychotherapy and sociotherapy may be essential aspects of the total treatment program.

The only fully adequate approach to cerebral syphilis is the prevention of syphilitic infection, or early detection and treatment where infection has taken place. In the United States, facilities are provided for the free diagnosis and treatment of syphilis; most states require examinations before marriage; and public education has been vigorously supported by governmental, educational, and religious agencies. It is also mandatory in all states for physicians to report cases of syphilis to local health authorities. Even so, a large number of cases go unrecorded. Partly this is due to the failure of many physicians to report them (Fleming et al., 1970).

In efforts directed toward finding and treating all infected cases, it has become common practice for patients with infectious syphilis to be interviewed for sex contacts. Every effort is then made to locate these individuals and screen them for possible syphilitic infection. In one study in a major urban center, only 11 patients out of 292 reported as having primary or secondary syphilis were unable or unwilling to identify at least one person with whom they had had sexual contact (Tarr & Lugar, 1960). A successful search was also conducted in a case involving a Sacramento, California, prostitute, named as a contact by an infected male; she, in turn, produced a list of 310 male contacts. Although they were chiefly interstate truck drivers scattered over 34 states, Canada, and Mexico, authorities were able to locate them and ask for blood tests (*Los Angeles Times*, 1970). In another case, cited by Strage (1971), an infected homosexual male was able to produce a file of nearly 1000 male contacts together with the details of their sexual acts and preferences.

To improve the efficiency of case-finding, investigators have extended interviews to include not only sex contacts of patients but also friends and acquaintances, whose sexual behavior is assumed to be similar to that of the patient; this is called *cluster testing*.

Although we now have the medical means to eradicate syphilis, it remains a major health problem in our society because its roots are social as well as medical. And with our changing sexual mores and increasing permissiveness, the rate of infection can be expected to increase—particularly among younger people—unless effective educational and public health measures are undertaken to combat the disease. With the cooperation of international and national agencies, better education, and more adequate facilities for diagnosis and treatment, there is every reason to believe that syphilis can eventually be controlled or even eliminated as a public health problem.

EPIDEMIC ENCEPHALITIS

Epidemic encephalitis was first described in 1917 as an inflammation of the brain caused by a virus. The disease was uncommon prior to an epidemic in Europe and the United States following World War I. It is again relatively rare in Western countries; however, it remains a serious problem in certain parts of Asia and Africa. Although no age group is immune, encephalitis is more common among children and young adults.

Clinical picture. During the acute phase of the disease, symptoms include fever, delirium, and stupor. Typically the individual is lethargic and appears to be sleeping all the time—although he can usually be awakened long enough to answer questions or take nourishment. As a consequence of the lethargy, the condition was once called *encephalis lethargica* and is now popularly known as *sleeping sickness*. Symptoms may also take the form of acute psychomotor excitement, in which the individual becomes restless, agitated, and irritable.

Although some children appear to make a satisfactory recovery, the aftereffects of epidemic encephalitis can be very serious. Previously well-behaved and cheerful children may become restless, aggressive, cruel, and generally unmanageable. They seem to lose their self-control and to be under a continual pressure of restless activity. Often they will state that they do not want to behave as they do, but that they cannot seem to help themselves. Without provocation, they may impulsively engage in destructive, homicidal, sexually aberrant, and other deviant behavior. As a result, such children usually require hospitalization. Other typical symptoms are hypersalivation, motor incoordination, and bizarreness of posture, such as leaning conspicuously backward or forward when walking. The precise relation of the symptoms to the neurological damage is not known. In children under 5, mental development may be severely retarded, and a child may not attain his normal intellectual status. Jervis (1959) reported that encephalitis accounted for some 5 percent of all institutionalized cases of mental retardation at that time. However, the incidence is much less today. In general, the older the child at the onset of the disease, the less severe the mental impairment.

In cases where the child becomes impulsive, aggressive, and hyperactive, there is residual brain damage that impairs inner controls and the organization of thought processes.[1] The following case illustrates many of the symptoms typically found in severe postencephalitic behavior disorders among children.

---

[1]Another infectious disease of the brain, cerebrospinal meningitis, may leave serious residual effects in children. Webb et al. (1968) reported that 18 percent of children who survive the high fever and acute infection of bacterial meningitis suffer seriously disabling aftereffects —including seizures, paralyses, and mental retardation.

"Harold is a boy of fifteen years whose behavior is so unpredictably and dangerously impulsive that his family cannot keep him at home. He must always live in an institution.

"He presents a strange, almost uncannily freakish appearance. He is short and squat in stature and has a short squarish head that is oversized for his body. He walks with an awkward, shambling gait, a little like a monkey. As you watch him, he sidles toward another child in a gingerly, apparently affectionate manner. Suddenly he grasps the child's finger and bends it backward mercilessly; then he slinks impishly away, laughing and chuckling. In a moment he raises his bitten nails to his mouth and stares at the cloudless sky as though abruptly transported, and mutters some incoherent remark about a 'terrible storm coming that will break all the limbs of the trees.' A few minutes later with tears streaming from his eyes he presents an appearance of genuine remorse. He puts his arms around the same child's neck and suddenly chokes the child painfully with a tremendous hug. When a teacher pries him away he tries to bite her hand. He murmurs to the teacher: 'I hurt you, didn't I? Can you whip? Whip me.' Perhaps a while later he may be seen to shuffle stealthily toward the same teacher and whisper to her in a childlike manner: 'I like you.' Then quick as a flash he may poke his finger into her eye and cry again: 'Can you whip? Whip me.'

". . . The most striking aspects of his behavior are his uncontrolled impulsive cruelties and his perverted craving to suffer pain himself. Like the rest of us, he wants love and affection, but he seeks it in a strange way. He torments and hurts others so they may do the same to him. He appears to derive an erotic pleasure from the pain which he provokes from others in lieu of love. To such injuries he adds those which he inflicts upon himself.

"This is a strange boy indeed. His disordered behavior is the consequence of an inflammatory illness of the brain, encephalitis, which complicated a contagious disease in infancy." (Menninger, 1946, pp. 41–42)

In adults, the aftereffects of epidemic encephalitis are usually not seriously impairing. In some cases, however, residual effects may include one or more of the following: (1) Parkinson's disease—also known as *paralysis agitans* and *shaking palsy*—which is a chronic, progressive disease of the central nervous system involving particularly the thalamus, basal ganglia, and reticular activating system; (2) tremors and ocular symptoms—including the loss of the blink reflex, which results in a staring and masklike expression; and (3) impulsive and aggressive behavior, which the individual is aware of but unable to control. In the third instance, the individual has been referred to as "master of what he says" but the "slave of what he does."

Treatment and outcomes. Epidemic encephalitis ordinarily can be arrested by antibiotics that kill the invading virus, and most children and adults make a complete or satisfactory recovery. As we have seen, however, in some cases there may be serious residual effects.

Formerly, once these residual effects were established, the outcome was unfavorable. Newer forms of drug therapy, however, may diminish hyperactivity and foster increased attention, learning ability, and self-control—particularly in children. Such treatment must include psychological, educational, and sociological measures, as well as medical procedures, if the residual potentialities of the child are to be realized.

DISORDERS WITH BRAIN TUMORS

In the writings of Felix Plater (1536–1614) we find the following rather remarkable account of "A Case of Stupor due to a Tumour in the Brain, Circular like a Gland":

"Caspar Bone Curtius, a noble knight, began to show signs of 'mental alienation' which continued through a period of two years until at last he became quite stupefied, did not act rationally, did not take food unless forced to do so, nor did he go to bed unless compelled, at table he just lay on his arms and went to sleep, he did not speak when questioned even when admonished, and if he did it was useless. Pituita dropped from his nose copiously and frequently: this condition continued for about six months, and finally he died. . . .

At the post mortem when the skull was opened and the lobes of the brain separated, a remarkable globular tumor was found on the upper surface of the Corpus Callosum, resembling a gland fleshly, hard and fungus-like, about the size of a medium sized apple, invested with its own membranes and having its own veins, lying free and without any connection with the brain itself. . . . This tumour, by its mass, produced pressure on the brain and its vessels, which caused stupor, torpor, and finally death. Some doctors who had seen this case earlier attributed it to sorcery, others just to the humors, but by opening the skull we made clear the abstruse and hidden cause." (1664)

A tumor is a new growth involving an abnormal enlargement of body tissue. Such growths are most apt to occur in the breast, the uterus, the prostate, or the intestinal tract, although they are sometimes found in the central nervous system. In adults, brain tumors occur with the greatest frequency during the 40's and 50's.

Some of these tumors are malignant, in that they destroy the tissue in which they arise; others are not destructive except by reason of the pressure they exert. Since the skull is a bony, unyielding container, a relatively small tumor in the brain may cause marked pressure and thus may interfere seriously with normal brain functioning.

About 1 percent of the autopsies in general hospitals have revealed brain tumors, as compared to 2 to 4 percent of those in mental hospitals (German, 1959; Patton & Sheppard, 1956; Wilson, 1940). Yet psychoses associated with brain tumors constitute less than 0.1 percent of all first admissions to mental hospitals. Apparently many brain tumors do not produce recognizable psychopathology.

CLINICAL PICTURE

The clinical picture that develops in cases of brain tumor is extremely varied and is determined largely by (1) the location, size, and rapidity of growth of the tumor, and (2) the personality and stress tolerance of the individual.

The brain tumor itself may result in both localized and general symptoms. Damage to a particular part of the brain may result in localized disturbances of sensory or motor functions. General symptoms appear when the tumor becomes large enough to result in greatly increased intracranial pressure. Common early symptoms are persistent headache, vomiting, memory impairment, listlessness, depression, and "choked disc"—a phenomenon due to swelling of the optic nerve when cerebrospinal fluid is forced into it by intracranial pressure.

As the tumor progresses and the intracranial pressure increases, there may be clouding of consciousness, disorientation for time and place, carelessness in personal habits, irritability, convulsive seizures, vomiting, sensorimotor losses, hallucinations, apathy, and a general impairment of intellectual functions. Terminal stages are usually similar to other types of severe brain damage, in which the patient is reduced to a vegetative stupor and eventual death.

The range of symptoms that may occur in brain tumor cases was demonstrated by Levin (1949) in an intensive study of 22 cases admitted to the Boston Psychopathic Hospital. These patients ranged in age from 22 to 65 years, the majority (73 percent) falling between the ages of 40 and 60 years. There were 11 males and 11 females. Prior to hospitalization the range of symptoms shown by these patients included those listed below.

SYMPTOMS PRIOR TO HOSPITALIZATION	NUMBER OF CASES
Memory impairment or confusion	13
Depression	9
Seizures	8
Headaches	8
Complaints of visual impairment	6
Drowsiness	6
Irritability	6
Indifference	5
Restlessness	4
Complaint of generalized weakness	4
Loss of sense of responsibility	3
Syncopal attacks	2
Paranoid ideas	2
Fearfulness	2
Tendency to be combative	2
Euphoria	2
Aphasia	2
Hypochondriacal tendencies	2

The interval between the onset of the symptoms and hospitalization varied from 1 week to 6 years, with an average interval of 17 months. In most cases, symptoms were evident 6 months or more prior to first admission. In this connection, it has been pointed out, however, that minor personality changes and depression often serve to mask the more definitive symptoms of a brain tumor—with the result that diagnosis and treatment are often delayed (Schwab, 1970).

The patient's emotional reaction to the organic damage and to the resulting intellectual impairment may vary. Initially, he may be overly irritable, drowsy, and mildly depressed. As the disorder progresses, however, he may have some insight into the seriousness of his condition and become severely depressed, anxious, and apprehensive. Patients who have less insight into their condition usually react to the brain damage and their failing functions by becoming expansive and euphoric. Such patients seem unconcerned about their illness and may joke and laugh in a most unrestrained and hilarious manner. Such reactions are apparently compensatory and are especially frequent in advanced stages when there is considerable brain damage or pressure.

Serious tumors, especially those with psychological complications, are most common in the frontal, temporal, and parietal lobes (McTaggart, Andermann & Bos, 1961; Soniat, 1951). Frontal-lobe tumors often produce subtle peculiarities, such as inability to concentrate, personal carelessness, a loss of inhibitions, and absentmindedness that later becomes a memory defect. Often, too, the individual becomes silly and prone to punning and general jocularity. In an analysis of 90 patients with frontal-lobe tumors, Dobrokhotova

(1968) found three common forms of emotional disorder: (1) the absence of spontaneity; (2) disinhibition and lability of affect—often with euphoria; and (3) forced emotions, which were abruptly expressed and terminated.

Tumors involving the special sensory areas in the brain may result in hallucinations of sight, hearing, taste, and smell. It has been estimated that about half of the patients with brain tumors evidence hallucinations sometime during the course of their illness. Visual hallucinations predominate and may involve dazzling, vividly colored flashes of light, as well as various kinds and sizes of animals and other objects. In temporal-lobe tumors, "Lilliputian hallucinations" are sometimes found, in which the patient sees small figures that he usually knows are not real. Such hallucinations apparently result from irritation of the visual pathways passing through the temporal lobe.

Similarly, irritation of the olfactory pathways may result in the perception of peculiar odors, such as rubber burning, for which there is no external stimulus. Auditory hallucinations may include buzzing, ringing, roaring, and occasionally voices and conversations.

The following excerpt from the case history of a 55-year-old man shows some of the milder symptoms commonly found in frontal-lobe tumors.

Several months prior to his hospitalization he had complained to his wife about frequent and severe headaches, which he attributed to tension over difficulties in getting along with his supervisor at work. About 3 months after the headaches appeared, he began to have occasional vomiting spells, which he also attributed to tension and an "upset stomach." Despite his wife's insistence, he refused to have a medical checkup. Shortly after this, his wife noticed that her husband "seemed preoccupied and absentminded a good deal of the time." He also became somewhat careless in his personal appearance and slovenly in his eating habits. On several occasions he became emotionally upset over trivial matters; sometimes he would joke about unhumorous topics, such as the death of someone in an automobile accident.

Some 9 months after the appearance of his persistent headaches, the man's wife was called in for a conference with his supervisor. The supervisor stated that her husband "didn't seem to be himself" and was becoming increasingly indifferent about the quality of his work. He had talked to him but "didn't seem to

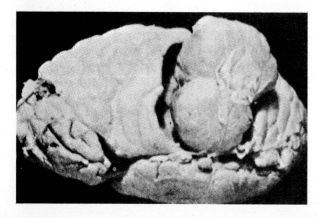

Brain tumors can cause a variety of personality alterations. Below is a picture of a meningioma—a tumor of one of the meninges, or coverings of the brain.

get through." He suggested that she encourage her husband to see a psychiatrist.

The wife agreed to carry out this suggestion, but her husband refused to see a psychiatrist or to admit that his personality had changed. Two evenings later, however, he had a convulsive seizure. His wife called a physician who had him hospitalized for observation. A thorough medical checkup revealed the presence of a growth in the right frontal lobe. Surgery proved successful and the patient made a good recovery and and was eventually able to resume his former employment.

Although such personality change is so common in brain-tumor cases that it has in the past been attributed directly to the tumor, we now realize that these symptoms are neither inevitable nor to be thought of as due solely to the tumor. We have stressed repeatedly that adjustive reactions must always be thought of as a function of both the stress situation (including biological, psychological, and sociocultural stresses) and the personality of the individual—his stability and level of stress tolerance. The greater an individual's maturity and stability, the greater the stresses he can successfully withstand. Nowhere is this more clearly brought out than in the tremendous range of reactions that we see in patients suffering from definite, observable, measurable stress in the form of brain pathology.

A most dramatic example of the importance of the patient's pre-illness personality in determining the psychological effects of brain pathology is provided in John Gunther's (1949) moving account of his son Johnny's courageous struggle against a malignant brain tumor. Johnny was 16 and in his junior year at preparatory school when the tumor was discovered. During the 14 months that preceded his death, he was subjected to two major operations and a variety of other treatment procedures.

Throughout his ordeal, Johnny never lost his courage, his ambition, his sense of humor, or his mental alertness. Although his strength and general physical condition deteriorated steadily, and he suffered increasing visual impairment, he fought to carry on a normal pattern of activity and to keep up with his studies by being tutored at home. Through tireless and determined effort, he managed to take and pass college entrance examinations—a 6-hour ordeal that followed an hour of standing in line—and to graduate with his class. By this time his physical impairment had become so great that it was a struggle simply to tie his shoelaces or even fasten his belt. At graduation late in May, he could only walk very slowly down the long aisle and grasp the diploma with his weak left hand. Less than a month later, death came to Johnny.

TREATMENT AND OUTCOMES

Treatment of brain-tumor cases is primarily a surgical matter and thus is outside the scope of our present discussion. However, it may be noted that the degree of recovery of the patient in such cases depends both on the size and location of the growth and on the amount of brain tissue that may have to be removed with the tumor. In some cases there seems to be full recovery, while in others there may be a residue of symptoms, such as partial paralysis and a reduction in intellectual level. Where tumors are well advanced and require extensive surgery, the mortality rate is high.

The following case, summarized from a report by Brickner, reveals a postoperative reduction in general intellectual capacity and the overcompensatory reaction of the patient to his changed life situation.

The patient was a man of 40 who had been a successful broker on the New York Stock Exchange. During the operation to remove his tumor, large portions of the frontal lobes of the brain were removed on both sides. As a result the patient's general adjustive capacities—including comprehension, judgment, restraint, memory, and learning capacity—were markedly lowered.

The following excerpt from Brickner's extensive case record on this man will serve to show his impaired intellectual capacity and his grandiose overcompensating reaction.

B.: One thing your illness lost you is the knowledge that you're not perfect.

A.: It's a damned good thing to lose.

B.: Do you really believe in your heart that you are perfect?

A.: Yes. Of course we all have faults. I have faults like everyone else.

B.: Name some of your faults.

A.: I don't think I have any.

B.: You just said you had.

A.: Well, they wouldn't *predominate* on the Exchange.

B.: I mean personal faults.

A.: Yes, I have personal faults. I never give a man an opportunity to do what he wants to do on the Exchange, if I know it.

B.: Is that a fault?

A.: That's being a good broker.

B.: Can you name a personal fault? Do you really believe you're perfect?

A.: You bet I do—pretty near perfect—they don't come much more perfect than I am. (1936, pp. 47–48)

German (1959) found that about 40 percent of all brain tumors are potentially curable; about 20 percent are capable of palliation for periods of 5 years or more; and the remainder are fatal within a short period of time. Some improvement in these figures, however, has more recently been noted (Cole, 1970). Ordinarily, the outcome depends heavily on early diagnosis and treatment—and there is some danger of delay through mistaken assessment of the clinical picture as of psychogenic, rather than organic, nature. But psychologists and psychiatrists are alert for the possibility of brain tumors—as well as other brain pathology—in neuroses and other psychopathology. Consequently, such cases are usually referred for neurological examination. And fortunately, newer methods of detecting and pinpointing brain tumors, as well as improved treatment procedures, are resulting in an improvement in outcomes.

DISORDERS WITH HEAD INJURY

Since ancient times brain injuries have provided a rich source of material for speculation about mental functions. Hippocrates pointed out that injuries to the head could cause sensory and motor disorders, and Galen included head injuries among the major causes of mental disorders.

Perhaps the most famous historical case is the celebrated American crowbar case reported by Dr. J. M. Harlow in 1868. Since it is of both historical and descriptive significance, it merits a few details:

"The accident occurred in Cavendish, Vt., on the line of the Rutland and Burlington Railroad, at that time being built, on the 13th of September, 1848, and was occasioned by the premature explosion of a blast, when this iron, known to blasters as a tamping iron, and which I now show you, was shot through the face and head.

"The subject of it was Phineas P. Gage, a perfectly healthy, strong and active young man, twenty-five years of age ... Gage was foreman of a gang of men employed in excavating rock, for the road way. ...

"The missile entered by its pointed end, the left side of the face, immediately anterior to the angle of the lower jaw, and passing obliquely upwards, and obliquely backwards, emerged in the median line, at the back part of the frontal bone, near the coronal suture.

... The iron which thus traversed the head, is round and rendered comparatively smooth by use, and is three feet seven inches in length, one and one fourth inches in its largest diameter, and weighs thirteen and one fourth pounds. ...

"The patient was thrown upon his back by the explosion, and gave a few convulsive motions of the extremities, but spoke in a few minutes. His men (with whom he was a great favorite) took him in their arms and carried him to the road, only a few rods distant, and put him into an ox cart, in which he rode, supported in a sitting posture, fully three quarters of a mile to his hotel. He got out of the cart himself, with a little assistance from his men, and an hour afterwards (with what I could aid him by taking hold of his left arm) walked up a long flight of stairs, and got upon the bed in the room where he was dressed. He seemed perfectly conscious, but was becoming exhausted from the hemorrhage, which by this time, was quite profuse, the blood pouring from the lacerated sinus in the top of his head, and also finding its way into the stomach, which ejected it as often as every fifteen or twenty minutes. He bore his sufferings with firmness, and directed my attention to the hole in his cheek, saying, 'the iron entered there and passed through my head.'" (1868, pp. 330, 331, 332)

Sometime later Dr. Harlow made the following report.

"His physical health is good, and I am inclined to say that he has recovered. Has no pain in head, but says it has a queer feeling which he is not able to describe. Applied for his situation as foreman, but is undecided whether to work or travel. His contractors, who regarded him as the most efficient and capable foreman in their employ previous to his injury considered the change in his mind so marked that they could not give him his place again. The equilibrium or balance, so to speak, between his intellectual faculties and animal propensities, seems to have been destroyed. He is fitful, irreverent, indulging at times in the grossest profanity (which was not previously his custom), manifesting but little deference for his fellows, impatient of restraint or advice when it conflicts with his desires, at times pertinaciously obstinate, yet capricious and vacillating, devising many plans of future operations, which are no sooner arranged than they are abandoned in turn for others . . . his mind is radically changed, so decidedly that his friends and acquaintances said he was 'no longer Gage.'" (1868, pp. 339–340)

Such changes in personality following frontal-lobe damage have been noted by laymen as well as doctors. In his book *Arctic Adventure*, Freuchen describes an old Eskimo, Agpaleq, whose gun exploded in his hand while he was shooting caribou and resulted in extensive destruction of the brain. The left frontal lobe was badly shattered in the accident and about a cupful of brain matter was lost.

"They cleaned out more with a spoon, after which Alequisaq sewed the skin together. . . . Agpaleq's recovery was slow, but almost complete. The accident resulted in peculiarity of habits rather than invalidism. During the remainder of his life he could sleep for a week or more at a time, and remain awake an equal length of time. When asleep, it was almost impossible for him to be awakened, and it became quite the custom for his neighbors to walk into his house and help themselves to whatever they might desire, including his wife. Agpaleq slept soundly through it all and never knew what practical jokes were played on him.

"He also became almost unbearably dirty, soiled himself and never cared. Prior to the accident he had been neat and clean, but afterward he was always smeared with grease or blood or both. His hands were filthy, his toes rotted away and filled the house with the most noisome stench. He could still hunt in his kayak, for he retained his heels and half of his feet, and was useful until the time of his death." (1935, p. 57)

Head injuries occur frequently, particularly as a result of falls, blows, and automobile and other

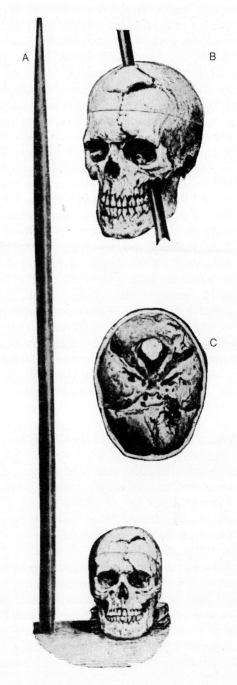

Harlow illustrated his famous crowbar case by these drawings, showing (A) the comparative sizes of the tamping iron and the cranium through which it passed; (B) a view of the cranium showing just where the iron passed through, and also a large section of the skull which was entirely torn away and later replaced; and (C) an upward view from inside the skull, giving the position and relative size of the hole that was made and showing a deposit of new bone partially closing it over.

accidents. It has been estimated that each year more than 1.5 million persons suffer head injuries in automobile accidents, and another 200,000 in industrial accidents (Earl, 1966). Many times bullets or other objects actually penetrate the cranium. Yet relatively few persons with head injuries find their way into mental hospitals, since many head injuries do not involve appreciable damage to the brain. Even when a head injury results in a temporary loss of consciousness, the damage to the brain is usually minor.

Most of us have received a blow on the head at one time or other, and in giving the case history of a mental patient, relatives often remember some such incident to which they attribute his difficulties. Patients, too, are apt to search their own childhood for evidence of having fallen on their heads or having been hit on the head. Apparently, blaming the alleged head injury for the difficulties is a convenient method of escaping the "disgrace" of a functional mental illness and at the same time avoiding any hereditary stigma to the family. Consequently, it should be emphasized that only when the brain injury is severe is it apt to leave any residual handicap.

GENERAL SYMPTOMS AND DYNAMICS

Head injuries usually give rise to immediate acute reactions, the severity of which depends on the degree and type of injury. These acute reactions may then clear up entirely or develop into chronic disorders.

Acute traumatic[1] disorders. Fortunately, the brain is an extraordinarily well-protected organ, but even so, a hard blow on the head may result in a skull fracture in which portions of bone press upon or are driven into the brain tissue. Even without a fracture, the force of the blow may result in small, pinpoint hemorrhages throughout the brain or in the rupturing of larger blood vessels in the brain.

The person rendered unconscious by a head injury usually passes through stages of stupor and confusion on his way to recovering clear consciousness (Symonds, 1962). This recovery of consciousness may be complete in the course of minutes, or it may take hours or days. In rare cases an individual may live for extended periods of time without regaining consciousness. The specific symptoms, of course, depend largely on the nature of the injury.

1. *Cerebral concussion* typically involves a mild head injury that disrupts circulatory and other brain functions and results in a slight clouding or momentary loss of consciousness. On regaining consciousness the individual may be somewhat confused and disoriented, have a loss of memory for the accident, and suffer from a headache. Severe psychological symptoms rarely occur, and the individual usually will recover within a few hours or days. However, a transitory post-concussion syndrome commonly consists of headache, dizziness, excessive fatigue, and inability to concentrate; and partial or total amnesia for the circumstances of the accident usually remain. This simple concussion syndrome is illustrated in the case of a football star who was knocked out in a head-on collision with an opposing player.

The player regained consciousness while being carried off the field but was disoriented and confused, and called signals as if he were still in the game. About an hour after his arrival at the hospital the mental confusion cleared up and he seemed normal except for complaints of a terrible headache and an inability to remember just what happened. For several days thereafter he suffered from headaches, feelings of fatigue, and difficulty in concentrating—but these symptoms were not severe and he shortly rejoined his team.

2. *Cerebral contusion* may occur if the injury to the head is so severe that the brain, normally anchored in a fixed position, is shifted within the skull and is pushed or compressed against the opposite side. In this sudden movement of the brain there may be an actual bruising of its surface against the cranium. Here, in addition to the symptoms that follow a concussion, there may be prolonged unconsciousness for hours or even days, followed by a train of more serious symptoms that may include delirium. When the patient regains clarity of mind, he usually complains of severe headaches, sensitivity to noise and light, and dizziness, nausea, and weakness. Even though these symptoms may, in the main, clear up in a few days or weeks, certain symptoms,

---

[1]The word *trauma* here refers to a physical wound or injury. We have previously used the term to refer to psychological wounds or shocks. This need not be confusing if we remember that stress may be biological or psychological.

such as irritability, may persist for a prolonged period. There may also be an impairment of intellectual and motor functions after the acute symptoms have cleared up.

Cerebral contusion is illustrated by the following case of a flier injured during a crash landing.

When taken to the hospital he was unconscious. Some 8 hours after the accident he returned to consciousness but was confused and mildly delirious. There was a gradual return to clarity over a period of the next 2 days, accompanied by complaints of headache, dizziness, and nausea, especially if he moved. He was also hypersensitive to noise and light. He was able to leave the hospital within a week but complained for several months of headaches and inability to tolerate noise.

3. *Cerebral laceration* is an actual rupture or tearing of the brain tissue. This often occurs in skull-fracture cases when a portion of the bone may be driven into the brain tissue. It may also result from injury by bullets or other objects that penetrate the cranium, or from the internal laceration of the brain, as in cases of severe contusion.

The immediate symptoms of cerebral laceration are similar to those in contusion—unconsciousness followed by confusion or delirium and a gradual return to clarity of mind. In addition to persistent headaches and related symptoms, there may be a residual impairment of intellectual and motor functions. This was illustrated in the crowbar case reported by Dr. Harlow.

During the coma that follows severe cerebral injury—including contusion and laceration—pulse, temperature, and blood pressure are affected and the patient's survival is uncertain. The duration of the coma is determined primarily by the extent of the injury. In severe cases, the patient may be unconscious for days or even weeks. If he survives, the coma is usually followed by delirium, in which he may manifest acute excitement and confusion, disorientation, hallucinations, and generally anxious, restless, and noisy activity. Often he talks incessantly in a disconnected fashion, with no insight into his disturbed condition. Gradually the confusion clears up and he regains contact with reality. Again, the severity and duration of residual symptoms will depend primarily on the nature and extent of the cerebral damage, the premorbid personality of the patient, and the life situation to which he will return.

BRAIN TRAUMA AND AMNESIA

Amnesia (loss of memory for previous experience) may result from brain trauma and damage—various labels being applied to designate specific types of memory loss. For example, in *traumatic amnesia* there is loss of memory for the situation surrounding the trauma; and often, brain trauma may also cause some degree of *retrograde amnesia* for events prior to the traumatic incident. Except in extreme cases the memory loss is not extensive and recovery tends to be orderly, with information more remote in time being remembered first and information that immediately preceded or involved the brain trauma being recovered gradually.

Retrograde amnesia resulting from cerebrovascular accidents and other severe types of brain trauma and damage may extend farther back in time. Thus a person may have no recollection of having gone to school or of having married and reared children. Such memory losses may be recovered eventually or they may be permanent. In addition, the individual may be subject to *anterograde amnesia*—inability to recall events that occurred after the accident or trauma. Here, new information is not registered and retained in memory storage in a way that facilitates its retrieval when the individual wishes to retrieve it. Talland (1967) described individuals suffering from anterograde amnesia as living in "... a world without continuity. With no memories of the recent past, amnesic patients lose their anchorage in time, and in their waking hours are as apt, as we are in dreams, to mistake the present for the past, or confuse two periods of the past with each other." (p. 46) The elderly man who thinks of himself as still being a star athlete in high school and who is looking forward to playing quarterback on the football team once he is released from the hospital is a good example of an anterograde amnesic.

Persons with retrograde and anterograde amnesia usually confabulate, or falsify information to fill in memory gaps; yet they make no systematic attempt to do so; nor do they try to cover up obvious contradictions. Interestingly enough, however, the confabulation generally has some relationship to their present life situations. In a study of 101 cases of acute brain injury—resulting from automobile crashes, shootings, and other severely incapacitating incidents—Weinstein and Lyerly (1968) reported that 60 subjects confabulated, usually about social relationships and personal identity. These investigators concluded, "While confabulation is ostensibly the fictitious narration of past events, it is also a condensed symbolic representation of current problems and relationships. The content is determined by the nature of the disability and those aspects of past experience that have been significant sources of identity." (p. 354)

In the most severe cases, the amnesic may suffer the loss of a sense of self-reference, a pattern which has been described by Talland as follows: "Perhaps the ultimate in amnesia is reached when a person correctly performs a required task, instantly forgets that he did so, and believes that the task was actually performed by the person who asked him to undertake it." (1967, p. 49) In behavioristic terms, the individual has become a completely "respondent organism," for he not only fails to see himself as the originator of his actions but tends to remain passive and indifferent until he receives instructions from others. His ability to follow these instructions will depend on whether he can retrieve from his limited memory the essential information for performing the action.

KEY TYPES OF EPILEPSY AND POSSIBLE RELATIONSHIP TO MALADAPTIVE BEHAVIOR

Epilepsy is a disorder of the nervous system caused by brain lesions or other pathology and characterized by disturbances in the rhythm of electrical discharges from the brain. Throughout man's recorded history, accounts of the disorder have appeared; and although its true incidence today in the United States is unknown, conservative estimates place the number of persons subject to epileptic seizures at between 2 and 3 million. Cases occur among all age groups, but more commonly in children than adults; in over half the known cases of epilepsy, the age at onset is under 15 years.

Epileptic seizures are infinitely varied in form, but they may, for practical purposes, be classified into the three main types described below. Typical EEG patterns for these three types are contrasted at right with recordings of normal brain waves.

1. Grand mal: "great illness." The most prevalent and spectacular form of epileptic seizure, grand mal, occurs in some 60 percent of the cases. Typically, the seizure is immediately preceded by an aura or warning, such as an unpleasant odor; and during an attack the individual loses consciousness and breathing is suspended. His muscles become rigid, jaws clenched, arms extended, and legs outstretched, and he pitches forward or slumps to the ground. With the return of air to the lungs his movements, instead of being rigid (tonic), become jerking (clonic). Muscular spasms begin, the head strikes the ground, the arms repeatedly thrust outward, the legs jerk up and down, the jaws open and close, and the mouth foams. Usually in about a minute the convulsive movements slow, the muscles relax, and the individual gradually returns to normality— in some cases after a deep sleep lasting from a few minutes to several hours. Another, less common, form of convulsive seizure, much like a modified grand-mal attack, is known as *Jacksonian epilepsy;* here, motor disturbances occurring in one region spread over the side in which they originate, and sometimes over the entire body.

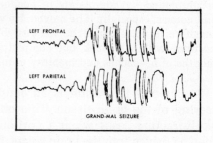

LEFT FRONTAL

LEFT PARIETAL

GRAND-MAL SEIZURE

2. Petit mal: "small illness." In petit-mal seizures there is usually a diminution, rather than a complete loss, of consciousness. The individual stops whatever he is doing, stares vacantly ahead or toward the floor, and then in a few seconds resumes his previous activity. In some cases, these seizures may occur several times a day; and, unlike grand-mal seizures, they rarely have an advance warning or aura. With onset usually occurring in childhood or adolescence, petit-mal attacks are rare after the age of 20.

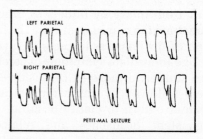

LEFT PARIETAL

RIGHT PARIETAL

PETIT-MAL SEIZURE

3. Psychomotor epilepsy. Psychomotor attacks occur in about 10 percent of child, and 30 percent of adult, epileptics. Attacks usually last from a few seconds to minutes, but in some rare cases they may last considerably longer. Their principal feature is a psychic disturbance, which varies greatly from one individual to another. Despite a lapse or clouding of consciousness, activity continues and the individual appears to be conscious; and during his attack he may perform routine tasks or some unusual or antisocial act. A very small percentage of cases may even involve self-mutilation or homicidal assault. The Flemish painter Van Gogh was subject to psychomotor attacks, for which he was later amnesic. On one occasion he cut off one of his ears, wrapped it in a sack, and presented it to a prostitute. In a more serious case, a brain-injured soldier subject to psychomotor epilepsy reported a dream in which he found himself trying to ward off attackers. Actually, he had beaten his 3-year-old daughter to death, but was completely amnesic for the tragic episode.

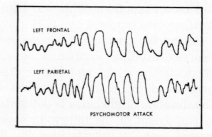

LEFT FRONTAL

LEFT PARIETAL

PSYCHOMOTOR ATTACK

Fortunately, newer drug medication makes it possible to prevent seizures in some 80 percent of epileptics. Often treatment procedures must also focus on helping the individual work through problems associated with his affliction, such as shame, self-pity, and withdrawal from social contacts. A well-ordered regimen of living, in which undue fatigue and alcoholic excesses are avoided, is also important in treatment.

Educational efforts by professional and lay organizations have succeeded in dispelling many misconceptions concerning epilepsy. The disorder is no longer considered indicative of impaired intelligence, criminal propensities, or insanity; and epileptics are no longer branded as poor employment risks—on the contrary, they show a relatively low incidence of on-the-job accidents. Also, legal restrictions on the operation of motor vehicles have been changed, so that epileptics are permitted to drive when it is established that they have been free of seizures (with or without medication) for 2 to 3 years. In general, most epileptics make adequate educational, marital, and occupational adjustments.

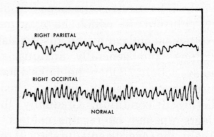

RIGHT PARIETAL

RIGHT OCCIPITAL

NORMAL

Based on Batchelor and Campbell (1969), Flor-Henry (1969), Jasper (1969), Noyes and Kolb (1968), Pryse-Phillips (1969), and Sutherland and Trait (1969).

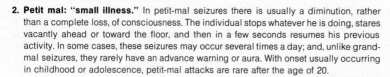

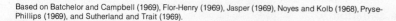

Some degree of bleeding, or *intracerebral hemorrhage*, occurs in most cases of head injury. In severe head injuries there is usually gross bleeding or hemorrhaging at the site of the damage. When the hemorrhaging involves small spots of bleeding—often microscopic sleeves of red cells encircling tiny blood vessels—the condition is referred to as *petechial hemorrhages.* There is some evidence of petechial hemorrhages in most brain injuries, but in fatal cases they are usually multiple or generalized throughout the brain. Professional boxers are likely to suffer such petechial hemorrhaging from repeated blows to the head; they may develop a form of encephalopathy (area or areas of permanently damaged brain tissue) from the accumulated damage of such injuries. Consequently, some former boxers may suffer from impaired memory, inability to concentrate, involuntary movements, and other symptoms—a condition popularly referred to as being "punch-drunk." Johnson (1969) has found abnormal EEG's in 10 of 17 retired boxers; and Earl (1966) has noted that two former welterweight champions suffered so much brain damage in their professional fights that confinement in mental institutions ended their careers before they reached the age of 30.

Chronic or post-traumatic disorders. Although many patients make a remarkably good recovery, even after severe brain injury, others show various residual *post-concussional* or *post-contusional* symptoms. Common aftereffects of moderate brain injury are chronic headaches, anxiety, irritability, dizziness, easy fatigability, and impaired memory and concentration. Where the brain damage is extensive, the patient's general intellectual level may be markedly reduced, especially where there have been severe frontal-lobe lesions. In addition, various specific neurological and psychological defects may follow localized brain damage: occipital-lobe lesions may impair vision, parietal-lobe lesions may result in sensory aphasia, and so on. Some 2 to 4 percent of head-injury cases develop post-traumatic epilepsy, usually within 2 years of the head injury but sometimes much later (Gibson, 1959). In general, the longer the period between the injury and the first convulsive seizure, the more likely they are to persist.

In a minority of brain-injury cases—some 2 to 3 percent—there are personality changes, such as those described in the historic cases of Phineas Gage and Agpaleq (O'Connell, 1961). Among older people and individuals who have suffered extensive damage to the frontal lobes, the symptom picture may be complicated by markedly impaired memory for recent events and by confabulation. This clinical picture is referred to as the *Korsakoff syndrome,* or the *amnesia-confabulatory syndrome.* We described this syndrome in some detail in our discussion of psychoses associated with alcoholism (page 410).

Where post-traumatic personality changes are concerned, we have no well-defined criteria to indicate the extent to which they are caused directly by the brain injury, or are secondary reactions to the injury. It is significant, how-

IMPAIRMENT OF LANGUAGE AND RELATED SENSORIMOTOR FUNCTIONS RESULTING FROM BRAIN DAMAGE

In many cases, brain damage results in fairly specific language and related sensorimotor functions. Among the more common of these are:

Auditory aphasia	Loss of ability to understand spoken words
Expressive aphasia	Loss of ability to speak required words
Nominal aphasia	Loss of ability to recall names of objects
Formulation aphasia	Loss of ability to formulate sentences
Paraphasia	Garbled speech, marked by inappropriate word use, transposed sounds, and ungrammatical sentences
Alexia (dyslexia)	Loss of ability to read (less severe in dyslexia)
Agraphia	Loss of ability to express thoughts in writing
Acalculia	Loss of ability to do simple arithmetic
Amusia	Loss of ability to produce or comprehend musical sounds
Apraxia	Loss of ability to perform simple voluntary acts

With reeducation, impaired or lost language and related sensorimotor functions can usually be recovered—either partially or totally.

ever, that such changes are much more likely to occur among marginally adjusted persons than among well-adjusted ones, and that an analysis of the premorbid personality of the patient often sheds considerable light on the post-traumatic personality changes. For example, Weinstein (1961) found that patients who related to others in a "narrow and rigid" fashion and followed stereotyped social roles were especially likely to develop post-concussion symptoms.

TREATMENT AND OUTCOMES

Immediate treatment for brain damage is primarily a medical matter and need not concern us in the present context except to note that prompt treatment may prevent further injury or damage—for example, when bone fragments or blood clots must be removed from the brain. In severe cases immediate medical treatment may have to be supplemented by a long-range program of reeducation and rehabilitation.

The great majority of patients suffering from mild concussion recover within a short time. In moderate brain injuries, a sizable number of patients recover promptly, a somewhat larger number suffer from headaches and other symptoms for prolonged periods, and a few patients develop chronic incapacitating symptoms. O'Connell (1961) has estimated that about 55 percent of such patients show post-concussional symptoms after 6 months, and 40 percent after 18 months.

In severe brain-injury cases, the prognosis is less favorable. Some patients may have to adjust to lower levels of occupational and social functioning, while others are so impaired intellectually that they can never adjust to conditions outside an institution. Often, however—even in cases where considerable amounts of brain tissue have been destroyed—patients with stable, well-integrated personalities are able to make a satisfactory adjustment. And in many cases there is improvement with time, due largely to reeducation and to the taking over of new functions by intact brain areas.

In general, the following factors indicate a favorable prognosis: (1) a short period of unconsciousness, (2) nonstrategic location of the brain lesion, (3) a well-integrated premorbid personality, (4) motivation to recover or make the most of residual capacities, (5) a favorable life situation to which to return, and (6), when necessary, an adequate program of retraining.

Various other factors may also have a direct bearing on the outcome of brain injuries. The results of brain damage in infancy, for example, differ from those in adolescence and adulthood, although in both instances the results may range from death to any number of neurological disorders, including epilepsy and mental retardation (Isaacson, 1970). Moreover, individuals who are also victims of alcoholism, drug dependence, arteriosclerosis, or any of a wide range of other organic conditions, have an unfavorable outlook. Alcoholics, in particular, are prone to head injuries and other accidents, and do not have good recovery records. Severe emotional conflicts sometimes appear to predispose an individual to accidents and also to delay recovery. Although malingering is thought to be rare in brain-injury cases, monetary compensation may be a factor in the exaggeration and maintenance of symptoms.

DISORDERS WITH TOXINS AND METABOLIC DISTURBANCES

Disturbances in cerebral functions may result from several types of toxins and a wide range of metabolic disorders—including nutritive deficiencies, endocrine imbalances, and the stress of surgery or childbirth. Before discussing such disturbances, it is relevant to note that the brain has a protective mechanism—known as the blood-brain barrier (BBB)—which screens the flow of substances from the blood to the central nervous system (Cole, 1970). While normally denying or restricting entry of harmful substances (for example, keeping 99.5 percent of LSD out of the brain), the BBB also permits ready access to substances essential for health and proper functioning. No other part of the body has a protective mechanism as specialized and efficient. However, a period of oxygen deprivation, as well as the presence of certain toxins, may impair the functioning of the BBB and adversely affect brain functioning, possibly causing brain damage.

TOXIC DELIRIA (PSYCHOSES)

The most common form of toxic psychosis is delirium accompanying various diseases, such as diphtheria, pneumonia, and euremia. Toxic deliria may also result from extreme exhaustion and from the ingestion of various metals, gases, and drugs. In these disorders there usually is an acute onset of the disturbance with delirium and often coma.

1. *Delirium accompanying disease.* The early symptoms of delirium usually consist of restlessness and uneasiness plus an increased sensitivity to noise and light. The individual's sleep may be troubled by frightening dreams. As the delirium progresses, consciousness becomes clouded and the individual becomes confused and disoriented for time and later for place and person. During this phase, attention and concentration are severely diminished, and he is unable to remember or interpret properly what he sees and hears. Often he has visual illusions or hallucinations which may be interwoven with unsystematized delusions.

Although some persons become emotionally elated and euphoric, the typical emotional reaction is fear and apprehension. The fears relate especially to the misinterpretation of sounds, which the individual perceives as threatening to his safety. A footstep may be that of a murderer who is stealthily approaching to kill him. As the delirium becomes more acute, the picture becomes one of increasing confusion, apprehension, and agitation. Often there are periods of drowsiness or coma alternating with the delirium. The degree of the delirium will, of course, depend to a large extent on the severity of the patient's illness—the degree of toxic disturbance. However, persons who have poorly integrated

personalities or who are marginally adjusted may become delirious with even mild fever.

Unless the toxic condition is very severe or prolonged, there usually is little or no actual damage to the brain, and the psychopathology is temporary and clears up rapidly (Levin, 1960; Noyes & Kolb, 1968).

2. *Exhaustion delirium.* Here we find acute confusion or delirium without infection or fever. Although not common, such reactions may occur under conditions of extreme physical exertion. Often there is a combination of physical exhaustion and starvation, as in the case of individuals who become lost in remote forest and desert areas and run out of food and water.

The onset usually is marked by insomnia, mild confusion, some clouding of consciousness, perplexity, vague fears, and fleeting hallucinations and delusions. The individual may see and hear rescuers, or he may see a lake, or tables loaded with food. Gradually his perceptions of his surroundings become increasingly distorted.

Sometimes the increasing confusion may be punctuated by a period of comparative clarity in which the person finds that he has been wandering in circles. This toxic-exhaustive state may continue for several days or even weeks, but usually clears up rapidly once the patient is given proper food and rest.

Admiral Byrd's record of his stay alone at the Bolling Advance Weather Base during the Antarctic winter night is a graphic and fascinating account of the thoughts and behavior of a man struggling desperately to survive in the face of cold, loneliness, monoxide poisoning, and exhaustion. The following brief excerpts are of dynamic interest.

"The next day, June 1, was a Friday. A black Friday for me. I awakened from a dream of horrors to find that I could hardly move. I realized that all I could reasonably hope for was to prolong my existence for a few days by hoarding my remaining strength; by doing the necessary things very slowly and with great deliberation.

"My first need was warmth and food. The fire had been out 12 hours; I had not eaten in 36. Performing every act in slow motion, I edged out of the bunk and worked into my clothes. Faintness seized me as I touched the floor, and for many minutes I sat in the chair just staring at the candle. Then I gained enough strength to light the stove. The flame burned red and smoky from faulty combustion. This fire was my enemy, but I could not live without it.

"My thirst was the tallest tree in a forest of pain. The tunnel where I cut ice to melt for water was a hundred miles away, but I started out. Soon I slipped and fell. My ice quarry was too far. I licked the tunnel wall until my tongue burned, and then scraped up half a bucket of dirty snow from the floor. It was still a soggy mass when I tried to drink. My hands were shaking and it spilled all over me. Then I vomited all that I had drunk. On the verge of fainting, I crawled up on my bunk to rest.

"Death had confronted me many times . . . . Now death was a stranger sitting in a darkened room, secure in the knowledge that he would be there when I was gone.

"Great waves of fear swept through me and settled deep within . . . .

"Afterwards, lying in the sleeping bag, I tried to analyze the possibilities. For five interminable days I had been lost on a great plateau of pain where all the passes were barred. I had suffered and struggled, hoped and stopped hoping . . . . Now I asked myself, What are your assets? What might be done that has not already been done?

"The first necessity was that to survive I must husband my strength. Second, to avoid further poisoning, I must use the stove sparingly and the gasoline pressure lamp—my one good light—not at all. And to build up my strength I must sleep and eat.

"But if I depended on this routine alone, I should go mad from the hourly reminders of my own futility. Something more—the will to endure these hardships—was necessary. That must come from deep inside me. But how? By taking control of my thoughts and dwelling only on those which would make for peace. A discordant mind, black with confusion and despair, would finish me off as thoroughly as the cold." (1938, pp. 175–190)

3. *Deliria associated with metals and gases.* A variety of metals and gases—such as lead and carbon monoxide—may result in toxic reactions and deliria.

In lead poisoning, early mild symptoms typically include fatigue, weakness, listlessness, and extreme irritability. The disorder is commonest among children, who may vomit, exhibit fear, and cry for no apparent reason. More severe cases are characterized by delirium, along with restlessness, confusion, insomnia, anxiety, hallucinations, tremors, and convulsions.

The inhalation of carbon monoxide in large amounts reduces the blood's capacity to take up oxygen—thus causing anorexemia (impaired func-

tioning of the nerve cells in the brain). Delirium or coma occurs in severe cases.

The delirious state in cases of lead poisoning, as well as carbon monoxide exposure, typically clears up in a matter of hours or days, although, of course, both types of poisoning may result in death. Where cases are severe but nonlethal, common residual symptoms are irritability, lack of emotional control, forgetfulness, confabulation, impaired judgment, and a general lowering of mental capacity. Among children, severe poisoning of either kind may cause convulsive seizures and mental retardation (Henderson, 1962; White & Fowler, 1960).

Deliria associated with drug intoxication were discussed in Chapter 12 and need not be considered here. However, it may be recalled that over 20 percent of all first admissions to general hospitals in large urban centers are now associated with drug intoxication.

Postoperative disturbances. Although observed since at least the sixteenth century, when noted in the writings of Ambroise Paré, psychological disturbances following general surgery are still somewhat of an enigma. In some instances these reactions are of a toxic-delirious type, and in others they involve anxiety, delusions, hallucinations, depression, bizarre behavior, and other psychopathology. Such disturbances appear to result from biological trauma, medication, and psychological stress. Constitutional factors also appear of significance—for example, elderly persons are particularly susceptible to delirious reactions following major surgery.

Postoperative psychoses have been reported by Lunde (1969) for 3 out of 9 heart transplant cases studied. In one case, the disturbance developed gradually several days after the operation, with the individual initially becoming belligerent toward the nurses, and over a period of weeks developing a rather extensive delusional system.

"He accused nurses and various other people of trying to kill him: whenever he did not receive his medication on time ('on time' meaning less than two minutes late or two minutes early), he decided that this was a plot to destroy him. . . .

"Being in reverse isolation, everyone who came into the room looked alike: each wore a gown, a cap, a mask, and gloves. There were literally dozens of people coming in day after day whom the patient could not identify, and he began to put these people into his delusional system. He felt that the masks were being worn so that he could not see the contemptuous, mocking, expressions on their faces. It helped to have the nurses and other people identify themselves each time they came into the room even if it was the third or fourth time that day. It also helped somewhat to provide this patient with newspapers and a TV set." (pp. 119–120)

This patient also was so anxious and disturbed that he suffered from insomnia and went for a week without more than a few hours' sleep. Obviously these symptoms posed serious problems for the physicians in charge of his case.

Lunde noted that in 2 of the 6 cases not manifesting psychoses, interesting personality changes took place. "One man literally decided that the day of his transplant was his new birthday, which he planned to celebrate from then on. He felt he had been born again and was 20 years old." (p. 120) This was a 42-year-old man who received the heart of a 20-year-old. In another case the recipient learned from the press that he had received the heart of a prominent local citizen and stated that "He felt an obligation to live up to the standards set by the man whose heart he had received. He hoped to become more like the donor." (p. 373) Lunde concluded that "as surgery becomes more radical and more vital organs are exchanged, distortions of personality can be expected, since personality and self-image are so closely tied to body image." (p. 121)

New surgical procedures—such as those involving organ transplants—pose a number of challenges in relation to the psychological, social, and ethical problems involved; and increasing attention and research effort are being devoted to these problems.

NUTRITIONAL DEFICIENCIES

Nutritional deficiencies have been shown to underlie certain types of psychopathology.

Vitamin and mineral deficiencies. Deficiencies in the vitamin B complex seem to be the type most commonly involved in the production of neuropsychiatric disorders. Perhaps the best known of these deficiencies is "beriberi," which once plagued people in the Far East who lived primarily on a diet of polished rice, deficient in vitamin B_1 (thiamine). "Beriberi" means "I cannot" and is an apt description of the lassitude,

weakened muscles, intestinal distress, depression, and lowered "will to do" which follow a deficiency in vitamin B_1.

In an early experiment, Brožek, Guetzkow, and Keys (1946) studied the personality changes in 8 normal young men who were maintained 161 days on a partially restricted intake of B-complex vitamins, followed by 23 days of acute deficiency and 10 days of thiamine supplementation. Little or no evidence of personality change was observed during the period of partial restriction, but consistent and striking deterioration occurred during the acute deficiency, with depression, loss of spontaneity, increased tension, hysteria, hypochondriasis, and increased emotionality. Adding thiamine to the diet produced rapid recovery.

A number of minerals—such as sodium chloride, copper, and calcium—are required for normal brain metabolism. Chronic conditions associated with a low concentration of salt in the blood may lead to a variety of mental symptoms: prominent are lassitude, apathy, apprehension, and depression. Severe hydration from lack of water may result in apathy, delirium, and stupor.

In addition to the vitamins, minerals, and chemicals we have mentioned, there are many others which—though less directly related to mental symptoms—are essential for bodily health and the maintenance of normal resistance to organic and psychological stress.

Semistarvation. Semistarvation occurs when there is a severe restriction of calorie intake over a prolonged period of time. Throughout man's history it has been the commonest type of nutritional deficiency.

A number of observations have been made regarding behavior under conditions of "natural starvation," stemming in the main from famines in the aftermath of wars and from the meager diet of prisoner-of-war and concentration-camp inmates. Observations of advanced stages of semistarvation during famines in Leningrad and other Russian cities during World War II emphasized a number of neurological, physical, and mental changes (Brožek & Grande, 1960). Asthenia was considered the principal mental syndrome, characterized by a slowing of thought processes, impaired ability to concentrate and sustain mental effort, a lowering of higher-level interests and feelings, increased irritability, and apathy with a tendency to daydreaming. Psychotic reactions were rare and occurred mostly in cases where caloric deficiency was complicated by infection, trauma, and related conditions. Writing on the basis of his experience in German POW camps, Leyton (1946) reported similar symptoms and also emphasized a marked reduction in sexual desire, lowered standards of cleanliness, loss of pride in personal appearance, and deterioration of ethical standards.

In Chapter 5 we noted the study on semistarvation carried out by Keys et al. (1950) on a group of 36 young conscientious objectors who volunteered for the experiment. These subjects underwent a 24-week semistarvation period during which they were maintained on a diet characteristic of European famine areas near the end of World War II. Physical changes included a 25 percent loss in body weight, a 40 percent decrease in basal metabolism, and a 30 percent reduction in body strength. The men became haggard, emaciated, subject to fainting attacks, and fatigued by the slightest exertion. Sexual urges and affectional responses decreased markedly. The outstanding mental symptoms were apathy, depression, loss of sense of humor, irritability, uncooperativeness, loss of pride in personal appearance, preoccupation with thoughts of food, and seriously impaired ability to concentrate on anything else. Most of the men worried about their declining intelligence and other functions, and their self-confidence was replaced by feelings of inferiority. So striking were these personality changes that Keys and his colleagues adopted the term *semistarvation neurosis*.

Unfortunately, many people in the world today still suffer from malnutrition, including vitamin and mineral deficiencies, and it can be readily seen that their condition has serious implications both on individual and social levels. Even in the United States, where food is plentiful, many people suffer the effects of "hidden starvation"— including lowered resistance to both biological and psychological stress—as a consequence of unbalanced and inadequate diets.

ENDOCRINE DISTURBANCES

The endocrine glands manufacture hormones, which are essential for normal physiological and psychological functioning. Consequently, under-

activity or overactivity of any endocrine gland may markedly affect psychological functioning, in addition to lowering general stress tolerance. Endocrine disturbances may also lead to physical anomalies that, in turn, contribute to adjustive difficulties. For example, pituitary "giants" or "midgets," bearded ladies, extremely fat persons, and other endocrine "freaks" are often subjected to curiosity, ridicule, and similar reactions from others, which make normal personality development and self-acceptance extremely difficult for them.

In the following discussion of thyroid and adrenal dysfunctions—the most common of the endocrine disorders associated with severe psychological disturbances—three points are well worth remembering: (1) endocrine dysfunction may contribute to psychopathology, as well as result from such pathology; (2) malfunction of any gland may have widespread effects on the functioning of other glands and other bodily organs and systems; and (3) glandular dysfunction may vary considerably in degree and its effects may differ widely, depending on the age, sex, and general personality makeup of the individual. It should also be reemphasized that the endocrine system is normally under the general control of the central nervous system.

Thyroid dysfunction. The best understood of the endocrine glands is the thyroid, which regulates bodily metabolism. Either oversecretion or undersecretion of the thyroid hormone *thyroxin* produces definite signs of physical pathology and/or psychopathology. For example, in an intensive study of 17 patients with thyroid dysfunction—10 with hyperthyroidism and 7 with hypothyroidism—Whybrow, Prange, and Treadway (1969) reported that 76 percent manifested profound disruption in psychological functioning. Actual psychotic symptoms occur in about 20 percent of such cases, but they are usually not severe; less than 1 percent of first admissions to mental hospitals involve disorders associated with thyroid dysfunction.

Oversecretion of thyroxin (hyperthyroidism) accelerates the metabolic processes and leads to weight loss, tremors, tenseness, insomnia, emotional excitability, and impairment in concentration and other cognitive processes. Where psychotic symptoms do occur, they commonly include intense anxiety, agitation, and transitory delusions and hallucinations. For example, Why-brow et al. (1969) cited the case of an individual who had visual hallucinations of "swarms of bees" flying toward her. In occasional cases there is a toxic reaction with delirium, and in other cases the thyroid dysfunction appears to precipitate an underlying schizophrenic or other psychotic pattern.

Pronounced thyroid deficiency in adulthood (hypothyroidism)—typically associated with an iodine deficiency—leads to a condition called *myxedema*. Here metabolism is slowed down and the individual typically puts on weight, becomes sluggish in action and thought, and shows impairment for recent memory, difficulty in concentrating, and other cognitive disturbances. Severe depression appears to be the most common psychotic disturbance associated with hypothyroidism. Whybrow et al. (1969) described a female patient who was seriously depressed, had frequent thoughts of suicide, and became preoccupied with memories of her son who had been killed in an automobile accident some years previously.

"She wished she had been the one killed. She dreamed of digging him from his grave with her bare hands and heard his voice calling her during the day. She felt she had been saved from a previous illness to be punished by her present one." (p. 55)

In general, the impairment in both cognitive and emotional functioning appears more severe in hypothyroidism than in hyperthyroidism. And although treatment of the latter leads to marked improvement, there is evidence that long-standing hypothyroidism may lead to a residual impairment in cognitive functioning (Richter, 1970; Whybrow et al., 1969). Fortunately, present methods of diagnosis are highly efficient, and early treatment has made severe cases of hypothyroidism extremely rare. The relation of hypothyroidism during early life to mental retardation will be discussed in Chapter 16.

Adrenal dysfunction. The adrenals are paired glands consisting of an outer layer called the *adrenal cortex* and an inner core called the *adrenal medulla*. The adrenal cortex secretes steroids that influence secondary sex characteristics as well as steroids that influence stress reactions. The adrenal medulla secretes the hormones adrenaline and noradrenaline (epinephrine and norepinephrine) during strong emotion. In Chapter 6 we noted that such emotional reactions may be useful in emergency situations but that when they are prolonged or become chronic, they can lead to a breakdown in adrenal function. The relation of such a breakdown of function to mental disorders is still uncertain.

Undersecretion or deficiency of the adrenal cortex results in *Addison's disease*—a disorder characterized by a variety of metabolic disturbances, including a lowering of blood pressure, body temperature, and basal metabolism and a darkening of the skin. The accompanying mental symptoms typically include lack of vigor, easy fatigability, depressed sexual functions, headaches, irritability, lassitude, and lack of ambition. More severe mental disturbances in Addison's disease are rare and appear to be related to the personality of the patient; however, there is evidence that disturbed brain metabolism plays a dominant role in some psychotic cases.

In the following case, the patient showed clear schizophrenic symptoms.

An 18-year-old male, manifesting his first episode of mental illness, complained of tension, irritability, and the conviction that he was being doped. His mental disorder had developed over a period of about 5 months without known precipitating stresses.

On his admission to a mental hospital, psychological assessment revealed psychomotor retardation, poverty of thought, and inappropriate smiling. Thought content centered about the notion that the lights outside the hospital were related to Sputnik and that the physicians were poisoning him with tablets. The patient was not hallucinated and was oriented as to time and also knew the year and month, but not the exact date. The medical examination was essentially normal.

Because of improvement following hospitalization, supportive psychotherapy was decided on as the method of treatment. After the first week, however, the patient showed rapid deterioration with grimacing, muteness, and the maintenance of postures for hours when left alone. These symptoms were sometimes interrupted by outbursts of destructiveness and combativeness. As a consequence, electroshock treatments were given, and the patient showed marked improvement. Thorazine was prescribed but had to be discontinued because of undesirable side effects, involving the swelling of the hands, wrists, and oropharynx. Eight days after the onset of the swelling, bronzing of the skin was noted and shortly thereafter the patient developed nausea, vomiting, abdominal pain, and

ABNORMALITIES ASSOCIATED WITH ENDOCRINE DYSFUNCTIONS

PINEAL Helps in regulating body's "biological clock"; may also pace sexual development.

PITUITARY Regulates growth, stimulates activities of other glands.
Dysfunctions
Gigantism—excessive pituitary hormone secretion during growth period, with extreme growth to height of 7 to 9 feet. Intelligence and affect not appreciably modified.
Midgetism—deficient pituitary hormone secretion in early life, preventing normal growth, but body correctly proportioned. Intelligence and affect not appreciably modified.
Acromegaly—excessive pituitary hormone secretion in adulthood, with thickening and elongating of body extremities, especially hands, feet, and jaw.

THYROIDS Influence metabolic rate, growth, and development of intelligence.
Dysfunctions
Cretinism—thyroid deficiency in infancy, with physical and mental dwarfing, heavy features.
Myxedema—thyroid deficiency in adulthood, with overweight, puffed physical features, general sluggishness.
Oversecretion—accelerated metabolic processes, tremors, tenseness, emotional excitability, weight loss. Psychotic symptoms, including delusions and hallucinations, may occur.

PARATHYROIDS Regulate calcium and phosphorous metabolism.
Dysfunction
Tetany (due to removal or destruction of parathyroids)—muscular twitches, tremors, cramps, convulsions.

THYMUS May play a role in sexual development and the body's immunity system.

ADRENALS Adrenal medulla secretes adrenaline and noradrenaline, which affect neural functioning and emotion; adrenal cortex secretes steroids (corticoids), which affect body activity and metabolism and influence stress reactions and the development of secondary sex characteristics.
Dysfunctions
Addison's disease—deficiency of deoxycortone from adrenal cortex, with increased fatigability, loss of appetite, anemia, listlessness, irritability, darkening of skin.
Cushing's syndrome—excessive secretion of cortisone, with muscle weakness, reduced sex drive, fatigability, and disfiguring bodily changes.
Feminism—hypersecretion of corticoids in a male, which causes increased estrogen output and development of female characteristics.
Virilism—hypersecretion of corticoids in a female, which causes increased androgen output and the development of male characteristics.
Puberty praecox—hypersecretion of corticoids in a child, which causes early sexual maturity.

ISLETS OF LANGERHANS Located in pancreas, secrete insulin, essential for metabolism of carbohydrates.
Dysfunctions
Diabetes—high level of blood sugar resulting from undersecretion of insulin; associated with transitory or chronic nervousness, irritability, anxiety, depression.
Hypoglycemia—low level of blood sugar resulting from oversecretion of insulin; associated with the same emotional effects as described for diabetes.

GONADS Vital to sexual development and reproduction; the ovaries (female) produce estrogens and progesterone, the testes (male) produce androgens (testosterone).
Dysfunctions
Eunuchism—castration of male before puberty, with development of secondary sex characteristics of female (musculature, bodily proportions, etc.).
Deficiency in development—as a result of insufficient gonadal hormone production during childhood, failure to develop secondary sex characteristics and sex drive.
Menopause or climacteric—marked reduction of gonadal hormone production in females and males, respectively, during middle age. May cause irritability, restlessness, hot flashes (in women), mental depression, and insomnia.

Pineal — Pituitary

Parathyroids

Thyroids

Thymus

Adrenals

Islets of Langerhans

Ovaries (female)

Gonads

Testes (male)

hypotension. Laboratory findings proved consistent with hypoadrenalism.

As the signs and symptoms of Addison's disease progressed, the patient's condition again deteriorated —the patient becoming withdrawn and tense and demonstrating blocking of thought processes and strong emotional ambivalence. Cortisone treatment was instituted, and within 48 hours the symptom picture cleared up. The patient was placed on a maintenance dosage of 12.5 mgm. of cortisone daily, and examination one year after discharge revealed no symptoms of either Addison's disease or schizophrenia.

The precise relation of Addison's disease to the mental reaction could not be ascertained, but the institution of hormonal therapy was closely followed by a remission of the schizophrenic symptoms. (Adapted from Wolff & Huston, 1959, pp. 365–368)

Hypersecretion of the adrenal cortex may lead to a number of rare and dramatic changes in secondary sex characteristics (Moon, 1961). An oversecretion of adrenal steroids in the male leads to the development of female characteristics —a condition referred to as *feminism*. On the other hand, an oversecretion of adrenal steroids in the female results in a deepening of voice, shrinking of breast, growth of beard, and other masculine changes—a condition referred to as *virilism*. In children the oversecretion of adrenal steroids accelerates puberty. The latter condition is referred to as *puberty praecox*, and children subject to it may develop adult stature and reach sexual maturity at a very early age. Although still immature in other areas of development, such youngsters are usually extensively and aggressively interested in sexual matters.

In cases of tumor or abnormal growth of the adrenal cortices, there may be an excessive secretion of cortisone. The resulting clinical picture is referred to as *Cushing's syndrome*. Typical symptoms include muscle weakness, fatigability, reduced sex drive, headache, and a number of disfiguring bodily changes, such as obesity, changes in skin color and texture, and spinal deformity. In some cases there is an excessive growth of body hair. Cushing's syndrome is relatively rare, occurring most often among young women. Reactive emotional disturbances are common among such individuals. The clinical picture not only varies markedly from one patient to another, but often varies in the same patient in the course of the disease.

Treatment in adrenal dysfunction is primarily a medical matter. Cortisone and drugs which suppress corticoid secretions are heavily relied on. In cases of tumor and related conditions, surgery may be indicated. With early detection and treatment the prognosis in adrenal disorders is usually highly favorable. As in other endocrine disorders, however, the psychiatric complications may not subside with the clearing up of the adrenal dysfunction, and additional therapy may be required.

A brief summary of the immediate symptoms associated with the dysfunction of the thyroid, adrenals, and other endocrine glands is shown on page 544.

POSTPARTUM (CHILDBIRTH) DISTURBANCES

It has been estimated that psychotic reactions occur in connection with at least 1 out of every 400 pregnancies—either before or after childbirth. About 10 to 15 percent occur during pregnancy, 60 percent during the first month after childbirth, and the others during the next 8 months. In a study of 100 women who became psychotic from 30 days prior to 90 days after delivery, Melges (1968) found the modal period to be 4 days after delivery.

Clinical picture. Symptoms in postpartum disturbances include rapidly fluctuating affective and confusional states and, in some cases, schizophrenic patterns. The affective states typically involve emotional lability and depression. Schizophrenic reactions appear to occur primarily in women who were marginally adjusted prior to pregnancy.

"The majority of such patients have a typical history of aloofness and introversion and may remain emotionally bound to their parents. The wife has often not achieved psychosexual maturity or a full emotional relation with her husband. During pregnancy such a patient is often morose, irritable and flighty, and these symptoms may progress to a schizophrenic episode before term. After delivery, the patient appears odd, preoccupied, and uncertain in her behavior and verbal productions. Frequently, indifference or open antagonism is expressed toward child and husband. Not uncommonly, the schizophrenic breakdown is acute, with confusion, apprehension, perplexity, paranoid delusions, and auditory hallucinations. Often the patient symbolically reveals her attitude toward the child by fearing or dreaming that he has been lost, kidnapped, or killed, or by denying her marriage and pregnancy. Features reminiscent of a toxic delirious state may cloud the diagnosis during the first few days." (Weiner & Steinhilber, 1961)

Psychotic depressive reactions are to be distinguished from milder depressions known colloquially as the "maternity blues" or the "disenchantment syndrome," which commonly occur on the mother's return home with the baby, and which are characterized by weeping, apathy, and fatigue. Usually such postpartum blues are short-lived, lasting no longer than 4 weeks (Melges, 1968; Yalom et al., 1968). However, in some cases such mild reactions may progress almost imperceptibly to deep depression, characterized by lethargy, psychomotor retardation, dejection, self-accusations of sin and unworthiness, and a marked sense of futility. A mother may express a lack of interest in her infant, have fears that it

may be harmed, and evidence considerable underlying hostility toward her husband. Such severe depressions constitute a hazard to the lives of both mother and infant; and suicide, infanticide, or both, may occur.

Manic reactions appear to be infrequent following childbirth, but involutional-type depressions with elements of depression, agitation, and suspiciousness may occur. Occasionally, delirious reactions are precipitated by infection, hemorrhage, exhaustion, or toxemia—particularly in marginally adjusted individuals. Here there is a clouding of consciousness, hallucinatory states, and some degree of confusion and disorientation. Formerly toxic-exhaustive psychoses were common following childbirth, but the introduction of antibiotics and improved obstetrical procedures has made these reactions relatively rare.

Dynamics. The stress in postpartum psychoses has numerous organic and psychological elements. Organic factors include metabolic reorganization incident to the pregnancy, the pain of delivery, and possible hemorrhage, lacerations, and infections. Protheroe (1969) has suggested that hormonal imbalance may lower stress tolerance and help "tip the balance" in an already susceptible person.

Except in unusual cases, however, the stress of childbirth, in and of itself, is not the primary cause of toxic delirium and psychotic decompensation. In most cases, stresses associated with pregnancy and adjustments that are attendant on assuming the role of mother serve as precipitating factors in an already unstable person or one particularly vulnerable to this type of stress situation. In fact, psychotic reactions indistinguishable from typical postpartum psychoses occasionally follow the adoption of a child.

In a study of 100 cases of puerperal psychoses, White et al. (1957) emphasized the following factors: (1) unstable marriage; (2) immaturity of patient; (3) long-standing maladjustment of patient; (4) unstable family history; (5) lack of desire for baby on part of wife or husband; (6) extra responsibility, particularly financial, imposed by birth of baby; (7) physical illness of mother or baby, including extreme fatigue resulting from caring for a sick baby; and (8) an unfavorable home situation after delivery, such as poor living conditions.

More recent studies have implicated similar

DESCRIPTIVE DATA CONCERNING 100 POSTPARTUM PSYCHIATRIC CASES

In his study of 100 postpartum psychiatric patients, Melges (1968) reported that his subjects ranged in age from 17 to 46, with a median age of 28. Most were high-school graduates, and a relatively high percentage—21 percent—had graduated from college. The median onset occurred 4 days after the baby's delivery, with 64 percent of the cases showing onset of symptoms within 10 days after delivery. Other findings pertaining to diagnoses, symptoms, and causes were as follows:

Diagnoses (number of patients)	Schizophrenic reaction: 51 Neurotic depressive reaction: 25 Sociopathic (personality) disorder: 11 Manic-depressive and other reactions: 13
Major symptoms (percentage of cases)	Irritability (95 percent) Confusion (92 percent) Disorientation for time (90 percent) Uneasiness (81 percent) Excitability, restlessness (63 percent)
Chief precipitating cause	Conflict over becoming a mother (observed in 63 percent of the subjects)
Chief predisposing causes (percentage of cases)	Feelings of ambivalence toward own mother (88 percent) Knowledge of postpartum psychoses among relatives (23 percent) Interpersonal conflict (15 percent)

As indicated by the data relating to symptoms and causes, subjects often manifested multiple symptoms, and a case might be attributable to multiple causes.

factors—emphasizing that mothers who developed postpartum psychoses had significantly more insecurity and stress in their backgrounds, in their marriages, and in their pregnancies (Larson & Evans, 1969; Melges, 1968). Many such mothers appeared to experience an identity confusion centering around a conflict in their role as mothers —in most cases repudiating this role and feeling "trapped." Often such a mother experiences strong guilt feelings because she does not enjoy her baby as society expects mothers to do. An immature, nonprotective, and rejecting reaction by the husband to his wife's pregnancy and to his own fatherhood may also markedly augment the stressfulness of the entire situation for the wife. Interestingly enough, the normality or legitimacy of the baby does not appear related to postpartum psychoses (Barzilai, Winnik & Davis, 1969).

Treatment and outcomes. Postpartum psychoses tend to be self-limiting, and with the assistance of modern treatment procedures well over 90 percent of these patients recover in a relatively short time. Although in many cases patients have been advised to avoid another pregnancy for 2 or 3 years, such counseling is now carefully weighed in relation to the individual and her life situation. However, follow-up studies have shown that from 25 to 50 percent of such mothers do have a recurrence of psychotic episodes on giving birth to other children (Martin, 1958; Poffenbarger et al., 1961; Protheroe, 1969).

At present, preventive measures call primarily for good obstetric care, preparing the mother psychologically for childbirth, and alleviating any undue stresses that the family situation may be placing on her.

Individual discussion with the obstetrician, and group discussions in prepartum clinics may help greatly in allaying fears and anxieties and preparing the expectant mother for childbirth and for her role as mother. Similar procedures have proven of value in helping the husband accept and prepare for his role as father.

PSYCHOSES OF THE AGED

"But worse than any loss of limb is the failing mind, which forgets the names of slaves, and cannot recognize the face of the old friend who dined with him last night, nor those of the children whom he has begotten and brought up." (Juvenal)

Such references to mental disturbances experienced by the aged and to the more dramatic aspects of apoplexy are found in the earliest scientific and literary works. Shakespeare's King Lear has been considered an example of senile dementia, and in *Gulliver's Travels* there is a famous passage picturing the progressive physical and mental decline in senility.

The increasing proportion of older people in our population has given rise to a great many psychological, sociological, and medical problems, among them the growing incidence of mental disorders associated with old age.[1] In 1970 an estimated 700,000 older persons in the United States were institutionalized for such disorders (Ford, 1970); and this figure says nothing of the many older people with less pronounced mental symptoms who were being cared for—or ignored —in the community.

Mental disorders among the aged run the entire gamut. Long-standing neurotic, alcoholic, or drug-dependent patterns may continue into old age, or may make their appearance during this life period for the first time. Any of the functional psychoses may also develop among older persons, with psychotic depressive states being the most common. However, the two major psychotic disorders of older people are *senile dementia* (associated with cerebral atrophy and degeneration) and *psychosis with cerebral arteriosclerosis*

---

[1]As we entered the decade of the 1970's, about 10 percent of our population was over 65, and the proportion continues to grow (Birren, 1970; *U.S. News and World Report*, 1971). The average life expectancy in the United States currently exceeds 70 years, and as we continue to conquer killing diseases, a life expectancy of 90 to 100 years may not be far distant. This is in striking contrast to the life expectancy of some 23 years in the days of the Roman Empire.

BRAIN SYNDROMES INVOLVED IN PRESENILE DEMENTIA

In a group of relatively rare diseases of the central nervous system accompanied by progressive mental deterioration—four of which are described below—the clinical pictures may resemble that of senile dementia, except that the disorders characteristically appear in younger persons. Despite considerable research, the etiology of these disorders remains unclarified.

Alzheimer's disease

Named for the German psychiatrist who first described it in 1907, Alzheimer's disease is thought to occur in about the ratio of 1 case for each 25 cases of senile dementia; the true incidence, however, is unknown. Differences from senile dementia are observable chiefly in: (1) the victims' earlier age at onset, usually in the 40's or 50's; (2) rapid progression, with especially severe brain and mental deterioration, often accompanied by tendencies toward overactivity, emotional distress, and agitation; and (3) frequent development of aphasias and apraxias. Typically, death occurs within 2 to 10 years—about 4 years on the average. Treatment is limited mainly to routine medical measures and custodial care.

Pick's disease

Even rarer than Alzheimer's disease, Pick's disease (first described by Arnold Pick of Prague in papers published in 1892) is a degenerative disorder of the nervous system, usually having its onset in persons between 45 and 50. Women are apparently more subject to Pick's disease than men, at a ratio of about 3 to 2. Onset is slow and insidious, involving difficulty in thinking, slight memory defects, easy fatigability, and often, character changes with a lowering of ethical inhibitions. At first there is a rather circumscribed atrophy of the frontal and temporal lobes; and as the atrophy becomes more severe, the mental deterioration becomes progressively greater and typically includes apathy and disorientation as well as severely impaired judgment and other intellectual functions. The disease usually runs a fatal course within 2 to 7 years. Treatment is limited mainly to routine medical measures and custodial care.

Parkinson's disease

Named after James Parkinson, who described it in 1817, Parkinson's disease rarely occurs before the age of 30, and in the great majority of cases occurs between the ages of 50 and 70. An estimated 1 to $1\frac{1}{2}$ million Americans are so afflicted. The disorder is characterized by rigidity and spontaneous tremors of various muscles, usually beginning in one arm and spreading gradually to the leg on the same side of the body, then to the neck and face, and last to the limbs on the other side. With time, the face becomes rigid and masklike, with speech becoming drawling and indistinct. Often there is a tendency to lean forward in walking, with the result that the individual appears to be running in order to keep from falling forward. Unless the progression of the disease is halted, the patient eventually becomes completely helpless and dependent on others. He may gradually withdraw from social interaction, become apathetic and indifferent, and show a general lessening of intellectual interest, activity, and flexibility. Although the psychological symptoms typically become more pronounced as the disease progresses, intelligence is little affected and these symptoms appear to be primarily a reaction to the affliction. Preliminary reports with a new drug called L-dopa indicate that it offers hope for improvement in about two thirds of the cases (Edwards, 1970; New York Academy of Science, 1969; also see illustration on page 549).

Huntington's chorea

Huntington's chorea was first described by the American neurologist George Huntington in 1872. With an incidence rate of about 5 cases per 100,000 persons, the disease usually occurs in individuals between 30 and 50. It is characterized by a chronic, progressive chorea (involuntary, irregular, twitching, jerking movements) with mental deterioration leading to dementia and death within 10 to 20 years. Interestingly enough, behavior deterioration often becomes apparent several years before the neurological manifestations. In a study of 21 cases, Bellamy (1961) found that in 6 patients the first indications of the disease had been behavior problems characterized by such symptoms as violence, depression, confusion, vagrancy, prostitution, paranoid thinking, and suicidal ideas and attempts. The remaining 15 patients—hospitalized with definite neurological signs—had also shown a history of personality changes, extending back 2 to 12 years. By the time of these patients' admission, typical symptoms included depression, hyperactivity, great irritability, poverty of thought and affect, memory failure, and defective attention and judgment. No effective treatment has as yet been developed, although a variety of drugs and surgical procedures may be used to alleviate the symptoms.

Based on Cotzias (1969), Edwards (1970), Noyes and Kolb (1968), Stang (1970), and Yahr (1969).

(associated with either blocking or ruptures in the cerebral arteries). These two disorders account for approximately 80 percent of psychotic disorders among older persons (Shakhmatov, 1968), and they will be our primary concern in the present discussion.

SENILE DEMENTIA

In senile dementia the degenerative brain changes of old age are accompanied by a clinical picture of mental deterioration, which may vary markedly in degree. Women slightly outnumber men, which might be expected, in view of the longer life span of women. The average age at first admission is about 75 for both sexes, although the onset of the disorder may occur at any time from the 60's to the 90's. Since many senile persons are cared for at home before the spouse or family decides on hospitalization, the mean age at onset of the disorder is lower than statistics on first admissions would indicate.

General clinical picture. The clinical picture in senile dementia may vary in severity, with the range extending from a mild organic brain syndrome—where there is difficulty concentrating and assimilating new material, a self-centering of interests, and a "childish" emotionality—to severe and progressive mental deterioration, a vegetative existence, and death.

The onset of senile dementia is usually gradual, involving a slow physical and mental letdown. In some cases the appearance of a physical ailment or some other situational stress is a dividing point, but usually the individual passes into a psychotic state almost imperceptibly, so that it is impossible to date the disorder's onset precisely. The clinical picture may vary markedly from one person to another, depending on the nature and extent of brain degeneration, the premorbid personality of the individual, and the particular stresses in his life situation.

Faulty reactions often begin with the individual's gradual withdrawal into himself, a narrowing of social and other interests, a lessening of mental alertness and adaptability, and a lowering of tolerance to new ideas and changes in routine. Often there is a self-centering of thoughts and activities and a preoccupation with the bodily functions of eating, digestion, and excretion. As these various changes—typical in lesser degree of many older people—become more severe, additional symptoms, such as impairment of memory for recent events, untidiness, impaired judgment, agitation, and periods of confusion, make their appearance. Specific symptoms may vary considerably from day to day; thus the clinical picture is by no means uniform until the terminal stages, when the patient is reduced to a vegetative level. There is also, of course, individual variation in the rapidity of progression of the disorder, and in some instances there may be a reversal of psychotic symptomatology and a partial or even good recovery.

Types of senile dementia. Senile reactions have been categorized into five types. It may be emphasized, however, that there is generally a considerable overlapping of symptoms from one type to another.

1. *Simple deterioration.* This is, as the name suggests, a relatively uncomplicated exaggeration of the "normal" changes of old age. The patient gradually loses contact with the environment and develops the typical symptoms of poor memory, tendency to reminisce, intolerance of change,

EFFECTS OF L-DOPA THERAPY

A man with Parkinson's disease has difficulty printing the date of the month before treatment with L-dopa (left). After three weeks on the drug his writing improves (center); and at the end of eight weeks a dramatic improvement can be seen (right).

Arthur Rothstein, *Look* magazine, © 1970

disorientation, restlessness, insomnia, and failure of judgment. This is the most common of the senile psychotic reactions, constituting about 50 percent of the entire group.

The following case—involving an engineer who had retired some 7 years prior to his hospitalization—is typical of simple senile deterioration.

During the past 5 years he had shown a progressive loss of interest in his surroundings and during the last year had become increasingly "childish." His wife and eldest son had brought him to the hospital because they felt they could no longer care for him in their home, particularly because of the grandchildren. They stated that he had become careless in his eating and other personal habits, was restless and prone to wandering about at night, and couldn't seem to remember anything that had happened during the day but was garrulous concerning events of his childhood and middle years.

After admission to the hospital, the patient seemed to deteriorate rapidly. He could rarely remember what had happened a few minutes before, although his memory for remote events of his childhood remained good. When he was visited by his wife and children, he did not recognize them, but mistook them for old friends, nor could he recall anything about the visit a few minutes after they had departed. The following brief conversation with the patient, which took place after he had been in the hospital for 9 months, and about 3 months prior to his death, shows his disorientation for time and person:

Dr.: How are you today, Mr. ——— ?
Pt.: Oh . . . hello . . . (looks at doctor in rather puzzled way as if trying to make out who he is).
Dr.: Do you know where you are now?
Pt.: Why yes . . . I am at home. I must paint the house this summer. It has needed painting for a long time but it seems like I just keep putting it off.
Dr.: Can you tell me the day today?
Pt.: Isn't today Sunday . . . why, yes, the children are coming over for dinner today. We always have dinner for the whole family on Sunday. My wife was here just a minute ago but I guess she has gone back into the kitchen.

2. *Paranoid reaction.* In this type of senile psychosis the main characteristic is a gradual formation of delusions, usually of a persecutory, erotic, or grandiose nature, and usually accompanied by related hallucinations. For example, the individual may develop the notion that his relatives have turned against him and are trying to rob and kill him. His suspicions are confirmed by the noxious gases he smells in his room, or by the poison he tastes in his food. Fortunately, such delusions are poorly systematized and rarely lead to overt physical attacks on his alleged persecutors. Grandiose delusions are usually minor in degree and may be obviously wish-fulfilling in nature. For example, Rothschild (1944) cited the case of an 84-year-old unmarried woman who had the delusion that she was married and the mother of two children.

In the early stages, the memory loss and other manifestations of senile degeneration are usually not so pronounced as in other types of senile reactions. Confusion and other disturbances of consciousness are not common, and often the individual remains oriented for time, place, and person.

The following case is typical of paranoid senile reactions.

A woman of 74 had been referred to a hospital after the death of her husband because she became uncooperative and was convinced that her relatives were trying to steal the insurance money her husband had left her. In the hospital she complained that the other patients had joined together against her and were trying to steal her belongings. She frequently refused to eat, on the grounds that the food tasted funny and had probably been poisoned. She grew increasingly irritable and disoriented for time and person. She avidly scanned magazines in the ward reading room but could not remember anything she had looked at. The following conversation reveals some of her symptoms:

Dr.: Do you find that magazine interesting?
Pt.: Why do you care? Can't you see I'm busy?
Dr.: Would you mind telling me something about what you are reading?
Pt.: It's none of your business . . . I am reading about my relatives. They want me to die so that they can steal my money.
Dr.: Do you have any evidence of this?
Pt.: Yes, plenty. They poison my food and they have turned the other women against me. They are all out to get my money. They even stole my sweater.
Dr.: Can you tell me what you had for breakfast?
Pt.: . . . (Pause) I didn't eat breakfast . . . it was poisoned and I refused to eat it. They are all against me.

Senile paranoid reactions are largely determined by the prepsychotic personality of the patient and tend to develop in individuals who have been suspicious and somewhat paranoid. Existing personality tendencies are apparently intensified by the senile degenerative changes and the stresses associated with old age. Approximately 30 percent of psychoses associated with senile brain disease take a paranoid form.

3. *The presbyophrenic type.* This senile psychosis is characterized by fabrication, a jovial, amiable mood, and marked impairment of memory. Such persons may appear superficially alert, and may talk volubly in a rambling, confused manner—filling in gaps in present memory with events that occurred 20 or 30 years before. They usually show a peculiar restlessness or excitability and engage in continual aimless activity; for example, an individual may fold and unfold pieces of cloth as if he were ironing, or he may collect various discarded objects with a great show of importance.

The presbyophrenic type of senile reaction apparently occurs most frequently in individuals who have been lively, aggressive, jovial, and extrovertive in their younger days. Such individuals make up less than 10 percent of all senile psychotics. Traditionally, the presbyophrenic type has had an unfavorable prognosis, since these individuals tend to exhaust themselves very rapidly.

The following conversation illustrates the jovial mood, impaired memory, and fabrication usually seen in these patients.

Dr.: How do you feel today, Mr. ——— ?
Pt.: Just fine, doctor. Just fine. Isn't that funny, doctor, I was just thinking about you. How are you today?
Dr.: Very well, thank you. How is your work progressing?
Pt.: Fine, doctor, just fine. I'm always busy here. I can't stand to sit and do nothing. When I first came here I was kind of worried because I didn't know exactly what was expected of me, but now that I have charge of the hospital laundry, it keeps me jumping.
Dr.: Are you well paid for your work?
Pt.: Oh, yes, doctor. Why, just the other day I got another raise. That shows how important my work is . . . the fifth raise in two years . . . not bad, doctor, eh?
Dr.: How long have you been working in the laundry?
Pt.: Well, let's see, doctor . . . I would say about 10 years . . . I had just graduated from high school . . . made good grades, you know, but jobs were scarce and I had to start at the bottom. I'm a hard worker though and now I am the superintendent. You can't keep a good man down, they always say.

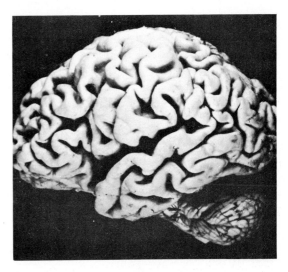

This is the brain of a 79-year-old man who had been hospitalized with a diagnosis of senile dementia; his symptoms included marked confusion, memory defects, especially for recent events, slight aphasia, paranoid ideation, and agitated depression. The cortex shows extensive, diffuse atrophy with a narrowing of the convolutions and a widening of the fissures throughout.

4. *Depressed and agitated types.* Here the individual is severely depressed and agitated and usually suffers from hypochondriacal and nihilistic delusions. Often he expresses morbid ideas about cancer, syphilis, and other diseases. Delusions of poverty are also common, and he may feel that he is headed for the poorhouse, that nobody wants him, and that he is a senseless burden on his children and just generally "in the way." In some cases, the person becomes self-accusatory and develops delusions of great sin. In many respects the symptoms resemble those in involutional reactions, and as in other psychotic depressions the possibility of suicide must be guarded against. This type constitutes less than 10 percent of senile reactions.

5. *Delirious and confused types.* In these cases there is a severe mental clouding in which the individual becomes extremely restless, combative, resistive, and incoherent. He recognizes no one and is completely disoriented for time and place. Such delirious states are often precipitated in old people by acute illness or by traumas, such as a broken leg or hip. Although transient delirious episodes often occur in senile dementia, chronic confusion and delirium are uncommon except in terminal states; they account for less than 10 percent of senile reactions.

With appropriate treatment, many persons with senile dementia show some alleviation of symptoms. In general, however, deterioration continues its downward course over a period of months or years. Eventually the patient becomes oblivious of his surroundings, bedridden, and reduced to a vegetative existence. Resistance to disease is lowered, and death usually results from pneumonia or some other infection.

PSYCHOSIS WITH CEREBRAL ARTERIOSCLEROSIS

Psychoses with cerebral arteriosclerosis are similar to senile psychoses, but there are certain differences in both anatomical and behavioral symptoms. The vascular pathology in cerebral arteriosclerosis involves a "hardening" of the arteries of the brain. Large patches of fatty and calcified material known as *senile plaques* accumulate at particular points in the inside layers of the blood vessels and gradually clog the arterial channel. Circulation becomes sluggish or may be blocked altogether by (1) the accumulation of

deposits; (2) *cerebral thrombosis*, in which a blood clot forms at a site where fatty and calcified materials have accumulated and blocks the vessel; or (3) an *embolism*, in which a fragment of hardened material is sloughed off the inside wall of the vessel and carried to a narrow spot where it blocks the flow of blood. There may then be a rupture in the blood vessel, with hemorrhage and intracranial bleeding.

Either blockage or rupture with hemorrhage may occur in large or small blood vessels anywhere in the brain. Of course, damage to a large vessel will do more harm than damage to a small one. When the narrowing or eventual blockage is gradual and involves small blood vessels, cerebral nutrition is impaired and there are areas of softening as the brain tissue degenerates. Such areas of softening are found in some 90 percent of patients suffering from arteriosclerotic brain disease (Yalom, 1960).

A sudden blocking or rupture in a small vessel is referred to as a *small stroke* and may result in a variety of transient psychological and physical symptoms, ranging from mental confusion and emotional lability to acute indigestion,

THREE CASES OF CEREBROVASCULAR PATHOLOGY

These pictures show cross sections of the brains of persons who suffered from cerebral arteriosclerosis. At the left is a section from the brain of a man who died at 43 after suffering from hypertension and two strokes that had resulted in some paralysis on both sides, emotional lability, and convulsions. The arrows indicate the areas where the cerebrovascular accidents and the specific brain damage occurred.

The center picture is of a section through the frontal lobes of a man who likewise suffered from two strokes; his strokes, however, were separated by an interval of 17 years. The arrow A points to a softening correlated with a recent stroke, which was associated with two months of paralysis on one side; the arrow B points to a cavity resulting from the earlier stroke, which had been associated with aphasia.

Arrows in the picture at right point to scattered emboli in another patient's brain, resulting in many tiny hemorrhages and widespread local damage.

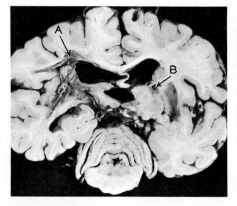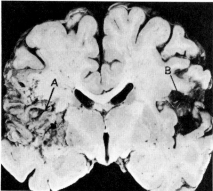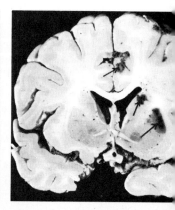

changes in handwriting, and unsteadiness in gait. Frequently, individuals suffer a succession of small strokes resulting in cumulative brain damage and gradual personality change.

When the blockage or rupture involves a large vessel, the individual suffers a major stroke (*cerebrovascular accident*—CVA). Here there is both focal and generalized impairment of brain function, resulting in coma or an acute confusional state. If the individual survives, his acute symptoms may largely clear up, but typically he will suffer some degree of residual brain damage.

It has been estimated that about 3 million persons in this country are handicapped or incapacitated by cerebral arteriosclerosis. The incidence and severity of psychopathology in these cases is not known. Although cerebral arteriosclerosis may occur in young adulthood or middle age, it usually has its onset in individuals after age 55. The average age of first admission approximates 74 for both sexes, with slightly more male than female first admissions. Although cerebral arteriosclerosis appears to be most common among persons on lower socioeconomic levels, it occurs in all economic groups.

Clinical picture. In about half the cases of psychosis with cerebral arteriosclerosis, symptoms appear suddenly (Yalom, 1960). Here individuals are usually admitted to a medical facility in an acute confusional state resulting from a cerebrovascular accident. Such persons show marked clouding of consciousness, disorientation for time, place, and person, incoherence, and often hemiplegia (paralysis of one side of the body). Rothschild (1956) reported such paralysis in about 50 percent of a large series of cases having an acute onset. Convulsive seizures are also relatively common and may precede the acute attack, occur at the same time, or appear at a later point in the illness. In severe cases the patient may die without a clearing of his confusional state.

Acute confusional states may last for days, weeks, or even months, with an eventual remission of the acute symptoms. In these cases, there may be varying degrees of residual brain damage and impairment in physical and mental functions. Often the individual is able to compensate for his brain damage, particularly with the help of special rehabilitative measures designed to alleviate physical handicaps and clear up possible aphasic conditions. Sometimes, however, there is a progressive loss of mental efficiency accompanied by other psychological symptoms, such as emotional lability, irritability, and hypochondriacal concern over bodily functions. In many cases, there appears to be an accentuation—following cerebrovascular accidents—of preexisting personality traits of a maladaptive nature (Soffer, 1968).

When the onset of the disorder is gradual, early symptoms may include complaints of weakness, fatigue, dizziness, headache, depression, memory defect, periods of confusion, and lowered efficiency in work. Often there is a slowing up of activity and a loss of zest in living. There may be a considerable delay between the appearance of such symptoms and the hospitalization of the individual.

By the time of hospitalization the clinical picture usually is similar to that in senile dementia. The memory defect has now increased, although it may be somewhat uneven—for example, it may be more severe when the patient is tired or under emotional stress. Emotional lability becomes pronounced and he may be easily moved to tears or highly irritable, with a tendency to "flare up" at the slightest provocation. Usually the flare-up is brief and ends with tears and repentance. Increased irritability may be accompanied by suspiciousness and poorly organized delusions of persecution. By this time, there is also a more pronounced impairment of concentration and general intellectual functioning. Interest in the outside world and in others is markedly reduced, as are the individual's initiative and work capacity. Judgment is impaired and in some instances there is a lowering of moral controls, with a tendency to sexual offenses involving children. Frequently, there are feelings of depression associated with some insight into failing physical and mental powers. As in cases with an acute onset, there may be marked fluctuations in the clinical picture, but the general course of the disease is in the direction of increasing deterioration and death.

Comparison with the clinical picture in senile dementia. The clinical aspects of senile dementia and psychosis with cerebral arteriosclerosis are so much alike that a differential diagnosis is frequently very difficult to make. In some cases, there is a mixture of the two disorders—a senile reaction may be superimposed on an arteriosclerotic condition or vice versa. However, mixed reactions are not nearly so common as might be expected, and usually one condition or the other predominates.

Among the clinically distinguishing features of these two disorders are: (1) senile dementia is usually gradual and progressive and lasts longer, while psychosis with cerebral arteriosclerosis is more apt to be brought on by a cerebrovascular accident and to run a brief and stormy course ending in death; (2) in senile dementia there is usually more pronounced intellectual impairment, and paranoid patterns are more common; (3) symptoms common in the arteriosclerotic group but less often seen in senile dementia are headaches, dizziness, convulsive seizures, depression, and strong emotional outbursts; and finally (4) the symptoms in cerebral arteriosclerotic reactions typically show more pronounced fluctuations. But although these differences are observable in early and intermediate states, with progressive intellectual deterioration all patients become very much alike.

DYNAMICS IN OLD-AGE PSYCHOSES

Early investigators seized on brain damage as the only important factor in the causation of both senile dementia and psychosis with cerebral arteriosclerosis. But in recent years, with the increased interest and attention devoted to mental disorders of old age, those early beliefs have undergone considerable revision.

Although cerebral damage alone, when sufficiently extensive, may produce marked mental symptoms, it has become evident that in most cases the organic changes are only one set of interactive factors. In the total clinical picture the prior personality organization of the individual and the stresses in his life situation are also of key importance. And since specific brain pathology, personality makeup, and stress factors vary from person to person, we find a somewhat different etiological pattern in each case.

The interplay of biological and psychosocial factors. When any psychotic disorder appears, there is always a search for possible hereditary and constitutional predisposing factors. A number of early studies showed a high incidence of senile and arteriosclerotic brain disease in the family backgrounds of elderly psychotics (Mayer-Gross, 1944; Post, 1944). However, from a comprehensive review of available findings—including his own extensive study on aging in twins—Kallmann (1961) concluded that it is unrealistic to search for a dominant genetic factor as the primary cause of the psychoses of old age. He contended that causal patterns include a long-standing deficit in adjustive plasticity, complicated by vascular and metabolic changes in the brain. This view, however, would not deny the influence of genetic factors on the rapidity of aging or exclude them from the causal pattern.

The effects of senile and arteriosclerotic degenerative changes on brain metabolism have been strongly emphasized in the etiological pattern. In cases involving cerebrovascular accidents, gross disturbances in circulatory and metabolic processes are apparent, and we have noted the confusional states and other symptoms that may result. However, in mental disorders having a gradual onset, much remains to be learned about the role of metabolic factors. Lowered oxygen consumption, vitamin deficiencies, endocrine malfunction, and other metabolic factors are being investigated, but as yet there are no definitive findings.

Nor does the extent of brain pathology ordinarily account for the psychotic disorders of old age, a point dramatically demonstrated by Gal (1959), who did a postmortem study of 104 patients ranging in age from 65 to 94 and found a lack of correlation between brain damage and behavior. Extensive cerebral damage was found in some patients who had manifested only mild mental symptoms, while minimal cerebral damage was found in others who had shown severe psychopathology. In general, it appears that undesirable personality traits—such as rigidity, compulsiveness, narrowness of interests, suspiciousness, social inadequacy, and poor adaptability to change—increase vulnerability to old-age psychoses more than does cerebral damage.

Other interactive factors in old-age psychoses are the many special stresses characteristic of old age, such as retirement, lowered income, physical impairment and fear of invalidism, and realization of impending death. The later years are often made more difficult by the death of one's mate, particularly for women, who tend to outlive their spouses by about 7 years.

The close link between physical and mental disorders in the aged was shown in the study by Bowman and Engle (1960). Among 534 persons aged 60 and over who were admitted for the first time to the psychiatric ward of a general hospital in San Francisco, it was found that 70 percent required daily care for physical disability, and that in more than 40 percent of the cases acute physical disorders had precipitated serious mental symptoms. It is unlikely that conditions have changed markedly, even though the study was made more than a decade ago.

With progressive cerebral impairment, of course, the role of psychosocial factors recedes as a determinant of behavior and the residual brain capacity shapes the response in greater measure. This point is well brought out by Ullman and Gruen in summarizing their findings with 84 patients who had suffered strokes and had showed mild, moderate, or severe degrees of cerebral deficit.

"Patients who have experienced mild strokes with little or no residual mental impairment react to the stress in their own idiosyncratic fashion. Some will integrate the experience successfully; others will become enmeshed in psychopathological maneuvers of varying severity. In patients with moderate or severe brain damage, the situation is quite different. Here the unique features of the stroke are highlighted, the chief of these being that the very organ governing the adaptation to stress is itself impaired. The resulting clinical picture has to be evaluated now, not only in terms of what the experience means to the patient, but also in terms of the capacity the patient has for evaluating the situation." (1961, p. 1009)

General sociocultural factors. The significance of sociocultural factors in senile and arteriosclerotic brain disorders is a matter of considerable speculation. In one interesting study, Carothers (1947) found a high rate of senile psychoses among natives in Kenya, Africa, but no psychoses associated with cerebral arteriosclerosis. On the other hand, other cross-cultural studies have shown varying rates of senile and arteriosclerotic brain disorders.

In our own society, the urban rate of first admissions to mental hospitals for both senile dementia and psychosis with cerebral arterio-sclerosis is approximately twice as high as the rural rate. But we do not know how much this indicates that urban living, with its faster pace, noise, crowds, and other stresses, is more conducive to the development of these disorders—and how much it indicates that more persons are cared for at home in rural areas. The picture is also complicated by the fact that in rural areas the older person enjoys higher social status and is generally able to work productively for a longer period.

In our urban industrial society the problems of old age have caught us largely unprepared. We have not provided ample conditions for utilizing the experience and wisdom of our older people; we have not even provided conditions necessary for them to live in reasonably respected and useful positions. (Group for the Advancement of Psychiatry, 1970). In fact, the term "role obsolescence" has been used to refer to society's attitude toward the older person's having outlived his usefulness. Thus, the attitude of modern urban society may contribute to the incidence of old-age psychoses.

Often the experience of an older person seems to have little relevance to the problems of younger generations, and he is deprived of active participation and decision making in both occupational and family settings. Not infrequently children assume a patronizing and protective attitude toward the aging parent, and in other ways tend to deprive him of dignity, responsibility, and a feeling of importance. Many parents are treated as unwanted burdens, and their children may secretly wish that they would die to relieve them of financial and other responsibilities. In a study of older people in France, De Beauvoir (1970) has pointed out that when the French go away for vacations, they sometimes deposit their aged parents in rest homes. Then, on their return home, they "forget" to pick them up, abandoning them like dogs in a kennel. In our own youth-oriented culture with its nuclear family, there is usually little place for the grandparents unless they are self-sufficient; and undoubtedly in the United States, too, many older people are "deposited" in rest or nursing homes to die, even though they may be in relatively good health. The effects of being cast aside simply for "being old" are likely to be particularly devastating for those suffering from prior cerebral impairment.

ADJUSTING TO THE STRESSES OF AGING

Reactions to aging and reaching the status of "senior citizen" are—as indicated by these pictures of a lonely, forgotten woman and a happy, socially active one—quite different in individual cases. How people react depends heavily on their personality makeup and on the challenges and frustrations of their life situations. A sense of status, self-identity, and meaning—all-important in every life period—are crucial in old age when they are perhaps most threatened.

Certain special stresses typically confronting the aged include: (1) retirement and reduced income, which often creates a feeling that one's usefulness is essentially over and activities are restricted; (2) reduction in physical attractiveness, which is particularly stressful for persons whose feelings of femininity or masculinity depend on their attractiveness to the opposite sex; (3) failing health and invalidism, now unalleviated by hope of full recovery; (4) isolation and loneliness, which is usually caused by the loss of contemporaries and loved ones, plus the neglect or indifference of others; and (5) the problem of meaning and death, at its most poignant for those who look back on their lives and say, "It all adds up to nothing." (Birren, 1970; Buhler, 1968)

A hint at the feeling of being sidelined in old age is conveyed in a song by the Beatles (1966):

When I get older, losing my hair, many years from now,
Will you still be sending me a Valentine,
Birthday greetings, bottle of wine?
If I've been out till quarter to three, would you lock the door?
Will you still need me, will you still feed me—
When I'm 64?

TREATMENT AND OUTCOMES

Whether or not to hospitalize the aged person who is mentally disordered is often a problem. Individuals manifesting such symptoms as confusion, violent and noisy behavior, depression, antisocial behavior, and disorientation for time, place, and person, usually require institutionalization. However, many investigators regard hospitalization as a last resource, feeling that the sudden change in environment and manner of living is highly stressful for the older person and may lead to a feeling of complete hopelessness (Lipscomb, 1971; Markson et al., 1971). Too frequently, the decision to hospitalize is based primarily on the fact that no other community facilities are available to assist the individual.

Effective treatment of the mental disorders of later life requires a comprehensive use of medical, psychological, and sociological procedures, as indicated by the needs of the individual.

Medical treatment ranges from surgical and specialized procedures to dietary and related measures—all designed to improve the physical health and psychological well-being of the elderly person. Antipsychotic and minor tranquilizing drugs have proven of marked value in controlling psychotic symptoms and emotional disturbances, but they are not effective in ameliorating the mental deterioration found in advanced cases of senile and arteriosclerotic brain disorders. One promising innovation is the exposure of patients to 100-percent oxygen at intervals during the day (Jacobs et al., 1969; Jacobs, Small & Winters, 1970). This approach appears to be particularly effective in reducing loss in memory efficiency—particularly for immediate events—in older persons.

There have been favorable reports on the use of both individual and group psychotherapy in treating mental disorders associated with old age, and additional research is needed for delineating the most effective psychological treatment procedures for older persons—particularly senile individuals and those with arteriosclerotic brain disorders. On hospital wards, "token economies"—in which desired behavior is rewarded by tokens that the patient can exchange for things he wants—have proven helpful and are regarded as promising (Atthowe & Krasner, 1968). A key aspect of such reinforcement procedures is that they parallel the demands of outside society and help counteract tendencies toward progressive institutional dependence and chronicity (Shean, 1971).

Sociotherapy with older patients is directed toward creating an environment in which the person can function successfully. In a hospital setting or nursing home this includes the provision of comfortable surroundings, together with stimulating activities that encourage the patient to utilize his capacities. Sociotherapy also includes working with the family in an attempt to help them understand the nature of the patient's disorder, to be supportive, and to show that they care. Where the patient is convalescing at home, follow-up visits by the social worker may be of great value in helping both the patient and his family to adjust.

Even seemingly minor innovations in treatment have shown promising results. In an interesting study, for example, Volpe and Kastenbaum (1967) worked with a group of older men who were so physically and psychologically incapacitated that they required around-the-clock nursing care. These men could perform no services for themselves, were agitated and incontinent, and had a record of striking at each other and tearing off their clothes. Some simple innovations were provided on the ward—games, cards, a record player, and a decorated bulletin board; the men were dressed in white shirts and ties; and at 2 P.M. each day they were served beer in 12-ounce bottles with crackers and cheese. Within a month there was a marked change in the group's behavior. The amount of medication needed dropped sharply, incontinent and agitated behavior markedly decreased, and social responsivity—as indicated by requests for and participation in parties and dances—markedly increased. The marked improvement of these men was attributed to their being treated with dignity as responsible individuals, and to the consequent *"expectancies of mutual gratification on the part of patients and staff members."* In essence, the expectations and demand characteristics of the ward had been changed from those of a medical to a social situation; the men were cared for in much the same way as in the era of moral treatment (Chapter 2).

Such programs show that the expectation and

reinforcement of "normal" social behaviors can bring about marked behavioral changes even in a relatively short time. Kahana and Kahana (1970) found that even such a simple measure as moving aged people from segregated to desegregated wards appeared to be beneficial for both young and old. The younger ones often tried to help the elderly, which provided them with a sense of purpose; while their active interest, in turn, increased the elderly individuals' sense of importance. Thus, the prognosis in the psychoses of old age is far from hopeless. Even without complete recovery many patients can return to their homes, and many others can remain in their homes while being treated in community clinics (Zimberg, 1969).

Although the outcome in cases of senile and arteriosclerotic brain disorders has traditionally been considered unfavorable, since the cerebral damage and psychopathology seemed irreversible once the psychosis was under way, recent evidence indicates that recovery or improvement is possible in about half of the cases when appropriate treatment is provided. For example, in one study, half of the patients in a group given intensive early treatment recovered sufficiently to leave the mental hospital, as compared with less than 10 percent of a control group given the usual geriatric treatment (Sklar & O'Neill, 1961). Similarly, Blau (1970) has pointed out that at the Boston State Hospital, which has an active treatment program for elderly patients and fosters aftercare in the community, almost half of the patients over 60 years of age are discharged within 6 months of their admission.

Interestingly enough, both the greatest number of deaths and the greatest number of improvements among hospitalized elderly psychotics occur during the first year after admission (Goldfarb, 1969). For patients who require continued care in the hospital, about 75 percent die within the first 5 years. In general, the following are considered favorable indicators with respect to outcome: (1) a well-integrated prepsychotic personality; (2) mild, rather than severe, cerebral pathology; (3) absence of such conditions as severe overweight, hypertension, and alcoholism; (4) average or above-average intelligence, education, and technical competence; and (5) a favorable life situation to which to return.

Increasingly aware of the problems confronting senior citizens, federal, state, and local groups are focusing on all aspects of growing old. Scientists in many areas of the biological and social sciences are investigating the pathological and the normal aspects of aging, and are exploring —in their respective fields—ways to minimize the aging process. Community centers and clinics for assisting older people with retirement and other problems are increasing. Specially designed housing developments for the elderly also are being established in many areas, although it is still too early to assess the impact such facilities will have on mental illness.

As Birren (1970) has pointed out, much more must be done in the way of setting up a system of flexible social supports for the aged in the community. At the present time, availability of psychological and medical assistance at community clinics is so limited that most elderly individuals who are admitted to mental hospitals are already in advanced stages of deterioration—not having received even a minimum of relevant treatment in the community.

But although society can do much to improve the status of the older person, the individual also needs to prepare himself for the problems typical of old age. He needs to face realistically the fact that he is getting older, and plan ahead for an active and useful life in his later years—a life that will take full advantage of the opportunities afforded to him. Of course, many of the adjustments of old age are highly specific to the situation of the given individual and hence cannot be fully anticipated, but at any age it is important to maintain mental flexibility and adaptability, establish new and satisfying interpersonal relationships, and continue to grow and fulfill one's potential. As Simmons (1960) has put it:

"The secret of success for anyone facing a long life . . . is to find for himself a suitable place in his society in which to age with grace and usefulness, and to participate tactfully and fully up to the very end if at all possible." (p. 63)

In short, old age does pose special problems, but it is by no means incompatible with meaning and self-fulfillment.

In this chapter we have examined acute and chronic disorders associated with known pathology of the brain or nervous system. Such disorders have a great variety of causes—some of them being syphilitic infection, brain tumors, head injuries, toxic poisoning, metabolic disturbances, and senile brain deterioration—and they may involve mild, moderate, or severe impairment of psychological functioning. In general, brain disorders typically involve such symptoms as impairment of orientation for time, place, and person; emotional shallowness and lability; and impairment of learning, comprehension, and judgment. There are significant differences in the clinical picture from one type of disorder to another, however, and also from one individual to another.

Three interrelated factors are of key importance in determining both the severity of symptoms and the likelihood of successful treatment: (1) the nature and extent of the organic pathology; (2) the personality and stress tolerance of the individual; and (3) his life situation—including the situation to which he returns if he has been hospitalized. As we have observed, the second and third factors are often as important as the first, except in cases of very severe brain damage or deterioration.

Mental Retardation

16

CLASSIFICATION AND CAUSES OF MENTAL RETARDATION

TYPES OF MENTAL RETARDATION ASSOCIATED WITH PHYSIOLOGICAL CAUSES

TREATMENT, OUTCOMES, AND PREVENTION

The American Psychiatric Association (1968) has defined *mental retardation* as "subnormal general intellectual functioning which originates during the developmental period and is associated with impairment of either learning and social adjustment or maturation, or both." (p. 14) The incidence of mental retardation in the United States is currently estimated to be about 6.5 million persons, or roughly 3 percent of the population (Albee, 1968; Isaacson, 1970; Wilkins, 1966). Figures vary, however, depending on exactly what criteria are used in classifying individuals as "mentally retarded." The most widely used measure of mental retardation is IQ, and statistics on incidence are generally based on a cutoff point of around IQ 70.[1] If a higher cutoff point is used, the number of individuals identified as mentally retarded will, of course, increase accordingly. Thus among men examined for military service, about 4.5 percent are rejected for mental retardation.

Epidemiological studies show that the incidence of mental retardation seems to increase sharply at age 5, with the number of cases peaking at age 15 and dropping off sharply thereafter (Gruenberg, 1966; Lemkau & Imre, 1968–1969; Payne, 1971; Richardson, 1969). The lower incidence of mental retardation at later ages may be partially explained by the fact that severe retardation is usually accompanied by a low life expectancy. For the most part, however, the changes in incidence with age appear to reflect changes in life demands. During early childhood, individuals with only a mild degree of intellectual impairment—who constitute the vast majority of mental retardates—are not obviously different from other children. They may be some-

[1]Most states have laws providing that individuals evidencing socially incompetent or disapproved behavior and with IQ's below 70 can be classified as mentally retarded and be committed to institutions.

what slow in learning to talk and in other aspects of development, but for the most part they appear to be relatively normal. Their subaverage intellectual functioning becomes apparent only when difficulties with schoolwork lead to a diagnostic evaluation. When adequate facilities are available for their education, children in this group are usually placed in special classes where they typically can master simple skills and achieve a satisfactory level of socially adaptive behavior. Following the school years, they usually make an acceptable adjustment in the community and thus lose the identity of mental retardates.

CLASSIFICATION AND CAUSES OF MENTAL RETARDATION

There has been growing criticism of the practice of identifying individuals as mentally retarded on the basis of IQ alone. For one thing, it is extremely difficult in many cases to make an accurate assessment of intellectual level. This is particularly true with brain-damaged children, who often possess genuine ability but have difficulty in making appropriate responses because of spasticity, athetosis, defective hearing or vision, or other impairments. Standardized intelligence tests are also likely to underestimate the ability of children who have been culturally deprived.

In any case, IQ is a measure of particular sets of intellectual abilities that are not always closely related to the kinds of adaptive behavior required for dealing with the problems of everyday life. Thus as Dybwad (1968) and others have pointed out, the criterion of low measured intelligence in defining mental retardation should be implemented by a second broad criterion, namely, the individual's ability to adapt to the demands of his life situation. Given the right kind of training, many people with IQ's well below 70 are able to support themselves and to get along creditably in the community; and certainly no useful purpose can be served by labeling such individuals as mental retardates. In short, *mental retardation*—like *insanity*—is essentially a legal term: it refers to a lack of intellectual ability sufficient to take care of oneself and to meet social demands and expectations.

DEGREES OF MENTAL RETARDATION

The classification system of the APA (1968) identifies five degrees of mental retardation, ranging from "borderline" retardation to "profound" retardation. Although this classification system is based primarily on the criterion of IQ level, it recognizes that IQ alone does not provide an adequate measure of an individual's adaptive behavioral capacity. As the APA manual states, in making a diagnosis of mental retardation or in evaluating its severity, "judgment should also be based on an evaluation of the [individual's] developmental history and present functioning, including academic and vocational achievement, motor skills, and social and emotional maturity." (p. 14)

1. *Borderline mental retardation (IQ 68–83)*. Individuals in this category are not usually included in incidence figures on mental retardation. However, they are slower in learning than most persons of normal intelligence, and also are more limited in ability to understand complex ideas and draw generalizations from what they have learned. Impairment usually involves verbal learning; there is little or no impairment of motor performance. In general, the deficiency is greater in rate of learning and ability to learn than in retaining what they have learned. In other respects, these individuals appear essentially normal. Most of them make adequate adjustments in the community, although they may need more

DIFFICULTIES AMONG MENTAL RETARDATES IN LEARNING LANGUAGE SKILLS

The basic learning processes of most mental retardates—aside from a minority with serious neurological defects—are not essentially different from those of normal children. However, retardates do learn at different rates than normal children and are less capable of mastering abstractions and complex concepts. This latter difficulty is especially apparent in the learning of language skills, in which the degree of abstraction is greater than in other kinds of learning. And in the essential process of sorting out relevant aspects of experience and applying a label to them—which the learning of language entails—a number of other skills are involved which enter into all kinds of learning. For example, the person obviously must be able to focus his attention appropriately, to categorize stimuli in his environment, to verbalize correctly, and to see the relationship between given sounds and categories of experience. Problems the retardate typically encounters in this process are associated with the following factors:

1. **Difficulty in focusing attention.** A number of studies have shown that a retardate's poor learning is often due to the fact that his attention is focused on irrelevant aspects of learning situations. Once he knows what stimulus dimensions are important—for example, attending to form when the shape of the letters is important in learning the alphabet—he may quickly master appropriate discrimination skills and show marked improvement in performance and learning.

2. **Deficiency in past learning.** Most formal learning requires prior learning. For example, a child on entering school will fall farther and farther behind if he has not previously learned basic verbal, conceptual, and problem-solving skills. Thus a number of programs have been established to help disadvantaged children of preschool age develop basic skills requisite for learning in school.

3. **Expectancy of failure—a self-fulfilling prophecy.** Because of having experienced more failure in learning attempts than other children, the mentally retarded child tends to begin tasks with a greater expectancy of failure and to engage in avoidance behavior as well. Often the child feels that forces beyond his control determine the outcome of his actions. Thus, if he should succeed in a task, he may not perceive his success as due to his own efforts or ability. He becomes passive, loses his initiative, and begins to rely too much on others. To counteract this tendency, learning experiences must be programmed into manageable components.

These learning difficulties are not exclusive to retardates, but they are common among them and suggest the most suitable paths to be followed in their education. That is, special education classes should be directed at helping retardates discriminate relevant from irrelevant stimuli in learning and problem-solving situations; it should associate new learning with the retardates' present information, needs, and life situations; and it should structure learning tasks in such a sequence that they can be readily mastered by the retardates. Such measures, of course, are useful in all educational settings, but are particularly important in training the mentally retarded.

Based on Bijou (1966), Hagen and Huntsman (1971), Karnes et al. (1970), MacMillan and Keogh (1971), and Ruch and Zimbardo (1971).

---

assistance from helping agencies than persons with higher levels of intelligence.

2. *Mild mental retardation (IQ 52–67).* If the borderline category is excluded, this group comprises the far largest number of those labeled mentally retarded (see chart, page 564). Their intellectual levels as adults are comparable to that of the average 8- to 11-year-old child. Their social adjustment often approximates that of the adolescent, although they tend to lack the normal adolescent's imagination, inventiveness, and judgment. Ordinarily they do not show signs of brain pathology or other physical anomalies. Often they require some measure of supervision due to limited ability to foresee the consequences of their actions. With early diagnosis, parental assistance, and special educational programs, the majority can adjust socially, master simple academic and occupational skills, and become self-supporting citizens.

3. *Moderate mental retardation (IQ 36–51).* In adult life, individuals classified as moderately retarded attain intellectual levels similar to that of the average 4- to 7-year-old child. While some of the brighter ones can be taught to read and write a little, and some manage to achieve a fair command of spoken language, the rate of learning is relatively slow among members of this group, and the level of conceptualizing extremely limited. Physically, they usually appear clumsy and ungainly, and they suffer from bodily deformities and poor motor coordination. A distinct minority is hostile and aggressive, but typically they present an affable and somewhat vacuous personality picture.

In general, with early diagnosis, parental help,

RELATIVE INCIDENCE OF MENTAL RETARDATION IN FOUR CATEGORIES
(excluding borderline cases)

Degree of Retardation	Approximate Number of Cases	Approximate Percent of Incidence
Mild	6,000,000	89
Moderate	380,000	6
Severe	227,000	3.5
Profound	68,000	1

and adequate opportunities for training, most of the moderately retarded can achieve partial independence in daily self-care, acceptable behavior, and economic usefulness in a family or other sheltered environment. Whether or not they require institutionalization usually depends on their general level of adaptive behavior and the nature of their home situation.

4. *Severe mental retardation (IQ 20–35).* This group comprises persons among whom motor and speech development are severely retarded, and sensory defects and motor handicaps are common. These individuals can develop limited levels of personal hygiene and self-help skills, which somewhat lessen their dependence, but all their lives they will be dependent on others for care. However, many profit to some extent from training and can perform simple occupational tasks under supervision.

5. *Profound mental retardation (IQ under 20).* Most of the mental retardates in this category are severely deficient in adaptive behavior and unable to master any but the simplest tasks. Useful speech, if it develops at all, is on a rudimentary level. Severe physical deformities, central nervous system pathology, and retarded growth are typical, and convulsive seizures, mutism, deafness, and other physical anomalies are common. These retardates must remain in custodial care all their lives. However, health and resistance to disease is lowered, and a short life expectancy is typical.

Moderate, severe, and profound cases of mental retardation usually are diagnosed in infancy because of physical malformations, grossly de-

layed habit training, and other obvious symptoms of abnormality. But although these individuals show a marked impairment of overall intellectual functioning, they may have considerably more ability in some areas than in others. Indeed, in very occasional cases—often referred to as involving "idiot savants"—seriously retarded persons may show a high level of skill in some specific aspect of behavior that does not depend on abstract reasoning. Thus a retardate may be able to remember the serial number on every dollar bill he is shown or has ever seen, or he may be able to tell the day of the week of a given date in any year, without resorting to paper and pencil. In other exceptional cases, a retardate may show considerable talent in art or music.[1] It may be emphasized, however, that such unusual abilities among mental retardates are rare.

In concluding this brief discussion of degrees of mental retardation, it should be noted that a prognosis of potential disability can, to some extent at least, be a self-fulfilling prophecy. All too often an assessment that shows severe limitations in ability is taken as implying that the abilities cannot be changed, and rehabilitative efforts are minimal, which tends to ensure the accuracy of the prognosis.

PHYSIOLOGICAL AND PSYCHOSOCIAL CAUSES OF MENTAL RETARDATION

In the present section we shall consider six categories of biological and psychosocial conditions that may lead to mental retardation, noting some of the possible interrelations between them. At one time it was believed that mental retardation was always a matter of heredity. Then, with the discovery that certain types of mental retardation were associated with underlying brain pathology, various other patterns of biological causation were identified. And in recent years, there has been a growing awareness that adverse

---

[1]Viscott (1970) has provided a detailed case study of "a musical idiot savant."

These pictures illustrate the extent to which even a severely mentally retarded child can be taught dancing and other forms of self-expression.

environmental conditions may also be primary or secondary etiological agents in many cases of mental retardation.

1. *Genetic-chromosomal factors.* Mental retardation tends to run in families. This is particularly true of mild retardation, which presumably is heavily influenced by the many genetic factors responsible for variations in intelligence. It may be noted, however, that poverty and sociocultural deprivation also tend to run in families—and that with early and continued exposure to such conditions, even the inheritance of above-average intellectual potential may not prevent subaverage intellectual functioning.

Genetic factors play a much clearer role in the etiology of such relatively rare types of mental retardation as PKU (page 574) and Down's syndrome (page 569). Here, specific genetic defects are responsible for metabolic alterations that adversely affect development of the brain. PKU is transmitted via a recessive gene and results in the lack of an enzyme needed to break down phenylalanine, an amino acid found in protein foods. And as noted in Chapter 6, Down's

syndrome (mongolism) is associated with an abnormal number of chromosomes. Genetic defects leading to metabolic alterations may, of course, involve many other developmental anomalies besides mental retardation. In general, mental retardation associated with genetic-chromosomal defects is moderate to severe in degree.

2. *Trauma or physical agent.* Isaacson (1970) has estimated that 1 baby in 1000 suffers brain damage that will prevent his reaching the intelligence level of a 12-year-old. Although normally the fetus is well protected by its fluid-filled bag, and its skull appears designed to resist delivery stresses, accidents do happen during delivery, as well as after birth. Difficulties in labor due to malposition of the fetus or other complications may damage the infant's brain at birth. Bleeding within the brain is probably the most common result of such birth trauma. *Anoxia* stemming from delayed breathing of the newborn infant or other causes is another type of birth trauma which may damage the brain. Anoxia may also occur after birth as a result of cardiac arrest associated with operations, heart attacks, or near drownings.

Mental retardation is an age-old problem which has claimed victims in every era and culture. This young victim, who sat for a portrait by Velázquez, resided in seventeenth-century Spain. He is identified as "El Niño de Vallecas."

Early severe postnatal head injuries, too, may occasionally result in mental retardation.

3. *Infections and toxic agents.* Mental retardation may be associated with a wide range of conditions due to infection. The fetus of a mother with certain virus diseases, such as German measles, may suffer brain damage; apparently, damage is greatest when the viral infection occurs during the first 8 weeks of pregnancy. The fetus of a mother with syphilis may suffer infection and varying degrees of brain damage. And, as in the case of epidemic encephalitis, brain damage may also result from infections occurring after birth.

A number of toxic agents, such as carbon monoxide and lead, also may cause brain damage during fetal development or after birth. In some instances, immunological agents, such as antitetanus serum or typhoid vaccine, may lead to brain damage. Similarly, certain drugs taken by the mother during pregnancy may sometimes lead

to congenital malformations, or an overdose of drugs administered to the infant may lead to toxicity and brain damage. In rare cases, brain damage results from incompatibility in blood types between mother and fetus—Rh and ABO incompatibility. Fortunately, early diagnosis and blood transfusions can now minimize the effects of this disorder.

4. *Ionizing radiation.* In the past decade a great deal of scientific attention has been focused on the damaging effects of radiation on the sex cells and other bodily cells and tissues. On the basis of figures published by the United States Federal Radiation Council (1962), it was estimated that as a result of weapons testing through 1962 there may ultimately be over 16 million cases of gross physical or mental defects from fallout and carbon-14 (Pauling, 1962). These figures apply to the world population. Ionizing radiation may act on the fertilized ovum directly or may produce gene mutations in the sex cells of either or both parents—which, in turn, may lead to defective offspring.

Recent reports appear more optimistic, but the long-range effects of nuclear testing in the atmosphere are not yet known. As we noted in Chapter 6, however, a higher than normal incidence of mental retardation—associated with small head circumference—has been reported among the children of survivors of Hiroshima and Nagasaki (Miller, 1970). The survivors, of course, were exposed to radiation from atom bombs dropped on those cities.

5. *Prematurity.* In follow-up studies of children born prematurely, weighing less than 1500 grams at birth, a high incidence of neurological disorders, including mental retardation, have been revealed (Kennedy, 1963; Knobloch, 1956; Rothchild, 1967). In fact, very small premature babies are 10 times more likely to be mentally retarded than normal infants.

6. *Malnutrition and other biological factors.* Experiments with lower animals, as well as observations of humans, have shown that deficiencies in certain vitamins, amino acids, and proteins during early development can result in irreversible physical and mental damage. Protein deficiencies in the mother's diet, as well as in the baby's diet after birth, have been pinpointed as particularly potent causes of lowered intelligence (Bladeslee, 1967; Dobbing, 1967).

A limited number of cases of mental retardation are also associated with other biological agents, such as brain tumors which either damage the brain tissue directly or lead to increased cranial pressure and concomitant brain damage. In some instances of mental retardation—particularly of the severe and profound types—the causes are uncertain or unknown, although extensive brain pathology is evident.

7. *Psychosocial (environmental) deprivation.* In the etiology of mild mental retardation, increasing emphasis is being placed on sociocultural factors rather than genetic or biological causes *per se*. It has been shown that 10 to 30 percent of school-age children in some disadvantaged areas are mentally retarded, as contrasted with only 1 or 2 percent in more prosperous neighborhoods. And of the estimated 6.5

THE "WILD BOY OF AVEYRON"

In 1800, long before the development of psychotherapy, Jean-Marc Itard attempted to inculcate normal human abilities in a "wild boy" who had been captured by peasants in the forest of Aveyron, France. The boy, who appeared to be between 10 and 12 years old, had been exhibited in a cage for about a year by his captors when Itard rescued him. From an examination of the scars on the boy's body, as well an observation of his personal habits, Itard concluded that he had been abandoned at the age of about 2 or 3.

At first Victor (as Itard named the boy) seemed more animal than human. He was oblivious to other human beings, could not talk, and howled and ate off the ground on all fours like an animal. He evidenced unusual sensory reactions; for example, he did not react if a pistol were fired next to his ear, but he could hear the cracking of a nut or the crackling of underbrush at a great distance. No adverse reaction seemed to result from his going unclothed even in freezing weather. Furthermore, he could reach into boiling water for a potato or pull hot chestnuts out of the fire with no apparent pain—nor did scar tissue develop. In fact, Victor had a fine velvety skin, despite his years of exposure.

Victor exhibited animal-like behavior in many ways. He had an obstinate habit of smelling any object that was given to him—even objects we consider void of smell. He knew nothing of love and perceived other human beings only as obstacles—in other words, like the wild animals he had known in the forest. He was typically indifferent and uncomplaining but, very occasionally, he showed a kind of frantic rage and became dangerous to those around him. He would be startled upon hearing forest sounds, and would evidence pleasure and interest in newly fallen snow, a still pond, and the sight of the moon. If he had any sense of self-identity, it was apparently more that of an animal than a human.

Philippe Pinel, Itard's teacher, diagnosed Victor's condition as congenital idiocy—concluding that the boy was incapable of profiting from training. But Itard, although only 25 years old and inexperienced in comparison with Pinel, disagreed; in his view, Victor's savage behavior was the result of early and lengthy isolation from other humans. He believed that human contact and intensive training would enable the boy to become a normal person, and, ignoring Pinel's advice, he began his now-famous attempt to civilize "the wild boy of Aveyron."

No procedures had yet been formulated which Itard could use in treating Victor; thus he developed a program based on principles which included the following: (1) without human contact a human infant—unlike a lower animal—cannot develop normally; (2) the instinct to imitate is the learning force by which our senses are educated, and this instinct is strongest in early childhood and decreases with age; and (3) in all human beings, from the most isolated savage to the most educated individual, a constant relationship exists between needs and ideas—the greater the needs, the greater the development of mental capacities to meet them.

In attempting to train Victor, Itard developed methods that have had considerable impact on the subsequent treatment of children with serious learning disabilities. Instructional materials were provided to broaden Victor's discrimination skills in touch, smell, and other sensory modalities, appropriate to his environment; language training was begun through the association of words with the objects Victor wanted; and modeling and imitation were used to reinforce Victor's learning of desired social behaviors.

Initial results were indeed promising. Victor learned to speak a number of words and could write in chalk to express his wants. He also developed affectionate feelings toward his governess, looking for her in her absence and expressing pleasure on her return.

In June 1801, Itard reported to the Academy of Science in Paris of the rapid progress in the first 9 months of training. But in November 1806, he could only report again on Victor's original savage state and his early rapid progress; for despite significant advances in several areas, Victor had not been made "normal" in the sense of becoming a self-directing and socially adjusted person. Being brought into the proximity of girls, for example, only upset the boy, leaving him restless and depressed, and Itard had to abandon his hope for a normal sexual response as a means of fostering Victor's motivation and socialization.

After devoting 5½ years to the task, Itard gave up the attempt to train "the wild boy of Aveyron." As for Victor, he lived to be 40, but never could speak more than a few words and never progressed appreciably beyond the achievements of that first year.

The story of Victor is of absorbing interest to both laymen and scientists. Recently a motion picture which portrays Itard's work with Victor—*The Wild Child*—was released by United Artists; while, in scientific circles, the lack of conclusive answers will keep psychologists and others puzzling over the question of whether Victor was a congenital mental defective, a brain-damaged child, a psychotic, or simply a child who had been so deprived of human contact during early critical periods of development that the damage he sustained could never be completely remedied. We shall probably never know whose assessment was correct—Pinel's or Itard's.

Based on Itard (1799; tr. Humphrey & Humphrey, 1932) and Silberstein and Irwin (1962).

EMOTIONAL DISTURBANCE
AND ANTISOCIAL BEHAVIOR
AMONG THE MENTALLY RETARDED

Incidence figures on emotional disturbance among the mentally retarded may vary not only with the criteria of emotional disturbance an investigator uses but also with the sample of retardates he chooses for study; however, studies suggest an incidence of 25 percent or possibly more (Chess & Korn, 1970; Menolascino, 1966, 1969; Philips, 1967).

The high incidence of emotional disorders among the mentally retarded is hardly surprising since, as a group, mentally retarded persons experience unusually difficult stresses—such as inability to understand the complexities of the world around them, and failure to meet the educational and other demands often placed upon them. The emotional problems resulting from myriad adaptive failures are likely to be exacerbated during adolescence, when the mental retardate develops the usual desires for peer-group identification, an eventual job, and love and marriage. At the same time he is faced with the realization that he is "different" and that there is little likelihood of his achieving the kind of life he sees modeled by normal adults.

Emotional disturbance in the mentally retarded often seems to stem primarily from the stress of being treated more like a "problem" than a person. Most mentally retarded individuals realize that other people regard them as inadequate. They are sensitive to being shunned by their peers and, even more so, to indications that their parents are dissatisfied with their progress or worried about their future. In the following case, the neurotic symptoms developed by a mentally retarded girl clearly reflect the particular pattern of her mother's concern.

"Helen, a 17-year-old adolescent, was socially isolated and withdrawn in her behavior. Her IQ was 68 and her school frequently reported that she could do better in her work but was withdrawn and disturbed. Her mother spent all of her free time with her, fearful that her daughter would get into trouble, that perhaps she would be attacked or be led into troublesome behavior. Helen developed phobic fears of being touched, avoided crowds, bathed frequently, and washed her hands throughout the day." (Philips, 1967, p. 33)

In cases of borderline and mild mental retardation, emotional disturbance quite frequently involves acting-out or delinquent behavior. Among mentally retarded boys, the most common patterns of delinquency are truancy, petty thievery, and minor aggressive acts, whereas among girls, the more usual problem is sexual promiscuity. But although the incidence of delinquency is disproportionately high among the mentally retarded, there is no evidence that mentally retarded persons are, "by nature," especially prone to aggressive or antisocial acts. Delinquent behavior among mentally retarded youths—as among youths of normal intelligence—seems generally to be the product of many interrelated factors, such as an inadequate home environment, school failure, undesirable peer-group associations, feelings of inadequacy, and a sense of being rejected by society as a whole. It may be noted, further, that many of these same factors have also been identified as possible causes of retarded intellectual development. Thus, the apparent relationship between mental retardation and delinquency may be partially explained by the fact that both problems often have similar patterns of causation.

million mentally retarded persons in the nation as a whole, three fourths are concentrated in our urban and rural slums (President's Committee on Mental Retardation, 1970).

The high incidence of mental retardation among the disadvantaged may be partially explained by heredity, since parents with low intellectual potential tend to be concentrated toward the bottom of the socioeconomic ladder. But investigators now realize that heredity is only one of many selective factors at work.[1] As might be expected, the incidence of fetal and birth difficulties is unusually high in poverty areas, where few women enjoy good prenatal and delivery care (Hurley, 1969; President's Committee on Mental Retardation, 1970; Scrimshaw, 1969). The rate of premature births, for example, is 3 times greater in the slums than it is in the country as a whole. Furthermore, some of the conditions that can cause mental retardation, such as malnutrition and lead poisoning, are almost exclusively problems of the poor. And finally, even when a child in the slums has been born with average or above-average intelligence, he is often reared in an environment in which lack of intellectual stimulation retards his mental development. As Eisenberg (1969) has described it:

"The urban slum child grows up in a home bereft of books and often of newspapers, restricted in geographic experience to the few blocks surrounding his dwelling, denied stimulating cultural vistas, and limited to learning a nonstandard language. His parents, like himself, are likely to have been earlier victims of limited educational exposure and to have cognitive styles which differ significantly from those modal for the larger society." (p. 396)

We have dealt with the socially disadvantaged child in some detail in Chapter 6, and need not pursue the topic at this point, beyond directing attention to the fact that a person's current level of intellectual functioning is based largely on previous learning. Since school requires such complex skills as being able to control one's attention, follow instructions, and recognize the meaning of a considerable range of words and

---

[1]For a thorough review of the relationship between poverty and mental retardation, the reader is referred to Baratz and Baratz (1970), Herzog and Lewis (1970), and Hurley (1969).

concepts, an individual is at a disadvantage from the beginning if his environment has deprived him of the opportunity to learn requisite background skills and be motivated toward further learning. Thus, it is not surprising that with each succeeding year these children tend to fall farther behind in school performance and relative ratings on intelligence tests—and that sooner or later some of them become labeled as mental retardates.

As a recent report by the American Psychological Association has noted:

"Mental retardation is primarily a psychosocial and psychoeducational problem—a deficit in adaptation to the demands and expectations of society evidenced by the individual's relative difficulty in learning, problem solving, adapting to new situations, and abstract thinking." (1970, p. 267)

This statement is not intended to minimize the possible role of genetic and other biological factors, to which the report gives due consideration. It merely recognizes the fact that in the vast majority of cases of mental retardation—some 85 percent—no neurological or physical dysfunction has been demonstrated. Clearly, it appears that efforts to understand and prevent mental retardation must place increasing emphasis on the role of environmental factors in either facilitating or impeding intellectual growth.

TYPES OF MENTAL RETARDATION ASSOCIATED WITH PHYSIOLOGICAL CAUSES

Mental retardation stemming primarily from biological causes can be classified into a number of recognizable clinical types. Several of the more common ones will be described in this section.

DOWN'S SYNDROME (MONGOLISM)

Down's syndrome, first described by Langdon Down in 1886, is the most common of the clinical conditions associated with moderate and severe mental retardation. The term *mongolism* has often been used in referring to this syndrome because persons so afflicted frequently have slanting eye slits with small folds covering the ends of the eyes nearest the nose. Twelve thousand persons with Down's syndrome are born in the United States annually (Benda, 1970).

A number of physical features are often found among children with Down's syndrome, but very few of these children have all of the characteristics that are commonly thought of as typifying this group. In addition to almond-shaped slanting eyes, in these children the face and nose are often flat and broad, as is the back of the head; and the tongue, which seems too large for the mouth, may show deep fissures. The iris of the eye is frequently speckled. The neck is often short and broad, as are the hands, which tend to have creases across the palms. The fingers are stubby and the little finger is often more noticeably curved than the other fingers. Well over 50 percent of these persons have cataracts, which are not congenital but tend to make their appearance when a child is about 7 or 8 (Falls, 1970). These cataracts aid in diagnoses, but fortunately they rarely become serious enough to warrant surgery. Interestingly enough, there appears to be little, if any, correlation between the number of physical symptoms of Down's syndrome and the degree of mental retardation.

Mongoloids are particularly susceptible to circulatory, gastrointestinal, and respiratory disorders. In approximately 10 percent of the cases there is an associated congenital heart defect; and there is some evidence that Down's syndrome predisposes these children to leukemia

(Heber, 1959; Miller, 1970). However, antibiotics, better medical care, and a more healthful and stimulating environment are increasing the life expectancy of many of the victims of this disorder.

The term *mongolian idiot* was widely used in the past, but it was misleading, inasmuch as most of these children show only moderate mental retardation. Despite their limitations, they are usually able to learn self-help skills, acceptable social behavior, and routine manual skills which enable them to be of assistance in a family or institutional setting. The social adjustment of mongoloid children is often helped by their tendency to be affectionate and relatively docile, although these traits are by no means universal. In a study of 77 children with Down's syndrome evaluated during a 3-year period at a state clinic, Wunsch (1957) found that about 51 percent exhibited unusually docile-affectionate behavior, while about 14 percent exhibited persistent aggressive-hostile behavior and the remaining 35 percent fell within the normal range.

Traditionally, the cause of mongolism was assumed to be faulty heredity. A number of studies demonstrated, however, that more than one case of mongolism in a family was very infrequent, occurring in less than 1 family in 100 (Southwick, 1939). As a consequence, a number of investigators turned to the study of metabolic factors and concluded that mongolism was probably due to some sort of glandular imbalance, most likely involving the pituitary gland (Benda & Farrell, 1954; Benda, 1956). Then, in 1959, the French scientists Lejeune, Turpin, and Gauthier found 47 chromosomes in several mongoloid cases, and research centered on possible chromosomal anomalies.

Subsequent studies have shown that about 95 percent of persons with Down's syndrome have 47 chromosomes instead of the normal complement of 46 (Lejeune, 1970; Robinson, 1961). Although there is usually an extra chromosome 21—resulting from nondisjunction, or failure to divide, during gametogenesis—there is a second type of Down's syndrome (mosaic type) in which the same individual shows this trisomy 21 in only a portion of the analysis of blood or skin cells, and the normal complement of 46 chromosomes in the remainder of the analysis. A third major type of chromosomal anomaly associated with this disorder is translocation, in which extra chromosomal material—a whole or a part of the chromosome—is attached to another chromosome. An estimate of the relative frequency of these various kinds of anomalies is provided by the survey by Johnson and Abelson (1968–1969). In those cases where karyotypic information was available, there were 254 cases of trisomy 21, 18 mosaic types, and 21 cases of chromosomal translocations.

The reason for the trisomy of chromosome 21 is not clear. In the majority of cases, the anomaly would appear to result from defective genes or something gone wrong in the mechanics of the growth process. The risk of Down's syndrome grows markedly with the age of the mother (Davis, 1968; Lejeune, 1970). A woman in her 20's has 1 chance in 2000 of having a mongoloid baby, whereas the risk for a woman in her 40's is 1 in 50. Thus it would appear that the nondisjunction of chromosome 21 is influenced by metabolic factors; but it is also possible that the older the mother, the greater the probability of exposure to radiation that may result in gene mutations. Further research is needed to clarify the causal picture.

Whatever the cause of the chromosomal anomaly, the end result is distortion in the growth process characteristic of this clinical syndrome.[1] Once mongolism occurs, the condition is irreversible. There is no known effective treatment. However, some preventive measures appear to be of value, one fairly recent development being the karyotyping of adults to see if they have chromosomal anomalies that increase the likelihood of abnormality in their children (Benda, 1970; Davis, 1968; Stimson, 1968). It should be noted that chromosomal analysis has been used in counseling not only to indicate dangers in having children, but also to provide assurance to prospective parents. When parents have had a child with Down's syndrome, they are naturally quite concerned about having further children. In such cases the mother's age and chromosomal analyses may indicate that the risk of abnormality in additional children is very small.

---

[1] Interestingly enough, McClure et al. (1969) have reported a case of autosomal trisomy in an infant chimpanzee who manifested clinical features remarkably similar to those in Down's syndrome among human infants.

THYROID DEFICIENCY (CRETINISM)

Cretinism provides a dramatic illustration of mental retardation resulting from endocrine imbalance. In this condition, the thyroid either has failed to develop properly or has undergone degeneration or injury; in either case, the infant suffers from a deficiency in thyroid secretion. Brain damage resulting from this insufficiency is most marked during the prenatal and early postnatal periods of rapid growth (Pickering & Fisher, 1958).

In the valleys of central Switzerland and other geographical areas of the world where iodine is deficient in the soil, and therefore in food grown on it, cretinism was formerly a common affliction. Pregnant women in such areas often gave birth to infants with defective thyroid glands which remained undeveloped or atrophied later. Because cretinism was observed to run in families in such areas it was once thought to be a heredi-tary disorder. In 1891, however, Dr. George Murray published his discovery that the injection of thyroid gland extract was beneficial in cases of *myxedema*—a disorder resulting from thyroid deficiency in adult life and characterized by mental dullness. This discovery, in turn, led to the treatment of cretinism with thyroid gland extract and to the realization that this condition, too, was the result of thyroid deficiency.

Although most cases of cretinism result from lack of iodine in the diet, thyroid deficiency may also occur as the result of birth injuries (involving bleeding into the thyroid) or in connection with infectious diseases, such as measles, whooping cough, or diphtheria. The resulting clinical picture will depend on the age at which the thyroid deficiency occurs, as well as on the degree and duration of the deficiency.

Typical descriptions of cretins involve cases in which there has been a severe thyroid deficiency from an early age—often before birth.

OTHER DISORDERS COMMONLY ASSOCIATED WITH MENTAL RETARDATION

CLINICAL TYPE	SYMPTOMS	CAUSES
No. 18 trisomy syndrome	Peculiar pattern of multiple congenital anomalies, the most common being low-set malformed ears, flexion of fingers, small mandible, and heart defects	Autosomal anomaly of chromosome 18
Tay-Sach's disease	Commonly, hypertonicity, listlessness, blindness, progressive spastic paralysis, and convulsions (death by the third year)	Disorder of lipoid metabolism, carried by a single recessive gene
Turner's syndrome	Webbing of the neck, increased carrying angle of forearm, and sexual infantilism	Sex chromosome anomaly
Klinefelter's syndrome	Vary from case to case, with only constant finding being the presence of small testes after puberty	Sex chromosome anomaly
Niemann-Pick's disease	Onset usually in infancy, with loss of weight, dehydration, and progressive paralysis	Disorder of lipoid metabolism
Bilirubin encephalopathy	Abnormal levels of bilirubin (a toxic substance released by red cell destruction) in the blood; choreoathetosis frequent	Often, Rh, A, B, O blood group incompatibility between mother and fetus
Rubella, congenital	Visual difficulties most common, with cataracts and retinal problems often occurring together with deafness and anomalies in the valves and septa of the heart	The mother's contraction of rubella (German measles) during the first few months of her pregnancy

Based on American Psychiatric Association (1968), Christodorescu et al. (1970), Donoghue, Abbas, and Gal (1970), Haddad and Wilkins (1959), Holub, Grumbach & Jailer (1958), Johnson et al. (1970), Koch (1967), Nielsen et al. (1970), Rundle (1962), Shapiro and Ridler (1960), Smith et al. (1962), and Stimson (1961).

Such a cretin has a dwarflike, thick-set body and short, stubby extremities. His height is usually just a little over 3 feet—the shortness accentuated by slightly bent legs and a curvature of the spine. He walks with a shuffling gait that is easily recognizable. His head is large, with abundant black, wiry hair; his eyelids are thick, giving him a sleepy appearance; his skin is dry and thickened and cold to the touch. Other pronounced physical symptoms include a broad, flat nose, large and flabby ears, a protruding abdomen, and failure to mature sexually. The cretin reveals a bland personality, and his thought processes tend to be sluggish. Most cretins fall within the severe and moderate categories of mental retardation, depending on the extent of brain damage. In cases with less pronounced physical signs of cretinism, the degree of mental retardation is usually less severe. A diagnosis of hypothyroidism is verified by finding a reduced level of protein-bound iodine in the blood, retarded skeletal growth (measured by X rays of the wrist), and elevated levels of blood cholesterol (Koch, 1967).

Early treatment with thyroid extract can produce striking results, and there are many instances of children restored to normal intellectual and personality levels. The success of treatment depends on the age at onset and the disorder's severity and duration. Smith, Blizzard, and Wilkins (1957) have shown that early treatment is essential, and that children not treated until after the first year of life may have permanently impaired intelligence. In long-standing cases, thyroid treatment may have some ameliorating effects, but the damage to the nervous system and to general physical development is beyond repair.

As a result of public health measures on both national and international levels—with respect to the use of iodized salt and the early detection and correction of thyroid deficiency—severe cases of cretinism have become practically nonexistent in the United States and most other countries.

CRANIAL ANOMALIES

Mental retardation is associated with a number of conditions in which there are relatively gross alterations in head size and shape, and where the etiology has not been definitely established. In craniosynostosis, for example, in contrast to the newborn's usual separability of cranial bones, which allows for the skull to stretch as the brain grows, the sutures or joints are fused together. Brain anomaly may result, especially in rarer cases in which all the joints are fused prematurely. The most common form of craniosynostosis involves the central suture that runs from the front to the back of the skull (Koch, 1967). The head cannot broaden, and brain growth results in unusual lengthening of the skull and a narrow-headed appearance. Surgery to provide expansion joints as needed has yielded good results in such cases.

Other conditions in which head size and shape are altered include *macrocephaly, microcephaly,* and *hydrocephalus.* In macrocephaly there is an increase in the size and weight of the brain, an enlargement of the skull, and visual impairment, convulsions, and other neurological symptoms resulting from the abnormal growth of glia cells which form the supporting structure for brain tissue. Microcephaly and hydrocephalus will be described in somewhat greater detail.

Microcephaly. The term *microcephaly* means "small-headedness." It refers to a type of mental retardation resulting from impaired development of the brain and a consequent failure of the cranium to attain normal size. In an early study of postmortem examinations of brains of microcephalics, Greenfield and Wolfson (1935) reported that practically all cases examined showed development to have been arrested at the fourth or fifth month of fetal life. Fortunately, this condition is extremely rare.

The most obvious characteristic of the microcephalic is his small head, whose circumference rarely exceeds 17 inches, as compared with the normal of approximately 22 inches. Penrose (1963) also described microcephalics as being invariably short in stature but having relatively normal musculature and sex organs. Beyond these characteristics, microcephalics differ considerably from each other in appearance, although there is a tendency for the skull to be cone-shaped, with a recession of the chin and forehead (Tredgold & Tredgold, 1952). Microcephalics have traditionally been thought to be inclined toward hyperactivity and restlessness, but good-natured and easy to get along with; however, Brandon,

 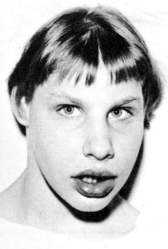 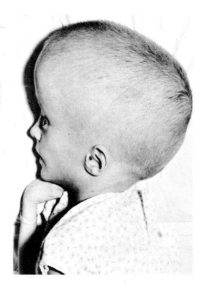

These children show three of the types of mental retardation associated with physiological causes. At the left is a 6-year-old mongoloid boy with the characteristic round head, slanting eyes with thick eyelids, small mouth with fissured lips, and short neck. In the center is a microcephalic girl with the usual cone-shaped skull and receding chin and forehead. On the right is a hydrocephalic boy whose face is of normal size in contrast with the greatly enlarged back part of his head.

Kirman, and Williams (1959) failed to find any consistent qualities of temperament in a group they studied. Microcephalics fall within the profound, severe, and moderate categories of mental retardation. The majority show little language development and are extremely limited in mental capacity.

Microcephaly may result from a variety of causes (Cowie, 1960). It is thought that so-called true or primary microcephaly may be transmitted via a single autosomal recessive gene (American Psychiatric Association, 1968). The evidence here is rather meager, however, and the precise nature of the genetic defect or defects remains to be clarified. Whether or not there is a characteristic chromosomal anomaly in microcephaly is not known.

Microcephaly may also result from a wide range of nongenetic factors that impair brain development, including intrauterine infections and pelvic irradiation of the mother during the early months of pregnancy (Cowie, 1960; Koch, 1967). A number of cases of microcephaly in Hiroshima and Nagasaki resulting from atom bomb explosions were noted by Miller (1970). As yet, no medical treatment has been developed

that is effective once the faulty brain development has occurred. Preventive possibilities are centered on the avoidance of infection and radiation during pregnancy.

Hydrocephalus. Hydrocephalus is a relatively rare condition in which the accumulation of an abnormal amount of cerebrospinal fluid within the cranium causes damage to the brain tissues and enlargement of the cranium.

In a number of congenital cases of hydrocephalus, the head is either already enlarged at birth or begins to enlarge soon thereafter, presumably as a result of a prenatal disturbance in the formation, absorption, or circulation of the cerebrospinal fluid (Dugdale & Patterson, 1968; Heber, 1959). The disorder can develop, however, in infancy or early childhood following the development of a brain tumor, subdural hematoma, meningitis, or other such conditions (Koch, 1967). Here the condition seems to result from a blockage of the cerebrospinal pathways and an excessive accumulation of fluid in certain brain areas, rather than from a failure in the mechanisms for forming or absorbing the fluid (Laurence, 1960).

The clinical picture in hydrocephalus depends on the extent of neural damage, which, in turn, depends on the age at onset and the duration and severity of the disorder. In chronic cases the chief symptom is the gradual enlargement of the upper part of the head out of all proportion to the face and the rest of the body. The face remains relatively normal, but the protruding skull gives the appearance one might expect in a race of super geniuses. While the expansibility of the skull helps minimize destructive pressure on the brain, serious brain damage occurs nonetheless, leading to intellectual impairment and such other effects as convulsions and impairment or loss of sight and hearing. The degree of intellectual impairment varies, being severe or profound in advanced cases.

A good deal of attention has been directed to the surgical treatment of hydrocephalus, and with early diagnosis and treatment this condition can usually be arrested with a minimum of brain damage (Laurence, 1969). Unfortunately, some cases do not respond to treatment, and in "expanding" hydrocephalus there is a progressive physical and mental deterioration, ending in the death of the patient.

Both of these sisters were afflicted with PKU, but the youngest one, at the left, was immediately placed on a special diet and the course of the disease was arrested.

PHENYLKETONURIA (PKU)

Phenylketonuria is a rare metabolic disorder, occurring in about 1 in 20,000 births; and mental retardates in institutions who suffer from PKU number about 1 in 100 (*The Sciences*, 1970). The baby appears normal at birth but lacks an enzyme needed to break down phenylalanine, an amino acid found in protein foods. When this condition is undetected, the phenylalanine builds up in the blood and damages the brain. The disorder usually becomes apparent between 6 and 12 months after birth, although such symptoms as vomiting, a peculiar odor, infantile eczema, and seizures may become apparent during the early weeks of life (Partington, 1961). Often the first symptoms noticed are signs of mental retardation, which may be moderate to severe, depending on the degree to which the disease has progressed. Motor incoordination and other neurological manifestations relating to the severity of brain damage are also common, and often there is a pale coloring to eyes, skin, and hair of untreated PKU patients.

PKU was identified in 1934 when a Norwegian mother sought to learn the reason for her child's mental retardation and peculiar musty odor. She consulted with many physicians to no avail until Dr. Asbjorn Folling found phenylpyruvic acid in the urine and concluded that the child had a disorder of phenylalanine metabolism (Centerwall & Centerwall, 1961).

Most older PKU patients show severe to profound mental retardation, with the median IQ of untreated adult phenylketonurics being about 20. Curiously, however, a number of PKU patients have PKU relatives with less severely affected intelligence. And Perry (1970) has reported the cases of two untreated PKU patients with superior intelligence. The preceding findings have made PKU somewhat of an enigma. It is still thought to result from metabolic alterations involving recessive genes, and 1 person in 70 is thought to be a carrier (Hsia, 1959; Kalter, 1962; *The Sciences*, 1970). However, there may be varying degrees of PKU, or possibly another genetic factor may ameliorate the destructive potential of the enzyme defect.

Methods for the early detection of PKU have been developed, and a diet low in phenylalanine is prescribed. Because brain differentiation is relatively complete by the age of 6, the dietary limitation can usually be reduced at this point. With early diagnosis and treatment—preferably before an infant is 6 months old—the deterioration process can usually be arrested, so that levels of intellectual functioning may range from normal down to about 80. However, a few patients suffer mental retardation despite restricted phenyl-alanine intake. It would appear that both the promptness and the consistency of treatment are crucial in determining the extent of intellectual impairment (*The Sciences*, 1970).

TREATMENT, OUTCOMES, AND PREVENTION

The need is apparent for alleviating adverse biosocial conditions and for maximizing the learning and adaptive capacities of mentally retarded individuals through specially designed educational programs. A number of recent programs have, in fact, demonstrated that significant positive changes in adaptive capacity are possible through such special rehabilitative measures.

TREATMENT AND OUTCOMES

Fortunately, as we have seen, most mental retardates do not need to be institutionalized. For those who do, however, state institutions for the mentally retarded are often desperately over-crowded, and in many instances are no better than prisoner-of-war camps (President's Committee on Mental Retardation, 1970). Moreover, most private facilities are beyond the means of the average family.

Woeful inadequacy also characterizes the educational and training facilities needed by the majority of mental retardates who do not require institutionalization. It has been estimated that 2 million mentally retarded persons who could use job training and become self-supporting members of their community are not getting this training (Humphrey, 1970). Thus, literally "hundreds of thousands of retarded persons who could

The loneliness and pathos which mark the shadowy world of many institutionalized mental retardates argue compellingly for the provision of meaningful and constructive treatment programs.

be trained and educated to useful work and life in American society are being wasted" (President's Committee on Mental Retardation, 1970). In fact, the majority of mentally retarded persons in the United States are never reached by any services directed toward their specific needs.

The negative side of this picture has been emphasized here to contrast sharply with what can be done about mental retardation. Classes for mild retardates—who are capable of some degree of achievement in such academic subjects as reading and arithmetic—concentrate on a functional program that usually emphasizes social skills, budgeting and money matters, and the development of simple occupational skills. These programs have succeeded in helping many mild retardates become independent, productive members of the community. Classes for the moderately and severely retarded usually have more limited objectives, but they emphasize development of self-care and other skills that will enable retardates to function adequately and be of assistance in either a family or institutional setting. In far more cases than had been realized, simple job skills can also be learned by these retardates (Dybwad, 1968). For example, Clark, Kivitz, and Rosen (1969) reported on a special project undertaken at the Elwyn Institute in Pennsylvania.

The goal of this program was the successful discharge to independent living in the community of the institutionalized mental retardate. The entire staff was oriented toward rehabilitation; emphasis was placed on the development of practical vocational skills; special programs provided remedial teaching and the learning of socialization skills; and counseling and assessment assured the individualization of training to meet each retardate's needs. As a result of this program, many mentally retarded persons who had been institutionalized for from 2 to 49 years were discharged and obtained skilled or semiskilled jobs in the community while coping successfully with everyday problems. Some married and had families, and none had to be readmitted to the institution. (p. 82)

Operant conditioning methods are being used increasingly to teach a wide variety of skills to retarded children. Typically, target areas of improvement are mapped out, such as improvement in personal grooming, social behavior, basic academic skills, and simple occupational skills. Within each area, specific skills are divided into simple components that can be learned and reinforced before more complex behaviors are required. Target areas are not selected arbitrarily, of course, but realistically reflect the requirements of the mental retardate's life situation. Training that builds on step-by-step progression and is guided by such realistic considerations can lead to substantial progress even by children previously regarded as uneducable.

Although much remains to be learned about the most effective educational and training procedures to use with the mentally retarded—particularly the moderate and severe types—new techniques, materials, and specially trained teachers have produced encouraging results. One interesting technological innovation now in exploratory use is the "talking typewriter" (Irwin, 1969). The machine works as follows:

"As a handicapped child, Jane, is seated, a recorded voice may say: 'Hello . . . Today we're going to play a game. You'll write the word CAT . . . First, type the letter C—a green key.' Jane sees C pictured in the window and looks for the green C key on the keyboard. Every other key but C is locked, so when she presses a wrong key, nothing registers and she tries again. When she strikes the right key, the letter appears on the screen and is spoken aloud by the voice. Then Jane hears, 'Now type A—a yellow letter.' ' . . . and T—a blue letter.'

"Finally the voice announces: 'You have typed the word CAT, CAT, CAT . . . look, this is the word CAT,' after which the picture of a cat is flashed on the screen. When she has typed the word a few times, Jane reads it into the microphone. The voice: 'Very good, you've finished the lesson for today.' Jane has begun to write and read." (Irwin, 1969, p. 32)

One problem that often inflicts great anxiety on parents is whether or not to institutionalize their mentally retarded child. In general, the ones who are institutionalized fall into two groups: (1) those who, in infancy and childhood, manifest severe mental retardation and associated physical impairment, and who enter the institution at an early age, and (2) those who, in adolescence, usually have no physical impairments but show mild mental retardation and fail to adjust socially, eventually requiring institutionalization for delinquent or other acting-out behavior.

REDUCTION OF SEVERELY MALADAPTIVE BEHAVIOR IN A MENTALLY RETARDED GIRL

Mary was a severely retarded as well as emotionally disturbed girl who entered behavior therapy at the age of $12\frac{1}{2}$ years. She was hyperactive and exhibited such negativistic, destructive, and other behaviors that assessment of her intellectual level was not possible prior to treatment. Paul and Miller (1971), who have reported the case, described her behavior.

"She picked up objects off the therapist's desk, threw them and whenever possible would run out of the room. When placed in the playroom she methodically began pulling toys from the shelves and throwing them on the floor. She did not seem to express any particular interest in any of the objects she handled; however, she did seem fascinated by a hole in the floor in which she spat and dropped various articles." (p. 19)

Investigation of Mary's background revealed that even before her first birthday she was brought to a psychiatric clinic for evaluation. Her parents were concerned about her habit of sitting with her legs outstretched and rocking back and forth for prolonged periods. Then after a severe ear infection at the age of 2, Mary ceased to respond to sounds although audiological tests showed no hearing loss. Shortly thereafter, Mary was diagnosed as brain damaged with moderate to severe mental retardation.

At the age of 5, Mary could not speak, and the groaning sounds she made did not appear to be communicative. A hyperactive child, she frequently engaged in spitting behavior and threw things such as books. Over the years she developed tantrums, deliberately hurt herself, destroyed objects, habitually disrobed (she had to be dressed in clothes which she could not easily unfasten), smeared feces, and gave way to bizarre laughter. When about 9 years of age, she was placed in her first nonbehavioral therapy program;

however, neither this form of therapy nor drug medication proved effective.

Behavior therapy in Mary's case was directed toward reducing such target behaviors as spitting, throwing objects (including feces), and self-destructive acts, plus certain other negative behaviors, including destruction of property and hitting people. When Mary behaved in a desired way, she was given bits of sweet, dry cereal as positive reinforcement. When she behaved in a negative way, the aversive consequence was to be put in the T.O. (time out) room. She was generally kept in the T.O. room for 3 minutes, but if she threw a tantrum, the timing did not begin until the tantrum was over. Since she did not like the T.O. room, this aversive procedure proved very effective. On the other hand, social disapproval had no effect as an aversive stimulus and was not used.

Mary attended three 15-minute therapy sessions each week; and after the first 20 sessions the outcome appeared favorable. As indicated in the two graphs below, she spent progressively less time in the T.O. room (under a minute per session), and a correspondingly longer time engaged in positive behavior (nearly the entire session).

Mary's improved behavior extended beyond the therapy sessions, being noted both in the school at the state training facility and in the cottage where she lived. Her increased attention and cooperation made it possible to assess her mental age (2.11) and IQ (23). Now that she could be helped, it was hoped that she would be able to continue to learn.

For a full description of the time-out procedure, the reader is referred to Zeilberger, Sampsen, and Sloan (1968).

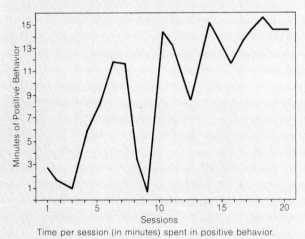

Time per session (in minutes) spent in positive behavior.

Time per session (in minutes) spent in T.O.

The families of those in the first group come from all socioeconomic levels, whereas a significantly higher percentage of the families of those in the second group come from lower educational and occupational strata.

Studies suggest that, in general, mentally retarded children are likely to show better emotional and mental development in a reasonably favorable home situation than in an institution. Centerwall and Centerwall (1960) compared 32 mongoloid children who were kept at home for at least 2½ years after birth with a control group who had been placed in an institution shortly after birth. They found that the children reared at home were superior in physical development, had higher measurable IQs, and functioned at

THERAPEUTIC PYRAMIDS AND THE "DOUBLE-CHANGE" PHENOMENON

A boy, Randy, and his therapist, Dawn, shared an exciting experience which is the subject of the following unusual case study by Whalen and Henker.

"Randy is an 11-year-old boy who lives in a state hospital. He is profoundly retarded; his estimated IQ is 32. Although there are 70 children on his ward, he spends most of his time alone, staring into space or passively watching what is going on around him. He often stands with his arms extended, oscillating his fingers and moving his head from side to side while making bizarre grimaces and clicking sounds with his tongue or teeth. He doesn't speak. He doesn't play. He has neither friends nor enemies among the other children.

"About 11 o'clock each morning Randy can be found stationed by the front door to his ward, eagerly scanning the faces of all who enter. He is waiting for his therapist, Dawn. To those who know and observe Randy, it is remarkable that he seems to know when it is time for his therapy session. He correctly anticipates this event, even though he cannot ask questions or understand explanations, and he certainly has never learned the significance of a clock.

"When Dawn arrives, Randy becomes visibly excited. His mannerisms stop and his smile broadens as his young therapist greets him and escorts him to a special room in another building. She pretends to carry on a conversation with Randy by taking two roles, asking him questions and then answering them for him. Randy's facial expressions and gestures seem to indicate that he is participating, although on a nonverbal level. More importantly, he receives more verbal stimulation in this short period than during the remainder of the day on his overcrowded, understaffed hospital ward.

"While delivering a monologue about the day's events, Dawn prepares for the session. Simple toddlers' toys are pulled out of a cupboard—a 'busy box,' a few blocks, a pounding board, and a hammer. A box of sugared cereal and a carton of chocolate yogurt are opened, and Randy is given a taste of each. Then Dawn announces, loudly, that it is time to go to work. The first item on today's agenda is a review of what Randy learned in the past week. Dawn says, 'Look at me, Randy.'

When his attention is secured, she quickly claps her hands and says, 'You do it.' As Randy imitates the simple response, Dawn exclaims, 'Good boy!' and gives Randy a spoonful of yogurt, which is for him a special treat. Dawn then goes through some other activities that, by this time in therapy, are relatively simple for Randy—raise your hand, dial the phone, throw the ball, pound the pegboard. For each task she uses the same sequence of procedures: secure attention, present the training stimulus (a nonverbal demonstration or a verbal direction), elicit the response, and then administer the rewards—praise, physical affection, and food.

"After this warm-up phase, Dawn tries a much harder task, a verbal direction which involves two discriminations. She places a block and a hammer on the table in front of Randy and asks him to hand her the hammer. Randy must choose both the correct object and the correct act. He first picks up the hammer and begins to pound the table. Although he has learned to respond to the direction 'Hand me . . .' and the label, 'Hammer,' he can't yet link the two together. He performs the only response he has ever learned involving a hammer—he pounds the table. Dawn says, 'No,' replaces the hammer, and repeats her verbal request. This time she includes a nonverbal prompt—she holds out her hand. Randy seems to understand the desired act but not the correct object as he places the block in her hand. Again Dawn says 'No' and shakes her head. Next time, she gives Randy more help. She places the hammer on top of the block and holds out her hand as she says, 'Give me the hammer.' With these cues, Randy makes the correct response and Dawn is delighted. Enthusiastic praise and a big hug accompany his food treat.

"Now Dawn settles into the difficult and often tedious job of 'fading the prompts' and teaching Randy to respond to the verbal direction alone, with no gestures or other artificial cues. To achieve this goal she must demand slightly more from Randy on each trial; she must help him less and less. If she prompts too completely or too frequently, he will show no improvement. But if her demands are too great, he may stop responding entirely. She must allow him enough time to practice his new response, but she must change the training task before he becomes too bored or frustrated. In short, multiple therapeutic decisions must be made at each stage of the learning sequence."

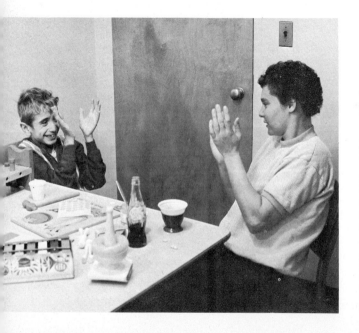
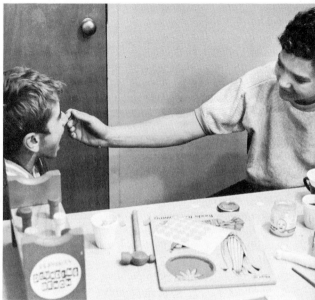

The remedial approach described in this situation is widely used in behavior therapy with mental retardates; what is unusual and dramatic about it is that Dawn, the therapist, is also mentally retarded. Both she and Randy resided in the same state institution for mental retardates.

Dawn dressed appropriately and seemed normal in appearance and movement. However, her vocabulary was very limited and her speech poorly articulated—at times being almost unintelligible. Her case history was replete with special-incident reports: she had thrown chairs through windows, run away, and destroyed property. She also had frequently engaged in physical and verbal assaults on companions as well as on hospital personnel, and her diagnosis of congenital cerebral defect was accompanied by the label "passive aggressive character with psychotic episodes." Though only mildly retarded (her IQ was 60), she was kept from family care placement by her unsuitable social behavior. She had been institutionalized for 11 of her 24 years.

Dawn's therapy sessions with Randy were part of a systematic research study of the "therapeutic pyramid concept"—in which professional therapists prepare moderately retarded adolescents and young adults to teach severely retarded children in simple social behaviors. Behavior therapy techniques are used in the training of "assistants," who use analogous methods with their younger "trainees." The key goal is to facilitate improvement in both assistants and trainees—in other words, to bring about a "double change."

And indeed this double-change phenomenon did occur in the case of Randy and Dawn. Randy learned to imitate gestures, respond to simple verbal requests, and relate to another person. And Dawn, for her part, acquired both occupational and social skills. As an assistant, she learned to arrive at work regularly and on time, assume responsibility, take pride and find satisfaction in her work, earn a salary, and manage her money. She also learned to relate to members of the research staff. In addition, she became uncomfortable about her poor articulation and tendency to "mouth off," and asked for help in improving her behavior. The ultimate consequence of her participation in the pyramid project came in her release from the hospital. She since has been reported adjusting well to her foster home.

As might be expected, research with therapeutic pyramids has shown that the greatest gains are achieved by assistants like Dawn, even though the results have been favorable for trainees as well. Among the assistants, gains have commonly been observed in improving speech skills, developing interpersonal competencies, developing a sense of personal responsibility, and building self-esteem. The success of the initial pyramid project has led to the initiation of similar programs in outpatient clinics, foster-care homes, and special schools.

Based on previously unpublished material by Carol K. Whalen, University of California at Irvine, and Barbara Henker, University of California at Los Angeles. Sources also include Guerney (1969) and Whalen and Henker (1971).

Successful imitation of Dawn's hand-clapping motion earns Randy a new treat.

higher intellectual levels. Lyle (1959; 1960) found that institutionalized retardates, in comparison with those raised at home, were especially deficient in tasks requiring verbal skills. It has also been shown that female retardates in institutions have a more negative self-attitude and consider themselves of less value than do those who remain at home (Guthrie et al., 1963). As a consequence of such considerations, institutionalization is not recommended where the child makes a satisfactory adjustment at home and in any special training school that he may attend during the day. The effect of institutionalization on a mentally retarded youth depends heavily, of course, on the institution's facilities as well as on the youth himself. It must be recognized, too, that many mental retardates do not have families in a position to care for them.

For institutionalized mental retardates who become ready to attempt an adjustment in the community and have no families, many cities have developed programs of foster home placement. Such placements require careful supervision and the education of the foster parents concerning the youth's needs and limitations.

Adolescents and young adults suffering from moderate to mild degrees of mental retardation—both those who are making the transition from institutional to community life and those who reside with their families—appear to benefit from the use of "sheltered workshops" in the community. In such sheltered workshops individuals who cannot compete successfully in modern industry can learn and perform simple occupational tasks under supervision. With the assistance of their families, they may thus find it possible to live reasonably satisfying and constructive adult lives.

In light of the statement of the President's Committee on Mental Retardation (1970) to the effect that with timely and suitable training, " . . . three quarters of the nation's retarded people could become self-supporting . . . and another 10 to 15 percent could become partially self-supporting," it is important for society to be concerned with the retardate's long-range life adjustment, as well as with his immediate schooling. Increasing automation is making it extremely difficult for him to compete in the labor market, and often he will need help in adjusting to the problems of our technical, complex, and rapidly changing society. The eventual outcome for most mild and moderate mental retardates thus appears to depend heavily on the type of community program that society is willing to provide. Unfortunately, special education programs now reach only about 1 in 5 mentally retarded children, and state-provided vocational rehabilitation programs for the mildly retarded reach a relatively small minority of persons needing them (Albee, 1968; Humphrey, 1970; President's Committee on Mental Retardation, 1970).

GENERAL PREVENTIVE MEASURES

The problem of preventing mental retardation involves the question of genetic factors as well as a wide range of biochemical, neurophysiological, and psychosocial conditions. Inevitably, it is an interdisciplinary problem concerned with human development in general.

Until rather recently the most hopeful approach to the prevention of mental retardation has been through routine health measures for the pregnant mother, precautions against the possibility of intrauterine or birth damage, and the use of various diagnostic measures to ensure the early detection and correction of abnormalities. With such health measures and a normal and stimulating environment after birth, many kinds of mental retardation that were once thought to be hereditary and inevitable have proved to be preventable.

New frontiers in prevention. Since the mid-1950's, two new frontiers have opened up in the field of prevention—one in genetics, the other in sociocultural approaches. Work in genetics has revealed the role of chromosomal anomalies in faulty development, and tests have been devised to identify parents who have these anomalies, thus making it possible to provide them with genetic counseling. There are now over 200 clinics in the United States where such counseling is available.

The second horizon in prevention involves the alleviation of sociocultural conditions which deprive children of the necessary stimulation, motivation, and opportunity for normal learning and mental development. As the late President Kennedy pointed out:

"Studies have demonstrated that large numbers of children in urban and rural slums, including pre-

"BUILDING MINDS THROUGH ART"

One approach to "building minds" utilized by the Exceptional Children's Foundation in Los Angeles is through art classes. Of particular significance are the opportunities students are provided for expressing themselves in their own ways and styles, and the increased self-confidence and coping ability they achieve in the process. For some students, participation in the classes and in the much broader educational program of the Foundation have resulted in "graduation" to classes in the public schools or to jobs (Shoshone, 1971; *Today's Health,* 1968).

The four paintings below are representative of the students' work. The two photos at left are of the classroom, one of them showing the art teacher discussing a student's work with him. Through special showings and exhibits, the paintings and other artwork of these students have won wide acclaim.

A mirror leads to wonderful discoveries of self by a child in a community-sponsored program to minister to the educational needs of handicapped preschoolers, including the mentally retarded.

school children, lack the stimulus necessary for proper development in their intelligence. Even when there is no organic impairment, prolonged neglect and a lack of stimulus and opportunity for learning can result in the failure of young minds to develop. Other studies have shown that, if proper opportunities for learning are provided early enough, many of these deprived children can and will learn and achieve as much as children from more favored neighborhoods. The self-perpetuating intellectual blight should not be allowed to continue." (1963, p. 286)

Broad spectrum approach. President Kennedy's report directed the attention of the nation to the tragic and costly problem of mental retardation. As a consequence, considerable research effort has been expended in dealing with this problem, and currently the following "keys to future progress" are being emphasized (American Psychological Association, 1970; President's Committee on Mental Retardation, 1970):

1. *Prevention.* High priority is given to prevention of mental retardation through the application of existing knowledge. General health, welfare, education, and urban renewal programs should contribute to the overall effort. More adequate medical care for the mother and baby, improved nutrition, specialized educational programs, and greater social and economic opportunities are expected to reduce mental retardation to the low incidence that has been achieved in some other countries.

2. *Community services.* The need for a new and comprehensive approach to facilities and services for the mentally retarded is stressed, with the emphasis being placed on community-centered agencies that will provide a coordinated range of diagnostic, health, educational, employment, rehabilitation, welfare, and related services. This phase of the program includes the training of needed personnel.

3. *Research.* Emphasis is placed on the facilitation and acceleration of research on all phases of the problem: etiology, educational procedures, social effects on the family, psychological effects on the individual, and the changing role and functions of community and state services and agencies.

This "broad spectrum" approach seems practical in terms of both immediate action and long-range improvement with respect to understanding, diagnosis, and treatment. It should go far toward helping us achieve the 75-percent reduction in the incidence of mental retardation, which the President's Committee on Mental Retardation (1970) cited as a realistic goal.

In this chapter we have dealt with mental retardation, which is a major problem in our society, directly affecting at least 3 percent of the population. Initially, we noted the changes in our views of *mental retardation;* that is, the criteria by which retardation is measured today include not only intelligence level but also the ability to adapt to requirements of everyday living. In dis-cussing degrees of mental retardation, we noted that the great majority of retardates fall within the borderline-to-mild range, with only a distinct minority manifesting more severe retardation.

In discussing the causes of mental retardation, we considered the significance of various genetic and biological anomalies and then noted the increasing attention being given to the role of poverty and early psychosocial deprivation in the etiological picture, since three fourths of the nation's mental retardates come from homes that are socially, economically, and culturally disadvantaged. We then proceeded to a consideration of the various clinical types of mental retardation associated with biological causes.

In the concluding section of the chapter, we considered both traditional and innovative approaches in the training of mental retardates and emphasized the current view that the vast majority of mentally retarded persons can become not only self-respecting but self-supporting members of the community if given appropriate training early enough. Finally, dealing with the problem of preventing mental retardation, we noted two new frontiers—one in genetics, where it has become possible to identify parents with chromosomal anomalies and provide them with genetic counseling, and the other in sociocultural approaches, aimed at alleviation of environmental conditions that contribute so heavily to the incidence of mental retardation in our society.

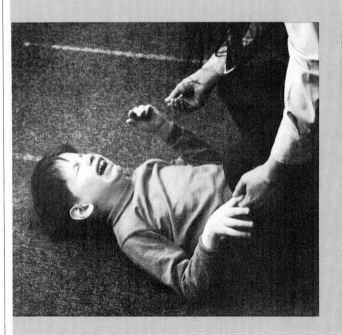
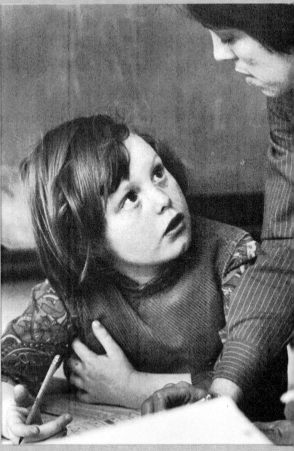

Behavior Disorders of Childhood

17

COMPARISON OF MALADAPTIVE BEHAVIOR IN CHILDHOOD AND LATER LIFE PERIODS

TYPES OF CHILDHOOD BEHAVIOR DISORDERS

PROBLEMS IN TREATMENT AND PREVENTION

"An estimated 500,000 American children are afflicted with psychoses and borderline psychotic conditions. Another million suffer from other severe mental disorders. Of the 50 million elementary school children in the United States, it is estimated that between 10 and 12 percent have moderate to severe emotional problems requiring some kind of mental health care. Among the 15 million youngsters in the United States who are being reared in poverty, one out of three has emotional problems that need attention." (NIMH, 1970, p. 7)

It is apparent from the preceding statement that maladaptive behavior among children includes a wide range of disorders and constitutes a major problem in our society. Only fairly recently, however, have childhood behavior disorders become the focus of special attention and study. During the nineteenth century, the usual approach was to apply the classification of adult mental disorders to "the insanity of children," with little attempt being made to differentiate between the symptoms and dynamics of psychopathology in children as opposed to adults. Maladaptive patterns relatively specific to childhood, such as the "runaway reaction" and the "hyperactive reaction," received virtually no attention at all.

An important step forward came in 1896 with Witmer's founding of the first psychological clinic at the University of Pennsylvania, which provided services for children as well as adolescents and adults. It is of interest to note that of the first two children treated at the clinic, one had a "speech disorder" and the other was a "chronic bad speller." In 1906 Witmer founded a journal, *The Psychological Clinic*, in which he and his students published case reports on a wide range of behavior problems of children. The goal was not to apply a diagnostic label to the child, but to study and understand the child's behavior so that appropriate educational procedures or treatment could be undertaken.

A closely related development was that of the child guidance movement. In 1909 the Juvenile Psychopathic Institute was founded in Chicago under the direction of William Healy, a psychiatrist. This institute fostered the view that the antisocial behavior of children could be modified with psychological methods. As a result of the pioneering work of Healy and Witmer, child guidance clinics were established throughout the United States, and by 1940 had become an accepted feature of the mental health field.

In the last two decades, marked strides have been made in understanding, assessing, and treating the maladaptive behavior patterns of children. But as we shall see, our facilities are woefully inadequate in relation to the magnitude of the task. In the final section of this chapter, we shall give detailed consideration to the problems of both treatment and prevention. First, however, we shall consider the general characteristics of maladaptive behavior in children and describe some of the disorders that are relatively specific to the childhood period.

COMPARISON OF MALADAPTIVE BEHAVIOR IN CHILDHOOD AND LATER LIFE PERIODS

Since personality differentiation, developmental tasks, and typical life stresses differ for childhood, adolescence, and adulthood, we would expect to find some differences in maladaptive behavior patterns for these life periods. For example, schizophrenia and depressive reactions are found in childhood as well as in later life periods, but there are differences in the clinical pictures.[1] In addition, there are certain disorders, ranging from severe separation anxiety to sleepwalking and enuresis, that are almost exclusively problems of childhood.

There is no sharp line of demarcation, of course, between the maladaptive behavior patterns of childhood and those of adolescence, nor between those of adolescence and adulthood. Thus although our focus in this chapter will be on the behavior disorders of children, we shall find some inevitable overlapping with those of later life periods. In this context, it is useful to emphasize the basic continuity of an individual's behavior over the years as he attempts to cope with the problems of living. The following comment by Lois Murphy, based on her intensive and long-range studies of children, is directly relevant:

"Seldom do we think of the child as a small human being, carrying on his own struggle to make sense out of life, to meet his own needs, to master the challenges presented by life—but differing from adults especially in the proportion of newness to which he is exposed." (1962, p. 1)

The points outlined below focus on both differences and similarities between maladaptive behavior patterns of childhood and those of later life periods.

1. *The clinical pictures for specific disorders may vary markedly, according to age.* As we have noted, the clinical pictures in given disorders may vary markedly in childhood from those shown in adolescence and adulthood. For example, while withdrawal and inability to relate to others are characteristic of childhood schizophrenia, delusions and hallucinations are not. Similarly, the suicidal impulses commonly found in adolescent and adult depression are fairly rare in childhood depression.

In children, too, the cognitive patterns in certain maladaptive patterns may vary considerably from those at other age levels. For example, if a child attempts suicide it may be for the purpose of rejoining a dead parent, a sibling, or a pet (Keeler, 1970). By the very young, suicide may be undertaken without any real understanding that death is final. As Seiden (1970) has put it, "Without the realization that death is final, a child measures his own life's value with a defective yardstick." (p. 29)

2. *Developmental level and degree of dependency markedly influence the clinical picture in childhood disorders.* Since personality differenti-

---

[1] Fish et al. (1968) have attempted a classification of schizophrenic reactions in children under 5, and Poznanski and Zrull (1970) have described depressive reactions in children ranging in age from 3 to 12.

Themes of a macabre or frightening nature characterize the drawings of a student who attended a facility for emotionally disturbed children at the University of California at Los Angeles. These drawings are representative of his work and appear to reflect a deep inner disturbance.

ation in childhood is not as advanced as in adolescence or adulthood, the child has not as clear-cut a view of himself and his world as he will at a later age. He is not as far along toward self-understanding and the development of a stable sense of identity, and is immature with respect to being guided by inner reality, possibility, and value controls. The immediate moment—since it is less moderated by considerations of the past or future, in the sense of "plans for the future" or an overall averaging of experience—tends to be disproportionately important to him. Thus the child often has more difficulty in coping with stressful events than he may have later when he has a better understanding of himself and his world and can see events in a broader perspective. It should also be noted that the child is highly dependent on others and that this dependency, though serving in some ways as a buffer against

stress, also makes him highly vulnerable to rejection and to disappointment and failure.

Because of their inexperience with life and their lack of self-sufficiency, then, children are more easily upset by seemingly minor problems than the average adult. However, they typically also recover more quickly from their hurts. Thus the emotional disturbances of childhood are likely to be relatively short-lived, undifferentiated, and changeable compared to those of later life periods.

3. *Underlying emotional problems are commonly masked in childhood.* Often childhood depressive reactions and other emotional problems are "masked." Among older children, for example, "acting out"—through disobedience, running away, delinquent behavior, or other maladaptive behavior—may mask an underlying depression (Lesse, 1968; Poznanski & Zrull, 1970). In a study of 14 cases of children manifesting

serious depression, the latter investigators noted not only such symptoms as sadness and frequent crying, but also withdrawal and episodic, violent outbursts.

Of course, the masking of emotional problems is by no means restricted to children. Depression, which was cited in the preceding example, may commonly be masked in adolescents by under-achievement and dropping out of school, delin-quency, aggressive outbursts, hypochondriacal concerns, and running away; and depression may similarly be masked in adults by inability to sleep and hypochondriacal concerns. But child-hood emotional disturbances are typically less differentiated and more changeable, and often no clear pattern of psychopathology emerges even in a child whose behavior is chronically mal-adaptive.

TYPES OF CHILDHOOD BEHAVIOR DISORDERS

The specific childhood disorders we shall discuss in this section are:

Autism

Hyperactive (hyperkinetic) reaction

Unsocialized aggressive reaction

Overanxious and withdrawal reactions

Runaway reaction

Stuttering

Minor "developmental" disorders such as enuresis, sleepwalking, and nail-biting

With the exception of autism, these disorders are less stable than most of the abnormal behavior patterns we have discussed in earlier chapters, and also less resistant to treatment. Often they are referred to simply as *emotional disturbances*, to indicate that the child is not so much "ill" as having problems in living with which he needs assistance. If such assistance is not received, however, the developmental disorders of child-hood sometimes merge almost imperceptibly into more serious and stable disorders during later life.

AUTISM

The boy is 5 years old. When spoken to, he turns his head away. Sometimes he mumbles unintelligibly. He is neither toilet trained nor able to feed himself. He actively resists being touched. He dislikes sounds. He cannot relate to others, and avoids looking anyone in the eye. He often engages in routine manipulative activities, such as dropping an object, picking it up, and dropping it again. While seated, he often rocks back and forth in a rhythmic motion for hours. Any change in routine is highly upsetting to him. He is in a school for severely psychotic children at UCLA. His diagnosis is childhood autism.

Autism in infancy and childhood was first de-scribed by Kanner (1943). It occurs with a fre-quency of approximately 1 or 2 cases per 10,000 of the general population, and is 3 or 4 times more frequent among males than females. The children come from all socioeconomic levels, ethnic backgrounds, and family patterns; how-ever, the educational and occupational status of parents of autistic children is usually average or above (Ritvo & Ornitz, 1970; Treffert, 1970).

Clinical picture. In autism, the child seems apart or aloof from the earliest stages of life; con-sequently, this disorder is often referred to as "early infantile autism." Mothers remember such babies as never being "cuddly," never reaching out when being picked up, never smiling or look-ing at them while being fed, and never appearing to notice the comings and goings of other persons. The absence or severely restricted use of speech is characteristic. If speech is present in an autistic child, it is almost never used to communicate except in the most rudimentary fashion, as by his saying "yes" when asked if he wants some-thing to eat. Often the autistic child shows an active aversion to auditory stimuli, crying even at the sound of his mother's voice. However, the pattern is not always consistent: autistic children "may at one moment be severely agitated or pan-icked by a very soft sound while at another time be totally oblivious to loud noise." (Ritvo &

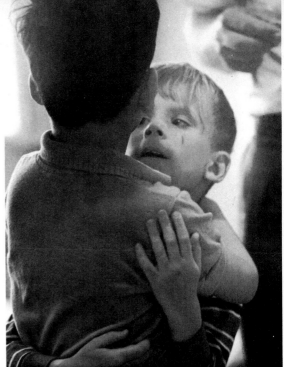

BEHAVIOR THERAPY IN THE TREATMENT OF AUTISM

At the University of California at Los Angeles, Ivar Lovaas and his associates have pioneered in the application of behavior-therapy techniques to the treatment of autistic children. Their approach is based on the seemingly old-fashioned concept that "when a child is bad he should be punished, and when he is good he should be rewarded." "Punishment" for maladaptive behavior is meted out immediately and inexorably, and includes slaps and, in extreme cases, electric shock. Rewards for adaptive behavior are also given immediately, and consist of tangible reinforcers such as food, as well as social approval and affection.

The first of these two pictures (above left) shows Chuck, an autistic boy, rocking back and forth while mutely contemplating nothing. The second picture shows the first big breakthrough with Chuck—eliciting a simple, friendly hug. After 6 weeks of treatment, Chuck had shown remarkable progress; he had learned to show affection and was able for the first time to talk in simple phrases.

Since these pictures were made, various refinements in treatment procedures have been developed utilizing additional data obtained through working with such children. But despite the marked progress which many of them show initially, only a small percentage of autistic children ever become "normal"—in the sense of being able to cope with the educational and other demands of everyday life and eventually taking their places as self-supporting and productive members of society. However, with this approach, the first barriers toward treating autistic children have been surmounted.

Life (1965), Lovaas (1967), Lovaas et al. (1972)

Ornitz, 1970, p. 6) Bizarre and repetitive movements are commonly observed. Finally, the concept of self seems to be blurred and undifferentiated, a condition Bettelheim (1967) has referred to as the "absence of I" or "the empty fortress."

In contrast to the behavior just described, considerable interest in the manipulation of objects is often shown by autistic children, who may become quite skillful at fitting objects together. Thus, their performance on puzzles or form boards may be average or even above. However, even in the manipulation of objects, difficulty with meaning is apparent. For example, when pictures are to be arranged in an order that tells a story, there is a marked deficiency in performance. When an autistic child's preoccupation with an object, such as a toy or a light switch, is disturbed, or when anything familiar in his environment is altered even slightly—including the furniture—he may have a violent temper tantrum, or he may continue crying until the familiar sameness is restored.

Because the clinical picture in infantile autism tends to blend almost imperceptibly with that of childhood schizophrenia, a differential diagnosis is often difficult or impossible to make. However,

JOEY: A "MECHANICAL BOY"

These four pictures were drawn by Joey, a schizophrenic boy who entered the Sonia Shankman Orthogenic School of the University of Chicago at the age of 9. His unusual case history has been reported by Bettelheim (1959).

Joey had been reared by parents in an utterly impersonal way, and he presumably denied his own emotions because they were unbearably painful. Apparently not daring to be human in a world which he felt had rejected him, Joey withdrew into a world of fantasy and perceived himself as a machine that "functioned as if by remote control." This idea is brought out in the drawing on the left—a self-portrait in which Joey depicts himself as an electrical robot. Bettelheim interpreted this portrait as symbolizing Joey's rejection of human feelings.

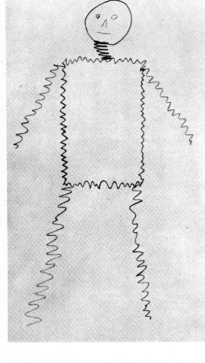

So elaborately constructed and acted out was Joey's mechanical character that: "Entering the dining room, for example, he would string an imaginary wire from his 'energy source'—an imaginary electric outlet—to the table. There he 'insulated' himself with paper napkins and finally plugged himself in. Only then could Joey eat, for he firmly believed that the 'current' ran his ingestive apparatus." (p. 117)

Joey's performance was convincing—so much so that others found themselves responding to him as a mechanical boy rather than as a human being: ". . . one had to look twice to be sure there was neither wire nor outlet nor plug. Children and members of our staff spontaneously avoided stepping on the 'wires' for fear of interrupting what seemed the source of his very life." When his machinery was idle, Joey "would sit so quietly that he would disappear from the focus of the most conscientious observation. Yet in the next moment he might be 'working' and the center of our captivated attention." (p. 117)

In his report on Joey, Bettelheim alluded to the painfully slow process by which Joey was eventually able to establish true relations with other human beings. Three of the drawings (left to right below) depict part of the process. In the earliest of the three, Joey portrays himself "as an electrical 'papoose,' completely enclosed, suspended in empty space and operated by wireless signals." In the next one, he apparently demonstrates increasing self-esteem, for although he is still operated by wireless signals, he is much larger in stature. In the final drawing, Joey depicts "the machine which controls him," but in this one, unlike the previous drawings, "he has acquired hands with which he can manipulate his immediate environment." (p. 119)

When Joey was 12—three years after he had entered the school—". . . he made a float for our Memorial Day parade. It carried the slogan: 'Feelings are more important than anything under the sun.' Feelings, Joey had learned, are what make for humanity; their absence, for a mechanical existence. With this knowledge Joey entered the human condition." (p. 127)

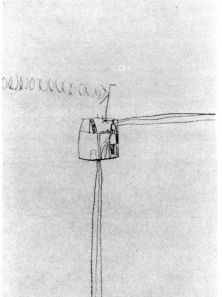

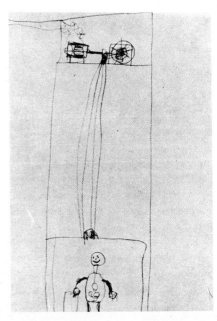

the schizophrenic child typically undergoes a period of seemingly normal development before evidencing withdrawal, thought disturbances, and inappropriate affect, and often he appears concerned and anxious about his relationships with persons and the world about him (Ritvo et al., 1970; Treffert, 1970). The autistic child, in contrast, is seemingly oblivious to his social environment from the start. As Bettelheim (1969) has stated it, "while the schizophrenic child withdraws from the world, the autistic child fails to ever enter it." (p. 21)

Dynamics. No brain pathology has been delineated in infant or childhood autism (Treffert, 1970); and since it does not run in families, it cannot be attributed directly to a hereditary defect. The possibility remains, however, that defective genes—resulting, for example, from radiation or effects of other mutagens on the mother during pregnancy—may play a key role in the etiological pattern. Thus, while Judd and Mandell (1968) failed to find significant chromosomal abnormalities in a carefully selected group of 11 autistic children, subtler genetic defects cannot be ruled out. In fact, most investigators believe that autism begins with some type of inborn defect—presumably one that interferes with the infant's ability to process incoming stimulation.

In his early studies of childhood autism, Kanner (1943) concluded that an innate disorder in the child is exacerbated by a cold and unresponsive mother, the first factor resulting in social withdrawal and the second tending to maintain the isolation syndrome. Rutter (1968) concluded that the innate disorder is a basic inability to comprehend sounds or language—to filter, integrate, categorize, and attach meaning to such stimuli—which results in the child's social withdrawal. The child's ritualistic and compulsive behavior then presumably represents an adaptation to the primary comprehension defect. Freedman (1971), noting the high incidence of autistic disturbances in congenitally blind children, has suggested that very early deprivation of meaningful sensory experience may result in gross, and apparently irreversible, personality disturbances.

On the basis of their intensive study of 53 autistic children, Clancy and McBride (1969) have suggested that the usual picture of the autistic child as lacking in language ability and being wholly withdrawn is probably oversimplified. They found that at least some autistic children *do* comprehend language, even though they may not use it to express themselves. These investigators also pointed to the occasional normal commencement of language development, followed by its disappearance as the autistic process becomes manifest. And perhaps even more significantly, they concluded that autistic children are very much aware of—and actively involved with—their environment:

"Autistic children actively seek to arrange the environment on their terms, and so as to exclude certain elements, e.g., intervention from other people, and variety in any aspect of routine. They show a high degree of skill in manipulating people for their ends, and again this skill is usually obvious in the first year of life. In a socially inverted manner the children are as active and resourceful as normal children." (p. 243)

These investigators then arrived at a conclusion that supports the earlier one of Kanner (1943):

"We suggest that the initial defect operates to interfere with the process by which bonds form. We see the child and his family, particularly the mother, contributing mutually to this abnormal affiliative process, so that the child is incorporated into the family system in such a way that the autistic process is reinforced and promoted. We suggest that predisposing and initiating factors may be involved in establishing the autistic process which then effectively isolates the child on his own terms. This is seen in the child's active resistance to intrusion by others, the maternal feelings of rejection, the use of 'cutoff' behaviours by the child, and the development of a high degree of manipulative skill in ordering his world." (Clancy & McBride, 1969, p. 243)

Although parental rejection is often cited as a key factor in the development of autism, its exact etiological significance is by no means clear. In fact, Wolff and Morris (1971) failed to find the parents of autistic children to be "emotional refrigerators," although they did suggest the need for further study of interaction patterns in families with an autistic child. As Harlow (1969) has somewhat wryly pointed out, it is often extremely difficult to pinpoint cause and effect in studying relationships between mother and child:

"Possibly . . . some children are rendered autistic by maternal neglect and insufficiency, but it is even more likely that many more mothers are rendered autistic because of an inborn inability of their infants to respond affectionately to them in any semblance of an adequate manner." (p. 29)

Clearly, much remains to be learned about the dynamics of childhood autism. It would appear, however, that this disorder does begin with an inborn defect or defects, regardless of what other etiological factors subsequently become involved.

Treatment and outcomes. Remedial teaching which utilizes behavior modification techniques—such as modeling, shaping, and reinforcement—has been heavily relied on in the treatment of autistic children (Bandura, 1969; Lovaas et al., 1972; Schopler et al., 1971). However, the results have not been encouraging. In a one-year study of the programmed teaching of autistic children, Fischer and Glanville (1970) found that 11 of 14 autistic children were able to complete only 10 percent of a specially developed program; and the other 3 were able to complete no more than 30 to 40 percent of it. These investigators concluded that "the majority of autistic children in our group require, on average, some ten years of teaching before they are ready to commence a normal school curriculum, assuming that the present rate of improvement is maintained." (p. 94)

Bettelheim (1967; 1969) has reported some success in treating autistic children with a program of warm, loving acceptance, and compliance with many of their demands. The love and permissiveness are accompanied by reinforcement procedures. Taking a somewhat different approach and treating the family rather than the child individually, Clancy and McBride (1969) reported successful outcomes with 12 of the 53 children in their study. Other studies have led to variable findings, but as Halpern (1970) has pointed out, "Without special help, autistic children are unable to pattern experience beyond primitive organizational levels" (p. 665).

In summary, whatever the causal pattern or whatever the treatment procedure, the prognosis in childhood autism is unfavorable. Even intensive long-term care in a clinical treatment facility may have very minimal results; and considerably less than one fourth of these children attain even marginal adjustment in later life. Comparable outcomes appear to be characteristic of childhood schizophrenia.

HYPERACTIVE (HYPERKINETIC) REACTION

Hyperactivity is a common presenting symptom among children seen at child guidance clinics and related facilities. It occurs with the greatest frequency before the age of 8 and tends to become less frequent and of shorter duration thereafter (Jenkins, 1969). Typically, it disappears by the middle teens. The hyperactive syndrome is much more frequent among boys than girls.

Clinical Picture. Hyperkinesis—excessive or exaggerated muscular activity—is the key element in a clinical picture that usually also includes some or all of the following:

Short attention span
Easy distractibility
Impulsiveness
Poor motor coordination
Low frustration tolerance
Emotional instability and changeable moods
Hypersensitivity
Lack of inhibition

These children tend to talk incessantly and to be socially uninhibited and immature. They do not appear to be anxious, although their overactivity, restlessness, and distractibility are sometimes interpreted as indications of anxiety. Usually they do poorly in school—commonly evidencing specific learning disabilities, such as difficulty in learning to read or in learning other basic school subjects.

The following case, involving an 8-year-old girl, reveals a somewhat typical clinical picture:

The subject was referred to a community clinic because of overactive, inattentive, and disruptive behavior. Her school achievement was poor. She was a problem to her teacher and to other students because of her hyperactivity and uninhibited behavior. Both at school and at home she had periodic temper outbursts. Despite her inferior school achievement, she had above-average intelligence. However, she felt inadequate and insecure, and had a devaluated self-image. Neurological tests revealed nothing significant. She was labeled as a hyperactive child.

Dynamics. There are no known genetic or chromosomal defects associated with hyperactivity (Warren et al., 1971). However, there is a higher-than-average number of premature births among hyperactive children, a substantial number of whom show so-called soft neurological signs—

such as perceptual motor coordination deficits (Caputo & Mandell, 1970; Wikler, Dixon & Parker, 1970). Such individuals are commonly assumed to be suffering from "minimal brain dysfunction," or MBD. This view has been supported and extended by Jenkins in his statement that "the hyperkinetic reaction implies an immature malfunctioning of the central nervous system." (1970, pp. 140–141) The evidence, however, is inadequate for the conclusion that all or even the majority of hyperactive reactions are associated with irregularities or alterations in brain processes. Hyperactivity is a relatively nonspecific symptom in children, and may occur in the anxious, depressed, schizophrenic, and autistic, as well as in those evidencing brain damage or minimal brain dysfunction. The concept of MBD is a controversial one, and is discussed in the illustration below.

Typically, the hyperactive reaction becomes manifested very early in life. Where it develops in later childhood, family and related stresses are likely to be key factors leading to anxiety and emotional upset. In any event, labeling a child as "hyperactive" may not indicate much in the way of etiology or appropriate treatment procedures. It would appear that in such cases a thorough assessment is essential for an understanding of the clinical picture and the formulation of an appropriate treatment program.

Because of their learning and performance difficulties with formal intellectual tasks, some of these children are mistakenly diagnosed as mentally retarded. However, in a comparison of the IQs of a sample of hyperactive children and a control group of normal children, Burks (1960) found no differences. That such children are especially susceptible to psychological disorders—particularly alcoholism—in later adolescence was reported by Morrison (1970) in a follow-up study of 50 hyperactive children. But since he also reported that 24 percent of the fathers were considered probable or actual alcoholics, it is difficult to say whether the alcoholism was learned from faulty parental models or resulted from hyperactivity, or both.

MINIMAL BRAIN DYSFUNCTION (MBD)

In a three-part study sponsored by the U.S. Department of Health, Education, and Welfare (Clements, 1966; Paine, 1969; Chalfant and Scheffelin, 1969), children with minimal brain dysfunction (MBD) have been described as

". . . of near average, average, or above average general intelligence with certain learning and/or behavioral disabilities ranging from mild to severe, which are associated with deviations of function of the central nervous system. These deviations may manifest themselves by various combinations of impairment in perception, conceptualization, language, memory, and control of attention, impulse, or motor function. These aberrations may arise from genetic variations, biochemical irregularities, perinatal brain insults or other illnesses or injuries sustained during the years which are critical for the development and maturation of the central nervous system, or from other unknown organic causes." (Paine, 1969, p. 53)

The ten outstanding characteristics of children with MBD are considered, in order of frequency, to be: (1) hyperactivity, (2) perceptual-motor impairments, (3) emotional lability, (4) general coordination deficits, (5) disorders of attention (short attention span, distractibility, perseveration), (6) impulsivity, (7) disorders of memory and thinking, (8) disorders of speech and hearing, (9) specific learning disabilities (reading, writing, spelling, and arithmetic), and (10) neurological signs, including EEG irregularities.

Although the concept of MBD is widely used, it remains somewhat controversial. Criticism has been directed especially at the practice of inferring that children have MBD simply because they display "typical symptoms" (e.g., poor perceptual-motor coordination,

difficulty in learning to read, attention problems, and hyperactivity) without conducting tests to determine if they actually have a neurological defect. It has also been pointed out that the intellectual, emotional, and behavioral manifestations of minimal brain dysfunction may vary greatly from child to child. For example, children with MBD do not necessarily have reading difficulties, nor are they necessarily hyperactive; in fact, they sometimes evidence a low level of motor activity. In their study on the relationship between MBD and school performance, Edwards, Alley, and Snider (1971) found "no evidence that a diagnosis of MBD, based on a pediatric neurological evaluation . . . is a useful predictor of academic achievement." (p. 134)

On the other hand, the specific "symptoms" of young children with serious learning problems are often so remarkably similar that the concept of a neurological learning disability syndrome can hardly be ruled out. In effect, the "computers" of some children seem to function atypically in the processing of auditory and visual information; and it seems likely in such cases that neurological evaluation would reveal brain dysfunction—or even actual brain damage. Even a clear diagnosis of brain dysfunction or damage may not be particularly useful, of course, unless the precise nature of the disorder can be determined, as well as its significance for behavior, treatment, and outcome.

Based on Chalfant and Scheffelin (1969), Clements (1966), Edwards, Alley, and Snider (1971), Friedman (1968–1969), Geschwind (1971), Gunderson (1971), Hertzig, Bortner, and Birch (1969), Paine (1969), Pollack (1969), Serf and Freundl (1971), Silver (1971), Tarnopol (1970), Tymchuk, Knights, and Hinton (1970), and Werry (1968).

DRUG THERAPY WITH CHILDREN

A number of important questions have been raised concerning the increasing use of drugs in the treatment of certain behavior disorders of children. The principal ones appear to include:

1. **Who is being selected for treatment?** Few investigators would question the usefulness of amphetamines or related drugs for treating hyperactivity, but many question the adequacy of assessment procedures used in identifying children who actually need medication. For example, a clear-cut distinction is not always made between the child who appears to need chemotherapy because of minimal brain dysfunction (MBD) and the child whose inattention and restlessness may be the result of hunger, crowded classrooms, irrelevant curriculum content, or anxiety and depression stemming from a pathogenic home situation.

2. **Are drugs sometimes being used simply to "keep peace in the classroom"?** Those who raise this question point to the possibility that children who manifest bewilderment, anger, restlessness, or lethargy at school may only be showing a normal reaction to educational procedures which fail to spark their interest or meet their needs. To label such children as "sick"—e.g., as evidencing hyperactivity, or some other behavior disorder—and to treat them through medication, these investigators maintain, is to sidestep the difficult and expensive alternative of providing better schools. Possibly such an approach also reinforces the notion—all too prevalent in our culture—that if things are not going well, all the individual has to do is take some type of drug.

3. **Do the drugs have harmful side effects?** Even in the small dosages usually prescribed for children, drugs sometimes have undesirable side effects. In the case of the amphetamines, the side effects appear to be minimal—even being self-correcting to some extent, in that the drug may "speed up" the child if he does not need "slowing down." However, such symptoms as decreased appetite, dizziness, headache, and insomnia have been reported in some cases with other stimulants, such as methylphenidate-hydrochloride (Ritalin). Minor tranquilizers also may have adverse side effects, including lethargy. And even with drugs that seem to produce no immediate side effects, the possibility of adverse long-range effects resulting from sustained usage during early growth and development should not be overlooked.

The consensus among investigators seems to be that drug therapy for children should be used with extreme caution, and only with those children for whom other alternatives simply do not work, such as the hyperactive child who shows definite indications of MBD and cannot control his behavior without drug therapy. It is also considered important that drug therapy be undertaken only with the informed consent of the parent, as well as the child if he is old enough, and that the child not be given the sole responsibility for taking his medication—a procedure that can lead to drug abuse. At the same time, there is a need to avoid exaggerated public attitudes against the use of drug therapy for children who genuinely need it. Finally, children who do benefit from drug therapy may also need other therapeutic measures for dealing with coexisting problems, such as learning deficiencies and psychological, interpersonal, and family difficulties.

Based on Eisenberg (1971), Freedman (1971), Ladd (1970), Rapoport (1971), and Witter (1971).

Treatment and outcomes. Traditionally, it has been customary to avoid unnecessarily stimulating and stressful situations in dealing with the hyperactive child. A program involving parental, educational, and medical factors is commonly indicated. Jenkins (1969) has pointed out that

"When hyperkinetic children develop in a strong, understanding, and stable home, they usually become adequately trained and socialized, although their training requires more than the usual amount of patience, repetition, firmness, and consistency. In an unstable, inconsistent home they tend to develop increasing conflict with their parents and to get out of control." (p. 69)

Freibergs and Douglas (1969) have reported on the importance of providing these children with positive and consistent reinforcement in learning. When only partial reinforcement was used, the children regressed in both learning and performance. Behavior-modification techniques that feature consistent positive reinforcement and the programming of learning materials and tasks in such a way as to minimize error and maximize immediate feedback have been reported to be of great value by Hewett (1968) and other investigators—particularly when these techniques are combined with appropriate medication.

Interestingly enough, cerebral stimulants—e.g., the amphetamines—typically have a quieting effect on hyperactive children. Such medication decreases their overactivity and distractibility and at the same time increases their attention span and concentration. As a consequence, they are often able to function much better at home and at school. In fact, many hyperactive children who have not been acceptable in regular classes are enabled to function and progress in a relatively normal manner. The medication does not appear to affect their intelligence, but rather to help them use their basic capacities more effectively (NIMH, 1971). Although such drugs do not "cure" the hyperactivity, they have been found beneficial in about half to two thirds of the cases in which medication appears warranted (Freedman et al., 1971).

Even without treatment, hyperactive reactions tend to clear up by the middle teens, although Weiss et al. (1971) have noted that in some cases residual learning and emotional problems may persist. The reason for the change in hyperactivity during the teens is not as yet understood. Since hyperactive children pose the majority of behavior problems in the schools, however, a good deal of current research effort is being devoted to this disorder.[1]

UNSOCIALIZED AGGRESSIVE REACTION

In his extensive study of the behavior problems of 1500 children seen at the Institute for Juvenile Research, Jenkins (1968) labeled 445 cases as unsocialized aggressive reaction. In many ways similar to the psychopathic personality pattern we have described for adolescents and adults (Chapter 11), this reaction is much more common among boys than girls.

Clinical picture. Although the following case is not necessarily typical of the unsocialized aggressive reaction, it does describe many of the symptoms commonly found in this type of disorder.

"This 9-year-old, wiry, active boy wore a 'crewcut' with an ever ready, engaging smile. From the beginning of each interview he led things, with careful attention to the responses of the interviewer. In addition to fire-setting he was chronically truant, had vandalized the school, and had set off a fire alarm in school. Speaking about the alarm, he noted, 'This kid dared me to do it and I didn't think it was hooked up.' In the clinic waiting room he got two boys to fight by informing one that the other was saying things about him, and then quickly assumed the role of peacemaker when an adult appeared. He spoke of his love for 'little kids,' and conspicuously held his baby sister in the waiting room, although his mother was unencumbered beside him. In the playroom he chose the activities and frequently seemed to have a program for what he wanted to do that day. This boy was enuretic. His main wish was for 'a gang—for protection.'" (Vandersall & Weiner, 1970, pp. 68–69)

In general, unsocialized aggressive children manifest such characteristics as overt or covert hostility, disobedience, physical and verbal aggressiveness, quarrelsomeness, vengefulness, and destructiveness. Lying, solitary stealing, and temper tantrums are common. Such children tend to be sexually uninhibited and inclined toward sexual aggressiveness. A minority may engage in fire-setting, solitary vandalism, and even homicidal acts. In the Vandersall and Weiner study (1970), the case was cited of a 7-year-old boy who set a fire under the crib of his 9-month-old sister. Financially, the damage from acts of vandalism committed each year by such children—particularly vandalism of public school buildings—runs into the millions of dollars.

Dynamics. There appears to be general agreement among investigators that the family setting of the unsocialized aggressive child is typically characterized by rejection, harsh and inconsistent discipline, and general frustration. Frequently the parents are unstable in their marital relationships, are emotionally disturbed or sociopathic, and provide the child with little in the way of consistent guidance, acceptance, or affection. Often the child is overtly rejected—he was unwanted and he knows it. In a disproportionate number of cases the child lives in a home broken by divorce or separation and is likely to have a stepparent (Bratfos, 1967; Shamsie, 1968). Not infrequently a single case may be characterized by rejection, harsh and inconsistent punishment, and actual physical abuse. Jenkins (1968) reported this pattern, plus the use of bribery by parents in their efforts to control their children's behavior. Thus, we appear to be dealing here with pathogenic family patterns that result in a basic defect in the child's socialization and in his tendency to act out frustrations in hostile, antisocial behavior.

Treatment and outcomes. The treatment of the unsocialized aggressive child is likely to be ineffective unless some means can be found for modifying the child's life setting. This is difficult where the parents are maladjusted and in conflict between themselves. And often an overburdened mother who is separated or divorced and working simply does not have the time or inclination to learn and practice a more adequate maternal role. The circumstances may call for removal of the child from the home and his placement in a foster home or institution, with the expectation that he later can be returned home if intervening therapy with the parents appears to justify it. Unfortunately, when the child is taken from his

---

[1]For further reading concerning the treatment of the hyperactive child, the following sources are most helpful: Benson (1969), Browning and Stover (1970), Fargo, Behrens, and Nolen (1970), Hewett (1968), and Woody (1969).

home he often interprets this as further rejection—not only by his parents but by society as well. And unless the changed environment offers a warm, kindly, acceptant—and yet consistent and firm—setting, the child is likely to make little progress.

By and large, society tends to take a punitive, rather than rehabilitative, attitude toward the antisocial aggressive youth. Thus, the emphasis is on punishment and on "teaching the child a lesson." Many such individuals are "treated" in indifferent or punitive correctional institutions that actually appear to intensify rather than correct the behavior. Where treatment is unsuccessful, the end product is likely to be a psychopathic personality with a long future of antisocial, aggressive behavior ahead of him. In an intensive longitudinal study of antisocial aggressive behavior in childhood, Robins (1968) found that

such behavior is highly predictive of sociopathic behavior in later adolescence and adulthood.

The advent of behavior therapy techniques has, however, made the outlook much brighter for children manifesting unsocialized aggressive reactions. Particularly important is training of the mother—or, when feasible, both parents—in control techniques, so that the parents function as therapists in reinforcing desirable behavior and modifying environmental conditions that may be reinforcing the maladaptive behavior. The change effected in the parents' overt reactions to the child's positive behavior, as well as to his negative behavior, may finally open up an avenue to a real change in their perception of and feelings toward the child, and to their positive acceptance of him.

RUNAWAY REACTION

In his study of 1500 children evidencing behavior disorders, Jenkins (1968) reported an incidence of 67 cases of running away from home. Boys appear to slightly outnumber girls in this type of disorder. The magnitude of the problem is indicated by the fact that there are an estimated 600,000 runaway youths in the U.S. during any given year (*Newsweek*, 1971).

Clinical picture. Again, the following case is not necessarily typical, but does serve to illustrate this reaction pattern.

Joan, an attractive girl who looked older than her 12 years, came to the attention of juvenile authorities when her parents reported her as a "runaway." Twice before she had run away from home, but no report had been filed. In the first instance she had gone to the home of a girl friend and returned two days later; in the second she had hitchhiked to another city with an older boy, and returned home about a week later.

Investigation revealed that the girl was having difficulty in her school adjustment and was living in a family situation torn by bickering and dissension. In explaining why she ran away from home, she stated simply that "I just couldn't take it anymore—all that quarreling and criticism, and no one really cared anyway."

For many children running away becomes a repetitive pattern. For example, an older boy may run away as often as once a week and either

---

TOKEN REINFORCEMENT PROGRAMS IN THE CLASSROOM

During the last decade there has been a systematic attempt to use token reinforcement programs in the classroom as a form of therapy—for example, in modifying the behavior of hyperactive children manifesting behavior disorders which interfere with their own learning and that of other students.

The basic essentials of such a token reinforcement program typically involve: (1) instructions to the class concerning behaviors that will be reinforced; (2) a method of making a potentially reinforcing stimulus—e.g., a token—contingent upon given behavior; and (3) rules governing the exchange of tokens for back-up reinforcers, such as low-calorie candy or the privilege of listening to music through earphones. These essentials must be adapted, of course, to the particular classroom setting, the children, the teacher, and the parents.

Usually there is a "fading" in the actual use of tokens and tangible back-up reinforcers, for when more positive and constructive behaviors have been established they may usually be maintained by praise and related intangible reinforcement which would not have been effective initially.

In an extensive review of such token reinforcement programs in classroom settings, O'Leary and Drabman (1971) have found them generally effective in achieving such stated objectives as (1) reducing hyperactive and disruptive behaviors; (2) increasing attention, study behavior, and academic achievement; and (3) improving interpersonal and other competencies. Often such programs also yield secondary gains, such as increased attendance. These investigators, on the basis of their findings, suggest that the long-range effectiveness of the programs merit further research and implementation.

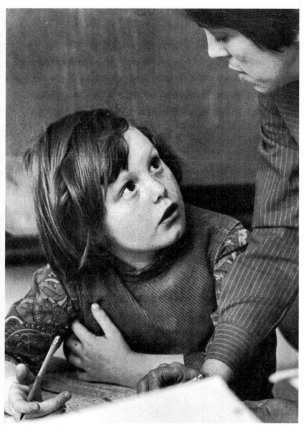

These pictures are of children labeled "emotionally disturbed or disturbing" or "socially discordant," and show them interacting with their teacher-counselors and each other. All are participants in "Project Re-Ed," which, as its name implies, is designed to reeducate children and foster more adaptive behavior on their part. The project is sponsored by the National Institute for Mental Health, the George Peabody College for Teachers, and the Mental Health Departments of the States of North Carolina and Tennessee.

Based on the philosophy that the child's problems are the product of the environment, Project Re-Ed's program is designed both to reeducate the environment to fit the child and to reeducate the child to fit the environment. Its two schools, Cumberland House in Nashville and Wright School in Durham, are viewed neither as dumping grounds where children who bother their parents can be sent and forgotten, nor snug nests where the children can do as they wish; rather they are places which emphasize the learning of more adaptive behavior through utilization of a group-oriented environment. No physical discipline is used, except that a child who misbehaves has to leave the group and go to the "quiet room" until he is ready to join his friends. For the few months of the child's stay at either school, the group—counselors and fellow pupils—constitute his world (*Transaction*, 1968).

return voluntarily or be brought back by juvenile authorities. Almost 50 percent of all arrests and detentions of adolescent girls involve running away; and although the actual incidence among male adolescents is not known, it amounts to many thousands each year.

Adolescent runaways sometimes stay with other families, but many appear to gravitate toward large cities where they join up with other teen-agers and share "pads." Others end up in "colonies" where they camp out in remote areas. In such settings they quite frequently become involved in drug abuse or deviant sexual behavior, resulting in their arrest by juvenile authorities and often in their return to their parents. For example, Mary—a 14-year-old runaway—had not been heard from by her parents for more than a year when they learned from juvenile authorities that she had been picked up for prostitution in a distant city. Mary subsequently was released to her parents on a probationary basis, with the understanding that the family would seek psychological counseling.

Dynamics. Jenkins (1970; 1971) views the unsocialized aggressive reaction and the runaway reaction as opposite sides of the same coin. In both instances, the child feels rejected by his parents and in an aversive life situation. However, while one child acts out his frustrations through aggressive antisocial behavior, the other runs away.

Often the specific reasons for runaway behavior are unclear. In many instances young people who are asked, "Why did you run away?" respond simply, "I don't know!" Usually, however, the precipitating factors appear to lie in the home and life situation of the youth. Such factors may include family dissension and conflict, overrestrictive parents, rejecting parents, and parents who just make life so miserable for the youth that his running away is an escape reaction.

Usually in runaway reactions there is a history of pathogenic family conditions, including parental rejection; but in some cases the family appears to be in a state of relative tranquillity until some event or series of events upsets its equilibrium and precipitates a crisis. For example, a sudden change in parental attitudes toward a child and his subjection to severe criticism for failing to live up to parental expectations may lead to the dramatic response of running away.

Running away may occur as an isolated incident or as part of a history of "crisis-flight" responses to which some young people and even adults resort in highly stressful situations (Hiatt & Spurlock, 1970). Here it may be emphasized that a situation which constitutes a relatively minor stress for one family may precipitate a serious crisis for another, depending on the strengths and vulnerabilities of the individual members and the life style of the family itself.

Treatment and outcomes. Treatment of the child runaway is similar to that for individuals manifesting other disorders of early life, with family therapy usually being an essential aspect. In some instances—as in those involving parental abuse, unconcern, or lack of cooperation—juvenile authorities may place the child in a foster home. The outcome will depend on the severity of the original situation and the success of efforts to modify the child's life situation so that it is no longer aversive to him.

OVERANXIOUS AND WITHDRAWAL REACTIONS

Although overanxious and withdrawal reactions are classified separately by the APA, they have so much in common that we shall deal with them under one heading. Jenkins (1968) classified 287 of his 1500 cases as reactions of these types, both of which are much more common among boys than girls.

Clinical picture. In general, the overanxious and the withdrawal reactions of childhood appear to share the following characteristics:

Oversensitivity
Unrealistic fears
Shyness and timidity
Pervasive feelings of inadequacy
Sleep disturbances
Fear of school

However, the child labeled as suffering from the overanxious reaction typically attempts to cope with his fears by becoming overdependent on others for help and support, while the child manifesting the withdrawal reaction apparently attempts to minimize his anxiety by turning away from reality and withdrawing into himself.

1. *Overanxious reaction.* The overanxious reaction is characterized by unrealistic fears, oversensitivity, self-consciousness, nightmares, and chronic anxiety. The child lacks self-confidence, is apprehensive in new situations, and tends to be immature for his age. Such children often are described by their parents as prone to worry, shy, sensitive, nervous, submissive, and easily discouraged and moved to tears. Typically they are overdependent, particularly on their parents. The following case involving "school phobia" illustrates the clinical picture in the overanxious reaction of childhood.

Johnny was a highly sensitive 6-year-old boy who suffered from myriad fears, nightmares, and chronic anxiety. He was terrified of being separated from his mother, even for a brief period. When the mother tried to enroll him in kindergarten, he became so upset when she left the room that the principal arranged for her to remain in the classroom. But after two weeks this had to be discontinued and Johnny had to be withdrawn from kindergarten, since his mother could not leave him even for a few minutes.

Later when his mother attempted to enroll him in the first grade, Johnny manifested the same intense anxiety and unwillingness to be separated from her. At the suggestion of the school counselor, the mother brought Johnny to a community clinic for assistance with the problem. The therapist who initially saw Johnny and his mother was wearing a white clinic jacket, and this led to a severe panic reaction on Johnny's part. His mother had to hold him to keep him from running away, and he did not settle down until the therapist removed his jacket. Johnny's mother explained that "He is terrified of doctors, and it is almost impossible to get him to a physician even when he is sick."

2. *Withdrawal reaction.* The withdrawal reaction is similar to the overanxious reaction, but here the child attempts to minimize his anxiety by turning inward—in effect detaching himself from a seemingly dangerous and hostile world. The results of this defensive strategy have been described by Jenkins (1969):

"In turning away from objective reality, these children turn away from the normal practice of constantly checking their expectations against experience. With such turning away, their capacity to distinguish fact from fancy tends to deteriorate. They function inefficiently and fail to develop effective patterns of behavior." (p. 70)

Children manifesting the withdrawal reaction tend toward seclusiveness, timidity, and inability to form close interpersonal relationships. Often they appear listless and apathetic and are prone to daydreaming and unrealistic fantasies. The following case is fairly typical:

Tommy was a small, slender, 7-year-old boy from a middle-class family. He was enrolled in the second grade at school but failed to function adequately in the classroom. In referring him to the school counselor, the teacher described him as being withdrawn, shy, oversensitive, and unable to make friends or to participate in classroom activities. During recess he preferred to remain in the classroom and appeared preoccupied with his thoughts and fantasies. He was seriously retarded in reading achievement and other basic school subjects. Psychological assessment showed that he was superior in intelligence but suffered from extreme feelings of inadequacy and a pervasive attitude of "I can't do it."

Dynamics. Various factors have been emphasized as being of etiological significance in both the overanxious and the withdrawal reactions of childhood. The more important of these appear to be:

1. Unusual constitutional sensitivity, easy conditionability by aversive stimuli, and the building up and generalization of "surplus fear reactions." In Chapter 8 we noted this pattern in the etiology of anxiety neuroses in adults.

2. The undermining of the child's feelings of adequacy and security by early illnesses, accidents, or losses that involve pain and discomfort. The traumatic effect of such experiences is often due partly to the child's finding himself in unfamiliar situations, as during hospitalization.

3. The "modeling" effect of an overanxious and protective parent who sensitizes the child to the dangers and threats of his world. Often the parent's overprotectiveness communicates a lack of confidence in the child's ability to cope, thus reinforcing his feelings of inadequacy.

4. The failure of an indifferent or detached parent to provide adequate guidance for his child's development. Although the child is not necessarily rejected by such a parent, neither is he adequately supported in mastering essential competencies and in gaining a positive view of himself. Repeated experiences of failure, stemming from poor learning skills, may lead to subsequent patterns of anxiety or withdrawal in the face of "threatening" situations.

Sometimes a child is made to feel that he must earn his parents' love and respect through outstanding achievement, especially in school. Such a child tends to be overcritical of himself and to feel intensely anxious and devaluated when he perceives himself as failing. Unlike the child who rejoices in his achievements, this child is a "perfectionist who does equally well but is left with a feeling of failure because he thinks he should have done better." (Krebs & Krebs, 1970, p. 40)

5. Inadequate interpersonal patterns, which typically extend beyond the family. The withdrawal reaction, in particular, "occurs in children who have found human contact more frustrating than rewarding." (Jenkins, 1970, p. 141) For the overanxious child, too, interpersonal patterns appear often to be unsatisfactory, although perhaps less aversive on the average than for the withdrawn child.

The various etiological patterns that we have been discussing in relation to the overanxious and withdrawal reactions of childhood can obviously occur in differing degrees and combinations. However, all of them are consistent with the view that these disorders result essentially from maladaptive learning.

Treatment and outcomes. Although the overanxious and withdrawal reactions of childhood may continue into adolescence and young adulthood—the first tending toward neurotic avoidance behavior and the latter toward increasingly idiosyncratic thinking and behavior—this is not typically the case. For as the child grows and his world widens in school and peer-group activities, he is likely to benefit from such corrective experiences as making friends and succeeding at given tasks. Teachers, who have become more and more aware of the needs of both the overanxious and the shy, withdrawn child—and of ways of helping them—often are able to ensure a child's success experiences and to foster constructive interpersonal relationships. Behavior-therapy procedures, employed in structured group experiences within educational settings, can help speed up and ensure favorable outcomes. Such procedures include desensitization, assertion training, and help with mastering essential competencies.

Behavior therapy has also proven highly effective in the treatment of children manifesting severe anxiety or withdrawal reactions. Montenegro (1968) has described the successful treatment of two young children manifesting pathological separation anxiety. The overall treatment program for one of the youngsters, a 6-year-old boy named Romeo, included the following procedures:

1. Exposure of the child to a graded series of situations involving the actual fear-arousing stimulus—that is, separation from the mother for increasingly longer intervals
2. The use of food during these separations as an anxiety inhibitor—which might involve taking the child to the hospital cafeteria for something to eat
3. Instruction of the parents on how to reduce the child's excessive dependence on the mother—for example, through letting him learn to do things for himself

After ten consecutive sessions, Romeo's separation anxiety was reduced to the point that he could stay home with a competent baby-sitter for an hour, and then increasingly longer. During the summer he was enrolled in a vacation church school, which he enjoyed; and when the new semester began at public school, he entered the first grade and made an adequate adjustment. It may be emphasized that the cooperation of the parents—particularly the mother—was a key factor in the treatment program.

STUTTERING

Stuttering is a speech disorder that involves a blocking or repetition of, or sometimes a struggling with, speech sounds. The term *stuttering* is synonymous with the older term *stammering*, which is gradually falling into disuse. The speaking behavior of the stutterer may vary from mild difficulty with initial syllables of certain words, as in "D-d-d-don't do that," to violent contortions and momentary inability to utter any sound at all. Most stutterers can speak fluently under ordinary circumstances; the blocking tends to occur at moments of important or stressful communication.

Every era has had its quota of these speech sufferers. Some of the more illustrious names on the roster are those of Moses, Aristotle, Vergil, Demosthenes, Charles Lamb, and Clara Barton. In our contemporary world, stuttering has been observed in diverse cultures—among the Bantu of South Africa and the Polynesians of the South Pacific, as well as among members of Oriental and Western societies (Aron, 1962; Lemert, 1962; 1970).

In the Western world an estimated 40 to 50 million children stutter badly; and in the United States stutterers include 3 million or more people, most of them children (Beech, 1967; Sheehan, 1970). More male than female children stutter, in a ratio of about 4 or 5 to 1.

Clinical picture. Most stuttering begins early in life—the onset occurring before the age of 6 in 90 percent of the cases, and the highest incidence being between the ages of 2 and 4. Words starting with consonants rather than vowels, words that are long rather than short, and words occurring early in a sentence rather than later are most likely to be stuttered (Taylor, 1966). Speech sounds that require the greatest articulatory effort, such as *b*, *d*, *s*, and *t*, are especially troublesome.

The entire performance of the stutterer represents an "internal struggle" to speak. After the momentary disturbance, however, speech becomes smooth and fluent until the next stumbling block. The stutterer's difficulty may vary considerably from one situation to another. Typically, stuttering increases both in severity and frequency in situations where the stutterer feels inferior, self-conscious, or anxious. On the other hand, most stutterers can articulate normally or with minimal difficulty when singing, whispering, or when they cannot hear the sound of their own voice.

On the basis of his early experiences as a stutterer, and also of his later studies in this field, Sheehan (1970) has pointed out that "for the child or adult who has developed the problem called stuttering, the production of a spoken word can be fraught with dread and difficulty." (vii) Similarly, Beech (1967) has pointed out that in a world organized around efficient verbal communication, stuttering can be highly stressful and self-devaluating.

"What insuperable difficulties confront the stutterer when he has to explain something to his boss, when he tries to propose marriage, or when he simply wants to buy an airplane ticket—while a restive queue forms behind him. What agony of mind must characterize the young stutterer in the classroom, eager to answer but fearing the crushing humiliation of another 'block,' wanting to join in a variety of games but knowing the ridicule which all too often greets his efforts to speak! Every day of his life the severe stutterer must brace himself against situations he cannot cope with and cannot avoid." (p. 49)

Dynamics. Stuttering has proved to be a most baffling disorder. Attempts to explain it have, in the main, focused on the following factors:

1. *Genetic and neurological factors.* In comparing a large group of children who stuttered with a matched group of nonstutterers, Johnson (1961) found that 9 times as many of the former had siblings or parents—mostly fathers—who stuttered. Although stuttering does appear to run in families, Johnson did not rule out the role of learning, pointing out that parents who are or have been stutterers may exert a detrimental influence on the speech fluency of their children. We shall comment on this point shortly.

As a group, stutterers show no evidence of brain damage or abnormal brain functioning. Brain damage causes a different type of speech or language disorder called *aphasia*—defined as a loss or impairment of ability to use language because of brain lesions. The aphasic's difficulty, as we noted in Chapter 15, is not in "getting his words out" but rather in understanding spoken words and in finding the word he wishes to use.

Another neurological view has implicated aberrations in auditory feedback. The experimental delay—or even complete withholding—of auditory feedback greatly reduces or even eliminates severe stuttering (Perkins, 1970). Although the relation of these research findings to the etiology of stuttering remains to be clarified, Dinnan, McGuiness, and Perrin (1970) have concluded from their studies that "in certain cases stuttering may be the result of minute physical imperfections in the feedback loop of the hearing mechanism." (p. 30)

2. *Learned behavior.* Currently, most investigators agree that learning is the primary factor in the etiology of stuttering. The question then arises as to the nature of such learning. Emphasizing parental standards for speech fluency, Johnson (1961) has pointed to parents who worry about the child's speech, attempt to correct his mistakes, and "tighten up" when he is speaking. Presumably their behavior—particularly during the early critical period of speech development—causes the child to develop doubts and anxieties about his ability to speak fluently. This pattern is then repeatedly reinforced by actual speech difficulties in social situations. Thus, Johnson has referred to the origin of stuttering as being in the ear of the parent rather than the tongue of the child. Although Glasner (1970) has noted that many children subjected to such parental patterns do not become stutterers, Johnson's approach seems to be supported by the fact that the child who gets through the early critical period of speech development is unlikely to become a stutterer at a later age.

The potential importance of the learning process in the etiology of stuttering has been demonstrated experimentally by Flanagan, Goldiamond, and Azrin (1959), using operant conditioning procedures. The normally fluent subject received continual electric shock, but blockage of fluent speech turned off the shock for 10 seconds; and each additional disfluency in speech that occurred during this 10-second interval further delayed the electroshock. Eventually the subject avoided the aversive stimulation almost entirely by con-

tinuous disfluent speech. As Bandura (1969) has pointed out, however, "it is exceedingly improbable that parents of stutterers continuously punish their children's fluent verbal patterns, but respond nonpunitively whenever their children block and stutter." (p. 323)

Although the precise ways in which stuttering may be learned require further study, Sheehan et al. (1962) have pointed to the importance of reinforcement in stuttering once it has been learned. According to this model, the stutterer has learned to fear the speech situation and wishes to avoid it; yet social necessity requires him to face it. Presumably he "blocks" when the two tendencies are equal in strength. A vicious circle thus develops in which (a) fear and anxiety lead to moments of blocking in speech, (b) the act of completing a stuttered utterance terminates the specific incident, and (c) the accompanying tension reduction tends to reinforce the stuttering. This pattern is well illustrated by an excerpt from a self-description by an adult stutterer:

"When I'm in the situation, I lose all contact with the world around me. I'm completely riveted on this one thing—on my struggles with the stammering. Along with that, there is a real feeling of anxiety and a feel-

In a study investigating stuttering as an approach-avoidance conflict, stutterers were asked to draw whatever they felt most adequately represented their behavior before, during, and after a moment of stuttering. The drawings of one subject, reproduced below, clearly show his high tension just before and during the block and his relief afterward. Guilt, shame, dejection, and anger were also frequently expressed, and in many cases the feelings continued after the block (Sheehan et al., 1962).

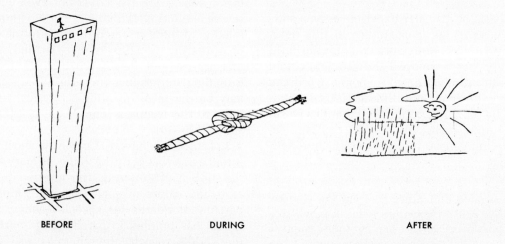

BEFORE   DURING   AFTER

ing of real tension. Following it, there is a reduction in the tension, a feeling of embarrassment and shame—almost a feeling of relief that the act is over." (Sheehan, 1970, p. 16)

3. *Stress and role behavior.* All of us have probably experienced blocking of thought and speech in stage fright or in situations where we have had to make unexpected introductions. In these situations it is probably safe to say that we were self-conscious and tense. Defective responses under these conditions are very common. Perhaps we may generalize here and say that any stressful situations that lead to severe feelings of inadequacy, self-consciousness, anxiety, fear, and tension also tend to impair psychomotor coordination and performance—and this may include speech functions. Why such stressful situations affect such speech functions far more in some persons than others is not known—although it may relate to the constitutional vulnerability of specific organ systems, including those involved in speech. For example, the child who has been subjected to disruptive factors while learning the difficult motor coordinations needed for speech may be especially vulnerable to later speech difficulties.

Sheehan (1970) has also pointed to the potential importance of role behavior in stuttering. This role behavior may take two different forms, but the eventual result is the same. In the first form the stutterer plays a "false role," in that he attempts to conceal his stuttering, as by assuming a foreign accent or a regional dialect. Even when this enables him to deceive others about his being a stutterer—at least temporarily—he is likely to experience guilt and doubt. These feelings, in turn, lead him to work even harder at denying his role as a stutterer and concentrating on his false role as a normal speaker. Ironically, however, the stutterer is usually able to be most fluent when he is not trying to keep from stuttering; and he has the greatest difficulty when he is trying to avoid disfluent speech. Thus, his false role sooner or later fails in its protective function—confronting him in turn with the view of himself as a stutterer and confirming him in the role of stutterer. In the second form, the individual simply views himself as a stutterer and hence plays that role. "I am a stutterer" becomes a permanent part of his self-concept—a view that is reinforced each time stuttering occurs. And presumably the expectations and reactions of those around him tend to further perpetuate the stuttering role and behavior.

Sheehan makes it clear that accepting the fact that one is a stutterer may have either positive or negative effects. If a person views his stuttering as self-devaluating and a chronic affliction about which he can do nothing, the result is negative. On the other hand, in accepting the fact that he is a stutterer, he has defined his problem. Like the alcoholic who recognizes his drinking problem, the stutterer can begin to cope with his problem if he recognizes it rather than denying or trying to conceal it. Of utmost importance in this regard is the point that in recognizing his problem he does not feel devaluated or obligated to play the role of a stutterer. Modern therapy places strong emphasis on self-acceptance, but not on self-resignation.

Treatment and outcomes. The following plea for help, written by a high-school youth, reveals the emotional upset that may be caused by stuttering, and the need for effective therapy.

"I have stuttered since childhood, and it is spoiling my whole life. Is there any hope that I can overcome this affliction? Isn't there anything that can be done for boys like me?" (Greene, 1946, p. 120)

Fortunately, since this letter was written marked advances have been achieved in the treatment of stuttering. As Sheehan (1970) has noted, there are not only many different ways in which stuttering can begin, but also many different ways in which it can be overcome:

"Stuttering is not a unitary disorder but a cluster of disorders of varying degrees of complexity and relatedness. Stuttering is a bog one can enter from many different pathways, and from which one may find a variety of exits." (p. 262)

Treatment for stuttering has taken such varied forms as aversive conditioning, desensitization, rhythm exercises, assertion training, hypnosis, social reinforcement of fluency, voice masking, and the delay of auditory feedback. These methods fall into two general categories: those involving direct elimination of the stuttering, and those involving acceptance and then elimination. For example, methods such as Demosthenes' speaking with pebbles in his mouth, aversive conditioning, and the delay of auditory feedback fall into the first category. Here, the attempt is to achieve fluency by means of some special technique, with the hope that this fluency will generalize to the individual's life situation. The second approach is based on the view that stuttering is an approach-avoidance conflict that produces a vicious circle. The first step here is for the stutterer to accept himself for a while, and then he can become fluent. This fluency, in turn, reduces avoidance and tends to break up the vicious circle, at which point self-assertion, social reinforcement, and other therapy approaches may be effective in maintaining the speech fluency.

Fortunately, about 4 out of 5 cases of stuttering clear up spontaneously (Sheehan & Martyn, 1970). Such recovery ordinarily occurs by the middle or late teens. Even in long-established cases, with appropriate treatment most stutterers can be completely relieved of their symptoms or be greatly helped. The term *appropriate* is important here, because a method that may be effective with one stutterer may be ineffective with another.

OTHER "DEVELOPMENTAL" DISORDERS

As in the case of stuttering, the behavior disorders we shall deal with here—enuresis, nail-biting, tics, and sleepwalking—typically involve a single outstanding symptom, rather than a more pervasive maladaptive pattern.

Enuresis. The term *enuresis* refers to the habitual involuntary discharge of urine after the age of 3. It may occur during the day, but is most common at night (bed-wetting). Among older children the enuresis often occurs in conjunction with dreams in which a child imagines he is urinating in a toilet, only to awaken and discover that he has wet the bed. The enuresis may vary in frequency, from nightly to occasional instances when the individual is under considerable stress or is unduly tired. Commonly, enuresis occurs from 2 to 5 times a week. An estimated 5 million children and adolescents in the United States suffer from the inconvenience and embarrassment of this disorder (Linde, 1966).

Although enuresis may result from a variety of organic conditions, most investigators have pointed to (1) faulty learning, resulting in the failure to acquire a needed adaptive response—that is, inhibition of reflex bladder emptying; (2) personal immaturity, associated with or stemming from emotional problems; and (3) disturbed family interactions, particularly involving conditions leading to sustained anxiety and/or hostility. In some instances a child may regress to bed-wetting when a new baby enters the family and replaces him as the center of attention; or he may resort to bed-wetting when he feels hostile toward his parents and wants to get even with them, since such behavior annoys and upsets them.

In general, treatment methods for enuretic children fall into two categories—drug therapy and conditioning procedures. Drug therapy usually involves the use of tranquilizers as well as drugs that tend to inhibit reflex bladder emptying. However, it has met with only limited success. Conditioning methods commonly utilize an electrified mattress that rings an alarm at the first few drops of urine, thus awakening the child and eliciting a reflex inhibition to micturition.

Although conditioning procedures have been effective in the treatment of enuresis, some concern has been expressed about the high relapse rate—variously reported as between 30 and 80 percent. However, with the use of intermittent rather than continuous reinforcement, the relapse rate can be markedly reduced. Fortunately, the incidence of enuresis tends to decrease markedly with age. Among 6-year-olds, an estimated 16 percent are enuretic, compared with only 3 percent of adolescents and 1 percent or less of young adults (Murphy et al., 1971).

Nail-biting. Probably about a fifth of all children bite their fingernails at one time or other. The incidence appears to be highest among stutterers, children reared in institutions, and children confronted with stressful demands. Although about as many girls as boys bite their nails at early ages, males outnumber females in later age groups, apparently because females are more interested in grooming.

Nail-biting typically appears to be a method of tension reduction, often associated with feelings of anxiety and/or hostility (Coleman & McCalley, 1948; Coleman & Seret, 1950). In general, it would appear that the tension-reducing value of nail-biting in stressful situations lies in giving the individual "something to do." In this view, nail-biting represents a learned maladaptive habit which is reinforced and maintained by its tension-reducing properties.

Little attention has been devoted to the treatment of nail-biting. While mild tranquilizers may prove helpful, it is generally agreed that restraint and bitter-tasting applications have yielded poor results. Behavior therapy should prove effective, but there has been a dearth of research evidence on the topic. Of course, initial development of this habit in a child may be checked by helping the child feel more adequate and secure, especially if he is going through some particularly difficult stress period.

Tics. A tic is a persistent, intermittent muscle twitch or spasm, usually limited to a localized muscle group. The term *tic* is used rather broadly to include blinking the eye, twitching the mouth, licking the lips, shrugging the shoulders, twisting the neck, clearing the throat, blowing through the nostrils, grimacing, and many other responses. In some instances, as in clearing the throat, the individual may be aware of the tic when it occurs, but usually he performs the act so habitually that he does not notice it. In fact, he may not even realize that he has a tic unless someone brings it to his attention. Tics occur most frequently between the ages of 6 and 14.

An adolescent who had wanted very much to be a teacher told the school counselor that he was thinking of giving up his plans. When asked the reason, he explained that several friends told him he had a persistent twitching of the mouth muscles when he answered questions in class. He had been unaware of this muscle twitch, and even after being told about it, could not tell when it took place. However, he became acutely self-conscious, and was reluctant to answer questions or enter into class discussions. As a result, his general level of tension increased, and so did the frequency of the tic—which now became apparent even when he was talking to a friend. Thus, a vicious circle had been established, but proved amenable to treatment by conditioning and self-assertive techniques.

Although tics may have an organic basis, the great majority are psychological in origin—usually stemming from self-consciousness or tension in social situations. Unfortunately, a tic often leads to a vicious circle in which the individual's awareness of the tic increases his tension in social situations because others can so readily notice it. Tics have been successfully treated by means of drugs, psychotherapy, and conditioning techniques.

Sleepwalking (somnambulism). Statistics are meager but it would appear that some 5 percent of children experience regular or periodic sleepwalking episodes.

The child usually goes to sleep in a normal manner, but arises during the second or third hour thereafter and carries out some act (Taves, 1969). This walk may take him to another room of the house or even outside, and may involve

TREATMENT OF SLEEPWALKING UTILIZING CONDITIONING PROCEDURES

Bobby, a 7-year-old boy, walked in his sleep on an average of four times a week. His mother kept a record, indicating that Bobby's sleepwalking episodes were associated with night-mares, perspiring, and talking in his sleep. During the actual sleepwalking Bobby usually was glassy-eyed and unsteady on his feet. On one occasion he started out the front door. The sleep-walking had commenced about 6 weeks before the boy was brought for therapy, and usually an episode would begin about 45 to 90 minutes after he had gone to bed.

During treatment the therapist learned that just before each sleepwalking episode Bobby usually had a nightmare about being chased by "a big black bug." In his dream Bobby thought "the bug would eat off his legs if it caught him." (Clement, 1970, p. 23) Bobby's sleepwalking episodes usually showed the following sequence: after his nightmare began, he perspired freely, moaned and talked in his sleep, tossed and turned, and finally got up and walked through the house. He was amnesic for the sleepwalking episode when he awakened the next morning.

Assessment data revealed no neurological or other medical problems and indicated that Bobby was of normal intelligence. However, he was found to be "a very anxious, guilt-ridden little boy who avoided performing assertive and aggressive behaviors appropriate to his age and sex." (p. 23) Assertive training and related measures were used but were not effective. The therapist then focused treatment on having Bobby's mother awaken the boy each time he showed signs of an impending episode. Washing Bobby's face with cold water and making sure he was fully awake, the mother would return him to bed, where he was "to hit and tear up a picture of the big black bug." At the start of the treatment program, Bobby had made up several of these drawings.

Eventually, the nightmare was associated with awakening, and Bobby learned to wake up on most occasions when he was having a bad dream. Clement considered the basic behavior therapy model in this case to follow that used in the conditioning treatment for enuresis, where a waking response is elicited by an intense stimulus just as micturition is beginning and becomes associated with and eventually prevents nocturnal bed-wetting.

rather complex activities. He finally returns to bed, and in the morning remembers nothing that has taken place. During the sleepwalking, the child's eyes are partially or fully open, he avoids obstacles, hears when spoken to, and ordinarily responds to commands, such as to return to bed. Shaking the child will usually awaken him, and he will be surprised and perplexed at finding himself in an unexpected place. Such sleepwalking episodes usually last from 15 minutes to a half hour.

The risk of injury during sleepwalking episodes is illustrated by the following case study.

"Last Fall, 14-year-old Donald Elliot got up from his bunk in his sleep, looked in the refrigerator, then, still asleep, walked out the back door. It would have been just another sleepwalking episode except that Donald was in a camper-pickup truck traveling 50 miles an hour on the San Diego Freeway. Miraculously, he escaped with cuts and bruises. But his experience,

and that of many other sleepwalkers, disproves one of the myths about somnambulism; that people who walk in their sleep don't hurt themselves." (Taves, 1969, p. 41)

The dynamics of sleepwalking are not fully understood. Kales et al. (1966) have shown that sleepwalking takes place during NREM (non-rapid eye movement) sleep, and hence presumably does not represent the acting out of a dream, as is commonly believed. In general, it would appear that sleepwalking is related to some anxiety-arousing situation that has just occurred or is expected to occur in the near future.

Very little attention has been given to the treatment of sleepwalking, although Clement (1970) has described the successful treatment—utilizing conditioning procedures—of a 7-year-old boy (see page 605). A good deal of additional research in this area is needed before we can generalize concerning treatment procedures.

PROBLEMS IN TREATMENT AND PREVENTION

We have referred to the increasing use of conditioning techniques in the treatment of childhood disorders, and in this trend we can see the decreasing dependence on psychoanalysis and other traditional long-term psychotherapeutic approaches, which have met with limited success. However, short-term psychotherapy still plays a crucial role in many cases, and sociotherapy is important in the alleviation of pathogenic family or other sociocultural conditions that are causing or maintaining the child's behavior problem.

In concluding our review of the behavior disorders of childhood, let us note: (1) certain problems that are relatively specific to the treatment of children; and (2) the advent of a new era in child therapy and prevention of disorders, with emphasis on a "Child's Bill of Rights" and the social commitment to provide conditions conducive to the optimal development of our youth.

PROBLEMS ASSOCIATED WITH THE TREATMENT OF CHILDREN

We have already discussed—in Chapter 6—the need for the early detection and correction of faulty behaviors and developmental trends in childhood. Here we shall briefly review certain points that are relatively specific to the treatment of children.

1. *The child's inability to seek assistance.* The great majority of emotionally disturbed children who need assistance are not in a position to ask for it themselves, or to transport themselves to and from child guidance clinics. Thus, unlike the adult or the adolescent, who usually can seek help during crisis periods, the child is dependent, primarily on his parents. They must realize when he needs professional help, and take the initiative in seeking it for him. Many children, of course, come to the attention of treatment agencies as a consequence of school referrals, delinquent acts, or parental abuse.

2. *The high incidence of pathogenic family patterns.* Another key factor in dealing with the behavior disorders of childhood is the high incidence of parents who are poorly equipped for child rearing. The Joint Commission on the Mental Health of Children of the American Orthopsychiatric Association (1968) has estimated that 25 percent of the children in our society come from inadequate homes. Since the care of the child is traditionally the responsibility of the parents, and local and state agencies intervene only in extreme cases—usually involving physical abuse—these children are obviously at a disadvantage. Not only are they deprived from the standpoint of environmental influence on their personality development, but they also lack parents who perceive their need for help and who actively seek and participate in treatment programs.

3. *Treatment of the parents as well as the child.* Since most of the behavior disorders specific to childhood appear to grow out of pathogenic family patterns, it usually is essential for the parents, as well as the child, to receive treatment. As we have noted, in some instances the child may be removed from his family setting, or the treatment program may focus on the parents rather than on the child, including the training of parents in the use of shaping and reinforcement procedures. Increasingly, the treatment of children has come to mean family therapy, in which one or both parents as well as the child or siblings participate in all phases of the program. For working mothers without husbands and for parents who basically reject the child, treatment may pose a difficult problem. It may also pose a problem for poorer families who lack transportation as well as money. Thus, both parental and economic factors help determine which emotionally disturbed children will receive assistance.

4. *The problem of placing the child outside the family.* Most communities have juvenile facilities which, day or night, will provide protective care and custody for child victims of unfit homes, abandonment, abuse, neglect, and related conditions. Depending on the home situation and the special needs of the child, he will either be returned to his parents or removed from his home. In the latter instance, four types of facilities are commonly relied on: (a) a foster home; (b) a private institution for the care of children; (c) a county or state institution; or (d) the home of relatives. Of course, the quality of the foster home or other placement is a crucial consideration.

It is apparent from the preceding discussion that much hinges on the availability of treatment facilities for children. The Joint Commission on the Mental Health of Children (1968), noting that some 15 to 20 percent of our nation's children

This picture of a cruel and aggressive cat and a submissive mouse was drawn by John——, an emotionally disturbed boy who grew up in a broken home in a socially disadvantaged area of Los Angeles. He was admitted to the children's division of a state mental hospital, where he drew the picture. In it, he depicted the world—symbolized by the cat—as a terrifying place. He saw himself as the mouse—helpless and inadequate. After 6 months in the hospital, John showed marked improvement and was admitted to a "Boy's-Town" type of facility which had a controlled, but more natural, environment. At last report, John was making a successful adjustment in his new setting and was continuing to gain needed competencies and self-confidence.

receive no health services or almost none, called for a change in bringing services directly to the areas needing them:

"We feel very strongly that no real progress will be made even if the available quantity of services is greatly expanded, unless a radical break is made with traditional ways in which services are organized and delivered . . . The child treatment centers of the future will have to be located and oriented to the population they serve." (p. 408)

As we turn to the even more basic problem of prevention, we may note that McGraw (1970) has marshalled evidence that such services must be available to the individual early in life if they are to be effective. The mother should be provided with adequate care during pregnancy, and adequate educational and health services should be available to the child from the cradle on.

CHILD ADVOCACY PROGRAMS

In mid-1969 there were over 55 million children under 14 years of age in our society (Sussex, 1970); this would indicate that a massive social commitment is needed to provide our youth not only with adequate treatment facilities, but also with conditions that foster their optimal development. At present, however, both treatment facilities and preventive programs are extremely inadequate. To illustrate, in 1970 not a single community in the United States provided adequate health services for its children (Lourie et al., 1970). In fact, the National Institute of Mental Health (1970) pointed out that "less than 1 percent of the disturbed youngsters in the United States receive any kind of treatment, and less than half of these receive adequate help." (p. 7)

In its final report—*Crisis in Child Mental Health: Challenge for the 1970's*—the Joint Commission on the Mental Health of Children (1970) referred to our lack of commitment to our children and youth as a "national tragedy." The Commission's report concludes:

"Either we permit a fifth of the nation's children to go down the drain—with all that this implies for public disorder and intolerable inhumanity—or we decide, once and for all, that the needs of children have first priority on the nation's resources." (p. 408)

In 1971, a positive step toward dealing with the rights of children and ensuring their access to needed services was taken by the President of the United States when, acting on the recommendation of the Joint Commission on the Mental Health of Children, as well as that of the White House Conference on Children, he established the National Center for Child Advocacy.

The National Center for Child Advocacy has as its objective the implementation and follow-up of the top priorities, or "overriding concerns," that were enumerated at the White House Conference on Children, held in Washington, D.C., in December 1970 (Chandler, 1971; Close, 1971).[1]

The first seven of these priorities bear mention here:

---

[1] *The Report to the President, White House Conference on Children,* is available from the Superintendent of Documents, Government Printing Office, Washington, D.C. 20402 (1970, 457 pp., $4.75).

1. The establishment of comprehensive family-oriented health programs, which would include health services, day care, and early childhood education
2. The development of realistic programs to eliminate racism, which handicaps so many of our children
3. The reordering of national priorities, starting with a guaranteed basic family income to provide adequately for the needs of children
4. Improvement of our system of justice to ensure timely and positive response to the needs of children
5. Establishment of a national child health care program financed by the federal government to ensure needed and comprehensive care for all children
6. The development of a system for the early identification of children with special needs, to ensure prompt delivery of appropriate treatment
7. The establishment of a federal agency for child advocacy in which all ethnic, cultural, racial, and related groups would be fully represented (Close, 1971, p. 44)

Lest the objectives of child advocacy programs and the priorities we have listed seem unrealistic or impossible of attainment, we might appropriately draw attention to the "Child's Bill of Rights," formulated by the New York State Youth Commission (1970). This bill seeks for every child, regardless of race, color, or creed:

"1. The right to the affection and intelligent guidance of understanding parents
2. The right to be raised in a decent home in which he or she is adequately fed, clothed, and sheltered
3. The right to live in a community in which adults practice the belief that the welfare of their children is of primary importance
4. The right to early diagnosis and treatment of physical handicaps and mental and social maladjust-

ments—at public expense whenever necessary" (p. 32)

In Chapter 21 we shall deal with the goals and programs of government and private organizations directly involved in the movement for comprehensive health care and with efforts toward fostering self-actualization and social progress.

In this chapter our focus has been primarily on behavior disorders specific to childhood—including autism, hyperactive reaction, runaway reaction, and other developmental disorders, such as stuttering and enuresis. We excluded from consideration transient situational, neurotic, psychotic, and other mental disorders that occur in other life periods as well as childhood, and that have been covered in preceding chapters.

We noted that it was not until the turn of the century that attention began to be directed toward the study of childhood disorders, and that during the intervening period great strides have been made in understanding and treating them. We have seen that particular emphasis is being placed on the use of behavior modification techniques in treating childhood disorders, and that early detection and correction of faulty behaviors and developmental trends is considered crucial.

We concluded this chapter by noting some of the special problems associated with the treatment of childhood behavior disorders, by commenting on the seeming lack of genuine commitment to the welfare of our children and youth, and by briefly discussing the important concept of child advocacy programs.

Maladaptive Behavior of Groups

18

WAR AND THREAT OF WAR

PREJUDICE AND DISCRIMINATION AGAINST GROUPS

OVERPOPULATION AND ECOLOGICAL VIOLATIONS

UNCONTROLLED SOCIAL CHANGE

With the fantastic pictures of man's first landing on the moon—and of the earth viewed from the perspective of man in space—the realization was brought home to hundreds of millions of people that our earth itself is a spaceship on which we are the astronauts. Unfortunately, it has also become obvious that our spacecraft is in serious jeopardy. As Dr. Brown of the California Institute of Technology has expressed it:

"Our ship has an efficient life-support system which produces our food, purifies our air, and processes our wastes. Our main trouble is that the size of the ship remains constant and the capacity of its processing units increases but very slowly while the population of astronauts increases with frightening rapidity. And not only does the population increase but the per capita volume of waste increases as well. We are poisoning ourselves often to the point of death. We must add to this the unhappy fact that the astronauts of this ship fight with each other and kill each other using weapons which steadily become more powerful and effective." (1967, p. 15)

Thus in our consideration of what behaviors are maladaptive for man, we must broaden our focus from individual and family patterns to larger groups whose structures and behavior can affect us all.

In labeling group behavior as *maladaptive*, we shall utilize the same general criteria which we have applied to individual behavior. Thus we shall assume: (1) that man's survival and actualization are worthwhile, and (2) that group behavior can be evaluated in terms of its consequences for these objectives. Again we must go beyond a consideration of prevailing social norms, since it is clear that many societies have had norms which turned out to be maladaptive. In addition, many of the patterns of group behavior which we have considered adaptive in the past —such as conquering our natural environment —now raise problems or have clearly become maladaptive in our time. Seemingly, the events on our spacecraft have reached a "critical point" which does not permit us to function in the future as we have in the past—not if we are to survive.

We cannot begin to deal with all maladaptive group behavior in the present chapter. The most we can do is consider some of the key dimensions in a few specific maladaptive patterns that are of crucial importance to all of us, clarify some of the possible consequences of different courses of group action, and note some of the efforts that are being made to improve the prospects for the human enterprise.

WAR AND THREAT OF WAR

If we look closely at a spaceship produced by modern science and technology, we note that it is designed to achieve certain objectives, that its crew is specified, and that discipline and cooperation are essential to its very existence. But if we look closely at the spaceship Earth, we see some disturbing differences. The crew is hurtling through space with no known goals or reliable navigational guides, and discipline and cooperation are precarious at best. In fact, violent conflict breaks out with alarming frequency, and the threat of global warfare is a continuing menace.

THE COSTS OF WAR

Throughout recorded history, wars have cost man dearly in terms of their inevitable accompaniments—death, mutilation, grief, destruction of material resources, privation, and social disorganization. And over the centuries, they have become increasingly costly and ever more destructive. The war between our states, during a period when our population was far lower than it is today, cost half a million lives. In 1945 the nations of the world concluded a war that had cost 40 million or more lives. The holocaust created by the bomb dropped on Hiroshima in the last week of that war—with estimates of the death toll reaching as high as 200,000 people —has been vividly described:

". . . an explosion filled the sky as though a piece of sun had broken off, a bolt of white-hot terror that twisted steel into unimaginable shapes, melted iron bridges, and incinerated more flesh than has ever been condemned at one time and in one place throughout the history of the human race." (Cousins, 1970, p. 38)

And now we have thermonuclear bombs thousands of times as powerful as the bomb that turned Hiroshima into a scene of epic desolation.

The psychological costs of war in terms of guilt, dehumanization, and irrational behavior—on the part of both the civilian population and the participants—have never been adequately assessed. The psychiatrist Gerald Caplan (1971), working with returning veterans from the war in Southeast Asia, has reported that a significant proportion suffer from "depression, social alienation, anger and resentment, emotional irritability, poor control over aggression, alcoholism, and drug addiction." (p. 11) In view of the relatively unique nature of this war, it is doubtful that these findings can be generalized to veterans of other wars, but the experience of regarding other human beings as quarry to be hunted down and destroyed is hardly calculated to prepare men to live together cooperatively on their spaceship. Even our civilian population has recently grown accustomed—if not desensitized—to the idea of "free-fire" zones where anything that moves may be fired upon; to "body-counts" of enemy dead as a criterion of "success"; to "acceptable losses"; and to special hospital wards for the mutilated survivors. Those doing the fighting have been exposed to such brutalizing experiences that an officer could refer to throwing villagers in a ditch and shooting them as "no big deal."

The costs of war also include the diversion of natural resources, productive capacity, trained minds, and dollars to promote death instead of

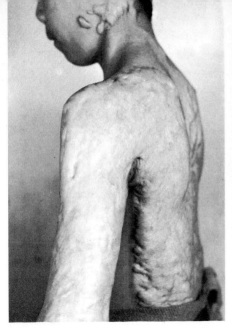

Effects of the atomic bomb on Hiroshima that day and on one survivor two years later. Some who seemed unharmed at the time developed leukemia later and died. Twenty-five years after the holocaust, some survivors were still hospitalized; others suffered frequent illnesses or needed periodic blood transfusions.

life. For example, between 1964 and 1970 over 200 billion dollars per year were spent by the countries of the world on arms and armed forces —money sorely needed for building a better life for the peoples of the world. Thus war, regardless of the perspective from which we view it, is an extremely costly way of trying to resolve human problems.

The preceding statement is in no way intended to minimize the necessity for national defense in our troubled world or to detract from the heroism of the many brave and dedicated men and women who have sacrificed their lives in warfare to achieve and maintain the freedom we now enjoy in our society. Rather our intent is to suggest that we must work out better and more rational means of dealing with our problems if man is to prosper or even survive.

PSYCHOLOGICAL BASES OF AGGRESSION

Since man is the only species—other than ants —that engages in warfare and other acts of collective violence against his own kind, the question has inevitably arisen as to what characteristics of man make him prone to this pattern of behavior. Among the answers that have been offered are the following.

Aggression as an instinctual part of man's nature.[1] In addressing his troops during World War II, General George Patton made the following statement:

"Men! This stuff we hear about Americans wanting to stay out of this war—not wanting to fight—is a lot of bullshit. Americans love to fight, traditionally. All real Americans love the sting of clash of battle. . . ."

No doubt leaders of military units have made similar statements to their men throughout the history of warfare. In fact, General Sherman is reputed to have said, "It is a good thing war is so terrible; otherwise men would love it too much."

Many people other than military leaders have viewed aggression as inherent in man's nature. Freud, for example, depicted man as essentially a predatory animal.

". . . men are not gentle, friendly creatures, wishing for love, who simply defend themselves if they are attacked, but . . . a powerful measure of desire for aggressiveness has to be reckoned with as part of their instinctual endowment. The result is that their neighbor is to them not only a possible helper or sexual object, but also a temptation to them to gratify their aggressiveness . . . to seize his possessions, to humiliate him, to cause him pain, to torture and to kill him. . . .

"Anyone who calls to mind the atrocities of the early migrations, of the invasions of the Huns or by the so-called Mongols under Genghis Khan and Tamurlane, of the sack of Jerusalem by the pious crusaders, even indeed the horrors of the last world-war, will have to bow his head humbly before the truth of this view of man." (1930, pp. 85–86).

---

[1]While our discussion will focus on acts involving physical aggression, it may be emphasized that people's physical and psychological integrity can also be violated in other ways, for example, in brainwashing or political repression.

According to Freud, the energy that fuels the aggressive instinct in man gradually accumulates, and if it cannot be discharged in small amounts or in socially constructive ways, it will eventually be discharged in extreme aggression or violence.

Viewing man in historical perspective, Toynbee (1970) has emphasized the thin veneer that separates civilized man from savagery:

"There is a persistent vein of violence and cruelty in human nature. Man has often striven to rid himself of what he recognizes as being a hideous moral blemish,

WAR CRIMES AND INDIVIDUAL RESPONSIBILITY

Slightly over 25 years ago, 22 of the most powerful men in Germany's Third Reich were summoned before an international tribunal of judges (two from each of the victorious Big Four powers) to answer for their actions in World War II. One interesting facet of the Nuremberg Trials, as they were called, was the fact that not only military leaders but also cabinet members, industrialists, and persons from other ranks were tried with the men who had actually ordered or done the shooting. Another facet was establishment of the principle that the individual is responsible for his acts during wartime, even though he is acting under orders.

The principles under which the trials were held were contained in the Charter of Nuremburg, affirmed by the General Assembly of the United Nations in 1945. In 1950, the International Law Commission, containing experts on international law from all the major legal systems in the world, was directed to draw up a formulation of these principles. Its report delineates three kinds of crimes punishable under international law—crimes against peace, war crimes, and crimes against humanity. This formulation offers the most complete set of guidelines we have regarding the relationship between such crimes and personal responsibility:

Principle I. Any person who commits an act which constitutes a crime under international law is responsible therefor and liable to punishment.

Principle II. The fact that internal law does not impose a penalty for an act which constitutes a crime under international law does not relieve the person who committed the act from responsibility under international law.

Principle III. The fact that a person who committed an act which constitutes a crime under international law acted as Head of State or responsible government official does not relieve him from responsibility under international law.

Principle IV. The fact that a person acted pursuant to order of his Government or of a superior does not relieve him from responsibility under international law, provided a moral choice was in fact possible for him.

Principle V. Any person charged with a crime under international law has the right to a fair trial on the facts and law.

Principle VI. The crimes hereinafter set out are punishable as crimes under international law:
  a. Crimes against peace:
    (i) Planning, preparation, initiation or waging of a war of aggression or a war in violation of international treaties, agreements or assurances;
    (ii) Participation in a common plan or conspiracy for the accomplishment of any of the acts mentioned under (i).
  b. War crimes:
    Violations of the laws or customs of war which include, but are not limited to, murder, ill-treatment or deportation to slave-labour or for any other purpose of civilian population of or in occupied territory, murder or ill-treatment of prisoners of war, of persons on the seas, killing of hostages, plunder of public or private property, wanton destruction of cities, towns, or villages, or devastation not justified by military necessity.
  c. Crimes against humanity:
    Murder, extermination, enslavement, deportation and other inhuman acts done against any civilian population, or persecutions on political, racial or religious grounds, when such acts are done or such persecutions are carried on in execution of or in connexion with any crime against peace or any war crime.

Principle VII. Complicity in the commission of a crime against peace, a war crime, or a crime against humanity as set forth in Principle VI is a crime under international law.[1]

It was anticipated that these general guidelines would be made more specific as competent domestic and international tribunals heard cases in the future. Although victors had been passing judgment on the acts of enemy citizens in the Nuremburg Trials, it was assumed that principles were involved that transcended the victor's classic "right" to punish a vanquished enemy—that "war crimes" are crimes regardless of what country's citizens commit them.

[1] Adopted by the United Nations International Law Commission at its second session, A/1316, part III, *Yearbook of the International Law Commission, 1950,* vol. II, pp. 374 and ff. (United Nations Publication, Sales No.: 1957 v. 3, vol. II).

unworthy of human nature's better side. Sometimes man has fancied that he has succeeded in civilizing himself.

"The Romans fancied this when, in the fourth century B.C., they substituted constitutional government for class war. After that, Roman political life was unstained by bloodshed for nearly a quarter of a millennium. But the spell was broken when, in the fateful year 133 B.C., Tiberius Gracchus was lynched—by senators, of all people.

"The Romans were horrified at what they had done. They had violated a taboo against violence that had come to seem to be quite securely established, but their horror did not bring them to their senses. During the next 100 years, violence in the Roman world went from bad to worse: violence committed by right against left; by masters against slaves; by citizens against subjects. . . ." (p. 3)

The ethologist Lorenz (1966) has suggested that in the course of evolution from infrahuman forms, man has lost the instinctual controls that protect other animals from members of their own species. He has noted that many animals make a great show of aggression toward other members of their species, but that the weaker animal usually withdraws or signals submission. For example, a defeated wolf will bare his throat to the victor, and the stronger animal then will discontinue the attack. But man has no such instinctive mechanism.

Thus many investigators view man as nature's ultimate word on the subject of the armed predator. And in view of the long chain of violence and cruelty extending from the most ancient times to today's headlines, it is not surprising that aggression has long been perceived as an inherent part of man's basic nature—to be held in check but never eliminated completely.

Aggression as a response to frustration. Closely related to the view of aggression as an inborn instinct is the frustration-aggression hypothesis formulated by the psychologists Miller and Dollard (1941). According to this hypothesis, aggression is a logical and expected consequence of frustration, its purpose being to remove or destroy the obstacle to need-gratification.

The frustration-aggression hypothesis has undergone considerable revision over time. One revision views aggressive behavior as based on both an inner readiness to aggress (as a result of frustration) and external cues which provide a target and release the aggressive behavior (Berko-

witz, 1965; Janis et al., 1969). These internal and external forces presumably operate in an additive manner. If one is weak, the other must be strong for aggression to occur. The strength of the inner readiness to aggress depends on factors such as the intensity and arbitrariness of the frustration, while the strength of external cues or releasers depends upon conditions such as the anticipated consequences of the aggressive action.

The interaction of inner feelings of frustration and external cues is well depicted on a group level in ghetto riots. The frustration component in this case has been well described by Clark (1967):

"A central fact emerges from the murky background of the present urban eruptions; a society of affluence has raised the expectations and aspirations of the poor but has bypassed them, thereby increasing their frustration and anger, their bitterness, hostility. . . ." (p. 31)

In this case the external targets are objects symbolizing the white racist society, which is perceived as the source of the frustration; and the specific release mechanism is the absence of adequate social controls, with a low level of expectation of punishment for participants (Ilfeld, 1969; Rosenthal, 1971). Presumably, many wars could also be explained in terms of this frustration-aggression model.

Recently, the frustration-aggression hypothesis has also been modified by the recognition that learning plays a key role not only in what aggressive responses are used but whether aggressive responses are made at all. Thus through learning, frustration may come to lead to any of a variety of responses, including constructive and peaceful ones.

Aggression as learned coping behavior. The early studies of Bandura and Walters (1963) and a number of later investigators have shown that aggressive behavior is readily learned through the observation and imitation of aggressive models and that it can be reinforced and maintained by a variety of rewarding conditions.

"Physically aggressive behavior can be learned in accordance with the tenets of learning theory just like any other response. Aggressive habits are acquired largely through imitation . . . or through the direct rewarding of aggressive responses. Preceding frustration is not required." (Ilfeld, 1969, p. 678)

WHY DO THEY DO IT?

Despite the horror of war and the long-lasting suffering and waste it causes, the momentum of a war, once undertaken, is sustained by several potent psychological processes.

1. **Purpose and meaning.** During wartime the individual typically becomes part of an important undertaking in which the stakes are high for him and presumably for his country. For many young people, it is the first time life has taken on real purpose and meaning. In a religious or ideological war, one has a great feeling of self-righteousness: he is preserving the truth and right against the forces of evil.

2. **Remoteness of the enemy.** With modern weapons, most soldiers never see the human beings they are killing; this is particularly true for air force personnel on bombing missions. Face-to-face encounters with the enemy are becoming increasingly rare in modern warfare.

3. **Negative image of the enemy.** The enemy comes to be seen as wrong, cruel, inferior, and less than human; the soldier rationalizes that killing and mutilating such a being is not cause for guilt. In assessing the lessons learned from the My Lai massacre, Opton (1971) noted a soldier's statement that many men in his company would not think of killing a man: "I mean a white man—a human so to speak."

4. **Atrocities committed by the enemy.** Witnessed or reported atrocities by the enemy, plus the experience of seeing many of one's buddies killed and mutilated, are seen as justifying ruthlessness on one's own part and may elicit both fear and hostility which, in turn, promote further aggression simply as a matter of survival. In essence, it becomes a matter of "kill or be killed."

5. **Habituation effect of killing in wartime.** In war, people become habituated to cruelty and killing, to seeing victims in terms of statistics. Dead bodies become objects rather than dead human beings who once had dreams, aspirations, and potential for creative achievement.

Other psychological factors include pressures not to let down one's buddies and pride in doing one's job skillfully and effectively. Some of these factors were dealt with in Chapter 7 in our discussion of combat exhaustion. The end result of all these factors is to provide multiple reinforcements for conformity and participation and a general acceptance of the legitimacy of killing under these circumstances.

Violence is standard fare in television, movies, newspapers, and other mass media to which our youth are constantly exposed. The National Commission on the Causes and Prevention of Violence issued an official statement noting that:

"Children begin to absorb the lessons of television before they can read or write. . . . In a fundamental way, television helps to create what children expect of themselves and others, and what constitutes the standards of civilized society. . . . Yet we daily permit our children during their formative years to enter a world

. . . of routine demonstrations of killing and maiming." (1969b, p. 393)

In fact, Buckhout et al. (1971) have estimated that the average child television viewer in our society sees some 12,000 or more violent deaths—as well as a multitude of other cruel and aggressive actions—before he is 14 years old. And this says nothing of the plethora of war toys—automatic rifles, tanks, fighter planes, and so on—which are so popular in the imaginary war games played by children.

Of course, children are also taught to discriminate between the violence portrayed in the mass media and violence in their own personal behavior. Parental or social disapproval and punishment make it clear that such behavior is not acceptable in everyday life. And some investigators believe that watching violence on TV or playing war games can serve as a safety valve by providing vicarious release of pent-up frustrations and hostilities. However, the opportunity it provides for maladaptive learning must also be considered.

Bandura, Ross, and Ross (1963) have concluded that a child exposed to violent models will learn aggressive actions as a part of his behavior repertoire. Later, under certain conditions, such actions may be brought into operation.

"From our knowledge of the effects of punishment on behavior, the responses in question would be expected to retain their original strength and could reappear on later occasions in the presence of appropriate eliciting stimuli, particularly if instigation is high, the instruments for aggression are available, and the threat of noxious consequences is reduced." (pp. 9–10)

The implications of this conclusion for civil violence as well as for cruel and inhuman acts committed by soldiers in wartime seem far-reaching. As with other kinds of learned behavior, models help supply the repertoire of responses available to the individual, and the anticipated consequences guide what response he makes at a given time.

TOWARD PREVENTING WAR

Despite the incompleteness of our knowledge, much of what we have learned about changing or preventing individual aggression seems relevant also to understanding and coping with group violence and war.

Preventing group aggression. Although the hypotheses concerning the causes of aggression suggest different ways of attempting to prevent it, they do tend to supplement each other. Thus we would expect that aggression could be lowered or prevented by a combination of the following: (1) reducing the tendency to aggress by reducing the causes of frustration, especially frustration perceived as arbitrary, unfair, and self-devaluating; (2) providing nonaggressive models for children, formal instruction and practice in constructive ways of coping with frustration, and positive reinforcement of constructive behavior when it occurs; and (3) assuring that aggression is surely, swiftly, and fairly punished. Explicitly, the emphasis is on alleviating the causes of frustration and fostering constructive rather than aggressive responses when frustration does occur. Implicitly, it means preventive work in devising an environment in which no group feels unfairly shut out from benefits available to other groups, and in which no group believes that it can meet its needs at the expense of other groups.

Clearly, aggression is not the only motivation that leads to group conflict and war. Fear, economic pressure, ambition for power, greed, rivalry, and ideological fervor have often been key factors in precipitating wars. Other psychosocial factors, such as misinformation, faulty perceptions of reality, cultural acceptance of war as a means of resolving group conflicts, and rationalizations justifying war have often played tragic roles. And in recent years, the spiraling arms race has contributed its share to war and the threat of war.

Reversing the cycle of aggression and counteraggression. The typical reaction to aggression is counteraggression, and the typical reaction to fear of aggression is preparation for counteraggression. In both cases there is likely to be an escalation, whether of violence or preparation for violence, with a deterioration in the chances for peace and an increase in the chances of violent conflict. As Janis et al. (1969) have pointed out, "Intergroup hostility between labor and management, between rival political groups, and between rival nations is frequently built up by a series of aggressive and counteraggressive moves." (p. 169)

On the international level, this process has been occurring during the last several decades in a spiraling arms race by the superpowers which has led to ever more deadly destructive capacity. The paradoxical nature of this arms race was pointed out over 30 years ago by Joad (1939):

". . . If, as they maintain, the best way to preserve peace is to prepare for war, it is not altogether clear why all nations should regard the armaments of other nations as a menace to peace. However, they do so regard them, and are accordingly stimulated to increase their armaments to overtop the armaments by which they conceive themselves to be threatened. . . . These increased arms being in their turn regarded as a menace by nation A whose allegedly defensive armaments have provoked them, are used by nation A as a pretext for accumulating yet greater armaments wherewith to defend itself against the menace. Yet these greater armaments are in turn interpreted by neighbouring nations as constituting a menace to themselves and so on. . . ." (p. 69)

With the development of the atom bomb, Winston Churchill saw some hope of resolving this para-

A REMEDY FOR AGGRESSIVENESS?

In September 1971, American Psychological Association President Kenneth Clark suggested that antisocial aggression, including war, might be prevented by chemicals inserted in specific brain centers. He particularly emphasized the possibility of administering such drugs to political leaders to prevent them from making aggressive decisions, but he also suggested that such chemicals might be useful for people generally for preventing cruelty and violence. The aim would be to control people's "baser instincts" without turning them into robots or impairing their creative and evaluative abilities (Clark, 1971).

Critics were quick to point out that there might be serious problems in getting a president—much less a dictator—to submit to such treatment and in setting up a procedure for giving the drug to him, as well as in preventing the general public from being victimized. More basic, however, was their reminder that destructive violence commonly involves learned and reinforced behavior rather than a simple instinctual response. It seems highly improbable that chemical changes could ever solve the complex problems of interpersonal and group aggression, especially without affecting our capacity for more desirable forms of behavior. In any event, chemicals such as Clark recommended have not yet been found.

Significantly, soon after Clark's address was given, there were speeches in the U.S. Congress opposing the use of government funds for research aimed at finding such a means of behavior control. Probably most of us would be skeptical of and opposed to other people's power to use chemicals in order to "keep us in line."

dox when he said that "mankind might be able to maintain a precarious peace through mutual terror."

But the paradox has continued, and it is not proving easy to stop the arms race, to start a rollback in armaments, or to implement the powers of the United Nations Security Council as an international mediating and peacekeeping agency. However, some progress has been made in recent years, including the banning of nuclear weapons tests in the atmosphere, under water, and in outer space. A treaty on the nonproliferation of nuclear weapons has been signed by most countries. And negotiations on the limitation of strategic arms have been undertaken. But real progress toward limiting the development and stockpiling of ever more lethal weapons of mass destruction has yet to be made.

Lawrence (1971) has emphasized the need to work through the United Nations in mobilizing world opinion in the "endeavor to put an end to nuclear armaments—to abolish these weapons wherever they are in existence today and to forbid the making thereafter of all instruments of mass murder." (p. 96) This will not be an easy endeavor, but as York (1970) has concluded, "I am equally sure that unless we nerve ourselves to make the attempt, and make it soon, we are quite simply doomed." (p. 41)

In concluding our immediate discussion of war and threat of war, it seems appropriate to quote the following message from the people of Hiroshima to the people of America. It was delivered by their mayor in 1970, 25 years after the atomic bomb was dropped on their city.

"The people of Hiroshima ask nothing of the world except that we be allowed to offer ourselves as an exhibit for peace. We ask only that enough people know what happened here and how it happened and why it happened, and that they work hard to see that it never happens anywhere again.

"We are sick at heart as we look out at the world and see that nations are already fighting the initial skirmishes that can grow into a full war. We know that stopping the war is not a simple thing and that there are grave questions that have to be solved before the world can have true peace.

"But we also know that some nation must take leadership in building the type of peace that will last. And we are looking to America for that leadership. America can call for world law, and all the world will listen. Leaders of some nations may not want to listen, but their people will hear. Let the call go forth from America for a federation of the nations strong enough to prevent war, and a thrill will be known in the hearts of people everywhere.

"This is the best hope for averting a war which would see thousands of Hiroshimas. And this is the message the people of Hiroshima respectfully but urgently put before you." (Cousins, 1970, p. 45)

PREJUDICE AND DISCRIMINATION AGAINST GROUPS

"We hold these truths to be self-evident, that all men are created equal, that they are endowed by their creator with certain inalienable rights; that among these rights are life, liberty, and the pursuit of happiness."
Declaration of Independence, July 4, 1776

Despite the ideals expressed in our Declaration of Independence, our society has a long history of group prejudice and discrimination. There has been racial prejudice, with cruel discrimination against Indians, blacks, and Mexican Americans; religious prejudice, with discrimination against

Irish-Catholics, Jews, and Mormons; and prejudice leading to discrimination against countless other groups regarded as "different" and inferior —homosexuals, ex-convicts, alcoholics, and even women and young people.[1]

In Chapter 6, we alluded to the damaging effects

---

[1]As used in the present context *prejudice* refers to any attitude toward other individuals or groups which is based on inadequate and selective sources of information, while *discrimination* refers to overt acts that deny equal status or opportunity to persons on the basis of their membership in certain groups. Usually, of course, prejudice and discrimination go together.

of racial prejudice and discrimination on an individual's early development as well as to the stressful life situation it creates for its victims in adult life. In the present section, we shall attempt to deal with group prejudice and discrimination in a broader social context, emphasizing its pernicious role in wasted human potential and destructive group divisiveness.

THE SCOPE OF THE PROBLEM

In 1740 the state of South Carolina passed legislation providing that:

"All negroes . . . mulattoes, or mestizos, who are or shall hereafter be in the province, and all their issue and offspring, born or to be born, shall be and they are hereby declared to be and remain forever hereafter absolute slaves. . . ." (Tannenbaum, 1947, pp. 66–67)

Thus blacks were considered simply as property, not as human beings—a practice which Hallie (1970) has referred to as "a legal formulation of the essence of cruelty." (p. 298)

The practical implementation of such cruelty is illustrated by the following advertisement which appeared at a later date in the *New Orleans Bee:*

"Negroes for sale.—A Negro woman, 24 years of age, and her two children, one eight and the other three years old. Said negroes will be sold separately or together, as desired. The woman is a good seamstress. She will be sold low for cash, or exchanged for groceries.

"For terms, apply to Matthew Bliss and Co., 1 Front Levee." (Tannenbaum, 1947, p. 77)

Although the practice of slavery ended over a hundred years ago, the roots of racism were deeply imbedded in our social fabric and have proven exceedingly difficult to eradicate. Even today, tremendous educational and economic gaps remain and in some cases have increased between black and white people in our society. It is in this historical perspective that we must view the emerging "black consciousness" and the struggle of the black minority for the equal rights and opportunities guaranteed in our Constitution.

The blacks have suffered most from racial prejudice and discrimination, but they have not been alone.

"Afro-Americans, Mexican-Americans (Chicanos), Asian-Americans, and Native-Americans (Indians) have contributed to the development of this nation since its inception. Yet, today, a man of color knows that his color or origin represents agony, suffering, and degradation at the hands of the white man." (Allen et al., 1971, p. 94)

The preceding conclusion was arrived at after a review of the historical evidence and present social situation by a group of "concerned students" representing all skin colors.[1] One of these students expressed his own feelings very poignantly:

"Step into my shoes; wear my skin;
See what I see; feel what I feel
And then you shall know,
Who I am, what I am, and why I am."

Patrick Tamayo
(p. 94)

The actual effects of racial prejudice and discrimination may take many forms, depending on the nature and degree of discrimination and the individuals or groups involved. One thing they have in common, however, is the curtailment of people's rights as human beings, with all that this implies in terms of suffering and wasted potential. And it is small comfort to be told that such discrimination is found in Britain, Israel, Nigeria, the Soviet Union, South Africa, and other countries as well as the United States. Like other forms of cruelty and tyranny, racism debases all those involved—the victims, those who victimize, and those who function as accessories by standing idly by.

Although group prejudice and discrimination have been most obviously directed against racial, ethnic, and religious minorities, many "less visible" groups have also been victims. Older people in our society are commonly treated as though they were an alien race to which the young and middle-aged are unrelated and will never belong. The physically handicapped are another group that suffer from discrimination (President's

---

[1] The material they gathered together is reprinted in a section called "Out of the Third World Experience" in Buckhout et al., 1971.

Committee on Employment of the Handicapped, 1971). Opportunities for rehabilitation training and gainful employment are severely limited for this sizable segment of our society, particularly for the "disabled disadvantaged," whose physical handicaps are exacerbated by racial, educational, and related social problems.

In addition there are several million former convicts who are excluded from holding public office as well as from many occupations because of their criminal record—without regard to the nature of their offense or the fact that they have supposedly "paid their debt to society." They must pay taxes but are not permitted to vote, a situation which they perceive as "taxation without representation." The Gay Liberation Front is convinced that homosexuals are the most harassed and discriminated-against minority in America. In 1971, a group called Insane Liberation was formed in New York City to combat what its members perceive as discriminatory and oppressive treatment of the mentally ill by many psychologists and psychiatrists as well as by society as a whole (Gilluly, 1971). And recently, we have heard the complaints of the Women's Liberation Movement and witnessed a well-organized campaign to achieve equality for women legally, economically, politically, and socially.

Probably most of us feel "put upon" by computer data banks which invade our privacy; by the ever spiraling burden of inflation and the "money squeeze"; and by a vast, impersonal bureaucracy which seems intent on reducing us to ciphers in a "controlled environment." Thus Lerner (1970) has concluded—perhaps somewhat facetiously—that we are showing signs of becoming a "paranoid" society.

When we broaden our perspective to include a global view, we see widespread examples of racial, political, religious, economic, and other discriminatory practices against particular groups, with all the suffering, resentment, conflict, and possible violence that such discrimination engenders.

LEARNING AND MAINTENANCE OF GROUP PREJUDICE AND DISCRIMINATION

All forms of group prejudice and discrimination are based on learning, and they are maintained because they are reinforced. However, the specific details vary considerably in different situations.

For purposes of brevity, our present discussion will focus primarily on the learning and maintenance of prejudice and discrimination against other races. But the principles we shall deal with also apply, in varying degrees and combinations, to other forms of group prejudice and discrimination.

Learning and the prejudiced community. Prejudice is a learned attitude; discrimination is a learned response. Both may result from unpleasant experiences with members of the groups involved, but such learning appears rare. In fact, direct contact and shared experience more often work in the other direction.

More commonly, prejudice and discrimination are learned from other people who serve as models and from playing expected roles in social institutions which practice discrimination. This point has been well illustrated by the findings of Coles (1967), who studied children's art and found that it reflected the adult models and culture of the larger society.

"Each of these children has learned to identify himself, somewhat, by his or her skin color—learned so during the first two or three years of life. What they have learned about their skin has been but the beginning of what they will learn. Yet, when they finally know what color they possess and what color they lack, they know something about their future. As one little Negro girl in Mississippi said after she had drawn a picture of herself: 'That's me, and the Lord made me. When I grow up my momma says I may not like how He made me, but I must always remember that He did it, and it's His idea. So when I draw the Lord He'll be a real big man. He has to be to explain about the way things are.'" (p. 71)

But the more basic question may be raised as to how a prejudiced community gets started in the first place. Attempts to answer this question have included such factors as: (1) discomfort or fear in the presence of people who seem different, with a tendency to see and describe them in overly simplified and overly generalized conceptual categories that become stereotypes, accepted and passed on without challenge; (2) the need to enhance the cohesiveness of the group and the self-image of its members by excluding outsiders and considering them as inferior; (3) economic factors,

A BLACK GIRL

These drawings were made by a 6-year-old black girl during her first year in an integrated school. The black children are drawn as smaller, less distinct, and less complete than the white children and are not smiling or surrounded by a pleasant scene. These drawings make it clear that even at this age a black child recognizes the prevailing discrepancies in the life space and outlook for black and white children.

Meers, a psychoanalyst who has been studying the effects of ghetto life on black children, has found impaired intellectual functioning, distortions of perception and memory, and gross self-devaluation and self-hatred, with an alternation between an acting out of anxieties and an apathetic withdrawal. He likens the latter to the fatalistic despondency and apathy found among prisoners-of-war who have given up hope. He suggests that repression or denial may be necessary for psychological survival of children exposed to such a high incidence of injuries, separations, deaths in the family, early sexual seduction, chronic insecurity, and violence of all kinds around them, in addition to pervasive racial discrimination. According to Meers, "The existing miseries of the inner cities . . . are nurturing severe pathological character disorders. The ghettoized black children's defensiveness against caring for others, their depersonalization of relationships, and their sado-masochistic resolutions of hurt and despair, appear to prepare them for retaliation against their own communities, and the social system at large, with potential for indiscriminate destructiveness of themselves and others." (McDaniel, 1972)

A WHITE GIRL   A BLACK BOY   A WHITE BOY

in which there are advantages to the ruling group in exploiting the outsiders, as in the institution of slavery, or in situations in which the outside group is seen as representing an economic threat; (4) the projection of frustrations and hostilities onto minority group members as a form of scapegoating and tension-release for the ruling group; and (5) the operation of psychological defense mechanisms such as rationalization. For example, a slave holder could rationalize behavior clearly inconsistent with his humanitarian principles by seeing his slaves as childish and irresponsible (thus in need of direction and control) or as less than human (thus to be treated more as animals or objects than as people).

In a given situation, many such factors may combine in the establishment of a prejudiced community. Once such a community comes into being, it tends to be self-perpetuating.

Maintenance of the prejudiced community. As we have seen, we all tend to become competent at seeing our world in accordance with our

THE ULTIMATE DANGER OF PREJUDICE

"In Germany, the Nazis first came for the Communists, and I didn't speak up because I was not a Communist. Then they came for the Jews, and I did not speak up because I was not a Jew. Then they came for the trade unionists, and I didn't speak up because I wasn't a trade unionist. Then they came for the Catholics and because I was a Protestant, I didn't speak up. Then they came for ME. . . . By that time there was no one to speak for anyone."

Martin Niemoller (1968)

This confession was made by a prominent Protestant clergyman in Germany. It carries a warning for us all of the consequences of standing idly by while others are victimized by prejudice and discrimination.

existing assumptions and in resolving discrepancies by such mechanisms as denial and rationalization. Thus, inaccurate and prejudicial views tend to be perpetuated in our thinking, and the prejudiced person selectively perceives those instances that tend to support his views and ignores the exceptions or interprets them to fit his convictions.

On a group level, the factors that have led to the establishment of the prejudiced community usually operate to maintain it. Where prejudice and discrimination enhance the cohesiveness and self-image of the group, they tend to be reinforced; likewise, where they yield economic or other gains, they are reinforced. Behavior that brings physical and psychological gains is notoriously easy to rationalize as being not only justified but quite logical, natural, and perhaps even righteous. As Hallie (1970) has noted, we look at the maiming of others—both psychologically and physically—"with disgust and horror, and yet we find it easy to justify in a hundred expediential and even religious ways." (p. 303)

By all these means, group prejudice and discrimination, both explicit and unrecognized, come to be built in systematic ways into the established institutions and agencies of the community and are then maintained and perpetuated through social norms and sanctions. The final irony occurs when even those who are discriminated against foster the stereotypes of prejudice by accepting the social roles and inferior status accorded to them and coming to believe in the validity of the prejudice and discrimination against them—in essence introjecting and identifying with the values of the "aggressor."

ELIMINATING GROUP PREJUDICE AND DISCRIMINATION

Throughout man's history and in most parts of the world, group prejudice and discrimination have been regarded as inevitable and accepted without question. In fact, it would appear that the capacity of societies to mangle people who cannot protect themselves is virtually without limit. Slavery still exists in some parts of the world, and in some countries government policies and even constitutions are frankly and intentionally discriminative. But the blind acceptance of the "inevitability" of prejudice and discrimination is rapidly giving way, and aspirations for equality and a better way of life have spread to even the most isolated peoples on our planet.

In our own country—as a consequence of both our democratic heritage and our technological and economic resources—this awakening has been strong and the demands for change insistent, particularly with respect to the crucial problem of prejudice and discrimination against our racial minorities. Unfortunately, this is proving to be a tremendously difficult problem to solve. As we have seen, the roots of racism go deep into our social fabric and are fed by custom, conflicting economic interests, unrecognized reinforcement for many individuals and groups, difficulties in communicating, and long-accumulated frustration, resentment, and mistrust.

In the present section, we shall confine our discussion to two key facets of the problem of racism as it relates to our black minority: (1) the issue of segregation as a solution, and (2) the efforts now being made toward overcoming prejudice through building an integrated society. Again the principles that emerge offer clues to dealing with other kinds of prejudice and discrimination.

Is separatism the answer? The Report of the U.S. National Advisory Commission on Civil Disorders (Kerner Commission) begins with the following statement: "This is our basic conclusion: Our nation is moving toward two societies, one black, one white—separate and unequal." (1968, p. 1) Such a trend could eventually lead to a policy of apartheid, such as that practiced in South Africa. Is that what we want?

The "Civil Rights Movement" of the 1960's, spearheaded by Dr. Martin Luther King, Jr., had integration as its goal. Though nonviolent protest failed to bring equality, the emerging black consciousness enabled blacks to reject the old stereotypes about themselves and to take pride in their racial identity. It was only one step further for some blacks to reject the idea of joining whites who had so long rejected them, feeling that they would never be accepted as full equals anyway and that to integrate would endanger their newfound identity. And so the conviction grew among both blacks and whites that black people need a period of autonomy during which to develop economic and political power and to experience the feelings of adequacy and self-respect that go with control of their own affairs.

Many of those who have studied the problem over the years take a dim view of separatism as a means of achieving racial equality. Pettigrew (1969) sees the move toward separatism as a sure way to maintain and further increase prejudice, discrimination, and segregation:

"First, isolation prevents each group from learning of the common beliefs and values they do in fact share. . . . Second, isolation leads in time to the evolution of genuine differences in beliefs and values, again making interracial contact in the future less likely." (p. 50)

Similarly, Klineberg (1971) has concluded that to deliberately "cultivate separatism, to insist on it as a right, is to play into the hands of the most bigoted white racists." (p. 123)

To assume that racial integration is out of reach in our time and should not be sought may well become a self-fulfilling prophecy which moves us toward the "two societies, separate and unequal" that the Kerner Commission feared. And there is evidence that the movement toward black separatism has tended to foster a kind of black racism. It is hard to see how adding black racism to white racism can be adaptive for either the individual or society. Pettigrew (1969) has stated the case very bluntly:

CIVIL DISORDERS IN THE URBAN GHETTOS

The summer of 1967 brought riots, violence, and widespread destruction to many American cities, and with them shock, fear, and bewilderment to many people. As a consequence, the President established the National Advisory Commission on Civil Disorders to study the causes of these riots and propose ways in which further riots could be prevented. This commission concluded that "White racism is essentially responsible for the explosive mixture which has been accelerating in our cities since the end of World War II." According to its report (1968), known popularly as the "Kerner Commission Report," the ingredients of this mixture included:

1. Pervasive discrimination and segregation in education, employment, and housing, which effectively excluded large numbers of black people from participating in the benefits of economic progress.

2. Black in-migration to the large cities with white exodus, resulting in a massive and growing concentration of impoverished blacks in our large cities. This, in turn, created a crisis of deteriorating services and facilities and unmet needs.

3. The black ghetto, where both poverty and segregation destroy opportunity and enforce failure. Among the results have been high rates of crime, violence, drug abuse, broken homes, dependency on welfare, and resentment and hostility against white society.

4. The police, not merely as a "spark factor" but as concrete representatives of white racism, repression, and power, in the eyes of many blacks. There has been a widespread belief that there is a "double standard" of protection and justice—one for blacks and one for whites.

5. The frustration of powerlessness, leading a substantial number of blacks to the conviction that there was no effective alternative to violence as a means of "moving the system."

Added to these grievances have been the difficulties of black veterans returning from the war in Southeast Asia. Fendrich and Pearson (1970) found that 76 percent of a representative sampling of these young veterans felt alienated from the broader society. These investigators and others have pointed to the cruel irony of black and white youth fighting and dying together for a society that still is too often unable to seat them in the same classrooms or provide equal opportunities in jobs or housing.

But despite the urgent need for a change in direction, a Commission of the National Urban Coalition, in an extensive survey three years after the Kerner Report, found that most of the changes in the nation's ghettos had been for the worse, with more deteriorated housing, higher rates of unemployment, crime, and drug abuse, inadequate school programs further curtailed, and hostility toward the police and the "white racist society" as great as ever (Harris & Lindsay, 1971).

"To prescribe more separatism because of discomfort, racism, conflict, or autonomy needs is like getting drunk to cure a hangover. The nation's binge of apartheid must not be exacerbated but alleviated." (p. 66)

Toward an integrated society. If we may assume, at least tentatively, that separatism is not the answer, the question arises as to how we can build an integrated community in which all residents are respected.

Three lines of attack appear to be involved: (1) utilizing intervention programs in infancy and early childhood directed toward preventing the damaging effects of racism on early development; (2) utilizing the mass media, education, and other social institutions to change established attitudes and to foster the view that racism is personally and socially maladaptive; and (3) attempting, through intergroup relationships, the delineation of common purposes and goals, and improved communication, to change the established patterns of discriminatory behavior. And while laws cannot abolish prejudice, legislation should not be overlooked as a means of creating conditions in which prejudice and discrimination are likely to be overcome or prevented from developing.

The evidence so far suggests that of the three general approaches, the third—changing behavior first—brings the quickest and most dramatic results. Over two decades ago Deutsch and Collins (1951) reported marked changes in the attitudes of white housewives who had lived in biracial housing projects. One wrote:

"I thought I was moving into the heart of Africa. . . . I had always heard about how they were . . . they were dirty, drink a lot . . . were like savages. Living with them, my ideas have changed altogether. They're just people . . . they're not any different." (p. 99)

Many of our young people serving in the Peace Corps or living on college campuses where there is a racial mixture have reported similar experiences.

Many gains have been made since the early 1960's in education, in access to the ballot box, in fair employment and higher-level job opportunities, in enrichment programs in ghetto areas, and in wider public acceptance of the urgency of change. Surveys show that only about a fifth of Americans today subscribe to the racist beliefs and attitudes that were long accepted without question by white citizens generally, and that the vast majority of young people in this country today reject racial discrimination wherever they recognize it (Cartter, 1971; Pettigrew, 1969). Thus progress is being made on many fronts toward fulfilling our American dream of freedom and equality.

But despite the gains that have been made and many hopeful signs for the future, progress has been agonizingly slow relative to the need and to the hopes of those who for the first time have seen not only "civil rights" but full "social justice" as a right and a possibility. In this country, as throughout the world, we are witnessing a "revolution of rising expectations" among those who see others enjoying affluence and opportunity and no longer accept sickness, poverty, and limited opportunity as their inevitable lot. Psychologically, it does little good to be better off than your parents if those around you are still vastly better off than you are. So long as marked discrepancies in opportunity exist, we can expect dissatisfaction to be strong and vocal among those who feel left behind or discriminated against in our society.

OVERPOPULATION AND ECOLOGICAL VIOLATIONS

It took hundreds of thousands of years to produce a population of some 250 million human beings by the year A.D. 1, and it took 1600 years for this population to double to 500 million. But the next doubling took only 250 years and the one after that only 75 years. By 1970, the world population had reached about 3½ billion, with twice that many expected by the end of the century. In fact, if present trends continue, the world's population will reach an estimated 15 billion by the year 2025 and 30 billion by the year 2050 (Clarke, 1967; Dyck, 1971; Kahn, 1970).

Thus our population growth is following not a linear pattern but rather a geometric or exponential one. At this rate, it would be less than a century before there would be 10 people living on earth for every one at present.

Actually, scientists are in general agreement that this will not occur—that with foreseeable technology in the next hundred years, even 14 billion people could not be sustained (Forrester, 1971). The implication is that some time in the next 60 years the present rate will slow and may even be reversed—by circumstances, if not by our planning.

We need not peer very far into the future to see that the population explosion will have increasingly important results for the entire fabric of man's economic, political, and social life. And accompanying the population problem is the interrelated problem of ecological violations. We are polluting our air, soil, and water at an alarming rate—thus upsetting the balance between us and our environment which is essential for our survival. Since the life-support system of our spacecraft Earth is limited, there are corresponding limits on the number of astronauts that it can accommodate before it will become uninhabitable. Thus the problems of overpopulation and ecological violations that we shall be dealing with in this section are of crucial importance for the quality of human life and even for the very survival of the human species.

EFFECTS OF OVERPOPULATION

A number of serious problems stem from overpopulation. In this section, we shall deal with maladaptive behavior associated with two of these—overcrowding and inadequate physical resources. Then, in the next section, we shall take up the problem of ecological imbalance that will result from excessive demands on our life-support system.

Overcrowding. Experimentation with animals has shown that they experience many pathological effects from overcrowding. In a pioneering study of a baboon colony living in the London Zoo under rather crowded and disorganized conditions, Zuckerman (1932) observed many instances of brutality, bloody fighting, and apparently senseless violence. In some instances, females were torn to pieces; and none of the infants survived to maturity. Initially, it was concluded that such behavior stemmed from the violent nature of baboons. But later studies of baboons showed that in their natural African habitat they lived in well-organized and peaceful groups. Their only aggressive behavior was directed toward intruders and predators.

In an interesting series of studies, Calhoun (1962) showed that when a colony of rats were given adequate food and nesting materials but put in a confined area with about twice the normal population density, many forms of abnormal sexual and social behavior appeared. Maternal behavior was so disrupted that few of the young survived. Many of the male rats also showed abnormal behavior; some made indiscrimate sexual advances toward males, females, and juveniles; some showed extreme passivity, moving through the colony like "somnambulists"; and still others "went beserk," attacking others without provocation and in some cases becoming cannibalistic. Even when a few of the healthiest males and females were moved to uncrowded surroundings, they continued to produce smaller than normal litters, and none of their offspring survived to maturity.

In a review of the effects of overcrowding upon lower animals, the National Institute of Mental Health (1969) challenged the legend that population explosions among the lemming, an Arctic rodent, are followed by a reckless migration which ends when the animals throw themselves into the sea. In a crowded area being observed by a Swedish scientist, for example, the lemmings did not migrate; rather they went through a period of tension or hysteria and then they began dying in their holes or other shelters for unexplained reasons. Other observers have reported similar findings for lemmings in Alaska and other areas. In summarizing these and other available research studies on lower animals, the report of the NIMH concluded:

". . . there is abundant evidence that among animals, at least, crowded living conditions and their immediate consequence, a greatly increased level of interaction with other members of the population, impose a stress that can lead to abnormal behavior, reproductive failure, sickness, and even death." (p. 20)

POPULATION CONTROL—NOT WHETHER BUT HOW

A team of scientists at the Massachusetts Institute of Technology has utilized a computer to predict the long-term effects of current trends and to simulate the outcomes of alternative policies with regard to five fundamental variables. All their projections indicate that the present world population growth will slow greatly very soon.

For example, based on present trends (top), population peaks at about 2020 and then declines because of a depletion of natural resources. According to this projection, quality of life (a variable assumed to be increased by food and material standard of living and decreased by pollution and crowding) has already started a downward path.

But in another projection (bottom), based on a 75 percent reduction in use of natural resources in 1970 through more effective technology without affecting the material standard of living, we see an accelerating pollution crisis, until population, after a peak in about 2030, falls to about a sixth of that level within 20 years. We would have saved ourselves from one fate only to fall prey to another. Thereafter,

quality of life would rise sharply for those who survived, but 30 to 40 years later, population and pollution would both start rising rapidly again.

Forrester (1971), the director of this set of simulations, suggests that a country with a high level of industrialization may not be sustainable—that industrialization "may be a more fundamental disturbing force in world ecology than is population. In fact, the population explosion is perhaps best viewed as a result of technology and industrialization." (p. 11)

Forrester is convinced that our greatest challenge now is to manage an orderly change from growth to an equilibrium in balance with the earth's finite resources, and to do so without causing great suffering or being left with an unacceptably low quality of life. With our increasing capacity to create our own environment—and hence to shape our future—computer projections such as these are an invaluable tool for helping us to anticipate the long-term effects of the various things we are doing or could do to improve or worsen conditions in our society and on our spaceship.

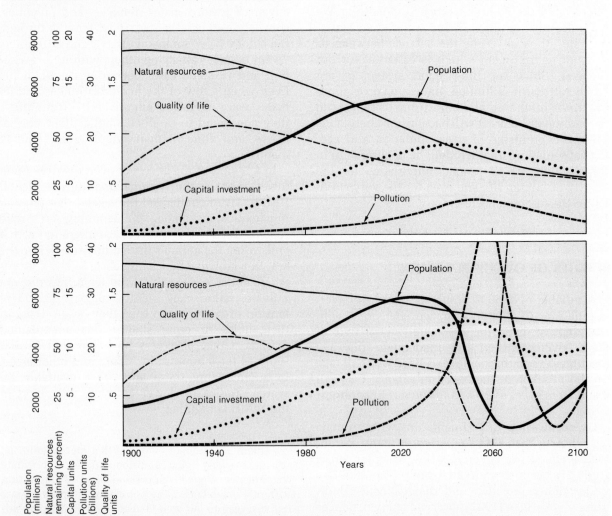

It is risky, of course, to assume that conclusions drawn from animal studies will be found to apply on the human level. In fact, we would expect that such stressful conditions would be less disruptive to man, with his great capacity for adaptability, than to species whose normal functioning is largely dependent on built-in mechanisms. On the other hand, it is widely assumed that overcrowding does have profound effects on human beings, and the violence, disorganization, and other pathology associated with congested urban centers are generally thought to be due in part to overcrowding.

Of the little research to date on the effects of overcrowding on human beings, two studies may be cited briefly. In one, a French research team found that when available space in a dwelling was below 10 square meters per person, the incidence of physical and psychological pathology was doubled (Hall, 1966). The second study was of 91 male married Filipinos living in the Samaloc area of Manila (Marsella, Escudero & Gordon, 1970). Many of these men lived in one-room shacks with less than a square meter of space per person; but even the more affluent who lived in larger houses were frequently overcrowded by virtue of the number of persons living in the dwelling. The amount of estimated space per person approximated 5 square meters among lower-class subjects and 16 square meters among upper-class subjects. Under these conditions of overcrowding, three distinct patterns emerged.

1. *Psychosomatic disorders and alienation.* A wide range of psychosomatic symptoms were reported as well as feelings of being lonely and alienated. Since Filipinos seek security through interdependence rather than independence, these symptoms occurring in a crowded house were considered tantamount to complete insecurity.
2. *Arousal, withdrawal, and passivity.* The arousal symptoms seemed to convey feelings of anger, hostility, and general frustration. Since the culture emphasizes "smooth interpersonal relations," withdrawal and apathy were interpreted as attempts to control emotions in socially accepted ways.
3. *Anxiety and eruptive violence.* Many individuals showed a high level of tension and anxiety, apparently related to feelings of alienation and insecurity. Loss of temper and eruptive violence were also common.

In commenting on their findings, the investigators noted that poverty as well as overcrowding may have contributed to the first two patterns. For example, where people live in shacks with barely enough room to lie down to sleep at night, with an almost complete lack of privacy, and with an inevitable future of physical and psychological want, such patterns as alienation, arousal, and withdrawal might reflect the long-continued privation. However, statistical analysis showed that overcrowding in and of itself was still an important variable. And the third pattern—anxiety and eruptive violence—cut across socioeconomic lines and appeared directly due to the overcrowding.

While it is possible that some individuals and groups can adjust to much higher population densities than can others, it would appear that the sheer number of people will determine many of the adjustive demands made on man in the future and may lead to serious psychological problems (Waggoner, 1970). And with the continuing trend toward congregating in large urban centers, the combination of overcrowding and accelerating change may prove overly stimulating and highly disruptive for many people in our society—including the more affluent as well as the poor.

Poverty. When population outruns available resources, the result is poverty, malnutrition, and frequently starvation. In our own affluent society, we have the potential to provide everyone with adequate nutrition, but we are far from winning the "war on poverty." In 1970 there were over a million persons on welfare in New York City alone; in our country as a whole, about 25½ million people were living below the government-set "poverty line,"[1] and some 15 million Americans were actually suffering from hunger and malnutrition (Hollings, 1971a; Pasamanick, 1971). Although over half of those below the poverty line were white, the incidence of poverty was proportionately three times greater among blacks than whites—approximately 32 percent of blacks, as contrasted with 10 percent of whites. Roughly the same ratio holds for Mexican-Americans as for blacks.

---

[1]In 1970, a nonfarm family of four or more persons with an income of less than $3968 per year—slightly over $300 per month—was considered to be living below the "poverty line."

Testifying before the U.S. Commission on Civil Rights in 1967, a resident described a ghetto slum as "a quagmire, a big quicksand . . . just like you step in something, you just sink and you can't get out of it. . . . I mean you can live here for millions and millions of years and you will see the same place, same time and same situation. It's just like time stops here." (p. 6)

A recent national survey found that one third of the children up to 6 years of age in our rural slums and urban ghettos were suffering from growth retardation due to malnutrition (Hollings, 1971b). Our failure to take effective measures to rectify this situation has been referred to by the sociologist Pasamanick as "murderous":

"How much research is necessary to demonstrate that . . . poverty can kill and maim you and degrade your children?" . . . Adequate food intake is not and never was problematic. Where do we stand as a society approaching the third millennium, rich and powerful, but indicted and condemned for killing thousands, maiming hundreds of thousands of children each year in full knowledge of what we have done and continue to do . . . ?" (1971, p. 24)

It is apparent that poverty also exacts its toll from the adult poor in terms of such conditions as inferior and crowded living quarters, reduced occupational opportunities, and limited access to recreational pursuits. But as Irelan and Besner (1967) have pointed out, what is not so obvious are the psychological consequences of the life style of the adult poor: (1) a sense of powerlessness and insecurity, of limited alternatives and little control over their lives or the workings of the larger society; (2) pervasive frustration and isolation, stemming partly from deprivation but also from seeing the affluence around them and being unable to participate in it; and (3) meaninglessness, as a result of feelings of helplessness, isolation, and lack of hope for a better future.

"Constant, fruitless struggle with these conditions is likely to produce estrangement—from society, and from other individuals, even from oneself. The wholeness of life which most of us experience—the conjunction of values, knowledge, and behavior which gives life unity and meaning—is less often felt by the poor. They see life rather as unpatterned and unpredictable, a congeries of events in which they have no part and over which they have no control." (1967, p. 3)

In summary, these investigators concluded that the very poor individual "does not grasp the structure of the world in which he lives, cannot understand his place in it, and never knows what to expect from it." (p. 4) For large numbers of people in a society to live under conditions of such acute physical and psychological privation is maladaptive in the extreme, both for the individuals and for the larger society.

On a global level, as in our own society, the problems of overpopulation and poverty are inextricably intertwined with political, economic, and other social problems. But until the population explosion is brought under control in the underdeveloped countries, there is not only the spectre of widespread famine but little probability that most people in the world will secure the housing, health care, and education to which they aspire. Economic gains in many underdeveloped countries have been nullified by population increases; in fact, such population increases often outstrip the gains, so that the net effect is greater poverty than before. It seems absolutely essential that we not only utilize the limited resources on our spacecraft more effectively but that we stabilize the world population at a level compatible with its life-support system as soon as possible.

VIOLATIONS OF ECOLOGICAL BALANCE

Bengelsdorf (1970) has contrasted the wastefulness of industrial society with the natural ecological balance maintained by nature:

"Unlike industrialized man, nature abhors waste. Miserly nature runs a taut, thrifty spaceship. Everything is reclaimed and recycled. Plants and animals die and are decomposed into reusable molecules that become parts of new plants and animals. And nature recycles its water—from oceans and clouds to rain, to rivers, and back to oceans." (p. 7)

Although our spaceship comes equipped with limited resources and certain built-in laws of geology and biology, the laws of economics are made by man. For example, there is no natural law to the effect that we must burn over 8 million gallons of gasoline each day in the city of Los Angeles alone or that we must have jetliners with a fuel capacity measured in thousands of gallons. Yet we have long accepted pretty much without question three assumptions about our relationship to our planet: (1) that our environment exists primarily for us to conquer and enjoy; (2) that our planet has infinite resources; and (3) that technological and economic growth are synonomous with "progress" and are worth whatever they cost.

The unfortunate consequences of such attitudes have been nowhere more apparent than in the United States. Americans discard some 8 million automobiles, 30 million tons of paper, 26 billion bottles, and 48 billion tin cans each year (*The Sciences*, 1970). Each day they contribute another

We have been slow to realize that our technology, in giving us unprecedented material conveniences, was also giving us by-products that we did not anticipate or want. In fact, many of our most serious problems today are the unexpected side effects of solutions to previous problems.

billion pounds of refuse to a pollution problem of staggering proportions involving our air, our soil, and our water. Americans have also contributed generously to the "orbiting junkyard" in the stratosphere.

In addition, the United States is using up the mineral resources of our planet at an incredible pace. In the last 30 years, we have used more non-renewable fuels, minerals, and other natural resources than were used in the entire world in all previous history. Americans make up less than 6 percent of the world's population, yet we use over 40 percent of the world's scarce or non-replacable resources; and if the present trend continues, the figure will rise to 80 percent by 1985 (Ehrlich, 1968; 1970; Frederick, 1968). Every American baby puts roughly 50 times as much stress on the earth's life-support system as a baby born in India (*U.S. News and World Report*, 1970).

Ecological disaster threatens not only the United States but countries throughout the world. Since 1950, overfishing and pollution have killed 40 percent of marine life in the oceans (Cousteau, 1971). When we stop to realize that 70 percent of the earth's surface is water, we can readily see the grim proportions of the ecological problem. In addition, pollution has altered the climate in some localities and may be having detrimental long-range effects on global climate (Landsberg, 1970; Report of the Study of Critical Environmental Problems, 1970).

"Ecological illnesses" resulting from pollution of the air have been recognized for some time. We are beginning to realize that even noise pollution can affect both our efficiency and our basic physiological functioning (Kryter, 1970). And beyond all these forms of pollution are the dangers arising from the development and stockpiling of ever more powerful weapons of mass destruction and the increasing problem of protection from radioactive and poisonous substances such as strontium-90 and mercury, many of which can get into the food chain. Radioactive wastes created this year from nuclear power reactors will be dangerous for up to a million years, and fool-proof methods of storage have yet to be developed. Do we have a right to leave these wastes on our planet for future generations?

There is no guarantee that man will survive. In the long history of the animal world, survival of species is not the general rule. Over two thirds of the animal species that ever existed are now extinct. The dinosaur lasted some 150 million years or so; man has been around only for about 2 million years and already is an endangered species. Yet despite the dawning of this awareness, he is so far persisting in behavior that is clearly maladaptive and may have fatal results.

COPING WITH OVERPOPULATION AND ECOLOGICAL PROBLEMS

The psychologist Leon Rappoport (1971) has somewhat facetiously pointed out that

"The population and pollution problems may cancel each other out over time, since pollution will begin killing off more and more people. Maybe some men will *adapt* in the Darwinian sense, and all the rest will die out. Thus a new type of man may emerge in our species —'coughing' to be sure."

Famine, pestilence, and war may also solve the overpopulation problem ultimately, if man simply lets events run their course.

Assuming that mankind prefers less painful and costly solutions, it is apparent that he is going to have to come to grips with the problems of population and ecology. And he is going to have to do so soon. In fact, Ehrlich (1970) has concluded that the decade of the '70's represents the last chance for man. Although others take a somewhat less gloomy view, there seems to be general agreement among scientists that the solutions of these problems cannot be delayed for long. The longer we wait, the fewer our options will be and the harder it will be to undo the damage we are causing to our environment.

From an encouraging viewpoint, we see an increasing awareness of the problems of population and ecology throughout the world. In many of the underdeveloped countries, including China and India, well-organized programs to control population growth are now under way. The United Nations' 1972 Stockholm conference, with some 130 nations in attendance, is the first global conclave to deal with the full range of our planet's environmental problems. A global monitoring system for ecological threats is under consideration. Such a system would provide information regarding both naturally occurring changes in our

PSYCHOLOGICAL ASPECTS OF THE POPULATION PROBLEM

It is possible that the desire to have and rear children has a strong biological basis in human nature. Clearly, having children can be very meaningful and self-actualizing for both men and women. Yet little is known about the extent to which learned values affect these reactions. This question has an important bearing on the problem of controlling population growth, for it may determine the extent to which we can rely on education to solve our problem.

The limited research available in this area is concerned primarily with the role of psychological factors in the effectiveness of various contraceptive methods. For example, Kutner and Duffy (1971) concluded that intrauterine devices tended to be more successful than oral contraceptives for women who were impulsive, immature, or irresponsible and also to be less guilt-inducing, although for some women there seemed to be harmful side effects. Since use of the "pill" requires that the woman take continuing active responsibility for contraception, it is most likely to be a successful method in cases where women are willing and able to take this responsibility. There is some evidence that "forgetting" may be enhanced by marital conflict (Bakker & Dightman, 1964).

The psychological effects of birth-control practices on people accustomed to social mores that encourage large families—as in most underdeveloped countries—remain largely unexplored. It seems likely that in a group setting that reinforces child-bearing and large families, members of both sexes are likely to feel unfulfilled if they do not have children. On the other hand, in a group setting that reinforces small families or perhaps not bearing children at all, both men and women would appear quite capable of making the adjustment.

The psychosocial dimensions of the problem, however, are far more complicated then the preceding observations might imply. For example, if society decides that population controls are needed, how should such controls be formulated and administered? Would controls discriminate against the socially disadvantaged, who both in this country and elsewhere tend now to have the largest families? Many fear that they would; some even see birth-control programs as a form of genocide.

A basic question here, of course, is whether society can rely on voluntary measures. Is the answer to be found in programs like those that have been used in India, in which both education and financial inducements are used but the decision to cooperate in birth-control measures is voluntary? Or will the answer be found in the view that parenthood may eventually have to be considered a privilege to be earned rather a natural right? Should people have to have certain qualifications to be certified to become parents? What would be the effects on individuals and on their marriages of being told that they were not eligible to be parents?

The problem of population control raises enormously complex questions—biological, psychological, social, and ethical. Yet there is no time to lose. Even if we had a world-wide program today for achieving "zero population growth," the present population might approximately double in the thirty years or so it could be expected to take to get the curve of increase to level off. Experts agree that the present fantastic rate of population growth cannot continue much longer. If we are to have the luxury of choosing the method of control on our spaceship we must act quickly.

environment and man-made effects on it; this information would then provide a basis for the formulation of effective corrective and preventive measures.

In our own society, various corrective measures have already been introduced, such as: (1) reduction of the wasteful consumption of non-renewable resources; (2) reduction of pollution and the recycling of wastes; and (3) encouragement of the voluntary limitation of family size.

The 1970 census figures in our own country indicate that our population growth had already slowed to manageable proportions during the 1960's, with a trend toward smaller families—about 2.5 children per woman, compared with about 3.4 in 1950. But though families are getting smaller, there are more of them. Thus we can still expect an increase in our population from about 205.4 million people in 1970 to 232.4 million in 1980. For the population to remain the same, a decline in the fertility rate to about 2.1 must be achieved. This would presumably lead to a leveling off of our population at 267 million in the year

2037. One organization that is fostering this trend is called ZPG—Zero Population Growth. Its basic aim is to convince young married couples that it is their duty to society not to have more than two children. In fact, it has been suggested that by 1980 the "mother of the year" may well be someone who has adopted two children and done a good job of rearing them, rather than someone who has had children of her own.

The solution of the problems of overpopulation and ecological violations will require the coordinated efforts of political and industrial leaders as well as scientists and laymen. And if the efforts are to succeed, it will require that many of us change our attitudes, broaden our loyalties, and make a personal commitment to helping solve these crucial problems. McNamara (1970) has elaborated on this point very succinctly:

"There are really no material obstacles to a sane, manageable response to the world's developmental needs. The obstacles lie in the minds of men. We have simply not thought long enough and hard enough about the fundamental problems of the planet. Today we are in fact an inescapable community, united by the forces of communication and interdependence in our new technological order.

"The conclusion is inevitable. We must apply at the world level that same moral responsibility, that same sharing of wealth, that same standard of justice and compassion without which our own national societies would surely fall apart. We can meet this challenge if we have the wisdom and moral energy to do so. But if we lack these qualities, then I fear we lack the means of survival on this planet." (p. 5)

McNamara went on to point out that if only 6 percent of the sum spent annually on armaments were devoted to developmental aid, we would be within sight of a reasonable beginning for assistance to the developing countries of the world and for reduction of the global population growth to a manageable 1 percent. And, of course, another 6 percent might help materially in the introduction of needed ecological measures. Thus again we glimpse the complex interaction of variables relating to war, population, and ecology.

UNCONTROLLED SOCIAL CHANGE

All life involves change. We grow up, marry, have children, shift social roles, undergo operations, face the death of parents, and adjust to numerous other major and minor changes as we go through life. Indeed, our society—as well as the subgroups within it—is constantly changing. Change *per se* need not cause difficulty. In fact, we are a society that is used to change, and in the main we have regarded it as beneficial.

But though change is a constant companion of the history and lives of man, cultural change in the past ordinarily took place at a relatively leisurely pace. For example, a century and a half passed between the patenting of the first typewriter in England in 1714 and its appearance on the commercial market. Now new technological innovations are applied and sweep through society with less and less time lag, leading, in turn, to ideas for further innovations. Thus the cycle of technological and social change is both self-perpetuating and self-accelerating. Perhaps the full impact of this point is brought home when we realize that more scientific, technological, and social changes have taken place in the last 75 years than in all of man's preceding history. There are many people living today whose life span encompasses the flight of the first airplane by the Wright brothers, the first transatlantic flight, the development of jet aircraft that can fly faster than sound, and now the development of spaceships that have landed man on the moon.

In this final section of the chapter we shall focus on the accelerating pace of technological and social change and the conflicts and maladaptive behavior apparently fostered by too-rapid change. We shall attempt to view the nature and effects of such change not only in our own society but in the broader perspective of the spaceship Earth.

"FUTURE SHOCK"

A number of investigators have raised the question of whether the human organism is equipped either physiologically or psychologically to cope with the supercharged rate of change in our "manic society." As Keniston (1963) has expressed it:

"The human capacity to assimilate such innovation is limited. Men can of course adjust to rapid change—that is, make an accommodation to it and go on living—but truly to assimilate it involves retaining some sense of connection with the past, understanding the relationship of one's position to one's origins and one's destinations, maintaining a sense of control over one's own life in a comprehensible universe undergoing intelligible transformations. This assimilation becomes increasingly difficult in a time like our own." (p. 74)

There would appear to be limits to the resilience of the human organism to assimilate change;

such limits evidently apply to both the complexity and the rate of change. When these limits are exceeded, the results can be seriously detrimental or even disastrous on both individual and group levels.

Excessive pace and complexity of social change. Toffler (1970) has proposed the term *future shock* to describe the result of social change that has become too fast for people to assimilate; in essence, the future will have arrived too soon.

From the few studies that have been made in the past, such as that of Murphy (1965), it would appear that social change is likely to be particularly stressful when certain conditions are present:

"1. when the tempo is accelerated and especially when major dimensions of change occur within the life span of a single generation,

"2. when [change] involves pervasive reorientation about basic values and assumptions,

"3. when [change] is experienced at the outset of a cycle when few guides and models exist,

"4. when there has been little formal training and preparation in the skills and techniques necessary to accomplish the new tasks,

"5. if there are serious ambiguities about what the change is leading to,

"6. if [change] involves new roles or values that are imperfectly integrated into or incompatible with the rest of the sociocultural system,

"7. if [change] involves expectations that are prone to be frustrated given the pre-existing pattern of life, and

"8. if [change] involves expansion rather than substitution and creates a sense of 'overloading.'" (pp. 279–280)

Murphy does not regard this list as all-embracing but offers it simply as a set of parameters or guidelines for assessing the probable stressfulness of particular social changes.

In times of rapid change, cultural mores and social institutions that were accepted yesterday may be rejected today. Margaret Mead (1971) has pointed out that in New Guinea some young people whose parents were cannibals are studying medicine. The rapidity and complexity of social change in our own society with respect to "educational obsolescence" has been well delineated by Glass (1970):

"The obsolescence of education in rapidly developing fields of knowledge has become about equal in rate to the obsolescence of an automobile. In 5 to 7 years it is due for a complete replacement. Consequently, our times, to a degree quite generally unrecognized, demand a major reconstitution of the educational process, which must become one of lifelong renewal." (p. 1041)

Similarly, Toffler (1971) has referred to the increasing obsolescence of our family patterns. People who got married in the 1900's could look forward to 30 years together on the average; with the increasing life span, the time has been extended to 50 years. Thus marital partners today are expected to make it together for a much longer period despite the rate and multiplicity of changes in our society—in jobs, in the sexual patterns around them, in leisure-time pursuits, in values, life styles, and so on—all of which tend to make it more difficult for a husband and wife to grow together over the years.

"My own hunch is that most people will try to go blindly through the motions of the traditional marriage, and try to keep the traditional family going, and they'll fail. And the consequence will be a subtle but very significant shift to much more temporary marital arrangements, an intensification of the present pattern of divorce and remarriage . . . to the point at which we accept the idea that marriages are not for life." (p. 35)

Whether or not this particular prediction is borne out, we can readily see that uncontrolled technological and social change can have pervasive effects on individuals, on institutions, and on societies. It would appear that in the decades ahead we must prepare ourselves to learn, unlearn, and relearn constantly; to expect and accept changing institutions, relationships, and ground rules; and to adapt and readapt at an ever increasing tempo.

Reactions to future shock. We have noted the work of Seyle (1969) on the "diseases of adaptation"—such as cardiovascular disorders, peptic ulcers, and hypertension—associated with the stresses of contemporary life. In fact, Ford (1970) has emphasized the role of accelerating social change in producing new sources of stress that lead not only to physical disease, disability, and death, but also to alienation and mental disorders. McCall and Simmon (1966) have found that in cases of serious conflict between old and new cultural patterns, many individuals tend to exhibit either a dedication to alternative belief systems, such as social movements, religions, or ideologies, or a profound disillusionment with and alienation from the mainstream of the society.

In his own analysis, Toffler (1970) has described the results of future shock as involving a wide range of possible symptoms. For some people, it can lead to a hardening or rigidification of established attitudes—to a reactionary posture. In the face of uncertainty and change, such individuals seemingly guard against the fears generated by novelty and change by simply "putting on blinders" and clinging to the old. Others may react with anxiety, confusion, withdrawal, alienation, or erratic swings in life style. And for some who keep trying to adapt to changes that come too fast, there may be a breakdown of organized behavior, with irrational violence. Thus Toffler has concluded that future shock may well be the most important mental health hazard of the future.

We cannot predict all the effects of the accelerating social changes on our institutions, but there can be no doubt that every major social institution in our country—church, school, family, military, and governmental—is going through a period of conflict and crisis. Also, as White (1970) has pointed out, the pressure on our leaders is enormous and increasing. "The pace of change forces us to make decisions faster than we can sort out right from wrong." (p. 521) Crisis piles on crisis, decisions must be made on inadequate information, and too often the action taken is simply a reaction to the present emergency rather than part of a coherent plan for the future.

CULTURES IN COLLISION

The phrase "cultures in collision" refers not only to the competing ideologies of the superpowers and the conflicts between old and new ways in the developing countries but also to the differing value orientations in our own society. Our world is undergoing a period in which multiple conflicts and crises seem to be the order of the day. This trend has been described by the psychologist Hadley Cantril (1958):

"As more and more people throughout the world become more and more enmeshed in a scientific age, its psychological consequences on their thought and behavior become increasingly complicated. The impact comes in a variety of ways: people begin to feel the potentialities for a more abundant life that modern technology can provide; they become aware of the inadequacies of many present political, social, and religious institutions and practices; they discern the threat which existing power and status relationships may hold to their own development; they vaguely sense the inadequacy of many of the beliefs and codes accepted by their forefathers and perhaps by themselves at an earlier age.

"The upshot is that more and more people are acquiring both a hope for a 'better life' and a feeling of frustration and anxiety that they themselves may not experience the potentially better life they feel should be available to them. They search for new anchorages, for new guidelines, for plans of action which hold a promise of making some of the dreams come true, some of their aspirations become experientially real." (pp. vii–viii)

During the decade and a half since this observation was made, we have continued to see the conflict and turmoil that result as old social patterns and values give way to new ones—or sometimes mainly to confusion as the old is rejected before there is something adequate to take its place.

In our own society, there has been a widespread questioning of traditional social norms and values and the emergence of a "counterculture," with ongoing experimentation in alternative life styles. Although the term *counterculture* perhaps implies a greater gulf between old and new than actually exists, there seem to be certain characteristic value differences that Slater (1970) has portrayed as follows:

"The old culture, when forced to choose, tends to give preference to property rights over personal rights, technological requirements over human needs, competition over cooperation, violence over sexuality, concentration over distribution, the producer over the consumer, means over ends, secrecy over openness . . . and so on. The new counterculture tends to reverse all of these priorities." (p. 31)

Other differences include an emphasis on gratification now rather than in the future, on feelings rather than intellect, on personal expression over social convention, on interpersonal relationships over achievement, and on intensity of experience rather than restraint in colors, sex, and other matters.

Griffith (1971) has attempted to identify certain qualities of the new orientation that might be expected to survive the winnowing and synthesis that will result from this culture collision. We can list these qualities in the form of four basic questions that the "new ethic" has raised:

1. *The question of honesty.* The new ethic emphasizes honesty in personal conduct, business, and politics. All too often our society has been deluged with "campaign oratory" in which candidates for political office have made promises they had no intention of keeping; business, via the advertising media, has made exaggerated claims for products or minimized the dangers associated with their use; and adults in all walks of life have raised a credibility gap in the discrepancy between what they profess to believe in and how they act.

2. *The question of personal ambition vs. humanity.* There is an old saying to the effect that "We pray to God on Sunday, and prey on our fellow men the rest of the week." The new ethic emphasizes respect for the integrity and humanity of others in all that one does. Thus, personal ambition—perhaps to be the most celebrated criminal lawyer or the most prominent architect —gives way to the use of one's professional training to improve the urban environment or to ensure legal rights for the poor. In short, the aim is not to erect a personal monument to oneself but to contribute to a better life for all.

3. *The question of technological growth as progress.* We have long equated technological growth with progress, assuming that greater productivity would bring us a richer life. The advocates of the new ethic believe that material achievement beyond a certain point is an inadequate criterion of progress and that in the pursuit of material wealth we have sacrificed our humanity. In fact, it is clear that our elaborate technology has brought not only blessings but serious unforeseen threats to mankind.

4. *The question of racial equality.* The aim of the new ethic is to move toward an easier and more equal relationship between racial groups and elimination of the institutional racism in our society. It puts top priority on the goals of equality and justice for all. In essence, it points to the time when Americans will again refer to themselves as "we the people."

The new ethic is deeply concerned with the need for eliminating poverty, providing adequate education for all for life today and tomorrow, and using one's time meaningfully in ways commensurate with one's potentialities. It is concerned with how people can regain feelings of personal identity and control over their lives. It insists that meaningful social roles must be available for all —young, middle-aged, and old. It holds that such realities can come only through a more participatory democracy which will help to ensure the freedom of the individual and his chance to share in decisions that affect his life.

In essence, America is not only a society, a culture, and a way of life; it is also a way of looking at our world and its future. It is a country founded on very idealistic premises—a *dream* for mankind. And not only the younger generation but an

---

DO WE NEED A NEW KIND OF PATRIOTISM?

Among wide segments of the population, "patriotism" has come to be seen as a self-righteous chauvinism, a glorying in past exploits, and a rationalization for selfish advancement of our country's interests with disregard for the interests of others. In a thought-provoking article, Ralph Nader (1971) has proposed a new kind of patriotism based on the following principles:

1. Patriotism should be rooted in the beliefs and conscience of the individual. If the "consent of the governed" is to have any meaning, it must be based upon the agreement and participation of an informed citizenry.

2. Love of country should include working to improve one's country by taking constructive action against racism, pollution, and other conditions that weaken it and prevent it from attaining its potential or living up to its ideals.

3. Acts that despoil, pollute, desecrate, or otherwise damage our country are unpatriotic. If it is unpatriotic to tear down the flag, it is also unpatriotic to engage in behavior that violates the principles for which the flag stands.

4. A patriotism equated with military exploits and wartime support of one's own country is too limited. Patriotism must also include the duty to advance our ideals toward a better community, country, and world. If patriotism is to have a "manifest destiny," it must be in building a world in which mankind is bound together by the bonds of love and peace.

Implicit in the preceding principles is the concept of patriotism as involving the duty to question and challenge current practices and to dissent from the majority if necessary in order to correct injustice and mistakes. As expressed by a loyal immigrant citizen, Carl Schurz: "Our country . . . when right, to be kept right. When wrong, to be put right."

CONFLICT ON THE CAMPUS

Perhaps nowhere have the strains of rapid social change been more evident than in the conflict and even violence on our college campuses. In many respects, these outbreaks appear to have had even more complex causes than the riots in the urban ghettos.[1]

Fearful that "If colleges and universities will not govern themselves, they will be governed by others," the American Council on Education established a Special Committee on Campus Tensions consisting of both distinguished lay leaders and representatives of the educational community. Its report, submitted in 1970, identified a range of conditions, both on and off campus, as associated with campus conflict and violence. Among these were:

1. **Obsolete educational practices.** Many students have contended that colleges and universities, as constituted, were incapable of providing an education relevant to life in our contemporary world.

2. **Breakdown of traditional authority.** Many students had lost respect for educational authority as traditionally held and administered—authority which they perceived as rigid and autocratic and were rebelling against, demanding a voice in their own education.

3. **Tremendous growth in the size of our institutions of higher learning.** Many students have felt they were being treated like numbers in a computer rather than as individual human beings with their own unique identities and needs.

4. **Generational conflict.** Rapid social change has increased the usual generation gap and made meaningful communication between students and "the Establishment" difficult or impossible. Thus the students tended to act out rather than talk out their frustrations.

5. **Social malaise.** The tensions on campuses reflected the troubles of society at large, especially the growing opposition to the unpopular and costly war in Vietnam and to unjust institutional practices in our society.

The latter point was also emphasized in the report of the National Commission on the Causes and Prevention of Violence (1969a):

"Today's intelligent, idealistic students see a nation which has achieved the physical ability to provide food, shelter and education for all, but has not yet devised social institutions that do so. They see a society, built on the principle that all men are created equal, that has not yet assured equal opportunity in life. They see a world of nation-states with the technical brilliance to harness the ultimate energy but without the common sense to agree on methods of preventing mutual destruction." (pp. 210-211)

As Altbach and Laufer (1971) have pointed out, these issues are not superficial ones but frame broad questions "about the nature of advanced industrial society, the processes of social change within it, the impact of such societies on youth." (p. ix) And to some of our youth, violent protest has seemed the only way to be heard on issues about which they were deeply concerned.

Many of the same conclusions were reported by still another group, the National Commission on Campus Unrest (1970). It blamed both "the Establishment" and a minority of students for the violence that had occurred. In commenting on specific episodes, such as the shootings at Jackson State and Kent State in 1970, it warned that "A nation driven to use the weapons of war upon its own youth is a nation on the edge of chaos."

Fortunately, we have seen a tapering off of destructive violence on our campuses as both students and administrators have come to realize that violent confrontations are counterproductive. Resentments have lessened and cooperation has increased as new channels have been opened for students to be heard and to have a voice in decisions affecting them.

---

[1]For a detailed discussion of student unrest and violence in the United States and other countries, the reader is referred to *The Annals of the American Academy of Political and Social Science*, May 1971, Vol. 395. The entire issue is devoted to these concerns.

---

increasing number of Americans from all walks of life are questioning our implementation of this dream and are demanding changes more in harmony with its vision.

Although we are all involved in this collision of cultures, it is the younger generation who are bearing the brunt of the conflict:

"Young people are at the vortex of modern social change. Whether they initiate change or react to it, they are paying an increasingly heavy toll." (Ford, 1970, p. 261)

While the great majority of those who are concerned about constructive social change are trying to work "within the system," a sizable segment

have become alienated from the broader society and see no meaningful role for themselves in it. Some are experimenting with communal living in an attempt to build, in small personal communities, the values they feel are lacking in the larger society. Others pay lip service to high ideals but live an escapist and hedonistic existence. A few have gone to the other extreme of nihilistic destructive violence.

Nor is the ferment only or even primarily an American phenomenon. In all parts of the world, cultures are in collision as old habits are changed and old ideas and institutions are challenged. And throughout the world it is the youth who are most centrally involved in the search for adequate answers to the difficult problems of our time.

TOWARD COPING WITH UNCONTROLLED CHANGE

The historian Genovese (1970) has described the problems created by the pressures of accelerating social change in our society as follows:

"When a growing portion of the nation's youth loudly proclaim its defection from everything . . . when black people find themselves trapped between failure of a promised integration and white resistance . . . when the richest nation in world history cannot keep its water and air clean, much less eliminate poverty; when great cities are acknowledged to be ungovernable, not to mention unliveable; when the country is racked with fear, foreboding, and hopelessness—then we had better declare a state of spiritual crisis, for the alternative would be to declare that irrationality, decadence, and disorder constitute our normal and preferred national condition." (p. 25)

Admittedly the United States has faced periods of internal crisis before. However, there seems little historical precedent for the accelerating social change and accompanying value conflicts with which we are now confronted.

The solution to the problem of change does not appear to lie in trying to "set the clock back" or in trying to prevent change, but rather: (1) in learning to guide and control the pace of change in ways that will enhance the quality of life rather than detract from it; (2) in preparing people for anticipated change in terms of what to expect and what to do—and in helping them acquire the understanding and competencies they will require; and (3) in providing opportunities for people to take a more active and participatory role in guiding the direction of the changes that affect them. Toffler (1970) has suggested the formation of a new type of institution along the lines of an "anticipatory democracy," in which people can participate in establishing priorities and guiding and controlling social change.

Following a similar line of thought and focusing particularly on our young people, Eisenberg (1970) has expressed it this way:

"The energy, idealism, and intelligence of youth are the prime resources of each nation; if these resources are to be wisely spent, our youth must be involved in the mainstream of national life. Youth is impatient—as it should be—with excuses for perpetuating evil. In the excess of its zeal, it sometimes abandons reason. But he who does not lose his mind over certain things has no mind to lose.

"To label unrest as 'sick' is no more than a sophisticated version of the rage of adults at the effrontery of the child who pointed out that the Emperor had no clothes on. In part, adult fury stems from the very accuracy of the charges the young lodge against us. This is not to say that the correctness of the accusation warrants abject surrender by our generation; the young

Shock and disbelief at Kent State in May 1970.

PARADOXES OF OUR TIME

The paradox of technology	While modern technology has enabled us to land men on the moon and return them safely to earth, it has not enabled us yet to solve many critical problems on earth, some of which have been caused or exacerbated by technology itself.
The paradox of speed	Our high-speed automobiles are slowed to a crawl during many hours of the day on our crowded urban freeways, and high-speed jet travel, involving the crossing of multiple time zones, tends to upset the circadian rhythms, as we noted in Chapter 14.
The paradox of communication	Via communication satellites and mass media, we have developed highly advanced communication facilities and techniques; yet "communication gaps" prevent or distort our understanding of each others' ideas and motives.
The paradox of affluence	The United States is the most affluent nation in the world and in history; yet we have upwards of 25 million people living below the government-set poverty line, are curtailing school programs and urban renewal programs for lack of funds, and are adding each year to an already mammoth national debt.
The paradox of equality	In a society based on the principle of freedom, equality, and justice for all, we find widespread group prejudice and discrimination with limited opportunities and unequal justice for the poor and the "different."
The paradox of child care	Although we loudly proclaim our devotion to the well-being of our children, our actions belie our words, as we have seen in Chapter 17. In fact, we spend more on alcohol and automobiles than we do on our children's education. We also fail to assure them adequate medical, psychological, and related services.
The paradox of defense	The security our costly military defense system should provide is offset by the spiraling arms race, the proliferation of nuclear weapons, and the increase in the number of "superpowers."
The paradox of values	In a society founded on principles which have brought unprecedented well-being and opportunity to a majority of its citizens, we find a sizable number of youth and adults feeling alienated and dehumanized and rejecting an achievement orientation.

have no greater wisdom than we possess, and a great deal less practicality. But it is to say that resort to harsh punishment will perpetuate angry rebellion and block meaningful change." (p. 1692)

If we are to achieve our dream as a people, each one needs to do not only "his thing" but "his part." Cynicism and hopelessness could destroy us just as surely as thermonuclear bombs. We need to remind ourselves that both young and old, in the broader view, are parts of the generation living at this moment of history. The task of preserving human life and improving its quality is laid on us all.

In this chapter we have dealt with maladaptive behavior of groups. In labeling group behavior *maladaptive*, we have utilized the same criteria that we applied throughout to individual behavior: namely, its consequences for the well-being and actualization of the individual and the group. We have briefly described some of the specific problems or maladaptive patterns which must be dealt with if we are to keep our spaceship habitable for man. Among these are war and threat of war, group prejudice and discrimination, overpopulation and ecological violations, and uncontrolled social change. We have also noted some of the dimensions that appear relevant to coping with these problems as well as some of the efforts that are currently being made in this direction.

In Part Four, which follows, we shall complete our discussion of abnormal behavior. Chapter 19 will deal with the problems of assessing maladaptive behavior and Chapter 20 with contemporary approaches to treatment. In Chapter 21, we shall pursue further a basic theme of the present chapter: the need to find better ways of preventing maladaptive behavior if we are to build a "good future" for man on our troubled spacecraft.

Modern Methods of Assessment, Treatment, and Prevention

Part Four

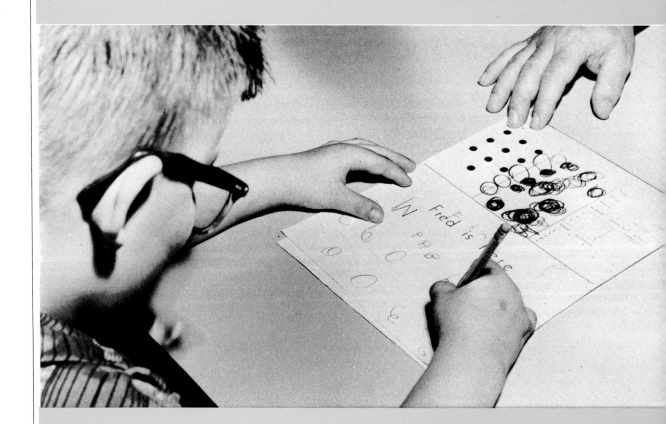

The Problem of Assessment

19

INTERDISCIPLINARY SOURCES OF ASSESSMENT DATA

PROBLEMS AND PROGRESS IN ASSESSMENT

Clinical assessment is concerned with identifying the nature and severity of maladaptive behavior on the part of the individual or group, and with understanding the conditions which have caused and/or are maintaining the maladaptive behavior.

On an individual level, assessment information provides a working model of the individual and his life situation which can be used for formulating a sound treatment program. The working model may be relatively comprehensive or limited to identification of the key problems and the specific conditions that are maintaining or exacerbating these problems. In either event, it then provides a basis for making decisions concerning hospitalization, the use of drugs, the role of psychotherapy, the modification of family patterns, and related aspects of possible treatment programs. Where feasible, these decisions are made with the consent and cooperation of the patient, though in cases of severe disorder they may have to be made without his participation.

Decisions about therapy are most likely to be sound if they are based on valid assessment data. Assessment information also provides objective measures that can be compared with measures obtained after treatment. In this way, dependence on subjective inference about processes going on inside the individual is minimized.

On a group level, assessment information provides a comparable model of group structure and functioning. In assessing the maladaptive behavior of a disturbed family, for example, attention may focus on role behavior, communication patterns, decision-making processes, and other aspects of the family interaction and functioning. In this case, analysis of the group patterns does not preclude the clinical assessment of the individual family members, but the focus is on the family as a social system. Such assessment data, in turn, provide a basis for planning modifications in group organization and behavior, usually with the consent and cooperation of group members.

Traditionally, "identifying the nature and severity of the individual's maladaptive behavior" has included assigning him to a category in accord with a currently accepted system of classification. This classification has then helped to determine whether he should be hospitalized and what kind of treatment is most likely to be helpful. Assessment data have also been used: (1) to provide a basis for predicting the probable outcome in discussing the situation with the individual, his family, or the group; (2) to check on the effectiveness of an ongoing treatment program to see if modifications may be indicated; (3) to detect pathological trends before a disorder becomes acute or to anticipate possible problems and help people prevent them; (4) to assure comparability of groups when evaluating the effectiveness of different programs of treatment or prevention.

As we have seen, however, putting a patient in a category and giving him a label may have undesirable and unintended effects both on his perception of himself and on others' perceptions of his capabilities. Labels intended to be merely descriptive may also come to be regarded as explanations of the problem. Because the results of assessment are subject to misunderstanding and misuse, because some of the measures conven-

tionally taken during original assessment have not been predictive or helpful in later treatment, and because assessment takes precious time, there has been a tendency to cut down on the amount of information that is gathered before treatment begins. Later, if a need for particular information becomes apparent, it can be obtained. On the other hand, without initial measures, there is no "baseline" against which to evaluate measures obtained later. In any case, instead of giving routine batteries of tests, there is now a focus on getting the particular information needed for the individual problem so that a treatment program that has proven effective with this type of problem can be selected.

Initially in this chapter we shall review some of the more commonly used assessment procedures—medical, psychological, and group—and show how assessment data are integrated into a coherent clinical picture or model for use in making decisions about treatment. Then we shall note some of the problems and trends in clinical assessment, including the "antitest" revolt, the issue of confidentiality and informed consent, and the use of computers in clinical assessment.

INTERDISCIPLINARY SOURCES OF ASSESSMENT DATA

Since a wide range of factors may play important roles in causing and maintaining maladaptive behavior, assessment typically involves the coordinated use of medical, psychological, and sociocultural assessment procedures.

The nature and comprehensiveness of clinical assessments vary, of course—depending in any given case upon the individual or group under study and the facilities of the treatment agency. Assessment by phone in a suicide prevention center, for example, is quite different from assessment aimed at determining whether a particular hospitalized patient should participate in an encounter group. Clinical assessment usually focuses on the target behaviors and conditions

that appear relevant to understanding and treating the particular individual or group. Our attempt here will be to provide a perspective about the collection and use of clinical data, with emphasis on psychological assessment.

MEDICAL EVALUATION

For the medical evaluation, data are collected relevant to the individual's general physical state and any physical pathology that may have a bearing on his maladaptive behavior. Most often this procedure is used for individuals referred for particular problems, though in the case of the

Head Start program, there was a systematic survey of the physical problems of the children participating in the project. Medical data may also be collected concerning adverse physical conditions —such as malnutrition—in entire societies.

The medical evaluation may include the following procedures.

1. *General physical examination.* The physical examination consists of the kinds of procedures most of us have experienced in getting a "medical checkup." Typically, a medical history is obtained and the major systems of the body are examined.

2. *Neurological examination.* Since brain pathology is involved in some psychopathology, a specialized neurological examination is commonly given in addition to the general medical examination. This may involve the use of electroencephalography to check on brain-wave patterns.

3. *Special diagnostic techniques.* Where EEG's reveal *dysrhythmias*—abnormal brain-wave patterns—or where other data indicate the possibility of brain pathology, a variety of specialized techniques may be utilized in an attempt to arrive at a precise diagnosis of the nature and extent of the problem.

Medicine and allied sciences are contributing many new procedures of value in assessing conditions that can affect brain functioning. Radioactive isotopes can help locate brain lesions and other types of nervous system disturbances; techniques have been developed for the early detection of PKU and other rare metabolic disorders; and new methods have made it a simple matter to detect the use of heroin and other drugs of dependence. And as we have seen, new techniques have made it increasingly easy to identify genetic and chromosomal abnormalities. These techniques not only make it possible to diagnose conditions such as Down's syndrome in mental retardation, but also permit *preventive assessment.* For example, potential parents may be examined to see if they carry particular genetic aberrations that may adversely affect their offspring.

PSYCHOLOGICAL ASSESSMENT

In psychological assessment there is a systematic attempt to construct a psychosocial model of the individual and his life situation for help in understanding how his maladaptive behavior developed and is maintained, and how it should be treated. This model is intended to provide an intelligible picture of his personality makeup, his present and potential level of functioning, and the stresses and resources in his life situation.

A wide range of psychological assessment procedures may be utilized, among the most important of which are the following:

Interviewing. The interview is probably the oldest method of psychological assessment. For centuries, men have assumed that they could "size up" another person by talking to him for a period of time.

In formal assessment, the interview usually involves a face-to-face conversation between two people, conducted in such a way that the clinician can obtain information about various aspects of the life situation, behavior, and personality makeup of the subject. The interview may vary from a simple set of questions designed to gather factual information—as in an *intake* or *case history* interview—to a more complex situation called a *stress interview,* in which questions are asked or tasks assigned under specially contrived, stressful conditions to see how the person functions intellectually and emotionally under difficult conditions. And, of course, there is the *therapeutic interview,* in which both assessment and therapy may take place.

In order to minimize sources of error—such as a possible tendency for the subject to say what he thinks the interviewer wants to hear rather than what he actually thinks or feels—interview assessment is often carefully structured in terms of goals, content to be explored, and the type of relationship the interviewer attempts to establish with the subject. Here, the use of rating scales may help focus and score the interview data. For example, the subject may be rated on a three-point scale with respect to self-esteem, anxiety, and various other characteristics. The structured interview is particularly effective in giving an overall impression of the subject and his life situation and in revealing specific problems or crises—such as marital difficulties, drug dependence, or suicidal fantasies—which may require immediate therapeutic intervention.

Psychological tests. Psychological tests are specialized assessment procedures for ascertaining such characteristics of an individual as intellectual capacity, motive patterns, self-concept, perception of the environment, role behaviors, values, level of anxiety or depression, coping patterns, and general personality integration. Our psychological tests are far from perfect tools and often focus on variables within the subject at the expense of important conditions in his life situation. Their value depends heavily upon the competence of the clinician who interprets them. In general, however, they are useful diagnostic tools for psychologists in much the same way that biochemical tests, such as the Wassermann, are useful to physicians. In both cases, pathology may be revealed in persons who appear on the surface to be quite normal, or a general impression of "something wrong" can be checked against more precise information.

1. *Intelligence tests.* There is a wide range of intelligence tests from which the clinician can choose. The Wechsler Intelligence Scale for Children (WISC) and the Stanford-Binet Intelligence Scale are widely used in clinical settings for measuring the intellectual capacity of children. Probably the most commonly used test for measuring adult intelligence is the Wechsler Adult Intelligence Scale (WAIS). It includes both verbal and performance material and consists of ten subtests with one alternative subtest. A brief description of two of the subtests—one verbal and one performance—will serve to illustrate the type of functions the WAIS measures:

General information. This subtest consists of questions designed to tap the individual's range of information on material that is ordinarily encountered. For example, the individual is asked to tell how many weeks there are in a year, to name the colors in the American flag, and to tell who wrote *Hamlet.*

Picture completion. This subtest consists of 21 cards showing pictures, each with a part missing. The task for the subject is to indicate what is missing. This test is designed to measure the individual's ability to discriminate between essential and nonessential elements in a situation (Wechsler, 1955, pp. 33–35).

Analysis of scores on the various subtests reveals the individual's present level of intellectual functioning. In addition, the subject's behavior in the test situation may reveal much relevant information, as when he is very apprehensive about not doing well, vacillates in his responses,

seeks continual reassurance from the clinician, or is so disturbed that he cannot concentrate on the tasks presented.

2. *Personality tests.* There are a great many tests designed to measure facets of personality makeup other than intellectual capacity. It is convenient to group these tests into two broad categories—*projective* and *nonprojective.*

Projective tests rely upon various ambiguous stimuli, such as inkblots, rather than specific test questions and answers. Through his interpretations of ambiguous material, the individual reveals a good deal about his conflicts, motives, intellectual level, coping techniques, and other aspects of his personality makeup. Thus projective tests place greater emphasis upon the ways in which learning and self-structure lead the individual to organize and perceive the information presented to him. Prominent among the many projective tests in common usage are the Rorschach Test, the Thematic Apperception Test (TAT), and the Sentence Completion Test.

The Rorschach Test is named after the Swiss psychiatrist Hermann Rorschach, who initiated experimental use of inkblots in personality assessment in 1911. The test utilizes ten inkblot pictures to which the subject responds in succession after being instructed somewhat as follows (Klopfer & Davidson, 1962):

People may see many different things in these inkblot pictures; now tell me what you see, what it makes you think of, what it means to you.

The following excerpts are taken from the responses of a subject to the sample inkblot shown here.

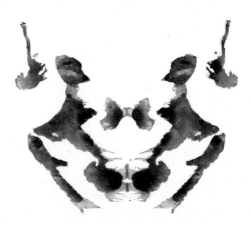

"This looks like two men with genital organs exposed. They have had a terrible fight and blood has splashed up against the wall. They have knives or sharp instruments in their hands and have just cut up a body. They have already taken out the lungs and other organs. The body is dismembered . . . nothing remains but a shell . . . the pelvic region. They were fighting as to who will complete the final dismemberment . . . like two vultures swooping down. . . ."

From this response and other test results, this subject was diagnosed as an antisocial personality with strong hostility.

Interestingly enough, there is evidence that typical responses to this inkblot have changed in the past twenty years, apparently reflecting cultural changes in our society and changing patterns in perception of sexual identity among young people. In the 1950's, most individuals of both sexes described the figures as male, and men who saw the figures as female were judged to be effeminate or perhaps homosexual. Today, however, among individuals of both sexes, especially under age 25, there is an increasing tendency to see feminine figures (Brown, 1971). This discovery highlights the problem of interpreting the significance of particular test responses in a rapidly changing society and the constant need for checking on the validity of criteria used.

The Thematic Apperception Test (TAT) was introduced in 1935 by its coauthors, Morgan and Murray of the Harvard Psychological Clinic. It utilizes a series of simple pictures about which the subject is instructed to make up stories. For example, one picture shows a young woman with a worried expression and an older woman in the background. Again the material is sufficiently ambiguous and unstructured that the individual tends to project his own conflicts and worries into it.

Another projective procedure which has proven useful in personality assessment is the sentence completion test. There are a number of such tests designed for children, adolescents, and adults. The material consists of the beginnings of sentences which the subject is asked to complete, as for example:

1. I wish _____ .
2. My mother _____ .
3. Sex _____ .
4. I hate _____ .
5. People _____ .

Since sentence completion tests are more structured than the Rorschach and most other projective tests, the examiner can pinpoint topics he feels should be explored in understanding the subject's personality makeup and problems.

Nonprojective personality tests—more structured than the projective ones—typically utilize the questionnaire, self-inventory, or rating-scale technique of measurement. One of the major clinical nonprojective tests is the Minnesota Multiphasic Personality Inventory, or MMPI. This test consists of over 500 items covering topics from physical condition to moral and social attitudes. Sample items are:

"_____ I sometimes keep on at a thing until others lose their patience with me."
"_____ Bad words, often terrible words, come into my mind and I cannot get rid of them."
"_____ I often feel as if things were not real."
"_____ Someone has it in for me." (Hathaway & McKinley, 1951, p. 28)

The subject checks those items that apply to him. His responses are then compared with the responses that schizophrenics, hysterics, or other types of patients have made; similarities in pattern provide a guide for appropriate treatment. The test also has built-in measures for detecting defensiveness or intentional falsification on the part of the person taking the test.

A second major nonprojective approach is called the Q sort. Here, a large number of statements are prepared concerning various traits, behavior patterns, or situations. For example, there might be statements like: "Is highly tense and anxious most of the time," and "Views sex as evil and strives to inhibit his sexual impulses." The subject is asked to sort these statements into piles graded from "highly typical" of him to "highly untypical." A variety of statistical techniques can then be used to evaluate the results of the sorting.

A third nonprojective approach utilizes the statistical technique of factor analysis in constructing personality tests that measure important and relatively independent personality traits. Here the goal is to measure one trait at a time with maximum precision and objectivity; a personality profile can then be drawn showing the degree to which specific traits are characteristic of the given subject and how their strengths compare. The

PERSONALITY PROFILES

By combining the test results of many people who show a particular type of maladaptive behavior, it is possible to discover whether they have a characteristic pattern of personality traits that distinguishes them from the general population. For example, this is a composite profile based on the scores of 937 drug addicts serving prison terms. The measures were obtained on the Sixteen Personality Factor Questionnaire. This profile is interpreted as indicating lower-than-average emotional stability (Factor C) and higher-than-average unrealistic thinking (Factor M) and guilt proneness (Factor O).

Since the testing was done entirely on prison inmates, we do not know whether this profile is representative of all drug addicts. Also, it must be borne in mind that such profiles are only descriptive: they indicate a probability of finding certain traits associated with certain behavior but do not tell us whether either one caused the other.

PERSONALITY PROFILE OF DRUG ADDICTS

FACTOR Primary	TRAIT DESCRIPTION for scores on left side of grid	CENTILE RANK	TRAIT DESCRIPTION for scores on right side of grid
A	RESERVED, critical		OUTGOING, warmhearted
B	LESS INTELLIGENT		MORE INTELLIGENT
C	EMOTIONALLY LESS STABLE		EMOTIONALLY STABLE
E	SUBMISSIVE, accommodating		AGGRESSIVE, assertive
F	SERIOUS, quiet		HAPPY-GO-LUCKY, enthusiastic
G	LESS RIGID, casual		STAID, persevering
H	TIMID, shy		VENTURESOME, uninhibited
I	TOUGH-MINDED, realistic		SENSITIVE
L	TRUSTING, adaptable		SUSPICIOUS
M	PRACTICAL, careful		IMAGINATIVE, impractical
N	UNSOPHISTICATED, naïve		SHREWD, sophisticated
O	CONFIDENT, serene		APPREHENSIVE, worrying
Q_1	CONSERVATIVE, traditional		EXPERIMENTING, analytical
Q_2	GROUP ADHERENT		SELF-SUFFICIENT
Q_3	FOLLOWS OWN URGES		CONTROLLED
Q_4	RELAXED		HIGH TENSION LEVEL
Secondary			
Q_I*	INTROVERSION		EXTRAVERSION
Q_{II}*	LOW ANXIETY		HIGH ANXIETY
Q_{III}*	RESPONSIVE EMOTIONALITY		TOUGH POISE
Q_{IV}*	SUBDUED GROUP ADHERENCE		INDEPENDENCE
	LOW NEUROTICISM		HIGH NEUROTICISM

CENTILE RANK scale: 00% 10% 20% 30% 40% 50% 60% 70% 80% 90% 100%

*Roman subscripts denote 'second-order' traits, which are derived from weighted combinations of the first-order trait scores and are broader and more extensive in their effects.

The Scenotest being administered here by Dr. Gerdhild von Staabs, the psychiatrist who developed it, is a diagnostic and therapeutic device for use with emotionally disturbed children. The young patients are encouraged to arrange and play out scenes with characters chosen from a large assortment of flexible dolls, animals, and furniture. The boy shown here had been referred because of theft and truancy; in the scene at the left (played early in therapy) he is showing a mother preoccupied with a younger child (his baby brother) while a grandmother tells stories to older children, perhaps indicating the boy's wish that all children be given equal attention. As therapy proceeded and the boy came to feel more loved and more fairly treated, the truancy and thefts stopped. Near the end of therapy, he acted the scene at the right, in which two dogs are racing; the bigger one wins, but the little one gets a consolation prize.

Comrey Personality Scale (1970), which measures key dimensions of personality, is an example of a test designed and used in this way.

Many other psychological tests are available for clinical use to reveal the subject's abilities, interests, aptitudes, temperament, anxiety level, self-concept, values, and other facets of his personality makeup. Some in common use are the Sixteen Personality Factor Questionnaire, the Kuder Preference Record, the "F-scale" (of manifest anxiety), and the Kahn Test of Symbol Arrangement. There are also a number of specialized tests such as the Bender Gestalt Test, which tests perception of form and thus may be used to diagnose particular kinds of brain damage.

Direct observation of the subject's behavior and life situation. Psychological tests, for the most part, try to identify consistent traits of the individual, characteristics that he takes with him wherever he goes. Increasingly, however, it has been recognized that much behavior is situation-specific and that all behavior is influenced in important ways by the situation in which it occurs. In fact, as we have seen, some psychologists hold that behavior is controlled entirely by the reinforcement contingencies provided by the environment. In any case, greater emphasis is now being given in assessment to (1) looking at how the individual interacts with those around him and (2) identifying environmental conditions that have caused or are maintaining maladaptive behavior.

Direct observation of the subject's behavior has always been an important procedure in psychological assessment. In the past, however, such observations have usually been confined to clinic or hospital settings and the main purpose has been to find out more about the individual's internal psychological processes.

In a hospital setting a brief description made of the subject's behavior on admission is usually put into the record, and periodically more detailed observations are made on the ward. These descriptions include concise notations of relevant information about the subject's personal hygiene, emotional behavior, delusions or hallucinations, motor activity, sexual behavior, aggressive or suicidal tendencies, and so on. To facilitate these observations, rating scales are commonly used which enable the recorder to indicate not only

GROUP ASSESSMENT OF INTERPERSONAL TRAITS

Pictured here is an innovative group technique called the GAIT (Group Assessment of Interpersonal Traits), developed by Goodman (1971). It can be used for a number of purposes, including screening of would-be encounter-group participants and assessment of individuals seeking to serve as nonprofessional or paraprofessional therapists.

After an initial "warm-up" involving brief interaction among group members, each member is instructed to write down two personal concerns which he is willing to discuss within the group setting. One person is then chosen as "the discloser"; he reads aloud one of the problems he has written down. The first member to respond becomes "the understander," and a 5-minute interaction between these two individuals takes place, with the other group members observing but taking no part. At the end of the time, the discloser then has 30 seconds in which to describe to the group the interaction that has occurred. This procedure continues in "round-robin" fashion until each member has participated as both discloser and understander.

Finally, all the group members rate each other and are rated by staff observers on such characteristics as acceptance-warmth, degree of openness, rigidity, and capacity for understanding. Research has shown a relationship between high scores on certain of these dimensions and effectiveness in working with emotionally disturbed children, as gauged by improvement on the part of the patients (Rappaport, Chinsky & Cowen, 1971).

The GAIT is an example of an innovative assessment procedure that shows marked promise. It will require further evaluation before the extent and range of its usefulness can be determined—during which process it is likely to undergo further refinement.

the presence or absence of a trait or behavior but also the prominence of it. The following is an example of such a rating-scale item; the observer is to check the most appropriate alternative.

Sexual behavior:

_____ 1. Sexually assaultive: aggressively approaches males or females with sexual intent.

_____ 2. Sexually soliciting: exposes genitals with sexual intent, makes overt sexual advances to other patients or staff, masturbates openly.

_____ 3. No overt sexual behavior: not preoccupied with discussion of sexual matters.

_____ 4. Avoids sex topics: made uneasy by discussion of sex, becomes disturbed if approached sexually by others.

_____ 5. Excessive prudishness about sex: considers sex filthy, condemns sexual behavior in others, becomes panic-stricken if approached sexually.

Observation of the subject's behavior may be made not only for original assessment purposes but also for later checking on the course or outcome of treatment procedures.

Recently, a good deal of attention has focused on observing the subject's behavior in his real-life setting. For example, a child who has been showing behavior problems may be observed at school, in his peer group, and in his home. Here the purpose is to obtain a sampling of his behavior in ordinary situations in order to understand the problems he is facing, the coping patterns he is using, and the environmental conditions that may be reinforcing his maladaptive behavior. It may turn out that the parents are paying attention to the child only when he engages in undesirable behavior, thus unwittingly reinforcing such behavior even though they are punishing it by scoldings or spankings. Such a "functional analysis of behavior" involves study of both the conditions that precede and stimulate the behavior and the consequences that reinforce it.

In situations where it may not be feasible to observe the subject's behavior in everyday situations—as when he is institutionalized—an entire family may be asked to meet together in the clinic or hospital where their interactions and difficulties can be observed and studied.

In cases where the type of direct observation of the subject's behavior and life situation described above is not feasible, a social worker may obtain relevant data in visits to the subject's home, talks with family members and others who are important to the subject, and observation of the stresses and resources in the subject's life situation. Even in cases where considerable data concerning the subject's life situation may be collected in the structured interview or in psychological tests, the collection of supplemental observational data is regarded as desirable.

Extending the use of such data a bit further, the worker may analyze future situations with which the subject is likely to be confronted. For example, a patient with little education and a history of chronic unemployment might improve sufficiently to leave the institution but be little better off than before unless his treatment had included training in job skills. Thus knowledge of the individual's life situation not only helps in understanding his present maladaptive behavior but is often essential for planning a treatment program that will enable him to meet future challenges in more adaptive ways.

INTEGRATION OF ASSESSMENT DATA

As assessment data are collected, their significance must be interpreted so that they can be integrated into a coherent "working model" for use in planning or changing treatment.

In a clinic or hospital setting, assessment data are usually evaluated in a staff conference attended by members of the interdisciplinary team (perhaps a psychiatrist, a clinical psychologist, a social worker, and other mental health personnel) who have gathered the data and are concerned with the decision to be made concerning treatment. By putting together all the information they have gathered, they can see whether the findings complement each other and form a definitive clinical picture or whether there are gaps or discrepancies that necessitate further investigation.

The decisions made on the basis of assessment data may have far-reaching implications for the persons or groups under study. The staff decision may determine whether a depressed person will be hospitalized or permitted to remain with his family; whether divorce will be accepted as a solution to an unhappy marriage or a further attempt will be made to salvage the marriage; or whether an accused person will be declared competent to stand trial. Thus a valid decision, based

ASSESSMENT OF ENVIRONMENTAL CONTINGENCIES

Assessment of the environmental contingencies maintaining the maladaptive behavior of a 7-year-old boy has been described by Bijou (1965). The boy had been brought to a clinic by his mother because of overly demanding behavior.

During the first four assessment sessions, the mother was asked to play with her son in the clinic playroom as she would at home. Two observers recorded the behaviors of both mother and son, first using general observations to delineate their overall behavior patterns and then noting the frequency of occurrence of cooperative and demanding behaviors on the part of the child and the mother's reaction to each. This record showed that the mother responded more frequently to the demanding behavior than to the cooperative behavior, leading to the hypothesis that she was reinforcing and maintaining the demanding behavior by her responses.

During the next four sessions, this hypothesis was tested. For two sessions the mother was under instructions to ignore the child except when a flashing red light was turned on. While the light was on, she was to respond to the child in any way that seemed natural to her except that she was limited to only one action or statement. The light remained off when the child made demands but was turned on each time he behaved cooperatively. Under these conditions, the frequency of the child's demands diminished and that of his cooperative behavior increased.

In the final two sessions, the mother was asked to revert to her former way of interacting with the child. The demanding behavior increased again and the cooperative behavior decreased.

This assessment procedure made it possible to formulate an effective treatment program focused on teaching the mother to use her own responses more appropriately at home in guiding her son's behavior.

on accurate assessment data, is of far more than theoretical importance.

At the time of the original assessment, integration of all the data may lead to agreement on a tentative diagnostic label—such as *schizophrenia* from the APA classification. In the case of marital, family, or larger group assessment, no accepted classification of maladaptive behavior is available and usually a concise summary of the assessment data is made. In any case, the findings of each member of the interdisciplinary team, as well as the recommendations for treatment, are entered in the case record, so that it will always be possible to check back and see why a certain course of therapy was undertaken, how accurate the clinical assessment was, and how valid the treatment decision turned out to be.

New assessment data collected during the course of therapy provide feedback on its effectiveness as well as a basis for making needed modifications in an ongoing treatment program. As we have noted, clinical assessment data are also commonly used in evaluating the final outcome of therapy as well as in comparing the relative effectiveness of different therapeutic and preventive approaches.

ASSESSMENT OF GROUPS (SOCIAL SYSTEMS)

In group assessment, the focus is on the group as a social system instead of on particular individuals within the group. Here too, interviewing, observing, testing, and other psychological procedures may be used, but in this case the primary concern is with social roles, communication processes, interpersonal patterns, and other aspects of the group's structure and functioning.

What information should be gathered for group assessment? There is an almost complete lack of research on assessment of the adaptiveness of group functioning. In fact, even the guidelines for such research are lacking. Hence our discussion will be brief and confined primarily to questions that seem directly relevant to assessing the nature and extent of maladaptive behavior in small groups, such as marital and family groups. Most of the questions we shall raise, however, relate to larger groups as well as smaller ones.

Five sets of variables related to group functioning can be explored by means of answers to the following questions.[1]

1. *What is the structure or organization of the group?* Here we are concerned with social roles available to and enacted by group members, communication patterns in the group, power relationships in the group, norms and values of the group, and the number and characteristics of group members.

2. *What is the field setting of the group?* Our chief concerns here are the specific physical and sociocultural environment of the group, the status and role of the group in the community and larger social milieu, adverse effects of the environment on the group, and possible sources of environmental support available to the group.

3. *What are the tasks and problems faced by the group?* In this area we are dealing with specific questions related to the goals of the group, the

needs of members that the group is expected to meet, any special stresses or crises confronting the group, and the competencies required by the group for dealing with its tasks and problems.

4. *How does the group function?* This question relates to the actual functioning of communication processes, the handling of conflicts among group members, the making of decisions by the group, the emotional climate established in the group, and the ways the group coordinates and uses its resources in coping with its problems.

5. *How effectively does the group cope with its problems and meet the needs of its members and the larger society?* Our inquiry now concerns itself with the outcomes of the group's efforts toward coping with internal and external stresses, the quality of interpersonal relationships within it, the need gratification and opportunities for personal growth it provides, and its contribution to the community or society of which it is a part.

In answering these questions, a wide range of assessment techniques may be used, including videotaping of interactional patterns to permit more precise analysis, drawing on data from epidemiological studies, and observing "high-risk" groups over a period of time to delineate conditions that may be causing problems.

What group behavior is maladaptive? Unfortunately, we have fewer guidelines for such an evaluation on the group level than on the individual level. What some persons might view as a satisfactory marital or family accommodation, others would view as highly maladaptive. Thus on the one hand, we may utilize subjective criteria, such as feelings of satisfaction or discomfort experienced by group members, as well as the more general criterion of fostering or blocking personal and social well-being and growth.

On the other hand, we do have considerable evidence on which to make judgments. For example, in earlier chapters, we discussed such evidence in connection with fraudulent and maladjustive "negotiated contracts" in interpersonal relationships; inadequate, disturbed, and other pathogenic family patterns; and destructive violence, group prejudice, and alienation or exclusion of some subgroups from the mainstream of the society. The adverse consequences of such

---

[1]This scheme is an adaptation and extension of one proposed by Sundberg and Tyler (1962).

group patterns for the individual members, the group as a whole, and even the larger social systems of which the group is a part, are well documented. Thus in evaluating the answers to the five key questions we have just reviewed, we can have considerable confidence in identifying certain patterns or trends as maladaptive—in some cases dangerously so if allowed to continue.

PROBLEMS AND PROGRESS IN ASSESSMENT

We have mentioned the trend in recent years toward spending less time on psychological assessment as an initial diagnostic tool and regarding it instead as a resource to be drawn on as needed at any time during treatment. There have also been basic challenges to long-established testing procedures, while at the same time the use of computers and other innovative approaches has increased. In concluding our discussion of clinical assessment, we shall briefly review some of the challenges and some of the innovations.

THE "ANTITEST" REVOLT

The *antitest revolt* refers to the development of attitudes of suspiciousness and hostility among the general public toward psychological testing. This revolt has been fueled by concern over the invasion of privacy—the right of the client to confidentiality in discussing his problems with mental health professionals—and over the possible misuse of test information. Additional impetus has derived from concern over the cultural bias of many psychological tests, and overuse of such tests for arbitrarily labeling people and assigning them to psychiatric categories.

The issue of confidentiality. Tests and other psychological assessment procedures often elicit very personal information. The implicit or explicit agreement of the professional clinician to keep this information confidential is a basic component in the client-professional relationship. In fact, the loss of confidentiality would seriously endanger the very relationship on which professional mental health personnel must rely if they are to render effective service.

In theory, the safeguarding of confidentiality appears simple, and in the field of law any information supplied by the client to his attorney is held inviolate unless the client consents to its release. In the mental health field, however, it is not so simple. For one thing, it may be advisable to share such information with parents, teachers, or other personnel who will be involved in planning and carrying out treatment. In addition, there are a number of special circumstances in which the disturbed person's right to confidentiality may be abridged, as when there is reason to believe that he may be dangerous to himself or others, or when legal authorities request such information. In fact, under some circumstances, professional mental health personnel are obligated to reveal information to legal authorities and are themselves subject to fine or imprisonment for failure to do so.

Most authorities agree that getting free and informed consent from the client is the safest method of preventing invasion of privacy (Noble, 1971). It is recommended that before assessment is undertaken, the client should be informed of the limits of confidentiality; then, if he takes part in assessment, his participation is presumably based on free and informed consent. This procedure may, of course, restrict his disclosure of information that he feels might be detrimental to him—information that might have helped the therapist in treatment. In addition, informed consent is far from a fail-safe precaution in that the client may not realize how powerful modern psychological assessment procedures can be in revealing information that he might wish to withhold, or even in revealing facets of his personality of which he himself may be unaware.

Another problem is that if such information gets into a computerized data system, it may become available to a wide range of persons and may influence the individual's opportunities for employment or promotion on the job and adversely affect many other aspects of his life. In addition, the privilege of withholding consent is not retroactive. Some persons have found that assessment information recorded during high-school or college years has been raised to question their reliability for employment years later. And we are well aware of what usually happens to persons with a history of psychiatric treatment who later seek political office. As Grossman (1971) has pointed out, "There is no predicting the ultimate use and misuse of permanent records of this nature." (p. 97)

Clinical psychologists have been instrumental in getting "privileged communication" laws passed in some states which protect the client's right to privacy concerning information he communicates to licensed psychologists or psychiatrists. But the issue of confidentiality is a complex matter that is far from resolution.

The issue of cultural bias. We have commented briefly on the detrimental effects of rigid labeling even where the label is an accurate description of the individual's current behavior. Where labels are applied on the basis of psychological tests that do not give valid measures, a doubly dangerous situation is created. Where the results of such tests are used to put an individual into a cubby-hole that ever after limits the opportunities open to him, testing is not serving the function for which it was developed and is doing serious harm.

Most psychological tests have been designed by middle-class psychologists for prediction of performance valued by middle-class people, and many have been standardized on white subjects from predominantly intermediate or upper socio-economic levels. It would be expected that those from other backgrounds might be handicapped in taking such tests and that their scores would not be a fair measure of their potential.

The issue of cultural bias in tests has been of special concern in the movement toward greater equality of opportunity for our racial minorities during the last decade. In 1971 the U.S. Supreme Court ruled that employers should not require individuals to pass a standardized intelligence test as a condition of employment unless such a test could be shown to be directly related to job performance. It is widely believed that in the past such tests have, in effect, been used as a means

of excluding minority-group individuals from certain jobs where employers have traditionally given preference to whites.

As yet, no completely culture-free psychological test has been developed. Such tests must have content of some kind, and the meaning any content will have for the person being tested depends partly on his previous experience. Even nonverbal psychological tests are not completely free of this dependence on past experience. A great deal of research effort, however, has gone into attempts to develop tests of intelligence and other abilities that are "culture fair." One interesting attempt in this direction is that of Ertle at Ottawa University (1971), who has shown that the speed of brain-wave responses to flashes of light correlates dependably with general intelligence as measured by conventional psychological tests. This finding, if it is replicated, might be developed as a means of assessing the general intellectual capacity of not only subjects from diverse cultural backgrounds but also very young subjects.

Minority groups sometimes charge cultural bias in testing on still other grounds. A test on which a ghetto resident does poorly may, in fact, give an accurate prediction of how he will perform on a job requiring middle-class behavior and attitudes, while failing to reveal many skills and abilities that he does have. Is he therefore to be rejected unless he can be taught to show the middle-class behavior and attitudes? The problem here is in what the objectives of tests should be—whether they should be for screening out those who do not conform to the current accepted mold or for identifying more diverse kinds of talents. Many of those who have been denied equal opportunity in the past see tests as a way of continuing to exclude them, a way of maintaining the status quo.

Theoretical and practical criticisms by clinicians. An even more basic challenge to the use of psychological tests in clinical assessment has stemmed from psychologists' own questioning of the long-accepted assumption that maladjustive behavior could best be understood by looking within the individual at his traits and characteristics. The whole concept of putting a person in a category and giving him a label places the emphasis on internal causation of his behavior. The development of tests to assess these continuing inner characteristics was a logical extension of this concept. Although the contributing influence of the environment was never denied, more or less stable traits within the individual were assumed to account for the consistency in his behavior.

As we have seen, evidence from two sources has been altering this view: (1) The study of groups as social systems has repeatedly shown the extent to which social goals and norms, role requirements, and other group-created conditions determine the feelings, behavior, and even observed abilities of the individual members, although their behavior may remain consistent so long as their social setting remains the same. (2) The dramatic changes in behavior brought about by changes in reinforcement contingencies have demonstrated how inconstant many supposed "inner characteristics" may be.

Both these developments call into question the concept of entities within the individual. Although they do not demonstrate that internal conditions can be disregarded, their net effect has been to lower clinician's expectations of what tests will be able to predict. Of the time now allotted to the psychological assessment of the individual, a far higher proportion is given to assessment of his transactions with his social environment. Much of the behavior observed does not fit anywhere in the established classification scheme, and the result is a further disenchantment with classification and labeling in general.

USE OF COMPUTERS AND OTHER INNOVATIVE APPROACHES

Perhaps the most dramatic innovation in clinical assessment during the last decade has been the increasing sophistication and use of computers in individual assessment. A second major innovative approach has been the use of models —often with computer assistance—in the assessment of social systems.

Use of computers in individual assessment. In individual assessment, computers are used primarily in two ways: (1) to put together all the information that has been gathered previously through interviews, tests, rating scales, and so on, from either the subject or others, and (2) to gather information directly from the subject.

By comparing the incoming information with data previously stored in its memory banks, the computer can perform a wide range of assessment functions. It can supply a diagnosis, evaluate the risk of certain kinds of behavior, suggest the most appropriate form of treatment, predict the outcome, and print out a summary report concerning the subject.

Over time, the computer builds an increasingly large data base covering many cases, which enables continual refinement of its probability statements. Interestingly enough, the computer is superior to individual clinicians in many of these functions. Goldberg (1970) demonstrated that a computer, programmed with the assessment strategies utilized by 29 clinical psychologists, was more proficient than the individual clinicians in differentiating between neurotic and psychotic individuals on the basis of MMPI profiles. Similarly, Mirabile, Houck, and Glueck (1970) demonstrated that a computer could outperform clinicians in selecting from among three chemotherapy programs for psychotic subjects. In predicting the risk of suicidal or assaultive behavior, the computer appears to be far superior to individual clinicians (Sletten, Altman & Ulett, 1971). A computer can save valuable time in helping the clinician to make gross discriminations which he can then test and refine by more precise tools as he puts the computer's findings into the context of the particular situation under consideration.

In making predictions for an individual, the computer uses an *actuarial* procedure much like that used by life-insurance companies in predicting risks. Its conclusions are only statements of probability, based on what has happened to a large number of other, supposedly similar, people. For such an approach to work successfully, two conditions are of critical importance: (1) there must be consistent and objective criteria for interpreting test responses and other data; and (2) these criteria must have an adequate statistical base: that is, they must have been derived from information gathered on a large sample of subjects similar to the one being assessed. Both these conditions, in turn, imply a stable world, one that does not change in relevant particulars. To the extent that there has been change in the "real world" since the computer was programmed, its conclusions are subject to possible error.

Innovations in assessment of social systems. Since one major trend in modern social science

COMPUTER SUMMARIES OF MMPI INFORMATION

In a 3-year research and treatment program in delinquency control conducted at the Center for the Study of Crime, Delinquency, and Corrections at Southern Illinois University at Carbondale, delinquent-prone high-school boys were identified and given several kinds of help, including "Big-Brother" counselors and different kinds of individual and group therapy. Assessment included the MMPI, responses from which were sent to the Institute of Clinical Analysis in Glendale, California, for analysis by computer. This procedure provided a computer report on each subject tested. Computer scoring of a test like the MMPI eliminates the variation that otherwise would occur through differences in the subjective judgments of different scorers. Although MMPI data alone are not definitive, they are useful when combined with other information.

On the basis of all the information collected, precise treatment goals were formulated for each individual. The hypothesis was that if treatment was successful, the individual's MMPI scores on a post-treatment testing would change accordingly.

The computer print-outs and graphs shown here summarize the case of a 15-year-old boy who had been referred by school guidance personnel because of problem behaviors, including drug abuse, truancy, and running away from home. At the time of referral, he was characterized as anxious, fearful, self-devaluated, negative in his attitude toward others, and suffering from serious inner conflicts. His MMPI scores were higher than normal for all but one of the clinical scales, and his Multiphasic Index[1] indicated a high level of overall emotional disturbance.

The primary treatment objectives set for this boy were to reduce his anxiety and help him establish a realistic self-concept. Treatment included individual reality therapy (see page 680), group counseling for the family, and monetary and social reinforcement contingent upon appropriate behaviors or approximations of such behaviors. For example, he was exposed to a variety of social situations and rewarded for participating rather than withdrawing.

Several months later, his scores were in the normal range on all but two of the clinical scales of the MMPI. He showed more confidence in himself, markedly reduced anxiety, and a more positive view of his world, but there still were indications of mild to moderate emotional disturbance (Pooley, 1971).

---

[1]The Multiphasic Index is an index of basic anxiety that functions like a fever thermometer in indicating the individual's "emotional temperature." It is derived from selected, especially dependable MMPI scores.

COMPUTER SUMMARY BEFORE TREATMENT

"MI, Emotional Disturbance Index . . . 149

Range 65 to 150. Scores of 90 and up reflect increasing degrees of emotional or personality disorder, i.e., 90 to 99 mild to mod.—100 to 115 mod. to marked—116 to 150 marked. . . .

Probability of low disturbance 1%

Probability of moderate disturbance 84%

Probability of marked disturbance 15%

Interpretation . . .

The MI, Multiphasic Index, reflects an emotional disorder of marked severity. Responses are inappropriate, unrealistic and self-defeating.

This pattern is usually considered an adolescent maladjustment reaction. It is often associated with delinquency, usually the result of ineptness, misunderstanding, emotional conflicts, or simply following the gang. These persons are over-dependent but act the opposite. They fear close emotional ties because of possible rejection. Their behavior is often irresponsible and their expectations are unrealistic. There is a history of family problems, sexual confusion, poor ego-identification and difficulty with authority. They tend to be non-conforming, unpredictable and impulsive.

Special coping problems . . .

Schizoid dissociation or fantasy is strongly indicated. There is evidence suggesting a paranoid trend. There is blocking of deep or positive emotional response, hostile reaction to rejection, and unresolved resentment toward stringent authority surrogates. . . . Investigate suicidal or self-destructive thoughts or plans. Alcohol proneness is indicated. Investigate history concerning excessive drinking."

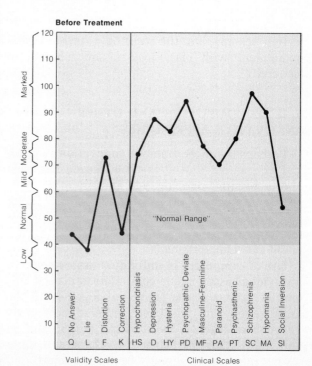

Before Treatment

Validity Scales   Clinical Scales

COMPUTER SUMMARY AFTER TREATMENT

"MI, Multiphasic Index . . . 96   Mild to moderate
                                             elevation

Probability of significant disturbance 36%

Two separate and distinct methods of appraising emotional conflict are shown on scores above. Either score may suggest a disorder but clinical significance is greater when both scores are elevated.

MI interpretation . . .
The MI, Multiphasic Index, reflects a mild degree of emotional conflict. Resilience or the ability to make satisfactory adjustments is fair to medium.

Summary . . .
Significant signs of emotional disorder are revealed.
Personality trait or character disorder is the most likely diagnostic classification.
There is little or no call for help which indicates a wish for self-sufficiency. Defenses appear quite adequate. However, good coping ability is probably over-estimated. This suggests more willful intent than tough resilience.

Validity . . .
Responses are not polarized in the direction of favorability or unfavorability which indicates the subject presents a reasonably candid picture of himself on the test.

Personality description . . .
There is a persistent tendency toward behavior problems . . . rationalization of irresponsible, asocial urges, difficulty with authority, and lack of social conformity. Some lowered morale, worry or self-doubt is admitted. Increased drive reflects a need to meet competitive demands and overcome frustration. . . ."

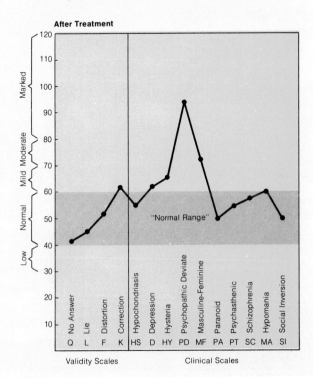

is toward increased emphasis on social systems —marital dyads, families, communities, organizations, and even societies—a good deal of research attention is being focused on ways of analyzing such systems. In the course of our discussion, we have already noted some of the forms this attention has taken, including observing marital and family interactions, experimentally manipulating reinforcement patterns in parent-child interactions, and studying patterns of communication, effective use of resources, and so on in other groups. All these techniques are ways of assessing interpersonal interactions as a basis for making improvements in the functioning of the system.

Another innovative technique that appears to offer great future promise involves the construction of computer models of social systems. Computers then simulate the actual functioning of the system. This not only permits detailed analysis of the system in operation, but also makes it possible to study the effects different changes would have on the overall operation of the system. An example of this use of computers in assessment was given on page 626. Simulations of complex social systems are handicapped today by our inadequate knowledge of many of the key variables that affect their functioning. Only as all these variables are included can the computer simulation be an accurate replica of the "real-world" social processes.

In the present chapter, we have attempted to gain an overall perspective on clinical assessment. Toward this end we noted the nature and uses of clinical assessment and then dealt briefly with the interdisciplinary sources utilized in collecting relevant assessment data as well as with methods of integrating and interpreting such data. In the final section of the chapter, we noted some of the problems, such as the antitest revolt, which have surrounded clinical assessment procedures; and we completed the chapter with a brief review of innovative approaches which are leading to advances in clinical assessment. Throughout, we emphasized the trend away from the assessment of individuals to the assessment of individual-environment relations and social systems, together with the trend away from the use of assessment data for labeling to its use in treatment and prevention.

Contemporary Approaches to Therapy

20

BIOLOGICAL THERAPY

PSYCHOTHERAPY

SOCIOCULTURAL APPROACHES TO THERAPY

CURRENT ISSUES AND TRENDS IN TREATMENT

Therapy is directed toward the modification of maladaptive behavior and the fostering of adaptive behavior. There are, of course, a great many other approaches to behavior change, such as formal education, political propaganda, and brainwashing. In therapy, however, the primary goal is to help an individual and/or group achieve more effective coping behavior.

The concept of therapy is not a new one. Throughout recorded history, men have tried to help each other with problems of living—including mental disorders—in both informal and formal ways. In Chapter 2 we noted the wide range of procedures that have been advocated for helping the mentally disturbed—from trephining and exorcism to incarceration and torture, from understanding and kindliness to the most extreme cruelty.

In the twentieth century marked advances have been made in the treatment of maladaptive behavior. These include the development, on a biological level, of methods for correcting or alleviating brain pathology and related organic conditions that impair thought, feeling, and action; on a psychological level, of a variety of methods for modifying maladaptive behavior, fostering more effective coping techniques, and opening channels for growth—methods applicable to married couples and families as well as to individuals; and on a sociocultural level, of methods for correcting or alleviating pathological social conditions and the maladaptive behaviors of entire communities or even societies.

In view of the complexity of human behavior and our lack of adequate knowledge concerning man, it is perhaps inevitable that marked differences in viewpoints concerning therapy should have arisen. Thus some therapists rely primarily upon chemotherapy or other biological approaches; others rely primarily upon behavior therapy or other psychological approaches; and still others focus on general sociocultural measures. Of course, even if there were complete agreement among therapists, all maladaptive behavior would not be treated in the same way. To be effective, any treatment program should be formulated in relation to the needs and potentialities of the given individual or group; and often this requires an interdisciplinary therapeutic approach.

In the present chapter, we shall examine the major biological, psychosocial, and sociocultural approaches to therapy. Then we shall deal with certain issues and trends that have emerged in recent years. Throughout our discussion, we shall attempt to provide the reader with a broad perspective concerning the goals, procedures, and outcomes of contemporary therapy.

BIOLOGICAL THERAPY

Biological approaches to therapy may embrace practically any branch of medicine, depending on the needs of the particular individual. Special diets may be prescribed for those suffering from malnutrition, brain surgery for those with tumors, tranquilizers for agitated individuals, and a number of emergency measures for those suffering from acute drug intoxication. In this section we shall focus on three biological treatment techniques: (1) chemotherapy, (2) electrotherapy, and (3) brain-wave therapy.

CHEMOTHERAPY

During the last two decades there has been an extraordinary acceleration in the use of chemicals in the treatment of abnormal behavior, often with dramatic results. This psychopharmacological revolution has come about as our expanding knowledge of the role of biochemistry in brain pathology and of the effects of given drugs has made possible the development of new drugs for achieving specific therapeutic objectives. In the present context we shall note the major types of drugs used in chemotherapy and attempt to gain a perspective on the advantages and limitations of this therapeutic approach.

Types of drugs used in chemotherapy. The most commonly used drugs in chemotherapy fall into three major categories: (1) the antipsychotic drugs, or major tranquilizers, (2) the antianxiety drugs, or minor tranquilizers, and (3) the antidepressant drugs. As we have seen,

these drugs are often used in combination, depending on the needs and reactions of the particular individual.

1. *Antipsychotic drugs.* For centuries the root of the plant *rauwolfia* (snakeroot) has been used in India for the treatment of mental disorders; and in 1943, the *Indian Medical Gazette* reported improvement in manic reactions, schizophrenia, and other types of psychopathology following the use of *reserpine*, a drug derived from rauwolfia. Reserpine was first used in the United States in the early 1950's, after it was found to have a calming effect on mental patients (Kline, 1954). Early enthusiasm for the drug was tempered, however, by the finding that it may produce low blood pressure, nasal congestion, and other undesirable side effects. Consequently reserpine has now been largely replaced by other major tranquilizing drugs, such as the phenothiazines.

The phenothiazines—also introduced in the early 1950's—have remained the most popular of the major tranquilizing drugs. Two of these drugs, chlorpromazine and trifluoperazine HCl (marketed as Thorazine and Stelazine, respectively), have proved highly successful in calming psychotics manifesting emotional tension, disordered thought processes, and motor hyperactivity. Often the acutely agitated individual calms down within 48 hours after the beginning of treatment; and within two weeks, hallucinations and delusions are usually eliminated or alleviated. Even chronic schizophrenics, as we have noted, may experience some relief of symptoms and take a more active interest in their environment. The phenothiazines are considered relatively safe drugs, but they sometimes have undesirable side effects such as jaundice, drowsiness, and fainting spells. Usually such difficulties clear up with an adjustment in dosage. However, other more subtle complications may arise when phenothiazine drugs are used on an outpatient basis. For example, they do not mix well with alcohol.

Other antipsychotic drugs include the butyrophenones and the thioxanthenes—common trade names being Haldol and Taractan, respectively. These drugs have effects similar to the phenothiazines and increase the therapist's choice of drugs for meeting the needs of given individuals.

2. *Antianxiety drugs.* Besides the major antipsychotic drugs, there are a number of minor tranquilizers, or antianxiety drugs, that have been introduced in recent years. In fact, such names as Miltown, Librium, and Valium—trade names used for meprobamate, chlordiazepoxide hydrochloride, and diazepam, respectively—have become household words.

Minor tranquilizers are commonly used for reducing tension and anxiety in normal individuals during periods of severe stress as well as in the treatment of neurotic and psychosomatic disorders. Minor tranquilizers may also be used as part of the total treatment program for psychotics and for persons who have formerly been addicted to alcohol or other drugs. Both with normal individuals undergoing crises and with persons being treated for more severe psychopathology, the minor tranquilizers are frequently used in place of barbiturates or other sedatives to help induce relaxation and sleep.

Although the mild tranquilizers are considered to have minimal side effects, they are not without their complications. They commonly produce drowsiness, and when the medication is stopped after prolonged, heavy dosage there may be severe withdrawal symptoms—including insomnia, tremors, hallucinations, and convulsions. In general, these drugs are contraindicated for women during pregnancy, for children under 6 years of age, for depressed persons, and for individuals engaged in hazardous occupations that require alertness. As in the case of the major tranquilizers, they should not be used in combination with alcohol.

3. *Antidepressants.* Although the tranquilizing drugs have proven highly beneficial in treating many types of disorders, they are largely ineffective for persons with depressive reactions. In such cases the need is for a "mood elevator"—something that will energize rather than tranquilize. The first drug to be tried for this purpose was *iproniazid*, a drug being tested in the treatment of tuberculosis. It was noted that tubercular patients treated with the drug became euphoric, optimistic, and zestful—often to the extent of not getting enough rest. Dr. Nathan Kline tried the drug on depressed patients at New York's Rockland State Mental Hospital and found that in most cases their gloom lifted in a matter of days. Further tests confirmed its effectiveness as an antidepressant, but unfortunately it was found to have dangerous side effects—particularly liver toxicity—which prohibited its use.

The discovery of the antidepressant effects of iproniazid, however, led to the study of other monoamine oxidase inhibitors (MAO inhibitors), several of which were found to be effective antidepressants with minimal side effects. Among the more widely used of these have been *phenelzine* (Nardil) and *isocarboxazid* (Marplan). A second category of antidepressants includes the tricyclic derivatives, such as Tofranil and Imipramine.

Because of the effectiveness of the antidepressant drugs, the use of electroshock in the treatment of depression has been greatly reduced. However, the more rapidly acting of the antidepressant drugs must be used with caution because of possible undesirable side effects, including anxiety and agitation; thus electroshock is often the preferred method of treatment for severely depressed and possibly suicidal individuals, where it is important to clear up the depression as rapidly as possible.

Chemotherapy in perspective. With the advent of modern chemotherapy there has been a reduction in the seriousness and chronicity of many types of psychopathology, particularly the psychoses. Chemotherapy has made it possible for many individuals to function in their family and community setting who would otherwise require hospitalization; it has led to the earlier discharge of those who do require hospitalization and to the greater effectiveness of aftercare programs; and it has made restraints and locked wards largely methods of the past. All in all, chemotherapy not only has outmoded more drastic forms of treatment, but has led to a much more favorable hospital climate for patients and staff alike.

However, there are a number of complications and limitations in the use of chemotherapy. Aside from possible undesirable side effects, the problem of matching drug and dosage to the needs of a given individual is often a difficult one; and it is often necessary to change medication in the course of treatment. In addition, as many investigators have pointed out, tranquilizers and antidepressants tend to alleviate symptoms rather than bring the individual to grips with personal or situational factors that may be reinforcing maladaptive behaviors. Although the reduction in anxiety, disturbed thinking, and other symptoms may tempt therapists to regard a patient as "recovered," it would appear essential to include psychotherapy and sociotherapy in the total treatment program if such gains are to be maintained or improved upon.

ELECTROTHERAPY

In this section we shall elaborate briefly on three forms of therapy which involve the influence of electric current on the functioning of the central nervous system. These are: (1) electroshock therapy, (2) electrosleep therapy, and (3) the surgical implantation of microcircuitry.

Electroshock therapy (EST). The groundwork for the development of electroshock therapy was laid in 1935, when a Budapest psychiatrist, Von Meduna, observed that there seemed to be a much lower incidence of epilepsy among schizophrenics than in the population as a whole. He also noted that schizophrenic symptoms tended to disappear temporarily following convulsions in those patients who did suffer from epilepsy. Accordingly, he set out to produce epileptic-like convulsions in his schizophrenic patients by chemical means. He first tried administering camphor and oil, but this did not work out well because the convulsions might occur at any time within the next two or three days. He then tried metrazol, but this drug induced intense fear in the patients and resulted in a high incidence of

fatalities. Considered a "barbaric" form of treatment, metrazol therapy was shortly abandoned.

In 1938 two Italians, Cerletti and Bini, introduced the use of electroshock for the artificial production of convulsive seizures in mental patients. The patient lay on a padded couch with electrodes attached to his head, and an electric current of 70 to 130 volts was administered for a fraction of a second. This shock resulted in convulsions similar to grand-mal seizures of epileptics, after which the patient was unconscious for several minutes. A muscle relaxant was usually administered to minimize the intensity of seizure activity and the danger of bone fractures. Electroshock procedures have since been refined to the extent that convulsions are either minimal or completely eliminated. A number of such treatments may be given over a period of days or weeks.

Although electroshock therapy (also called electroconvulsive therapy) did not prove effective in the treatment of schizophrenics, it was found to be highly effective in the treatment of depressives, with immediate improvement rates as high as 90 percent or more. But how it works remains a matter of conjecture. One popular view holds that the electroshock somehow—possibly as a consequence of chemical alterations—"clears the circuits" in the nervous system, enabling the individual to think more rationally. A related view holds that the retrograde amnesia following the electroshock—which may blot out memory for the few minutes or even hours preceding treatment—is responsible for the therapeutic effect, possibly by interrupting maladaptive memory and thought sequences (Dawson, 1971; Ostow, 1968). Some behavior therapists have even suggested that electroconvulsive therapy is so noxious that it acts as a negative reinforcer to "crazy" or depressed behavior, so that the individual changes his behavior to avoid more punishment.

The fact is that EST is used because it works, even though we do not yet understand *how* it works. But as we have noted, recent advances in chemotherapy have reduced the use of EST; and it is now used chiefly for the rapid alleviation of depression in suicidal individuals.

Electrosleep therapy. Although it has received little attention in this country, electrosleep, or *cerebral electrotherapy*, has been the subject of extensive research in the U.S.S.R. In this procedure, a soft mask containing electrodes is placed over the upper part of the individual's face. A mild electric current—just enough to cause a slight tingling sensation—is administered. The individual does not lose consciousness or experience convulsions; he may or may not fall asleep during the treatment. Usually, half-hour treatments are administered daily for one or two weeks.

Using an American-made instrument modeled after a Russian device, Rosenthal and Wulfson (1970) reported favorable preliminary results with a group of more than 40 outpatients suffering from chronic anxiety, depressive states, and associated insomnia.

"With this population of patients who were previously refractory to standard medication therapy, we found to our surprise, that approximately two thirds showed a rapid and relatively complete remission of symptoms. The most immediate effect was an almost total and complete improvement in the nighttime insomnia; the patients reported sleeping through the night following the first, second, or third treatment. Improvements in anxiety and depressive symptoms were usually seen by the fifth treatment." (p. 534)

Adequate research data concerning the lasting effectiveness of electrosleep therapy are not yet available, although international efforts to evaluate this form of treatment are under way (Wageneder, Iwanovsky & Dodge, 1969). It may well prove to be a useful treatment in and of itself or as an adjunct to a broader treatment program.

Implantation of microcircuitry. One of the new frontiers in brain research involves the electrical stimulation of the brain (ESB) in an attempt to learn more about how various brain areas function. For example, electrical stimulation of the hypothalamus in human beings can produce a whole gamut of emotional responses, from euphoria to terror.

Such findings have led to research in the use of microcircuitry to control pathological brain functioning, such as may result in epileptic seizures or behavioral disturbances. In Chapter 4, for example, we noted the use of microcircuitry in bringing about changes in a brain-damaged girl's emotions and behavior. Delgado (1970), a pioneer in this field, has suggested that the

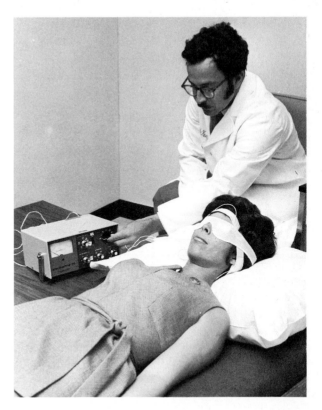

American interest in electrosleep techniques, first developed in Russia, is growing steadily. The battery-operated transistor device shown here passes a light current through the brain. Favorable results have been reported in cases of chronically anxious, depressed, and insomniac individuals who had failed to respond to antidepressants or antianxiety drugs; researchers are currently investigating the applicability of the technique to psychosomatic disorders such as asthma and hypertension.

surgical implantation of microcircuitry to stimulate given brain areas might be of great help in the treatment of individuals manifesting such symptoms as chronic agitation, homicidal impulses, or suicidal behavior. In fact, it is not beyond the realm of possibility that manic-depressive individuals might one day be able to control extreme mood swings with ESB.

BRAIN-WAVE THERAPY

Waking EEG's show a continuous series of brain waves which wax and wane in frequency of occurrence. A number of these brain waves have been identified and labeled in terms of the number of cycles per second and the amplitude

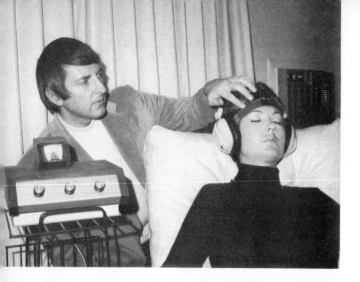

Researchers at the University of Colorado Medical Center have been investigating the applicability of bio-feedback techniques to psychosomatic disorders and anxiety problems. Portable BFT systems like the one shown here have proved valuable in teaching claustrophobics and stutterers to relax without the aid of tranquilizers (Trotter, 1971).

of the wave—e.g., alpha, beta, delta, and theta rhythms. The dominance of a given wave pattern appears to be related to specific functions of the brain and types of consciousness.

Alpha waves, which have a rhythm of 8 to 12 cycles per second and an amplitude of up to 40 microvolts, are associated with an alert state that is devoid of concrete visual imagery and is accompanied by feelings of tranquility and a lack of tension and anxiety. Alpha waves occur intermittently—the typical individual slipping in and out of alpha from about 5 to 30 times per minute. In contrast, beta waves—which fall into a fast-paced 14 to 28 cycles per second—tend to occur when the individual is attempting to solve a problem or is worrying about something; they are usually accompanied by feelings of tension.

Most persons are, of course, unaware of their brain-wave patterns and unable to control them consciously. Pioneering studies in the conscious control of alpha waves were conducted in 1958 by Joseph Kamiya. His initial experiments involved placing subjects in a darkened room and monitoring their brain waves. The subjects were instructed to close their eyes and guess whether they were in an alpha or a nonalpha state whenever they heard a bell ring. After each guess they were told whether they were right or wrong. With this type of feedback, the subjects learned in a few sessions to discriminate between alpha and nonalpha states. Even more remarkable, once they had learned to make this discrimination, they could voluntarily switch alpha rhythms on or off. Kamiya (1968) later found he could speed up the process of learning by sounding a feedback tone whenever alpha waves were occurring. Other investigators using similar bio-feedback training (BFT) procedures have obtained comparable results (Gustaitis, 1971; Rorvik, 1970).

In our discussion of psychosomatic disorders, we noted the possible therapeutic value of learning to regulate blood pressure and other functions of the autonomic nervous system. Similar interest has been expressed in the possible therapeutic use of brain-wave control as well as in illuminating and possibly expanding the processes of consciousness. Investigators have shown that dedicated Zen and Yogi meditators are capable not only of raising and lowering their blood pressure, body temperature, and related functions but also of controlling their brain waves. In fact, Hirai and Kasamatsu (1966) of Tokyo University found a high correlation between brain-wave control and the proficiency rating of Zen masters. During meditation, the EEG of Zen masters showed prominent alpha activity. Those with 20 years or more of Zen practice also showed prolonged patterns of theta activity—the theta wave having a rhythm of only 5 to 7 cycles per second. The significance of the latter rhythm is still the subject of research.

It has been suggested that bio-feedback training—which has also been referred to as "electronic Yoga"—could alleviate many psychosomatic ills, help overcome anxiety and tension, reduce the need for tranquilizers and other drugs, and enhance mental functioning, including creativity and access to new dimensions of inner experiencing. Although many questions remain unanswered, a number of portable BFT devices are, in fact, already being marketed. The self-control and manipulation of brain waves, like self-experimentation with LSD, may have incipient dangers, however—among them the possibility that malfunctioning of the device could lead to the conditioning and maintenance of maladaptive rather than adaptive states. In addition, it seems unlikely that learning to deal effectively with life's problems can ever be achieved simply through the control of inner states of feeling and consciousness.

PSYCHOTHERAPY

Psychotherapy is not completely new or far removed from the ken of any of us. As Alexander pointed out:

". . . Everyone who tries to console a despondent friend, calm down a panicky child in a sense practices psychotherapy. He tries by psychological means to restore the disturbed emotional equilibrium of another person. Even these commonsense, everyday methods are based on the understanding of the nature of the disturbance, although on an intuitive and not a scientific understanding. . . . Methodological psychotherapy to a large degree is nothing but a systematic, conscious application of methods by which we influence our fellow men in our daily life. The most important difference is that intuitive knowledge is replaced by the well established general principles of psychodynamics." (1946, p. 110)

We shall see, however, that these "well established principles" are not always as well grounded scientifically as we might hope.

In general, psychotherapy aims toward personality growth in the direction of maturity, competence, and self-actualization. This usually involves the achievement of one or more of the following specific goals: (1) increased insight into one's problems and behavior, (2) a better delineation of one's self-identity, (3) resolution of handicapping or disabling conflicts, (4) changing of undesirable habits or reaction patterns, (5) improved interpersonal or other competencies, (6) the modification of inaccurate assumptions about oneself and one's world, and (7) the opening of a pathway to a more meaningful and fulfilling existence.

These goals are by no means easy to achieve. Often an individual's distorted environmental perspective and unhealthy self-concept are the end products of faulty parent-child relationships reinforced by many years of life experiences. In other instances, adequate occupational, marital, or social adjustment requires major changes in the person's life situation in addition to psychotherapy. It would be too much to expect that the psychotherapist could intervene and in a short period of time undo the entire past history of the individual and prepare him to cope with a difficult life situation in a fully adequate manner.

The psychotherapist does have certain assets on his side, however, the major one being the inner drive of the individual toward integrity and health. Although this inner drive is often obscured in severely disturbed patients, the majority are anxious, unhappy, and discouraged, and are eager to cooperate in any program that holds hope for improvement. Some degree of cooperation on the part of the individual receiving help is considered essential if psychotherapy is to have much chance of success.

Psychotherapy with severely disturbed individuals usually takes place in a hospital or inpatient clinic setting. The various psychotherapeutic procedures we shall be discussing, however, are by no means confined to inpatients. Most of those who receive psychotherapy for neuroses, alcoholism, or personality disorders do so on an outpatient basis—either in an outpatient clinic or with psychiatrists or clinical psychologists in private practice.

In the discussion that follows, we shall deal with the differing systematic viewpoints, goals, and procedures of the major forms of psychotherapy. The illustration on page 664 provides an overview of some of the key dimensions or characteristics of this rather complex area of study.

PSYCHOANALYTIC THERAPY

As developed by Freud, psychoanalytic therapy is an intensive, long-term procedure for uncovering repressed memories, motives, and conflicts—presumably stemming from problems in early psychosexual development—and helping the individual resolve them in the light of adult reality. It is felt that gaining insight into such repressed material will free the individual from the need to squander his energies on repressive defense mechanisms, thus opening the way for better personality integration and more effective living.

KEY DIMENSIONS OF PSYCHOTHERAPY

The forms of psychotherapy discussed on the following pages can be classified in a number of ways. For example, some, like behavior therapy, are based on the theory that changes in behavior will lead to changes in attitude, while others place primary emphasis upon changing attitudes, with the expectation that this will lead to changed behavior patterns. Listed below are a few "key dimensions" that will be useful to bear in mind as we examine the various approaches to psychotherapy.

1. **Individual/group.** In individual or one-to-one therapy, the therapist treats one person at a time. The effectiveness of such therapies depends to a great extent upon the patient-therapist relationship. In group therapy, several persons are treated at the same time in a group setting. Here the interactions and relationships of the group members to one another are important aspects of therapy. Many of the approaches to therapy to be discussed in this chapter can be adapted to either type of setting.

2. **Brief/long term.** The historical leader among psychotherapies—standard psychoanalysis—is a long-term process involving several sessions a week over a period of years. However, many of the newer forms of therapy, including modified psychoanalytic approaches, are designed to shorten the length of time required. For example, a marathon encounter group is an intensive group experience which may last for only a few days.

3. **Supportive/depth.** The main concerns of so-called supportive therapy are to reassure the individual, provide needed guidance, and reinforce existing coping patterns. Depth therapy, on the other hand, is concerned with helping the individual work through deep conflictual material or highly traumatic and painful experiences to achieve better personality integration and more effective coping patterns. Supportive therapy is usually brief, while depth therapy may be either brief or long term.

4. **Directive/nondirective.** Therapists differ widely with respect to the amount of responsibility they place upon the individual being treated as contrasted with the degree to which they themselves direct the course of therapy. In directive therapy, the therapist takes an "active" role, asking questions and offering interpretations; in nondirective therapy, the major responsibility is placed on the client, and the therapist may simply try to help him clarify and understand his feelings and values.

5. **Segregated/total push.** In segregated therapy a person sees a therapist periodically in an attempt to work through particular problems, but little attempt may be made to relate the therapy to his overall life situation. In total push or milieu therapy, the therapy program is directly concerned with the individual's entire life situation. This typically involves working with other members of his family and often with professional agencies in the community.

6. **Crisis intervention/personal growth.** Crisis intervention therapy is designed to help an individual cope with an immediate stress situation which is approaching or perhaps exceeding the limits of his adjustive capacities. In personal growth oriented therapy, the primary focus is on fostering increased self-understanding, sensory awareness, and other avenues toward the fulfillment of potentialities. As we shall see, growth-fostering techniques may be used with "normal" individuals as well as the mentally disturbed.

7. **Eliminating maladaptive patterns/developing competencies.** In some cases, therapy is directed primarily toward the elimination of phobias or other maladaptive patterns; while in other cases, therapy is directed primarily toward the development of needed competencies. Systematic desensitization in dealing with a phobia of heights would be an example of the former, while assertive training in helping an individual establish more satisfying relationships with members of the opposite sex would be an example of the latter. Often, of course, these approaches are used simultaneously.

8. **Inner control of behavior/outer control of behavior.** In some instances, psychotherapy is aimed at establishing environmental control of the individual's behavior through principles of reinforcement—as in the example of behavioral contracting on page 675. In other instances, the primary goal of psychotherapy is to change the individual's value assumptions in such a way as to foster the inner cognitive control of behavior. Of course, external controls may be used as an emergency measure with the expectation that inner controls will eventually be developed and take over.

There are some therapists who faithfully adhere to a particular systematic approach, but these are in the minority. The great majority of psychotherapists can best be described as *eclectic*—that is, they attempt to be flexible, utilizing whatever concepts and procedures seem best suited to the needs of a given individual.

Techniques and process. Psychoanalytic therapy is not easy to describe, and the problem is complicated by the fact that most people have some more-or-less inaccurate conceptions of psychoanalysis based on cartoons, movies, and television dramas. Perhaps the simplest starting point in our present discussion is to describe the four basic techniques of psychoanalytic therapy: free association, dream interpretation, analysis of resistance, and analysis of transference. Then we shall note some of the changes that have taken place in psychoanalytic therapy since Freud.

1. Free association. The "basic rule" of psychoanalysis is that the individual being treated must say whatever comes into his mind, regardless of how personal, painful, or seemingly irrelevant it may be. Usually he sits comfortably in a chair or lies in a relaxed position on a couch and allows his mind to wander freely, giving a running account of his thoughts, feelings, and desires. The therapist usually takes a position behind him, so as not to be a distraction or disrupt the free flow of associations.

It is important to note that Freud did not view free associations as simply a random matter, but maintained that they are determined like other events. As we have seen, he also thought that the conscious represents a relatively small part of the mind, while the unconscious, like the submerged part of an iceberg, is much the larger portion. Thus the task of the therapist is to identify accurately the materials repressed beneath the surface in the unconscious domain. The therapist then interprets this material to the individual, guiding him toward increased insight into the underlying motives and conflicts of which he has been unaware.

2. *Dream interpretation.* Another important procedure for uncovering unconscious material is dream analysis. When a person is asleep, repressive defenses are lowered and forbidden desires and feelings may find an outlet in dreams. For this reason dreams have been referred to as the "royal road to the unconscious." But some motives are so unacceptable to the individual that even in dreams they are not revealed openly but are expressed in disguised or symbolic form. Thus a dream has two kinds of content: *manifest* content, which is the dream as it appears to the dreamer, and *latent* content, composed of the actual motives which are seeking expression but are so painful or unacceptable that they are disguised.

The actual process by which the latent content of the dream is transformed into the less painful manifest content is called *dream work.* In dream interpretation, it is the task of the therapist to uncover these disguised meanings by studying the symbols that appear in the manifest content of the dream. For example, the following dream was that of a petite, attractive girl who had never had a problem with her weight.

"I was walking down this street and I saw this booth and it said 'help fat people' or something like this, and it was full of ugly fat people. This is nice repetition. I would be interested in finding out what this fatness is, ah, what it represents, ah, 'help ugly fat people reduce,' it said. 'Pay here and we will give you

the means' or something like this. So I went up and paid a lot of money and, ah, went away. I didn't refuse it. That was the end of the dream." (Breger, 1967, p. 20)

Without attempting a complete analysis of the dream, the analyst noted that when the girl was asked to express her associations to the dream, she stated that she had secretly had an abortion about a year previously, and spoke with regret about having lost the child. Thus Breger interpreted the "ugly" aspects of the fat people in her dream as symbolizing the guilt she experienced over her pregnancy and abortion.

3. *Analysis of resistance.* During the process of free association or of associating to dreams, an individual may evidence resistance—an unwillingness or inability to relate certain thoughts, motives, or experiences. For example, he may be talking about an important area in his life and then suddenly switch topics, perhaps stating that "it really isn't that important," or that "it is too absurd to discuss"; or he may give some glib interpretation to his associations. In some instances resistance may be evidenced by coming late to an appointment, or even "forgetting" an appointment altogether. Since resistance prevents painful and threatening material from entering awareness, it must be broken down if the individual is to face his problems and conflicts and deal with them in a realistic manner.

4. *Analysis of transference.* As patient and therapist interact, the relationship between them may become complex and emotionally involved. Often a person carries over and applies to the therapist attitudes and feelings that developed in his relations with significant others in the past, perhaps reacting to the analyst as he did to his mother or father, and feeling the hostility and rejection that he once felt toward his real parent.

By recognizing the transference relationship, the therapist may provide the individual with the experience of having a "good" father. It thus becomes possible for the individual to work though his conflicts in regard to his own father and to overcome feelings of hostility and self-devaluation stemming from his father's rejection. In essence, the pathogenic effects of an undesirable early relationship are counteracted by working through a similar emotional conflict in a therapeutic setting. Since the person's reliving of his own pathogenic past in a sense re-creates

THE USE OF HYPNOSIS IN PSYCHOTHERAPY

Hypnosis was known among the ancient Egyptians and other early peoples, but its modern use in psychotherapy dates from the time of Mesmer (see pages 50–51). Since that time, there have been periodic fluctuations in the popularity of hypnosis in psychotherapy, and differing viewpoints have arisen concerning the exact nature of hypnotic phenomena. In general, hypnosis may be defined as an altered state of consciousness involving extreme suggestibility. Hypnotic induction procedures are designed to bring about a heightened state of selective attention in which the subject "tunes out" irrelevant stimuli and concentrates solely upon the hypnotist's suggestions. The induction of hypnosis and some of the therapeutic uses to which it has been put may be briefly outlined as follows:

1. Induction of hypnosis. Hypnosis may be induced by a variety of techniques, most of which involve the following factors: (a) enlisting the cooperation of the subject and allaying any fears of hypnosis; (b) having the subject assume a comfortable position and relax completely; (c) narrowing and focusing the subject's attention, perhaps by having him fix his gaze on some bright object; and (d) directing the subject's activities by means of reinforced suggestions. The latter often involves establishing the assumption that normal bodily reactions have in fact come about at the direction of the hypnotist. For example, the subject may be directed to gaze upward toward a light or other object, and then be told that his eyelids feel slightly heavy. This is a normal reaction to the strain of looking upward, but the subject interprets it as being due to the instructions of the hypnotist; thus the way is paved for the acceptance of additional suggestions.

Not everyone can be readily hypnotized—although it would appear that with training most persons are amenable to hypnosis—and there are varying degrees in the depth of the hypnotic state which is induced. The latter may vary from light hypnosis in which the subject becomes drowsy and tends to follow simple directions to deep hypnosis in which complete anesthesia may be produced and surgical operations may be performed without the subject's experiencing pain. During hypnosis, the subject may open his eyes and move about without any disturbance in the hypnotic state. With training, some persons can elicit a state of autohypnosis without the presence of a hypnotist. For example, Sacerdote (1966) found that some terminal cancer patients can bring pain under control by self-hypnosis, so that they no longer need to rely on morphine or other pain-reducing drugs.

2. Recall of buried memories. Traumatic experiences that have been repressed from consciousness may be recovered under hypnosis. This technique was occasionally used in treating combat-exhaustion cases during World War II. Under hypnosis, the amnesic soldier could relive his battle experience, thus discharging the emotional tensions associated with it and permitting the experience to be assimilated into his self-structure. Civilian shock reactions involving amnesia may be similarly handled.

3. Age regression. Closely related to memory recall is hypnotic age regression. The hypnotized subject may be told that he is now a six-year-old child again and will subsequently act, talk, and think very much as he did at the age of six years. Even such characteristics as handwriting will become increasingly childish

an an individual is regressed through successively younger ages. Regression to the age just preceding the onset of phobias often brings to light the traumatic experiences that precipitated them. Here again the traumatic experience may be relived in order to desensitize the subject to it.

4. Dream induction. Dreams can be induced through hypnosis, although some investigators consider hypnotic dreams to more nearly resemble fantasies than nocturnal dreams. In this connection, it may be pointed out that there is little similarity between EEG recordings of sleeping and hypnotized persons (Ruch & Zimbardo, 1971). In any event, hypnotic dreams may be used to explore intrapsychic conflicts along the lines of dream analysis worked out by Freud. Perhaps the particular value of such dreams is that the therapist can suggest the theme about which he wants the dreams to center, using them much like projective techniques in exploring the individual's inner conflicts.

5. Posthypnotic suggestion. One of the hypnotic phenomena most widely used in psychotherapy is posthypnotic suggestion. Here suggestions made by the therapist during the hypnotic state may be carried over into the waking state, with the subject remaining unaware of their source. For example, the subject may be told that he will no longer have a desire to smoke when he comes out of the hypnotic state. While such suggestions do carry over into the waking state, their duration is usually short. That is, the individual may again experience a desire to smoke in a few hours or a few days. This time factor can be partially compensated for, however, by regular reinforcement of the posthypnotic suggestion in booster sessions.

Some investigators attribute the altered state of consciousness in hypnosis to the subject's strong motivation to meet the demand characteristics of the situation. Barber (1969) has shown that many of the behaviors induced under hypnosis can be replicated in nonhypnotized subjects simply by giving instructions which they are strongly motivated to follow. On the other hand, O'Connell, Shor, and Orne (1970), on the basis of their extensive study of age regression in hypnotized and nonhypnotized subjects, have warned that "the equivalence of waking and hypnotic phenomena which seem the same cannot simply be taken for granted." (p. 30) Other investigators have offered dramatic evidence indicating that the pain response can be brought almost completely under hypnotic control, permitting a degree of pain reduction well beyond that produced in nonhypnotized subjects (McGlashin, Evans & Orne, 1969; Zimbardo, Rapaport & Baron, 1969).

In connection with the use of hypnosis in therapy, it may be pointed out that such drugs as sodium pentothal can be used to produce phenomena similar to those manifested in the hypnotic trance. This form of biological therapy is referred to as *narcoanalysis* or *narcosynthesis*. In Chapter 7 we noted the use of sodium pentothal in the treatment of severe cases of combat exhaustion involving amnesia.

his real-life neuroses, this experience is often referred to as a *transference neurosis.*

It is not possible here to consider at length the complexities of transference relationships, but it may be stressed that the patient's attitudes toward the therapist do not always follow simple patterns. Often the patient is ambivalent—distrusting the therapist and feeling hostile toward him as a symbol of authority, but at the same time seeking acceptance and love. In addition, the problems of transference are by no means confined to the patient, for the therapist may also have a mixture of feelings toward the patient. This is known as *countertransference* and must be recognized and handled properly by the therapist. For this reason, it is considered important that the therapist have an understanding of his own motives, conflicts, and "weak spots," and all psychoanalytic therapists have themselves undergone psychoanalysis.

Particularly during the early stages, psychoanalytic therapy is directed toward uncovering unconscious desires and conflicts and helping the person integrate them into the conscious dimension of his personality. However, the new insights achieved by the patient do not automatically generalize to his day-to-day relationships. Thus as the therapy progresses toward its terminal phase, it is increasingly directed toward furthering his emotional reeducation and helping ensure the generalization of new insights and behaviors to his real-life situation.

Changes in psychoanalytic therapy since Freud. Although some psychoanalysts still adhere to standard long-term therapy—which may take years—most analysts have worked out modifications in procedure designed to shorten the time and expense required. Most neo-Freudian therapists place more emphasis on the individual's current interpersonal relationships and life situation and less on his childhood experiences, also playing down Freud's emphasis on repressed sexual desires and conflicts.

Despite such modifications, psychoanalytic therapy is still commonly criticized for being relatively time-consuming and expensive, for being based upon a biased model of man, and for lacking experimental evidence of its effectiveness. Because it expects the individual to achieve insight and major personality change, it is also limited in its applicability. For example, it is best suited for persons who are average or above in intelligence and who do not suffer from severe psychopathology. However, many individuals do feel that they have profited from psychoanalytic therapy—particularly in terms of greater self-understanding, relief from inner conflict and anxiety, and improved interpersonal relationships.

BEHAVIOR THERAPY

It has been over 50 years since Watson's experiment with little Albert, described in Chapter 3, but it was not until the 1960's that behavior therapy really came into its own. The major reason for the long delay was the dominant position of psychoanalysis in the fields of clinical psychology and psychiatry. In recent years, however, the therapeutic potentialities of behavior therapy techniques have been strikingly demonstrated in dealing with a wide variety of maladaptive behaviors, and there have been literally thousands of research publications dealing with the systematic application of learning principles to the modification of maladaptive behavior—on group as well as individual levels.

The behavioristic model views the maladjusted person—unless there is brain pathology—as differing from other people only in that (1) he has learned faulty coping patterns which are being maintained by some kind of reinforcement, and/or (2) he has failed to acquire needed competencies for coping with the problems of living. Thus behavior therapy specifies the maladaptive behaviors to be modified and the adaptive behavior to be achieved as well as the specific learning principles or procedures to be utilized. Rather than exploring inner conflicts and attempting cognitive change, behavior therapists attempt to modify behavior directly by manipulating environmental contingencies—that is, by the use of reward and punishment. Their techniques include punishment for maladaptive responses, removal of reinforcers which are maintaining maladaptive behaviors, safe exposure to feared situations, and positive reinforcement for learning new competencies. Behavior therapy techniques seem especially effective in altering maladaptive

These two autistic boys were enrolled in an intensive behavior therapy program at the UCLA Neuropsychiatric Institute. Here they are shown receiving immediate positive reinforcement in the form of food for their social interactions in a play setting. Other techniques used included punishment and modeling. The boy on the right, mute and self-destructive when he entered the program, was able to return home in less than a year, and two years later was doing first-grade work at a special school. A number of other children in the program made similar gains.

behavior when the reinforcement is administered immediately following the desired response, and when the person knows what is expected and why the reinforcement is given. The ultimate goal, of course, is not only to achieve the desired responses but to bring them under the control and self-monitoring of the individual.

We have cited other examples of the application of behavior therapy in the chapters on neuroses and other patterns of abnormal behavior. In the present section, we shall elaborate briefly upon the key techniques of behavior therapy and then note the expanding role of this approach to the treatment of maladaptive behavior.

Simple extinction. Since learned behavior patterns tend to weaken and disappear over time if they are not reinforced, the simplest way to eliminate a maladaptive pattern is often to remove the reinforcement for it. This is especially true in situations where maladaptive behavior is being reinforced unknowingly by others.

Billy, a 6-year-old first grader, was brought to a psychological clinic by his parents because he "hated school," and his teacher had told them that his showing-off behavior was disrupting the class and making

him unpopular. It became apparent in observing Billy and his parents during the initial interview that both his mother and father were noncritical and approving of everything he did. After further assessment, a three-phase program of therapy was undertaken: (1) the parents were helped to discriminate between showing-off behavior and appropriate behavior on Billy's part; (2) the parents were instructed to show a loss of interest and attention when Billy engaged in showing-off behavior while continuing to evidence their approval of appropriate behavior; and (3) Billy's teacher was instructed to ignore Billy, insofar as it was feasible, when he engaged in showing-off behavior and to devote her attention at those times to children who were behaving more appropriately.

Although Billy's showing-off behavior in class increased during the first few days of this therapy program, it diminished markedly thereafter when it was no longer reinforced by his parents and teacher. As his maladaptive behavior diminished, he was better accepted by his classmates, which, in turn, helped reinforce more appropriate behavior patterns and change his negative attitude toward school.

Inadvertent reinforcement may also encourage delusions and other psychotic behavior. As Ruch and Zimbardo (1971) have pointed out,

"It is standard procedure in many mental hospitals for the staff to ask patients frequently how they are feeling. This may focus the patient's attention on his emotional state and provide the expectation that the 'appropriate' behavior is to be thinking and talking about one's feelings, unusual symptoms, hallucinations, and so on. In fact, the more bizarre the symptoms and verbalizations, the more attention may be shown by the staff in their efforts to understand the 'dynamics' of the case. One patient, asked by an interviewer if there was 'anything else that was bothering him,' responded, 'You mean *halicinations* or *sublimitions?*' " (p. 631)

Maladaptive behaviors may not extinguish readily, since such responses have often been sustained for long periods by intermittent reinforcement. For this reason Wolpe (1969) considers it important that the cessation of reinforcement be both abrupt and complete. In many cases, extinction is used along with the positive reinforcement of more adaptive responses. Ayllon and Michael (1959) cited a case in which nurses on a psychiatric ward were instructed to *ignore* the delusional statements of patients and to *reinforce* normal statements. Thereafter, there was a marked drop in psychotic statements and an increased incidence of more normal and adaptive behavior.

Systematic desensitization. In the preceding section we dealt with the extinction of behavior that is being *positively reinforced*. Behavior that is being *negatively reinforced*—reinforced by the successful avoidance of a painful situation—is harder to deal with. In this case, since the individual becomes anxious and withdraws at the first sign of the painful situation, he never gets a chance to find out whether the aversive consequences he fears are still in operation. In addition, his avoidance is anxiety reducing and hence is itself reinforced.

One commonly used technique for extinguishing negatively reinforced behavior involves eliciting an antagonistic or competing response. Since it is difficult to feel both pleasant and anxious at the same time, the method of desensitization is aimed at teaching the client to emit a response which is inconsistent with anxiety while in the presence (real or imagined) of the anxiety-producing stimulus. The prototype of this approach is the classic experiment of Mary Cover Jones (1924), cited in Chapter 3, in which she successfully eliminated a small boy's conditioned fears of a white rabbit and other furry animals.

The term *systematic desensitization* has been applied to a specific approach developed by Wolpe[1] (1961; 1963; 1969). On the assumption that most neurotic patterns fundamentally are conditioned anxiety responses, Wolpe attempts to train the client to remain calm and relaxed in situations that formerly produced anxiety—since "the autonomic effects that accompany deep relaxation are diametrically opposed to those characteristic of anxiety." (1969, p. 96)

Wolpe's model is elegant in its simplicity, and the carrying out of his method is equally straightforward.

1. *Training in relaxation.* The first step in therapy is training the individual to relax. This is usually done in the first six sessions and consists of having him contract and then gradually relax different muscles until he achieves a state of complete relaxation. The basic technique follows the principles of "progressive relaxation" outlined by Jacobson (1938) and is described in detail by Wolpe (1969). Other techniques that are sometimes used to facilitate complete relaxation include meditation, hypnosis, and drugs (Bandura, 1969; Brady, 1967; Todd & Kelley, 1970).

2. *The construction of hierarchies.* During the early sessions of therapy, time is also spent constructing a hierarchy of the individual's anxieties. This anxiety hierarchy is a list of related stimuli ranked in descending order according to the amount of anxiety they evoke in the client. For example, if a client is overly possessive or jealous of her husband, she describes the situations in which she feels this jealousy. The highest anxiety-producing situation might be observing him at a cocktail party talking intimately with an attractive woman. Further down the list might be hearing him comment favorably about a waitress; and the lowest anxiety-evoking stimulus might be noticing him look casually at a young female hitchhiker. In some instances the anxiety is easier to quantify, as in the case of acrophobia or of a student's examination anxiety; and, of course, anxiety may focus around more than one theme, as when the client shows a variety of phobias.

3. *Desensitization procedure.* When the client has mastered the relaxation techniques and the therapist has established an appropriate anxiety hierarchy, the actual process of desensitization begins. While the client relaxes completely in a comfortable chair with his eyes closed, the therapist describes a series of scenes to him, directing him to imagine himself experiencing each situation. The first scene presented is a neutral one. If the client remains calm and relaxed, the lowest scene on the hierarchy is presented; then the therapist moves progressively up the hierarchy until the client indicates that he is experiencing anxiety and the scene is terminated. Treatment continues until the client is able to remain in a relaxed state while vividly imagining the scenes that formerly evoked the greatest anxiety.

---

[1]In an attempt to clarify the confusion in terminology relating to desensitization, Van Egeren (1971) has noted that *reciprocal inhibition* has been applied in classical neurophysiology to momentary, reversible inhibition of one nerve process by another, as in the inhibition of antagonistic skeletal muscles. *Counterconditioning* implies the permanent inhibition of a reaction by means of an incompatible or antagonistic response—as, for example, in the inhibition of anxiety in a fear-arousing situation by the repetitive presentation of food. Wolpe, although referring to his method of desensitization as involving reciprocal inhibition, achieves long-lasting changes in response by means of planned repetition, and thus, in effect, produces counterconditioning.

The usual duration of a desensitization session is 15 to 30 minutes, and the sessions are ordinarily given 2 to 3 times per week. The overall therapy program may, of course, take a number of weeks or even months.

A number of variants of systematic desensitization have been utilized. Migler and Wolpe (1967) have successfully used a tape recorder to enable a client to carry out the desensitization process at home. Paul and Shannon (1966) used group desensitization techniques with college students manifesting severe anxiety and disablement in public-speaking situations; a two-year follow-up study showed that improvement had been maintained or had increased (Paul, 1968). A variation of this technique involves "marathon" desensitization groups in which the entire desensitization program is compressed into a few days of intensive treatment (Suinn, 1970). *In vivo* desensitization, in which the client is asked to expose himself in reality to situations to which he has just been desensitized in imagination, appears to accelerate the desensitization procedure and may be the method of choice for individuals who do not respond to imagined anxiety-eliciting situations in the same way they

POSITIVE REINFORCEMENT THROUGH TIME PROJECTION

A unique therapeutic approach that combines aspects of desensitization procedure with hypnotic time projection and positive reinforcement has been developed by Lazarus (1968b). In commenting on the role of time in therapy, Lazarus has noted that "The truism 'time heals' ignores the fact that the passage of time *per se* is not therapeutic, but that psychological healing occurs because time permits new or competing responses to emerge." (p. 86) The following case report describes the way this process was hastened in treating a young woman for neurotic depression:

"Miss C. H., a 23-year-old art student, became acutely depressed when her boy friend informed her that he intended marrying one of her classmates. She became sleepless, anorexic, restless, and weepy. Previously she had been a most talented and enthusiastic student; now she was unable to concentrate on her work, had stopped attending classes, and had become apathetic and listless. After 10 days, her parents persuaded her to consult a psychiatrist who prescribed amphetamines and barbiturates, whereupon she made a suicidal attempt by swallowing all her pills. Fortunately, the dose was not lethal. She refused to seek further psychiatric help, but her family physician nevertheless requested the writer to conduct a home visit.

"It was difficult to establish rapport but the patient was finally responsive to emphatic statements of sympathy and reassurance. She agreed to see the writer at his consulting room on the following day. A behavioral inquiry revealed that prior to her unrequited love relationship, she had enjoyed painting, sculpting, and practicing the guitar. She also went horse-riding and displayed some interest in symphony concerts. During the 10 months of her love affair, she had exchanged all of these activities for 'stock-car racing, amateur dramatics and a few wild parties.'

"As the patient proved highly susceptible to hypnotic techniques, a trance state was induced and the following time projection sequence was applied:

"'It is almost 3:15 P.M. on Wednesday, April 14, 1965. (This was the date of the actual consultation.) Apart from sleeping, eating, etc., how could you have occupied these 24 hr? You could have gone horse-riding for a change. or taken your guitar out of mothballs . . . (5-sec pause) . . . Let's push time forward another 24 hr. You are now 48 hr ahead in time. Enough time has elapsed to have started a painting and done some sculpting. You may even have enjoyed a ride in the country and attended a concert. Think about these activities; picture them in your mind; let them bring a good feeling of pleasant associations, of good times . . . (5-sec pause) . . . Let's advance even further in time. A whole week has gone by, and another, and yet another. Now these past three weeks into which you have advanced have been busy and active. Reflect back for a moment on three weeks of enjoyable activity . . . (10-sec pause) . . . Now you move further forward in time. Days are flying past; time advances; days become weeks; time passes; weeks become months. It is now 6 months later. It's the 14th of October, 1965. Look back on the past 6 months, from April to October. Think about the months that separate April from October. What have you done during May, June, July, August, and September? (Pause of 5 sec) . . . Now six months ago, going back to April, you were very upset. In retrospect, how do you feel? Think back; reflect over an incident now more than 6 months old. If it still bothers you, signal to me by raising your left index finger.'

"As the patient did not raise her finger, she was told that she would recall the entire time projection sequence and return back in time to April 14, feeling as she did during October. She was then dehypnotized and asked to recount her feelings. (If she had signalled, the time projection sequence would have been continued, up to 2-yr ahead.) She stated: 'How can I put it in words? Let me just explain it in three ways. First, I feel kind of foolish; second, there are lots of pebbles on the beach; and number three, there's something inside that really wants to find an outlet on canvas. Does that make sense?'

"Miss C. H. was interviewed a week later. She reported having enjoyed many productive hours, had regained her appetite, and had been sleeping soundly. There were some minor episodes of 'gloom' which responded to self-induced imagery, similar to the therapeutic time-projection sequence. She cancelled her subsequent appointments, stating that she had completely overcome her depression. This impression was confirmed by her parents and the referring physician. A follow-up after a year revealed that she had been exposed to a series of disappointments which often led to temporary bouts of depression (none, however, as severe as that which had led her to therapy)." (pp. 86–87)

do to real-life situations (Garfield et al., 1967; Wolpe, 1969).

Wolpe (1969) has noted three types of problems that may contraindicate desensitization training in certain cases: (1) difficulties in relaxation, (2) misleading or irrelevant hierarchies, and (3) inadequacies of imagery. Desensitization procedures have, however, been used successfully in dealing with a wide range of maladaptive behaviors, including examination anxieties, phobias, generalized fears, neurotic anxieties, impotence, and frigidity.

Wilkins (1971) has raised some interesting questions regarding the traditional assumptions underlying systematic desensitization as a form of therapy, suggesting that its effectiveness is due not so much to "the traditionally stated mutual antagonism between muscle relaxation and anxiety" as to social and cognitive variables, including the patient-therapist relationship, expectancy of therapeutic gain, information feedback, and learning through instructed imagination. He concludes that:

"Strong trends in the research evidence indicate that neither relaxation training nor hierarchy construction are necessary for successful therapy outcome. It appears that the only necessary element of the desensitization procedure is the cognitive element of instructed imagination of fear-relevant scenes." (p. 316)

Implosive therapy. Another method of behavior therapy used increasingly in recent years is implosive therapy, which was mentioned earlier in our discussion of neuroses. Like systematic desensitization, this approach regards neurotic behavior as involving the conditioned avoidance of anxiety-arousing stimuli, and the client is asked to imagine and relive aversive scenes associated with his anxiety.

In this case, rather than trying to banish anxiety from the treatment sessions, the therapist deliberately attempts to elicit a massive flood, or "implosion," of anxiety (Hogan & Kirschner, 1967; Hussain, 1971; Stampfl & Levis, 1967). With repeated exposure in a "safe" setting where no harm is forthcoming, the stimulus loses its power to elicit anxiety and the neurotic avoidance behavior is extinguished.

Stampfl and Levis (1967), who are among the foremost developers of this approach, devote the first two or three therapy sessions to ascertaining the nature of the anxiety-arousing stimuli. The ensuing procedure is described as follows:

"Once the implosive procedure is begun, every effort is made to encourage the patient to 'lose himself' in the part that he is playing and 'live' the scenes with genuine emotion. . . . The scenes which contain the hypothesized cues are described at first by the therapist. The more involved and dramatic the therapist becomes in describing the scenes, the more realistic the presentation, and the easier it is for the patient to participate. At each stage of the process an attempt is made by the therapist to attain a maximal level of anxiety evocation from the patient. When a high level anxiety is achieved, the patient is held on this level until some sign of spontaneous reduction in the anxiety-inducing value of the cues appears (extinction). The process is repeated, and again, at the first sign of spontaneous reduction of fear, new variations are introduced to elicit an intense anxiety response. This procedure is continued until a significant diminution in anxiety has resulted. . . . Between sessions the patient is instructed to reenact in his imagination the scenes which were presented during the treatment session." (p. 500)

As in the case of systematic desensitization, hypnosis or drugs may be used to enhance suggestibility, and here too *in vivo* procedures may be used with individuals who do not imagine scenes realistically. For example, a client with a phobia of airplanes may be instructed to take a short flight on a commercial airliner. This is another means of exposing the client to the anxiety-eliciting stimulus and demonstrating to him that the consequences he had feared do not occur.

Reports on the effectiveness of implosive therapy have generally been quite favorable. In fact, a number of therapists consider implosive therapy superior to systematic desensitization in the treatment of neurotic phobias, since it results in more rapid improvement (Barrett, 1969; Boulougouris, Marks & Marset, 1971; Hogan & Kirschner, 1967, 1968; Hussain, 1971). However, some investigators have reported unfavorable as well as favorable results with implosive therapy (Mealiea, 1967; Wolpe, 1969). In general, it would appear that most patients respond favorably to implosive therapy, that some others do not respond, and that a few suffer an exacerbation of their phobias. The latter finding suggests a need for caution in the use of this method, particularly since it involves procedures that may be highly traumatic.

Assertive training. Assertive training has been used as a method of desensitization as well as a means of developing more effective coping techniques. It appears particularly useful in helping individuals who have difficulties in interpersonal situations because of conditioned anxiety responses which prevent them from "speaking up" for what they consider to be appropriate and right. Such inhibition may lead to continual inner turmoil, particularly if the individual feels strongly about the situation. Assertive training may also be indicated in cases where an individual consistently allows other people to take advantage of him or maneuver him into situations which he finds uncomfortable.

The expression of assertive behavior—first by role-playing in the therapy setting and then by practice in real-life situations—is guided by the therapist. Often attention is focused on developing more effective interpersonal skills; in some instances, the client is taught to use techniques of "gamesmanship" or "lifemanship" in situations where he seems at a disadvantage. For example, he may learn to ask the other person such questions as "Is anything wrong? You don't seem to be your usual self today." Such questions put the focus on the other person without indicating an aggressive or hostile intent on the part of the speaker. Of course, the assertive response need not be aggressive; situations calling for affectionate or other positive responses may also elicit intense or inappropriate anxiety. In any event, each act of assertion inhibits the anxiety associated with given interpersonal situations, and therefore weakens the maladaptive anxiety response patterns. At the same time, it tends to foster more adaptive interpersonal behaviors.

Although assertive training is a highly useful therapeutic procedure in certain types of situations, it does have limitations. For example, Wolpe (1969) has pointed out that it is largely irrelevant for phobias involving nonpersonal stimuli. It may also be of little use in some types of interpersonal situations; for instance, if an individual is rejected by some individual who is important to him, assertive behavior may tend to aggravate rather than resolve the problem. However, in interpersonal situations where maladaptive anxiety can be traced to lack of self-assertiveness, this type of therapy appears particularly effective.

Aversion therapy. This approach involves the modification of undesirable behavior by the old-fashioned method of punishment. Punishment may involve either the removal of positive reinforcers or the use of aversive stimuli, but the basic idea is to reduce the "temptation value" of stimuli that elicit undesirable behavior. The most commonly used aversive stimulus is electric shock, although drugs may also be used. As we shall see, however, punishment is rarely employed as the sole method of treatment.

Apparently the first formal use of aversion therapy was made by Kantorovich (1930), who administered electric shocks to alcoholics in association with the sight, smell, and taste of alcohol. Since that time aversion therapy has been used in the treatment of a wide range of maladaptive behaviors, including smoking, drinking, overeating, drug dependence, gambling, and various sexual deviations, including fetishism and homosexuality. Since we have described the use of aversion therapy in the course of our discussion of abnormal behavior patterns, we shall restrict ourselves here to a review of a few brief examples and principles.

A leading exponent of punishment to inhibit maladaptive behavior is Lovaas, who has worked mostly with severely disturbed autistic children. He has found punishment by electric shock to be effective even in extreme cases of self-destructive behavior among such children. In one case a 7-year-old autistic boy, diagnosed as severely retarded, had to be kept in restraints 24 hours a day because he would continually beat his head with his fists or bang it against the walls of his crib, inflicting serious injuries. Though it is difficult to understand why punishment should reduce the frequency of self-destructive behavior, electric shock following such behavior was nevertheless quite effective, bringing about complete inhibition of this maladaptive behavior pattern in a relatively short time (Bucher & Lovaas, 1967). In earlier chapters we have noted that irrational and maladaptive thoughts—obsessions, delusions, and hallucinations—may also be minimized or extinguished by means of electric shock or other aversive control measures.

Aversion therapy for alcoholism by means of nausea-producing drugs was introduced by Voegtlin (1940). Since then, a large number of studies have been carried out, using a wide range of drugs. In one such approach, the combination of alcohol and an emetic is administered daily for a period of 7 to 10 days. If the treatment is effective, alcohol alone will then produce severe nausea. A related aversive procedure involves putting alcoholics on daily doses of disulpherim (Antabuse), a drug which is not aversive by itself, but causes severe nausea if alcohol is drunk later. Knowledge of this effect tends to inhibit further drinking behavior, although it is possible for the alcoholic to stop taking the drug for several days and then resume drinking.

Continued abstinence over a period of years is obtained in up to 50 percent of alcoholics treated by drug-related aversive therapy. This rate is encouraging, considering the relatively low rate of remission from alcoholism when aversive procedures are not utilized (Bandura, 1969). It should be emphasized, however, that a recovered alcoholic remains an alcoholic in the sense that he cannot take a drink without activating a chain of excessive drinking behavior.

A number of investigators have raised the issue of the "intensity dilemma" in aversion therapy. They point out that while aversive procedures depend heavily on the intensity of the noxious stimuli, limitations must be placed on the intensity of such stimuli, for both practical and ethical reasons. Thus renewed interest has centered on the earlier suggestion of Lazarus (1968a) that it is not the *intensity* of the aversive stimulus *per se*, but the *incompatibility* of the response elicited by the aversive stimulus and the maladaptive behavior that should be emphasized.

The use of punishment may be strongly resented or willingly accepted, depending upon the way the subject perceives the intent of the punishing agent; that is, whether the agent is applying sanctions mainly for his own convenience or to help modify behavior that the subject himself recognizes as maladaptive and harmful. Thus it is desirable to be sure that alternative forms of adaptive behavior are clearly delineated and to administer the punishment in such a way that the individual does not feel personally rejected but is helped to see that the aversive consequences are associated only with particular maladaptive behaviors—that punishment is not being used in an arbitrary and vindictive fashion.

Aversion therapy is primarily a way of stopping maladaptive responses for a period of time during which there is an opportunity for changing a life style by encouraging more adaptive alternative patterns which will prove reinforcing in themselves. This point is particularly important, since otherwise the client may simply refrain from maladaptive responses in "unsafe" therapy situations, where such behavior leads to immediate aversive results, but retain them in "safe" real-life situations, where there is no fear of immediate discomfort.

The systematic use of positive reinforcement. Systematic programs for the application of behavior therapy are achieving notable success, particularly in institutional settings. Response shaping, modeling, and token economies are among the most widely used of such techniques.

1. *Response shaping.* Positive reinforcement is often used in response shaping; that is, in establishing a response that is not initially in the individual's behavior repertoire. This technique has been used extensively in working with the behavior problems of children. The following case reported by Wolf, Risley, and Mees (1964) is illustrative:

A 3-year-old autistic boy lacked normal verbal and social behavior. He did not eat properly, engaged in self-destructive behavior such as banging his head and scratching his face, and manifested ungovernable tantrums. He had recently had a cataract operation, and required glasses for the development of normal vision. He refused to wear his glasses, however, and broke pair after pair.

The technique of shaping was decided upon to counteract the problem of glasses. Initially, the boy was trained to expect a bit of candy or fruit at the sound of a toy noisemaker. Then training was begun with empty eyeglass frames. First the boy was reinforced with the candy or fruit for picking them up, then for holding them, then for carrying them around, then for bringing the frames closer to his eyes, and then for putting the empty frames on his head at any angle. Through successive approximation, he finally learned to wear his glasses up to twelve hours a day.

2. *Modeling.* Response shaping can be tedious and time-consuming, especially when complex responses are to be learned. Such responses can be acquired much more readily if the subject observes a model and is then reinforced for imitating the model's behavior. As we have noted, modeling and imitation are used in various forms of behavior therapy. For example, in Chapter 8 we noted a study by Bandura (1969) involving treatment for snake phobia via the modeling of progressively more fear-eliciting interactions with a large king snake. Here it was found that live modeling combined with instruction and guided participation was the most effective desensitization treatment, resulting in the elimination of snake phobias in over 90 percent of the cases.

Another interesting example of the modeling-imitation-reinforcement paradigm is the program based on the "therapeutic pyramid concept," in which moderately retarded adolescents and young adults are trained, via behavior-therapy techniques, to help professional therapists teach basic verbal and nonverbal skills to severely retarded children (Whalen & Henker, 1971). As described in Chapter 16, the goal of this program is to facilitate improvement in both the assistants and the younger retardates—to bring about a "double change"—and early results have been promising.

3. *Token economies.* Approval and other intangible reinforcers often prove ineffective in behavior therapy programs, especially those dealing with severely maladaptive behavior. In such instances, appropriate behaviors may be rewarded with tangible reinforcers in the form of tokens which can later be exchanged for desired objects or privileges. In our discussion of schizophrenia and other maladaptive patterns, we have already noted the use of token economies in establishing desired behavior. In working with schizophrenics, for example, Ayllon and Azrin (1968) found that using the commissary, listening to records, and going to movies were considered

A token-economy program has been used with good results on the exit wards at New Castle State Hospital in Indiana. Patients about to be discharged are assigned to various types of jobs within the hospital, in laboratory workshops, or perhaps in domestic situations off the hospital grounds. They receive payment in points which can be exchanged at the hospital's "Point Store" for personal articles, coffee, or cigarettes or used to "rent" private living quarters. The young men pictured on the left are assembling cardboard dividers in the hospital's Industrial Laboratory Workshop—work performed on a contract basis for local industries and for which they are paid in cash as well as in points. Shown on the right is one of the private rooms on the female exit ward. Such quarters are in great demand despite the fact that they are comparatively "expensive."

USING BEHAVIORAL CONTRACTING WITH DISTURBED CHILDREN AND ADOLESCENTS

Behavioral contracting is one reinforcement technique that has recently been used in attempts to modify the behavior of delinquent youngsters. By definition, a behavioral contract is a written agreement governing the exchange of positive reinforcements among two or more persons (Krumboltz & Thoresen, 1969, p. 87). Such contracts detail the responsibilities of each party and the privileges to be gained by fulfillment of these responsibilities. In some instances the parties to the contract are the client and the therapist or counselor; in other cases the counselor negotiates a contract between other parties, such as an adolescent and his parents or summer campers and camp administrators.

In working with disruptive children in the classroom, for example, a contract among child, parents, teacher, and principal may specify that the child has the privilege of remaining in the classroom only so long as he behaves in accordance with the responsibilities set forth by the contract. The teacher agrees to send the child home immediately whenever he breaks the contract, and the parents consent to this action. A week or two of such systematic exclusion under the provisions of a behavioral contract is usually enough to establish the desired patterns of classroom behavior, at least in elementary-school children (Krumboltz & Thoresen, 1969, p. 88).

An example of behavioral contracting within a family concerns a 16-year-old girl, Candy, who had been admitted to a psychiatric hospital following alleged exhibitionism, drug abuse, truancy from home, and promiscuity (Stuart, 1971). Candy's parents also complained that she was chronically antagonistic in her verbal exchanges with them and was near failing in her schoolwork. Because of the cost of private psychiatric care, they requested that she be made a ward of the juvenile court. They were advised that their allegations would probably not stand up in court and agreed to let her remain at home under the terms of a behavioral contract.

An initial contract, based on unrealistic parental demands, failed when Candy consistently violated its terms by sneaking out at night to visit local communes. A court order was obtained, proscribing Candy from entering the communes, and it was made clear to her that any violation would result in prosecution of the commune members for contributing to the delinquency of a minor. A new, more permissive contract between Candy and her parents was then negotiated, and a monitoring form containing a checklist of chores, curfew conditions, and bonus time for each day of the month was provided. A few of the provisions of the new contract are reprinted here.

PRIVILEGES	RESPONSIBILITIES
"In exchange for the privilege of going out at 7:00 p.m. on one weekend evening without having to account for her whereabouts	Candy must maintain a weekly average of "B" in the academic ratings of all of her classes and must return home by 11:30 p.m.
"In exchange for the privilege of going out a second weekend night	Candy must tell her parents *by 6:00 p.m.* of her destination and her companion, and must return home by 11:30 p.m.
"In exchange for the privilege of having Candy complete household chores and maintain her curfew	Mr. and Mrs. Bremer agree to pay Candy $1.50 on the morning following days on which the money is earned." (Stuart, 1971, p. 9)

Further provisions set for certain bonuses and sanctions:

"If Candy is 31–60 minutes late	she loses the privilege of going out the following day and does forfeit her money for the day.
"Candy may go out on Sunday evenings from 7:00 to 9:30 p.m. and either Monday or Thursday evening	if she abides by all the terms of this contract from Sunday through Saturday with a total tardiness not exceeding 30 minutes which must have been made up. . . ." (p. 9)

Behavioral contracting proved to be a constructive means of structuring the interaction between Candy and her parents, and Candy's behavior improved steadily. By removing the issues of privileges and responsibilities from the realm of contention, many intrafamilial arguments were avoided, and those that did occur tended to be tempered by the specified options. Through the contract, privileges such as money and free time were established as effective environmental contingencies in fostering desired behavior (p. 11).

highly desirable activities by most patients. Consequently, these activities were chosen as reinforcers for socially appropriate behavior. To participate in any of them, the patient had to earn a number of tokens by appropriate ward behavior. As we have seen, token economies have been used to establish adaptive behaviors ranging from elementary responses such as eating and making one's bed to the daily performance of responsible hospital jobs. In the latter instance, the token economy resembles the outside world where the individual is paid for his work in tokens (money) which he can then exchange for desired objects and activities.

The use of tokens as reinforcers for appropriate behavior has a number of distinct advantages: (a) the number of tokens earned by the patient can be equated with the amount of desired behavior which he manifests; (b) tokens are not readily subject to satiation and hence tend to maintain their incentive value; (c) tokens can reduce the delay which often occurs between appropriate performance and reinforcement; (d) the number of tokens earned and the way in which they are "spent" are largely up to the patient, and (e) tokens tend to bridge the gap between the institutional environment and the demands and rewards that are encountered in the outside world.

The ultimate goal in token economies, as in other programs of extrinsic reinforcement, is not only to achieve desired responses but to bring such responses to a level where their adaptive consequences will be reinforcing in their own right—thus enabling natural rather than artificial reward contingencies to maintain the desired behavior. For example, extrinsic reinforcers may be used initially to help children overcome reading difficulties, but once the child becomes proficient in reading skills, these skills will presumably provide their own intrinsic reinforcement.

Evaluation of behavior therapy. As compared with psychoanalytic and other interview psychotherapies, behavior therapy appears to have three distinct advantages. First is the precision of the treatment approach. The target behaviors to be modified are specified, the methods to be used are clearly delineated, and the results can be readily evaluated. Second is the economy of time, cost, and personnel. Behavior therapy usually gets results in a short period of time, leading to faster relief of personal distress for the individual, as well as financial savings. In addition, more people can be treated by a given therapist. Third is the dependence on explicit principles of learning. Since the personality, interpretive ability, and interpersonal skills of the therapist play a relatively minor role, the training of therapists is easier and shorter. This also makes it possible for behavior therapy methods to be mastered and used by paraprofessionals.

The effectiveness of behavior therapy must be evaluated in terms of the type of behavior being treated as well as the specific methods used. Like other forms of psychotherapy, behavior therapy has proven relatively unsuccessful in the treatment of such patterns as childhood autism, schizophrenia, and severe depression—although considerable improvement is often shown in such cases. Similarly, different kinds of behavior therapy vary in their effectiveness for particular problems: desensitization seems most useful in treating conditioned avoidance re-

sponses, aversive techniques in establishing impulse control, and modeling combined with positive reinforcement in the acquisition of complex responses. But although behavior therapy is not a "cure-all," it has proven effective in the treatment of a wide range of maladaptive behaviors, typical reports indicating a success rate of well over 50 percent and sometimes as high as 90 percent, depending largely on the type of maladaptive pattern being treated.

HUMANISTIC-EXISTENTIAL THERAPIES

"For this is the journey that men make: to find themselves. If they fail in this, it doesn't matter much what else they find."

James Michener (1949, p. 488)

The humanistic and existential viewpoints and therapies have emerged as a "third force" in psychology during the last two decades. To a large extent, they have developed in reaction to the psychoanalytic and behavioristic viewpoints, which many feel do not accurately take into account either the existential problems or the full potentialities of contemporary man. In a society dominated by computerized technology and mass bureaucracy, proponents of the humanistic-existential therapies see psychopathology as stemming in many cases from problems of alienation, depersonalization, loneliness, and the lack of a meaningful and fulfilling existence, which are not met either by delving into forgotten memories or by correcting specific responses.

The humanistic-existential therapies follow some variant of the general philosophies spelled out in Chapter 3. They are based on the assumption that man has the freedom to control his own behavior—that he can reflect upon his problems, make choices, and take positive action. Whereas the behavior therapist sees himself as a "behavioral engineer," responsible for changing specific behaviors by appropriate modifications in the environment, humanistic-existential therapists feel that the individual himself must take most of the responsibility in the course of therapy, with the therapist serving as counselor, guide, and facilitator. The basic theme is well expressed in the above quotation from James Michener's early novel, *The Fires of Spring*.

Client-centered therapy. The client-centered therapy of Carl Rogers (1951; 1961; 1964) has been by far the most widely used humanistic approach to therapy. Viewing man as essentially good and rational, this approach recognizes that the individual may be hampered in achieving his inherent potentialities for growth by evading experiences which threaten his self-concept. This process of self-defense ultimately leads to an incongruence between the individual's conscious experience and his actual "gut" reactions and hence results in lowered integration, impaired personal relationships, and maladjustment.

The primary objective of Rogerian therapy is to resolve this incongruence—to help the client become able and willing to be *himself*. To this end, a psychological climate is established in which the client can feel unconditionally accepted, understood, and valued as a person. This frees him to explore his real feelings and thoughts and to accept them as part of himself. As his self-concept becomes more congruent with his experiencing, he becomes more self-accepting, more open to experience, and a better integrated person.

The therapist's task is not to direct the course of therapy by asking questions or giving answers. Rather, he restates in his own words what the client has been saying and helps clarify the client's true feelings about it. The therapist does not offer interpretations, nor does he attempt to lead the client beyond the boundaries of his or her current awareness. The following excerpt from a counselor's second interview with a young woman will serve to illustrate these techniques of reflection and clarification:

Alice: "I was thinking about this business of standards. I somehow developed a sort of a knack, I guess, of —well—habit—of trying to make people feel at ease around me, or to make things go along smoothly. . . .
Counselor: In other words, what you did was always in the direction of trying to keep things smooth and to make other people feel better and to smooth the situation.
Alice: Yes. I think that's what it was. Now the reason why I did it probably was—I mean, not that I was a good little Samaritan going around making other people happy, but that was probably the role that fell easiest for me to play. I'd been doing it around home so much. I just didn't stand up for my own

convictions, until I don't know whether I have any convictions to stand up for.
Counselor: You feel that for a long time you've been playing the role of kind of smoothing out the frictions or differences or what not . . . .
Alice: M-hm.
Counselor: Rather than having any opinion or reaction of your own in the situation. Is that it?
Alice: That's it. Or that I haven't been really honestly being myself, or actually knowing what my real self is, and that I've been just playing a sort of false role. Whatever role no one else was playing, and that needed to be played at the time, I'd try to fill it in."

(Rogers, 1951, pp. 152–153)

The idea that "the doctor knows best" is notably missing from this form of therapy; the therapist does not offer advice, resort to moral exhortation, or suggest "right" ways of behaving. Instead, he restricts himself to reflecting and clarifying the patient's feelings and attitudes in such a way as to promote self-understanding, positive action, and personal growth.

Existential therapy. Existential therapy can best be understood in terms of certain fundamental concepts on which it rests—concepts stemming from the existential model of man which we reviewed in Chapter 3.

First of all, this approach to therapy emphasizes the importance of existence itself, of the human situation as experienced by the individual. Second, the existentialists are deeply concerned about the predicament of modern man, the breakdown of traditional faith, the alienation and depersonalization of man in contemporary culture, and the lack of meaning in many people's lives. Third, existential therapists see man as having a high degree of freedom and thus as capable of doing something about his predicament. Unlike other living creatures, he has the ability to be aware of, reflect upon, and question his existence. And fourth, they consider that man's freedom confronts him with the responsibility for *being*—for deciding what kind of person he shall be, for defining and actualizing himself and establishing his own values.

Existential therapists do not follow any rigidly prescribed procedures, but emphasize the uniqueness of the individual and his "way-of-being-in-the-world." They stress the importance of *confrontation*—challenging the individual directly with questions concerning the meaning and

purpose of his existence—and the encounter—
the complex relationship which is established
between two interacting human beings in the
therapeutic situation. In contrast to the revival
of former interpersonal relationships, as in the
concept of transference, existential therapy calls
for the therapist to share himself—his feelings,
his values, and his existence—and not to let the
client respond to him as anything other than he
really is (May, 1969). For example, the existential therapist might respond to the statement,
"I hate you just like I hated my father," by saying
"I am not your father, I am me, and you have to
deal with me as Dr. S., not as your father." The
focus is on the here and now—on what the individual is choosing to do, and therefore be, at
this moment in time. This sense of immediacy,
of the urgency of experience, is the touchstone
of existential therapy and sets the stage for clarifying and choosing alternative ways of being.

The existential approach is illustrated by the
treatment of Hilda, a 29-year-old woman whose
case was diagnosed as "chronic undifferentiated
schizophrenia." This was the third time she had
been hospitalized for mental illness.

"Prior to this current hospitalization she had been
unemployed; had 'floated around and almost starved.'
Her relationships with females were negative and hostile; with men, always rather 'shady, mistress types
of things.' She expressed feelings of failure, inadequacy, anger and dread. She was loud, boisterous,
brutally frank and blistering to anyone who 'crossed'
her. . . .

"The questions that interested me most were: What
was her world? What was she to herself? I decided to
attempt to meet her in her world, hoping to achieve
some understanding of her—she had had the gamut of
traditional types of treatment. I knew that I would
have to encounter her where she was before she would
be able to accept me as a helping person, who was—
in essence—criticizing her way of being. My 'treatment goal' was, therefore, to encounter her in her
own world, which seemed to be constructed upon a
series of negative reflections which made unauthentic
being in the world the only existence possible for her.
I further sought to explore and understand her system,
so that I might attempt to lead her, or point her, toward
the possibility of orienting herself to the hopeful
timelessness of a true future, instead of to the futile
finiteness of her factual past. . . .

"We then began to explore, in earnest, 'the world
of Hilda,' as she termed it, and I followed where she

led. She proved to be unsure of where she had been
or where she was. As she grew more and more related
to me, I began to ask her: 'Where are you?' It was
not very long before she stopped saying 'in the nut-
tery . . .'; and started telling me things which made
me wonder if she were not trying to give me something; trying to tell me about Hilda. She began to
disorganize but could write:

" 'I'm glad I'm young in heart. You're at this time
my strongest contact with reality. You are it. This
"epistle" represents my "search for reality." Ha, ha.
Let's call it that: one fool's search . . .'

" '. . . It is as if I'm a girl alone in an attic. With
no air to breath, or only at certain times . . .'

"Finally, she evaluated my relationship to her:

" '. . . I wanted to give you my illness . . . but
you don't want it. You want me to just lose it and
work it out of my system, but I'm giving it to you
in written form instead . . . Keep watching the light
up there above San Francisco like a beacon! Guide
me, please guide me out of this . . . I'm mesmerized
today . . . Now I'm going ashore, the bridge will be
my vehicle . . .'

"Shortly after this 'prophecy,' she became so disorganized that I could not read her writings, nor follow her arguments. However, I tried, spending time
with her almost every day. She was put on an increased dosage of Thorazine but still managed to get
to group meetings and to our interviews. Even in her
disorganization, she clung to her relationship with
me, and managed to write:

" '. . . I must listen when you talk, I'm not always
there . . .'

"She had encountered me, perhaps long before I became fully aware of it. The idea of love—love without purpose—was emerging from deep within her. On
800 milligrams of tranquilizer, she gradually became
less disorganized. With a burst of unbelievable energy,
she began to plan for a 'future'; took hospital jobs, as
she said, 'fighting to stay awake.'

"When the patients on her ward elected her president of the government group, she got up and ran out
of the room, crying violently. I felt that I had lost;
she had recoiled from letting herself be liked. But she
returned to the room, accepting the role of president.
Later she was to write:

" 'Well here I am with time on my hands, you in
my heart and getting well on my mind . . . I'm very
selfish about getting well. I've been hurt and hindered
enough. I must not keep confusing hurt with masochism because that is what I do. It is too bad I ever
heard of all those terms. They have been very seductive . . . You can keep your glorious terms, I'll take
romance—a continual romance with life, good or bad
. . . Love, to me, is beauty with eyes open, ears open,
head open . . .'

"She was in the midst of turning from her future-less, pseudo-world of distortions to the world of possibility, in which one could find hope and meaning; in which one could establish an authentic relationship!

"One of the last things she wrote, before she gave up writing, was a poem which began:

Glorious night all is right

No time for flight too tired to fight . . .

and ended:

I'm awake I'm awake

A happy wake for a former fake . . .

"Hilda remained on leave for one year, received her discharge and managed extremely well for approximately another year. She experienced a slight relapse and was rehospitalized elsewhere for about three months. After this, she once again returned to the community." (Curry, 1962, pp. 129–135)

Gestalt therapy. The term *gestalt* means "whole," and gestalt therapy emphasizes the unity of mind and body—placing strong emphasis upon the integration of thought, feeling, and action. One of the newer and more innovative approaches, gestalt therapy was developed by Frederick Perls (1967; 1969).

Though gestalt therapy is commonly used in a group setting, the emphasis is on the individual. The therapist works intensively with one individual at a time, attempting to help him perceive those aspects of himself and of his world which are "blocked out." To increase awareness of self and of areas of avoidance, the individual may be asked to act out fantasies concerning his feelings and conflicts or to act out one part of the conflict in one chair and then switch chairs to take the part of the "adversary." This technique of working through unresolved conflicts is called "taking care of unfinished business." We all go through life, according to Perls, with unfinished or unresolved traumas and conflicts. We carry the excess baggage of these unfinished situations into new relationships and tend to act out our tensions in our relations with other people. If we are able to complete our past unfinished business, we shall then have much less psychological tension to cope with and be more realistically aware of ourselves and our world.

The individual is completely on his own in the therapeutic process, even though he may be expressing himself in front of the group. Denied the use of his usual techniques for avoiding self-awareness, he is brought to an "impasse," in which he must confront his feelings and conflicts. According to Perls, "In the safe emergency of the therapeutic situation, the neurotic discovers that the world does not fall to pieces if he gets angry, sexy, joyous, mournful." (1967, p. 311) Thus he finds that he can, after all, get beyond the impasse on his own.

In Perls' approach to therapy, a good deal of emphasis is placed on dreams:

". . . all the different parts of the dream are fragments of our personalities. Since our aim is to make every one of us a wholesome person, which means a unified person, without conflicts, what we have to do is put the different fragments of the dream together. We have to *re-own* these projected, fragmented parts of our personality, and *re-own* the hidden potential that appears in the dream." (1967, p. 67)

In the following dialog, taken from the transcript of a "dreamwork seminar," Perls (Fritz) helps a young woman (Linda) interpret the meaning of her dream:

Linda: I dreamed that I watch. . . a lake. . . drying up, and there is a small island in the middle of the lake, and a circle of. . . porpoises—they're like porpoises except that they can stand up, so they're like porpoises that are like people, and they're in a circle, sort of like a religious ceremony, and it's very sad—I feel very sad because they can breathe, they are sort of dancing around the circle, but the water, their element, is drying up. So it's like a dying—like watching a race of people, or a race of creatures, dying. And they are mostly females, but a few of them have a small male organ, so there are a few males there, but they won't live long enough to reproduce, and their element is drying up. And there is one that is sitting over here near me and I'm talking to this porpoise and he has prickles on his tummy, sort of like a porcupine, and they don't seem to be a part of him. And I think that there's one good point about the water drying up, I think—well, at least at the bottom, when all the water dries up, there will probably be some sort of treasure there, because at the bottom of the lake there should be things that have fallen in, like coins or something, but I look carefully and all that I can find is an old license plate. . . That's the dream.

Fritz: Will you please play the license plate.

L: I am an old license plate, thrown in the bottom of a lake. I have no use because I'm no value—although I'm not rusted—I'm outdated, so I can't be used as a license plate. . . and I'm just thrown on the rubbish heap. That's what I did with a license plate, I threw it on a rubbish heap.

F: Well, how do you feel about this?

L: (quietly) I don't like it. I don't like being a license plate—useless.

F: Could you talk about this. That was such a long dream until you come to find the license plate, I'm sure this must be of great importance.

L: (sighs) Useless. Outdated. . . The use of a license plate is to allow—give a car permission to go. . . and I can't give anyone permission to do anything because I'm outdated. . . In California, they just paste a little—you buy a sticker—and stick it on the car on the old license plate. (faint attempt at humor) So maybe someone could put me on their car and stick this sticker on me, I don't know. . .

F: Okeh, now play the lake.

L: I'm a lake. . . I'm drying up, and disappearing, soaking into the earth. . . (with a touch of surprise) *dying*. . . But when I soak into the earth, I become a part of the earth—so maybe I water the surrounding area, so. . . even in the lake, even in my bed, flowers can grow (sighs). . . New life can grow. . . from me (cries). . .

F: You get the existential message?

L: Yes. (sadly, but with conviction) I can paint—I can create—I can create beauty. I can no longer reproduce, I'm like the porpoise. . . but I. . . I'm. . . I. . . keep wanting to say I'm *food*. . . I. . . as water becomes. . . I water the earth, and give life—growing things, the water—they need both the earth and water, and the. . . and the air and the sun, but as the water from the lake, I can play a part in something, and producing—feeding.

F: You see the contrast: On the surface, you find something, some artifact—the license plate, the artificial you—but then when you go deeper, you find the apparent death of the lake is actually fertility. . .

L: And I don't need a license plate, or a permission, a license in order to. . .

F: (gently) Nature doesn't need a license plate to grow. You don't have to be useless, if you are organismically creative, which means if you are involved.

L: And I don't need permission to be creative. . . Thank you. (Perls, 1969, 81–82)

In gestalt therapy sessions, the focus is on the more obvious elements of the person's behavior. Such sessions are often called "gestalt awareness training," since the therapeutic results of the experience stem from the process of becoming more aware of one's total self and one's environment. Gestalt therapy has become a widely used form of therapy, perhaps because it blends many of the strong points of psychoanalysis (working

through intrapsychic conflicts), behaviorism (the focus on overt behavior), and the humanistic-existential orientation (the importance of self-awareness and personal growth).

Other humanistic-existential therapies. Two other forms of therapy which may be roughly classified as humanistic-existential therapies merit brief consideration.

1. *Rational therapy.* This approach stems from the work of Ellis (1958), who has pointed out that in our society we learn many beliefs during early life which tend to be continually reinforced through a sort of self-dialog. For example, an individual may continually tell himself that: "It is necessary to be loved and approved by everyone"; "One should be thoroughly adequate and competent in everything he does"; or "It is catastrophic when things are not as one would like them to be." Such "mistaken ideas" inevitably lead to ineffective and self-defeating behavior.

The task of psychotherapy thus becomes one of unmasking the client's self-defeating ideas and verbalizations, helping him understand their role in causing and maintaining his difficulties, and helping him change his faulty assumptions and verbalize more constructive ones to himself. Thus rational therapy places heavy emphasis upon cognitive change, for it is only in this way that "psychotherapists can help their clients live the most self-fulfilling, creative, and emotionally satisfying lives. . . ." (Ellis, 1958, p. 35)

2. *Reality therapy.* As formulated by Glasser (1965), reality therapy assumes that in early life the individual develops a basic sense of right and wrong which provides the basis for his later values. Difficulties arise when the individual's actual behavior is in conflict with this basic sense of right and wrong.

Therapy focuses on helping the individual clarify his basic values and evaluate his current behavior and future plans in relation to these values. Presumably there is little difficulty in helping the client formulate a clear set of values; these are often influenced by the values of the therapist, who in this form of therapy is considered to function as a moral agent and model. However, difficulties may arise in helping the individual learn to live responsibly; that is, in accordance with his values. The latter task is achieved largely by helping him perceive the aversive consequences of living irresponsibly and the satisfactions and sense of personal fulfillment that accrue from living in accordance with one's basic values.

Favorable results have been reported for both rational and reality therapy. Of particular interest is Glasser's (1967) report of successful results with reality therapy in dealing with delinquents.

Evaluation of the humanistic-existential therapies. The humanistic-existential therapies have been criticized for their lack of a highly systematized model of man, their lack of agreed-upon therapeutic procedures, and their vagueness about what is supposed to happen between client and therapist. It is these very features, however, which are seen by many proponents of this approach as contributing to its strength and vitality. There is no highly systematized model of man, because man cannot be reduced to an abstraction, and any attempt at doing so only results in diminishing his status. Similarly, because of the uniqueness of each person, it is impossible to suggest what techniques should be used with all, or even most, individuals.

In any event, many of the humanistic-existential concepts—the uniqueness of man, his untapped potentialities, his present predicament, his quest for meaning and fulfillment, his conflict between being and nonbeing, and his existential anxiety—have had a major impact on our contemporary views of man and of psychotherapy.

INTERPERSONAL THERAPY: MARITAL AND FAMILY THERAPY, TRANSACTIONAL ANALYSIS

In Chapter 3 we noted the emphasis of the interpersonal viewpoint on the role of faulty communications, interactions, and relationships in maladaptive behavior. This viewpoint has had an important impact on other approaches to therapy—particularly on the behavioristic and humanistic-existential therapies. For example, in behavior therapy we have seen the emphasis on modifying social reinforcements that may be maintaining maladaptive responses; and in humanistic-existential therapy we have seen the concern with such problems as lack of acceptance, relatedness, and love in the individual's life.

In many cases, however, disordered interpersonal relationships are at the very center of an individual's problems. Such cases require therapeutic techniques which focus on relationships rather than individuals. In this section we shall explore the growing fields of marital and family therapy and then examine in some detail the popular interpersonal technique of transactional analysis.

Marital therapy. The large numbers of people seeking assistance with problems centering around their marriage situation have made this a growing field of therapy. Typically the partners are seen together, and therapy focuses on clarifying and improving the interactions and relationships between them.

Attempts to achieve this goal include a wide range of concepts and procedures. Some therapists emphasize mutual need gratification, social role expectations, communication patterns, and similar interpersonal factors. Not surprisingly, it has been shown that happily married couples tend to differ from unhappily married couples in that they talk more to each other, keep channels of communication open, make more use of nonverbal techniques of communication, and show more sensitivity to each other's feelings and needs (Navran, 1967). Faulty role expectations often play havoc with marital adjustment. For example, Paul (1971) cited the case of a couple who came for marital therapy when the 39-year-old husband was about to divorce his wife to marry a much younger woman. During therapy he broke into sobs of grief as he recalled the death of his Aunt Anna, who had always accepted him as he was and created an atmosphere of peace and contentment. In reviewing this incident, the husband realized that his girl friend represented his lifelong search for another Aunt Anna. This led to a reconciliation with his wife, who was now more understanding of his needs, feelings, and role expectations.

One of the difficulties in marital therapy is the intense emotional involvement of the marital partners, which makes it difficult for them to perceive and accept the realities of their relationship. Often, wives can see clearly what is "wrong" with their husbands but not with themselves; while husbands usually have remarkable "insight" into their wives' flaws but not their own. To help correct this problem, videotape recordings have been used increasingly to recapture

MARITAL COUNSELING IN A WILDERNESS SETTING

A unique program for marital counseling has been developed by Dr. Hugh Allred of Brigham Young University. Dr. Allred found in his work with family relationships that many couples experiencing marital problems avoid the difficult and often painful task of working through their problems by becoming preoccupied with jobs, community responsibilities, and similar activities. Personal relationships often become routine and mechanical, and when their children are grown the couples often find they are strangers. He felt that this pattern could be counteracted by bringing couples together in circumstances where they would be forced to cooperate in overcoming problems, hopefully strengthening their marital relationships.

Following a brief course in wilderness survival, the five couples in the experimental program, accompanied by the therapist, set out on a 3-mile hike up a steep, narrow trail on a remote mountain in Utah. The hike began in a chilling rain; the next morning there was snow on the ground, and the remaining 8 days of the experiment were all rainy. Each couple was equipped only with a knife, a change of clothing, a sleeping bag, and a tin can to cook in and eat from. They built lean-tos for sleeping, gathered their own firewood, and ate whatever plants and forms of animal life they were able to collect. To survive on the mountaintop, the partners had to cooperate and to communicate.

While much of the communication and interaction was informal, two hours each day were devoted to group discussion of the quality of their marriages, utilizing concepts from two textbooks on marriage and family relationships. For another two hours, the couples took turns role playing their marital problems —often with husband and wife reversing their roles. Feedback was used to guide practice in more effective ways of relating to each other. Additional time was provided by the therapist for private marital counseling. The goal throughout was to help the couples understand their marital difficulties, learn more effective means of coping with their problems, and build more satisfying marriages in terms of happiness and growth for both partners.

Admittedly the sample was too small to draw any definitive conclusions concerning the efficacy of this procedure in marital counseling, and certainly it would not be appropriate for all couples experiencing marital problems. The reports of the participants were most positive, however. For example, one husband reported that for the first time he understood his wife's feelings and his own tendency to dominate her in the marital relationship. Another couple reported that they had never gotten to the roots of their marital problems until they underwent the wilderness experience; the nine days of roughing it had given them a feeling of mutual accomplishment and had brought them closer together emotionally than they had ever been before. A benefit commented on by several couples was the realization that their problems were not unique, that others shared many of the same problems. On the last night the couples sat around the campfire exchanging light-hearted conversation and planning a "class reunion" the next year (Allred, 1971a, 1971b).

crucial moments of intense interaction between the marital partners. Watching these tapes then fosters fuller awareness of the nature of their interactions. Thus the husband may realize for the first time that he tries to dominate rather than listen to his wife and consider her needs and expectations; or a wife may realize that she is continually nagging and undermining her husband's feelings of worth and esteem. Alger and Hogan (1969) describe an instance of such revelation:

"The husband saw himself for the first time as cringing and servile before his wife. . . . As he watched the screen his reaction was so intense that sweat stood out on his forehead. He said that he couldn't stand to watch it again. He did, however, watch several more times, and then determined to stand up to his wife regardless of the consequences. Since then he has been able to persist in this determination, with the result that a more respectful relationship between them continues to develop." (p. 91)

Other relatively new and innovative approaches to marital therapy merit brief mention. Olson (1970) has reported success in training marital partners to use Rogerian nondirective techniques in helping their spouses clarify their feelings and interactions. Behavior therapy has been used to bring about desired changes in the marital relationship by teaching the spouses to reinforce desired behavior and to withdraw reinforcement for undesirable behavior. Such therapy may involve one or both spouses. Goldstein and Francis (1969) worked with five graduate student wives, attempting in each case to help the wife alter a specified undesirable behavior of her husband which she had been unsuccessful in altering previously. Initially the wives were trained to record the undesirable behavior each time it occurred in order to establish a base rate. Then they were taught techniques for extinguishing the undesirable behavior and establishing a desired alternative response. This procedure was successful in modifying the husbands' undesirable behavior without actually involving them in the therapy situation.

Family therapy. Therapy for the family group overlaps with marital therapy but has somewhat different roots. While marital therapy developed in response to the large number of clients who came for assistance with marital problems, family therapy had its roots in the finding that many people who showed marked improvement in therapy—often in institutional settings—had a relapse upon their return home. It soon became apparent that many of these people came from disturbed family settings which required modification if they were to maintain their gains.

A pioneer in the field of family therapy has described the problem as follows:

"Psychopathology in the individual is a product of the way he deals with his intimate relations, the way they deal with him, and the way other family members involve him in their relations with each other. Further, the appearance of symptomatic behavior in an individual is necessary for the continued function of a particular family system. Therefore changes in the individual can occur only if the family system changes, and resistance to change in the individual centers in the influence of the family as a group." (Haley, 1962, p. 70)

This viewpoint led to an important concept in the field of psychotherapy; namely, that the problem of the "identified patient" is often only a symptom of a larger family problem. A careful study of the family of a disturbed child may reveal that the child is merely reflecting the pathology of the family unit. If the child is seen alone in therapy, he may be able to work out some of his problems; but when he goes back home, he will have to face the same pathological circumstances which led to his problems in the first place.

In family therapy, as in marital therapy, family members are usually seen together. Again, however, there are many variations in therapy arrangements as well as in specific procedures. In fact, after an extensive review of the field, the Group for the Advancement of Psychiatry (1970) concluded that "Family therapy today is not a treatment method in the usual sense; there is no generally agreed-upon set of procedures followed by practitioners who consider themselves family

There are a number of specialized therapeutic techniques for use with children, which may be used either in conjunction with family therapy or in individual treatment programs. Among these is *play therapy,* in which children are encouraged to express themselves spontaneously. Provided with a "family" of dolls, the four-year-old on the left is able to structure the family situation in ways that reflect his feelings about his own parents and siblings and his place in the family. The boy on the right is free in the therapeutic setting to express his hostility toward his brother without fear of reprisal. Such techniques provide the child with an outlet for pent-up feelings as well as an opportunity to experiment with new ways of handling his problems.

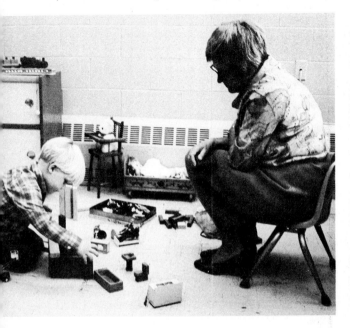

therapists." (p. 572) However, most family therapists share the view that the family is a causal agent in individual psychopathology and hence should be directly involved in therapy.

Perhaps the most widely used approach to family therapy is the "conjoint family therapy" of Satir (1967). Her emphasis is on improving faulty communications, interactions, and relationships among family members and fostering a family system which better meets the needs of family members. The following example shows Satir's emphasis in family therapy upon the problem of faulty communication.

Husband: She never comes up to me and kisses me. I am always the one to make the overtures.

Therapist: Is this the way you see yourself behaving with your husband?

Wife: Yes, I would say he is the demonstrative one. I didn't know he wanted me to make the overtures.

Th: Have you told your wife that you would like this from her—more open demonstration of affection?

H: Well, no, you'd think she'd know.

W: No, how would I know? You always said you didn't like aggressive women.

H: I don't, I don't like *dominating* women.

W: Well, I thought you meant women who make the overtures. How am I to know what you want?

Th: You'd have a better idea if he had been able to *tell* you. (Satir, 1967, pp. 72–73)

At the other extreme of the continuum with regard to methods, but still concerned with faulty relationships, are the behavioristically oriented therapists. For example, Huff (1969) has suggested that the task of the therapist involves helping the family switch from punishment to reward, reducing the aversive value of the family for the identified patient as well as that of the patient for other family members. "The therapist does this by actively manipulating the *relationship* between members so that the relationship changes to a more positively reinforcing and reciprocal one." (p. 26)

As in the case of marital therapy, videotape recordings have been increasingly used in family therapy to enhance awareness of interactive patterns. Another recent innovation in family therapy is the use of workshops in which several families remain together for a certain period of time, usually over a weekend. Stoller

(1967) described a workshop experience as follows:

"Families come to the workshop with ready-made relationships, but they have not learned to talk about them. As initial shyness and family chauvinism wear off, the interplay begins. . . .

"There are rules: Regardless of which family they belong to, group members are expected to respond to each other directly, and to express their perceptions as clearly as possible. As families get to know one another, they become aware of the implicit contractual arrangements which determine their behavior. The workshop . . . is a microcosm of the difficulties that families encounter at home; experimenting with new and more fruitful ways of dealing with these problems is a major goal of the session." (p. 33)

It has become common in family therapy to have cotherapists, usually one male and one female.

Transactional analysis. Eric Berne (1964) developed an innovative technique of interpersonal therapy based on the notion that our personalities are composed of three "ego states"— Child, Adult, and Parent—which correspond very roughly to Freud's id, ego, and superego. Our Parent is that part of our behavior which we have incorporated from our own parents or from other parental models whom we have inadvertently learned to emulate. Statements such as "You shouldn't eat so much" or "Put on a sweater if you're going outside in the cold" are examples of our Parent talking. Such statements may be appropriate when spoken to a child, but if they are used with a spouse, it may well be that the speaker is playing too active a Parent role. Our Child is that part of us which is a carry-over from our childhood feelings. "I'll eat as much as I want, and don't always yell at me!" is an example of the Child responding to the first Parent above. A Child response to the second command might be simply to break down and cry—behavior possibly appropriate for a real child, but not for a mature adult. Finally, the Adult in each of us is that part of us which processes information rationally and appropriately for the present unique set of circumstances. An Adult response to the Parent's sweater command might be, "I really don't think it is cold enough for a sweater."

In transactional analysis, the therapist analyzes the interactions among group members (often married couples) and helps the participants understand the ego states in which they are communicating with each other. As long as each participant reacts to the other in the way that he is being addressed, e.g., as a Child to a Parent, the transactions may continue indefinitely. Many couples find out that they have been having "complementary" transactions for years, but that they have always been communicating as mother to son or father to daughter. However, when one party decides to discontinue playing Child to the spouse's Parent, the game ceases, and conflicts develop that must be worked out. Since analysis is done in a group setting, other members are encouraged to participate; the method of their participation often invites analysis of how they, in turn, communicate with other people.

Berne characterized many of our social interactions as "games"—not because they are played "for fun," but because they are played according to a set of unspoken rules. In *Games People Play* (1964), he described a number of these games, many of which are deadly serious and even destructive in their effects.

1. *Why Don't You—Yes But (YDYB)*. This is considered the prototype game in transactional analysis and involves what is commonly referred to as "gamesmanship" or "one-up-manship." The game is perpetrated by A who adopts a docile stance toward B (the victim) and presents some personal problem in such a way that B is induced to offer advice—e.g., to adopt a counterstance of Therapist. Once the advice has been offered, A responds by saying "Yes, but . . . ," and proceeds to add additional information about his problem that renders B's advice erroneous or irrelevant. At this point B may come back with an alternative solution, still believing that A is sincere in offering him the Therapist role. A again follows the same procedure and "shoots" B down again. This game may go on for several rounds until B finally realizes he has been defeated and is forced to assume a self-effacing stance, perhaps acknowledging that A "sure has a tough problem." In this game, A has perpetrated a transactional role reversal in which he achieves competitive satisfaction at B's expense. A has, so to speak, "put B down."

2. *Wooden Leg*. This game involves the adoption of a "sick" role—much like that in conversion hysteria. In essence, the individual asks "What do you expect from a person with a 'wooden leg'?" e.g., a personality deficiency, physical deformity, or slum background.

As we have seen, our society relaxes its demands on persons who are "sick"—who are temporarily or permanently incapable of meeting usual social standards of performance by virtue of some serious misfortune or handicap. It is a "helpless" game played by the Child who wants sympathy but does not really want to get better. The payoff is, "Oh yes, I understand; don't worry, we'll take care of you and give you whatever comfort you need." Of course, this kind of game is maladaptive in that the individual—whether or not he has an actual handicap—avoids acquiring the competencies and sense of responsibility needed for independence and self-direction.

3. *Now I've Got You, You Son of a Bitch (NIGYSOB)*. This game involves an aggressive payoff in which the perpetrator adopts a self-effacing stance that invites competitive exploitation from his victim. Since there is presumably "a little larceny in all of us," the victim unwisely accepts the proffered role and initiates a program of exploitation. The perpetrator plays along for a while, but at a certain point suddenly reverses his stance and reveals the exploitation; with an appropriate show of anger and indignation, he assumes his justly deserved aggressive position of NIGYSOB. The victim, in turn, is forced into the apologetic and devaluating role of guilty self-effacement.

By analyzing the "games" we play, transactional analysis makes us aware of our basic coping patterns and their consequences in terms of our interpersonal relationships and life adjustment. In holding up a mirror so that we can see our behavior for what it really is, transactional analysis reveals how we often unthinkingly manipulate and harm other people as well as ourselves. And as a form of therapy, it holds out the possibility of eliminating the subterfuge and deceit with which we deal with one another and of achieving more authentic, meaningful, and satisfying interpersonal relationships and life styles.

In concluding our discussion of interpersonal therapy, it may be emphasized that in the latter half of the twentieth century we are confronted with serious problems in human relations as well as technological change. Although we still lack much needed research data concerning the effectiveness of these therapies, it is interesting to note the increasing emphasis on interpersonal relationships rather than individual "deviance." We shall see a continuation and extension of this orientation when we discuss encounter groups and the human potential movement.

GROUP THERAPY AND
THE ENCOUNTER GROUP

Treatment of patients in groups received a good deal of impetus in the military during World War II, when psychotherapists were in short supply. It was found to be effective in dealing with a variety of problems, and group therapy rapidly became an important therapeutic approach in civilian life. In fact, all the major systematic approaches to psychotherapy that we have discussed—psychoanalysis, behaviorism, and so on—have been applied in group as well as individual settings.

Traditional group psychotherapy. Group therapy has traditionally involved a relatively small group of patients in a clinic or hospital setting, using a variety of procedures depending upon the age, needs, and potentialities of the patients and the orientation of the therapists. The degree of patient participation in the group process varies in different types of groups. At one extreme is *didactic group therapy*, which consists of the presentation of more or less formal lectures and visual materials to patients as a group. For example, a group of alcoholic patients may be shown a film depicting the detrimental effects of excessive drinking on the human body, with a group discussion afterwards. While this approach by itself has not proved effective in combating alcoholism, it is often a useful adjunct to other forms of group therapy. And we have already seen that organizations such as Alcoholics Anonymous may function both as group treatment settings and sources of continuing support.

Psychodrama is an interesting form of group therapy based upon role-playing techniques. The patient, assisted by staff members or other patients, is encouraged to act out problem situations in a theater-like setting. This technique frees the individual to express his anxieties and hostilities or relive traumatic experiences in a situation which simulates real life but is more sheltered. The goal is to help the patient achieve emotional catharsis, increased understanding, and improved interpersonal competencies. This form of therapy has proved beneficial for the patients who make up the audience as well as for those who participate on the stage (Sundberg & Tyler, 1962).

Transactional analysis is another form of therapy that is frequently used in group settings. Group therapy may also be completely unstructured, as in activity groups where children with emotional problems are allowed to act out their aggressions without interference.

Encounter-group therapy. In recent years the entire field of group therapy has been changed by the advent of encounter groups, and it seems appropriate to end our discussion of psychotherapy with an account of this increasingly popular form of group therapy. Some encounter groups stem from the sensitivity training or T-groups started over 20 years ago at the National Training Laboratories in Bethel, Maine; others stem from patterns developed at the Esalen Institute in California, Synanon, and similar "growth centers."

Some encounter groups are directed toward helping normal individuals learn more about how their feelings and behavior affect themselves and others, while other groups are directed primarily toward the treatment of personal problems and hence tend to be an extension of traditional group therapy. It is these therapeutically oriented encounter groups with which we are presently concerned, although many of the aspects of group process described here are characteristic of both types of group.

1. *Format and goals.* There has always been a great deal of flexibility and experimentation in encounter groups, and a variety of formats have emerged. Thus there are leaderless groups of drug addicts, marathon groups in which the participants are conventionally clad and marathons in the nude, and encounter groups involving the confrontation of members of conflicting groups in the community.

Usually the encounter group consists of some 6 to 12 participants with one or two group leaders and the physical setting is relatively bare, permitting maximum freedom of movement and activity. Specific goals in encounter-group therapy vary considerably, depending on the nature and orientation of the group. However, the focus is on providing an intensive group experience which helps members work through emotional problems and achieve more adaptive coping techniques. The group situation, with its intensive give-and-take, is much closer to social reality than is traditional individual therapy; in fact, it typically goes beyond conventional social

Group therapy is a theme whose variations are almost endless. The informal "rap session" for drug addicts and the nude encounter group shown here are but two examples of the ways in which people come together to share in the therapeutic process. But whatever the setting or the background of the participants, the emphasis is likely to be on direct, honest expression and interaction as a means to personal growth.

reality in terms of the honesty and frankness it demands in interpersonal interactions.

The encounter-group leader—more appropriately described as a leader-participant since his function is not highly directive—is usually responsible for screening group members and for scheduling meetings. He is also responsible for establishing a climate of "psychological safety" in which each member feels safe to drop his façade, to express his feelings, and to try out new ways of interacting with others. He may also serve as a model by expressing his own feelings openly and honestly and accepting expressions of hostility or other negative feelings directed toward him without becoming defensive. He encourages group members to give descriptive

feedback (such as "it made me uncomfortable when you said that") rather than evaluative feedback (such as "you are really obnoxious"). It is also the responsibility of the group leader to see that confrontations among group members are resolved in a constructive way, and in general to serve as a resource person when the group needs guidance or comes to an impasse.

2. *Group process.* The emphasis in encounter groups is on the removal of masks, the free and honest expression of feelings, and the resolution of confrontations and other interactions that emerge within the group. This in turn requires prompt and honest feedback, both negative and positive, from other group members. Usually a good deal of support and affection develops within the group for members who are experiencing periods of crisis.

Nonverbal techniques may be used as "warming-up" exercises to facilitate awareness and group interaction. Such techniques include *eyeball-to-eyeball*, in which two participants gaze into each other's eyes for 60 to 90 seconds; the *blind mill*, in which all of the group members walk around with their eyes closed, learning how to communicate by touch; and *trusting exercises*, in which participants take turns being lifted and passed around the circle formed by other group members. Partial or total disrobing has also been used, and is reported to enhance feelings of spontaneity and confidence rather than eliciting sexual excitement.

Verbal techniques also may be used to facilitate group interaction, to provide feedback, and to focus on personal problems. One method is to have a member occupy the "hot seat" while the others provide feedback about their reactions to him and his behavior. A variation of this technique is called *positive and negative bombardment*, in which the members are instructed to say only negative or positive things about the person on the "hot seat," with the proviso that they must be sincere. This may help the member gain a remarkably different impression of him-

EVENTS IN ENCOUNTER GROUPS

Just what is it that goes on in an encounter group? On the basis of his extensive work with such groups, Rogers (1970) has delineated a pattern of events which is typical of the group process. An adaptation of his analysis is presented below.

1. **Milling around.** As the group leader makes it clear that group members have unusual freedom but also responsibility for the direction of the group, there tends to be an initial period of confusion, frustration, awkward silences, and "cocktail-party talk"—polite surface interaction intermixed with questions about who is in charge of the group and what its purpose is.

2. **Resistance to personal expression or exploration.** Initially, members tend to portray only their "public selves"; only fearfully and gradually do they begin to reveal aspects of the private self. The difficulty which a member may experience in dropping his façade is well summarized in the following statement by a group member:

"There is a self which I present to the world and another one which I know more intimately. . . . My inner self, by contrast with the image I present to the world, is characterized by many doubts. The worth I attach to this inner self is . . . very dependent on how others are reacting to me. At times this private self can feel worthless." (p. 16)

3. **Description of negative feelings.** Interestingly enough, the first expression of feelings concerning the here-and-now interaction in the group tends to involve negative feelings directed toward the group leader or other group members.

"In one group in which members introduced themselves at some length, one woman refused, saying that she preferred to be known for what she was in the group and not in terms of her status outside. Very shortly after this, a man in the group attacked her vigorously and angrily for this stand, accusing her of failing to cooperate, of keeping herself aloof from the group, of being unreasonable. It was the first *current personal feeling* brought into the open in that group." (p. 18)

4. **Expression and exploration of personally meaningful material.** Despite the resistance to revealing one's private self, the voicing of critical or angry feelings, and the initial confusion, the event most likely to occur next is for some member to take the gamble of revealing some significant aspect of himself—perhaps a seemingly hopeless problem of communication between himself and his wife. Apparently this member has come to realize that this is in effect "his" group, and he can help shape its direction; apparently also the fact that negative feelings have been expressed in the group without catastrophic results tends to foster a climate of trust.

5. **The expression of immediate interpersonal feelings in the group.** Although this may occur at any point in the group process, it involves the explicit expression of feelings, positive or negative, experienced at the moment by one member toward another. Examples would be:

"'I feel threatened by your silence.' . . . 'I took an instant dislike to you the first moment I saw you.' 'To me you're like a breath of fresh air in the group.' 'I like your warmth and your smile.' 'I dislike you more every time you speak up.'" (p. 21)

Each of these immediate expressions of feeling is usually explored in the increasing climate of trust which is developing in the group.

6. **Development of a healing capacity in the group and the beginning of change.** One fascinating aspect of the intensive group experience is the manner in which some group members evidence a spontaneous capability for responding to the pain and suffering of others in a therapeutic way—thus paving the way for change. This point is well illustrated in the following excerpt from a group session in which one member (Art) has been talking about his "shell" and his difficulty in accepting himself:

"Art: 'When that shell's on it's, uh . . .'
Lois: 'It's on!'
Art: 'Yeah, it's on tight.'
Susan: 'Are you always so closed in when you're in your shell?'
Art: 'No, I'm so darn used to living with the shell, it doesn't even

self than he had before. Here we are reminded of the words of the poet Robert Burns:

O wad some Pow'r the giftie gie us
To see oursels as ithers see us!

Most encounter-group therapists consider such warming-up exercises as useful in getting people to "open up" and to develop feelings of trust and mutual support. Other therapists consider any type of structured technique to be "gimmicky" and counterproductive and prefer to allow group interaction to take its natural course. So far,

there is no conclusive evidence as to which approach works best.

Encounter group experiences may be intensified by the use of the *marathon* format in which the group meets for a live-in weekend with only a brief break for sleep. The "opening-up" process appears to be hastened by the continuous contact as well as the lowering of inhibitions that accompanies fatigue. Presumably the participants are too tired to play games, and there is more immediacy, openness, and honesty of expression. This approach also helps members focus on the immediate group experience—on the here and now rather than the past or future. Thus the

---

bother me. I don't even know the real me. I think I've, well, I've pushed the shell away more here. When I'm out of my shell—only twice—once just a few minutes ago—I'm really me, I guess. But then I just sort of pull in a cord after me when I'm in my shell, and that's almost all the time. And I leave the front standing outside when I'm back in the shell.'
Facilitator: 'And nobody's back in there with you?'
Art: (Crying) 'Nobody else is in there with me, just me. I just pull everything into the shell and roll the shell up and shove it in my pocket. I take the shell, and the real me, and put it in my pocket where it's safe. I guess that's really the way I do it—I go into my shell and turn off the real world. And here—that's what I want to do here in the group, y'know—come out of my shell and actually throw it away.'
Lois: 'You're making progress already. At least you can talk about it.'
Facil.: 'Yeah. The thing that's going to be hardest is to stay out of the shell.'
Art: (Still crying) 'Well, yeah, if I can keep talking about it I can come out and stay out, but I'm gonna have to, y'know, protect me. It hurts. It's actually hurting to talk about it.'" (p. 26)

Here the understanding and support of group members is helping Art take the crucial initial steps toward self-acceptance. This healing capacity may extend beyond the regular group sessions, as when a few members remain after the session is over to offer support and therapeutic assistance to a member they sense is experiencing serious difficulties.

7. Dropping of façades, confrontations, and feedback. As the group sessions continue, many things are occurring simultaneously and it is difficult to organize them into any coherent pattern: the various threads and stages overlap and interweave. As time goes on, the group finds it increasingly unacceptable for any member to hide behind a mask or façade, refusing to reveal himself to the group as he really is. In a general sense, the group *demands* that each individual be himself.

Often this results in a direct confrontation between two group members. Such confrontations are often negative in tone, as in the following excerpt:

"Norma: (Loud sigh) 'Well, I don't have *any* respect for you, Alice. *None!* (Pause) There's about a hundred things going through my mind I want to say to you, and *by God* I hope I get through 'em all.'" (p. 31)

Norma continued to elucidate her feelings toward Alice in no uncertain terms. As is often the case in such confrontations, however, these two women eventually came to a more understanding acceptance of each other.

In the *basic encounter* with other group members, individuals come into more direct, honest, and closer contact than is customary in ordinary life. This is likely to provide the individual with a good deal of totally new feedback concerning himself and his effects on others.

8. Expression of positive feelings and behavior change. Rogers states that "an inevitable part of the group process seems to be that when feelings are expressed and can be accepted in a relationship, then a great deal of closeness and positive feeling results. Thus as the sessions proceed, an increasing feeling of warmth and group spirit and trust is built up, not out of positive attitudes only but out of a realness which includes both positive and negative feeling." (pp. 34–35)

He concludes that while there are certain risks inherent in the intensive encounter group experience, there is also great therapeutic potential, as evidenced by the following statement written by a member to his group:

"I have come to the conclusion that my experiences with you have profoundly affected me. I am truly grateful. This is different than personal therapy. None of you *had* to care about me. None of you had to seek me out and let me know of things you thought would help me. None of you had to let me know I was of help to you. Yet you did, and as a result it has far more meaning than anything I have so far experienced. When I feel the need to hold back and not live spontaneously, for whatever reasons, I remember that twelve persons just like those before me now said to let go and be congruent, be myself and of all unbelievable things they even loved me more for it. This has given me the *courage* to come out of myself . . . ." (p. 33)

ENCOUNTER GROUP "CASUALTIES"

Encounter groups encourage, support, and frequently pressure members toward increased awareness of feelings, interpersonal patterns, and potential for change. The result is often a more positive self-concept, increased competency, and the opening of pathways toward personal growth. Unfortunately, failure in the face of group pressure can be a crushing experience, confirming and intensifying an individual's negative self-evaluation.

"I was not in the mood for 'encountering' and was almost forced to. I don't trust anyone in the group and felt threatened by it. I came away feeling insecure and having many self doubts without being able to resolve them within the group. I overheard another member of the group describing my actions with his roommate, and he was reinforcing my own self doubts about myself. I didn't want to participate, was forced to participate unnaturally and then was emotionally upset by the experience for several days afterwards. . . ." (Yalom & Lieberman, 1971, p. 23)

This student continued to feel helpless, disgusted with himself, anxious, and less trustful of others for months after his group experience. He was among the 16 "encounter group casualties" identified by Yalom and Lieberman (1971). A casualty was defined as a person who became more psychologically depressed or evidenced more maladaptive effects persisting through the time of a follow-up interview 8 months later.

The major tragedy uncovered by the study was the suicide of a student shortly after the second meeting of his group. This suicide was not considered an encounter group casualty, because the person had a long history of emotional difficulties and his suicide could not necessarily be attributed to his group experience. Nevertheless, his suicide note vividly illustrates the extreme difficulty that a vulnerable person can have in an encounter group:

"I felt great pain that I could not stop any other way. It would have been helpful if there had been anyone to understand and care about my pain, but there wasn't. People did not believe me when I told them about my problems or pain or else that it was just self pity; or if there had been someone to share my feelings with, but all they said was that I was hiding myself, not showing my true feelings, talking to myself. They kept saying this no matter how hard I tried to reach them. This is what I mean when I say they do not understand or care about my pain; they just discredited it or ignored it and I was left alone with it. I ask that anyone who asks about me see this; it is my only last request." (p. 19)

Three of the encounter group casualties who had psychotic experiences during or shortly after the termination of the group experience simply seemed unable to handle the input overload —the intensive emotional stimulation, feedback about unrecognized aspects of self, and pressure to "open up"—when their need at the time was for support of their tenuous inner control. There are some encounter group leaders who do not see decompensation of old personality structure as necessarily negative, but view the journey through despair and loss of organized self as providing the potential for more positive personality reorganization. The majority of group leaders, however, do not share this view of the purpose of encounter group therapy and seek to protect vulnerable individuals from the potential dangers inherent in excessive group pressure.

marathon encounter group has been called a "pressure cooker" because of the emotional tension it builds up and the reduced amount of time apparently required to achieve therapeutic goals.

3. *Termination and reentry.* The term *reentry* refers to the return of group members from the new climate of the encounter group to the everyday world. It is often difficult for the individual to return to the mundane patterns of everyday life, where his new understandings and ways of behaving may not be readily accepted. For example, there is considerable risk in being completely open with others and giving honest feedback in family, work, or social groups.

As yet there is no simple strategy for overcoming the reentry problem. Some group leaders utilize a final session of the group for "reflections," during which participants share their feelings about the group experience and how it may carry over into their lives. In some cases, follow-up sessions are scheduled. Of course, for many encounter groups there is no set termination date. For example, encounter groups for alcoholics and drug addicts may be more or less continuous, with the membership changing over time as new members enter the group and old ones leave it.

Evaluation of encounter-group therapy. Although we shall not attempt to assess the advantages and pitfalls of encounter groups, a few comments seem in order. The potency of this approach is indicated by the fact that a group of strangers can learn, in a relatively short period of time, to function with a high degree of honesty, trust, and supportiveness. Participants frequently attest that the intensive group experience has had a profound influence on their lives. A typical reaction upon termination of the group is "I feel I know each of you better and feel closer to you than to most people I have known or worked with for years."

On the other hand, professionals have pointed with concern to the lack of scientific data concerning the actual effects of encounter-group therapy, the lack of adequate screening of group members, and the lack of adequate training of many group leaders. They point to the possibilities of short-term change and subsequent discouragement after reentry into the world of reality, of the aggravation of personal problems that are brought out but not adequately resolved in the group, and of the development of sexual involvements among group members which may jeopardize their marriages. Similarly, one hears references to "encounter freaks" who wander like lost souls from one encounter group to another, always seeking intimacy and belonging which they never really capture.

Several studies have related emotional disturbances to encounter group experiences (Kane, Wallace & Lipton, 1971; Laken, 1970; Stone & Tieger, 1971). In a systematic study of 18 encounter groups for undergraduates, Yalom and Lieberman (1971) found that 16 of the 170 students who completed the group sessions suffered significant psychological damage as a direct consequence of the group experience (see illustration, page 690). The majority of students in the groups studied reported a positive change in themselves and a favorable attitude toward the group experience. Nevertheless, the fact that 16 "ordinary" college students (nearly 10 percent of the small group studied) were adversely affected by the group experience raises some important questions about what might be expected in a setting where all the members are there because they have been judged to be "emotionally disturbed."

Perhaps any potential adverse effects of encounter-group therapy can be minimized by ensuring the qualifications of group leaders and by the more careful screening of participants for different types of groups. In this context it is encouraging to note that the American Psychological Association has established a commission to recommend a code of ethics for the accreditation of group leaders.

SOCIOCULTURAL APPROACHES TO THERAPY

Sociocultural approaches to therapy typically involve the modification of the individual's life situation in order to provide a more supportive or therapeutic environment. Such modification can take many forms, some of which we have already mentioned. It may involve changing parental behavior that is reinforcing and maintaining a child's maladaptive behavior; it may involve foster-home care for children who are abused by their parents; it may involve the hospitalization of an emotionally disturbed child or adult; or it may involve the placement of criminal offenders in a "correctional" or penal institution.

The term *sociotherapy* has traditionally been used for approaches focusing on the role of the social worker in helping individuals who have been hospitalized make a successful readjustment. This has involved helping the individual's family deal with financial problems, preparing them for his return home, and giving other assistance in smoothing the way for the individual's eventual return to his family and community setting. Recently, however, it has been acknowledged that probation officers and related mental health personnel play a major role in sociotherapy. In addition, the concept of sociotherapy has expanded from concern with the individual's immediate family setting to concern with the broader community and social system in which people live and function. Thus clinical psychologists and psychiatrists have now "begun to see an intimate relationship between their roles with individuals and the bringing about of changes in the social institutions in which such individuals are born, grow or fail to grow, struggle, and succeed or perish." (Peck, 1970, p. 436)

In the present section we shall be concerned with the role of the mental hospital, community mental health services, and the therapeutic modification of communities and larger social systems.

INSTITUTIONALIZATION AND AFTERCARE

As we have seen, it is sometimes necessary to remove persons—children, adolescents, adults, and the aged—from their family and community settings and place them in mental hospitals for treatment. Typically the sequence of events involves (1) admission to the hospital, (2) assessment and treatment, and (3) discharge and aftercare. Assessment procedures were discussed in Chapter 19; here we shall focus on treatment procedures and aftercare.

The mental hospital as a therapeutic community. Any of the traditional forms of therapy that we have been discussing may, of course, be used in the hospital setting. In more and more mental hospitals, however, these techniques are being supplemented by an effort to make the hospital environment itself a *therapeutic community*. That is, all the ongoing activities of the hospital are brought into the total treatment program, and the environment, or *milieu*, is a crucial aspect of therapy. The aim is to get patients back into their family and community settings as soon as possible.

In the therapeutic community, as few restraints as possible are placed on the freedom of the patient, and the orientation is toward encouraging patients to take responsibility for their behavior as well as to participate actively in their treatment programs. Open wards permit patients the use of grounds and premises. Self-government programs confer "citizenship" on them, giving them responsibility for managing their own affairs and those of the ward. All hospital personnel are oriented toward treating the patients as human beings who merit consideration and courtesy. A number of studies have shown the beneficial effects of such staff attitudes on everyone concerned, staff and patients alike.

The interaction among patients—whether in encounter groups, social events, or other activities—is planned in such a way as to be of therapeutic benefit. In fact, it is becoming apparent that often the most beneficial aspects of the

---

PSYCHOTHERAPEUTIC AIDS

There are a number of procedures which have proved of therapeutic value, particularly in hospital settings, but which are usually considered aids or adjuncts to the total therapy program rather than as systematic approaches to psychotherapy.

1. **Bibliotherapy.** Books, pamphlets, and other reading material are often of value in helping the patient realize that others have problems similar to his and in increasing his self-understanding and motivation to improve. Specific reading materials are usually selected in terms of the needs and intellectual abilities of the patient.

   Related to this type of therapy is the practice of providing patients or prison inmates with the opportunity to take extension or correspondence courses for credit, and in some instances to attend educational institutions including colleges.

2. **Audio-visual aids.** Videotape playbacks of excerpts from marital, encounter group, and other forms of therapy are often extremely helpful in reviewing and integrating critical events and processes in therapy sessions. In addition, there are many fine films dealing with alcoholism, drug abuse, and other maladaptive patterns which can be utilized in overall treatment programs.

3. **Occupational therapy.** This may involve constructive work which contributes to the operation of the hospital or clinic, formal training in actual job skills, or the supervision of the patient in a therapeutic role in helping other patients—often

with the expectation that the patient may later become a paraprofessional in a specific mental health area.

4. **Social events.** Many mental hospitals and clinics have a regular schedule of social events including dances, teas, and "cocktail hours." In some instances patients may operate a closed-circuit television program featuring items of interest to patients. In addition, theatrical productions may be put on by patients. Such social events help the patients feel less isolated and more involved in their environment.

5. **Athletics.** Regularly scheduled athletic events for patient participation may include softball, basketball, and other team sports. Where facilities are available, a physical conditioning program may be worked out to meet individual needs.

6. **Music therapy.** Patients are commonly provided the opportunity for both listening to music and playing an instrument—often as part of a musical group. Traditional music and folk singing have been found especially effective in fostering patient interest and group cohesiveness.

7. **Art therapy.** Painting, clay sculpturing, and other art media may facilitate the communication of feelings and assist in the resolution of inner conflicts, as may creative writing of prose or poetry. In addition, patients commonly experience a sense of pride and accomplishment in their creative productions. In some instances, art exhibitions are held and prizes awarded; and there may be competition between different hospital or clinic facilities in such exhibitions.

THE HOSPITALIZATION SYNDROME

Although individuals differ markedly in their response to hospitalization, we have noted that some who reside in large mental hospitals over long periods of time tend to adopt a passive role and become "colonized," losing the self-confidence and motivation required for reentering the outside world. In fact, a sizable number of chronic patients become adept at manipulating their symptoms and making themselves appear "sicker" than they are in order to avoid the possibility of discharge from the sheltered hospital environment. This pattern is not ordinarily considered to be the result of hospitalization alone, but rather is attributed to an interaction between the patient and the hospital milieu. The following are some of the steps which have been delineated in the development of this hospitalization or, as it is also called, *social breakdown* syndrome.

1. **Deficiency in self-concept.** A precondition for the development of the social breakdown syndrome is the presence of severe self-devaluation and inner confusion concerning social roles and responsibilities.

2. **Social labeling.** During an acute crisis period in the person's life he has probably been labeled as dangerous to himself or others and involuntarily sent to a mental hospital, perhaps legally certified as being incompetent and lacking in self-control.

3. **Induction into the "sick" role.** Admission procedures, diagnostic labeling, and treatment by staff members and

other patients all too often initiate the individual into the role of a "sick" person—helpless, passive, and requiring care and external control.

4. **Atrophy of work and social skills.** In institutions that serve primarily as "storage bins" for the emotionally disturbed, basic work and social skills may atrophy through disuse. And during prolonged hospitalization, technological changes in the outside world may exacerbate the obsolescence of an individual's work skills.

5. **Development of the chronic sick role.** Eventually the confused and devaluated patient becomes a full member of the sick community in which passive dependence and "crazy" behavior are not only common but expected. Now he has been "colonized"—he has learned and adopted the chronic sick role.

In spite of the current emphasis on short-term hospitalization and intensive aftercare, there is still a "hard core" of chronic patients who remain relatively untouched by these new procedures. However, the staffs of our large mental hospitals are becoming more aware of this problem of chronicity and are introducing various corrective procedures for remotivation and resocialization, as well as stressing a recovery-expectant attitude.

Based on Bandura (1969), Braginsky et al. (1968), Goffman (1962), Paul (1969), and Zusman (1967).

---

therapeutic community are the interactions among the patients themselves. Differences in social roles and backgrounds may make empathy between staff and patients difficult, but fellow patients have "been there"—they have had similar problems and breakdowns and have experienced the anxiety and humiliation of being labeled "mentally ill" and hospitalized. Thus constructive and helping relationships frequently develop among patients in a warm, encouraging milieu.

As we have seen, a highly successful method for helping chronic patients take increased responsibility for their behavior has been the use of token economies as part of the total milieu approach. Such programs are effective both in shaping various socially desirable behaviors and in helping bridge the gap between the hospital environment and the world outside.

It must always be remembered that the ultimate goal of hospitalization is to enable the patient to resume his place in society. There is always the danger that the mental hospital may become a permanent refuge from the world,

either because it offers total escape from the demands of everyday living or because it encourages patients to settle into a chronic "sick" role (see illustration at top of page). To avoid this, hospital staffs try to establish close ties with the family and community and to maintain a "recovery-expectant" attitude. Between 70 and 85 percent of patients labeled as psychotic and admitted to mental hospitals can now be discharged within a few weeks, or at most months, and with adequate aftercare the readmission rate can be markedly reduced.

Provisions for aftercare. Even where hospitalization or other institutional approaches have modified maladaptive behavior and perhaps fostered needed occupational, interpersonal, and related skills, the readjustment of the individual in his community setting may still be a very difficult one. We have noted that up to 45 percent of schizophrenic patients are readmitted within a year after their discharge. Adequate aftercare programs can help smooth the transition from institutional to community life and markedly reduce the number of relapses.

The last decade has seen a marked trend toward the establishment of *halfway houses* which provide needed aftercare and help former patients function adequately in the community. Typically such halfway houses are not run by professional mental health personnel, but by the residents themselves.

In a pilot program with a group of newly released mental patients, Fairweather and his colleagues (1969) demonstrated that these patients could function in the community in a patient-run halfway house. Initially a member of the research staff coordinated the daily operations of the lodge, but he was shortly replaced by a lay person. The patients were given full responsibility for operating the lodge, for regulating each other's behavior, for earning money, and for purchasing and preparing food. They established a handyman service which produced over $50,000 in less than three years. The proceeds were apportioned according to each person's productivity and responsibility. The only professional assistance they received was in the formal periodic consultations with a member of the research team to supply needed information concerning any personal or organizational problems that arose, to evaluate the group's recommended solutions, and to assess the group's overall functioning.

Forty months after their discharge, a comparison was made of these ex-patients and a comparable group of 75 patients who had been discharged at the same time but had not had the halfway house experience. Whereas most members of the halfway house were able to hold income-producing jobs, to manage their daily lives, and to adjust in the outside world, the majority of those who had not had the halfway house experience were unable to adjust to life on the outside.

Similar halfway houses have been established for alcoholics and drug addicts and other persons attempting to make an adjustment in the community after institutionalization. Such establishments may be said to be specialized in the sense that all residents share similar backgrounds and problems, and this seems to contribute to their effectiveness.

One of the chief problems of halfway houses is that of gaining the acceptance and support of the community. As Jansen (1969) has pointed out, "They must develop a rather complete integration into the community in which they are situated so that community residents, through contact with the house and its residents, will make it their concern." (p. 24)

COMMUNITY MENTAL HEALTH SERVICES

As the trend toward treatment in the family and community setting—rather than in large state mental hospitals—has gathered impetus, we have seen the development of community mental health facilities throughout the country. Where such facilities are available to provide immediate assistance to the individual or the family, many crises can be rapidly alleviated. Thus the family is not disrupted, nor does the individual have to be sent to a distant institution and, later, face the problem of return to family and community.

An interesting illustration of this trend is found in the study of Langsley (1968) and his co-workers who tried intercepting certain patients at the point of hospital entry and returning them to their homes instead for a type of family crisis treatment under the supervision of trained therapists. These individuals, selected on a random basis, exhibited a wide range of mental disorders including schizophrenia and severe depression. Most of them were successfully treated at home with the participation of family members. Only about 20 percent of the first 75 eventually entered a mental hospital during a 6-month period. And those eventually hospitalized spent only a third as much time in the hospital as did a control group not treated at home before hospitalization.

This approach is not without its problems. The family must be willing to participate in therapy, and the home must provide a supportive environment and not one which reinforces and maintains the maladaptive behavior. Qualified therapists must be available in the community, and the resistance of family members as well as neighbors to having a "mentally ill" person in their midst must be overcome. However, this approach tends to shift the criterion for hospitalization from the severity of the individual's symptoms to the degree of family support and the availability of therapeutic supervision outside the hospital setting.

Community mental health centers. In 1963 President Kennedy sent a message to Congress calling for "a bold new approach" to mental illness. From this message came the Community Mental Health Centers Act providing federal assistance to communities for constructing such centers. Since that time, over 400 mental health centers have been built, providing services for

COMMUNITY MENTAL HEALTH CENTER SERVICES

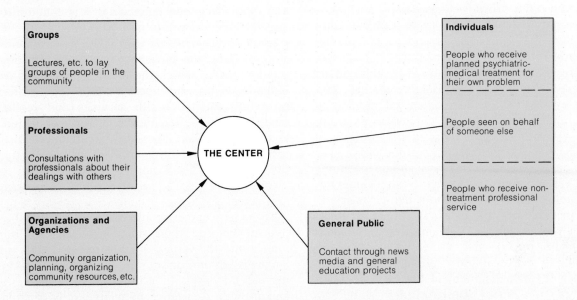

A community mental health center usually serves a population of between 75,000 and 200,000. It touches the lives of this population in a number of ways, as suggested in the diagram. Depending upon the needs of the particular community and the resources available, such a center may offer a number of services in addition to the five basic services listed in the text. These may include diagnostic services, rehabilitation, precare and aftercare, training of professional mental health workers, and research and evaluation. Whatever the extent of its services, the focus is on *continuity of care*, permitting the patient to receive the type of treatment he needs at the time he needs it (Person, 1969).

millions of Americans in their home communities. These centers offer at least five types of services to local residents and institutions: (1) *inpatient care* for persons requiring short-term hospitalization; (2) *partial hospitalization,* with day hospitalization for patients able to return home evenings, or night hospitalization for patients able to work but in need of further care; (3) *outpatient therapy* permitting patients to live at home and go about their daily activities; (4) *emergency care* with psychiatric services around the clock; and (5) *consultation and education* for members of the community. These services are provided without discrimination for all who need them—young or old, well-to-do or indigent.

These community mental health centers are highly flexible and have a number of advantages. For example, the emotionally disturbed individual need no longer face the choice between being admitted to a distant hospital or receiving no treatment at all. If his disturbance is severe he can enter the center's inpatient facility for short-term hospitalization; if he can remain on the job or in his family with supportive care, he can enter partial hospitalization; and if outpatient therapy is sufficient for his needs, he can obtain it at the center. In addition, such community centers usually utilize an interdisciplinary approach to therapy, involving psychiatrists, psychologists, social workers, nurses, and other mental health personnel. Finally, such centers have many resources at their disposal, thus enabling the individual to obtain most or all of the needed services at one agency instead of traveling around the city from one place to another.

Free clinics. While free clinics are not an official part of the federally assisted mental health centers, the rise of the free-clinic concept deserves special mention. At the start of the hippie movement in the 1960's, many young people developed serious psychological and physical problems, often associated with the heavy use of psychedelic and other drugs. Yet because of their rejection of the "Establishment," they were reluctant to utilize the usual private and public mental health facilities.

In response to the need for free, anonymous treatment facilities, the Haight-Ashbury and Berkeley Free Clinics were organized and staffed by volunteer physicians, psychiatrists, psychologists, and other health personnel. Clients were not charged for treatment; no information was given out to parents or relatives; and no questions were asked about drug usage, sexual behavior, or truancy. This freedom from being "hassled" appeared to have a constructive effect on these young people, whose problems were associated with feeling oppressed by a society they perceived as being hypocritical and "uptight."

Since the establishment of the free clinics in San Francisco, many similar clinics—staffed by local volunteer professionals and nonprofessionals—have opened throughout the country. The philosophy of these clinics is to provide free medical and psychological services with no questions asked. The lay volunteers act as aides and often conduct "rap sessions" with troubled youngsters. The atmosphere of these clinics focuses on the "youth culture"—psychedelic posters, poetry on the walls, and bright colors all around. Young people between the ages of 11 and 20 flock to these free clinics by the thousands, to talk to a gynecologist about birth control or to a "shrink" about how to get down from a bad trip. Although such clinics may appear to be less than adequate in some respects, the fact is that many of the people they serve would not be amenable to counseling or treatment except in such a setting. In this way the free clinics supplement the more formally organized and run community mental health centers.

Neighborhood service centers. During the last decade, a number of programs have developed in which imaginative and concerned members of the community are attempting to cope with the joint problems of unemployment and mental health in the inner cities. This approach has been referred to under the rubric of "new careers

program." For example, one type of new career in a ghetto area is that of community spokesman, in which a member of the community becomes a communication link between the undereducated and often desperate members of his community and the many separate and often uncoordinated welfare and service agencies. With governmental support, programs have been established in some inner cities in which these new careerists have helped set up and operate store-front centers providing mental health services and related facilities. These neighborhood service centers, as they are called, are readily available to local residents and provide a variety of services, so that the individual need not risk being labeled as "mentally ill" or a "drug addict" in seeking assistance.

These new careerists often are especially effective in helping their neighbors because they understand the values and customs and "talk the language" of the community. Rather than remaining behind desks, they often make home visits and provide assistance in many kinds of situations—from helping a family find a new dwelling to making funeral arrangements. In addition to providing assistance during crisis periods, the new careers program has been instrumental in developing community-action groups that focus on alleviating unemployment, poor housing, drug addiction, violence, and other community-wide problems.

MODIFYING LARGER SOCIAL SYSTEMS

It is now being recognized that not only the immediate family but larger groups and institutions in the society may behave in maladaptive ways and/or may be pathogenic for the individuals within them. Thus there has been increasing concern not only with providing community-based facilities for treating individuals and families but also with approaches to modifying maladaptive conditions in organizations, institutions, and larger social systems.

One approach to therapeutic intervention with larger groups originated in a project of the Connecticut Interracial Commission begun in 1946 under the direction of Kurt Lewin. Lewin and his colleagues arranged a series of discussion groups in which black and white leaders could get together to air their differences. Because of Lewin's long-standing interest in group processes, he also appointed observers to be present at the meetings and record their comments on the group interaction. The conferees insisted that they too be allowed to participate in the postmortem sessions, and found the feedback both informative and exciting, particularly when it focused on their own behavior. The experience of these groups led to the establishment of the National Training Laboratories in Bethel, Maine, now known as the NTL Institute for Applied Behavioral Science.

The NTL combines research in basic group processes with offering practical help to various groups and individuals through intensive group experiences, particularly sensitivity training. T-groups, as they are called, have been directed especially toward men and women in responsible business, government, and civic organizations and toward professional people who are directly involved in supervising, helping, or dealing with people in special ways—such as business executives, physicians, clergymen, youth leaders, teachers, lawyers, police officers, psychologists, and social workers. "Labs" held each year for selected groups incorporate sensitivity training with lectures on organizational functioning and growth, the study of relationships between as well as within groups, and related supplementary experiences.

Two other approaches to therapeutic intervention on larger group levels may be mentioned. The first, which started about the same time as sensitivity training, involves the establishment of psychological consulting firms for helping organizations in the selection and training of personnel and in the resolution of organizational problems. From this approach has stemmed a second: the idea of "performance contracting," in which a psychological consulting firm is brought in as a "troubleshooter" to a school system or other social system with the objective of correcting maladaptive functioning. For example, a community may contract with such a firm to take over operation of the local schools. Under the terms of the contract, the firm guarantees to produce certain results—say to bring the reading level of

all students up to or above national norms. The firm is paid for its services in proportion to its success in meeting these objectives.

This is a relatively new field, however, and as yet there has been little research concerning therapeutic intervention in larger social systems. It may be expected that many of the techniques used in therapy with family systems will also be applicable to larger social systems: (1) removing reinforcers that tend to foster and maintain the maladaptive behavior, (2) utilizing aversive consequences to eliminate maladaptive behaviors while providing positive reinforcement for desired behaviors, (3) providing clear-cut and meaningful social roles as well as constructive role models, (4) ensuring the effective functioning of communication processes, and (5) obtaining the cooperation and participation of group members in planning and carrying out desired change. These principles may be applied to the system as a whole or to malfunctioning subsystems within the larger social system.

But as we move from the family to larger social systems, the problems of therapeutic intervention become much more complex. A change in one subsystem to correct one glaring problem may have far-reaching consequences on the entire system that the planners have not fully anticipated; and in some cases changes that seem adaptive in the short run may prove to be maladaptive in the longer perspective. For example, health measures in underdeveloped countries, which seem intuitively to be a highly desirable undertaking, may bring about greater misery than before if the resulting reduction in the death rate is not accompanied by a reduction in the birth rate and provision of a more adequate food supply. Thus there has been an increasing recognition that the needed solutions to problems of social systems may be "counterintuitive"— counter to what we would expect intuitively. Yet only as we anticipate the joint effects of many variables can we make accurate predictions.

As we saw in Chapter 18, one modern technique that is helping social scientists "rehearse" the effects of particular interventions or combinations of interventions is computer simulation. Although some people feel that we do not yet know enough about all the key variables to place confidence in such simulation, Forrester (1971) has pointed out that we are in fact taking far-reaching actions now on the basis of predictions made on far less dependable evidence.

". . . what justification can there be for the apparent assumption that we do not know enough to construct models but believe we do know enough to directly design new social systems by passing laws and starting new social programs? I am suggesting that we now do know enough to make useful models of social systems. Conversely, we do not know enough to design the most effective social systems directly without first going through a model-building experimental phase. But I am confident, and substantial supporting evidence is beginning to accumulate, that the proper use of models of social systems can lead to far better systems, laws, and programs." (p. 54)

CURRENT ISSUES AND TRENDS IN TREATMENT

In this chapter we have described a variety of treatment orientations and procedures, commenting on some of the current trends in the field of therapy. We shall close by examining some of the issues and trends that are on the "growing edge" of this field, including: (1) crisis intervention, (2) the use of paraprofessionals, (3) the problem of evaluating "success" in psychotherapy, (4) the issue of values, and (5) the human potential movement. We shall keep our discussion of each one brief.

CRISIS INTERVENTION

Crisis intervention has emerged as a response to a widespread need for immediate help for individuals and families confronted with highly stressful situations. Often such people are in a state of acute turmoil and feel overwhelmed and incapable of dealing with the stress by themselves. In such instances they do not have time to wait for the customary initial therapy appointment, nor are they usually in a position to continue therapy over a sustained period. They need immediate assistance.

To meet this need, two modes of therapeutic intervention have been developed: (1) short-term crisis therapy involving face-to-face discussion, and (2) the telephone "hot line." These forms of crisis intervention are usually handled either by professional mental health personnel or by paraprofessionals.

Short-term crisis therapy. The sole concern of short-term crisis therapy is the current problem with which the individual or family is having difficulty. In essence, the therapist tries to provide as much help as he can or as the client will accept.

Although the treatment of medical problems may involve crisis intervention, we are concerned here with personal or family problems of an emotional nature. In such crisis situations the therapist is usually very active, helping clarify the problem, suggesting plans of action, providing reassurance, and otherwise giving needed information and support. Strong emphasis is usually placed on mobilizing the support of other family members. Often this enables the person to avoid hospitalization and disruption of the family life. Crisis intervention may also involve bringing other mental health or medical personnel into the treatment picture.

Most individuals and families who need short-term crisis therapy do not continue in treatment for more than one to six sessions. Often, in fact, they come to the therapist or clinic for an "emotional band-aid," and after receiving needed guidance and support do not return.

The "hot line." As we noted in Chapter 10, the Suicide Prevention Center in Los Angeles has opened up a whole new approach to dealing with people in crises. All major cities in the United States and most smaller ones have developed some form of telephone hot line to help individuals undergoing periods of deep stress. While suicide prevention is the most dramatic problem, the range of problems that people call about is virtually unlimited—from breaking up with a boyfriend to being on a bad drug trip.

As with other crisis intervention, the person on the other end of the hot line is confronted with the problem of rapidly assessing "what's wrong" and "how bad it is." But even if his assessment is accurate and he does everything within his power to help the individual—within the confines imposed by the telephone—the caller may become extremely upset while talking about his problem and hang up without leaving his name, telephone number, or address. This can be a deeply disturbing experience for the therapist—particularly if, for example, the caller has announced that he has just swallowed a lethal dose of sleeping pills. Even in less severe cases, it often happens that the hot-line therapist never learns whether the caller took positive action or solved his problem.

For this reason, crisis intervention is probably the most discouraging for the therapist of any treatment approach that we have discussed. Despite the high frustration level of this work, however, crisis intervention therapists fill a crucial need in the mental health field—particularly for the young people who make up the majority of their clients (Browning, Tyson & Miller, 1971). For thousands of individuals in desperate trouble, an invaluable social support is provided by the fact that there is somewhere they can go for immediate help or someone they can call who will listen to their problems and try to help them. Thus it is not surprising that we are witnessing the proliferation of crisis intervention services and telephone hot lines.

THE USE OF PARAPROFESSIONALS

"It is now acknowledged that professional manpower cannot meet the mental health needs of the population through the use of present methods, and that there is no reasonable hope that such manpower can be increased sufficiently to do so in the future." (Guerney, 1969, p. 1)

While many professionals in the field of mental health believe that only extensively trained and experienced personnel are qualified to undertake the complex task of therapeutic intervention, it is becoming increasingly obvious that there are simply not enough of them to do the job. Thus we find more and more interest in the possibilities of training housewives, teachers, clergymen, police officers, nurses, and college students in therapy procedures, either within clinical or hospital settings or within the context of their usual professional situations (Cowen et al., 1967; Matarazzo, 1971). As Halleck (1971) has pointed out, "there are many relatively uneducated but otherwise intelligent and sensitive persons in all strata of our society who could and would make excellent therapists if they were properly trained." (p. 100)

This innovative approach to implementing mental health manpower has stemmed in part from increasing sophistication in the use of behavior-therapy techniques, which can be mastered in a relatively short period by such nonprofessionals as parents, teachers, and student volunteers. Such individuals are increasingly being used as systematic reinforcing agents in modifying the maladaptive behavior of children either on an individual basis or in token-economy programs.

In a pioneering study, Rioch and his associates (1963) reported positive results from a program designed to show that carefully selected lay persons could be trained within two years to function as therapists. The trainees were eight women in their 40's, married and with children; each was encouraged to develop an approach best suited to her own philosophical orientation and personality. The individuals whom they treated encompassed a wide range of ages and disorders, though most were emotionally disturbed adolescents.

Below is the list of guidelines presented to lay counselors trained in an experimental community mental health program in Susanville, California (Goodall, 1971):

1. "Notice the concept of blame whether it is directed at self or others. Point it out to the family members when it occurs and discuss the consequences of this behavior as it affects the other members.
2. "Do not accept 'I am as I am' statements. Consider persons capable of changing.
3. "Try to truly listen to other persons, not just be quiet until you can talk. Listen to and observe nonverbal means with which persons shut up others. Verbalize your observation descriptively, not critically.

College students, like this girl, and other volunteer workers can do a great deal to augment the programs of mental hospitals and other institutions. One important function is simply to provide companionship and social interaction for patients who might otherwise have only minimal contact with overworked staff members.

4. "Do not give advice—do not present solutions to others. One goal of therapeutic intervention is to allow persons to become responsible for themselves and aware of the consequences of their actions.
5. "Do not create dependency on yourself by taking over this responsibility. You clarify, they solve.
6. "Do not take sides with any family member. Each person contributes equally to the maladjustment; i.e., each person can break up a fight he is involved in.
7. "Give equal attention to each family member, whether adult or child.
8. "Do not become absorbed with historical excuses or reasons for present problems; that is a dead end. Focus on what is happening now to maintain the situation and permit the persons to explore what could be done to change it.
9. "Ask the family member to consider how he himself should act differently to help the other person, rather than waiting for the other person to change." (p. 32)

Currently there would appear to be three primary nontraditional sources of mental health workers.

1. *Community college trainees.* The junior or community college is a relatively new development in our educational system. This institution may offer a two-year program leading to an Associate of Arts (AA) degree with specialized training in some mental health area; or it may provide opportunities for the upgrading and extension of skills on the part of hospital attendants, nurses, police officers, and other personnel already working in this area or related fields. In one AA program, the graduate, called a *mental health technologist,* is prepared to function as an allied professional in a clinic or hospital facility (Matarazzo, 1971). Other colleges and universities have established four-year programs along similar lines. Such programs are roughly analogous to the training of paramedical personnel in the field of medicine.

2. *Lay volunteers.* The use of lay volunteers in working with mental patients goes back many years, but it has only been in recent years that this approach has been subjected to systematic study and evaluation. Ewalt (1967) and Guerney (1969) have provided extensive descriptions of the use of lay volunteers in assisting in various programs for the mentally retarded and emotionally disturbed. The contribution such lay volunteers can make is well illustrated in a study by Katkin and his colleagues (1971). They utilized female volunteers who functioned primarily in a supportive role in providing posthospital therapy for mental patients. In comparison with a control group of patients who had a recidivism rate of 34 percent within a one-year period, the recidivism rate in the experimental group was only 11 percent. Yet the program did not involve extensive training, but relied primarily on supervision the volunteers received while working with the patients.

3. *Former patients.* Perhaps the most creative and exciting work being done in implementing mental health manpower is the use of former mental patients, prison inmates, delinquents, drug addicts, or other previously disturbed individuals to treat those with similar problems. We have also commented on the use of actual patients who are progressing favorably in helping those who are more seriously disturbed and the "pyramid approach" in which the less severely mentally retarded assist in the training of more severely retarded individuals. And as we have seen (Chapter 16), these "therapists" often get as much benefit from giving therapy as their trainees do from receiving it.

This approach has sometimes been described as "the blind leading the blind"; but it would appear that there is much to be said for the understanding and therapeutic potential of someone who has "been there." There is mounting evidence that former drug addicts can help addicts, that recovered psychotics can help disturbed patients, and that ex-convicts can become good probation officers. We have already noted the recruitment of a sizable number of former addicts as regular staff members in treatment centers, and the establishment of halfway houses in which former mental patients support each other in their return to community life.

In essence, we appear to be creating a new breed of therapist who will ordinarily be a resident of the community in which he serves, who will have lived much the same kind of life as his clients, and who will understand and be able to communicate with them because he speaks their language.

EVALUATION OF "SUCCESS" IN PSYCHOTHERAPY

In recent years there has been a good deal of questioning of the value of psychotherapy. Despite the fact that hundreds of thousands of people undergo some form of psychotherapy each year, we have surprisingly little scientific data to show how often such therapeutic intervention is successful. While attempts have been made to assess and compare the outcomes of various forms of therapy, the wide variations among therapists, patients, goals, procedures, and definitions of success have made it virtually impossible to reach any valid conclusions. Some investigators have questioned whether any form of psychotherapy is effective; others have concluded that while the participants may undergo a profound experience, the outcomes are at best uncertain. In his presidential address to the American Psychological Association (1970), George Albee questioned whether clinical psychology could or should survive as part of the field of scientific psychology; and, in fact, some

major universities have stopped offering degrees in this field.

What are some of the problems involved in evaluating the success of psychotherapy? Attempts at evaluation generally depend on one or more of the following sources of information: (1) the therapist's impression of changes that have occurred, (2) the patient's reports of change, (3) reports from the patient's family or friends, (4) comparison of pre- and post-treatment personality test scores, and (5) measures of change in selected overt behaviors.

Unfortunately, each of these sources has serious limitations. Since the therapist quite naturally wants to see himself as competent and successful, he is not the best judge of his own effectiveness. Furthermore, he can inflate his improvement rate by consciously or unconsciously encouraging difficult patients to discontinue therapy with him. It has also been somewhat facetiously remarked that the therapist often thinks the patient is getting better because he is getting used to the patient's symptoms. The patient, too, is an unreliable source concerning the outcomes of therapy. He may not only want to think that he is getting better but may report that he is being helped in an attempt to please the therapist. Family and relatives may also tend to see the improvement they had hoped for, although they often seem to be more realistic than the therapist or patient in their long-term evaluations. Psychological tests may show change but are likely to focus on certain measures in which the therapist is interested. Such tests are not necessarily valid predictors of how the client will behave in real-life situations, nor do they give any indication of whether changes are likely to be enduring.

Changes in selected behaviors appear to be the safest measure of outcome, but even this criterion is subject to limitations. Changes in the therapy situation may not generalize to other life situations. In addition, the changes selected reflect the goals of the individual therapist. For example, one therapist may consider therapy "successful" if a patient becomes more manageable on the ward; another, if an individual becomes a more growth-oriented and self-directing person.

To complicate matters further, such terms as "recovery," "marked improvement," and "fair improvement" are open to considerable differences in interpretation, and there is always the possibility that spontaneous improvement or "regression toward the mean"—which in essence means a change in the direction of less deviant behavior—will be attributed to the particular form of treatment used. In spite of these difficulties, however, it is possible to study the effectiveness of various treatment approaches separately—determining what procedures work best with various types of individuals. In the course of our discussion of abnormal behavior patterns we have mentioned a number of such studies, most of which have demonstrated positive outcomes from psychotherapy.

In this context, it is relevant to ask what happens to people who do not obtain formal treatment. In view of the many ways that people can help each other, it is not surprising that there may be considerable improvement without therapeutic intervention. Some forms of psychopathology, such as manic-depressive reactions and some types of schizophrenia, appear to run a fairly predictable course even without treatment; and there are many instances in which disturbed persons improve over time for reasons that are not apparent.

But even if many emotionally disturbed individuals would improve over time without psychotherapy, it seems clear that psychotherapy can often accelerate such improvement or ensure desired behavior change that might not otherwise occur. Thus we can summarize by saying that the experience of psychotherapy usually appears to have a beneficial effect.

But the issue of evaluation remains a vital one. Controlled programs of research and evaluation are essential. Rotter (1971) has issued a stern warning:

"It seems to me that if psychologists are not more active and explicit in their evaluation of techniques of intervention, they will find themselves restrained from the outside (as are drug companies by the FDA) as a result of their own failure to do what ethical and scientific considerations require. Clinical psychologists must become more concerned with formal and informal studies of the effects of their own methods of treatment . . . and the ethical considerations involved in practicing a method of intervening in other people's lives." (p. 2)

THE ISSUE OF VALUES

Many persons—both inside and outside the mental health professions—have come to see psychotherapy primarily as an attempt to get people adjusted to a "sick" society. As Halleck (1971) has described it, "therapy is the handmaiden of the status quo." (p. 30) Such charges, of course, bring us back to the question we raised in Chapter 1: What do we mean by "abnormal"? Our answer to that question must be made in the light of our values.

Mental health professionals have further been accused of concentrating on individual dynamics and ignoring social injustices and inequities that foster and maintain maladaptive behavior. Hallowitz (1970) has pointedly asked:

"Is it possible that we have been so preoccupied with the inner conflicts of our patients that we have neglected doing something about those other forces in our society that have contributed to, exacerbated, or perhaps even produced the individual pathology?" (p. 424)

Critics go on to charge that the mental health profession is geared to help middle-class individuals who come from relatively favorable environmental conditions, rather than those who have been thwarted and emotionally crippled by adverse economic and social conditions. As Sager (1968) has expressed it:

"The social conditions of the ghetto, the intertwisted network of social agencies that decide the fate of its residents, combine to repel or overwhelm us. Confrontation with the dead-end plight of a family or with the desperate inability of an individual to extricate himself from his crushing environment forces us to realize that our therapeutic task, when performed in keeping with the models we were taught, is equally hopeless." (p. 421)

In a broader perspective, of course, we are concerned with the complex and controversial issue of the role of values in science. For psychotherapy is not a system of ethics but a set of tools to be used at the discretion of the therapist. Thus mental health professionals are confronted with the same kind of question that confronts scientists in general. Should the physical sci-

IS INVOLUNTARY COMMITMENT A CRIME?

The individual who feels the need for intensive therapeutic assistance with emotional problems can voluntarily enter any of a wide range of hospital facilities. Usually such patients have the right to leave whenever they wish. A sizable number of patients are involuntarily committed by court order, however, after psychiatric and/or psychological examination and observation. Here we are not referring to persons labeled as criminally insane and committed to maximum security institutions, but rather to individuals who are considered potentially dangerous to themselves or others and are committed by court order to regular mental hospitals. In such cases, the patient is not free to leave the hospital against medical advice—that is, before the staff feels he is ready to be discharged.

A number of investigators have emphasized the dehumanizing and other adverse effects of involuntary commitment and "total institutionalization" on the patient.

"On admission to the institution, people are characteristically deprived of most of their personal possessions, their civil rights, their social status, their accustomed satisfactions, their privacy, and their individuality, so that they can be handled expeditiously in large groups. Throughout the period of institutionalization, the patient's behavior is closely regulated and accommodated to fixed hospital routines. Under these types of organizational contingencies, initiative, self-reliance, and self-determination . . . are generally extinguished. . . ." (Bandura, 1969, pp. 261–262)

With such procedures in mind, Szasz has referred to involuntary hospitalization as "the crime of commitment."

"Involuntary mental hospitalization remains today what it has been ever since its inception in the 17th Century: an extra-legal, quasi-medical form of social control for persons who annoy or disturb others and whose nonconformity cannot be controlled through the criminal law. To be sure the rhetoric has changed . . . . But the social reality remains the same: commitment is still punishment without trial, imprisonment without time limit, and stigmatization without hope of redress." (1969, p. 57)

In essence, Szasz views involuntary commitment as a form of social control which identifies and immobilizes those with deviant ideas in much the same way that the inquisitors of medieval times identified and tortured witches. This phenomenon, of course, has been noted in certain communist countries where writers whose views are in disagreement with established doctrine are sent to mental hospitals for "treatment" rather than to prisons for punishment.

Such charges may seem overly dramatic, and they ignore the question of what should be done about persons who are in fact incompetent and/or potentially dangerous to themselves and others. They do, however, draw attention to the fact that such evaluations should be made with extreme care and proper legal safeguards to protect the individual from infringement of his civil rights. And, of course, the dehumanizing aspects of involuntary hospitalization should be minimized.

---

entist who helps develop thermonuclear weapons be morally concerned about how they are used? Similarly, should the psychologist or behavioral scientist who develops powerful techniques of behavior control be concerned about how they are used?

Many psychologists and other scientists try to sidestep this issue by insisting that science is value free—that it is concerned only with gathering "facts," not with how they are applied. But the increasing social awareness of today's mental health professional has brought into sharp focus ethical questions concerning his role as therapist and value model as well as his role as an agent for maintaining the status quo or fostering social change. For therapy takes place in a context which involves the values of the therapist, his client, and the society in which they live. There are strong pressures on the therapist—from parents, schools, courts, and other social institutions—to help people adjust to "the world as it is." At the same time there are many

counterpressures, particularly from young people who are seeking support in their attempts to become authentic persons rather than blind conformists.

The dilemma in which the contemporary therapist often finds himself is well illustrated by the following case example.

A 15-year-old high-school sophomore is sent to a therapist because her parents have discovered that she has been having sexual intercourse with her boyfriend. The girl tells the therapist that she thoroughly enjoys such relations and feels no guilt or remorse over her behavior, even though her parents strongly disapprove. In addition, she reports that she is acutely aware of the danger of becoming pregnant and is very careful to take contraceptive measures.

What is the role of the therapist? Should he encourage her to conform to the mores of society and postpone the gratification of her sexual needs until she is older and more mature? Or, if he believes that what she is doing is not harmful to others, even though it is contrary to parental and social norms, should he help her adjust to the pattern of sexual behavior which she has chosen?

It becomes apparent that there are diametrically opposed ways of dealing with the same problems in therapy. Society must enforce conformity to certain norms if it is to maintain its organization and survive. But how does one distinguish between those norms which are relevant and valid and those which are irrelevant and outmoded? It is often up to the individual therapist to decide what path to take, and this requires value decisions on his part concerning what is best for the individual and for the larger society. Thus mental health professionals find themselves confronted with the problem of "controlling the controller"; that is, of developing ethical standards and societal safeguards to prevent misuse of the techniques they have developed for modifying individual and group behavior.

THE HUMAN POTENTIAL MOVEMENT

Recently we have seen a great deal of experimentation with procedures designed to increase the self-understanding and awareness of essentially normal people and help them find pathways to enriched experience and to more meaningful human relationships. The basic idea underlying this "human potential movement" is that the average person actually utilizes only a fraction of the creativity, feeling, and experiencing of which he is capable. The primary objective is to help individuals learn to become more spontaneous and creative, drop their façades and be more authentic in their interactions with others, and try out new ways of feeling, communicating, and being.

A wide range of techniques for achieving this objective are being explored—including exercises in relaxation and sensory awareness; nude

RELIGION AND PSYCHOTHERAPY

Although some colleges and universities have courses in the psychology of religion, most do not; and psychology as a field of science has tended to simply ignore religion and its role in man's life. But much as psychologists are beginning to realize the necessity for social relevance in other areas, many are taking an interest in the role of religion in man's existence. In this connection, many psychotherapists are recognizing the emotional support that religion can give to disturbed and unhappy people, and a number of large churches are employing mental health professionals as full- or part-time members of the church staff.

A great variety of religious movements are springing up among young people today. One example is the rapidly growing "Jesus Movement." Apparently young people are sincerely searching for answers to the value problems with which they are confronted and for a meaningful and fulfilling way of life. For many of these young people, religious faith supplies values to live by as well as a meaning they have failed to find through other channels. The late Dr. Reinhold Niebuhr has been quoted as saying, "Religious faith is basically a trust that life, however difficult and strange, has ultimate meaning." (*Los Angeles Times*, 1971, p. 1)

The following is a statement made by a student who felt that he had found the solution in religious faith to rather severe emotional difficulties, including inner conflict, confusion, anxiety, and guilt. During his freshman year in college, he became acquainted with a group of students who seemingly "had something different

in their lives—a joy and enthusiasm I had never known." Although he was skeptical of their approach, he decided to give it a try.

"I can honestly say that I have never been the same since! Christ has given me a new meaning and purpose for living, a genuine joy and lasting peace within. He has freed me from the guilt that used to plague me and replaced discouragement with hope. . . . He has given me the power to live the kind of life I have always wanted to live."

This statement was made during his senior year in college, and is indicative of the enduring nature of the change he experienced.

Man lives in a vast universe in which distance is sometimes measured in terms of trillions of light years, and to pretend that we understand the nature of this universe or the forces in it would be grandiose indeed. It would be equally foolish to ignore the fact that many people do undergo major changes in values and life style after spiritual experiences in which they feel that somehow they can tune into or open their hearts to forces in the universe that are much greater than they can hope to understand. Of course, many so-called hard-headed scientists would explain away such experiences as the product of naivety or wishful thinking but other equally hard-headed scientists would not. In any event, it is of interest to note that the great religious philosophies of the world share many value precepts in common, including the importance of love, peace, brotherhood, and the Golden Rule.

sensitivity training; Tai Chi (meditation in movement); dance; meditation; body massage; the celebration of life as a religious experience; seminars on love, sex, Zen Buddhism, Yoga, and many other topics; gestalt therapy workshops; transactional analysis; and encounter groups. Although there is no fixed format, group interaction is usually strongly emphasized; most of our conventional ideas about thinking, feeling, and relating to each other come under scrutiny; and a great deal of freedom is provided for exploring new pathways in experiencing.

Although the human potential movement was initially quite apart from psychotherapy—stemming from attempts to counteract an alleged overemphasis on intellectual development at the expense of emotional and social development in our society—the two may blend imperceptibly in such settings as gestalt workshops and encounter groups. In the latter context, Rogers (1967) has pointed out that

"It seems evident from our review of the group process that in a climate of freedom, group members move toward becoming more spontaneous, flexible, closely related to their feelings, open to their experience, and closer and more expressively intimate in their interpersonal relationships. If we value this type of person and this type of behavior, then clearly the group process is a valuable process. If, on the other hand, we place a value on the individual who is effective in suppressing his feelings, who operates from a firm set of principles, who does not trust his own reactions and experiences but relies on authority, and who remains aloof in his interpersonal relationships, then we would regard the group process, as I have tried to describe it, as a dangerous force." (p. 275)

The human potential movement is but one aspect of the growing concern with creating a healthier society. With its emphasis on fostering greater self-understanding, increased sensory awareness, enriched emotional experiencing, and more intimate and fulfilling personal relationships, it may well represent a counterforce to dehumanization in our age of impersonal mass bureaucracy.

Just as we look on Cro-Magnon man as extremely primitive in his personal, emotional, and social development, so may people of the twenty-first century look back at us as extremely primitive in terms of the actualization of our human potentialities. In any event, the human potential movement, together with the growing social consciousness of mental health personnel, appears to augur well for the future. Whether these trends will have sufficient strength and impact to counteract the negative forces in our society remains to be seen. But they do appear to be providing momentum in a constructive direction.

In this chapter we have discussed a wide range of approaches to therapy—biological, psychosocial, and sociocultural—examining both standard techniques and new developments. We have noted the general trend toward an interdisciplinary approach to treatment, and we have also commented on more specific trends. Among the latter were the increasing emphasis on the use of behavior therapy in modifying specific maladaptive behaviors and on the humanistic-existential therapies in fostering self-understanding and personal growth. We have also noted the new emphasis on interpersonal and encounter-group therapies as well as the increasing concern with modifying pathological social conditions which foster the development and maintenance of maladaptive behavior. And in the closing sections we have glanced briefly at some of the issues and trends of concern in the field of therapy today. In our final chapter, which now follows, we shall take up the problem of preventing mental disorders and fostering comprehensive health; the problem of building a good future for man; and the challenge these problems pose for all of us who share the dream of a better society in a better world.

Action for Mental Health and a Better World

21

PERSPECTIVES ON PREVENTION

ORGANIZED EFFORTS FOR MENTAL HEALTH

HORIZONS IN MENTAL HEALTH

"Some men look at the way things are and say why.
I dream things that never were and say why not."
Robert F. Kennedy (1968)

As modern psychology, psychiatry, and allied fields have become established and sophisticated sciences, they have directed their efforts toward preventing as well as assessing and treating abnormal behavior. Just as medical science developed vaccines and antitoxins for treating smallpox and diptheria, so the contemporary social sciences are attempting to formulate and apply principles that can help us prevent maladaptive behavior and foster a better world for man. Such efforts are taking place on international as well as national and local levels, and by governmental, professional, and voluntary citizen groups.

What we have said in earlier chapters concerning the causation of abnormal behavior has, of course, direct implications for its prevention. We know that metabolic deficiencies as well as sociocultural deprivation underlie certain types of mental retardation, and it has become possible to detect and correct many of these conditions before development is seriously arrested. Unfortunately, we lack sufficient knowledge about the causes of the functional psychoses and other forms of maladaptive behavior to be equally positive and specific in preventing them. However, as our understanding of maladaptive behavior is continually augmented by new scientific findings, we are becoming increasingly capable of preventing the unhappiness and waste of human potentials that mental disorders inevitably exact.

In this, our final chapter, we shall examine the nature of preventive measures and the scope of organized efforts for mental health; and we shall suggest some of the contributions that the individual can make to prevent mental disorders and help build a better world for man on the spaceship Earth.

PERSPECTIVES ON PREVENTION

In the prevention of mental disorders we are concerned with two key tasks: seeking out and eradicating the causes of mental disorders, and establishing conditions which foster positive mental health. Preventive measures thus run the gamut from programs directed toward known and specific causal agents to programs aimed at more general social advances.

In our present discussion we shall utilize the concepts of primary, secondary, and tertiary prevention, which we introduced briefly in Chapter 7 in connection with military psychology and psychiatry.

PRIMARY PREVENTION

Primary prevention includes all measures designed to foster healthy development and effective coping behavior—on biological, psychological, and sociocultural levels.

1. *Physical health measures.* Preventive physical health measures begin with help in family planning and include both prenatal and postnatal care. A good deal of current emphasis is being placed on guidance in family planning— how many children to have, when to have them in relation to marital and other family conditions, and even whether to have children at all. Such guidance may include genetic counseling, in which chromosomal maps may be made for potential parents to assess their risk of having defective children.

Breakthroughs in research on the genetic code may make it possible for man to correct faulty genes, thus providing him with fantastic new power to prevent hereditary pathology. But while this would help ensure a healthy beginning in life, it would not minimize the crucial importance of adequate prenatal and postnatal care—including medical supervision to ensure adequate nutrition for the expectant mother, obstetric care at the time of delivery, and follow-up postnatal care.

2. *Psychological health measures.* Our definition of *normality* as "optimal development and functioning" implies opportunities for learning needed competencies—physical, intellectual, emotional, and social. As we have seen, failure to develop the skills required for effective problem solving, for handling emotions constructively, and for establishing satisfying interpersonal relationships places the individual at a serious disadvantage in coping with life problems.

A second crucial psychological health measure involves acquiring an accurate frame of reference—in terms of reality, possibility, and value assumptions. We have seen repeatedly that when an individual's assumptions about himself or his world are inaccurate, his behavior is likely to be maladaptive. Likewise, inability to find satisfying values that foster a meaningful and fulfilling life constitutes a fertile source of maladjustment and mental disorders.

Psychological health measures also ordinarily require preparation of the individual for the types of problems he is likely to encounter during given life stages. For example, childbirth usually has a great deal of emotional significance to both parents. As we have seen, pregnancy and childbirth may disturb family equilibrium or exacerbate an already disturbed marital situation. Thus family planning may involve psychological as well as physical health considerations. Similarly, the individual needs to be prepared adequately for other developmental tasks characteristic of given life periods, including old age.

3. *General sociocultural measures.* With our growing realization of the importance of pathological social conditions in producing maladaptive behavior, increased attention is being focused on broad sociocultural measures that will foster the healthy development and effective functioning of all members of the group.

This trend is reflected in a wide spectrum of social measures ranging from public education and social security to economic planning. More specifically, it involves such measures as housing projects to eradicate slums, social legislation

PREVENTIVE INTERVENTION IN A HIGH SCHOOL

An example of "primary prevention" in a school setting is the Student Schools Effectiveness Committee (SSEC) at the public high school in Ansonia, Connecticut, which was set up by joint action of the school's psychological consultant and the school administration. Its purposes are to (1) assess the attitudes and needs of the students; (2) promote general interest in and commitment to the school by increasing the students' participation in and influence on school affairs; and (3) mobilize support for needed changes in the school. Every week its 15 members—who were selected by student government representatives—meet with the consultant to discuss the quality of life at the school and formulate ideas for improving it. Among the topics discussed are dress codes, discipline, student government, racism, and the curriculum. The group has become an important force in working toward constructive change in the school and has provided a powerful and meaningful channel for personal growth for the members.

One program in which the group has taken part was a collaborative student-faculty program set up to fulfill the state's requirement for drug education. Unlike many drug-education programs, which are based on scare tactics and seen by students as propaganda, the Ansonia program was aimed at preparing students to make their own decisions intelligently by providing an opportunity for honest dialogue, a sharing of experiences, and an analysis of the personal and social dynamics of drug use.

The SSEC was asked to nominate teachers whom students especially liked and trusted, and from these nominations 8 teachers were selected to attend a summer session of the Drug Dependence Institute at nearby Yale University. Then, in the fall, "communication groups" of students were set up, each containing an ethnic mix of both sexes. These groups held weekly meetings over a period of 10 to 15 weeks with one of the trained teachers (left).

A further unusual feature of the program was a series of small-group sessions involving other faculty members, set up to interpret the program to them after some friction due to misunderstanding. Each small group contained one of the teachers in the program (right). The discussions held by these groups generated better understanding and acceptance of the program, as well as useful new ideas which were incorporated into the program (Trickett, 1971).

to ensure more equal educational and job opportunities, programs such as Head Start to prevent later educational and personal problems, Medicare and Medicaid to better meet the health needs of people, and ecological planning to cope with our multiple environmental problems. Such sociocultural measures must, of course, take into consideration the future stresses and health problems we are likely to encounter in our rapidly changing society.

As the National Institute of Mental Health has summarized the matter, "In the final analysis, the mental health of each citizen is affected by the maturity and health of our society—from the smallest unit to the largest." (1969, p. 120)

SECONDARY PREVENTION

Secondary prevention emphasizes the early detection and prompt treatment of maladaptive behavior in the individual's family and commu-

THE TIME TO MANAGE A CRISIS IS BEFORE THE CONFRONTATION

This unusual picture was taken in Austin, Texas, in May 1970—the same week that four students were killed by National Guard action at Kent State University. Here, too, feelings had run high at news of the Cambodian invasion, and on Tuesday, in a spontaneous demonstration following the Kent State announcement, there was some rock-throwing and use of tear gas. There was fear that things might get out of hand in a parade being planned for Friday in defiance of the city council's refusal to grant a permit.

Intelligent preventive measures, initiated long before the crisis, were an important factor in preventing further violence. The members of the police force were highly selected and well trained: many had taken courses in psychology, sociology, and community relations, and some had received special training in managing civil disturbances without overreaction. Students from the University of Texas Law School had gone on patrol with police officers and fed back their impressions. Members of the psychology faculty had helped design the police training program and were at the time conducting a consultation project with the police department.

During the tense three days, a number of people with varied knowledge and expertise worked together to keep channels of communication open, building on the trust relationships that already existed to help each side see the other as being in a difficult position and as basically reasonable and well intentioned. Meanwhile, the faculty supported the students and worked with them to prevent violence: students were taught ways to deal with tear gas and mace and were urged not to respond to provocation; 300 faculty and students volunteered to act as marshals, and it was decided to march on the sidewalk, which was legal. Even so, those at the center of the effort found it "a chilling experience to observe both parties to a confrontation preparing for combat, each hoping and wishing that its preparations will prove unnecessary." (Mann & Iscoe, 1971, p. 111)

At the last minute, a group of law students, aided by professors and community legal talent, succeeded in getting a restraining order against enforcement of the parade ordinance. In the end, 20,000 students, faculty, and even some parents marched peacefully in support of numerous worthy causes—even including "higher pay for Austin police." The spirit that prevailed is reflected in the picture. It was felt generally that extreme polarization and violence had been prevented only because communication channels and relationships of trust had been established previously on which those working during the crisis could build.

nity setting. Thus it is concerned with the incidence and scope of maladaptive behavior in specific populations, with the early detection of such behavior, with the variety and availability of mental health facilities, and with crisis intervention.

Science has found that most contagious physical diseases can be brought under control once their distribution and modes of communication are discovered via epidemiological studies. In Chapter 15, for example, we noted the application of the epidemiological approach to the early detection and eradication of syphilis in a major urban area. Epidemiological studies are also helping investigators obtain information concerning the incidence and distribution of various maladaptive behaviors in our society. For example, epidemiological studies have shown that areas with a high concentration of residences occupied by other than husband-wife families—

single people, groups, or female-headed households—are likely to have many people with problems, as are neighborhoods in which there is a high turnover. In a generally homogeneous area, those who are different are a high-risk group. School dropouts, working mothers, aged persons living alone, and disabled persons also tend to be high-risk groups (Redick, Goldsmith & Unger, 1971).

Epidemiological studies tell us what to look for and where to look; the next step is to deal with these trouble spots. Since 1950 we have witnessed a marked increase in the variety and availability of mental health facilities in the United States. The new comprehensive community mental health centers are of particular significance, since they mark a distinct trend away from the traditional state mental hospital approach. As we have seen, such centers are designed to provide both inpatient and outpatient treatment, partial hospitalization on either a day or a night basis, and emergency services 24 hours a day—in essence, to provide individuals and families with the type of care they need when they need it and close to home. Further, the community mental health center makes it possible to elicit the active participation of members of the community in planning the treatment programs that will best meet the needs of its particular population and in serving as nonprofessional volunteers.

As hoped from the beginning, there are wide differences in the services offered by different centers, even those in the same city, and often a center will have "satellites" or "outposts" that offer particular kinds of help in particular neighborhoods. For example, the South Central Community Mental Health Center in Atlanta has 5 satellites, each with its own staff and orientation. One concentrates on children's services, another on drug problems; still another, in a public housing development, tries to encourage a sense of community by promoting neighborhood projects, including a cooperative food store and a course on how residents can organize themselves politically. The South Central center has also helped make arrangements with a nearby college for a 2-year training program for mental health technicians (Holden, 1971).

We have dealt with the nature of life crises and crisis intervention in earlier chapters and need not go into detail again here. However, it may be emphasized that such crises may confront individuals of all ages, as well as family groups, communities, and even entire societies. A common problem of children receiving assistance at community mental health centers involves transient situational reactions to special stresses or crises. Similarly, we have noted the trauma that divorce can bring to a family, or that racial conflict can bring to a community.

Emergency services for all manner of emotional problems are increasingly available not only in the community mental health centers and the psychiatric wards of general hospitals but also via the "hot lines" described in earlier chapters. These telephone services bring help to many troubled people who would never present themselves at a mental health facility. Callers seek help with a wide range of problems including personal relationships, drugs, sex, family conflicts, legal questions, loneliness, and abortion.

It is not possible, of course, to prevent crises altogether, nor would we wish to avoid all stress and challenge. *The Happy Prince* by Oscar Wilde (1888) illustrates the problems likely to befall the person who attempts to avoid all the troubles consequent to life. Successful mastery of challenges and crises is needed for individual and group growth. On the other hand, failure to deal adequately with crises can lead to the breakdown of individual or group functioning. Thus crisis intervention must be considered a crucial aspect of secondary prevention.

School is one of the chief arenas where a child tests himself to find out what he can do. Success experiences in school, especially in the early years, are vitally important if children are to gain the self-confidence they will need all their lives for meeting new challenges. Often, however, children with special problems experience failure because their needs are not recognized and taken into account in the instructional program.

The Learning Center in the Ray Public School in Chicago, shown here, was opened with federal funds in 1968 to offer special programs for slow learners and children with special talents. It offered something to intrigue every kind of student—from crocheting (with practical mathematics thrown in) to computer programming by talented older children of question-and-answer games they had created for use by younger children in learning reading and arithmetic. Two large rooms housed the group, and the staff included 3 paid teachers and 30 volunteers.

The Learning Center's success in devising individual instruction and in raising achievement levels attracted country-wide attention and brought many visitors. But despite its success and the great need for its services, funds could not be found for its continuation past the end of 1971, and it was closed.

TERTIARY PREVENTION

Despite crisis intervention and other secondary preventive measures, some persons do require hospitalization for emotional disorders. Tertiary prevention involves prompt and intensive inpatient treatment for such disorders. Its aim is to prevent the disorder from becoming chronic and to enable the individual to return to his home setting as soon as possible. Project Re-Ed, described on page 597, is an example of tertiary prevention with children. Here children too disturbed to be treated at home spend several months in a special environment designed to help them learn more adaptive behavior.

In many cases, intensive inpatient treatment can be given in the local community mental health center or in a nearby general hospital. But even where the individual requires treatment in a state mental hospital—which is usually a considerable distance from his home—the emphasis is on brief hospitalization and long-range follow-up care. Such follow-up care becomes the primary responsibility of community mental health facilities and personnel as well as of the person's family and of the community as a whole. It seeks to ensure that the individual will be helped make an adequate readjustment and return to full participation in his home and community setting with a minimum of delay and difficulty.

Even in a society as affluent as ours, the comprehensive preventive approach that we have outlined—involving primary, secondary, and tertiary prevention—places a heavy strain on our resources. However, the alternative would be even more costly in both financial and human terms. Fortunately, as we noted in Chapter 4, there is a strong trend in our society toward the comprehensive public health concept—the goal advanced by the World Health Organization of "a sound mind, in a sound body, in a sound society."

ORGANIZED EFFORTS FOR MENTAL HEALTH

With increasing public awareness of the magnitude and severity of our contemporary mental health problem, a large number of governmental, professional, and lay organizations have joined in a concerted attack on mental disorders—a broad-based attack directed toward better understanding, more effective treatment, and long-range prevention. This trend is apparent not only in our society but also in many other countries. And international as well as national and local organizations and measures are involved.

GOVERNMENTAL, PROFESSIONAL, AND LAY ORGANIZATIONS

Traditionally, dealing with mental disorders has been primarily the responsibility of state and local agencies. During World War II, however, the extent of mental disorders in the United States was brought to public attention when a large number of young men—2 out of every 7

recruits—were rejected for military service for psychiatric reasons. This discovery, in turn, led to a variety of organized measures for coping with the mental health problem.

The government and mental health. Aware of the need for more research, training, and services in the field of mental health, Congress in 1946 passed its first comprehensive mental health bill, the National Mental Health Act, which laid the basis for the federal government's present mental health program.

The 1946 bill provided for the establishment of a National Institute of Mental Health (NIMH) in or near Washington, D.C., to serve as a central research and training center and headquarters for the administration of a grant-in-aid program. The grant-in-aid feature was designed to foster research and training elsewhere in the nation and to help state and local communities expand and improve their own mental health services. New powers were conferred on NIMH in 1956, when Congress, under Title V of the Health

Amendments Act, authorized the Institute to provide "mental health project grants" for experimental studies, pilot projects, surveys, and general research having to do with the understanding, assessing, treating, and aftercare of mental disorders.

Today NIMH is the largest single source of financial support for research and training in mental health and for upgrading mental health services. Its role is largely that of an enabler: most of its funds are allocated for programs and activities initiated and carried out by others. Federal grants through NIMH help graduate schools defray teaching costs and provide stipends for students for training in medicine, psychiatry, psychology, nursing, social work, public health, and other specialties. Similar grants help hospitals reorganize and improve their facilities and move toward smaller, community-based units. Pilot projects and demonstrations supported by NIMH funds have pioneered and tested innovative methods in prevention, therapy, and rehabilitation, and publications of many kinds put out by NIMH are disseminating new information to mental health workers of all types throughout the country.

One recent pioneering effort of NIMH has been in the development of 2-year training programs for mental health workers in junior and community colleges for which the Associate of Arts degree is awarded. Curricula vary but generally include (1) general education courses in humanities, physical sciences, and social sciences; (2) courses in mental health-related areas such as psychology and social work; and (3) courses providing practical experience in agencies serving mental health needs. The first such program began at Purdue with NIMH support as recently as 1966; by 1970, the idea had caught on to the extent that there were at least 45 such programs, only a few of which had required grants from NIMH to get started.

In addition to this facilitation of study, training, and service by others, NIMH itself operates several centers for the study of particular mental health problems. These serve as focal points for research on causes, prevention, and treatment of particular problems and for training of personnel. Included here are separate centers for studies of suicide prevention, narcotic and drug abuse, metropolitan problems, crime and delinquency, epidemiology, schizophrenia, child and family mental health, and mental health and social problems.

NIMH is only one of the federal agencies working in the mental health field. Among the numerous others concerned with related problems are: National Center for Health Services Research and Development, Community Health Service, National Institute of Environmental Health Sciences, National Institute of Child Health and Human Development, and Youth Development and Delinquency Prevention Administration.

A central concept in the federal government's mental health program, as we have seen, is that of comprehensive care in the community. This concept was first implemented by legislation in 1963 which outlined a national program for mental health and a related program to combat mental retardation. The next milestone came in 1967 with the Report of the National Commission on Community Mental Health Services, which further emphasized the concept of mental health as a community affair and supplied additional guidelines for the community mental health movement; it led to the passage two years later of the Community Mental Health Centers Act which provided for the construction and staffing of community mental health centers throughout the nation. Since 1970 we have seen the advent of a number of new programs, including the establishment of a National Center for Child Advocacy.

Although the federal government provides leadership and financial aid, the states and localities actually plan and run most programs. In addition, the states establish, maintain, and supervise their own mental hospitals and clinics. A number of states have also pioneered, through their own legislation, in the development of community mental health centers, rehabilitation services in the community for ex-patients, and facilities for dealing with alcoholism, drug abuse, and other special mental health problems. A significant trend has been in the development of state "Community Mental Health Services Acts," by which states provide grants-in-aid to localities for the development and expansion of local mental health services. Usually the programs also provide consultant services to schools, courts, and welfare agencies.

Through the combination of federal grants and state funds, a wide range of vital mental health

PROFESSIONAL ORGANIZATIONS CONCERNED WITH MENTAL HEALTH

American Psychological Association (APA)	An association of professionally trained psychologists. Its purpose is to advance psychology as a science, as a profession, and as a means of promoting human welfare. It has 30 divisions concerned with various special areas within psychology, and it establishes and monitors standards for the training and practice of psychologists in mental health areas.
American Psychiatric Association (APA)	An association of medically trained psychiatrists. Its purpose is to further study of the nature, treatment, and prevention of mental disorders; to help set, improve, and maintain standards of practice and service in mental hospitals, clinics, general hospital psychiatric units, and institutions for the mentally retarded; to further psychiatric research and education; and to foster enlightened views with regard to the social and legal aspects of psychopathology and the role of psychiatry in fostering human welfare.
American Medical Association (AMA)	An association of physicians who are members of constituent state medical associations. In addition to its myriad other functions, it is concerned with mental disorders as a general health problem and with fostering research, education, and legislation to advance comprehensive health efforts in the United States.
American Psychoanalytic Association (APA)	An association of analytically trained psychiatrists. It sets standards for the training of psychoanalysts, fosters research, and is concerned with the alleviation of social problems.
American Sociological Association (ASA)	An association of sociologists, social scientists, and other professional persons interested in research, teaching, and application of sociology. Its sections on Social Psychology, Medical Sociology, and Criminology have special pertinence to mental health.
National Association of Social Workers (NASW)	An association of professionally trained social workers, organized to promote the quality and effectiveness of social work and to foster mental health. It establishes and monitors standards for training and practice, encourages research, and interprets the role of social work in the community.
American Nurses Association (ANA) and National League for Nursing (NLN)	An association of registered nurses concerned with high standards of professional practice. Two of its clinical conference groups (one on Psychiatric Nursing Practice and one on Maternal and Child Health Nursing) have special mental health concerns. A Coordinating Council unites its program with that of the National League for Nursing, a voluntary organization of professional, semi-professional, and lay persons and of institutions and organizations; the National League is the principal standard-setting group in the nursing field.
American Occupational Therapy Association (AOTA)	A society of registered occupational therapists administering medically supervised activities to physically or mentally ill persons. It maintains standards of education and training, makes surveys and recommendations on request, and works with its state association in the preparation and certification of occupational therapy volunteer assistants.

facilities and activities has been made possible, including financing of badly needed basic research in the field of mental disorders.

Professional organizations and mental health. There are a number of professional organizations in the mental health field. Some of the most influential of these are listed in the chart above.

One of the most important functions of these organizations is to set and maintain high professional and ethical standards within their special areas. This function may include: (1) establishing and reviewing training qualifications for professional and paraprofessional personnel; (2) setting standards and procedures for accreditation of undergraduate and graduate training programs; (3) setting standards for accreditation of clinic,

hospital, or other service operations and carrying out inspections to see that the standards are followed; and (4) investigating reported cases of unethical or unprofessional conduct, and taking disciplinary action where necessary.

A second key function of these professional organizations involves communication and information exchange within their fields via meetings, symposia, workshops, refresher courses, and related activities. In addition, all such organizations sponsor programs of public education as a means of advancing the interests of their professions, drawing attention to mental health needs, and attracting students to careers in their professional fields.

A third key function of professional organiza-

National Rehabilitation Association (NRA)	An association of physicians, counselors, therapists, and others (including organizations) concerned with rehabilitation of the physically and mentally handicapped. Reviews existing services and makes recommendations for improved rehabilitation programs.
American Orthopsychiatric Association (AOA)	An organization of psychiatrists, psychologists, social workers, sociologists, and members of other disciplines working in a collaborative approach to the study and treatment of human behavior, primarily in clinical settings. The AOA encourages research and is directly concerned with fostering human welfare.
National Council for Family Relations (NCFR)	Primarily composed of and directed toward practitioners serving couples and families through counseling, therapy, education, and community service. The NCFR fosters research and the application of its findings to practice.
American Association on Mental Deficiency (AAMD)	An interdisciplinary association of doctors, educators, administrators, social workers, psychologists, psychiatrists, and others interested in assisting the mentally retarded. It works with the American Psychiatric Association in setting standards for hospitals and schools for the mentally retarded.
Council for Exceptional Children (CEC)	Made up largely of professional workers in fields dealing with mentally retarded, physically handicapped, and emotionally disturbed children. Fosters research and its applications, education, and social legislation relating to exceptional children.
Group for the Advancement of Psychiatry (GAP)	An invitational association of limited membership (approximately 185 psychiatrists at any one time). Members are organized into small committees for the purpose of studying and reporting on various aspects of psychiatry and on the applications of current knowledge. Its influential, action-directed reports are often developed through consultation and collaboration with experts from many other disciplines.
American Association for the Advancement of Science (AAAS)	Composed of scientists from many disciplines. Its objectives include furthering the work and mutual cooperation of scientists, improving the effectiveness of science and its contribution to human welfare, and increasing understanding and appreciation of the importance and promise of scientific methods in human progress.

Most of these organizations sponsor national conventions, workshops, symposia, and public educational programs and publish journals in their respective areas. They are also concerned with broad social problems as well as with the special problems in their professional areas.

tions, which is receiving increasing attention, is that of applying their insights and methods to contemporary social problems. The tenor of this approach is indicated by the theme of the 1969 convention of the American Psychological Association which was "Psychology and the Problems of Society." In his presidential address to the convention, George A. Miller stated, "We must somehow incorporate our hard-won knowledge more effectively into the vast social changes that we all know are coming—that must come if our nation and other nations are to survive and flourish." (p. 178) Similarly, the 1970 convention of the American Orthopsychiatric Association, whose membership includes psychologists, psychiatrists, and social workers, gave top priority

to its Council on Social Issues. And in his presidential address to the American Psychiatric Association in 1970, Raymond Waggoner urged the need for psychiatrists to be concerned about problems of racism, overpopulation, social commitment, and man's "search for a future":

"In sum, I plead for a psychiatry that is involved with fundamental social goals. I plead for a psychiatry that will eschew isolation altogether and assume its proper role in advancing the total health of our nation. I plead for a psychiatry that is at once concerned with individual liberty and communal responsibility. And I ask of psychiatrists that they be not only pragmatists but also dreamers with a vision of the future." (p. 8)

Composed as they are of qualified personnel, professional mental health organizations are in a unique position to serve as consultants on mental health problems and programs not only on the national level but also on state and local levels. Increasingly, they are establishing closer liaison with one another as well as with both governmental and voluntary agencies concerned with mental health.

Role of voluntary mental health organizations and agencies. While professional mental health personnel and organizations can give expert technical advice in regard to mental health needs and programs, real progress in helping plan and implement these programs must come from an informed and concerned citizenry. In fact, it has been repeatedly stated that it has been non-professionals who have blazed the trail in the mental health field.

The best-known voluntary mental health agency is the National Association for Mental Health (NAMH). It was founded in 1950 by the merger of the National Committee for Mental Hygiene, the National Mental Health Foundation, and the Psychiatric Foundation; and it was further expanded in 1962 by amalgamation with the National Organization for Mentally Ill Children. Through its national governing body and more than 1000 state and local affiliates, the NAMH works for the improvement of conditions and services in community clinics and mental hospitals; it helps recruit, train, and place volunteers for service in treatment and aftercare; and it works for enlightened mental health legislation and provision of needed facilities and personnel. It also carries on special educational programs aimed at helping people understand mental disorders and fostering positive mental health.

With a program and organization similar to that of the NAMH, the National Association for Retarded Children (NARC) works to reduce the incidence of mental retardation, to seek community and residential treatment centers and services for the retarded, and to carry on a program of education aimed at better public understanding of the retardate and greater support for legislation on the retardate's behalf. The NARC also fosters scientific research into mental retardation, the recruitment and training of volunteer workers, and sound programs of community action. On the local level, it is especially interested in forming groups of parents of retarded children, in order to help such parents better understand, accept, and deal with their children's limited capabilities.

These and other voluntary health organizations, such as Alcoholics Anonymous, are particularly American in their development of extensive programs of research, service, and training of volunteers financed by public donations. To succeed in their objectives, of course, they need the backing of a wide constituency of knowledgeable and involved citizens.

INTERNATIONAL EFFORTS FOR MENTAL HEALTH

Mental health is a major problem not only in the United States but in the rest of the world as well. Indeed, many of the unfavorable conditions in this country with regard to the causes and treatment of mental disorders are greatly magnified in developing countries throughout the world.

It was the knowledge of this great unmet need that served to bring about the formation of several international organizations at the end of World War II. We shall briefly review here the World Health Organization and the United Nations Educational, Scientific, and Cultural Organization (both agencies of the United Nations), as well as the World Federation for Mental Health.

The World Health Organization (WHO). It is the general function of the World Health Organization to formulate recommendations concerning physical and mental health to be carried out by member states of the United Nations. The Canadian psychiatrist Brock Chisholm, the first Director-General, said: "The desperate need of the human race at this most precarious stage of its development is for understanding of man and for the development of methods by which he can learn to live in peace with his kind." (1948, p. 543) Chisholm then called for study of the psychological conditions that stand in the way of man's physical and mental well-being.

A WHO Expert Committee on Mental Health had its first meeting in 1949 to formulate the principles that should govern the activities of WHO in the mental health field. In view of the very great needs and the shortage of professional personnel and facilities throughout the world, the Committee considered that it would be impossible to provide adequate facilities for therapy for mental disorders within the foreseeable future. As a consequence, the Committee placed its first emphasis upon the study and eradication of physical diseases like malaria, syphilis, and cardiovascular diseases, and upon improving the general physical health and welfare of the people of the world, while developing and applying mental health resources as rapidly as conditions permitted.

This committee, which has a rotating membership, has conducted studies and issued reports on a variety of mental disorders, on pathological social conditions, and on the development of community mental health facilities. It has made mental health consultants available to member states and has provided training grants and sponsored conferences and workshops both worldwide and local in scope. In 1968 the report of the WHO Project on International Classification of Mental Disorders was published; as we noted in Chapter 1, this forms the basis for our present classification scheme. A fuller summary of this formulation appears on the endsheets at the back of the book.

WHO has headquarters in Geneva and regional offices for Africa, the Americas, Southeast Asia, Europe, the Eastern Mediterranean, and the Western Pacific. Hence its activities extend into areas with diverse physical environments, types of social organization, and mental health facilities. In its work, WHO does not try to impose a predetermined plan on this diversity; rather it works toward identifying the basic needs of each country or region and then delineating the most useful efforts to be made. In helping member states through consultation or other assistance, WHO also strives to make its services available over a period of several years to ensure continuity and success for the programs that are undertaken. Since its inception, WHO has made many significant contributions to the fostering of physical and mental health among the peoples of the world.

The United Nations Educational, Scientific, and Cultural Organization (UNESCO). The constitution of UNESCO contains a statement which seems to strike many people with the force of a conversion: "Since wars begin in the minds of men, it is in the minds of men that the defenses of peace must be constructed." UNESCO seeks

"... to contribute to peace and security by promoting collaboration among the nations through education, science, and culture in order to further universal respect for justice, for the rule of law and for the human rights and fundamental freedoms for all." (1945)

Not all UN members belong to UNESCO and several nonmembers do (there were 126 members in 1972). UNESCO elects a Director-General,

UNESCO ACTIVITIES

UNESCO has sponsored a large number of studies and projects which are relevant to mental health. Only a few can be mentioned here.

1. **Studies of international tensions.** Examples of major works that have resulted from these studies are *Tensions that Cause Wars,* edited by Hadley Cantril; *The Human Dimension in International Relations,* by Otto Klineberg; and *In the Minds of Men,* by Gardner Murphy. These works have contributed to our understanding of the causes of war and suggest potential avenues toward world peace.

2. **Studies of racial discrimination and racial tensions.** These studies have culminated in a series of works published under the titles *Race and Society, The Race Question in Modern Science,* and *The Race Question and Modern Thought.* These works document the harmfulness of racial discrimination to the total structure of any society where it is practiced.

3. **Studies on differences in national cultures and on attitude formation and change.** Analyses of national "stereotypes" —ready-made conceptions of what people of different countries are like—and suggestions as to how the peoples of the world may be helped to understand each other better are some of the contributions from the studies in these important areas.

4. **Investigations of the influence of technological change on attitudes, living patterns, values, and relationships among people and groups.** The focus of these studies has been on the effects of stresses created by rapid change, especially their influence on mental health.

5. **Programs to foster understanding among peoples by travel, student exchange programs, fellowships, exhibitions, and other means.** Through educational efforts directed toward both people and governments throughout the world, UNESCO has sought to foster worldwide acceptance of the principles set forth in the United Nations Declaration on Human Rights.

UNESCO is also actively participating in a campaign for world literacy, hoping ultimately to achieve universal primary education in developing countries where many children do not now attend school. In this effort, modern technological resources may be teamed with age-old methods. For example, it will soon be possible for educational programs originating in Bombay, India, to be beamed throughout the country via a NASA satellite. In this way programs especially planned to meet local needs can be delivered to remote areas despite teacher shortages and poor transportation.

chooses an Executive Board, and holds a General Conference every two years at which a budget for the next two years is established and the contributions to be made by the member states are set. For 1971 and 1972 the budget was set at over 83 million dollars. The UNESCO programs are divided into four main sectors: (1) education, (2) natural sciences, (3) social and human sciences and culture, and (4) communication. On many problems UNESCO works cooperatively with other agencies—sometimes as instigator or catalyst, sometimes as consultant, sometimes as one of several cooperating groups. For example, the use of a NASA satellite for educational broadcasting in India, mentioned on page 717, was arranged by UNESCO and implemented by an American corporation.

UNESCO is also working to provide better opportunities for young people to participate actively in the social, economic, and cultural life of their own countries and of the world and is helping in the training of scientists and technicians, as well as in developing scientific research in developing countries. Thus on many fronts UNESCO is working for the progress of education, culture, and research and for the intellectual and moral unity of mankind in a peaceful world.

Perhaps the most appropriate conclusion to such a brief description of the multitudinous activities of WHO and UNESCO on behalf of mental health and social progress is a reminder of the early note of "careful urgency" sounded by Klineberg (1949):

"Our goal is, of course, research leading to action. There is a real and obvious danger in action which is premature. There is an equal danger in delaying action until it is too late. Our major difficulty lies in steering the proper course somewhere in between." (p. 10)

The problem of mental health on a world level is even more complex than the one we face in this country, and the formulation and application of effective measures on an international scale are correspondingly more difficult.

The World Federation for Mental Health. The World Federation for Mental Health was established in 1948 at an international congress of nongovernmental organizations and individuals concerned with mental health. Its purpose is to further cooperation at the international level between governmental and nongovernmental mental health agencies, and its membership now extends to more than 50 countries.

The Federation has been granted consultative status by both WHO and UNESCO, and it assists the UN agencies by collecting information on mental health conditions all over the world. Recently, its efforts have been focused on aiding developing countries through consultation with local mental health groups, holding regional workshops, and trying to combat the low priority often given to mental health planning in the emerging countries.

We have now seen something of the maze of local, national, and international measures for mental health. It is the first time in history that mental health problems have been viewed as having discoverable causes and as being amenable to treatment and prevention by scientific means, and it is also the first time that a systematic attack has been waged against these problems on a worldwide level. Many people now believe the statement Julian Huxley (1959) made over a decade ago, that through the advances of modern science and technology "human life could gradually be transformed from a competitive struggle against blind fate into a great collective enterprise, consciously undertaken . . . for greater fulfillment through the better realization of human potentialities." (p. 409)

LIMITATIONS IN MENTAL HEALTH EFFORTS

In contrast to the potential we now see and to the progress that has been achieved during the last half century in the understanding, treatment, and prevention of mental disorders is the inescapable fact that many limitations still exist, some of them caused by short-sightedness rather than by ignorance. Even in our own country, minimal mental health standards are far from being met, and often the standards themselves are open to question. In fact, the organization and delivery of mental health services in the United States is today lagging behind that of Israel, Sweden, and various other countries.

Limitations in personnel. There is a serious inadequacy in the number of professional and paraprofessional personnel to deal with the mental health problems of the more than 200 million people in our society. For example, in 1970 there were only 25,000 psychiatrists and about 7000 clinical psychologists in the United States, with comparable shortages of personnel in social work, psychiatric nursing, and other mental health fields. The personnel shortage is particularly acute for work with children.

The ratio is even more inadequate in most of the developing countries. For example, India, with an enormous population, still has only a handful of professionally trained mental health personnel; other developing countries have comparable or even more severe shortages of personnel.

Limitations in facilities. Despite the dramatic reduction in the number of patients in mental hospitals, many of the buildings still used to house mental patients are badly deteriorated and obsolete. Furthermore, the construction of the new community mental health centers required as a result of the shift toward local treatment has lagged badly; this, of course, affects the delivery of services to both young people and adults. Thus the recognized need for early detection and correction of behavior disorders before they become more severe and disabling is not being adequately met in most American communities. And, of course, facilities in the developing countries are practically nonexistent or at best woefully inadequate.

Limitations in research. In relation to the magnitude and social importance of mental disorders in our society, research in the area of mental health is very inadequately financed. In fact, we spend over 150 times as much money on alcohol as on research in mental health. And in the developing countries, very little research is being carried on. Yet it is apparent that a key factor in the effectiveness of the mental health movement is the research upon which its concepts and procedures are based.

There is evidence that the progress in mental health and community facilities made in the 1960's has lost its momentum as we have become more concerned with environmental problems than with mental health. Our mental health programs today suffer from both duplications and great gaps and thus often seem more a collection of bits and pieces than the integrated system we need, in which facilities will be matched against needs. In fact, Roe (1970) has proposed that the community mental health centers should be broadened to become full community resource centers, in which educational, occupational, legal, financial, and other services would be available—as well as mental health services—in order to help people cope with the many kinds of problems and crises that arise in everyday living. As we have seen, some multipurpose centers are available in disadvantaged urban

MENTAL HEALTH WORKERS

"Mental health workers" include people with a wide variety of skills. Below is a listing of the kinds of staff members working in 205 community mental health centers in 1969. The figures show the proportions of the different types of workers and include both full-time and part-time staff members, as well as trainees and volunteers (NIMH, 1970).

Discipline	Total Staff
Psychiatrists	1,981
Other physicians	325
Psychologists (master's degree and above)	1,145
Other psychologists	169
Social workers (master's degree and above)	1,728
Other social workers	633
Registered nurses	2,344
Vocational rehabilitation counselors and assistants	233
Occupational therapists and assistants	546
Recreational therapists and assistants	359
Other professionals, including teachers	1,364
Licensed practical nurses, nurses aides, attendants, psychiatric technicians or aides	3,815
Other nonprofessional mental health workers	2,601
All other personnel (clerical, fiscal, maintenance, etc.)	4,301
Total, all personnel	**21,544**

communities, and as the federal government's programs for better general health care for all citizens gather momentum, it seems likely that multipurpose centers will become more common.

Of course, neither the community mental health center nor a more general community service center will be the final or complete answer to our problems of mental health and effective living. Ultimately, we are faced with the problem of values and of the priorities we wish to place on the use of our resources in building a future world for man.

HORIZONS IN MENTAL HEALTH

The question has arisen as to whether we or any other technologically advanced nation can achieve mental health in isolation from the rest of the world, however great our efforts. Mental disorders, wars, international tensions, racism, poverty, and similar problems are interrelated. What happens to the rest of the world affects us also, both directly and indirectly. The possibility of nuclear war breeds anxiety about the future in the minds of all of us, and our military defenses against perceived threats in other parts of the world absorb vast funds and energy which otherwise might be turned to health, education, and a better quality of life for our citizens at home.

Thus it would appear that every measure undertaken to reduce international conflict and improve the condition of mankind makes its contribution to our own nation's programs for social progress and mental health. Without slackening our efforts at home, we shall probably find it increasingly essential to participate in international measures toward reducing group tensions and promoting mental health and a better world for man. These measures will require understanding, concern, and moral commitment from our citizens.

TOWARD A "GOOD FUTURE" FOR MAN

As we saw in Chapter 18, our present task, speaking broadly, is to learn to plan for the effective running of our spaceship before it is too late. This will require planning on community, national, and international levels.

To some people in our society, social planning seems contrary to the American way of life and the ideal of individual freedom. Yet as the NIMH (1969) has pointed out, "Social planning does not imply authoritarian control; a planned society does not mean a closed society. Techniques are now emerging to guarantee that planning will enhance, not diminish, the power and influence of individuals in controlling their destinies and achieving their personal goals. 'Advocacy planning' and 'participatory democracy' provide for the inclusion of all interested groups and individuals in the planning and decision-making process." (p. 117) In fact, to be planless in our complex, interdependent, and rapidly changing world is to invite—and perhaps ensure—disaster.

The "futurists." As Shepherd (1971) has pointed out, "Man may be headed for extinction, like the dinosaur." He adds, however, "Unlike the dinosaur, man has options." (p. 15)

Recently a growing number of scientists and organizations have become involved in delineating what man's options are—in delineating various possible futures for our own country and for mankind. In May 1970, 100 scientists from 16 nations met to discuss "Environment and Society in Transition." The conference was jointly sponsored by the American Division of the World Academy of Arts and Science and the American Geographical Society. On a more permanent basis, various scientific groups have been set up by the federal government, by our military establishments, by major universities, and by private foundations. These groups are composed of scientists from diverse fields and devote full time to considering the range of future alternatives open to us and the possible consequences of given alternatives. As we have already seen, the use of computers to simulate changes in social systems and to ascertain both the short-term and long-term consequences of the changes on the total system is receiving increasing emphasis.

Although these futurists are not comparable to psychotherapists on an individual or small-group level, they do provide somewhat the same functions in the society in helping people recognize the alternatives available to them and visualize the probable consequences of different choices. Perhaps the chief message of the futurists is that man is not trapped by some absurd fate but can and must choose his own destiny. Thus it is essential that he carefully explore and weigh all the alternatives he can see. It has even been suggested, somewhat facetiously, that various types of future worlds be portrayed on television, allowing the public to vote on the future of their choice.

Sounding a more somber note, many scientists and others are seriously worried about the possibility that some elite minority may someday plan and exercise control over the rest of us, using the very techniques provided by behavioral scientists. We have been forewarned of this possibility by such frightening "utopias" as those depicted in Huxley's *Brave New World* (1932), Orwell's *1984* (1949), and Skinner's *Walden Two* (1948). More recently, in fact, Skinner has argued in *Beyond Freedom and Dignity* (1971) that freedom is not only illusory but actually a dangerous goal to seek and that comprehensive control of individual behavior through systematic reinforcement is man's best hope.

It will be no easy task to ensure that science is used to enlarge rather than restrict the life of the ordinary man. Recognizing the overarching need to safeguard ourselves against the misuse of control, scientists are becoming increasingly concerned with the value orientations upon which our choices among alternative "futures" will be based.

The enduring problem of values. We are all concerned not only with *whether* man will survive but also with *how*—with the quality of life that will be possible. It will not be enough to preserve man for a future world of "unsanity" or lockstep regimentation or bare subsistence. As man consciously takes his future into his own hands, it is critical that he first consider the entire range of options open to him and then make wise value judgments in choosing among these alternatives.

Thus again we are confronted with the question of *why*. Why these goals rather than other goals? Why these means rather than other means? The answers to these questions involve value judgments. Although science can specify the conditions that will foster passivity, creativity, or other personality traits, it is our values that determine the kind of children we want to rear, the kind of lives we want to live, and the type of world we want to live in.

IS AN ENGINEERED SOCIETY THE ANSWER?

Considerable controversy has been stirred by B. F. Skinner's book *Beyond Freedom and Dignity* (1971). In it, Skinner argues that our values of freedom and dignity not only have been based on false assumptions about choice and free will but are endangering our survival. In his view, we must give up these values because they are preventing us from engineering an environment that will make us behave as we should. He envisions a society in which all men behave for the good of others because the reinforcements induce them to, and since the most effective reinforcements are positive rather than negative ones, he expects a safer, more pleasant situation for all concerned under such a system.

Many questions are raised by this proposal. There is the practical question of who would do the controlling and decide what was good for the society. There is the moral question of whether some should decide what others should do and have enough power to manipulate them into doing it. There is the reality question of whether, in fact, all relevant interpersonal behavior *could* be controlled by such an engineered society—and how it would be possible to ensure against error on the part of the controllers and provide for necessary changes in the system in the light of changing environmental conditions. There is the philosophical question of how, if behavior is determined, we could change our direction by decision and planning: how could we do on a social level what we lack the autonomy to do as individuals? And if we could, there is the existential question of what it would do to people's sense of self-worth and experience of meaning to see themselves as objects manipulated for their own good, with no possibility of controlling their own destiny.

Although it is clear that consequences do guide behavior and that social inducements and pressures strongly influence what we do, the basic behavioristic assumptions of determinism and environmental control are by no means accepted by all, as we have seen. One immediate effect of Skinner's proposal (as in the case of Clark's proposal for chemical control, referred to on page 617) was pressure in Congress to cut off public funds for research that might lead to such control of the individual by the society. Again it would appear that people accustomed to democratic values do not take readily to the notion of external compulsion even "for their own good."

From the alternatives we see open to us, we make choices in terms of what we consider desirable or undesirable, good or bad—that is, in terms of our value judgments. Where we lack values for making such choices, are confused about our values, or put our faith in false values, the results are likely to be destructive and maladaptive. Although it would be both arrogant and premature to attempt a formulation of values or value premises to be used as guides in making our choices, it would appear that we are likely to have to come to grips with the following tentative value assumptions as minimal essentials:

1. A belief in the worth of the individual and of man's survival
2. A belief that personal growth and social progress are possible and worthwhile
3. A belief in equal justice and in providing opportunities for each person to fulfill his potentialities
4. A belief in the value of the "truth" that we try to approach by means of scientific inquiry
5. A belief in the right and responsibility of each person to have a voice in decisions that will affect his life
6. A belief in brotherly love and other fundamental ethical tenets of the world's religious philosophies
7. A belief in the inevitability and desirability of social change and in the possibility of achieving it in ways that will safeguard man's hard-won gains from the past
8. A belief in the reciprocal need of individuals for a "good" society and of society for "good" individuals
9. A belief in mankind as a functional part of the universe with potentialities for evolution that can be fulfilled
10. A belief in the responsibility of each individual for carrying forward the progress made by preceding generations and for contributing his part to creating a good future for man

These value assumptions are not universally accepted, and, being assumptions, they are not subject to proof. They are suggested here simply as guidelines that may merit consideration by a generation of youth who are seeking a new ethic that can match the impact of science on society. If we have no faith in the worth of the individual, in the possibility or value of social progress, or in the potentiality of a meaningful role in the universe for man, then these value assumptions will be useless. However, man does not easily adopt the doctrine of despair so vividly portrayed in the lines of Shakespeare that life is

"a tale
Told by an idiot, full of sound and fury,
Signifying nothing." (*Macbeth*, V, v, 26–28)

As man embarks upon the great adventure of shaping his own future, let us hope that he will learn to change what needs to be changed while preserving what is valid out of his heritage from the past. For it has taken many thousands of years to achieve the imperfect level of freedom and opportunity that we have reached in our society. As Haskins (1968) has pointed out, we must be continually aware of the danger that "in embracing new and experimental courses on myriad fronts of movement with the ardor that we must, we do not at the same time discard long-tested values and long-tried adaptive courses, which, if they are lost, will only have, one day, to be rewon—and probably at enormous cost."

In any event, this book can go no further toward a value orientation. Beyond this point, each of us must make his own value judgments and choices.

THE INDIVIDUAL'S CONTRIBUTION

> "Each man can make a difference,
> and each man should try."
> John F. Kennedy

When students become aware of the tremendous scope of the mental health problem both nationally and internationally and the woefully inadequate facilities for coping with it, they often ask, "What can I do?" This is not an idle question, for much of the progress that has been achieved in the treatment of mental disorders has resulted from the work of concerned citizens rather than professional mental health personnel. Thus it seems appropriate to suggest for interested students a few of the lines of action that they can profitably take where valuable contributions can be made.

Many opportunities in mental health work are open to trained personnel, both professional and paraprofessional. Social work, psychiatric nursing, counseling psychology, clinical psychology, and psychiatry are all rewarding in both monetary and spiritual terms. And as we have seen, the personnel shortage is great in all these fields. In addition, there are many occupations—ranging from law enforcement to teaching and the ministry—that can and do play a key role in the mental health and well-being of people. Professional training in all these fields now includes many undergraduate and graduate courses that offer opportunities for students to work in local communities helping citizens assess and meet their needs through community organization. These "outreach" courses are excellent opportunities for students to receive training in understanding the needs and concerns of people and the possible community resources.

A citizen can find many ways to be of direct service if he is familiar with national and international resources and programs and invests the effort necessary to become cognizant of his community's special needs and problems. Whatever his occupation—as student, teacher, lawyer, homemaker, businessman, or trade-unionist—his interests are at stake, directly and indirectly. For although the mental health of a nation may be manifested in many ways—in its purposes, courage, moral responsibility, scientific and cultural achievements, and quality of daily life—its health and resources derive ultimately from the individuals within it. In a participatory democracy, it is they who plan and implement its goals.

Besides accepting some measure of responsibility for the mental health of others through the quality of his own interpersonal relationships, there are several other constructive courses of action open to each citizen, including: (1) serving as a volunteer in a mental hospital, community mental health center, or youth service organization; (2) joining with other members of the community to work toward enlightened public education, racial tolerance, religious freedom, and responsible government; (3) supporting and helping others understand the need for expanded mental health facilities for all age groups; and (4) becoming acquainted with the crucial need of using science to create conditions conducive to man's fulfillment and exerting whatever influence he has toward this objective.

All of us are concerned with mental health for personal as well as altruistic reasons, for we want to overcome the harassing problems of contemporary living and find our share of happiness in a meaningful and fulfilling life. To do so, we may sometimes need the courage to admit that our problems are too much for us. When existence seems futile or the going becomes too difficult, it may help to remind ourselves of the following basic facts, which have been emphasized in the course of the present text.

1. From time to time each of us has serious difficulties in coping with the problems of living.

2. During such crisis periods, we may need psychological and related assistance.

3. Such difficulties are not a disgrace; they can happen to anyone if the stress is sufficiently severe.

4. The early detection and correction of maladaptive behavior is of great importance in preventing the development of more severe or chronic conditions.

5. Preventive measures—primary, secondary, and tertiary—are the most effective long-range approach to the solution of both individual and group mental health problems.

To recognize these facts is essential because statistics show that almost all of us will have to deal with severely maladaptive behavior or mental disorder in ourselves or those close to us in the course of our lives. The interdependence among us and the loss to us all, individually and collectively, when any one of us fails to achieve his potential are eloquently expressed in the famous lines of John Donne (1624):

"No man is an island, entire of itself; every man is a piece of the continent, a part of the main. If a clod be washed away by the sea, Europe is the less, as well as if a promontory were, as well as if a manor of thy friends or of thine own were: any man's death diminishes me, because I am involved in mankind, and therefore never send to know for whom the bell tolls; it tolls for thee."

Acknowledgments and References

The reference list includes not only the sources from which the author has drawn material, but also acknowledgments of the permission granted by authors and publishers to quote directly from their works.

Journal abbreviations

ACTA PSYCHIATR. SCANDIN.—*Acta Psychiatrica Scandinavica*
AIR UNIVER. QUART. REV.—*Air University Quarterly Review*
AMER. ED. RES. J.—*American Educational Research Journal*
AMER. J. DIS. CHILD.—*American Journal of Diseases of Children*
AMER. J. MED. SCI.—*American Journal of Medical Science*
AMER. J. MENT. DEF.—*American Journal of Mental Deficiency*
AMER. J. NURS.—*American Journal of Nursing*
AMER. J. ORTHOPSYCHIAT.—*American Journal of Orthopsychiatry*
AMER. J. PSYCHIAT.—*American Journal of Psychiatry*
AMER. J. PSYCHOTHER.—*American Journal of Psychotherapy*
AMER. J. PUB. HLTH.—*American Journal of Public Health*
AMER. PSYCHOLOGIST—*American Psychologist*
AMER. SCIEN.—*American Scientist*
AMER. SOC. REV.—*American Sociological Review*
ANN. N.Y. ACAD. SCI.—*Annals of the New York Academy of Science*
ANN. AMER. ACAD. POLIT. SOC. SCI.—*Annals of the American Academy of Political and Social Science*
ANNU. REV. PSYCHOL.—*Annual Review of Psychology*
ARCH. GEN. PSYCHIAT.—*Archives of General Psychiatry*
ARCH. NEUROL.—*Archives of Neurology*
ARCH. NEUROL. PSYCHIAT.—*Archives of Neurology and Psychiatry*
ARCH. PEDIAT.—*Archives of Pediatrics*
BEHAV. RES. THER.—*Behavior Research and Therapy*
BRIT. J. CRIM.—*British Journal of Criminology*
BRIT. J. EDUC. PSYCHOL.—*British Journal of Educational Psychology*
BRIT. J. MED. PSYCHOL.—*British Journal of Medical Psychology*
BRIT. J. OPHTHALMOL.—*British Journal of Ophthalmology*
BRIT. J. PSYCHIAT.—*British Journal of Psychiatry*
BRIT. MED. J.—*British Medical Journal*
BULL. MENNINGER CLIN.—*Bulletin of the Menninger Clinic*
CALIF. MED.—*California Medicine*
CANAD. NURSE.—*Canadian Nurse*
CANAD. PSYCHIAT. ASSN. J.—*Canadian Psychiatric Association Journal*
CHARACT. & PERS.—*Character and Personality*
CHILD DEVELOP.—*Child Development*
CONN. MED.—*Connecticut Medicine*
DEVELOP. PSYCHOL.—*Developmental Psychology*
DIS. NERV. SYS.—*Diseases of the Nervous System*
GEN. PSYCHIAT.—*General Psychiatry*
GENET. PSYCHOL. MONOGR.—*Genetic Psychology Monographs*
GROUP PSYCHOTHER.—*Group Psychotherapy*
HARVARD ED. REV.—*Harvard Educational Review*
HUMAN DEVELOP.—*Human Development*
INTER. J. ADDICTIONS—*International Journal of the Addictions*
INTER. J. GROUP PSYCHOTHER.—*International Journal of Group Psychotherapy*
INTER. J. OFFEN. THER.—*International Journal of Offender Therapy*
INTER. J. PSYCHIAT.—*International Journal of Psychiatry*
INTER J. PSYCHOANAL.—*International Journal of Psychoanalysis*
J. ABNORM. PSYCHOL.—*Journal of Abnormal Psychology*
J. ABNORM. SOC. PSYCHOL.—*Journal of Abnormal and Social Psychology*
J. AMER. ACAD. CHILD PSYCHIAT.—*Journal of the American Academy of Child Psychiatry*
J. ARK. MED. SOC.—*Journal of the Arkansas Medical Society*

J. BEHAV. RES. EXP. PSYCHIAT.—*Journal of Behavior Research and Experimental Psychiatry*
J. CHILD PSYCHOL. PSYCHIAT.—*Journal of Child Psychology and Psychiatry*
J. CHRON. DIS.—*Journal of Chronic Diseases*
J. CLIN. CONS. PSYCHOL.—*Journal of Clinical and Consulting Psychology*
J. CLIN. ENDOCRINOL.—*Journal of Clinical Endocrinology*
J. CLIN. PSYCHOPATH.—*Journal of Clinical Psychopathology*
J. COMPAR. PHYSIOL. PSYCHOL.—*Journal of Comparative and Physiological Psychology*
J. COUNS. PSYCHOL.—*Journal of Counseling Psychology*
J. CRIM. LAW—*Journal of Criminal Law*
J. CRIM. LAW, CRIMINOL. POLICE SCI.—*Journal of Criminal Law, Criminology, and Police Science*
J. CRIM. PSYCHOPATH. PSYCHOTHER.—*Journal of Criminal Psychopathology and Psychotherapy*
J. EXP. ANAL. BEHAV.—*Journal of Experimental Analysis of Behavior*
J. EXP. PSYCHOL.—*Journal of Experimental Psychology*
J. EXP. RES. PERSON.—*Journal of Experimental Research in Personality*
J. FOREN. MED.—*Journal of Forensic Medicine*
J. GEN. PSYCHOL.—*Journal of General Psychology*
J. GENET. PSYCHOL.—*Journal of Genetic Psychology*
J. GERIAT. PSYCHOL.—*Journal of Geriatric Psychology*
J. HLTH. SOC. BEHAV.—*Journal of Health and Social Behavior*
J. IND. MED. ASS.—*Journal of the Indiana Medical Association*
J. INT. COLL. SURGEONS—*Journal of the International College of Surgeons*
J. LEARN. DIS.—*Journal of Learning Disabilities*
J. MARR. FAM.—*Journal of Marriage and the Family*
J. MENT. DEF. RES.—*Journal of Mental Deficiency Research*
J. MENT. SCI.—*Journal of Mental Science*
J. NERV. MENT. DIS.—*Journal of Nervous and Mental Disease*
J. PERSONAL.—*Journal of Personality*
J. PERS. SOC. PSYCHOL.—*Journal of Personal and Social Psychology*
J. PSYCHIAT.—*Journal of Psychiatry*
J. PSYCHIAT. RES.—*Journal of Psychiatric Research*
J. PSYCHOL.—*Journal of Psychology*
J. PSYCHOSOM. MED.—*Journal of Psychosomatic Medicine*
J. PSYCHOSOM. RES.—*Journal of Psychosomatic Research*
J. REHAB.—*Journal of Rehabilitation*
J. SEX RES.—*Journal of Sex Research*
J. SOC. ISSUES—*Journal of Social Issues*
J. SPEC. ED.—*Journal of Special Education*
J. SPEECH HEAR. DIS.—*Journal of Speech and Hearing Disorders*
J. SPEECH HEAR. RES.—*Journal of Speech and Hearing Research*
MARYLAND ST. MED. J.—*Maryland State Medical Journal*
MED. J. AUSTRAL.—*Medical Journal of Australia*
MENT. HLTH. PROG. REP.—*Mental Health Program Reports*
MENT. HYG.—*Mental Hygiene*
MONOGR. SOC. RES. CHILD DEVELOP.—*Monographs of the Society for Research in Child Development*
NAV. MED. BULL.—*Navy Medical Bulletin*
N.C. MED. J.—*North Carolina Medical Journal*
NEW ENGL. J. MED.—*New England Journal of Medicine*
N.Y. ST. J. MED.—*New York State Journal of Medicine*
PSYCHIAT. SOC. SCI. REV.—*Psychiatry and Social Science Review*
PSYCHOANAL. QUART.—*Psychoanalytic Quarterly*
PSYCHOANAL. REV.—*Psychoanalytic Review*
PSYCHOL. BULL.—*Psychology Bulletin*

PSYCH. TODAY—*Psychology Today*

PSYCHOSOM. MED.—*Psychosomatic Medicine*

PUBL. MASS. MED. SOC.—*Publication of the Massachusetts Medical Society*

QUART. J. STUD. ALCHOL.—*Quarterly Journal of Studies in Alcoholism*

SAT. REV.—*Saturday Review*

SCI. J.—*Science Journal*

SCIENTIF. AMER.—*Scientific American*

SMITH COLL. STUD. SOC. WORK—*Smith College Studies in Social Work*

SOC. PSYCHIAT.—*Social Psychiatry*

SOC. SCI. RES. COUNCIL BULL.—*Social Science Research Council Bulletin*

SOCIOL. QUART.—*Sociological Quarterly*

1. Abnormal Behavior in Our Times

ALLPORT, G. *Pattern and growth in personality.* New York: Holt, Rinehart & Winston, 1961.

AMERICAN PSYCHIATRIC ASSOCIATION. *Diagnostic and statistical manual of mental disorders.* Washington, D.C.: APA, 1968.

AMERICAN PSYCHOLOGICAL ASSOCIATION. *Ethical standards of psychologists.* Washington, D.C.: APA, 1963.

BANDURA, A. *Principles of behavior modification.* New York: Holt, Rinehart & Winston, 1969.

BLUEMEL, C. S. *War, politics, and industry.* Denver: World Press, 1948.

BOEHM, W. W. The role of psychiatric social work in mental health. In A. M. Rose (Ed.), *Mental health and mental disorder.* New York: Norton, 1955.

BORN, W. Great artists who suffered from mental disorders. *Ciba Symposia,* 1946, **7,** 225–233.

BUGENTAL, J. F. T. *Challenges of humanistic psychology.* New York: McGraw-Hill, 1967.

CANTRIL, H. A fresh look at the human design. In J. F. T. Bugental (Ed.), *Challenges of humanistic psychology.* New York: McGraw-Hill, 1967. Pp. 13–20.

CARSON, R. *Interaction concepts of personality.* Chicago: Aldine, 1969.

COX, R. *Youth into maturity.* New York: Mental Health Materials Center, 1970.

EDWARDS, J. Sinners in the hands of an angry God. *The works of President Edwards in eight volumes,* Vol. 7. Worcester: Isiah Thomas, 1809.

ELINSON, J., PADILLA, E., & PERKINS, M. E. *Public image of mental health services.* New York: Mental Health Materials Center, 1967.

ENGLISH, H. B., & ENGLISH, A. *A comprehensive dictionary of psychological and psychoanalytical terms.* London: Longmans, Green, 1958.

GIOVANNONI, J. M., & GUREL, L. Socially disruptive behavior of ex-mental patients. *Arch. gen. Psychiat.,* 1967, **17,** 146–153.

HESS, A. E. Medicare and mental illness. *Amer. J. Psychiat.,* 1966, **123,** 174–176.

JAHODA, M. *Current concepts of positive mental health.* New York: Basic Books, 1958.

JUDA, A. The relationship between highest mental capacity and psychic abnormalities. *Amer. J. Psychiat.,* 1949, **106,** 296–307.

KAPLAN, A. A philosophical discussion of normality. *Arch. gen. Psychiat.,* 1967, **17,** 325–330.

LOMBROSO, C. *Man of genius.* New York: Scribner's, 1891.

MAC KINNON, D. W. The nature and nurture of creative talent. *Amer. Psychologist,* 1962, **17,** 484–495.

MARKS, J. *Genius and disaster.* New York: Greenberg, 1925.

MASLOW, A. Self-actualization and beyond. In J. F. T. Bugental (Ed.), *Challenges of humanistic psychology.* New York: McGraw-Hill, 1967. Pp. 279 ff.

MENNINGER, K. *The human mind.* (3rd ed.) New York: Knopf, 1945.

NATIONAL COMMISSION ON COMMUNITY HEALTH SERVICES. *Health is a community affair.* Boston: Harvard Univer. Press, 1967.

NATIONAL INSTITUTE OF MENTAL HEALTH. Cited in *Psychiatric News,* 1969, **4**(2), 19.

PECK, R. Measuring the mental health of normal adults. *Genet. Psychol. Monogr.,* 1959, **60,** 197–255.

ROBINSON, E. A. "Richard Cory" is reprinted by permission of Charles Scribner's Sons from *The Children of the Night* by Edwin Arlington Robinson (1897).

ROGERS, C. The process of the basic encounter group. In J. F. T. Bugental (Ed.), *Challenges of humanistic psychology.* New York: McGraw-Hill, 1969. Pp. 261–278.

SABAHIN, M. Psychiatric perspectives on normality. *Arch. gen. Psychiat.,* 1967, **17,** 285–294.

SARBIN, T. R., & MANCUSO, J. C. Failure of a moral enterprize. *J. clin. cons. Psychol.,* 1970, **35,** 159–173.

SEWELL, W. S. (Ed.) *Famous personalities.* Philadelphia: Blakiston, 1943.

TERMAN, L. M., & ODEN, M. H. *The gifted group at mid-life.* Vol. 5. Stanford, Calif.: Stanford Univer. Press, 1959.

ULLMANN, L. P., & KRASNER, L. *Case studies in behavior modification.* New York: Holt, Rinehart & Winston, 1965.

ULLMANN, L. P., & KRASNER, L. *Psychological approach to abnormal behavior.* Englewood Cliffs, N.J.: Prentice-Hall, 1969.

UNITED STATES DEPARTMENT OF HEALTH, EDUCATION AND WELFARE. National health survey. *Roche Report,* 1971, **1**(9), 2.

UNITED STATES PUBLIC HEALTH SERVICE. NIMH reports continued drop in patient population. *Psychiatric News,* 1969, **4**(10), 16.

UNITED STATES PUBLIC HEALTH SERVICE. Population dip in institutions cited in report. *Psychiatric News,* 1970, **5**(5), 28.

WHITWELL, J. R. *Historical notes on psychiatry.* London: H. K. Lewis, 1936.

WORLD HEALTH ORGANIZATION. Wide research needed to solve the problem of mental health. *World ment. Hlth.,* 1960, **12.**

YOLLES, S. Patient release hits peak. *Science News,* 1967, **92**(5), 107.

ZILBOORG, G., & HENRY, G. W. *A history of medical psychology.* New York: Norton, 1941.

2. Historical Perspectives and the Medical Model

ADAMS, H. B. "Mental illness" or interpersonal behavior? *Amer. Psychologist,* 1964, **19,** 191–197.

BARTON, W. E. Family care and outpatient psychiatry. *Amer. J. Psychiat.,* 1959, **115,** 642–645.

BENNETT, A. E. Mad doctors. *J. nerv. ment. Dis.,* 1947, **106,** 11–18.

BROMBERG, W. *The mind of man.* New York: Harper, 1937.

BROWNE, E. G. *Arabian medicine.* New York: Macmillan, 1921.

CAMPBELL, D. *Arabian medicine and its influence on the Middle Ages.* New York: Dutton, 1926.

CASTIGLIONI, A. *Adventures of the mind.* New York: Knopf, 1946.

COCKAYNE, T. O. *Leechdoms, wort cunning, and star craft of early England.* London: Longman, Green, Longman, Roberts & Green, 1864–1886.

DEUTSCH, A. *The mentally ill in America.* New York: Columbia Univer. Press, 1946.

DUMONT, M. P., & ALDRICH, C. K. Family care after a thousand years—a crisis in the tradition of St. Dymphna. *Amer. J. Psychiat.,* 1962, **119,** 116–121.

GLOYNE, H. F. Tarantism. *American Imago,* 1950, **7,** 29–42.

GUTHRIE, D. J. *A history of medicine.* Philadelphia: Lippincott, 1946.

HEWITT, R. T. Critique of M. P. Dumont & C. K. Aldrich: Family care after a thousand years—a crisis in the tradition of St. Dymphna. *Amer. J. Psychiat.,* 1962, **119,** 120–121.

KARNOSH, L. J., & ZUCKER, E. M. *Handbook of psychiatry.* St. Louis: C. V. Mosby, 1945. Reprinted by permission.

LEWIS, N. D. C. *A short history of psychiatric achievement.* New York: Norton, 1941.

LOWREY, L. G. *Psychiatry for social workers.* New York: Columbia Univer. Press, 1946.

MENNINGER, R. W. The history of psychiatry. *Dis. nerv. System,* 1944, **5,** 52–55.

MORA, G. Paracelsus' psychiatry. *Amer. J. Psychiat.,* 1967, **124,** 803–814.

PLATO. *The laws.* Vol. 5. G. Burges (Tr.). London: George Bell & Sons, n.d.

POLVAN, N. Historical aspects of mental ills in Middle East discussed. *Roche Reports*, 1969, **6**(12), 3.

RABKIN, L. Y. *Psychopathology and literature*. San Francisco: Chandler, 1966.

REES, T. P. Back to moral treatment and community care. *J. ment. Scien.*, 1957, **103**, 303–313. In H. B. Adams, "Mental illness" or interpersonal behavior? *Amer. Psychologist*, 1964, **19**, 191–197.

ROSEN, G. Emotion and sensibility in ages of anxiety. *Amer. J. Psychiat.*, 1967, **124**, 771–784.

RUSSELL, W. L. A psychopathic department of an American general hospital in 1808. *Amer. J. Psychiat.*, 1941, **98**, 229–237.

SELLING, L. S. *Men against madness*. New York: Garden City Books, 1943.

SIGERIST, H. E. *Civilization and disease*. Ithaca, N.Y.: Cornell Univer. Press, 1943.

STONE, S. Psychiatry through the ages. *J. abnorm. soc. Psychol.*, 1937, **32**, 131–160.

TOURNEY, G. A history of therapeutic fashions in psychiatry, 1800–1966. *Amer. J. Psychiat.*, 1967, **124**, 784–796.

WHITE, A. D. *A history of the warfare of science with theology in Christendom*. New York: Appleton, 1896.

WHITE, R. W. Abnormalities of behavior. *Annu. Rev. Psychol.*, 1959, **10**, 265–286.

WHITWELL, J. R. *Historical notes on psychiatry*. London: H. K. Lewis, 1936.

ZILBOORG, G., & HENRY, G. W. *A history of medical psychology*. New York: Norton, 1941.

3. Psychosocial Models

AYLLON, T., & MICHAEL, J. The psychiatric nurse as a behavioral engineer. *J. exp. Anal. Behav.*, 1959, **2**, 323–334.

BANDURA, A. *Principles of behavior modification*. New York: Holt, Rinehart & Winston, 1969.

BROWN, J. F., & MENNINGER, K. A. *Psychodynamics of abnormal behavior*. New York: McGraw-Hill, 1940.

BUGENTAL, J. F. T. *Challenges of humanistic psychology*. New York: McGraw-Hill, 1967.

CARSON, R. *Interaction concepts of personality*. Chicago: Aldine, 1969.

GILLULY, R. H. A new look at the meaning of reality. *Science News*, 1971, **99**, 335–337.

GORDON, J. S. Who is mad? Who is sane? The radical psychiatry of R. D. Laing. *Atlantic*, 1971, **227**(1), 50–66.

ISAACS, W., THOMAS, J., & GOLDIAMOND, I. Application of operant conditioning to reinstate verbal behavior in psychotics. *J. speech hear. Dis.*, 1960, **25**, 8–12.

JAMES, W. *The principles of psychology*. Vols. 1 & 2. New York: Holt, 1890.

JONES, M. C. A laboratory study of fear: The case of Peter. *Pedagogical Seminary*, 1924, **31**, 308–315.

KOESTLER, A. *The invisible writing*. New York: Macmillan, 1954.

LAING, R. D. *The politics of experience*. New York: Ballantine, 1967.

LAING, R. D., & ESTERSON, A. *Sanity, madness, and the family*. London: Tavistock, 1964.

LENNARD, H. L., & BERNSTEIN, A. *Patterns in human interaction*. San Francisco: Jossey-Bass, 1969.

LOVAAS, O. I., FRIETAG, G., GOLD, V. J., & KASSORLA, I. C. Experimental studies in childhood schizophrenia. *J. exper. Child Psychol.*, 1965, **2**, 67–84.

MASLOW, A. H. *Toward a psychology of being*. New York: Van Nostrand, 1962.

MASLOW, A. H. Toward a humanistic biology. *Amer. Psychologist*, 1969, **24**(8), 734–735.

MORRIS, M. G. Psychological miscarriage: An end to mother love. *Transaction*, 1966, **3**(2), 8–13.

PAVLOV, I. P. *Lectures on conditioned reflexes*. Vol. 2. W. H. Gantt (Ed. & tr.). New York: International Publ., 1941.

RABKIN, R. Uncoordinated communication between married partners. *Family Process*, 1967, **6**(1), 10–15.

ROGERS, C. R. *On becoming a person*. Boston: Houghton Mifflin, 1961.

SELLING, L. S. *Men against madness*. New York: Garden City Books, 1943.

SKINNER, B. F. *Walden two*. New York: Macmillan, 1948.

SKINNER, B. F. *Science and human behavior*. New York: Macmillan, 1953.

SKINNER, B. F. *Beyond freedom and dignity*. New York: Knopf, 1971.

SULLIVAN, H. S. *The interpersonal theory of psychiatry*. H. S. Perry & M. L. Gawel (Eds.). New York: Norton, 1953.

THORNDIKE, E. L. *The psychology of learning*. New York: Teachers College, 1913.

WAHLER, R. G. Behavior therapy for oppositional children: Love is not enough. Paper presented at Eastern Psychological Assn. meeting, Washington, D.C., April 1968.

WATSON, J. B., & RAYNOR, R. Conditioned emotional reactions. *J. exper. Psychol.*, 1920, **3**, 1–14.

WATZLAWICK, P., BEAVIN, J., & JACKSON, D. D. *Pragmatics of human communication*. New York: Norton, 1967.

WOLPE, J. Conditioned inhibition of craving in drug addiction. *Behav. Res. Ther.*, 1965, **2**, 285–288.

4. Sociocultural and Interdisciplinary Approaches

ADAMS, H. B. "Mental illness" or interpersonal behavior? *Amer. Psychologist*, 1964, **19**, 191–197.

BENEDICT, R. Anthropology and the abnormal. *J. gen. Psychol.*, 1934, **10**, 59–82.

BERRIEN, F. K. *General and social systems*. New Brunswick, N.J.: Rutgers Univer. Press, 1968.

BERTALANFFY, L. V. The world of science and the world of value. In J. F. T. Bugental (Ed.), *Challenges of humanistic psychology*. New York: McGraw-Hill, 1967. Pp. 335–344.

BERTALANFFY, L. V. General systems theory. In W. Buckley (Ed.), *Modern systems research for the behavioral scientist*. Chicago: Aldine, 1968. Pp. 11–30.

BUCKLEY, W. (Ed.) *Modern systems research for the behavioral scientist*. Chicago: Aldine, 1968.

CARSON, R. *Interaction concepts of personality*. Chicago: Aldine, 1969.

CLINE, E. W. The view from here. *LACPA Newsletter*, 1970, **9**(3), 5.

COLEMAN, J. C. *Psychology and effective behavior*. Glenview, Ill.: Scott, Foresman, 1969.

COLLIER, R. M. Selected implications from a dynamic regulatory theory of consciousness. *Amer. Psychologist*, 1964, **19**(4), 265–269.

FARIS, R. E. L., & DUNHAM, W. *Mental disorders in urban areas*. Chicago: Univer. of Chicago Press, 1939.

HYDE, R. W., & KINGSLEY, D. V. Studies in medical sociology. I. *New Engl. J. Med.*, 1944, **231**, 543–548.

JACO, E. G. *The social epidemiology of mental disorders*. New York: Russell Sage Found., 1960.

LENNARD, H. L., & BERNSTEIN, A. *Patterns in human interaction*. San Francisco: Jossey-Bass, 1969.

MALINOWSKI, B. *Sex and repression in savage society*. New York: Humanities, 1927.

MEAD, G. H. *Mind, self, and society*. C. Q. Boots (Ed.). Chicago: Univer. of Chicago Press, 1934.

MILLER, D. H. Worlds that fail. *Trans-action*, 1966, **4**(2), 36–41.

MILLER, J. G. Living systems: Basic concepts. *Behav. Sci.*, 1965, **10**, 193–237. [a]

MILLER, J. G. Living systems. Structure and process. *Behav. Sci.*, 1965, **10**, 337–379. [b]

RAPHLING, D. L., & LION, J. Patients with repeated admissions to a psychiatric emergency service. *Commun. ment. Hlth. J.*, 1970, **6**(4), 313–318.

ROE, A. Community resources centers. *Amer. Psychologist*, 1970, **25**, 1033–1040.

SMITH, M. B. The revolution in mental-health care—a "bold new approach"? *Trans-action*, 1968, **5**(5), 19–23.

SZASZ, T. S. The myth of mental illness. *Amer. Psychologist*, 1960, **15**(2), 113–118.

SZASZ, T. S. *The myth of mental illness.* New York: Harper & Row, 1961.

SZASZ, T. S. The crime of commitment. *Psych. Today,* 1969, **2**(10), 55–57.

WILLIAMS, G. J. The psychologist as child advocate. *Clinical Psychologist,* 1970, **23**(4), 7–8.

5. Personality Development and Adjustment

ARONSON, E., & CARLSMITH, J. M. The effect of the severity of threat on the devaluation of forbidden behavior. *Amer. Psychologist,* 1962, **17**, 300.

BANDURA, A., & WALTERS, R. H. *Social learning and personality development.* New York: Holt, Rinehart & Winston, 1963.

BARD, M. The price of survival for cancer victims. *Trans-action,* 1966, **3**(3), 10–14.

BARTHOL, R. P., & KU, N. D. Regression under stress to first learned behavior. *J. abnorm. soc. Psychol.,* 1959, **59**, 134–136.

BEADLE, G. W. The new genetics. *Britannica book of the year.* Chicago: Britannica, 1964.

BERGER, R. J. Morpheus descending. *Psych. Today,* 1970, **4**(1), 33–36.

BETTELHEIM, B. Individual and mass behavior in extreme situations. *J. abnorm. soc. Psychol.,* 1943, **38**, 417–452.

BLUESTONE, H., & MC GAHEE, C. L. Reaction to extreme stress. *Amer. J. Psychiat.,* 1962, **119**, 393–396.

BOMBARD, A. *The voyage of the Hérétique.* New York: Simon and Schuster, 1954.

BOOTZIN, R. R., & NATSOULAS, T. Evidence for perceptual defense uncontaminated by response bias. *J. pers. soc. Psychol.,* 1965, **1**, 461–468.

BUSS, A. H. *The psychology of aggression.* New York: Wiley, 1961.

BUSS, A. H. Physical aggression in relation to different frustrations. *J. abnorm. soc. Psychol.,* 1963, **67**, 1–7.

CANTRIL, H. A fresh look at the human design. In J. F. T. Bugental (Ed.), *Challenges of humanistic psychology.* New York: McGraw-Hill, 1967.

CHODOFF, P. The Germàn concentration camp as a psychological stress. *Arch. gen. Psychiat.,* 1970, **22**(1), 78–87.

COUSINS, S. (pseud.) *To beg I am ashamed.* New York: Vanguard, 1938.

DEMENT, W. Effects of dream deprivation. *Science,* 1960, **131**, 1705–1707.

DEMENT, W. Paper presented at meeting of American Academy of Psychoanalysis. New York, December 7–9, 1963.

DUFFY, E. *Activation and behavior.* New York: Wiley, 1962.

ELKIND, D. Piaget and Montessori. *Harvard Ed. Rev.,* 1967, **37**(4), 535–545.

ERICKSON, M. H. Experimental demonstrations of the psychopathology of everyday life. *The Psychoanalytic Quarterly,* 1939, **8**, 342–345. Reprinted by permission.

FARBER, M. *Theory of suicide.* New York: Funk and Wagnalls, 1968.

FENZ, W. D., & EPSTEIN, S. Stress: In the air. *Psych. Today,* 1969, **3**(4), 27–28, 58–59.

FESTINGER, L. Cognitive dissonance. *Scientif. Amer.,* 1962, **207**, 93–107.

FOWLER, W. The problems of deprivation and developmental learning. *Merrill-Palmer Quart.,* 1970, **16**(2), 141–162.

FRANKL, V. E. *Man's search for meaning.* Boston: Beacon, 1959.

FRIEDMAN, P. Some aspects of concentration camp psychology. *Amer. J. Psychiat.,* 1949, **105**, 601–605.

FROMM, E. *The sane society.* New York: Rinehart, 1955.

GAGNE, R. M. Contributions of learning to human development. *Psychiat. Rev.,* 1968, **74**(3), 177–191.

GESELL, A. Human infancy and the embryology of behavior. In A. Weider (Ed.), *Contributions toward medical psychology.* New York: Ronald, 1953. Pp. 51–74.

GESELL, A., & ARMATRUDA, C. S. *Developmental diagnosis: Normal and abnormal child development.* (2nd ed.) New York: Harper, 1947.

HAMBURG, D. A., & ADAMS, J. E. A perspective on coping behavior. *Arch. gen. Psychiat.,* 1967, **17**, 277–284.

HARDY, K. R. An appetitional theory of sexual motivation. *Psychol. Rev.,* 1964, **71**, 1–18.

HARLOW, H. F., & HARLOW, M. Learning to love. *Amer. Scien.,* 1966, **54**, 244–272.

HARLOW, H. F., & HARLOW, M. The young monkeys. *Psych. Today,* 1967, **1**(5), 40–47.

HAYTHORN, W. W., & ALTMAN, I. Together in isolation. *Trans-action,* 1967, **4**(3), 18–22.

HEBB, D. O. The American revolution. *Amer. Psychologist,* 1960, **15**, 735–745.

HELSON, H. Some problems in motivation. In D. Levine (Ed.), *Nebraska symposium on motivation.* Lincoln: Univer. of Nebr. Press, 1966. Pp. 137–182.

HOLMES, D. S. Dimensions of projection. *Psychol. Bull.,* 1968, **69**, 248–268.

HUNT, J. MC V. *Intelligence and experience.* New York: Ronald Press, 1961.

HUXLEY, A. Human potentialities. In R. E. Farson (Ed.), *Science and human affairs.* Palo Alto, Calif.: Science and Behavior Books, 1965.

HUXLEY, J. *Evolution in action.* New York: Harper, 1953.

ILFELD, F. W., JR. Overview of the causes and prevention of violence. *Arch. gen. Psychiat.,* 1969, **20**, 675–689.

ILG, F. L., & AMES, L. B. *Child behavior.* New York: Harper, 1955.

JACOBSON, B., & KALES, A. Deep sleep needed for best health. *Univer. Calif. Bull.,* 1967, **15**, 168.

JONES, A., & MC GILL, D. The homeostatic character of information drive in humans. *J. exper. Res. Person.,* 1967, **2**(1), 25–31.

KANTER, R. M. Communes. *Psych. Today,* 1970, **4**(2), 53–57, 78.

KATZ, J. L., WEINER, H., GALLAGHER, T., & HELLMAN, L. Stress, distress, and ego defenses. *Arch. gen. Psychiat.,* 1970, **23**, 131–142.

KEYS, A., BROŽEK, J., HENSCHEL, A., MICKELSON, O., & TAYLOR, H. L. *The biology of human starvation.* Minneapolis: Univer. Minn. Press, 1950.

KORNER, I. N. Hope as a method of coping. *J. clin. cons. Psychol.,* 1970, **34**(2), 134–139.

KOVACH, J. K. Critical period or optimal arousal? *Develop. Psychol.,* 1970, **3**, 88–97.

LACEY, J. I. Somatic response patterning and stress: Some revisions of activation theory. In M. H. Appley & R. Trumbull (Eds.), *Psychological stress.* New York: Appleton-Century-Crofts, 1967. Pp. 14–37.

LANGDON, G., & STOUT, I. *These well-adjusted children.* New York: John Day, 1951.

LAZARUS, R. S. *Psychological stress and the coping process.* New York: McGraw-Hill, 1966.

MALMO, R. B. Activation: A neurophysiological dimension. *Psychol. Rev.,* 1959, **66**, 367–386.

MASLOW, A. H. Toward a humanistic biology. *Amer. Psychologist,* 1969, **24**(8), 734–735.

MASLOW, A. H., & MURPHY, G. (Eds.) *Motivation and personality.* New York: Harper, 1954, 1969.

MASSERMAN, J. H. *Principles of dynamic psychiatry.* (2nd ed.) Philadelphia: W. B. Saunders Company, 1961. Reprinted by permission.

MC CLEARN, G. E. Behavioral genetics. *Merrill-Palmer Quart.,* 1968, **14**(1), 9–24.

MEAD, M. *Male and female.* New York: Morrow, 1949.

MILLER, J. G. Information input and psychopathology. *Amer. J. Psychiat.,* 1960, **116**, 695–704.

MILLER, J. G. Living systems: Basic concepts. *Behav. Sci.,* 1965, **10**, 193–237.

MILLER, N. E., & DOLLARD, J. *Social learning and imitation.* New Haven, Conn.: Yale Univer. Press, 1941.

MORRIS, G. O., WILLIAMS, H. L., & LUBIN, A. Misperception and disorientation during sleep deprivation. *Arch. gen. Psychiat.,* 1960, **2**, 247–254.

NARDINI, J. E. Survival factors in American prisoners of war of the Japanese. *Amer. J. Psychiat.,* 1952, **109**, 241–248.

NELSON, H. Sleep: It's the kind you get—not how much. *Los Angeles Times,* April 3, 1967, II, 6.

NIEDERLUND, W. G. Comments on E. Wind's "The confrontation with death." *Psyche, Stutgart,* 1968, **22**(6), 442–446.

PETERSON, C. R., & BEACH, L. R. Man as an intuitive statistician. *Psychol. Bull.*, 1967, **68**(1), 29–46.

PFEIFFER, J. *The cell.* New York: Time-Life Books, 1964.

PIAGET, J. *The origins of intelligence in children.* Paris: Delachaux & Niestle, 1936. (Republished—New York: International Univer. Press, 1952.

RICHARDS, I. A. The secret of feedforward. *Sat. Rev.*, 1968, **51**(5), 14–17.

ROGERS, C. R. *Becoming a person.* Austin: Hogg Found. Ment. Hlth., Univer. Texas, 1958.

ROGERS, C. R. The process of the basic encounter group. In J. F. T. Bugental (Ed.), *Challenges of humanistic psychology.* New York: McGraw-Hill, 1967. Pp. 261–278.

ROGERS, C. R. The group comes of age. *Psych. Today*, 1969, **3**(7), 27–31, 58–61.

ROGERS, C. R. *Carl Rogers on encounter groups.* New York: Harper & Row, 1971.

ROHRER, J. H. Interpersonal relations in isolated small groups. In B. E. Flaherty (Ed.), *Psychophysiological aspects of space flight.* New York: Columbia Univer. Press, 1961. Pp. 263–271.

SCHULTZ, D. P. *Sensory restriction.* New York: Academic Press, 1965.

SCOTT, J. P. The progress of primary socialization in canine and human infants. *Monogr. soc. res. Child Develop.*, 1963, **28**(1), 1–47.

SEARS, R. R., MACCOBY, E. E., & LEVIN, H. *Patterns of child rearing.* Evanston, Ill.: Row, Peterson, 1957.

SIMON, H. A. Motivational and emotional controls of cognition. *Psychol. Rev.*, 1967, **74**(1), 29–39.

SIMON, H. A., & NEWELL, A. Human problem solving: The state of theory in 1970. *Amer. Psychologist*, 1971, **26**(2), 145–159.

SOLOMON, P., & KLEEMAN, S. Sensory deprivation. *Amer. J. Psychiat.*, 1971, **127**(11), 1546–1547.

SOLOMON, P., KUBZANSKY, P. E., LEIDERMAN, P. H., MENDELSON, J. H., TRUMBUL, R., & WEXLER, D. (Eds.) *Sensory deprivation: A symposium held at Harvard Medical School in 1958.* Cambridge, Mass.: Harvard Univer. Press, 1961.

SOLOMON, R. L. Punishment. *Amer. Psychologist*, 1964, **19**, 239–253.

SONNENBORN, T. M. The new genetics. *Science and Technology*, 1962, **1**(9), 66–74. Reprinted by permission.

SPENCE, D. P. Subliminal perception and perceptual defense. *Behav. Sci.*, 1967, **12**(3), 183–193.

WATSON, J. D. *Molecular biology of the gene.* New York: Benjamin, 1965.

WATZLAWICK, P., BEAVIN, J., & JACKSON, D. D. *Pragmatics of human communication.* New York: Norton, 1967.

WEISS, P. A., & TAYLOR, A. C. Shuffled cells can reconstruct same organs. *Sci. Newsletter*, 1960, **78**, 263.

WHITE, R. W. Motivation reconsidered. *Psychol. Rev.*, 1959, **66**, 297–333.

WHITE, W. A. Medical philosophy from the viewpoint of a psychiatrist. *Psychiatry*, 1947, **10**, 77–98, 191–210.

WILSON, E. B. *The cell in development and heredity.* (3rd ed.) New York: Macmillan, 1925.

WOLF, S., & RIPLEY, H. S. Reactions among Allied prisoners of war subjected to three years of imprisonment and torture by the Japanese. *Amer. J. Psychiat.*, 1947, **104**, 180–193.

WOOLDRIDGE, D. E. *Mechanical man: The physical basis of intelligent life.* New York: McGraw-Hill, 1968.

6. Causative Factors in Abnormal Behavior

AINSWORTH, M. D. The effects of maternal deprivation. In World Health Organization, *Deprivation of maternal care: A reassessment of its effects.* Geneva: WHO, 1962. Pp. 97–165.

ANTHONY, J. E. A clinical evaluation of children with psychotic parents. *Amer. J. Psychiat.*, 1969, **126**(2), 177–184.

ASCH, S. E. Opinions and social pressure. *Scientif. Amer.*, 1955, **193**(5), 31–35.

BANDURA, A. Social learning through imitation. In M. R. Jones (Ed.), *Nebraska symposium on motivation.* Lincoln: Univer. Nebr. Press, 1962. Pp. 211–269.

BANDURA, A., ROSS, D., & ROSS, S. A. Imitation of film-mediated aggressive models. *J. abnorm. soc. Psychol.*, 1963, **66**, 3–11.

BARATZ, S. S., & BARATZ, J. C. Early childhood intervention: The social science base of institutional racism. *Harvard Ed. Rev.*, 1970, **40**(1), 29–50.

BARKER, R. G., WRIGHT, B. A., & GONICK, M. R. Adjustment to physical handicap and illness. *Soc. Sci. Res. Council Bull.*, 1946, **55**, 1–372.

BATESON, G. Minimal requirements for a theory of schizophrenia. *Arch. gen. Psychiat.*, 1960, **2**, 477–491.

BEACH, F. A., & JAYNES, J. Effects of early experience upon the behavior of animals. *Psychol. Bull.*, 1954, **51**, 239–263.

BECKER, E. Toward a comprehensive theory of depression. *J. nerv. ment. Dis.*, 1962, **135**, 26–35.

BECKER, W. C. Consequences of different kinds of parental discipline. In M. L. Hoffman & L. W. Hoffman (Eds.), *Review of child development research.* Vol. 1. New York: Russell Sage Found., 1964. Pp. 169–208.

BERES, D., & OBERS, S. J. The effects of extreme deprivation in infancy on psychic structure in adolescence. In R. S. Eissler et al. (Eds.), *The psychoanalytic study of the child.* Vol. 5. New York: International Univer. Press, 1950. Pp. 212–235.

BERNABEU, E. P. The effects of severe crippling on the development of a group of children. *Psychiatry*, 1958, **21**, 169–194.

BILLER, H. B. Father absence and the personality development of the male child. *Develop. Psychol.*, 1970, **2**, 181–201.

BLADESLEE, A. L. Nutritional time bomb. *Today's Health*, 1967, **45**(6), 7.

BLAU, A., SLAFF, B., EASTON, K., WELKOWITZ, J., SPRINGARN, J., & COHEN, J. The psychogenic etiology of premature births. *Psychosom. Med.*, 1963, **25**, 201–211.

BOWEN, M. A family concept of schizophrenia. In D. D. Jackson (Ed.), *The etiology of schizophrenia.* New York: Basic Books, 1960.

BOWLBY, J. Separation anxiety. *Inter. J. Psychoanal.*, 1960, **41**, 89–93.

BRATFOS, O. Parental deprivation in childhood and type of future mental disease. *Acta Psychiatr. Scandin.*, 1967, **43**(4), 453–461.

BUHLER, C. *Psychology for contemporary living.* New York: Hawthorn Books, 1969.

BULLARD, D. M., GLASER, H. H., HEAGARTY, M. C., & PIVCHEK, E. C. Failure to thrive in the neglected child. *Amer. J. Orthopsychiat.*, 1967, **37**, 680–690.

BYRNE, D., OLIVER, L., & REEVES, K. The effects of physical attractiveness, sex, and attitude similarity on interpersonal attraction. *J. Personal.*, 1968, **36**(2), 259–271.

CAPUTO, D. V., & MANDELL, W. Consequences of low birth weight. *Develop. Psychol.*, 1970, **3**, 363–383.

CARSON, R. C. *Interaction concepts of personality.* New York: Aldine, 1969.

CHESS, S., THOMAS, A., & BIRCH, H. G. *Your child is a person.* New York: Viking, 1965.

CHESS, S., THOMAS, A., BIRCH, H. G., & HERTZIG, M. Implications of a longitudinal study of child development for child psychiatry. *Amer. J. Psychiat.*, 1960, **117**, 434–441.

CLARK, K. B. *Dark ghetto: Dilemmas of social power.* New York: Harper & Row, 1965.

CLARK, K. B. Explosion in the ghetto. *Psych. Today*, 1967, **1**(5), 31–38.

CLOSE, K. Giving babies a healthy start in life. *Children*, 1965, **12**(5), 179–184.

COHEN, S. A. Studies in visual perception and reading in disadvantaged children. *J. learning Disab.*, 1969, **10**, 498–507.

COOPERSMITH, S. *The antecedents of self-esteem.* San Francisco: Freeman, 1967.

CORTÉS, J. B., & GATTI, F. M. Physique and propensity. *Psych. Today*, 1970, **4**(5), 42–44, 82, 84.

DAMON, A., & POLEDNAK, A. P. Physique and serum pepsinogen. *Human Biology*, 1967, **39**(4), 355–367.

DAVIDS, A., & DE VAULT, S. Maternal anxiety during pregnancy and childbirth. *Psychosom. Med.*, 1962, **24**, 464–470.

DAVIDSON, M. A., MC INNES, R. G., & PARNELL, R. W. The distribution of personality traits in seven-year-old children. *Brit. J. educ. Psychol.,* 1957, **27,** 48–61.

DAVIS, D. C. Predicting tomorrow's children. *Today's Health,* 1968, **46**(1), 32–37.

DAWSON, R. E., DE CHARMS, R., MONTGOMERY, R., & TALBOT, G. The American underclass: Red, white, and black. *Trans-action,* 1969, **6**(4), 9.

DEARING, G. P. Russians support genetic basis for schizophrenia. *Psychiatric News,* 1969, **4**(8), 18.

DENENBERG, V., ROSENBERG, K., HALTMEYER, G., & WHIMBEY, A. Programming life histories: Effects of stress in ontogency upon emotional reactivity. *Merrill-Palmer Quart.,* 1970, **15,** 109–116.

DENNIS, W. Spaulding's experiment on the flight of birds repeated with another species. *J. compar. physiol. Psychol.,* 1941, **31,** 337–348.

DENNIS, W. Causes of retardation among institutional children: Iran. *J. genet. Psychol.,* 1960, **96,** 47–59.

DEPARTMENT OF HEALTH, EDUCATION AND WELFARE, CHILDREN'S BUREAU. *Health of children of school age.* Washington, D.C.: Govt. Printing Office, 1965.

DEUR, J. I., & PARKE, R. D. Effects of inconsistent punishment on aggression in children. *Develop. Psychol.,* 1970, **2,** 403–411.

DEUTSCH, M., ET AL. *The disadvantaged child.* New York: Basic Books, 1967.

DEVOR, G. M. Children as agents in socializing parents. *Family Coordinator,* 1970, **19**(3), 208–212.

DOBBING, J. Growth of the brain. *Sci. J.,* 1967, **3**(5), 81–86.

DOBZHANSKY, T. The present evolution of man. *Scientif. Amer.,* 1960, **203**(3), 206–217.

DOUGLAS, J. W. B., ROSS, J. M., HAMMOND, W. A., & MULLIGAN, D. G. Delinquency and social class. *Brit. J. Crim.,* 1966, **6,** 294–302.

DOUVAN, E., & ADELSON, J. *The adolescent experience.* New York: Wiley, 1966.

DURANT, W., & DURANT, A. *Rousseau and revolution.* New York: Simon & Schuster, 1967.

EARL, H. G. 10,000 children battered and starved: Hundreds die. *Today's Health,* 1965, **43**(9), 24–31.

EIDUSON, B. T., EIDUSON, S., & GELLER, E. Biochemistry, genetics, and the nature-nurture problem. *Amer. J. Psychiat.,* 1962, **119,** 342–350.

EINSTEIN, G., & MOSS, M. Some thoughts on sibling relationships. *Social Casework,* 1967, **48**(9), 549–555.

EISENBERG, J. F. Crowded animals neither fight nor mate. *Science News,* 1967, **92**(23), 542.

EISENBERG, L. Child psychiatry: The past quarter century. *Amer. J. Orthopsychiat.,* 1969, **39,** 389–401.

EISENDRATH, R. M. The role of grief and fear in the death of kidney transplant patients. *Amer. J. Psychiat.,* 1969, **126,** 381–387.

EYSENCK, H. J. *Behavior therapy and the neuroses.* London: Pergamon Press, 1960.

EYSENCK, H. J., & RACHMAN, S. *The causes and cures of neuroses.* San Diego: Knapp, 1965.

FENZ, W. D., & EPSTEIN, S. Stress: In the air. *Psych. Today,* 1969, **3**(4), 27–28, 58–59.

FISHER, S., BOYD, I., WALKER, D., & SHEER, D. Parents of schizophrenics, neurotics, and normals. *Arch. gen. Psychiat.,* 1959, **1,** 149–166.

FLYNN, W. R. Frontier justice: A contribution to the theory of child battery. *Amer. J. Psychiat.,* 1970, **127**(3), 375–379.

FROMM-REICHMANN, F. Loneliness. *Psychiatry,* 1959, **22,** 1–15.

GARDNER, J. W. The abused child. *McCalls,* Sept. 1967, pp. 97, 143.

GLUECK, S., & GLUECK, E. *Family environment and delinquency.* Boston: Houghton Mifflin, 1962.

GLUECK, S., & GLUECK, E. *Non-delinquents in perspective.* Cambridge: Harvard Univer. Press, 1968.

GOERTZEL, V., & GOERTZEL, M. *Cradles of eminence.* Boston: Little, Brown, 1962.

GRAY, P. H. Theory and evidence of imprinting in human infants. *J. Psychol.,* 1958, **46,** 155–166.

GURIN, G., VEROFF, J., & FELD, S. *Americans view their mental health.* New York: Basic Books, 1960.

HARLOW, H. F. The heterosexual affectional system in monkeys. *Amer. Psychologist,* 1962, **17,** 1–9.

HARLOW, H. F., & SUOMI, S. J. Nature of love—simplified. *Amer. Psychologist,* 1970, **25**(1), 161–168.

HARMELING, P. C. Therapeutic theater of Alaska Eskimos. *Group Psychother.,* 1950, **3,** 74–76.

HEINSTEIN, M. I. Expressed attitudes and feelings of pregnant women and their relation to physical complications of pregnancy. *Merrill-Palmer Quart.,* 1967, **13,** 217–236.

HELFER, R. E., & KEMPE, C. H. (Eds.) *The battered child.* Chicago: Univer. of Chicago, 1968.

HERSHER, L., MOORE, U., RICHMOND, J. B., & BLAUVELT, H. The effects of maternal deprivation during the nursing period on the behavior of young goats. *Amer. Psychologist,* 1962, **17,** 307.

HESS, R. D., & SHIPMAN, V. C. Early experience and the socialization of cognitive modes in children. *Child Develop.,* 1965, **36,** 869–886.

HUGHES, G. R. Self-resignation: A mighty foe. *J. Rehab.,* 1960, **265,** 18–19.

HUNT, J. MC V. Traditional personality theory in the light of recent evidence. *Amer. Scien.,* 1965, **53,** 80–95.

HURLEY, J. R. Parental acceptance-rejection and children's intelligence, *Merrill-Palmer Quart.,* 1965, **11**(1), 19–32.

HURLOCK, E. B. *Developmental psychology.* (3rd ed.) New York: McGraw-Hill, 1968.

JACKSON, D. *Etiology of schizophrenia.* New York: Basic Books, 1960.

JENKINS, R. L. Psychiatric syndromes in children and their relation to family background. *Amer. J. Orthopsychiat.,* 1966, **36,** 450–457.

JENKINS, R. L. The varieties of children's behavioral problems and family dynamics. *Amer. J. Psychiat.,* 1968, **124,** 1440–1445.

JOINT COMMISSION ON THE MENTAL HEALTH OF CHILDREN. *Amer. J. Orthopsychiat.,* 1968, **38,** 402–409.

KADUSHIN, A. Reversibility of trauma: A follow-up study of children adopted when older. *Social Work,* 1967, **12**(4), 22–23.

KAGAN, J., & MOSS, H. A. *Birth to maturity.* New York: Wiley, 1962.

KAISER FOUNDATION HEALTH PLAN, INC. *Planning for health.* Summer 1970, 1–2.

KALLMANN, F. J. *Heredity in health and mental disorder.* New York: Norton, 1953.

KALLMANN, F. J. The use of genetics in psychiatry. *J. ment. Scien.,* 1958, **104,** 542–549.

KARNES, M., TESKA, J. A., & HODGINS, A. S. The effects of four programs of classroom intervention on the intellectual and language development of 4-year-old disadvantaged children. *Amer. J. Orthopsychiat.,* 1970, **40,** 58–76.

KELLER, S. The social world of the urban slum child. *Amer. J. Orthopsychiat.,* 1963, **33,** 823–831.

KENISTON, K. College students and children in developmental institutions. *Children,* 1967, **14**(1), 2–7.

LANGNER, T. S., & MICHAEL, S. T. *Life stress and mental health.* Vol. 20. New York: Free Press, 1963.

LENNARD, H. L., & BERNSTEIN, A. *Patterns in human interaction.* San Francisco: Jossey-Bass, 1969.

LENNON, J., & MC CARTNEY, P. *Nowhere man.* Copyright © 1967 Northern Songs Limited. Used by Permission. All Rights Reserved.

LESSAC, M., & SOLOMON, R. L. Effects of early isolation on the later adaptive behavior of beagles. *Develop. Psychol.,* 1969, **1**(1), 14–25.

LEVY, D. M. Maternal overprotection. In N. D. C. Lewis & B. L. Pacella (Eds.), *Modern trends in child psychiatry.* New York: International Univer. Press, 1945.

LINDZEY, G., LYKKEN, D. T., & WINSTON, H. D. Infantile trauma, genetic factors, and adult temperament. *J. abnorm. soc. Psychol.,* 1960, **61,** 7–14.

LOPER, M. L. Trauma of child beating. *Los Angeles Times,* Oct. 12, 1970, IV, 1, 11.

LOYD, G. F. Finally, facts on malnutrition in the United States. *Today's Health,* 1969, **47**(9), 32–33.

LU, Y. C. Contradictory parental expectations in schizophrenia. *Arch. gen. Psychiat.,* 1962, **6,** 219–234.

MAHER, B. A. Personality, problem-solving and the Einstellung-effect. *J. abnorm. soc. Psychol.*, 1957, **54**, 70–74.

MAHER, B. A. *Principles of psychopathology.* New York: McGraw-Hill, 1966.

MAIER, N. R. F. *Frustration.* New York: McGraw-Hill, 1949.

MAY, R. Love and will. *Psych. Today*, 1969, **3**(3), 17–64.

MC CORD, W., MC CORD, J., & ZOLA, I. K. *Origins of crime.* New York: Columbia Univer. Press, 1959.

MC DAVID, J. W., & HARARI, H. *Social psychology.* New York: Harper & Row, 1968.

MC DONALD, R. L., GYTHER, M., & CHRISTAKOR, A. Relations between maternal anxiety and obstetric complications. *Psychosom. Med.*, 1963, **25**, 357–363.

MC KUSICK, V. A., & RIMOIN, D. L. General Tom Thumb and other midgets: With biographical sketches. *Scientif. Amer.*, 1967, **217**(10), 102–106.

MECHANIC, D. *Students under stress.* New York: Free Press, 1962.

MILLER, G. A., GALANTER, E., & PRIBAM, K. H. *Plans and the structure of behavior.* New York: Holt, Rinehart & Winston, 1960.

MILLER, J. G. Sensory overloading. In B. E. Flaherty (Ed.), *Psychophysiological aspects of space flight.* New York: Columbia Univer. Press, 1961. Pp. 215–224.

MILLER, J. G. Living systems: Basic concepts. *Behaviorial Science*, 1965, **10**, 193–237.

MILLER, N. E. Liberalization of basic S–R concepts. In S. Koch (Ed.), *Psychology: A study of a science.* Vol. 2. New York: McGraw-Hill, 1959.

MILLER, R. W. Delayed radiation effects in atomic-bomb survivors. *Science*, 1969, **166**(3905), 569–573.

MISHLER, E. G., & WAXLER, N. E. Family interaction process and schizophrenia: A review of current theories. *Merrill-Palmer Quart.*, 1965, **11**, 269–316.

MOLTZ, H. Imprinting: Empirical basis and theoretical significance. *Psychol. Bull.*, 1960, **57**, 291–314.

MOORE, T. Language and intelligence: A longitudinal study of the first eight years. II. Environmental correlates of mental growth. *Human Develop.*, 1968, **11**, 1–24.

NATIONAL INSTITUTE OF MENTAL HEALTH. *The mental health of urban America.* Washington, D.C.: Public Hlth. Serv. Publ. No. 1906, 1969.

PACKARD, V. *The sexual wilderness.* New York: David McKay, 1968.

PALMORE, E. Work and happiness. *Science News*, 1970, **97**, 589.

PASAMANICK, B., & KNOBLOCH, H. Brain damage and reproductive causality. *Amer. J. Orthopsychiat.*, 1960, **5**(1), 57–72.

PASAMANICK, B., & KNOBLOCH, H. Epidemiologic studies on the complications of pregnancy and the birth process. In G. Caplan (Ed.), *Prevention of mental disorders in children.* New York: Basic Books, 1961. Pp. 74–94.

POLLACK, J. H. Five frequent mistakes of parents. *Today's Health*, 1968, **46**(5), 14–15, 26–29.

PRESIDENT'S COMMITTEE ON MENTAL RETARDATION. *Los Angeles Times*, Sept. 30, 1968, II, 6.

PRINGLE, M. L. K. *Deprivation and education.* New York: Humanities Press, 1965.

PROVENCE, S., & LIPTON, R. C. *Infants in institutions.* New York: International Univer. Press, 1962.

PRUGH, D. G., & HARLOW, R. G. "Masked deprivation" in infants and young children. In World Health Organization, *Deprivation of maternal care.* Geneva: WHO, 1962. Pp. 9–29.

RADIN, N. Some impediments to the education of disadvantaged children. *Children*, 1968, **15**(5), 170–176.

REISEN, A. H. The development of visual perception in men and chimpanzee. *Science*, 1947, **106**, 107–108.

RENNE, K. S. Correlates of dissatisfaction in marriage. *J. Marr. Fam.*, Feb. 1970, 54–67.

RIBBLE, M. A. Infantile experience in relation to personality development. In J. McV. Hunt (Ed.), *Personality and the behavior disorders.* Vol. 2. New York: Ronald, 1944. Pp. 621–651.

RIBBLE, M. A. Anxiety in infants and its disorganizing effects. In N. D. C. Lewis & B. L. Pacella (Eds.), *Modern trends in child psychiatry.* New York: International Univer. Press, 1945.

RIESMAN, D. (in collaboration with R. Denney & N. Glazer). *The lonely crowd: A study of the changing American character.* New Haven: Yale Univer. Press, 1950.

RIESMAN, D. The young are captives of each other. *Psych. Today*, 1969, **3**(5), 28–31.

ROBBINS, N. H. Will arbitration ease the crowded divorce docket? *Family Coordinator*, 1970, **19**(4), 374–376.

ROGERS, C. M., & DAVENPORT, R. K. Effects of restricted rearing on sexual behavior of chimpanzees. *Develop. Psychol.*, 1969, **1**(3), 200–204.

ROSENTHAL, M. J. The syndrome of the inconsistent mother. *Amer. J. Orthopsychiat.*, 1962, **32**, 637–644.

ROTHSCHILD, B. F. Incubator isolation as a possible contributing factor to the high incidence of emotional disturbance among prematurely born persons. *J. genet. Psychol.*, 1967, **110**(2), 287–304.

SAGER, C. J. Alienation "can be said to epitomize our times." *Roche Reports*, 1968, **5**(8), 1–2, 11.

SATIR, V. *Conjoint family therapy.* (rev. ed.) Palo Alto, Calif.: Science and Behavior Books, 1967.

SCHAEFER, E. S., & BAYLEY, N. Consistency of maternal behavior from infancy to preadolescence. *J. abnorm. soc. Psychol.*, 1960, **61**, 1–6.

SCHEIN, E. H. The first job dilemma. *Psych. Today*, 1968, **1**(10), 26–37.

SCIENCE JOURNAL. Editorial. Feb. 1967, p. 11.

SCOTT, R. Head start before home start? *Merrill-Palmer Quart.*, 1967, **13**, 317–322.

SCRIMSHAW, N. S. Early malnutrition and central nervous system function. *Merrill-Palmer Quart.*, 1969, **15**, 375–388.

SEAMAN, M. Antidote to alienation. *Trans-action*, 1966, **3**(4), 35–39.

SEARS, R. R. Relation of early socialization experiences to aggression in middle childhood. *J. abnorm. soc. Psychol.*, 1961, **63**, 466–492.

SEARS, R. R., MACCOBY, E. E., & LEVIN, H. *Patterns of child rearing.* Evanston, Ill.: Row, Peterson, 1957.

SELYE, H. *The stress of life.* New York: McGraw-Hill, 1956.

SELYE, H. Stress. *Psych. Today*, 1969, **3**(4), 24–26.

SERGOVICH, F., VALENTINE, G. H., CHEN, A. T., KINCH, R., & SMOUT, M. Chromosomal abberations in 2159 consecutive newborn babies. *New Engl. J. Med.*, 1969, **280**(16), 851–854.

SHAW, C. R., & SCHELKUN, R. F. Suicidal behavior in children. *Psychiatry*, 1965, **28**, 157–168.

SHELDON, W. H. *The varieties of temperament.* New York: Harper, 1942.

SHELDON, W. H. (with the collaboration of C. W. Dupertuis & E. McDermott). *Atlas of men.* New York: Harper, 1954.

SKEELS, H. M. Adult status of children with contrasting early life experiences. *Monogr. Soc. res. Child Develop.*, 1966, **31**(3).

SMITH, M. S., & BISSELL, J. S. The impact of Headstart: The Westinghouse-Ohio Headstart evaluation. *Harvard Ed. Rev.*, 1970, **40**, 51–104.

SONTAG, L. W., STEELE, W. G., & LEWIS, M. The fetal and maternal cardiac response to environmental stress. *Human Develop.*, 1969, **12**, 1–9.

SPREY, J. On the institutionalization of sexuality. *J. Marr. Fam.*, 1969, **31**, 432–440.

STABENAU, J. R., TUPIN, J., WERNER, M., & POLLIN, W. A comparative study of families of schizophrenics, delinquents, and normals. *Psychiatry*, 1965, **28**, 45–59.

TERR, L. A family study of child abuse. *Amer. J. Psychiat.*, 1970, **127**, 665–671.

TIME. On being an American parent. Dec. 15, 1967.

TOMAN, W. Birth order rules all. *Psych. Today*, 1970, **4**(7), 45–49, 68–69.

TURNER, C., DAVENPORT, R., & ROGERS, C. The effect of early deprivation on the social behavior of adolescent chimpanzees. *Amer. J. Psychiat.*, 1969, **125**(11), 85–90.

VAN DEN BERGHE, P. L. Poverty as underdevelopment. *Trans-action*, 1969, **6**(9), 3–4, 31.

WATSON, J. D. *Molecular biology of the gene.* New York: Benjamin, 1965.

WATZLAWICK, P., BEAVIN, J., & JACKSON, D. D. *Pragmatics of human communication*. New York: Norton, 1967.

WERNER, E. E. Sex differences in correlations between children's IQs and measures of parental ability and environmental ratings. *Develop. Psychol.*, 1969, **1**, 280–285.

WESTMAN, J. C., CLINE, D. W., SWIFT, W. J., & KRAMER, D. A. Complexities of divorce studied in regard to impact on children. *Roche Reports*, 1969, **6**(7), 3.

WINDER, C. L., & RAU, L. Parental attitudes associated with social deviance in preadolescent boys. *J. abnorm. soc. Psychol.*, 1962, **64**, 418–424.

WINICK, C. The beige epoch: Depolarization of sex roles in America. *Annals Amer. Acad. Polit. Soc. Sci.*, 1968, **376**, 18–24.

WITMER, H. L. National facts and figures about children without families. *J. Amer. Acad. Child Psychiat.*, 1965, **4**, 249–253.

WOLFE, T. *Look homeward angel*. New York: Scribners, 1929.

YARROW, L. J. Separation from parents during early childhood. In M. L. Hoffman & L. W. Hoffman (Eds.), *Review of child development research*. Vol. 1. New York: Russell Sage Found., 1964. Pp. 89–136.

YARROW, L. J. Conceptual perspectives on the early environment. *J. Amer. Acad. Child Psychiat.*, 1965, **4**, 168–185.

7. Transient Situational Disorders

ADLER, A. Neuropsychiatric complications in victims of Boston's Cocoanut Grove disaster. *JAMA*, 1943, **123**, 1098–1101.

ARCHIBALD, H. C., LONG, D. M., MILLER, D., & TUDDENHAM, R. D. Gross stress reaction in combat—a 15-year follow-up. *Amer. J. Psychiat.*, 1962, **119**, 317–322.

ARCHIBALD, H. C., & TUDDENHAM, R. D. Persistent stress reaction after combat. *Arch. gen. Psychiat.*, 1965, **12**(5), 475–481.

BARTEMEIER, L. H., KUBIE, L. S., MENNINGER, K. A., ROMANO, J., & WHITEHORN, J. C. Combat exhaustion. *Journal of Nervous and Mental Disease*, 1946, **104**, 385–389, 489–525. Copyright © 1946, The Williams & Wilkins Co., Baltimore, Md., 21202, U.S.A.

BELL, E., JR. The basis of effective military psychiatry. *Dis. nerv. System*, 1958, **19**, 283–288.

BETTELHEIM, B. Individual and mass behavior in extreme situations. *J. abnorm. soc. Psychol.*, 1943, **38**, 417–452.

BETTELHEIM, B. *The informed heart*. New York: Free Press, 1960.

BLOCH, H. S. Army clinical psychiatry in the combat zone—1967–1968. Reprinted from *The American Journal of Psychiatry*, volume **126**, pages 289–298, 1969. Copyright 1969, the American Psychiatric Association.

BOURNE, P. G. Military psychiatry and the Vietnam experience. *Amer. J. Psychiat.*, 1970, **127**(4), 481–488.

CHAMBERS, R. E. Discussion of "Survival factors. . . ." *Amer. J. Psychiat.*, 1952, **109**, 247–248.

CHODOFF, P. The German concentration camp as a psychological stress. *Arch. gen. Psychiat.*, 1970, **22**(1), 78–87.

CHOLDEN, L. Some psychiatric problems in the rehabilitation of the blind. *Bull. Menninger Clin.*, 1954, **18**, 107–112.

EITINGER, L. Pathology of the concentration camp syndrome. *Arch. gen. Psychiat.*, 1961, **5**, 371–379.

EITINGER, L. Concentration camp survivors in the postwar world. *Amer. J. Orthopsychiat.*, 1962, **32**, 367–375.

EITINGER, L. *Concentration camp survivors in Norway and Israel*. New York: Humanities Press, 1964.

EITINGER, L. (with F. Askevold). Psychiatric aspects. In A. Strom (Ed.), *Norwegian concentration camp survivors*. New York: Humanities Press, 1968. Pp. 45–84.

EITINGER, L. Psychosomatic problems in concentration camp survivors. *J. psychosom. Res.*, 1969, **13**, 183–190.

FARBER, I. E., HARLOW, H. F., & WEST, L. J. Brainwashing, conditioning, and DDD (debility, dependency and dread). *Sociometry*, 1956, **19**, 271–285.

FITZGERALD, R. Reactions to blindness. *Arch. gen. Psychiat.*, 1970, **22**(4), 370–379.

FRANKL, V. E. *Man's search for meaning*. Boston: Beacon Press, 1959.

FRIEDMAN, P. The effects of imprisonment. *Acta Medica Orientalia, Jerusalem*, 1948, 163–167.

FRIEDMAN, P., & LINN, L. Some psychiatric notes on the Andrea Doria disaster. *Amer. J. Psychiat.*, 1957, **114**, 426–432.

FRITZ, C. E. Disasters compared in six American communities. *Human Organization*, 1957, **16**(2), 6–9.

GLASS, A. J. Psychotherapy in the combat zone. *Amer. J. Psychiat.*, 1954, **110**, 725–731.

GLASS, A. J., ARTISS, K. L., GIBBS, J. J., & SWEENEY, V. C. The current status of Army psychiatry. *Amer. J. Psychiat.*, 1961, **117**, 673–683.

GOLDSMITH, W., & CRETEKOS, C. Unhappy odysseys: Psychiatric hospitalization among Vietnam returnees. *Amer. J. Psychiat.*, 1969, **20**, 78–83.

GRINKER, R. R. An essay on schizophrenia and science. *Arch. gen. Psychiat.*, 1969, **20**, 1–24.

GRINKER, R. R., & SPIEGEL, J. P. *War neuroses*. Philadelphia: Blakiston, 1945.

HAFNER, H. Psychological disturbances following prolonged persecution. *Soc. Psychiat.*, 1968, **3**(3), 80–88.

HAMBURG, D. A., & ADAMS, J. E. A perspective on coping behavior. *Arch. gen. Psychiat.*, 1967, **17**(3), 277–284.

HASTINGS, D. W., WRIGHT, D. G., & GLUECK, B. C. *Psychiatric experiences of the Eighth Air Force*. New York: Josiah Macy, Jr., Found., 1944.

HAUSMAN, W., & RIOCH, D. M. Military psychiatry. *Arch. gen. Psychiat.*, 1967, **16**, 727–739.

HAYES, F. K. Military aeromedical evacuation and psychiatric patients during the Vietnam War. *Amer. J. Psychiat.*, 1969, **126**(5), 658–666.

HAYTHORN, W. W., & ALTMAN, I. Together in isolation. *Trans-action*, 1967, **4**(3), 18–22.

HINKLE, L. E., JR., & WOLFF, H. G. Communist interrogation and indoctrination of "enemies of the states." *Arch. neurol. Psychiat.*, 1956, **76**, 115–174.

HIRSCHBERG, C. Neurology and psychiatry: Psychoneuroses in military personnel. *Amer. J. med. Sci.*, 1944, **208**, 119–132.

HOROWITZ, M. J. Psychic trauma. *Arch. gen. Psychiat.*, 1969, **20**, 552–559.

HUNTER, E. *Brain-washing in Red China*. New York: Vanguard, 1954.

KARPE, R., & SCHNAP, I. Nostopathy—a study of pathogenic homecoming. *Amer. J. Psychiat.*, 1952, **109**, 46–51.

KEISER, L. *The traumatic neurosis*. Philadelphia: Lippincott, 1968.

KINKEAD, E. *In every war but one*. New York: Norton, 1959.

KLEMER, R. H. *Marriage and family relationships*. New York: Harper & Row, 1970.

KNIGHT, R. P. The treatment of the psychoneuroses of war. *Bull. Menninger Clin.*, 1943, **7**, 148–155.

LEOPOLD, R. L., & DILLON, H. Psychoanatomy of a disaster: A long term study of post-traumatic neuroses in survivors of a marine explosion. *Amer. J. Psychiat.*, 1963, **119**, 913–921.

LIFTON, R. J. Home by ship: Reaction patterns of American prisoners of war repatriated from North Korea. *Amer. J. Psychiat.*, 1954, **110**, 732–739.

LIFTON, R. J. *Thought reform and the psychology of totalism: A study of "brainwashing" in China*. New York: Norton, 1961.

LINDEMANN, E. Symptomatology and management of acute grief. *Amer. J. Psychiat.*, 1944, **101**, 141–148.

LUDWIG, A. O., & RANSON, S. W. A statistical follow-up of treatment of combat-induced psychiatric casualties. I and II. *Military Surgeon*, 1947, **100**, 51–62, 169–175.

MC DAVID, J. W., & HARARI, H. *Social psychology: Individuals, groups, societies*. New York: Harper & Row, 1968.

MC ELROY, R. B. Psychoneuroses, combat-anxiety type. *Amer. J. Psychiat.*, 1945, **101**, 517–520.

MC NEEL, B. H., & DANCEY, T. E. The personality of the successful soldier. *Amer. J. Psychiat.*, 1945, **102**, 337–342.

MENNINGER, W. C. *Psychiatry in a troubled world*. New York: Macmillan, 1948.

MODLIN, H. C. The trauma in "traumatic neurosis." *Bull. Menninger Clin.*, 1960, **24**, 49–56.

MODLIN, H. C. The postaccident anxiety syndrome: Psychosocial aspects. *Amer. J. Psychiat.*, 1967, **123**, 1008–1021.

MULLIN, C. S., JR. Some psychological aspects of isolated antarctic living. *Amer. J. Psychiat.*, 1960, **117**, 323–325.

NARDINI, J. E. Survival factors in American prisoners of war of the Japanese. Reprinted from *The American Journal of Psychiatry*, volume **109**, pages 241–248, 1952. Copyright 1952, the American Psychiatric Association.

NARDINI, J. E. Navy psychiatric assessment program in the antarctic. *Amer. J. Psychiat.*, 1962, **119**, 97–105. [a]

NARDINI, J. E. Psychiatric concepts of prisoners of war confinement. The William C. Porter Lecture—1961. *Military Medicine*, 1962, **127**, 299–307. [b]

NOBLE, D., ROUDEBUSH, M. E., & PRICE, D. Studies of Korean War casualties. I. Psychiatric manifestations in wounded men. *Amer. J. Psychiat.*, 1952, **108**, 495–499.

ORWELL, G. *1984*. New York: Harcourt, 1949.

OSWALD, P., & BITTNER, E. Life adjustment after severe persecution. *Amer. J. Psychiat.*, 1968, **124**(10), 1393–1400.

PETERSON, D. B., & CHAMBERS, R. E. Restatement of combat psychiatry. *Amer. J. Psychiat.*, 1952, **109**, 249–254.

POLNER, M. Vietnam War stories. *Trans-action*, 1968, **6**(1), 8–20. Copyright © November 1968 by Transaction, Inc., New Brunswick, New Jersey.

RAKER, J. W., WALLACE, A. F. C., & RAYMER, J. F. *Emergency medical care in disasters*. Disaster Study No. 6, Natl. Acad. of Sciences, Natl. Res. Coun. Publ. No. 457, Washington, D.C., 1956.

ROHRER, J. H. Interpersonal relations in isolated small groups. In B. E. Flaherty (Ed.), *Psychophysiological aspects of space flight*. New York: Columbia Univer. Press, 1961.

SATLOFF, A. Psychiatry and the nuclear submarine. *Amer. J. Psychiat.*, 1967, **124**(4), 547–551.

SAUL, L. J. Psychological factors in combat fatigue. *Psychosom. Med.*, 1945, **7**, 257–272.

SCHEIN, E. H. The Chinese indoctrination program for prisoners of war: A study of attempted "brainwashing." *Psychiatry*, May 1956, 149–172.

SCHEIN, E. H., SCHNEIER, I., & BARKER, C. H. *Coercive persuasion*. New York: Norton, 1961.

SEGAL, H. A. Initial psychiatric findings of recently repatriated prisoners of war. *Amer. J. Psychiat.*, 1954, **111**, 358–363.

SERXNER, J. An experience in submarine psychiatry. *Amer. J. Psychiat.*, 1968, **125**(1), 25–30.

SHEPS, J. G. A psychiatric study of successful soldiers. *JAMA*, 1944, **126**, 271–273.

SOBEL, MAJ. R. Anxiety-depressive reactions after prolonged combat experience—the old sergeant syndrome. *Bull. U.S. Army Med. Dept.*, *Combat Psychiat. Suppl.*, Nov. 1949, 137–146.

STERN, R. L. Diary of a war neurosis. *Journal of Nervous and Mental Disease*, 1947, **106**, 583–586. Copyright © 1947, The Williams & Wilkins Co., Baltimore, Md., 21202, U.S.A.

STRANGE, R. E., & BROWN, D. E., JR. Home from the wars. *Amer. J. Psychiat.*, 1970, **127**(4), 488–492.

STRASSMAN, H. D., THALER, M. B., & SCHEIN, E. H. A prisoner of war syndrome: Apathy as a reaction to severe stress. *Amer. J. Psychiat.*, 1956, **112**, 998–1003.

THOMPSON, G. N. Post-traumatic psychoneurosis—a statistic survey. *Amer. J. Psychiat.*, 1965, **121**, 1043–1048.

TROSSMAN, B. Adolescent children of concentration camp survivors. *Canadian Psychiat. Assn. J.*, 1968, **13**(2), 121–123.

TUOHY, W. Battlefield psychiatrist sees task as twofold. *Los Angeles Times*, March 2, 1967, I, 34. [a]

TUOHY, W. Drugs fight shell shock in Vietnam. *Los Angeles Times*, July 30, 1967, F, 12–13. [b]

TUOHY, W. Combat fatigue: U.S. lessens its toll in Vietnam. *Los Angeles Times*, Dec. 1, 1968, A, 1.

WATZLAWICK, P., BEAVIN, J., & JACKSON, D. D. *Pragmatics of human communication*. New York: Norton, 1967.

WEST, L. J. Psychiatric aspects of training for honorable survival as a prisoner of war. *Amer. J. Psychiat.*, 1958, **115**, 329–336.

WHITE, GEN. T. D. The inevitable climb to space. *Air Univer. quart. Rev.*, 1958–1959, **10**(4).

WILLIAMS, A. H. A psychiatric study of Indian soldiers in the Arakan. *Brit. J. med. Psychol.*, 1950, **23**, 130–181.

WOLFF, H. G. Stressors as a cause of disease in man. In J. M. Tanner (Ed.), *Stress and psychiatric disorder*. London: Oxford, 1960.

YINGER, J. M. *Toward a field theory of behavior*. New York: McGraw-Hill, 1965.

8. Neuroses

ABSE, D. W. Hysteria. In S. Arieti (Ed.), *American handbook of psychiatry*. Vol. 1. New York: Basic Books, 1959. Pp. 272–292.

ARIETI, S. A re-examination of the phobic symptoms and of symbolism in psychopathology. *Amer. J. Psychiat.*, 1961, **118**, 106–110.

BANDURA, A. *Principles of behavior modification*. New York: Holt, Rinehart & Winston, 1969.

BANDURA, A., BLANCHARD, E. B., & RITTER, B. Relative efficacy of desensitization and modeling approaches for inducing behavioral, affective, and attitudinal changes. *J. Pers. soc. Psychol.*, 1969, **13**, 173–179.

BEARD, G. M. *A practical treatise on nervous exhaustion (neurasthenia), its symptoms, nature, sequences, treatment.* (5th ed.) New York: E. B. Treat, 1905.

BERGIN, A. E. Some implications of psychotherapy research for therapeutic practice. In G. E. Stollak, B. G. Guerney, Jr., & M. Rothberg (Eds.), *Psychotherapy research: Selected readings*. Chicago: Rand McNally, 1966. Pp. 118–129.

BERNE, E. *Games people play*. New York: Grove Press, 1964.

BLANCHARD, W. Stimulus response: Ecstasy without agony is baloney. *Psych. Today*, 1970, **3**, 8–10, 64.

BROWN, W. L. Psycho-iconography of the office neurotic. *Clinical Symposia*, 1957, **9**(5), 173–175. © Copyright 1957, by CIBA Pharmaceutical Products, Inc. From *CIBA Clinical Symposia*, by Walter L. Brown.

CAROTHERS, J. C. The African mind in health and disease. *A study in ethnopsychiatry*. Geneva: World Organization, 1953, No. 17.

CAROTHERS, J. C. Culture, psychiatry, and the written word. *Psychiatry*, 1959, **22**, 307–320.

CARSON, R. B. *Interaction concepts of personality*. Chicago: Aldine, 1969.

CATTELL, R. B., & SCHEIER, I. H. *The meaning and measurements of neuroticism and anxiety*. New York: Ronald, 1961.

CATTELL, R. B., SCHEIER, I. H., & LORR, M. Recent advances in the measurement of anxiety, neuroticism, and the psychotic syndrome. *Ann. N.Y. Acad. Sci.*, 1962, **93**, 840–850.

COLEMAN, J. C. *Abnormal psychology and modern life.* (3rd ed.) Glenview, Ill.: Scott, Foresman, 1964.

COMBS, A. W., & SNYGG, D. *Individual behavior.* (rev. ed.) New York: Harper, 1959.

COON, G., & RAYMOND, A. *A review of the psychoneuroses at Stockbridge*. Stockbridge, Mass.: Austin Riggs Foundation, 1940. From "Talks to Patients" by Dr. Austen Fox Riggs. Copyright 1915, 1930, 1937 by Austen Fox Riggs, M.D. Reprinted from Appendix A, *A Review of the Psychoneuroses at Stockbridge* by G. P. Coon and Alice Raymond, copyright 1940. Reprinted by permission of Austen Riggs Center, Inc., G. P. Coon, and Alice Raymond.

DENKER, P. G. The prognosis of insured neurotics. *N.Y. St. J. Med.*, 1939, **39**, 238–247.

EIDUSON, B. T. The two classes of information in psychiatry. *Arch. gen. Psychiat.*, 1968, **18**, 405–419.

ELIOT, T. S. *The cocktail party*. Reprinted by permission of Harcourt Brace Jovanovich, Inc., and Faber and Faber Ltd.

EYSENCK, H. J. New ways in psychotherapy. *Psych. Today*, 1967, **1**(2), 39–47.

EYSENCK, H. J. Release and symptom substitution after different types of psychotherapy. *Behav. Res. Ther.*, 1969, **7**, 283–287.

FRANKEL, A. S. Treatment of a multisymtomatic phobic by a self-directed, self-reinforced imagery technique: A case study. Reprinted from the *Journal of Abnormal Psychology*, 1970, Vol. **76**, pp. 496–499, "Treatment of a Multisymptomatic Phobic by a Self-Directed Self-Reinforced Imagery Technique" by A. S. Frankel, by permission of the American Psychological Association.

GOODWIN, D. W., GUZE, S. B., & ROBBINS, E. Follow-up studies in obsessional neurosis. *Arch. gen. Psychiat.*, 1969, **20**, 182–187.

GUILFORD, J. P. *Personality.* New York: McGraw-Hill, 1959.

GUZE, S. B. The diagnosis of hysteria: What are we trying to do? *Amer. J. Psychiat.*, 1967, **124**(4), 491–498.

GUZE, S., WOODRUFF, R. A., & CLAYTON, P. J. Hysteria and antisocial behavior: Further evidence of an association. *Amer. J. Psychiat.*, 1971, **127**(7), 957–960.

HALLECK, S. L. Hysterical personality traits. *Archives of General Psychiatry*, 1967, **16**, 750–757. Copyright *Archives of General Psychiatry*, 1967. Reprinted by permission.

HALPERN, H. J. Hysterical amblyopia. *Bull. U.S. Army Med. Dept.*, 1944, No. 72, 84–87.

HAMMER, H. Astasia-abasia: A report of two cases at West Point. *Amer. J. Psychiat.*, 1967, **124**(5), 671–674.

HOGAN, R. A., & KIRCHNER, J. H. Preliminary report of the extinction of learned fears via short-term implosive therapy. *J. abnorm. Psychol.*, 1967, **72**, 106–109.

IRONSIDE, R., & BATCHELOR, I. R. C. The ocular manifestations of hysteria in relation to flying. *Brit. J. Ophthalmol.*, 1945, **29**, 88–98.

JENKINS, R. L. Psychiatric syndromes in children and their relation to family background. *Amer. J. Orthopsychiat.*, 1966, **36**, 450–457.

JENKINS, R. L. The varieties of children's behavioral problems and family dynamics. *Amer. J. Psychiat.*, 1968, **124**(10), 1440–1445.

JENKINS, R. L. Classification of behavior problems of children. *Amer. J. Psychiat.*, 1969, **125**(8), 1032–1039.

JONES, M. C. A laboratory study of fear: The case of Peter. *Pedagogical Seminary*, 1924, **31**, 308–315.

JORDAN, B., & KEMPLER, B. Hysterical personality: An experimental investigation of sex-role conflict. *J. Abnorm. Psychol.*, 1970, **75**, 172–176.

KENYON, F. E. Hypochondriasis: A survey of some historical, clinical, and social aspects. *Inter. J. Psychiat.*, 1966, **2**, 308–325.

KERCKHOFF, A. C., & BACK, K. W. The bug. *Psych. Today*, 1969, **3**(1), 46–49.

KERRY, R. J. Phobia of outer space. *J. ment. Sci.*, 1960, **106**, 1383–1387.

KIDSON, M. A., & JONES, I. H. Psychiatric disorders among aborigines of the Australian Western Desert. *Arch. gen. Psychiat.*, 1968, **19**, 413–417.

KIERSCH, T. A. Amnesia: A clinical study of ninety-eight cases. *Amer. J. Psychiat.*, 1962, **119**, 57–60.

KLINE, N. S. Drug treatment of phobic disorders. *Amer. J. Psychiat.*, 1967, **123**(11), 1447–1450.

KOHL, R. N. Pathologic reactions of marital partners to improvement of patients. *Amer. J. Psychiat.*, 1962, **118**, 1036–1041.

KNOFF, W. A history of the concept of neurosis, with a memoir of William Cullen. *Amer. J. Psychiat.*, 1970, **127**(1), 80–84.

KORA, T. Morita therapy. *Intern. J. Psychiat.*, 1965, **1**, 611–640.

KRAINES, S. H. *The therapy of the neuroses and psychoses.* (3rd ed.) Philadelphia: Lea & Febiger, 1948. Reprinted by permission.

LACEY, J. I. Somatic response patterning and stress: Some revisions of activation theory. In M. H. Appley & R. Trumbull (Eds.), *Psychological stress: Issues in research.* New York: Appleton-Century-Crofts, 1967. Pp. 14–37.

LADER, M., & MATHEWS, A. Physiological changes during spontaneous panic attacks. *J. psychosom. Res.*, 1970, **14**(4), 377–382.

LANCASTER, E., & POLING, J. *Final face of Eve.* New York: McGraw-Hill, 1958.

LANG, P. J., STROUFE, L. A., & HASTINGS, J. E. Effects of feedback and instructional set on the control of cardiac-rate variability. *J. exp. Psychol.*, 1967, **75**, 425–431.

LESSING, L. Science takes a closer look at man. *Fortune*, 1970, **81**, 113–114.

LIEBSON, I. Conversion reaction: A learning theory approach. *Behav. Res. Ther.*, 1969, **7**, 217–218.

LIEF, H. I. Generic and specific aspects of phobic behavior. *Inter. J. Psychiat.*, 1968, **6**, 470–473.

LIPMAN, R. S., RICKELS, K., COVI, L., DEROGATIS, L. R., & UHLENHUTH, E. H. Factors of symptom distress. *Arch. gen. Psychiat.*, 1969, **21**, 328–338.

LIPTON, S. Dissociated personality: A case report. *Psychiatric Quarterly*, 1943, **17**, 35–36. Permission granted by *Psychiatric Quarterly*.

MADDI, S. R. The existential neurosis. *J. abnorm. Psychol.*, 1967, **72**, 311–325.

MALAN, D. H., BACAL, H. A., HEALTH, E. S., & BALFOUR, F. H. G. A study of psychodynamic changes in untreated neurotic patients. *Brit. J. Psychiat.*, 1968, **114**, 525–551.

MALMO, R. B. Emotions and muscle tension: The story of Anne. *Psychology Today*, 1970, **3**(10), material adapted from pages 64–67, and 83. Copyright © Communications/Research/Machines, Inc. Reprinted by permission.

MARKS, I. M. Agoraphobic syndrome (phobic anxiety state). *Arch. gen. Psychiat.*, 1970, **23**(6), 538–553.

MASSERMAN, J. H. *Principles of dynamic psychiatry.* (2nd ed.) Philadelphia: W. B. Saunders Company, 1961. Reprinted by permission.

MATHER, M. D. The treatment of an obsessive-compulsive patient by discrimination learning and reinforcement of decision-making. *Behav. Res. Ther.*, 1970, **8**(3), 315–318.

MC GUIRE, R. J., & VALLANCE, M. Aversion therapy by electric shock: A simple technique. *Brit. med. J.*, 1964, **1**, 151–153.

MENNINGER, K. A. *The human mind.* (3rd ed.) New York: Knopf, 1945. From pages 41–42, 139–140 in *The Human Mind*, by Karl Menninger. Copyright 1930, 1937, 1945 and renewed 1958, 1965 by Karl Menninger. Reprinted by permission of Alfred A. Knopf, Inc.

MILLER, N. E. Learning of visceral and glandular responses. *Science*, 1969, **163**(3866), 434–445.

MOWRER, O. H. "Sin": The lesser of two evils. *Amer. Psychologist*, 1960, **15**, 301–304.

MOWRER, O. H. Civilization and its malcontents. *Psych. Today*, 1967, **1**, 49–52.

MUCHA, T. F., & REINHARDT, R. F. Conversion reactions in student aviators. Printed in original form in *The American Journal of Psychiatry*, volume **127**, pages 493–497, 1970. Copyright 1970, the American Psychiatric Association.

MURPHY, G. *Personality.* New York: Harper, 1947.

NEMIAH, J. C. Obsessive-compulsive reaction. In A. M. Freedman & H. I. Kaplan (Eds.), *Comprehensive textbook of psychiatry.* Baltimore: Williams & Wilkins, 1967. Pp. 912–928.

O'NEILL, M., & KEMPLER, B. Approach and avoidance responses of the hysterical personality to sexual stimuli. *J. abnorm. Psychol.*, 1969, **74**, 300–305.

PARKIN, A. Neurosis and schizophrenia. III. Clinical considerations. *Psychiat. Quart.*, 1966, **40**, 405–428.

PARRY-JONES, W., SANTER-WESTSTRATE, H. G., & CRAWLEY, R. C. Behavior therapy in a case of hysterical blindness. *Behav. Res. Ther.*, 1970, **8**(1), 79–85.

PAUL, G. L. Outcome of systematic desensitization. II. In C. M. Franks (Ed.), *Assessment and status of the behavior therapies.* New York: McGraw-Hill, 1968. Pp. 105–159.

PITTS, F. N., JR., & MC CLURE, J. N., JR. Lactate metabolism in anxiety neurosis. *New Engl. J. Med.*, 1967, **277**, 1329–1336.

POLLIN, W., ALLEN, M. G., HOFFER, A., STABENAU, J. R., & HRUBEC, Z. Psychopathology in 15,909 pairs of veteran twins. *Amer. J. Psychiat.*, 1969, **126**, 597–609.

PORTNOY, I. The anxiety states. In S. Arieti (Ed.), *American handbook of psychiatry. Vol. 1.* New York: Basic Books, 1959. Pp. 307–323.

RACHMAN, S. Systematic desensitization. *Psychol. Bull.*, 1967, **67**, 93–103.

RICKELS, K., GORDON, P. E., MECKELNBURG, R., SABLOSKY, L., WHALEN, E. M., & DION, H. Iprindole in neurotic depressed general practice patients: A controlled study. *Psychosomatics*, 1968, **9**, 208–214.

ROGERS, C. The group comes of age. *Psych. Today*, 1969, 3(7), 8–10, 64.

ROSENTHAL, S. H., & WULFSOHN, N. L. Electrosleep—a clinical trial. *Amer. J. Psychiat.*, 1970, **127**(4), 533–534.

SALZMAN, L. Obsessions and phobias. *Inter. J. Psychiat.*, 1968, **6**, 451–468.

SHAPIRO, S. B. A theory of ego pathology and ego therapy. *J. Psychol.*, 1962, **53**, 81–90.

SKINNER, B. F. In M. H. Hall, An interview with "Mr. Behaviorist" B. F. Skinner. *Psych. Today*, 1967, **1**, 21–23.

SLATER, E., & WOODSIDE, M. *Patterns of marriage*. London: Cassell, 1951.

SNAITH, R. P. A clinical investigation of phobias. *Brit. J. Psychiat.*, 1968, **114**, 673–697.

SOLOMON, P., LEIDERMAN, P. H., MENDELSON, J., & WEXLER, D. Sensory deprivation. *Amer. J. Psychiat.*, 1957, **114**, 357–363.

STAMPFL, T. G., & LEVIS, D. J. Essentials of implosive therapy: A learning-therapy-based psychodynamic behavioral therapy. *J. abnorm. Psychol.*, 1967, **72**, 496–503.

STEELE, J. The hysteria and psychasthenia constructs as an alternative to manifest anxiety and conflict-free ego functions. *J. abnorm. Psychol.*, 1969, **74**, 79–85.

STEVENSON, L. Processes of "spontaneous" recovery from the psychoneuroses. *Amer. J. Psychiat.*, 1961, **117**, 1057–1064.

TERHUNE, W. B. The phobic syndrome—its nature and treatment. *J. Ark. Med. Soc.*, 1961, **58**, 230–236.

THIGPEN, C. H., & CLECKLEY, H. A case of multiple personality. *J. abnorm. soc. Psychol.*, 1954, **49**, 135–151.

THIGPEN, C. H., & CLECKLEY, H. M. *Three faces of Eve*. New York: McGraw-Hill, 1957.

WALLERSTEIN, E., DYKYJ, R., & NODINE, J. H. Fluphenazine and amitriptyline in the anxious depressed patient. *Amer. J. Psychiat.*, 1967, **124**(3), 397–403.

WEISS, E., & ENGLISH, O. S. *Psychosomatic medicine*. Philadelphia: W. B. Saunders, 1943.

WOLPE, J. *Psychotherapy by reciprocal inhibition*. Stanford: Stanford Univer. Press, 1958.

WOLPE, J. For phobia: A hair of the hound. *Psychol. Today*, 1969, **3**, 34–37.

9. Schizophrenia and Paranoia

AKERFELDT, S. Oxidation of N, N-Dimethyl-p-phenylenediamine by serum from patients with mental disease. *Science*, 1957, **125**(1), 117–119.

ALANEN, Y. O. The mothers of schizophrenic patients. *Acta Psychiatrica Neurologica Kbh.*, 1958, **33**(Suppl. No. 124), 359.

ALANEN, Y. O. From the mothers of schizophrenic patients to interactional family dynamics. In D. Rosenthal & S. S. Kety (Eds.), *The transmission of schizophrenia*. Elmsford, N.Y.: Pergamon Press, 1968. Pp. 201–212.

AL-ISSA, I. Problems in the cross-cultural study of schizophrenia. *J. Psychol.*, 1969, **71**(1), 143–151.

AMERICAN ORTHOPSYCHIATRIC ASSOCIATION. Communication from American Orthopsychiatric Association to Joint Commission on the Mental Health of Children. *Amer. J. Orthopsychiat.*, 1969, **39**(3), 383–388.

ANTHONY, E. J. The developmental precursors of adult schizophrenia. In D. Rosenthal & S. Kety (Eds.), *The transmission of schizophrenia*. Elmsford, N.Y.: Pergamon, 1968. Pp. 293–316.

ARIETI, S. Schizophrenia: The manifest symptomatology, the psychodynamic and formal mechanisms. In S. Arieti (Ed.), *American handbook of psychiatry*. Vol. 1. New York: Basic Books, 1959. Pp. 455–484.

ARONSON, J., & POLGAR, S. Pathogenic relationships in schizophrenia. *Amer. J. Psychiat.*, 1962, **119**, 222–227.

ATTHOWE, J. M., JR., & KRASNER, L. Preliminary report on the application of contingent reinforcement procedures (token economy) on a "chronic" psychiatric ward. *J. abnorm. Psychol.*, 1968, **73**, 37–43.

AYLLON, T., & AZRIN, N. H. The measurement and reinforcement of behavior of psychotics. *J. exper. Anal. Behav.*, 1965, **8**, 357–384.

BANDURA, A. *Principles of behavior modification*. New York: Holt, Rinehart & Winston, 1969.

BANNISTER, D. Schizophrenia: Carnival mirror of coherence. *Psych. Today*, 1971, **4**(8), 66–69, 84.

BATESON, G. Cultural problems posed by a study of schizophrenic process. In A. Auerback (Ed.), *Schizophrenia: An integrated approach*. New York: Ronald, 1959. Pp. 125–264.

BATESON, G. Minimal requirements for a theory of schizophrenia. *Arch. gen. Psychiat.*, 1960, **2**, 477–491.

BECK, S. J. Families of schizophrenic and of well children: Methods, concepts, and some results. *Amer. J. Orthopsychiat.*, 1960, **30**, 247–275.

BECKER, E. Toward a theory of schizophrenia. External objects and the creation of meaning. *Arch. gen. Psychiat.*, 1962, **7**, 170–181.

BECKETT, P. G., SENF, R., FROHMAN, C. E., & GOTTLIEB, J. S. Energy production and premorbid history in schizophrenia. *Arch. gen. Psychiat.*, 1963, **8**, 155–162.

BETTELHEIM, B. *Truants from life: The rehabilitation of emotionally disturbed children*. Glencoe, Ill.: Free Press, 1955.

BLACKER, K. H., JONES, R., STONE, G., & PFEFFERBAUM, D. Chronic users of LSD: The "acidheads." *Amer. J. Psychiat.*, 1968, **125**(3), 341–351.

BLISS, E. L., CLARK, L. D., & WEST, C. D. Studies of sleep deprivation: Relationship to schizophrenia. *Arch. neurol. Psychiat.*, 1959, **81**, 348–359.

BORN, W. Artistic behavior of the mentally deranged; and Great Artists who suffered from mental disorders. *Ciba Symposia*, 1946, **8**, 207–216, 225–232.

BOWEN, M. Family relationships in schizophrenia. In A. Auerback (Ed.), *Schizophrenia: An integrated approach*. New York: Ronald, 1959. Pp. 147–178.

BOWEN, M. A family concept of schizophrenia. In D. D. Jackson (Ed.), *The etiology of schizophrenia*. New York: Basic Books, 1960. Pp. 346–372.

BOWERS, M. The onset of psychosis—A diary account. *Psychiatry*, 1965, **28**, 346–358. Permission granted by author and The William Alanson White Psychiatric Foundation.

BOWERS, M. Pathogenesis of acute schizophrenic psychosis. Reprinted by permission of *Archives of General Psychiatry*, September 1968, volume **19**, number 3, pages 349, 350, 352, and 353.

BRODEY, W. M. Some family operations and schizophrenia. *Arch. gen. Psychiat.*, 1959, **1**, 379–402.

BROEN, W. E., JR. *Schizophrenia: Research and theory*. New York: Academic Press, 1968.

BROOKS, G. W., DEANE, W., & HUGEL, R. Some aspects of the subjective experience of schizophrenia. *Dis. nerv. Sys.*, 1968, **29**(5), 78–82.

BUBER, M. Distance and relation. *Psychiatry*, 1957, **20**, 97–104.

BURTON, A. Schizophrenia and existence. *Psychiatry*, 1960, **23**, 385–394.

BUSS, A. H., & BUSS, E. H. (Eds.) *Theories of schizophrenia*. New York: Atherton, 1969.

CAFFEY, E. M., GALBRECHT, C. R., & KLETT, C. J. Brief hospitalization and aftercare in the treatment of schizophrenia. *Arch. gen. Psychiat.*, 1971, **21**(1), 81–86.

CAMERON, N. Paranoid conditions and paranoia. In S. Arieti (Ed.), *American handbook of psychiatry*. New York: Basic Books, 1959. Pp. 508–539.

CAMERON, N., & MARGARET, A. Experimental studies in thinking. I. Scattered speech in the responses of normal subjects to incomplete sentences. *J. exper. Psychol.*, 1949, **39**(5), 617–627.

CAMERON, N., & MARGARET, A. *Behavior pathology*. Boston: Houghton Mifflin, 1951.

CAROTHERS, J. C. The African mind in health and disease. In *A study in ethnopsychiatry*. Geneva: World Health Organization, 1953, No. 17.

CAROTHERS, J. C. Culture, psychiatry, and the written word. *Psychiatry*, 1959, **22**, 307–320.

CARSON, R. *Interaction concepts of personality*. Chicago: Aldine, 1969.

CHRISTIAN, H. A. *Psychiatry for practitioners*. New York: Oxford Univer. Press, 1936.

COPELAND, J. Aspects of mental illness in West African students. *Soc. Psychiat.*, 1968, **3**(1), 7–13.

CURRY, A. E. The world of a schizophrenic woman. Reprinted from *The Psychoanalytic Review*, Vol. **49**, No. 1, 1962, through the courtesy of the Editors and the Publisher, National Psychological Association for Psychoanalysis, New York, N.Y.

DEARING, G. P. Russians support genetic basis for schizophrenia. *Psychiatric News*, 1969, **4**(8), 18.

DELGADO, J. M. R. Electronic pacing of behavior: Brain research, treatment tool. *Roche Reports*, 1969, **6**(7), 1–2, 8.

DELGADO, J. M. R. ESB. *Psych. Today*, 1970, **3**(12), 48–53.

DEMENT, W. C. A new look at the third stage of existence. *Stanford M. D.*, 1968–1969, **8**, 208.

DEMENT, W. C., ZARCONE, V., FERGUSON, J., COHEN, H., PIVIK, T., & BARCHAS, J. Some parallel findings in schizophrenic patients and serotonin-depleted cats. Paper presented at the Schizophrenia Conference, Nov. 1968.

DEWALD, P. A. Folie a deux and the function of reality testing. *Psychiatry*, 1970, **33**(3), 390–392. Copyright 1970 The William Alanson White Psychiatric Foundation, Inc. Reprinted by special permission of The William Alanson White Psychiatric Foundation, Inc.

DIAMOND, B. L. Sirhan B. Sirhan: A conversation with T. George Harris. *Psych. Today*, 1969, **3**(4), 48–56.

DRIEMEN, P. M., & MINARD, C. Preleave planning: Effect upon rehabilitation. *Arch. gen. Psychiat.*, 1971, **24**(1), 87–90.

DUPONT, R. L., JR., & GRUENBAUM, H. Willing victims: The husbands of paranoid women. *Amer. J. Psychiat.*, 1968, **125**(2), 151–159.

EISENBERG, L. The interaction of biological and experiential factors in schizophrenia. In D. Rosenthal & S. S. Kety (Eds.), *The transmission of schizophrenia*. Elmsford, N.Y.: Pergamon Press, 1968. Pp. 403–409.

ENDERS, L. J., & FLINN, D. E. Clinical problems in aviation medicine: Schizophrenic reaction, paranoid type. *Aerospace Medicine*, 1962, **33**, 730–732. Reprinted by permission.

FABREGA, H., SWARTZ, J. D., & WALLACE, C. A. Ethnic differences in psychopathology. *Arch. gen. Psychiat.*, 1968, **19**, 218–226.

FEINBERG, I., BRAUN, M., KARESKO, R., & GOTTLIEB, F. Stage 4 sleep in schizophrenia. *Arch. gen. Psychiat.*, 1969, **21**(3), 262–266.

FEINSILVER, D. Communication in families of schizophrenic patients. *Arch. gen. Psychiat.*, 1970, **22**(2), 143–148.

FENZ, W. D., & VELNER, J. Physiological concomitants of behavior indexes in schizophrenia. *J. abnorm. Psychol.*, 1970, **76**(1), 27–35.

FIELD, M. J. *Search for security: An ethnopsychiatric study of rural Ghana*. Evanston: Northwestern Univer. Press, 1960.

FISCHER, J. Negroes and whites and rates of mental illness: Reconsideration of a myth. *Psychiatry*, 1969, **32**(4), 428–446.

FLECK, S. Family dynamics and origin of schizophrenia. *Psychosomatic Medicine*, 1960, **22**, 337–339. Reprinted by permission of Harper & Row, Inc.

FLECK, S., LIDZ, T., & CORNELISON, A. R. Comparison of parent-child relationships of male and female schizophrenic patients. *Arch. gen. Psychiat.*, 1963, **8**, 1–7.

FORGUS, R., & DE WOLFE, A. Perceptual selectivity in hallucinatory schizophrenics. *J. abnorm. Psychol.*, 1969, **74**(3), 288–292.

FREEMAN, T. On the psychopathology of schizophrenia. *J. ment. Sci.*, 1960, **106**, 925–937.

GALTON, F. *Inquiries into human faculty and its development*. London: Macmillan, 1883.

GARMEZY, N. The prediction of performance in schizophrenia. In P. H. Hock & J. Zubin (Eds.), *Psychopathology of schizophrenia*. New York: Grune & Shatton, 1966. Pp. 129–181.

GARMEZY, N., CLARKE, A. R., & STOCKNER, C. Child rearing attitudes of mothers and fathers as reported by schizophrenic and normal patients. *J. abnorm. soc. Psychol.*, 1961, **63**, 176–182.

GERARD, D. L., & SIEGEL, J. The family background of schizophrenia. *Psychiat. Quart.*, 1950, **24**, 47–73.

GILLULY, R. H. A new look at the meaning of reality. *Science News*, 1971, **99**, 335–337.

GOLDSTEIN, M. J., JUDD, L. K., RODNICK, E. H., & LA POLLA, A. Psychophysiological and behavioral effects of phenothiazine administration in acute schizophrenics as a function of premorbid states. *J. psychiat. Res.*, 1969, **6**, 271–287.

GOLDSTEIN, M. J., RODNICK, E. H., & JUDD, L. K. Schizoid therapy. *Newsweek*, June 7, 1971, 77–78.

GOOD, H. S. Fifteen days adrift on a raft: A clinical evaluation of five survivors. *Nav. med. Bull.*, 1943, **41**, 367–373.

GOODWIN, D. W., ALDERSON, P., & ROSENTHAL, R. Clinical significance of hallucinations in psychiatric disorders. *Arch. gen. Psychiat.*, 1971, **21**(1), 76–80.

GORDON, J. S. Who is mad? Who is sane? R. D. Laing: In search of a new psychiatry. *Atlantic*, 1971, **227**(1), 50–66. From "Who Is Mad? Who Is Sane? R. D. Laing: In Search of a New Psychiatry?" Copyright © 1970, by THE ATLANTIC MONTHLY COMPANY, Boston, Mass. Reprinted with permission.

GOTTESMAN, I., & SHIELDS, J. Schizophrenia in twins: 16 years' consecutive admissions to a psychiatric clinic. *Brit. J. Psychiat.*, 1966, **112**, 809–818.

GOTTLIEB, J. S., FROHMAN, C. E., & BECKETT. P. G. S. A theory of neuronal malfunction in schizophrenia. *Amer. J. Psychiat.*, 1969, **126**(2), 149–156.

GRALNICK, A. Folie a deux—the psychosis of association; a review of 103 cases and the entire English literature, with case presentations. *Psychiat. Quart.*, 1942, **14**, 230–263.

GRANT, V. W. Paranoid dynamics: A case study. Reprinted from *The American Journal of Psychiatry*, volume **113**, pages 143–148, 1956. Copyright 1956, the American Psychiatric Association.

GREEN, H. *I never promised you a rose garden*. New York: Holt, Rinehart & Winston, 1964.

GREGORY, I. *Psychiatry, biological and social*. Philadelphia: W. B. Saunders, 1961.

GRINKER, R. R., SR. An essay on schizophrenia and science. *Arch. gen. Psychiat.*, 1969, **20**, 1–24.

GRINSPOON, L., EWALT, J. R., & SHADER, R. Psychotherapy and pharmacotherapy in chronic schizophrenia. *Amer. J. Psychiat.*, 1968, **124**(12), 1645–1652.

HALEY, J. The family of the schizophrenic: A model system. *J. nerv. ment. Dis.*, 1959, **129**, 357–374.

HALEY, J. Direct study of child-parent interactions. III. Observation of the family of the schizophrenic. *Amer. J. Orthopsychiat.*, 1960, **30**, 460–467.

HEATH, R. G. A biochemical hypothesis on the etiology of schizophrenia. In D. D. Jackson (Ed.), *The etiology of schizophrenia*. New York: Basic Books, 1960.

HEATH, R. G., KRUPP, I. M., BYERS, L. W., & LILJEKVIST, J. I. Schizophrenia as an immunologic disorder. *Arch. gen. Psychiat.*, 1967, **16**(1), 1–33.

HEATH, R. G., MARTENS, S., LEACH, B. E., COHEN, M., & ANGEL, C. Effect on behavior in humans with the administration of taraxein. *Amer. J. Psychiat.*, 1957, **114**, 14–24.

HEATH, R. G., MARTENS, S., LEACH, B. E., COHEN, M., & FEIGLEY, C. A. Behavioral changes in nonpsychotic volunteers following the administration of taraxein, the substance obtained from serum of schizophrenic patients. *Amer. J. Psychiat.*, 1958, **114**, 917–920.

HESTON, L. Psychiatric disorders in foster home reared children of schizophrenic mothers. *Brit. J. Psychiat.*, 1966, **112**, 819–825.

HESTON, L. L. The genetics of schizophrenic disease. *Science*, 1970, **167**, 249–256.

HILLYER, J. *Reluctantly told*. New York: Macmillan, 1926.

HIMWICH, H. E. Study backs biochemical etiology in schizophrenia. *Psychiatric News*, 1970, **5**(10). 15.

HOAGLAND, H. Some consideration of the role of the adrenal cortex in the origin of the psychoses. *J. nerv. ment. Dis.*, 1954, **119**, 75–76.

HOFFER, A., & POLLIN, W. Schizophrenia in the NAS–NRC panel of 15,909 veteran twin pairs. *Arch. gen. Psychiat.*, 1970, **23**(5), 469–477.

HOFFMAN, J. L. Psychotic visitors to government offices in the national capital. *Amer. J. Psychiat.*, 1943, **99**, 571–575.

HOLLISTER, L. E. Drug-induced psychoses and schizophrenic reactions: A critical comparison. *Ann. N.Y. Acad. Sci.*, 1962, **96**, 80–92.

HORWITT, M. K. Fact and artifact in the biology of schizophrenia. *Science*, 1956, **124**(3), 429–430.

JACO, E. G. *The social epidemiology of mental disorders.* New York: Russell Sage Found., 1960.

KALLMANN, F. J. *Heredity in health and mental disorder.* New York: Norton, 1953.

KALLMANN, F. J. The use of genetics in psychiatry. *J. ment. Sci.*, 1958, **104**, 542–549.

KAUFMAN, I., FRANK, T., HEIMS, L., HERRICK, J., REISER, D., & WILLER, L. Treatment implications of a new classification of parents of schizophrenic children. *Amer. J. Psychiat.*, 1960, **116**, 920–924.

KETY, S. S. Recent biochemical theories of schizophrenia. In D. D. Jackson (Ed.), *The etiology of schizophrenia.* New York: Basic Books, 1960. Pp. 120–145.

KIMMICH, R. A. Ethnic aspects of schizophrenia in Hawaii. *Psychiatry*, 1960, **23**, 97–102.

KLAF, F. S. Female homosexuality and paranoid schizophrenia. *Arch. gen. Psychiat.*, 1961, **4**, 84–86.

KLAF, F. S., & DAVIS, C. A. Homosexuality and paranoid schizophrenia: A survey of 150 cases and controls. *Amer. J. Psychiat.*, 1960, **116**, 1070–1075.

KORANYI, E. K., & LEHMANN, H. E. Experimental sleep deprivation in schizophrenic patients. *Arch. gen. Psychiat.*, 1960, **2**, 534–544.

KRAMER, M. Cross-national study of diagnosis of the mental disorders: Origin of the problem. *Amer. J. Psychiat.*, 1969, **125**(10, Suppl.), 1–10.

KRINGLEN, E. *Heredity and environment in the functional psychosis: An epidemiological-clinical twin study.* Oslo: Universitsforlaget, 1967.

LACEY, J. I. Somatic response patterning and stress: Some revisions of activation theory. In M. H. Appley & R. Trumbull (Eds.), *Psychological stress: Issues in research.* New York: Appleton-Century-Crofts, 1967. Pp. 14–37.

LAING, R. D. *The politics of experience.* New York: Pantheon, 1967. [a]

LAING, R. D. Schizophrenic split. *Time*, Feb. 3, 1967, 56. [b]

LAING, R. D. *The divided self.* New York: Pantheon, 1969.

LAING, R. D. Quoted in J. S. Gordon, Who is mad? Who is sane? R. D. Laing: In search of a new psychiatry. *Atlantic*, 1971, **227**(1), 50–66.

LAING, R. D., & ESTERSON, A. *Sanity, madness, and the family.* London: Tavistock, 1964.

LEMERT, E. M. Paranoia and the dynamics of exclusion. *Sociometry*, 1962, **25**, 2–25.

LEVITZ, L., & ULLMANN, L. P. Manipulation of indications of disturbed thinking in normal subjects. *J. cons. clin. Psychol.*, 1969, **33**(6), 633–641.

LEWINSON, T. S. Dynamic disturbances in the handwriting of psychotics; with reference to schizophrenic, paranoid, and manic-depressive psychoses. Reprinted from *The American Journal of Psychiatry*, volume 97, pages 102–135, 1940.

LIDZ, T. The family, language, and the transmission of schizophrenia. In D. Rosenthal & S. S. Kety (Eds.), *The transmission of schizophrenia.* Elmsford, N.Y.: Pergamon Press, 1968. Pp. 175–184.

LIDZ, T., CORNELISON, A. R., FLECK, S., & TERRY, D. Intrafamilial environment of the schizophrenic patient. I. The father. *Psychiatry*, 1957, **20**, 329–342.

LIDZ, T., CORNELISON, A. R., TERRY, D., & FLECK, S. Irrationality as a family tradition. *Arch. neurol. Psychiat.*, 1958, **79**, 305–316.

LIDZ, T., FLECK, S., ALANEN, Y. O., & CORNELISON, A. R. Schizophrenic patients and their siblings. *Psychiatry*, 1963, **26**, 1–18.

LIEF, A. (Ed.) *The commonsense psychiatry of Dr. Adolf Meyer.* New York: McGraw-Hill, 1948.

LUBY, E. D., GRISELL, J. L., FROHMAN, C. E., LEES, H., COHEN, B. D., & GOTTLIEB, J. S. Biochemical, psychological, and behavioral responses to sleep deprivation. *Ann. N.Y. Acad. Sci.*, 1962, **96**, 71–78.

MC GHIE, A., & CHAPMAN, J. Disorders of attention and perception in early schizophrenia. *British Journal of Medical Psychology*, 1961,

34, 103–116. Reprinted by permission of the authors and the British Psychological Society.

MEARES, A. *The door of serenity.* Springfield, Ill.: Thomas, 1958.

MEDNICK, S. A. Breakdown in individuals at high risk for schizophrenia: Possible predispositional perinatal factors. *Mental Hygiene*, 1970, **54**(1), 50–63.

MEDNICK, S. A. Birth defects and schizophrenia. *Psych. Today*, 1971, **4**(11), 48–50, 80–81.

MEDNICK, S. A., & MC NEIL, T. F. Current methodology in research on the etiology of schizophrenia: Serious difficulties which suggest the use of the high-risk-group method. *Psychol. Bull.*, 1968, **70**, 681–693.

MENNINGER, K. Diagnosis and treatment of schizophrenia. Reprinted with permission from the *Bulletin of the Menninger Clinic*, vol. **12**, pp. 101–104, copyright 1948 by The Menninger Foundation.

MILLER, C. Worlds that fail. *Trans-action*, 1966, **4**(2), 36–41.

MILNER, K. O. The environment as a factor in the aetiology of criminal paranoia. *J. ment. Sci.*, 1949, **95**, 124–132.

MISHLER, E., & WAXLER, N. Family interaction and schizophrenia: Alternative frameworks of interpretation. In D. Rosenthal & S. S. Kety (Eds.), *The transmission of schizophrenia.* Elmsford, N.Y.: Pergamon Press, 1968. Pp. 213–222.

MODLIN, H. C. Psychodynamics and the management of paranoid states in women. *Arch. gen. Psychiat.*, 1963, **8**(3), 263–268.

MOORE, R. A., & SELZER, M. L. Male homosexuality, paranoia, and the schizophrenias. *Amer. J. Psychiat.*, 1963, **119**, 743–747.

MURPHY, H. B. Cultural factors in the genesis of schizophrenia. In D. Rosenthal & S. S. Kety (Eds.), *The transmission of schizophrenia.* Elmsford, N.Y.: Pergamon Press, 1968. Pp. 137–152.

OFFORD, D. R., & CROSS, L. A. Behavioral antecedents of schizophrenia. *Arch. gen. Psychiat.*, 1969, **21**, 267–283.

OVERSTREET, H. *The mind alive.* New York: Norton, 1954.

PAUL, G. L. Chronic mental patients: Current status—future directions. *Psychol. Bull.*, 1969, **71**, 81–94.

PAVLOV, I. P. *Conditioned reflexes and psychiatry.* (Trans. & ed. W. H. Gant.) New York: Inter. Publ., 1941.

PLANANSKY, K., & JOHNSTON, R. The incidence and relationship of homosexual and paranoid features in schizophrenia. *J. ment. Sci.*, 1962, **108**, 604–615.

POLLIN, W., ALLEN, M. G., HOFFER, A., STABENAU, J. R., & HRUBEC, Z. Psychopathology in 15,909 pairs of veteran twins. *Amer. J. Psychiat.*, 1969, **126**(5), 43–56.

RETTERSTOL, N. Paranoid psychoses associated with impending or newly established fatherhood. *Acta Psychiatr. Scandin.*, 1968, **44**(1), 51–61.

RIN, H., & LIN, T. Y. Mental illness among Formosan aborigines as compared with the Chinese in Taiwan. *J. ment. Sci.*, 1962, **108**, 134–146.

RODNICK, E. H. The psychopathology of development: Investigating the etiology of schizophrenia. *Amer. J. Orthopsychiat.*, 1968, **38**, 784–798.

ROSEN, H., & KIENE, H. E. Paranoia and paranoiac reaction types. *Diseases of the Nervous System*, 1946, **7**, 330–337. Reprinted by permission of the Physicians Postgraduate Press.

ROSENBAUM, C. P. Patient-family similarities in schizophrenia. *Arch. gen. Psychiat.*, 1961, **5**, 120–126.

ROSENTHAL, D., & KETY, S. S. (Eds.) *The transmission of schizophrenia.* Elmsford, N.Y.: Pergamon Press, 1968.

ROSENTHAL, D., WENDER, P. H., KETY, S. S., SCHULSINGER, F., WELNER, J., & OSTERGAARD, L. Schizophrenics' offspring reared in adoptive homes. In D. Rosenthal & S. S. Kety (Eds.), *The transmission of schizophrenia.* Elmsford, N.Y.: Pergamon Press, 1968. Pp. 377–391.

RUBIN, L. S. Autonomic dysfunction in psychoses: Adults and autistic children. *Arch. gen. Psychiat.*, 1962, **7**, 1–14.

RUBINSTEIN, E. A., & COELHO, G. V. Mental health and behavioral sciences: One federal agency's role in the behavioral sciences. *Amer. Psychologist*, 1970, **25**(6), 517–523.

RUESCH, J., BRODSKY, C., & FISCHER, A. The acute nervous breakdown. *Arch. gen. Psychiat.*, 1963, **8**, 197–207.

RUTNER, I., & BUGLE, C. An experimental procedure for the modification of psychotic behavior. *J. cons. clin. Psychol.*, 1969, **33**(6), 651–653.

SACHAR, E. J., KANTER, S., BUIE, D., ENGLE, R., & MEHLMAN, R. Psycho-endocrinology of ego disintegration. *Amer. J. Psychiat.*, 1970, **126**(8), 1067–1078.

SALZMAN, L. Paranoid state—theory and therapy. *Arch. gen. Psychiat.*, 1960, **2**, 679–693.

SARVIS, M. A. Paranoid reactions: Perceptual distortion as an etiological agent. *Arch. gen. Psychiat.*, 1962, **6**, 157–162.

SCHOOLER, C., & FELDMAN, S. E. *Experimental studies of schizophrenia.* Goleta, Calif.: Psychonomic Press, 1967.

SCHULTZ, D. P. *Sensory restriction.* New York: Academic Press, 1965.

SCHWARTZ, D. A. A re-view of the "paranoid" concept. *Gen. Psychiat.*, 1963, **8**, 349–361.

SEBASTIANI, J., & FOY, J. Psychotic visitors to the White House. *Amer. J. Psychiat.*, 1965, **122**(6), 679–686.

SHAKOW, D. On doing research in schizophrenia. *Arch. gen. Psychiat.*, 1969, **20**(6), 634–635.

SHORE, P. A., PLETSCHER, A., TOMICH, E. G., CARLSSON, A., KUNTZMAN, R., & BRODIE, B. B. Role of brain serotonin in reserpine action. *Ann. N.Y. Acad. Sci.*, 1957, **66**, 609–615.

SINGER, M. Address delivered at Mt. Zion Hospital and Medical Center, San Francisco, Sept. 12, 1960. Reported in C. P. Rosenbaum, Patient-family similarities in schizophrenia. *Arch. gen. Psychiat.*, 1961, **5**, 120–126.

SINGER, M., & WYNNE, L. C. Differentiating characteristics of the parents of childhood schizophrenics, childhood neurotics and young adult schizophrenics. *Amer. J. Psychiat.*, 1963, **120**, 234–243.

SINGER, M., & WYNNE, L. C. Thought disorder and family relations of schizophrenics. III. Methodology using projective techniques. *Arch. gen. Psychiat.*, 1965, **12**, 182–200. [a]

SINGER, M., & WYNNE, L. C. Thought disorder and family relations of schizophrenics. IV. Results and implications. *Arch. gen. Psychiat.*, 1965, **12**, 201–212. [b]

SOMMER, R., & OSMOND, H. The schizophrenic no-society. *Psychiatry*, 1962, **25**, 244–255.

STABENAU, J. R., TUPIN, J., WERNER, M., & POLLIN, W. A comparative study of families of schizophrenics, delinquents, and normals. *Psychiatry*, 1965, **28**, 45–59.

STEPHENS, J., ASTRUP, C., & MAGNUM, J. Prognostic factors in recovered and deteriorated schizophrenics. *Amer. J. Psychiat.*, 1966, **122**(10), 1116–1121.

STRAUSS, J. S. Hallucinations and delusions as points on continua function. *Arch. gen. Psychiat.*, 1969, **21**(5), 581–586.

TAYLOR, A. Sex ratios of newborns: Associated with prepartum and postpartum schizophrenia. *Science*, 1969, **164**(3880), 723–724.

TURNER, R., DOPKEEN, L., & LABRECHE, G. Marital status and schizophrenia: A study of incidence and outcome. *J. abnorm. Psychol.*, 1970, **76**(1), 110–116.

VITOLS, M. M. The significance of the higher incidence of schizophrenia in the Negro race in North Carolina. *N.C. med. J.*, 1961, **22**(4), 147–158.

VORONIN, L. G. Some results of comparative physiological investigations of higher nervous activity. *Psychol. Bull.*, 1962, **59**, 161–195.

WAHL, C. W. Some antecedent factors in the family histories of 568 male schizophrenics of the United States Navy. *Amer. J. Psychiat.*, 1956, **113**, 201–210.

WILL, O. A., JR. Human relatedness and the schizophrenic reaction. *Psychiatry*, 1959, **22**, 205–223.

WYNNE, L. C. Methodologic and conceptual issues in the study of schizophrenics and their families. In D. Rosenthal & S. S. Kety (Eds.), *The transmission of schizophrenia.* Elmsford, N.Y.: Pergamon Press, 1968. Pp. 185–200.

WYNNE, L. C., RYCKOFF, I. M., DAY, J., & HIRSCH, S. I. Pseudo-mutuality in the family relations of schizophrenia. *Psychiatry*, 1958, **21**, 205–220.

YERBURY, E. C., & NEWELL, N. Genetic and environmental factors in psychoses of children. *Amer. J. Psychiat.*, 1943, **100**, 599–605.

YOLLES, S. F. Unraveling the mystery of schizophrenia. *Today's Health*, 1967, **45**, 42, 82–84.

ZILFERSTEIN, I. Speaking prose without knowing it. *Inter. J. Psychiat.*, 1968, **6**(5), 366–370.

ZUBOWICZ, G. What is adequate treatment for schizophrenia? *Roche Reports*, 1969, **6**(5), 5, 11.

10. Major Affective Disorders and Suicide

AMERICAN PSYCHIATRIC ASSOCIATION. *Diagnostic and statistical manual of mental disorders.* 2nd ed. Washington, D.C.: APA, 1968.

ANDERSON, D. B., & MC CLEAN, L. J. (Eds.) *Identifying suicide potential.* New York: Behavioral Publications, 1971.

ARIETI, S. Manic-depressive psychosis. In S. Arieti (Ed.), *American handbook of psychiatry.* New York: Basic Books, 1959. Pp. 419–454.

BALDESSARINI, R. J., & STEPHENS, J. H. Lithium carbonate for affective disorders. *Arch. gen. Psychiat.*, 1970, **22**(1), 72–77.

BECK, A. T. *Depression: Clinical, experimental, and theoretical aspects.* New York: Harper & Row, 1967.

BECK, A. T. The meaning of depression. *Science News*, 1969, **96**(24), 554.

BECKER, E. *The revolution in psychiatry: The new understanding of man.* New York: Free Press, 1964.

BECKER, J. Achievement related characteristics of manic-depressives. *J. abnorm. soc. Psychol.*, 1960, **60**, 334–339.

BECKER, J., & ALTROCCHI, J. Peer conformity and achievement in female manic-depressives. *J. abnorm. Psychol.*, 1968, **73**(6), 585–589.

BIBRING, E. The mechanisma of depression. In P. Greenacre (Ed.), *Affective disorders.* New York: International Univer. Press, 1953.

BLAINE, G., & CARMEN, L. Causal factors in suicidal attempts by male and female college students. *Amer. J. Psychiat.*, 1968, **125**(6), 146–149.

BLINDER, M. G. The pragmatic classification of depression. *Amer. J. Psychiat.*, 1966, **123**, 259–269.

BOGARD, H. M. Follow-up study of suicidal patients seen in emergency room consultation. *Amer. J. Psychiat.*, 1970, **126**(7), 1017–1020.

BRATFOS, O., & HAUG, J. O. The course of manic-depressive psychosis: A follow-up investigation of 215 patients. *Acta Psychiatr. Scandin.*, 1968, **44**(1), 89–112.

BUNNEY, W., BRODIE, H., MURPHY, D., & GOODWIN, F. Studies of alpha-methl-para-tyrosine, L-dopa, and L. trypitophan in depression and mania. *Amer. J. Psychiat.*, 1971, **127**(7), 48–56.

BUNNEY, W. E., PAUL, M. I., & CRAMER, H. Biological trigger of "switch" from depression to mania may be CAMP. *Roche Reports*, 1971, **1**(6), 1–2, 8. Reprinted by permission of Dr. W. E. Bunney, Jr., and Dr. M. I. Paul.

CAROTHERS, J. C. A study of mental derangement in Africans, and an attempt to explain its peculiarities, more especially in relation to the African attitude of life. *J. ment. Sci.*, 1947, **93**, 548–597.

CAROTHERS, J. C. Frontal lobe function and the African. *J. ment. Sci.*, 1951, **97**, 12–48.

CAROTHERS, J. C. The African mind in health and disease. In *A study in ethnopsychiatry.* Geneva: World Health Organization, 1953, No. 17.

CAROTHERS, J. C. Culture, psychiatry, and the written word. *Psychiatry*, 1959, **22**, 307–320.

COWEN, J. R. Depression. *Psychiatric Quarterly*, 1959, **33**, 351. Reprinted by permission of the *Psychiatric Quarterly*.

DARBONNE, A. R. Suicide and age: A suicide note analysis. *J. cons. clin. Psychol.*, 1969, **33**, 46–50.

DE FLEUR, M. L., D'ANTONIO, W. V., & DE FLEUR, L. B. *Sociology: Man in society.* Glenview, Ill.: Scott, Foresman, 1971.

DIZMANG, L. H. Suicide found epidemic among Indian teenagers. *Psychiat. News*, 1970, **5**(10), 17.

DORZAB, J., BAKER, M., CADORET, R., & WINOKUR, G. Depressive disease: Familial psychiatric illness. *Amer. J. Psychiat.*, 1971, **127**(9), 48–60.

DURKHEIM, E. *Suicide: A study in sociology.* Trans. J. A. Spaulding & G. Simpson. Ed. G. Simpson. New York: Free Press, 1951. Originally published 1897.

EASSON, W. M., & STEINHILBER, R. M. Murderous aggression by children and adolescents. *Arch. gen. Psychiat.*, 1961, **4**, 1–9.

EATON, J. W., & WEIL, R. J. *Culture and mental disorders: A comparative study of the Hutterites and other populations.* Glencoe, Ill.: Free Press, 1955.

ENGEL, G. L. Anxiety and depression withdrawal: The primary affects of unpleasure. *Inter. J. Psychoanal.*, 1962, **43**, 89–97.

ENGLISH, O., & FINCH, S. M. *Introduction to psychiatry.* New York: Norton, 1954.

FARBEROW, N. L., & LITMAN, R. E. A comprehensive suicide prevention program. Suicide Prevention Center of Los Angeles, 1958–1969. Unpublished final report DHEW NIMH Grants No. MH 14946 & MH 00128. Los Angeles, 1970.

FARBEROW, N. L. & SHNEIDMAN, E. S. (Eds.) *The cry for help.* New York: McGraw-Hill, 1961.

FARBEROW, N. L., SHNEIDMAN, E. S., & LEONARD, C. Suicide among general medical and surgical hospital patients with malignant neoplasms. Veterans Administration, Dept. of Medicine and Surgery, *Medical Bulletin* MB–9, Feb. 25, 1963, 1–11.

FIELD, M. J. *Search for security: An ethnopsychiatric study of rural Ghana.* Evanston: Northwestern Univer. Press, 1960.

FOLSOM, J. C. Kind firmness technique. *Science News*, 1969, **95**(22), 517–540.

FRANK, J. The role of hope in psychotherapy. *J. Psychiat.*, 1968, **5**, 383–395.

FRIEDMAN, A. S. Minimal effects of severe depression on cognitive functioning. *J. abnorm. soc. Psychol.*, 1964, **69**, 237–243.

GIBSON, R. W. The family background and early life experience of the manic-depressive patient: A comparison with the schizophrenic patients. *Psychiatry*, 1958, **21**, 71–90.

GIBSON, R. W., COHEN, M. B., & COHEN, R. A. On the dynamics of the manic-depressive personality. *Amer. J. Psychiat.*, 1959, **115**, 1101–1107.

GOLD, H. R. Observations on cultural psychiatry during a world tour of mental hospitals. *Amer. J. Psychiat.*, 1951, **108**, 462–468.

GOLDSMITH, W., & CRETEKOS, C. Unhappy Odysseys: Psychiatric hospitalization among Vietnam returnees. *Arch. gen. Psychiat.*, 1969, **20**, 78–83.

GOLDSTEIN, I. B. The relationship of muscle tension and autonomic activity to psychiatric disorders. *Psychosom. Med.*, 1965, **27**, 39–52.

GOODWIN, F. K., MURPHY, D. L., & BUNNEY, W. E., JR. Lithium-carbonate treatment in depression and mania. *Arch. gen. Psychiat.*, 1969, **21**(4), 486–496.

GREENSPAN, K., SCHILDKRAUT, J. J., GORDON, E. K., LEVY, B., & DURELL, J. Catecholamine metabolism in affective disorders. *Arch. gen. Psychiat.*, 1969, **21**(6), 710–716.

GREGORY, I. *Psychiatry, biological and social.* Philadelphia: W. B. Saunders, 1961.

GRINKER, R. An essay on schizophrenia and science. *Arch. gen. Psychiat.*, 1969, **20**(1), 1–24.

HAGGERTY, H. Pre-psychotic personality traits in women with involutional melancholia. *Smith Coll. Stud. soc. Work*, 1941, **12**, 191–192.

HALL, J. C., BLISS, M., SMITH, K., & BRADLEY, A. Suicide gestures, attempts found high among poor. *Psychiat. News*, July 1, 1970, p. 20.

HARTMANN, E. Longitudinal studies of sleep and dream patterns in manic-depressive patients. *Arch. gen. Psychiat.*, 1968, **19**, 312–329.

HAVIGHURST, R. J. Suicide and education. In E. S. Shneidman (Ed.), *On the nature of suicide.* San Francisco: Jossey-Bass, 1969. Pp. 53–67.

HELLER, A., ZAHOUREK, R., & WHITTINGTON, H. Effectiveness of antidepressant drugs: A triple blind study comparing imipramine, desipramine, and placebo. *Amer. J. Psychiat.*, 1971, **127**(8), 132–135.

HENDERSON, D., & GILLESPIE, R. D. *A textbook of psychiatry for students and practitioners.* New York: Oxford Univer. Press, 1950.

HENDIN, H. Black suicide. *Arch. gen. Psychiat.*, 1969, **21**, 407–422.

HES, J. P. Manic-depressive illness in Israel. *Amer. J. Psychiat.*, 1960, **116**, 1082–1086.

HILL, D. General discussion. In J. M. Tanner (Ed.), *Stress and psychiatric disorder.* Oxford: Blackwell, 1960. Pp. 121–129.

HILL, D. Depression: Disease, reactions, or posture? *Amer. J. Psychiat.*, 1968, **125**(4), 445–457.

HOEDEMAKER, F. S. Psychotic episodes and postpsychotic depression in young adults. *Amer. J. Psychiat.*, 1970, **127**(5), 66–70.

JACO, E. G. *The social epidemiology of mental disorders.* New York: Russell Sage Found., 1960.

JANOWSKY, D. S., LEFF, M., & EPSTEIN, R. Playing the manic game. *Arch. gen. Psychiat.*, 1970, **22**, 252–261.

JENNER, F. A., GJESSING, L. R., COX, J. R., DAVIES-JONES, A., & HULLIN, R. P. A manic-depressive psychotic with a 48 hour cycle. *Brit. J. Psychiat.*, 1967, **113**(501), 859–910.

JOHNSON, W. B. Euphoric and depressed moods in normal subjects. I. *Charact. & Pers.*, 1937, **6**, 212–216.

KALLMANN, F. J. Genetic aspects of psychoses. In *The biology of mental health and disease* (27th annual conference of the Milbank Memorial Fund). New York: Harper, 1952.

KALLMANN, F. J. *Heredity in health and mental disorder.* New York: Norton, 1953.

KALLMANN, F. J. The use of genetics in psychiatry. *J. ment. Sci.*, 1958, **104**, 542–549.

KARNOSH, L. J. (with collaboration of Zucker, E. M.) *Handbook of psychiatry.* St. Louis: Mosby, 1945. Reprinted by permission of the C. V. Mosby Co.

KASTENBAUM, R. Psychological autopsy: A case commentary. *Bulletin of Suicidology*, 1970, **7**, 33–35.

KATKIN, E. S., SASMOR, D., & TAN, R. Conformity and achievement-related characteristics of depressed patients. *J. abnorm. Psychol.*, 1966, **71**(6), 407–412.

KENDELL, R. Relationship between aggression and depression. *Arch. gen. Psychiat.*, 1970, **22**, 308–318.

KIDSON, M., & JONES, I. Psychiatric disorders among aborigines of the Australian Western Desert. *Arch. gen. Psychiat.*, 1968, **19**, 413–422.

KIEV, A. New directions for suicide prevention centers. *Amer. J. Psychiat.*, 1970, **127**(1), 87–88.

KING, L., & PITTMAN, G. Six-year follow-up of affect disorders in adolescents traced. *Roche Reports*, 1970, **7**(5), 3.

KOPIN, I. J. Brain biochemistry and human behavior. *Inter. J. Psychiat.*, 1967, **4**(3), 223–224.

KORNER, I. Hope as a method of coping. *J. clin. cons. Psychol.*, 1970, **34**(2), 134–139.

KRAEPELIN, E. *Clinical psychiatry.* (6th ed.) New York: Macmillan, 1937. Originally published 1899.

LANZKRON, J. Murder as a reaction to paranoid delusions in involutional psychosis and its prevention. *Amer. J. Psychiat.*, 1961, **118**, 426–429.

LAZARUS, A. P. Learning theory in the treatment of depression. *Behav. Res. Ther.*, 1968, **8**, 83–89.

LEFF, M. J., ROATCH, J. F., & BUNNEY, W. E., JR. Environmental factors preceding the onset of severe depressions. *Psychiatry*, 1970, **33**(3), 298–311. Reprinted by special permission of Dr. William E. Bunney, Jr., and The William Alanson White Psychiatric Foundation, Inc.

LEHMANN, H. E. Clinical perspectives on anti-depressant therapy. *Amer. J. Psychiat.*, **124**(11, Suppl.), 12–21.

LIPTON, M. A. Affective disorders: Progress but some unresolved questions remain. *Amer. J. Psychiat.*, 1970, **127**(3), 357–358.

LORR, M., & KLETT, C. J. Cross-cultural comparison of psychotic syndromes. *J. abnorm. Psychol.*, 1969, **74**(4), 531–543.

LUNN, D. Hawaii meeting highlights transcultural psychiatry. *Psychiat. News*, July 1, 1970, 9.

LYNN, E. J., SATLOFF, A., & TINLING, D. Mania and the use of lithium: A three-year study. *Amer. J. Psychiat.*, 1971, **127**(9), 96–100.

MANDELL, A. J. Chemical bases of depression. *Science News*, 1969, **96**(24), 554.

MANDELL, A. J. Biochemical findings said to support Freud's ideas. *Psychiat. News*, Jan. 1970, 21.

MASSERMAN, J. H. *Principles of dynamic psychiatry.* Philadelphia: W. B. Saunders Company, 1961. Reprinted by permission.

MC GEE, L. L., & HILTNER, S. The role of the clergy. In H. L. P. Resnik (Ed.), *Suicidal Behavior: Diagnosis and management.* Boston: Little, Brown and Company, 1968. Pp. 468–469. Reprinted by permission.

MELGES, F., & BOWLBY, J. Types of hopelessness in psychopathological process. *Arch. gen. Psychiat.*, 1969, **20**, 690–699.

MENDELS, J., & HAWKINS, D. R. Sleep and depression. *Arch. gen. Psychiat.*, 1968, **19**(4), 445–452.

MEYER, A. *Collected papers of Adolf Meyer.* 4 vols. Baltimore: John Hopkins Press, 1948–1952.

MOTTO, J. A. Langley Porter receives grant to study depression and suicide. Univer. of California: *University Bulletin*, 1969, **17**(36), 180.

MURPHY, H. B. M., WITTKOWER, E. D., & CHANCE, N. A. Crosscultural inquiry into the symptomatology of depression: A preliminary report. *Inter. J. Psychiat.*, 1967, **3**(1), 6–15.

NATIONAL INSTITUTE OF MENTAL HEALTH. Psychiatrists suicide prone. *Science News*, 1969, **95**(16), 380.

NELSON, H. New treatment for suicidal depression called successful. *Los Angeles Times*, Dec. 22, 1970, II, 1–2.

NELSON, H. County suicide rate up sharply among young. *Los Angeles Times*, Jan. 26, 1971, II, 1.

NEUGARTEN, B. L. A new look at menopause. *Psych. Today*, 1967, **1**(7), 67–69.

NEW ZEALAND DEPARTMENT OF HEALTH. *Annual report of the medical statistician on the mental health statistics of New Zealand for the year 1960.* Wellington: Author, 1960.

OLDS, S. Menopause—something to look forward to? *Today's Health*, 1970, **48**(5), 48–49, 74–76, 79–80.

PALMER, H. D. Involutional psychoses: Melancholia. *Pub. Hlth. Rep.* (Suppl. No. 168), Washington, D.C., 1942, 118–124.

PARKER, N., & BURTON-BRADLEY, B. G. World's lowest suicide rate reported in New Guinea. *Roche Reports*, 1967, **4**(6), 1.

PAYKEL, E. S., MYERS, J., DIENELT, M., KLERMAN, G., LINDENTHAL, J., & PEPPER, M. Life events and depression. *Arch. gen. Psychiat.*, 1969, **21**, 753–760.

POLLACK, B. Clinical findings in the use of tofranil in depressive and other psychiatric states. *Amer. J. Psychiat.*, 1959, **116**, 312–317.

POLLACK, J. H. "I want out"—teen suicides. *Today's Health*, 1971, **49**(1), 69–71.

POLLIN, W., ALLEN, M. G., HOFFER, A., STABENAU, J. R., & HRUBEC, Z. Psychopathology in 15,909 pairs of veteran twins: Evidence for a genetic factor in the pathogenesis of schizophrenia and its relative absence in psychoneurosis. *Amer. J. Psychiat.*, 1969, **126**(5), 43–56.

POZNANSKI, E., & ZRULL, J. P. Childhood depression. *Arch. gen. Psychiat.*, 1970, **23**(1), 8–15.

REICH, T., CLAYTON, P. J., & WINOKUR, G. Family history studies: The genetics of mania. *Amer. J. Psychiat.*, 1969, **125**(10), 1358–1369.

RENNIE, T. A. C., & FOWLER, J. B. Prognosis in manic-depressive psychoses. *Amer. J. Psychiat.*, 1942, **98**, 801–814.

RESNIK, H. L. P., & DIZMANG, L. H. Observations on suicidal behavior among American Indians. *Amer. J. Psychiat.*, 1971, **127**(7), 882–887.

RINGEL, E. Suicide prevention in Vienna. In H. L. P. Resnik (Ed.), *Suicidal behaviors: Diagnosis and management.* Boston: Little, Brown, 1968. Pp. 381–390.

ROBINS, E., MURPHY, G. E., WILKINSON, R. H., GASSNER, S., & KAYES, J. Some clinical considerations in the prevention of suicide based on a study of 134 successful suicides. *Amer. J. Pub. Hlth.*, 1959, **49**, 888.

ROGOW, A. A. Private illness and public policy: The cases of James Forrestal and John Winant. *Amer. J. Psychiat.*, 1969, **125**(8), 1093–1097.

ROSEN, D. H. The serious suicide attempt: Epidemiological and follow-up study of 886 patients. *Amer. J. Psychiat.*, 1970, **127**(6), 64–70.

ROSENTHAL, S. H. The involutional depressive syndrome. *Amer. J. Psychiat.*, 1968, **124**(11, Suppl.), 21–34.

ROSS, M. Suicide among college students. *Amer. J. Psychiat.*, 1969, **126**(2), 220–225.

RUDESTAM, K. E. Stockholm and Los Angeles: A cross-cultural study of the communication of suicidal intent. *J. cons. clin. Psychol.*, 1971, **36**(1), 82–90.

SCHILDKRAUT, J. J. The catecholamine hypothesis of affective disorders: A review of supporting evidence. *Amer. J. Psychiat.*, 1965, **122**(5), 509–522.

SCHILDKRAUT, J. J. Catecholamine hypothesis of affective disorders. *Inter. J. Psychiat.*, 1967, **4**(3), 203–217.

SCHRUT, A. Some typical patterns in the behavior and background of adolescent girls who attempt suicide. *Amer. J. Psychiat.*, 1968, **125**(1), 107–112.

SCOTTISH HOME AND HEALTH DEPARTMENT. *Scottish health statistics.* Edinburgh: Her Majesty's Stationery Office, 1961.

SEIDEN, R. H. Campus tragedy: A study of student suicide. *J. abnorm. Psychol.*, 1966, **71**(6), 389–399.

SEIDEN, R. H. We're driving young blacks to suicide. *Psych. Today*, 1970, **4**(3), 24–28.

SHAEFER, H. H., & MARTIN, P. L. Behavioral therapy for "apathy" of hospitalized schizophrenics. *Psychol. Rep.*, 1966, **19**, 1147–1158.

SHAFFER, L. Fear and courage in aerial combat. *J. cons. Psychol.*, 1947, **11**, 137–143.

SHNEIDMAN, E. S. Fifty-eight years. In E. S. Shneidman (Ed.), *On the nature of suicide.* San Francisco: Jossey-Bass, 1969. Pp. 1–30.

SHNEIDMAN, E. S., PARKER, E., & FUNKHOUSER, G. R. You and death. *Psych. Today*, 1970, **4**(3), 67–72.

SLATER, E. T. O. Genetics in psychiatry. *J. ment. Sci.*, 1944, **90**, 17–35.

SLOTTEN, I. W., ALTMAN, H., & ULETT, G. A. Computer spots patients likely to elope or think of suicide. *Roche Reports*, 1971, **1**(6), 1–2.

SNYDER, F., SCOTT, J., KARACAN, I., & ANDERSON, D. Presumptive evidence of REMS deprivation in depressive illness. *Psychophysiology*, 1968, **4**(3), 382.

SPIELBERGER, C. D., PARKER, J. B., & BECKER, J. Conformity and achievement in remitted manic-depressive patients. *J. nerv. ment. Dis.*, 1963, **137**, 162–172.

STANLEY, E. J., & BARTER, J. T. Adolescent suicidal behavior. *Amer. J. Orthopsychiat.*, 1970, **40**(1), 87–96.

STAR, J. Suicide. *Look*, Aug. 22, 1966, 60–62.

STOTLAND, E. *The psychology of hope.* San Francisco: Jossey-Bass, 1969.

TAIT, C. D., & BURNS, G. C. Involutional illnesses: A survey of 379 patients, including follow-up study of 114. *Amer. J. Psychiat.*, 1951, **108**, 27–36.

THOMAS, K. The Berlin syndrome. *Time*, March 30, 1970, 92.

TITLEY, W. B. Prepsychotic personality of involutional melancholia. *Arch. neurol. Psychiat.*, 1936, **36**, 19–33.

TONKS, C., PAYKEL, E., & KLERMAN, G. Clinical depression among Negroes. *Amer. J. Psychiat.*, 1970, **127**(3), 329–335.

TUCKMAN, J., KLEINER, R., & LAVELL, M. Emotional content of suicide notes. Reprinted from *The American Journal of Psychiatry*, volume **116**, pages 59–63, 1959. Copyright 1959, the American Psychiatric Association.

ULLMANN, L. P., & KRASNER, L. *Psychological approach to abnormal behavior.* Englewood Cliffs, N.J.: Prentice-Hall, 1969.

VAN DER VELDE, C. Effectiveness of lithium carbonate in the treatment of manic-depressive illness. *Amer. J. Psychiat.*, 1970, **127**(3), 345–351.

VOGEL, G., & TRAUB, A. Further studies on REM deprivation of depressed patients. *Psychophysiology*, 1968, **5**(2), 239.

WATKINS, C., GILBERT, J. E., & BASS, W. The persistent suicidal patient. *Amer. J. Psychiat.*, 1969, **125**, 1590–1593.

WEISMAN, A. D. "Life-threatening behavior" identified by suicidologist. *Psychiat. News*, 1970, **5**(18), 5.

WEISZ, S. Types of depressive reactions. *Dis. nerv. Sys.*, 1947, **8**, 212–216.

WHYBROW, P. C., & MENDELS, J. Toward a biology of depression: Some suggestions from neurophysiology. *Amer. J. Psychiat.*, 1969, **125**(11), 45–54.

WILSON, W. P., & WILSON, N. J. The neurophysiology of affective disorders. *Dis. nerv. Sys.*, 1968, **29**(2), 105–107.

WINOKUR, G., CADORET, R., DORZAB, J., & BAKER, M. Depressive disease. *Arch. gen. Psychiat.*, 1971, **24**(2), 135–144.

WORLD HEALTH ORGANIZATION. Suicides rising. *Science News*, 1967, **92**(10), 229.

WYATT, R. J., FRAM, D. H., KUPFER, D., & SNYDER, F. Total prolonged drug-induced REM sleep suppression in anxious-depressed subjects. *Arch. gen. Psychiat.*, 1971, **24**(2), 145–155.

ZUNG, W. W. K. Evaluating treatment methods for depressive disorders. *Amer. J. Psychiat.*, 1968, **124**(11), 40–47.

ZUNG, W. W. K. A cross-cultural survey of symptoms in depression. *Amer. J. Psychiat.*, 1969, **126**(1), 116–121.

11. Sociopathic Disorders, Delinquency, and Crime

ABDULLAH, S., JARVIK, L., KATO, T., JOHNSTON, W., & LANZKRON, J. Extra Y chromosome and its psychiatric implications. *Arch. gen. Psychiat.*, 1969, **21**(4), 497–501.

ABRAMSON, R. Fingerprints may be keys to criminality: Symposium on biology of violence hears latest findings in chromosomal research. *Los Angeles Times*, Dec. 31, 1969, I, 6.

ALSOP, J. Cosa Nostra bigger than president's attack on it. *Los Angeles Times*, April 25, 1969, II, 10.

AMERICAN PSYCHIATRIC ASSOCIATION. *Diagnostic and statistical manual.* (2nd ed.) Washington, D.C.: APA, 1968.

ANDERSON, R. E. Where's Dad? Paternal deprivation and delinquency. *Arch. gen. Psychiat.*, 1968, **18**(6), 641–649.

ANDRY, R. G. Paternal and maternal roles and delinquency. *WHO Publ. Hlth. Paper*, 1962, **14**, 31–44.

ARIEF, A. J., & BOWIE, C. G. Some psychiatric aspects of shoplifting. *J. clin. Psychopath.*, 1947, **7**, 565–576.

BACH-Y-RITA, G., LION, J. R., CLIMENT, C. E., & ERVIN, F. R. Episodic dyscontrol: A study of 130 violent patients. *Amer. J. Psychiat.*, 1971, **127**(11), 1473–1478.

BACON, M. K., CHILD, I. L., & BARRY, H., III. A cross-cultural study of correlates of crime. *J. abnorm. soc. Psychol.*, 1963, **66**, 291–300.

BALOGH, J. The wings of an angel. *Trans-action*, 1965, **2**(2), 41.

BANAY, R. S. Immaturity and crime. Reprinted from *The American Journal of Psychiatry*, volume **100**, pages 170–177, 1943.

BANAY, R. S. *Wanted—an institute of criminal science.* Yearbook of the National Probation Association, 1945.

BANDURA, A. *Principles of behavior modification.* New York: Holt, Rinehart & Winston, 1969.

BANDURA, A., & WALTERS, R. H. *Adolescent aggression.* New York: Ronald, 1959.

BANDURA, A., & WALTERS, R. H. *Social learning and personality development.* New York: Holt, Rinehart & Winston, 1963.

BARKER, G. H., & ADAMS, W. R. Comparison of the delinquencies of boys and girls. *J. crim. Law*, 1962, **53**, 470–475.

BARKER, J. C., & MILLER, M. Aversion therapy for compulsive gamblers. *J. nerv. ment. Dis.*, 1968, **146**(4), 285–302.

BEDNAR, R. L., ZELHART, P. F., GREATHOUSE, L., & WEINBERG, S. Operant conditioning principles in the treatment of learning and behavior problems with delinquent boys. *J. couns. Psychol.*, 1970, **17**(6), 492–497.

BENNETT, I. *Delinquent and neurotic children: A comparative study.* New York: Basic Books, 1961.

BERES, D., & OBERS, S. J. The effects of extreme deprivation in infancy on psychic structure in adolescence: A study in ego development. In R. S. Eissler et al. (Eds.), *Psychoanalytic study of the child.* Vol. 5. New York: International Univer. Press, 1950.

BERGLER, E. *The psychology of gambling.* New York: Hill & Wang, 1957.

BERRY, J. R. What makes a gambling addict? *Today's Health*, 1968, **46**(10), 20–23.

BLACKHURST, A. E. Mental retardation and delinquency. *J. spec. Ed.*, 1968, **2**(4), 379–391.

BLAKE, G. Community treatment plan aids delinquents. Five year experiment. *Los Angeles Times*, Jan. 26, 1967, I, 6.

BLOCH, H. A. The dilemma of American gambling: Crime or pastime?

In H. A. Bloch (Ed.), *Crime in America.* New York: Philosophical Library, 1961. Pp. 333–351.

BLUEMEL, C. S. *War, politics, and insanity.* Denver: World Press, 1948. Reprinted by permission of Mrs. C. S. Bluemel.

BOLEN, D. W., & BOYD, W. H. Gambling and the gambler. *Arch. gen. Psychiat.*, 1968, **18**(5), 617–630.

BORKOVEC, T. D. Autonomic reactivity to sensory stimulation in psychopathic, neurotic, and normal juvenile delinquents. *J. cons. clin. Psychol.*, 1970, **35**, 217–222.

BOYD, W. H., & BOLEN, D. W. The compulsive gambler and spouse in group psychotherapy. *Inter. J. group Psychother.*, 1970, **20**, 77–90.

BUCHARD, J. D. Systematic socialization: A programmed environment for the rehabilitation of antisocial retardates. *Psychol. Rec.*, 1967, **17**, 461–476.

BURDMAN, M. Realism in community-based correctional services. *Ann. Amer. Acad. Polit. Soc. Sci.*, 1969, **381**, 71–80.

BURGER, W. Speeding up justice—the President's plan. *U.S. News and World Report*, March 27, 1971, p. 37.

BURKS, H. L., & HARRISON, S. I. Aggressive behavior as a means of avoiding depression. *Amer. J. Orthopsychiat.*, 1962, **32**, 416–422.

BUSS, A. H. *Psychopathology.* New York: Wiley, 1966.

CAPUTO, D. V., & MANDELL, W. Consequences of low birth weight. *Develop. Psychol.*, 1970, **3**(3), 363–383.

CASH, J. R. 8 lines from the lyrics of "San Quentin." Copyright © 1970 House of Cash, Inc., P.O. Box 508, Hendersonville, Tennessee 37075. Used by permission.

CHIRICOS, T. G., & WALDO, G. P. Punishment as a deterrent. *Science News*, 1970, **98**(11), 220.

CHRISS, N. C. Conjugal visits: Is the prisoner helped or hurt? *Los Angeles Times*, April 17, 1969, I, 1.

CLARKE, J. The precipitation of juvenile delinquency. *J. ment. Sci.*, 1961, **107**, 1033–1034.

CLONINGER, C. R., & GUZE, S. Psychiatric illness and female criminality: The role of sociopathy and hysteria in the antisocial woman. *Amer. J. Psychiat.*, 1970, **127**(3), 303–311. [a]

CLONINGER, C. R., & GUZE, S. B. Female criminals: Their personal, familial, and social backgrounds. *Arch. gen. Psychiat.*, 1970, **23**(6), 554–558. [b]

CLOWARD, R. A., & OHLIN, L. E. *Delinquency and opportunity: A theory of delinquent gangs.* New York: Free Press, 1963.

COHEN, A. K. *Delinquent boys: The culture of the gang.* New York: Free Press, 1955.

COHEN, H. L., FILIPCZAK, J., BIS, J., COHN, J., GOLDIAMOND, I., & LARKIN, P. *Case II-Model: A contingency-oriented 24-hour learning environment in a juvenile correctional institution.* Silver Springs, Md.: Educational Facility Press, 1968.

COHEN, J., & HANSEL, M. *Risk and gambling: A study of subjective probability.* New York: Philosophical Library, 1956.

COLE, K. E., FISHER, G., & COLE, S. Women who kill. *Arch. gen. Psychiat.*, 1968, **19**(1), 1–8.

CORTÉS, J. B., & GATTI, F. M. Physique and propensity. *Psych. Today*, 1970, **4**(3), 42–44, 82–84.

CRESSEY, D. R. To fight organized crime: Define it. *University Bulletin* (Univer. of Calif.), 1967, **15**(39), 176.

CRESSEY, D. R. *Theft of the nation: The structure and operations of organized crime in America.* New York: Harper & Row, 1969.

CRICHTON, R. *The great imposter.* New York: Random House, 1959. Summarized from *The Great Imposter*, by Robert Crichton. © Copyright 1959 by Robert Crichton. Used by permission of Random House, Inc.

DAVIS, A. J. Sexual assaults in the Philadelphia prisons and sheriff's vans. *Trans-action*, 1968, **6**(2), 28–35.

DEVEREAUX, G. Psychodynamics of Mohave gambling. *American Imago*, 1950, **7**, 55–56.

DRUMMOND, W. J. San Quentin: An inside view of its turmoil. *Los Angeles Times*, March 18, 1971, I, 1, 3.

DUNCAN, J. W., & DUNCAN, G. M. Murder in the family: A study of some homicidal adolescents. Reprinted from *The American Journal of*

Psychiatry, volume **127**, pages 1498–1502, 1971. Copyright 1971, the American Psychiatric Association.

ELKIND, D. Middle-class delinquency. *Mental Hygiene*, 1967, **51**, 80–84.

ENNIS, P. H. Crime, victims, and the police. *Trans-action*, 1967, **4**(7), 36–44.

EYSENCK, H. J. *Behaviour therapy and the neuroses.* London: Pergamon Press, 1960.

FENZ, W. D. Heart rate responses to a stressor: A comparison between primary and secondary psychopaths and normal controls. *J. exp. Res. Person.*, 1971, **5**(1), 7–13.

FINE, R. H., & FISHMAN, J. J. Institutionalized girl delinquents. *Dis. nerv. Sys.*, 1968, **29**(1), 17–27.

FINKELSTEIN, B. Offenses with no apparent motive. *Dis. nerv. Sys.*, 1968, **29**(5), 310–314.

GIBBENS, T. C. N. Psychosomatic aspects of the recidivist population. *J. psychosom. Res.*, 1969, **13**(3), 253–256.

GLAUS, A. The handling of criminal psychopaths in Switzerland. *Inter. J. offen. Ther.*, 1968, **12**(1), 29–36.

GLUECK, S., & GLUECK, E. T. *Physique and delinquency.* New York: Harper, 1956.

GLUECK, S., & GLUECK, E. T. *Family environment and delinquency.* Boston: Houghton Mifflin, 1962. •

GLUECK, S., & GLUECK, E. T. Delinquency prediction method reported highly accurate. *Roche Reports*, 1969, **6**(15), 3.

GORDON, R. A. Issues in the ecological study of delinquency. *Amer. soc. Rev.*, 1967, **32**(6), 927–944.

GOSHEN, C. E. Transcultural studies: A state prison population of youthful offenders. *Adolescence*, 1969, **4**(15), 401–430.

GREENACRE, P. Conscience in the psychopath. *Amer. J. Orthopsychiat.*, 1945, **15**, 495–509.

GREENBERG, H., & BLANK, H. R. Murder and self-destruction by a twelve-year-old boy. *Adolescence*, 1970, **5**(20), 391–396.

GUTTMACHER, M. S. *The mind of the murderer.* New York: Farrar, Straus, 1960.

GUZE, S. B., GOODWIN, D. W., & CRANE, J. B. Criminality and psychiatric disorders. *Arch. gen. Psychiat.*, 1969, **20**, 592–597.

HALLECK, S. American psychiatry and the criminal. *Inter. J. Psychiat.*, 1968, **6**(3), 185–218.

HARE, R. D. Psychopathy, autonomic functioning and the orienting response. *J. abnorm. Psychol.*, 1968, **73**(Monogr. Suppl. 3, part 2), 1–24.

HEAVER, W. L. A study of forty male psychopathic personalities before, during, and after hospitalization. *Amer. J. Psychiat.*, 1943, **100**, 342–346.

HENLEY, A. Muggers of the mind. *Today's Health*, 1971, **49**(2), 39–41, 71.

HOOVER, J. E. The story of crime in U.S. *U.S. News and World Report*, Oct. 7, 1968, 61–68.

HUNTER, H. Chromatin-positive and XYY boys in approved schools. *Lancet*, 1968, **1**(7545), 816.

JACOBS, P. A., BRUNTON, M., & MELVILLE, M. M. Aggressive behavior, mental sub-normality, and the XYY male. *Nature*, 1965, **208**, 1351–1352.

JARVIK, L. F. Over 100 violent persons found to have extra Y chromosome. *Roche Reports*, 1968, **5**(10), 3.

JENKINS, R. L. Classification of behavior problems of children. *Amer. J. Psychiat.*, 1969, **125**, 1032–1039.

KARABIAN, W. Overnight visits by girlfriends of prisoners backed. *Los Angeles Times*, June 2, 1971, I, 3.

KAUFMAN, I. Crimes of violence and delinquency in schizophrenic children. *J. Amer. Acad. Child Psychiat.*, 1962, **1**(2), 269–283.

KLEIN, M. W. Impressions of juvenile gang members. *Adolescence*, 1968, **3**(9), 53–78.

KONOPKA, G. Adolescent delinquent girls. *Children*, 1964, **11**(1), 21–26. Poem by delinquent girl, which has been published in The adolescent girl in conflict (Prentice-Hall, 1966), reprinted by permission.

KONOPKA, G. Rehabilitation of the delinquent girl. *Adolescence*, 1967, **2**(5), 69–82. Reprinted by permission of Libra Publishers, Inc.

LANGNER, H. P. The making of a murderer. *Amer. J. Psychiat.*, 1971, **127**(7), 126–153.

LERMAN, P. Child convicts. *Trans-action*, 1971, **8**(9–10), 35–44.

LIFE. The kid with the bad eye. 1951, **30**(5), 17–21.

LINDNER, R. M. Psychopathic personality and the concept of homeostasis. *J. clin. Psychopath. Psychother.*, 1945, **6**, 517–521.

LOMBROSO-FERRERO, G. *Criminal man.* New York: Putnam's, 1911.

LOOMIS, S., ROBERT, P. J., & HUNCHE, S. Prediction of EEG abnormalities in adolescent delinquents. *Arch. gen. Psychiat.*, 1967, **17**(4), 494–497.

MAHER, B. A. *Principles of psychopathology.* New York: McGraw-Hill, 1966.

MAC DONALD, J. M. A psychiatric study of check offenders. *Amer. J. Psychiat.*, 1959, **116**, 438–442.

MC CORD, W., & MC CORD, J. *Origins of crime.* New York: Columbia Univer. Press, 1959.

MC GEE, R. A. What's past is prologue. *Ann. Amer. Acad. polit. soc. Sci.*, 1969, **381**, 1–10.

MELGES, F. T., & BOWLBY, J. Types of hopelessness in psychopathological process. *Arch. gen. Psychiat.*, 1969, **20**, 690–699.

MENNINGER, K. *The crime of punishment.* New York: Viking Press, 1968.

MENNINGER, K. Prison systems in U.S. are a shambles, Menninger says. *Los Angeles Times*, May 23, 1971, I, B, 22.

MITCHELL, J. N. Where war against crime is being won. *U.S. News and World Report*, March 22, 1971, 38–42.

MONTAGU, A. Chromosomes and crime. *Psych. Today*, 1968, **2**(5), 42–49.

MURPHY, P. V. Crime and its causes—a need for social change. *Los Angeles Times*, Dec. 13, 1970, H, 1–2.

NATIONAL INSTITUTE OF MENTAL HEALTH. Study says XYY males not proved violence prone. *Psychiatric News*, 1970, **5**(17), 19.

NIXON, R. The shame of the prisons. *Time*, Jan. 18, 1971, 46–55.

O'NEAL, P., ROBINS, L. N., KING, L. J., & SHAEFER, J. Parental deviance and the genesis of sociopathic personality. *Amer. J. Psychiat.*, 1962, **118**, 1114–1124.

PRINCE, W. H., & WHATMORE, P. B. Behavior disorders and patterns of crime among XYY males identified at a maximum security hospital. *Brit. med. J.*, 1967, **1**(5537), 533–536.

QUAY, H. C. Psychopathic personality as pathological stimulation seeking. *Amer. J. Psychiat.*, 1965, **122**(2), 180–183.

RACHMAN, S., & TEASDALE, J. *Aversion therapy and behavior disorders: An analysis.* Coral Gables, Fla.: Univer. of Miami Press, 1969.

RAWITCH, R. Jail releases without bond prove a success. *Los Angeles Times*, Jan. 4, 1971, II, 1.

ROBINS, E. Antisocial and dyssocial personality disorders. In A. M. Freedman & H. I. Kaplan (Eds.), *Comprehensive textbook of psychiatry.* Baltimore: Williams & Wilkins, 1967. Pp. 951–958.

ROBINS, L. N. *Deviant children grown up: A sociological and psychiatric study of sociopathic personality.* Baltimore: Williams & Wilkins, 1966.

ROSTEN, R. A. Some personality characteristics of compulsive gamblers. Unpublished dissertation, UCLA, 1961.

ROSWELL, H. F., & FISHMAN, J. J. Institutionalized girl delinquents. *Dis. nerv. Sys.*, 1968, **29**(1), 17–27.

RUSHING, W. A. *Deviant behavior and social process.* Chicago: Rand McNally, 1969.

SCHARFMAN, M., & CLARK, R. W. Delinquent adolescent girls: Residential treatment in a municipal hospital setting. *Arch. gen. Psychiat.*, 1967, **17**(4), 441–447.

SCHWARTZ, B. The effect in Philadelphia of Pennsylvania's increased penalties for rape and attempted rape. *J. crim. Law, Criminol. police Sci.*, 1968, **59**(4), 509–515.

SERGOVICH, F. R. Quoted in I. Bengelsdorf, What's a half-chromosome more or less? Why, plenty! *Los Angeles Times*, April 2, 1970, II, 7.

SERGOVICH, F., VALENTINE, G. H., CHEN, A. T., KINCH, R., & SMOUT, M. Chromosomal aberrations in 2159 consecutive newborn babies. *New Engl. J. Med.*, 1969, **280**(16), 851–854.

SHAINBERG, D. Motivations of adolescent military offenders. *Adolescence*, 1967, **2**(6), 244–254.

SHERROD, B. *Dallas Times Herald*, n.d. Quoted in D. Bolen & W. H. Boyd, Gambling and the gambler. *Arch. gen. Psychiat.*, 1968, **18**(5), 617–630.

SHORE, M. F., & MASSINO, J. L. The alienated adolescent: A challenge to the mental health profession. *Adolescence*, 1969, **4**(13), 19–34.

SKRZYPEK, G. J. Effect of perceptual isolation on anxiety, complexity preference, and novelty preference in psychopathic and neurotic delinquents. *J. abnorm. Psychol.*, 1969, **74**, 321–329.

SILVERMAN, H. Determinism, choice, responsibility, and the psychologists role as an expert witness. *Amer. Psychologist*, 1969, **24**(1), 5–9.

SMALL, I., SMALL, J., ALIG, V., & MOORE, D. Passive-aggressive personality disorder: A search for a syndrome. *Amer. J. Psychiat.*, 1970, **126**, 97–107.

SMALL, J. G. The organic dimensions of crime. *Arch. gen. Psychiat.*, 1966, **15**(1), 82–89.

SMITH, R. L. Strange tales of medical imposters. *Today's Health*, 1968, **46**(10), 44–47, 69–70.

STAIN, K. B., & SARBINETA, T. Future time perspective: Its relation to the socialization process and the delinquent role. *J. cons. clin. Psychol.*, 1968, **32**(3), 257–264.

STOJANOVICH, K. Antisocial and dyssocial. *Arch. gen. Psychiat.*, 1969, **21**(5), 561–567.

STOTLAND, E. *The psychology of hope.* San Francisco: Jossey-Bass, 1969.

STOTT, D. H. Evidence for a congenital factor in maladjustment and delinquency. *Amer. J. Psychiat.*, 1962, **118**, 781–794.

STRINE, G. Compulsive gamblers pursue elusive dollar forever. *Los Angeles Times*, March 30, 1971, III, 1, 6.

SUTHERLAND, E. H., & CRESSEY, D. R. *Principles of criminology.* (7th ed.) Philadelphia: Lippincott, 1966.

TANAY, E. Psychiatric study of homicide. *Amer. J. Psychiat.*, 1969, **125**(9), 146–152.

THORNE, F. C. The etiology of sociopathic reactions. *Amer. J. Psychother.*, 1959, **13**, 319–330.

TIME. Young man with a gun. Jan. 22, 1951, 19–20.

TIME. Billy's last words. Dec. 22, 1952.

TIME. The shame of the prisons. Jan. 18, 1971, 46–55.

UNIFORM CRIME REPORTS. Federal Bureau of Investigation, United States Department of Justice, 1971.

U.S. NEWS AND WORLD REPORT. Crime expense now up to 51 billion a year. Oct. 26, 1970, 30–34.

VELDE, R. W. Half of serious crimes laid to juvenile delinquents. *Los Angeles Times*, April 4, 1971, I, 2.

VICTOR, R., & KRUG, C. "Paradoxical intention" in the treatment of compulsive gambling. *Amer. J. Psychother.*, 1967, **21**, 808–814.

VOSS, H. L., & HEPBURN, J. R. Patterns in criminal homicide in Chicago. *J. crim. Law, Criminol. police Sci.*, 1968, **59**(4), 499–508.

WEINER, S. The XYY syndrome. In A. Montagu, Chromosomes and crime. *Psych. Today*, 1968, **2**(5), 42–49.

WELCH, J. P., BORGAONKAR, D. S., & HERR, H. M. Psychopathy, mental deficiency, aggressiveness, and the XYY syndrome. *Nature*, 1967, **214**(5087), 500–501.

WILKINS, W. L. *The identification of character and behavior disorders in the military life.* U.S. Navy Medical Neuropsychiatric Research Unit, San Diego 52, California. Washington, D.C.: Navy Department, Bureau of Medicine and Surgery, 1961.

WIRT, R. D., BRIGGS, P. F., & GOLDEN, J. Delinquency prone personalities. III. The sociopathic personality: Treatment. *Minnesota Med.*, 1962, **45**, 289–295.

WOLFGANG, M. E. Who kills whom? *Psych. Today*, 1969, **3**(5), 54–56, 72–75.

WOLFGANG, M. E. Violence and human behavior. In M. Wertheimer (Ed.), *Confrontation: Psychology and the problems of today.* Glenview, Ill.: Scott, Foresman, 1970. Pp. 169–180.

YABLONSKY, L. The delinquent gang as a near-group. *Social Problems*, 1959, **7**, 108–117.

YABLONSKY, L. *The violent gang.* New York: Macmillan, 1962.

YABLONSKY, L. Where is science taking us? *Sat. Rev.*, 1963, **46**(5), 54–56.

12. Alcoholism and Drug Dependence

AASE, J. M., LAESTADIUS, N., & SMITH, D. W. LSD-dosed mothers have normal infants in Seattle. *Psychiatric News*, 1971, **6**(1), 6.

ABELSON, P. H. Death from heroin. *Science*, 1970, **168**, 1289.

AL-ANON FAMILY GROUP. *What's next?—asks the husband of an alcoholic.* New York: Author, 1966.

ALPERT, M., & SILVERS, K. Perceptual characteristics in distinguishing auditory hallucinations in schizophrenia and acute alcoholic psychoses. *Amer. J. Psychiat.*, 1970, **127**(3), 74–78.

ALSOP, S. Worse than My Lai. *Newsweek*, May 24, 1971, 108.

AMERICAN MEDICAL ASSOCIATION. *Test your A. Q. (alcohol quotient).* Chicago: AMA, 1965.

AMERICAN MEDICAL ASSOCIATION, Department of Mental Health. The crutch that cripples: Drug dependence. Part I. *Today's Health*, 1968, **46**(9), 11–12, 70–72. [a]

AMERICAN MEDICAL ASSOCIATION, Department of Mental Health. The crutch that cripples: Drug dependence. Part II. *Today's Health*, 1968, **46**(10), 12–15, 73–75. [b]

AMERICAN MEDICAL ASSOCIATION, Committee on Alcoholism and Drug Dependency. *The illness called alcoholism.* Chicago: AMA, 1969.

AUSUBEL, D. P. Causes and types of narcotic addiction: A psychosocial view. *Psychiat. Quart.*, 1961, **35**, 523–531.

BALES, R. F. Cultural differences in rates of alcoholism. *Quart. J. Stud. Alcohol.*, 1946, **6**, 480–499.

BANDURA, A. *Principles of behavior modification.* New York: Holt, Rinehart & Winston, 1969.

BATESON, G. The cybernetics of "self": A theory of alcoholism. *Psychiatry*, 1971, **34**(1), 1–18.

BENGELSDORF, I. S. Alcohol, morphine addictions believed chemically similar. *Los Angeles Times*, March 5, 1970, II, 7. [a]

BENGELSDORF, I. S. Amphetamines are a case of a truly dangerous drug. *Los Angeles Times*, March 19, 1970, II, 7. [b]

BENGELSDORF, I. S. Another "prohibition" that probably wouldn't work. *Los Angeles Times*, June 18, 1970, II, 7. [c]

BEWEY, T. H. Legal addiction said to reduce new addicts. *Psychiatric News*, 1970, **5**(17), 9.

BLACKER, K. H., JONES, R. T., STONE, G. C., & PFEFFERBAUM, D. Chronic users of LSD: The "acidheads." *Amer. J. Psychiat.*, 1968, **125**(3), 97–107.

BLOCK, M. S. Medical treatment of alcoholism. In Council on Mental Health of the American Medical Association, Committee on Alcoholism, *Manual on alcoholism.* Chicago: AMA, 1962. Pp. 7–33.

BLUM, R. *Society and drugs.* Vol. 1. San Francisco: Jossey-Bass, 1969.

BLUM, R. Many roads lead to the hard drugs. *Los Angeles Herald Examiner*, March 9, 1970, A, 11.

BOEHM, G. At last—a nonaddicting substitute for morphine? *Today's Health*, 1968, **46**(4), 69–72.

BREKHMAN, I. I., & SAM, Y. A. Psychoactive preparations used by paleoasiatic peoples. *Roche Report*, 1967, **4**(8), 3.

CALAHAN, D. *Problem drinkers: A national survey.* San Francisco: Jossey-Bass, 1970.

CHAFETZ, M. E. A new day of hope for alcoholics. *Amer. J. Psychiat.*, 1971, **127**(2), 118–119.

CHINLUND, S. The female addict. *Science News*, 1969, **95**(14), 578.

CISIN, I., & CALAHAN, D. The big drinkers. *Newsweek*, July 6, 1970, 57.

CITRON, P. Study cites fatality risk in methamphetamine use. *Psychiatric News*, 1970, **6**(18), 3.

CLAESON, E., & CARLSSON, C. Swedish scientists link alcohol to brain disorder. *Psychiatric News*, 1971, **6**(4), 20.

CLARK, D., HUGHES, R., & NAKASHIMA, E. Behavioral effects of marijuana. *Arch. gen. Psychiat.*, 1970, **23**(3), 193–198.

COMMISSION OF INQUIRY INTO THE NON-MEDICAL USE OF DRUGS. *Interim report.* Ottawa, Canada: Crown, 1970.

CULLITON, B. J. Pot facing stringent scientific examination. *Science News*, 1970, **97**(4), 102–105.

CURLEE, J. Alcoholism and the "empty nest." *Bull. Menninger Clin.*, 1969, **33**(3), 165–171.

DAVIES, D. L. Normal drinking in recovered alcohol addicts. *Quart. J. Stud. Alcohol.*, 1962, **23**, 94–104.

DEPARTMENT OF HEALTH, EDUCATION AND WELFARE. *Report—March 1970.* Washington, D.C.: Govt. Printing Office, 1970.

DISHOTSKY, N. I., LOUGHMAN, W. D., MOGAR, R. E., & LIPSCOMB, W. R. LSD and genetic damage. *Science*, 1971, **172**(3982), 431–440.

DOLE, V. P. In the course of professional practice. *N.Y. St. J. Med.*, 1965, **65**(7), 927–931.

DOLE, V. P., & NYSWANDER, M. The miracle of methadone in the narcotics jungle. *Roche Report*, 1967, **4**(11), 1–2, 8, 11.

DOLE, V. P., NYSWANDER, M., & WARNER, A. Successful treatment of 750 criminal addicts. *JAMA*, 1968, **206**, 2709–2711.

DOLE, V. P., & ROBINSON, J. W. Methadone treatment of randomly selected criminal addicts. *New Engl. J. Med.*, 1969, **280**(25), 1372–1375.

DREW, L. R. Alcoholism as a self-limiting disease. *Quart. J. Stud. Alcohol.*, 1968, **29**(4–A), 956–967.

ELLINWOOD, E. H. Assault and homicide associated with amphetamine abuse. *Amer. J. Psychiat.*, 1971, **127**(9), 90–95.

ELLISON, B. Robert Young's toughest role. *Today's Health*, 1971, **49**(5), 25–27, 59–60.

EMPLOYERS INSURANCE OF WAUSAU. Question Number 7. L971, 1971.

EWING, J. A., & BAKEWELL, W. E. Diagnosis and management of depressant drug dependence. *Amer. J. Psychiat.*, 1967, **123**, 909–917.

FISHER, G. Psychodelic drug usage: Psychological and socio-political considerations. *California School Health*, 1968, **4**, 40–54.

FORT, J. P., JR. Heroin addiction among young men. *Psychiatry*, 1954, **17**, 251–259.

FRANKS, C. M. Conditioning and conditioned aversion therapies in the treatment of the alcoholic. *Inter. J. Addictions*, 1966, **1**, 61–98.

FREEDMAN, D. X. On the use and abuse of LSD. *Arch. gen. Psychiat.*, 1968, **18**, 330–347.

FURLONG, B. How "speed" kills athletic careers. *Today's Health*, 1971, **49**(2), 30–33.

GALLUP, G. Drugs on campus. *Newsweek*, Jan. 25, 1971, p. 52.

GEARING, F. R. Methadone project called success after five years. *Psychiatric News*, 1970, **5**(12), 18.

GILBERT, J. G., & LOMBARDI, D. N. Personality characteristics of young male narcotic addicts. *J. couns. Psychol.*, 1967, **31**, 536–538.

GOLDSTEIN, S. G., & LINDEN, J. D. Multivariate classification of alcoholics by means of the MMPI. *J. abnorm. Psychol.*, 1969, **74**, 661–669.

GOMBERG, E. Etiology of alcoholism. *J. cons. clin. Psychol.*, 1968, **37**(1), 18–20.

GOODWIN, D. W., CRANE, J. B., & GUZE, S. B. Alcoholic "blackouts": A review and clinical study of 100 alcoholics. *Amer. J. Psychiat.*, 1969, **126**(2), 77–84.

GOSS, A., & MOROSKO, T. Alcoholism and clinical symptoms. *J. abnorm. Psychol.*, 1969, **74**, 682–684.

GREENBERG, R., & PEARLMAN, C. Delirium tremens and dreaming. *Amer. J. Psychiat.*, 1967, **124**(2), 37–46.

GREENBLATT, D. J., & SHADER, R. I. Meprobamate: A study of irrational drug use. *Amer. J. Psychiat.*, 1971, **127**(10), 1297–1303.

GRIFFITH, J. A study of illicit amphetamine drug traffic in Oklahoma City. Reprinted from *The American Journal of Psychiatry*, volume **123**, pages 560–569, 1966. Copyright 1966, the American Psychiatric Association.

HABER, J. Robert Young: Welby has the right Rx for life. *Los Angeles Times Calendar*, Feb. 21, 1971, 13, 27.

HARRIS, E. M. "Pot" users said more alienated than non-users. *Psychiatric News*, 1971, **6**(2), 4.

HAZLETT, B. Two who played with death—and lost the game. *Los Angeles Times*, March 2, 1971, II, 1, 5.

HEKIMIAM, L. J., & GERSHON, S. Characteristics of drug abusers admitted to a psychiatric hospital. *JAMA*, 1968, **205**(3), 125–130.

HEW. Physical damage of pot yet unproven, says HEW. *Psychiatric News*, 1971, **6**(7), 3.

HOFFMAN, A. LSD discoverer disputes "chance" factor in finding. *Psychiatric News*, 1971, **6**(8), 23–26.

HOLLISTER, L. E. Marijuana in man: Three years later. *Science*, 1971, **172**(3978), 21–29.

HOROWITZ, M. J. Flashbacks: Recurrent intrusive images after the use of LSD. *Amer. J. Psychiat.*, 1969, **126**(4), 147–151.

HORTON, D. The functions of alcohol in primitive societies: A cross-cultural study. *Quart. J. Stud. Alcohol.*, 1943, **4**, 199–320.

HUGHES, H. E. Senator fears 40,000 GI addicts as criminals. *Los Angeles Times*, May 29, 1971, I, 3.

HUXLEY, A. *The doors of perception and heaven and hell.* New York: Harper & Row, 1954.

INGERSOLL, J. E. Drug menace: How serious? *U.S. News and World Report*, May 25, 1970, 38–42.

IRWIN, T. Attacking alcohol as a disease. *Today's Health*, 1968, **46**(9), 21–23, 72–74.

ISBELL, H., & CHRUSCIEL, T. L. *Dependence liability of "non-narcotic" drugs.* Geneva: World Health Organization, 1970.

JAFFE, J. Study supports effectiveness of methadone. *Psychiatric News*, 1970, **5**(4), 30. [a]

JAFFE, J. Whatever turns you off. *Psych. Today*, 1970, **3**(12), 43–44, 60–62. [b]

JAFFE, J. Psychiatrist cites virtues, ills of methadone use. *Psychiatric News*, 1971, **6**(2), 20.

JAFFE, J. H., & SENAY, E. C. Methadone and l-methadyl acetate: Use in management of narcotics addicts. *JAMA*, 1971, **216**(8), 1303–1305.

JARVIK, M. E. The psychopharmacological revolution. *Psych. Today*, 1967, **1**(1), 51–58.

JELLINEK, E. M. Phases of alcohol addiction. *Quart. J. Stud. Alcohol.*, 1952, **13**, 673–678.

JELLINEK, E. M. Phases of alcohol addiction. In G. D. Shean (Ed.), *Studies in abnormal behavior*. Chicago: Rand McNally, 1971. Pp. 86–98.

JONES, B., & PARSONS, O. A. Impaired abstracting ability in chronic alcoholics. *Arch. gen. Psychiat.*, 1971, **24**(1), 71–75.

JONES, M. Personality correlates and antecedents of drinking patterns in adult males. *J. cons. clin. Psychol.*, 1968, **32**(1), 2–12.

JONES, M. C. Personality antecedents and correlates of drinking patterns in women. *J. cons. clin. Psychol.*, 1971, **36**(1), 61–69.

KAPLAN, J. The new prohibition. *Los Angeles Times*, June 21, 1970, VII, 3.

KATZ, M. M., WASKOW, E. E., & OLSSON, J. Characteristics of the psychological state produced by LSD. *J. abnorm. Psychol.*, 1968, **73**(1), 1–14.

KAUFMAN, J., ALLEN, J. R., & WEST, L. J. Runaways, hippies, and marijuana. *Amer. J. Psychiat.*, 1969, **126**(5), 163–166.

KEEHN, J. D., & WEBSTER, C. D. Behavior therapy and behavior modification. *Canadian Psychologists*, 1969, **10**, 68–73.

KEELER, M. K. Search for insight in heavy marijuana users. *Psychiatric News*, 1970, **5**(6), 42.

KING, L. J., MURPHY, G., ROBINS, L., & DARVISH, H. Alcohol abuse: A crucial factor in the social problems of Negro men. *Amer. J. Psychiat.*, 1969, **125**(12), 96–104.

KLETT, C. J., POINT, P., HOLLISTER, L., CAFFEY, E., & KAIM, S. Evaluating changes in symptoms during acute alcohol withdrawal. *Arch. gen. Psychiat.*, 1971, **24**(2), 174–178.

LASEGUE, C. Le delire alcoolique n'est pas un delire, mais un reve. *Arch. gen. Med.*, 1881, **88**, 513–536.

LIPSCOMB, W. Drug use in a black ghetto. *Amer. J. Psychiat.*, 1971, **127**(9), 86–89.

LOS ANGELES POLICE DEPARTMENT. *Youth and narcotics.* Reprinted by Los Angeles City School District, 1952, pp. 3–4.

MAC KAY, J. R. Clinical observations on adolescent problem drinkers. *Quart. J. Stud. Alcohol.*, 1961, **22**, 124–134.

MASSETT, L. Marijuana and behavior: The unfilled gaps. *Science News*, 1970, **97**(6), 156–158.

MC ARTHUR, G. All GIs leaving Vietnam to be given tests for heroin usage. *Los Angeles Times*, June 19, 1971, I, 1, 11.

MC CLELLAND, D. C. The power of positive drinking. *Psych. Today*, 1971, **4**(8), 40–41, 78–79.

MC CORD, W., & MC CORD, J. A longitudinal study of the personality of alcoholics. In D. J. Pittman & C. R. Snyder (Eds.), *Sociology, culture, and drinking patterns*. New York: Wiley, 1962.

MC CORD, W., MC CORD, J., & SUDEMAN, J. *Origins of alcoholism*. Stanford: Stanford Univer. Press, 1960.

MC GLOTHIN, W. H., & ARNOLD, D. O. LSD revisited. *Arch. gen. Psychiat.*, 1971, **24**(1), 35–49.

MC GLOTHIN, W. H., ARNOLD, D. O., & ROWAN, P. K. Marijuana use among adults. *Psychiatry*, 1970, **33**(4), 433–443.

MC GLOTHIN, W. H., & WEST, L. J. The marijuana problem: An overview. *Amer. J. Psychiat.*, 1968, **125**, 368–373.

MEISSNER, W. W. Memory function in the Korsakoff syndrome. *J. nerv. ment. Dis.*, 1967, **145**(2), 106–122.

MELGES, F., TINKLENBERG, J., HOLLISTER, L., & GILLESPIE, H. Temporal disintegration and depersonalization during marijuana intoxication. *Arch. gen. Psychiat.*, 1970, **23**(3), 204–210.

MIKURIYA, T. H. On smoking pot. *Trans-action*, 1969, **7**(2), 8, 10.

MIRIN, S. M., SHAPIRO, L. M., MEYER, R. E., PILLARD, R. G., & FISHER, S. Casual versus heavy use of marijuana: A redefinition of the marijuana problem. *Amer. J. Psychiat.*, 1971, **127**(9), 1134–1141.

MOORE, R. A. Legal responsibility and chronic alcoholism. *Amer. J. Psychiat.*, 1966, **122**, 748–756.

MOSKIN, J. R. Drugs: We are just plain ignorant. *Look*, Oct. 6, 1970, 108–112.

MOTHNER, I. How can you tell if your child is taking drugs? *Look*, April 7, 1970, 42, 44.

MURPHY, M., & STEELE, R. H. GI heroin epidemic reported in Vietnam. *Los Angeles Times*, April 20, 1971, I, 1, 7.

NATIONAL INSTITUTE OF MENTAL HEALTH. Socio-technical systems: An exploration of alternative approaches to the prevention and control of alcoholism. Unpublished report, 1971.

NELSON, H. Study compares drug dangers. *Los Angeles Times*, Oct. 6, 1969, I, 3, 25.

NEWSWEEK. The heroin plague: What can be done? July 5, 1971, 27–32.

NIXON, R. War on addiction. *Los Angeles Times*, June 20, 1971, J, 5.

PERKINS, M. E., & BLOCH, H. I. Studies question therapy limited to methadone use. *Psychiatric News*, 1970, **5**(12), 3, 18.

PUTNAM, P. L., & ELLINWOOD, E. H., JR. Narcotic addiction among physicians: A ten-year follow-up. *Amer. J. Psychiat.*, 1966, **122**, 745–747.

QUINN, W. F. Large numbers of M.D.'s found turning to drugs. *Psychiatric News*, 1970, **5**(17), 23.

RAMER, B. S., ZASLOVE, M., & LANGAN, J. Is methadone enough? The use of ancillary treatment during methadone maintenance. *Amer. J. Psychiat.*, 1971, **127**(8), 80–84.

REESE, J. Marijuana: Is it time for a change in our laws? *Newsweek*, Sept, 7, 1970, 20–22, 27–32.

REINERT, R. E., & BOWEN, W. T. Social drinking following treatment for alcoholism. *Bull. Menninger Clin.*, 1968, **32**(5), 280–290.

RINKEL, M. Psychodelic drugs. *Amer. J. Psychiat.*, 1966, **122**, 1415–1416.

ROE, A., BURKS, B., & MITTELMANN, B. Adult adjustment of foster children of alcoholic and psychotic parentage and the influence of the foster home. *Memorial Section on Alcohol Studies*, No. 3. New Haven: Yale Univer. Press, 1945.

RORVIK, D. M. Do drugs lead to violence? *Look*, April 7, 1970, 58–61.

ROSE, A., & BURKS, B. Roundup of current research: Is the child really the father of the man? *Trans-action*, 1968, **5**(6), 6.

RUBINGTON, E. Two types of drug use. *Inter. J. Addictions*, 1968, **3**(2), 301–318.

SCHAEFER, H. H. Accepted theories disproven. *Science News*, 1971, **99**(11), 182.

SCHER, J. Patterns and profiles of addiction and drug abuse. *Arch. gen. Psychiat.*, 1966, **15**, 539–551.

SIEGLER, M., OSMOND, H., & NEWELL, S. Models of alcoholism. *Quart. J. Stud. Alcohol.*, 1968, **29**(3–A), 571–591.

SMART, R., & JONES, D. Illicit LSD users: Their personality characteristics and psychopathology. *J. abnorm. Psychol.*, 1970, **75**, 286–292.

STEWART, R. B., FINGER, K., & CLUFF, L. Drug interactions in a pill-popping age. *Science News*, 1971, **99**(22), 365.

STUDENT, V., & MATOVA, A. Development of psychic disorders in wives of alcoholics. *Ceskoslovenská Psychiatrie*, 1969, **65**(1), 23–29.

SZARA, S. The hallucinogenic drugs—curse or blessing. *Amer. J. Psychiat.*, 1967, **123**, 1513–1518.

TARTER, R. E., & PARSONS, O. A. Conceptual shifting in chronic alcoholics. *J. abnorm. Psychol.*, 1971, **77**(1), 71–75.

TAVEL, M. E. A new look at an old syndrome: Delirium tremens. *Arch. int. Med.*, 1962, **109**, 129–134.

UNGERLEIDER, J. T., FISHER, D. D., FULLER, M., & CALDWELL, A. The "bad trip"—the etiology of the adverse LSD reaction. *Amer. J. Psychiat.*, 1968, **124**(11), 41–48.

VOGLER, R. E., LUNDE, S. E., JOHNSON, G. R., & MARTIN, P. L. Aversion conditioning with chronic alcoholics. *J. cons. clin. Psychol.*, 1970, **34**(3), 302–307.

WALLER, J. A. Alcohol still leads drugs in auto accidents. *Psychiatric News*, 1971, **6**(8), 30.

WARNER, A. Successful treatment of 750 criminal addicts. *JAMA*, 1968, **206**, 2709–2711.

WEEKS, G. C., & LAWRENCE, F. E. Characteristics of patients at the Central Indiana alcoholism clinic. *J. Ind. med. Ass.*, 1961, **54**, 1506–1511.

WEIL, T. E., ZINBERG, E., & NELSON, J. M. Clinical and psychological effects of marijuana in man. *Science*, 1968, **162**, 1234–1242.

WEINGOLD, H., LACHIN, J. M., BELL, A. H., & COXE, C. Depression as a symptom of alcoholism: Search for a phenomenon. *J. abnorm. Psychol.*, 1968, **73**(3), 195–197.

WESTERMEYER, J. Use of alcohol and opium by the Meo of Laos. *Amer. J. Psychiat.*, 1971, **127**(8), 1019–1023.

WILWERTH, J. Armed forces: As common as chewing gum. *Time*, March 1, 1971, 14–16.

WINOKUR, G., REICH, T., RIMMER, J., & PITTS, F. N., JR. Alcoholism. III: Diagnosis and familial psychiatric illness in 259 alcoholic probands. *Arch. gen. Psychiat.*, 1970, **23**(2), 104–111.

WITCOVER, J. Addict-veterans: A national concern. *Los Angeles Times*, June 13, 1971, I, B, 4.

WOOD, H., & DUFFY, E. Psychological factors in alcoholic women. *Amer. J. Psychiat.*, 1966, **123**(3), 341–345.

YOLLES, S. Pop drugs: The high as a way of life. *Time*, Sept. 26, 1969, 74.

ZAKS, M. Study supports effectiveness of methadone. *Psychiatric News*, 1970, **5**(4), 30.

13. Sexual Deviations

ABEL, G. G., LEVIS, D. J., & CLANCY, J. Aversion therapy applied to taped sequences of deviant behavior in exhibitionism and other sexual deviations: A preliminary report. *J. behav. Res. exp. Psychiat.*, 1970, **1**(1), 59–66.

ACHILLES, N. The development of the homosexual bar as an institution. In J. H. Gagnon & W. Simon (Eds.), *Sexual deviance*. New York: Harper & Row, 1967. Pp. 228–244.

ADAMS, M. S., & NEEL, J. V. Children of incest. *Pediatrics*, 1967, **40**, 55–62.

ADLER, P. *A house is not a home*. New York: Rinehart, 1953.

AMIR, M. *Patterns in forcible rape*. Chicago: Univer. of Chicago Press, 1971.

APFELBERG, B., SUGAR, C., & PFEFFER, A. Z. A psychiatric study of 250 sex offenders. *Amer. J. Psychiat.*, 1944, **100**, 762–770.

AVERY, P., & AVERY, E. Some notes on wife swapping. In H. Grunwald (Ed.), *Sex in America*. New York: Bantam, 1964. Pp. 248–254.

BAGLEY, C. Incest behavior and incest taboo. *Social Problems*, 1969, **16**(4), 505–519.

BAKER, H. J. Transsexualism—problems in treatment. *Amer. J. Psychiat.,* 1969, **125**, 118–124.

BANDURA, A. *Principles of behavior modification.* New York: Holt, Rinehart & Winston, 1969.

BARTELL, G. D. *Group sex: A scientist's eyewitness report on the American way of swinging.* New York: Peter H. Wyden, 1971.

BENJAMIN, H. *The transexual phenomenon.* New York: Julian Press, 1966.

BENTLER, P. M., & PRINCE, C. Personality characteristics of male transvestites. III. *J. abnorm. Psychol.,* 1969, **74**(2), 140–143.

BENTLER, P. M., & PRINCE, C. Psychiatric symptomology in transvestites. *J. clin. Psychol.,* 1970, **26**(4), 434–435.

BENTLER, P. M., SHEARMAN, R. W., & PRINCE, C. Personality characteristics of male transvestites. *J. clin. Psychol.,* 1970, **126**(3), 287–291.

BERG, A. *The sadist.* O. Illner & G. Godwin (Tr.). New York: Medical Press of New York, 1954.

BERGLER, E. Analysis of an unusual case of fetishism. *Bull. Menninger Clin.,* 1947, **2**, 67–75.

BIEBER, I., DAIN, H., DINCE, P., DRELLECH, M., GRAND, H., GRUNDLACH, R., KREMER, M., RITKIN, A., WILBUR, C., & BIEBER, T. *Homosexuality: A psychoanalytic study.* Adapted from *Homosexuality* by Irving Bieber, M.D., & Associates, Basic Books, Inc., Publishers, New York, 1962.

BRANCALE, R., ELLIS, A., & DOORBAR, R. Psychiatric and psychological investigations of convicted sex offenders: A summary report. *Amer. J. Psychiat.,* 1952, **109**, 17–21.

BRILL, A. A. Necrophilia. *J. crim. Psychopath.,* 1941, **2**, 51–73, 433.

BRYAN, J. H. Apprenticeships in prostitution. *Social Problems,* 1965, **12**, 287–297.

BRYAN, J. H. Occupational ideologies and individual attitudes of call girls. *Social Problems,* 1966, **13**, 441–450.

BUCKNER, H. T. The transvestic career path. *Psychiatry,* 1970, **33**(3), 381–389.

CAVALLIN, H. Incestuous fathers: A clinical report. *Amer. J. Psychiat.,* 1966, **122**(10), 1132–1138.

CLARK, D. F. A note on avoidance conditioning techniques in sexual disorders. *Behav. Res. Ther.,* 1965, **3**, 203–206.

COHEN, M., & SEGHORN, T. Sociometric study of the sex offender. *Journal of Abnormal Psychology,* 1969, **74**(2), 249–255. Copyright 1969 by the American Psychological Association and reproduced by permission.

COOPER, A. J. A clinical study of "coital anxiety" in male potency disorders. *J. psychosom. Res.,* 1969, **13**(2), 143–147.

CRAFT, M. Boy prostitutes and their fate. *Brit. J. Psychiat.,* 1966, **112**(492), 1111–1114.

DANK, B. M. Coming out in the gay world. *Psychiatry,* 1971, **34**, 180–197. Copyright 1971 The William Alanson White Psychiatric Foundation, Inc. Reprinted by special permission of the author and The William Alanson White Psychiatric Foundation, Inc.

DAVENPORT, W. Sexual patterns and their regulation in a society of the Southwest Pacific. In F. Beach (Ed.), *Sex and behavior.* New York: Wiley, 1965.

DAVIS, A. J. Sexual assault in the Philadelphia prisons and sheriff's vans. *Trans-action,* 1968, **6**(2), 28–35.

DAVISON, G. C. Elimination of a sadistic fantasy by a client-controlled counterconditioning technique: A case study. *J. abnorm. Psychol.,* 1968, **73**, 84–90.

DENGROVE, E. Behavior therapy of the sexual disorders. *J. sex Res.,* 1967, **3**, 49–61.

DE RIVER, J. P. *The sexual criminal.* Springfield, Ill.: Thomas, 1949.

DUNHAM, H. W. *Crucial issues in the treatment and control of sexual deviation in the community.* Lansing, Mich.: State Dept. of Mental Hlth., 1951.

EAST, W. N. Sexual offenders. *J. nerv. ment. Dis.,* 1946, **103**, 626–666.

EHRENREICH, G. A. Headache, necrophilia, and murder: A brief hypnotherapeutic investigation of a single case. *Bull. Menninger Clin.,* 1960, **24**, 273–287.

ESSELTYN, T. C. Prostitution in the United States. *Ann. Amer. Acad. Polit. Soc. Sci.,* 1968, **376**, 123–135.

EVANS, D. R. An exploratory study into the treatment of exhibitionism by means of emotive imagery and aversive conditioning. *Canadian Psychologist,* 1967, **8**, 162.

EVANS, R. B. Childhood parental relationships of homosexual men. *J. cons. clin. Psychol.,* 1969, **33**(2), 129–135.

FBI. *Uniform crime reports.* Washington, D.C.: Govt. Printing Office, 1971.

FENICHEL, O. *The psychoanalytic theory of neurosis.* New York: Norton, 1945.

FERSTER, C. B. Reinforcement and punishment in the control of homosexual behavior by social agencies. In H. J. Eysenck (Ed.), *Experiments in behavior therapy.* London: Pergamon, 1965. Pp. 189–207.

FISHER, G. Psychological needs of heterosexual pedophiliacs. *Dis. nerv. Sys.,* 1969, **30**, 419–421.

GAGNON, J. H., & SIMON, W. (Eds.) *Sexual deviance.* New York: Harper & Row, 1967.

GAGNON, J. H., & SIMON, W. Sexual deviance in contemporary America. *Ann. Amer. Acad. Polit. Soc. Sci.,* 1968, **376**, 106–122.

GEBHARD, P. H., GAGNON, J. H., POMEROY, W. B., & CHRISTENSON, C. V. *Sex offenders: An analysis of types.* New York: Harper & Row, 1965.

GIBBENS, T. C. N. Trends in juvenile delinquency. *WHO Publ. Hlth. Paper,* 1961, **5**, 56.

GRANT, V. W. A case study of fetishism. *J. abnorm. soc. Psychol.,* 1953, **48**, 142–149.

GRECO, M. C., & WRIGHT, J. C. The correctional institution in the etiology of chronic homosexuality. *Amer. J. Orthopsychiat.,* 1944, **14**, 295–308.

GREEN, R. Childhood cross-gender identification. *J. nerv. men. Dis.,* 1968, **147**(5), 500–509.

GREEN, R. Guidelines to the management of the transsexual patient. *Roche Reports,* 1971, **11**(8), 3, 6.

GUNDLACH, R. H. Childhood parental relationships and the establishment of gender roles of homosexuals. *J. cons. clin. Psychol.,* 1969, **33**(2), 136–139.

HARTMAN, A. A., & NICOLAY, R. C. Sexual deviant behavior in expectant fathers. *J. abnorm. Psychol.,* 1966, **71**(3), 232–234.

HIRSCHFELD, M. *Sexual anomalies.* New York: Emerson Books, 1956.

HIRSCHI, T. The professional prostitute. *Berkeley Journal of Sociology,* 1962, **7**, 37–41, 47–48.

HOFFMAN, M. Homosexual. *Psych. Today,* 1969, **3**(2), 43–45, 70.

HOOKER, E. The adjustment of the male overt homosexual. *Journal of Projective Techniques,* 1957, **21**, 18–31.

HOOKER, E. The homosexual community. In *Proceedings of the XIV International Congress of Applied Psychology.* Vol. II. *Personality research.* Copenhagen: Munksgaard, 1962. Reprinted by permission.

HUMPHREYS, L. Tearoom trade: Impersonal sex in public places. *Trans-action,* 1970, **7**(3), 10–25.

JACKMAN, N. R., O'TOOLE, R., & GEIS, G. The self-image of the prostitute. *Sociol. Quart.,* 1963, **4**(2), 150–161.

KALLMANN, F. J. *Heredity in health and mental disorder.* New York: Norton, 1953.

KENNEDY, F., HOFFMAN, H. R., & HAINES, W. H. A study of William Heirens. Printed in original form in *The American Journal of Psychiatry,* volume **104**, pages 113–121, 1947. Copyright 1947, the American Psychiatric Association.

KINSEY, A. C., POMEROY, W. B., & MARTIN, C. E. *Sexual behavior in the human male.* Philadelphia: W. B. Saunders, 1948.

KINSEY, A. C., POMEROY, W. B., & MARTIN, C. E. Concepts of normality and abnormality in sexual behavior. In P. H. Hoch & J. Zubin (Eds.), *Psychosexual development in health and disease.* New York: Grune & Stratton, 1949. Pp. 11–32.

KINSEY, A. C., POMEROY, W. B., & MARTIN, C. E. *Sexual behavior in the human female.* Philadelphia: W. B. Saunders, 1953.

KLAF, F. S., & BROWN, W. Necrophilia: Brief review and case report. *Psychiat. Quart.,* 1958, **32**, 645–652.

KONOPKA, G. Adolescent delinquent girls. *Children*, 1964, **11**(1), 21–26.

KOPP, S. B. The character structure of sex offenders. *Amer. J. Psychother.*, 1962, **16**, 64–70.

KRAFFT-EBING, R. V. *Psychopathica sexualis*. New York: Pioneer Publications, 1950.

KREMER, M., & RITKIN, A. H. The early development of homosexuality: A study of adolescent lesbians. *Amer. J. Psychiat.*, 1969, **126**(1), 91–96.

KUSHNER, M. The reduction of a long-standing fetish by means of aversive conditioning. In L. P. Ullmann & L. Krasner (Eds.), *Case studies in behavior modification*. New York: Holt, Rinehart & Winston, 1965. Pp. 239–242.

LAMBERD, W. G. The treatment of homosexuality as a monosymptomatic phobia. *Amer. J. Psychiat.*, 1969, **126**, 94–100.

LAVIN, N. I., THORPE, J. G., BARKER, J. C., BLAKEMORE, C. B., & CONWAY, C. G. Behavior therapy in a case of transvestitism. *J. nerv. men. Dis.*, 1961, **133**, 346–353.

LINDZEY, G. Some remarks concerning incest, the incest taboo, and psychoanalytic theory. *Amer. Psychologist*, 1967, **22**(12), 1051–1059.

LOS ANGELES TIMES. Woman awarded damages in cable car sex accident. May 3, 1970, F, 5.

MAC KINNON, J. The homosexual woman. Reprinted from *The American Journal of Psychiatry*, volume **103**, pages 661–664, 1947. Copyright 1947, the American Psychiatric Association.

MAC NAMARA, D. E. J. Sex offenses and sex offenders. *Amer. Acad. Polit. Soc. Sci.*, 1968, **376**, 148–155.

MANOSEVITZ, M. Early sexual behavior in adult homosexual and heterosexual males. *J. abnorm. Psychol.*, 1970, **76**(3), 396–402.

MARKS, I. M., & GELDER, M. G. Transvestism and fetishism: Clinical and psychological changes during faradic aversion. *Brit. J. Psychiat.*, 1967, **113**, 711–729.

MARSHALL, D. S. Too much in Mangaia. *Psych. Today*, 1971, **4**(9), 43–47, 68.

MASSETT, L. Homosexuality: Changes on the way. *Science News*, 1969, **96**(24), 557–559.

MASTERS, W. H., & JOHNSON, V. E. *Human sexual response*. Boston: Little, Brown, 1966.

MASTERS, W. H., & JOHNSON, V. E. *Human sexual inadequacy*. Boston: Little, Brown, 1970.

MC CONAGHY, N. Aversive therapy of homosexuality: Measures of efficacy. *Amer. J. Psychiat.*, 1971, **127**(9), 141–144.

MICHAUX, M. H., & MICHAUX, W. W. Psychodiagnostic follow-up of a juvenile sex murderer. *Psychoanal. Rev.*, 1963, **50**, 93–113.

MILLER, M. Homosexual's story: No more quiet desperation. *Los Angeles Times*, Jan. 31, 1971, F, 2.

MONEY, J., & ALEXANDER, D. Psychosexual development and absence of homosexuality in males with precocious puberty. *J. nerv. ment. Dis.*, 1969, **148**(2), 111–123.

MONEY, J., & BRENNAN, J. G. Sexual dimorphism in the psychology of female transexuals. *J. nerv. ment. Dis.*, 1968, **147**(5), 487–499.

MONEY, J., HAMPSON, J. G., & HAMPSON, J. L. Imprinting and the establishment of gender role. *Arch. Neurol. Psychiat.*, 1957, **77**, 333–336.

MONEY, J., & PRIMROSE, C. Sexual dimorphism and dissociation in the psychology of male transexuals. *J. nerv. ment. Dis.*, 1968, **147**(5), 472–486.

MOSHER, D. L., & CROSS, H. J. Sex guilt and premarital sexual experiences of college students. *J. cons. clin. Psychol.*, 1971, **36**(1), 27–32.

NADLER, R. P. Approach to psychodynamics of obscene telephone calls. *N.Y. St. J. Med.*, 1968, **68**(1), 521–526.

NAMH. NAMH supports repeal of homosexual status. *Psychiatric News*, 1971, **6**(3), 1.

NEWMAN, L. E. Transsexualism in adolescence: Problems in evaluation and treatment. *Arch. gen. Psychiat.*, 1970, **23**(2), 112–121.

OLLENDORFF, R. *The juvenile homosexual experience*. New York: Julian Press, 1966.

PACKARD, V. *The sexual wilderness*. New York: David McKay, 1968.

PAULY, I. B. The current status of the change of sex operation. *J. nerv. ment. Dis.*, 1968, **147**(5), 460–471.

PFEIFFER, E., VERWOERDT, A., & WANG, H. Sexual behavior in aged men and women. *Arch. gen. Psychiat.*, 1968, **19**(6), 753–758.

POLLACK, J. H. They're cracking down on the telephone nuts . . . and you can help. *Today's Health*, 1970, **48**(5), 24–27, 66–67.

PRESIDENT'S COMMISSION ON LAW ENFORCEMENT AND ADMINISTRATION OF JUSTICE. *The challenge of crime in a free society*. Washington, D.C.: Govt. Printing Office, 1967.

RACHMAN, S. Sexual fetishism: An experimental analogue. *Psychol. Rec.*, 1966, **16**, 293–296.

RAPHLING, D. L., CARPENTER, B. L., & DAVIS, A. Incest. *Archives of General Psychiatry*, 1967, **16**(4), 505–511. Copyright 1967, American Medical Association.

REVITCH, E., & WEISS, R. G. The pedophiliac offender. *Dis. nerv. Sys.*, 1962, **23**, 73–78.

SAGHIR, M. T., ROBINS, E., & WALBRAN, B. Homosexuality. I. Sexual behavior of the female homosexual. *Arch. gen. Psychiat.*, 1969, **20**, 192–201. [a]

SAGHIR, M. T., ROBINS, E., & WALBRAN, B. Homosexuality. II. Sexual behavior of the male homosexual. *Arch. gen. Psychiat.*, 1969, **21**(2), 219–229. [b]

SALZMAN, L. Sexuality: Changing standards. *Time*, May 16, 1969, p. 50.

SCHARFMAN, M. A., & CLARK, R. W. Delinquent adolescent girls. *Arch. gen. Psychiat.*, 1967, **17**(4), 441–447.

SENOUSSI, A. E., COLEMAN, D. R., & TAUBER, A. S. Factors in male impotence. *J. Psychol.*, 1959, **48**, 3–46.

SHOPE, D. F., & BRODERICK, C. B. Level of sexual experience and predicted adjustment in marriage. *J. Marr. Fam.*, 1967, **29**(3), 424–427.

SIMON, W., & GAGNON, J. H. The lesbians: A preliminary overview. In W. Simon & J. H. Gagnon (Eds.), *Sexual deviance*. New York: Harper & Row, 1967. Pp. 247–282.

SNORTUM, J. R., MARSHALL, J. E., GILLESPIE, J. E., MC LAUGHLIN, J. P., & MOSBERG, L. Family dynamics and homosexuality. *Psychol. Rep.*, 1969, **24**(3), 763–770.

SONENSCHEIN, D. The ethnography of male homosexual relationships. *J. sex Res.*, 1968, **4**(2), 69–83.

STOLLER, R. J. Transvestites' women. Reprinted from *The American Journal of Psychiatry*, volume **124**, pages 333–339, 1967. Copyright 1967, the American Psychiatric Association.

STURUP, G. K. Treatment of sexual offenders in Herstedvester, Denmark: The rapists. *Acta Psychiatr. Scandin.*, 1968, **44**(Suppl. 204), 1–62.

SUTHERLAND, S., & SCHERL, D. L. Patterns of response among victims of rape. *American Journal of Orthopsychiatry*, 1970, **49**(3), 503–511. Copyright, the American Orthopsychiatric Association, Inc. Reproduced by permission.

SWANSON, D. W. Adult sexual abuse of children: The man and circumstances. *Dis. nerv. Sys.*, 1968, **29**(10), 677–683.

TIME. Reflections on the sad profession. Aug. 23, 1971, pp. 34–35.

TOFFLER, A. Family '71: Is the family obsolete? *Look*, 1971, **35**(2), 35.

WEINBERG, S. K. *Incest behavior*. New York: Citadel Press, 1955.

WERTHAM, F. *The show of violence*. New York: Doubleday, 1949.

WITSCHI, E., & MENGERT, W. F. Endocrine studies on human hermaphrodites and their bearing on the interpretation of homosexuality. *Journal of Clinical Endocrinology*, 1942, **2**, 279–286. Used by permission of J. B. Lippincott Company.

WITZIG, J. S. The group treatment of male exhibitionists. *Amer. J. Psychiat.*, 1968, **125**, 75–81.

WOLPE, J. *The practice of behavior therapy*. New York: Pergamon Press, 1969.

YALOM, I. D. Group therapy of incarcerated sexual deviants. *J. nerv. ment. Dis.*, 1961, **132**, 158–170.

YOUNG, W. *Eros denied: Sex in western society*. New York: Grove Press, 1964. Copyright © 1964 by Wayland Young. Reprinted by permission of Grove Press, Inc. and George Weidenfeld & Nicolson Ltd.

YOUNG, W. Prostitution. In J. H. Gagnon & W. Simon (Eds.), *Sexual deviance*. New York: Harper & Row, 1967. Pp. 105–133.

14. Psychosomatic Disorders

ALEXANDER, F. *Psychosomatic medicine.* New York: Norton, 1950.

ALVAREZ, W. C. Chocolate "candy" for X rays, a clue to migraines, an anti-senility drug. *Look,* Sept. 22, 1970, 13–14.

BACHRACH, A. J., ERWIN, W. J., & MOHR, J. P. The control of eating behavior in an anorexic by operant conditioning techniques. In L. P. Ullmann & L. Krasner (Eds.), *Case studies in behavior modification.* New York: Holt, Rinehart & Winston, 1965. Pp. 153–163.

BAHNSON, C. B. Psychophysiologic complementarity in malignancies: Past work and future vistas. *Ann. N.Y. Acad. Sci.,* 1969, **164**(2), 319–333.

BAHNSON, C., & SOLOMON, G. F. Study links cancer to emotional stress. *Los Angeles Times,* April 6, 1971, II, 5.

BASEDOW, H. *The Australian aboriginal.* London: Adelaide, 1927.

BLEEKER, E. Many asthma attacks psychological. *Science News,* 1968, **93**(17), 406.

BLOCK, J. Parents of schizophrenic, neurotic, asthmatic, and congenitally ill children. *Arch. gen. Psychiat.,* 1969, **20**, 659–674.

BRADY, J. V. Personal communication to F. L. Ruch & P. G. Zimbardo, 1970. In F. L. Ruch & P. G. Zimbardo, *Psychology and life.* (8th ed.) Glenview, Ill.: Scott, Foresman, 1971. P. 48.

BRADY, J. V., PORTER, R. W., CONRAD, D. G., & MASON, J. W. Avoidance behavior and the development of gastroduodenal ulcers. *J. exp. Anal. Behav.,* 1958, **1**, 69–73.

BULATOV, P. K. The higher nervous activity in persons suffering from bronchial asthma. In Problems of interrelationship between psyche and soma in psychoneurology and general medicine. *Institute Bechtereva,* 1963, 317–328. (*Inter. J. Psychiat.,* Sept. 1967, p. 245.)

CANNON, W. B. "Voodoo" death. *American Anthropologist,* 1942, **44**(2), 169–181.

CRISP, A. H. Premorbid factors in adult disorders of weight, with particular reference to primary anorexia nervosa (weight phobia). *J. psychosom. Med.,* 1970, **14**(1), 1–22.

DAVIES, M. Blood pressure and personality. *J. psychosom. Res.,* 1970, **14**(1), 89–104.

DAY, G. The psychosomatic approach to pulmonary tuberculosis. *Lancet,* May 12, 1951, p. 6663.

DI CARA, L. V. Learning in the autonomic nervous system. *Scientif. Amer.,* 1970, **222**(1), 30–39.

DUNBAR, F. *Psychosomatic diagnosis.* New York: Harper, 1943.

DUNBAR, F. *Emotions and bodily changes.* 4th ed. New York: Columbia Univer. Press, 1954.

EITINGER, L. Psychosomatic problems in concentration camp survivors. *J. psychosom. Res.,* 1969, **13**(2), 183–190.

ELLIS, E. F. Asthma—the demon that thrives on myths. *Today's Health,* 1970, **48**(6), 63–64.

ENGEL, G. L., & ADLER, R. Psychological factors in organic disease. *Ment. Hlth. Prog. Rep.,* U.S. Department of Health, Education and Welfare, Feb. 1967, 1–23.

FARIS, R. E. L., & DUNHAM, H. W. *Mental disorders in urban areas.* Chicago: Univer. Chicago Press, 1939.

FINNERTY, F. A. Hypertension among black women. *Science News,* 1971, **99**(7), 116.

FRENCH, J. D., PORTER, R. W., CAVANAUGH, E. B., & LONGMIRE, R. L. Experimental gastroduodenal lesions induced by stimulation of the brain. *Psychosom. Med.,* 1957, **19**, 209–220.

GOLDBERG, E. M. *Family influences and psychosomatic illness.* London: Tavistock Publ. Ltd., 1959.

GRAHAM, D. T. Some research on psychophysiologic specificity and its relation to psychosomatic disease. In R. Roessler & N. S. Greenfield (Eds.), *Physiological correlates of psychological disorder.* Madison: Univer. Wisconsin Press, 1962. Pp. 221–238.

GREEN, E., GREEN, A., & WALTERS, D. Voluntary control of internal states: Psychological and physiological variables. *Journal of TransPersonal Psychology,* 1970, **1**(1), 1–26.

GREGORY, I., & ROSEN, E. *Abnormal psychology.* Philadelphia: W. B. Saunders, 1965.

HINKLE, L. E., & WOLFF, H. G. Health and social environment. In A. Leighton, J. Calusen & R. Wilson (Eds.), *Exploration in social psychiatry.* Garden City, N.Y.: Basic Books, 1957. Pp. 105–137.

HOKANSON, J. E., & BURGESS, M. The effects of three types of aggression on vascular process. *J. abnorm. soc. Psychol.,* 1962, **64**, 446–449.

JACOBS, M. A., SPILKEN, A. Z., NORMAN, M. M., & ANDERSON, L. S. Life stress and respiratory illness. *Psychosom. Med.,* 1970, **32**, 233.

JACOBS, M. A., SPILKEN, A. Z., NORMAN, M. M., & ANDERSON, L. S. Patterns of maladaptive and respiratory illness. *J. psychosom. Res.,* 1971, **15**(1), 63–72.

JOHNSON, J. In G. Getze (Ed.), High blood pressure—the unknown killer. *Los Angeles Times,* Nov. 12, 1971, II, 1, 5.

KAHN, R. L. Stress: From 9 to 5. *Psych. Today,* 1969, **3**(4), 34–38.

KAMIYA, J. Conscious control of brain waves. *Psych. Today,* 1968, **1**(11), 56–61.

KIDSON, M., & JONES, I. Psychiatric disorders among aborigines of the Australian Western Desert. *Arch. gen. Psychiat.,* 1968, **19**(4), 413–417.

KNAPP, P. H. The asthmatic and his environment. *J. nerv. ment. Dis.,* 1969, **149**(2), 133–151.

LANG, P. Autonomic control. *Psych. Today,* 1970, **4**(5), 37–41.

LANG, P. J., STROUFE, L. A., & HASTINGS, J. E. Effects of feedback and instructional set on the control of cardiac-rate variability. *J. exp. Psychol.,* 1967, **75**, 425–431.

LEBEDEV, B. A. Corticovisceral psychosomatics. *Inter. J. Psychiat.,* 1967, **4**(3), 241–246.

LEONARD, A. G. *The lower Niger and its tribes.* London: Barnes & Noble, 1906.

LE SHAN, L. An emotional life-history pattern associated with neoplactic disease. *Ann. N.Y. Acad. Sci.,* 1966, **125**, 780–793.

LIPTON, E. L., STEINSCHNEIDER, A., & RICHMOND, J. B. Psychophysiologic disorders in children. In L. W. Hoffman & M. L. Hoffman (Eds.), *Review of child development research.* Russell Sage Foundation, 1966. Pp. 169–220.

MASON, E. E., & ITO, C. Gastric bypass. *Annals of Surgery,* 1969, **170**, 329–339.

MATARAZZO, R. G., MATARAZZO, J. D., & SASLOW, G. The relationship between medical and psychiatric symptoms. *J. abnorm. soc. Psychol.,* 1961, **62**(1), 55.

MILLER, N. E. Learning of visceral and glandular responses. *Science,* 1969, **163**(3866), 434–445.

MITCHELL, K. R., & MITCHELL, D. M. Migraine: An exploratory treatment application of programed behavior therapy techniques. *J. psychosom. Res.,* 1971, **15**(2), 137–157.

MURPHY, J. M., & HUGHES, C. C. The use of psychophysiological symptoms as indicators of disorder among Eskimos. In J. M. Murphy & A. Leighton (Eds.), *Approaches to cross-cultural psychiatry.* New York: Cornell Univer. Press, 1965. Pp. 108–160.

MUSAPH, H. Aggression and symptom formation in dermatology. *J. psychosom. Res.,* 1969, **13**(3), 257–264.

MUTTER, A. Z., & SCHLEIFER, M. J. The role of psychological and social factors in the onset of somatic illness in children. *Psychosom. Med.,* 1966, **28**, 333.

NECHELES, H. A blood factor in peptic ulcers. *The Sciences,* 1970, **10**(9), 15–16.

NEMIAH, J. C. Emotions and gastrointestinal disease. In H. Lief, V. F. Lief & N. R. Lief (Eds.), *The psychological basis of medical practice.* New York: Hoeber, 1963. Pp. 233–244.

OLDS, S. Say it with a stomach ache. *Today's Health,* 1970, **48**(11), 41–43, 88.

PARKES, C. M., BENJAMIN, B., & FITZGERALD, R. G. Broken hearts: A statistical study of increased mortality rate among widowers. *Brit. med. J.,* 1969, **1**, 740.

PASAMANICK, B. Prevalence and distribution of psychosomatic conditions in an urban population according to social class. *Psychosom. Med.,* 1962, **24**, 352–356.

PEDDER, J. R. Psychosomatic disorder and psychosis. *J. psychosom. Res.*, 1969, **13**(4), 339–346.

PENICK, S., FILION, R., FOX, S., & STUNKARD, A. J. Behavior modification in the treatment of obesity. *Psychosom. Med.*, 1971, **33**(1), 49–55.

PURCELL, K., MUSER, J., MIKLICH, D., & DIETIKER, K. E. A comparison of psychologic findings in variously defined asthmatic subgroups. *J. psychosom. Res.*, 1969, **13**(1), 67–71.

RAHE, R. H., & HOLMES, T. H. Life crisis and major health change. *Psychosom. Med.*, 1966, **28**, 774.

REES, L. The importance of psychological, allergic and infective factors in childhood asthma. *J. psychosom. Res.*, 1964, **7**, 253–262.

RENNIE, T. A. C., & SROLE, L. Social class prevalence and distribution of psychosomatic conditions in an urban population. *Psychosom. Med.*, 1956, **18**, 449–456.

ROSENTHAL, S., & WULFSOHN, N. Electrosleep—a clinical trial. *Amer. J. Psychiat.*, 1970, **127**(4), 175–176.

RUCH, F. L., & ZIMBARDO, P. G. *Psychology and life.* (8th ed.) Glenview, Ill.: Scott, Foresman, 1971.

SARGENT, J. Mystic migraine treatment. *Science News*, 1971, **100**(3), 42.

SAWREY, W. L., & SAWREY, J. M. Conditioned fear and restraint in ulceration. *J. compar. physiol. Psychol.*, 1964, **57**, 150–151.

SCHACHTER, S. Eat, eat. *Psych. Today*, 1971, **4**(11), 44–47, 78–79.

SCHWAB, J. J. Comprehensive medicine and the concurrence of physical and mental illness. *Psychosomatics*, 1970, **11**(6), 591–595.

SCHWAB, J. J., MC GINNIS, N. H., NORRIS, L. B., & SCHWAB, R. B. Psychosomatic medicine and the contemporary social scene. *Amer. J. Psychiat.*, 1970, **126**(11), 108–118.

SCHWARTZ, G. E., SHAPIRO, D., & TURSKY, B. Learned control of cardiovascular integration in man through operant conditioning. *Psychosom. Med.*, 1971, **33**(1), 57–62.

SELYE, H. *The stress of life.* New York: McGraw-Hill, 1956.

SELYE, H. Stress. *Psych. Today*, 1969, **3**(4), 24–26.

SENAY, E. C., & REDLICH, F. C. Cultural and social factors in neuroses and psychosomatic illnesses. *Social Psychiatry*, 1968, **3**(3), 89–97.

SOLOMON, G. F. Emotion, stress, the central nervous system, and immunity. *Ann. N.Y. Acad. Sci.*, 1969, **164**(2), 335–343.

SOLOMON, G. F. Study links cancer to emotional stress. *Los Angeles Times*, April 6, 1971, II, 5.

STAMLER, J. In G. Getze (Ed.), High blood pressure—the unknown killer. *Los Angeles Times*, Nov. 12, 1971, II, 1, 5.

STEIN, J. *Neurosis in contemporary society: Process and treatment.* Belmont, Calif.: Brooks/Cole, 1970.

STEINMANN, M. New discoveries about how immunity works. *Life*, 1971, **70**(20), 54.

STERNBACH, R. A. Psychosomatic diseases. In G. D. Shean (Ed.), *Studies in abnormal behavior.* Chicago: Rand McNally, 1971. Pp. 136–154.

STUART, R. B. A three-dimensional program for the treatment of obesity. *Behav. Res. Ther.*, 1971, **9**, 177–186.

SZYRYNSKI, V. Defective "psychological weaning" in psychosomatic pathology. *Psychosomatics*, 1960, **1**, 22–25.

TIME. Shocks to stop sneezes. June 17, 1966, p. 72.

TRIESMAN, M. Mind, body, and behavior: Control systems and their disturbances. In P. London & D. Rosenhan (Eds.), *Foundations of abnormal psychology.* New York: Holt, Rinehart & Winston, 1968. Pp. 460–518.

TURNBULL, J. W. Asthma conceived as a learned response. *J. psychosom. Res.*, 1962, **6**, 59–70.

WARREN, W. A study of anorexia nervosa in young girls. *J. child Psychol. Psychiat.*, 1968, **9**(1), 27–40.

WEITZMAN, E. D., & LUCE, G. Biological rhythms: Indices of pain, adrenal hormones, sleep, and sleep reversal. In NIMH, *Behavioral sciences and mental health.* Washington, D.C.: Govt. Printing Office, 1970.

WENAR, C., ET AL. *Origins of psychosomatic and emotional disturbances: A study of mother-child relationships.* New York: Harper, 1962.

WITTKOWER, E. D., & SOLYOM, L. Models of mind-body interaction. *Inter. J. Psychiat.*, 1967, **4**(3), 225–233.

WOLF, S., & WOLFF, H. G. Psychosomatic aspects of peptic ulcers. *Scope*, 1946, **11**, 4–9. Used with permission of The Upjohn Company, Kalamazoo, Michigan.

WOLF, S., & WOLFF, H. G. *Human gastric functions.* New York: Oxford Univer. Press, 1947.

WOLFF, H. G. *Headache and other head pain.* Cambridge: Oxford University Press, 1948. Used by permission of Oxford University Press.

WOLFF, H. G. Life stress and cardiovascular disorders. *Circulation*, 1950, **1**, 187–203.

WOLFF, H. G. Life stress and bodily disease. In A. Weider (Ed.), *Contributions toward medical psychology.* Vol. 1. Copyright © 1953 The Ronald Press Company, New York. Used with permission.

WOLPE, J. For phobia: A hair of the hound. *Psych. Today*, 1969, **3**(1), 34–37.

15. Organic Brain Syndromes

AMERICAN MEDICAL ASSOCIATION. *VD is still a world problem.* Chicago: AMA, 1969.

ATTHOWE, J., JR., & KRASNER, L. Preliminary report on the application of contingent reinforcement procedures (token economy) on a "chronic" psychiatric ward. *J. abnorm. Psychol.*, 1968, **73**, 37–43.

BARZILAI, S., WINNIK, H. Z., & DAVIS, M. Postpartum mental disturbances. *Harefuah: J. Israel med. Ass.*, 1969, **76**(3), 104–106.

BATCHELOR, I., & CAMPBELL, R. *Henderson and Gillespie's textbook of psychiatry for students and practitioners.* (10th ed.) New York: Oxford Univer. Press, 1969.

BEATLES. *When I'm sixty-four*, by J. Lennon & P. McCartney. Copyright © 1967 Northern Songs Limited. Used by Permission. All Rights Reserved.

BELLAMY, W. E., JR. Huntington's chorea. *N.C. med. J.*, 1961, **22**, 409–412.

BIRREN, J. E. The abuse of the urban aged. *Psych. Today*, 1970, **3**(10), 37–38.

BLAU, D. The course of psychiatric hospitalization in the aged. *J. geriat. Psychol.*, 1970, **3**(2), 210–223.

BOWMAN, K. M., & ENGLE, B. Geriatrics. *Amer. J. Psychiat.*, 1960, **116**, 629–630.

BRICKNER, R. M. *The intellectual functions of the frontal lobes.* New York: Macmillan, 1936.

BROŽEK, J., GUETZKOW, H., & KEYS, A. A study of personality of normal young men maintained on restricted intakes of vitamins of the B complex. *Psychosom. Med.*, 1946, **8**, 98–109.

BROŽEK, J., & GRANDE, F. Abnormalities of neural function in the presence of inadequate nutrition. In J. Field (Ed.), *Handbook of physiology. Section I: Neurophysiology.* Vol. 3. Baltimore, Md.: Williams & Wilkins, 1960. Pp. 1891–1910.

BRUETSCH, W. L. Neurosyphilitic conditions. In S. Arieti (Ed.), *American handbook of psychiatry.* Vol. 2. New York: Basic Books, 1959. Pp. 1003–1020.

BUHLER, C. The course of human life as a psychological problem. *Human Develop.*, 1968, **11**, 184–200.

BYRD, R. E. *Alone.* New York: Putnam, 1938. Reprinted by permission of G. P. Putnam's Sons from *Alone* by Admiral Richard E. Byrd. Copyright 1938 by Richard E. Byrd. Copyright renewed 1966 by Marie A. Byrd.

CAROTHERS, J. C. A study of mental derangement in Africans, and an attempt to explain its peculiarities, more especially in relation to the African attitude to life. *J. ment. Sci.*, 1947, **93**, 548–597.

COLE, W. New insights into the brain's defenses. *Today's Health*, 1970, **48**(1), 50–53.

CORTZIAS, G. C. Progress in Parkinson's disease. *The Sciences*, 1969, **9**(7), 20–23.

DE BEAUVOIR, S. The terrors of old age. *Newsweek*, Feb. 9, 1970, p. 54.

DOBROKHOTOVA, T. A. On the pathology of the emotional sphere in tumorous lesion of the frontal lobes of the brain. *Zhurnal Nevropatologii i Psikhiartrii*, 1968, **68**(3), 418–422.

EARL, H. G. Head injury: The big killer. *Today's Health*, 1966, **44**(12), 19–21.

EDWARDS, C. C. L-dopa: Limited approval. *Newsweek,* June 15, 1970, p. 91.

FETTERMAN, J. L. *Practical lessons in psychiatry.* Springfield, Ill.: Charles C Thomas, 1949. From Fetterman, J. L., *Practical Lessons in Psychiatry,* 1949. Courtesy of Charles C Thomas, Publisher, Springfield, Illinois.

FLEMING, W., BROWN, W., DONAHUE, J., & GRANIGIN, P. National survey of venereal disease treated by physicians in 1968. *JAMA,* 1970, **211,** 1827–1830.

FLOR-HENRY, P. Temporal lobe epilepsy: Etiological factors. *Amer. J. Psychiat.,* 1969, **126**(3), 400–403.

FORD, A. B. Casualties of our time. *Science,* 1970, **167**(3196), 256–263.

FREUCHEN, P. *Arctic adventure.* New York: Rinehart, 1935.

GAL, P. Mental disorders of advanced years. *Geriatrics,* 1959, **14,** 224–228.

GAZZANIGA, M. The split brain in man. *Scientif. Amer.,* 1967, **217**(2), 24–29.

GERMAN, W. J. Initial symptomatology in brain tumors. *Conn. Med.,* 1959, **23,** 636–637.

GIBSON, J. Mental effects of head injury. *Canad. Nurse,* 1959, **55,** 118–119.

GIBSON, J. General paralysis. *Canad. Nurse,* 1960, **55,** 118–119.

GOLDFARB, A. I. Predicting mortality in the institutionalized aged. *Arch. gen. Psychiat.,* 1969, **21,** 172–176.

GROUP FOR THE ADVANCEMENT OF PSYCHIATRY. GAP hits neglect of geriatric patients. *Psychiatric News,* 1970, **5**(16), 1, 16.

GUNTHER, J. *Death be not proud.* New York: Harper, 1949.

HARLOW, J. M. Recovery from the passage of an iron bar through the head. *Publ. Mass. med. Soc.,* 1868, **2,** 327.

HENDERSON, D. K. *Textbook of psychiatry for students and practitioners.* (9th ed.) London: Oxford Univer. Press, 1962.

ISAACSON, R. L. When brains are damaged. *Psych. Today,* 1970, **3**(8), 38–42.

JACOBS, E. A., SMALL, S. M., & WINTERS, P. Oxygen for senility symptoms. *Science News,* 1970, **97**(21), 506.

JACOBS, E., WINTERS, P. M., ALVIS, H. J., & SMALL, S. M. Hyperbaric oxygen: Temporary aid for senile minds. *JAMA,* 1969, **209,** 1435–1438.

JASPER, H. (Ed.) *Basic mechanisms of the epilepsies.* Boston: Little, Brown, 1969.

JERVIS, G. A. The mental deficiencies. In S. Arieti (Ed.), *American handbook of psychiatry.* Vol. 2. New York: Basic Books, 1959. Pp. 1289–1316.

JOHNSON, J. The EEG in the traumatic encephalography of boxers. *Psychiatrica Clinica,* 1969, **2**(4), 204–211.

JUVENAL. *Satires.* G. G. Ramsay (Tr.) Cambridge, Mass.: Harvard Univer. Press.

KAHANA, B., & KAHANA, E. Changes in mental status of elderly patients in age-integrated and age-segregated hospital milieus. *J. abnorm. Psychol.,* 1970, **75,** 177–181.

KALLMANN, F. J. Genetic factors in aging: Comparative and longitudinal observations on a senescent twin population. In P. H. Hoch & J. Zubin (Eds.), *Psychopathology of aging.* New York: Grune & Stratton, 1961. Pp. 227–247.

KEMBLE. *Idols and invalids.* New York: Doubleday, 1936.

KEYS, A., BROŽEK, J., HENSCHEL, A., MICKELSON, O., & TAYLOR, H. L. *The biology of human starvation.* Minneapolis: Univer. Minn. Press, 1950.

LARSON, V. L., & EVANS, T. Social stresses implicated in most postpartum psychoses. *Roche Reports,* 1969, **6**(6), 2.

LEVIN, M. Bromide hallucinosis. *Arch. gen. Psychiat.,* 1960, **2,** 429–433.

LEVIN, S. Brain tumors in mental hospital patients. *Amer. J. Psychiat.,* 1949, **105,** 897–900.

LEYTON, G. B. The effects of slow starvation. *Lancet,* 1946, **251,** 73–79.

LIPSCOMB, C. F. The care of psychiatrically disturbed elderly patients in the community. *Amer. J. Psychiat.,* 1971, **127**(8), 107–114.

LOS ANGELES TIMES. Prostitute's diary aids in syphilis hunt. April 1, 1970, III, 16.

LOS ANGELES TIMES. Venereal disease out of control. April 16, 1971, II, 10.

LUNDE, D. T. Psychiatric complications of heart transplants. *Amer. J. Psychiat.,* 1969, **126**(3), 117–121.

MARKSON, E., KOWH, A., CUMMING, J., & CRUMMIN, E. Alternatives to hospitalization for psychiatrically ill geriatric patients. *Amer. J. Psychiat.,* 1971, **128**(8), 95–102.

MARTIN, M. E. Puerperal mental illness: A follow-up study of 75 cases. *Brit. med. J.,* 1958, **2,** 733–777.

MAYER-GROSS, W. Arteriosclerotic, senile, and presenile psychoses. *J. ment. Sci.,* 1944, **90,** 316–327.

MC TAGGART, A. N., ANDERMANN, F., & BOS, C. A survey of cerebral tumors presented at a psychiatric institution. *Canad. Psychiat. Ass. J.,* 1961, **6,** 333–338.

MELGES, F. T. Postpartum psychiatric syndromes. *Psychosom. Med.,* 1968, **30,** 95–108.

MENNINGER, K. *The human mind.* New York: Knopf, 1946. From pages 41–42, 139–140 in *The Human Mind,* by Karl Menninger. Copyright 1930, 1937, 1945 and renewed 1958, 1965 by Karl Menninger. Reprinted by permission of Alfred A. Knopf, Inc.

MOON, H. E. (Ed.) *The adrenal cortex.* New York: Harper, 1961.

NEW YORK ACADEMY OF SCIENCES. Progress in Parkinson's disease. *The Sciences,* 1969, **9**(7), 20–24.

NOYES, A., & KOLB, L. C. *Modern clinical psychiatry.* (7th ed.) Philadelphia: W. B. Saunders Company, 1968. Used by permission.

O'CONNELL, B. Postcontusional syndrome. *J. Foren. Med.,* 1961, **8,** 122–130.

PARRAN, T. *Shadow on the land.* New York: Reynal & Hitchcock, 1937.

PATTON, R. B., & SHEPPARD, J. A. Intracranial tumors found at autopsy in mental patients. *Amer. J. Psychiat.,* 1956, **113,** 319–324.

POFFENBARGER, R. S., FRAMINGHAM, W. H., STEINMETZ, C. H., POOLER, B. G., & HYDE, R. T. The picture puzzle of the postpartum psychosis. *J. chron. Dis.,* 1961, **13,** 161–173.

POST, F. Some problems arising from a study of mental patients over the age of sixty years. *J. ment. Sci.,* 1944, **90,** 554–565.

PROTHEROE, C. Puerperal psychoses: A long term study. *Brit. J. Psychiat.,* 1969, **115**(518), 9–30.

PRYSE-PHILLIPS, W. *Epilepsy.* London: Bristol-Wright, 1969.

PUSEY, W. A. *The history and epidemiology of syphilis.* Springfield: Charles C Thomas, 1933.

RICHTER, C. P. *The role of biological clocks in mental and physical health.* Washington, D.C.: Pub. Hlth. Serv., 1970. Pp. 245–271.

ROTHSCHILD, D. The role of the premorbid personality in arteriosclerotic psychoses. *Amer. J. Psychiat.,* 1944, **100,** 501–505.

ROTHSCHILD, D. Senile psychoses and psychoses with cerebral arteriosclerosis. In O. J. Kaplan (Ed.), *Mental disorders in later life.* (2nd ed.) Stanford: Stanford Univer. Press, 1956.

RUCH, F. L., & ZIMBARDO, P. G. *Psychology and life.* (8th ed.) Glenview, Ill.: Scott, Foresman, 1971.

SCHWAB, J. J. Comprehensive medicine and the concurrence of physical and mental illness. *Psychosomatics,* 1970, **11**(6), 591–595.

SHAKHMATOV, N. F. Clinico-statistical study of the psychoses of old age. *Zhurnal Nevropatologii i Psikhiartrii,* 1968, **68**(2), 220–226.

SHEAN, G. D. (Ed.) *Studies in abnormal behavior.* Chicago: Rand McNally, 1971. Pp. 438–439, 475–476.

SIMMONS, L. Aging in preindustrial societies. In C. Tibbitts (Ed.), *Handbook of social gerontology.* Chicago: Univer. Chicago Press, 1960. Pp. 63–87.

SKLAR, J., & O'NEILL, F. J. Experiments in intensive treatment in a geriatric ward. In P. H. Hoch & J. Zubin (Eds.), *Psychopathology of aging.* New York: Grune & Stratton, 1961. Pp. 266–273.

SOFFER, A. What you should know about strokes. *Today's Health,* 1968, **46**(8), 40–41, 71–72.

SONIAT, T. L. L. Psychiatric symptoms associated with intracranial neoplasms. *Amer. J. Psychiat.,* 1951, **108,** 19–22.

STANG, R. R. The etiology of Parkinson's disease. *Dis. nerv. Sys.,* 1970, **31**(6), 381–390.

STAPLETON, K. One of 10 L.A. youths to get VD in 1971. *Los Angeles Herald Examiner,* April 5, 1970, A, 1–3.

STRAGE, M. VD: The clock is ticking. *Today's Health,* 1971, **49**(4), 16–18, 69–71.

SUTHERLAND, J. M., & TRAIT, H. *The epilepsies: Modern diagnosis and treatment.* Edinburgh: Livingstone, 1969.

SYMONDS, C. Concussion and its sequelae. *Lancet,* 1962, **1**, 1–5.

TALLAND, G. Amnesia: A world without continuity. *Psych. Today,* 1967, **1**(1), 43–50.

TARR, J. D., & LUGAR, R. R. Early infectious syphilis: Male homosexual relations as a mode of spread. *Calif. Med.,* 1960, **93**, 35–37.

ULLMANN, M., & GRUEN, A. Behavioral changes in patients with strokes. *Amer. J. Psychiat.,* 1961, **117**, 1004–1009.

U.S. NEWS AND WORLD REPORT. "Senior power"—a growing force in politics. May 24, 1971, pp. 66–77.

U.S. PUBLIC HEALTH SERVICE. *Syphilis—modern diagnosis and management.* (Publication No. 743) Washington, D.C.: Govt. Printing Office, 1961.

VOLPE, A., & KASTENBAUM, R. TLC. *Amer. J. Nurs.,* 1967, **67**, 100–103.

WEBB, W. W., SELF, S. H., PATE, J. E., & SOLOMON, A. H. The sequelae of acute bacterial meningitis: A possible clue to early school problems. *J. spec. Ed.,* 1968, **2**(4), 293–296.

WEINER, A., & STEINHILBER, R. The postpartum psychoses. *J. Int. Coll. Surgeons,* 1961, **36**, 490–499.

WEINSTEIN, E. A. Psychiatric aspects of head injury. *N.Y. J. Med.,* 1961, **61**, 1879–1883.

WEINSTEIN, E., & LYERLY, O. G. Confabulation in severe brain injury cases. *Arch. gen. Psychiat.,* 1968, **18**(9), 348–354.

WHITE, H. H., & FOWLER, F. D. Chronic lead encephalopathy: A diagnostic consideration in mental retardation. *Pediatrics,* 1960, **25**, 309–315.

WHITE, M. A., PROUT, C. T., FIXSEN, C., & FOUNDEUR, M. Obstetrician's role in postpartum mental illness. *JAMA,* 1957, **165**, 138–143.

WHYBROW, P. C., PRANGE, A. J., & TREADWAY, C. R. Mental changes accompanying thyroid gland dysfunction. *Arch. gen. Psychiat.,* 1969, **20**, 48–63.

WILSON, S. A. K. *Neurology.* Vol. 2. Baltimore: Williams & Wilkins, 1940.

WOLFF, H. D., & HUSTON, P. E. Schizophrenia associated with Addison's disease. *Amer. J. Psychiat.,* 1959, **116**, 365–367.

YAHR, M. D. Progress in Parkinson's disease. *The Sciences,* 1969, **9**(7), 20–23.

YALOM, I. D. Organic brain diseases of senility. *Maryland St. med. J.,* 1960, **9**, 781–787.

YALOM, I. D., LUNDE, D. T., MOOS, R. H., & HAMBURG, D. A. "Postpartum blues" syndrome. *Arch. gen. Psychiat.,* 1968, **18**, 16–27.

ZIMBERG, S. Outpatient geriatric psychiatry in an urban ghetto with nonprofessional workers. *Amer. J. Psychiat.,* 1969, **125**(12), 111–119.

16. Mental Retardation

ALBEE, G. W. Needed—a revolution in caring for the retarded. *Transaction,* 1968, **5**, 37–42.

AMERICAN PSYCHIATRIC ASSOCIATION. *Diagnostic and statistical manual of mental disorders.* (2nd ed.) Washington, D.C.: APA, 1968.

AMERICAN PSYCHOLOGICAL ASSOCIATION. Psychology and mental retardation. *Amer. Psychologist,* 1970, **25**, 267–268.

BARATZ, S., & BARATZ, J. C. Early childhood intervention: The social science base of institutional racism. *Harvard Ed. Rev.,* 1970, **40**(1), 29–50.

BENDA, C. E. Mongolism: A comprehensive review. *Arch. Pediat.,* 1956, **73**, 391–407.

BENDA, C. E. Down's syndrome: Beginning of end. *Roche Reports,* 1970, **7**(15), 1, 5.

BENDA, C. E., & FARRELL, M. Metabolic studies in mongolism: Discussion. *Amer. J. Psychiat.,* 1954, **111**, 144–145.

BIJOU, S. W. A functional analysis of retarded development. In N. R. Ellis (Ed.), *International review of research in mental retardation.* Vol. 1. New York: Academic Press, 1966. Pp. 1–19.

BLADESLEE, A. L. Nutritional time bomb. *Today's Health,* 1967, **45**(6), 7.

BRANDON, M. W. G., KIRMAN, B. H., & WILLIAMS, C. E. Microcephaly. *J. ment. Sci.,* 1959, **105**, 721–747.

CENTERWALL, S. A., & CENTERWALL, W. R. Study of children with mongolism reared in the home compared to those reared away from the home. *Pediatrics,* 1960, **25**, 678–685.

CENTERWALL, W. R., & CENTERWALL, S. A. Phenylketonuria (Folling's disease): The story of its discovery. *Journal of the History of Medicine,* 1961, **16**, 292–296.

CHESS, S., & KORN, S. Temperament and behavior disorders in mentally retarded children. *Arch. gen. Psychiat.,* 1970, 23(2), 122–130.

CHRISTODORESCU, D., COLLINS, S., ZELLINGHER, R., & TAUTU, C. Psychiatric disturbances in Turner's syndrome: Report of three cases. *Psychiatrica Clinica,* 1970, **3**(2), 114–124.

CLARK, G. R., KIVITZ, M. S., & ROSEN, M. Program for mentally retarded. *Science News,* 1969, **96**, 82.

COWIE, V. The genetics and sub-classification of microcephaly. *J. ment. Def. Res.,* 1960, **4**, 42–47.

DAVIS, D. C. Predicting tomorrow's children. *Today's Health,* 1968, **46**, 32–37.

DOBBING, J. Growth of the brain. *Sci. J.,* 1967, **3**(5), 81–86.

DONOGHUE, E. C., ABBAS, K. A., & GAL, E. The medical assessment of mentally retarded children in hospital. *Brit. J. Psychiat.,* 1970, **117**(540), 531–532.

DUGDALE, A. E., & PATTERSON, H. S. Detection of hydrocephalus in infancy. *Med. J. Austral.,* 1968, **1**(24, Suppl.).

DYBWAD, G. Who are the mentally retarded? *Children,* 1968, **15**, 43–48.

EISENBERG, L. Child psychiatry: The past quarter century. *Amer. J. Orthopsychiat.,* 1969, **39**, 389–401.

FALLS, H. F. Ocular changes in Down's syndrome help in diagnosis. *Roche Reports,* 1970, **7**(16), 5.

GREENFIELD, J. C., & WOLFSON, J. M. Microcephalia vera. *Arch. neurol. Psychiat.,* 1935, **33**, 1296–1316.

GRUENBERG, E. M. Epidemiology of mental illness. *Inter. J. Psychiat.,* 1966, **2**, 78–126.

GUERNEY, B. G., JR. (Ed.) *Psychotherapeutic agents: New roles for nonprofessionals, parents, and teachers.* New York: Holt, Rinehart & Winston, 1969.

GUTHRIE, G. M., BUTLER, A., & GORLOW, L. Personality differences between institutionalized and non-institutionalized retardates. *Amer. J. ment. Def.,* 1963, **67**, 543–548.

HADDAD, H. M., & WILKINS, L. Congenital anomalies associated with gonadal aplasia: Review of 55 cases. *Pediatrics,* 1959, **23**, 885–902.

HAGAN, J. W., & HUNTSMAN, N. J. Selective attention in mental retardation. *Develop. Psychol.,* 1971, **5**(1), 151–160.

HEBER, R. A manual on terminology and classification in mental retardation. *Amer. J. ment. Def.,* 1959, **64**, Monogr. Suppl. No. 2.

HEBER, R. Modifications in the manual on terminology and classification in mental retardation. *Amer. J. ment. Def.,* 1961, **65**, 499–500.

HERZOG, E., & LEWIS, H. Children in poor families: Myths and realities. *Amer. J. Orthopsychiat.,* 1970, **40**(3), 375–387.

HOLUB, D. A., GRUMBACH, M. M., & JAILER, J. W. Seminiferous tubule dysgenesis (Klinefelter's syndrome) in identical twins. *J. clin. Endocrinol. Metabolism,* 1958, **18**, 1359–1368.

HSIA, D. Y. *Inborn errors of metabolism.* Chicago: Year Book, 1959.

HUMPHRY, H. Training mentally retarded can be a good investment. *Los Angeles Times,* Feb. 16, 1970, II, 9.

HURLEY, R. *Poverty and mental retardation: A causal relationship.* New York: Random, 1969.

IRWIN, T. The wondrous machine that salvages backward kids. *Today's Health,* 1969, **47**, 31–33, 71.

ISAACSON, R. L. When brains are damaged. *Psych. Today,* 1970, **3**(4), 38–42.

ITARD, J. *The wild boy of Aveyron.* Paris, 1799. G. Humphrey & M. Humphrey (Tr.) New York: Century, 1932.

JOHNSON, H. R., MYHRE, S. A., RIWALCABA, R. H. A., THULINE, H. C., & KELLEY, V. C. Effects of testosterone on body image and behavior in Klinefelter's syndrome: A pilot study. *Develop. Med. child Neurol.,* 1970, **12**(4), 454–460.

JOHNSON, R. C., & ABELSON, R. B. Intellectual, behavioral, and physical characteristics associated with trisomy, translocation, and mosaic types of Down's syndrome. *Amer. J. ment. Def.*, 1968–1969, **73**, 852–855.

KALTER, H. Paper delivered at symposium on phenylketonuria. Institute for Postgraduate Education, Cincinnati, Nov. 16, 1961. Reported Ross Laboratories, *Currents in Publ. Hlth.*, 1962, 2.

KARNES, M. B., TESKA, J. A., & HODGINS, A. S. The effects of four programs of classroom intervention on the intellectual and language development of 4-year-old disadvantaged children. *Amer. J. Orthopsychiat.*, 1970, **40**, 58–76.

KENNEDY, J. F. Message from the President of the United States relative to mental illness and mental retardation. *Amer. Psychologist*, 1963, **18**, 280–289.

KNOBLOCH, H. Neuropsychiatric sequelae of prematurity: A longitudinal study. *JAMA*, 1956, **161**, 581–585.

KOCH, R. The multidisciplinary approach to mental retardation. In A. A. Baumeister (Ed.), *Mental retardation: Appraisal, education, and rehabilitation*. Chicago: Aldine, 1967. Pp. 20–38.

LAURENCE, K. M. Hydrocephalus and disability. *Cerebral Palsy Bull.*, 1960, **2**, 170–179.

LAURENCE, K. M. Neurological and intellectual sequelae of hydrocephalus. *Arch. Neurol.*, 1969, **20**(1), 73–81.

LEJEUNE, J. Down's syndrome explained as error in meiotic process. *Roche Reports*, 1970, **7**(15), 1–2.

LEMKAU, P. V., & IMRE, P. D. Results of a field epidemiologic study. *Amer. J. ment. Def.*, 1968–1969, **73**, 858–863.

LYLE, J. G. The effect of an institution environment upon the verbal development of institutional children. I. Verbal intelligence. *J. ment. Def. Res.*, 1959, **3**, 122–128.

LYLE, J. G. The effect of an institution environment upon the verbal development of institutional children. II. Speech and language. III. The Brooklands residential family unit. *J. ment. Def. Res.*, 1960, **4**, 1–13, 14–23.

MAC MILLAN, D. L., & KEOGH, B. K. Normal and retarded children's expectancy for failure. *Develop. Psychol.*, 1971, **4**(3), 343–348.

MC CLURE, H. M., BELDEN, K. M., PIEPER, W. A., & JACKSON, C. B. Autosomal trisomy in a chimpanzee: Resemblance to Down's syndrome. *Science*, 1969, **165**(3897), 1010–1012.

MENOLASCINO, F. J. The façade of mental retardation: Its challenge to child psychiatry. *Amer. J. Psychiat.*, 1966, **122**, 1227–1235.

MENOLASCINO, F. J. Emotional disturbance in mentally retarded children. *Amer. J. Psychiat.*, 1969, **126**(2), 168–176.

MILLER, R. Does Down's syndrome predispose children to leukemia? *Roche Reports*, 1970, **7**(16), 5.

NIELSEN, J., BJARNASON, S., FRIEDRICH, U., FROLAND, A., HANSEN, V. H., & SORENSEN, A. Klinefelter's syndrome in children. *J. child Psychol. Psychiat.*, 1970, **11**(2), 109–120.

PARTINGTON, M. W. The early symptoms of phenylketonuria. *Pediatrics*, 1961, **27**, 465–473.

PAUL, H. A., & MILLER, J. R. Reduction of extreme deviant behavior in a severely retarded girl. *Training School Bulletin*, 1971, **67**(4), 193–197. Reprinted by permission from *The Training School Bulletin*, American Institute for Mental Studies, Vineland, New Jersey.

PAULING, L. Genetic effects of weapons tests. *Bulletin of the Atomic Scientists*, 1962, **18**(10), 15–18.

PAYNE, J. S. Prevalence survey of severely mentally retarded in Wyandotte County, Kansas. *Training School Bulletin*, 1971, **67**(4), 193–197.

PENROSE, L. S. *Biology of mental defect*. (3rd ed.) New York: Grune & Stratton, 1963.

PERRY, T. The enigma of PKU. *The Sciences*, 1970, **10**(8), 12–16.

PHILIPS, I. Psychopathology and mental retardation. *Amer. J. Psychiat.*, 1967, **124**, 29–35.

PICKERING, D. E., & FISHER, D. A. Therapeutic concepts relative to hypothyroidism in childhood. *J. chron. Dis.*, 1958, **7**, 242–263.

PRESIDENT'S COMMITTEE ON MENTAL RETARDATION. *The decisive decade*. Washington, D.C.: Govt. Printing Office, 1970.

RICHARDSON, S. A. Retarded children. *Trans-action*, 1969, **6**(10), 6, 8.

ROBINSON, A. The human chromosomes. *Amer. J. Dis. Child.*, 1961, **101**, 379–398.

ROTHCHILD, B. F. Incubator isolation as a possible contributing factor to the high incidence of emotional disturbance among prematurely born persons. *J. genet. Psychol.*, 1967, **110**(2), 287–304.

RUCH, F. L., & ZIMBARDO, P. G. *Psychology and life*. (8th ed.) Glenview, Ill.: Scott, Foresman, 1971.

RUNDLE, A. T. Etiological factors in mental retardation. I. Biochemical. II. Endocrinological. *Amer. J. ment. Def.*, 1962, **67**, 61–77.

THE SCIENCES. The enigma of PKU. 1970, **10**(8), 12–16.

SCRIMSHAW, N. S. Early malnutrition and central nervous system function. *Merrill-Palmer Quart.*, 1969, **15**, 376–388.

SHAPIRO, A., & RIDLER, M. A. The incidence of Klinefelter's syndrome in a mental deficiency hospital. *J. ment. Def. Res.*, 1960, **4**, 48–50.

SHOSHONE, R. Director of Exceptional Children's Foundation. Personal communication to author, 1971.

SILBERSTEIN, R. M., & IRWIN, H. Jean-Marc-Gaspard Itard and the savage of Aveyron: An unsolved diagnostic problem in child psychiatry. *J. Amer. Acad. Child Psychiat.*, 1962, **1**(2), 314–322.

SMITH, D. W., BLIZZARD, R. M., & WILKINS, L. The mental prognosis in hypothyroidism in infancy and childhood. *Pediatrics*, 1957, **19**, 1011–1020.

SMITH, D. W., PATAU, K., THERMAN, E., & INHORN, S. L. The no. 18 trisomy syndrome. *J. Pediat.*, 1962, **60**, 513–527.

SOUTHWICK, W. E. Time and stage in development at which factors operate to produce mongolism. *Amer. J. Dis. Child.*, 1939, **117**, 68–69.

STIMSON, C. W. Human cytogenetics and its clinical application to mental retardation. *Amer. J. ment. Def.*, 1961, **65**, 713–725.

STIMSON, C. W. Understanding the mongoloid child. *Today's Health*, 1968, **46**, 56–59.

TODAY'S HEALTH. Building minds through art. 1968, **46**(12), 28–31.

TREDGOLD, A. F., & TREDGOLD, R. F. *Textbook of mental deficiency*. London: Baillière Tindall & Cox, 1952.

U.S. FEDERAL RADIATION COUNCIL. *Health implications of fallout from nuclear weapons testing through 1961*. Washington, D.C.: Author, 1962.

VISCOTT, D. S. A musical idiot savant. *Psychiatry*, 1970, **33**(4), 494–515.

WHALEN, C. K., & HENKER, B. A. Pyramid therapy in a hospital for the retarded. *Amer. J. ment. Def.*, 1971, **75**(4), 414–434.

WILKINS, W. L. Mental and educational retardation. In I. A. Berg & L. A. Pennington (Eds.), *An introduction to clinical psychology*. (3rd ed.) New York: Ronald Press, 1966. Pp. 226–247.

WUNSCH, W. L. Some characteristics of mongoloids evaluated in a clinic for children with retarded mental development. *Amer. J. ment. Def.*, 1957, **62**, 122–130.

ZEILBERGER, J., SAMPSON, S., & SLOAN, H., JR. Modification of a child's behavior problem in the home with the mother as therapist. *J. appl. behav. Anal.*, 1968, **1**, 47–53.

17. Behavior Disorders of Childhood

ARON, M. L. The nature and incidence of stuttering among a Bantu group of school-going children. *J. speech hear. Dis.*, 1962, **27**, 116–128.

BANDURA, A. *Principles of behavior modification*. New York: Holt, Rinehart & Winston, 1969.

BEECH, R. Stuttering and stammering. *Psych. Today*, 1967, **1**(3), 48–51.

BENSON, F. A. M. (Ed.) *Modifying deviant social behaviors in various classroom settings*. Eugene, Ore.: Univer. Oregon Press, 1969.

BETTELHEIM, B. Joey: A "mechanical boy." *Scientific American*, 1959, **200**, 116–127. From "Joey: A 'Mechanical Boy'" by Bruno Bettelheim. Copyright © March 1959 by Scientific American, Inc. All rights reserved.

BETTELHEIM, B. *The empty fortress*. New York: Free Press, 1967.

BETTELHEIM, B. Laurie. *Psych. Today*, 1969, **2**(12), 24–25, 60.

BRATFOS, O. Parental deprivation in childhood and type of future mental disease. *Acta Psychiatr. Scandin.*, 1967, **43**(4), 453–461.

BROWNING, R. M., & STOVER, D. O. *Behavior modification and child treatment.* Chicago: Aldine, 1970.

BURKS, H. F. The hyperkinetic child. *Exceptional Children*, 1960, **27**, 18–26.

CAPUTO, D. V., & MANDELL, D. Consequences of low birth weight. *Develop. Psychol.*, 1970, **3**(3), 363–383.

CHALFANT, J. C., & SCHEFFELIN, M. A. *Central processing dysfunctions in children: A review of research.* INNDS monogr. no. 9. Washington, D.C.: Govt. Printing Office, 1969.

CHANDLER, B. A. The White House Conference on Children—a 1970 happening. *Family Coordinator*, 1971, **20**(3), 195–208.

CLANCY, H., & MC BRIDE, G. The autistic process and its treatment. *J. child Psychol. Psychiat.*, 1969, **10**(4), 233–244.

CLEMENT, P. Elimination of sleepwalking in a seven-year-old boy. *J. cons. clin. Psychol.*, 1970, **34**(1), 22–26.

CLEMENTS, S. D. *Minimal brain dysfunction in children—terminology and identification.* Washington, D.C.: HEW, 1966.

CLOSE, K. Selecting priorities at the White House Conference on Children. *Children*, 1971, **18**(2), 42–48.

COLEMAN, J. C., & MC CALLEY, J. E. Nail-biting and mental health: A survey of the literature. *Ment. Hyg.*, 1948, **32**, 428–454.

COLEMAN, J. C., & SERET, C. The role of hostility in fingernail biting. *Psychological Service Center Journal*, 1950, **2**, 238–244.

DINNAN, J. A., MC GUINESS, E., & PERRIN, L. Auditory feedback—stutterers versus nonstutterers. *J. learn. Dis.*, 1970, **3**(4), 30–34.

EDWARDS, R. P., ALLEY, G. R., & SNIDER, W. Academic achievement and minimal brain dysfunction. *J. learn. Dis.*, 1971, **4**(3), 134–138.

EISENBERG, L. Principles of drug therapy in child psychiatry with special reference to stimulant drugs. *Amer. J. Orthopsychiat.*, 1971, **4**(3), 371–379.

FARGO, G. A., BEHRENS, C., & NOLEN, P. (Eds.) *Behavior modification in the classroom.* Belmont, Calif.: Wadsworth, 1970.

FISCHER, I., & GLANVILLE, B. W. K. Programmed teaching of autistic children. *Arch. gen. Psychiat.*, 1970, **23**(1), 90–94.

FISH, B., SHAPIRO, T., CAMPBELL, M., & WILE, R. A classification of schizophrenic children under five years. *Amer. J. Psychiat.*, 1968, **124**(10), 109–117.

FLANAGAN, B., GOLDIAMOND, I., & AZRIN, N. H. Instatement of stuttering in normally fluent individuals through operant procedures. *Science*, 1959, **130**, 979–981.

FREEDMAN, D. A. Congenital and perinatal sensory deprivation: Some studies in early development. *Amer. J. Psychiat.*, 1971, **127**(11), 1539–1545.

FREEDMAN, D. X., & MEMBERS OF DRUG PANEL. The use of stimulant drugs in treating hyperactive children. *Children*, 1971, **18**(3), 111.

FREIBERGS, V., & DOUGLAS, V. I. Concept learning in hyperactive and normal children. *J. abnorm. Psychol.*, 1969, **74**(3), 388–395.

FRIEDMAN, R. Utility of the concept of brain damage for the school psychologist. *J. school Psychol.*, 1968–1969, **7**(4), 27–32.

GESCHWIND, N. The organization of language and the brain. *Mental Health Digest,* 1971, **3**(4), 1–5.

GLASNER, P. J. Developmental view. In J. Sheehan (Ed.), *Stuttering: Research and therapy.* New York: Harper & Row, 1970. Pp. 242–259.

GREENE, J. S. Hope for the stutterer. *Hygeia*, 1946, **24**(2), 120–121.

GUNDERSON, B. F. Diagnosis of learning disabilities: The team approach. *J. learn. Dis.*, 1971, **4**(2), 107–113.

HALPERN, W. The schooling of autistic children: Preliminary findings. *Amer. J. Orthopsychiat.*, 1970, **40**(4), 665–671.

HARLOW, H. A brief look at autistic children. *Psychiat. soc. Sci. Rev.*, 1969, **3**(1), 27–29.

HERTZIG, M. E., BORTNER, M., & BIRCH, H. G. Neurologic findings in child educationally designated as brain damaged. *Amer. J. Orthopsychiat.*, 1969, **39**(3), 437–446.

HEWETT, F. M. *The emotionally disturbed child in the classroom: A developmental strategy for educating children with maladaptive behavior.* New York: Allyn & Bacon, 1968.

HIATT, C., & SPURLOCK, R. E. Geographical flight and its relation to crisis theory. *Amer. J. Orthopsychiat.*, 1970, **40**(1), 53–57.

JENKINS, R. L. The varieties of children's behavioral problems and family dynamics. *Amer. J. Psychiat.*, 1968, **124**(10), 134–139.

JENKINS, R. L. Classification of behavior problems of children. *Amer. J. Psychiat.*, 1969, **125**(8), 68–75.

JENKINS, R. L. Diagnostic classification in child psychiatry. *Amer. J. Psychiat.*, 1970, **127**(5), 140–141.

JENKINS, R. L. The runaway reaction. *Amer. J. Psychiat.*, 1971, **128**(2), 168–173.

JOHNSON, W. *Stuttering and what you can do about it.* Minneapolis: Univer. Minn. Press, 1961.

JOINT COMMISSION ON THE MENTAL HEALTH OF CHILDREN. Position statement: Statement of the American Orthopsychiatric Association on the work of the Joint Commission on the Mental Health of Children. *Amer. J. Orthopsychiat.*, 1968, **38**(3), 402–409.

JOINT COMMISSION ON THE MENTAL HEALTH OF CHILDREN. *Crisis in child mental health: Challenge for the 1970's.* New York: Harper & Row, 1970.

JUDD, L., & MANDELL, A. Chromosome studies in early infantile autism. *Arch. gen. Psychiat.*, 1968, **18**(4), 450–457.

KALES, A., PAULSON, M. J., JACOBSON, A., & KALES, J. Somnambulism: Psychophysiological correlates. *Arch. gen. Psychiat.*, 1966, **14**(6), 595–604.

KANNER, L. Autistic disturbances of affective content. *Nervous Child,* 1943, **2**, 217–240.

KEELER, W. Child suicide. *The Sciences*, 1970, **10**(9), 28–32.

KREBS, M., & KREBS, R. Are you raising a perfectionist? *Today's Health*, 1970, **48**(8), 39–41.

LADD, E. T. Pills for classroom peace? *Sat. Rev.*, Nov. 21, 1970, 66–68, 81–82.

LEMERT, E. M. Stuttering and social structure in two Pacific societies. *J. speech hear. Dis.*, 1962, **27**, 3–10.

LEMERT, E. M. Sociological perspective. In J. Sheehan (Ed.), *Stuttering: Research and therapy.* New York: Harper & Row, 1970. Pp. 172–187.

LESSE, S. The multivariant masks of depression. *Amer. J. Psychiat.*, 1968, **124**(11), 35–40.

LIFE. Screams, slaps, and love. 1965, **58**(18), 90–101.

LINDE, S. M. What parents need to know about bed-wetting. *Today's Health*, Aug. 1966, 50–51, 75.

LOURIE, R., STUBBLEFIELD, R., HIRSCHBERG, C., & PUGH, D. Psychiatrists clarify Joint Commission report on children. *Roche Reports*, 1970, **7**(13), 1–3, 11.

LOVAAS, O. I. Behavior therapy approach to treating childhood schizophrenia. In J. Hill (Ed.), *Minnesota Symposium on Child Development.* Minneapolis: Univer. Minn. Press, 1967.

LOVAAS, O. I., KOEGEL, R., SIMMON, J., & STEVEN, J. Some generalization and followup measures on autistic children in behavior therapy. *J. appl. behav. Anal.*, 1972, in press.

MC GRAW, M. Major challenges for students of infancy and early childhood. *Amer. Psychologist*, 1970, **25**, 754–756.

MONTENEGRO, H. Severe separation anxiety in two preschool children: Successfully treated by reciprocal inhibition. *J. child Psychol. Psychiat.*, 1968, **9**(2), 93–103.

MORRISON, J. Hyperactivity: Links with alcoholism. *Science News*, 1970, **97**(21), 507.

MURPHY, L. *The widening world of childhood.* New York: Basic Books, 1962.

MURPHY, S., NICHOLS, J., EDDY, R., & UMPHRESS, A. Behavioral characteristics of adolescent enuretics. *Adolescence*, 1971, **6**(21), 1–18.

NATIONAL INSTITUTE OF MENTAL HEALTH, United States Department of Health, Education, and Welfare. Mental Health Publication No. 5027. Washington, D.C.: Govt. Printing Office, 1970.

NATIONAL INSTITUTE OF MENTAL HEALTH. Amphetamines approved for children. *Science News*, 1971, **99**(4), 240.

NEWSWEEK. Prostitutes: The new breed. July 12, 1971, p. 78.

NEW YORK STATE YOUTH COMMISSION. The abused child. *The Sciences*, 1970, **10**(5), 5–8, 29–32.

O'LEARY, K. D., & DRABMAN, R. Token reinforcement programs in the classroom: A review. *Psychol. Bull.*, 1971, **5**(6), 379–398.

PAINE, R. S. *Minimal brain dysfunction.* National Project on Learning Disabilities. Publ. Hlth. Publ. No. 2015. Washington, D.C.: Govt. Printing Office, 1969.

PERKINS, W. H. Physiological studies. In J. Sheehan (Ed.), *Stuttering: Research and therapy.* New York: Harper & Row, 1970. Pp. 190–238.

POLLACK, M. Suspected early minimal brain damage and severe psychopathology in adolescence. *Adolescence,* 1969, **4**(15), 361–384.

POZNANSKI, E., & ZRULL, J. Childhood depression. *Arch. gen. Psychiat.,* 1970, **23**(1), 8–15.

RAPOPORT, R. Just a little pill to keep the kid quiet? *West* (*L.A. Times* Publ.), April 25, 1971, 38–42.

RITVO, E., & ORNITZ, E. A new look at childhood autism points to CNS disease. *Roche Reports,* 1970, **7**(18), 6–8.

RITVO, E., ORNITZ, E., WALTER, R. D., & HANLEY, J. Correlation of psychiatric diagnosis and EEG findings: A double-blind study of 184 hospitalized children. *Amer. J. Psychiat.,* 1970, **126**(7), 112–120.

ROBINS, L. N. *Deviant children grown up: A sociological and psychiatric study of sociopathic personality.* Baltimore: Williams & Wilkins, 1968.

RUTTER, M. Concepts of autism: A review of the research. *J. child Psychol. Psychiat.,* 1968, **9**(1), 1–25.

SCHOPLER, E., BREHM, S. H., KINSBOURNE, M., & REICHLER, R. J. Effect of treatment structure on development in austistic children. *Arch. gen. Psychiat.,* 1971, **24**(5), 415–421.

SEIDEN, R. Child suicide. *The Sciences,* 1970, **10**(9), 28–32.

SERF, G. M., & FREUNDL, P. C. Memory and attention factors in specific learning disabilities. *J. learn. Dis.,* 1971, **4**(2), 94–106.

SHAMSIE, S. J. (Ed.) *Adolescent psychiatry.* Pointe Claire, Quebec: Schering Corp., 1968.

SHEEHAN, J. G. (Ed.) *Stuttering: Research and therapy.* New York: Harper & Row, 1970.

SHEEHAN, J. G., CORTESE, P. A., & HADLEY, R. G. Guilt, shame, and tension in graphic projections of stuttering. *Journal of Speech and Hearing Disorders,* 1962, **27**, 129–139. Used by permission.

SHEEHAN, J. G., & MARTYN, M. Stuttering and its disappearance. *J. speech hear. Dis.,* 1970, **13**(2), 279–289.

SILVER, L. B. A proposed view on the etiology of the neurological learning disability system. *J. learn. Dis.,* 1971, **4**(3), 123–133.

STONE, H. *Foster care in question.* New York: Child Welfare League of America, 1970.

SUSSEX, J. N. The relationship between child psychiatry and general psychiatry. *Amer. J. Psychiat.,* 1970, **127**(5), 138–139.

TARNOLPOL, L. Delinquency and minimal brain dysfunction. *J. learn. Dis.,* 1970, **3**(4), 200–208.

TAVES, I. Is there a sleepwalker in the house? *Today's Health,* 1969, **47**(5), 41, 76.

TAYLOR, I. K. What words are stuttered. *Psychol. Bull.,* 1966, **65**(4), 233–242.

TRANS-ACTION. Helping "socially discordant" children. 1968, **5**(5), 24–27.

TREFFERT, D. A. Epidemiology of infantile autism. *Arch. gen. Psychiat.,* 1970, **22**, 431–438.

TYMCHUK, A. J., KNIGHTS, R. M., & HINTON, G. C. The behavioral significance of differing EEG abnormalities in children with learning and/or behavior problems. *J. learn. Dis.,* 1970, **3**(11), 547–552.

VANDERSALL, T. A., & WEINER, J. M. Children who set fires. *Arch. gen. Psychiat.,* 1970, **22**(1), 63–71.

WARREN, R., KARDUCK, W., BISSARATID, S., STEWART, M., & SLY, W. The hyperactive child syndrome. *Arch. gen. Psychiat.,* 1971, **24**(2), 161–162.

WEISS, G., MINDE, K., WERRY, J. S., DOUGLAS, V., & NEMETH, E. Studies on the hyperactive child. VIII. *Arch. gen. Psychiat.,* 1971, **24**(5), 409–421.

WERRY, J. S. Studies on the hyperactive child. *Arch. gen. Psychiat.,* 1968, **19**(1), 9–16.

WIKLER, A., DIXON, J. F., & PARKER, J. B. Brain function in problem children and controls: Psychometric, neurological, and electroencephalographic comparisons. *Amer. J. Psychiat.,* 1970, **127**(5), 94–105.

WITTER, C. Drugging and schooling. *Trans-action,* 1971, **8**(9–10), 30–34.

WOLFF, W. M., & MORRIS, L. A. Intellectual personality characteristics of parents of autistic children. *J. abnorm. Psychol.,* 1971, **77**(2), 155–161.

WOODY, R. H. *Behavioral problem children in the schools.* New York: Appleton-Century-Crofts, 1969.

18. Maladaptive Behavior of Groups

ALLEN, L. S., ET AL. Out of the third world experience. In R. Buckhout et al. (Eds.), *Toward social change.* New York: Harper & Row, 1971. Pp. 94–96.

ALTBACH, P. G., & LAUFER, R. S. Student protest. *Ann. Amer. Acad. Polit. Soc. Sci.,* 1971, **395**, iv–viii.

AMERICAN COUNCIL ON EDUCATION, Special Committee on Campus Tensions. Campus tensions: Analysis and recommendations. *Amer. Psychologist,* 1970, **25**(8), 694–767.

BAKKER, C. B., & DIGHTMAN, C. R. Psychological factors in fertility control. *Fertil. and Steril.,* 1964, **15**, 559.

BANDURA, A., ROSS, D., & ROSS, S. A. Imitation of film-mediated aggressive models. *J. abnorm. soc. Psychol.,* 1963, **66**(1), 3–11.

BANDURA, A., & WALTERS, R. *Social learning and personality development.* New York: Holt, Rinehart & Winston, 1963.

BENGELSDORF, I. S. Dear student: Our spaceship earth's in trouble; so are we. *Los Angeles Times,* April 16, 1970, II, 7.

BERKOWITZ, L. The concept of aggressive drive: Some additional considerations. In L. Berkowitz (Ed.), *Advances in experimental social psychology.* Vol. 2. New York: Academic Press, 1965.

BROWN, H. Where wonder is taking us: Caltech and the world of science. *Los Angeles Times,* Dec. 10, 1967, 5.

BUCKHOUT, R., & 81 CONCERNED BERKELEY STUDENTS. (Eds.) *Toward social change.* New York: Harper & Row, 1971. Four line poem by Patrick Tamayo. Copyright © 1971 by Harper & Row, Publishers, Inc. Reprinted by permission of the publishers.

CALHOUN, J. B. Population density and social pathology. *Scientif. Amer.,* 1962, **206**(2), 139–150.

CANTRIL, H. *The politics of despair.* New York: Basic Books, 1958.

CAPLAN, G. Home from the war. *New Republic,* Jan. 30, 1971, 11.

CARTTER, A. M. All sail and no anchor. *The Key Reporter,* 1971, **36**(2), 2–3, 8.

CLARK, K. B. Explosion in the ghetto. *Psych. Today,* 1967, **1**(5), 31–38, 62–64.

CLARK, K. The pathos of power: A psychological perspective. *Amer. Psychologist,* 1971, **26**(12), 1047–1057.

CLARKE, R. People and proteins. *Sci. J.,* 1967, **3**(4), 3.

COLES, R. *Children of crisis: A study of courage and fear.* Boston: Little, Brown, 1967.

COUSINS, N. Hiroshima. *Look,* Aug. 11, 1970, pp. 38, 43–45. Reprinted by permission of Norman Cousins.

COUSTEAU, J. Issue of the year: The environment. *Time,* Jan. 4, 1971, pp. 21–22.

DEUTSCH, M., & COLLINS, M. E. *Interracial housing: A psychological evaluation of a social experiment.* Minneapolis: Univer. Minn. Press, 1951.

DYCK, A. J. Ethical aspects of population policy. In R. Buckhout et al. (Eds.), *Toward social change.* New York: Harper & Row, 1971. Pp. 407–415.

EHRLICH, P. *The population bomb.* New York: Ballantine, 1968.

EHRLICH, P. People pollution. *Audubon,* 1970, **72**(5), 4–9.

EISENBERG, L. Student unrest: Sources and consequences. *Science,* 1970, **167**(3926), 1688–1692.

FENDRICH, J., & PEARSON, M. Black veterans return. *Trans-action,* 1970, **7**(5), 32–37.

FORD, A. Casualties of our time. *Science,* 1970, **167**(3916), 256–263.

FORRESTER, J. W. *World dynamics.* Cambridge, Mass.: Wright-Allen, 1971. Copyright © 1971 by Wright-Allen Press, Inc. Used by permission.

FREDERICK, C. *Affluence in jeopardy: Minerals and our political economy.* San Francisco: Freeman-Cooper, 1968.

FREUD, S. *Civilization and its discontents.* London: Hogarth, 1930.

GENOVESE, E. D. A massive breakdown. *Newsweek,* July 6, 1970, 25–27.

GILLULY, R. H. A new look at the meaning of reality. *Science News,* 1971, **99**(20), 335–337.

GLASS, B. Educational obsolescence. *Science,* 1970, **170**(3962), 1041.

GRIFFITH, T. Putting it back together. *Life,* 1971, **70**(1), 85–94.

HALL, E. T. *The hidden dimension.* New York: Doubleday, 1966.

HALLIE, P. P. Sadean and institutional cruelty. In F. Korten, S. Cook & J. Lacey (Eds.), *Psychology and the problems of society.* Washington, D.C.: Amer. Psychol. Assn., 1970. Pp. 295–303.

HARRIS, F., & LINDSAY, J. *Report of the Commission on the Cities in the 70's.* Natl. Urban Coalition, 1971.

HOLLINGS, E. Hunger survey finds retarded growth in slum-area children. *Los Angeles Times,* March 11, 1971, I, 5. [a]

HOLLINGS, E. Hunger survey finds retarded growth in slum-area children. *Los Angeles Times,* March 25, 1971, I, 1, 23. [b]

ILFELD, F. W. Overview of the causes and prevention of violence. *Arch. gen. Psychiat.,* 1969, **20**(6), 675–689.

IRELAN, L. M., & BESNER, A. Low-income outlook on life. In L. M. Ireland (Ed.), *Low-income life styles.* Washington, D.C.: Govt. Printing Office, 1967. Pp. 1–12.

JANIS, I. L., MAHL, G. R., KAGAN, J., & HOLT, R. *Personality: Dynamics, development, and assessment.* New York: Harcourt, Brace & World, 1969.

JOAD, C. E. M. *Why war?* Harmondsworth: Penguin Special, 1939.

KAHN, H. The Malthusian score. *Time,* 1970, **96**(8), 1.

KENISTON, K. Social change and youth in America. In E. H. Erikson (Ed.), *Youth: Change and challenge.* New York: Basic Books, 1963.

KLINEBERG, O. Black and white in international perspective. *Amer. Psychologist,* 1971, **26**(2), 119–128.

KRYTER, K. D. *The effects of noise on man.* New York: Academic Press, 1970.

KUTNER, S. J., & DUFFY, T. J. A psychological analysis of oral contraceptives and the intrauterine device. In R. Buckhout et al. (Eds.), *Toward social change.* New York: Harper & Row, 1971. Pp. 401–404.

LANDSBERG, H. E. Man-made climatic changes. *Science,* 1970, **170,** 1265–1274.

LAWRENCE, D. Can nuclear weapons be abolished? *U.S. News and World Report,* Sept. 27, 1971, p. 96.

LERNER, M. Life, liberty, and the pursuit of paranoia. *Los Angeles Times,* July 2, 1970, II, 7.

LORENZ, K. *On aggression.* New York: Harcourt, Brace & World, 1966.

MARSELLA, A. J., ESCUDERO, M., & GORDON, P. The effects of dwelling density on mental disorders in Filipino men. *J. Hlth. soc. Behav.,* 1970, **11**(4), 288–293.

MC CALL, G. J., & SIMMON, J. L. *Identities and interaction.* New York: Free Press, 1966.

MC DANIEL, C. The ghetto nightmare. *The Christian Century,* 1972, **89**(1), 15–16.

MC NAMARA, R. S. McNamara paints grim picture of world plight. *Los Angeles Times,* Sept. 22, 1970, I, 5.

MEAD, M. Family future. *Trans-action,* 1971, **8**(1), 50–53.

MILLER, N. E., & DOLLARD, J. *Social learning and imitation.* New Haven, Conn.: Yale Univer. Press, 1941.

MURPHY, J. M. Social science concepts and cross-cultural methods for psychiatric research. In J. M. Murphy & A. H. Leighton (Eds.), *Approaches to cross-cultural psychiatry.* New York: Cornell Univer. Press, 1965. Pp. 251–284.

NADER, R. We need a new kind of patriotism. *Life,* 1971, **71**(2), 4.

NATIONAL ADVISORY COMMISSION ON CIVIL DISORDERS. *Report.* Washington, D.C.: Govt. Printing Office, 1968.

NATIONAL COMMISSION ON CAMPUS UNREST. *Report.* Washington, D.C.: Govt. Printing Office, 1970.

NATIONAL COMMISSION ON THE CAUSES AND PREVENTION OF VIOLENCE. *The politics of protest.* Washington, D.C.: Govt. Printing Office, 1969. [a]

NATIONAL COMMISSION ON THE CAUSES AND PREVENTION OF VIOLENCE. *Violence and the media.* Staff Report, Vol. 9. Washington, D.C.: Govt. Printing Office, 1969. [b]

NATIONAL INSTITUTE OF MENTAL HEALTH. *The mental health of urban America.* Washington, D.C.: Govt. Printing Office, 1969.

NIEMOLLER, M. Speech given in 1966. Cited in B. Mandelbaum (Ed.), *Choose life.* New York: Random House, 1968.

OPTON, E. Lessons of My Lai. In R. Buckhout et al. (Eds.), *Toward social change.* New York: Harper & Row, 1971. Pp. 176–186.

PASAMANICK, B. Inaction on hunger called "murderous." *Psychiatric News,* 1971, **6**(7), 1, 24.

PETTIGREW, T. W. Racially separate or together? *J. soc. Issues,* 1969, **25**(1), 43–70.

PRESIDENT'S COMMITTEE ON EMPLOYMENT OF THE HANDICAPPED. Committee urges action on disabled disadvantaged. *Psychiatric News,* 1971, **6**(4), 13.

RAPPOPORT, L. Personal communication, 1971.

REPORT OF THE STUDY OF CRITICAL ENVIRONMENTAL PROBLEMS. *Man's impact on the global environment.* Cambridge, Mass.: MIT Press, 1970.

REPORT OF THE U.S. NATIONAL ADVISORY COMMISSION ON CIVIL VIOLENCE. Washington, D.C.: Govt. Printing Office, 1968.

ROSENTHAL, M. Where rumor raged. *Trans-action,* 1971, **8**(4), 34–38.

THE SCIENCES. The effluent society, 1970, **10**(6), 5–10.

SELYE, H. Stress. *Psych. Today,* 1969, **3**(4), 24–26.

SLATER, P. E. Cultures in collision. *Psych. Today,* 1970, **4**(2), 31–32, 66–68.

TANNENBAUM, F. *Slave and citizen: The Negro in America.* New York: Knopf, 1947.

TOFFLER, A. *Future shock.* New York: Random House, 1970.

TOFFLER, A. Is the family obsolete? *Look,* Jan. 26, 1971, p. 35.

TOYNBEE, A. Human savagery cracks thin veneer. *Los Angeles Times,* Sept. 6, 1970, C, 3.

U.S. COMMISSION ON CIVIL RIGHTS. *A time to listen . . . a time to act.* Washington, D.C.: Author, 1967.

U.S. NEWS AND WORLD REPORT. The drive to stop population growth. March 2, 1970, p. 37.

WAGGONER, R. W. The presidential address: Cultural dissonance and psychiatry. *Amer. J. Psychiat.,* 1970, **127**(1), 1–8.

WHITE, T. *The making of the president: 1968.* New York: Pocket Books, 1970.

YORK, H. F. We can reverse the arms race. *Life,* 1970, **69**(24), 40–41.

ZUCKERMAN, S. *The social life of monkeys and apes.* London: Kegan Paul, 1932.

19. The Problem of Assessment

BIJOU, S. W. Experimental studies of child behavior, normal and deviant. In L. Krasner & L. P. Ullmann (Eds.), *Research in behavior modification: New developments and implications.* New York: Holt, Rinehart & Winston, 1965. Pp. 56–81.

BROWN, F. Changes in sexual identification and role over a decade and their implications. *J. Psychol.,* 1971, **77,** 229–251.

COMREY, A. *Comrey personality scales.* San Diego: Educational Industrial Testing Service, 1970.

ERTLE, J. I.Q. testing by brain wave. *Science News,* 1971, **100**(3), 42.

GOLDBERG, L. R. Man versus model of man. *Psychol. Bull.,* 1970, **73**(6), 422–432.

GOODMAN, G. Systematic selection of psychotherapeutic talent: The group assessment of interpersonal traits. In S. Golann & C. Eisdorfer (Eds.), *Handbook of community psychology and mental health.* New York: Appleton-Century-Crofts, 1971.

GROSSMAN, M. Insurance reports as a threat to confidentiality. *Amer. J. Psychiat.,* 1971, **128**(1), 96–100.

HATHAWAY, S. R., & MC KINLEY, J. C. *The Minnesota multiphasic personality inventory.* Rev. ed. New York: Psychol. Corp., 1951.

KLOPFER, B., & DAVIDSON, H. *The Rorschach technique: An introductory manual.* New York: Harcourt Brace Jovanovich, Inc., 1962.

MIRABILE, C. S., HOUCK, J., & GLUECK, B. C., JR. Computer beats clinician in prognosis contest. *Psychiatric News*, 1970, **5**(18), 18.

NOBLE, J. H. Protecting the public's privacy in computerized health and welfare information systems. *Social Work*, 1971, **16**(1), 35–41.

POOLEY, R. *An experiment in delinquency prevention and control.* Carbondale: Southern Illinois University, 1971. From "An Experiment in Delinquency Prevention and Control" by Richard Pooley. Reprinted by permission of the author.

RAPPAPORT, J., CHINSKY, J., & COWEN, E. *Innovations in helping chronic patients: College students in a mental institution.* New York: Academic Press, 1971.

SLETTEN, I. W., ALTMAN, H., & ULETT, G. A. Routine diagnosis by computer. *Amer. J. Psychiat.*, 1971, **127**, 1147–1152.

SUNDBERG, N. D., & TYLER, L. E. *Clinical psychology.* New York: Appleton-Century-Crofts, 1962.

WECHSLER, D. *Manual for the Wechsler Adult Intelligence Scale.* New York: Psychol. Corp., 1955.

20. Contemporary Approaches to Therapy

ALBEE, G. W. The uncertain future of clinical psychology. *Amer. Psychologist*, 1970, **25**, 1071–1080.

ALEXANDER, F. Individual psychotherapy. *Psychosom. Med.*, 1946, **8**, 110–115.

ALGER, I., & HOGAN, P. Enduring effects of videotape playback experience on family and marital relationships. *Amer. J. Orthopsychiat.*, 1969, **39**, 86–94.

ALLRED, G. H. Hardships help in marriage course on mountaintop. *Los Angeles Times*, June 28, 1971, I, 1, 11. [a]

ALLRED, G. H. Personal correspondence, 1971. [b]

AYLLON, T., & AZRIN, N. H. *The token economy: A motivational system for therapy and rehabilitation.* New York: Appleton-Century-Crofts, 1968.

AYLLON, T., & MICHAEL, J. The psychiatric nurse as a behavioral engineer. *J. exp. Anal. Behav.*, 1959, **2**, 323–334.

BANDURA, A. *Principles of behavior modification.* New York: Holt, Rinehart & Winston, 1969.

BARBER, T. X. *Hypnosis: A scientific approach.* New York: Van Nostrand Reinhold, 1969.

BARRETT, C. L. Systematic desensitization versus implosive therapy. *J. abnorm. Psychol.*, 1969, **74**, 587–592.

BERNE, E. *Games people play.* New York: Grove Press, 1964.

BOULOUGOURIS, J. C., MARKS, I. M., & MARSET, P. Superiority of flood to desensitization for reducing pathological fear. *Behav. Res. Ther.*, 1971, **9**, 7–17.

BRADY, J. P. Drugs in behavior therapy. Paper presented at the Sixth Annual Meeting of the American College of Neuropsychopharmacology, San Juan, Puerto Rico, December 1967.

BRAGINSKY, B. M., HOLZBERG, J., RIDLEY, D., & BRAGINSKY, D. Patient styles of adaptation to a mental hospital. *J. Person.*, 1968, **36**, 393–398.

BREGER, L. Function of dreams. *J. abnorm. Psychol. Monogr.*, 1967, **72**(5), 1–28.

BROWNING, C., TYSON, R. L., & MILLER, S. I. Crisis patients found younger, self-referred. *Psychiatric News*, 1971, **6**(8), 21.

BUCHER, B., & LOVAAS, O. I. Use of aversive stimulation in behavior modification. In M. R. Jones (Ed.), *Miami symposium on the prediction of behavior 1967: Aversive stimulation.* Coral Gables: Univer. Miami Press, 1968. Pp. 77–145.

COWEN, E. L., GARDNER, E. A., & ZAX, M. (Eds.) *Emergent approaches to mental health problems.* New York: Appleton-Century-Crofts, 1967.

CURRY, A. E. The world of a schizophrenic woman. Reprinted from *The Psychoanalytic Review.* Vol. **49**, No. 1, 1962, through the courtesy of the Editors and the Publisher, National Psychological Association for Psychoanalysis, New York, N.Y.

DAWSON, R. G. Retrograde amnesia and conditioned emotional response incubation reexamined. *Psychol. Bull.*, 1971, **75**(4), 278–285.

DELGADO, J. M. R. ESB. *Psych. Today*, 1970, **3**(12), 48–53.

ELLIS, A. Rational psychotherapy. *J. gen. Psychol.*, 1958, **59**, 35–49.

EWALT, P. L. (Ed.) *Mental health volunteers: The expanding role of the volunteer in hospital and community mental health service.* Springfield, Ill.: Charles C Thomas, 1967.

FAIRWEATHER, G. W., SANDERS, D. H., MAYNARD, H., & CRESSLER, D. L. *Community life for the mentally ill: An alternative to institutional care.* Chicago: Aldine, 1969.

FORRESTER, J. W. Counterintuitive behavior of social systems. *Technology Review*, 1971, **73**(3), 53–68.

GARFIELD, Z. H., DARWIN, P. L., SINGER, B. A., & MC BREARTY, J. F. Effect of "in vivo" training on experimental desensitization of a phobia. *Psychol. Rep.*, 1967, **20**, 515–519.

GLASSER, W. *Reality therapy.* New York: Harper & Row, 1965.

GLASSER, W. Reality therapy—a new approach. In O. H. Mowrer (Ed.), *Morality and mental health.* New York: Rand McNally, 1967. Pp. 126–134.

GOFFMAN, E. *Asylums.* Chicago: Aldine, 1962.

GOLDSTEIN, M. K., & FRANCIS, B. Behavior modification of husbands by wives. Paper presented at annual meeting of National Council on Family Relations, Washington, D.C., 1969.

GOODALL, K. Homemade mental health. *Psychology Today*, 1971, **5**(7), 30–32. From "Homemade Mental Health" by Kenneth Goodall. Reprinted from *Psychology Today* Magazine, December, 1971. Copyright © Communications/Research/Machines, Inc.

GROUP FOR THE ADVANCEMENT OF PSYCHIATRY. *The field of family therapy.* Rep. No. 78, 1970, pp. 525–644.

GUERNEY, B. G., JR. (Ed.) *Psychotherapeutic agents: New roles for nonprofessionals, parents, and teachers.* New York: Holt, Rinehart & Winston, 1969.

GUSTAITIS, R. The alpha gambit. *Los Angeles Times*, Aug. 8, 1971, pp. 7–8.

HALEY, J. Whither family therapy. *Family Process*, 1962, **1**, 69–100.

HALLECK, S. Therapy is the handmaiden of the status quo. *Psych. Today*, 1971, **4**(11), 30–32, 98–100.

HALLOWITZ, E. The challenge to the group psychotherapist created by a society in flux. *Inter. J. group Psychother.*, 1970, **20**, 423–434.

HIRAI, T., & KASAMATSU, A. An electroencephalographic study of the Zen meditation. *Fol. Psychiat. Neurol., Japan.*, 1966, **20**, 315–336.

HOGAN, R. A., & KIRSCHNER, J. H. Preliminary report of the extinction of learned fears via short term implosive therapy. *J. abnorm. Psychol.*, 1967, **72**, 106–109.

HOGAN, R. A., & KIRSCHNER, J. H. Implosive, eclectic verbal and bibliotherapy in the treatment of fears of snakes. *Behav. Res. Ther.*, 1968, **6**, 167–171.

HUFF, F. W. A learning theory approach to family therapy. *Family Coordinator*, 1969, **18**(1), 22–26.

HUSSAIN, M. Z. Desensitization and flooding in treatment of phobias. *Amer. J. Psychiat.*, 1971, **127**(11), 85–90.

JACOBSON, E. *Progressive relaxation.* Chicago: Univer. Chicago Press, 1938.

JANSEN, E. U.S. urged to duplicate British halfway "hostels." *Psychiatric News*, 1969, **4**(2), 24.

JONES, M. C. A laboratory study of fear: The case of Peter. *Pedagogical Seminary*, 1924, **31**, 308–315.

KAMIYA, J. Conscious control of brain waves. *Psych. Today*, 1968, **1**(11), 56–60.

KANE, F. J., WALLACE, C. D., & LIPTON, M. A. Emotional disturbance related to T-group experience. *Amer. J. Psychiat.*, 1971, **127**(7), 954–956.

KANTOROVICH, F. An attempt at associative reflex therapy in alcoholism. *Psychol. Abstracts*, 1930, **4282**.

KATKIN, S., GINSBURG, M., RIFKIN, M., & SCOTT, J. Effectiveness of female volunteers in the treatment of outpatients. *J. couns. Psychol.*, 1971, **18**(2), 97–100.

KLINE, N. S. Use of *Rauwolfia sepentina* in neuropsychiatric conditions. *Ann. N.Y. Acad. Sci.*, 1954, **54**, 107–132.

KRUMBOLTZ, J. D., & THORESEN, C. E. (Eds.) *Behavioral counseling.* New York: Holt, Rinehart & Winston, 1969. Pp. 87–89.

LAKEN, M. T-group promiscuity tales split psychologist camp. *Psychiatric News*, 1970, **5**(14), 9.

LANGSLEY, D. Treatment goes home. *Science News*, 1968, **94**(6), 133.

LAZARUS, A. A. Aversion therapy and sensory modalities. *Perception and Motor Skills*, 1968, **27**, 178. [a]

LAZARUS, A. A. Learning theory and the treatment of depression. Reprinted with permission from Arnold A. Lazarus, "Learning Theory and the Treatment of Depression," *Behaviour Research and Therapy*, Vol. **6**, No. 1, copyright 1968, Pergamon Press. [b]

LOS ANGELES TIMES. Noted moralist dies. June 2, 1971, I, 1.

MATARAZZO, J. D. Some national developments in the utilization of nontraditional mental health manpower. *Amer. Psychologist*, 1971, **26**(4), 363–372.

MAY, R. *Love and will*. New York: Norton, 1969.

MC GLASHIN, T. H., EVANS, F. J., & ORNE, M. T. The nature of hypnotic analgesic and placebo response to experimental pain. *Psychosom. Med.*, 1969, **31**, 227–246.

MEALIEA, W. L., JR. The comparative effectiveness of systematic desensitization and implosive therapy in the elimination of snake phobia. Unpublished doctoral dissertation, University of Missouri, 1967.

MICHENER, J. A. *The fires of spring*. New York: Random House, 1949.

MIGLER, B., & WOLPE, J. Automated desensitization. *Behav. Res. Ther.*, 1967, **133**, 5.

NAVRAN, L. Communication and adjustment in marriage. *Family Process*, 1967, **6**(2), 173–182.

O'CONNELL, R., SHOR, E., & ORNE, M. T. Hypnotic age regression: An empirical and methodological analysis. *J. abnorm. Psychol.*, 1970, **76**(3), 1–32.

OLSON, D. H. Marital and family therapy. *J. Marr. Fam.*, 1970, **32**(4), 501–538.

OSTOW, M. Amnesia termed the therapeutic element of electroshock. *Roche Report*, 1968, **5**(11), 3.

PAUL, G. L. Two-year follow-up of systematic desensitization in therapy groups. *J. abnorm. Psychol.*, 1968, **73**, 119–130.

PAUL, G. L. Chronic mental patient: Current status—future direction. *Psychol. Bull.*, 1969, **74**, 199–204.

PAUL, G. L., & SHANNON, D. T. Treatment of anxiety through systematic desensitization in therapy groups. *J. abnorm. Psychol.*, 1966, **71**, 124.

PAUL, N. The family as patient. *Time*, May 31, 1971, p. 60.

PECK, H. B. A small-group approach to individual and institutional change. *Inter. J. group Psychother.*, 1970, **20**, 435–449.

PERLS, F. S. Group vs. individual therapy. *ETC*, 1967, **34**, 306–312.

PERLS, F. S. *Gestalt therapy verbatim*. Lafayette, California: Real People Press, 1969. Reprinted by permission.

PERSON, P. H. *A statistical information system for community health centers*. Washington, D.C.: NIMH, 1969.

RIOCH, M. J., ELKES, C., FLINT, A. A., USDANSKY, B. S., NEWMAN, R. G., & SILBER, E. National Institute of Mental Health pilot study in training mental health counselors. *Amer. J. Orthopsychiat.*, 1963, **33**, 678–689.

ROGERS, C. R. *Client-centered therapy*. Boston: Houghton Mifflin, 1951. Reprinted by permission of Houghton Mifflin Company and Constable & Company Limited.

ROGERS, C. R. *On becoming a person: A client's view of psychotherapy*. Boston: Houghton Mifflin, 1961.

ROGERS, C. R. Toward a modern approach to values. *J. abnorm. soc. Psychol.*, 1964, **68**(2), 160–167.

ROGERS, C. R. The process of the basic encounter group. In J. F. T. Bugental (Ed.), *Challenges of humanistic psychology*. New York: McGraw-Hill, 1967. Pp. 261–276.

ROGERS, C. R. *Carl Rogers on encounter groups*. New York: Harper & Row, 1970. From pp. 16, 18, 21, 26, 31, 35, 33 in *Carl Rogers on Encounter Groups* by Carl R. Rogers. Copyright © 1970 by Carl R. Rogers. Reprinted by permission of Harper & Row, Publishers, Inc. and Penguin Books Ltd.

RORVIK, D. M. Brain waves. *Look*, Oct. 6, 1970, pp. 88–94.

ROSENTHAL, S. H., & WULFSOHN, N. L. Electrosleep—a clinical trial. *Amer. J. Psychiat.*, 1970, **127**(4), 175–176.

ROTTER, J. B. On the evaluation of methods of intervening in other people's lives. *Clin. Psychologist*, 1971, **24**(3), 1–2.

RUCH, F. L., & ZIMBARDO, P. G. *Psychology and life*. (8th ed.) Glenview, Ill.: Scott, Foresman, 1971.

SACERDOTE, P. Hypnosis in cancer patients. *Amer. J. clin. Hypnosis*, 1966, **9**, 100–108.

SAGER, C. J. The group psychotherapist: Bulwark against alienation. *Amer. J. group Psychother.*, 1968, **18**, 419–431.

SATIR, V. *Conjoint family therapy*. (rev. ed.) Palo Alto: Science and Behavior Books, 1967.

STAMPFL, T. G., & LEVIS, D. J. Essentials of implosive therapy: A learning-theory-based psychodynamic behavioral therapy. *J. abnorm. Psychol.*, 1967, **72**, 496–503.

STOLLER, F. H. The long weekend. *Psych. Today*, 1967, **1**, 28–33.

STONE, W. N., & TIEGER, M. E. Screening for T-groups. *Amer. J. Psychiat.*, 1971, **127**(11), 1485–1490.

STUART, R. B. Behavioral contracting within the families of delinquents. *J. behav. Ther. exp. Psychiat.*, 1971, **2**, 1–11.

SUINN, R. M. Marathon desensitization groups. *Behav. Res. Ther.*, 1970, **8**(1), 97–98.

SUNDBERG, N. D., & TYLER, L. E. *Clinical psychology*. New York: Appleton-Century-Crofts, 1962.

SZASZ, T. The crime of commitment. *Psych. Today*, 1969, **2**(10), 55–57.

TODD, F. J., & KELLEY, R. J. The use of hypnosis to facilitate conditioned relaxation responses. *J. behav. Ther. exp. Psychiat.*, 1970, **1**(4), 295–298.

TROTTER, R. J. Listen to your head. *Science News*, 1971, **100**, 314–316.

VAN EGEREN, L. F. Psychophysiologic aspects of systematic desensitization. *Behav. Res. Ther.*, 1971, **9**(1), 65–77.

VOEGTLIN, W. L. The treatment of alcoholism by establishing a conditioned reflex. *Amer. J. med. Sci.*, 1940, **199**, 802–810.

WAGENEDER, F. M., IWANORSKY, A., & DODGE, C. H. Electrosleep and electroanesthesia. *Foreign Science Bulletin*, 1969, **5**, 1–104.

WHALEN, C. K., & HENKER, B. A. Pyramid therapy in a hospital for the retarded. *Amer. J. ment. Def.*, 1971, **75**(4), 414–434.

WILKINS, W. Desensitization: Social and cognitive factors underlying the effectiveness of Wolpe's procedure. *Psych. Bull.*, 1971, **76**, 311–317.

WOLF, M., RISLEY, T., & MEES, H. Application of operant conditioning procedures to the behavior problems of an autistic child. *Behavior Research and Therapy*, 1964, **1**, 305–312. Permission granted by Maxwell International Microforms Corporation.

WOLPE, J. The systematic desensitization treatment of neuroses. *J. nerv. ment. Dis.*, 1961, **132**, 189–203.

WOLPE, J. Quantitative relationships in the systematic desensitization of phobias. *Amer. J. Psychiat.*, 1963, **119**, 1062.

WOLPE, J. *The practice of behavior therapy*. New York: Pergamon, 1969.

YALOM, I. D., & LIEBERMAN, M. A. A study of encounter group casualties. *Arch. gen. Psychiat.*, 1971, **25**, 16–30.

ZIMBARDO, P. G., RAPAPORT, C., & BARON, J. Pain control by hypnotic induction of motivational states. In P. Zimbardo (Ed.), *The cognitive control of motivation*. Glenview, Ill.: Scott, Foresman, 1969. Pp. 136–152.

ZUSMAN, J. The social breakdown syndrome. *Inter. J. Psychiat.*, 1967, **3**, 216–237.

21. Action for Mental Health and a Better World

CHISHOLM, B. The future of psychiatry. *Amer. J. Psychiat.*, 1948, **104**, 543.

DONNE, J. Meditation XVII. *Devotions upon emergent occasions*. London, 1624.

HASKINS, C. P. *Report to the president, 1966–1967*. Washington, D.C.: Carnegie Institute, 1968.

HOLDEN, C. Community mental health centers: Storefront therapy and more. *Science*, 1971, **174**(4015), 1219–1221.

HUXLEY, A. *Brave new world.* New York: Harper & Row, 1932.

HUXLEY, J. The future of man. *Bull. atom. Scientists*, 1959, **15**, 402–409.

KENNEDY, R. F. Edward Kennedy's eulogy to Robert Kennedy. *Vital speeches*, 1968, **34**(1).

KLINEBERG, O. The UNESCO project on international tensions: A challenge to the sciences of man. *Inter. soc. Sci. Bull.*, 1949, **1**, 1–2.

MANN, P. A., & ISCOE, I. Mass behavior and community organization: Reflections on a peaceful demonstration. *Amer. Psychologist*, 1971, **26**, 108–113.

MILLER, G. A. Relevance in Washington. *Science News*, 1969, **96**(10), 177–178.

NATIONAL INSTITUTE OF MENTAL HEALTH. *The mental health of urban America.* Washington, D.C.: Govt. Printing Office, 1969.

NATIONAL INSTITUTE OF MENTAL HEALTH. *Staffing patterns in community mental health centers.* Washington, D.C.: NIMH, Office of Program Planning and Evaluation, 1970.

ORWELL, G. *1984.* New York: Harcourt Brace Jovanovich, Inc., 1949.

REDICK, R. W., GOLDSMITH, H. F., & UNGER, E. L. *1970 census data used to indicate areas with different potentials for mental health and related problems.* Chevy Chase, Md.: NIMH, Mental Health Statistics Series C, 1971.

ROE, A. Community resources centers. *Amer. Psychologist*, 1970, **25**, 1033–1040.

SHEPHERD, J. Rebirth. *Look*, 1971, **35**(1), 15.

SKINNER, B. F. *Walden two.* New York: Macmillan, 1948.

SKINNER, B. F. *Beyond freedom and dignity.* New York: Knopf, 1971.

TRICKETT, E. Personal communication, 1971.

UNESCO. *Constitution.* Paris: UNESCO, 1945.

WAGGONER, R. W. The presidential address: Cultural dissonance and psychiatry. *Amer. J. Psychiat.*, 1970, **127**(1), 1–8.

WILDE, O. *The happy prince and other tales.* 1888. Ann Arbor, Mich.: Univer. Microfilms, 1967.

Picture Credits

Cover and front endsheets Painting by Curt Stenvert, Vienna, Austria. Photo from the artist.

2 Black Star/Claus Meyer

5 The Bettmann Archive, Inc.

8 The Folger Shakespeare Library (left)
The Bettmann Archive, Inc. (right)

21 The Porcupine Family, Inc.

24 The Bettmann Archive, Inc. (upper left)
Historical Pictures Service (lower left)
The Bettmann Archive, Inc. (right)

30 The Bettmann Archive, Inc. (upper left)
Historical Pictures Service (lower left)
The Bettmann Archive, Inc. (right)

34 The Bettmann Archive, Inc. (upper left and right)
Culver Pictures, Inc. (lower)

35 The Bettmann Archive, Inc.

38 From *A History of Medical Psychology*, by Gregory Zilboorg and W. Henry, W. W. Norton, 1941, used by permission.

40 Historical Pictures Service (upper left and right)
The Bettmann Archive, Inc. (lower)

41 The Bettmann Archive, Inc. (upper)
Culver Pictures, Inc. (lower left)
Historical Pictures Service (lower right)

44 The Bettmann Archive, Inc.

48 Tom Medcalf and Joseph Meinike

55 The Bettmann Archive, Inc. (left and center)
Dr. Karl Menninger, courtesy of the Menninger Clinic Foundation (right)

60 James Ballard

63 The Bettmann Archive, Inc. (far left)
Historical Pictures Service (center left)
Courtesy of Dr. B. F. Skinner (center right)
Courtesy of Dr. Albert Bandura (far right)

68 The Bettmann Archive, Inc. (far left)
Courtesy of the W. P. Laughlin Foundation (center left)
Hugh L. Wilkerson (center right)
Courtesy of Dr. Carl R. Rogers (far right)

70 The Bettmann Archive, Inc. (far left)
Historical Pictures Service (center left)
Courtesy of Dr. Rollo May, photo by Bernard Gotfryd (center right)
John Haynes (far right)

73 Courtesy of The William Alanson White Psychiatric Foundation, Inc. (left)
Courtesy of Grove Press (right)

76 From the film "Journey Into Self," courtesy of Western Behavioral Sciences Institute (left)
Pix, Inc. (right)

77 Photograph by John Scotfield, © 1962 National Geographic Society

79 Fritz Goro, *Life* Magazine, © Time, Inc. (left)
Photograph by John Scotfield, © 1962 National Geographic Society (right)

80 Courtesy of Dr. Margaret Mead

82 The Bettmann Archive, Inc.

83 Courtesy of Dr. Thomas S. Szasz

84 © 1970 Harper and Row, Inc.—VIOLENCE AND THE BRAIN

85 From the film "Journey Into Self," courtesy of Western Behavioral Sciences Institute (left)
Pix, Inc. (right)

87 Courtesy of Dr. James G. Miller

92 NASA (left)
Monkmeyer Press Photo Service (right)

93 Courtesy of Metropolitan Crusade of Mercy

101 Wisconsin Regional Primate Research Center

117 Allan Grant (upper left)
Department of the Navy (upper right)
NASA (lower left)
Courtesy of Chicago's Alcoholic Treatment Center, 1969 Annual Report; City of Chicago (lower right)

133 Courtesy of Dr. John Romano, Dr. Jules Masserman, and the W. B. Saunders Company

136 Wide World Photos (left)
Benedict J. Fernandez (right)

139 Courtesy of Dr. James L. German III

140 Culver Pictures, Inc.

146–147 Allan Grant

152 Ken Heyman (left)
Wide World Photos (right)

155 From J. Plokker, *Art from the Mentally Disturbed*, courtesy of Mouton & Company, n.v. Publishers, THE HAGUE

158 Courtesy of Dr. Albert Bandura and The American Psychological Association

edited by Leonard P. Ullmann and Leonard Krasner. Copyright © 1965 by Holt, Rinehart and Winston, Inc. Reproduced by permission of Holt, Rinehart and Winston, Inc.

516 "Time" by William Gropper. Photo by Sy Friedman/Zodiac (left) American Psychiatric Association (right)

517 From *Boyd's Pathology for the Surgeon*, 8th Edition, by William Anderson, © 1967, W. B. Saunders Company.

522 F. Jahnel, "Pathologische Anatomie der progressiven Paralyse," in O. Bumke, *Handbuch der Geisteskrankheiten*, Vol. 11, copyright 1930. Reprinted by permission of Springer-Verlag. (left) H. H. Merritt, R. D. Adams & H. C. Solomon, *Neurosyphilis.* New York: Oxford University Press, 1946. Reprinted by permission. (right)

530 From *Boyd's Pathology for the Surgeon*, 8th Edition, by William Anderson, © 1967, W. B. Saunders Company.

533 American Psychiatric Association

536 Louis P. Thorpe and Barney Katz, *The Psychology of Abnormal Behavior.* Copyright © 1948 The Ronald Press Company, New York.

551–552 N. Malamud, *Atlas of Neuropathology*, University of California Press, 1957. Originally published by the University of California Press; reprinted by permission of The Regents of the University of California.

556 Daniel Ransohoff (left) Ken Heyman (right)

560 Rick Winsor/Woodfin Camp, Inc. (left) Photograph by Martin Weaver for the National Association for Mental Health, London (right)

561 Stephen Deutch

565 Rick Winsor/Woodfin Camp, Inc.

566 "El Niño de Vallecas" by Velazquez, Prado Museum. Photo from MAS.

573 Courtesy of Dr. Clemens E. Benda (left) Courtesy of Dixon State School, Dixon, Illinois (center and right)

574 Courtesy of the National Association for Retarded Children, Inc.

575 Stephen Deutch

578 Courtesy of Carol K. Whalen, University of California at Irvine and Barbara Henker, University of California at Los Angeles

580 Courtesy of Los Angeles Exceptional Children's Foundation

581 Photos by Charles Conrad

582 Fletcher Drake/Pix, Inc.

584 Esther Bubley (left) Jack Corn/Image (right)

585 Allan Grant

589 Allan Grant

590 Courtesy of Dr. Bruno Bettelheim

597 Jack Corn/Image

607 Courtesy of John Harris, Children's Division, Camarillo State Mental Hospital, Camarillo, California

610 United Press International (left) Leif Skoogfors (right)

611 Paul Sequeira

613 Official U.S. Air Force Photo

621 From *Children of Crisis: A Study of Courage and Fear* by Robert Coles. Copyright 1964, 1965, 1966, 1967 by Robert Coles. By permission of Atlantic-Little, Brown and Company.

628 Bruce Davidson/Magnum

629 Federal Water Quality Administration (left) New York Times Photo (right)

640 Courtesy Hans Huber, Publishers, Berne (upper) Courtesy of The Merrill-Palmer Institute by Donna J. Harris (lower)

641 Courtesy of Dr. Gerald Goodman, University of California at Los Angeles

644 Courtesy Hans Huber, Publishers, Berne

646 "Personality Profile of Drug Addicts" from *IPAT'S Personality Profile Series.* Reprinted by permission of Institute for Personality and Ability Testing.

647 Courtesy of Dr. Gerdhild von Staabs

648 Courtesy of Dr. Gerald Goodman, University of California at Los Angeles

656 Allan Grant (left) Josiah Hornblower/Globe Photos

657 Michael Semak

661 Courtesy of the University of Texas Medical School at San Antonio

662 Courtesy of Dr. Thomas Budzynski, University of Colorado Medical School

668 Allan Grant

674 Courtesy of Dr. Loren C. Fitzhugh, New Castle State Hospital

683 Tom Medcalf (left) Photo by Edward Clark, courtesy of *Life*, © 1952, Time, Inc. (right)

687 The Porcupine Family, Inc. (upper) J. M. Vincent/Camera Five (lower)

700 Michael Semak

706–707 NASA

709 Courtesy of Linda Hughes, Yale Psycho-Educational Clinic

710 Jack Wait/Austin American Statesman

711 Reprinted with permission from The *Chicago Daily News.* Photo by John White

Glossary

Abnormal. Maladaptive behavior detrimental to the individual and/or the group. (14)

Abnormal sexual behavior. Sexual behavior which is maladaptive for the individual and/or the group. (452)

Abreaction. Expression of pent-up emotions.

Abulia. Impairment of ability to initiate voluntary action and make decisions.

Acalculia. Loss of ability to perform mathematical operations. (537)

Acromegaly. Progressive disease associated with hyperfunction of the pituitary; characterized by permanent enlargement of the skeleton, hands, feet, and face. (544)

Acrophobia. Morbid fear of high places. (227)

Acting-out. Defense mechanism in which individual reduces anxiety, hostility, or other unpleasant emotions by permitting their expression in overt behavior. (134)

Activation (arousal). Energy mobilization required for organism to pursue its goals and meet its needs. (111)

Actualization strivings. Strivings toward growth and fulfillment. (109)

Actuarial approach. Application of probability statistics to human behavior, as in insurance. (653)

Acute alcoholic hallucinosis. State of alcoholic intoxication characterized by auditory hallucinations. (410)

Acute brain disorder. Temporary impairment of brain function, as in cases of vitamin deficiency. (518)

Adaptability. Flexibility in meeting changed circumstances or demands. (118)

Addison's disease. Disease of the adrenal glands characterized by an anemic, emaciated condition and a brownish coloration of the skin. (543)

Adequacy feelings. Feeling of being confident or capable. (107)

Adjustive behavior. Behavior by which the individual attempts to deal with stress and meet his needs, including efforts to maintain harmonious relationships with the environment. (118)

Adjustment. Outcome of the individual's efforts to deal with stress and meet his needs. (121)

Adrenal cortex. Outer layer of the adrenal glands; secretes the adrenal steroids and other hormones. (543)

Adrenal glands. Endocrine glands located at the upper end of the kidneys; consist of inner adrenal medulla and outer adrenal cortex. (543)

Adrenaline. Hormone secreted by the adrenal medulla during strong emotion; causes such bodily changes as an increase in blood sugar and a rise in blood pressure. Also called *epinephrine*. (543)

Affect. Any experience of emotion or feeling. (321)

Affective reaction. Psychosis characterized by severe disturbance of mood or feeling. (321)

Aftercare. Follow-up therapy after release from a hospital. (308)

Age regression. Inducing a hypnotized subject to evidence behavior of an earlier life period. (666)

Aggravated assault. Physical assault with intent to commit bodily injury to another. (391)

Aggression. Response to frustration by attacking either the source of frustration or a substitute. (153)

Agitated depression. Type of psychotic depressive reaction characterized by both severely depressed mood and hyperactivity. (343)

Agitation. Marked restlessness and psychomotor excitement. (203)

Agnosia. Loss or impairment of ability to recognize familiar objects.

Agoraphobia. Morbid fear of large, open places. (227)

Agraphia. Loss of ability to write words even though they are understood. (537)

Akinesia. Loss or impairment of motor functions.

Alarm reaction. First stage of the general-adaption-syndrome, characterized by the mobilization of defenses to cope with a stressful situation. (180)

Alcoholic deterioration. Personality deterioration, including impaired judgment, associated with alcoholism. (408)

Alcoholic intoxication. State reached when alcohol content of blood is 0.1 percent or above. (407)

Alcoholics Anonymous. Organization composed of ex-alcoholics for treatment of alcoholism via personal, religious, and social rehabilitation. (419)

Alcoholism. Physiological dependence on alcohol. (406)

Algophobia. Irrational fear of pain. (227)

Alienation. Lack or loss of relationships to others. (165)

Alpha waves. Brain waves having a rhythm of between 8 and 12 cycles per second and associated with an alert state accompanied by feelings of tranquility. (662)

Alzheimer's disease. A presenile dementia. (548)

Ambivalence. Simultaneous existence of contradictory emotional attitudes toward the same person, e.g., love and hate. (121)

Ambivert. Personality type intermediate between introvert and extrovert.

Amblyopia. Visual weakness or dimness without associated organic pathology of the eye structure. (240)

Ambulatory schizophrenic. Mild schizophrenic who is not hospitalized and continues to live and function in the community. (292)

Amnesia. Total or partial loss of memory. (243)

Amok. A state of frenzy often accompanied by homicidal tendencies. (78)

Amphetamine. One type of drug that produces a psychologically stimulating and energizing effect. (437)

Amusia. Loss of ability to comprehend or produce musical sounds. (537)

Amygdala. Area in the brain whose damage results in excessive sexual behavior. (460)

Anal stage. In psychoanalytic theory, stage of psychosexual development in which behavior is presumably focused on anal pleasure and activities. (54)

Analgesia. Loss or impairment of pain sensibility. (236)

Analytic psychology. The school or system of psychology developed by Carl Jung. (55)

Androgen. Hormone which regulates development of male sexual characteristics. (488)

Anesthesia. Loss or impairment of sensitivity (usually to touch but often applied to sensitivity to pain and other senses as well). (236)

Anomie. Without relationship or feeling of belonging. (164)

Anorexia (nervosa). Loss or severe diminishment of appetite. (514)

Anoxia. Lack of sufficient oxygen. (145)

Anterograde amnesia. Loss of memory for events following trauma or shock. (535)

Antianxiety drugs. Drugs which are used primarily for alleviating anxiety. (659)

Antidepressant drugs. Drugs which are used primarily to elevate mood and relieve depression. (659)

Antisocial (psychopathic) personality. Personality disorder involving a marked lack of ethical or moral development. (366)

Anxiety. Generalized feelings of fear and apprehension. (121)

Anxiety-defense model. Assumption that abnormal behavior patterns are based on extreme defenses against anxiety. (182)

Anxiety hierarchy. Ranking of anxiety-eliciting situations utilized in systematic desensitization therapy. (669)

Anxiety neurosis. Type of neurosis characterized by chronic anxiety and apprehension. (221)

Aphasia. Loss or impairment of ability to communicate and understand language symbols—involving loss of power of expression by speech, writing, or signs, or loss of ability to comprehend written or spoken language—resulting from brain injury or disease. (537)

Aphonia. Loss or marked impairment of voice without associated or organic pathology. (236)

Approach-avoidance conflict. Type of stress situation involving both positive and negative features. (115)

Apraxia. Loss of ability to perform purposeful movements. (537)

Argyll-Robertson pupil or **sign.** Failure of the pupillary reflex to light, a diagnostic sign in general paresis. (46)

Arousal. See **Activation.**

Arteriosclerosis. Degenerative thickening and hardening of the walls of the arteries, occurring usually in old age. (552)

Assertive training. Behavior therapy technique for helping individuals become more self-assertive in interpersonal relationships. (672)

Astasia-abasia. Inability to stand or walk without the legs wobbling about and collapsing, although the person has normal control of legs while sitting or lying down; no associated organic pathology. (236)

Asthenic personality. Personality disorder characterized by low energy level, easy fatigability, and lack of enthusiasm. (371)

Astraphobia. Morbid fear of lightning, thunder, and storms. (227)

Ataxia. Muscular incoordination, particularly of the arms and legs. See **Locomotor ataxia.** (241)

Athetosis. Recurring involuntary, tentacle-like movements of the hands and feet, usually associated with brain pathology. (562)

Atonicity. Lack of normal muscle tone.

Atrophy. Wasting away or shrinking of a bodily organ. (522)

Attitude. A consistent, learned, emotionalized predisposition to respond in a particular way to a given object, person, or situation. (487)

Auditory aphasia. Loss of ability to understand spoken words. (537)

Aura. Subjective sensations, such as a peculiar odor, preceding an epileptic seizure. (536)

Autism. Disorder beginning in infancy characterized by inability of child to relate to others or form normal self-concept. (588)

Automatic writing. Writing without full conscious awareness or control. (245)

Automation. The use of machines to control machines. (385)

Automatism. Performance of repetitive acts of a nonhabitual and non-reflex nature without conscious intent or supervision. (242)

Autonomic nervous system. The section of the nervous system that regulates the internal organs; consists primarily of ganglia connected with the brain stem and spinal cord and may be subdivided into the sympathetic and parasympathetic systems. (518)

Autonomic reactivity. Individual's characteristic degree of emotional reactivity to stress. (505)

Autonomy. Self-reliance; the sense of being an individual in one's own right. (97)

Autosome. Any chromosome other than those determining sex. (139)

Aversion therapy. Form of behavior therapy in which punishment or aversive stimulation is used to eliminate undesired responses. (672)

Avoidance conditioning. Form of conditioning in which the subject learns to behave in a certain way in order to avoid an unpleasant stimulus. (61)

"Bad trip." An unpleasant or traumatic experience while under the influence of a hallucinogenic drug, such as LSD. (444)

Bedlam. Popular corruption of the name of the early London asylum of St. Mary of Bethlehem. (37)

Behavior control. Shaping and manipulation of behavior by drugs, persuasion, and other techniques. (61)

Behavior therapy. Therapeutic procedures based primarily on application of principles of respondent and operant conditioning. (667)

Behavioral contract. A contract, often between family members, stipulating privileges and responsibilities. (675)

Behavioral sciences. The various interrelated disciplines, including psychology, sociology, and anthropology, that focus on human behavior. (81)

Behaviorism. School of psychology restricting itself primarily to study of man's overt behavior. (57)

Benign. Of a mild, self-limiting, recoverable nature; not malignant.

Bestiality. Sexual relations with animals. (478)

Beta waves. Brain waves having a rhythm of 14 to 28 cycles per second and associated with problem solving and feelings of tension. (662)

Biochemical disorders. Disorders involving disturbances in metabolic processes. (538)

Bio-feedback. Feedback information concerning blood pressure and other bodily processes under control of the autonomic nervous system. (510)

Biological clocks. The 24-hour rhythmic fluctuations in metabolic processes of plants and animals. Also called *circadian cycles.* (504)

Bisexual. Individual who enjoys sexual relations with members of either sex. (482)

Blocking. Involuntary inhibition of recall, ideation, or communication (including sudden stoppage of speech). (600)

Brain pathology. Diseased or disordered condition of the brain. (518)

Brain stem. Structures lying between the spinal cord and the cerebrum. (518)

Brainwashing. Intensive form of propaganda conducted under highly stressful conditions, as in a prisoner-of-war camp. (210)

Brain waves. Minute oscillations of electrical potential given off by neurons in the cerebral cortex and measured by the electroencephalograph. (661)

Brain-wave therapy. The attempt to use alpha or other brain waves for psychotherapeutic purposes. (661)

Broca's area. Area in frontal lobe of cerebral hemisphere above the fissure of Sylvius which plays important role in speech. (518)

Cardiovascular. Pertaining to the heart and blood vessels. (498)

Castrating. Refers to any source of injury to or deprivation of the genitals, or, more broadly, to a threat to the masculinity or femininity of the individual. (54)

Catalepsy. A condition in which the muscles are waxy and semirigid, tending to maintain the limbs in any position in which they are placed. (78)

Catastrophic reaction. Severe disintegration of personality organization under excessive stress. (204)

Catharsis. Discharge of emotional tension associated with repressed traumatic material, e.g., by "talking it out." (52)

Censorship. In psychoanalytic theory, the functioning of the ego and superego in preventing dangerous impulses or desires from entering consciousness. (54)

Central nervous system (CNS). The brain and spinal cord. See also **Peripheral nervous system.** (519)

Cerebral arteriosclerosis. Hardening of the arteries in the brain. (552)

Cerebral concussion. Mild head injury that disrupts brain functions. (534)

Cerebral contusion. Brain damage resulting from head injury severe enough to shift brain and compress it against skull. (534)

Cerebral cortex. The surface layers of the cerebrum. (518)

Cerebral syphilis. Syphilitic infection of the brain. (520)

Cerebral thrombosis. The formation of a clot or thrombus in the vascular system of the brain. (552)

Cerebrovascular accident (CVA). Blockage or rupture of large blood vessel in brain leading to both focal and generalized impairment of brain function. Also called *stroke.* (553)

Cerebrum. Main part of brain; divided into left and right hemispheres. (518)

Character disorder. See **Sociopathic disorder.**

Chemotherapy. Use of drugs in treatment of mental disorders. (658)

Child advocacy. Movement or agencies concerned with protecting rights and ensuring well-being of children. (608)

Chlorpromazine. One of the major tranquilizing drugs. (658)

Chorea. A pathological condition characterized by jerky, irregular, involuntary movements. See also **Huntington's chorea.** (548)

Chromosomal map. Photograph showing number and arrangement of chromosomes for a given individual. (140)

Chromosomes. Chainlike structures within cell nucleus that contain genes. (139)

Chronic. Referring to relatively permanent maladaptive pattern or condition. (518)

Classical (respondent) conditioning. Basic form of learning in which a previously neutral stimulus is paired with a stimulus that elicits the desired response. (59)

Claustrophobia. Irrational fear of small enclosed places. (227)

Client-centered psychotherapy. A nondirective approach to psychotherapy developed chiefly by Carl Rogers and based on his personality theory. (677)

Climacteric. The life period associated with the menopause in women and various related glandular and bodily changes in men. (544)

Clinical picture. The total available diagnostic picture, including symptoms, stresses, dynamics, and so on. (189)

Clinical psychology. Field of psychology concerned with the understanding, assessment, treatment, and prevention of maladaptive behavior. (21)

Clonus. Rapid, oscillatory movements in which muscular rigidity and relaxation rapidly follow each other; occurs following tonic phase in grand-mal epilepsy. (536)

Cluster testing. Interviewing the associates of a person who has contracted venereal disease, whose sexual patterns are assumed to be similar to those of subject. (527)

Cognitive dissonance. Condition existing when new information is contradictory to one's assumptions. (107)

Cognitive processes. Those processes by means of which an individual becomes aware of objects and situations or represents them to himself. Include learning, reasoning, remembering, imagining, problem solving, and decision making. (97)

Coitus. Sexual intercourse. (456)

Collective unconscious. Term used by Carl Jung to refer to that portion of the unconscious which he considered common to all mankind. (55)

Coma. Profound stupor with unconsciousness. (428)

Compensation. The ego-defense mechanism by means of which an undesirable trait is covered up by exaggerating a desirable trait. May also refer to the correction of an organic deficit by increased functioning of another organ. (134)

Complex. Group of emotionally toned attitudes, desires, or memories which are partially or totally repressed. (54)

Compromise reaction. A response to frustration in which the individual partially relinquishes his original goal; often involves a lowering of his level of aspiration or the acceptance of substitute goals. (125)

Compulsion. An irrational and repetitive impulse to perform some act. (231)

Computer assessment. Use of computers in assessing diagnostic data. (653)

Computer model. Use of computer to simulate group functioning. (654)

Conative. Striving or purposive; related to motivation.

Conceived values. The individual's conception of the ideal values. (174)

Concussion. See **Cerebral concussion.**

Conditioned inhibition. Process by which an organism or individual is conditioned not to respond to some stimulus which formerly produced a response.

Conditioning. See **Classical conditioning** and **Operant conditioning.**

Confabulation. The filling in of memory gaps with false and often irrelevant details. (519)

Confidentiality. Commitment on part of professional person to keep information he obtains from a client confidential. (651)

Conflict. Simultaneous arousal of two or more incompatible motives. (115)

Congenital. Existing at birth or before birth but not necessarily hereditary. (144)

Conscience. The functioning of an individual's system of moral values in the approval or disapproval of his own thoughts and actions. Equivalent to Freudian concept of superego. (53)

Consciousness. Awareness of inner and/or outer environment. (67)

Constitution. The relatively constant biological makeup of the individual, resulting from the interaction of heredity and environment. (142)

Continuous reinforcement. Reward or reinforcement given regularly after each correct response. (60)

Control group. A group of subjects compared with experimental group in assessing effects of independent variables. (22)

Convulsion. Pathological, involuntary, muscular contractions. (536)

Corpus callosum. Nerve fibers that connect the two cerebral hemispheres. (518)

Correlational studies. Studies dealing with the extent to which two or more variables co-vary. (80)

Counseling psychology. Branch of psychology in which the psychologist tries to help another person solve certain adjustment problems, usually pertaining to education, marriage, or occupation. (21)

Counterculture. Emerging culture in conflict with established culture in a given society. (635)

Countertransference. Arousal by the client of feelings of transference on the part of the analyst during the course of psychoanalytic therapy. (677)

Covert. Concealed, disguised, not directly observable. (157)

Crazy. Mentally disordered (term not used in scientific circles). (13)

Cretinism. Condition arising from thyroid deficiency in early life and marked by mental retardation and distinctive physical characteristics. (571)

Criminal responsibility. Legal question of whether an individual should be permitted to use insanity as a defense after having committed some criminal act. (402)

Crisis. Stress situation which approaches or exceeds adaptive capacities of individual or group. (118)

Crisis intervention. Various methods for rendering therapeutic assistance during a crisis period in an individual's life. (698)

Critical period. Period of development during which organism most needs certain inputs or is most ready for acquisition of a given response. (101)

Cross-tolerance. Tolerance for other drugs which are similar to one for which the individual has developed tolerance through use. (413)

Cultural bias. Use of assessment criteria which are biased in favor of a given group. (652)

Culture-free test. Test designed to eliminate the effects of cultural differences on performance. (652)

Cunnilingus. Use of the tongue or mouth in erotic play with female genitals. (482)

Cyclothymic (affective) personality. Behavior pattern characterized by alternating and recurring periods of depression and elation. (370)

Day hospital. A community-based mental hospital where the patients are treated during the day, returning to their homes at night. (19)

Decompensation. Ego or personality disorganization under excessive stress. (180)

Defense mechanism. See **Ego-defense mechanism.**

Defense-oriented reaction. Reaction involving one's feelings of adequacy and worth rather than objective handling of the stress situation. (126)

Deficiency motivation. Motivation directed primarily toward maintaining or restoring physiological or psychological equilibrium rather than toward personal growth. (103)

Delinquency. Antisocial or illegal behavior by a minor. (379)

Delirium. State of mental confusion characterized by clouding of consciousness, disorientation, restlessness, excitement, and often hallucinations. (539)

Delirium tremens. Acute delirium associated with prolonged alcoholism; characterized by intense anxiety, tremors, and hallucinations. (409)

Delusion. Strong belief opposed to reality but maintained in spite of logical persuasion and strong evidence to the contrary. (270)

Delusional system. An internally coherent, systematized pattern of delusions. (312)

Dementia. Severe mental disorder involving impairment of mental ability; not congenital. (548)

Dementia praecox. Older term for schizophrenia. (268)

Denial of reality. Ego-defense mechanism by means of which the individual protects himself from unpleasant aspects of reality by refusing to perceive them. (126)

Deoxyribonucleic acid (DNA). Principal component of the genes. (95)

Dependent variable. In an experiment, the factor which the hypothesis predicts will change with changes in the independent variable. (22)

Depersonalization. Loss of sense of personal identity, often with a feeling of being something or someone else. (104)

Depression. Emotional state of dejection, gloomy ruminations, feelings of worthlessness and guilt, and usually apprehension. (252)

Depressive stupor. Extreme degree of depression characterized by marked psychomotor underactivity. (329)

Desensitization. Therapeutic process by means of which reactions to traumatic experiences are reduced in intensity by repeatedly exposing the individual to them in mild form, either in reality or in fantasy. (261)

Desire. To wish for or want some object or condition related to psychobiological needs. (231)

Deterioration. Degeneration of mental abilities due to brain pathology. Sometimes used more broadly to include any impairment of intellectual functions, whether of functional or organic origin. (522)

Developmental task. A competency that is considered essential to master during a particular life period, e.g., learning to talk during infancy. (100)

Deviant behavior. Behavior which deviates markedly from the average or norm; usually pathological in nature as used in abnormal psychology. (15)

Diagnosis. Determination of the nature and extent of a specific disease. (641)

Didactic group therapy. Group therapy consisting of more or less formal group lectures and discussions. (686)

Diplopia. Double vision; seeing one object as two. (231)

Directive therapy. Type of therapeutic approach in which the therapist supplies direct answers to problems and takes much of the responsibility for the progression of therapy. (664)

Discrimination learning. Learning to interpret and respond differently to two or more similar stimuli. (61)

Diseases of adaptation. Stomach ulcers and other disease conditions resulting from the stresses of life. (181)

Disintegration. Loss of organization or integration in any organized system. (181)

Disorganization. Severely impaired integration. (285)

Disorientation. Mental confusion with respect to time, place, or person. (104)

Displacement. Transfer of an emotional attitude or symbolic meaning from one object or concept to another. As an ego-defense mechanism, the redirection of emotional charges to less dangerous objects, e.g., hostility aroused by one's boss may be taken out on one's wife. (129)

Dissociation. Separation or "isolation" of mental processes in such a way that they become split off from the main personality or lose their normal thought-affect relationships. (243)

Dissociative reaction. Psychoneurotic reaction characterized by amnesia, fugue, somnambulism, or multiple personality. (243)

Dizygotic (fraternal) twins. Twins that develop from two separate eggs. (283)

DNA. Deoxyribonucleic acid, the principal component of the genes. (95)

Dominant gene. A gene whose hereditary characteristics prevail in the offspring. (141)

Don Juan. Legendary roué, seducer, and profligate. (9)

Double-approach conflict. Type of conflict in which individual is confronted with choosing between two or more desirable alternatives. (116)

Double-avoidant conflict. Type of conflict in which individual is confronted with choosing between two or more aversive alternatives. (116)

Double-bind. Situation in which an individual will be disapproved for performing a given act and equally disapproved if he does not perform it. (156)

Down's syndrome. See **Mongolism.**

Dream analysis. Psychoanalytic technique involving the interpretation of the patient's dreams. (665)

Drive. Internal conditions directing organism toward a specific goal, usually involving biological rather than psychological motives. (62)

Drug abuse. Use of a drug to extent that it interferes with health and/or occupational or social adjustment. (405)

Drug addiction. Continual use of and physiological dependence upon habit-forming drugs. (405)

Drug culture. Subculture centering around the use of psychedelic or other drugs. (420)

Drug dependence. Physiological and/or psychological dependence on a drug. (424)

Drug habituation. Psychological but not physiological dependence on a drug. (405)

Drug therapy. See **Chemotherapy.**

Dual personality. See **Multiple personality.**

Dyad. A two person group. (654)

Dynamic. Pattern of interactive factors underlying a particular event or condition. (191)

Dysfunction. Impairment or disturbance in the functioning of an organ. (238)

Dysgraphia. Impaired ability to write because of ataxia, tremors, or similar conditions. (237)

Dyslexia. Impairment of the ability to read. (537)

Dysrhythmia. Disturbance in rhythm. (643)

Dyssocial personality. Behavior pattern characterized by criminal values but good ego strength. (396)

Echolalia. Meaningless repetition of words by the individual, usually of whatever is said to him. (279)

Echopraxia. Automatic imitation by the individual of another person's movements or mannerisms. (279)

Eclectic therapy. Psychotherapy based on elements of various theories or procedures. (664)

Ecology. Study of mutual relations between organisms and their physical environment. (629)

Economy, principle of. Theory that the individual meets stress in the simplest way possible. (119)

Edema. Watery swelling of tissues. (212)

Ego. In psychoanalytic theory, the rational subsystem of the personality which mediates between id and superego demands and reality. More generally, the individual's self-concept. (53)

Ego-defense mechanism (reaction). Type of reaction designed to maintain the individual's feelings of adequacy and worth rather than to cope directly with the stress situation; usually unconscious and reality distorting. (126)

Ego-ideal (self-ideal). The person or "self" the individual thinks he could and should be. (97)

Ego involvement. Perception of a situation in terms of its potential effect on the individual.

Egocentric. Preoccupied with one's own concerns and relatively insensitive to the concerns of others. (219)

Electra complex. In psychoanalytic theory, an excessive emotional attachment (love) of the daughter for the father. (54)

Electroencephalograph (EEG). Instrument for recording brain potentials. (622)

Electroencephalogram (EEG). Recording of the minute electrical oscillations (brain waves) emitted by the cerebral cortex. (662)

Electroshock treatment. Use of electricity to produce convulsions and unconsciousness; most widely used form of convulsive therapy. (660)

Electrotherapy. Methods of therapy which involve the influence of electric current on the central nervous system. (660)

Embolism. Lodgment of a blood clot in a blood vessel too small to permit its passage. (552)

Emotion. Complex state of feeling involving conscious experience, internal and overt responses, and power to motivate the organism to action. (120)

Emotional immaturity. Failure to develop normal adult degrees of independence and self-reliance, with consequent use of immature adjustive patterns and inability to maintain equilibrium under stresses which most people can meet satisfactorily. (138)

Emotional insulation. Ego-defense mechanism in which the individual reduces the tensions of need and anxiety by withdrawing into a shell of passivity. (130)

Emotional lability. See **Lability.**

Empathy. Ability to understand and to some extent share the state of mind of another person. (72)

Encephalitis. Inflammation of the brain. (527)

Encephalitis lethargica. Sleeping sickness. (527)

Encephalography. Examination of the brain and mapping of the result. (662)

Encounter. Term applied to the interaction between client and therapist (in existential therapy) or between patients (in encounter-group therapy). (678, 689)

Encounter group. Small group designed to provide an intensive interpersonal experience focusing on feelings and group interactions; used in therapy or to promote personal growth. (686)

Endocrine glands. Ductless glands which secrete hormones directly into the lymph or blood stream. (544)

Endogeneous factors. Factors originating within the organism that affect behavior. (286)

Energizer. Drug which has a stimulating effect.

Engram. Hypothesized physiological change in nervous system thought to be responsible for memory.

Entrophy. Deterioration and eventual disintegration or death of a living system. (89)

Enuresis. Bed-wetting; involuntary discharge of urine. (604)

Environmental evaluation. Way in which the individual views the world—its dangers, pleasures, etc.

Enzyme. Catalyst regulating metabolic activities. (500)

Epidemic encephalitis. Disease of the brain believed to be caused by a filterable virus. (527)

Epidemiology. Study of the distribution of physical or mental disorders in a population. (79)

Epilepsy. Group of disorders varying from momentary lapses of consciousness to generalized convulsions. (536)

Epileptic furor. See **Psychomotor epilepsy.**

Equilibrium. Steady state; balance. (103)

Erogenous zones. Those parts of the body which when stimulated give rise to sexual feelings, e.g., lips, breasts, sex organs. (54)

Erotic. Pertaining to sexual stimulation and gratification. (454)

Estrogens. Female hormones produced by the ovaries. (544)

Ethnic group. Group of people who are treated as distinctive in terms of culture and group patterns. (78)

Etiology. Causation; the systematic study of the causes of disorders. (138)

Eugenics. Science concerned with conditions that affect inborn or hereditary qualities of a race or group in direction of either improvement or degeneracy.

Eunuch. Castrated male. (544)

Euphoria. Exaggerated feeling of well-being and contentment. (455)

Excitation. Process whereby activity is elicited in a nerve. (284)

Exhaustion delirium. Delirious condition resulting from severe fatigue or exhaustion. (539)

Exhibitionism. Public display or exposure of genitals for conscious or unconscious purpose of sexual excitement and pleasure. (462)

Existential anxiety. Anxiety concerning one's ability to find a satisfying and fulfilling way of life. (70)

Existential model. A psychosocial model of man that emphasizes the importance of being and personal fulfillment. (69)

Existential psychotherapy. Therapy based on existential concepts, emphasizing the development of a sense of self-direction and meaning in one's existence. (676)

Existentialism. View of man which emphasizes man's responsibility for himself and for becoming the kind of person he should be. (69)

Exogenous. Originating from or due to external causes. (278)

Exophthalmic goiter (Graves' disease). Disorder of the thyroid characterized by enlargement of this gland, protrusion of the eyeballs, and various mental symptoms. (544)

Exorcism. Various techniques practiced in ancient and medieval times for casting the "evil spirit" out of the mentally ill, based on the concept that mental illness was caused by demons or evil spirits. (32)

Expanded consciousness. Sensation produced by psychedelic drugs or meditation in which individual feels his mind is opened to new types of experience. (442)

Experimental neurosis. Neurotic behavior produced in animals by inescapable conflicts and other types of stress. (57)

Explosive personality. Type of personality disorder or behavior pattern characterized by gross outbursts of rage and physical or verbal aggression. (370)

Expressive aphasia. Loss of ability to speak required words. (537)

External frustration. Environmental obstacle to goals and need satisfactions. (115)

Extinction. Gradual disappearance of conditioned response when it is no longer reinforced. (668)

Extrapunitive. Characterized by a tendency to evaluate the source of frustrations as external and to direct hostility outward.

Extrovert. Personality type characterized by interests directed toward the external environment of people and things rather than toward inner experiences and oneself; outgoing, sociable. (55)

Fabrication. Relating imaginary events as if they were true without intent to deceive; confabulation. (522)

Familial. Pertaining to characteristics which tend to run in families and have a higher incidence in certain families than in the general population. (158)

Family therapy. Form of interpersonal therapy focusing on relationships within the family. (682)

Fantasy. Daydream; also, an ego-defense mechanism by means of which the individual escapes from the world of reality and gratifies his desires in fantasy achievements. (127)

Faulty learning model. Model which attributes abnormal behavior to faulty learning. (183)

Feedback. Knowledge of results of one's behavior; used in judging appropriateness of one's responses and making corrections where indicated. (123)

Feeling. The pleasure and pain dimension of emotion or bodily functions. (68)

Fellatio. Insertion of penis into the mouth for purposes of sexual gratification. (482)

Fetishism. Sexual deviation in which the individual achieves sexual gratification by means of an object (hair, handkerchief, panties) which symbolizes the person to whom it belongs. (466)

Fetus. Embryo after the sixth week following conception. (565)

Field properties. Characteristics of the environment surrounding a living system. (88)

Fixation. Unreasonable or exaggerated attachment to some person or arresting of emotional development on a childhood or adolescent level.

Flashback. The recurrence of a drug experience without further ingestion of the drug, usually of a negative nature following a "bad trip." (441)

Flight of ideas. Rapid succession of ideas without logical association or continuity. (325)

Flooding. Anxiety-eliciting technique used in implosive therapy. (671)

Focal lesion. Lesion in a particular area of the brain. (537)

Folie a deux. A psychotic interpersonal relationship involving two people; e.g., husband and wife both become psychotic with similar symptomatology. (291)

Formulation aphasia. Loss of ability to formulate sentences. (537)

Frame of reference. The reality, ethical, and possibility assumptions which form the individual's "cognitive map" for interpreting and coping with his world. (97)

Fraternal twins. Dizygotic twins; fertilized by separate germ cells, thus not having same genetic inheritance. May be of the same or opposite sex. (283)

Fraudulent interpersonal contract. Violation of rules or norms governing healthy interpersonal relationships. (74)

Free association. Psychoanalytic procedure for probing the unconscious in which individual gives a running account of his every thought and feeling. (664)

Free-floating anxiety. Anxiety not referable to any specific situation or cause. (221)

Frigidity. Lack or reduction of sexual desire in a woman; inability to experience sexual pleasure or gratification. (459)

Frontal lobe. Portion of the brain active in reasoning and other higher thought processes. (518)

Frustration. Thwarting of a need or desire. (115)

Frustration tolerance. See **Stress tolerance.**

Fugue. Dissociative reaction in which the individual leaves his present life situation and establishes a somewhat different mode of life in another locale. Although he is amnesic for his past life, his other abilities are unimpaired and he appears normal to those around him. (243)

Functional. Having no demonstrable organic basis or etiology; psychogenic. (267)

Functional psychoses. Severe mental disorders attributed primarily to psychological stress. (267)

Furor. Transitory outbursts of excitement or anger during which the individual may be quite dangerous. (536)

Future shock. Condition brought about when social change proceeds so rapidly that the individual cannot cope with it adequately. (633)

Gamblers Anonymous. Voluntary organization of ex-gamblers patterned along the lines of Alcoholics Anonymous. (378)

Gamete. Male or female germ cell; contains only half the number of chromosomes found in other cells of the body. (139)

"Gay." Slang term referring to homosexuals. (484)

Gender identity. Individual's identification of himself as male or female; usually occurs by about 3 years of age. (493)

General-adaptation-syndrome. Reaction of the individual to excessive stress; consists of the alarm reaction, the stage of resistance, and the stage of exhaustion. (181)

General paresis. Mental disorder associated with syphilis of the brain. (520)

General systems theory. A comprehensive theoretical model embracing all living systems. (87)

Generalization. Tendency of a response that has been conditioned to one stimulus to become associated with other similar stimuli. (61)

Generalized reinforcer. Reinforcer such as money which may influence a wide range of stimuli and behaviors. (60)

Genes. Ultramicroscopic areas of DNA which are responsible for transmission of hereditary traits. (95)

Genetic code. Means by which DNA controls the sequence and structure of proteins manufactured within each cell and also makes exact duplicates of itself. (95)

Genetic counseling. Use of chromosomal maps to counsel potential parents concerning the possibility of defective offspring. (580)

Genetics. Science of heredity. (95)

Genital stage. In psychoanalytic theory, the final stage of psychosexual development involving shift from autoeroticism to heterosexual interest. (54)

Genitalia. Organs of reproduction, especially the external organs. (54)

Geriatrics. Science of the diseases and treatment of the aged. (547)

Germ cells. Reproductive cells (female ovum and male sperm) which unite to produce a new individual. (139)

Gerontology. Science dealing with the study of old age. (547)

Gestalt psychology. School of psychology which emphasizes patterns rather than elements or connections taking the view that the whole is more than the sum of its parts. (679)

Gestalt therapy. Type of psychotherapy emphasizing the wholeness of the person and integration of thought, feeling, and action. (679)

Gigantism. Abnormally tall stature resulting from hyperfunctioning of the pituitary. (544)

Glioma. Tumor. (528)

Glove anesthesia. Area of anesthesia approximating the area of hand and wrist that would be covered by a glove. Formerly common in hysterical (conversion) reactions. (236)

Goal. Object or condition for which an individual strives. (109)

Gonads. The sex glands. (544)

Gonorrhea. Type of venereal desease. (526)

Grand mal epilepsy. Type of epilepsy characterized by generalized convulsive seizures. (536)

Graves' disease. See **Exophthalmic goiter.**

Group therapy. Psychotherapy with two or more individuals at the same time. (686)

Guilt. Feelings of culpability arising from behavior or desires contrary to one's ethical principles. Involves both self-devaluation and apprehension growing out of fears of punishment. (167)

Habit. Any product of learning, whether it is a customary or transitory mode of response. (439)

Halfway house. Facility which provides aftercare following institutionalization, seeking to ease the individual's adjustment to the community. (694)

Hallucination. Sense perception for which there is no appropriate external stimulus. (271)

Hallucinogens. Drugs or chemicals capable of producing hallucinations. (439)

Hedonism. Doctrine that pleasure is the primary good or value in life. (636)

Hemi-. Prefix meaning *half.*

Hemophobia. Pathological fear of blood. Also called *hematophobia.* (227)

Hemiplegia. Paralysis of one lateral half of the body. (553)

Hereditary potential. Individual's genetic potentialities for development. (94)

Heredity. Genetic transmission of characteristics from parents to their children. (94)

Hermaphroditism. Anatomical sexual abnormality in which an individual has well-developed sex organs of both sexes. (448)

Heterosexuality. Sexual interest in a member of the opposite sex. (451)

Hierarchy of needs. The concept that needs arrange themselves in a hierarchy in terms of importance or "prepotence," from the most basic biological needs to those psychological needs concerned with self-actualization. (112)

High-risk group. Group showing great vulnerability to physical or mental disorders. (362)

Holistic. A systematic approach to science involving the study of the whole or total configuration; the view of man as a unified psychobiological organism inextricably immersed in a physical and sociocultural environment. (88)

Homeostasis. Tendency of organisms to maintain conditions making possible a constant level of physiological functioning. (103)

Homicide. Illegal killing of another person; murder. (393)

Homosexuality. Sexual preference for member of one's own sex. (481)

Hostility. Emotional reaction or drive toward the destruction or damage of an object interpreted as a source of frustration or threat. (120)

Human potential movement. Movement concerned with enrichment of experience, increased sensory awareness, and fulfillment of human potentials. (704)

Huntington's chorea. Incurable disease, presumably of hereditary origin, which is manifested in jerking, twitching movements and mental deterioration. (548)

Hydrocephalus. Organic condition associated with brain damage and mental retardation. (573)

Hydrotherapy. Use of hot or cold baths, ice packs, etc., in treatment. (28)

Hyper-. Prefix meaning *increased.*

Hyperalgesia. Increased sensitivity to pain. (236)

Hyperesthesia. Excessive sensitivity. (236)

Hyperkinesis. Excessive or exaggerated muscular activity. (145)

Hyperkinetic (hyperactive) reaction. Disorder of childhood characterized by overactivity, restlessness, and distractibility. (592)

Hypersensitivity. Oversensitivity. (193)

Hypertension. High blood pressure. (498)

Hypesthesia. Partial loss of sensitivity. (236)

Hypnagogic. Pertaining to drowsiness or a sleep-like or trance-like state. (666)

Hypnoanalysis. Analytic psychotherapy carried out under hypnosis. (666)

Hypnosis. Trance-like mental state induced in a cooperative subject by suggestion. (666)

Hypnotherapy. Use of hypnosis in psychotherapy. (666)

Hypnotic regression. Process by which a subject is brought to relive, under hypnosis, early forgotten or repressed experiences. (666)

Hypo-. Prefix meaning *decreased.*

Hypochondriacal delusions. Delusions concerning various horrible disease conditions, such as the belief that one's brain is turning to dust. (271)

Hypochondriacal neurosis. Condition dominated by preoccupation with bodily processes and fear of presumed diseases. (247)

Hypomania. Mildest form of manic reaction, characterized by moderate psychomotor overactivity. (324)

Hypothalamus. Key structure at the base of the brain; important in temperature regulation, emotion, and motivation. (518)

Hypothesis. Statement or proposition, usually based on observation, which is tested in an experiment; may be denied or supported by experimental results but never conclusively proved. (414)

Hysteria. Older term used to include conversion and dissociative neurotic reactions; involves the appearance of symptoms of organic illness in the absence of any related organic pathology. (235)

Hysterical neurosis. Disorder characterized by involuntary psychogenic loss of motor or sensory function. (235)

Hysterical personality. Personality pattern characterized by excitability, emotional instability, and self-dramatization. (370)

Id. In psychoanalytic terminology, the reservoir of instinctual drives; the most inaccessible and primitive stratum of the mind. (53)

Ideal self. The individual's concept of himself as he thinks he should be. (50)

Identical twins. Monozygotic twins; developed from a single fertilized egg. (283)

Identification. Ego-defense mechanism in which the individual identifies himself with some person or institution, usually of an illustrious nature. (133)

Idiot. Older term referring to severe and profound degrees of mental retardation (IQ below 24). (564)

Illusion. Misinterpretation of sensory data; false perception. (539)

Imbecile. Older term referring to moderate to severe degrees of mental deficiency (IQ of 35–49). (563)

Implosive therapy. Type of behavior therapy in which desensitization is achieved by eliciting a massive "flood" or implosion of anxiety. (671)

Impotence. Inability of male to achieve orgasm. (459)

Imprinting. Form of learning which occurs very early in life, particularly in animals, and determines specific behavior patterns.

Impulse. Tendency to action. (54)

Impulsiveness. Tendency to act without thinking. (241)

Inadequate family. Family characterized by inability to cope with ordinary problems of family living. (159)

Incest. Sexual relations between close relatives such as father and daughter or brother and sister. (472)

Incompetent. Legal designation of an individual as incapable of managing his affairs with ordinary prudence because of mental illness or deficiency. (99)

Incorrigibility. Repetitive delinquent behavior. (379)

Independent variable. Factor whose effects are being examined in an experiment; it is manipulated in some way while the other variables are held constant.

Individuation. Pattern of development from the general to the specific; characteristic of human maturation. (99)

Infantilism. Persistence of infantile emotional attitudes and patterns into adult life. (153)

Inferiority complex. Strong feelings of inadequacy and insecurity which color an individual's entire adjustive efforts. (146)

Inhibition. Conscious restraint of impulse or desire. (119)

Innate. Inborn. (94)

Inner controls. Reality, value, and possibility assumptions which serve to inhibit dangerous or undesirable behavior; could also apply to conditioned avoidance reactions. (97)

Inpatient. Hospitalized mental patient. (695)

Insanity. Legal term for mental disorder, implying lack of responsibility for one's acts and inability to manage one's affairs. (13)

Insight. Clinically, the individual's understanding of his illness or of the motivations underlying his behavior; in general psychology, the sudden grasp or understanding of meaningful relationships in a situation. (218)

Instinct. Inborn tendency to particular behavior pattern under certain conditions in absence of learning; characteristic of species. (615)

Instrumental (operant) conditioning. Type of conditioning in which the subject is reinforced for making a predetermined response, such as pressing a lever. (59)

Integration. Organization of parts (psychological, biological functions) to make a functional whole. (167)

Integrative properties. Tendency of living systems to maintain their organization and functional integrity. (88)

Integrity. Quality of being unified and honest with self and others. (172)

Intellectualization. Ego-defense mechanism by which the individual achieves some measure of insulation from emotional hurt by cutting off or distorting the emotional charge which normally accompanies hurtful situations. (130)

Interdisciplinary (multidisciplinary) approach. Integration of various scientific disciplines in understanding, assessing, treating, and preventing mental disorders. (81)

Intermittent reinforcement. Reinforcement given intermittently rather than after every response. (60)

Internal frustration. Barrier to goals and need satisfactions arising from personal limitations or attitudes of the individual. (115)

Interpersonal accommodation. A reciprocal process of give and take meant to promote satisfactory interpersonal relationships. (73)

Intrapsychic conflict. Psychoanalytic concept referring to conflict between id, ego, and superego. (54)

Introjection. Incorporation of qualities or values of another person or group into one's own ego structure with a tendency to identify with them and to be affected by what happens to them. (133)

Intropunitive. Responding to frustration by tending to blame oneself. (129)

Introvert. Personality type characterized by the direction of interest toward oneself and one's inner world of experiences. (55)

In vivo. Taking place in a real-life situation as opposed to the therapeutic or laboratory setting. (670)

Involutional melancholia (involutional psychotic reaction). Depressive psychotic reaction characterized by depression, agitation, and apprehension. (343)

Ionizing radiation. Form of radiation, such as an X ray, that causes the formation of ions in substances through which it passes. Often used in the treatment of cancer. Major cause of gene mutations. (139)

Isolation. Ego-defense mechanism by means of which contradictory attitudes or feelings which normally accompany particular attitudes are kept apart, thus preventing conflict or hurt. (130)

Jacksonian epilepsy. Muscle spasms usually restricted to a small group of muscles or to one half of the body, although occasionally the entire body may become involved. Consciousness is usually retained. (536)

Juvenile delinquency. Legally prohibited behavior committed by minors. (379)

Juvenile paresis. General paresis in children; usually of congenital origin. (524)

Klinefelter's syndrome. Type of mental retardation associated with sex chromosome anomaly. (571)

Korsakoff's psychosis. Psychosis usually associated with chronic alcoholism and characterized by disorientation, gross memory defects, and confabulation. (410)

Labeling. Assigning an individual to a particular diagnostic category, such as schizophrenia. (61)

Lability. Instability, particularly with regard to affect. (519)

Latent. Inactive or dormant. (54)

Latent content. In psychoanalytic theory, repressed wishes that are indirectly expressed in the manifest content of dreams. (665)

Law of effect. Principle that responses that have rewarding consequences are strengthened and those that have aversive consequences are weakened or eliminated. (58)

Learning. Modification of behavior as a consequence of experience. (101)

Lesbian. Female homosexual. (487)

Lesion. Destruction of a portion of the brain. (537)

Level of aspiration. Standard by which the individual judges success or failure of his behavior. (114)

Libido. In general psychoanalytic terminology, the instinctual drives of the id. In a narrow sense, the drive for sexual gratification. (53)

Life crisis. Stress situation that approaches or exceeds the individual's adjustive capacity. (509)

Life history method. Technique of psychological observation in which the development of particular forms of behavior is traced by means of records of the subject's past or present behavior. (643)

Life style. The general pattern of assumptions, motives, cognitive styles, and coping techniques that characterize the behavior of a given individual and give it consistency. (114)

Limbic system. Group of structures in brain associated with such functions as attention, flight and defense, remembering, and emotion. (518)

Locomotor ataxia. Muscular incoordination usually resulting from syphilitic damage to the spinal-cord pathways. (522)

Logic-tight compartments. Form of intellectualization in which contradictory desires or attitudes are "sealed off" in separate areas of consciousness. (130)

Low adaptation energy. Low constitutional energy. (180)

Lunacy. Legal term roughly synonymous with insanity. The term originates from the Latin word *luna* (moon); the moon was presumed to be the cause of certain types of mental illness. (36)

Lycanthropy. The delusion of being a wolf. (31)

Lysergic acid diethylamide-25 (LSD). A potent hallucinogen. (432)

Macrocephalic. Having an abnormally large cranium. (573)

Madness. Nontechnical synonym for mental illness. (6)

Maintenance strivings. Strivings directed toward maintenance of physiological and psychological equilibrium and integration. (103)

Major tranquilizers. Antipsychotic drugs, such as the phenothiazenes. (658)

Maladaptive behavior. Behavior which is detrimental to well-being of the individual and/or group. (13)

Maladjustment. A more or less enduring failure of adjustment; lack of harmony with self or environment. (17)

Malinger. To fake illness or disability symptoms consciously. (239)

-mania. Suffix denoting a compulsive or morbid preoccupation with some impulse or activity; e.g., compulsive stealing is called kleptomania. (322)

Manic-depressive psychoses. Group of psychotic disorders characterized by prolonged periods of excitement and overactivity (mania) or by periods of depression and underactivity (depression) or by alternation of the two. (322)

Manifest content. In psychoanalytic theory, the apparent meaning of a dream; masks the latent content. (665)

Mannerism. Recurring stereotyped gesture, posture, or movement. (280)

Marathon encounter group. Intensive group experience lasting for 2 or more days with only brief breaks for sleep. (689)

Marijuana. Drug derived from the plant *cannabis indica*; often used in cigarettes called "reefers." (444)

Marital schism. Marriage characterized by severe chronic discord which threatens continuation of marital relationship. (292)

Marital skew. Marriage maintained at expense of distorted relationship. (292)

Marital therapy. Therapy directed toward improving communication and interaction between marital partners. (681)

Masked deprivation. Rejection of child by mother; does not involve separation. (148)

Masked disorder. "Masking" of underlying depression or other emotional disturbance by delinquent behavior or other patterns seemingly unrelated to the basic disturbance. (587)

Masochism. Sexual deviation in which an individual obtains sexual gratification from having pain inflicted upon him. (477)

Mass hysteria. Group outbreak of hysterical reactions. (238)

Massed practice. Use of concentrated learning periods.

Masturbation. Self-stimulation of genitals for sexual gratification. (455)

Maternal deprivation. Lack of adequate care and stimulation by the mother or mother surrogate. (146)

Maturation. Process of development and body change resulting from heredity rather than learning. (98)

Maturity, emotional. Degree to which an individual manifests behavior appropriate to his age and intelligence levels. (99)

Megalomania. Delusions of grandeur. (312)

Melancholia. Mental disorder characterized by severe depression. (322)

Meninges. Membranes which envelop the brain and spinal cord. (522)

Meningitis. Inflammation of the meninges. (52)

Mental age (MA). An individual's degree of mental development as measured against standardized norms. (247)

Mental deficiency. Synonym for mental retardation; the latter term is now preferred. (561)

Mental disease. Mental disorder associated with an organic disease of the nervous system. (13)

Mental disorder. Entire range of abnormal behavior patterns. (13)

Mental hygiene. Scientific field primarily concerned with healthy personality development and the prevention of mental disorders. (247)

Mental illness. Once used synonymously with mental disorder but now ordinarily restricted to psychoses. (13)

Mental retardation. Below-normal intelligence, usually meaning an IQ below 68. (561)

Mental retardate. An individual who is mentally retarded. (561)

Mescaline. One of the hallucinogenic drugs. (439)

Mesmerism. Theories of "animal magnetism" (hypnosis) formulated by Anton Mesmer. (50)

Methadone. An orally administered narcotic which kills the craving for heroin and paves way for rehabilitation of heroin addicts. (431)

Metrazol. Drug which produces epileptiform convulsions; formerly used in the treatment of certain psychotic reactions. (660)

Microcephaly. Form of mental retardation characterized by abnormally small cranium and retarded development of brain. (573)

Migraine headache. Type of psychosomatic disorder characterized by recurrent headaches, usually on one side of head only, and associated with emotional tension. (501)

Milieu. The immediate environment, physical or social or both; sometimes used to include the internal state of an organism. (692)

Military psychology. Field of psychology that deals with psychological problems in the armed forces. (200)

Minimal brain dysfunction (MBD). Controversial term referring to various "soft" neurological signs presumably indicative of malfunctioning of brain. (593)

Minor tranquilizers. Antianxiety drugs such as the meprobramates. (659)

Model psychoses. Psychotic-like states produced by various hallucinogenic drugs such as LSD. (439)

Modeling. Form of learning in which individual learns by watching someone else (the model) perform the desired response. (61)

Modus operandi. Manner or mode of behavior; a criminal's typical pattern of performing his crimes. (396)

Mongolism (Down's syndrome). Form of mental retardation associated with chromosomal anomalies. (569)

Monophobia. Irrational fear of being alone. (227)

Monozygotic twins. Identical twins, developed from one fertilized egg. (283)

Monte Carlo fallacy. Belief of gambler after successive losses that his luck is bound to change. (377)

Mood. Affective state of relatively long duration; usually less intense than typical emotional reactions.

Moral moron. One who fails to develop adequate moral values. (367)

Moral nihilism. Doctrine which denies any objective or real ground for moral beliefs, and holds that individual is not bound by obligation to others or society. (70)

Moral therapy. Therapy based on provision of kindness, understanding, and favorable environment; prevalent during early part of 19th century. (43)

Morbid. Unhealthy, pathological. (52)

Morita therapy. Treatment of neuroses involving deprivation of external stimulation. (260)

Moron. Term formerly used to refer to mild degrees of mental retardation. (564)

Motivation. Often used as a synonym for drive or activation; implies that the organism's actions are partly determined in direction and strength by its own inner nature. (110)

Motivational selectivity. Influence of motives on perception and other cognitive processes. (112)

Motivational sequence. Need-goal-means-satisfaction sequence. (103)

Motive. Internal condition which directs action toward some goal; term usually used to include both the drive and the goal to which it is directed. (113)

Multiple personality. Type of dissociative reaction characterized by the development of two or more relatively independent personality systems in the same individual. (245)

Mutant gene. Gene that has undergone some change in structure. (140)

Mutation. Change in the composition of a gene, usually causing harmful or abnormal characteristics to appear in the offspring. (139)

Mutism. Refusal or inability to speak. (236)

Mysophobia. Morbid or irrational fear of dirt or contamination. (227)

Myxedema. Disorder due to thyroid deficiency in adult life, characterized by mental dullness. (543)

Narcissism. Self-love. (293)

Narcolepsy. Abnormal reaction characterized by transient, compulsive states of sleepiness. (437)

Narcotherapy (narcoanalysis, narcosynthesis). Psychotherapy carried on while the patient is under the influence of a narcotic drug, such as sodium amytal or pentothal. (658)

Narcotic drugs. Drugs such as morphine which lead to physiological dependence and increased tolerance. (424)

Narcotics Anonymous. An organization of ex-drug addicts similar to Alcoholics Anonymous. (433)

Necrophilia. Morbid sexual interest in corpses. (478)

Need. Biological or psychological condition whose gratification is necessary for the maintenance of homeostasis or for self-actualization. (104)

Need-satisfaction sequences. Behavior leading to the gratification of needs, with accompanying pleasure or satisfaction. (109)

Negativism. Form of aggressive withdrawal which involves refusing to cooperate or obey commands, or doing the exact opposite of what has been requested. (272)

Negotiated maladjustment contract. Maintenance of interpersonal relationship because one of parties agrees to abide by deviant and undesirable rules and norms. (74)

Neonate. Newborn infant. (148)

Neoplasm. Tumor. (529)

Nervous breakdown. Refers broadly to lowered integration and inability to deal adequately with one's life situation. (12)

Nervousness. State of emotional tension, restlessness, and hypersensitivity. (189)

Neurasthenic neurosis. Neurotic disorder characterized by complaints of chronic weakness, easy fatigability, and lack of enthusiasm. (250)

Neurology. Field concerned with study of brain and nervous system and disorders thereof. (643)

Neuron. Individual nerve cell. (145)

Neuropsychiatry. Broadly speaking, the scientific field concerned with the diagnosis, treatment, and prevention of psychiatric disorders. (188)

Neurosis. Emotional disturbance characterized by exaggerated use of avoidance behavior and defense mechanisms against anxiety. (217)

Neurosyphilis. Syphilis affecting the central nervous system. (520)

Neurotic-depressive reaction. Psychoneurotic reaction characterized by marked, persistent dejection and discouragement. (252)

Neurotic nucleus. Basic personality characteristics underlying neurotic disorders. (218)

Neurotic paradox. Failure of neurotic patterns to extinguish despite their self-defeating nature. (219)

"New" criminal. Individual who commits criminal acts for "kicks" rather than material gain. (397)

Night hospital. Mental hospital in which an individual may receive treatment during all or part of the night while carrying on his usual occupation in the daytime. (19)

Nihilistic delusion. Fixed belief that everything is unreal, that nothing really exists. (271)

Nomadism. Withdrawal reaction in which the individual continually attempts to escape frustration by moving from place to place or job to job. (608)

Nominal aphasia. Loss of ability to recall the names of objects. (537)

Nondirective therapy. An approach to psychotherapy in which the therapist refrains from advice or direction of the therapy. See also **Client-centered psychotherapy.** (664)

Normal. Conforming to the usual or norm. (10)

Normal distribution. Tendency for most members of a population to cluster around a central point or average with respect to a given trait, with the rest spreading out to the two extremes. (10)

Norm. Standard based on measurement of a large group of persons; used for comparing the scores of an individual with those of others in a defined group.

Nosology. Naming and classification of diseases. (217)

NREM sleep. Stages of sleep not characterized by the rapid eye movements that accompany dreaming. (104)

Nurture. Environmental surroundings or care of the young. (94)

Nyctophobia. Morbid fear of darkness. (227)

Nymphomania. Excessive sexual desire in females. (460)

Obsession. Persistent idea or thought which the individual recognizes as irrational but cannot get rid of. (231)

Obsessive-compulsive neurosis. Disorder characterized by persistent intrusion of unwanted desires, thoughts, or actions. (231)

Obsessive-compulsive personality. Personality disorder characterized by excessive concern with conformity and adherence to ethical values. (370)

Occipital lobe. Portion of cerebrum concerned with visual function. (518)

Occupational therapy. Use of occupational training or activity in psychotherapy. (692)

Ocholophobia. Morbid fear of crowds. (227)

Oedipus complex. Desire for sexual relations with parent of opposite sex, specifically that of a boy for his mother. (54)

Olfactory hallucinations. Hallucinations involving the sense of smell, as of poison gas. (271)

Operant conditioning. Form of learning in which the correct response is reinforced and becomes more likely to occur. (59)

Opium. Narcotic drug which leads to physiological dependence and the building up of tolerance; derivatives are morphine, heroin, paregoric, and codeine. (424)

Oral stage. First stage of psychosexual development in Freudian theory, in which mouth or oral activities are primary source of pleasure. (54)

Organic brain syndromes. Mental disorders associated with organic brain pathology. (517)

Organic psychosis. Psychosis associated with organic brain pathology. (517)

Organic viewpoint. Concept that all mental disorders have an organic basis. (45)

Orientation. Individual's ability to comprehend the environment with reference to time, place, and person.

Orthopsychiatry. Field combining the resources of several disciplines, including psychiatry, psychology, and social work. (715)

Outpatient. An ambulatory patient who visits a hospital clinic for examination and treatment, as distinct from a hospitalized patient. (695)

Outpatient clinic. Clinic where patients are treated on a nonhospitalized basis. (695)

Ovaries. Female gonads. (544)

Overanxious reaction. Disorder of childhood characterized by chronic anxiety, unrealistic fears, sleep disturbances, and exaggerated autonomic responses. (598)

Overloading. Subjecting organism to excessive stress, e.g., forcing the organism to handle or "process" an excessive amount of information. (175)

Overprotection. Shielding a child to the extent that he becomes too dependent on the parent. (151)

Overt behavior. Activities which can be observed by an outsider. (159)

Ovum. Female gamete or germ cell. (139)

Panic. Severe personality disorganization involving intense anxiety and usually either paralyzed immobility or blind flight. (228)

Paralysis agitans. See **Parkinson's disease.**

Paramnesia. False memory in which the individual "remembers" events that did not occur. (411)

Paranoia. Psychosis characterized by a systematized delusional system. (311)

Paranoid personality. Individual showing abortive paranoid reaction characterized by projection (as a defense mechanism), suspiciousness, envy, extreme jealousy, and stubbornness. (370)

Paranoid state. Transient psychotic disorder in which the main element is a delusion, usually persecutory or grandiose in nature. (316)

Paraphasia. Garbled speech. (537)

Paraprofessional. Individual who has been trained in mental health services, but not at the professional level. (699)

Paresthesia. Exceptional sensations, such as tingling. (236)

Paresis. General paresis; an organic psychosis caused by syphilitic infection of the brain. (520)

Parkinson's disease (Paralysis agitans). Progressive disease characterized by a masklike, expressionless face and various neurological symptoms. (548)

Passive-aggressive personality. Personality pattern characterized by passively expressed aggressiveness. (371)

Pathogenic. Pertaining to conditions which lead to pathology. (161)

Pathological intoxication. Severe cerebral and behavioral disturbance in an individual whose tolerance to alcohol is extremely low. (409)

Pathology. Diseased or abnormal physical or mental condition; also the science which deals with such conditions. (13)

Pathophobia. Morbid fear of disease. (227)

Pederasty. Sexual intercourse between males via the anus. (482)

Pedophilia. Sexual deviation in which an adult engages in or desires sexual relations with a child. (468)

Peer group. Social group of equivalent age and status. (96)

Perceptual defense. Selective perception; the unconscious screening out of unpleasant or threatening perceptions. (112)

Perceptual filtering. Processes involved in selective attention to aspects of the great mass of incoming stimuli which continually impinge on organism. (269)

Performance contract. Agreement in which one party must perform a specified service successfully or forfeit payment, as when a firm contracts to improve the reading level of pupils in a given school system. (697)

Peripheral nervous system. Nerve fibers passing between the central nervous system and the sense organs, muscles, and glands. (519)

Perseveration. Persistent continuation of a line of thought or activity once it is under way. Clinically, inappropriate repetition. (593)

Personality. The unique pattern of traits which characterizes the individual. (93)

Personality dynamics. Cognitive and other processes involved in personality functioning and adjustment. (97)

Perversion. Deviation from normal. (451)

Pervert. A sexual deviate. (451)

Petit mal. Relatively mild form of epilepsy involving a temporary partial lapse of consciousness. (536)

Phallic stage. In psychoanalytic theory, the stage of psychosexual development during which genital exploration and manipulation occur. (54)

Phallic symbol. Any object which resembles the erect male sex organ. (469)

Phenylketonuria (PKU). Type of mental retardation resulting from a metabolic deficiency. (574)

Phobia. Irrational fear; the individual may realize its irrationality but nevertheless be unable to dispel it. (227)

Phobic neurosis. Disorder characterized by intense fear of an object or situation which the individual consciously realizes poses no real danger to him. (227)

Photophobia. Morbid fear of strong light. (236)

Physiological dependence. Type of drug dependence involving withdrawal symptoms when drug is discontinued. (427)

Physiology. Study of the functioning of living organisms and their parts. (22)

Pick's disease. Form of presenile dementia. (548)

Pineal gland. Small gland at the base of the brain which helps regulate body's biological clock and may also pace sexual development. (544)

Pituitary gland. Endocrine gland associated directly with growth. (544)

Placebo. An inactive drug administered in such a way that individual thinks he is receiving an active medication. (242)

Play therapy. Use of play activities in psychotherapy with children. The counterpart for adults is recreational therapy. (683)

Pleasure centers. Areas of the brain where stimulation is known or presumed to be pleasurable in nature. Also called *reward centers.* (84)

Pleasure principle. In psychoanalysis, the demand that an instinctual need be immediately gratified regardless of reality. (99)

Possession. Ancient term for mental illness, based on the belief that the patient was "possessed" by an evil spirit. (32)

Post-hypnotic suggestion. Suggestion given during hypnosis to be carried out by the subject after he is brought out of hypnosis. (666)

Postpartum disturbances. Emotional disturbances associated with childbirth. (545)

Postraumatic disorders. Residual symptoms following traumatic experience. (537)

Precipitating cause. The particular stress which precipitates a disorder. (184)

Predisposing cause. Factor which lowers the individual's stress tolerance and paves the way for the appearance of a disorder. (184)

Predisposition. Likelihood that an individual will develop certain symptoms under given stress conditions. (141)

Prejudice. Emotionally toned conception favorable or unfavorable to some person, group, or idea. (163)

Prematurity. Birth of an infant before the end of normal period of pregnancy. (566)

Premorbid. Existing prior to onset of mental disorder. (549)

Prenatal. Before birth. (145)

Presenile dementia. Senile brain deterioration occurring at an early age and accompanied by mental disorder. (548)

Pressure. Demand made on an organism. (116)

Primary cause. Cause without which a disorder would not have occurred. (345)

Primary impotence. Form of impotence in which male has never been able to sustain an erection long enough to have successful intercourse. (459)

Primary mental abilities. Relatively independent abilities, such as verbal comprehension and numerical ability, which make up "general intelligence." (101)

Primary prevention. Establishing conditions designed to prevent occurrence of mental disorders. (708)

Primary reaction tendencies. Constitutional tendencies apparent in infancy, such as sensitivity and activity level. (94)

Primary reinforcer. Reinforcing stimulus whose value is intrinsic, such as food. (60)

Privileged communication. Freedom from the obligation to report to the authorities information concerning legal guilt revealed by a client or patient; enjoyed by lawyers, by clergymen, and in some states by other professionals. (651)

Prognosis. Prediction as to the probable course and outcome of a disorder. (650)

Projection. Ego-defense mechanism in which individual attributes his own unacceptable desires and impulses to others. (128)

Projective technique. Any psychological technique for the diagnosis of personality organization utilizing relatively unstructured stimuli which reveal the individual's basic attitudes, conflicts, and so on. (644)

Promiscuity. Repeated sexual episodes with different partners; referred to as sexual delinquency in girls under 18. In view of changing sexual mores, no longer a very meaningful term. (457)

Prostitution. Sexual intercourse for financial gain. (478)

Pseudo-community. Delusional social environment developed by a paranoiac. (316)

Pseudo-mutuality. Relationship among family members that appears to be mutual, understanding, and open, but in fact is not. (293)

Psychedelic drugs. "Mind expanding" drugs, such as LSD, which often result in hallucinations. (432)

Psychiatric evaluation. Medical, psychological, and sociological data used in the diagnosis of mental disorders. (643)

Psychiatric nursing. Field of nursing primarily concerned with mental disorders. (21)

Psychiatric social work. Field of social work primarily concerned with the mentally ill. (21)

Psychiatrist. Medical doctor who specializes in the diagnosis and treatment of mental disorders. (21)

Psychiatry. Field of medicine concerned with understanding, assessing, treating, and preventing mental disorders. (21)

Psychic pain. Synonym for *anxiety*. (53)

Psychic trauma. Stressful experience of a severely traumatic nature. (148)

Psychoanalysis. Theoretical model and therapeutic approach developed by Freud. (52)

Psychoanalytic model. Model of man, developed primarily by Freud, emphasizing role of repression and unconscious processes in mental disorders. (50)

Psychobiology. Broad, eclectic approach to human behavior fostered by Adolf Meyer, emphasizing the pluralistic determinants of behavior and the necessity for maintaining a holistic approach. (82)

Psychodrama. Psychotherapeutic technique worked out by J. L. Moreno in which the acting of various roles is a cardinal part of the therapy. (686)

Psychogenic. Of psychological origin: originating in the psychological functioning of the individual. (243)

Psychological assessment. Psychometric and other personality and behavior assessment data used in the diagnosis of mental disorders. (643)

Psychological need. Need emerging out of environmental interactions, e.g., the need for social approval. (106)

Psychological test. Standardized procedure designed to measure the subject's performance on a specified task. (643)

Psychology. Science of human behavior. (49)

Psychomotor. Involving both psychological and physical activity. (536)

Psychomotor epilepsy. State of disturbed consciousness in which the individual may perform various actions, sometimes of a homicidal nature, for which he is later amnesic. (536)

Psychoneurosis. See **Neurosis.**

Psychopathic (antisocial) personality. Sociopathic disorder characterized by lack of moral development and inability to show loyalty to other persons or groups. (366)

Psychopathology. Mental disorder. (13)

Psychopharmacological drugs. Drugs used in treatment of mental disorders. (85)

Psychophysiologic disorders. See **Psychosomatic disorders.**

Psychosexual development. Freudian view of development as involving a succession of stages, each characterized by a dominant mode of achieving libidinal pleasure. (54)

Psychosis. Severe personality disorder involving loss of contact with reality and usually characterized by delusions and hallucinations. Hospitalization is ordinarily required. (267)

Psychosocial deprivation. Lack of needed stimulation and interaction during early life. (162)

Psychosocial development. Development of the individual in his relationships to others. (107)

Psychosomatic (psychophysiologic) disorders. Physical symptoms, which may involve actual tissue damage, resulting from continued emotional mobilization under stress; usually involve single organ system under autonomic nervous system innervation. (499)

Psychotherapy. Treatment of mental disorders by psychological methods. (663)

Puberty. Stage of physical development when reproduction first becomes possible. (54)

Puberty praecox. Oversecretion of adrenal hormones in childhood, resulting in pathologically early sexual maturity. (544)

Punishment. Application of aversive stimulation in response to behavior considered undesirable. (233)

Pyrophobia. Morbid fear of fire. (227)

Q-sort test. A personality inventory in which subject, or someone evaluating him, sorts a number of statements into piles according to their applicability to the subject. (645)

Racism. Prejudice and discrimination directed toward individuals or groups because of their racial background. (619)

Random sample. Sample drawn in such a way that each member of the population has an equal chance of being selected.

Randomization. Selection of experimental groups by chance or at random in the hope of eliminating any selective factor which might affect the results of the experiment.

Rape. To force sexual relations upon another person. (469)

Rapport. Interpersonal relationship characterized by a spirit of cooperation, confidence, and harmony. (85)

Rating scale. Device for evaluating oneself or someone else in regard to specific traits. (643)

Rational psychotherapy. Form of psychotherapy which encourages patient to substitute rational for irrational assumptions in his inner dialogue with himself. (680)

Rationalization. Ego-defense mechanism in which the individual thinks up "good" reasons to justify what he has done, is doing, or intends to do. (127)

Reaction formation. Ego-defense mechanism in which individual's conscious attitudes and overt behavior are opposite to his repressed unconscious wishes. (128)

Reaction sensitivity. Sensitization or tendency to perceive certain elements of a total situation, as a result of acquired attitudes and previous experience. (143)

Reactive depression (neurotic depressive reaction). Continued depression in the face of loss or environmental setback. (252)

Reality assumptions. Assumptions which relate to the gratification of needs in the light of environmental possibilities, limitations, and dangers. (99)

Reality principle. Awareness of the demands of the environment and adjustment of behavior to meet these demands. (99)

Reality testing. Behavior aimed at testing or exploring the nature of the individual's social and physical environment; often used more specifically to refer to the testing of the limits of permissiveness of his social environment. (107)

Reality therapy. Form of therapy based on assumption that emotional difficulties arise when an individual violates his basic sense of right and wrong. (680)

Recessive gene. Gene which is effective only when paired with an identical gene. (141)

Recidivism. A shift back to one's original behavior (often delinquent or criminal) after a period of treatment or rehabilitation. (401)

Reciprocal inhibition. Technique of desensitization used in behavior therapy in which responses antagonistic to anxiety are paired with anxiety-eliciting stimuli. (669)

Recompensation. Increase in integration or inner organization. Opposite of *decompensation*. (182)

Reentry. Return from the openness of an encounter group to the real world, which is presumably less open and honest. (690)

Referral. Sending or recommending an individual and/or family for psychiatric assessment and/or treatment. (189)

Regression. Ego-defense mechanism in which the individual retreats to the use of less mature responses in attempting to cope with stress and maintain ego integrity. (132)

Rehabilitation. Use of reeducation rather than punishment in dealing with criminal offenders. (401)

Reinforcement. In classical conditioning, the process of following the conditioned stimulus with the unconditioned stimulus; in operant conditioning, the rewarding of desired responses. (59)

Rejection. Lack of acceptance of another person, usually referring to such treatment of a child by his parents. (151)

Reliability. Degree to which a test or measuring device produces the same result each time it is used to measure the same thing. (652)

REM sleep. Stage of sleep involving rapid eye movements (REM), associated with dreaming. (104)

Remission. Marked improvement or recovery appearing in the course of a mental illness; may or may not be permanent. (338)

Repression. Ego-defense mechanism by means of which dangerous desires and intolerable memories are kept out of consciousness. (127)

Reserpine. One of the early antipsychotic drugs, now largely supplanted by newer drugs. (658)

Resistance. Tendency to maintain symptoms and resist treatment or uncovering of repressed material. (665)

Respondent conditioning. See **Classical conditioning.**

Reticular activating system (RAS). Fibers going from the reticular formation to higher brain centers and presumably functioning as a general arousal system. (518)

Reticular formation. Neural nuclei and fibers in the brain stem which apparently play an important role in arousing and alerting the organism and in controlling attention. (518)

Retrograde amnesia. Loss of memory for events during a circumscribed period prior to brain injury or damage. (535)

Reverse tolerance. Situation in which a decreased amount of some psychoactive drug brings about the effects formerly achieved by a larger dose. (413)

Rigid control. Coping patterns involving reliance upon inner restraints, such as inhibition, suppression, repression, and reaction formation. (126)

Rigidity. Tendency to follow established coping patterns, with failure to see alternatives or extreme difficulty in changing one's established patterns. (219)

Role. See **Social role.**

Role distortion. Violation of expected role behavior in an undesirable way. (292)

Role obsolescence. Condition occurring when the ascribed social role of a given individual is no longer of importance to the social group. (555)

Role playing. Form of psychotherapy in which the individual acts out a social role other than his own or tries out a new role for himself. (686)

Rorschach test. Projective personality test making use of inkblots. (644)

Sadism. Sexual deviation in which sexual gratification is obtained by the infliction of pain upon others. (474)

St. Vitus' dance. Hysterical chorea of common occurrence during the Middle Ages. (31)

Sample. Group upon which measurements are taken; should normally be representative of the population about which an inference is to be made.

Satyriasis. Excessive sexual desire in males. (460)

Scapegoating. Displacement of aggression onto some object, person, or group other than the source of frustration. (621)

Schizoid personality. Personality pattern characterized by shyness, oversensitivity, seclusiveness, and often eccentricity. (370)

Schizophrenia. Psychosis characterized by the breakdown of integrated personality functioning, withdrawal from reality, emotional blunting and distortion, and disturbances in thought and behavior. (273)

Secondary cause. Factor which contributes to a mental illness but which in and of itself would not have produced it, as distinct from the *primary cause.* (387)

Secondary impotence. Condition in which male is capable of successful intercourse but manifests impotence 25 percent or more of the time. (459)

Secondary prevention. Preventive techniques focusing on early detection and correction of maladaptive patterns within context of individual's present life situation. (709)

Secondary reinforcer. Reinforcement provided by a stimulus that has gained reward value by being paired with a primary reinforcing stimulus. (60)

Security. Maintenance of conditions necessary to need gratification. (107)

Sedative. Drug used to reduce tension and induce relaxation and sleep. (432)

Self (ego). The integrating core of the personality which mediates between needs and reality. (97)

Self-acceptance. Being satisfied with one's attributes and qualities while remaining aware of one's limitations. (107)

Self-actualization. Fulfillment of one's potentialities as a human being. (109)

Self-concept. The individual's sense of his own identity, worth, capabilities, and limitations. (97)

Self-devaluation. Lowered feelings of worth and self-esteem. (132)

Self-differentiation. Degree to which the individual achieves a sense of unique identity apart from the group. (97)

Self-direction. Basing one's behavior on inner assumptions rather than external contingencies. (66)

Self-esteem. Feeling of personal worth. (108)

Self-evaluation. Way in which the individual views himself—his worth, adequacy, etc. (97)

Self-fulfillment. Living a meaningful, actualizing, and fulfilling life. (65)

Self-ideal. See **Ego-ideal.**

Self-identity. Individual's delineation and awareness of his continuing identity as a person. (108)

Self-recrimination. Self-condemnation and blame. (154)

Self-theory. Personality theory which utilizes the self-concept as the integrating core of personality organization and functioning. (65)

Self-worth. The individual's evaluation of himself as a person. (108)

Senile. Pertaining to old age. (548)

Senile dementia. A form of psychosis caused in part by deteriorative brain changes due to aging. (548)

Sensitivity training group (T-group). One type of small group designed to provide intensive group experience and foster self-understanding and personal growth. (686)

Sensory awareness. Openness to new ways of experiencing and feeling. (705)

Sensory deprivation. Restriction of sensory stimulation below the level required for normal functioning of the central nervous system. (102)

Sentence-completion test. Form of projective technique utilizing incomplete sentences which the subject is to complete. (645)

Sequelae. Symptoms remaining as the aftermath of a disorder. (213)

Sexual delinquency. Repeated transient coital experience by a girl under 18 years of age. (457)

Sexual deviate. Individual who manifests nonconforming sexual behavior, often of a pathological nature. (451)

Shaping. Form of instrumental conditioning used in training animals; at first, all responses resembling the desired one are reinforced, then only the closest approximations, until finally the desired response is attained. Also called *approximation*. (61)

Sheltered workshops. Workshops where mentally retarded or otherwise handicapped individuals can engage in constructive work in the community. (579)

"Shock" reaction. Transient personality decompensation in the face of sudden acute stress. (188)

Shock therapy. Use of electroshock or related methods in treating mental disorders. (660)

Siblings. Offspring of the same parents. (156)

Sick role. Protected role provided by society via medical model for individual suffering from severe physical or mental disorder. (83)

Situation stress reaction (acute). Superficial maladjustment to newly experienced life situations which are especially difficult or trying. (204)

Situational test. Test which measures performance in a simulated life situation. (648)

Social feedback. Exchange of error-reducing information among members of a group.

Social norms. Group standards concerning behaviors viewed as acceptable or unacceptable. (611)

Social pathology. Abnormal patterns of social organization, attitudes, or behavior; undesirable social conditions which tend to produce individual pathology. (161)

Social role. Behavior expected of individual occupying given position in group. (73)

Social sanction. Punishment by group for violation of social norms. (111)

"Social" self. The façade the individual displays to others as contrasted with his private self. (50)

Socioeconomic status. Position on social and economic scale in community; determined largely by income and occupational level. (162)

Sociogenic. Having its roots in sociocultural conditions or causes. (161)

Sociopathic disorder. Lack of social responsibility and inability to conform to prevailing social norms even when such norms are adaptive. (365)

Sociotherapy. Treatment of interpersonal aspects of the individual's life situation. (691)

Sodium pentothal. Barbiturate drug sometimes used in psychotherapy to produce a state of relaxation and suggestibility. (127)

Sodomy. Sexual intercourse via the anus. (482)

Somatic. Pertaining to the body. (142)

Somatic weakness. Special vulnerability of given organ systems to stress. (503)

Somatotype. Physique or build of a person, as assessed by various theories relating temperament to physical characteristics. (142)

Somnambulism. Sleepwalking. (605)

Sour grapes mechanism. Form of rationalization in which the individual denies the hurt of frustration by concluding that what he wanted is not worth having after all. (128)

Spasm. Intense, involuntary, usually painful contraction of a muscle or group of muscles. (427)

Spasticity. Marked hypertonicity or continual overcontraction of muscles, causing stiffness, awkwardness, and motor incoordination. (562)

Special vulnerability. Low tolerance for specific types of stress. (138)

Sperm. Male gamete or germ cell. (139)

Spontaneous recovery. Spontaneous remission. Also, in conditioning, the return of a conditioned response which has once been extinguished. (263)

Spontaneous remission. Recovery of a mental patient without treatment or with minimal treatment. (263)

S-R psychologists. Psychologists who emphasize the role of stimulus-response (S-R) connections in learning. Also called *associationists*. (57)

Stage of exhaustion. Third and final stage in the general-adaptation-syndrome, in which the organism is no longer able to resist continuing stress; may result in death. (181)

Stage of resistance. Second stage of the general-adaptation-syndrome. (181)

Startle reaction. Sudden involuntary motor reaction to intense unexpected stimuli; may result from mild stimuli if person is hypersensitive. (189)

Statutory rape. Sexual intercourse with a minor. (469)

Stereotype. A generalized notion of how people of a given race, religion, or other group will appear, think, feel, or act. (622)

Stereotypy. Persistent and inappropriate repetition of phrases, gestures, or acts. (231)

Stimulants. Drugs that tend to increase feelings of alertness, reduce feelings of fatigue, and enable individual to stay awake over sustained peiods of time. (432)

Stimulus generalization. The spread of a conditioned response to some stimulus similar to, but not identical with, the conditioned stimulus. (61)

Stress. Any adjustive demand that requires coping behavior on part of individual or group. (115)

Stress-decompensation model. Model of abnormal behavior which emphasizes progressive disorganization of behavior under excessive stress. (183)

Stress interview. Interview of a subject under simulated stress conditions. (643)

Stress tolerance (frustration tolerance). Nature, degree, and duration of stress which an individual can tolerate without undergoing serious personality decompensation. (178)

Stroke. See **Cerebrovascular accident.**

Stupor. Condition of lethargy and unresponsiveness, with partial or complete unconsciousness. (279)

Stuttering (stammering). Speech disorder characterized by blocking and repetition of initial sounds of words. (600)

Subconscious. Pertaining to mental activities of which the individual is not aware; term no longer in common use. (54)

Subcortical structures. Structures of the brain lying under the cortex. (518)

Subcultural delinquent. Individual whose delinquency is associated with membership in a delinquent subculture. (386)

Sublimation. Ego-defense mechanism by means of which frustrated sexual energy is partially channeled into substitutive activities. (54)

Substitution. Acceptance of substitute goals or satisfactions in place of those originally sought after or desired. (125)

Superego. Conscience; ethical or moral dimensions (attitudes) of personality. (53)

Suppression. Conscious forcing of desires or thoughts out of consciousness; conscious inhibition of desires or impulses. (127)

Surrogate. Substitute parental figure. (101)

Symbol. Image, object, or activity that is used to represent something else. (310)

Symbolism. Representation of one idea or object by another. (310)

Sympathetic division. Division of the autonomic nervous system which is active in emergency conditions of extreme cold, violent effort, and emotions. (518)

Syncope. Temporary loss of consciousness resulting from cerebral anemia. (529)

Syndrome. Group or pattern of symptoms which occur together in a disorder and represent the typical picture of the disorder.

Syphilophobia. Morbid fear of syphilis. (227)

System. An assemblage of interdependent parts, living or nonliving. (89)

Systematic desensitization. A behavior therapy technique for eliminating anxiety responses. (669)

Tachycardia. Rapid pulse. (503)

Tactual hallucinations. Hallucinations involving the sense of touch, such as feeling cockroaches crawling over one's body. (271)

Tarantism. Type of hysterical dancing occurring in epidemic form during the Middle Ages. (31)

Task-oriented reaction. Realistic rather than ego-defensive approach to stress. (123)

Temporal lobe. Portion of cerebrum located in front of occipital lobe and separated from frontal and parietal lobes by the fissure of Sylvius. (518)

Tension. Condition arising out of the mobilization of psychobiological resources to meet a threat; physically, involves an increase in muscle tonus and other emergency changes; psychologically, is characterized by feelings of strain, uneasiness, and anxiety. (181)

Tertiary prevention. Preventive techniques focusing on short-term hospitalization and intensive aftercare when an emotional breakdown has occured, with aim of returning individual to his family and community setting as soon as possible. (712)

Testosterone. Male sex hormone. (544)

Therapeutic. Pertaining to treatment or healing. (657)

Therapeutic community. The hospital environment used for therapeutic purposes. (692)

Therapy. Treatment; application of various treatment techniques. (657)

Theta wave. Brain wave having a frequency of only 5 to 7 cycles per second. (662)

Threat. Real or imagined danger to individual or group. (126)

Thymus. Gland of uncertain function located in neck and upper thorax; usually atrophies in human adults. (544)

Thyroids. Endocrine glands located in neck which influence body metabolism, rate of physical growth, and development of intelligence. (544)

Thyrotoxic. Pertains to oversecretion of thyroxin. (544)

Thyroxin. Hormone secreted by the thyroid glands. (544)

Tic. Intermittent twitching or jerking, usually of facial muscles. (236)

Token economy. Reinforcement technique often used in hospital or institutional settings in which individuals are rewarded for socially constructive behavior with tokens that can then be exchanged for desired objects or activities. (307)

Tolerance. Physiological condition in which increased dosage of an addictive drug is needed to obtain effects previously produced by smaller dose. (413)

Tonic. Pertaining to muscle tension or contraction; muscle tone. (536)

Toxemia. Pathological condition resulting from poison in the blood. (546)

Toxic. Poisonous. (539)

Toxic deliria (psychoses). Severe disturbances in cerebral functions resulting from toxins. (539)

Trait. Characteristic of individual which can be observed or measured. (102)

Trance. Sleeplike state in which the range of consciousness is limited and voluntary activities are suspended; a deep hypnotic state. (666)

Tranquilizers. Drugs used for antipsychotic purposes and/or reduction of anxiety and tension. See also **Major tranquilizers, Minor tranquilizers.** (434)

Transactional analysis. Form of interpersonal therapy based on interaction of "Child," "Adult," and "Parent" ego states. (684)

Transference. Process whereby client projects attitudes and emotions applicable to another significant person onto the therapist; emphasized in psychoanalytic therapy. (665)

Transient situational disorder. Temporary mental disorder developing under conditions of overwhelming stress, as in military combat or civilian catastrophes. (187)

Transsexualism. Identification of oneself with members of opposite sex, as opposed to acceptance of one's sexual identity. (493)

Transvestism. Persistent desire to dress in garments of the opposite sex and feeling of discomfort when dressed in clothing of one's own sex; persistent association of sexual excitement with dressing in clothes of the opposite sex. Also called *transvestitism*. (492)

Trauma. Severe psychological or physiological stress resulting in injury or wound. (148)

Traumatic. Pertaining to a wound or injury. (148)

Traumatic neurosis. See **"Shock" reaction.**

Tremor. Repeated fine spastic movement. (236)

Tube feeding. Feeding patients by inserting a flexible tube through the nostrils into the throat and pouring liquids directly into the esophagus. (514)

Turner's syndrome. Form of mental retardation associated with sex chromosome anomaly. (571)

Unconscious. Lack of awareness; in Freudian theory, that portion of the psyche which is a storehouse of repressed or forgotten memories and desires which are not directly accessible to consciousness but may be brought into consciousness when ego restraints are removed, as in hypnosis. (54)

Unconscious motivation. Motivations for an individual's behavior of which he is unaware. (113)

Unconscious process. Psychological event not in conscious awareness.

Undoing. Ego-defense mechanism by means of which the individual performs activities designed to atone for his misdeeds, thereby, in a sense, "undoing" them. (131)

Vacillate. To waver or fluctuate between two or more alternatives. (533)

Vaginismus. A condition of sexual inadequacy in female in which the outer third of the vagina involuntarily clamps tightly shut when attempts are made to enter. (459)

Validity. Extent to which a measuring instrument actually measures what it was designed to measure. (652)

Values. Assumptions concerning good and bad, right and wrong. (70)

Vasomotor. Pertaining to the walls of the blood vessels. (552)

Vegetative. Withdrawn or deteriorated to the point where the individual leads a passive, vegetable-like existence. (503)

Verbigeration. Prolonged and monotonous repetition of meaningless words and phrases. (280)

Vertigo. Dizziness. (240)

Vicarious living. Attempt to evade efforts toward self-fulfillment by repressing one's own individuality and identifying with some hero or ideal. (129)

Vicious circle. Chain reaction in which individual resorts to an unhealthy defensive reaction in trying to solve his problems, which only serves to complicate them and make them harder to solve. (168)

Virilism. Accentuation of masculine secondary sex characteristics, especially in a woman or young boy, caused by overactivity of the adrenal cortex. (544)

Viscera. Internal organs. (503)

Visual hallucinations. Hallucinations involving sense of sight. (271)

Voyeurism. Achievement of sexual pleasure through clandestine "peeping," usually watching other persons disrobe and/or engage in sexual activities. (466)

Wassermann test. Serum test used in the diagnosis of syphilis. (46)

Withdrawal. Intellectual, emotional, or physical retreat. (598)

Withdrawal symptoms. Wide range of symptoms evidenced by addicts when the drug on which they are physiologically dependent is not available. (427)

Word hash. Jumbled or incoherent use of words by psychotic or disoriented individuals. (325)

Working through. Confronting and dealing with a problem situation until satisfactory adjustments are achieved and established. (169)

Worry. Persistent concern about past behavior or about anticipated dangers in the present or future. (4)

X chromosome. Sex-determining chromosome; all female gametes contain X chromosomes, and if fertilized ovum has also received an X chromosome from its father it will be female. (139)

Y chromosome. Sex-determining chromosome found in half of the total number of male gametes; uniting with X chromosome always provided by female produces a male offspring. (139)

Zoophobia. Morbid fear of animals. (227)

Zygote. Fertilized egg cell formed by union of male and female gametes. (139)

Name Index

Subject Index